Conte[nts]

- 2 — President
- 3 — Chairman
- 4 — Tips on u[sing]
- 6 — Discoveri[ng]
- 7 — National Garden Scheme 2024 donations
- 8 — The impact of our donations on nursing
- 10 — Gardens and health: access for all
- 12 — Open your garden and be part of an inspiring community
- 16 — The importance of community gardens
- 22 — Gardens for wildlife

26 Gardens Open in England

26	Bedfordshire	412	Nottinghamshire
34	Berkshire	424	Oxfordshire
42	Buckinghamshire	442	Shropshire
54	Cambridgeshire	454	Somerset & Bristol
70	Cheshire & Wirral	476	Staffordshire & W Midlands
86	Cornwall	484	Suffolk
104	Cumbria	496	Surrey
116	Derbyshire	512	Sussex
132	Devon	550	Warwickshire
156	Dorset	564	Wiltshire
182	Essex	578	Worcestershire
198	Gloucestershire	592	Yorkshire
218	Hampshire		
240	Herefordshire		
252	Hertfordshire		
264	Isle of Wight		
270	Kent		
294	Lancashire		
314	Leicestershire & Rutland		
326	Lincolnshire		
336	London		
370	Norfolk		
384	North East		
396	Northamptonshire		

614 Gardens Open in the Channel Islands

616 Gardens Open in Northern Ireland

624 Gardens Open in Wales

- 625 — Carmarthenshire & Pembrokeshire
- 634 — Ceredigion
- 640 — Glamorgan
- 650 — Gwent
- 658 — Gwynedd
- 666 — North East Wales
- 672 — Powys

- 684 — Plant Heritage collections in our gardens
- 687 — Acknowledgments

Published by the National Garden Scheme
A company limited by guarantee.
Registered in England & Wales.
Charity No. 1112664.
Company No. 5631421

Registered & Head Office:
Hatchlands Park, East Clandon,
Guildford, Surrey, GU4 7RT.
01483 211535 www.ngs.org.uk

© The National Garden Scheme 2025

Foreword

A year ago, I ended my foreword looking ahead to the show garden the National Garden Scheme was due to have at Chelsea Flower Show 2024. Looking back to the event it is wonderful that all our expectations were achieved – and more. The garden, designed by Tom Stuart-Smith and fully funded by Project Giving Back, won a gold medal and its sheer beauty inspired both visitors to the show and everyone who saw it on television.

Perhaps most importantly, it gave the National Garden Scheme a unique opportunity to raise its public profile and widen knowledge about its charitable activities – the amazing annual support it gives to nursing and health charities – which you can read more about on page 8.

We know this had an impact for the rest of 2024 because our gardens once again raised a record total of more than £4 million. Looking ahead to 2025 I am confident that this will continue so that our brilliant owners, who put in so much work to open their gardens, will again be rewarded by increased numbers of visitors and increased funds raised.

I am hugely impressed that our gardens succeed in increasing the annual funds raised at the same time as remaining resolutely affordable – such an important strength that the National Garden Scheme has always had. In 2025 the average admission to all gardens will still be less than £6 (and children go free in nearly all). That means that in most gardens you will be able to buy a ticket and refreshments for less than £10 – what better way to spend an afternoon! And in so many gardens, you will enjoy an absolutely delicious tea with homemade cake.

I am looking forward to visiting some new gardens that I'm sure will inspire us all to be more creative at home. And very soon when the first snowdrops appear we can start visiting National Garden Scheme gardens again.

Dame Mary Berry
National Garden Scheme President

Who's who

Patron
His Majesty King Charles III

President
Dame Mary Berry

Vice-Presidents
Elizabeth Anton
Angela Azis
Ann Budden
Daphne Foulsham MBE
A Martin McMillan OBE
Heather Skinner
Penny Snell CBE

Chairman
Rupert Tyler

Deputy Chairman
Sue Phipps

Hon Treasurer
Andrew Ratcliffe

Trustees
Arit Anderson
Richard Barley MBE
Atty Beor-Roberts
Lucy Hall
Maureen Kesteven
Professor John Newton OBE
Susan Paynton
Mark Porter
Vernon Sanderson
Debbie Thomson
Alison Wright

Chief Executive
George Plumptre

Ambassadors
Emma Bridgewater CBE
Danny Clarke
Alan Gray
Joe Swift
Rachel de Thame
Jo Whiley

Chairman's message

As we look to a new season of garden visiting, with all the enjoyment but also the occasional challenges this will bring, a vital part of my role as Chairman of the National Garden Scheme is to thank the wide array of people involved.

First, I am delighted to thank His Majesty The King, for agreeing to continue as Patron of the National Garden Scheme, the position in which he so generously supported us as Prince of Wales for 20 years from 2002–2022.

We are also very fortunate to have as our President, Dame Mary Berry who has written a new foreword for this edition of the *Garden Visitor's Handbook* and does so much else to support us.

This year, as previously, nearly 3,300 gardens will open for the National Garden Scheme, with its unique combination of offering huge enjoyment to visitors and raising substantial sums of money for our beneficiary charities. They will be supported by some 550 volunteers in our teams in England, Wales, Northern Ireland and the Channel Islands – many of whom also open their own gardens. This group represent the heart of the National Garden Scheme, responsible for so much of not only the charity's fundraising but also its distinctive character and I offer huge thanks to you all. You are all supported by the fantastic small team at our Surrey central office who are brilliantly led by George Plumptre. As a garden owner myself, I know how much they do.

Amongst our various supporters I particularly want to single out and thank our long-term core sponsor, Rathbones. Through a series of changing names but always with the same commitment, they have given generous funding to the National Garden Scheme for more than 30 years and we are immensely grateful for their long-term support.

Last, but not least, I want to thank all of you who are going to visit our gardens. In the coming weeks and months you will help us raise enough to once again donate more than £3 million to our beneficiaries before the end of the year.

Rupert Tyler
Chairman

Tips on using your Handbook

This book lists all the gardens opening for the National Garden Scheme. They are arranged alphabetically in county sections, each including a map, calendar of opening dates and details of each garden with illustrations of some.

Symbols explained

NEW Gardens opening for the first time this year or re-opening after a long break.

◆ Garden also opens on non-National Garden Scheme days. (Gardens which carry this symbol contribute to the National Garden Scheme either by opening on a specific day(s) and/or by giving a guaranteed contribution.)

♿ Wheelchair access to at least the main features of the garden.

🐕 Dogs on short leads welcome.

✽ Plants usually for sale.

⋅)) Card payments accepted.

NPC Plant Heritage National Plant Collection.

🛏 Gardens that offer accommodation.

☕ Refreshments are available, normally at a charge.

🪑 Picnics welcome.

D Garden designed by a Fellow, Member, Pre-registered Member, or Student of The Society of Garden Designers.

🚌 Garden accessible to coaches. Coach sizes vary so please contact the garden owner or County Organiser in advance to check details.

Group Visits Group organisers may contact the county organiser or a garden owner direct to organise a group visit to a particular county or garden. Otherwise contact the National Garden Scheme office on 01483 211535.

Children must be accompanied by an adult.

Photography is at the discretion of the garden owner; please check first. Photographs must not be used for sale or reproduction without prior permission of the owner.

Funds raised In most cases all funds raised at our open gardens come to the National Garden Scheme. However, there are some instances where income from teas or a percentage of admissions is given to another charity.

Toilet facilities are not guaranteed at all gardens.

If you cannot find the information you require from a garden owner or county organiser, call the National Garden Scheme office on 01483 211535.

RATHBONES

WHEN YOU'RE READY TO WRITE THE NEXT CHAPTER IN YOUR WEALTH STORY, RELY ON RATHBONES.

A TRUSTED PARTNER FOCUSED ON YOU AND YOUR FINANCIAL GOALS.
FOR INDIVIDUALS AND FAMILIES.

rathbones.com

The value of investments and the income from them may go down as well as up and you may not get back what you originally invested.

Rathbones is a trading name of Rathbones Investment Management Limited which is authorised by the Prudential Regulation Authority and regulated by the Financial Conduct Authority and the Prudential Regulation Authority.

Discovering the nation's best gardens

The National Garden Scheme gives visitors unique access to thousands of exceptional private gardens and raises impressive amounts of money for nursing and health charities through admissions, teas and cake.

Thanks to the generosity of garden owners, volunteers and visitors we have donated over £74 million to nursing and health charities since we were founded in 1927. In 2024 we donated a record £3,501,227.

Originally established to raise funds for district nurses, we are now the most significant charitable funder of nursing in the UK and our beneficiaries include Macmillan Cancer Support, Marie Curie, Hospice UK, Parkinson's UK, The Queen's Nursing Institute and Carers Trust. Year by year, the cumulative impact of our donations grows incrementally, helping our beneficiaries make their own important contribution to the nation's health and care.

The National Garden Scheme doesn't just open beautiful gardens for charity, we are passionate about the physical and mental health benefits of gardens too. We run a Community Garden Grants programme and fund projects which promote gardens and gardening as therapy. In 2017 we launched our annual Gardens and Health Week to raise awareness of the topic

Our funding also supports the training of gardeners and offers respite to horticultural workers who have fallen on difficult times.

With over 3,300 gardens opening across England, Wales, Northern Ireland and the Channel Islands there are plenty for you to discover. Most gardens open on one or more specific dates but many also open by arrangement, offering the facility for you to book a private visit.

Browse the pages of this *Garden Visitor's Handbook* and start to discover some of the stunning gardens just waiting to be explored in the year ahead.

Pictured: Naman Chaudhary, National Garden Scheme volunteer, London

YOUR GARDEN VISITS HELP CHANGE LIVES

NATIONAL Open GARDEN SCHEME

In 2024 the National Garden Scheme donated £3,501,227 to our beneficiaries, providing critical support to nursing and health charities.

- **Marie Curie** £450,000
- **Macmillan Cancer Support** £450,000
- **Hospice UK** £450,000
- **Carers Trust** £350,000
- **The Queen's Nursing Institute** £500,000
- **Parkinson's UK** £350,000

SUPPORT FOR GARDENERS
- English Heritage £125,000
- Perennial £100,000
- National Botanic Garden, Wales £26,000
- Bankside Open Spaces Trust £21,000
- Professional Gardeners' Trust £20,000
- Garden Museum £10,000
- Support for Community Gardens £232,000

GARDENS AND HEALTH CHARITIES
- Maggie's £122,227
- Horatio's Garden £90,000
- Army Benevolent Fund £80,000
- John King Brain Tumour Trust £50,000
- Cancer Help Preston £50,000
- The Country Trust £25,000

Thank you!
To find out more visit **ngs.org.uk/beneficiaries**

Charity number: 1112664

DONATE

The impact of our donations on nursing

Originally established to raise funds for district nurses, the National Garden Scheme is now the most significant charitable funder of nursing in the UK and our beneficiaries include Macmillan Cancer Support, Marie Curie, Hospice UK, Parkinson's UK, The Queen's Nursing Institute and Carers Trust.

Thanks to the generosity of garden owners, volunteers and visitors we have donated over £74 million to nursing and health charities since we were founded in 1927. In 2024 the lion's share of the record £3,501,227 donation went to our major long-term beneficiaries who are all leading providers of nursing and healthcare, in particular community and specialist nursing, cancer, palliative, and end of life care.

In the current state of the wider UK health and care landscape the impact of our donations has never been more important, ensuring that our beneficiary charities can continue to make a crucial contribution to the health of the nation. As a group, our beneficiaries are a significant force, and our support helps them continue their individual and joint activities.

We have continued to have a special impact with some beneficiaries by funding specific projects that benefit both their staff and patients or other service users. With The Queen's Nursing Institute (QNI) we have continued to fund their Executive Nurse Leadership programme which trains and equips senior community nurses to take on some of the highest roles in the nursing profession. Previously these roles have rarely been filled by community nurses. Also, with the QNI we continue to fund their Elsie Wagg scholarships. These are named after the QNI Trustee who had the original idea to establish the National Garden Scheme in 1927. They fund nurses to develop garden projects at their place of work, such as a GP's surgery, a care home or homeless hostel for the benefit of patients and their families. And with Marie Curie we continue to support their Nightingale Challenge which funds Marie Curie nurses to gain qualifications which enable their career progression, thereby helping ensure that nurses stay in the profession and do not leave.

National Garden Scheme funding has also helped to fund 23 new nurse and allied health professional posts for Parkinson's UK to bring better care, treatments and quality of life to those living with the condition. Over 9,000 people living with Parkinson's, who did not previously have access to specialist care, are now reached thanks to our funding and we will continue to support Parkinson's UK's ambitious strategy to support an additional 30 new nurse posts and 30 new allied health professional roles between 2023–2025.

Our funding in 2024 has helped:

- Care for 66,000 people in nine Marie Curie Hospices
- Provide guidance on what to expect when a person is dying to 129,032 people through our support for Hospice UK
- Support 3,000 Queen's Nurses
- Provide specialist care for 9,000 people living with Parkinson's
- Support 26,081 unpaid carers and their families through Carers Trust

Opposite: A Queen's Nurse at work in the community. Photo © Kate Stanworth/QNI

Gardens and health: access for all

Our Gardens and Health Programme raises awareness of the physical and mental health benefits of gardens and gardening for everyone. Celebrated in May each year with a dedicated Gardens and Health Week, we also work to promote gardens and health throughout the year, linking service users from our beneficiaries with free garden visits, and funding gardens and health projects.

The charities we fund create gardens with health benefits and promote gardens and gardening as therapy. They include Horatio's Garden, which builds beautiful, accessible gardens in NHS spinal injury centres. Since our support began in 2015 the National Garden Scheme has donated over £600,000 and we have committed funding to complete all eleven gardens at spinal injury units across the country. The latest donation of £90,000 in 2024 is the second of two for Horatio's Garden Northern Ireland which, along with six others, hosted an open day for us in 2024.

Another of our Gardens and Health beneficiaries is Maggie's which creates cancer support centres combining the best architects and landscape designers to build a strong connection between the outside and inside space. Our 2024 RHS Chelsea Show Garden, designed by Tom Stuart-Smith and funded by Project Giving Back, is being relocated to the new Maggie's in Cambridgeshire and our donation of £122,227 in 2024 included £22,227 raised from the sale of pictures by our Chelsea Flower Show artist in residence, Tyga Helme, and the plant sale held after the show in June. Five Maggie's also hosted open days for us in 2024 and over 48,000 people affected by cancer were reached by Maggie's centres supported by the National Garden Scheme.

The Army Benevolent Fund is the third of our larger Garden and Health beneficiaries to which we give ongoing support. It funds the provision of horticultural-related assistance to soldiers, veterans and their immediate families to help improve their health and wellbeing, and our donation of £80,000 in 2024 helped support 700 people.

The National Garden Scheme also gives one-off grants to charities providing gardens as part of their therapy or care. In 2024 we donated £27,300 to Thrive for the creation of a new sanctuary garden for vulnerable older people in London, and £48,000 to Sue Ryder to complete the gardens at its Leckhampton Court Hospice in Gloucestershire.

In addition, we also provide funding for community gardening projects that support the health and wellbeing of local communities and groups. In 2024 we funded 89 projects with a total of £232,000. From social welfare and gardening projects that help the isolated, the disabled and the disenfranchised, to support for community orchards, food banks and social prescribing projects at GP surgeries, the funding provides a much-needed boost to those working on, or initiating, community garden projects throughout England, Wales and Northern Ireland. Many of the funded community projects in turn open for the National Garden Scheme completing a virtuous circle of giving and giving back.

Opposite: Head Gardener Alex and patient enjoying garden therapy in Horatio's Garden Midlands
Photo © Eva Nemeth

Above: Thrive's new sanctuary garden created for vulnerable older people in London

Open your garden and be part of an inspiring community

The success of the National Garden Scheme and the significant amounts of money it donates to its beneficiary charities would not be possible without the dedicated support of the charity's garden owners and volunteers. In 2024, 3,372 gardens opened across England, Wales, Northern Ireland and the Channel Islands supported by 582 volunteers, all contributing to our record donation total of over £3.5 million.

The enthusiasm, expertise and generosity of our garden owners is at the heart of everything the charity achieves. While there are many things that inspire people to open their gardens there is an almost universal sense of joy among garden owners in sharing their gardens.

Kerrie Lloyd-Dawson and Pete Stevens, who open their garden at 43 Mardley Hill in Hertfordshire, have opened their garden for the last 12 years. "In our previous garden we opened for our village open gardens and really enjoyed it. We bought 43 Mardley Hill specifically to create a new garden together and hoped that the National Garden Scheme might take us on. They did and we've been opening now for over a decade.

"Opening our garden for the public is so rewarding, not only because of the fundraising, but also because we can see how much pleasure our visitors get from visiting our garden. Many go away inspired to create something new in their own garden, often armed with a plant purchase. A couple of people have even brought us plants that they thought we ought to have. It's a very social, collaborative experience, and it's also great motivation to get all those gardening jobs done!" says Kerrie.

Opposite: Ginny Fairfax who is opening her garden at Kirky Cottage, Northumberland on 15 June 2025. Photo © Val Corbett

Above: Kerrie Lloyd-Dawson and Pete Stevens who are opening their garden at 43 Mardley Hill on 26 May 2025. Photo © Jiaji Wu

For Ginny Fairfax opening two successive gardens in Northumberland since 1991 has become a thing of joy. From novice gardener to accomplished plantswoman most of the plants in Ginny's garden have a history of coming from a friend's garden or have been gifted to her. It is the sharing of these plants that is her biggest joy.

"Many of the plants self-seed in the gravel or can be propagated so I'm always selling them," she says. "So many young people visit who are desperate to get started and they want their gardens to look like mine – so I help them. And the plants, if being rehomed locally, usually settle in well.

"You make all sorts of friends of different ages when you share your garden, all with the shared interest of wanting to have a lovely garden. It's so satisfying to know that the plants that have given you so much joy go on to create similar levels of joy for other people too."

For Wayne Amiel, who gardens in South London and has welcomed visitors to 35 Turret Grove since 2012, opening his garden brings new people and new conversations. "I love sharing my garden, and the conversations it prompts about gardens and gardening," he says. "I meet such wonderful people, the joy it gives to others and the money it raises for so many good causes is very special. I've been visiting National Garden Scheme gardens since my childhood and I never thought I would have a garden in the 'yellow book'. I know most people use the website now but for me, the thrill of being in the Garden Visitor's Handbook never goes away."

"Whether a garden opens once or over a number of decades every garden is important," says Chairman, Rupert Tyler, who has opened his own garden at 51 The Chase in Clapham since 2009. "We owe an enormous debt of gratitude to all of our garden owners and all the volunteers who support them. Without their combined dedication and passion, we would not have become the most significant charitable funder of nursing charities in the UK or been able to give £3,501,227 to our beneficiaries in 2024.

"As we head towards our centenary in 2027, we would like to thank everyone who has helped create such a vibrant, inspiring and enduring community that gives so much pleasure to visitors and raises so much money for good causes, and to invite you to consider opening your own garden for the charity too."

Above: Wayne Amiel in his garden at 35 Turret Grove, London – open with the National Garden Scheme on 20 July 2025

We're looking for new gardens

Join our community of like-minded individuals all passionate about gardens. Our portfolio of gardens is diverse, from country estates and cottage gardens to urban oases and allotments. So, whatever its style or size, if your garden has quality, character and interest we'd love to hear from you.

For more information:
email hello@ngs.org.uk,
call us on 01483 211535
or contact your local
volunteer team.

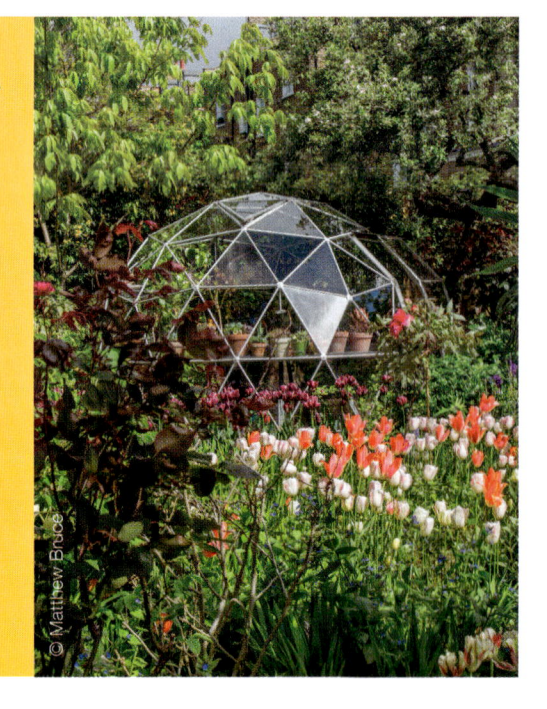

Bonhams

AUCTIONEERS SINCE 1793

Bring it to Bonhams
We'll sell it to the world

With a strong market for Jewellery, Watches, Fine Art, Collectables and Asian Art, there has never been a better time to sell at auction.

ENQUIRIES
01564 776 151
sarah.priest@bonhams.com

sell.bonhams.com

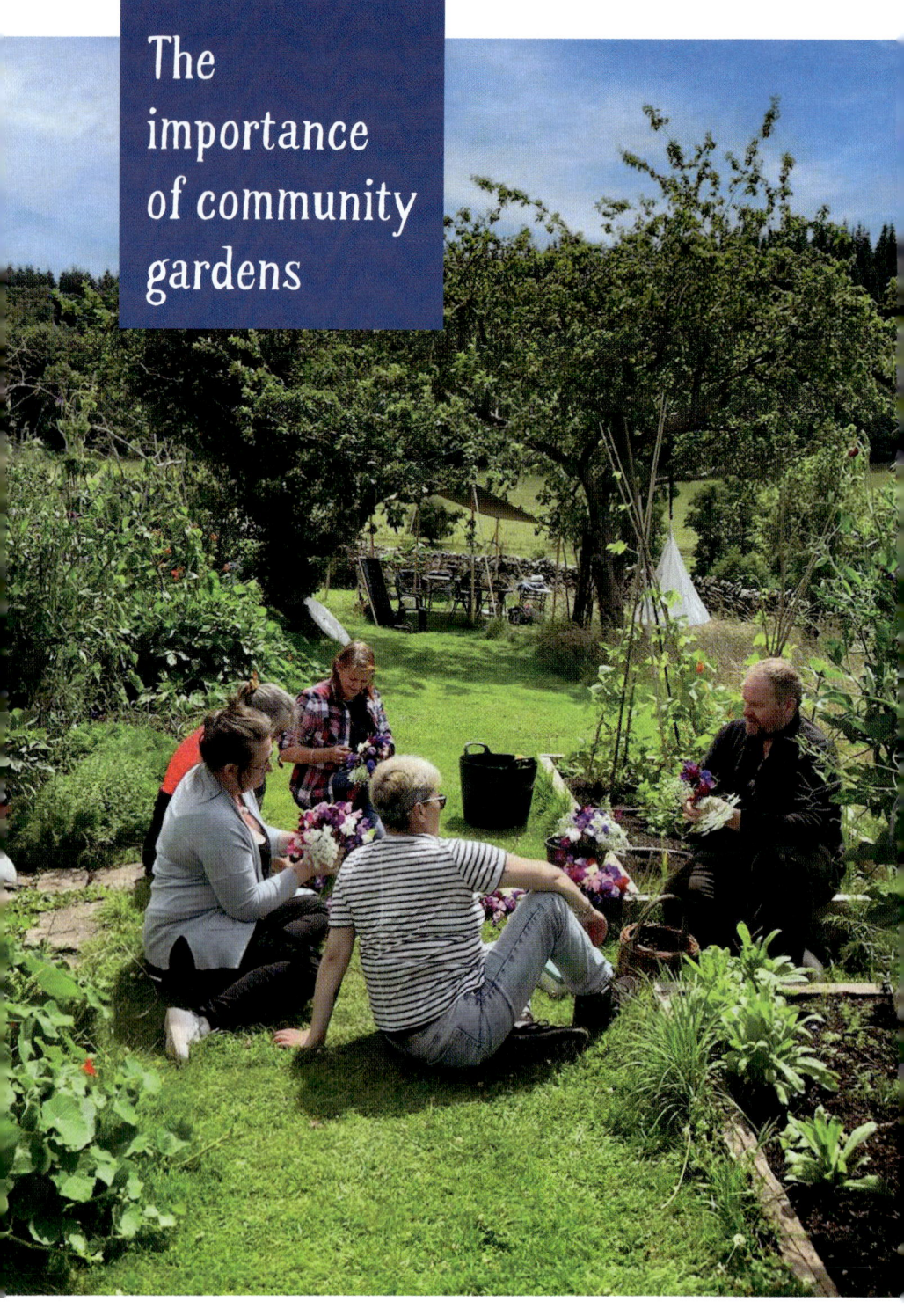

The importance of community gardens

Over recent years there has been a ground swell of interest and research supporting the importance that gardens and green spaces can play in the health and wellbeing of communities. It is a trend that the National Garden Scheme recognised in 2011 when we launched our Community Garden Grants programme. Today, as part of the charity's wider Gardens and Health programme, over £893,000 has been donated to support almost 400 community gardens, with £232,000 of that total donated in 2024 funding 89 projects.

The 2024 funding was announced in April. Many of the applications received centred on the growing of food for communities and those helping others to learn to grow food. Commenting, Chief Executive of the National Garden Scheme, George Plumptre said: "At a time when the cost-of-living crisis is forcing many people to find innovative ways to support themselves, their families and their communities, our Community Garden Grants are providing even more of a helping hand to thousands of people across the UK."

Others cited the benefits to the physical and mental wellbeing of their local community including dozens supporting children, and people with dementia. Applications also came from a broad spectrum of society. "Community gardens help to reduce isolation, build friendships and give people a sense of purpose and hope, so it is easy to see why people get involved. We are delighted to provide ongoing support to so many inspirational projects," adds George Plumptre.

Many of the funded community projects in turn open for the National Garden Scheme completing a virtuous circle of giving and giving back.

In 2025 you can visit grantee gardens such as Rhubarb Farm in Nottinghamshire, a 2-acre horticultural social enterprise that provides training and volunteering opportunities to ex-offenders, drug and alcohol misusers, older people, school students, people with mental and physical ill health and learning disabilities. The project opens its gates through the National Garden Scheme on dates in June, July and August. See page 420 for more details.

Or the Pakistan Association Liverpool (PAL) Wellbeing Garden which received a £4,900 Community Garden Grant to help expand the garden. Established in 1977, PAL has served as a community hub for different generations who integrate as equals under one roof, regardless of race, creed, and religion. The PAL Wellbeing Garden opens in 2025 for the National Garden Scheme as part of the Canning Georgian Quarter group gardens on 22 June. See page 300 for more details.

These inspiring projects, and hundreds more like them, demonstrate the importance of gardens to community health and wellbeing.

Above: Young gardeners at Wicor Primary School share the joy of their community garden
Opposite: Social and therapeutic gardening activities are delivered by The Fathom Trust in the Brecon Beacons

Alongside our Community Garden Grants programme, we also launched the NGS Elsie Wagg (Innovation) Scholarship in partnership with The Queen's Nursing Institute (QNI) in 2021. Open to all nurses working in the community there are five scholarships available for the best applications each year. The projects, which receive £5,000 each must be community gardens that promote the health benefits of gardening and garden visiting.

Named after Elsie Wagg, the QNI council member who originally had the idea to open gardens to raise funds for charity, which led to the creation of the National Garden Scheme in 1927, the QNI has a long track record of supporting nurses to develop and implement their own ideas to improve the nursing care of the people they look after in the community. Each scholarship comes with a year-long programme of individual and group support, as well as funding to implement the project to improve healthcare.

Since the Scholarship began £75,000 has supported 15 projects. The most recent include: The Sanctuary Garden Project in Gloucestershire, aimed at providing a safe outdoor space for female patients at a community mental health hospital; The Green Wellbeing Project in Staffordshire that helps improve mental health and wellbeing for care home residents; the Botanical Brothers Project in East London that aims to provide a safe space for fathers and male carers to talk freely about their mental health and wellbeing while participating in horticultural activities; The New Longton Wellbeing Garden Project in Lancashire which allows patients and staff at a care home to access gardening as part of therapeutic appointments, and the Grow Together Share Together Project which brings different generations together in a shared garden space within the grounds of Dorking Community Hospital in Surrey.

The experiences shared by participants in these projects is universally positive and helps build strong, cohesive and healthy communities.

Above, right: A Father benefits from the Botanical Brothers project in East London

One participant from a current QNI nurse-led project said:

"I want to say how the garden has done me good. I've found something that I enjoy ... something that I care about and something that allows me to care about me. Something that gives me some peace from all of the chaos that comes with hustling and searching for that thing to take me out of my misery. Gardening takes me out of my misery. Even if only for the 10 minutes that my mind and body allows. Thank you for giving money so Kendra can do this. So I can do this."

To find out more about the Gardens and Health programme, including recent funding for nurse-led community projects and our Community Garden Grants visit our website **ngs.org.uk**

Pass on your love of gardens
with a gift in your will

Leaving a gift to the National Garden Scheme will help us ensure that everyone can experience the joy of garden visiting and inspire a passion for gardens in future generations.

For more information or to speak to a member of our team call **01483 211535** email **giftinwill@ngs.org.uk** or visit **ngs.org.uk/giftinwill**

Scan for more information

Spread the word

Perennial is the UK's only horticultural charity dedicated to helping everyone working with plants, trees, flowers or grass through our free, confidential helpline and support services.

> "Life without gardens and green spaces is unimaginable. These cherished havens wouldn't exist without the dedicated people who support them, and sometimes, those people need support too."
>
> Alan Titchmarsh, President, Perennial

Find out more or donate
perennial.org.uk

115 - 117 Kingston Road, Leatherhead, Surrey, KT22 7SU. A company limited by guarantee. A company limited by guarantee. Registered in England & Wales no: 8828584. Charity no: 1155156. Registered in Scotland, Charity no: SC040180. VAT no. 9912541 09. Gardeners' Royal Benevolent Society (trading as Perennial) is authorised and regulated by the Financial Conduct Authority under FRN: 694883.

Helping people in horticulture
Perennial

21

STIHL

**PREMIUM TOOLS.
BATTERY-POWERED.
FROM STIHL.**
—

ONE BATTERY. MANY TOOLS.

Cut, mow, saw or clear around the garden with STIHL's AK System battery-powered tools. German engineering combined with powerful performance and just one battery which fits every tool.

Discover our range of premium garden tools at your nearest STIHL Approved Dealer or at www.stihl.co.uk

AK SYSTEM

BATTERY POWER. BY STIHL.

Gardens for wildlife

Many of us recognise the importance of gardens to our own physical and mental wellbeing but gardens are important for another reason: they provide vital sustenance and connectivity for the wildlife around us too. Gardens help to create a mosaic of habitats and green corridors for wildlife to move across as well as homes for hundreds of species from insects and amphibians to birds and mammals.

Above: 84 Higham Street, Walthamstowe, London
Opposite, from top: The Tythe Barn in Oxfordshire, Hogchester Farm, Dorset

There are 23 million gardens in the UK, and each one, whatever their size, can play a part in reversing biodiversity loss, and making just a few changes can really help give nature a much-needed boost.

Over the last few years hundreds of gardens that open for the National Garden Scheme have reflected the need for change by wilding parts, or all, of their gardens. From wildflower meadows, ponds and insect hotels to native tree planting and green roofs, there are plenty of inspirational gardens to visit in 2025.

For example, the Tythe Barn in Oxfordshire is a ½ acre garden designed by RHS Chelsea award winner Sarah Naybour. It's a delightful garden designed with wildlife in mind, with bee-friendly planting in the formal garden leading to a woodland area along with a 2½ acre wildflower meadow with apiary. There's honey for sale when it opens on Sunday 8 June too.

For other rewilding inspiration visit Hogchester Farm in rural Dorset, which has been able to preserve wild meadows and wilding areas now filled with local flora and fauna. Open on Sunday 13 July it's a great family day out. Or visit the Walled Garden at Knepp in West Sussex which opens on 21 June and has been transformed into a garden for biodiversity. Along with designers Tom Stuart-Smith and James Hitchmough they have applied some of the principles learned from rewilding the wider landscape to this smaller space to create a mosaic of dynamic habitats for wildlife. The croquet lawn is now a riot of humps and hollows, hosting almost 1,000 species of plants.

For urban inspiration the garden at 84 Higham Street in Walthamstow, London which opens for the National Garden Scheme on 6 July is a must for visitors who want to see just how exciting the garden of a semi-detached house can be! In such an urban location the large pond and small woodland hideaway are an oasis for wildlife.

Water is the life blood of any garden and water features help support a wide variety of water loving plants and attract wildlife too and with over 2,000 gardens mentioning water in their descriptions there are plenty of ideas to explore when you visit gardens with the National Garden Scheme this year.

Don't worry if the idea of wilding your garden seems daunting, the biodiversity study carried out at the famous garden at Great Dixter (which supports the National Garden Scheme) showed that the most biodiverse parts of the garden were the thickly planted ornamental borders where the density of plant species attracted a corresponding density of insect and animal species. Proof that you don't have to dig up your borders to accommodate wildlife.

COBRA

One of the UK's largest ranges of garden machinery

Create a lawn that is the envy of your neighbours with a brand new lawn tractor or lawnmower from Cobra. At the heart of these powerful, stylish machines is a choice of cut sizes and either electric, cordless or petrol engines powered by Briggs & Stratton, Honda and Loncin.

Cobra have over 65 lawnmowers in their portfolio including a comprehensive range of powerful 40V and Twin 40V cordless models including the 'Which?' award winning Cobra MX51S80V cordless lawnmower. Whatever your gardening needs, Cobra has a lawnmower for you.

AWARD WINNER — BEST BUY
MX51S80V

80V MAX LITHIUM-ION — POWERED BY BRIGGS & STRATTON — Expertly Powered By COBRA — POWERED BY HONDA

Model Shown: Cobra MX51S80V

For your nearest dealer visit: **www.cobragarden.co.uk** or call: **0115 986 6646**   *Promotional prices only at participating dealers

You feed the family, we'll feed the lawn

GreenThumb provide a year-round premium lawn care experience.

We seed them, feed them, even control the weeds. So, you don't have to.

For a **FREE** lawn analysis visit **greenthumb.co.uk** to contact our local team.

GreenThumb
LAWN TREATMENT SERVICE

BEDFORDSHIRE

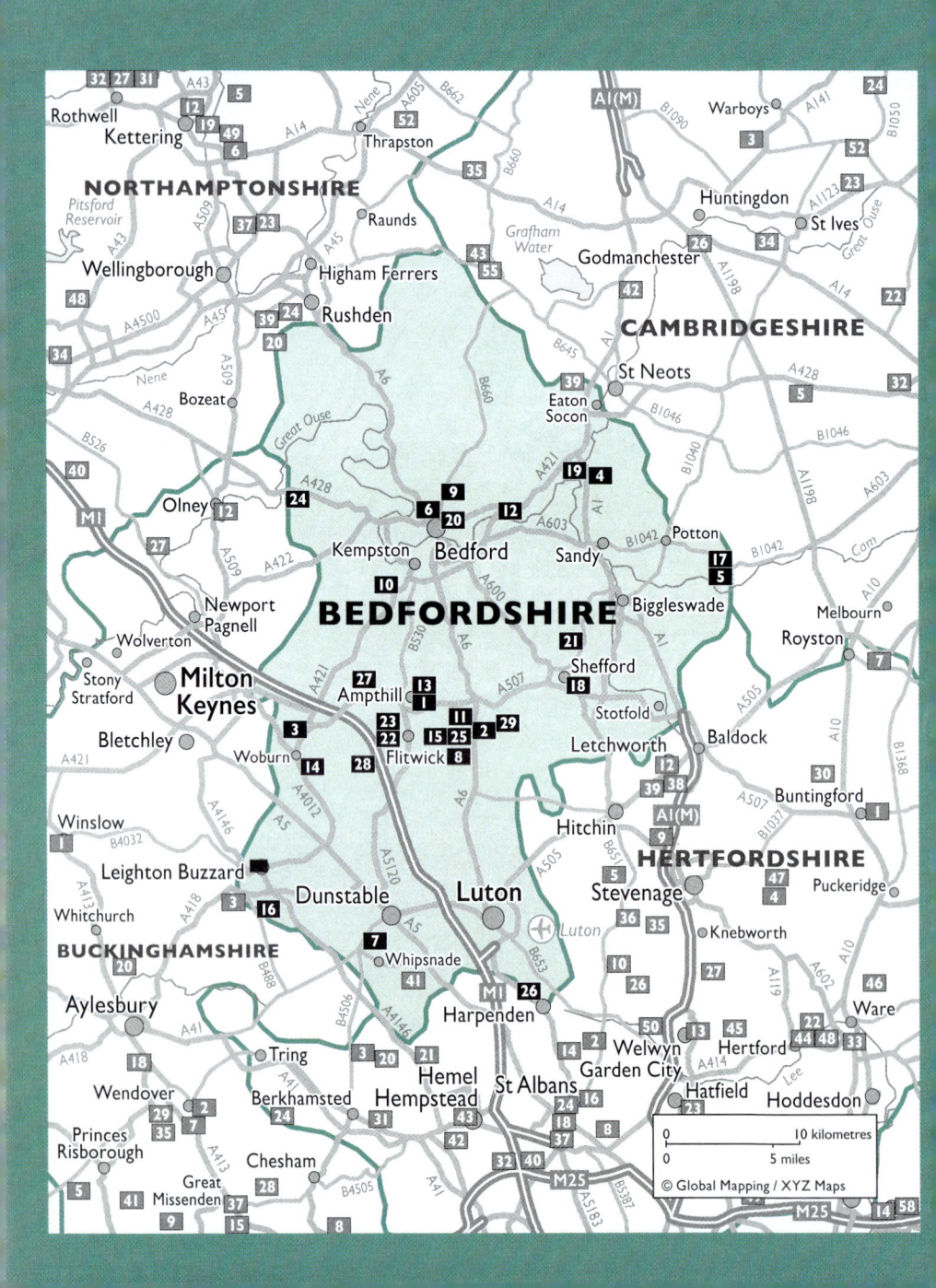

VOLUNTEERS

Acting County Organiser
Indi Jackson
07973 857633
indi.jackson@ngs.org.uk

County Treasurer
Colin Davies
07811 022211
colin.davies@ngs.org.uk

Booklet Co-ordinators
Indi Jackson
(as above)

Alex Ballance
alexballance@yahoo.co.uk

Press Officer
Position Vacant

Talks
Christopher Bamforth Damp
chrisdamp@mac.com

Photographer
Venetia Barrington
venetiajanesgarden@gmail.com

Assistant County Organisers
Alex Ballance
(as above)

Natalie Jeffs
natalie.jeffs@ngs.org.uk

Facebook
Indi Jackson
(as above)

@bedfordshire.ngs

OPENING DATES

All entries subject to change. For latest information check www.ngs.org.uk
Map locator numbers are shown to the right of each garden name.

February
Snowdrop Openings
Sunday 16th
♦ King's Arms Garden ... 13
Sunday 23rd
Townsend Farmhouse ... 23

March
Sunday 16th
NEW 8 Abbey Close ... 1

April
Sunday 20th
Steppingley Village Gardens ... 22
Monday 21st
Steppingley Village Gardens ... 22
Saturday 26th
22 Elmsdale Road ... 10
Sunday 27th
22 Elmsdale Road ... 10

May
Saturday 10th
The Old Rectory, Wrestlingworth ... 17
Sunday 11th
The Old Rectory, Wrestlingworth ... 17
Saturday 17th
Church Farm ... 8
Sunday 18th
Church Farm ... 8
Sunday 25th
Steppingley Village Gardens ... 22
Monday 26th
Steppingley Village Gardens ... 22
Saturday 31st
Hollington Farm ... 11

June
Sunday 1st
Ash Trees ... 3
Hollington Farm ... 11
Southill Park ... 21
Saturday 7th
12 Queen Elizabeth Close ... 18
Sunday 8th
12 Queen Elizabeth Close ... 18
Saturday 14th
Mill Lane Gardens ... 15
Sunday 15th
Mill Lane Gardens ... 15
Turvey Village Gardens ... 24
Sunday 22nd
NEW Roxton Village Gardens ... 19
Saturday 28th
Old Church House ... 16
Sunday 29th
Old Church House ... 16

July
Friday 4th
Bedford Heights ... 6
Saturday 5th
40 Leighton Street ... 14
Saturday 12th
NEW Witts End Gardens ... 28
Sunday 13th
NEW Witts End Gardens ... 28
Sunday 27th
NEW Brooklands ... 7

August
Friday 1st
♦ The Walled Garden ... 26
Saturday 2nd
Beck House ... 5
Sunday 3rd
Beck House ... 5
Thursday 14th
♦ Wrest Park ... 29
Monday 25th
15 Douglas Road ... 9
Sunday 31st
NEW 29 Tyburn Lane ... 25

September

Sunday 7th
Howbury Hall Garden 12

October

Saturday 25th
Townsend Farmhouse 23

Sunday 26th
◆ King's Arms Garden 13

By Arrangement

Arrange a personalised garden visit with your club, or group of friends, on a date to suit you. See individual garden entries for full details.

NEW 8 Abbey Close	1
10 Alder Wynd	2
1c Bakers Lane	4
Beck House	5
Church Farm	8
1a St Augustine's Road	20
NEW Willow Cottage	27

The National Garden Scheme donated over £3.5 million to our nursing and health beneficiaries from money raised at gardens open in 2024.

The Old Rectory, Wrestlingworth

THE GARDENS

1 NEW 8 ABBEY CLOSE
Ampthill, Bedford, MK45 2SH.
Mrs Ann Vickers, 07776 387106.
Outskirts of Ampthill. A507 bypass to 2nd r'about for Maulden/Flitwick. Take 1st L Abbey Ln. After passing tidy tip take 2nd R hand turn into Oliver St. Abbey Cl is on the bend.
Sun 16 Mar (1-4). Adm £5, chd free. Visits also by arrangement in Apr for groups of up to 15.
A mature, town garden with scented spring bulbs, colourful early flowering perennials, budding shrubs and trees with sprouting new leaves. A variety of evergreen shrubs also offer an interesting mix of foliage. There is a small pond providing a home to frogspawn and tadpoles. Wheelchair access onto patio, remainder of garden is gravelled.
& ❁))

2 10 ALDER WYND
Silsoe, MK45 4GQ. David & Frances Hampson, 01525 861356, mail@davidhampson.com. *N of Luton, S of Bedford. From Barton Rd, turn into Obelisk Way, R at the sch & 1st L into Alder Wynd.* Visits by arrangement 20 July to 30 Sept for groups of up to 20. Adm £7, chd free. Light refreshments.
Created from scratch in the autumn of 2014, the owners have had to contend with the realities of building a garden on a modern housing estate. The garden is courtyard in style and formed from a series of raised beds and green oak structures. Visitors can expect plantings of bananas, gingers, bamboos and *Tetrapanax*, along side traditional herbaceous perennials grasses and clematis. Find the bespoke, quirky greenhouse and a small water feature which adds a subtle background noise. The garden can easily be accessed by wheelchair.
& ❁ ☕))

3 ASH TREES
Green Lane, Aspley Guise, Milton Keynes, MK17 8EN. John & Teresa. *About 10m from Milton Keynes and 2m from J13 M1. Green Ln is off Wood Ln. Yellow signs indicate where to turn. Some on-road parking in Wood Ln. Disabled or mobility parking only at house.* **Sun 1 June (10-4.30). Adm £6, chd free.**
Medium sized, secluded village garden, walled in with borrowed treescape and hidden in a private lane. Herbaceous borders, shrubs, trees, bulbs, and fruit inc apricot and peach. There is a unique garden arch sculpture created for a Hampton Court show garden. Seats in quiet spots amongst the plants. Children and wheelchairs welcome as are dogs on leads. Garden is flat with reasonable access for wheelchairs and walkers.
& 🐕 ☕ 🪑))

4 1C BAKERS LANE
Tempsford, Sandy, SG19 2BJ.
Juliet & David Pennington, 01767 640482, juliet.pennington01@gmail.com. *1m N of Sandy on A1 & Station Rd is on the E side. Bakers Ln is 300 yds down Station Rd on L. Parking on Station Rd & Knott's Farm Shop car park.* Visits by arrangement 2 Feb to 30 Nov. Adm £6, chd free.
Enchanting, wildlife friendly garden where each month of the year has something exciting to offer. Winter borders planted with colourful cornus and evergreen shrubs, underplanted here with snowdrops and hellebores. Gravel areas are carpeted with miniature cyclamen. It develops through the seasons culminating in early autumn with a spectacular show of sun-loving herbaceous plants. Plant sale of exotic and unusual plants. No refreshments but visitors are welcome to bring a picnic to enjoy in the garden. Regret, no dogs. Much of the garden can be accessed by wheelchair.
& ❁ 🪑))

5 BECK HOUSE
Water End, Wrestlingworth, Sandy, SG19 2HA. Donal & Victoria McKenna, 07803138390, tory.mckenna@btinternet.com. *Halfway between Cambridge & Bedford. From High St, Wrestlingworth turn into Water End (opp 8 and 10 High St). Garden at far end of Water End.* **Sat 2, Sun 3 Aug (2-5). Adm £8, chd free.** Home-made teas. Visits also by arrangement June to Sept for groups of 10 to 40.
A 2½ acre garden created over 40 years with various formal and informal areas divided by hedges and shrub borders. Features inc topiary yew avenue, circular dahlia garden with small pond, parterre with English roses, herbaceous borders, courtyard, herb and vegetable gardens, rose and clematis pergola walk. Woodland garden. Wheelchair accessible but there are some slopes to access upper part of garden.
& ❁ ☕))

6 BEDFORD HEIGHTS
Brickhill Drive, Bedford, MK41 7PH. *N Bedford. Plenty of free parking is available. Our visitors car park, also called car park 1, is at the front of the building. Additional car parking is available in car park 2.* **Fri 4 July (11-3). Adm £5. Light refreshments in Graze Café.**
Originally built by Texas Instruments, a Texan theme runs throughout the building and gardens. The entrance simulates an arroyo or dry riverbed, and is filled with succulents and cacti, plus a mixture of grasses and herbaceous plants, many of which are Texan natives. There are also three courtyard gardens, where less hardy plants thrive in the almost frost-free environment. No wheelchair access to two of the courtyards but can be viewed from a platform.
& ❁ 🚗 ☕))

7 NEW BROOKLANDS
Bottom Drive, Wellhead, Dunstable, LU6 2JS. Paul Randall. *½m W of Dunstable, very close to Dunstable Gliding Club. Main parking in the nearby field. Limited disabled & mobility parking in the driveway.* **Sun 27 July (11-5). Adm £6, chd free.** Light refreshments.
A ½ acre hardy exotic garden. Many mature palms, yuccas, *cycas*, bananas and bamboos. Around 3000 succulent plantings, all growing in ground- very few pots! 20 varieties of *Agave*, the largest is now over 5ft tall. 28 *Aeonium* cultivars. *Echeverias*, *Aloes*, *Crassula*, *Haworthia* and *Sedum*. Large *Sempervivum* collection. Feature koi pool and goldfish ponds. A chalk stream borders the end of the garden. A well-maintained winding brick path runs through almost all of the garden and allows good wheelchair access.
& ❁ ☕ 🪑))

Our donation to the Army Benevolent Fund supported 700 individuals with front line services and horticultural related grants in 2024.

BEDFORDSHIRE

8 CHURCH FARM
Church Road, Pulloxhill, Bedford, MK45 5HD. Sue & Keith Miles, 07941 593152. *7m from M1 J12. Parking by kind permission of The Cross Keys Pub, Pulloxhill High St, MK45 5HB (approx 500yds from garden). Yellow signs from the Cross Keys to Church Rd & past parish church.* **Sat 17, Sun 18 May (2-5). Adm £7, chd free. Visits also by arrangement June to Aug for groups of 10 to 20. Adult groups only. Adm inc refreshments.**
Mixed colourful formal planting to the rear of the house leading to a gravel yard with drought tolerant borders and large topiary subjects (topiary award winner). Beyond the farmyard is a wildlife pond, kitchen garden and wildflower orchard with a rose walk. Cut flower area and countryside views. Fairy glade across meadows. Livestock may be present in adjoining fields so regret no dogs. Winner of the Henchman Choice Award for outstanding topiary 2024.

9 15 DOUGLAS ROAD
Bedford, MK41 7YF. Peter & Penny Berrington. *B660 Kimbolton Rd, turn into Avon Dr, R into Tyne Cres, & Douglas Rd on R.* **Mon 25 Aug (2-5). Adm £5, chd free. Light refreshments.**
This medium sized town garden has a series of outdoor rooms, separated by hedges, fences and arches. There is seating for visitors to relax and enjoy the peace and seclusion. A circular cottage garden with a central decorative fire pit, separated by plum and apple trees from vegetables and herbs grown in raised beds. The pond is home to newts, snails and midwife toads. Wheelchair access to most parts of the garden.

10 22 ELMSDALE ROAD
Wootton, Bedford, MK43 9JN. Roy & Dianne Richards. *Follow signs to Wootton, turn R at The Cock Pub, follow to Elmsdale Rd.* **Sat 26, Sun 27 Apr (1-5). Adm £5, chd free. Home-made teas.**
Topiary garden greets visitors before they enter a genuine Japanese Feng Shui garden inc bonsai. Large collection of Japanese plants, Koi pond, lily pond and a Japanese Tea House. The garden was created from scratch by the owners about 20 years ago and has many interesting features inc Japanese lanterns and a Kneeling Archer terracotta soldier from China. Free-flying parrot.

11 HOLLINGTON FARM
Flitton Hill, Maulden, Bedford, MK45 2BE. Susan & John Rickatson. *Off A507 between Clophill & Ampthill- take Silsoe/Flitton then bear R & follow yellow signs.* **Sat 31 May, Sun 1 June (2-5.30). Adm £7, chd free. Cream Teas and cakes served 2pm - 4.30pm.**
Two acre country garden developed around an old farmhouse over a 30 year period. Trees and shrubs are now mature impressive specimens. Semi formal areas near the house inc a small parterre, pergola, pond and borders. In outer parts there is a small woodland planted in the 1990's and a farm wildflower meadow on Flitton Hill with views over the River Flit valley. Play areas for children. Wheelchair access, some steps and slopes.

12 HOWBURY HALL GARDEN
Howbury Hall Estate, Renhold, Bedford, MK41 0JB. Julian Polhill & Lucy Copeman, www.howburyfarmflowers.co.uk. *Leave A421 at A428/Gt Barford exit towards Bedford. Entrance to house & gardens ½m on R. Parking in field.* **Sun 7 Sept (2-5). Adm £6, chd free. Home-made teas.**
A late Victorian garden with mature trees, sweeping lawns and herbaceous borders. The large walled garden is a working garden, where one half is dedicated to growing a large variety of vegetables whilst the other is run as a cut flower business. Large collection dahlias in September. There are also several varieties of Bedfordshire heritage apple trees and an avenue of pears. Gravel paths and lawns may be difficult for smaller wheelchairs.

13 ♦ KING'S ARMS GARDEN
Brinsmade Road, Ampthill, Bedford, MK45 2PP. Ampthill Town Council, www.ampthill-tc.gov.uk/amenities/kings-arm-garden. *Free parking in Waitrose car park limited time. Entrance opp Market Square Cafe, down King's Arms Path, 2nd gate on the R.* **For NGS: Sun 16 Feb, Sun 26 Oct (2-4). Adm £5, chd free. Light refreshments. For other opening times and information, please visit garden website.**
Small woodland garden of about 1½ acres created by plantsman, the late William Nourish. Trees, shrubs, bulbs and many interesting collections throughout the year. Since 1987, the garden has been maintained by 'The Friends of the Garden' on behalf of Ampthill Town Council. Charming woodland garden with mass plantings of snowdrops and early spring bulbs. Beautiful autumn colours in October. Wheelchair friendly path running around most of the garden.

14 40 LEIGHTON STREET
Woburn, MK17 9PH. Rita Chidley. *500yds from centre of village L side of road. Limited on- road parking outside house.* **Sat 5 July (2-5). Adm £5, chd free. Home-made teas.**
Large cottage style garden with an abundance of perennials, roses, climbers, vegetables, trees and two ponds with fish. There are several 'rooms' with interesting features to explore and many quiet seating areas. Hanging baskets and a large selection of pots of unusual and tender plants.

GROUP OPENING

15 MILL LANE GARDENS
Mill Lane, Greenfield, Bedford, MK45 5DG. *In the centre of Greenfield off High St. From Flitwick, Mill Ln is on L in the centre of the village. Room for disabled parking only at each garden. On road parking, please park with consideration to our neighbours.* **Sat 14, Sun 15 June (1-5). Combined adm £8, chd free. Home-made teas at 69 Mill Lane.**

NEW   13 MILL LANE
Shirley Dickinson.

68 MILL LANE
Chris Boon.

69 MILL LANE
Pat Rishton.

70 MILL LANE
Lesley & Neil Arthur.

71 MILL LANE
Carol Mcclurg.

Greenfield is an attractive and varied Bedfordshire village close to Flitwick and Ampthill. There are houses of many different character inc several thatches and a recently refurbished village pub. Mill Lane was previously the centre of a fruit growing area and was famous for its strawberry fields. The five gardens are interesting and varied inc cottage garden style perennials, courtyards, fruit gardens and ponds, both ornamental and for wildlife. River Flit runs through two of the gardens where the river banks are maintained to nurture wildlife. Most of the gardens are accessible to wheelchairs but there are some steps, banks and gravel paths. Plenty of seating provided. 69 & 71 Mill Lane fully accessible. Regret, no dogs.

& ✿ ☕))

16 OLD CHURCH HOUSE
Grove, Leighton Buzzard, LU7 0QU. Rob King. *Off the B488 S of Leighton Buzzard. Take the turning signed Grove. Garden at end of a narrow single track lane. Caution as tight blind bend half way down.* **Sat 28, Sun 29 June (1-5). Adm £6, chd free. Tea, coffee & cake.**
This varied and colourful, sunny garden surrounds a pretty converted C13 church. There is a small wildflower meadow and wildlife pond, many generously sized herbaceous borders and island beds, filled with a wide variety of cottage garden plants. Beautiful views across open pasture. Plenty of places to sit and relax with home-made refreshments, then enjoy walk on the adjacent canal footpath. Garden accessed via gravel driveway.

& 🐕 ✿ ☕))

17 THE OLD RECTORY, WRESTLINGWORTH
Church Lane, Wrestlingworth, Sandy, SG19 2EU. Josephine Hoy. *Garden is at top of Church Ln, which is well signed, behind the church.* **Sat 10, Sun 11 May (2-5). Adm £8, chd free.**
A four acre garden full of colour and interest. The owner has a free style of gardening sensitive to wildlife. Beds overflowing with tulips, alliums, bearded iris, peonies, poppies, geraniums and much more. Beautiful mature trees and many more planted in the last 30 years inc a large selection of *Betulas*. Gravel gardens, box hedging and clipped balls, woodland garden and wildflower meadows. Wheelchair access may be restricted to grass paths.

& 🐕 ✿ 🪑))

18 12 QUEEN ELIZABETH CLOSE
Shefford, SG17 5LE. Kasey Brock. *Turn off Ivel Rd into Queen Elizabeth Rd and follow round to L.* **Sat 7, Sun 8 June (2-5). Adm £5, chd free.**
A small town garden with a jungle like feel. This garden is all about foliage, with the emphasis on leaf shapes and textures, some more unusual and quirky than others. The whole garden has been designed to make you feel like you've been transported to somewhere far more exotic.

))

GROUP OPENING

19 NEW ROXTON VILLAGE GARDENS
Roxton, Bedford, MK44 3ED. *S of St Neots. At the A1, Black Cat r'about follow road signs to Roxton. Follow signs for parking at the playing field.* **Sun 22 June (1-5). Combined adm £8, chd free. Home-made teas.**

NEW CHAPEL VIEW
Chris & Sharon Evans.

NEW 36 HIGH STREET
Mandy & Steve Andrew.

HILL FARM HOUSE
Anna and Julian Chillingworth.

NEW 34 PARK ROAD
Paul & Margaret Gale.

An opportunity to visit Roxton and see four very different gardens, one an old garden replanted and landscaped over the last eight years, another well established over many years with an orchid house, whilst two others offer a rural aspect and have been completely redesigned in the last few years. You will see across the gardens a wide range of ornamentals, specimen trees, shrubs and vegetables being grown. Fresh home-made teas are on offer and an opportunity to visit the unique thatched C18 Congregational Chapel.

☕))

32 BEDFORDSHIRE

20 1A ST AUGUSTINE'S ROAD
Bedford, MK40 2NB. **Chris Bamforth Damp**, 01234 353730, chrisdamp@mac.com. *St Augustine's Rd is on L off Kimbolton Rd as you leave the centre of Bedford.* **Visits by arrangement July to Sept. Adm £6, chd free. Home-made teas.**
A colourful town garden with herbaceous borders, climbers, a greenhouse and a pond. Planted in cottage garden style with traditional flowers, the borders overflow with late summer annuals and perennials inc salvias and rudbeckia. The pretty terrace next to the house is lined with ferns and hostas. The owners also make home-made chutneys and preserves which can be purchased on the day. The garden is wheelchair accessible.

21 SOUTHILL PARK
Southill, Biggleswade, SG18 9LL. **Mr & Mrs Charles Whitbread.** *On the outskirts of the village. 5m from the A1.* **Sun 1 June (2-5). Adm £6, chd free. Cream teas.**
Southill Park first opened its gates to National Garden Scheme visitors in 1927 as one of the inaugural NGS gardens. This is a large garden with mature trees and flowering shrubs, herbaceous borders, a formal rose garden, sunken garden, ponds and kitchen garden. It is on the south side of the 1795 Palladian house. The parkland

was designed by Lancelot 'Capability' Brown. A large conservatory houses the tropical collection.

GROUP OPENING

22 STEPPINGLEY VILLAGE GARDENS
Steppingley, Bedford, MK45 5AT. *Follow signs to Steppingley, pick up yellow signs from village centre.* **Sun 20, Mon 21 Apr (2-5). Combined adm £8, chd free. Sun 25, Mon 26 May (12-5). Combined adm £10, chd free. Home-made teas at Townsend Farmhouse. Hot Dogs at Village Hall on 25th & 26th May. Easter Egg Hunt for Children on 20th & 21st April.**

21 CHURCH END
Christine and Steve Ovenden.
Open on all dates

THE CROFT
Stephen Cook.
Open on Sun 25, Mon 26 May

MIDDLE BARN
John & Sally Eilbeck.
Open on all dates

1 PARK FARM COTTAGE
Tim & Tally Clift.
Open on Sun 25, Mon 26 May

37 RECTORY ROAD
Bill & Julie Neilson.
Open on Sun 25, Mon 26 May

TOP BARN
Tim & Nicky Kemp.
Open on all dates

TOWNSEND FARMHOUSE
Hugh & Indi Jackson.
Open on all dates
(See separate entry)

Steppingley is a picturesque Bedfordshire village on the Greensand Ridge, close to Ampthill, Flitwick and Woburn. Although a few older buildings survive, most of Steppingley was built by the 7th Duke of Bedford between 1840 and 1872. Seven gardens in the village offer an interesting mix of planting styles and design to inc pretty courtyards, cottage garden style perennial borders, three large wildlife ponds and several small ponds, a Victorian well, a shell grotto, glasshouses, vegetable gardens and country views. Livestock inc chickens, ducks and fish.

23 TOWNSEND FARMHOUSE
Rectory Road, Steppingley, Bedford, MK45 5AT. **Hugh & Indi Jackson.** *Follow directions to Steppingley village and pick up yellow signs from village centre.* **Sun 23 Feb (2-4). Adm £6, chd free. Home-made teas. Evening opening Sat 25 Oct (5.30-8.30). Adm £10, chd free. Home-made cakes and savouries. Opening with Steppingley Village Gardens on Sun 20, Mon 21 Apr, Sun 25, Mon 26 May.**
Country garden with tree lined driveway. Large selection of spring bulbs, colourful perennials, roses and flowering shrubs. Pretty cobbled courtyard with a glasshouse housing large selection of house plants. A Victorian well 30 metres deep, viewed through a glass top. Large wildlife pond and a shell grotto. A spectacular evening of lanterns, diya lamps and flower rangoli in late October.

GROUP OPENING

24 TURVEY VILLAGE GARDENS
High Street, Turvey, Bedford, MK43 8EP. *Follow arrow signs from village centre. Parking in field behind Chantry House.* **Sun 15 June (1.30-5). Combined adm £9, chd free. Home-made teas in medieval church of All Saints.**

1c Bakers Lane

BEDFORDSHIRE

CHANTRY HOUSE
Sheila & Anthony Ormerod.
GABLE END
Chris & Wendy Knell.
7 THE GREEN
Paul & Rosemary Gentry.
NEW MILL LODGE
Jane & Tim Brewster.
PEPPERS
Liz & Mark Upex.

The historic village of Turvey lies beside the River Great Ouse and is recorded in Domesday Book of 1086 as a parish in the Hundred of Willey. Five gardens in the village offer a varied mix of design and interest. Chantry House is a 1½ acre garden, approached by a drive bounded by mature yew and box cloud hedges where the medieval church of All Saints overlooks the garden at this point. A south facing lawn is flanked by high rose covered walls and interspersed by herbaceous beds. 7 The Green has a wide terrace with comfortable seating and a myriad of planted pots overlooks a central lawn and flowerbeds. Gable End has four distinct areas with a range of planting inc fruit and vegetables. Peppers is a small, informal village garden with mixed planting aimed at attracting wildlife and achieving year-round interest. At Mill Lodge there are informal, cottage garden-style borders packed with flowers, herbs and foliage plants, many pots and containers, and several fruit trees. Wheelchair access via gravel paths and few shallow distanced steps.
♿ ❀ ☕ 🔊

25 NEW 29 TYBURN LANE
Pulloxhill, Bedford, MK45 5HG.
Mr Mark Bamber. *Drive to the High St in the village of Pulloxhill. Parking is available in the field beyond the Crosskeys Pub. The garden is less than 5 mins on foot from the pub, in Tyburn Ln, off Church Rd.* **Sun 31 Aug (2-5). Adm £5, chd free.**
A large and young garden with views of the countryside beyond. It is composed of component garden zones, hosting a mix of diverse fruit and ornamental trees. There are perennial beds, dahlia beds, roses, a kitchen garden, and a 365ft long and narrow border. Two ponds interlinked by a dry river with water sprinklers, create a pleasing ambience in the garden. Two parking spaces on front drive for blue badge holders.
♿ 🐕 🔊

26 ♦ THE WALLED GARDEN
Luton, LU1 4LF. Luton Hoo Estate, 01582 721443, office@lutonhooestate.co.uk, www.lutonhooestate.co.uk. *Just outside Harpenden. From A1081 turn into West Hyde Rd. After 100 metres turn L through black gates, follow signs to Walled Garden.* **For NGS: Fri 1 Aug (11-3). Adm £7, chd free. For other opening times and information, please phone, email or visit garden website.**
The five acre Luton Hoo Estate Walled Garden was designed by Capability Brown and established by noted botanist and former Prime Minister, Lord Bute, in the late 1760s. The Walled Garden is now the focus of an incredible volunteer project and continues to be researched, restored, repaired and re-imagined for the enjoyment of all. Unique service buildings inc a vinery, fernery and propagation houses. Exhibition of Victorian tools. Uneven surfaces reflect the age and history of the site.
♿ 🐕 ❀ 🚗 ☕ 🔊

27 NEW WILLOW COTTAGE
Lombard Street, Lidlington, MK43 0RP. Erika Maass, 07957 684968, erikamaass99@googlemail.com.
2m from Ampthill, Flitwick and Marston. Follow sign for Lidlington from A507, continue straight. Turn L after the church and follow road to row of 4 cottages. **Visits by arrangement 16 June to 27 July for groups of 8 to 10. Adm £5, chd free. Tea, coffee & cake.**
Willow Cottage was originally part of the Duke of Bedford estate, known for their generously sized gardens enabling tenants to grow additional food. Over the years the garden has changed into a cottage style garden with a mixture of shrubs, perennials, raised beds and a rose garden.
☕ 🔊

GROUP OPENING

28 NEW WITTS END GARDENS
Witts End, Eversholt, Milton Keynes, MK17 9DZ. *Follow signs from Eversholt Rd and village centre. Parking at Willow Lodge.* **Sat 12, Sun 13 July (2-5). Combined adm £6, chd free. Home-made teas at Willow Lodge.**

WILLOW LODGE
Catherine Doherty.

NEW WITTS END CLOSE
Anna Blomfield.

The village of Eversholt is situated in rural Mid-Bedfordshire in an area of land that was in the old kingdom of Mercia. The village was named after the wild boar which used to live in this part of the country and indeed the boar's head is still used as the emblem of the village. Two village gardens open as a group, offering a mix of style and design. Witts End Close is set around a historic dwelling from the 1600's and is a cottage garden with views of the surrounding fields. Willow Lodge is a collaborative vegetable garden, tended by four local people, each sharing in the toil and the spoils of the produce. Established 10 years ago, it is largely organic with a no dig approach.
❀ ☕ 🔊

29 ♦ WREST PARK
Silsoe, Bedford, MK45 4HR.
English Heritage. *¾ m E of Silsoe off A6. 10m S of Bedford.* **For NGS: Evening opening Thur 14 Aug (5.30-7.30). Adm £20, chd free. Pre-booking essential, please email fundraising@english-heritage.org.uk or visit www.english-heritage.org.uk/visit/places/wrest-park/events for information & booking. Light refreshments. For other opening times and information, please email or visit garden website.**
With an exclusive tour with our Head Gardener and expert gardens team, explore diverse gardens showcasing French, Dutch, Italian and English styles side by side, inc formal parterres, a kitchen garden, and a lush rose garden. Fancy French curves and bold Italian geometry provide an opportunity for contrast through Wrest Park's dynamic bedding displays, surrounded by beautiful park and woodland.
☕

In 2024, our donations to Carers Trust meant that 26,081 unpaid carers were supported across the UK.

BERKSHIRE

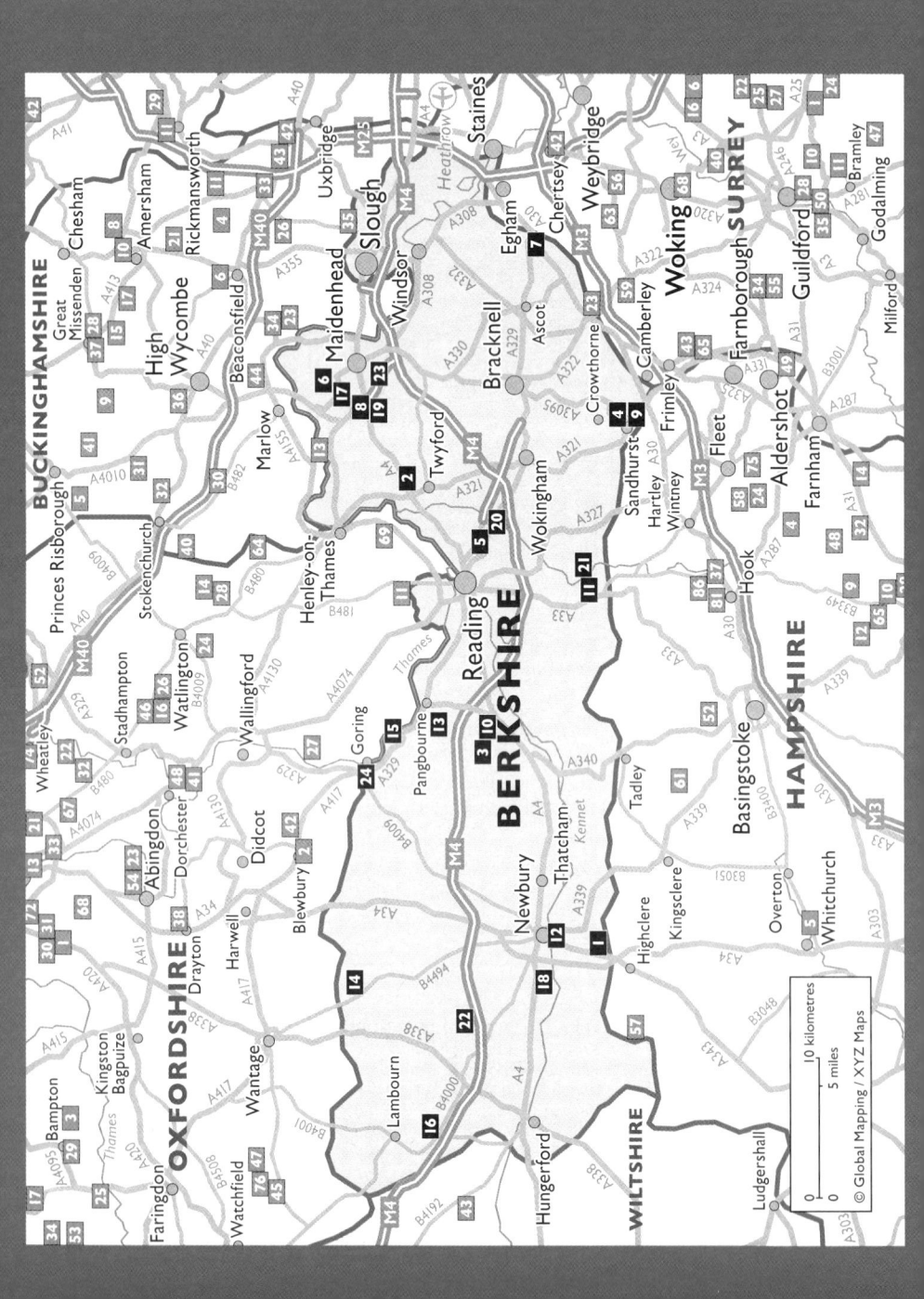

VOLUNTEERS

County Organiser
Heather Skinner
01189 737197
heather.skinner@ngs.org.uk

County Treasurer
Carolyn Clark
07701 016961
carolyn.clark@ngs.org.uk

Booklet Co-ordinator
Heather Skinner
(as above)

Assistant County Organisers
Claire Fletcher
claire.fletcher@ngs.org.uk

Carolyn Foster
07768 566482
candrfoster@btinternet.com

Rebecca Thomas
01491 628302
rebecca.thomas@ngs.org.uk

Bob Weston
01635 550240
bob.weston@ngs.org.uk

@BerksNationalGardenScheme
@BerksNGS
@nationalgardenschemeberkshire

OPENING DATES

All entries subject to change.
For latest information check
www.ngs.org.uk

Map locator numbers are shown to the right of each garden name.

January

Tuesday 14th
St Timothee — 17

Thursday 16th
St Timothee — 17

February
Snowdrop Openings

Wednesday 5th
◆ Welford Park — 22

March

Saturday 15th
Stubbings House — 19

Sunday 16th
Stubbings House — 19

April

Tuesday 1st
St Timothee — 17

Thursday 3rd
St Timothee — 17

Sunday 13th
Deepwood Stud Farm — 8
The Old Rectory, Farnborough — 14

Wednesday 30th
Rooksnest — 16

May

Saturday 10th
Stubbings House — 19

Sunday 11th
Stubbings House — 19

Saturday 17th
Wynders — 24

Sunday 18th
6 Beverley Gardens — 2
The Old Rectory, Farnborough — 14
Stockcross House — 18
Wynders — 24

June

Sunday 1st
NEW Bradfield College — 3

Wednesday 4th
61 Sutcliffe Avenue — 20

Thursday 5th
61 Sutcliffe Avenue — 20

Sunday 8th
13 Broom Acres — 4
Dorset Cottage — 9
St Timothee — 17

Thursday 12th
St Timothee — 17

Sunday 15th
6 Beverley Gardens — 2

Wednesday 25th
The Old Rectory, Farnborough — 14
Rooksnest — 16

Sunday 29th
13 Broom Acres — 4
Dorset Cottage — 9
Swallowfield Village Gardens — 21

July

Sunday 6th
6 Beverley Gardens — 2
Island Cottage — 12

Friday 18th
Wembury — 23

Tuesday 29th
Wembury — 23

Wednesday 30th
The Old Rectory, Farnborough — 14

August

Sunday 3rd
The Old Rectory, Lower Basildon — 15

Thursday 14th
NEW Coworth Park — 7

Friday 15th
Wembury — 23

Sunday 17th
Belvedere 1
13 Broom Acres 4
Stockcross House 18

September
Sunday 7th
13 Broom Acres 4
Deepwood Stud Farm 8
Dorset Cottage 9

November
Tuesday 4th
St Timothee 17
Thursday 6th
St Timothee 17

February 2026
Wednesday 4th
◆ Welford Park 22

By Arrangement
Arrange a personalised garden visit with your club, or group of friends, on a date to suit you. See individual garden entries for full details.

Belvedere 1
13 Broom Acres 4
68 Church Road 5
Compton Elms 6
Deepwood Stud Farm 8
Dorset Cottage 9
Handpost 11
Island Cottage 12
Lower Bowden Manor 13
Rooksnest 16
Stockcross House 18
Wembury 23

In 2024 we awarded £232,000 in Community Garden Grants, supporting 89 community garden projects.

Coworth Park

THE GARDENS

1 BELVEDERE
Garden Close Lane, Newbury, RG14 6PP. Noushin Garrett, 07500 925270, noushin.garrett@gmail.com. *7m S of M4 J13. Take A34 exit Highclere/Wash Common, then A343 towards Newbury. Sorry, due to narrow lane no parking at garden. Parking at St George's Church, Wash Common RG14 6NU with 600 metres walk to garden.* **Sun 17 Aug (1-4.30). Adm £5, chd free.** Visits also by arrangement 2 Aug to 1 Oct for groups of 20+.
A garden of 2½ acres consisting of herbaceous borders, rose garden, fruit trees with woodland, bamboo and rhododendron walks. A formal parterre garden with dahlias.
✿))

2 6 BEVERLEY GARDENS
Wargrave, Reading, RG10 8ED. Patricia Vella & Jon Black. *A4 from Maidenhead take B477 to Wargrave, turn R into Silverdale Rd. A4 from Reading take A321 into Wargrave, turn R at lights, ¼ m turn L into Silverdale Rd, Beverley Gardens is on R.* **Sun 18 May, Sun 15 June, Sun 6 July (1-5). Adm £4, chd free. Tea, coffee & cake.**
The main garden has primarily exotic and Mediterranean planting with small paths through some of the beds, inviting you to take a closer look. This leads into a kitchen garden with greenhouse, chickens and ducks. There is a small woodland garden with stumpery and fire pit. The garden has plenty of places to sit and relax. Wheelchair access over gravel drive leading to a level garden with some bark paths. No access through main beds.
♿ ✿ ☕))

3 NEW BRADFIELD COLLEGE
Bradfield, Reading, RG7 6AU. www.bradfieldcollege.org.uk. *From M4 J12 take A4 W towards Theale. At 2nd r'about turn R on A340 N towards Pangbourne, then 1st L signed Bradfield. Continue straight for 2m.* **Sun 1 June (1-4). Adm £5, chd free. Light refreshments in Stunt Pavilion.**
To celebrate our 175th Anniversary, Bradfield College is proud to open its gardens for the NGS. Set in the Pang Valley, the beautifully tended grounds are surrounded by brick and flint buildings dating from 1850. Features inc Quad and Sunken Gardens, and a rare chance to view inside the College's Greek Theatre and St Andrew's Church, now converted into a stunning Study Centre.
☕))

4 13 BROOM ACRES
Sandhurst, GU47 8PN. Sunil Patel, 07974 403077, garden@sunilpatel.co.uk, www.sunilpatel.co.uk. *Between Crowthorne & Sandhurst. From Crowthorne/Sandhurst road turn E into Greenways, then 1st R into Broom Acres. Street parking.* **Sun 8 June (1-5). Combined adm with Dorset Cottage £7, chd free. Home-made teas. Sun 29 June (1-5). Combined adm with Dorset Cottage £7, chd free. Sun 17 Aug (1-5). Adm £5, chd free. Sun 7 Sept (1-5). Combined adm with Dorset Cottage £7, chd free. Home-made teas on all dates but served at Dorset Cottage on 29 June & 7 Sept.** Visits also by arrangement 15 June to 15 Sept for groups of 20 to 40.
A spellbinding ¼ acre, suburban, romantic style garden with shrubbery, exotics, specimen trees, scented climbers and mixed herbaceous borders. Densely planted and decadently flowering, a feast for all the senses. Come for the garden, stay for the magic and discover why romance remains compelling, timeless and enduring.
☕))

5 68 CHURCH ROAD
Earley, Reading, RG6 1HU. Pat Burton, 07809 613850, patsi777@virginmedia.com. *E of Reading. Off A4 at Shepherd's House Hill, turn into Pitts Ln, into Church Rd, across r'about, 4th property on L.* **Visits by arrangement July & Aug for groups of 5 to 25. Tea, coffee & cake.**
A fascinating urban garden with changing elements throughout the seasons. Different areas showcase a variety of interesting plants, pergola, outdoor dining room and summerhouse. The working greenhouse is home to alpines grown year-round. Tiered areas of hostas and an abundance of summer bedding along with specimen container plants.
🐕 ☕

6 COMPTON ELMS
Marlow Road, Pinkneys Green, Maidenhead, SL6 6NR. Alison Kellett, kellettaj@gmail.com. *Situated at end of gravel road located opp & in between Berkshire Aesthetics & The Golden Ball Pub & Kitchen on the A308.* **Visits by arrangement 26 Mar to 9 Apr for groups of 15 to 35. Adm £12, chd free. Light refreshments inc.**
A delightful spring garden set in a sunken woodland, lovingly recovered from clay pit workings. The atmospheric garden is filled with snowdrops, primroses, hellebores and fritillaria, interspersed with anemone and narcissi under a canopy of ash and beech.
🐕 ☕

7 NEW COWORTH PARK
London Road, Ascot, SL5 7SE. www.dorchestercollection.com/ascot/coworth-park. *3m E of Ascot. Hotel is accessed from London Rd. Visitors are invited to arrive from 12pm & 2.30pm as the garden tours will start promptly at 12.30pm & 3pm.* **Thur 14 Aug (12.30-5). Adm £25. Pre-booking essential, please visit www.ngs.org.uk for information & booking. Two hour timed slots at 12.30pm & 3pm. Cream tea inc with the tour.**
A rare opportunity to enjoy a guided tour with the Head Gardener at Coworth Park, followed by a cream tea in the Drawing Room. Set amongst 240 acres of gardens, parkland, paddocks and woodland. Highlights inc the beautiful terrace and rose gardens bordered by lavender, a sunken garden, weeping lime trees, and a stunning 10 acre wildflower meadow. Please email hello@ngs.org.uk in advance of any dietary or allergy requirements.
🛏 ☕

In 2024, we celebrated 40 years of continuous funding for Macmillan Cancer Support equating to more than £19.5 million.

Bradfield College

☐ DEEPWOOD STUD FARM
Henley Road, Stubbings, nr Maidenhead, SL6 6QW. Mr & Mrs E Goodwin, 07878 911064, ed.goodwin@deepwood.co. *2m W of Maidenhead. M4 J8/9 take A404M N. 2nd exit for A4 to Maidenhead. L at 1st r'about on A4130 Henley, approx 1m on R.* **Sun 13 Apr, Sun 7 Sept (2-5). Adm £6, chd free. Tea, coffee & cake.** Visits also by arrangement 31 Mar to 21 Sept for groups of 12 to 30.
4 acres of formal and informal gardens within a 25 acre stud farm. A formal rose garden with fountain, a walled herbaceous border with windows through which to admire the views and horses, two rock gardens, and hot plant terrace. Small lake with Monet style bridge and pergola. Several neo-classical follies and statues. A planted woodland area with a winding path. Partial wheelchair access.
&♿ ☕))

☐ DORSET COTTAGE
22 Albion Road, Sandhurst, GU47 9BP. Sarah & Paul Merrill, 01252 873530, sarah.merrill@yahoo.co.uk. *Albion Rd is N off Yorktown Rd in Sandhurst. Turning is opp Boots chemist. Street parking on Albion Rd or Wellington Rd.* **Sun 8, Sun 29 June, Sun 7 Sept (1-5). Combined adm with 13 Broom Acres £7, chd free. Home-made teas on all dates but at 13 Broom Acres on 8 June.** Visits also by arrangement 3 June to 25 July for groups of 12 to 25.
Discover this attractive suburban secret garden behind a pretty red brick cottage. Inviting paths weave around a curving island bed surrounded by long borders packed with interesting plants reflecting the passion of its owner. Features inc rose and clematis covered arches, pots with gunnera, figs, hostas and ferns. Towering palms, acers and magnolia trees offer shelter and seclusion. Wheelchair access to most of the garden via a grass path.
&♿ ☕))

☐ ♦ ENGLEFIELD HOUSE GARDEN
Englefield, Theale, Reading, RG7 5EN. Lord & Lady Benyon, 01189 302504, peter.carson@englefield.co.uk, www.englefieldestate.co.uk. *6m W of Reading. M4 J12. Take A4 towards Newbury. 2nd r'about take A340 to Pangbourne. After ⅙m entrance on the L.* **For opening times and information, please phone, email or visit garden website.**
The 12 acre garden descends dramatically from the hill above the historic house through woodland where mature native trees mix with rhododendrons and camellias. Drifts of spring and summer planting are followed by striking autumn colour.

BERKSHIRE

Stone balustrades enclose the lower terrace with lawns, roses and mixed borders. A stream meanders through the woodland. Open every Monday from Apr-Sept (10am-6pm) and Oct-Mar (10am-4pm). Please check the Englefield Estate website for any changes before travelling. Wheelchair access to some parts of the garden.

11 HANDPOST
Basingstoke Road, Swallowfield, Reading, RG7 1PU. Faith Ramsay, 07801 239937, faith@mycountrygarden.co.uk, www.mycountrygarden.co.uk. *From M4 J11, take A33 S. At 1st T-lights turn L on B3349 Basingstoke Rd. Follow road for 2¾m, garden on L, opp Barge Ln. Car sharing preferred. Parking on-site limited for up to 15 cars.* **Visits by arrangement 14 May to 22 Aug for groups of 10 to 40. Adm £12, chd free. Tea or coffee & home-made cake inc. Donation to Thrive.** 4 acre designer's garden with many areas of interest. Features inc four lovely long herbaceous borders attractively and densely planted in different colour sections, a formal rose garden, a cutting garden, an old orchard with a grass meadow, pretty pond and peaceful wooded area. Large variety of plants, trees and a productive fruit and vegetable patch. Regret, no dogs allowed. Largely wheelchair accessible with some gravel areas.

12 ISLAND COTTAGE
West Mills, Newbury, RG14 5HT. Karen Swaffield, karen@lockisland.com. *7m from M4 J13. Park in town centre car parks. Walk past St Nicholas Church or between Côte Restaurant & Holland & Barrett to canal. 200yds to swing bridge & follow signs. Limited side road parking.* **Sun 6 July (2-5). Adm £4, chd free. Home-made teas. Visits also by arrangement 1 June to 29 Sept for groups of 6 to 25.**
A pretty, small waterside garden set between the River Kennet and the Kennet and Avon Canal. Interesting combinations of colour and texture to look rather than walk through, although visitors are welcome to do that too. A deck overlooks a sluiceway towards a lawn and border. Started from scratch in 2005 and mostly again after the floods of 2014. Trying high planters this yr. Home-made teas unless very wet weather. Cream teas and carrot cake a speciality!

13 LOWER BOWDEN MANOR
Bowden Green, Pangbourne, RG8 8JL. Juliette & Robert Cox-Nicol, 07552 217872, robert.cox-nicol@orange.fr. *1½m W of Pangbourne. Directions provided on booking.* **Visits by arrangement 13 Jan to 5 Dec for groups of 6 to 50. Adm £10, chd free. Tea with cake by prior request.**
A 7 acre designer's garden with stunning views and where structure predominates. Specimen trees show contrasting bark and foliage. A marble 'Pan' plays to a pond with boulders and boulder shaped evergreens. Versailles planters with standard topiaries line a rill. A stumpery leads to the orchard's carpet of daffodils and later a wave of white hydrangeas. Steps and gravel, but most areas accessible. Dogs welcome on leads.

14 THE OLD RECTORY, FARNBOROUGH
Wantage, OX12 8NX. Mrs Michael Todhunter. *4m SE of Wantage. Take B4494 from Wantage, after 4m turn L at sign for Farnborough. Follow NGS signs.* **Sun 13 Apr, Sun 18 May, Wed 25 June, Wed 30 July (2-5). Adm £7, chd free. Home-made teas. Donation to Farnborough PCC.**
8 acre garden with a series of immaculately tended garden rooms. Herbaceous borders, arboretum, secret garden, roses, vegetables, pool, bog gardens and woodland, with an explosion of rare and interesting plants, beautifully combined for colour and texture. Stunning views and once home to John Betjeman (memorial window by John Piper in church). Specialist plants and home-made preserves for sale. Wheelchair access over gravel paths.

15 THE OLD RECTORY, LOWER BASILDON
Church Lane, Lower Basildon, Reading, RG8 9NH. Charlie & Alison Laing. *2m NW of Pangbourne on A329. Into Lower Basildon, 200yds past petrol station, turn R down lane to church & follow signs to parking.* **Sun 3 Aug (2-5). Adm £5, chd free. Home-made teas at adjacent St Bartholomew's Church.**
A 2 acre garden based around mature trees (notably cedar, magnolia and mulberry) with a pond and crinkle crankle wall. Plantings inc fruit trees, white border, rose and peony beds, herbaceous long border and substantial kitchen garden. In AONB the garden also benefits from proximity to listed church (site of memorial to Jethro Tull) and Thames river walks. Wheelchair access over level site, but grass is uneven and some gravel paths.

16 ROOKSNEST
Ermin Street, Lambourn Woodlands, RG17 7SB. Rooksnest Estate, 07787 085565, gardens@rooksnest.net. *2m S of Lambourn on B4000. From M4 J14, take A338 Wantage Rd, turn 1st L onto B4000 (Ermin St). Rooksnest signed after 3m.* **Wed 30 Apr, Wed 25 June (11-3.30). Adm £6, chd free. Light refreshments. Visits also by arrangement 1 Apr to 26 June for groups of 15 to 50. Advance payment may be required for group visits.**
Approx 10 acre, exceptionally fine traditional English garden. Rose garden, herbaceous garden, pond garden, herb garden, fruit, vegetable and cutting garden and glasshouses. Many specimen trees and fine shrubs, orchard and terraces. Garden designed by Arabella Lennox-Boyd. Limited WC facilities. Most areas have step free wheelchair access, although surfaces consist of gravel and mowed grass.

Our donation to Marie Curie this year equates to 17,496 hours of nursing care or 43 days of care in one of their nine hospices.

40 BERKSHIRE

17 ST TIMOTHEE
Darlings Lane, Pinkneys Green, Maidenhead, SL6 6PA. Sarah & Sal Pajwani, www.instagram.com/sarahpajwani. *1m N of Maidenhead. M4 J8/9 to A404M, 3rd exit onto A4 to Maidenhead. L at 1st r'about to A4130 Henley Rd. After ½ m turn R onto Pinkneys Dr. At Pinkneys Arms pub turn L into Lee Ln. Follow NGS signs.* **Sun 8 June (11-4). Adm £7, chd free. Home-made teas. Talk & Walk events inc home-made teas, start promptly at 10.30am on Tue 14, Thur 16 Jan, Tue 1, Thur 3 Apr, Thur 12 June, Tue 4, Thur 6 Nov (10.30-12.30). Adm £20. Pre-booking essential, please visit www.ngs. org.uk for information & booking.**
A 2 acre country garden planted for year-round interest with a variety of different colour themed borders each featuring a wide range of hardy perennials, bulbs, shrubs and ornamental grasses. Also inc a box parterre, wildlife pond, rose terrace, areas of long grass and beautiful mature trees, all set against the backdrop of a 1930s house. This year there will be one open day (8 June) and a series of Talk & Walk events on a variety of topics; The Winter Garden (14 Jan), Creating a Garden for All Seasons (16 Jan, 3 Apr, 12 Jun & 6 Nov), The Joy of Spring Bulbs (1 Apr), Grasses and the Autumn Garden (4 Nov). Events start promptly with an illustrated slideshow talk and home-made teas followed by time to explore the garden.

♿ ✿ 🚌 ☕ 🔊))

18 STOCKCROSS HOUSE
Church Road, Stockcross, Newbury, RG20 8LP. Susan & Edward Vandyk, 01488 608810, Info@stockcrosshousegarden.co.uk, www.stockcrosshousegarden. co.uk. *3m W of Newbury. M4 J13, A34(S). After 3m exit A4(W) to Hungerford. At 2nd r'about take B4000, 1m to Stockcross, 2nd L into Church Rd. Coach parking available.* **Sun 18 May, Sun 17 Aug (11-5). Adm £6, chd free. Home-made teas & gluten free option. Visits also by arrangement 23 Apr to 3 Sept for groups of 20 to 40. Wednesdays only.**
Romantic 2 acre garden set around a listed former Victorian rectory, created over the last 31 yrs. Features deep mixed borders with succession planting and emphasis on both height and strong complementary colour combinations. A wisteria clad pergola, an orangery, a folly with a reflecting pond, a croquet lawn and pavilion, naturalistic planting and a pond on the lower level, a small stumpery, and a kitchen garden. Plants from garden for sale. Partial wheelchair access with some gravelled areas.

♿ ✿ 🚌 ☕ 🔊))

19 STUBBINGS HOUSE
Stubbings Lane, Henley Road, Maidenhead, SL6 6QL. Mr & Mrs D Good, www.stubbingsnursery.co.uk. *Located on the outskirts of Maidenhead, just mins from the M4 J8/9 & M40 J4. From A404(M) W of Maidenhead, exit at A4 r'about & follow signs to Maidenhead. At the small r'about turn L towards Stubbings. Take the next L onto Stubbings Ln.* **Sat 15, Sun 16 Mar, Sat 10, Sun 11 May (10-4). Adm £5, chd free. Light refreshments (additional charges apply).**
Parkland garden accessed via adjacent retail plant centre. Set around C18 Grade II listed house (not open), home to Queen Wilhelmina of Netherlands in WW2. Large lawn with ha-ha and woodland walks. Notable trees inc historic cedars and araucaria. March brings an abundance of daffodils and in May a 60 metre wall of wisteria. Attractions inc a C18 icehouse and access to adjacent NT woodland. On site café offering breakfast, snacks, cream teas and seasonal lunches. Wheelchair access to a level site with firm gravel paths.

♿ 🐕 ✿ ☕

20 61 SUTCLIFFE AVENUE
Earley, Reading, RG6 7JN. Sue & Dave Wilder. *3m SE of Reading. Road: On Wokingham Rd (A329) from E, pass Showcase Cinema, then L at Nisa (Meadow Rd), then R into Sutcliffe Ave; from W, turn R at Nisa. Train: Earley stn, then 10 min walk.* **Wed 4, Thur 5 June (10.30-5). Adm £3.50, chd free. Tea, coffee & cake.**
A characterful urban wildlife friendly garden imaginatively rewilded. The garden offers the relaxing sense of a walk in the countryside. An inviting path winds past wildflower islands, through a rose covered arch, to a pollinators paradise garden and small pond. Tree trunks creatively recycled and a chicken run are added features. Wheelchair access to the bottom of garden.

♿ ☕

GROUP OPENING

21 SWALLOWFIELD VILLAGE GARDENS
The Street, Swallowfield, RG7 1QY. *5m S of Reading. From the M4 J11 take the A33 S. At the 1st T-lights turn L on B3349 signed Swallowfield. As you enter village follow signs for parking & directions to buy tickets & maps.* **Sun 29 June (2-5.30). Combined adm £9, chd free. Home-made teas at Brambles.**

5 BEEHIVE COTTAGE
Ray Tormey.

BRAMBLES
Sarah & Martyn Dadds.

BRIERLEY HOUSE
Jean & Terry Trinder.

BROOKSIDE COTTAGE
Jackie & Graham King.

5 CURLYS WAY
Carolyn & Gary Clark.

9 FOXBOROUGH
Jeremy Bayliss.

HOLLYTREE COTTAGE
Sue & Roger Henderson.

LAMBS FARMHOUSE
Eva Koskuba.

NORKETT COTTAGE
Jenny Spencer.

PRIMROSE COTTAGE
Patricia Armitage.

SWALLOWFIELD ALLOTMENTS
SPAA - Swallowfield Parish Allotment Association.

SWALLOWFIELD COTTAGE
Toni & Brian Carter.

WESSEX HOUSE
Val Payne.

Swallowfield is offering 12 gardens plus allotments (30 plots) to visit with 8 gardens in the village itself and 4 gardens and the allotments just outside. The 8 village gardens can be reached on foot from the village parking with the 4 gardens and allotments outside the village requiring a car or bicycle. Each garden is different and provides its own character and interest. Swallowfield nestles in the countryside by the Blackwater and Loddon rivers with an abundance of wildlife and lovely views. See website for info about individual gardens. Plants for sale. Wheelchair access to many gardens, however some have gravel drives, slopes and uneven ground.

♿ ✿ ☕ 🔊))

BERKSHIRE

22 ◆ WELFORD PARK
Welford, Newbury, RG20 8HU.
Mrs J H Puxley, 01488 608691,
contact@welfordpark.co.uk,
www.welfordpark.co.uk. *6m NW of Newbury. M4 J13, A34(S). After 3m exit for A4(W) to Hungerford. At 2nd r'about take B4000, after 4m turn R signed Welford. Car park entrance on Newbury-Lambourn road.* **For NGS: Wed 5 Feb (11-5). Adm £11, chd £4. Soup & hot lunches available, with home-made cakes, hot & cold drinks in large tent. For 2026: Wed 4 Feb. For other opening times and information, please phone, email or visit garden website.**
One of the finest natural snowdrop woodlands in the country and a wonderful display of hellebores, galanthus cultivars, and winter flowering shrubs throughout the extensive gardens. This is a NGS 1927 pioneer garden on the River Lambourn set around Queen Anne House (not open). Also, the stunning setting for Great British Bake Off. WC facilities. Child friendly, and dogs welcome on leads. Coach parties please book in advance. A wheelchair friendly route has been made, please follow the signs and avoid damp areas near the river, deep wood chip paths and bridges.
& 🐐 ❋ 🚗 🛏 ☕))

23 WEMBURY
Altwood Close, Maidenhead, SL6 4PP. Carolyn Foster, 07768 566482, candrfoster@btinternet.com. *W side of Maidenhead, S of A4. M4 J8/9, then A404M J9B, 3rd exit to A4 to Maidenhead, R at 1st r'about, 2nd L onto Altwood Rd, then 5th R, follow NGS signs.* **Fri 18, Tue 29 July, Fri 15 Aug (10.30-4). Adm £4.50, chd free. Pre-booking essential, please visit www.ngs.org.uk for information & booking. Home-made teas. Two hour timed slots at 10.30am & 2pm. Visits also by arrangement July & Aug for groups of 10 to 20.**
A wildlife friendly, plant lover's cottage garden with borders generously planted with bulbs, perennials, grasses and shrubs for successional interest for every season. Productive vegetable garden and greenhouses. Many pots and baskets with seasonal annuals and tender perennials, especially salvias.
& ❋ ☕))

24 WYNDERS
Rectory Road, Streatley, Reading, RG8 9QA. Marcus & Emma Francis, www.instagram.com/marcusfrancis21. *From Streatley, N on A329 Wallingford Rd. Fork L onto A417 Wantage Rd, then fork L again along Rectory Rd. After golf course, downhill & parking will be signed. Wynders is on L after stables.* **Sat 17, Sun 18 May (10-4). Adm £4, chd free. Tea, coffee & cake.**
Densely planted ¾ acre garden surrounded by stunning countryside. Over 60 roses, 150ft long border, formal garden, gravel garden, cutting beds, and entertainment for children. Free roaming wildfowl and waterfowl. Classic and modern sports cars on display. Something for everyone. Partial wheelchair access over gravel drive, please call in advance for reserved disabled parking.
& 🐐 ❋ 🚗 ☕))

In 2024, National Garden Scheme funding for Perennial supported 1,367 people working in horticulture.

Swallowfield Allotments, Swallowfield Village Gardens

BUCKINGHAMSHIRE

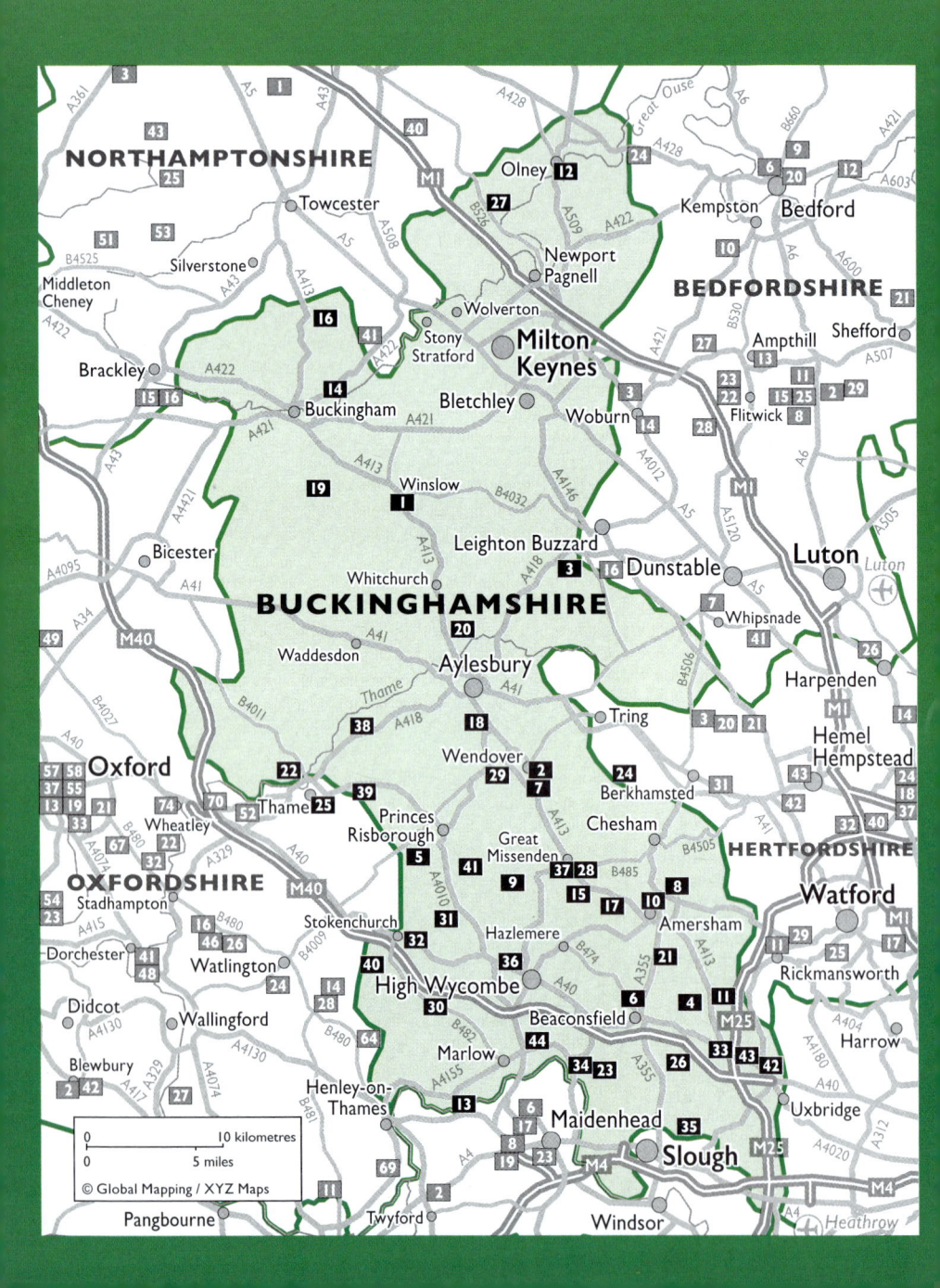

BUCKINGHAMSHIRE 43

VOLUNTEERS

County Organiser
Maggie Bateson
01494 866265
maggiebateson@gmail.com

County Treasurer
Tim Hart
01494 837328
timgc.hart@btinternet.com

Publicity
Sandra Wetherall
01494 862264
sandracwetherall@gmail.com

Social Media
Stella Vaines
07711 420621
stella@bakersclose.com

Booklet Co-ordinator
Maggie Bateson
(as above)

Assistant County Organisers
Judy Hart
01494 837328
judy.elgood@gmail.com

Mhairi Sharpley
01494 782870
mhairisharpley@btinternet.com

Stella Vaines
(as above)

@BucksNGS
@BucksNGS

OPENING DATES

All entries subject to change.
For latest information check
www.ngs.org.uk
Map locator numbers are
shown to the right of each
garden name.

February
Sunday 16th
Hollydyke House 17

March
Wednesday 19th
Montana 24

April
Sunday 13th
Long Crendon Gardens 22
Sunday 20th
Overstroud Cottage 28
Sunday 27th
Abbots House 1
◆ Stoke Poges Memorial
    Gardens 35

May
Sunday 11th
The Plough 29
Tuesday 13th
Red Kites 31
Sunday 18th
18 Brownswood Road 6
The White House 42
Monday 19th
◆ Ascott 3
Wednesday 21st
Montana 24
Sunday 25th
Foscote Manor 14
Tyringham Hall 38
Monday 26th
Glebe Farm 16
The Plough 29

June
Sunday 1st
Tythrop Park 39
Saturday 7th
Acer Corner 2
◆ Cowper & Newton Museum
    Gardens 12
Horatio's Garden 18
Sunday 8th
Acer Corner 2
◆ Cowper & Newton Museum
    Gardens 12
Long Crendon Gardens 22
Saturday 14th
St Michaels Convent 33
Sunday 15th
Bledlow Manor 5
Old Keepers 26
Wednesday 18th
The Walled Garden, Wormsley 40
Thursday 19th
Cornfield Cottage 11
Saturday 21st
Old Park Barn 27
Sunday 22nd
Old Park Barn 27
Sunday 29th
18 Copperkins Lane 10

July
Thursday 3rd
NEW Lilies 20
Saturday 5th
Little Missenden Gardens 21
Sunday 6th
Little Missenden Gardens 21
Sunday 13th
Fressingwood 15
Tuesday 15th
Red Kites 31
Wednesday 16th
Montana 24
Saturday 19th
NEW Wardrobes House 41
Sunday 20th
Chiltern Forage Farm 9
Sunday 27th
NEW Rackleys 30

BUCKINGHAMSHIRE

August

Wednesday 6th
Danesfield House 13

Sunday 24th
◆ Nether Winchendon House 25

October

Saturday 18th
Acer Corner 2

Sunday 19th
Acer Corner 2

By Arrangement

Arrange a personalised garden visit with your club, or group of friends, on a date to suit you. See individual garden entries for full details.

Abbots House	1
Acer Corner	2
Beech House	4
Bledlow Manor	5
18 Brownswood Road	6
Cedar House	7
Chesham Bois House	8
Glebe Farm	16
Kingsbridge Farm	19
Magnolia House	23
Montana	24
Old Park Barn	27
Overstroud Cottage	28
Red Kites	31
Robin Hill	32
The Shades	34
1 Talbot Avenue	36
Touchwood	37
Wind in the Willows	43
NEW Woodlands House	44

Wind in the Willows

# THE GARDENS

1 ABBOTS HOUSE
10 Church Street, Winslow, MK18 3AN. Mrs Jane Rennie, 01296 712326, jane@renniemail.com. *9m N of Aylesbury. A413 into Winslow. From town centre take Horn St & R into Church St, L fork at top. Entrance through door in wall, Church Walk. Parking in town centre & adjacent streets.* **Sun 27 Apr (12.30-5). Adm £5, chd free. Home-made teas.** Visits also by arrangement 2 May to 31 July for groups of 6 to 16.
Behind red brick walls a ¾ acre garden on four different levels, each with unique planting and atmosphere. Lower lawn with white wisteria arbour and pond, upper lawn with rose pergola and woodland, pool area with grasses, Victorian kitchen garden, glasshouse and wild meadow. Spring bulbs in wild areas and woodland, many tulips in April, remaining areas peak in June/July. Water feature, sculptures and many pots. Rennie's award-winning Winslow Cider is available. Partial wheelchair access due to steps leading to garden levels. Guide dogs and medical-aid dogs only.
&. ✿ ☕ ♨)

2 ACER CORNER
10 Manor Road, Wendover, HP22 6HQ. Jo Naiman, 07958 319234, jo@acercorner.com, www.acercorner.com. *3m S of Aylesbury. Follow A413 into Wendover. L at clock tower r'about into Aylesbury Rd. R at next r'about into Wharf Rd, continue past schools on L, garden on R.* **Sat 7, Sun 8 June, Sat 18, Sun 19 Oct (2-5). Adm £4, chd free. Home-made teas.** Visits also by arrangement 1 May to 24 Oct.
Garden designer's garden with Japanese influence and large collection of *Acer palmatum* Japanese maples. The enclosed front garden is Japanese in style. Back garden is divided into three areas; patio area recently redesigned in the Japanese style, densely planted area with many acers and roses, also a corner which inc a productive greenhouse and interesting planting. There are over 70 acers in the garden.
🐕 ✿ ☕ ♨)

3 ♦ ASCOTT
Ascott Estate, Wing, Leighton Buzzard, LU7 0PP. The National Trust. *2m SW of Leighton Buzzard, 8m NE of Aylesbury. Via A418. Buses: 150 Aylesbury to Milton Keynes, 250 Aylesbury & Milton Keynes. Access is via the visitors entrance, use postcode LU7 0ND.* **For NGS: Mon 19 May (11.30-5). Adm £11.90, chd £5.90. Pre-booking essential, please email info@ascottestate.co.uk or visit www.ascottestate.co.uk for information & booking. Adm subject to change. NT members are required to pay to enter the gardens on NGS days.** For other opening times and information, please email or visit garden website.
Combining Victorian formality with natural planting and modern design. Terraced lawns with specimen and ornamental trees and panoramic views to the Chilterns. Naturalised bulbs, mirror image herbaceous borders and impressive topiary inc a unique box and yew sundial. Ascott House is closed on NGS Days. The Pavilion Tearoom will be open until 15 mins before closing, serving a range of hot and cold refreshments. Pathways are gravel and grass. Manual wheelchairs are available to use for your visit, please contact the Estate Office to reserve in advance.
&. ✿ 🚗 ☕

4 BEECH HOUSE
Long Wood Drive, Jordans, nr Beaconsfield, HP9 2SS. Sue & Ray Edwards, 01494 875580, raychessmad@hotmail.com. *2m NE of Beaconsfield. From A40, L to Seer Green & Jordans for approx 1m, turn into Jordans Way on R, Long Wood Dr 1st L. From A413, turn into Chalfont St Giles, straight ahead until L signed Jordans, 1st L Jordans Way.* **Visits by arrangement Mar to Sept for groups of up to 50. Adm £5, chd free.**
2 acre garden created over the last 37 yrs with a wide range of flowering and foliage plants in a variety of habitats. Bulbs, perennials, shrubs, roses and grasses together with trees planted for their flowers, foliage, ornamental bark and autumn display give a continual display. Two attractive meadows combine long flowering season in a wildlife friendly environment are a popular feature. Extensive collection of plants, meadow gardens established over 32 yrs always attract attention and discussion. Wheelchair access dependent upon weather conditions.
&. 🐕 🚗 ☕ 🎪

5 BLEDLOW MANOR
Off Perry Lane, Bledlow, nr Princes Risborough, HP27 9PA. Lord & Lady Carrington, melaniedoughty@carington.co.uk, www.carington.co.uk/gardens. *9m NW of High Wycombe, 3m SW of Princes Risborough. ½m off B4009 in middle of Bledlow village. For SatNav use postcode HP27 9PA.* **Sun 15 June (2-5). Adm £8, chd free. Home-made teas.** Visits also by arrangement May to Sept.
The present garden covering around 12 acres inc the walled kitchen garden crisscrossed by paths with vegetables, fruit, herbs and flowers. The sculpture garden, the replanted granary garden with fountain and borders, as well as the individual paved gardens and parterres divided by yew hedges and more. The Lyde water garden formed out of old cress beds fed by numerous springs. Partial wheelchair access via steps or sloped grass to enter gardens.
&. 🚗 ☕ ♨)

6 18 BROWNSWOOD ROAD
Beaconsfield, HP9 2NU. John & Bernadette Thompson, 07879 282191, tbernadette60@gmail.com. *From New Town turn R into Ledborough Ln, L into Sandleswood Rd, 2nd R into Brownswood Rd.* **Sun 18 May (1.30-5). Adm £4, chd free.** Visits also by arrangement 17 Mar to 14 Sept for groups of up to 35.
A plant filled garden designed by Barbara Hunt. A harmonious arrangement of arcs and circles introduces a rhythm that leads through the garden. Sweeping box curves, gravel beds, brick edging and lush planting. A restrained use of purples and reds dazzle against a grey and green background.
☕

48,000 people affected by cancer were reached by Maggie's centres supported by the National Garden Scheme over the last 12 months.

BUCKINGHAMSHIRE

7 CEDAR HOUSE
Bacombe Lane, Wendover,
HP22 6EQ. Sarah Nicholson,
01296 622131, sarahhnicholson@
btinternet.com. *5m SE Aylesbury.
From Gt Missenden take A413 into
Wendover. Turn L for Ellesborough
Rd, and watch for signs for Bacombe
Ln. Parking for 10 cars only.* **Visits
by arrangement 10 Feb to 8 Sept
for groups of 10+. Adm £5, chd
free. Tea, coffee & cake.**
A plantsman's garden in the Chiltern
Hills with a great variety of trees,
shrubs and plants. A sloping lawn
leads to a natural swimming pond
with wild flowers inc native orchids.
A lodge greenhouse and a good
collection of half-hardy plants in
pots. Local artist's sculptures can be
viewed. Picnics welcome on prior
request. Wheelchair access over
gentle sloping lawn.

8 CHESHAM BOIS HOUSE
85 Bois Lane, Chesham Bois,
Amersham, HP6 6DF. Julia
Plaistowe, 01494 726476,
plaistowejulia@gmail.com,
cheshamboishouse.co.uk. *1m N
of Amersham-on-the-Hill. Follow
Sycamore Rd (main shopping centre
road of Amersham), which becomes
Bois Ln. Do not use SatNav once in
lane as you will be led astray.* **Visits
by arrangement Mar to Aug. Adm
£6, chd free. Tea, coffee & cake.**
3 acre beautiful garden with
primroses, daffodils and hellebores
in early spring. Interesting for most of
the yr with lovely herbaceous borders,
rill with small ornamental canal, walled
garden, old orchard with wildlife pond,
and handsome trees some of which
are topiary. It is a peaceful oasis.
Wheelchair access via gravel at front
of house.

9 CHILTERN FORAGE FARM
Spring Coppice Lane,
Speen, Princes Risborough,
HP27 0SU. Emma Plunket,
www.plunketgardens.com. *Follow
signs to gate at top of the hill & park
in field; trainers or walking shoes for
uneven ground.* **Sun 20 July (2.30-
5). Adm £5, chd free.**
Tours at 2.30pm and 4pm of this
project in attractive hillside setting.
Pasture being restored to grassland
meadows and planted with fruit. Tips
for foraging, encouraging wild flowers
and creation of wildlife habitats. On
calm sunny day great for spotting
butterflies and moths. Enjoy cool
drinks in shady seating and share our
identification tips, survey findings and
field guides.

10 18 COPPERKINS LANE
Amersham, HP6 5QF. Chris
Ludlam. *1m N of Amersham. 15 min
walk from Amersham Tube/Train stn.
Off Amersham/Chesham road A416.
Parking on road only, please park
with consideration to neighbours.*
**Sun 29 June (12-6). Adm £5,
chd free. Pre-booking essential,
please visit www.ngs.org.uk for
information & booking. Home-
made teas.**
A fabulous compact ½ acre garden
with lawn, herbaceous borders, wild
flowers, orchard, vegetable beds,
treehouse, summerhouse and pool.
Originally designed as a white garden,
it now inc purple, blue and pink
colours. Plenty of roses, grasses,
salvia, nepeta, peony, delphinium,
lupin, geranium, foxglove, allium,
lavender, astrantia, ornamental trees
inc davidia, and many perovskia
varieties. Wheelchair access over
deep gravel path, plus two sloped
tiled paths on entry.

11 CORNFIELD COTTAGE
Roberts Lane, Chalfont St
Peter, Gerrards Cross, SL9 0QR.
Debbie & Stewart Walker. *In the
hamlet of Horn Hill, 1½ m from the
centre of Chalfont St Peter. Take
Rickmansworth Ln to Horn Hill Village
Hall, turn R into Roberts Ln. Cornfield
Cottage is 300 metres on L. Limited
car parking opp the house & at Horn
Hill Village Hall.* **Thur 19 June (2-5).
Adm £4.50, chd free. Home-made
teas.**
A beautiful rural garden in a quiet
country lane. The borders are
planted with scented roses and bee
and butterfly friendly flowers inc
honeysuckle, delphiniums and sweet
peas. Seating areas provide enjoyable
views of the garden at different times
of the day. A natural arch leads to
a paddock with a small vegetable
garden, orchard, wildflower beds
and wood with a seasonal spring
fed pond. Disabled parking opp the
house or on the drive can be booked.
The entrance gate to the garden is
800mm wide.

**12 ♦ COWPER & NEWTON
MUSEUM GARDENS**
Orchard Side, Market
Place, Olney, MK46 4AJ.
Cowper & Newton Museum,
01234 711516, house-manager@
cowperandnewtonmuseum.org.uk,
www.cowperandnewtonmuseum.
org.uk. *5m N of Newport Pagnell.
12m S of Wellingborough. On A509.
Please park in public car park in East
St.* **For NGS: Sat 7, Sun 8 June
(11-4.30). Adm £4, chd free. Home-
made teas.** For other opening times
and information, please phone,
email or visit garden website.
The tranquil Flower Garden of C18
poet William Cowper, who said
'Gardening was of all employments,
that in which I succeeded best', has
plants introduced prior to his death
in 1800, many mentioned in his
writings. The Summerhouse Garden,
now a Kitchen Garden, inc heritage
vegetables organically grown, also
herb and medicinal beds and the
summerhouse Cowper called his
'verse manufactory'. Features inc
lacemaking demonstrations, local
artists painting and live musical
entertainment. Wheelchair access on
mostly hard paths.

13 DANESFIELD HOUSE
Henley Road, Marlow, SL7 2EY.
Danesfield House Hotel,
www.danesfieldhouse.co.uk. *3m
from Marlow. On the A4155 between
Marlow & Henley-on-Thames. Signed
on the LHS Danesfield House Hotel
& Spa.* **Wed 6 Aug (10-4). Adm £5,
chd free. Pre-booking essential,
please phone 01628 891010 or
email amoorin@danesfieldhouse.
co.uk for information & booking.**
The gardens at Danesfield were
completed in 1901 by Robert Hudson,
the Sunlight Soap magnate who built
the house. Since the house opened
as a hotel in 1991, the gardens have
been admired by several thousand
guests each yr. However, in 2009
it was discovered that the gardens
contained outstanding examples of
pulhamite in both the formal gardens
and the waterfall areas. The 100 yr old
topiary is also outstanding. Part of the
grounds inc an Iron Age fort. Tours
with the Gardener at 10.30am and
1.30pm only (max 30 per tour). Lunch
and afternoon tea in the Orangery
Restaurant (pre-booking required).
Wheelchair access on gravel paths
through parts of the garden.

BUCKINGHAMSHIRE 47

Little Missenden Gardens

14 FOSCOTE MANOR

Foscott, Buckingham, MK18 6AE. Kate Pryke. *Just outside Maids Moreton, NE of Buckingham. The postcode takes you to a small hamlet of cottages. For Foscote Manor, continue across the cattle grid into the fields & you will see the gates of the Manor House.* **Sun 25 May (2-5). Adm £10, chd free. Home-made teas inc.**

A restored walled kitchen garden with vegetables, fruit, herbs and flowers as the centre piece of this 40 acre estate. The surrounding waterway is bordered by a wildflower meadow, attracting heron, egret and kingfisher. Behind the walled garden, the back drive leads to ancient woodland sprouting a carpet of spring bulbs, and the lake which is home to Canada geese, swans and heron.

15 FRESSINGWOOD

Hare Lane, Little Kingshill, Great Missenden, HP16 0EF. John & Maggie Bateson. *1m S of Great Missenden, 4m W of Amersham. From the A413 at Chiltern Hospital, turn L signed Gt & Lt Kingshill. Take 1st L into Nags Head Ln. Turn R under railway bridge, then L into New Rd & continue to Hare Ln.* **Sun 13 July (2-5.30). Adm £5, chd free. Home-made teas.**

Thoughtfully designed and structured garden with year-round colour and many interesting features inc herbaceous borders, a shrubbery with ferns, hostas, grasses and hellebores. Small formal garden, pergolas with roses and clematis. A variety of topiary and small garden rooms. A central feature incorporating water with grasses and an old olive tree. Large bonsai collection.

16 GLEBE FARM

Lillingstone Lovell, Buckingham, MK18 5BB. Mr David Hilliard, 01280 860384, thehilliards@talk21.com, sites.google.com/site/glebefarmbarn. *Off A413, 5m N of Buckingham & 2m S of Whittlebury. From A5 at Potterspury, turn off A5 & follow signs to Lillingstone Lovell. From A413 Lillingsone Lovell is situated between Lillingstone Dayrell & Whittlebury.* **Mon 26 May (1.30-5). Adm £4, chd free. Home-made teas.** Visits also by arrangement 2 June to 30 June for groups of 6 to 12. Guided tour of garden & refreshments for group visits.

A large cottage garden with an exuberance of colourful planting and winding gravel paths, amongst lawns and herbaceous borders on two levels. Ponds, a wishing well, vegetable beds, a knot garden, a

The White House

BUCKINGHAMSHIRE 49

small walled garden and an old tractor feature. Everything combines to make a beautiful garden full of surprises. Greenhouses to look in, and seating areas and lawns to sit on. Wheelchair access to some flat areas of garden.

17 HOLLYDYKE HOUSE
Little Missenden, HP7 0RD.
Bob & Sandra Wetherall. *Off A413 between Great Missenden & Amersham. Parking, please use field adjacent to house, weather permitting.* **Sun 16 Feb (11-4). Adm £4, chd free. Light refreshments. Opening with Little Missenden Gardens on Sat 5, Sun 6 July.**
3 acre garden surrounds Hollydyke House (not open) with year-round interest. During February we hope to see hellebores, crocus and carpets of snowdrops. You will be able to appreciate the structure in winter with the trees, colourful barks, seed heads and grasses. Wheelchair access on gravel paths.

18 HORATIO'S GARDEN
National Spinal Injuries Centre (NSIC), Stoke Mandeville Hospital, Mandeville Road, Stoke Mandeville, Aylesbury, HP21 8AL. Amy Moffett, www.horatiosgarden.org.uk. *The closest car park for Horatio's Garden is at Stoke Mandeville Hospital, Car Park B, opp Asda (charges may apply).* **Sat 7 June (2-5). Adm £5, chd free. Tea, coffee & cake in the garden room.**
Opened in September 2018, Horatio's Garden at the National Spinal Injuries Centre, Stoke Mandeville Hospital is designed by Joe Swift. The fully accessible garden for patients with spinal injuries has been part funded by the NGS. The beautiful space is cleverly designed to bring the sights, sounds and scents of nature into the heart of the NHS. Everything is high quality and carefully designed to bring benefit to patients who often have lengthy stays in hospital. The garden features a contemporary garden room, designed by Andrew Wells as well as a stunning Griffin Glasshouse. We also have a wonderful wildflower meadow. Please come along and meet the Head Gardener and volunteer team, and taste our delicious tea and home-made cake! The garden is fully accessible, having been designed specifically for patients in wheelchairs or hospital beds.

19 KINGSBRIDGE FARM
Steeple Claydon, MK18 2EJ. Mr & Mrs Tom Aldous, 01296 730224. *3m S of Buckingham. Halfway between Padbury & Steeple Claydon. Xrds signed to Kingsbridge Only.* **Visits by arrangement 1 Mar to 15 July for groups of 6+. Adm £7, chd free.**
A stunning, exceptional 6 acre garden, constantly evolving! Main lawn is enclosed by softly curving, colour themed herbaceous borders with gazebo, topiary, clipped yews, pleached hornbeams leading to ha-ha and countryside beyond. A natural stream with bog plants and nesting kingfishers, meanders serenely through shrub and woodland gardens, with many walks. A garden to visit again and again.

20 NEW LILIES
High Street, Weedon, Aylesbury, HP22 4NS. Mr & Mrs George Anson. *²⁄₃ m N of Aylesbury. From Aylesbury A413 N towards Buckingham, follow for ²⁄₃ m, passing a R turn signed Weedon/Aston Abbots & continue until you see horse sign on the L & then turn R into High St.* **Thur 3 July (2-5). Adm £7, chd free.**
Since the C17, a house and grounds have been recorded on the site of Lilies in Buckinghamshire. Rebuilt in 1870, the current owners have lovingly restored and renovated the house (not open) and surrounding gardens. There are several acres of formal lawns and gardens, with mature specimen trees. The woodlands, large walled garden, and flower meadow complete the picture. Wheelchair access over lawn with some paved/soil pathways and a shallow gravelled approach.

---

70 inpatients and their families are being supported at the newly opened Horatio's Garden Northern Ireland, thanks to National Garden Scheme donations.

GROUP OPENING

21 LITTLE MISSENDEN GARDENS
Amersham, HP7 0RD. *On A413 between Great Missenden & Old Amersham. Please park in signed car parks.* **Sat 5, Sun 6 July (2-6). Combined adm £8, chd free. Home-made teas at Hollydyke House & St John the Baptist Church.**

HOLLYDYKE HOUSE
Bob & Sandra Wetherall.
(See separate entry)

KINGS BARN
Mr & Mrs Playle.

LITTLE MISSENDEN CE INFANT SCHOOL
Little Missenden School.

MANOR FARM HOUSE
Evan Bazzard.

MILLARD'S BARN
Rosemary Higgs.

MISSENDEN HOUSE
Sara Jane Ambrose.

MISSENDEN LODGE
Mr & Mrs R Kimber.

TOWN FARM COTTAGE
Mr & Mrs Tim Garnham.

THE WHITE HOUSE
Mr & Mrs Harris.

A variety of gardens set in this attractive Chiltern village in an AONB. You can start off at one end of the village and wander through stopping off halfway for tea at the beautiful Anglo-Saxon church built in 975. The church has recently received a lottery grant for restoration and many medieval wall paintings have been found. Tours will be given of these discoveries. The gardens reflect different style houses inc several old cottages, converted barns, Elizabethan and Georgian houses (houses not open). There are herbaceous borders, shrubs, trees, old-fashioned roses, hostas, topiary, Koi and lily ponds, kitchen gardens, play areas for children and the River Misbourne runs through a few. Some gardens are highly colourful and others just green and peaceful. Beekeeper at Hollydyke House. Partial wheelchair access to some gardens due to gravel paths and steps.

GROUP OPENING

22 LONG CRENDON GARDENS
Long Crendon, HP18 9AN. *2m N of Thame. Park in the village as there is no parking at most individual gardens, although there is limited parking at 25 Elm Trees.* **Sun 13 Apr, Sun 8 June (2-6). Combined adm £6, chd free. Home-made teas in Church House, High St (Apr) & St Mary's Church (June).**

BAKER'S CLOSE
Mr & Mrs Peter Vaines.
Open on Sun 13 Apr

BARRY'S CLOSE
Mr & Mrs Richard Salmon.
Open on Sun 13 Apr

NEW 50 CHILTON ROAD
Pete & Karen Bromley.
Open on Sun 8 June

COP CLOSE
Sandra & Tony Phipkin.
Open on all dates

25 ELM TREES
Carol & Mike Price.
Open on all dates

MANOR FARM BUNGALOW
Tracy Russell & David Newman.
Open on Sun 13 Apr

MANOR HOUSE
Mr & Mrs West.
Open on Sun 13 Apr

TOMPSONS FARM
Mr & Mrs T Moynihan.
Open on Sun 8 June

Six gardens open Sun 13 Apr. Baker's Close: 1000s of daffodils, tulips, shrubs and wild area. Barry's Close: spring flowering trees, borders and water garden. Cop Close: daffodils, tulips, borders and bog garden. 25 Elm Trees: cottage style organic garden planted to encourage wildlife. Manor Farm Bungalow: wildlife garden with natural swimming pond. Manor House: a large garden with views to the Chilterns, two ornamental lakes, a variety of spring bulbs and shrubs. Four gardens open Sun 8 June. Cop Close with mixed borders, vegetable garden, wildflower bank and damp garden. 50 Chilton Road (New): medium garden, large pond and wildlife area. Tompsons Farm: a large woodland garden with large lake and herbaceous borders. 25 Elm Trees: cottage style organic garden planted to encourage wildlife and all round colour. Partial wheelchair access only at Barry's Close and Manor House in April, and Tompson's Farm and Manor Farm Bungalow in June.

23 MAGNOLIA HOUSE
Grange Drive, Wooburn Green, Wooburn, HP10 0QD. Elaine & Alan Ford, 01628 525818, lanforddesigns@gmail.com, sites.google.com/site/lanforddesigns. *On A4094 2m SW of A40 between Bourne End & Wooburn. From Wooburn Church, direction Maidenhead, Grange Dr is on L before r'about. From Bourne End, L at 2 mini r'abouts, then 1st R.* **Visits by arrangement Apr to July for groups of up to 25. Visits can be combined with The Shades next door. Light refreshments.**
½ acre garden with mature trees inc large magnolia. Cacti, fernery, stream, water wheel, two ponds, greenhouses, aviary, 10,000 snowdrops, hellebores, bluebells and over 60 varieties of hosta. Small Japanese style area. Child friendly. Constantly being changed and updated. Partial wheelchair access.

24 MONTANA
Shire Lane, Cholesbury, HP23 6NA. Diana Garner *3m NW of Chesham. From Chesham drive up the Vale to Cholesbury common, turn onto Cholesbury Rd by cricket club, 1st L is Shire Ln. From Tring head towards Wigginton past Champneys, Cholesbury Rd next R.* **Wed 19 Mar, Wed 21 May, Wed 16 July (11-2). Adm £4, chd free. Pre-booking essential, please phone 01494 758347 or email montana@cholesbury.net for information & booking. Home-made teas. Visits also by arrangement 2 Mar to 31 July for groups of up to 35.**
A peaceful large woodland garden planted by the owner with rare and unusual flowering trees, shrubs, perennials and loads of bulbs. Shade loving herbaceous plants, kitchen garden and meadow with apiary. Gate leads to old brickyard, now 3 acre mixed deciduous wood: level paths, large fernery planted in a clay pit, acers and an avenue of thousands of daffodils. Lots of seats to enjoy the quiet. An unmanicured garden high in the Chiltern Hills. Surrounding fields have been permanent pasture for more than 100 yrs. Covered open barn for teas in wet weather. The majority of paths in the garden and wood are wheelchair friendly and flat.

25 ◆ NETHER WINCHENDON HOUSE
Nether Winchendon, nr Aylesbury, HP18 0DY. Mr Robert Spencer Bernard, 01844 290101, Contactus@netherwinchendonhouse.com, www.nwhouse.co.uk. *6m SW of Aylesbury, 6m from Thame. Approx 4m from Thame on A418, turn 1st L to Cuddington, turn L at Xrds, downhill turn R & R again to parking by house.* **For NGS: Sun 24 Aug (2-5.30). Adm £4, chd free. Pre-booking essential, please visit www.ngs.org.uk for information & booking. Cream teas in village church. For other opening times and information, please phone, email or visit garden website.**
Nether Winchendon House has fine, and rare trees set in an inspiring and stunning landscape with parkland. The south lawn runs down to the River Thame. A Founder NGS Member (1927). Enchanting and romantic Mediaeval and Tudor House, one of the most romantic of the historic houses of England and listed Grade I. Dogs on leads welcome. Picturesque small village with an interesting church.

26 OLD KEEPERS
Village Lane, Hedgerley, SL2 3UY. Rob Cooper, www.instagram.com/oldkeepersgarden. *Parking in village hall on Kiln Ln, postcode SL2 3UU.* **Sun 15 June (12.30-4.30). Adm £5, chd free. Cream teas.**
Described by visitors as 'a real gardener's garden'. A fairly new 1½ acre garden set around a Grade II listed former brickmaker's cottage (not open). The garden features borders packed full of perennials, a small meadow, and a small orchard, creating a haven for wildlife, with over 20 different types of butterfly spotted in 2023. We designed the garden ourselves, carefully placing benches and perching spots to make the most of the beautiful views of the garden and village. It's the perfect setting to enjoy a coffee and cake.

27 OLD PARK BARN

Dag Lane, Stoke Goldington, MK16 8NY. Emily & James Chua, 07833 118903, emilychua51@yahoo.com. *4m N of Newport Pagnell on B526. Park on High St. A short walk up Dag Ln. Accessible parking for 4 cars nr garden via Orchard Way. Please contact us for coach parking details.* **Sat 21, Sun 22 June (1.30-5). Adm £6, chd free. Home-made teas. Visits also by arrangement 7 June to 7 July for groups of 10 to 40.**
A garden of almost 3 acres made from a rough field over 25 yrs ago. A series of terraces cut into the sloping site create the formal garden with long and cross vistas, lawns and deep borders. The aim is to provide interest throughout the yr with naturalistic planting and views borrowed from the surrounding countryside. Beyond this there is a wildlife pond, stream, grass, meadow, and woodland gardens. Partial wheelchair access.

& ❀ 🚗 ☕ 🔊

28 OVERSTROUD COTTAGE

The Dell, Frith Hill, Great Missenden, HP16 9QE. Mr & Mrs Jonathan Brooke, 01494 862701, susanmbrooke@outlook.com. *½m E Great Missenden. Turn E off A413 at Great Missenden onto B485 Frith Hill to Chesham Rd. White Gothic cottage set back in lay-by, 100yds uphill on L. Parking on R at church.* **Sun 20 Apr (2-5). Adm £4, chd free. Cream teas at parish church. Visits also by arrangement May & June for groups of up to 20.**
Artistic chalk garden on two levels. Collection of C17/C18 plants inc auricula, hellebores, bulbs, pulmonarias, peonies, geraniums, herbs and succulents. Many antique species and rambling roses. Potager and lily pond. Blue and white ribbon border. Cottage was once C17 fever house for Missenden Abbey. Features inc a garden studio with painting exhibition (share of flower painting proceeds to NGS).

❀ ☕

29 THE PLOUGH

Chalkshire Road, Terrick, Aylesbury, HP17 0TJ. John & Sue Stewart. *2m W of Wendover. Entrance to garden & car park signed off B4009 Nash Lee Rd. 200yds E of Terrick r'about. Access to garden from field car park.* **Sun 11, Mon 26 May (1-5). Adm £5, chd free. Home-made teas.**

Formal garden with open views to the Chiltern countryside. Designed as a series of outdoor rooms around a listed former C18 inn (not open) inc border, parterre, vegetable and fruit gardens and organic orchard with wild flowers. Delicious home-made teas in our barn and adjacent entrance courtyard. Jams and apple juice made with fruits from the garden for sale. Cash only please.

🐕 ❀ ☕

30 NEW RACKLEYS

Marlow Road, Cadmore End, High Wycombe, HP14 3PP. Nick & Wendy Sargent, rackleys.co.uk. *Rackleys Chiltern Hills is situated 5½m from Marlow & 9½m from Henley upon Thames. In Marlow head SE on A4155 Marlow Rd, take 1st exit Dean St/Marlow Rd B482, after 5½m turn L. From M40 J5 exit to Stokenchurch on A40, after ½m turn R into Marlow Rd B482, after 4m turn R.* **Sun 27 July (2-5.30). Adm £6, chd free. Tea, coffee & cake. Wine, beer & soft drinks.**
Rackleys was a farm built in the 1700s and has been lovingly restored into a wedding and events venue. It is set in 7 acres of stunning gardens with sweeping views over the Chilterns. The gardens boast a wide range of flowering trees and shrubs as well as roses, herbaceous perennials and bulbs that provide continuous colour throughout the yr. Wheelchair access to the meadow is via a grass pathway.

& ❀ 🚗 ☕ 🔊

© Tom Hampson

BUCKINGHAMSHIRE

31 RED KITES
46 Haw Lane, Bledlow Ridge, HP14 4JJ. Mag & Les Terry, 01494 481474, lesterry747@gmail.com. *4m S of Princes Risborough. Off A4010 halfway between Princes Risborough & West Wycombe. At Hearing Dogs sign in Saunderton turn into Haw Ln, then ¾m on L up the hill.* **Tue 13 May, Tue 15 July (2-5). Adm £6, chd free. Home-made teas. Visits also by arrangement 15 May to 4 Sept for groups of 20+.** This Chiltern hillside garden of 1½ acres is planted for year-round interest and has superb views. Lovingly and beautifully maintained, there are several different areas to relax in, each with their own character. Wildflower orchard, mixed borders, pond, vegetables, woodland area and a lovely hidden garden. Many climbers used in the garden change significantly through the seasons.

32 ROBIN HILL
Water End, Stokenchurch, High Wycombe, HP14 3XQ. Caroline Renshaw & Stuart Yates, 07957 394134, info@cazrenshawdesigns.co.uk. *2m from M40 J5 Stokenchurch. Turn off A40 just S of Stokenchurch towards Radnage, then 1st R to Waterend & then follow signs.* **Visits by arrangement 26 May to 31 July for groups of 15 to 30. Adm £5, chd free. Home-made teas.** Garden designer's own garden at the start of The Chilterns. Informal planting with a variety of trees, woodland edge plants, shade borders, shrubs, perennials and grass borders blending into pastureland, now restored to a beautiful long grass meadow. Mature cherry orchard, chickens, and vegetable garden. Planting constantly evolving to better suit our changing climate and enhance biodiversity. Wheelchair access if dry over mainly flat and lawned garden, but no paths.

33 ST MICHAELS CONVENT
Vicarage Way, Gerrards Cross, SL9 8AT. Sisters of the Church, stmichaelsconvent.sistersofthechurch.org. *15 min walk from Gerrards Cross stn. 10 mins from East Common buses. Parking in nearby street, limited parking at St Michael's.* **Sat 14 June (2-4.30). Adm by donation. Home-made teas.** St Michael's Convent is home to the Sisters of the Church and the Society of the Precious Blood. The garden is a place for quiet, reflection, and to gaze upon beauty, and inc a walled garden with vegetables, labyrinth and pond, a shady woodland dell and a chapel. Enjoy the colourful borders, beds and mature majestic trees. Come and see, and spend time being!

34 THE SHADES
High Wycombe, HP10 0QD. Pauline & Maurice Kirkpatrick, 01628 522540. *On A4094 2m SW of A40 between Bourne End & Wooburn. From Wooburn Church, direction Maidenhead, Grange Dr is on L before r'about. From Bourne End, L at 2 mini r'abouts, then 1st R.* **Visits by arrangement Apr to July for groups of up to 25. Combined visit with Magnolia House.** The Shades drive is approached through mature trees, areas of shade loving plants, beds of shrubs, 60 various roses and herbaceous plants. The rear garden with natural well surrounded by plants, shrubs and acers. A green slate water feature and scree garden with alpine plants completes the garden. Light refreshments at Magnolia House. Partial wheelchair access.

35 ♦ STOKE POGES MEMORIAL GARDENS
Church Lane, Stoke Poges, Slough, SL2 4NZ. Buckinghamshire Council, 01753 523744, memorial.gardens@buckinghamshire.gov.uk, www.buckinghamshire.gov.uk. *1m N of Slough, 4m S of Gerrards Cross. Follow signs to Stoke Poges & from there to the Memorial Gardens. Car park opp main entrance, disabled visitor parking in the gardens. Weekend disabled access through churchyard.* **For NGS: Sun 27 Apr (1-4.30). Adm £6, chd free. Tea, coffee & cake. For other opening times and information, please phone, email or visit garden website.** Unique 22 acre Grade I registered garden constructed 1934-9 with a contemporary garden extension. Rock and water gardens, sunken colonnade, rose garden, 500 individual gated gardens, beautiful mature trees and newly landscaped areas. Guided tours every hour. Guide dogs only.

36 1 TALBOT AVENUE
Downley, High Wycombe, HP13 5HZ. Mr Alan Mayes, 01494 451044, alan.mayes2@btopenworld.com. *From Downley T-lights off West Wycombe Rd, take Plomer Hill turn off, then 2nd L into Westover Rd, then 2nd L into Talbot Ave.* **Visits by arrangement 28 Apr to 30 Sept for groups of up to 20. Adm £4, chd free. Tea.** A Japanese garden, shielded from the upper garden level by Shoji screens. A winding path leads you over a traditional Japanese bridge by a pond and waterfall, inviting you through a moongate to reveal a purpose built tea house, all surrounded by traditional Japanese planting inc maples, cherry blossom trees, azaleas and rhododendrons. Ornamental grasses and bamboo complement the hard landscaping with feature cloud tree and checkerboard garden path.

37 TOUCHWOOD
Grimms Hill, Great Missenden, HP16 9BG. Katharine Hersee, 07801 948650, kjhersee@gmail.com. *If coming up Grimms Hill from Great Missenden end, house is after 1st LH-bend on L. If coming downhill from Prestwood, house is ¾ of the way down Grimms Hill on RH-side. Parking for 10 cars on drive.* **Visits by arrangement Tue 11 to Thur 13 Feb & Mon 24 to Wed 26 Feb for groups of 10 to 25. Adm £10, chd free. Tea, coffee & cake inc. Advanced notice required for special dietary requirements.** A 2 acre garden containing drifts of common snowdrops as well as a few unusual ones. Strong structure provided by terracing, walls and topiarised yew hedging. Your visit will start with a short illustrated talk about snowdrop varieties before you explore the snowdrops lining a shrubbery path, woodland path and rockery. Naturalised snowdrops also line the lawn on either side of the driveway. The visit will end with tea and cakes. Other early spring bulbs and shrubs may also be in flower, although this is seasonally dependent.

BUCKINGHAMSHIRE

38 TYRINGHAM HALL
Upper Church Street, Cuddington, Aylesbury, HP18 0AP. Mrs Sherry Scott MBE. *R at Cuddington Xrd (Upper Church St), 100 metres Tyringham Hall on RH-bend.* **Sun 25 May (2-5). Adm £5, chd free. Home-made teas.**
Medieval house that will be partly open. A large garden with extensive lawns, water garden with underground springs, vegetable garden, tennis court and swimming pool. Colourful varieties of flowers are planted around the garden with mature trees offering shade where needed. Many seating areas around the garden. Parking at garden for wheelchair visitors only.
&♿ 🐕 ☕

39 TYTHROP PARK
Kingsey, HP17 8LT. Nick & Chrissie Wheeler. *2m E of Thame, 4m NW of Princes Risborough. Via A4129, at T-junction in Kingsey turn towards Haddenham, take L turn on bend. Parking in field on L.* **Sun 1 June (2-5.30). Adm £8, chd free.**
10 acres of garden surrounds a C17 Grade I listed manor house (not open). This large and varied garden blends traditional and contemporary styles, featuring pool borders rich in grasses with a green and white theme, walled kitchen and cutting garden with large greenhouse at its heart, box parterre, deep mixed borders, water feature, rose garden, wildflower meadow and many old trees and shrubs.
♿ D ☕ 🔊

SPECIAL EVENT

40 THE WALLED GARDEN, WORMSLEY
Wormsley, Stokenchurch, High Wycombe, HP14 3YE. Wormsley Estate. *Leave M40 at J5. Turn towards Ibstone. Entrance to estate is ¼m on R. NB: 20mph speed limit on estate. Please do not drive on grass verges. Disabled parking onsite.* **Wed 18 June (10-3). Adm £8, chd free. Pre-booking essential, please visit www.ngs.org.uk for information & booking. Home-made teas.**
The Walled Garden at Wormsley Estate is a 2 acre garden providing flowers, vegetables and tranquil contemplative space for the family. For many yrs the garden was neglected until Sir Paul Getty purchased the estate in the mid 1980s. In 1991 the garden was redesigned and has changed over the yrs, but remains true to the original brief. Wheelchair access to grounds, but no disabled WC facilities.
♿ ☕

41 NEW WARDROBES HOUSE
Woodway, Princes Risborough, HP27 0NL. Tara Leaver. *Located off the A4010 just S of Princes Risborough, on the LHS on road leading to Lacey Green & before Wardrobes Ln. No access from Wardrobes Ln.* **Sat 19 July (1-5). Adm £7, chd free. Pre-booking essential, please visit www.ngs.org.uk for information & booking. Tea, coffee & cake.**
Located on the edge of the Chiltern Hills with long reaching views, these 3 acre gardens surround a C18 Georgian Manor House built for the First Earl of Burlington (not open). Over recent yrs they have been remodelled to inc formal and vegetable gardens, a classic water garden, large greenhouse and more informal areas. There are a variety of mature trees inc a holm oak and yew.
☕ 🔊

42 THE WHITE HOUSE
Village Road, Denham Village, UB9 5BE. Mr & Mrs P G Courtenay-Luck. *3m NW of Uxbridge, 7m E of Beaconsfield. Signed from A40 or A412. Parking in Village Rd. The White House is in centre of village, opp St Mary's Church. Chiltern Line Train Stn, Denham.* **Sun 18 May (2-5). Adm £7, chd free. Cream teas.**
Well established 6 acre formal garden in picturesque setting. Mature trees and hedges with River Misbourne meandering through lawns. Shrubberies, flower beds, rockery, rose garden and orchard. Large walled garden. Herb garden, vegetable plot and Victorian greenhouses. Wheelchair access with gravel entrance and paved path into gardens.
♿ 🐕 ❀ ☕ 🔊

43 WIND IN THE WILLOWS
Moorhouse Farm Lane, Off Lower Road, Higher Denham, UB9 5EN. Ron James, 07740 177038, r.james@company-doc.co.uk. *6m E of Beaconsfield. Turn off A412, approx ½ m N of junction with A40 into Old Rectory Ln. After 1m enter Higher Denham straight ahead. Take lane next to the community centre & Wind in the Willows is the 1st house on L.* **Visits by arrangement Mar to Sept for groups of 10+. Donation to Higher Denham Community CIO (Garden Upkeep Fund).**
3 acre wildlife friendly, year-round garden, comprising informal woodland and wild gardens, separated by streams lined by iris, primulas and astilbe. Over 350 shrubs and trees, many variegated or uncommon, marginal and bog plants and a bed of stripy roses. Stunning was the word most often used by visitors. 'Best private garden I have visited in 20 yrs of NGS visits' said another. Although unlikely to be seen on a busy day, 65 species of bird and 13 species of butterfly have been seen in and over the garden, which is also home to the now endangered water vole (Water Rat in the book Wind in the Willows), as well as frogs and toads. Wheelchair access over gravel paths and spongy lawns.
♿ ❀ ☕ 🔊

44 NEW WOODLANDS HOUSE
Winchbottom Lane, Marlow, SL7 3RN. Jan Mash, 07928 432337, woodlandshouse-marlow@outlook.com. *Little Marlow. Winchbottom Ln is off the A4155 towards Bourne End. Single track lane parking in field.* **Visits by arrangement July & Aug for groups of 10 to 30. Adm £12. Home-made teas inc.**
A country garden with a series of rooms each with their own planting style inc a formal box parterre with gazebo, a knot garden, a pool garden with grasses and perennials. A Victorian style glasshouse with scented pelargoniums and a garden with raised beds of dahlias and herbs, two stumperies with hellebores and ferns, woodland and meadow walks with wonderful views, and a labyrinth.
🚗 ☕

CAMBRIDGESHIRE

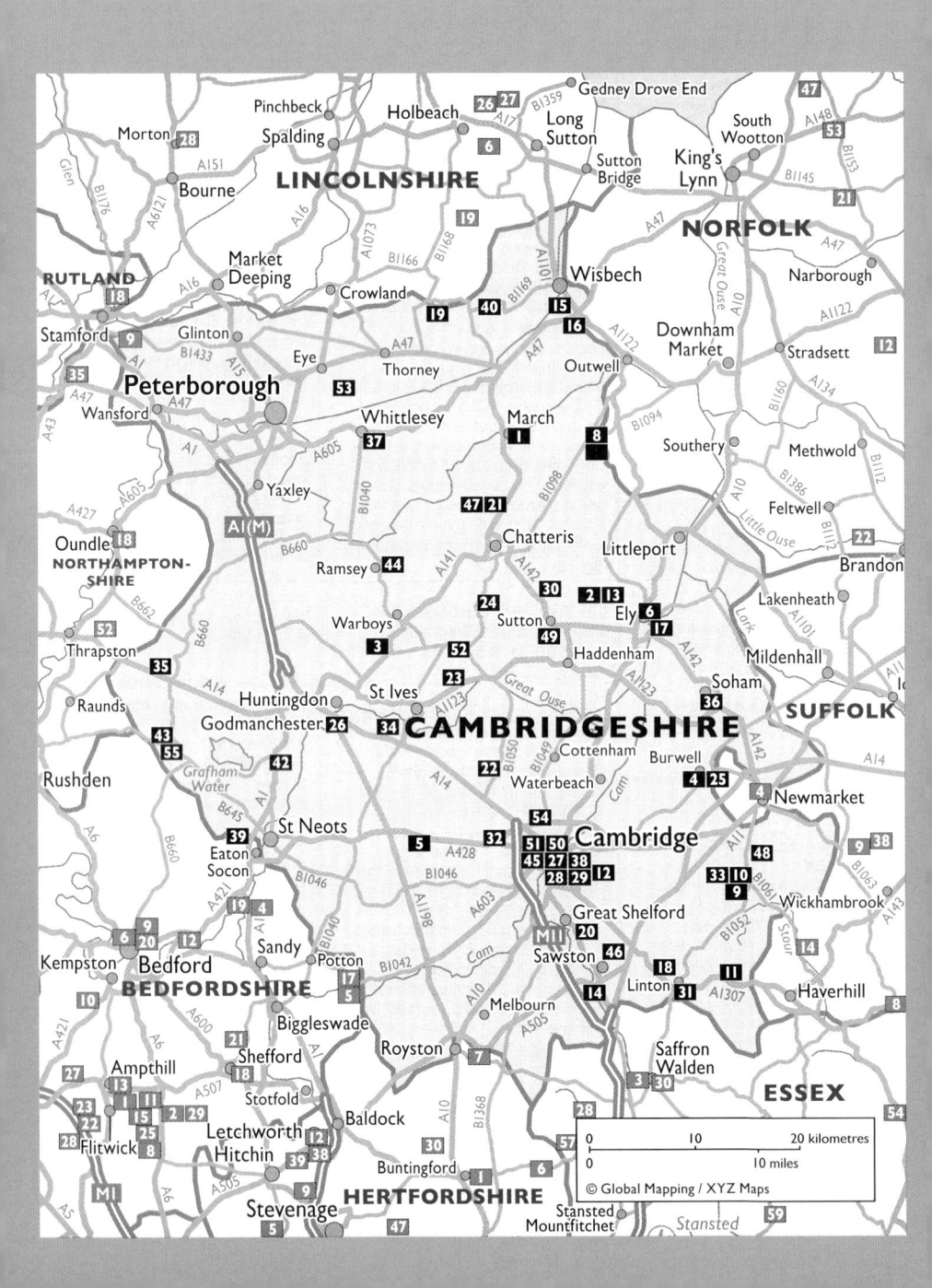

VOLUNTEERS

County Organiser
Jenny Marks 07956 049257
jenny.marks@ngs.org.uk

Deputy County Organiser
Pam Bullivant 01353 667355
pam.bullivant@ngs.org.uk

County Treasurer
Position Vacant

Booklet Coordinator
Jenny Marks (As above)

Publicity
Penny Miles 07771 516448
penny.miles@ngs.org.uk

Social Media
Hetty Dean
hetty.dean@ngs.org.uk

Assistant County Organisers
Claire James 07815 719284
claire.james@ngs.org.uk

Jacqui Latten-Quinn 07941 279571
jacqui.quinn@ngs.org.uk

Penny Miles (As above)

Jane Pearson 07890 080303
jane.pearson@ngs.org.uk

Barbara Stalker 07800 575100
barbara.stalker@ngs.org.uk

Carolyn Thompson 01353 778640
carolyn.thompson@ngs.org.uk

Annette White 01638 730876
annette.white@ngs.org.uk

National Garden Scheme Cambs
@GardenCambs
cambsngs

OPENING DATES

All entries subject to change. For latest information check
www.ngs.org.uk

Extended openings are shown at the beginning of the month.

Map locator numbers are shown to the right of each garden name.

January

Every day from Thursday 2nd
Robinson College 45

February

Snowdrop Openings

Every day
Robinson College 45

Sunday 16th
Clover Cottage 11

Sunday 23rd
Clover Cottage 11

March

Every day
Robinson College 45

Sunday 2nd
Clover Cottage 11

Sunday 30th
Netherhall Manor 36

April

Every day until Monday 21st
Robinson College 45

Saturday 12th
Heath Fruit Farm 23

Sunday 13th
Trinity College Fellows' Garden 50
Trinity Hall - Wychfield Site 51

Tuesday 29th
Madingley Hall 32

May

Every Saturday and Sunday
23A Perry Road 42

Sunday 4th
Chaucer Road Gardens 7
Netherhall Manor 36

Monday 5th
Chaucer Road Gardens 7

Sunday 18th
Linton Gardens 31
Molesworth House 35
Sutton Gardens 49

Saturday 24th
Coveney & Wardy Hill Gardens 13
NEW 41A New Road 37

Sunday 25th
Cambourne Gardens 5
Coveney & Wardy Hill Gardens 13
Island Hall 26
NEW 41A New Road 37
Willow Holt 53

Monday 26th
Willow Holt 53

Saturday 31st
NEW Fountain Court 21
NEW Springfield 47

June

Every Saturday and Sunday
23A Perry Road 42

Sunday 1st
Clover Cottage 11
Cottage Garden 12
Duxford Gardens 14

Sunday 8th
Burwell Village Gardens 4
38 Chapel Street 6
Clover Cottage 11
Ely Open Gardens 17
NEW Fountain Court 21
Isaacson's 25
The Old Rectory 40
NEW Springfield 47

Saturday 14th
6 Finch's Close 20

Sunday 15th
6 Finch's Close 20

Saturday 21st
Preachers Passing 43

Sunday 22nd
Christchurch Village Gardens 8
Old Farm Cottage 39
Preachers Passing 43

Saturday 28th
Leisure Land 30
Wrights Farm 55

CAMBRIDGESHIRE

Sunday 29th
Bramble Lodge	2
King's College Fellows' Garden and Provost's Garden	27
Leisure Land	30
NEW 41A New Road	37
Wrights Farm	55

July

Every Saturday and Sunday
23A Perry Road	42

Wednesday 2nd
Madingley Hall	32

Sunday 6th
NEW Broughton Village Gardens	3
Elm House	16
Green End Farm	22
38 Kingston Street	28
73 Kingston Street	29
Sawston Gardens	46

Every day from Wednesday 9th
Robinson College	45

Saturday 19th
Twin Tarns	52

Sunday 20th
NEW Stetchworth and Dullingham Gardens	48
Twin Tarns	52

Saturday 26th
38 Norfolk Terrace	38

Sunday 27th
NEW 41A New Road	37
38 Norfolk Terrace	38

129,032 people were able to access guidance on what to expect when a person is dying through the National Garden Scheme's support for Hospice UK this year.

August

Every Saturday and Sunday
23A Perry Road	42

Every day until Friday 15th
Robinson College	45

Sunday 3rd
Netherhall Manor	36

Sunday 10th
Netherhall Manor	36

Thursday 14th
◆ Elgood's Brewery Gardens	15

Sunday 17th
Bramble Lodge	2

Saturday 30th
Wrights Farm	55

Sunday 31st
Wrights Farm	55

September

Every Saturday and Sunday to Sunday 7th
23A Perry Road	42

Every Monday to Friday
Robinson College	45

Every Saturday and Sunday
Robinson College	45

Sunday 7th
◆ The Manor, Hemingford Grey	34

Saturday 13th
Ramsey Walled Garden	44

October

Every day
Robinson College	45

November

Every day
Robinson College	45

December

Every day until Monday 22nd
Robinson College	45

Our donation in 2024 has enabled Parkinson's UK to fund 3 new nursing posts this year directly supporting people with Parkinson's.

By Arrangement

Arrange a personalised garden visit with your club, or group of friends, on a date to suit you. See individual garden entries for full details.

Beaver Lodge	1
Bramble Lodge	2
Bustlers Cottage, Duxford Gardens	14
38 Chapel Street	6
Church Lane House	9
Church View	10
Clover Cottage	11
NEW Farm Lodge	18
Fenleigh	19
Horseshoe Farm	24
Isaacson's	25
41 Main Street	33
Molesworth House	35
NEW 41A New Road	37
Newnham Farmhouse, Burwell Village Gardens	4
The Old Baptist Chapel, Sutton Gardens	49
The Old Rectory	40
Pavilion House, Stetchworth and Dullingham Gardens	48
3 Roman Close, Burwell Village Gardens	4
Twin Tarns	52
The Windmill	54

The Briars, Broughton Village Gardens

THE GARDENS

1 BEAVER LODGE
Henson Road, March, PE15 8BA.
Mr & Mrs Nielson-Bom,
01354 656185,
beaverbom@gmail.com. *A141 to Wisbech Rd into March, L into Westwood Ave, at end, R into Henson Rd, property on R opp sch playground.* **Visits by arrangement 2 May to 30 Sept for groups of up to 20. Adm £7.50, chd free.**
An impeccable oriental garden with more than 120 large and small bonsai trees, acers, pagodas, oriental statues, water features and pond with koi carp, creating a peaceful and relaxing atmosphere. Described by visitors as an oasis of peace and tranquillity. The garden is divided into three different sections: The Mediterranian garden, pond area and a collection of acers. Seating area near waterfall finishes the scene.

2 BRAMBLE LODGE
Gravel End, Coveney, Ely,
CB6 2DN. Mrs Kathryn Kerridge,
07956 854091,
kerridgek@gmail.com. *3½m NW of Ely. From A142 or A10 Ely bypass, follow signs for Coveney. Garden is off Gravel End, behind 10a.*
Sun 29 June, Sun 17 Aug (2-5). Adm £5, chd free. Tea, coffee & cake. Visits also by arrangement May to Aug for groups of 10+.
Bramble lodge is hidden from the road with panoramic views of open farmland and large fen skies. A medium sized garden, it has been designed and built entirely from scratch over 15 years by the owners from a bramble, nettle and rubble field on the site of an old pig farm. It has swirling borders filled with familiar favourites and some unusual species of perennials, shrubs, roses and hydrangeas. Mainly lawn, except secret garden which is gravel.

GROUP OPENING

3 **NEW** BROUGHTON VILLAGE GARDENS
Causeway Road, Broughton, Huntingdon, PE28 3AS. Susannah Cameron. *Approx. 7½m NE of Huntingdon. From A141 take turning signposted towards Broughton. Follow road into the village, approx. 1½m. Gardens located on Bridge Rd, The Causeway and School Rd.* **Sun 6 July (11-6). Combined adm £6, chd free. Tea, coffee & cake in Broughton Village Hall. WC are located in the village hall. Payments for refreshments will be cash only.**

NEW **THE BRIARS**
Mike & Elaine Fisher.

NEW **LYCHGATE**
Mr & Mrs R Probyn.

NEW **MAGNOLIA COTTAGE**
Susannah Cameron.

Three village gardens of different sizes and character. Lychgate Cottage is a secluded cottage garden, developed over the last 10 years from an existing framework. Inc herbaceous borders, vegetable patch, pond area, orchard, stumpery, wildflower meadow and plenty of untidy corners for the wildlife. The Briars is a mature cottage garden with a backdrop of open countryside. Mixed borders of roses, perennials and grasses surround interesting seating areas. Designed and built entirely from scratch over 25 years. Magnolia Cottage was a scruffy chicken run in 2010. Now a sheltered, lush cottage garden with a difference, inc many traditional plants and a surprising array of exotics with a backdrop of interesting trees.

Wrights Farm

CAMBRIDGESHIRE

GROUP OPENING

4 BURWELL VILLAGE GARDENS
Burwell, CB25 0HB. *10m NE of Cambridge, 4m NW of Newmarket via the B1102/ B1103.* **Sun 8 June (12-5). Combined adm £8, chd free. Home-made teas at Isaacson's, open nearby. Home-made cakes inc gluten & nut free options.**

9 THE BRIARS
Ms Marianne Hall and Mr Tony Hollyer.

3 FIELD VIEW
Mr and Mrs Farrow

NEWNHAM FARMHOUSE
Mr and Mrs Quentin Cooke, 07802 857150, q.cooke@ntlworld.com.
Visits also by arrangement 29 Mar to 28 Sept for groups of 8+.

3 ROMAN CLOSE
Mrs Dove, 07437 581674, lizdove11@icloud.com.
Visits also by arrangement 1 May to 1 Sept for groups of up to 6.

SPRING VIEW
Colin Smith
[NPC]

3 Roman Close has a small, pretty modern cottage garden, with roses perennials and annuals. Pots and hanging baskets. Spring View has the National Collection of Yucca, for the specialist plantsman huge diversity of form and sizes, drought tolerant planting plus other species. 9 The Briars is environmentally friendly with a pond, flowers and vegetables, featuring a living wall. Newnham Farmhouse has a walled garden surrounding a C16 thatched cottage, with over 70 Japanese acers. Packed borders and a wildflower lawn, not just grass. Ponds front and back and a few interesting sculptures. See also Isaacsons' separate listing; a plantsman's garden of striking diversity in a series of different zones and incorporating medieval plants, in the grounds of a clunch stone former lodging range dating from 1340. 3 Field View is a new build lockdown garden with modern planting and design, secluded entertaining areas and borrowed vistas, wildflowers and young trees.

GROUP OPENING

5 CAMBOURNE GARDENS
Great Cambourne, CB23 6AH. *8m W of Cambridge on A428. From A428, take Cambourne junc into Great Cambourne. From B1198, enter village at Lower Cambourne & drive through to Great Cambourne. Follow yellow signs via either route to start at any garden.* **Sun 25 May (11-5). Combined adm £7, chd free. Tea, coffee & cake at 13 Fenbridge.**

13 FENBRIDGE
Lucinda & Tony Williams.

128 GREENHAZE LANE
Fran & John Panrucker.

8 LANGATE GREEN
Steve & Julie Friend.

5 MAYFIELD WAY
Debbie & Mike Perry.

NEW 20 MILLER WAY
Mr Ed Savory.

43 MONKFIELD LANE
Penny Miles.

A unique and inspiring modern group, all created from new build in just a few years. This selection of six demonstrates how imagination and gardening skill can be combined in a short time to create great effects from unpromising and awkward beginnings. The grouping inc a foliage garden with collections of maple and hosta; a suntrap garden for play, socialising and colour; gardens with ponds, a vegetable plot and many other beautiful borders showing their owners' creativity and love of growing fine plants well. Cambourne is one of Cambridgeshire's newest communities, and this grouping showcases the happy, vibrant place our town has become. Excellent examples of beauty and creativity in a newly built environment.

6 38 CHAPEL STREET
Ely, CB6 1AD. Peter & Julia Williams, 01353 659161, peterrcwilliams@btinternet.com. *Entering Ely from Cambridge (A10), pass Cathedral Green (on your R) take 1st L (Downham Rd) towards Ely College. Chapel St is 1st R. Alternatively enter Chapel St from Lynn Rd (300yds).* **Sun 8 June (12-6). Combined adm with Ely Open Gardens £10, chd free.**

Visits also by arrangement Mar to Sept.
Approx ½ acre, with many unusual plants. Year-round interest. Gravel garden, well-stocked colourful rockery, herbaceous borders raised vegetable beds, soft fruit and figs, pergolas with many climbing roses. Numerous pots on terraces. Front garden has wide variety of roses, flowering *Prunus*, *Philadelphus*, Judas tree. Secluded and tranquil level garden near city centre. Wide variety of unusual plants, year-round. Well established quince often producing 500 or more fruits. Of special note cut-leaf elder, *Solanum rantonnetii*, *Viburnum x hillieri* Winton.

GROUP OPENING

7 CHAUCER ROAD GARDENS
Cambridge, CB2 7EB. *1m S of Cambridge. Off Trumpington Rd (A1309), nr Brooklands Ave junc. Parking available at MRC Psychology Dept on Chaucer Rd.* **Sun 4, Mon 5 May (2-5). Combined adm £8, chd free. Home-made teas at Upwater Lodge.**

NEW 8 CHAUCER ROAD
Tim Spiers and Camilla Worth.

12 CHAUCER ROAD
Mr & Mrs Bradley.

16 CHAUCER ROAD
Mrs V Albutt.

UPWATER LODGE
Mr & Mrs George Pearson.

Chaucer Road Gardens are fine examples of large Edwardian gardens tucked away on the south side of Cambridge. They are all very different in size and character, some with glimpses of a bygone age. There are magnificent old trees, fine lawns, ponds and a water meadow with river frontage and rare breed sheep. Planting is varied, sometimes unusual, and in constant flux. Home-made cakes with garden fruit. Wheelchair access consists of some gravel areas and grassy paths with fairly gentle slopes.

GROUP OPENING

8 CHRISTCHURCH VILLAGE GARDENS
Christchurch, PE14 9PQ. *5m E of March, 10m N of Ely on the Cambridgeshire/Norfolk border. Midway between March and Welney.* **Sun 22 June (12-4). Combined adm £8, chd free. Home-made teas at Christchurch Community Centre.**

THE GREEN
Pauline Hutchins.

OAKLANDS
Sandra Kay.

THE OLD SCHOOL HOUSE
Philippa Pearson.

SANDHURST
Stuart Turner.

The Old School House is a developing plantswoman's and designer's garden with traditional and contemporary planting, many perennials, a sunny walled border and shady borders. The Green is a traditional cottage garden with small trees, a summerhouse, roses and mixed planting. Sandhurst is a large country garden begun over 30 years ago with island beds, inspired by Alan Bloom's garden at Bressingham, Norfolk. Perennials inc 50 different hardy geraniums, 60 *Hemerocallis* and 70 hostas. Oaklands has cottage garden style planting with shrubs and many perennials inc hostas and hardy geraniums. There's a water feature, two raised beds for vegetables, a greenhouse and patio. Some gravel paths and small level changes, generally all gardens can be accessed.
&♿ ❀ ☕ 🔊

9 CHURCH LANE HOUSE
Church Lane, Westley Waterless, CB8 0RL. Mrs Lucy Crosby, 07908 622292, lucycrosby.vet@gmail.com, www.thegardencompanion.co.uk. *5m S of Newmarket. Located on the L side corner of Church Ln.* **Visits by arrangement 19 May to 30 Sept for groups of 5+. Two nearby gardens may also be available to visit, depending on dates.**
Set in just under an acre, our garden offers a wildlife pond, herbaceous borders, Victorian style greenhouse and kitchen garden, orchard and wildflower meadow. There are borders dedicated to cut flowers and dye plants. This is a family friendly garden, shared with chickens, guinea pigs and bees with plenty of seating areas to take in the views. Wheelchair access is mostly via lawns.
♿ ❀ ☕ 🔊

10 CHURCH VIEW
Main Street, Westley Waterless, CB8 0RQ. Diana Hall, 07974 667298, boohall@icloud.com. *On Main St opp the turning into Church Ln.* **Visits by arrangement 19 May to 30 Sept for groups of 5+. Two nearby gardens may also be available to visit, depending on dates.**
A country garden which inc a small flower farm. There are many old fashioned scented roses, both shrub and climbing. As well as the garden herbaceous borders, there are raised growing beds and two polytunnels. The garden inc a wildlife pond and flowering plant-filled pots. The farm growing area changes season by season. Wide sloping concrete paths from front to back.
♿ ❀ ☕ 🔊

11 CLOVER COTTAGE
50 Streetly End, West Wickham, CB21 4RP. Mr Paul & Mrs Shirley Shadford, 07538 569191, shirleyshadford@live.co.uk. *3m from Linton, 3m from Haverhill & 2m from Balsham. From Horseheath turn L, from Balsham turn R, thatched cottage opp triangle of grass next to old windmill.* **Sun 16, Sun 23 Feb, Sun 2 Mar (2-4). Adm £3, chd free. Light refreshments. Sun 1, Sun 8 June (12-4.30). Adm £4, chd free. Tea, coffee & cake.** Visits also by arrangement 14 Feb to 29 June.
In winter find a flowering cherry tree, borders of snowdrops, aconites, *Iris reticulata*, hellebores and miniature *Narcissus* throughout the packed small garden which has inspiring ideas on use of space. Pond and arbour, raised beds of fruit and vegetables. In summer arches of roses and clematis, hardy geraniums, delightful borders of English roses and herbaceous plants. Charming patio. Snowdrops, hellebores and spring flowering bulbs for sale for the winter opening. Plants also for sale in June.
❀ 🚗 ☕

12 COTTAGE GARDEN
79 Sedgwick Street, Cambridge, CB1 3AL. Rosie Wilson. *Off Mill Rd, S of the railway bridge.* **Sun 1 June (2-6). Adm £4, chd free. Home-made teas.**
Small, long, narrow and planted in the cottage garden style with over 38 roses, some on arches and growing through trees. Particularly planned to encourage wildlife with small pond, mature trees and shrubs. Perennials and some unusual plants interspersed with sculptures.
❀

GROUP OPENING

13 COVENEY & WARDY HILL GARDENS
Coveney, Ely, CB6 2DN. *From A142 or A10 Ely bypass, follow signs for Coveney, then for Wardy Hill. From A142 sp Witcham.* **Sat 24, Sun 25 May (1-5). Combined adm £6, chd free. Home-made teas.**

DROVERS
Mr David C Guyer.

1A THE GREEN
Mrs Kate Bullen.

THE HEY CHAPEL
Mr Peter Ross.

TOADS ACRE
Ms Naomi Laredo.

Four medium sized gardens, in the fenland parish of Coveney overlooking Ely Cathedral. Whilst passing through Coveney, do visit the C13 church and award winning wildlife churchyard. The gardens, this year, are all in Wardy Hill where there is a welcoming free cuppa and cakes to buy at Hey Chapel, which has winding paths to view the cathedral and a splendid vegetable garden, down through a series of rooms with arched roses and wildlife ponds. On the Green 1a, is a new build house and garden with a more modern feel of arbours, interesting herbaceous borders and water feature. Across the Green is Toadsacre, ⅔ acres of Heritage Orchard and mature tree walks with a Potage terrace and an ideal place for another cuppa. Drovers is based on a Chinese pleasure garden philosophy but with English naturalist planting that wanders by a wildlife pond, beneath mature trees to a rose garden and potted terrace.
☕ 🔊

CAMBRIDGESHIRE

GROUP OPENING

14 DUXFORD GARDENS
Duxford, CB22 4RP. *All gardens are close to the centre of the village of Duxford. S of the A505 between M11 J10 & Sawston. Street parking.* **Sun 1 June (2-6). Combined adm £8, chd free. Home-made teas at Bustlers Cottage (cream teas) and in St Peter's Church (in aid of church roof).**

BUSTLERS COTTAGE
John & Jenny Marks,
07956 049257,
jenny.marks@ngs.org.uk.
Visits also by arrangement 2 June to 31 July for groups of 10 to 30.

2 GREEN STREET
Mr Bruce Crockford.

5 GREEN STREET
Jenny Shaw.

16 ICKLETON ROAD
Claire James.

OLD LACEYS
Dr G Hinks.

THE RECTORY

ROBYNET HOUSE
Gordon Lister.

31 ST PETER'S STREET
Mr David Baker.

Eight gardens of different sizes and character. 2 Green St is packed with plants and flowers, 5 Green St is an enclosed garden which was planted to be easily managed and require little maintenance without compromising on colour and interest. 31 St Peter's St, on a steep slope, is filled with surprises, and a dry rockery. Bustlers Cottage has a cottage garden inc vegetables, many trees and places to sit. Stop here for a home-made cream tea and buy some plants. The gardener at 16 Ickleton Rd is a plantaholic, unable to refuse room to an unusual plant, and has a fascinating garden as a result. This may be the last opportunity to visit this garden- not to be missed. The garden at Robynet House, with its many rooms, fountain, stream and glorious planting is picture perfect and inspiring. In St John's St, the garden at number 38, Old Laceys, is a cottage garden with some formal touches, inc a cloud pruned Pyracantha. Opposite Old Laceys a grass maze has been mown into the lawn at the Rectory. Wheelchair access, some gravel paths and a few steps, mostly avoidable.

15 ♦ ELGOOD'S BREWERY GARDENS
72 North Brink, Wisbech, PE13 1LW. Elgood & Sons Ltd, 01945 583160, info@elgoods-brewery.co.uk, www.elgoods-brewery.co.uk. *1m W of town centre. Leave A47 towards Wisbech Centre. Cross river to North Brink. Follow river & brown signs to brewery & car park beyond signposted The Hop Rooms.* **For NGS: Thur 14 Aug (11-4). Adm £5, chd free. Light refreshments inc cakes and sausage rolls served in The Hop Rooms.** For other opening times and information, please phone, email or visit garden website.

Approx four acres of peaceful garden featuring 250 year old specimen trees providing a framework to lawns, lake, rockery, herb garden and maze. Wheelchair access to visitor centre and most areas of the garden.

16 ELM HOUSE
Main Road, Elm, Wisbech, PE14 0AB. Mrs Diana Bullard. *2½m SW of Wisbech. From A1101 take B1101, signed Elm, Friday Bridge. Elm House is ⅓m on L.* **Sun 6 July (2-5). Adm £5, chd free. Tea, coffee & cake.**
Elm House has a lovely walled garden with arboretum, many rare trees and shrubs, mixed perennials and a three acre flower meadow. Children and guide dogs welcome. Most paths suitable for wheelchair users. Uneven surfaces in meadow.

8 Chaucer Road, Chaucer Road Gardens

GROUP OPENING

17 ELY OPEN GARDENS
Chapel Street, Ely, CB6 1AD. *14m N of Cambridge. Parking is available at Barton Rd, The Grange Council Offices, St.Mary's St, Brays Ln & Newnham St. On street parking only at 1 Merlin & 1 Robins Dr.* **Sun 8 June (12-6). Combined adm with 38 Chapel Street £10, chd free. Homemade teas at Ely Methodist Church and 1 Merlin Drive. Ice creams and apple juice available at Bishop of Huntingdon's Garden.**

BISHOP OF HUNTINGDON'S GARDEN
Dagmar, Bishop of Huntingdon.

THE BISHOP'S HOUSE
The Bishop of Ely.

42 CAMBRIDGE ROAD
Mr & Mrs J Switsur.

1 MERLIN DRIVE
Dr Chris Wood.

1 ROBINS CLOSE
Mr Brian & Mrs Ann Mitchell.

A delightful and varied group of gardens in the historic cathedral city. The Bishop's House, adjoining Ely Cathedral, has a wild area, beehives and a formal rose garden. The Bishop of Huntingdon's garden is a family garden with a pond, herbaceous borders and an orchard. 1 Merlin Drive and 1 Robins Close are both gardens with attractive mixed plantings. The former has a collection of subtropical plants, and ferns, the latter has raised beds, a vegetable plot and a small dry garden. 42 Cambridge Road is a large, appealing town garden with delightful planting, fig-trees and a greenhouse leading to a vegetable area. Map showing all garden locations is provided. Wheelchair access to areas of most gardens.

18 NEW FARM LODGE
High Street, Hildersham, Cambridge, CB21 6BU. Mrs Athene Hunt, 01223 891412, huntcam2015@gmail.com. *7m S of Cambridge. Exit 9 or 10 off M11. Off A1307, next to the Village Hall, between the river and the Pear and Olive, opp Hall Farm.* **Visits by arrangement 24 June to 30 Sept for groups of up to 20. Tuesdays, Thursdays and weekends preferred. Adm £7.50, chd free. Tea, coffee & cake.**
This secluded garden is just under an acre. The house stands in the centre and the borders wrap around it, giving opportunities for planting schemes in the different aspects. There is a woodland walk, a shady dell with a hidden table and bench, semi wild areas, a kitchen garden, fruit trees, compost bays and an extensive patio with a wealth of home propagated mediterranean and unusual plants. Parking on gravel drive, level with patio. Easy access to lawn areas. Please contact in advance if a visitor has mobility concerns.

Springfield

CAMBRIDGESHIRE 63

19 FENLEIGH
Inkerson Fen, off Common Rd, Throckenholt, PE12 0QY. Jeff & Barbara Stalker, 07800 575100, barbara.stalker@ngs.org.uk. *Halfway between Gedney Hill & Parson Drove. Postcode for SatNavs takes you within 200 metres, then follow NGS signage.* **Visits by arrangement May to Aug for groups of up to 40. Adm £5, chd free. Tea, coffee & cake.**
A fish pond dominates this large garden surrounded with planting. Patio with pots and raised beds and an undercover BBQ. Small wooded area, polytunnels and corners of the garden for wildlife.

20 6 FINCH'S CLOSE
Stapleford, Cambridge, CB22 5BL. Prof & Mrs S Sutton. *4m S of Cambridge. From the London Rd (A1301) turn into Bury Rd (by the Rose PH), then turn 2nd L into Bar Ln and 3rd L into Finch's Close.* **Sat 14, Sun 15 June (1-6). Adm £3, chd free. Tea, coffee & cake.**
Clever use of limited space, with a series of raised beds in the vegetable garden next to fruit trees and greenhouse. The borders around the lawn and wildlife pond are stocked with shrubs and perennial planting whilst a bird-feeding station is the centrepiece of the lawn. There are musical references throughout the garden. Designated a Wildlife Friendly garden by the BCN Wildlife Trust in 2023.

21 NEW FOUNTAIN COURT
48 Benwick Road, Doddington, March, PE15 0TG. Mr Hilton Fisher. *4m from March, 300 metres from Doddinton village centre. Doddington is situated off A141 between March and Chatteris. In Doddington drive until clock tower. Turn down Benwick Rd (B1093). Fountain Court is approx 300 metres on the L.* **Sat 31 May, Sun 8 June (11-5.30). Combined adm with Springfield £7.50, chd free.**
Garden developed over last eight years from blank canvas. Front garden has planted borders. Explore the small courtyard garden with dovecote and the terrace with an aviary, formal garden with roses, Edwardian Lily pond and new summerhouse surrounded by specimen trees. There is also a small vegetable garden with raised beds. Gates to Informal garden with gypsy caravan and bantams.

22 GREEN END FARM
Over Road, Longstanton, Cambridge, CB24 3DW. Sylvia Newman, www.sngardendesign.co.uk. *From A14 head towards Longstanton. At r'about take 2nd exit, at next r'about turn L. Garden 200 metres on L.* **Sun 6 July (11-4). Adm £5, chd free. Light refreshments.**
A developing garden that's beginning to blend well with the farm. An interesting combination of new and established spaces executed with a design eye. An established orchard with beehives; two wildlife ponds. An outside kitchen and social space inc pool, productive kitchen and cutting garden. Doves, chickens, bees and sheep complete the picture.

23 HEATH FRUIT FARM
The Heath, Bluntisham, Huntingdon, PE28 3LQ. Rob and Mary Bousfield, www.heathfruitfarm.co.uk. *4m N of St Ives. Drive out of Bluntisham at Wood End; garden on R after water towers. From St Ives to Wheatsheaf, at X-roads take The Heath on your R. Garden on L after a few bends.* **Sat 12 Apr (10-2). Adm £4, chd free. Home-made teas.**
A traditional orchard of 25 acres, boasting a range of apples, pears, apricots, plums, gages and cherries. Visit for a tour in the spring to behold a magnificent array of blossom and buzzing bees, while brown hares gambol around in springtime madness. Guided tours on the hour focusing on fruit growing, wildlife and the history of a Cambridgeshire orchard. Dogs allowed but must be kept on a lead. We are looking forward to welcoming you to our orchard. Bring your wellies and waterproofs just in case.

24 HORSESHOE FARM
Chatteris Road, Somersham, Huntingdon, PE28 3DR. Neil & Claire Callan, 01354 693546, nccallan@yahoo.co.uk. *9m NE of St Ives, Cambs. Easy access from the A14. Situated on E side of B1050, 4m N of Somersham Village. Parking for 8 cars on the drive.* **Visits by arrangement 17 May to 29 June for groups of up to 20. Adm £5, chd free. Home-made teas.**
This ¾ acre plant-lovers' garden has a large pond with summerhouse and decking, bog garden, alpine troughs, mixed rainbow island beds with over 40 varieties of bearded irises, water features, a small hazel woodland area, wildlife meadow, secret corners and a lookout tower for wide Fenland views and bird watching.

25 ISAACSON'S
6 High Street, Burwell, CB25 0HB. Dr Richard & Dr Caroline Dyer, 01638 601742, richard@familydyer.com. *10m NE of Cambridge, 4m NW of Newmarket. Behind a tall yew hedge with topiary, & grass triangle, at the S end of the village where Isaacson Rd turns off the High St. Approx 400 yds S of the church.* **Sun 8 June (12-5). Adm £8, chd free. Home-made teas. Open nearby Burwell Village Gardens. Tea, coffee, home-made cake and scones available. Visits also by arrangement 26 Apr to 29 June for groups of 15 to 30. Adm inc refreshments.**
A plantsman's garden warmed and sheltered by the medieval walls of a C14 house (the oldest in Burwell), richly diverse in format and planting. There are 'theatres' (auricula, pinks), hints of Snowdonia, the Mediterranean, a French potager and traditional English. Throughout there are many interesting, unusual and rare plants. Around each corner a new vista surprises. Some assistance with wheelchair over bark or gravel will be required.

26 ISLAND HALL
Godmanchester, PE29 2BA. Grace Vane Percy, 01480 459676, enquire@islandhall.com, www.islandhall.com. *1m S of Huntingdon (A1). 15m NW of Cambridge (A14). In centre of Godmanchester next to free Mill Yard car park.* **Sun 25 May (10.30-4.30). Adm £6, chd free. Home-made teas.**
Three acre grounds, tranquil riverside setting with mature trees. Chinese bridge over Saxon Mill Race to embowered island with wildflowers. Garden restoration begun in 1983 to mid C18 formal design, with box hedging, clipped hornbeams, parterres, topiary, beautiful vistas over the borrowed landscape of Portholme. The ornamental island has been replanted with Princeton elm avenue *(Ulmus americana)*.

CAMBRIDGESHIRE

27 KING'S COLLEGE FELLOWS' GARDEN AND PROVOST'S GARDEN
Queen's Road, Cambridge, CB2 1ST. Provost & Scholars of King's College, tinyurl.com/kingscol. *Entry by gate at junc of Queen's Rd & West Rd or at King's Parade. Parking at Lion Yard, short walk, or some pay & display places in West Rd & Queen's Rd.* **Sun 29 June (10.30-4.30). Adm £10, chd free. Tea, coffee & cake.** Fine example of a Victorian garden with rare specimen trees. Rond Pont entrance leads to a small woodland walk, herbaceous and sub-tropical borders, rose pergola, kitchen/allotment garden and orchard. The Provost's Garden opens with kind permission, offering a rare glimpse of an Arts and Crafts design. Chance to view the new wildflower meadow created on the former Great Lawn. Tickets available to purchase on the day at the college shop in King's Parade. Wheelchair access to garden over gravel paths.
&♿ ☕ 🔊

28 38 KINGSTON STREET
Cambridge, CB1 2NU. Wendy & Clive Chapman. *Central Cambridge. Off Mill Rd, W of railway bridge.* **Sun 6 July (2-5). Combined adm with 73 Kingston Street £5, chd free.**
A tiny courtyard garden with contrasts between deep shade and sunlit areas. Raised beds and pots of various sizes with a range of perennial and annual planting. Please note there is a small step into garden.
♿ 🔊

29 73 KINGSTON STREET
Cambridge, CB1 2NU. Ed Pearson & Karina Michel. *Off Mill Rd, Cambridge. Enter via Hooper St. Back gate is a short walk from the front of the house. Follow the signs.* **Sun 6 July (2-5). Combined adm with 38 Kingston Street £5, chd free. Home-made teas.**
A contemporary, sunken urban space, this patio garden contains a small pond and tiered planters and pots with naturalistic planting. The focal point is a Himalayan birch tree offering shade for the concrete benches. Hints of Mexican planting add an interesting accent in a cosy sanctuary.
☕ 🔊

30 LEISURE LAND
Mepal, Ely, CB6 2AX. David & Mary Gowing. *From Ely take the A142, sp March. Stay on the A142 and cross the Mepal bridge. Turn immed R onto Engine Bank. Drive past the large brick building and turn immed L onto a single track for 800m.* **Sat 28, Sun 29 June (11-4). Adm £5, chd free. Light refreshments.**
Nestled in the fenland landscape, Leisure Land has been developed by its owners over the last five years, creating a quiet oasis within the fenland. 11 acres of lake, ponds and woodland to explore. Take a wander and find surprises: a fairy walk, sculptures, an area for quiet reflection and much more. Bring a friend, children, family. Take a picnic, have fun and relax in this natural environment. A delightful way to spend a summer's afternoon.
🐕 ☕ 🪑

GROUP OPENING

31 LINTON GARDENS
Linton, CB21 4HS. *On A1307 between Cambridge & Haverhill, parking at Linton Village College.* **Sun 18 May (1-5). Combined adm £7, chd free. Home-made teas in the Maltings Courtyard at 94 High Street.**

15 BALSHAM ROAD
Lucy & Tom Wylie.

CHALKLANDS COMMUNITY GARDEN

94 HIGH STREET
Rosemary Wellings.

NEW THE HOLLIES
Hilary and Edwin Green.

QUEENS HOUSE
Michael & Alison Wilcockson.

30 SYMONDS LANE

Several gardens in the village of Linton. Near the top of the High Street, close to the junction with the A1307, is Queens House, with garden 'rooms' separated by hedging and graced by statuary reflecting the age of the house, Elizabethan and Georgian. At the other end of the High Street, the garden behind the Gallery Above at 94 High Street is small and perfectly formed, and accessed via a courtyard where teas are served, and all manner of interesting things go on. 30 Symonds Lane is a small, long Edwardian plot planted as a cottage garden and because of the enormous walnut tree in the middle, the garden is at its best in late spring. The community garden at Chalklands is a riot of colour and joy, and a modern family garden at 15 Balsham Road shows how beauty in a garden can also accommodate a family's needs. 36 Symonds Lane is an established garden which contains a surprising number of acid-loving plants and a newly planted wildflower area with mature trees as backdrop. Some on-street parking throughout the village, and in the car park next to the Health Centre, reached from Coles Lane.
♿ ☕ 🔊

32 MADINGLEY HALL
Cambridge, CB23 8AQ. University of Cambridge, 01223 746222, reservations@madingleyhall.co.uk, www.madingleyhall.co.uk. *4m W of Cambridge. 1m from M11, J13. Located in the centre of Madingley village. Entrance adjacent to mini r'about.* **Tue 29 Apr (2-3.30). Adm £20, chd free. Tea, coffee & cake. Evening opening Wed 2 July (6-7.30). Adm £25, chd free. Light refreshments. Pre-booking essential, please visit www.ngs.org.uk for information & booking.**
Enjoy a tour of this historic garden with a member of the garden team. C16 Hall set in eight acres of attractive grounds landscaped by Capability Brown. Features inc landscaped walled garden with hazel walk. Historic meadow, topiary, mature trees and wide variety of hardy plants.
🐕 ❄ 🪑 ☕ 🔊

33 41 MAIN STREET
Westley Waterless, CB8 0RQ. Maurice Biggins, 07866 057829, mauricebiggins74@gmail.com. *10m E of Cambridge, 5m S of Newmarket. Parking along the Main St and part way up Church Ln.* **Visits by arrangement 19 May to 30 Sept for groups of 5+. Two nearby gardens may also be available to visit, depending on dates.**
Inspired by the gardens of Piet Oudolf and Beth Chatto, the owner has spent the last 10 years creating a beautiful tapestry of colour in his garden in Westley Waterless. Using contemporary design principles and with wildlife in mind, the garden has year-round interest inc drought-tolerant prairie-style borders, pond, topiary, herb garden, fruit trees,

CAMBRIDGESHIRE 65

greenhouse and raised vegetable beds. Access on gravel and paths via a wheelchair ramp.
&

34 ♦ THE MANOR, HEMINGFORD GREY
Hemingford Grey, PE28 9BN. Mrs D S Boston, 01480 463134, diana_boston@hotmail.com, www.greenknowe.co.uk. *4m E of Huntingdon. Off A1307. Parking for NGS opening day only, in field of double bends between Hemingford Grey & Hemingford Abbots. This will be signed. Entrance to garden via small gate off river towpath.* **For NGS: Sun 7 Sept (2-5). Adm £6, chd free. Home-made teas.** **For other opening times and information, please phone, email or visit garden website.**
Garden designed by author Lucy Boston, surrounds C12 manor house on which Green Knowe books based (house by appt). Three acre cottage garden with topiary, snowdrops, old roses, extensive collection of irises inc Dykes Medal winners and Cedric Morris var., herbaceous borders with scented plants. Meadow with mown paths. Enclosed by river, moat and wilderness. Variety of annuals for late flowering. Gravel paths throughout. Wheelchair users are encouraged to use the lawns.
&

35 MOLESWORTH HOUSE
Molesworth, PE28 0QD. John & Gilly Prentis, 07771 918250, gillyprentis@gmail.com. *10m W of Huntingdon off the A14. Next to the church in Molesworth.* **Sun 18 May (2-6). Adm £5, chd free. Home-made teas.** **Visits also by arrangement 1 Apr to 1 July.**
Molesworth House is an old three acre rectory garden with everything that you would both expect and hope for, given its Victorian past. Every corner offers a surprise to its traditional setting, a very happy and relaxed garden - come and see for yourself. A humble gem and amazing tropical greenhouse built by the garden owner awaits your discovery. Accessible to wheelchair users, although there is some gravel.
&

36 NETHERHALL MANOR
Tanners Lane, Soham, CB7 5AB. Timothy Clark. *6m Ely, 6m Newmarket. Enter Soham from Newmarket, Tanners Ln 2nd R 100yds after cemetery. Enter Soham from Ely, Tanners Ln 2nd L after War Memorial.* **Sun 30 Mar, Sun 4 May, Sun 3, Sun 10 Aug (2-5). Adm £4, chd free. Home-made teas.**
Unusual garden appealing to those with historical interest in individual collections of plant groups: March-old primroses, daffodils, Victorian double flowered hyacinths and first garden hellebore hybrids. May-old English tulips, Crown Imperials. Aug-Victorian *Pelargonium, Heliotrope, Calceolaria,* Red list for Plant Heritage. Margery Fish's Country Gardening and Mary McMurtrie's Country Garden Flowers, Historic Plants 1500-1900. Author's books for sale. Wheelchair access good as it is a flat garden.
&

37 NEW 41A NEW ROAD
Whittlesey, Peterborough, PE7 1SU. Miss Emma Bates, 07766 474631, emma@news.co.uk. *Follow SatNav directions for PE7 1SU. From Whittlsey, take A605 E towards Eastrea. At r'about, take 3rd exit onto B1093 then 2nd L to Inhams Rd. New Rd is 1st turning on L.* **Sat 24, Sun 25 May, Sun 29 June, Sun 27 July (12-4.30). Adm £3, chd free. Tea, coffee & cake.** **Visits also by arrangement 1 Mar to 28 Sept for groups of 5 to 10.**
Suburban nature garden situated on the edge of the village with fields and woodland close by. Created over several years, with wildlife the priority, the majority of the garden was over grown brambles. The garden is split into three sections to create interest, each with a different theme. Dogs welcome. Lattersey Nature Reserve at the end of the road.

38 38 NORFOLK TERRACE
Cambridge, CB1 2NG. John Tordoff & Maurice Reeve. *Central Cambridge. A603 East Rd turn R into St Matthews St to Norfolk St, L into Blossom St & Norfolk Terrace is at the end.* **Sat 26, Sun 27 July (11-5). Adm £3, chd free. Light refreshments.**
This lavish Moroccan style paved courtyard garden, in the middle of the city, has masses of colour in raised beds and pots, backed by oriental arches. The ornamental pool defined by its patterned tiles offers the soothing splash of water. There will be a display of recent paintings by John Tordoff and handmade books by Maurice Reeve.

39 OLD FARM COTTAGE
Staploe, St Neots, PE19 5JA. Sir Graham & Lady Fry. *Approx 1m W of St Neots. Going S on Great North Rd in St Neots, turn R into Duloe Rd. Under A1 through Duloe village. Follow the road to Staploe. Last house on the L.* **Sun 22 June (1-5). Adm £5, chd free. Tea, coffee & cake.**
Terraced and formal flower beds surrounding a thatched house and leading to three acres of orchard, grassland, woodland and wetland maintained for wildlife. Present owners have planted some non-native trees, inc ornamental cherries, *loquat, Metasequoia, Ginkgo, Pawlonia* and Monkey Puzzle, extended the area of native woodland and created a wildflower meadow. Wheelchair access: Gravel, uneven ground and one steep slope.
&

40 THE OLD RECTORY
312 Main Road, Parson Drove, Wisbech, PE13 4LF. Helen Roberts, 07818 070641, yogahelen@talk21.com. *SW of Wisbech. From Peterborough on A47 follow signs to Parson Drove, L after Thorney Toll. From Wisbech follow the B1166 through Leverington Common.* **Sun 8 June (11-4). Adm £5, chd free. Tea, coffee & cake.** **Visits also by arrangement May to July for groups of 10+.**
This garden represents the personality of this Georgian house (not open), classical and formal at the front and friendly and a bit crazy at the back. A walled cottage style of about an acre with an abundance of plants and roses leading onto wildflower meadows with walking paths. There are also three ponds each one also with a different personality.
&

The National Garden Scheme donated £281,000 in 2024 to support those looking to work in horticulture as well as those struggling within the industry.

42 23A PERRY ROAD
Buckden, St Neots, PE19 5XG. David & Valerie Bunnage. *5m S of Huntingdon on A1. From A1 Buckden r'about take B661, Perry Rd approx 300yds on L.* **Every Sat and Sun 3 May to 7 Sept (2-4). Adm £5, chd free. Pre-booking essential, please visit www.ngs.org.uk for information & booking.** Approx an acre of many garden designs inc Japanese, interlinked by gravel paths. A plantsmans garden featuring 155 acers and unusual shrubs. Quirky with interesting features and some narrow paths. Regret, not suitable for wheelchairs. WC available.

43 PREACHERS PASSING
55 Station Road, Tilbrook, Huntingdon, PE28 0JT. Keith & Rosamund Nancekievill. *Tilbrook 4½m S of J16 on A14. Station Rd in Tilbrook can be accessed from the B645 or B660. Preachers Passing faces the small bridge over the River Til at a sharp bend in Station Rd with All Saints church behind it.* **Sat 21, Sun 22 June (10.30-4.30). Adm £5, chd free. Tea, coffee & cake. Home-made ice cream and soft drinks also available.** A ¾ acre garden fits into its pastoral setting. Near the house, parterre, courtyard and terrace offer formality; but beyond, prairie planting leads to a wildlife pond, rock gardens, meadow, stumpery, rose garden and copse. Enjoy different views from arbour, honeysuckle-covered swing or scattered benches. Deciduous trees and perennials give changing colour. There are open spaces and hidden places.

Our donation to the Army Benevolent Fund supported 700 individuals with front line services and horticultural related grants in 2024.

Church Lane House

CAMBRIDGESHIRE 67

44 RAMSEY WALLED GARDEN
Wood Lane, Ramsey, Huntingdon, PE26 2XD. Ramsey Abbey Walled Garden CIO, www.ramseywalledgarden.org. *Just N of Ramsey Town Centre. Follow B1096 out of Ramsey. Just after last house on R, turn R opp cemetery. Take track to Ramsey Rural Museum. Park under trees. See map on Ramsey Walled Garden website.* **Sat 13 Sept (2-5). Adm £5, chd free. Light refreshments at Ramsey Rural Museum. The museum is volunteer run. Parking is close by.**
A Victorian Walled Garden, located within the grounds of Ramsey Abbey, has been restored by volunteers and is an enchanting secret in the heart of Ramsey. Dating back to 1840, this one acre garden is dedicated to growing fruit, vegetables and flowers. Features inc a magnificent 33m glasshouse, an apple tunnel planted with Cambridgeshire varieties, a dahlia border and a collection of salvias. The garden is wheelchair accessible but is 450m from the car parking area along a grass path. Motorised buggies can access the garden.

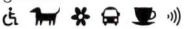

♿ 🐾 ❄ 🚗 ☕ 🔊

45 ROBINSON COLLEGE
Grange Road, Cambridge, CB3 9AN. Warden and Fellows, www.robinson.cam.ac.uk/about-robinson/gardens/national-gardens-scheme. *Garden at main Robinson College site, report to Porters' Lodge. There is only on-street parking.* **Daily weekdays (10-4), weekends (2-4) from Fri 2 Jan. Closed Mon 21 April - Tue 8 July, Fri 15 Aug – Sun 31 Sept, Mon 22 - Wed 31 Dec. Adm £5, chd free. Pre-booking essential, please visit www.ngs.org.uk for information & booking.**
10 original Edwardian gardens linked to central wild woodland water garden focused on Bin Brook, with small lake at heart of site, giving a feeling of park and informal woodland, while keeping the sense of older more formal gardens beyond. Mature stately trees frame central wide lawn running down to the lake. Much original planting is still intact. More recent planting inc bulbs and commemorative trees. No picnics. Children must be accompanied at all times. Tickets must be booked on line in advance. Please collect guidebook from Porters' Lodge. In 2025 essential building and garden maintenance may affect part of the gardens, and some of the suggested garden walking route may not be accessible. Occasionally parts or all of the gardens may be closed for safety reasons involving work by contractors and maintenance staff. Regret no dogs. Ask at Porters' Lodge for wheelchair access.

♿ ☕

GROUP OPENING

46 SAWSTON GARDENS
Sawston, CB22 3HY. *5m SE of Cambridge. Midway between Saffron Walden & Cambridge on A1301.* **Sun 6 July (1-5). Combined adm £7, chd free. Home-made teas in Mary Challis Garden, 68 High Street. Refreshments served from 1.30-4.00pm.**

34 CAMBRIDGE ROAD
Mrs Mary Hollyhead.

20 LONDON ROAD
Linda and David Ambrose.

◆ **MARY CHALLIS GARDEN**
A M Challis Trust Ltd, 01223 560816, chair@challistrust.org.uk, www.challistrust.org.uk.

11 MILL LANE
Tim & Rosie Phillips.

NEW 124 WOODLAND ROAD
Mrs Helen Velioglu.

10 WYNEMARES
Mr Lee Kirby.

Six gardens in this large South Cambs village. New for 2025, 124 Woodland Road has an attractive well laid out and well maintained colourful rear garden, with wonderful views across fields to the Gog Magog hills. 11 Mill Lane is an attractive C16/C19 house with an impressive semi-circular front lawn edged with roses and mixed borders, and a secluded sun-dappled garden at the rear. The two acre Mary Challis Garden has a tranquil setting in the heart of the village, with extensive lawns, wildflower meadow, herbaceous borders, orchard, vegetable beds, vinehouse and beehives. 10 Wynemares presents colourful and creative plantings in a small developing garden. The long rear garden at 20 London Road had a design makeover in 2023, with winding gravel paths and plants chosen to encourage wildlife. Large mature trees border the long garden at 34 Cambridge Road, with attractive borders, greenhouse, raised vegetable beds and fruit trees. Nearly all parts of the gardens are accessible by wheelchair, with the exception of 20 London Road, and steps limit access at 124 Woodland Road.

♿ 🐾 ❄ ☕ 🪑 🔊

---

47 NEW SPRINGFIELD
Benwick Road, Doddington, March, PE15 0TY. Jan & Jon Holdich. *Approx 1m from Doddington. From Doddington toward Benwick on the B1093, look for handwritten Springfield sign on L just after the layby on the bend. What3words app: indicated.stop. hometown.* **Sat 31 May, Sun 8 June (11-5.30). Combined adm with Fountain Court £7.50, chd free. Tea, coffee & cake at Springfield. Home-made cakes, pizza and savouries.**
A 2½ acre informal and relaxed, meandering garden with many areas to explore inc large natural pond with bridges, an orchard, vegetable plot and polytunnel. Wander through the meadow and wildflower areas, and discover woodland paths with established trees. Developed over 30 years. Many different seating areas to enjoy sun or shade. Good wheelchair access via gravel drive and grass paths.

♿ ❄ ☕ 🪑 🔊

Our 2024 donation to The Queen's Nursing institute now helps support over 3,000 Queen's Nurses working in the community in England, Wales, Northern Ireland, the Channel Islands and the Isle of Man.

GROUP OPENING

48 NEW STETCHWORTH AND DULLINGHAM GARDENS
Stetchworth and Dullingham, CB8 9TN. *3m S of Newmarket and 12m E of Cambridge. Stetchworth garden and teas in centre of the village. Dullingham gardens are in the centre and edge of village.* **Sun 20 July (2-5.30). Combined adm £6, chd free. Home-made teas at Stetchworth church.** A short stroll from The Dove House.

NEW THE DOVE HOUSE
Mr & Mrs T Gross.

NEW DULLINGHAM RAILWAY STATION
Network Rail, Managed by Greater Anglia.

PAVILION HOUSE
Mrs Gretta Bredin, 07776 197709, gretta@thereliablesauce.co.uk.
Visits also by arrangement Apr to Sept for groups of 5 to 12.

NEW TILBROOK FARMHOUSE
Mike and Kate Sumpster.

The one acre Dove House garden, professionally designed by the owner, has colour-themed herbaceous borders, formal yew hedges, roses, greenhouse and small orchard. The whole garden encircles a large natural pond with water lilies. The delightful south facing 30 year old one acre garden at Pavilion House has traditional colour-themed borders, expansive rural views, wildflower walk, and stunning vegetable potager used and changes daily so never looks perfect. The lovely old Tilbrook Farmhouse has a charming new small modern garden, rare chalk stream, hot and gravel borders, colourful grasses, Annabelle hydrangeas, lavenders, roses, a covered pergola over the patio and a dry shade area. Dullingham Station offers a garden of sumptuous borders with a wide variety of mixed, colourful wildlife-friendly plants, a pond and insect hotel - all created and cared for by Station Adopters since 2019, to raise the spirits of waiting passengers or those looking out from trains. At Dullingham Station exhibition of 1950's and 1960's certificates won by the station for Best Display on the platforms, and old photographs of the station buildings as they were. Three of the gardens are fully accessible (one with gravel paths).The Dove House is partially accessible, with ramps, but also steps in some areas.

& 🐕 🚗 ☕ 🔊

GROUP OPENING

49 SUTTON GARDENS
89 The Row, Sutton, Ely, CB6 2QQ. *6m W of Ely. From Ely take A142 to March, turn L at r'about to B1381 towards Earith. Parking at Brooklands Centre and along The Row.* **Sun 18 May (1-5). Combined adm £6, chd free. Tea, coffee & cake in The Glebe (to the rear of St Andrew's Church).**

NEW THE BIRCHES
Sue and Colin Frost.

61 HIGH STREET
Ms Kate Travers & Mr Jon Megginson, 01353 778427, katetravers@outlook.com.
🛏

THE OLD BAPTIST CHAPEL
Janet Porter & Steve Newton, 01353 777493, janet.porter@cantab.net.
Visits also by arrangement June & July.

87 THE ROW
Mrs Alison Beale.

89 THE ROW
Andrew Thompson.

The Old Baptist Chapel is a garden created around an C18 building converted to a family home. It inc the adjacent burial ground. The emphasis is on year-round interest and minimal maintenance. 61 The High Street is a tiny shaded garden with a host of features: interesting trees, herb and vegetable plots, water features, a greenhouse, boxes for birds, bats and bugs, and a large collection of acers. 87 The Row is a spacious family garden with pergola, herbaceous beds, shrub border, mature native trees, vegetable beds and fruit trees. 89 The Row is an informal garden on a slight slope with a variety of planted areas inc mature trees, shrubs, fernery, herbaceous, a small vegetable plot and a greenhouse. Scented plants are important throughout the garden. 4a The Row, the garden surrounds the house and has mixed planting for year-round interest. The garden incorporates a very steep bank at the rear which demonstrates gardening on a difficult site.

☕ 🔊

50 TRINITY COLLEGE FELLOWS' GARDEN
Queen's Road, Cambridge, CB3 9AQ. Master and Fellows of Trinity College, www.trin.cam.ac.uk/about/gardens. *Short walk from city centre. At the Northampton St/Madingley Rd end of Queen's Rd, close to Garret Hostel Ln. What3words app: foods.tables.tags.* **Sun 13 Apr (1-4). Adm £5, chd free. Tea, coffee & cake. Special dietary requirements are catered for.**
Historic gardens of about eight acres with specimen trees, mixed borders, drifts of spring bulbs and informal lawns with notable influences throughout from Fellows over the years. Across chalk stream Bin Brook to Burrell's Field, some modern planting styles nestled amongst accommodation blocks in smaller intimate gardens, plus a new woodland walk and mixed fruit orchard. Members of the Gardens Team will be on hand to answer any questions and serve homemade cakes and drinks. Wheelchair access via some gravel and bark chip paths.

& ❀ ☕ 🔊

51 TRINITY HALL - WYCHFIELD SITE
Storey's Way, Cambridge, CB3 0DZ. The Master & Fellows, www.trinhall.cam.ac.uk/about/gardens. *1m NW of city centre. Turn into Storey's Way from Madingley Rd (A1303) & follow the yellow signs. Limited on-road parking is available.* **Sun 13 Apr (11-2). Adm £5, chd free. Tea, coffee & cake in the Sports Pavilion.**
A beautiful, large garden that complements the interesting and varied architecture. The Edwardian Wychfield House and its associated gardens contrast with the recent, contemporary development located off Storey's Way. Majestic trees, tulips and spring flowers on the cherry mound, shady, under-storey, woodland planting and established lawns work together to provide an inspiring garden. Wheelchair access via gravel paths. Some steps in garden.

& ❀ ☕ 🔊

52 TWIN TARNS
6 Pinfold Lane, Somersham, PE28 3EQ. Michael & Frances Robinson, 07938 174536, mikerobinson987@btinternet.com. *Easy access from the A14. 4m NE of St Ives. Turn onto Church St. Pinfold Ln is next to the church. Please park on Church St as access is narrow & limited.* **Sat 19, Sun 20 July (1-5). Adm £6, chd free. Cream teas. Visits also by arrangement May to Aug for groups of up to 25.**
One acre wildlife garden with formal borders, kitchen garden and ponds. There is a large rockery to discover and mini woodland to explore. Wander through the wildflower meadow, rose walk, character bridge and greenhouses. We also have a veranda and treehouse. The garden is adjacent to C13 village church.

&. ❀ ☕ ♪))

53 WILLOW HOLT
Willow Hall Lane, Thorney, Peterborough, PE6 0QN. Angie & Jonathan Jones, www.instagram.com/angiecjones45. *4m E of Peterborough. Turn S from A47 between Thorney and Eye. Sign post Willow Hall. Go 1.8m, we are on the R.* **Sun 25, Mon 26 May (11-5). Adm £5, chd free. Tea, coffee & cake.**
Two acres, part farm field and part old gravel diggings were combined as a building plot in 1960. In 1992 the current owners began a 30 year transformation from nettle bed and local tip to a peaceful garden of mature trees, wildflower meadow, wildlife ponds, bridges, scrap metal sculptures and a varied and impressive collection of plants and shrubs. Largely accessible for wheelchair users.

&. ❀ ☕ 🪑 ♪))

54 THE WINDMILL
10 Cambridge Road, Impington, CB24 9NU. Pippa & Steve Temple, 07775 446443, mill.impington@ntlworld.com, www.impingtonmill.org. *2½ m N of Cambridge. Off A14 at J32, B1049 to Histon, L into Cambridge Rd at T-lights, follow Cambridge Rd round to R, the Windmill is approx 400yds on L.* **Visits by arrangement. Adm inc guided tours of garden or windmill. Adm £10, chd free. Light refreshments inc coffee, tea, wine and nibbles. Discuss refreshments when booking.**
Over a period of 25 years, an acre and a half of wilderness has been transformed into a haven of peace and tranquillity. Gorgeous views stretching across the garden from all angles highlight differing seasonal beds with specific palettes of colour. The design follows the dictates of the Mill at the centre of the garden with an orchard (for cogs), workshops and mill specific work spaces. The Windmill (an C18 smock on C19 tower on C17 base on C16 foundations) is being restored.

&. ❀ 🚗 ☕

55 WRIGHTS FARM
Tilbrook Road, Kimbolton, Huntingdon, PE28 0JW. Russell & Hetty Dean. *13m SW of Huntingdon. ¼m W of Kimbolton on the B645. Do not follow SatNav, not accessed from lay-by.* **Sat 28, Sun 29 June, Sat 30, Sun 31 Aug (11-4). Adm £6, chd free. Home-made teas.**
A substantial garden in a rural setting taking advantage of countryside views. Varied borders with bee and butterfly friendly planting. Formal walled vegetable garden with raised beds, potting shed and greenhouses. Mediterranean style courtyard with dry garden. Newly designed and planted front garden with tropical greenhouse. Courtyard garden to annexe with raised borders and green roof seating area. Wildlife pond. Predominantly flat, but with some gravel surfaces and grass paths.

&. 🐕 ❀ ☕ ♪))

Fenleigh

CHESHIRE & WIRRAL

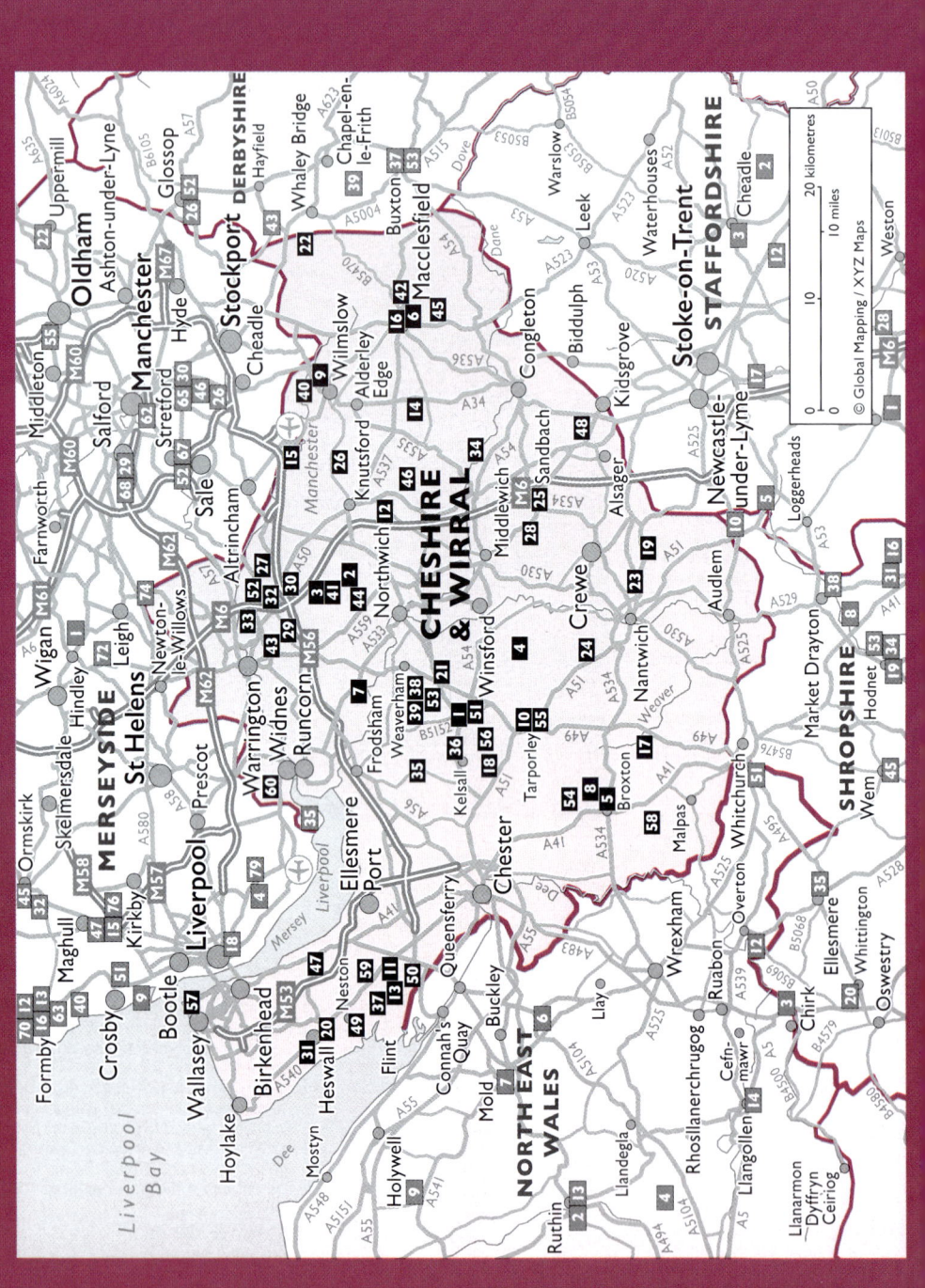

CHESHIRE & WIRRAL 71

VOLUNTEERS

County Organiser
Janet Bashforth
07809 030525
jan.bashforth@ngs.org.uk

County Treasurer
John Hinde
0151 353 0032
johnhinde059@gmail.com

Booklet Co-ordinator
Sharon Maher
0151 837 1321
sharon.maher@ngs.org.uk

Booklet Advertising
Richard Goodyear
richard.goodyear@ngs.org.uk

Social Media & Publicity
Jacquie Denyer
jacquie.denyer@ngs.org.uk

Photographer
Liz Mitchell 01260 291409
liz.mitchell@ngs.org.uk

Assistant County Organisers
Sue Bryant 01619 283819
suewestlakebryant@btinternet.com

Jean Davies 01606 892383
mrsjeandavies@gmail.com

Linda Enderby 07949 496747
linda.enderby@ngs.org.uk

Sandra Fairclough 0151 342 4645
sandrafairclough51@gmail.com

Richard Goodyear (see above)

Juliet Hill 01829 732804
t.hill573@btinternet.com

Romy Holmes 01829 732053
romy@holmes-email.co.uk

Mike Porter 07951 606906
porters@mikeandgailporter.co.uk

 @National Garden Scheme Cheshire & Wirral

 CheshireWirrNGS

 @ngscheshirewirral

OPENING DATES

All entries subject to change.
For latest information check
www.ngs.org.uk

Map locator numbers are shown to the right of each garden name.

January

Sunday 26th
Briarfield 11

February

Snowdrop Openings

Every Sunday to Sunday 16th
Briarfield 11

Sunday 23rd
Bucklow Farm 12

April

Friday 4th
NEW HMP Thorn Cross 29

Saturday 5th
NEW HMP Thorn Cross 29

Sunday 6th
Briarfield 11
NEW HMP Thorn Cross 29
Parm Place 44

Monday 14th
◆ Arley Hall & Gardens 3

Saturday 19th
◆ Poulton Hall 47

Sunday 20th
◆ Poulton Hall 47

Sunday 27th
Hill Farm 28
Norley Court 39

May

Thursday 1st
◆ Cholmondeley Castle Gardens 17

Friday 2nd
NEW HMP Thorn Cross 29

Saturday 3rd
All Fours Farm 2
NEW HMP Thorn Cross 29

Sunday 4th
All Fours Farm 2
NEW HMP Thorn Cross 29
Laskey Farm 33
◆ Stonyford Cottage 53

Monday 5th
All Fours Farm 2
Laskey Farm 33

Friday 9th
Bolesworth Castle 8

Saturday 10th
Bolesworth Castle 8
64 Carr Wood 15
Highbank 25
◆ Lane End Cottage Gardens 32

Sunday 11th
Highbank 25
◆ Lane End Cottage Gardens 32
Tiresford 55

Saturday 17th
10 Statham Avenue 52

Sunday 18th
Manley Knoll 35
10 Statham Avenue 52
Tirley Garth Gardens 56

Saturday 24th
Bankhead 5
◆ Mount Pleasant 36

Sunday 25th
Norley Court 39
The Old Parsonage 41

Monday 26th
The Old Parsonage 41

Thursday 29th
15 Park Crescent 43

June

Sunday 1st
NEW Deva, 3 Weaverham Road 21
Tattenhall Hall 54

Friday 6th
NEW HMP Thorn Cross 29

Saturday 7th
Drake Carr 22
NEW HMP Thorn Cross 29
One House Walled Garden 42
◆ Peover Hall Gardens 46

CHESHIRE & WIRRAL

Sunday 8th
Drake Carr	22
24 Eastern Road	23
Hill Farm	28
NEW HMP Thorn Cross	29
One House Walled Garden	42
♦ Peover Hall Gardens	46
Sandymere	51

Saturday 14th
Laskey Farm	33
10 Statham Avenue	52
Willaston Grange	59

Sunday 15th
18 Dee Park Road	20
NEW Deva, 3 Weaverham Road	21
Laskey Farm	33
10 Statham Avenue	52

Wednesday 18th
♦ Capesthorne Hall	14
18 Dee Park Road	20

Saturday 21st
All Fours Farm	2
2 Ashcroft Cottages	4
♦ Bluebell Cottage Gardens	7
NEW The Nuthouse, 2 Carlton Avenue	40

Sunday 22nd
♦ Abbeywood Gardens	1
All Fours Farm	2
♦ Bluebell Cottage Gardens	7
18 Dee Park Road	20
The Homestead	30
NEW The Nuthouse, 2 Carlton Avenue	40

Friday 27th
NEW Blakelow Farm	6

Saturday 28th
NEW Blakelow Farm	6

Sunday 29th
NEW Blakelow Farm	6
Burton Village Gardens	13
15 Park Crescent	43

July

Friday 4th
NEW HMP Thorn Cross	29

Saturday 5th
NEW HMP Thorn Cross	29

Sunday 6th
NEW HMP Thorn Cross	29
Parm Place	44
The Wonky Garden	60

Thursday 10th
5 Cobbs Lane	19

Saturday 12th
5 Cobbs Lane	19
Laskey Farm	33

Sunday 13th
Laskey Farm	33
Rose Brae	49

Saturday 19th
NEW 187 Victoria Road	57

Sunday 20th
The Homestead	30
Norley Bank Farm	38
Norley Court	39
NEW 187 Victoria Road	57

Saturday 26th
2 Ashcroft Cottages	4

Sunday 27th
2 Ashcroft Cottages	4
The Firs	24
Norley Bank Farm	38

August

Friday 1st
NEW HMP Thorn Cross	29

Saturday 2nd
NEW HMP Thorn Cross	29

Sunday 3rd
The Firs	24
NEW HMP Thorn Cross	29

Monday 4th
Norley Bank Farm	38

Saturday 9th
♦ Lane End Cottage Gardens	32

Sunday 10th
Chinook Cottage	16
♦ Lane End Cottage Gardens	32

Saturday 16th
2 Ashcroft Cottages	4

Sunday 17th
2 Ashcroft Cottages	4
The Wonky Garden	60

Sunday 24th
Laskey Farm	33

Monday 25th
Laskey Farm	33

September

Friday 5th
NEW HMP Thorn Cross	29

Saturday 6th
NEW HMP Thorn Cross	29

Sunday 7th
2 Ashcroft Cottages	4
NEW HMP Thorn Cross	29

Tuesday 16th
♦ Ness Botanic Gardens	37

Sunday 28th
♦ Abbeywood Gardens	1

October

Sunday 5th
Bucklow Farm	12

Sunday 12th
♦ The Lovell Quinta Arboretum	34

Saturday 18th
Parvey Lodge	45

February 2026

Sunday 22nd
Bucklow Farm	12

By Arrangement

Arrange a personalised garden visit with your club, or group of friends, on a date to suit you. See individual garden entries for full details.

All Fours Farm	2
2 Ashcroft Cottages	4
Bankhead	5
Bolesworth Castle	8
Bollin House	9
Bowmere Cottage	10
Briarfield	11
Clemley House	18
18 Dee Park Road	20
The Firs	24
Higher Dam Head Farm	26
166 Higher Lane	27
Hill Farm	28
The Homestead	30
Inglewood	31
Laskey Farm	33
Norley Bank Farm	38
Norley Court	39
Parm Place	44
Parvey Lodge	45
Rosewood	50
Sandymere	51
10 Statham Avenue	52
Tattenhall Hall	54
Trustwood, Burton Village Gardens	13
The Well House	58
The Wonky Garden	60

THE GARDENS

1 ♦ ABBEYWOOD GARDENS
Chester Road, Delamere, Northwich, CW8 2HS. The Rowlinson Family, 01606 889477, info@abbeywoodestate.co.uk, www.abbeywoodestate.co.uk. *11m E of Chester. On the A556 facing Delamere Church.* **For NGS: Sun 22 June, Sun 28 Sept (9-4). Adm £6.50, chd free. Light refreshments. Restaurant in Garden.** For other opening times and information, please phone, email or visit garden website.
Superb setting near Delamere Forest. Total area 45 acres inc mature woodland, new woodland and new arboretum all with connecting pathways. Approx 4½ acres of gardens surrounding large Edwardian house. Vegetable garden, exotic garden, chapel garden, pool garden, woodland garden, lawned area with beds.
& 🐕 ✿ 🚗 🏠 ☕

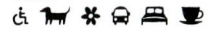

2 ALL FOURS FARM
Colliers Lane, Aston by Budworth, Northwich, CW9 6NF. Mr & Mrs Evans, 01565 733286, www.curbishleysroses.co.uk. *M6 J19, take A556 towards Northwich. Turn immed R, past The Windmill pub. Turn R after approx 1m, follow rd, garden on L after approx 2m. Direct access available for drop off & collection for those with limited mobility.* **Sat 3, Sun 4, Mon 5 May, Sat 21, Sun 22 June (10-4). Adm £5, chd free. Tea, coffee & cake.** Visits also by arrangement 3 May to 29 June for groups of 30+. £9.00 entry on group bookings inc tea & cake. Coaches welcome.
A traditional and well established country garden with a wide range of roses, hardy shrubs, bulbs, perennials and annuals. You will also find a small vegetable garden, pond and greenhouse as well as vintage machinery and original features from its days as a working farm. The garden is adjacent to the family's traditional rose nursery. The majority of the garden is accessible by wheelchair.
& ✿ 🚗 ☕

3 ♦ ARLEY HALL & GARDENS
Arley, Northwich, CW9 6NA. Viscount Ashbrook, 01565 777353, enquiries@arleyhallandgardens.com, www.arleyhallandgardens.com. *10m from Warrington. Signed from J9 & 10 (M56) & J19 & 20 (M6) (20 min from Tatton Park, 40 min to Manchester). Please follow the brown tourist signs.* **For NGS: Mon 14 Apr (10-5). Adm £12, chd £6. Tea, coffee & cake in The Gardener's Kitchen Cafe.** For other opening times and information, please phone, email or visit garden website.
Within Arley's 8 acres of formal garden there are many different areas, each with its own distinctive character. Beyond the Chapel is The Grove, a well established arboretum and a woodland walk of a further 6 or 7 acres. Gardens are mostly wheelchair accessible (steps in some areas). Parts of the estate have cobbles which can prove difficult for manual wheelchairs.
& 🐕 ✿ 🚗 🏠 ☕

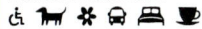

4 2 ASHCROFT COTTAGES
Wettenhall, Winsford, CW7 4DQ. Steve & Sue Redmond, 07763 923005, sredmond24707825@aol.com. *Between Winsford & Tarporley. From Winsford follow Hall Lane for approx 2m. From Tarporley direction, follow signs for Eaton, pick up Hickhurst Lane until it meets Winsford Rd, turn L. We are 500 metres on L.* **Sat 21 June, Sat 26, Sun 27 July, Sat 16, Sun 17 Aug, Sun 7 Sept (11-5). Adm £6, chd free. Tea, coffee & cake.** Visits also by arrangement 10 May to 30 Aug for groups of 6 to 36.
A ¾ acre garden full of wonder and intrigue. Come and immerse yourself amongst large herbaceous borders, mature shrubs, grasses and a large wildlife pond with waterfall. From novice to expert you'll find something new at every turn, our garden mixes both kitchen and ornamental planting with free range hens. If you want something with the wow factor this is the garden for you. Partial access for wheelchairs.
& 🐕 ✿ 🚗 ☕ 🏠 ᴗ))

5 BANKHEAD
Old Coach Road, Barnhill, Chester, CH3 9JL. Simon & Sian Preston, 07970 794456, sian@simonpreston.org. *Turn L off A41 10m S of Chester into Old Coach Rd. House is on L at top of the road, just before the junction with A534.* **Sat 24 May (1-5). Adm £7, chd free. Light refreshments.** Visits also by arrangement 26 May to 29 June for groups of 10 to 25.
Two acres of terraced gardens developed from Victorian times with spectacular views south and west over the Dee valley towards the Welsh hills. Rose garden, herbaceous borders, large pond with Japanese style garden, rhododendrons and azaleas. Small orchard and vegetable garden. Shetland ponies and chickens. Some steps to main terrace but wheelchair users can reach most areas on paths with slight inclines. Parking close to the garden for disabled access.
& ☕ ᴗ))

6 NEW BLAKELOW FARM
Blakelow Road, Macclesfield, SK11 7ED. Christine Tacon & William Thomas-Davies. *1m from centre of Macclesfield. Look for electric metal gates on a sharp bend on the sloping part of Blakelow Rd, on L if going downhill. Adjacent to wooden gates leading to riding stables. What3words app: flames.back.flies.* **Fri 27, Sat 28 June (10-4.30); Sun 29 June (10-3.30). Adm £6, chd free. Cream teas in the garden, served from the conservatory. A limited number of visitors can come inside the conservatory if cold or wet.**
10 acre hillside garden with views over Macclesfield. Wildflower areas, a pond, orchard, vegetable plots, dry stone walls, sedum roofs, both established and new tree planting, flower borders around the house, chickens and doves. Mown paths will take you round the garden whilst you listen to the birdsong. It is too big to keep it all tidy but it is wildlife friendly. Around the house is flat, the drive is tarmac but the front is laid to grass. Most of the garden and some of the views can be seen from here.
& 🐕 ☕ ᴗ))

7 ♦ BLUEBELL COTTAGE GARDENS
Lodge Lane, Dutton, WA4 4HP. Sue Beesley, 01928 713718, info@bluebellcottage.co.uk, www.bluebellcottage.co.uk. *5m NW of Northwich. From M56 (J10) take A49 to Whitchurch. After 3m turn R at T-lights towards Runcorn/ Dutton on A533. Then 1st L. Signed with brown tourism signs from A533.* **For NGS: Sat 21, Sun 22 June (10- 5). Adm £5, chd free. Tea, coffee & cake. For other opening times and information, please phone, email or visit garden website.** South facing country garden wrapped around a cottage on a quiet rural lane in the heart of Cheshire. Packed with thousands of rare and familiar hardy herbaceous perennials, shrubs and trees. Unusual plants available at adjacent nursery. New walled garden with gorgeous brick 'Moongate', greenhouse and raised vegetable beds. The opening dates coincide with the peak of flowering in the herbaceous borders. Visitors are welcome to picnic in the meadow area adjacent to the car park or at the picnic benches in the nursery. The garden is on a gentle slope with wide lawn paths. All areas are accessible. We have a wider access accessible WC.

& ✿ 🚗 ☕ 🪑 ♪)

8 BOLESWORTH CASTLE
Tattenhall, CH3 9JJ. Mrs Anthony Barbour, 01829 782210, dcb@bolesworth.com. *8m S of Chester on A41. Enter via Production Gate A in Old Coach Rd & follow signs to park on the Showground. There is then a fairly strenuous walk from the car park up the Bridge Walk to access the start of the Rock Walk.* **Fri 9, Sat 10 May (10-5). Adm £10, chd £5. Light refreshments. Visit www.bolesworth.com/ gardenopening to buy reduced price early bird tickets in advance or pay full price on the gate. Visits also by arrangement 14 Apr to 30 May for groups of 10 to 40.** An enchanting well planted woodland garden stretching along the sandstone ridge above Bolesworth Castle featuring large leaf, species & hybrid rhododendrons, azaleas and camellias. Explore the paths on The Rock and find the Lion & Lamb Cave with its stunning view of the Welsh Hills and the skyline of Liverpool. Continue your walk through the castle gardens and round the lake. Steep drops so children must be carefully supervised at all times. Wonderful coffee & light refreshments from The Lost Barn Coffee Roasters. Dogs to be on leads at all times (please pick up after them).

🐕 ☕ 🪑 ♪)

9 BOLLIN HOUSE
Hollies Lane, Wilmslow, SK9 2BW. Angela Ferguson & Gerry Lemon, 07828 207492, fergusonang@doctors.org.uk. *From Wilmslow past stn & proceed to T-junction. Turn L onto Adlington Rd. Proceed for ½m, then turn R into Hollies Ln (just after One Oak Ln). Drive to the end of Hollies Ln & follow yellow signage. Park on Browns Ln (other side Adlington Rd) or Hollies Ln.* **Visits by arrangement 1 May to 20 July for groups of 8+. Adm £5, chd free. Tea & cake/biscuits. Cold drinks also available.** The garden has deep borders full of perennials, a wildflower meadow and a formal area with parterres and central water feature. The perennial wildflower meadow (with mown pathways and benches), attracts lots of bees, dragonflies and other insects and butterflies. There are views over the Bollin river valley and Alderley Edge to the south and over to White Nancy in the east. Bollin House is in an idyllic location with the garden, orchard and meadow dropping into the Bollin valley. The River Bollin flows along this valley and on the opp side the fields lead up to views of Alderley Edge. Ramps to gravel lined paths to most of the garden. Some mown pathways in the meadow.

& ✿ ☕

10 BOWMERE COTTAGE
5 Bowmere Road, Tarporley, CW6 0BS. Romy & Tom Holmes, 01829 732053, romy@holmes-email.co.uk. *10m E of Chester. From Tarporley High St (old A49) take Eaton Rd signed Eaton. After 100 metres take R fork into Bowmere Rd, Garden 100 metres on L.* **Visits by arrangement 9 June to 31 July for groups of 5 to 25. Adm £6, chd free. Tea, coffee & cake.** A colourful and relaxing 1 acre country style garden around a Grade II listed house. The lawns are surrounded by well-stocked herbaceous and shrub borders. Two plant filled courtyard gardens, a small vegetable garden, pergolas, rambling roses, clematis, hardy geraniums and hardy herbaceous plants make this a very traditional English garden.

🚗 ☕

11 BRIARFIELD
The Rake, Burton, Neston, CH64 5TL. Liz Carter, 07711 813732, carter.burton@ btinternet.com. *9m NW of Chester. Turn off A540 at Willaston-Burton Xrds T-lights & follow road for 1m to Burton village centre.* **Every Sun 26 Jan to 16 Feb (11-4). Sun 6 Apr (1-5). Home-made teas in the church just along the lane from the garden for April opening only. There will be no refreshments for the snowdrop openings. Adm £5, chd free. Opening with Burton Village Gardens on Sun 29 June. Visits also by arrangement 3 Feb to 28 Sept.** Tucked under the south side of Burton Wood the garden is home to many specialist and unusual plants, some available in plant sale. This 2 acre garden is on two sites, a short walk along an unmade lane. Trees, shrubs, colourful herbaceous, bulbs, alpines and water features compete for attention. Deliberately left untidy through the winter for wildlife, the snowdrops love it. Erythronium are a feature of the garden in April. Always changing, Liz can't resist a new plant! Rare and unusual plants sold (70% to NGS) from the drive each Thursday from 10am to 4pm, 20 February to end September. Check updates on Briarfield Gardens Facebook page: www.facebook.com/people/ Briarfield-Gardens-National-Garden-Scheme/100063468283490/.

✿ ☕

12 BUCKLOW FARM
Pinfold Lane, Plumley, Knutsford, WA16 9RP. Dawn & Peter Freeman. *2m S of Knutsford. M6 J19, A556 Chester. L at 2nd set of T-lights. In 1¼m, L at concealed Xrds. 1st R. From Knutsford A5033, L at Sudlow Ln, becomes Pinfold Ln.* **Sun 23 Feb, Sun 5 Oct (12.30-4). Adm £5, chd free. Light refreshments. Mulled wine, with usual tea, coffee & biscuits. 2026: Sun 22 Feb.** Donation to The Ticker Club.
Country garden with shrubs, perennial borders, rambling roses, herb garden, vegetable patch, meadow, wildlife pond/water feature and alpines. Landscaped and planted over the last 35 yrs with recorded changes. Free range hens. Carpet of snowdrops and

Blakelow Farm

spring bulbs. Leaf, stem, flowers and berries to show colour in autumn and winter. Cobbled yard from car park, but wheelchairs can be dropped off near gate.

& 🐕 ❄ ☕

GROUP OPENING

13 BURTON VILLAGE GARDENS
Burton, Neston, CH64 5SJ. *9m NW of Chester. Turn off A540 at Willaston-Burton Xrds T-lights & follow road for 1m to Burton. Parking well signed. Maps given to visitors. Buy ticket at first garden. Card reader at 4 Burton Manor Gardens only.* **Sun 29 June (11-5). Combined adm £6, chd free.** Home-made teas in the Sport and Social Club behind the village hall.

BRIARFIELD
Liz Carter.
(See separate entry)

NEW **4 BURTON MANOR GARDENS**
Rosemary & Anthony Hannay.

♦ **BURTON MANOR WALLED GARDEN**
Friends of Burton Manor Gardens CIO, 0151 336 6154, friendsofburtonmanorgardens. chessck.co.uk.

TRUSTWOOD
Peter & Lin Friend, 0151 336 7118, p.j.friend@icloud.com, www.trustwoodbnb.uk.
Visits also by arrangement May to Sept for groups of 5 to 15.

🚐

Only 2 years old, 4 Burton Manor Gardens is a tiny gem. It has everything you could want in a garden, interesting shrubs, a herbaceous border, cheerful pots and even tomatoes in the greenhouse and some veg. Close by is Burton Manor Walled garden with period planting and a splendid vegetable garden surrounding the restored Edwardian glasshouse. Paths lead past a sunken garden and terraces to views across the Cheshire countryside. Trustwood is a relaxed country garden, a haven for wildlife with emphasis on British native trees planted along the drive, the use of insect friendly plants and wildlife ponds. Briarfield is home to many unusual plants, some available in the plant sale at the house. The 1½ acre main garden invites exploration not only for its variety of plants but also for the imaginative use of ceramic sculptures. Such diversity, but we are all gardening on a light sandy, slightly acid soil. Briarfield is on a hillside with several flights of steps. Only partially accessible.

& ❄ 🚗 🚌 ☕))

The National Garden Scheme donated over £3.5 million to our nursing and health beneficiaries from money raised at gardens open in 2024.

4 ♦ CAPESTHORNE HALL

Congleton Road, Siddington, Macclesfield, SK11 9JY. Sir William & Lady Bromley-Davenport, 01625 861221, info@capesthorne.com, capesthorne.com/the-grounds-and-gardens. *5m W of Macclesfield. 7m S of Wilmslow. On A34. Free parking.* **For NGS: Wed 18 June (11-4.30). Adm £9, chd free. Lakeside Café offers delicious home-made light refreshments. Afternoon teas are available, pre-booking is required.** For other opening times and information, please phone, email or visit garden website.

Varied garden with daffodil lawn, azaleas, rhododendrons, herbaceous border, woodland walk and arboretum. The tranquil gardens at Capesthorne Hall alongside the adjoining lakes are full of colourful perennials merging with the more unusual C18 plants, shrubs and trees. A family Georgian Chapel, ice house, cascade and memorial garden are located within the grounds. Our landmark trail gives details of all the main architectural features within the grounds. A copy of the map and feature descriptions will be given out to each visitor. Uneven ground on the Woodland Walk, Wilderness Trail and the narrow pathway around the lower pool may be inaccessible to wheelchairs users.

♿ 🐕 🚌 🚗 ☕ 🔊

5 64 CARR WOOD

Hale Barns, Altrincham, WA15 0EP. Mr David Booth. *10m S of Manchester city centre. 2m from J6 M56: Take A538 to Hale Barns. L at 'triangle' by church into Wicker Lane & L at mini r'about into Chapel Lane & 1st R into Carr Wood.* **Sat 10 May (1-5). Adm £5, chd free. Tea, coffee & cake.**

²⁄₃ acre landscaped, south facing garden overlooking Bollin valley laid out in 1959 by Clibrans of Altrincham. Gently sloping lawn, woodland walk, seating areas and terrace, extensive mixed shrub and plant borders. Ample parking on Carr Wood. Wheelchair access to terrace overlooking main garden.

♿ ❀ ☕ 🔊

6 CHINOOK COTTAGE

96 Westminster Road, Macclesfield, SK10 3AJ. Miss Sara Wreford. *1m NW of Macclesfield. From Sainsburys r'about, turn L directly after Sainsburys entrance. The garden is down on the R, opp West Park/ Cemetery. There is more free parking at Bollinbrook shops just further along.* **Sun 10 Aug (12-4.30). Adm £4, chd free. Cream teas. Pimms, teas and coffees.**

A mature enclosed cottage garden of flowers, edibles and fruit trees. Patio screened by bamboo, ferns, crocosmia, foxgloves, poppies, pieris, lychnis and many pots. Lawn surrounded by mature trees and perennials. Mediterranean themed summerhouse. Long border of rhubarb, currants and berries. Front beds inc astrantia, hollyhocks, daphne, campsis. Small greenhouse enables propagation for 2 raised beds in side garden. Lots of seating areas to enjoy refreshments and Pimms. Mainly lawn with some inclines.

♿ ❀ ☕

Higher Dam Head Farm

CHESHIRE & WIRRAL   77

17 ♦ CHOLMONDELEY CASTLE GARDENS
Cholmondeley, Malpas, SY14 8AH. The Cholmondeley Gardens Trust, 01829 720203, eo@chol-estates.co.uk, www.cholmondeleycastle.com. 4m NE of Malpas SatNav SY14 8ET. Signed from A41 Chester-Whitchurch road & A49 Whitchurch-Tarporley road. **For NGS: Thur 1 May (10-5). Adm £8.50, chd £4. Fresh coffee, lunches & cakes daily with locally sourced produce located in the heart of the Gardens.** For other opening times and information, please phone, email or visit garden website.
Discover the romantic Temple and Folly Water Gardens, Glade, Arboretum, 100m long double herbaceous border walkway Lavinia Walk, ornamental woodland upon Tower Hill and the newly created Cholmondeley Rose Garden with 250 rose varieties. Large display of daffodils, magnificent magnolias and bluebell woodland. One of the finest features of the gardens are its trees, many of which are rare and unusual, with over 40 county champion trees. Partial wheelchair access.
&. ⛟ 🐕 ♨ ☕ ⛱

18 CLEMLEY HOUSE
Well Lane, Duddon Common, Tarporley, CW6 0HG. Sue & Tom Makin, 07790 610586, s_makingardens@yahoo.co.uk. *8m SE of Chester, 3m W of Tarporley. A51 from Chester towards Tarporley. 1m after Tarvin turn off, at bus shelter, turn L into Willington Rd. After community centre, 2nd L into Well Lane, 3rd house.* **Visits by arrangement 5 July to 31 Aug for groups of 10 to 50. Pls arrange food orders when booking visit. Adm £7, chd free. Cream teas. Home grown organic fruits used in jams & cakes. Gluten free by prior arrangement. Cash only for teas & plants.**
2 acre organic, wildlife friendly, gold award winning cottage garden. Orchard, 2 wildlife ponds, perennial wildflower meadow, fruit and vegetable areas, rose pergola and veranda, gazebo, shepherd's hut, summerhouse, barn owl and many other nest and bat boxes. Drought tolerant gravel garden and shade garden. New wild areas. The garden is a clear example of how an oasis for wildlife can be beautiful. Vegetables and soft fruits grown organically. Owner has qualified in garden design at Reaseheath College and worked in this field. Gravel paths may be difficult to use but most areas are flat and comprise grass paths or lawn.
&. ⛟ 🐕 ♨ ☕ ⛱

19 5 COBBS LANE
Hough, Crewe, CW2 5JN. David & Linda Race. *4m S of Crewe. M6 J16 r'about take A500 (Nantwich). Next r'about 1st exit Keele. Next r'about straight (Hough). After 1m L into Cobbs Ln. From A51 Nantwich bypass to A500 r'about 3rd exit (Shavington), after 3m (past White Hart), R into Cobbs Ln. Park at village hall (300 metres).* **Thur 10, Sat 12 July (11-5). Adm £5, chd free. Home-made teas at village hall 300 metres up Cobbs Lane. WC avail.**
A plant person's ⅔ acre garden with island beds, wide cottage style herbaceous borders with bark paths. A large variety of hardy and some unusual perennials. Interesting features, shrubs, grasses and trees, with places to sit and enjoy the surroundings. A water feature runs to a small pond, a wildlife friendly garden containing a woodland area bordered by a small stream.
🐕 ♨ ☕

20 18 DEE PARK ROAD
Dee Park Road, Wirral, CH60 3RQ. Mrs Shay & Mr Les Whitehead, 07778 309671, shaywhitehead@gmail.com. *J4 off M53. Follow signs for Brimstage, Heswall, follow to end. Turn L at r'about, take 1st L onto A540 to Chester, 1st R down Gayton Lane. Dee Park is on the bottom L.* **Sun 15, Wed 18, Sun 22 June (11-4.30). Adm £5, chd free. Tea, coffee & cake.** Visits also by arrangement 1 June to 1 July.
A long suburban garden backing onto private woodland. Mature garden laid to lawns, with mixed borders, leading on to numerous seating areas. The garden features a very unusual triple hexagonal greenhouse, which was originally purchased from the Liverpool Garden Festival site, c1984, before taking you through to a shaded wooded area where there are numerous different types of hosta on display. Wheelchair accessible with one step to negotiate.
&. ⛟ 🐕 ♨ ☕

21 NEW DEVA,
3 WEAVERHAM ROAD
Sandiway, Northwich, CW8 2NJ. Mr Andrew & Mrs Tracey Molyneux. *5m outside Northwich, towards Chester. Take A556 towards Chester. On entering Sandiway, pass the sandstone tower, go straight across T-lights positioning yourself ready to take the next R onto Weaverham Rd. 2nd Victorian house on L.* **Sun 1, Sun 15 June (10-3). Adm £4, chd free. Tea, coffee & cake.**
You are greeted at the front by a mature lavender garden, enclosed with a box hedge. To the side a walled yard with cordoned apple, pear and fig trees. Passing through a wrought iron gate a formal Victorian garden awaits with four separate beds. In the centre is a water feature. The garden is enclosed with hawthorn hedges.
&. ☕ ⛱

22 DRAKE CARR
Mudhurst Lane, Higher Disley, SK12 2AN. Alan & Joan Morris. *8m SE of Stockport, 10m NE of Macclesfield. From A6 in Disley centre turn into Buxton Old Rd, go up hill 1m & turn R into Mudhurst Lane. After ⅓m park on layby or grass verge. No parking at garden. Approx 150 metre walk.* **Sat 7, Sun 8 June (11-5). Adm £5, chd free. Home-made teas & gluten-free cakes.**
½ acre cottage garden in beautiful rural setting with natural stream running into wildlife pond with many native species. Surrounding C17 stone cottage, the garden, containing borders, shrubs and vegetable plot, is on several levels divided by grassed areas, slopes and steps. This blends into a boarded walk through bog garden, mature wooded area and stream-side walk into a wildflower meadow.
♨ ☕ ⛱

Our donation to the Army Benevolent Fund supported 700 individuals with front line services and horticultural related grants in 2024.

23 24 EASTERN ROAD
Willaston, Nantwich, CW5 7HT. Mr Roger & Mrs Rosemary Murphy. *1m E of Nantwich. From A51 Nantwich bypass follow sign into Willaston at Crewe Rd R'about. At the T junction turn R over the level Xing then immed turn L into Eastern Rd, garden is approx 100yds on R.* **Sun 8 June (11-4). Adm £5, chd free. Home-made teas.** South facing garden evolved over the last 6 yrs, mixed herbaceous borders inc trees, shrubs and climbers, raised bed, small vegetable plot, seating areas, summerhouse, greenhouse with succulent collection, pots and containers and other features.

24 THE FIRS
Old Chester Road, Barbridge, Nantwich, CW5 6AY. Richard & Valerie Goodyear, richard.goodyear@ngs.org.uk. *3m N of Nantwich on A51. After entering Barbridge turn R at Xrds after 100 metres. The Firs is 2nd house on L.* **Sun 27 July, Sun 3 Aug (11-4). Adm £5, chd free. Tea, coffee & cake.** Visits also by arrangement 4 June to 10 Aug for groups of 10 to 30.
Canalside garden set idyllically by a wide section of the Shropshire Union Canal with long frontage. Garden alongside canal with varied trees, shrubs and herbaceous beds, with some wild areas. All leading down to an observatory and Japanese torii gate at the far end of the garden with views across fields. Usually have nesting friendly swans with cygnets, moor hens and lots of ducks. Wheelchair access to main areas and to all unless the lawns are wet/soft.

25 HIGHBANK
110 Bradwall Road, Sandbach, CW11 1AW. Peter & Coral Hulland. *Approx 1m N of Sandbach town centre. The garden runs between Bradwall Rd & Twemlow Ave, but access & limited parking are on Twemlow Ave only (CW11 1GL).* **Sat 10, Sun 11 May (11-4). Adm £5, chd free. Light refreshments.**
Beautiful town garden, designed by Peter, an RHS Gold Medallist, on what was originally a builders yard of approx ⅓ acre. The current owners of 38 yrs have planted trees, many unusual shrubs and perennials, some being allowed to naturalise, encouraging biodiversity, wildlife and nesting birds. The garden is on different levels featuring lawns, pond, water features, greenhouse and many seating areas.

26 HIGHER DAM HEAD FARM
Damson Lane, Mobberley, WA16 7HY. Richard & Alex Ellison, 07785 288908, alex.ellison@talk21.com. *2m N E of Knutsford. 4m W of Alderley Edge. Turn off B5085 into Mill Lane at sign for Roebuck Inn. Damson Lane runs alongside the Roebuck car park and property lies 150yds further on R.* **Visits by arrangement 1 May to 1 Oct for groups of 10 to 50. Adm £6, chd free. Tea, coffee & cake.**
Two acre country garden with several box lined courtyards, large terracotta pots, deep herbaceous borders, pergola, wildflower orchard, walled vegetable garden, large glasshouse with extensive collection of succulents and cacti. Natural pond with waterside deck. Newly planted area of silver birch and grasses in modern style.

27 166 HIGHER LANE
Lymm, WA13 0RG. Trevor Holland & Marian Bingham, 07711 163411, tholland31755@yahoo.ca. *6m ESE of Warrington on E edge of Lymm, just off the A56. From M6, exit at J20, from M56 exit at J9 & follow signs to Lymm (B5158), R at T-junction onto A56 heading SE for 1½m on Higher Ln. Park on Higher Ln, garden 50yds on Whiteleggs Ln.* **Visits by arrangement 4 May to 14 Sept for groups of 5 to 20. Groups up to 12 can be served in the orangery when the weather is poor. Adm £5, chd free. Home-made teas. Barista coffees, sweet & savoury baked goods.**
Garden plot 110'x 80' on Whiteleggs Lane off Higher Lane with large summerhouse and orangery. Habitats and flowers for bees and wildlife. Wooded area of silver birch, maples, shrubs and pond, patio area with vine arbour and gravel garden, cottage garden with lawn and less mowed area for wild flowers. No parking on Whiteleggs Lane, parking only on Higher Lane on the side of the cottages.

28 HILL FARM
Mill Lane, Moston, Sandbach, CW11 3PS. Mrs Chris & Mr Richard House, 01270 526264, housecr2002@yahoo.co.uk. *2m NW of Sandbach. From Sandbach town centre take A533 towards Middlewich. After Fox pub take next L (Mill Lane) to a canal bridge & turn L. Hill Farm 400m on R just before post box.* **Sun 27 Apr, Sun 8 June (11-5). Adm £5, chd free. Light refreshments.** Visits also by arrangement 20 Apr to 28 Sept.
The garden extends to approx ½ acre and is made up of a series of gardens inc a formal courtyard with a pond and vegetable garden with south facing wall. An orchard and wildflower meadow were established about 6 yrs ago. A principal feature is a woodland garden which supports a rich variety of woodland plants. This was extended in April 2020 to inc a pond and grass/herbaceous borders. A level garden, the majority of which can be accessed by wheelchair.

29 NEW HMP THORN CROSS
Arley Road, Appleton, Warrington, WA4 4RL. Jade McDonnell. *Pls enter through the large wooden gates opp Appleton Thorn primary school.* **Fri 4, Sat 5, Sun 6 Apr, Fri 2, Sat 3, Sun 4 May, Fri 6, Sat 7, Sun 8 June, Fri 4, Sat 5, Sun 6 July, Fri 1, Sat 2, Sun 3 Aug, Fri 5, Sat 6, Sun 7 Sept (10-1). Adm £5. Pre-booking essential, please visit www.ngs.org.uk for information & booking. Light refreshments.**
HMP Thorn Cross is an open prison with large sprawling grounds which we are delighted to open for the enjoyment of the public. We have an impressive range of biodiversity inc beehives, ducks, newts, birds and more! We are extremely proud of our award-winning landscape, carefully maintained by the prisoners and look forward to welcoming visitors for a unique and once in a lifetime experience. Features inc pond, beehives, orchard, fields, flower displays, planting beds, extensive woodland and herbaceous borders. Pls note identity documentation will be required and we will contact you prior to your visit. Pls notify us in advance of any access requirements.

The Firs

30 THE HOMESTEAD
2 Fanners Lane, High Legh, Knutsford, WA16 0RZ. Janet Bashforth, 07809 030525, janbash43@sky.com. *J20 M6/J9 M56 at Lymm interchange take A50 for Knutsford, after 1m turn R into Heath Lane then 1st R into Fanners Lane. Follow parking signs.* **Sun 22 June, Sun 20 July (11-4). Adm £5, chd free.** Visits also by arrangement for groups of 10 to 40.
This compact gem of a garden has been created over the last 9 yrs by a keen gardener and plantswoman. Enter past groups of liquidambar and white stemmed birch. Colour themed areas with many perennials, shrubs and trees. Past topiary and obelisks covered with many varieties of clematis and roses, enjoy the colours of the hot border. A decorative greenhouse and pond complete the picture.

&. ✿ 🚗 ☕))

31 INGLEWOOD
4 Birchmere, Heswall, CH60 6TN. Colin & Sandra Fairclough, 07715 546406, sandrafairclough51@gmail.com. *6m S of Birkenhead. From A540 Devon Doorway/Clegg Arms r'about go through Heswall. ¼m after Tesco, R into Quarry Rd East, 2nd L into Tower Rd North & L into Birchmere.* **Visits by arrangement 14 Apr to 19 July for groups of 12 to 30. Adm £5, chd free. Home-made teas.**
Beautiful ½ acre garden with stream, large koi pond, 'beach' with grasses, wildlife pond and bog area. Brimming with shrubs, bulbs, acers, conifers, rhododendrons, hydrangeas, herbaceous plants and hosta border. Interesting features inc hand cart, wood carvings, bug hotel and Indian dog gates leading to a secret garden. Lots of seating to enjoy refreshments.

&. 🐕 ✿ ☕

32 ♦ LANE END COTTAGE GARDENS
Old Cherry Lane, Lymm, WA13 0TA. Imogen Sawyer, 01925 752618, imogen@laneendcottagegardens.co.uk, www.laneendcottagegardens.co.uk. *1m SW of Lymm. J20 M6/J9 M56/A50 Lymm interchange. Take B5158 signed Lymm. Turn R 100 metres into Cherry Corner, turn immed R into Old Cherry Lane.* **For NGS: Sat 10, Sun 11 May, Sat 9, Sun 10 Aug (10-5). Adm £5, chd £2.50. Tea, coffee & cake.** For other opening times and information, please phone, email or visit garden website.
Formerly a nursery, this 1 acre cottage garden is densely planted for year-round colour with many unusual plants. Features inc deep mixed borders, scented shrub roses, ponds, herb garden, walled orchard with trained fruit, shady woodland walk, sunny formal courtyard, vegetable garden and chickens. Wheelchair accessible WC. Disabled visitors can park by garden entrance. The garden is flat but some bark paths may be difficult if wet.

&. ✿ 🚗 ☕ 🏕

33 LASKEY FARM

Laskey Lane, Thelwall, Warrington, WA4 2TF. Howard & Wendy Platt, 07785 262478, howardplatt@lockergroup.com, www.laskeyfarm.com. *2m from M6/M56. From M56/M6 follow directions to Lymm. At T-junction turn L onto the A56 in Warrington direction. Turn R onto Lymm Rd. Turn R onto Laskey Lane.* **Sun 4, Mon 5 May, Sat 14, Sun 15 June, Sat 12, Sun 13 July, Sun 24, Mon 25 Aug (11-4). Adm £6, chd £1. Tea, coffee & cake.** Visits also by arrangement 1 May to 29 Aug for groups of 20 to 50. 1½ acre garden inc herbaceous and rose borders, vegetable area, a greenhouse, parterre and a maze showcasing grasses and prairie style planting. Interconnected pools for wildlife, specimen koi and terrapins form an unusual water garden which features a swimming pond. There is a treehouse plus a number of birds and animals. Family friendly, we offer a treasure hunt, and a mini menagerie consisting of chickens, guinea fowl and guinea pigs. Most areas of the garden may be accessed by wheelchair.

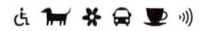

& 🐕 ✱ 🚗 ☕ 🔊

34 ♦ THE LOVELL QUINTA ARBORETUM

Swettenham, CW12 2LF. Tatton Garden Society, 01565 831981, admin@tattongardensociety.org.uk, lovellquintaarboretum.co.uk. *4m NW of Congleton. Turn off A54 N 2m W of Congleton or turn E off A535 at Twemlow Green, NE of Holmes Chapel. Follow signs to Swettenham. Park at Swettenham Arms. What3words app: twins.sheds.keepers.* **For NGS: Sun 12 Oct (1.30-4). Adm £5, chd free. Tea. Admission is cash only.** For other opening times and information, please phone, email or visit garden website.
This 28 acre arboretum has been established since the1960s and contains around 2,500 trees and shrubs, some very rare. National Collections of Quercus, Pinus and Fraxinus. A large selection of oaks plus autumn flowering, fruiting and colourful trees and shrubs. Newly restored lake. Waymarked walks. Refreshments at the adjacent Swettenham Arms. With care wheelchairs can access much of the arboretum on the mown paths.

& 🐕 🚗 NPC ☕ 🔊

35 MANLEY KNOLL

Manley Road, Manley, WA6 9DX. Mr & Mrs James Timpson. *3m N of Tarvin. On B5393, via Ashton & Mouldsworth. 3m S of Frodsham, via Alvanley.* **Sun 18 May (12-5). Adm £5, chd free. Tea, coffee & cake.** Arts & Crafts garden created in the early 1900s. Covering 6 acres, divided into different rooms encompassing parterres, clipped yew hedging, ornamental ponds and herbaceous borders. Banks of rhododendron and azaleas frame a far-reaching view of the Cheshire Plain. Also a magical quarry/folly garden with waterfall and woodland walks.

🐕 ✱ ☕ 🍽 🔊

36 ♦ MOUNT PLEASANT

Yeld Lane, Kelsall, CW6 0TB. Dave Darlington & Louise Worthington, 01829 751592, louisedarlington@btinternet.com, www.mountpleasantgardens.co.uk. *8m E of Chester. Off A54 at T-lights into Kelsall. Turn into Yeld Lane opp Farmers Arms pub, 200yds on L. Do not follow SatNav directions.* **For NGS: Sat 24 May (11-4). Adm £8, chd £5. Tea, coffee & cake.** For other opening times and information, please phone, email or visit garden website.
10 acres of landscaped garden and woodland started in 1994 with impressive views over the Cheshire countryside. Steeply terraced in places. Specimen trees, rhododendrons, azaleas, conifers, mixed and herbaceous borders; 4 ponds, formal and wildlife. Vegetable garden, stumpery with tree ferns, sculptures, wildflower meadow and Japanese garden. Bog garden, tropical garden. Sculpture trail and exhibition.

✱ 🚗 ☕

37 ♦ NESS BOTANIC GARDENS

Neston Road, Ness, Neston, CH64 4AY. The University of Liverpool, 0151 795 6300, nessgdns@liverpool.ac.uk, www.liverpool.ac.uk/ness-gardens. *10m NW of Chester. Off A540. M53 J4, follow signs M56 & A5117 (signed N Wales). Turn onto A540 follow signs for Hoylake. Ness Gardens is signed locally. 487 bus takes visitors travelling from Liverpool, Birkenhead etc.* **For NGS: Tue 16 Sept (10-5). Adm £8.50, chd £4.50. For other opening times and information, please phone, email or visit garden website.**
Looking out over the dramatic views of the Dee estuary from a lofty perch on the Wirral peninsula, Ness Botanic Gardens boasts 64 acres of landscaped and natural gardens overflowing with horticultural treasures. With a delightfully peaceful atmosphere, a wide array of events taking place, plus a café and gorgeous open spaces it is a great fun-filled day out for all the family. National Collections of Sorbus and Betula. Herbaceous borders, Rock Garden, Mediterranean Bank, Potager and conservation area. Wheelchairs and scooters are available to hire but advance booking is highly recommended.

& ✱ 🚗 NPC ☕

38 NORLEY BANK FARM

Cow Lane, Norley, Frodsham, WA6 8PJ. Margaret & Neil Holding, 07828 913961, neil.holding@hotmail.com. *Near Delamere forest. From the Tigers Head pub in the centre of Norley village keep the pub on L, carry straight on through the village for approx 300 metres. Cow Lane is on the R.* **Sun 20, Sun 27 July, Mon 4 Aug (11-5). Adm £6, chd free. Home-made teas. Some allergy free refreshments available.** Visits also by arrangement 14 July to 8 Aug for groups of 10+.
Wander past a flower meadow before entering the main garden. Here well-stocked herbaceous borders wrap around this traditional Cheshire farmhouse. Within an orchard are enclosed cut flower borders that surround a greenhouse and just beyond the house lies a vegetable garden. Walk past this to 2 wildlife ponds with a backdrop of pollinating flowers and stumpery. All set in 2 acres. WC available. Free range hens, donkeys and Coloured Ryeland sheep. Access in the main is possible for wheelchairs (though not the WC). There are some stone steps and a small number of narrow paths.

& 🐕 ✱ 🚗 ☕ 🔊

In 2024, our donations to Carers Trust meant that 26,081 unpaid carers were supported across the UK.

CHESHIRE & WIRRAL   81

39 NORLEY COURT
Marsh Lane, Norley, Frodsham, WA6 8NY. Clare Albinson, 07717 447465, Albinsonc@hotmail.com. *20 mins E of Chester. Close to Delamere Forest. A556 - Stoneyford Ln/ Cheese Hill/Cow Ln - L then R. A49 Acton Ln/Station Rd L at church next R into Marsh Ln. Norley Ct is top of hill. Parking on nearby roads or in field at bottom of steep hill.* **Sun 27 Apr, Sun 25 May (11-4.30). Tea, coffee & cake. Sun 20 July (11-4.30). Adm £6, chd free. Visits also by arrangement 14 Apr to 19 Oct for groups of up to 20.**
Norley Court is a large spring and summer garden with a bluebell wood, rhododendrons, azaleas, pieris, tulips, daffodils and kalmias. The red Embothriums flower against the Cheshire plain. Clematis, wisteria, roses, abutilon and jasmine abound. Many interesting and unusual trees along the banks inc cornus, a handkerchief tree, Judas trees, sorbus varieties, eucryphia, Katsura, maple varieties etc. Walled garden. Large display of rhododendrons and azaleas inc several perfumed rhododendrons. Bluebell wood. Wonderful views over Cheshire. Sunken gardens. Tremendous Autumn Colour. There is sloped access to most areas of the garden, though some are quite steep and grassed. Drop off at house for those with limited mobility.
&. 🐕 ✱ ☕ 🪑 »))

40 NEW THE NUTHOUSE, 2 CARLTON AVENUE
Wilmslow, SK9 4EP. Sue Ghori & Leo Worsick. *From Wilmslow town centre head towards Handforth on the old A34 (Manchester Rd). Continue to T-lights at Majestic Wines and turn L & then 1st R up to Carlton Ave.* **Sat 21, Sun 22 June (10.30-5). Adm £5, chd free. Light refreshments.**
A brick paved and pebbled substantial suburban garden with large wildlife fish pond . Many trees, inc 2 mature tulip trees, contorted hazel, several magnolia and over 80 various acers. There is a wisteria covered pergola and numerous places to sit and relax inc an arbour. Various hostas, clematis and herbaceous plants to admire.
✱ ☕ »))

41 THE OLD PARSONAGE
Back Lane, Arley Green, Northwich, CW9 6LZ. The Hon Rowland & Mrs Flower, www.arleyhallandgardens.com. *5m NNE of Northwich. 3m NNE of Great Budworth. M6 J19 & 20 & M56 J10. Follow signs to Arley Hall & Gardens. From Arley Hall follow signs to Old Parsonage which lies across park at Arley Green (approx 1m).* **Sun 25, Mon 26 May (2-5). Adm £6, chd free. Home-made teas.**
2 acre garden in attractive and secretive rural setting in secluded part of Arley Estate, with ancient yew hedges, herbaceous and mixed borders, shrub roses, climbers, leading to woodland garden and unfenced pond with gunnera and water plants. Rhododendrons, azaleas, meconopsis, cardiocrinum, plus some interesting and unusual trees. Wheelchair access over mown grass, some slopes and bumps and rougher grass further away from the house.
&. 🐕 ✱ ☕ »))

42 ONE HOUSE WALLED GARDEN
off Buxton New Road, Rainow, SK11 0AD. Louise Baylis. *2½ m NE of Macclesfield. Just off A537 Macclesfield to Buxton road. 2½ m from Macclesfield Station.* **Sat 7, Sun 8 June (10.30-4.30). Adm £5, chd free. Tea, coffee & cake.**
An historic early C18 walled kitchen garden, hidden for 60 yrs and restored by volunteers. This romantic and atmospheric garden has a wide range of vegetables, flowers and old tools. There is an orchard with friendly pigs, a wildlife area and pond, woodland walk with wildflowers and foxgloves and views and a traditional greenhouse with ornamental and edible crops. Small plant nursery.
🐕 ✱ ☕ 🪑

43 15 PARK CRESCENT
Appleton, Warrington, WA4 5JJ. Linda & Mark Enderby. *2½ m S of Warrington. From M56 J10 take A49 towards Warrington for 1½ m. At 2nd set of lights turn R into Lyons Lane, then 1st R into Park Crescent. N015 is last house on R.* **Thur 29 May, Sun 29 June (11.30-4.30). Adm £5, chd free. Light refreshments.**
An abundant garden containing many unusual plants, trees and a mini orchard. A cascade, ponds and planting encourage wildlife. There are raised beds, many roses in various forms and relaxed herbaceous borders. The garden has been split into distinct areas on different levels each with their own vista drawing one through the garden. You never know what is around the next hedge! The garden continues to evolve after 23 yrs. Mature trees surround the garden, and a large oak lies within which acts as a host to *Rosa filipedes 'Kiftsgate'*. In addition there are numerous acers, cornus, cercis and a Turkey fig trained along a wall.
🐕 ✱ 🚗 ☕ »))

44 PARM PLACE
12 High Street, Great Budworth, CW9 6HF. Jane Fairclough, 07770 612915, janefair@btinternet.com. *3m N of Northwich. Great Budworth on E side of A559 between Northwich & Warrington, 4m from J19 M56, also 4m from J19 M6. Parm Place is W of village on S side of High St.* **Sun 6 Apr, Sun 6 July (12-4). Adm £5, chd free. Visits also by arrangement 1 Apr to 17 Aug for groups of up to 50. Donation to Great Ormond Street Hospital.**
Well-stocked ½ acre plantswoman's garden with stunning views towards south Cheshire. Curving lawns, parterre, shrubs, colour coordinated herbaceous borders, roses, water features, rockery, gravel bed with some grasses. Fruit and vegetable plots. In spring large collection of bulbs and flowers, camellias, hellebores and blossom.
&. 🐕 🚗 ☕

45 PARVEY LODGE
Parvey Lane, Sutton, Macclesfield, SK11 0HX. Mrs Tanya Walker, 07789 528093, tanya.v.walker@gmail.com. *In the heart of the village of Sutton, we are close to Fairways Garden Centre, Sutton Hall & Sutton PO.* **Sat 18 Oct (11-4). Adm £5, chd free. Home-made teas. Light refreshments. Visits also by arrangement for groups of 10+.**
A beautiful privately owned 3 acre garden with different areas to explore. Formal garden, Himalayan Cedar majestically situated at the front of the house, plenty of acer, fruit trees, shaped box hedge, tennis court lawn, lots of bulbs, daffodils, rhododendron and camellia, birds and wildlife (deer). Best to visit in autumn for spectacular autumn colour. Most of the garden is wheelchair friendly.
&. 🐕 ☕ »))

CHESHIRE & WIRRAL

46 ◆ PEOVER HALL GARDENS
Over Peover, Knutsford, WA16 9HW. Mr & Mrs Brooks, 01565 654107, bookings@peoverhall.com, www.peoverhall.com. *4m S of Knutsford. Do not rely on SatNav. From A50/Holmes Chapel Rd at Whipping Stocks pub turn onto Stocks Lane. Follow R onto Grotto Ln ¼m turn R onto Goostrey Ln. Main entrance on R on bend through white gates.* **For NGS: Sat 7, Sun 8 June (2-5). Adm £7, chd free. There will be sweet treat refreshments to purchase. For other opening times and information, please phone, email or visit garden website.**
The extensive formal gardens to Peover Hall feature a series of 'garden rooms' filled with clipped box, water garden, Romanesque loggia, warm brick walls, unusual doors, secret passageways, beautiful topiary work and walled gardens, rockery, rhododendrons and pleached limes. Peover Hall, a Grade II* listed Elizabethan family house dating from 1585, provides a fine backdrop. The Grade I listed Carolean Stables, which are of significant architectural importance, will be open to view. Tours of Peover Hall will also be available over the weekend with Mr & Mrs Brooks.
🐕 ✿ 🚗 ☕))

47 ◆ POULTON HALL
Poulton Lancelyn, Bebington, Wirral, CH63 9LN. The Poulton Hall Estate Trust & Poulton Hall Walled Garden Charitable Trust, 07836 590875, info@poultonhall.co.uk, www.poultonhall.co.uk. *2m S of Bebington. From M53, J4 towards Bebington; at T-lights R along Poulton Rd; house 1m on R.* **For NGS: Sat 19, Sun 20 Apr (2-5). Adm £6, chd free. Cream teas may be booked in advance via our website. For other opening times and information, please phone, email or visit garden website.**
A quirky garden which children love. 3 acres, lawns fronting house, wildflower meadow. Surprise approach to walled garden, with reminders of Roger Lancelyn Green's retellings, Excalibur, Robin Hood and Jabberwock. Memorial sculpture for Richard Lancelyn Green by Sue Sharples. Rose, nursery rhyme, witch, herb and oriental gardens and Memories Reading room. Restored Excalibur garden. Level gravel paths. Separate wheelchair access (not across parking field). Disabled WC.
♿ 🐕 ✿ ☕

48 ◆ RODE HALL
Church Lane, Scholar Green, ST7 3QP. Randle & Amanda Baker Wilbraham, 01270 873237, enquiries@rodehall.co.uk, www.rodehall.co.uk. *5m SW of Congleton. Between Scholar Green (A34) & Rode Heath (A50).* **For opening times and information, please phone, email or visit garden website.**
Nesfield's terrace and rose garden with stunning view over Humphry Repton's landscape is a feature of Rode, as is the woodland garden with terraced rock garden and grotto. Other attractions inc the walk to the lake with a view of Birthday Island complete with heronry, restored ice house, working 2 acre walled kitchen garden and Italian garden. Fine display of snowdrops in February and bluebells in May. Snowdrop walks in February. Bluebell walks in May. Summer: Weds and Bank Holiday Mons until end of Sep, 10-5. Courtyard Kitchen offering wide variety of homemade cakes and lunches.
🐕 ✿ 🚗 ☕

49 ROSE BRAE
Earle Drive, Parkgate, Neston, CH64 6RY. Joe & Carole Rae. *11m NW of Chester. From A540 take B5134 at the Hinderton Arms towards Neston. Turn R at the T-lights in Neston & L at the Cross onto Parkgate Rd, B5135. Earle Drive is ½m on R.* **Sun 13 July (1.30-4.30). Adm £5, chd free. Tea, coffee & cake.**
An all season, half acre garden comprising bulbs, trees, shrubs, perennials and climbers. In July roses, clematis, hydrangeas, phlox and agapanthus predominate together with ferns, grasses, flowering trees, topiary, a bulb lawn and a formal pool with water lilies.
✿ ☕))

50 ROSEWOOD
Old Hall Lane, Puddington, Neston, CH64 5SP. Mr & Mrs C E J Brabin, 0151 353 1193, angela.brabin@btinternet.com. *8m N of Chester. From A540 turn down Puddington Lane, 1½m. Park by village green. Walk 30yds to Old Hall Lane, turn L through archway into garden.* **Visits by arrangement for groups of up to 40. Adm £4, chd free. Tea, coffee & cake.**
Year-round garden; thousands of snowdrops in Feb, camellias in autumn, winter and spring. Rhododendrons in April/May and unusual flowering trees from March to June. Autumn cyclamen in quantity from Aug to Nov. Perhaps the greatest delight to owners are 2 large *Cornus capitata*, flowering in June. Bees kept in the garden. Honey sometimes available.
♿ ✿ 🚗 ☕

51 SANDYMERE
Middlewich Road, Cotebrook, CW6 9EH. Sir John Timpson, rachelnorwood72@gmail.com. *5m N of Tarporley. On A54 approx 300yds W of T-lights at Xrds of A49/A54. What3words app: tolerable.pursue.education.* **Sun 8 June (12-4). Adm £7, chd free. Tea, coffee & cake.** Visits also by arrangement 1 May to 4 July. Refreshments are not included but picnics are welcome.
16 landscaped acres of beautiful Cheshire countryside with terraces, walled garden, extensive woodland walks and an amazing hosta garden. Turn each corner and you find another gem with lots of different water features inc a rill built in 2014, which links the main lawn to the hostas. Look out for our new Japanese themed garden. Partial wheelchair access.
♿ ✿ ☕))

70 inpatients and their families are being supported at the newly opened Horatio's Garden Northern Ireland, thanks to National Garden Scheme donations.

All Fours Farm

52 10 STATHAM AVENUE

Lymm, WA13 9NH. Mike & Gail Porter, 07951 606906, porters@mikeandgailporter.co.uk, www.youtube.com/watch?v=53zmVWfZa-s. *Approx 1m from J20 M6 /M56 interchange. From M/way follow B5158 to Lymm. Take A56 Booth's Hill Rd, L towards Warrington, R on to Barsbank Lane, pass under bridge, 50mtrs turn R onto Statham Ave. No 10 is 100mtrs on R. What3words app: smallest.plump.snooze.* **Sat 17, Sun 18 May, Sat 14, Sun 15 June (11-4). Adm £5, chd free. Home-made teas. Enjoy Gail's famous meringues with fresh fruit & cream.** Visits also by arrangement May to Aug for groups of 10 to 40.

Beautifully structured ¼ acre south facing terraced garden rising to the Bridgewater towpath. Hazel arch opens to clay paved courtyard with roses, clematis and herbs. Rose pillars lead to lush herbaceous beds and tranquil shaded areas, vibrant azaleas and rhododendrons in spring, peaceful, pastel shades in early summer and hydrangeas, fuchsias in late summer. Interesting garden buildings. A treasure hunt/quiz to keep the children occupied. Delicious refreshments to satisfy the grown ups.

53 ◆ STONYFORD COTTAGE

Stonyford Lane, Oakmere, CW8 2TF. Janet & Tony Overland, 07816 531358, info@stonyfordcottagegardens.co.uk, www.stonyfordcottagegardens.co.uk. *5m SW of Northwich. From Northwich take A556 towards Chester. ¾m past A49 junction turn R into Stonyford Lane. Entrance ½ m on L.* **For NGS: Sun 4 May (11-4). Adm £5, chd free.** For other opening times and information, please phone, email or visit garden website.

Set around a tranquil pool, this Monet style landscape has a wealth of moisture loving plants, inc iris and *Primula candelabra*. Drier areas feature unusual perennials, rarer trees and shrubs. Woodland paths meander through shade and bog plantings, along boarded walks, across wild natural areas with views over the pool to the cottage gardens.

Capesthorne Hall

Unusual plants available at the adjacent nursery. Open Tues - Fri, Apr - Oct 10-5pm. Some gravel paths.

54 TATTENHALL HALL
High Street, Tattenhall, Chester, CH3 9PX. Jen & Nick Benefield, Chris Evered & Jannie Hollins, 01829 770654, janniehollins@gmail.com. *8m S of Chester on A41. Turn L to Tattenhall, through village, turn R at Letters pub, past War Memorial on L through sandstone pillared gates. Park on road or in village car park.* **Sun 1 June (2-5). Adm £6, chd free. Home-made teas. Visits also by arrangement 31 Mar to 28 July.** Plant enthusiasts' garden around Jacobean house (not open). 4½ acres, wildflower meadows, interesting trees, large pond, stream, walled garden, colour themed borders, succession planting, spinney walk with shade plants, yew terrace overlooking meadow, views to hills. Glasshouse and vegetable garden. Wildlife friendly, sometimes untidy garden, interest year-round, always developing. Extensive collection of plants. Partial wheelchair access due to gravel paths, cobbles and some steps.

55 TIRESFORD
Tarporley, CW6 9LY. Susanna Posnett, 07989 306425. *Tiresford is on A49 Tarporley bypass. It is adjacent to the farm on R leaving Tarporley in the direction of Four Lane Ends T-lights.* **Sun 11 May (2-5). Adm £5, chd free. Home-made teas. Ice-Cream.** Established 1930s garden undergoing a major restoration project to reinstate it to its former glory. Fabulous views of both Beeston and Peckforton Castles offer a wonderful backdrop in which to relax and enjoy a delicious tea. This year we hope to realise our long term plan to recreate the kitchen garden and to repair the fountain amongst the new hot borders of the sunken garden. The house has been transformed into a stylish 6 bedroom B&B. There is parking for wheelchair users next to the house and access to a disabled WC in the house.

56 TIRLEY GARTH GARDENS
Mallows Way, Willington, Tarporley, CW6 0RQ. *2m N of Tarporley. 2m S of Kelsall. Entrance 500yds from village of Utkinton. At N of Tarporley take Utkinton Road. What3words app: shift.morphing. such.* **Sun 18 May (1-5). Adm £5, chd free. Home-made teas.** 40 acre garden, terraced & landscaped, designed by Thomas Mawson who is considered the leading exponent of garden design in early C20. It is the only Grade II* Arts & Crafts garden in Cheshire that remains complete and in excellent condition. The gardens are an important example of an early C20 garden laid out in both formal and informal styles. By early May the garden is bursting into flower with almost 3000 rhododendron and azalea, many 100 yrs old. Art Exhibition by local Artists.

57 NEW 187 VICTORIA ROAD
New Brighton, Wallasey, CH45 0JY. Mrs Sharon Maher & Mr Mike Costall. *Opp the side entrance to New Brighton Merseyrail train station.* **Sat 19, Sun 20 July (10-4). Adm £4, chd free. Tea, coffee & cake.** A small, front and rear suburban garden which is nonetheless packed with plants and ideas. Roses, hostas, auriculas, a fernery and a cottage garden bed. We also have an edible garden on a roof.

58 THE WELL HOUSE
Wet Lane, Tilston, Malpas, SY14 7DP. Mrs S H French-Greenslade, 01829 250332. *3m NW of Malpas. On A41, 1st R after Broxton r'about, L on Malpas Rd through Tilston. House on L.* **Visits by arrangement 10 Feb to 31 Aug. Pre-booked refreshments for small groups only.** 1 acre cottage garden, bridge over natural stream, spring bulbs, perennials, herbs and shrubs. Triple ponds. Adjoining ¾ acre field made into wildflower meadow; first seeding late 2003. Large bog area of kingcups and ragged robin. February for snowdrop walk. Victorian parlour and collector's items on show. Dogs on leads only.

59 WILLASTON GRANGE
Hadlow Road, Willaston, CH64 2UN. Anita & Mark Mitchell. *From Chester, take A540 (Chester High Rd) turning into B5151 to Willaston. Willaston Grange is 400 yards on R. From the village, take B5151 (Hadlow Rd). Willaston Grange is 800 yds on L.* **Sat 14 June (12-5). Adm £6, chd free. Home-made teas.** Fifteen years ago, Willaston Grange and gardens had been derelict for 3 years. A year of restoration work began. The gardens now extend to 6 acres with a small lake, a range of mature trees, herbaceous border, woodland and vegetable gardens, orchard and magical treehouse. The fully restored Arts & Crafts house makes for a perfect backdrop for a visit, along with afternoon teas and live music. Most areas accessible by wheelchair.

60 THE WONKY GARDEN
Ditton Community Centre, Dundalk Road, Widnes, WA8 8DF. Mrs Angela Hayler, 07976 373979, thewonkygarden@gmail.com, en-gb.facebook.com/thewonkygarden. *From the Widnes exit of the A533 turn L (Lowerhouse La) then L at the r'about. The Community Centre is ½ m up on the R. The garden entrance is on the far L of the building.* **Sun 6 July, Sun 17 Aug (11.30-3.30). Adm £5, chd free. Tea, coffee & cake. Visits also by arrangement 16 June to 26 Sept for groups of 10 to 30.** The flower garden is our show garden, the focus for horticultural therapy/nature based activities. It has large herbaceous borders, trees and shrubs, planting focussing on the senses and wildlife. We grow masses of edibles and cut flowers in the allotment (for gifting to our community) and The Yard has a massive greenhouse, workshop, activity shelter and Friendship Garden. The garden is designed and managed by a wonderful group of volunteers. We support many community groups and individuals of all ages and abilities inc schools, colleges and work experience. Our focus is on supporting physical and mental health, isolation and loneliness. An accessible path (1½ metres wide) extends from the car park through the herbaceous and children's nature garden and into the allotment and yard.

CORNWALL

ISLES OF SCILLY

Tresco
St Martin's
Bryher 59
Hugh Town
St Mary's
St Agnes

The Isles of Scilly lie about 28 miles or 45 kilometres south west of Land's End

Port Isaac
Trevose Head
32 Padstow
Wadebridge 22
Trenance
24 Newquay
45 31
Newquay
St Columb Major
Perranporth
Mitchell
Goonhavern
St Agnes
54
Probus
50
Truro
Tregony 28
47 48
Portreath
18
Redruth
46
11
St Ives
Camborne
60 55 Hayle
Penryn
St Mawes
St Just 57
6
Marazion
7 15 39
Falmouth
21
1 49
Helston
30 44 58 34
Sennen
Penzance
43 52
Falmouth Bay
Land's End 62
10
Porthleven
9 25
Mount's Bay
19
St Keverne
5
Mullion 61
Coverack
Lizard
56
Lizard Point

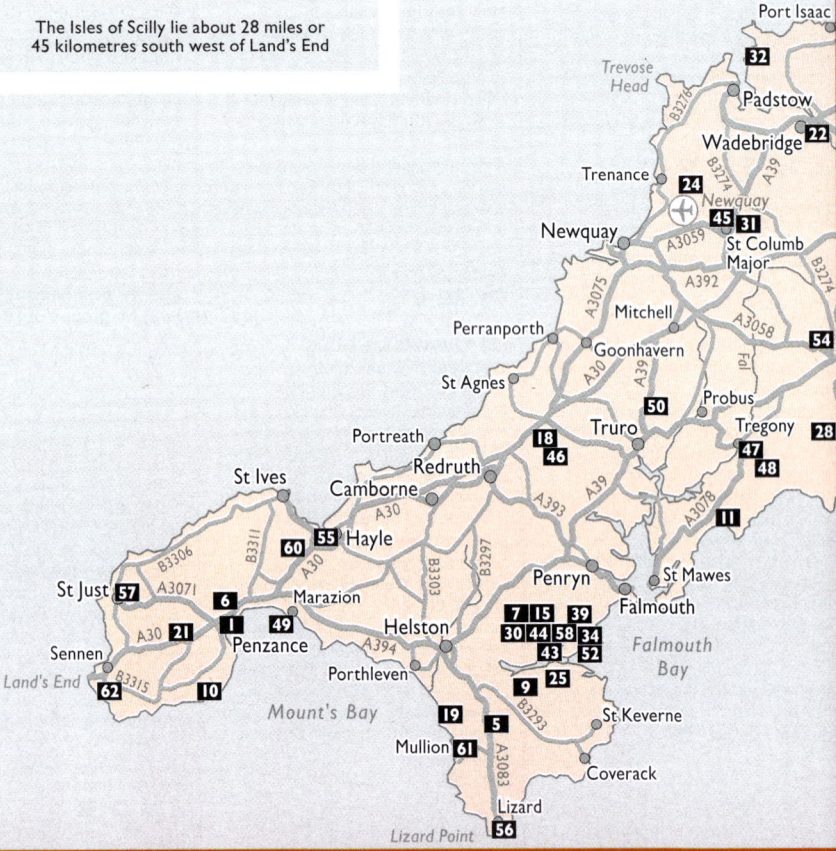

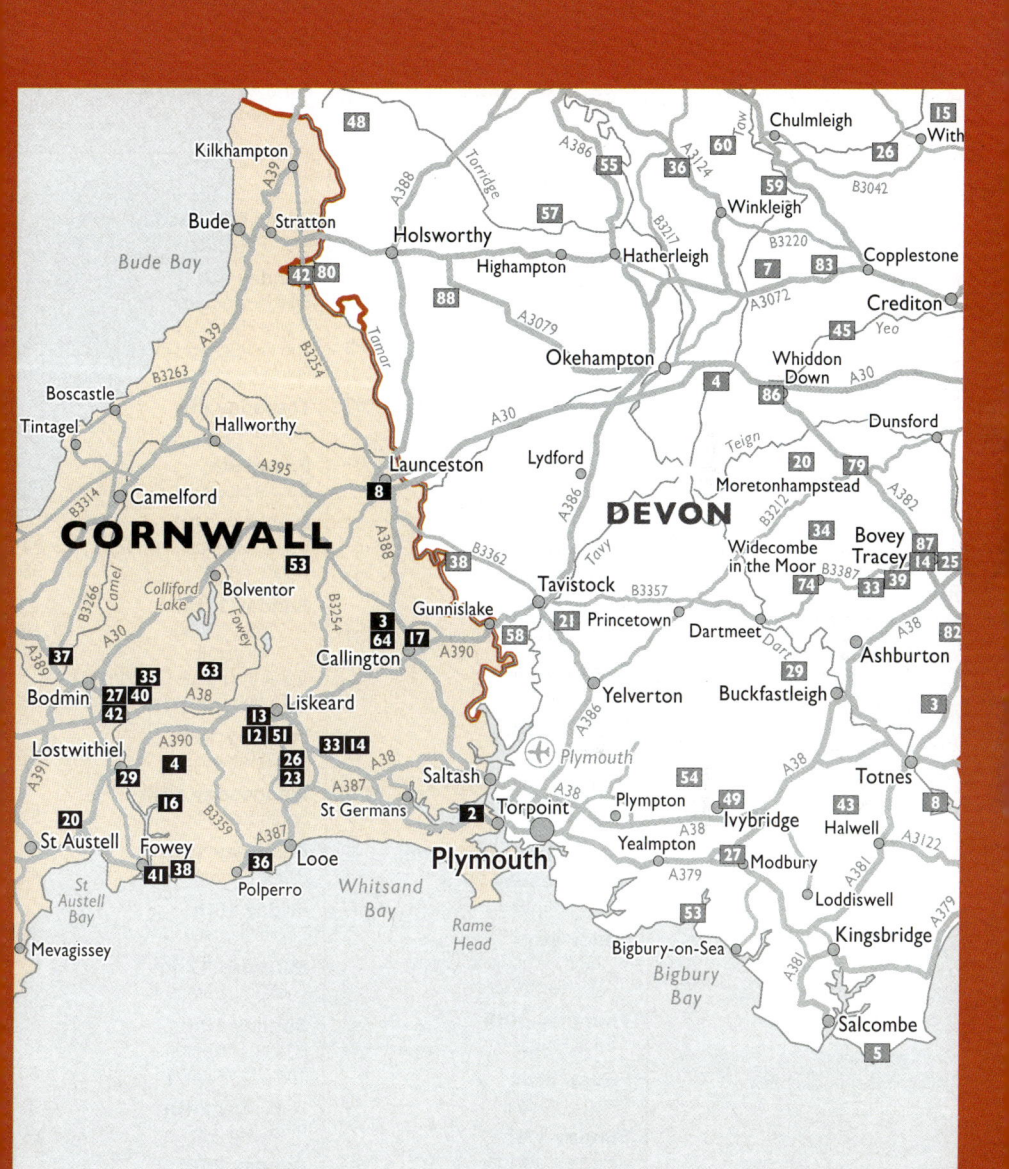

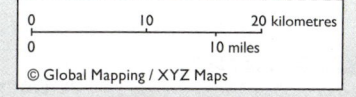

CORNWALL

CORNWALL

VOLUNTEERS

County Organiser
Sue Newton
07786 367610
sue.newton@ngs.org.uk

Claire Woodbine
07483 244318
claire.woodbine@ngs.org.uk

County Treasurer
Marie Tolhurst
marie.tolhurst@ngs.org.uk

Publicity
Laura Tucker
laura.tucker@ngs.org.uk

Social Media
Claire Wood
07921 153305
claire.wood@ngs.org.uk

Booklet Co-ordinator
Ian Gillbard 07969 440935
ian.gillbard@ngs.org.uk

Photographer
Keith Tucker
keith.tucker@ngs.org.uk

Assistant County Organisers
Kirsty Angwin
kirsty.angwin@ngs.org.uk

Caroline Cudmore 01726 882325
caroline.cudmore@ngs.org.uk

Sara Gadd 07814 885141
sara.gadd@ngs.org.uk

Ian Gillbard
(see above)

Sorcha Hitchcox
sorcha.hitchcox@ngs.org.uk

Libby Pidcock 01208 821303
libby.pidcock@ngs.org.uk

Graham Sykes 07719 711683
graham.sykes@ngs.org.uk

@CornwallNGS
@cornwall.ngs

OPENING DATES

All entries subject to change. For latest information check
www.ngs.org.uk

Extended openings are shown at the beginning of the month.

Map locator numbers are shown to the right of each garden name.

March

Thursday 13th
Trevina House 63

Friday 14th
Trevina House 63

Tuesday 25th
Lower Tregamere 31

Wednesday 26th
Lower Tregamere 31

Thursday 27th
Lower Tregamere 31

Friday 28th
Lower Tregamere 31

Saturday 29th
The Lodge 27

Sunday 30th
The Lodge 27

April

Every Wednesday from Wednesday 23rd
NEW Polventon 42

Friday 4th
◆ Antony Woodland Garden & Woodland Walk 2

Thursday 10th
Trevina House 63

Friday 11th
Trevina House 63

Sunday 13th
Higher Locrenton 23

Monday 14th
◆ Pencarrow 37

Friday 18th
◆ Boconnoc 4

Wednesday 23rd
Pinsla Garden 40

Thursday 24th
Pinsla Garden 40

Saturday 26th
◆ Chygurno 10

Sunday 27th
◆ Chygurno 10
Ethnevas Cottage 15
Rose Morran 45

May

Every Wednesday
NEW Polventon 42

Sunday 4th
East Down Barn 14
Navas Hill House 34
The Old School House 35
Pinsla Garden 40

Thursday 8th
Trevina House 63

Friday 9th
Trevina House 63

Saturday 10th
◆ The Japanese Garden 24
Trelan 55

Sunday 11th
NEW Fan Cottage 16
NEW Heycroft 22
Trebartha Estate Garden and Country Garden at Lemarne 53

Tuesday 13th
South Bosent 51

Wednesday 14th
South Bosent 51

Thursday 15th
Pinsla Garden 40

Friday 16th
Pinsla Garden 40

Saturday 17th
The Old Vicarage 36

Sunday 18th
Higher Locrenton 23
The Old Vicarage 36

Saturday 24th
Pinsla Garden 40

Sunday 25th
Lametton Mill 26

Wednesday 28th
Lametton Mill 26

Saturday 31st
Pinsla Garden 40

CORNWALL

June

Every Wednesday
NEW Polventon 42

Sunday 1st
NEW Boscrowan 6
Gardens Cottage 20

Wednesday 4th
♦ Kestle Barton 25

Sunday 8th
Treglyn 54
Trevesco 61

Wednesday 11th
Gardens Cottage 20
♦ Kestle Barton 25

Thursday 12th
Gardens Cottage 20
Trevina House 63

Friday 13th
Bucks Head House Garden 7
Dobwalls Gardens 12
Trevina House 63

Saturday 14th
Dobwalls Gardens 12
NEW Polruan Gardens 41

Sunday 15th
Alverton Cottage 1
Caervallack 9
Higher Locrenton 23
NEW Polruan Gardens 41
Trevilley 62

Monday 16th
Pinsla Garden 40

Tuesday 17th
Pinsla Garden 40

Wednesday 18th
♦ Kestle Barton 25

Saturday 21st
Fox Hollow 18

Sunday 22nd
Rose Morran 45

Tuesday 24th
Pinsla Garden 40

Wednesday 25th
♦ Kestle Barton 25

Friday 27th
Bucks Head House Garden 7

Saturday 28th
Lostwithiel Gardens 29
The Old Vicarage 36
♦ Roseland House 46
Trelan 55

Sunday 29th
NEW Boscrowan 6
Firste Park 17
Gwrythia 21
Lametton Mill 26
The Old Vicarage 36
♦ Roseland House 46

July

Every Wednesday
NEW Polventon 42

Wednesday 2nd
♦ Kestle Barton 25
Lametton Mill 26

Thursday 3rd
Dobwalls Gardens 12

Friday 4th
Dobwalls Gardens 12

Sunday 6th
Anvil Cottage 3
Gardens Cottage 20
Windmills 64

Wednesday 9th
♦ Kestle Barton 25

Thursday 10th
Trevina House 63

Friday 11th
Bucks Head House Garden 7
Trevina House 63

Saturday 12th
NEW Secret Garden 50

Sunday 13th
Crugsillick Manor 11
NEW Heycroft 22
Higher Locrenton 23
Menheniot Gardens 33
NEW Secret Garden 50

Wednesday 16th
♦ Kestle Barton 25

Saturday 19th
♦ Chygurno 10

Sunday 20th
♦ Chygurno 10

Wednesday 23rd
♦ Kestle Barton 25

Friday 25th
Bucks Head House Garden 7
Dobwalls Gardens 12

Saturday 26th
Dobwalls Gardens 12

Sunday 27th
Byeways 8
Lametton Mill 26

Wednesday 30th
♦ Kestle Barton 25
Lametton Mill 26

August

Wednesday 6th
♦ Kestle Barton 25

Friday 8th
Dobwalls Gardens 12

Saturday 9th
Dobwalls Gardens 12

Sunday 10th
NEW Heycroft 22

Wednesday 13th
♦ Bonython Manor 5
♦ Kestle Barton 25

Friday 15th
Bucks Head House Garden 7

Sunday 17th
NEW Fan Cottage 16

Wednesday 20th
♦ Kestle Barton 25

Sunday 24th
Lametton Mill 26

Wednesday 27th
♦ Kestle Barton 25
Lametton Mill 26

Friday 29th
Bucks Head House Garden 7

Sunday 31st
Rose Morran 45

September

Wednesday 3rd
Gardens Cottage 20
♦ Kestle Barton 25

Thursday 4th
Gardens Cottage 20

Sunday 7th
Treglyn 54

Wednesday 10th
♦ Kestle Barton 25

Thursday 11th
Trevina House 63

Friday 12th
Trevina House 63

CORNWALL

Sunday 14th
Towan House 52

Tuesday 16th
South Bosent 51

Wednesday 17th
◆ Kestle Barton 25
South Bosent 51

Wednesday 24th
◆ Kestle Barton 25

Sunday 28th
Trebartha Estate Garden and
    Country Garden at Lemarne 53

October

Wednesday 8th
Trevina House 63

Thursday 9th
Trevina House 63

Friday 10th
◆ Antony Woodland Garden &
    Woodland Walk 2

By Arrangement

Arrange a personalised garden visit with your club, or group of friends, on a date to suit you. See individual garden entries for full details.

Bucks Head House Garden 7
Caervallack 9
Crugsillick Manor 11
Dobwalls Gardens 12
Dove Cottage 13
East Down Barn 14
Ethnevas Cottage 15
NEW Fan Cottage 16
Firste Park 17
Fox Hollow 18
Garden Cottage 19
Gardens Cottage 20
Gwrythia 21
Higher Locrenton 23
9 Higman Close, Dobwalls
    Gardens 12
Lametton Mill 26
Lower Tregamere 31
Malibu 32
Navas Hill House 34
The Old Vicarage 36
Pendower House 38
Penwarne 39
NEW Polventon 42
Port Navas Chapel 43
Rose Morran 45
Roseland Parc 47
Rosevallon Barn 48
Towan House 52
Treglyn 54
Trelan 55
Tremichele 56
NEW Tremorran & The Angel 57
Trenarth 58
Tresithney 60
Trevilley 62
Trevina House 63

In 2024 we awarded £232,000 in Community Garden Grants, supporting 89 community garden projects.

Boscrowan

THE GARDENS

1 ALVERTON COTTAGE
Alverton Road, Penzance, TR18 4TG. David & Lizzie Puddifoot. *Next door to YMCA. About 600 metres from Penlee car park travelling towards A30. Morrab Gardens are also close to car park.* **Sun 15 June (2-6). Adm £5, chd free. Tea, coffee & cake.**
Alverton Cottage is a Grade II listed Regency house. The garden is modest in size though large for a Penzance garden, south facing and sheltered by mature trees. There is a large monkey-puzzle tree, a holm oak and many other trees. The garden was laid out in the 1860s, we have added succulents, a wildlife pond, a fernery, magnolias and have cleared and replanted since 2013. Off road disabled parking but wheelchair to garden terrace only.
& 🐕 ✱ ☕ »)

2 ◆ ANTONY WOODLAND GARDEN & WOODLAND WALK
Ferry Lane, Torpoint, PL11 2QA. Sir Richard Carew-Pole, 01752 815303, woodlandgarden@antonyestate.com, www.antonywoodlandgarden.com. *2m NW of Torpoint. From the main gate off A374, proceed along Ferry Lane past Antony House. Shortly after passing Antony House, you will see the car park on R, beneath the trees.* **For NGS: Fri 4 Apr, Fri 10 Oct (10.30-5). Adm £10, chd free. Tea, coffee & cake at 'Zinns Coffee in the Woodland', a quaint converted horse box, which offers a lovely selection of cakes, tea & artisan coffees.** For other opening times and information, please phone, email or visit garden website.
Antony Woodland Garden is one of the most beautiful gardens in SE Cornwall. A haven of serenity and peace, the perfect place for a pleasant walk, a family picnic, and to explore and enjoy a magnificent variety of plants. As an "International Camellia Garden of Excellence" it holds the National Collection of *Camellia japonica* Dogs are permitted on the Woodland Walk only. It has the most stunning array of magnolias, beautiful walks along the river's edge, contemporary sculpture and carpets of wild flowers, waiting to be discovered. Enjoy lunch or dinner at the Wilcove Inn, a nearby waterside pub (www.thewilcoveinn.com). Some woodland paths are wheelchair-accessible, but rainfall can make them muddy in areas. Pls check conditions before your visit.
& 🚗 NPC 🏠 ☕ 🧺 »)

3 ANVIL COTTAGE
South Hill, PL17 7LP. Geoff & Barbara Clemerson. *3m NW of Callington. Head N on A388 from Callington centre. After ½m L onto South Hill Rd (signed South Hill), straight on for 3m. Gardens on R just before St Sampson's Church.* **Sun 6 July (1.30-5). Combined adm with Windmills £6, chd free. Home-made teas. Gluten free refreshments available.**
Essentially, this is a plantsman's garden. Winding paths lead through a series of themed rooms with familiar, rare and unusual plants. Steps lead up to a raised viewpoint looking west towards Caradon Hill and Bodmin Moor. Other paths take you on a circular route through a rose garden, hot beds, a tropical area and a secret garden. In the rose garden there is a new flower bed with wildlife pond.
✱ ☕ 🧺

4 ◆ BOCONNOC
Lostwithiel, PL22 0RG. Fortescue Family, 01208 872507, events@boconnoc.com, www.boconnoc.com. *Off A390 between Liskeard & Lostwithiel. From East Taphouse follow signs to Boconnoc. Do not rely on SatNav, follow directions on Boconnoc website.* **For NGS: Fri 18 Apr (2-5). Adm £6, chd £3. Light refreshments in stable yard.** For other opening times and information, please phone, email or visit garden website.
20 acres surrounded by parkland and woods with magnificent trees, flowering shrubs and stunning views. The gardens are set amongst mature trees which provide the backcloth for exotic spring flowering shrubs, woodland plants, with newly planted magnolias and a fine collection of hydrangeas. Features inc bathhouse built in 1804, obelisk built in 1771, house dating from Domesday, deer park and C15 church.
& 🐕 🚗 🏠 ☕

5 ◆ BONYTHON MANOR
Cury Cross Lanes, Helston, TR12 7BA. Mr & Mrs Richard Nathan, 01326 240550, sbonython@gmail.com, www.bonythonmanor.co.uk. *5m S of Helston. On main A3083 Helston to Lizard Rd. Turn L at Cury Cross Lanes (Wheel Inn). Entrance 300yds on R.* **For NGS: Wed 13 Aug (2-4). Adm £11, chd free. Tea, coffee, fruit juices and home-made cakes.** For other opening times and information, please phone, email or visit garden website.
Magnificent 20 acre colour garden inc sweeping hydrangea drive to Georgian manor (not open). Herbaceous walled garden, potager with vegetables and picking flowers; 3 lakes in valley planted with ornamental grasses, perennials and South African flowers. A 'must see' for all seasons colour.
& 🐕 ✱ 🚗 🏠 ☕

6 NEW BOSCROWAN
Heamoor, Penzance, TR20 8UJ. David & Elizabeth Harris, 01736 332396, elizabeth@boscrowan.co.uk, www.boscrowan.co.uk. *1m NW of Penzance. Leaving the A30 r'about signed to Heamoor, continue through Heamoor to the end & turn R into Josephs Lane. ¼m down turn L up Bone Valley & Boscrowan turning is 200yds on L.* **Sun 1, Sun 29 June (2-6). Adm £6, chd free. Light refreshments.**
Boscrowan sits in a sheltered valley, surrounded by mature trees. The 1½ acre garden area features herbaceous borders, a formal front garden, large pond, a willow walk, orchard and gardens in the two holiday cottages. An antique revolving 'Boulton and Paul' summerhouse, large vegetable and flower cutting area are of further interest. Emphasis on wildlife friendly plants and changing climate.
& 🐕 ✱ 🏠 ☕ 🧺 »)

129,032 people were able to access guidance on what to expect when a person is dying through the National Garden Scheme's support for Hospice UK this year.

92 CORNWALL

7 BUCKS HEAD HOUSE GARDEN
Trengove Cross, Constantine, TR11 5QR. Deborah Baker, 07801 444916, deborah.fwbaker@gmail.com, www.instagram.com/bucks_head_garden. *5m SW of Falmouth. A394 towards Helston, L at Edgcumbe towards Gweek/Constantine. Proceed for 0.8m then L towards Constantine. Further 0.8m, garden on L at Trengove Cross.* **Fri 13, Fri 27 June, Fri 11, Fri 25 July, Fri 15, Fri 29 Aug (2-4.30). Adm £6, chd free. Tea, coffee & cake.** Visits also by arrangement 6 June to 19 Sept for groups of up to 25.
Enchanting cottage and woodland gardens of native and rare trees, shrubs and perennials, encouraging biodiversity. The site of 1½ acres is on a south facing Cornish hillside with panoramic views. Protected by essential windbreak hedging, the inspiring collection of plants has been chosen to create an intriguing woodland garden and increase biodiversity. During the summer months art works will be on display.
&. ✿ ☕ 🔊)

8 BYEWAYS
Dunheved Road, Launceston, PL15 9JE. Tony Reddicliffe. *Launceston town centre. 100yds from multi-storey car park past offices of Cornish & Devon Post into Dunheved Rd, 3rd bungalow on R.* **Sun 27 July (1-5.30). Adm £5, chd free. Tea, coffee & cake.**
Small town garden developed over 11 yrs by enthusiastic amateur gardeners. Herbaceous borders, rockery. Tropicals inc bananas, gingers and senecio. Stream and water features. Roof garden. Japanese inspired tea house and courtyard. Redeveloped area features Japanese inspired planting. Sunken area with planting. Fig tree and Pawlonia flank area giving secluded seating. Living pergola.
🐕 ✿ ☕

9 CAERVALLACK
St Martin, Helston, TR12 6DF. Matt Robinson & Louise McClary, 07795 560907, studio@mattrobinsonarchitecture.co.uk, www.mattrobinsonarchitecture.co.uk. *5m SE of Helston. Go through Mawgan village, over 2 bridges, past Gear Farm shop; go past turning on L, garden next farmhouse on L. Parking is in field opp entrance.* **Sun**

15 June (1.30-4). Adm £6, chd free. Tea & home-made cakes; scones, clotted cream & jam. Visits also by arrangement 25 Apr to 26 Sept for groups of up to 30. (Fridays only).
Romantic garden arranged into rooms, the collaboration between an artist and an architect. Colour and form of plants structured by topiary, hedging and architectural experiments in cob, brick, slate & concrete. Grade II listed farmhouse and ancient orchard. Roses and wisteria a speciality. 30 yrs in the making. 2 acre field turning into native grassland/woodland. Arts & Crafts cob walls and paving around herbaceous borders; heroic 54ft pedestrian footbridge, 5 sided meditation studio, cast concrete ponds and amphitheatre; coppice and wildflower meadow; mature orchard and vegetable plot. Topiary throughout.
🐕 ✿ 🚗 🛏 ☕ 🔊)

10 ♦ CHYGURNO
Lamorna, TR19 6XH. Dr & Mrs Robert Moule, 01736 732153, rmoule010@btinternet.com. *4m S of Penzance. Off B3315. Follow signs for Lamorna Cove, take the R fork in the road before the Wink pub. The garden is at the top of the hill on the L.* **For NGS: Sat 26, Sun 27 Apr, Sat 19, Sun 20 July (2-5). Adm £5, chd free.** For other opening times and information, please phone or email.
Beautiful, unique, 3 acre cliffside garden overlooking Lamorna Cove. Planting started in 1998, mainly southern hemisphere shrubs and exotics with hydrangeas, camellias and rhododendrons. Woodland area with tree ferns set against large granite outcrops. Garden terraced with steep steps and paths. Plenty of benches so you can take a rest and enjoy the wonderful views.
🐕 🍴

11 CRUGSILLICK MANOR
Ruan High Lanes, Truro, TR2 5LJ. Dr Alison Agnew & Mr Brian Yule, 07538 218201, alisonagnew@icloud.com. *On Roseland Peninsula. Turn off A390 Truro-St Austell road onto A3078 towards St Mawes. Approx 5m after Tregony turn 1st L after Ruan High Lanes towards Veryan, garden is 200yds on R.* **Sun 13 July (11-5). Adm £5, chd free. Tea, coffee, soft drinks, cakes & light lunches.** Visits also by arrangement 19 Apr to 30 Sept for groups of 10 to 30.

Parking is limited so pls discuss when booking.
2 acre garden, substantially re-landscaped and planted, mostly over last 12 yrs. To the side of the C17/C18 house, a wooded bank drops down to a walled kitchen garden and hot garden. In front, sweeping yew hedges and paths define oval lawns and broad mixed borders. On a lower terrace, the focus is a large pond and the planting is predominantly exotic flowering trees and shrubs. Wheelchair access to the central level of the garden, the house and cafe. Garden is on several levels connected by fairly steep sloping gravel paths.
&. 🐕 ✿ ☕

GROUP OPENING

12 DOBWALLS GARDENS
Dobwalls, Liskeard, PL14 4LX. 07539 256855, lloydadj@btinternet.com. *In Dobwalls at double mini r'about take road to Duloe. Yellow signs will then direct to both gardens.* **Fri 13, Sat 14 June, Thur 3, Fri 4, Fri 25, Sat 26 July, Fri 8, Sat 9 Aug (2-5.30). Combined adm £7, chd free. Home-made teas at South Bosent.** Visits also by arrangement 13 June to 31 Aug.

9 HIGMAN CLOSE
Jim Stephens & Sue Martin, 01579 321074.
Visits also by arrangement in Aug for groups of up to 30.

SOUTH BOSENT
Adrienne Lloyd & Trish Wilson. (See separate entry)

Two very different gardens within a few minutes drive from each other. 9 Higman Close, a constantly changing, multifaceted garden packed full of interesting plants but also colour, scent and form. Shady and sunny areas are exploited to the full and every effort made to create year-round interest. Sue's glasshouse is overflowing with cacti and succulents, some over 35 yrs old. All is on a scale readily relatable to small garden owners. Both owners are retired horticulturalists. The garden at South Bosent is developed from farmland with interesting plants as well as habitat for wildlife over a total of 9½ acres. Different areas inc mixed borders, woodland gardens, meadow, 6 ponds of varying sizes. In spring, the bluebell wood trail runs alongside

CORNWALL

the stream. Dogs on leads permitted at South Bosent. Partial wheelchair access at 9 Higman Close and main garden accessible at South Bosent.
♿ ❀ ☕ ♫

13 DOVE COTTAGE
Lantoom, Dobwalls, Liskeard, PL14 4LR. Becky Martin, 07871 368227, beckymartin1@hotmail.com. *Close to Liskeard. Do not use postcode for SatNav. In Dobwalls at double mini r'about take road to Duloe, About 20 metres after end-of-speed-limit sign turn L at football club. Follow concrete track.* **Visits by arrangement in Aug for groups of up to 30. Combined with 9 Higman Close. Adm £6, chd free. Home-made teas by prior arrangement. Charged separately and served in garden or house depending on weather.**
A densely planted small garden replanted from scratch in 2017. Divided into separate areas with different types of planting. Strong emphasis on colour. Narrow winding paths, shady pergola, deck with tropical planting, tiny sunroom, greenhouse, pots of succulents, lush green foliage area. Separate productive garden with vegetables, polytunnel and cutting patch.
❀ ☕

14 EAST DOWN BARN
Menheniot, Liskeard, PL14 3QU. David & Shelley Lockett, 07803 159662, davidandshelleylockett@btinternet.com. *S side of village nr cricket ground. Turn off A38 at Hayloft restaurant/railway stn junction & head towards Menheniot village. Follow NGS signs from sharp LH bend as you enter village.* **Sun 4 May (1-4.30). Adm £5, chd free. Home-made teas. Visits also by arrangement 1 Apr to 5 June for groups of 12 to 30.**
Garden laid down between 1986-1991 with the conversion of the barn into a home and covers almost ½ acre of east sloping land with stream running north-south acting as the easterly boundary. 3 terraces before garden starts to level out at the stream. Garden won awards in the early years under the stewardship of the original owners. Ducks are in residence in the stream so regret no dogs.
☕ ♫

15 ETHNEVAS COTTAGE
Constantine, Falmouth, TR11 5PY. Lyn Watson & Ray Chun, 01326 340076, ethnevas@outlook.com. *6m SW of Falmouth. Nearest main roads A39, A394. Follow signs for Constantine. At lower village sign, at bottom of winding hill, turn off on private lane. Garden ¾ m up hill.* **Sun 27 Apr (1-5). Adm £5, chd free. Tea, coffee & cake. Visits also by arrangement Mar to June.**
Isolated granite cottage in 2 acres. Intimate flower and vegetable garden. Bridge over stream to large pond and primrose path through semi-wild bog area. Hillside with grass paths among native and exotic trees. Many camellias and rhododendrons. Mixed shrubs and herbaceous beds, wildflower glade, spring bulbs. A garden of discovery with hidden delights.
🐕 ❀ ☕

16 NEW FAN COTTAGE
Piggy Lane, Lerryn, Lostwithiel, PL22 0PT. Lin Briggs, robetlin@btopenworld.com. *3m from Lostwithiel. Park in council car park (free). Turn R up hill, continue past pub (approx 50yds). Turn R under Bluebell Cottage. Continue on Piggy Lane to end (approx 50yds). Fan Cottage is on R.* **Sun 11 May, Sun 17 Aug (10-5). Adm £5, chd free. Visits also by arrangement May to Sept for groups of up to 15.**
A one acre garden in a stunning setting with views over the Lerryn River. Divided into different parts there is much to interest visitors inc raised vegetable patches, fruit and apple trees, greenhouses, shrubberies and borders, a wildlife pond, and a bonsai display. Plenty of seating and places to relax. Visitors are welcome to picnic or refreshments avail at nearby pub or shop. Regret no dogs. Some, but not all, of the garden is accessible by wheelchair.
♿ ❀ ☕ 🪑

17 FIRSTE PARK
Winsor Lane, Kelly Bray, Callington, PL17 8HD. Mrs Tina Monahan, 07866 997753, tina@firstepark.co.uk. *From Callington towards Kelly Bray, just before Swingletree pub, turn R into Station Rd, about ¼ m Firste Park is on the L top of Winsor Lane. Parking signposted in adjoining field.* **Sun 29 June (11-3). Adm £5, chd free.**

Tea, coffee & cake. Visits also by arrangement 1 June to 27 Sept.
1950s house with mature trees, flower gardens established about 5 yrs ago with just over 1 acre incorporating a waterfall, pond and lawned areas. Packed with many plants and shrubs inc over 100 named roses, several varieties of hydrangeas and perfumed plants in abundance. There is an outside kitchen area, pergolas, a fruit and vegetable garden with cut flowers which we also use for dried flowers. Most of the garden is accessible but some gravel pathways.
♿ ☕ 🪑 ♫

18 FOX HOLLOW
Station Road, Carnhot, Chacewater, Truro, TR4 8PA. Adele & Gary Peters-Float, devilishdel@btinternet.com. *Enter Blackwater, take lane next to Citroen garage signed Chacewater, Station Rd, 1m on R just before train viaduct. Ignore SatNav once on this lane. Park in lane, few extra spaces opp.* **Sat 21 June (11-4). Adm £5, chd free. Tea, coffee & cake. Visits also by arrangement June & July for groups of 10 to 20.**
Approx 1 acre garden rediscovered and lovingly redesigned over 9 yrs by the owners so the 4 generations living here can enjoy. Every year something new, with herbaceous beds, traditional cottage flowers, wildflower areas, vegetable garden and orchard. A garden of discovery, meandering paths lead to hidden upcycled treasures and seating areas with far-reaching views. Greenhouses with many plants. Most areas accessible to wheelchairs.
♿ 🐕 ❀ ☕

19 GARDEN COTTAGE
Gunwalloe, Helston, TR12 7QB. Dan & Beth Tarling, 01326 241906, bethgunwalloe@gmail.com, www.gunwalloecottages.co.uk. *Just beyond Halzephron Inn at Gunwalloe. Cream cottage with green windows.* **Visits by arrangement 1 Apr to 6 Oct. Adm £5, chd £5. Cream teas.**
Coastal cottage garden. Small garden with traditional cottage flowers, vegetable garden, greenhouse and meadow with far-reaching views. Instagram: seaview_gunwalloe.
🐕 ❀ 🚗 🅿 ☕

20 GARDENS COTTAGE
Prideaux, St Blazey, PL24 2SS. Sue & Roger Paine, 07786 367610, sue.newton@btinternet.com, en-gb.facebook.com/gardenscottageprideaux. *1m from railway Xing on A390 in St Blazey. Turn into Prideaux Rd opp Gulf petrol station in St Blazey (signed Luxulyan). Proceed ½ m. Turn R (signed Luxulyan Valley and Prideaux) & follow signs.* **Sun 1 (12-5), Wed 11, Thur 12 June, Sun 6 July, Wed 3, Thur 4 Sept (2-5). Adm £5, chd free. Home-made teas.** Visits also by arrangement 1 June to 7 Sept for groups of 10 to 30. Morning, afternoon or evening visits available.
A stunning landscape and a variety of planting styles define this country garden. Formal and informal areas are enhanced with sculpture, and with its abundant herbaceous borders, dry terraces, courtyard garden, woodland glade, wildlife pond, beehives, orchard, fruit garden and a productive (and beautiful) kitchen garden it's a plot that feels much bigger than its one and a half acres. Check our Facebook page for special events.

21 GWRYTHIA
Sancreed, Penzance, TR20 8QS. Maggie Feeny, 07840 288916, maggiefeeny@yahoo.com, www.maggiefeeny.co.uk. *4m W of Penzance. From Penzance A30 to Lands End, at Drift go R at Xrds to Sancreed Beacon Ancient Monument. Go 1½ m past Sancreed sign, go L up track for Gwrythia. Walkers pay on gate. Visitors in cars must pre book.* **Sun 29 June (2-5). Adm £5, chd free. Pre-booking essential, please visit www.ngs.org.uk for information & booking. Tea, coffee & cake.** Visits also by arrangement 29 June to 10 Aug for groups of 6 to 15. Weekdays only.
A three acre garden with meadows, wildlife ponds, mixed ornamental borders of grasses, perennials, shrubs, roses and annuals. Walk through an arch of an established hornbeam hedge into a vegetable garden with polytunnel, on to an artist's studio, and down through a small woodland. Gwrythia is gardened organically, with plants chosen for both their attraction to wildlife and plant lovers alike. One of the gardeners is a painter and potter, ceramic and resin sculpture can be seen dotted about the land.

22 NEW HEYCROFT
Trevanion Road, Wadebridge, PL27 7NZ. Joanna Milner. *South side of town past the cinema. Parking on Trevanion Rd, Trevanion Park, Trevanion Close & Brook Rd, or 2 spaces avail round the back off New Park to the R of the green garage.* **Sun 11 May, Sun 13 July, Sun 10 Aug (1-5). Adm £5, chd free.**
A small town garden divided into many different areas. Packed with many interesting features inc a pond, a very small (but proper) meadow, wisteria and fern tunnel, rockery, greenhouse, vegetable plot and some unusual plants. Developed over the last 14 yrs but still very much an ongoing project. The garden is on two levels with the front only accessible by steps.

23 HIGHER LOCRENTON
St Keyne, Liskeard, PL14 4RN. Ade & Elise Allen, 01579 342301, adelise.allen@btinternet.com. *Nr St Keyne Well, between Looe & Liskeard. By St Keyne Church, take the lane to St Keyne Well for ½ m. Turn L at Well. Higher Locrenton is 100 yds on R. Parking for 8 cars.* **Sun 13 Apr, Sun 18 May, Sun 15 June, Sun 13 July (2-5). Adm £5, chd free. Light refreshments £3 per person.** Visits also by arrangement Apr to Aug for groups of up to 20.
The garden is set in 2 acres on a hillside. It has been developed over the past 30 yrs and is part parkland, part 'plantsman' in style, featuring a wide variety of trees, shrubs and perennials. It is informally divided into a number of themed beds. A key aim has been to provide year-round interest in terms of atmosphere, form, colour and scent. Some parts of the garden can only be accessed via steps or somewhat steep gradients.

24 ♦ THE JAPANESE GARDEN
St Mawgan, TR8 4ET. Natalie & Stuart Ellison, 01637 860116, info@japanesegarden.co.uk, www.japanesegarden.co.uk. *6m E of Newquay. St Mawgan village is directly below Newquay Airport. Follow brown & white road signs on A3059 & B3276.* **For NGS: Sat 10 May (10-6). Adm £6, chd £3.** For other opening times and information, please phone, email or visit garden website.
Discover an oasis of tranquillity in a Japanese-style Cornish garden, set in approx 1 acre. Spectacular Japanese maples and azaleas, symbolic teahouse, koi pond, bamboo grove, stroll woodland, zen and moss gardens. A place created for contemplation and meditation. Adm free to gift shop, bonsai and plant areas. Refreshments available in the village a short walk from garden entrance. 90% wheelchair accessible, with uneven, gravel paths.

25 ♦ KESTLE BARTON
Manaccan, Helston, TR12 6HU. Karen Townsend, 01326 231811, info@kestlebarton.co.uk, www.kestlebarton.co.uk. *10m S of Helston. Leave Helston on A3083 towards Lizard. At the R'about take 1st exit onto B3293 & follow signs towards St Keverne; after Trelowarren turn L and follow the brown signs for appprox 4m.* **For NGS: Every Wed 4 June to 24 Sept (10.30-5). Adm by donation. Modest Tea Room in garden. Cash only honesty box. Tea, coffee, cakes, ice creams, apple juice from our own orchards.** For other opening times and information, please phone, email or visit garden website.
A delightful garden near Frenchmans Creek, on the Lizard, which is the setting for Kestle Barton Gallery; wildflower meadow, Cornish orchard with named varieties and a formal garden with prairie planting in blocks by James Alexander Sinclair. It is a riot of colour in summer and continues to delight well into late summer. Good wheelchair access & reasonably accessible WC. Dogs on leads welcome.

26 LAMETTON MILL
St Keyne, Liskeard, PL14 4SH. Mr Richard & Mrs Leigh Woods, 07812 103518, lamettonmill@btinternet.com, www.lamettonmill.co.uk. *The postcode brings you to our door. If you wish to travel by train we are across the road from the St Keyne Wishing Well Halt railway stn. What3words app: access.motoring.nicknames.* **Sun 25 May (11-4); Wed 28 May (1-4); Sun 29 June (11-4); Wed 2 July (1-4); Sun 27 July (11-4); Wed 30 July (1-4); Sun 24 Aug (11-4); Wed 27 Aug (1-4). Adm £5, chd free. Tea, coffee & cake.**

Rosevallon Barn

Visits also by arrangement 24 May to 27 Aug for groups of 6 to 25.
A newly created garden, planted during 2023, on the site of a former mill. Contains a variety of young specimen trees, herbaceous borders, an extensive collection of Intersectional (ITOH) peonies, roses, small pond and water feature. The garden is laid out on different levels on a gently sloping site with several seating areas to relax in sun or shade. There are gravel paths and some steps.

27 THE LODGE
Fletchersbridge, Bodmin, PL30 4AN. Mr Tony Ryde & Dr James Wilson. *2m E of Bodmin. From A38 at Glynn Crematorium r'about take road towards Cardinham & continue down to hamlet of Fletchersbridge. Park at Stable Art on R. Short walk to garden 1st R over river bridge.* **Sat 29, Sun 30 Mar (12-5). Adm £6, chd free. Cream teas. Also light lunches 12 noon till 2.30pm.**

3 acre riverside garden created since 1998, specialising in trees and shrubs chosen for their flowers, foliage and form, and embracing a Gothic lodge remodelled in 2016, once part of the Glynn estate. Water garden with ponds, waterfalls and abstract sculptures. Magnolias, camellias, and spring bulbs at their peak in late March with early rhododendrons and azaleas starting. Wheelchair access to gravelled areas around house and along left side of garden.

28 ♦ THE LOST GARDENS OF HELIGAN
Pentewan, St Austell, PL26 6EN. Heligan Gardens Ltd, 01726 845100, heligan.reception@heligan.com, www.heligan.com. *5m S of St Austell. From St Austell take B3273 signed Mevagissey, follow signs.* **For opening times and information, please phone, email or visit garden website.**

Lose yourself in the mysterious world of The Lost Gardens where an exotic sub-tropical jungle, atmospheric Victorian pleasure grounds, an interactive wildlife project and the finest productive gardens in Britain all await your discovery. Wheelchair access to Northern gardens. Wheelchairs available at reception foc but pre booking advised due to limited number.

48,000 people affected by cancer were reached by Maggie's centres supported by the National Garden Scheme over the last 12 months.

CORNWALL

GROUP OPENING

29 LOSTWITHIEL GARDENS
Park Road, Lostwithiel, PL22 0BU. Claire Wood. *Pls park considerately in Lostwithiel. Head along Quay St with the river on your L, take the path to the L of Duchy Motors heading to the 1st garden called Llawnroc (PL22 0BU) Look for yellow signs.* **Sat 28 June (11-4.30). Combined adm £7, chd free. Home-made teas at Llawnroc, Silverlake Cottage and Benbole House.**

NEW **BENBOLE HOUSE**
PL22 0DT. Mr Richard & Mrs Becks Trant.

4 BOWNDER LOWEN
PL22 0GB. Franco Szczepaniak.

7 GILBURY HILL
PL22 0GH. Claire Wood.

NEW **LANLIVERY COTTAGE**
PL22 0JP. Dr Caroline Yates.

NEW **LLAWNROC**
PL22 0BU. Evette Hall.

NEW **MEANDERS**
PL22 0BA. Mr Chris & Mrs Sheila Marwood.

NEW **SILVER LAKE COTTAGE**
PL22 0JP. Annette Walker.

An ancient stannary town, Lostwithiel dates back to the C12. A bustling and colourful little town with a strong sense of community and camaraderie. 7 great gardens, each with their own sense of style, most of them typically small-town gardens. They are guaranteed to inspire those who have their own small garden and showcase what can really be done with a town garden. The route between the gardens is not for the faint hearted as there will be some small but steep hills to walk between the gardens. We recommend that you park in the town and start at Llawnroc where a route map will be provided (maps will be provided at each garden but payments both cash and card can only be made at Llawnroc and 7 Gilbury Hill). You could always catch the train to Lostwithiel and walk from the station which is conveniently located.

☕ 🔊

Bucks Head House Garden

CORNWALL

31 LOWER TREGAMERE
Tregamere, St Columb, TR9 6DN. Annette & Stuart Taylor, 07977 712298, annette@kico.co.uk. *Approx 1m from St Columb Major. Take A30 to Indian Queens then A39 towards Wadebridge. 1½m after Trekenning r'about turn R signed St Columb Major. After ½m turn L signed Tregamere. Follow for ½m. 1st L into drive after bridge.* **Tue 25, Wed 26, Thur 27, Fri 28 Mar (1-4.30). Adm £5, chd free.** Visits also by arrangement 1 May to 26 Sept for groups of up to 10.

An evolving 2½ acre garden. Bisected by a river, where English formal style juxtaposes with woodland and oriental styles. Walk through tall redwoods and past magnificent old oaks to take in many unusual trees and shrubs. Catch the cherry blossoms in late spring, the colourful acers, or the autumnal display of the Katsuras. Experience the air of tranquillity the garden evokes.

32 MALIBU
Tristram Cliff, Polzeath, Wadebridge, PL27 6TP. Nick Pickles, 07944 414006, nickdpickles@gmail.com. *Travel via Pityme/Rock/Trebetherick past Oystercatcher pub on L. Take 2nd L signed Tristram Caravan Park/ Cracking Crab Restaurant. Then L signed Tristram Cliff, up to end house. Free parking for coast & beach.* **Visits by arrangement for groups of up to 25. Hosted by keen cook a variety of refreshments/parties can be catered for. Adm £5, chd free. Cream teas, coffee, cakes & light lunches/ suppers offered by prior agreement.**

Just yards away from the Coast Path with stunning views over the beach and Pentire headland, Malibu consists of a sheltered compact garden to the rear and a general interest front garden. An interesting mix of features, different rockeries and strong focus on succulents, ferns and herbaceous plants. Greenhouse with many plants make this a rounded garden experience. We welcome dogs on leads. Wheelchairs can access the front garden with ease. Rear garden can only be accessed with assistance. Ground floor WC available.

GROUP OPENING

33 MENHENIOT GARDENS
Menheniot Village, PL14 3RZ. *4m SE of Liskeard. From the A38 turn L at the Menheniot junction, drive 1¼m into the village, follow yellow signs to the sports pavilion and collect a comprehensive map of the gardens to be visited.* **Sun 13 July (2-5.30). Combined adm £5, chd free. Home-made teas at the Old School, adjacent to the village green at the end of the tour.**

Menheniot Gardens is a group of 5 gardens and 3 community spaces situated in an attractive old mining village all within a reasonable walking distance from the sports pavilion. They consist of cottage gardens, private gardens and community spaces. The village has an historical connection with the Royal Navy, with the captain of HMS Pickle, Lt. Lapenotiere, buried in the churchyard. HMS Pickle was at Trafalgar and was ordered back to England to inform King George III of the death of Nelson. The village has a Holy Well which is a short distance from St Lalluwy's Church which is also a place of interest. Wheelchair access to 6 of the 8 gardens.

34 NAVAS HILL HOUSE
Bosanath Valley, Mawnan Smith, Falmouth, TR11 5LL. Aline & Richard Turner, 01326 251233, alineturner@btinternet.com. *1½m from Trebah & Glendurgan Gardens. Head for Mawnan Smith, pass Trebah & Glendurgan Gardens then follow yellow signs. Don't follow SatNav which suggests you turn R before Mawnan Smith.* **Sun 4 May (2-5). Adm £5, chd free. 'All you can eat' cream teas with home-made cake served on the terrace £5.** Visits also by arrangement 6 May to 30 June.

8½ acre elevated valley garden with paddocks, woodland, kitchen garden and ornamental areas. The ornamental garden consists of 3 plantsman areas with specialist trees and shrubs, walled rose garden, water features and rockery. Young and established wooded areas with bluebells, camellia walks and young large leafed rhododendrons. Seating areas with views across wooded valley. There is plenty of parking at the property. There is usually some sort of musical entertainment around the tea area at about 3.30pm. Partial wheelchair access, some gravel and grass paths.

35 THE OLD SCHOOL HOUSE
Averys Green, Cardinham, Bodmin, PL30 4EA. Mike & Libby Pidcock. *Edge of Cardinham village. A30 to Cardinham. Xrds in village towards church on R. Pass cemetery, and tennis court on L, 3rd house on R after tennis court. Parking Parish Hall opp church or at tennis court.* **Sun 4 May (11-5). Adm £5, chd free. Open nearby Pinsla Garden.**

Cottage garden created in the grounds of a Victorian school by a passionate and enthusiastic gardener over 35 yrs. Not so much by design, but led by a love of plants and trying anything: herbaceous, annuals, bulbs, shrubs, trees, fruit cage, espalier apples, cut flower patch and some veg. Wildflower area, wildlife ponds, bird feeding stations, jungle corner, quirky containers. Plenty of seating.

Our 2024 donation to The Queen's Nursing institute now helps support over 3,000 Queen's Nurses working in the community in England, Wales, Northern Ireland, the Channel Islands and the Isle of Man.

CORNWALL

36 THE OLD VICARAGE
Talland, PL13 2JA. Rachel James & Iain Doubleday, 07966 195378, oldvicaragetalland@gmail.com, instagram.com/oldvicaragetalland. *Situated next to Talland Church & opp Talland Barton Farm. From Looe follow A387 towards Polperro for 1¼m & take L turn signed 'The Bay' & 'Tencreek'. Follow winding road for 1¼m. Entrance on L, just before Talland Church.* **Sat 17, Sun 18 May, Sat 28, Sun 29 June (1-4). Adm £5, chd free. Light refreshments. Visits also by arrangement 19 May to 27 June for groups of 8 to 18. Early booking advised as availability is limited.**
Vibrant 4 acre south-facing coastal garden, with varied stunning vistas of Talland Bay, the ancient Talland Church and surrounding hills. Mature Monterey pines lead directly to the SW Coast Path. Restoring this historic churchyard garden has been an ongoing labour of love since 2018. Paths and some steep steps wind through terraced gardens, with seating to rest and enjoy the wonderful views. Special features inc mature Monterrey pines, large magnolia and copper beech, a small vineyard, and recreational facilities inc a tennis lawn, pétanque, and sand pit for younger children. Main garden area around the house is accessed over gravel paths, with an accessible WC.

37 ◆ PENCARROW
Washaway, Bodmin, PL30 3AG. Molesworth-St Aubyn Family, 01208 841369, info@pencarrow.co.uk, www.pencarrow.co.uk. *4m NW of Bodmin. Signed off A389 & B3266. Free parking.* **For NGS: Mon 14 Apr (10-5). Adm £10, chd free. Tea, coffee & cake. The Peacock Cafe will be open all day. For other opening times and information, please phone, email or visit garden website.**
50 acres of tranquil, family-owned Grade II* listed gardens. Superb specimen conifers, azaleas, magnolias and camellias galore. Many varieties of rhododendron give a blaze of spring colour; blue hydrangeas line the mile-long carriage drive throughout the summer. Discover the Iron Age hill fort, lake, Italian gardens and granite rock garden. Dogs welcome, café and children's play area. Gravel paths, some steep slopes.

38 PENDOWER HOUSE
Lanteglos-by-Fowey, PL23 1NJ. Mr Roger Lamb, 07860 391959, rl@rogerlamb.com. *Nr Polruan off B3359 from East Taphouse. 2m from Fowey if using the Bodinnick ferry. Parking in NT Lantivet Bay car park. Yellow signs from B3359.* **Visits by arrangement 18 June to 16 July for groups of up to 30. Adm £6, chd free. Home-made teas.**
Set in the heart of Daphne du Maurier country in its own valley this established garden, surrounding a Georgian rectory, is now undergoing a revival having been wild and neglected for some years. It has formal herbaceous terraces, a cottage garden, orchard, ponds, streams and a C19 shrub garden with a fine collection of azaleas, camellias and rhododendrons plus rare mature specimen trees.

39 PENWARNE
Mawnan Smith, Falmouth, TR11 5PH. Mrs R Sawyer, penwarnegarden@gmail.com. *Located approx 1m N of Mawnan Smith.* **Visits by arrangement 24 Feb to 5 May for groups of 6 to 20. Adm £7.50, chd free. Please discuss refreshments when booking.**
Originally planted in the late C19, this 12 acre garden inc extensive plantings of camellias, rhododendrons and azaleas. Special features inc large magnolias and a number of fine mature trees inc copper beech, handkerchief tree and Himalayan cedar. The walled garden, believed to be the site of a medieval chapel, houses herbaceous planting, climbing roses and fruit trees. Historic house and gardens with many mature specimens.

40 PINSLA GARDEN
Glynn, nr Cardinham, Bodmin, PL30 4AY. Mark & Claire Woodbine, www.pinslagarden.wordpress.com. *3½m E of Bodmin. From A30 or Bodmin take A38 towards Plymouth, 1st L at r'about, go past Crematorium & Cardinham Woods turning. Continue towards Cardinham village, up steep hill, 2m on R.* **Wed 23, Thur 24 Apr (9-5). Sun 4 May (9-5), open nearby The Old School House. Thur 15, Fri 16, Sat 24, Sat 31 May, Mon 16, Tue 17, Tue 24 June (9-5). Adm £5, chd free.**
Surround yourself with deep nature. Pinsla is a tranquil cottage garden buzzing with insects enjoying the sheltered sunny edge of a wild wood. Lose yourself in an experimental tapestry of naturalistic growing and self seeding. There are lots of unusual planting combinations, cloud pruning, intricate paths, garden art and a stone circle. Sorry, no teas, but do bring a picnic, or use cafe close by. Partial wheelchair access as some paths are narrow and bumpy.

GROUP OPENING

41 NEW POLRUAN GARDENS
Polruan, PL23 1PZ. Mrs Sue Rowe, sjsherwood2@gmail.com. *A390 to East Taphouse. B3359 towards Looe. At Lanreath R to Lanteglos Highway. By old telephone box turn L at Whitecross. Park at St Saviour's pay car park (PL23 1PZ). Also car or foot ferries from Fowey. Tickets, map, teas in Village Hall.* **Sat 14, Sun 15 June (1-5.30). Combined adm £6, chd free. Tea, coffee & cake. Cash only.**
Polruan Gardens is a group of over 9 gardens dotted around our small, very hilly village. All have stunning views of the River Fowey estuary or sea. Our gardens show various styles of coastal planting and terracing to suit steep slopes and occasionally lots of steps! Woodland, ponds, roses, herbaceous borders, rhododendrons, summer planting, picnic areas and even a funicular railway and art studio.

42 NEW POLVENTON
Fletchers Bridge, Bodmin, PL30 4AN. Mr & Mrs D Watson, 07816 967340. *2m E of Bodmin. From A30 > A38 Plymouth. At r'bout 1st L past Crematorium, over bridge, past L turn to Cardinham Woods. Main road 500yds to Fletchers Bridge. Before Stable Arts, acute R turn. Polventon 100yds on L.* **Every Wed 23 Apr to 30 July (11-5). Adm £6, chd free. Pre-booking essential, please visit www.ngs.org.uk for information & booking. Tea, coffee & cake. Visits also by arrangement 23 Apr to 30 July**

for groups of up to 15. Limited parking.
Restored 1¼ acres bordered by mixed woodland and divided into different 'rooms'. A kitchen garden, mixed and cut flower borders, hydrangea walk, small waterfall, bog garden fed by natural springs, mature rhododendrons, camellias and azaleas, bluebells, adolescent Japanese acers, ornamental and specimen shrubs, and a peaceful woodland glade. Sloping areas, narrow paths, stout shoes recommended.

43 PORT NAVAS CHAPEL
Port Navas, Constantine, Falmouth, TR11 5RQ. Keith Wilkins & Linda World, 01326 341206, keithwilkins47@gmail.com. *2m E of Constantine, nr Falmouth.*

From the direction of Constantine, we are the 2nd driveway on R after the 'Port Navas' village sign. **Visits by arrangement for groups of up to 25. Adm £6, chd free. Refreshments by prior arrangement.**
Japanese style garden set in ¾ acre of woodland, next to the old Methodist Chapel, with ornamental ponds and waterfalls, rock formations, Tsukubai water feature, granite lanterns, woodland stream, geodesic dome and Zen garden. Partial wheelchair access to driveway and sloping grass areas.

44 ♦ POTAGER GARDEN
High Cross, Constantine, Falmouth, TR11 5RF. Mr Mark Harris, 01326 341258, enquiries@potagergarden.org, www.potagergarden.org. *5m SW of Falmouth. From Falmouth, follow signs to Constantine. From Helston, drive through Constantine & continue towards Falmouth.* **For opening times and information, please phone, email or visit garden website.**
Potager has emerged from the bramble choked wilderness of an abandoned plant nursery. With mature trees which were once nursery stock and lush herbaceous planting interspersed with fruit and vegetables Potager Garden aims to demonstrate the beauty of productive organic gardening. There are games to play, hammocks to laze in and boules and badminton to enjoy. Potager café serving vegetarian food all day.

4 Bownder Lowen, Lostwithiel Gardens

45 ROSE MORRAN
Talskiddy, St Columb, TR9 6EB. Peter & Jenny Brandreth, 07711 517159, jennybrandreth@yahoo.com. *2 m N of St Columb Major. From A39 take Talskiddy/St Eval turn. Then take 2nd R signed Talskiddy & follow yellow NGS signs.* **Sun 27 Apr, Sun 22 June, Sun 31 Aug (2-5). Adm £5, chd free. Tea, coffee & cake. Visits also by arrangement 26 Apr to 7 Sept for groups of 12 to 24.** Colour, shape and texture define this North Cornwall garden. The property and gardens extend to about an acre, with lawn, wild areas and Cornish hedges completing the 2 acre plot. Landscaped and planted over 12 yrs there is a mix of shrubs and trees interplanted with perennials to ensure year-round display. Vegetable beds and a polytunnel with tender plants make this a rounded garden visit. There are level areas to view and the whole garden is accessible via grass slopes but some are quite steep. There is one step to the inside WC.

46 ◆ ROSELAND HOUSE
Chacewater, TR4 8QB. Mr & Mrs Pridham, 01872 560451, charlie@roselandhouse.co.uk, www.roselandhouse.co.uk. *4m W of Truro. Park in village car park (100yds) or on surrounding roads.* **For NGS: Sat 28, Sun 29 June (1-5). Adm £5, chd free. Home-made teas. For other opening times and information, please phone, email or visit garden website.** The 1 acre garden is a mass of summer colour in late June and July when the National collection of *Clematis viticella cvs* is in flower. Other climbing plants abound lending foliage, flower and scent. Situated in the garden is a specialist climbing plant nursery which along with a Victorian conservatory and greenhouse is open. The garden features two ponds and lots of seating areas. Some slopes.

47 ROSELAND PARC
Tregony, Truro, TR2 5PD. Mr Bob Mehen (Head Gardener), RobertMehen@retirementvillages.co.uk. *Follow signs for Tregony from the A390. Roseland Parc is situated on the main street, just past the clock tower & Kings Arms pub.* **Visits by arrangement in Mar for groups of 10 to 20. Inc a spring tour of the gardens with the Head Gardener. Adm £5, chd free. Tea, coffee & biscuits inc in entry fee.** Set in 7½ acres of wooded grounds, Roseland Parc offers much that makes Cornish gardens so special in spring. Magnolias, rhododendrons and over 80 named varieties of camellias thrive in this historic setting. Drifts of daffodils, crocus and hellebores vie for admiration with tree ferns, exotic tropical planting and ponds. Approx half the gardens are accessible for wheelchair users.

48 ROSEVALLON BARN
Tregony, Truro, TR2 5TS. Jenny Ralph, 07971 436344, rosevallon@icloud.com. *From main road in Tregony turn into Cuby Close on opp side of the road from St Cuby. Follow lane for just over 1m, pass Pencoose, then turn R down lane onto farm track.* **Visits by arrangement 3 Mar to 30 June for groups of 5 to 20. Adm £5, chd free. Tea, coffee & cake.** Rural setting surrounded by farmland. Converted barn with 3 acres of garden planted by present owners. Small stream and pond fed from spring water, herbaceous borders, shrubs, coppice with snowdrops, bluebells, primroses, fritillary. Vegetables and fruit, wildflower meadow, gravel garden, year-round interest. Bricked drive and accessible grass areas.

SPECIAL EVENT

49 ◆ ST MICHAEL'S MOUNT
Marazion, TR17 0HS. James & Mary St Levan, www.stmichaelsmount.co.uk. *2½ m E of Penzance. ½ m from shore at Marazion by Causeway.* **For opening times and information, please visit garden website or www.ngs.org.uk for details of special pop up opening date.** Infuse your senses with colour and scent in the unique sub-tropical gardens basking in the mild climate and salty breeze. Clinging to granite slopes the terraced beds tier steeply to the ocean's edge, boasting tender exotics from places such as Mexico, the Canary Islands and South Africa. This year the St Aubyn Family will be opening the gardens again, but pre-booking is essential. Please visit St Michael's Mount website for details of pop-up opening and the link to book online. Last entry to the garden is 4pm. Aeoniums, aloes and agave rear out of the bedrock, succulents appear from the flower beds basking in the sun. Salvias, tulbaghia and pelargoniums provide binding threads through the East and West Terraces and the Walled Gardens hold their own surprises.

50 NEW SECRET GARDEN
Tresthick, Trispen, Truro, TR4 9AU. Alan & Caroline Rounsevell. *A39 from Truro. Exit Trispen/St Erme & turn immed R. Follow signs to end of the road & yellow signs to lane leading to garden. What3words app: trickster.slumped.bitter.* **Sat 12, Sun 13 July (12-5). Adm £5, chd free. Tea, coffee & cake.** Lovingly created during lockdown, transformed from a rubbish dump! An upcycled garden hidden within enclosed walls of an old farm building. Colourful tropical planting of bananas, cannas, agapanthus etc propagated on site. Sunken stone fire-pit, Mediterranean bistro kitchen, unique pergolas. Nearby raised beds for fruit and vegetable and overflowing polytunnel. Wide flat paths suitable for wheelchairs.

51 SOUTH BOSENT
Liskeard, PL14 4LX. Adrienne Lloyd & Trish Wilson. *2½ m W of Liskeard. From r'about at junction of A390 & A38 take exit to Dobwalls. At mini-r'about, R to Duloe, after 1¼ m at Xrds turn R. Garden on L after ¼ m.* **Tue 13, Wed 14 May, Tue 16, Wed 17 Sept (2-5). Adm £5, chd free. Home-made teas. Opening with Dobwalls Gardens on Fri 13, Sat 14 June, Thur 3, Fri 4, Fri 25, Sat 26 July, Fri 8, Sat 9 Aug.** This garden has been developed from farmland. The aim is to create a combination of interesting plants coupled with habitat for wildlife over a total of 9½ acres. There are several garden areas, woodland gardens, a meadow, ponds of varying sizes, inc a rill and waterfall. In spring, the bluebell wood trail runs alongside the stream. Main garden area accessible. No wheelchair access to bluebell wood due to steps.

CORNWALL 101

52 TOWAN HOUSE
Old Church Road, Mawnan Smith, Falmouth, TR11 5HX. Mr Dave & Mrs Tessa Thomson, 01326 250378, tandd.thomson@btinternet.com. *Approx 5m from Falmouth. On entering Mawnan Smith, fork L at the Red Lion pub. When you see the gate to Nansidwell, turn R into Old Church Rd. Follow NGS signs.* **Sun 14 Sept (2-5). Adm £6, chd free. Tea, coffee & cake. Visits also by arrangement 22 June to 7 Sept for groups of 5 to 15.**
Towan House is a coastal garden with some unusual plants and views to St Mawes, St Anthony Head lighthouse and beyond with easy access to the SW coast path overlooking Falmouth Bay. It is approximately ¼ acre and divided into 2 gardens, one exposed to the north and east winds, the other sheltered allowing tropical plants to flourish such as Hedychium, Corymbosa and cannas.

53 TREBARTHA ESTATE GARDEN AND COUNTRY GARDEN AT LEMARNE
Trebartha, Near North Hill, Launceston, PL15 7PD. The Latham Family. *6m SW of Launceston. Near junction of B3254 & B3257. What3words app: breathing.blown. zoomed. No coaches.* **Sun 11 May, Sun 28 Sept (2-5). Adm £8, chd free. Home-made teas.**
Historic landscape gardens featuring streams, cascades, rocks and woodlands, with fine veteran and champion trees, bluebells, ornamental walled garden; also visit Lemarne garden en route. Allow at least an hour for a circular walk. Some steep and rough paths, which can be slippery when wet. Stout footwear advised.

54 TREGLYN
Gover Valley, St Austell, PL25 5RD. Mrs Heather Beales, 01726 339040, keith.cats@gmail.com. *1m from St Austell town centre. SatNav use PL25 5RB (not D). Keep on Gover Rd which becomes an unmade single track lane (do not veer to R) & follow signs.* **Sun 8 June, Sun 7 Sept (1-5). Adm £5, chd free. Home-made teas served on vintage china. Outside seating & small covered area. Visits also by arrangement 1 June to 7 Sept for groups of 5 to 30.**

A tranquil woodland garden that celebrates Cornwall's unique industrial heritage. Deep in the Gover Valley on the site of old china clay works this wildlife friendly garden has been lovingly created to make the most of the many historical features. River/woodland walks, spring bluebells, formal planting, bog garden, exotic plant jungle, stumpery, leaf fed ponds, secluded seating areas and more. Quarries and Goblins Gold. Remains of industrial heritage accessible. Wheelchair access to lower garden area, lawns and refreshment areas.

55 TRELAN
Wharf Road, Lelant, St Ives, TR26 3DU. Nick Williams, 07817 425157, nick@nickgwilliams.com. *Close to St Uny Church, Lelant. Trelan Gardens are off Wharf Rd which leads to a car park on Dynamite Quay. Car park signed at the end of Wharf Rd & the gardens are 100m down on R.* **Sat 10 May, Sat 28 June (2-5). Adm £6, chd free. Tea, coffee & cake. Visits also by arrangement May to July for groups of 6 to 20.**
Trelan has a distinctly tropical feel. There is a swimming pond surrounded by lush vegetation, an Italianate sunken garden, a fern garden, numerous young trees and countless *Echium pininana*. There's also an echium root sculpture and lots of pathways. It is a feast for the eyes!

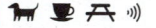

56 TREMICHELE
Housel Bay, The Lizard, Helston, TR12 7PG. Mike & Helen Painton, 01326 291370, paintonfam@btinternet.com. *On the Lizard peninsular approx 10m from Helston. Follow directions to Lizard village. Park on the village green, parking is by voluntary contribution. Walk along Beacon Terrace & follow signs for Housel Bay Hotel.* **Visits by arrangement May to Aug for groups of up to 15. Adm £5, chd free. Tea, coffee, cold drinks, home-made cake & cookies.**
A coastal garden, created in 2016, of approx 1 acre overlooking the Atlantic and the Lizard Lighthouse. It is a steep sloping garden divided into 3 terraces accessed by slopes or steps. A productive kitchen garden, with raised beds and fruit trees. Greenhouse and cold frames. A wildflower meadow with access to the coast path. Banks have a mix of planting inc hardy exotics.

57 NEW TREMORRAN & THE ANGEL
Truthwall, St. Just, Penzance, TR19 7QJ. Annie & Martin Henry Holland, 07768 166309, missanniehenry@hotmail.com, www.tremorran.co.uk/tremorran-and-the-angel-gallery.html. *Situated on the iconic B3306 coast road Lands End to St Ives ½ m outside of St Just. Opp the Botallack sign. What3words app: column.crabmeat.remit.* **Visits by arrangement 20 Apr to 20 Sept for groups of up to 30. Adm by donation. Cream teas. Coffee & biscuits in the morning, tea & cake in the afternoon.**
The garden is set in the grounds of Tremorran, a mine captain's house built in the early 1900s. A maze of paths lead to many 'rooms' furnished with seating and sculptures. A sloping pebble beach around the wildlife pond is planted with a variety of grasses and sea holly. Well-stocked borders contain trees, established shrubs, hydrangeas, rhododendrons, and herbaceous plants. Walk the labyrinth. Artist Studios.

58 TRENARTH
High Cross, Constantine, Falmouth, TR11 5JN. Lucie Nottingham, 01326 340444, lmnottingham@btinternet.com, trenarthgardens.com/garden. *6m SW of Falmouth. Main road A39/A394 Truro to Helston, follow Constantine signs. At High X garage turn L for Mawnan, 30yds on R down dead end Trenarth Lane. Trenarth is ½ m at end of lane.* **Visits by arrangement Jan to Sept. Adm £8, chd free. Tea, coffee & cake.**
4 acres round C17 farmhouse in peaceful pastoral setting. Year-round and varied. Emphasis on tender, unusual plants, structure and form. C16 courtyard, listed garden walls, holm oak avenue, yew rooms, vegetable garden, traditional potting shed, orchard, palm and gravel area SA veldt area, with close planting inc agapanthus, agave, dietes and dierama, woodland areas. Circular walk down ancient green lane via animal pond to Trenarth Bridge, returning through woods. Abundant wildlife. Bees in tree bole, lesser horseshoe bat colony, swallows, wildflowers and butterflies. Family friendly, children's play area, the Wolery, and plenty of room to run, jump and climb.

St Michael's Mount

CORNWALL 103

SPECIAL EVENT

59 ◆ TRESCO ABBEY GARDENS
Tresco, TR24 0QQ. Mr R A Dorrien-Smith, 01720 424108, gardenvisitorcentre@tresco.co.uk, www.tresco.co.uk. *28m SW Lands End. You can fly to neighbouring St. Mary's via fixed wing aircraft from Lands End, Newquay or Exeter, or can travel via ferry from Penzance. There is a short boat journey to Tresco from St. Mary's.* **For opening times and information, please phone, email or visit garden website or www.ngs.org.uk for details of special pop up opening date.**
Meander a myriad of winding paths through flowers of the King Protea and the handsome Lobster Claw, great blue spires of Echium, brilliant Furcraea, Strelitzia and shocking-pink drifts of Pelargonium. World renowned Tresco Abbey Garden is home to plants from every Mediterranean climate zone, flourishing just 28 miles off the coast of Cornwall. Augustus Smith established Tresco Abbey Garden in the C19 around the ruins of a Benedictine Abbey. Today, the garden is a sanctuary for some 2,000 specimens from across the southern hemisphere and subtropics, from Brazil to New Zealand; Myanmar to South Africa. Please note the gardens and cafe open at 10am and close at 4pm.

♿ 🐕 ✤ ☕

60 TRESITHNEY
Bowl Rock, Lelant, St Ives, TR26 3JE. Caroline Marwood, 07515 339400, carolinemarwood@me.com, www.facebook.com/Tresithney. *At Bowl Rock just off The Old Coach Rd between the A3074 & B3311. A 'Walking Garden' on The St Michael's Way between Carbis Bay & Trencrom Hill. Turn at Bowl Rock, between Lelant & St Ives. Marked with flag.* **Visits by arrangement May to Aug for groups of up to 20. Adm inc cream tea & cake, as well as guided tour. Adm £15, chd free.**
This is a unique 'Walking Garden' on the ancient St Michael's Way. The garden is approx 1½ acres with a variety of distinct areas, inc a rose garden, potager, fernery, orchard and wild areas. With beautiful views up to Trencrom Hill an Iron Age Hill Fort. Artist studio will also be open. Partial wheelchair access by using main path through centre of garden.

♿ 🐕 ✤ ☕ 🔊

61 TREVESCO
7 Commons Close, Mullion, Helston, TR12 7HY. Colin Read. *Situated on the W side of Mullion on the road to Poldhu Cove & Cury. ¼ m from village centre car parks.* **Sun 8 June (11-4). Adm £5, chd free. Tea, coffee & cake.**
This ¼ acre garden has been established over 15 yrs in a sub-tropical style with rare unusual plants. Many tender plants have been established without winter protection very successfully due to local climate. There is also a pond and two feature olive trees. Also there is a separate fruit and vegetable area.

✤ ☕

62 TREVILLEY
Sennen, Penzance, TR19 7AH. Patrick Gale & Aidan Hicks, 07970 060401, trevilley@btinternet.com, www.instagram.com/trevilley. *For walkers, Trevilley lies on the footpath from Trevescan to Polgigga & Nanjizal. On Open Day follow the signs into our parking field. If visiting by arrangement, Trevilley lies up a track outside Trevescan. If you reach a white house, reverse then enter our farmyard by the gate!* **Sun 15 June (2-5.30). Adm £6, chd free. Tea, coffee & cake. Visits also by arrangement in June for groups of 6 to 50. Smaller groups are welcome for the same adm fee as a group of six (£36).**
Eccentric, romantic and constantly evolving garden, as befits the intense creativity of its owners, carved out of an expanse of concrete farmyard over 20 yrs. Inc elaborate network of decorative cobbling, pools, container garden, vegetable garden, shade garden, the largely subtropical mowhay garden and both owners' studios but arguably its glory is the westernmost walled rose garden in England. Dogs are welcome on leads. The garden visit can form the climax of enjoying the circular coast path walk from Land's End to Nanjizal and back across the fields. Visitors may leave their cars with us while they take a walk across the fields to Nanjizal or Trevescan (where there is sometimes a cafe.).

🐕 ✤ 🚗 ☕ 🔊

63 TREVINA HOUSE
St Neot, Liskeard, PL14 6NR. Kevin & Sue Wright, 07428 102104, kevin@trevina.com, www.facebook.com/TrevinaInCornwall. *1m N of St Neot. From A38 turn off at Halfwayhouse pub. Head up hill to Goonzion Downs. Bear L & keep straight on towards Colliford Lake. From A30 take Colliford Lake/St Neot turning. Head towards St Neot.* **Thur 13, Fri 14 Mar, Thur 10, Fri 11 Apr, Thur 8, Fri 9 May, Thur 12, Fri 13 June, Thur 10, Fri 11 July, Thur 11, Fri 12 Sept, Wed 8, Thur 9 Oct (10.30-5). Adm £6, chd free. Visits also by arrangement Feb to Oct for groups of 5 to 30. Please car share if possible as very narrow lanes.**
The gardens at Trevina are both old and new. From a Victorian cottage garden with original cobbled paths to rewilded woodland. A trout pond occupies the site of a medieval fish pond and the site of a Cornish Round. There is a traditional kitchen garden and organic orchard. The gardens have colour and interest year-round, from the first snowdrops, bluebells, apple blossom and ripe apples in October.

🐕 ✤ ☕ 🔊

64 WINDMILLS
South Hill, Callington, PL17 7LP. Sue & Peter Tunnicliffe. *3m NW of Callington. Head N from Callington A388, after about ½ m turn L onto South Hill Rd (signed South Hill). Straight on for 3m, gardens on R just before church.* **Sun 6 July (1.30-5). Combined adm with Anvil Cottage £6, chd free. Home-made teas. Gluten free cakes available.**
Next to medieval church and on the site of an old rectory there are still signs in places of that long gone building. A garden full of surprises, formal paths and steps lead up from the flower beds to extensive vegetable and soft fruit area. More paths lead to a pond, past a pergola, and down into large lawns with trees and shrubs and chickens. Partial wheelchair access.

♿ ✤ ☕ 🪑

In 2024, we celebrated 40 years of continuous funding for Macmillan Cancer Support equating to more than £19.5 million.

CUMBRIA

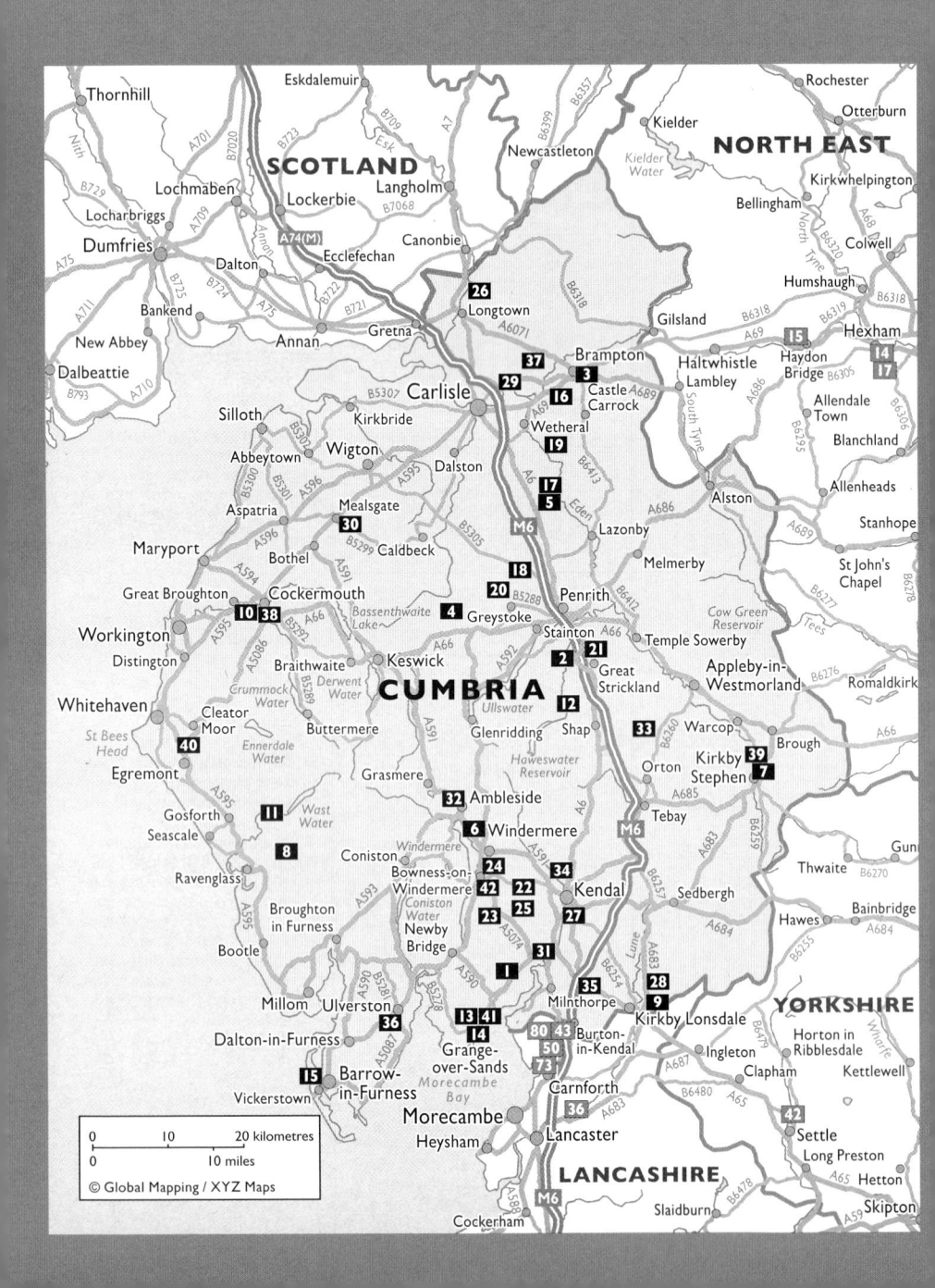

CUMBRIA 105

VOLUNTEERS

County Organiser
Alannah Rylands
01697 320413
alannah.rylands@ngs.org.uk

County Treasurer
Cate Bowman
01228 573903
cate.bowman@ngs.org.uk

Publicity – Social Media
Gráinne Jakobson
01946 813017
grainne.jakobson@ngs.org.uk

Booklet Co-ordinator
Cate Bowman
01228 573903
cate.bowman@ngs.org.uk

Assistant County Organisers
Carole Berryman
07808 974877
carole.berryman@outlook.com

Christine Davidson
07966 524302
christine.davidson@ngs.org.uk

Bruno Gouillon
01539 532317
brunog45@hotmail.com

Gráinne Jakobson (as above)

Liz Jolley
07948 472923
liz.jolley@ngs.org.uk

Belinda Quigley
07738 005388
belinda.quigley@ngs.org.uk

@CumbriaNGS
@CumbriaNGS
@ngscumbria

OPENING DATES

All entries subject to change.
For latest information check
www.ngs.org.uk

Map locator numbers are shown to the right of each garden name.

February

Friday 28th
◆ Swarthmoor Hall 36

March

Sunday 2nd
◆ Swarthmoor Hall 36

Sunday 23rd
◆ Rydal Mount and Gardens 32

Monday 31st
◆ Rydal Mount and Gardens 32

April

Tuesday 1st
◆ Rydal Mount and Gardens 32

Wednesday 2nd
◆ Rydal Mount and Gardens 32

Saturday 26th
Park House 28

Sunday 27th
Park House 28
Summerdale House 35

May

Sunday 4th
Low Fell West 23

Monday 5th
Low Fell West 23

Saturday 10th
Low Crag 22

Sunday 11th
Low Crag 22

Saturday 17th
Hazel Cottage 17

Sunday 18th
Hayton Village Gardens 16
Hazel Cottage 17

Matson Ground 24
Summerdale House 35

Saturday 24th
Galesyke 11

Sunday 25th
Galesyke 11

Thursday 29th
Cragwood Country House Hotel 6

Saturday 31st
Coombe Eden 5

June

Sunday 1st
Coombe Eden 5
Sprint Mill 34
Yewbarrow House 41

Friday 6th
◆ Swarthmoor Hall 36

Sunday 8th
Chapelside 4
◆ Hutton-In-The-Forest 18
◆ Swarthmoor Hall 36

Monday 9th
◆ Rydal Mount and Gardens 32

Tuesday 10th
◆ Rydal Mount and Gardens 32

Wednesday 11th
◆ Rydal Mount and Gardens 32

Saturday 14th
Hazel Cottage 17

Sunday 15th
Hazel Cottage 17
8 Oxenholme Road 27
5 Primrose Bank 29
Tithe Barn 37

Thursday 19th
NEW Grange Farm 12

Friday 20th
NEW Grange Farm 12

Saturday 21st
Eden Place 7
Esk Bank 8
NEW Grange Farm 12

Sunday 22nd
Askham Hall 2
Esk Bank 8
Ivy House 19
Yews 42

Saturday 28th
Eden Place 7
NEW The White House 38

CUMBRIA

July

Saturday 5th
NEW School House ... 33

Sunday 6th
Brampton East Gardens ... 3
Yewbarrow House ... 41

Thursday 10th
Larch Cottage Nurseries ... 21

Saturday 12th
27 Haverigg Gardens ... 15

Sunday 13th
27 Haverigg Gardens ... 15
Winton Park ... 39

August

Every day from Sunday 17th to Monday 25th
Fell Yeat ... 9

Sunday 3rd
Grange Fell Allotments ... 13
Yewbarrow House ... 41

Thursday 7th
Larch Cottage Nurseries ... 21

Saturday 9th
Galesyke ... 11

Sunday 10th
Abi and Tom's Garden Plants ... 1
Galesyke ... 11
Ivy House ... 19

Monday 25th
◆ Netherby Hall ... 26

Saturday 30th
Middle Blakebank ... 25

September

Thursday 4th
Larch Cottage Nurseries ... 21

Sunday 7th
Yewbarrow House ... 41

October

Sunday 19th
Low Fell West ... 23

By Arrangement

Arrange a personalised garden visit with your club, or group of friends, on a date to suit you. See individual garden entries for full details.

Eden Place ... 7
Esk Bank ... 8
Foinhaven ... 10
Galesyke ... 11
NEW Grange Farm ... 12
Grange Fell Allotments ... 13
Grange over Sands Hidden Gardens ... 14
27 Haverigg Gardens ... 15
Ivy House ... 19
Johnby Hall ... 20
Low Fell West ... 23
Matson Ground ... 24
8 Oxenholme Road ... 27
5 Primrose Bank ... 29
Quarry Hill House ... 30
Rose Croft ... 31
Sprint Mill ... 34
NEW 11 Tree Gardens, Brampton East Gardens ... 3
Woodend House ... 40
Yewbarrow House ... 41

Grange Farm

THE GARDENS

1 ABI AND TOM'S GARDEN PLANTS
Halecat Garden Nursery, Witherslack, Grange-over-Sands, LA11 6RT. Abi & Tom Attwood, www.abiandtom.co.uk. *20 mins from Kendal. From A590 turn N to Witherslack. Follow brown tourist signs to Halecat. Rail Grange-Over-Sands 5m, Bus X6 2m, NCR 70.* **Sun 10 Aug (10-5). Adm £4.50, chd free. Home-made teas.**
The 1 acre nursery garden is a fusion of traditional horticultural values with modern approaches to the display, growing and use of plant material. Our full range of perennials can be seen growing alongside one another in themed borders be they shady damp corners or south facing hot spots. The propagating areas, stock beds and family garden, normally closed to visitors, will be open on the NGS day. More than 1,000 different herbaceous perennials are grown in the nursery, many that are excellent for wildlife. For other opening times and information please visit our website. We are on a sloping site that has no steps but steep inclines in places.

2 ASKHAM HALL
Askham, Penrith, CA10 2PF. Charles Lowther, 01931 712350, hello@askhamhall.co.uk, www.askhamhall.co.uk. *5m S of Penrith. Turn off A6 for Lowther & Askham.* **Sun 22 June (11.30-7). Adm £7, chd free. Light refreshments. Donation to Penrith Red Squirrel Group.**
Askham Hall is a Pele Tower incorporating C14, C16 and early C18 elements in a courtyard plan. Opened in 2013 with luxury accommodation, a restaurant, outdoor heated pool and wedding barn. Splendid formal garden with terraces of herbaceous borders and topiary, dating back to C17. Meadow area with trees and pond, kitchen gardens and animal trails. Café serving wood-fired pizzas, cakes, hot and cold drinks with indoor and outdoor seating.

GROUP OPENING

3 BRAMPTON EAST GARDENS
Brampton, CA8 1EX. *Gardens located at the eastern side of Brampton, between the Co-op & the top of Station Rd. Parking around The Sands & Lanercost Rd area of Brampton. Community garden & Sands Terrace are to the W of The Sands. A map will be provided on entry to the first garden.* **Sun 6 July (1-5). Combined adm £5, chd free. Home-made teas at Ridge House. Visitors can picnic at the Community Garden, weather permitting. The Sands grassed area can also be used for picnics which also has a roofed shelter.**

25 EDMONDSON CLOSE
CA8 1GH. Mrs Penny Young.

LOVER'S LANE COMMUNITY GARDEN
CA8 1TN. www.facebook.com/Loverslanecommunitygarden.

RIDGE HOUSE
CA8 1EN. Mrs Vita Collins.

6 SANDS COTTAGES
CA8 1UQ. Ms Jane Streames.

NEW 10 TREE GARDENS
CA8 1TZ. Bill Parkin.

NEW 11 TREE GARDENS
CA8 1TZ. Shelagh Smith, 01697 742014, shelaghdavid.smith@gmail.com. **Visits also by arrangement 7 June to 21 June for groups of up to 6. Regret no children or dogs.**

A selection of gardens of differing sizes and styles. 25 Edmondson Close, created from scratch 12 yrs ago, features a productive organic vegetable area, espaliered apples, soft fruit, area set aside for wildlife inc small pond, greenhouse, ornamental pond and herbaceous borders. Ridge House is well established, with mature trees around a house built in 1833; in a traditional setting with relaxed naturalistic planting with self-seeders positively encouraged. Lover's Lane is a Community Garden currently with around 40 members. Their aim is to be inclusive and organic, and experiment with new ways of gardening in trial beds. 6 Sands Cottages is a communal back lane behind terraced cottages which has been transformed into a lovely space. Two more gardens in this terrace will also be open. 10 and 11 Tree Gardens are neighbours with small gardens, each with different approaches to their gardens.

4 CHAPELSIDE
Mungrisdale, Penrith, CA11 0XR. Tricia & Robin Acland. *12m W of Penrith. On A66 take minor rd N signed Mungrisdale (no NGS sign till turned!). After 2m, sharp bends, garden on L after tiny church on R. Use church car park at foot of our short drive.* **Sun 8 June (1-5). Adm £5, chd free.**
1 acre, windy garden below fell, round C18 farmhouse and outbuildings. Fine views. Tiny stream, large pond. Herbaceous, gravel, alpine and shade areas, bulbs in grass. Wide range of plants, many unusual. Relaxed planting regime, lively plant combinations. Run on organic lines. Art constructions in and out, local stone used creatively. There may be plants for sale. Good teas available nearby.

5 COOMBE EDEN
Armathwaite, Carlisle, CA4 9PQ. Belinda & Mike Quigley. *8m SE of Carlisle. Turn off A6 just S of High Hesket signed Armathwaite. Continue to bottom of hill where garden can be found on R turn for Lazonby.* **Sat 31 May, Sun 1 June (12-5). Adm £5, chd free. Home-made teas.**
A one acre garden of traditional and contemporary beds. A pretty beck runs through the lower garden with a Japanese style bridge and large rhododendrons. Many choice trees can be seen throughout the garden, Japanese acers, white birches, flowering dogwood and a growing rowan collection. A long herbaceous border, grassed areas and gravelled paths lead to a formal garden and potager.

Our donation to Marie Curie this year equates to 17,496 hours of nursing care or 43 days of care in one of their nine hospices.

6 CRAGWOOD COUNTRY HOUSE HOTEL
Ecclerigg, Windermere, LA23 1LQ. David Williams, 01539 488177, info@cragwoodhotel.co.uk, www.lakedistrictcountryhotels.co.uk/cragwood-hotel. *Leave the M6 at J36 & follow the A591 for 15m until you see Cragwood signed on the L. Cragwood is immed before the National Park Visitor Centre at Brockhole.* **Thur 29 May (11-4.30). Adm £5, chd free. Tea in one of our lounges or outside on our terrace.**
The gardens at Cragwood Country House are an integral part of the property's rich history and charm. The gardens were originally designed in the late C19 by the renowned landscape architect Thomas Hayton Mawson, who was known for his work in the Lake District and other parts of England. Mawson created a beautiful formal garden with carefully manicured lawns, elegant flower beds, and striking topiary, as well as a peaceful woodland walk and a charming rock garden. Over the years, the gardens have been carefully maintained and developed, with new features and plantings added to enhance their beauty and appeal. Today, the gardens at Cragwood are a highlight of any visit to the property, offering a tranquil and picturesque setting in which to relax and explore. There is a gradual slope to the left of reception. Also some gravel paths.

7 EDEN PLACE
Kirkby Stephen, CA17 4AP. J S Parrot Trust, kirstymahoney76@gmail.com. *¼ m N of Kirkby Stephen. Take the A685 Kirkby Stephen to Brough road. Cross the bridge & take R turn. Eden Place is 200 yds on R.* **Sat 21, Sat 28 June (10.30-5). Adm £5, chd free. Tea, coffee & cake.** Visits also by arrangement 14 June to 19 July.
3 acre garden with many large perennial borders and island beds enclosed by tall hedges. Part of the garden is made over to aviaries with exotic birds, some are free-flying. There is also a lake and a woodland walk through a conservation area.

8 ESK BANK
Eskdale Green, Holmrook, CA19 1UE. Pooja & Adrian Norton, 07947 146737, esk.bank@btinternet.com. *Take the A595 to Holmrook, turn off on the rd to Eskdale Green. Park at the Green Station. By train to Ravenglass for Eskdale, then take La'al Ratty steam train to the Green Station.* **Sat 21 June (11-5); Sun 22 June (11-4.30). Adm £5, chd free. Tea, coffee & cake.** Visits also by arrangement 7 June to 30 Aug for groups of 10+. At least two weeks notice required prior to visit.
Nestled in Eskdale, the ¾ acre cottage style garden is on a south-facing slope with 360 panoramic views of the valley. There is a mix of perennial beds and herbaceous borders with many roses and shrubs inc rhododendrons, magnolia and azaleas. There is a summerhouse and a large kitchen garden with a greenhouse. The sloping lawns have an orchard, wildflower borders and a small pond. Public WC available in Eskdale Green village next to shop.

9 FELL YEAT
Casterton, Kirkby Lonsdale, LA6 2JW. Mr C. Benson. *1m E of Casterton village. On the road to Bull Pot. Leave A65 at Devils Bridge, follow A683 for 1m, take the R fork to High Casterton at golf course, straight across at 2 sets of Xrds, house on L, ¼ m from no-through-rd sign.* **Daily Sun 17 Aug to Mon 25 Aug (11-4). Adm £4, chd free.**
Relaxed, natural 1 acre garden, the largest part of which was started 35 yrs ago. Planted with many unusual trees, shrubs and large collection of hydrangeas. Increasingly emphasis is on encouraging wildlife and creating a wilder feel. A wonderful breeding ground for owls, sparrowhawks and buzzards. Enjoy the meandering paths, fernery, maturing stumpery and new grotto house with rocks and ferns. Adjoining nursery specialising in ferns, hostas, hydrangeas and many unusual plants.

10 FOINHAVEN
Brigham, Cockermouth, CA13 0SY. Bill Wheeler, 01900 372921, junebill1@gmail.com. *2m W Cockermouth. Leave Cockermouth on A5086 & turn R at r'about on A66. 1st L for Brigham, Foinaven 100y on L after 30mph sign.* **Visits by arrangement Apr to Sept for groups of up to 10. Adm £4, chd free. Light refreshments.**
Cottage style, small garden in a village location. Densely planted around a chalet bungalow on sloping, half acre site. Wide range of small trees, shrubs and perennials. Pond, bog garden, rockeries and camomile lawn. Parking on site. Partial wheelchair access.

11 GALESYKE
Wasdale, CA20 1ET. Christine McKinley, 01946 726267, mckinley2112@sky.com. *In Wasdale valley, between Nether Wasdale village & the lake. From Gosforth, follow signs to Nether Wasdale & then to lake, approx 5m. From Santon Bridge follow signs to Wasdale then to lake, approx 2¼ m.* **Sat 24, Sun 25 May, Sat 9, Sun 10 Aug (10-5). Adm £5, chd free. Cream teas.** Visits also by arrangement.
4 acre garden combining formal areas, shrubberies and woodland, dissected by the River Irt which can be crossed by a suspension bridge. In spring the garden is vibrant with azaleas and rhododendrons, in summer by an impressive collection of colourful hydrangeas. Set in the heart of the Wasdale valley the garden has an unforgettable backdrop of the Screes and the high Lakeland fells. There is a magnificent Victorian sandstone sundial in the garden.

12 NEW GRANGE FARM
Bampton Grange, Penrith, CA10 2QR. Mrs Charlie Morison, 07977 518613, charlie@campbell-bell.com. *9m S of Penrith in beautiful Lowther Valley in Bampton Grange village. Close to Askham & M6. What3words app: define.nothing.dumplings Take lane on L of Crown & Mitre pub, follow lane round to L & we are last white house.* **Thur 19, Fri 20, Sat 21 June (10.30-4). Adm £5, chd free.** Visits also by arrangement 2 June to 30 June.
A rustic Cumbrian country garden designed by Peter Stott of Larch Cottage. The garden takes you on a journey along winding paths, alongside ponds and into the large and productive vegetable garden. The land beyond the walls of the garden becomes wilder as you journey through the rewilding area and along the bank of the River Lowther. Here

13 GRANGE FELL ALLOTMENTS
Fell Road, Grange-over-Sands, LA11 6HB. Mr Bruno Gouillon, 01539 532317, brunog45@hotmail.com. *Opp Grange Fell Golf Club. Rail 1.3m, Bus 1m X6, NCR 70.* **Sun 3 Aug (11-4). Adm £4.50, chd free. Tea, coffee & cake.** **Visits also by arrangement May to Aug for groups of 10 to 40.** The allotments are managed by Grange Town Council. Opened in 2010, 30 plots are now rented out and offer a wide selection of gardening styles and techniques. The majority of plots grow a mixture of vegetables, fruit trees and flowers. There are a few communal areas where local fruit tree varieties have been donated by plot holders with herbaceous borders and annuals.

GROUP OPENING

14 GRANGE OVER SANDS HIDDEN GARDENS
Grange-over-Sands, LA11 7AF. Bruno Gouillon, 01539 532317, brunog45@hotmail.com. *Off Kents Bank Rd, 3 gardens on Cart Lane then last garden up Carter Rd for Shrublands. Rail 1.4m; Bus X6; NCR 70.* **Visits by arrangement 19 May to 30 Sept for groups of 10 to 40. Combined adm £5.50, chd free. Tea, coffee & cake.** Donation to St Mary's Hopsice.
Four very different gardens hidden down narrow lanes off the road south out of Grange. Off Kents Bank Road, the 3 gardens on Cart Lane all back onto the railway embankment, providing shelter from the wind but also creating a frost pocket. The garden at 21 Cart Lane is a series of rooms designed to create an element of surprise with fruit and vegetables in raised beds. Elder Cottage is an organised riot of fruit trees, vegetables, shrubby perennials and herbaceous plants. Productive and peaceful. Hawthorne Cottage has been redesigned and replanted over the last 2 yrs to create a garden with colour and interest. Up the hill on Carter Rd, Shrublands is a ¾ acre garden situated on a hillside overlooking Morecambe Bay. Visitors with mobility issues can access Shrublands & 21 Cart Lane, but can only view Elder Cottage from the roadside & Hawthorne Cottage from the gate.

School House

Woodend House

15 27 HAVERIGG GARDENS
North Scale, Walney Island, Barrow-in-Furness, LA14 3TH. Jo & Brendan Sweeney, 01229 472726, jo@bjts.co.uk. *North end of Walney Island. A590 to Walney Island, R at end of the bridge, continue on through N Scale. We are the last road before the airport. Additional parking at N Scale Community Centre.* **Sat 12, Sun 13 July (10.30-4). Adm £4, chd free. Tea, coffee & cake.** Visits also by arrangement 17 May to 31 Aug. Colourful 300ft cottage style garden backing on to sheep fields with views to Blackcombe and the Coniston hills. Planting adapted to a coastal situation. Wildlife pond, woodland area, herbaceous borders, vegetable and fruit beds, a bee attracting slate scree front garden, two summerhouses, and many seating areas for relaxing. Plus an outside WC disguised as a Tardis!

GROUP OPENING

16 HAYTON VILLAGE GARDENS
Hayton, Brampton, CA8 9HR. www.facebook.com/NGSopengardens. *5m E of M6, J43 at Carlisle-towards Hexham. Signed: Hayton ½ m S of A69. 3m W of Brampton. Please park one side only & less centrally, leaving space for less able near Inn. Tickets sold East of village (Townhead), West & Middle with map. What3words app: romance.cooked.tango.* **Sun 18 May (12-5). Combined adm £5, chd free. Home-made teas in Hayton Village Primary School. Also cold refreshments in one of the gardens outside if suitable. Village green available for picnics. Cash only.** Donation to Hayton Village Primary School.

ARNWOOD
CA8 9JQ. Joanne Reeves-Brown.

BECK COTTAGE
CA8 9HR. Fiona Cox.

THE GARTH
CA8 9HR. Frank O'Connor & Linda Mages.

HEMPGARTH
CA8 9HR. Sheila & David Heslop.

KINRARA
CA8 9HR. Tim & Alison Brown.

MILLBROOK
CA8 9HT. M Carruthers.

STONECHATS
CA8 9HT. Anna & Mic Mayhew.

TOWNFOOT HOUSE
CA8 9HR. Alison Springall.

TOWNHEAD COTTAGE
CA8 9JQ. Chris & Pam Haynes.

WEST GARTH COTTAGE
CA8 9HL. Debbie Jenkins, www.westgarth-cottage-gardens.co.uk.

A picturesque valley of quality gardens of very varied size and styles, mostly around old stone cottages. Smaller and larger cottage gardens, courtyards and containers, woodland walks, exuberant borders, frogs, pools, colour and texture throughout. Spring bluebells, azaleas and wisteria. Home-made teas and sometimes live music at the school where the children create gardens annually within the main school garden (RHS award). Gardens additional to those listed also generally open or visible. The annual Scarecrow display/competition may also coincide which children will enjoy (pls check the website nearer to the date). Kinrara is owned by an artist and architect with multiple garden design experience and may open on additional dates in 2025 (pls visit www.ngs.org.uk for pop up dates). West Garth Cottage is owned by a professional artist/designer. Accessibility ranges from full to none. Furthest gardens require a half-mile walk (and back) or extra driving. Come early or late for easier parking.

&. * ♨ 🜨

17 HAZEL COTTAGE
Armathwaite, Carlisle, CA4 9PG. Mr D Ryland & Mr J Thexton. *8m SE of Carlisle. Turn off A6 just S of High Hesket signed Armathwaite, after 2m house facing you at T-junction. 1¼m walk from Armathwaite train stn.* **Sat 17, Sun 18 May, Sat 14, Sun 15 June (12-5). Adm £5, chd free. Home-made teas.**
Flower arrangers and plantsman's garden extending to approx 5 acres. Inc mature herbaceous borders, pergola, ponds and planting of disused railway siding providing home to wildlife. Many variegated and unusual plants. Varied areas, planted for all seasons, south facing, some gentle slopes, ever changing. Partial access for wheelchair users, small steps to WC area. Main garden planted on gentle slope.

&. 🐾 * 🚗 ♨

18 ♦ HUTTON-IN-THE-FOREST
Penrith, CA11 9TH. Lord & Lady Inglewood, 01768 484449, info@hutton-in-the-forest.co.uk, www.hutton-in-the-forest.co.uk. *6m NW of Penrith. On B5305, 2m from exit 41 of M6 towards Wigton.* **For NGS: Sun 8 June (10-5). Adm £10, chd free. Delicious home-made cakes & scones, light lunches & teas served in the Cloisters tearoom.** For other opening times and information, please phone, email or visit garden website.

Hutton-in-the-Forest is surrounded on two sides by distinctive yew topiary and grass terraces - which to the south lead to C18 lake and cascade. 1730s walled garden is full of old fruit trees, tulips in spring, roses and an extensive collection of herbaceous plants in summer. Our gravel paths can make it difficult to push a wheelchair in places.

&. 🐾 * 🚗 ♨ 🜨

19 IVY HOUSE
Cumwhitton, CA8 9EX. Martin Johns & Ian Forrest, 01228 561851, martinjohns193@btinternet.com. *6m E of Carlisle. At the bridge at Warwick Bridge on A69 take turning to Great Corby & Cumwhitton. Through Great Corby & woodland until you reach a T-junction. Turn R into village.* **Sun 22 June, Sun 10 Aug (1-5). Adm £5, chd free. Light refreshments. Visits also by arrangement Apr to Aug.**
Approx 2 acres of sloping fellside garden with meandering paths leading to a series of 'rooms': inc pond, fern garden, Acer terrace, shrubberies, herbaceous borders and grass and herb gardens. Copse with meadow leading down to beck. Trees, shrubs, ferns, grasses, bamboos, evergreens and perennials planted with emphasis on variety of texture and colour. Sadly unsuitable for wheelchairs. WC available.

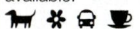

🐾 * 🚗 ♨

20 JOHNBY HALL
Johnby, Penrith, CA11 0UU. Henry & Anna Howard, 01768 483257, bookings@johnbyhall.com, www.johnbyhall.com. *Greystoke, Penrith. From Greystoke village green follow signs to Johnby, forking L as you leave the village. Gateway signed Johnby Hall after 1m on the L.* **Visits by arrangement 19 May to 11 July (Mon- Thurs only) Parking limited to 15 cars max so car shares encouraged. Adm by donation. Tea, coffee & cakes or biscuits.**
Large, very informal and natural mature garden around an ancient manor house. Intriguing courtyards are full of wild flowers and old roses; the 1683 walled garden is now an orchard. Wildflower lawns and meadows in summer, a bluebell walk through the beginnings of a pinetum with some unusual young specimens, and a field of free-range rare-breed pigs.

🐾 🚙 ♨

21 LARCH COTTAGE NURSERIES
Melkinthorpe, Penrith, CA10 2DR. Peter Stott, www.larchcottage.co.uk. *4m S of Penrith. From N leave M6 J40 take A6 S. From S leave M6 J39 take A6 N signed off A6.* **Thur 10 July, Thur 7 Aug, Thur 4 Sept (1-4). Adm £5, chd free. Refreshments available in our onsite restaurant, La Casa Verde.**
A unique nursery and garden designed and built over the past 40 yrs. The gardens inc lawns, flowing perennial borders, rare and unusual shrubs, trees, a small orchard and a kitchen garden. A natural stream runs into a small lake, a haven for wildlife and birds. At the head of the lake stands a small frescoed chapel designed and built by the owner for family use. Private Lower gardens, lake and Chapel (open on NGS open days), Japanese dry garden, pond, Italianesque columned garden for shade plants. Glass walled kitchen garden. Italianesque tumbled down walls act as a backdrop for the borders, showcasing rare and unusual shrubs, trees and stock plants. Accessible to wheelchair users although the paths are rocky in places.

&. * ♨

22 LOW CRAG
Crook, Kendal, LA8 8LE. Chris Dodd & Liz Jolley. *Halfway between Kendal (3m) & Windermere (4m). From Kendal turn off B5284 just before Sun Inn. Pass Ellerbeck Farm on R, continue ¼m. Low Crag is 3rd drive on L at Footpath sign. For parking follow signs.* **Sat 10, Sun 11 May (10-5.30). Adm £5, chd free. Tea, coffee & cake.**
A relaxed 2 acre nature-friendly garden using organic principles and set around former farmhouse. The more formal garden features yew hedge, herbaceous planting, arboretum, orchard, vegetable and herb garden. This transitions to compost area, pond, damson hedges, meadows - some scythed, and the greater landscape of the Lyth Valley. Long views with seating and viewpoints.

🐾 * ♨ 🜨))

23 LOW FELL WEST
Crosthwaite, Kendal, LA8 8JG. Barbie Handley, 07423 055928, barbie@handleyfamily.co.uk. 4½ m S of Bowness. Off A5074, turn W just S of Damson Dene Hotel. Follow lane for ½ m. **Sun 4 May (2-5); Mon 5 May (11-2); Sun 19 Oct (11-4). Adm £5, chd free. Light refreshments. Visits also by arrangement for groups of up to 30.**
This 2 acre woodland garden in the tranquil Winster valley has extensive views to the Pennines. The four season garden, restored since 2003, inc expanses of rock planted sympathetically with grasses, unusual trees and shrubs, climaxing for autumn colour. There are native hedges and areas of plant rich meadows. A woodland area houses a gypsy caravan and there is direct access to Cumbria Wildlife Trust's Barkbooth Reserve of Oak woodland, bluebells and open fellside. Wheelchair access to much of the garden, but some rough paths and steep slopes.
& ⛟ ✳ 🍵 🍴

24 MATSON GROUND
Windermere, LA23 2NH. Matson Ground Estate Co Ltd, 07831 831918, sam@matsonground.co.uk. ⅔ m E of Bowness. Turn N off B5284 signed Heathwaite. From E 100yds after Windermere Golf Club, from W 400yds after Windy Hall Rd. Rail 2½ m; Bus 1m, 6, 599, 755, 800; NCR 6 (1m). **Sun 18 May (1-5). Adm £6.50, chd free. Tea, coffee & cake. Visits also by arrangement 6 Jan to 15 Dec for groups of 5 to 30.**
2 acres of mature, south facing gardens. A good mix of formal and informal planting inc topiary features, herbaceous and shrub borders, wildflower areas, stream leading to a large pond and developing arboretum. Rose garden, rockery, topiary terrace borders, ha-ha. Productive, walled kitchen garden c1862, a wide assortment of fruit, vegetables, cut flowers, cobnuts and herbs. Greenhouse.
& ⛟ ✳ 🚗 🏠 🍵 🔊

25 MIDDLE BLAKEBANK
Underbarrow, Kendal, LA8 8HP. Christian Burrell & Stuart McGill, www.instagram.com/middleblakebank. *Lyth valley between Underbarrow & Crosthwaite. From Underbarrow take A5074 to Crosthwaite. The garden is on Broom Lane, a turning between Crosthwaite & Underbarrow signed Red Scar & Broom Farm What3words app: hampers.speedily.budget.* **Sat 30 Aug (11-4). Adm £5, chd free. Tea, coffee & cake.**
With meticulously considered grounds that inc formal planting areas, abundant borders, a wondrous orchard and a wildflower meadow, you will be sure to discover colour, texture, and creativity in whichever direction you look. Developed and nurtured by the previous owners, the gardens are now chaotically maintained by two, out-of-their depth novice gardeners.
⛟ 🍵 🏠 🔊

26 ◆ NETHERBY HALL
Longtown, Carlisle, CA6 5PR. Mr Gerald & Mrs Margo Smith, 01228 792732, events@netherbyhall.co.uk, netherbyhall.co.uk. *2m N of Longtown. Take Junction 44 from the M6 & follow the A7 to Longtown. Take Netherby Rd & follow it for about 2m. Netherby Hall is on L.* **For NGS: Mon 25 Aug (10-4). Adm £6, chd free. For other opening times and information, please phone, email or visit garden website.**
Netherby Hall Garden is 36 acres, consisting of a 1½ acre walled kitchen garden which produces fruit, vegetables and herbs for the Pentonbridge Inn restaurant, as well as herbaceous borders, traditional kidney beds amongst wonderful lawns, woodlands with many fine specimen trees, azaleas and rhododendrons, all set in a designed landscape bordering the River Esk. Ample parking. Carriage paths allow easy access around the Victorian pleasure grounds & walled garden.
& ⛟ 🏠 🍴 🔊

27 8 OXENHOLME ROAD
Kendal, LA9 7NJ. Mr John & Mrs Frances Davenport, 07496 029842, frandav8@btinternet.com. *SE Kendal. From A65 (Burton Rd, Kendal/Kirkby Lonsdale) take B6254 (Oxenholme Rd). No.8 is 1st house on L beyond red post box.* **Sun 15 June (10-4). Adm £5, chd free.**

Home-made teas. **Visits also by arrangement 18 Apr to 30 Sept for groups of 10+.**
Artist and potter's garden of approx ½ acre of mixed planting designed for year-round interest, inc two linked small ponds. Roses, grasses and colour themed borders surround the house, with a gravel garden at the front, as well as a number of woodland plant areas, some vegetables, fruit and orchard areas and lots of sitting spaces. Designed to attract birds and insects. John is a ceramic artist and Frances is a painter and paintings and pots are a feature of the garden display. We offer tea, coffee, biscuits and cakes to eat at seating around garden. Garden essentially level, but access to WC is up steps.
& ⛟ 🚗 🍵

28 PARK HOUSE
Barbon, Kirkby Lonsdale, LA6 2LG. Mr & Mrs P Pattison. *2½ m N of Kirkby Lonsdale. Off A683 Kirkby Lonsdale to Sedburgh road. Follow signs into Barbon Village.* **Sat 26, Sun 27 Apr (10.30-4.30). Adm £6, chd free. Cream teas.**
Romantic Manor House (not open). Extensive vistas. Formal tranquil pond encased in yew hedging. Meadow with meandering pathways, water garden filled with bulbs and ferns. Formal lawn, gravel pathways, cottage borders with hues of soft pinks and purples, shady border, kitchen garden. An evolving garden to follow.
⛟ ✳ 🍵

29 5 PRIMROSE BANK
Crosby-on-Eden, Carlisle, CA6 4QT. Mark & Cate Bowman, 01228 573903, cate.bowman@ngs.org.uk. *3m NE of Carlisle off A689. From M6 J44 take A689 towards Hexham. At the next r'about take the 1st turn towards Brampton/Hexham. Take the 2nd turn on R to Crosby on Eden. Park at the village hall.* **Sun 15 June (1-5). Adm £5, chd free. Home-made teas. Open nearby Tithe Barn. Visits also by arrangement 9 June to 22 June for groups of up to 30.**
A beautiful village garden of ⅓ acre, overlooking the river Eden and Hadrian's Wall footpath. Gravel paths take you through several garden rooms featuring an extensive vegetable garden, small orchard, rose garden, wildlife pond, wide mixed

Middle Blakebank

borders with espaliered crab apples on the boundary, rose clad pergolas and arches. Designed to be wildlife friendly. Gravel paths unsuitable for wheelchairs.

30 QUARRY HILL HOUSE
Boltongate, Mealsgate, Wigton, CA7 1AE. Mr Charles Woodhouse & Mrs Philippa Irving, 07785 934377, cfwoodhouse@btinternet.com. $^{1}/_{3}$ m W of Boltongate, 6m SSW of Wigton, 13m NW of Keswick, 10m E Cockermouth. M6 J41, direction Wigton, through Hesket Newmarket, Caldbeck & Boltongate on B5299, entrance gates to drive on R. On A595 Carlisle to Cockermouth turn L for Boltongate, Ireby. **Visits by arrangement Apr to Aug. Home-made teas.** Donation to Cumbria Community Foundation: Quarry Hill Grassroots Fund.

3 acre parkland setting, country house (not open), woodland garden with marvellous views of Skiddaw, Binsey and the Northern Fells and also the Solway and Scotland. Outstanding trees, some ancient and rare and many specimen, shrubs, herbaceous borders, potager vegetable garden.

31 ROSE CROFT
Levens, Kendal, LA8 8PH. Enid Fraser, 07976 977018, fraserenid@gmail.com. *Approx 4m from J36 on M6. From J36 take A590 toward Barrow. R turn Levens, at pub, follow road to garden on L, over Xrds, downhill. L turn signed 'PV Dobson'. Garden on R after Dobsons.* **Visits by arrangement 1 June to 7 Sept for groups of up to 20. Light refreshments, tea, soft drinks, biscuits. Adm £5, chd free.**

This 'secret' garden's richness in herbaceous plants, grasses, shrubs and trees belies the twin challenges of thin topsoil and an acutely sloping site. With grand views across the Lyth valley, steps and pathways carry down to lower-level lawns, streamside summerhouse and wild flowers. Long season of interest with designed elements providing bountiful displays well into late summer.

32 ♦ RYDAL MOUNT AND GARDENS
Rydal, Ambleside, LA22 9LU. Helen Green, 01539 433002, info@rydalmount.co.uk, www.rydalmount.co.uk. *Rydal Mount is located between Ambleside & Grasmere. Visitors will turn L up Rydal Hill to arrive at the Rydal Mount car park where there is limited parking.* **For NGS: Sun 23, Mon 31 Mar, Tue 1, Wed 2 Apr, Mon 9, Tue 10, Wed 11 June (10.30-4.30). Adm £5, chd free. Home-made scones & soup as well as tea, coffee & cold drinks avail in our tearoom. For other opening times and information, please phone, email or visit garden website.** Rydal Mount was the family home of William Wordsworth. Wordsworth considered himself as good a landscape gardener as a poet, and the Rydal Mount garden is the largest example of his design. The garden stretches over 5 acres and inc the terraces that Wordsworth built, informal herbaceous borders, trees planted by the poet and a wonderful range of traditional lakeland plants.

☕ 🪑

33 NEW SCHOOL HOUSE
Silver Street, Crosby Ravensworth, Penrith, CA10 3JA. Judith & Nigel Harrison. *Exit M6, J39 drive N to Shap on A6 & take the R turn at the Shap Chippy signed to Crosby Ravensworth, at T junction in the village turn L and park by church then follow signs to walk to garden.* **Sat 5 July (1-5). Adm £5, chd free. Tea, coffee & cake.**
A newly created medium sized cottage garden next to the River Lyvennet in a village setting. Next to the house is a formal garden of lawn, herbaceous borders and box hedging. Then we have a small orchard, and vegetable beds. A wilder area contains a meadow, a natural spring fed pond and a ditch as a flood mitigation measure. We also have a number of green roofs and a riverbank sitting area.

☕

34 SPRINT MILL
Burneside, Kendal, LA8 9AQ. Edward & Romola Acland, 01539 725168/07806 065602, mail@sprintmill.uk. *2m N of Kendal. From Burneside follow signs towards Skelsmergh for ½ m, then L into drive. From A6, about 1m N of Kendal follow signs towards Burneside, then R into drive. What3words app: segregate. petty.error.* **Sun 1 June (10.30-5). Adm £5, chd free. Refreshments are self-service by donation.** Variety of teas, good coffee & home-made cakes. Pls visit www.ngs.org.uk for details of pop up openings. **Visits also by arrangement.**
Unorthodox organically run garden, the wild and natural alongside provision of owners' fruit, vegetables and firewood. Idyllic riverside setting, 5 acres to explore inc wooded riverbank with hand-crafted seats. Large vegetable and soft fruit area, following no dig and permaculture principles. Hand tools prevail. Historic water mill with original turbine. The 3 storey building houses owner's art studio and personal museum, inc collection of old hand tools associated with rural crafts. Goats, hens, ducks, rope swing, very family friendly. Short walk to our flower-rich hay meadows. Access for wheelchairs to some parts of both garden and mill.

♿ 🐐 ☕ 🪑

35 SUMMERDALE HOUSE
Cow Brow, Nook, Lupton, LA6 1PE. David & Gail Sheals, www.summerdalegardennursery.co.uk/the-garden-1. *7m S of Kendal, 5m W of Kirkby Lonsdale. From J36 M6 take A65 towards Kirkby Lonsdale, at Nook take R turn Farleton. Location not signed on highway. Detailed directions available on our website.* **Sun 27 Apr, Sun 18 May (11-4.30). Adm £6, chd free. Home-made teas.**
1½ acre part-walled country garden set around C18 former vicarage. Several defined areas have been created by hedges, each with its own theme and linked by intricate cobbled pathways. Relaxed natural planting in a formal structure. Rural setting with fine views across to Farleton Fell. Large collection of auriculas with displays during the season.

🐐 ❀ ☕))

36 ♦ SWARTHMOOR HALL
Swarthmoor Hall Lane, Ulverston, LA12 0JQ. 01229 583204, info@swarthmoorhall.co.uk, www.swarthmoorhall.co.uk. *1m SW of Ulverston. A590 to Ulverston. Turn off to Ulverston railway stn. Follow Brown/blue tourist signs to Hall. Rail 0.9m. NCR70 & 700 (1m).* **For NGS: Fri 28 Feb, Sun 2 Mar (11-3); Fri 6, Sun 8 June (11-4).** Adm £2.50, chd free. Tea, coffee & cake. **For other opening times and information, please phone, email or visit garden website.**
Traditional English country garden surrounding a Grade II* C17 hall, the cradle of Quakerism. Cottage style borders, woodland garden, quiet garden dedicated to peaceful contemplation, ornamental vegetable garden and wildflower meadow with fabulous crocus display in late February/March. Please check the website for opening times for the Hall and Gardens. Our on site cafe offers a range of hot and cold drinks, fabulous cakes and scones, ice creams and other snacks. There is wheelchair access around one side of the hall and into all of the garden areas.

♿ 🐐 🚗 🛏 ☕))

37 TITHE BARN
Laversdale, Irthington, Carlisle, CA6 4PJ. Mr Gordon & Mrs Christine Davidson, 01228 573090, christinedavidson7@sky.com. *8m N E of Carlisle. ½ m from Carlisle Lake District Airport. From A6071 turn for Laversdale, from M6 J44 follow A689 Hexham/Brampton/Airport. Follow NGS signs.* **Sun 15 June (1-5). Adm £5, chd free. Open nearby 5 Primrose Bank.**
Set on a slight incline, the thatched property has stunning views of the Lake District, Pennines and Scottish Border hills. Planting follows the cottage garden style. The surrounding walls, arches, grottos and quirky features have all been designed and created by the owners. There is a peaceful sitting glade beside a rill and pond. This property also offers self-catering accommodation (sleeps 2) within the grounds of the garden.

🚗 🛏

38 NEW THE WHITE HOUSE
Brigham Road, Cockermouth, CA13 0AX. Jean & John Jowsey. *From Penrith turn R into C'mouth off A66 at Travel Lodge r'about. 3rd turn L into Brigham Rd. 40 metres along on L follow lane up to house. (NB foot access only up lane-no cars please).* **Sat 28 June (12-5). Adm £4.50, chd free. Home-made teas.**
The garden is a large urban plot slowly developed over the last 20 yrs, parts of which date back to Victorian times. High walls on most sides have provided shelter along with a pergola. Mixed borders of herbaceous perennials, shrubs and trees, a formal pond, a fruit and vegetable

area, small orchard, a stable yard with pots, planters and potting shed, a greenhouse and covered seating areas. Most areas are easily accessed but paths along pergola may prove difficult . A ramp provides access into the lower fruit and vegetable garden.

39 WINTON PARK
Appleby Road, Kirkby Stephen, CA17 4PG. Mr Anthony Kilvington, www.wintonparkgardens.co.uk. *2m N of Kirkby Stephen. On A685 turn L signed Gt Musgrave/Warcop (B6259). After approx 1m turn L as signed.* **Sun 13 July (11-4). Adm £6, chd free. Light refreshments.** 5 acre country garden bordered by the banks of the River Eden with stunning views. Many fine conifers, acers and rhododendrons, herbaceous borders, hostas, ferns, grasses, heathers and several hundred roses. Four formal ponds plus rock pool. Partial wheelchair access.

40 WOODEND HOUSE
Woodend, Egremont, CA22 2TA. Grainne & Richard Jakobson, 019468 13017, gmjakobson22@gmail.com. *2m S of Whitehaven. Take A595 from Whitehaven towards Egremont. On leaving Bigrigg take 1st turn L. Go down the hill. Garden is at the bottom of the road opp Woodend Farm.* **Visits by arrangement May to Sept for groups of up to 25.** A beautiful garden tucked away in a small hamlet. Meandering gravel paths lead around the garden with imaginative, colourful planting and quirky features. Take a look around a productive, organic potager using no-dig methods, wildlife pond, mini spring and summer meadows and sit in the pretty summerhouse. Designed to be beautiful year-round and wildlife friendly. The gravel drive and paths are difficult for wheelchairs but more mobile visitors can access the main seating areas in the rear garden.

41 YEWBARROW HOUSE
Hampsfell Road, Grange-over-Sands, LA11 6BE. Jonathan & Margaret Denby, 07733 322394, jonathan@bestlakesbreaks.co.uk, www.yewbarrowhouse.co.uk. *¼ m from town centre. Proceed along Hampsfell Rd passing a house called Yewbarrow to brow of hill then turn L onto a lane signed 'Charney Wood/Yewbarrow Wood' & sharp L again. Rail 0.7m, Bus X6, NCR 70.* **Sun 1 June, Sun 6 July, Sun 3 Aug, Sun 7 Sept (11-4). Adm £5, chd free. Light refreshments. Visits also by arrangement Mar to Oct for groups of 10 to 60.**
More Cornwall than Cumbria, according to Country Life, a colourful 4 acre garden filled with exotic and rare plants, with dramatic views over Morecambe Bay. Outstanding features inc the Orangery, the Japanese garden with infinity pool, the Italian terraces and the restored Victorian kitchen garden. Dahlias, cannas and colourful exotica are a speciality. Find us on YouTube.

42 YEWS
Storrs Park, Bowness-on-Windermere, LA23 3JR. Sir Christopher & Lady Scott, www.yewsestate.com. *1.4m S of Bowness-on-Windermere. On A5074 about 0.3m N of Blackwell, The Arts & Crafts House. Rail Windermere 3m, What3words app: ballots.speak.fractions.* **Sun 22 June (11-4.30). Adm £6.50, chd free. Tea, coffee & cake.** Donation to International Dendrology Society.
7 acre garden overlooking Windermere which has undergone extensive redevelopment since 2018. Formal gardens designed by Mawson and Avray Tipping inc sunken borders, rose garden and croquet lawn. Newly planted woodland walk, bog garden and renovated Yew maze. Naturalistic planting, areas left for wildlife and many fine trees. New kitchen garden built 2022 and original Messenger glasshouse. There is some level access to formal areas of the garden but only via gravel paths.

Yews

DERBYSHIRE

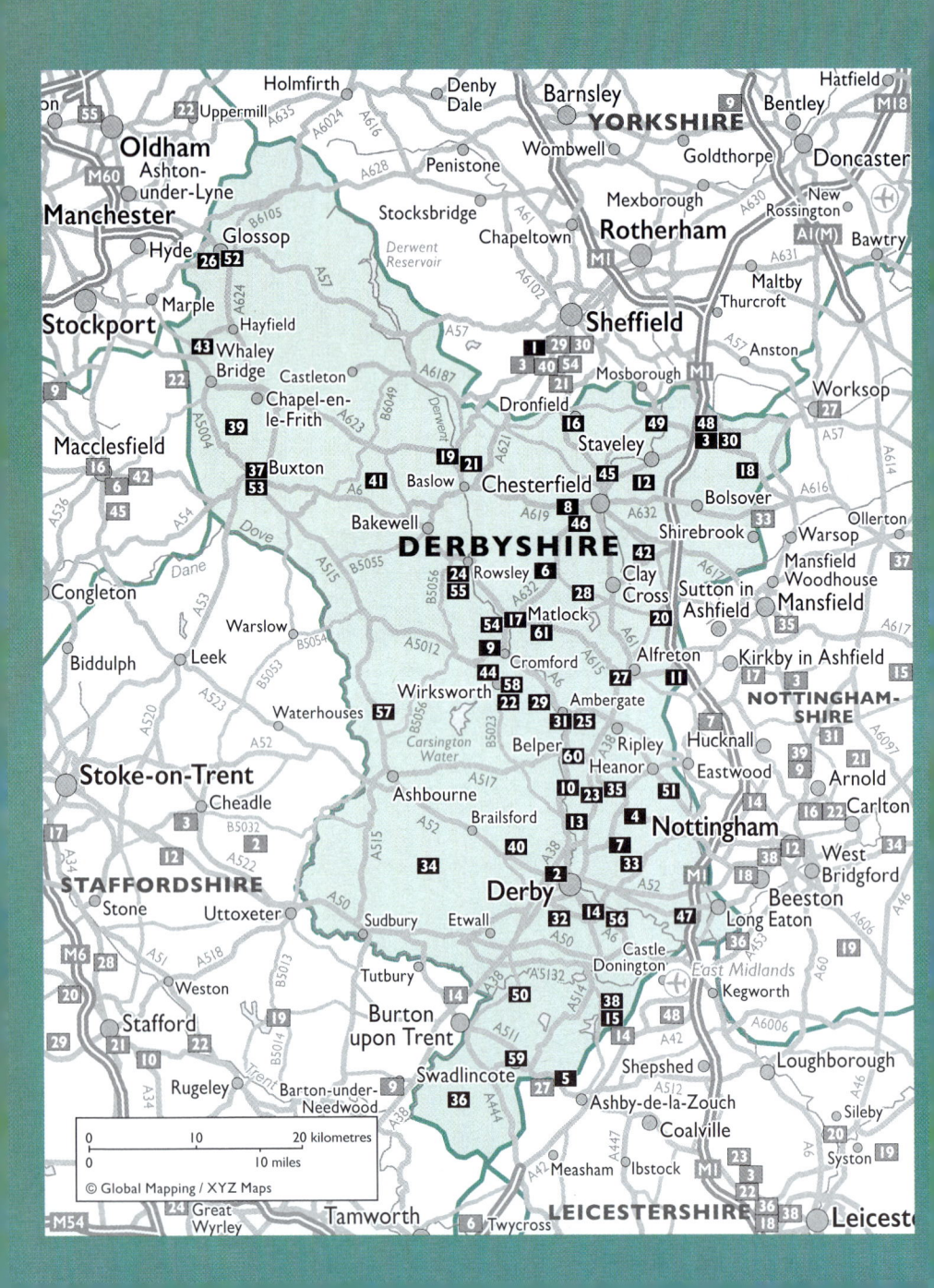

DERBYSHIRE

VOLUNTEERS

County Organiser
Hildegard Wiesehofer
07809 883393
hildegard@ngs.org.uk

County Treasurer
Anne Wilkinson
07831 598396
annelwilkinson@btinternet.com

Social Media
Tracy & Bill Reid
07932 977314
billandtracyreid@ngs.org.uk

Booklet Co-ordinators
Dave & Valerie Booth
07891 436632
valerie.booth1955@gmail.com

Group Visit Co-ordinator
Pauline Little
01283 702267
plittle@hotmail.co.uk

Assistant County Organisers
Dave & Valerie Booth
(See above)

Kathy Fairweather
07779 412702
kathy.fairweather@ngs.org.uk

Gill & Colin Hancock
01159 301061
gillandcolinhancock@gmail.com

Paul & Kathy Harvey
01629 822218
pandk.harvey@ngs.org.uk

Jane Lennox
07939 012634
jane@lennoxonline.net

Pauline Little
(See above)

Christine & Vernon Sanderson
01246 570830
christine.r.sanderson@uwclub.net

@ngsderbyshire
@DerbyshireNGS
@derbyshirengs

OPENING DATES

All entries subject to change. For latest information check www.ngs.org.uk
Map locator numbers are shown to the right of each garden name.

February
Snowdrop Openings
Saturday 15th
The Dower House   15
Sunday 16th
The Dower House   15
Dronfield Heritage Trust   16
NEW Meveril Lodge   39
Saturday 22nd
The Old Vicarage   44
Sunday 23rd
The Old Vicarage   44

March
Sunday 2nd
Coxbench Hall   13
Saturday 22nd
Chevin Brae   10

April
Sunday 13th
The Paddock   45
26 Stiles Road   56
Saturday 19th
◆ Cascades Gardens   9
Sunday 20th
12 Ansell Road   1
NEW 36 Edge Road   17
Yew Tree Bungalow   61
Monday 21st
12 Ansell Road   1
Wednesday 23rd
Greenacres   23
Sunday 27th
Barlborough Gardens   3

May
Sunday 4th
27 Wash Green   58
Monday 5th
Repton NGS Village Gardens   50
◆ Tissington Hall   57
Wednesday 7th
◆ Renishaw Hall & Gardens   49
Saturday 10th
The Old Vicarage   44
Sunday 11th
The Old Vicarage   44
26 Stiles Road   56
Saturday 17th
334 Belper Road   4
◆ Cascades Gardens   9
The Dower House   15
2 Haddon View   24
Sunday 18th
The Dower House   15
Fir Croft   19
2 Haddon View   24
Locko Park   33
NEW 3 School Woods Close   51
Saturday 24th
Longford Hall Farm   34
Sunday 25th
12 Ansell Road   1
Highfield House   27
Longford Hall Farm   34
NEW 60 Poplar Road   47
Monday 26th
12 Ansell Road   1
◆ Tissington Hall   57
Wednesday 28th
Fir Croft   19

June
Sunday 1st
88 Church Street West   11
The Smithy   53
Wednesday 4th
The Hollies   30
Saturday 7th
NEW Ford Lodge   20
The Smithy   53
Sunday 8th
334 Belper Road   4
NEW Ford Lodge   20
Gorsey Bank Gardens   22
The Smithy   53
13 Westfield Road   59

Wednesday 11th
The Hollies 30

Saturday 14th
Elmton Gardens 18
NEW Hillside 29
Holmlea 31
The Smithy 53

Sunday 15th
Elmton Gardens 18
Fir Croft 19
Holmlea 31
Repton NGS Village Gardens 50

Wednesday 18th
◆ Bluebell Arboretum and Nursery 5

Saturday 21st
12 Ansell Road 1
NEW Gorse Cottage 21

Sunday 22nd
12 Ansell Road 1
NEW Gorse Cottage 21
NEW 49 Middle Row 41

Saturday 28th
◆ Melbourne Hall Gardens 38

Sunday 29th
High Roost 26
Hill Cottage 28
58A Main Street 36
◆ Melbourne Hall Gardens 38
◆ Meynell Langley Trials Garden 40
NEW Slatelands House 52

July

Wednesday 2nd
◆ Renishaw Hall & Gardens 49

Sunday 6th
8 Curzon Lane 14
NEW 36 Edge Road 17
Yew Tree Bungalow 61

Saturday 12th
Barlborough Gardens 3
Longford Hall Farm 34
New Mills School 43

Sunday 13th
Barlborough Gardens 3
Longford Hall Farm 34
New Mills School 43
The Paddock 45

Wednesday 16th
◆ Bluebell Arboretum and Nursery 5

Saturday 19th
◆ Cascades Gardens 9
Marlborough Cottage 37

Sunday 20th
8 Curzon Lane 14
Marlborough Cottage 37
◆ Meynell Langley Trials Garden 40
26 Windmill Rise 60

Saturday 26th
12 Ansell Road 1
Byways 8
Stanton in Peak Gardens 55

Sunday 27th
12 Ansell Road 1
Byways 8
Greenacres 23
Stanton in Peak Gardens 55

August

Saturday 2nd
Ashbourne Road and District Allotments 2

Sunday 3rd
8 Curzon Lane 14
9 Hawkins Drive 25
9 Main Street 35
NEW Meveril Lodge 39
13 Westfield Road 59

Sunday 10th
Clarendon 12
Littleover Lane Allotments 32
Raiswells House 48

Monday 11th
◆ Tissington Hall 57

Wednesday 13th
◆ Bluebell Arboretum and Nursery 5

Saturday 16th
Chevin Brae 10

Sunday 17th
NEW 36 Edge Road 17
Yew Tree Bungalow 61

Monday 18th
◆ Tissington Hall 57

Saturday 23rd
The Hollies 30

Sunday 24th
◆ Meynell Langley Trials Garden 40
27 Wash Green 58

Monday 25th
Repton NGS Village Gardens 50
◆ Tissington Hall 57

September

Sunday 7th
Broomfield Hall 7
Coxbench Hall 13

Saturday 13th
Holmlea 31
The Old Vicarage 44

Sunday 14th
Holmlea 31
◆ Meynell Langley Trials Garden 40
The Old Vicarage 44

February 2026

Sunday 15th
NEW Meveril Lodge 39

By Arrangement

Arrange a personalised garden visit with your club, or group of friends, on a date to suit you. See individual garden entries for full details.

Askew Cottage, Repton NGS Village Gardens 50
334 Belper Road 4
Brierley Farm 6
Byways 8
10 Chestnut Way, Repton NGS Village Gardens 50
Chevin Brae 10
88 Church Street West 11
Coxbench Hall 13
8 Curzon Lane 14
The Dower House 15
Greenacres 23
High Roost 26
34 High Street, Repton NGS Village Gardens 50
Highfield House 27
Hill Cottage 28
The Hollies 30
Holmlea 31
Littleover Lane Allotments 32
9 Main Street 35
58A Main Street 36
Moorfields 42
The Old Vicarage 44
The Paddock 45
Park Hall 46
22 Pinfold Close, Repton NGS Village Gardens 50
Snitterton Hall 54
27 Wash Green 58
Yew Tree Bungalow 61

THE GARDENS

1 12 ANSELL ROAD
Ecclesall, Sheffield, S11 7PE. **Dave Darwent.** *Approx 3m SW of City Centre. Travel to Ringinglow Rd (88 bus), then Edale Rd (opp Ecclesall CofE Primary School). 3rd R - Ansell Rd. No 12 on L ¾ way down.* **Sun 20, Mon 21 Apr, Sun 25, Mon 26 May, Sat 21, Sun 22 June, Sat 26, Sun 27 July (11-5). Adm £4.50, chd free. Light refreshments inc vegan & GF options.**
Now in its 97th year since being created by my grandparents, this is a suburban mixed productive and flower garden retaining many original plants and features as well as the original layout but with the addition of seven water features and a small winter garden. Original rustic pergola with 90+ yr old roses. Then and now pictures of the garden in 1929 and 1950's vs present. Map of landmarks up to 55m away which can be seen from garden.

2 ASHBOURNE ROAD AND DISTRICT ALLOTMENTS
Mackworth Road, Derby, DE22 3BL. Ashbourne Road District Allotment Association Limited, www.araa.org.uk. *From Kedleston Rd turn onto Cowley St which becomes Mackworth Rd. From Ashbourne Rd turn onto Merchant St which becomes Mackworth Rd.* **Sat 2 Aug (11-3). Adm £5, chd free. Tea, coffee & cake.**
This beautiful allotment site is nestled quietly between two main roads leading into Derby city. It boasts of being over 100 yrs old with plots of all differing shapes and sizes. It houses a giant cockerel made from sheet metal and recycled tools, as well as a Growing Academy, packed polytunnels, starter plots, and is the 'home' of Radio Derby's Potty Plotters. The site has plots for you to venture onto and enthusiastic plot holders to chat to. There are 6 starter plots to inspect and main plots filled with flowers, vegetables and fruits in varying stages of growth and production. Bees to view and allotment things to buy. The main grass paths are flat and accessible with care.

60 Poplar Road

GROUP OPENING

🖸 BARLBOROUGH GARDENS
Clowne Road, Barlborough, Chesterfield, S43 4EH. Christine Sanderson, 07956 203184, christine.r.sanderson@uwclub.net, www.facebook.com/barlboroughgardens. *7m NE of Chesterfield. Off A619 between Chesterfield & Worksop. ½ m E M1, J30. Follow signs for Barlborough then yellow NGS signs. At De Rhodes Arms r'about take 3rd exit onto Clowne Rd S43 4EH - where 2 gardens located.* **Sun 27 Apr (11.30-4.30). Combined adm £5, chd free. Sat 12, Sun 13 July (11.30-4.30). Combined adm £7, chd free. Home-made teas. Cool drinks will also be available at 90 Boughton Lane at the July openings.**

90 BOUGHTON LANE
S43 4QF. Angela and Ian Cross.
Open on Sat 12, Sun 13 July

GREYSTONES BARN
S43 4EN. Kathryn and John Hardwick.
Open on Sat 12, Sun 13 July

THE HOLLIES
Vernon & Christine Sanderson.
Open on all dates
(See separate entry)

LINDWAY
S43 4TR. Thomas Pettinger.
Open on all dates

THE RED BRICK HOUSE
S43 4TS. Steven and Ashlyn Miller.
Open on Sat 12, Sun 13 July

19 WEST VIEW
S43 4HT. Mrs Pat Cunningham.
Open on Sat 12, Sun 13 July

Barlborough is an ancient village, steeped in history, perched on the top of yellow limestone scarp in the furthest North East corner of Derbyshire. The July weekend garden opening coincides with the 'Big Barlborough Festival' with lots of additional exhibitions and activities taking place. St James The Greater Church, an ancient place of worship will be open to visitors both afternoons of the July opening weekend. Six colourful gardens of different sizes and styles will be opening their garden gates. A map detailing the location of all six gardens, plus a community garden, will be issued with adm ticket.

More information can be found by visiting the Barlborough Gardens Facebook page. Packets of feed can be purchased at 90 Boughton Lane to feed the poultry. Partial wheelchair access at The Hollies, 90 Boughton Lane, Greystones Barn and 19 West View.

&. 🐕 ✤ 🚗 ☕

🖸 334 BELPER ROAD
Stanley Common, DE7 6FY. Gill & Colin Hancock, 01159 301061, gillandcolinhancock@gmail.com. *7m N of Derby. 3m W of Ilkeston. On A609, ¾ m from Rose & Crown Xrds (A608). Please park in field up farm drive.* **Sat 17 May, Sun 8 June (12-4). Adm £5, chd free. Visits also by arrangement 1 Apr to 21 June for groups of up to 30.**
Beautiful country garden with many attractive features inc a laburnum tunnel, rose and wisteria domes, old workmen's hut, wildlife pond. Take a walk through the 10 acres of woodland and glades to a ½ acre lake. Organic vegetable garden. See the lovely wisteria pergola in May and wild orchids and rose meadow in June. Plenty of seating to enjoy

Slatelands House

home-made cakes. Children welcome with plenty of activities to keep them entertained. Abundant wildlife.

5 ♦ BLUEBELL ARBORETUM AND NURSERY
Annwell Lane, Smisby, Ashby-de-la-Zouch, LE65 2TA. Robert Vernon, 01530 413700, sales@bluebellnursery.com, www.bluebellnursery.com. *1m NW of Ashby-de-la-Zouch. Arboretum is clearly signed in Annwell Ln (follow brown signs), ¼ m S, through village of Smisby off B5006, between Ticknall & Ashby-de-la-Zouch. Free parking.* **For NGS: Wed 18 June, Wed 16 July, Wed 13 Aug (9-4). Adm £6, chd free.** For other opening times and information, please phone, email or visit garden website.
Beautiful 9 acre woodland garden with a large collection of rare trees and shrubs. Interest throughout the year with spring flowers, cool leafy areas in summer and sensational autumn colour. Many information posters describing the more obscure plants. Adjacent specialist tree and shrub nursery. Please be aware this is not a wood full of bluebells, despite the name. The woodland garden is fully labelled and the staff can answer questions or talk at length about any of the trees or shrubs on display. Please wear sturdy, waterproof footwear during or after wet weather. Full wheelchair access however grass paths can become inaccessible after heavy rain.

6 BRIERLEY FARM
Mill Lane, Brockhurst, Ashover, Chesterfield, S45 0HS. Anne & David Wilkinson, 07831 598396, annelwilkinson@btinternet.com. *6m SW of Chesterfield, 4m NE of Matlock, 1½ m NW of Ashover. From the A632 turn W into Alicehead Rd, L into Swinger Ln, 2nd L into Brockhurst Ln & R into Mill Ln. Brierley Farm is the only house on the L.* **Visits by arrangement 9 June to 22 Aug for groups of 15 to 30. Adm £9. Home-made teas.**
This hillside site features two acre garden and lawns and three acre woodland with paths, with a bridge over a stream connecting the two. There are three linked ponds with raised stone-walled beds featuring seasonal planting from early spring through the summer and into the autumn.

7 BROOMFIELD HALL
Morley, Ilkeston, DE7 6DN. Derby College Group, www.facebook.com/BroomfieldPlantCentre. *4m N of Derby. 6m S of Heanor on A608, N of Derby.* **Sun 7 Sept (10-4). Adm £5, chd free. Tea, coffee & cake in a pop-up volunteer run, café.**
25 acres of constantly developing educational Victorian gardens/woodlands maintained by volunteers and students. Herbaceous borders, walled garden, themed gardens, rose garden, potager, prairie plantings, Japanese garden, tropical garden, winter garden, plant centre. Light refreshments, cacti, carnivorous, bonsai, fuchsia specialists and craft stalls. A gem of Derbyshire. Most of garden is accessible to wheelchair users and assistance is available if needed.

8 BYWAYS
7A Brookfield Avenue, Brookside, Chesterfield, S40 3NX. Terry & Eileen Kelly, 07414 827813, telkel1@aol.com. *1½ m W of Chesterfield. Follow A619 from Chesterfield towards Baslow. Please park carefully in Brookfield School Car Park, or neighbouring roads. Brookfield Ave is 2nd on R.* **Sat 26, Sun 27 July (11.30-4.30). Adm £4, chd free. Tea, coffee & cake inc gluten free option.** Visits also by arrangement 5 July to 16 Aug for groups of 10 to 25. Donation to Ashgate Hospice.
Three times winners of the Best Back Garden over 80 sqm, and also twice winners of Best Front Garden, Best Container Garden and Best Hanging Basket in Chesterfield in Bloom. Well established perennial borders inc helenium, monardas, phlox, grasses, acers. Rockery and many planters containing acers, pelargoniums, ferns and hostas. Large shady pergola with acers, hostas and ferns.

9 ♦ CASCADES GARDENS
Clatterway, Bonsall, Matlock, DE4 2AH. Alan & Alesia Clements, 07967 337404, alan.clements@cascadesgardens.com, www.cascadesgardens.com. *3m SW of Matlock. From Cromford A6 T-lights turn to Wirksworth. Turn R along Via Gellia, signed Buxton & Bonsall. After 1m turn R up hill towards Bonsall. Garden entrance at top of hill. Park in village car park.* **For NGS: Sat 19 Apr, Sat 17 May, Sat 19 July (12-4). Adm £8, chd £4. Home-made teas.** For other opening times and information, please phone, email or visit garden website.
The Meditation Garden and Bonsai centre: Fascinating 4 acre peaceful garden in spectacular natural surroundings with woodland, cliffs, stream, pond and an old limestone quarry. Inspired by Japanese gardens and Buddhist philosophy, secluded garden rooms for relaxation and reflection. Beautiful landscape with a wide collection of unusual perennials, conifers, shrubs and trees. Mostly wheelchair accessible. Gravel paths, some steep slopes.

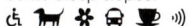

10 CHEVIN BRAE
Chevin Road, Milford, Belper, DE56 0QH. Dr David Moreton, 07778 004374, davidmoretonchevinbrae@gmail.com. *1½ m S of Belper. Coming from S on A6 turn L at Strutt Arms & cont up Chevin Rd. Park on Chevin Rd. After 300yds follow arrow to L up Morrells Ln. After 300yds Chevin Brae on L with silver garage.* **Sat 22 Mar, Sat 16 Aug (1-5). Adm £3, chd free. Home-made teas inc home-made cakes, pastries and biscuits, many of which feature fruit and jam from the garden.** Visits also by arrangement 3 Feb to 31 Oct for groups of up to 16.
A large garden, with swathes of daffodils in the orchard during spring. Extensive wildflower planting along edge of wood features aconites, snowdrops, wood anemones, fritillaries and dog tooth violets. Other parts of garden will have hellebores and early camellias. In the summer, the large flower borders and rose trellises give much colour, and the vegetable and fruit gardens are at their peak. The garden is accessed via steep steps and not suitable for people with mobility issues.

In 2024, National Garden Scheme funding for Perennial supported 1,367 people working in horticulture.

122 DERBYSHIRE

1 88 CHURCH STREET WEST
Pinxton, NG16 6PU. Rosemary Ahmed, 07842 141210. *Pinxton is approx 1m from J28 of the M1. At motorway island take B6019 towards Alfreton & take the 1st L Pinxton Ln which turns into Alfreton Rd, the garden is signposted from there.* **Sun 1 June (12-4.30). Adm £4, chd free. Light refreshments inc homemade cakes. Visits also by arrangement 17 May to 24 Aug for groups of up to 15.**
Plantwomans garden, developed over 25yrs to inc collections of hardy geraniums, agaves, ferns, persicaria and grasses. The garden has a quirky mix of salvage items. A wild lawn is a work in progress, a small rockery, upcycled garden room with mature grapevine, mixed borders and a large patio with displays of succulents.

2 CLARENDON
28 Clowne Road, Barlborough, Chesterfield, S43 4EN. Neil & Lorraine Jones. *7m NE of Chesterfield. 7 m W of Worksop, off J30 of M1. Clarendon and Raiswell House are within easy walking distance of each other; with 2 pubs in between.* **Sun 10 Aug (11.30-4.30). Combined adm with Raiswells House £5, chd free. Light refreshments at Raiswells House.**
A bay tree archway leads to the first of many seating areas, underneath a specimen Cedar. This leads to a triangular shaped front lawn and an artificial stream. A pathway of York stones then takes you down the side of the house to a very secluded rear garden full of specimen conifers, evergreen shrubs and acers. Plenty of comfortable seating to enjoy the vistas and the summer sunshine. Secret walkways meander around the perimeter of the garden leading to a gazebo, a pond with bridge and waterfall, a playhouse, a pear archway, vegetable planters and a greenhouse. Brass band playing during the afternoon. Partial wheelchair access.

3 COXBENCH HALL
Alfreton Road, Coxbench, Derby, DE21 5BB. Coxbench Hall Ltd, 01332 880200, office@coxbench-hall.co.uk, www.coxbench-hall.co.uk. *4m N of Derby close to A38. After going through Little Eaton, turn L onto Alfreton Rd for 1m, Coxbench Hall is on L next to Fox & Hounds pub between Little Eaton & Holbrook. From A38 take Kilburn turn & go towards Little Eaton.* **Sun 2 Mar (10-11.30am); Sun 7 Sept (2.30-4.30). Adm £3, chd free. Tea, coffee & cake inc home-made diabetic and gluten free cakes. Visits also by arrangement Feb to Oct for groups of up to 15.**
Former ancestral Georgian Home of the Meynell family, the gardens focus on sustainability, organic and wildlife friendly themes. There is a tropical style garden, ponds, hostas, fruits, C18 potting shed, veteran yew tree and hillside terraced garden of wildflowers and trees with a curved stone path incorporating reclaimed sleepers. A stoned path by the upper woodland overlooks the gardens below. Our wheelchair accessible gardens are developed to inspire the senses of our residents via different colours, textures and fragrances of plants. Block paved path around the edges of the main lawn. We regret no wheelchair access to woodland area.

4 8 CURZON LANE
Alvaston, Derby, DE24 8QS. John & Marian Gray, 01332 601596, maz@curzongarden.com, www.curzongarden.com. *2m SE of Derby city centre. From city centre take A6 (London Rd) towards Alvaston. Curzon Ln on L, approx ½ m before Alvaston shops.* **Sun 6, Sun 20 July, Sun 3 Aug (12.30-4.30). Adm £4, chd free. Tea, coffee & cake. Visits also by arrangement July & Aug for groups of 10 to 30.**
Mature garden with lawns, borders packed full with perennials, shrubs and small trees, tropical planting and hot border. Ornamental and wildlife ponds, greenhouse with different varieties of tomato, cucumber, peppers and chillies. Well-stocked vegetable plot. Gravel area and large patio with container planting.

5 THE DOWER HOUSE
Church Square, Melbourne, DE73 8JH. William & Griselda Kerr, 07799 883577, griseldakerr@btinternet.com, www.instagram.com/griselda.kerr. *6m S of Derby. 5m W of J23A M1. 4m N of J13 M42. When in Church Sq, turn R just before the church by a blue sign giving service times. Gates are 50 yds ahead.* **Sat 15 Feb (10-4.30); Sun 16 Feb (10-3.30); Sat 17, Sun 18 May (10-4.30). Adm £8, chd free. Tea, coffee & cake. Visits also by arrangement 1 Jan to 19 Dec for groups of 10+. No weekends or evening openings.**
Beautiful view of Melbourne Pool from balustraded terrace running length of 1829 house. Garden drops steeply by paths or steps to lawn with herbaceous borders and bank of some 60 shrubs. Numerous paths lead to different areas of the garden, providing varied planting opportunities inc a bog garden, glade, shrubbery, grasses, herb and kitchen garden, rose tunnel, arbour, orchard and small woodland. Hidden paths and different areas entice children to explore the garden with various animals such as a bronze crocodile and stone dragons to find. Children must be supervised by an adult at all times due to the proximity of water. This garden proudly provided plants for the National Garden Scheme's Show Garden at Chelsea Flower Show 2024. Wheelchair access to top half of the garden only. Shoes with a good grip are essential as slopes are steep. There is no parking within 50 yds.

6 DRONFIELD HERITAGE TRUST
High Street, Dronfield, S18 1PX. Mr Sam Reavy, 07814 140034, sam@dronfieldhallbarn.org, www.dronfieldhallbarn.org. *The Barn is located in the centre of Dronfield. Please follow the 'Garden Open for Charity' signs. 2 accessible spaces at front (High St). Free, unlimited parking at Sainsburys (S18 1NW) to the rear.* **Sun 16 Feb (11-3.30). Adm £4, chd free. Tea, coffee & cake.**
The garden is part of the Dronfield heritage centre, situated in the grounds of the original manor house of Dronfield. It was transformed from a muddy field to a much loved community space with mixed native flower beds, veteran trees, woodland border, small herb garden and a lawned play/ picnic area. Specialist Snowdrop sale. Garden tour and talk. The garden and barn are on one level however the garden is situated on a slope. There is hard standing path that runs top to bottom.

DERBYSHIRE

17 NEW 36 EDGE ROAD
Matlock, DE4 3NH. Mr David Pass. *Matlock town centre. From the rear M&S town centre car park go up Imperial Rd for about 150 metres. Garden is on corner of Imperial Rd/ Edge Rd - use the Edge Rd access.* **Sun 20 Apr, Sun 6 July, Sun 17 Aug (11-4). Adm £5, chd free. Tea, coffee & cake. Open nearby Yew Tree Bungalow.**
Matlock town centre garden of approx 1 acre. Beautifully designed and landscaped. Herbaceous borders, wildlife pond, mature trees, woodland walk, formal borders and many points of interest. Spectacular views of Riber Castle and the Derwent Valley. This garden is a real hidden gem.
& 🐾 ✳ ☕ 🔊

GROUP OPENING

18 ELMTON GARDENS
Elmton, Worksop, S80 4LS. *2m from Creswell, 3m from Clowne, 5m from J30, M1. From M1 J30 take A616 to Newark. Follow approx 4m. Turn R at Elmton signpost. At junc turn R, the village centre is in ½m.* **Sat 14, Sun 15 June (1-5). Combined adm £6, chd free. Cream teas at the Old Schoolroom next to the church. Food also available all day at the Elm Tree Inn.**

THE BARN CHALICO FARM
S80 4LS. Mrs Anne Merrick.
THE COTTAGE
S80 4LX. Judith Maughan & Roy Reeves.
ELM TREE COTTAGE
S80 4LS. Mark & Linda Hopkinson.
ELM TREE FARM
S80 4LS. Angie & Tim Caulton.
PEAR TREE COTTAGE
S80 4LS. Geoff & Janet Cutts.
PINFOLD
S80 4LS. Nikki Kirsop & Barry Davies.

Elmton is a lovely little village situated on a stretch of rare unimproved Magnesian limestone grassland with quaking grass, bee orchids and harebells all set in the middle of attractive, rolling farm land. It has a pub, which serves food all day, a church and a village green with award winning wildlife conservation area and a village Pinfold. The very colourful but different open gardens have wonderful views. They show a range of gardening styles, themed beds and several have a commitment to fruit and vegetable growing. Elmton received a gold award and was voted best small village for the 7th time and best wildlife and conservation area in the East Midlands in Bloom competition in 2019. Village trail with interpretation boards.
& 🐾 ✳ 🚗 ☕ 🔊

19 FIR CROFT
Froggatt Road, Calver, S32 3ZD. Dr S B Furness, www.alpineplantcentre.co.uk. *4m N of Bakewell. At junc of B6001 with A625 (formerly B6054), adj to Froggat Edge Garage.* **Sun 18, Wed 28 May, Sun 15 June (1-4). Adm by donation.**
World renowned plantsman's garden, large scree beds and rockery, extensive collection of alpines and dwarf conifers; many new varieties not seen anywhere else. Huge tufa wall planted with many rare alpines and sempervivums, water garden and cascade system. Garden currently undergoing renovation and replanting. Two National Collections. Superb views over the Dales. Wheelchair access to part of garden only.
& ✳ NPC

20 NEW FORD LODGE
Winkpenny Lane, Tibshelf, Alfreton, DE55 5RG. Richard and Jean Briley. *7 m S of Chesterfield. Off B6014, Tibshelf High St. Turn at the Crown Hotel and follow yellow signs. On street parking available in West View adj to Winkpenny Ln. Limited disabled parking by the house.* **Sat 7, Sun 8 June (1-5). Adm £4, chd free. Tea, coffee & cake.**
This small garden offers different 'garden rooms,' ranging from a formal area to our water themed, cottage and Mediterranean garden. There is a wide range of plants, from roses through to Abyssinian bananas and various grasses. Plenty of seating areas from which to enjoy the relaxing atmosphere whilst listening to the sound of the stream and perhaps enjoy afternoon tea and home-made cakes.
🐾 ☕ 🔊

21 NEW GORSE COTTAGE
Bar Road, Curbar, Hope Valley, S32 3YB. Mrs Caralyn Denver. *Off A623 in Curbar. Below Baslow & Curbar Edges. 6m N of Bakewell, 3m to Chatsworth. Turn off A623 at Bridge Inn onto Bar Ln. The garden is ½m up the hill. Parking by church or on lane. Limited disabled parking.* **Sat 21, Sun 22 June (1.30-4.30). Adm £4, chd free. Tea, coffee & cake inc vegan options.**
Delightful cottage garden bounded by mature trees, rhododendrons and far-reaching views to Chatsworth. Features inc a shady spring garden, mixed perennial borders, secret summerhouse, south facing patio and pond, home to newts and dragonflies. Beyond the hedge find a hidden seat to enjoy the kitchen garden, greenhouse and fruit trees, lovingly tended by the grandchildren. Wheelchair access to the patio, which overlooks part of the garden.
& 🐾 ✳ ☕ 🔊

The National Garden Scheme donated £281,000 in 2024 to support those looking to work in horticulture as well as those struggling within the industry.

GROUP OPENING

22 GORSEY BANK GARDENS
Brooklands Avenue, Wirksworth, Matlock, DE4 4AB. Miss Philippa Cooper. *At the southern edge of Wirksworth. From Duffield on B5023. R onto Water Ln immed after mini r'about, signed Hannage Brook Medical Centre. From Cromford on B5036/B5023 3rd L after pelican crossing. Parking on L off Hannage Way.* **Sun 8 June (11-4). Combined adm £7, chd free. Home-made teas at Watts House. Light refreshments at Fern Bank.**

2 BROOKLANDS AVENUE
DE4 4AB. Miss Philippa Cooper.

FERN BANK
DE4 4AD. Scott Thompson and Beccy Owen.

MILL COTTAGE
DE4 4AD. Kirstie and Andy Lyne.

WATTS HOUSE
DE4 4AR. Sue and Robert Watts.

A charming hillside hamlet at the southern edge of the historic market town of Wirksworth, set in the beautiful Derbyshire Dales. This group features four gardens which demonstrate contrasting design responses to challenging terrain with a wide variety of planting; 2 Brooklands Ave has been developed since 2019, using a naturalistic planting style, with many interesting and unusual plants. Fern Bank is a hidden gem set in a small former quarry, surrounded by farmland, with beautiful views. Mill Cottage is a secluded cottage style garden with mill stream and architectural features, with seating areas to enjoy the different aspects. Watts House is a delightful tranquil garden. The four gardens are within comfortable walking distance, although it is a steep uphill walk on tarmac to Mill Cottage and Fern Bank, but the gardens and spectacular views are well worth the effort. The walk to Watts House is relatively flat. Ticket sales at 2, Brooklands Avenue. Flights of steps in all the gardens. Watts House features Robert's sculptures, some previously exhibited at RHS Chatsworth. Fern Bank featured on Gardeners' World Sept 2024.
✤ 🐾 🍵))

23 GREENACRES
Makeney Road, Holbrook, Belper, DE56 0TF. Veronica Holtom, 07749 277927, veronica.cooke1@icloud.com. *5m N of Derby. Approach via Makeney Rd using the private drive for Holbrook Hall Care Home. Parking is on St Michael's FC car park. Disabled visitors may park at the house.* **Wed 23 Apr, Sun 27 July (12.30-4.30). Adm £6, chd free. Home-made teas. Visits also by arrangement 7 Apr to 29 Sept for groups of 8 to 35. Please pre-order gluten free & vegan options.**
Beautiful large garden in rural Derbyshire, wonderful countryside views. Wander among the pines, weeping birches, acers, oaks and beeches. Many camellias, shrubs, hellebores and spring bulbs. Spectacular mixed beds and borders, ornamental grasses, lily pond, rock garden, cascades and alpines. Colourful patio plants, sweeping lawns, lots of seating areas and walkways. There are few steps, but the majority of the site is level.
♿ 🐾 🚗 🍵))

24 2 HADDON VIEW
Birchover Road, Stanton-in-the-Peak, Matlock, DE4 2LR. Steve Tompkins. *At the top of the hill in Stanton in Peak, on road to Birchover. Stanton in Peak is 5m S of Bakewell. Turn off the A6 at Rowsley, or at the B5056 & follow signs up the hill.* **Sat 17, Sun 18 May (12.30-4.30). Adm £4, chd free. Tea, coffee & cake. Opening with Stanton in Peak Gardens on Sat 26, Sun 27 July.**
The 30 rhododendrons and azaleas make a lovely spring display. They surround the summerhouse and are part of the herbaceous borders. Other spring flowers inc marsh marigolds around the four ponds, and dog's-tooth violets in pink and yellow. Dramatic agaves, aeoniums, tulips and bedding plants fill the diverse range of pots on the patios. Tea, coffee and home-made cakes will be waiting!
🐾 🍵))

25 9 HAWKINS DRIVE
Ambergate, Belper, DE56 2JN. Carol and Martyn Taylor-Cockayne. *Just off the A610 at Ambergate between Belper & Matlock. From Derby at the A6 and A610 inter-section by the Hurt Arms, turn R onto the A610. After ½ m turn* R onto New Rd. After 100yds turn R onto Crich Ln. After 100yds turn R onto Hawkins Dr. **Sun 3 Aug (12-4). Adm £3.50, chd free. Home-made teas.**
A small yet busy garden with flowering shrubs and evergreens, perennials and annuals. Fern and heuchera beds provide a splash of colour. Terraced patio with a range of colourful planters. Two small wildlife ponds with log pile lodges, home to resident toads and frogs. Elevated view over the rooftops to Crich Chase.
✤ 🍵))

26 HIGH ROOST
27 Storthmeadow Road, Simmondley, Glossop, SK13 6UZ. Peter & Christina Harris, 01457 863888, harrispeter448@gmail.com. *¾ m SW of Glossop. From Glossop A57 to Manchester, L at 2nd r'about, up Simmondley Ln 1st top R turn. From Marple A626 to Glossop, in Ch'worth R up Town Ln past Hare & Hound pub 2nd L.* **Sun 29 June (12-4). Adm £4, chd free. Tea, coffee & cake. Visits also by arrangement 2 June to 6 July for groups of up to 30. Donation to Donkey Sanctuary.**
Garden on terraced slopes, views over fields and hills. Winding paths, archways and steps explore different garden rooms packed with plants, designed to attract wildlife. Alpine bed, gravel garden; vegetable garden, water features, statuary, troughs and planters. A garden which needs exploring to discover its secrets tucked away in hidden corners. Features inc a craft stall, children's garden quiz and lucky dip.
🐾 ✤ 🚗 🍵))

27 HIGHFIELD HOUSE
Wingfield Road, Oakerthorpe, Alfreton, DE55 7AP. Paul & Ruth Peat and Janet & Brian Costall, 07714 529098, highfieldhouseopengardens@hotmail.co.uk, www.highfieldhouse.weebly.com. *Rear of Alfreton Golf Club. A615 Alfreton-Matlock Rd.* **Sun 25 May (10.30-5). Adm £3, chd free. Home-made teas. Visits also by arrangement 15 Feb to 25 Feb and 20 May to 30 June for groups of 15+.**
Lovely country garden of approx 1 acre, incorporating a shady garden, woodland, pond, laburnum tunnel, orchard, herbaceous borders and vegetable garden. Home-made baked cakes and lunches available. Lovely

DERBYSHIRE 125

walk to Derbyshire Wildlife Trust nature reserve to see Orchids in June. Some steps, slopes and gravel areas.

28 HILL COTTAGE
Ashover Road, Littlemoor, Ashover, nr Chesterfield, S45 0BL. Jane Tomlinson & Tim Walls, 07946 388185, lavenderhen@aol.com. *1.8m from Ashover village, 6.3m from Chesterfield & 6.1m from Matlock. Hill Cottage is on Ashover Rd (also known as Stubben Edge Ln). Opp the end of Eastwood Ln.* **Sun 29 June (11-4). Adm £4, chd free. Tea, coffee & cake. Visits also by arrangement in July for groups of 5 to 15.**
Hill Cottage is a lovely example of an English country cottage garden. Whilst small, the garden has full, colourful and fragrant mixed borders with hostas and dahlias in pots along with a heart shaped lawn. A small gravel garden is a recent addition. A greenhouse full of chillies, tomatoes and scented pelargoniums and a small Potager. Views over a pastoral landscape to Ogston reservoir. A wide variety of perennials and annuals grown in pots and containers.

29 NEW HILLSIDE
Higg Lane, Alderwasley, Belper, DE56 2RB. Mr & Mrs Mandy and Mark Wilton. *4½m N of Belper. W onto B5035 from A6 at Whatstandwell, immed L to Alderwasley. Parking at Village Hall (WC available).* **Sat 14 June (10.30-4.30). Adm £5, chd free. Tea, coffee & cake.**
1.3 acre gently sloping garden with rural views. Recently replanted relaxed cottage style borders near the house give way to informal planting down the slope, terminating in a meadow with beehives. Extensive collection of mature trees and shrubs supplemented by new planting, inc cherries, acers, rhododendrons, camellias and magnolias. Alpine rockery adjacent to two ponds on differing levels.

30 THE HOLLIES
87 Clowne Road, Barlborough, Chesterfield, S43 4EH. Vernon & Christine Sanderson, 07956 203184, christine.r.sanderson@uwclub.net, www.facebook.com/barlboroughgardens. *7m NE of Chesterfield. Off A619 midway between Chesterfield & Worksop. ½m E M1, J30. Follow signs for Barlborough then yellow NGS signs. At De Rhodes Arms r'about take 3rd exit onto Clowne Rd. Garden at far end on L.* **Wed 4, Wed 11 June (1.30-4.30). Cream teas. Sat 23 Aug (12-4.30). Home-made teas. Adm £4, chd free. Opening with Barlborough Gardens on Sun 27 Apr, Sat 12, Sun 13 July. Visits also by arrangement 1 May to 25 Aug for groups of 10 to 25.**
The Hollies maximises the unusual garden layout and ine shade area, patio garden with Moroccan corner, cottage border plus fruit trees. A wide selection of home-made cakes on offer inc gluten free, sugar free, dairy free and vegan options. Home-made preserves for sale. Extensive view across arable farmland. An area of the garden, influenced by the Majorelle Garden in Marrakech, was achieved using upcycled items together with appropriate planting. This garden project was featured on an episode of "Love Your Garden". Partial wheelchair access - gravel paths on either side of the house lead to the patio area.

31 HOLMLEA
Derby Road, Ambergate, Belper, DE56 2EJ. Bill & Tracy Reid, 07932 977314, billandtracy.reid@gmail.com. *On the A6 in Ambergate - between Belper & Matlock. 9m N of Derby, 6m S of Matlock. Easy access from M1 J28. On A6 next to Bridge House Cafe. Additional Parking at Anila Restaurant opp Hurt Arms. Short walk from Ambergate Stn.* **Sat 14, Sun 15 June, Sat 13, Sun 14 Sept (11-4). Adm £5, chd free. Home-made teas. Refreshments self-service with honesty box. Gluten Free and Vegan options. Visits also by arrangement 16 June to 30 June and 15 Sept to 3 Oct for groups of 10+.**
Explore our 1½ acre garden, described by many visitors as unique. Wide variety of plants grown in different situations. Large kitchen garden inc cut flower patch, beautiful riverside walk and canal lock water feature. Family friendly with activities for kids. Pop-up ride on garden railway in June. Join us in September for a blaze of late season colour. Home-made teas in 'The Pavilion'. Adjacent to Shining Cliff Woods, SSI. Find us on Facebook and Instagram at 'Holmlea Gardens'. Wheelchair route around main features of the garden. Unfortunately the Riverside Walk is not suitable for wheelchairs.

32 LITTLEOVER LANE ALLOTMENTS
19 Littleover Lane, Normanton, Derby, DE23 6JF. Ms Amanda Sawford, 07883 010924, amanda.sawford@sky.com, www.littleoverlaneallotments.org.uk. *On Littleover Ln opp the junc with Foremark Ave. Off the Derby Outer Ring Rd (A5111). At the Normanton Park r'about turn into Stenson Rd then R into Littleover Ln. The main gates are on the L as you travel down the road.* **Sun 10 Aug (11-3). Adm £3.50, chd free. Tea, coffee & cake. Visits also by arrangement 3 Mar to 31 Oct for groups of 5 to 15.**
A quiet oasis just off Derby's Outer Ring Road, hidden away in a residential area. A private site of nearly 12 acres, established in 1920, cultivated in a variety of ways, inc organic, no dig and potager style. Come and chat with plot holders about their edibles and ornamentals. Many exotic and Heritage varieties cultivated. Later in the year produce can be available to sample. The many allotments showcase a wide variety of gardening styles and provide you with inspiration for your own garden. Disabled parking is available on site. All avenues are stoned, but the extensive site is on a slope and so some areas not easily accessible.

Our donation in 2024 has enabled Parkinson's UK to fund 3 new nursing posts this year directly supporting people with Parkinson's.

33 LOCKO PARK
Spondon, Derby, DE21 7BW. Lucy Palmer, www.lockopark.co.uk. *6m NE of Derby. From A52 Borrowash bypass, 2m N via B6001, turn to Spondon. SatNav use DE21 7BW Via Locko Rd. What3words app: shady. cheeks.judge.* **Sun 18 May (2-5). Adm £7, chd free. Home-made teas.**
An original 1927 open garden for the National Garden Scheme. A large garden, consisting of a pleasure garden and a rose garden. Extensive grounds featuring rhododendrons. House (not open) by Smith of Warwick with Victorian additions. Chapel (open) built by Charles II, with original ceiling. Tulip tree in the arboretum purported to be the largest in the Midlands. Large collection of rhododendron and azalea.

34 LONGFORD HALL FARM
Longford, Ashbourne, DE6 3DS. Liz Wolfenden, www. longfordhallfarmholidaycottages. co.uk. *From A52 take turn to Hollington. At T-junc (Long Ln) turn R & follow signs. Use drive with Longford Hall Farm sign at the entrance.* **Sat 24, Sun 25 May, Sat 12, Sun 13 July (2-5). Adm £5, chd free. Home-made teas.**
The garden consists of a large front garden, where shrubs such as hydrangeas, roses, ferns, grasses and hosta beds surround a modern pond and fountain. There is also a large pond with pontoon and a stumpery. The rear walled garden has traditional herbaceous borders and a modern rill feature. Most of the garden is on one level.

35 9 MAIN STREET
Horsley Woodhouse, Ilkeston, DE7 6AU. Ms Alison Napier, 01332 881629, ibhillib@btinternet.com. *3m SW of Heanor. 6m N of Derby. Turn off A608 Derby to Heanor Rd at Smalley, towards Belper, (A609). Garden on A609, 1m from Smalley turning.* **Sun 3 Aug (1.30-4.30). Adm £4, chd free. Cream teas. Visits also by arrangement 16 June to 14 Sept for groups of 12+.**
⅓ acre hilltop garden with lovely farmland views. Terracing, borders, lawns and pergola create space for an informal layout with planting for colour effect. Features inc large wildlife pond with water lilies, bog garden and small formal pool.

Emphasis on carefully selected herbaceous perennials mixed with shrubs and old fashioned roses. Gravel garden for sun loving plants and scree garden, both developed from former drive. Wide collection of homegrown plants for sale -please bring your own carrier bag. All parts of the garden accessible to wheelchairs. Wheelchair adapted WC.

36 58A MAIN STREET
Rosliston, Swadlincote, DE12 8JW. Paul Marbrow, 07596 629886, paulmarbrow@hotmail.co.uk. *Rosliston. If exiting the M42, J11 onto the A444 to Overseal follow signs Linton then Rosliston. From A38, exit to Walton-on-Trent, then follow Rosliston signs.* **Sun 29 June (12.30-4.30). Adm £5, chd free. Tea, coffee & cake. Visits also by arrangement 20 June to 15 Aug for groups of 5+. Refreshments inc in adm.**
¾ acre garden formed from a once open field over the last few years. The garden has developed into themed areas and is changing and maturing. Japanese, arid beach, bamboo grove with ferns, water gardens etc. The 100m² indoor garden for cacti, exotic and tender plants, is now becoming established as a mini Eden. Areas are easily accessible, although some are only for the sure of foot, advice signs will be situated on unsuitable routes.

37 MARLBOROUGH COTTAGE
Corbar Road, Buxton, SK17 6RQ. Sandra and Graham Jowett. *N of Buxton Town Centre. On N side of Corbar Rd. Directly opp junc with Marlborough Rd. Free on-street parking is readily available on Corbar Rd.* **Sat 19, Sun 20 July (10.30-4.30). Adm £4, chd free. Home-made teas inc gluten free options.**
Victorian gardener's cottage close to the centre of Georgian Buxton. ⅕ of an acre organic garden, reclaimed in the last seven years. It is 1100ft above sea level, surrounded by mature trees and a tranquil haven for wildlife. It has front and rear borders, herbs and a variety of containers and ornaments. It has a small wildlife pond, wildflowers, vegetable beds, soft fruit and a greenhouse. For wheelchair users, the front garden, side and rear patios are accessible. Access to other features is limited.

38 ◆ MELBOURNE HALL GARDENS
Church Square, Melbourne, Derby, DE73 8EN. Melbourne Gardens Charity, 01332 862502, info@melbournehall.com, www.melbournehall.com. *6m S of Derby. At Melbourne Market Place turn into Church St, go down to Church Sq. Garden entrance across visitor centre next to Melbourne Hall tea room.* **For NGS: Sat 28, Sun 29 June (1-5). Adm £10, chd £5. Light refreshments in Melbourne Hall Tearooms and locally. The Sitooterie serves takeaway coffee and ice cream from the courtyard. For other opening times and information, please phone, email or visit garden website.**
A 17 acre historic garden with an abundance of rare trees and shrubs. Woodland and waterside planting with extensive herbaceous borders. Meconopsis, candelabra primulas, various Styrax and *Cornus kousa*. Other garden features inc Bakewells wrought iron arbour, a yew tunnel and fine C18 statuary and water features. Discover 300 yr old trees, waterside planting, feature hedges and herbaceous borders. Don't forget to visit the pigs, alpacas, goats and various other animals in their garden enclosures. Gravel paths, uneven surface in places, some steep slopes.

39 NEW MEVERIL LODGE
Lesser Lane, Combs, High Peak, SK23 9UZ. Mrs Sally Williams. *5m N of Buxton. On Manchester Rd (B5470), Chapel-en-le-Frith, head down Combs Rd into Combs village until the Beehive Inn on R, turn L then R down Lesser Ln. Meveril Lodge is ½ m down.* **Sun 16 Feb (11-3); Sun 3 Aug (11-5). Adm £6, chd free. Tea, coffee & cake. 2026: Sun 15 Feb. Donation to Plant Heritage.**
A recently developed 1½ acre rural garden surrounded by a stream, divided into areas themed by colour and season, with an emphasis on scented plants. White, summer, dark, hot, frosted garden areas, and wildflower streamside walk, winter interest borders and kitchen garden. The garden has snowdrops, hellebores, and unusual trees and shrubs. Display of National Plant Collection of Peperomia. The paths around the garden are graveled, but mainly flat. The woodland streamside walk and hot gardens are not accessible by wheelchair.

DERBYSHIRE

40 ♦ MEYNELL LANGLEY TRIALS GARDEN

Lodge Lane (off Flagshaw Lane), Kirk Langley, Ashbourne, DE6 4NT. Robert & Karen Walker, 01332 824358, enquiries@meynellgardens.com, www.meynellgardens.com. *4m W of Derby, nr Kedleston Hall. Head W out of Derby on A52. At Kirk Langley turn R onto Flagshaw Ln (signed to Kedleston Hall) then R onto Lodge Ln. Follow Meynell Langley Gardens signs.* **For NGS: Sun 29 June, Sun 20 July, Sun 24 Aug, Sun 14 Sept (10-4). Adm £5, chd free.** For other opening times and information, please phone, email or visit garden website.

Completely re-designed during 2020 with new glasshouse and patio area incorporating water rills and small ponds. Wildlife and fish ponds also added. Displays and trials of new and existing varieties of bedding plants, herbaceous perennials and vegetable plants grown at the adjacent nursery. Over 180 hanging baskets and floral displays. Adjacent tearooms serving lunches and refreshments daily. Plant sales from adjacent nursery. Level ground, firm grass and some hard paths.

& 🐕 ✿ 🚗 ☕))

41 NEW ♦ 49 MIDDLE ROW

Cressbrook, Buxton, SK17 8SX. Ms Jane Money and Mr Chris Gilbert. *4 m NW of Bakewell. Midway between Litton and Monsal Head. Garden by phone box at top of village. Parking: Layby near Church 250 metre walk or limited roadside. Avoid white lines. What3words app: desire.aura. excavate.* **Sun 22 June (1.30-4.30). Adm £4, chd free. Tea, coffee & cake in the Cressbrook Club (next door). Gluten free and vegan options available.**

Steep, terraced, south facing, hillside garden in small, historic mill village, with glorious views over Monsal Dale. Formal side garden with Summerhouse, rose hedge and wisteria arch leads to surprise view over rockery, large, colourful herbaceous border and, further down, small herbaceous borders, two small ponds and wildlife area. Lower garden is accessed by steep steps with no handrail.

☕))

42 MOORFIELDS

261 Chesterfield Road, Temple Normanton, Chesterfield, S42 5DE. Peter, Janet & Stephen Wright, 01246 852306, peterwright100@hotmail.com. *4m SE of Chesterfield. From Chesterfield take A617 for 2m, turn on to B6039 through Temple Normanton, taking R fork signed Tibshelf, B6039. Garden ¼ m on R. Limited parking.* **Visits by arrangement 24 May to 20 July for groups of 12+. Light refreshments.**

Two adjoining gardens, each planted for seasonal colour, which during the late spring and early summer feature perennials inc alliums, lupins, camassias and bearded irises. The larger garden has mature, mixed island beds and borders, a gravel garden to the front, a small wildflower area, large wildlife pond, orchard, soft fruit beds and vegetable garden. Seasonal colour. Large wildlife pond. Open aspect with extensive views to mid Derbyshire.

✿ ☕

43 NEW MILLS SCHOOL
Church Lane, New Mills, High Peak, SK22 4NR. Mr Craig Pickering, www.newmillsschool.co.uk. *12m NNW of Buxton. From A6 take A6105 signed New Mills, Hayfield. At CofE Church turn L onto Church Ln. Sch on L. Parking on site.* **Sat 12, Sun 13 July (2-5). Adm £4, chd free. Tea, coffee & cake in School Library.**
Mixed herbaceous perennials/shrub borders, with mature trees and lawns and gravel border situated in the semi rural setting of the High Peak inc a Grade II listed building with four themed quads. The school was awarded highly commended in the School Garden 2019 RHS Tatton Show and won the Best High School Garden and the People's Choice Award. Ramps allow wheelchair access to most of outside, flower beds and into Grade II listed building and library.

44 THE OLD VICARAGE
The Fields, Middleton by Wirksworth, Matlock, DE4 4NH. Jane Irwing, 01629 825010, irwingjane@gmail.com. *Behind church on Main St & nr school. Travelling N on A6 from Derby turn L at Cromford, at top of hill turn R onto Porter Ln, at T-lights, turn R onto Main St. Park on Main St near DWT. Walk through churchyard. No parking at house.* **Sat 22, Sun 23 Feb, Sat 10, Sun 11 May (11-3.30); Sat 13, Sun 14 Sept (11-4). Adm £5, chd free. Home-made teas at the house. Visits also by arrangement 1 Mar to 14 Sept for groups of 5 to 20.**
Glorious garden with mixed flowering borders and mature trees in gentle valley with fantastic views to Black Rocks. All-season interest. Acid loving plants such as camellias and rhododendrons are grown in pots in courtyard garden. Tender ferns and exotic plants grown in fernery. Beyond is the orchard, fruit garden, vegetable patch and greenhouse, the home of honey bees, doves and hens. A garden designed to create a variety of different spaces in which to enjoy planting combinations from wide views over the countryside to enclosed and intimate places.

45 THE PADDOCK
12 Manknell Rd, Whittington Moor, Chesterfield, S41 8LZ. Mel & Wendy Taylor, 01246 451001, debijt9276@gmail.com. *2m N of Chesterfield. Whittington Moor just off A61 between Sheffield & Chesterfield. Parking at Victoria Working Mens Club, garden signed from here.* **Sun 13 Apr, Sun 13 July (11-5). Adm £4, chd free. Cream teas. Visits also by arrangement June to Aug for groups of 10 to 25.**
½ acre garden incorporating small formal garden, stream and koi filled pond. Stone path over bridge, up some steps, past small copse, across the stream at the top and back down again. Past herbaceous border towards a pergola where cream teas can be enjoyed.

46 PARK HALL
Walton Back Lane, Walton, Chesterfield, S42 7LT. Kim Staniforth, 07785 784439, kim.staniforth@btinternet.com. *2m SW of Chesterfield centre. From town on A619 L into Somersall Ln. On A632 R into Acorn Ridge. Park on field side only of Walton Back Ln.* **Visits by arrangement Apr to July for groups of 10+. Adm £7, chd free.**
Romantic low acre plantsmans garden, in a stunningly beautiful setting surrounding C17 house (not open) four main rooms, terraced garden, parkland area with forest trees, croquet lawn, sunken garden with arbours, pergolas, pleached hedge, topiary, statuary, roses, rhododendrons, camellias, several water features. Runner-up in Daily Telegraph Great British Gardens Competition 2018. Two steps down to gain access to garden.

47 NEW 60 POPLAR ROAD
Breaston, Derby, DE72 3BH. Mrs Frances O'Brien. *Situated between Derby and Nottingham. M1 J25 interchange with A52 Derby. Long Eaton turn. At mini r'about turn R, then 1st R to Breaston, Longmoor Ln. Turn L at Poplar Rd. Number 60 is on L. Or A6005 turn R Poplar Rd last on R.* **Sun 25 May (12-5). Adm £5, chd free. Tea, coffee & cake.**
Rambling roses and clematis climb through flowering fruit and conifer trees. Small flowering cornus and cersis trees. Ornamental ponds with mature fish. Plants with nectar rich flowers for bees and pollinators.

Perennial wildflower meadow. Natural pond for spawning newts and frogs. Beehives and wood stack for hedgehogs, mice and insects. Gardens with sculpture and glass art surround house. Accessible in most parts of garden. Ground is mainly lawn with access points to some areas rather narrow.

48 RAISWELLS HOUSE
Park Street, Barlborough, Chesterfield, S43 4ES. Mr Andrew & Mrs Rosie Dale. *7m NE of Chesterfield. 7 m W of Worksop, off J30 of M1. Clarendon and Raiswells House are within easy walking distance of each other, with 2 pubs in between.* **Sun 10 Aug (11.30-4.30). Combined adm with Clarendon £5, chd free. Light refreshments.**
A spacious ½ acre garden surrounded by fields and a woodland backdrop, designed to give a peaceful, calm, relaxing aura. Large borders are full of architectural foliage, trees, ferns, giant acanthus plants and a rose arch. There are five seating areas, all with dawn to dusk lighting, to enjoy different views of the garden. The summerhouse offers shade from the sunshine or shelter from the showers. Within the garden you will find a formal topiary courtyard, a Koi Pond and a children's play area. Brass band playing at Clarendon during the afternoon and with light refreshments available at Raiswells House. Partial access for wheelchairs.

49 ♦ RENISHAW HALL & GARDENS
Renishaw Park, Eckington, Sheffield, S21 3WB. Alexandra Hayward, 01246 432310, enquiries@renishaw-hall.co.uk, www.renishaw-hall.co.uk. *10m from Sheffield city centre. 3m from J30 on M1, well sign posted from J30 r'about. What3words app: bungalows.relished.staining.* **For NGS: Wed 7 May, Wed 2 July (10.30-4.30). Adm £10, chd free. Takeaway kiosk at the Gardens entrance plus at Renishaw's Café within courtyard.** For other opening times and information, please phone, email or visit garden website.
Renishaw Hall and Gardens boasts seven acres of stunning gardens created by Sir George Sitwell in 1885. The Italianate gardens feature various

rooms with extravagant herbaceous borders. Rose gardens, rare trees and shrubs, National Collection of Yuccas, sculptures, woodland walks and lakes create a magical and engaging garden experience. The National Garden Scheme openings coincide with the bluebells being in flower on Wed 7 May and the roses blooming on Wed 2 July. For a sumptuous Afternoon Tea in the Courtyard Café, prebooking is required. Please visit the website to book. www.renishaw-hall.co.uk. Mobility scooter and wheelchairs available to hire free of charge. Pre-booking is strongly advised. Wheelchair route and map around the formal gardens.

GROUP OPENING

50 REPTON NGS VILLAGE GARDENS
Repton, Derby, DE65 6FQ. *6m S of Derby. From A38/A50, S of Derby, follow signs to Willington, then Repton, then R at r'about towards Newton Solney to reach 10 Chestnut Way, other gardens signposted from the r'about.* **Mon 5 May, Sun 15 June, Mon 25 Aug (11-4). Combined adm £8, chd free. Light refreshments at 10 Chestnut Way in May, Askew Cottage in June, 34 High Street in Aug.**

ASKEW COTTAGE
DE65 6FZ. Louise Hardwick, 07970 411748, louise.hardwick@hotmail.co.uk, www.hardwickgardendesign.co.uk. Open on Mon 5 May, Sun 15 June Visits also by arrangement 1 May to 26 Sept for groups of 5 to 25.

10 CHESTNUT WAY
DE65 6FQ. Pauline Little, 07842 500673, plittle@hotmail.co.uk. Open on all dates Visits also by arrangement Feb to Oct for groups of 5 to 40. Adm inc drink and cake. Options such as soup available.

34 HIGH STREET
DE65 6GD. Adrian and Natalie Argyle, 01283 701277, nargyle@argylefrics.co.uk. Open on all dates Visits also by arrangement May to Aug for groups of up to 20.

22 PINFOLD CLOSE
DE65 6FR. Mr & Mrs O Jowett, 01283 701964, helen.jowett23@gmail.com. Open on Mon 5 May, Mon 25 Aug Visits also by arrangement 5 May to 25 Aug for groups of up to 10.

REPTON ALLOTMENTS
DE65 6FX. Mr A Topping. Open on Mon 5 May, Sun 15 June

Repton is a thriving village dating back to Anglo Saxon times. The village gardens are all very different, ranging from the very small to very large, several of them have new features for 2025. Askew Cottage is a professionally designed garden and has many structural features linked together by curving paths and is undergoing changes in the winter. 34 High Street is a traditional old-established garden at the rear of one of the historic village properties. 10 Chestnut Way is a plantaholic's garden which is always very popular. 22 Pinfold Close is a small garden but is packed full with a special interest in tropical plants and has an orchid house and conservatory. The award winning Repton Allotments is a small set of allotments currently undergoing a revival with community area, new polytunnel and attractive views across Derbyshire. Plenty of seating throughout. Some gardens have grass or gravel paths but most areas wheelchair accessible.

51 NEW 3 SCHOOL WOODS CLOSE
Shipley, Heanor, DE75 7JS. Sue and Phil Walker. *In between Heanor and Ilkeston. From Heanor, head towards Ilkeston. Turn R along bridle road to Shipley village. From Ilkeston, head towards Heanor. Turn L along bridle path to Shipley village. Follow Yellow NGS signs.* **Sun 18 May (12-5). Adm £3.50, chd free. Tea, coffee & cake.**
A small, level 20yr old garden in a semi-rural location adjacent to Shipley Country Park with lawns surrounded by established deep borders of herbaceous perennials, ferns, hostas and shrubs shaded by deciduous and coniferous trees. Flat lawns extend throughout the garden. Only a lower woodland path is inaccessible but it can be seen from the lawn.

52 NEW SLATELANDS HOUSE
Slatelands Road, Glossop, SK13 6LH. Mr Ian Laybourn. *Slatelands Rd is a cul-de-sac with barrier across road (house 50yds) Very limited parking if accessing from Pikes Ln/Hollincross Ln side. More parking if accessing from Primrose Ln/Turnlee Rd side.* **Sun 29 June (12-4). Adm £4, chd free. Tea, coffee & cake.**
Victorian mill-owner's residence built on rising ground. Steepest slope from road to house level is terraced stone retaining ilex balls, wild grasses with geraniums flowing down between. Rear slopes comprise stone walls, terraced beds, paths between, lawns, patio and a classic Derbyshire waterfall. Rich plantings bring a warmth of colour whilst seated and admiring the hills. Slightly steep and roughly cobbled drive gives access to house level. Main features of side plantings and rear slopes are viewable from here.

53 THE SMITHY
Church Street, Buxton, SK17 6HD. Roddie & Kate MacLean. *200 metres S of Buxton Market Place, in Higher Buxton. Located on access-only Church St, which cuts corner between B5059 & A515. Walk S from Buxton Market Place car park. Take slight R off A515, between Scriveners Bookshop & The Swan Inn.* **Sun 1, Sat 7, Sun 8, Sat 14 June (10.30-5). Adm £4, chd free.**
Small oasis of calm in the town centre, designed by its architect-owners. Pretty colour-themed borders and dappled tree cover. Many visitors comment about how the owners have optimised the use of the space without appearing to cram it all in. Herbaceous borders, wildlife pond, octagonal greenhouse, raised vegetable beds and several different seating areas for eating outdoors. Garden with many levels; steps at entrance and around the garden.

The National Garden Scheme donated over £3.5 million to our nursing and health beneficiaries from money raised at gardens open in 2024.

54 SNITTERTON HALL
Snitterton, Matlock, DE4 2JG. Simon Haslam & Kate Alcock, 01629 583311, simon@snitterton.org. *1m NW of Matlock. Turn off from A6 in Matlock at lights near Sainsbury's. Follow road round to R to Matlock Meadows. Stay on the road for ½m then turn L up a lane marked 'no through road'.* Visits by arrangement 1 Apr to 14 Sept for groups of up to 25. Weekdays preferred. Adm £12, chd free. Tea, coffee & cake.

Snitterton Hall is a Grade I listed late Elizabethan manor house. Its gardens extend to over four acres. While little of the original C16 and C17 gardens remain, there are areas of formal planting, a productive vegetable garden and more naturally planted areas extending into the surrounding countryside. Delightful collection of sculptures. The gardens are a real haven for wildlife. Lots of garden sculptures - particularly driftwood sculptures by James Doran-Webb and bronzes by Helen Sinclair.

GROUP OPENING

55 STANTON IN PEAK GARDENS
Stanton-in-the-Peak, Matlock, DE4 2LR. *At the top of the hill in Stanton in Peak. Stanton in Peak is 5m S of Bakewell. Turn off the A6 at Rowsley, or at the B5056 & follow signs up the hill.* Sat 26, Sun 27 July (12.30-4.30). Combined adm £5, chd free. Tea, coffee & cake at 2 Haddon View. At Woodend a pop-up pub serves draught real ale from a local brewery.

2 HADDON VIEW
Steve Tompkins.
(See separate entry)

WOODEND COTTAGE
DE4 2LX. Will Chandler.

Stanton in Peak is a hillside, stone village which is a Conservation Area in the Peak District National Park. Two beautiful cottage style gardens are open, both enjoying glorious views. Steve's garden at 2 Haddon View is at the top of the village and is crammed with plants. Follow the winding path up the garden with a few steps. There are cacti flowering in the greenhouse, lots of pots, herbaceous borders, three wildlife ponds with red and pink water lilies, a koi pond, lots of rhododendrons and a cosy summerhouse. Enjoy home-made cakes and refreshments on one of the patios. Just down the hill is Woodend, where Will has constructed charming roadside stone follies on a strip of raised land along the road. The hidden rear garden has diverse planting, an extended vegetable plot, and the 'pop-up' pub.

Brierley Farm

DERBYSHIRE

56 26 STILES ROAD
Alvaston, Derby, DE24 0PG. Mr Colin Summerfield & Karen Wild. *2m SE of Derby city centre. From city take A6 (London Rd) towards Alvaston. At Blue Peter Island take L into Beech Ave 1st R into Kelmoor Rd & 1st L into Stiles Rd.* **Sun 13 Apr, Sun 11 May (12-4). Adm £3, chd free. Home-made teas.**
Our small town garden is full of surprises. Pass through our ever growing wisteria tunnel and fernery to find ponds, a stream, a bluebell walk, and an eclectic mix of plants, vegetable plot and mature fruit trees, over 30 clematis, 12 acers, 3 wisterias and seating areas. Our front garden features an aubrietia wall, azaleas and clematis plus much more. Close to Elvaston Castle. Half of garden is wheelchair accessible, most can be appreciated from patio area.

57 ♦ TISSINGTON HALL
Tissington, Ashbourne, DE6 1RA. Sir Richard & Lady FitzHerbert, 01335 352200, sirrichard@tissingtonhall.co.uk, www.tissingtonhall.co.uk. *4m N of Ashbourne. E of A515 on Ashbourne to Buxton Rd in centre of the beautiful Estate Village of Tissington.* **For NGS: Mon 5, Mon 26 May, Mon 11, Mon 18, Mon 25 Aug (12-3). Adm £8, chd £4. Light refreshments at award winning Herbert's Fine English Tearooms. Tel 01335 350501.** For other opening times and information, please phone, email or visit garden website.
Large garden celebrating over 85 yrs in the National Garden Scheme, with stunning rose garden on west terrace, herbaceous borders and five acres of grounds. Features inc Tissington Craft Fairs at the Village Hall and Onawick Candle workshop also open in the village. Wheelchair access advice from ticket seller. Please seek staff and we shall park you nearer the gardens.

58 27 WASH GREEN
Wirksworth, Matlock, DE4 4FD. Paul & Kathy Harvey, 07811 395679, pandk.harvey@ngs.org.uk, www.facebook.com/27washgreen. *⅓ m E of Wirksworth centre. From Wirksworth centre, follow B5035 towards Whatstandwell. Cauldwell St leads over railway bridge to Wash Green, 200 metres up steep hill on L. Park in town or uphill from garden entry.* **Sun 4 May, Sun 24 Aug (11-4). Adm £5, chd free. Tea, coffee & cake inc gluten free options.** Visits also by arrangement 5 May to 28 Sept for groups of 6 to 30.
Beautiful large garden, with outstanding views of historic Wirksworth town, and the surrounding Ecclesbourne valley. Inner walled area has topiary, pergola and mixed borders. The larger part of the garden has sweeping lawns, large beds planted for year-round colour, wildlife pond with summerhouse, bog garden, areas of woodland and specimen trees. Also productive fruit and vegetable garden. Drop off at property entry for wheelchair access. The inner garden has flat paths with good views of whole garden.

59 13 WESTFIELD ROAD
Swadlincote, DE11 0BG. Val & Dave Booth. *5m E of Burton-on-Trent, off A511. Follow signs for Swadlincote. Turn R into Springfield Rd, take 3rd R into Westfield Rd.* **Sun 8 June, Sun 3 Aug (12-4). Adm £3.50, chd free. Home-made teas.**
A deceptive country-style garden in Swadlincote, a real gem. The garden is on two levels of approx ½ acre. Packed herbaceous borders designed for colour. Shrubs, baskets and tubs. Lots of roses. Greenhouses, raised-bed vegetable area, fruit trees and two ponds. Free range chicken area. Plenty of seating to relax and take in the wonderful planting from two passionate gardeners. The small top garden is accessible for wheelchairs, the lower garden can be accessed via a slope instead of the 7 steps.

60 26 WINDMILL RISE
Belper, DE56 1GQ. Kathy Fairweather. *From Belper Market Place take Chesterfield Rd towards Heage. Top of hill, 1st R Marsh Ln, 1st R Windmill Ln, 1st R Windmill Rise. Limited parking on Windmill Rise - disabled mainly.* **Sun 20 July (11.30-4.30). Adm £4, chd free. Light refreshments inc gluten free and vegan options.**
Behind a deceptively ordinary façade, lies a real surprise. A lush oasis, much larger than expected, with an amazing collection of rare and unusual plants. A truly plant lovers' organic garden divided into sections: woodland, Japanese, secret garden, cottage, edible, ponds and small stream. Many seating areas, inc a summerhouse in which to enjoy a variety of refreshments.

61 YEW TREE BUNGALOW
Thatchers Lane, Tansley, Matlock, DE4 5FD. Jayne Conquest, 07745 093177, jayneconquest@btinternet.com. *2m E of Matlock, off A615 in Tansley. On A615, 2nd R after Tavern at Tansley. Parking available in Charles Gregory & Sons Timber yard car park opp Tavern Inn.* **Sun 20 Apr, Sun 6 July, Sun 17 Aug (11.30-4). Adm £5, chd free. Home-made teas.** Visits also by arrangement 21 Apr to 16 Aug for groups of 6 to 30.
Plantswoman's ½ acre cottage style garden on a slope created by the present owners over 30 yrs. Many mixed borders planted with many choice and unusual trees, shrubs, herbaceous perennial, bulbs and annuals to provide year-round interest. Several seats to view different aspects of the garden. Shady area planted with a wide range of ferns. Vegetable and fruit garden. The garden is sloping but most of garden can be seen from the patio.

129,032 people were able to access guidance on what to expect when a person is dying through the National Garden Scheme's support for Hospice UK this year.

DEVON

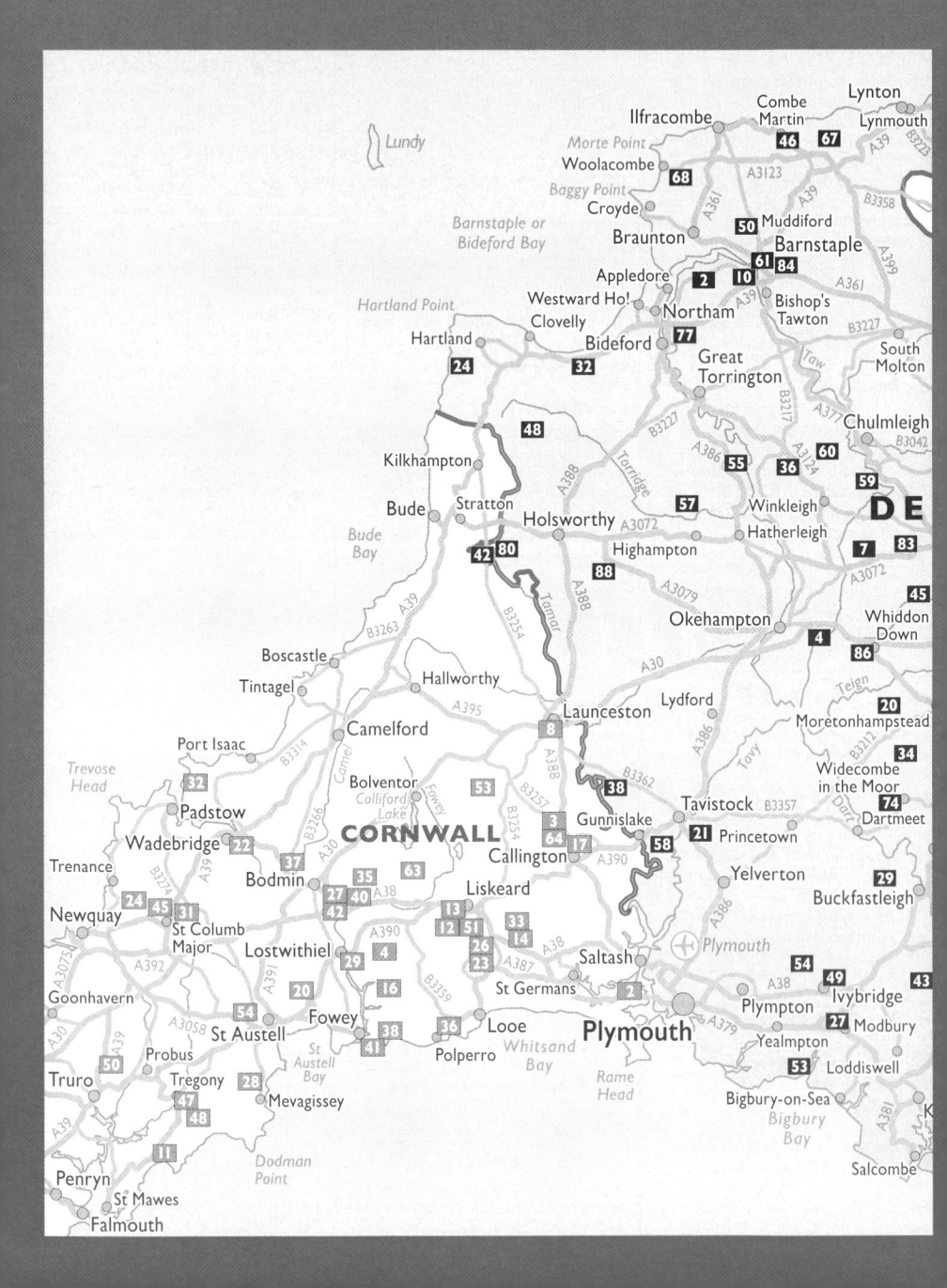

DEVON 133

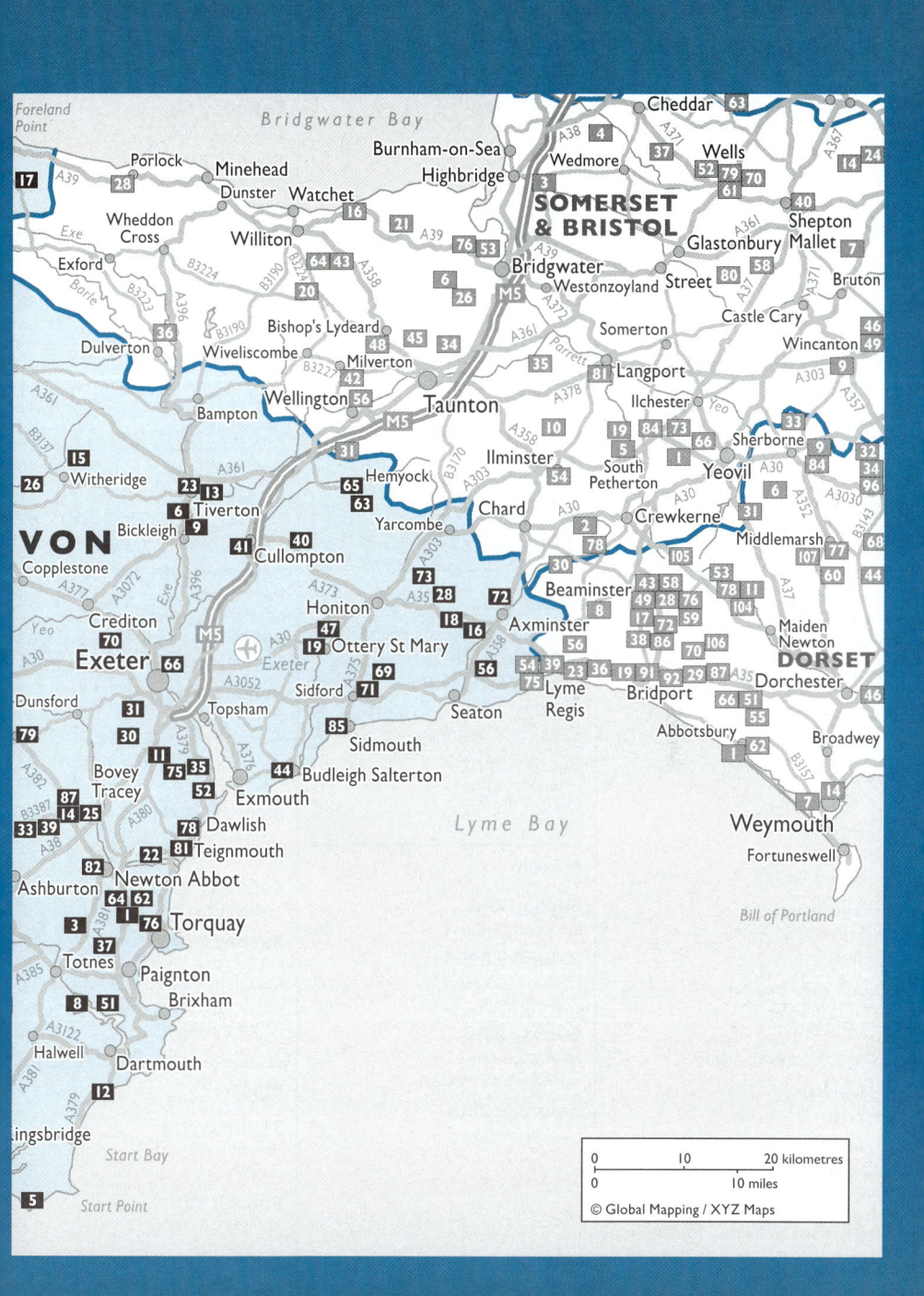

DEVON

VOLUNTEERS

County Organiser & Dartmoor
Miranda Allhusen 01647 440296
Miranda@allhusen.co.uk

County Treasurer
Nigel Hall 01884 38812
nigel.hall@ngs.org.uk

Publicity
Tracy Armstrong 07729 225549
tracygorsty@aol.com

Booklet Co-ordinator
Anne Sercombe 01626 923170
anne.sercombe@ngs.org.uk

Social Media
Neil Littleales 07722 321838
littleales@ngs.org.uk

Talks
Neil & Kerry Littleales
(as above and below)

Julia Tremlett 07715 718040
juliatremlett16@gmail.com

Assistant County Organisers

East Devon
Penny Walmsley 01404 831375
walyp_uk@yahoo.co.uk

Exeter
Jenny Phillips 01392 254076
jennypips25@hotmail.co.uk

Exmoor
Angela Percival 01598 741343
lalindevon@yahoo.co.uk

North Devon
Jo Hynes
hynesjo@gmail.com

North East Devon
Jill Hall 01884 38812
jill22hall@gmail.com

North West Devon
Kerry Littleales
07727 657246
kerry.littleales@ngs.org.uk

South Hams
Position Vacant

South West Devon
Naomi Hindley 07969 792360
naomi.hindley@ngs.org.uk

f @Devon NGS   @ngsdevon

Torbay
Tracy Armstrong (see left)

West Devon
Jan Gasper 01822 6111304
jan.gasper@ngs.org.uk

Central Devon
Rosie Moore 01837 847737,
devonrosie@yahoo.com

OPENING DATES

All entries subject to change.
For latest information check
www.ngs.org.uk
Map locator numbers are
shown to the right of each
garden name.

February

Snowdrop Openings

Friday 7th
Higher Cherubeer 36

Friday 14th
Higher Cherubeer 36

Saturday 15th
The Mount, Delamore 54

Sunday 16th
The Mount, Delamore 54

Sunday 23rd
East Worlington House 26
Higher Cherubeer 36

March

Sunday 2nd
East Worlington House 26

Saturday 22nd
Haldon Grange 30
Samlingstead 68

Sunday 23rd
Heathercombe 34
Upper Gorwell House 84

Saturday 29th
Haldon Grange 30

Sunday 30th
Bickham House 11
Chevithorne Barton 23
Haldon Grange 30

April

Saturday 5th
Haldon Grange 30

Sunday 6th
Andrew's Corner 4
Ashley Court 6
Haldon Grange 30

Saturday 12th
Haldon Grange 30
Little Dinworthy 48
Weston House 85

Sunday 13th
Andrew's Corner 4
Bickham House 11
Haldon Grange 30
Little Dinworthy 48
Weston House 85

Friday 18th
Musselbrook Cottage Garden 57
Pounds 63

Saturday 19th
Haldon Grange 30
Musselbrook Cottage Garden 57
Pounds 63
Regency House 65

Sunday 20th
Haldon Grange 30
Kia-Ora Farm & Gardens 41
Musselbrook Cottage Garden 57
Regency House 65

Monday 21st
Haldon Grange 30
Kia-Ora Farm & Gardens 41

Saturday 26th
Haldon Grange 30

Sunday 27th
Chevithorne Barton 23
Haldon Grange 30
Upper Gorwell House 84
Whitstone Farm 87

May

Saturday 3rd
Greatcombe 29
Haldon Grange 30

Sunday 4th
Andrew's Corner 4
Greatcombe 29

DEVON 135

Haldon Grange 30
Heathercombe 34
Kia-Ora Farm & Gardens 41

Monday 5th
Andrew's Corner 4
Greatcombe 29
Haldon Grange 30
Kia-Ora Farm & Gardens 41

Friday 9th
Avenue Cottage 8
Musselbrook Cottage Garden 57

Saturday 10th
Avenue Cottage 8
Haldon Grange 30
Heathercombe 34
Musselbrook Cottage Garden 57

Sunday 11th
Bickham House 11
Haldon Grange 30
Heathercombe 34
NEW Larapinta 42
Middle Well 51
Musselbrook Cottage Garden 57

Tuesday 13th
◆ Hotel Endsleigh 38

Friday 16th
The Blundell's School Garden 13
Sutton Mead 79

Saturday 17th
NEW Ashridge Court 7
The Blundell's School Garden 13
Haldon Grange 30
Haytor Gardens 33
Heathercombe 34
Little Dinworthy 48
Old Glebe 59
Sutton Mead 79
Weston House 85

Sunday 18th
NEW Ashridge Court 7
The Chantry 21
Haldon Grange 30
Haytor Gardens 33
Heathercombe 34
Kia-Ora Farm & Gardens 41
Little Dinworthy 48
Old Glebe 59
Sutton Mead 79
Weston House 85

Tuesday 20th
Heathercombe 34

Wednesday 21st
NEW Ashridge Court 7
◆ Goren Farm 28
Heathercombe 34

Thursday 22nd
NEW Ashridge Court 7
◆ Goren Farm 28
Heathercombe 34

Friday 23rd
◆ Goren Farm 28
Heathercombe 34

Saturday 24th
Abbotskerswell Gardens 1
◆ Goren Farm 28
Greatcombe 29
Haldon Grange 30
Heathercombe 34
NEW Journey's End 39
Old Crebor Farm 58

Sunday 25th
Abbotskerswell Gardens 1
Andrew's Corner 4
◆ Cadhay 19
The Chantry 21
Chevithorne Barton 23
◆ Goren Farm 28
Greatcombe 29
Haldon Grange 30
Heathercombe 34
NEW Journey's End 39
Kia-Ora Farm & Gardens 41
NEW Larapinta 42
◆ Mothecombe House 53
Sherwood 70
Upper Gorwell House 84

Monday 26th
Andrew's Corner 4
◆ Cadhay 19
◆ Goren Farm 28
Greatcombe 29
Haldon Grange 30
Kia-Ora Farm & Gardens 41
Old Crebor Farm 58

Tuesday 27th
◆ Goren Farm 28
Heathercombe 34

Wednesday 28th
◆ Goren Farm 28
Heathercombe 34

Thursday 29th
◆ Goren Farm 28
Heathercombe 34

Friday 30th
◆ Goren Farm 28
Heathercombe 34
Pounds 63
Torview 82

Saturday 31st
Bradford Tracy House 15
Brendon Gardens 17
Dunley House 25
◆ Goren Farm 28
Haldon Grange 30
Heathercombe 34
NEW The Old Rectory 60
Pounds 63
Regency House 65
South Wood Farm 73
Torview 82

June

Sunday 1st
Bickham House 11
Bradford Tracy House 15
Brendon Gardens 17
Dunley House 25
◆ Goren Farm 28
Haldon Grange 30
Heathercombe 34
High Garden 35
NEW The Old Rectory 60
Regency House 65
South Wood Farm 73
Torview 82

Monday 2nd
◆ Goren Farm 28

Tuesday 3rd
◆ Goren Farm 28

Wednesday 4th
◆ Goren Farm 28

Thursday 5th
◆ Goren Farm 28

Friday 6th
◆ Goren Farm 28
Southcombe Barn 74

Saturday 7th
◆ Goren Farm 28
Haldon Grange 30
Heathercombe 34
Higher Orchard Cottage 37
Rosebarn Gardens 66

Sunday 8th
◆ Docton Mill 24
◆ Goren Farm 28
Haldon Grange 30
Heathercombe 34
Higher Orchard Cottage 37
Kia-Ora Farm & Gardens 41
Rosebarn Gardens 66

Monday 9th
◆ Goren Farm 28

Tuesday 10th
◆ Goren Farm 28

DEVON

Wednesday 11th
- 🆕 Ashridge Court — 7
- ♦ Goren Farm — 28

Thursday 12th
- 🆕 Ashridge Court — 7
- ♦ Goren Farm — 28

Friday 13th
- ♦ Goren Farm — 28
- Musselbrook Cottage Garden — 57
- Regency House — 65
- Southcombe Barn — 74

Saturday 14th
- Ash Park — 5
- 🆕 Ermecot House — 27
- ♦ Goren Farm — 28
- Heathercombe — 34
- Musbury Barton — 56
- Musselbrook Cottage Garden — 57
- Regency House — 65
- Stone Farm — 77
- Teignmouth Gardens — 81
- Whiddon Goyle — 86

Sunday 15th
- Ash Park — 5
- 🆕 Ermecot House — 27
- ♦ Goren Farm — 28
- Heathercombe — 34
- Musbury Barton — 56
- Musselbrook Cottage Garden — 57
- Stone Farm — 77
- Teignmouth Gardens — 81
- Whiddon Goyle — 86

Monday 16th
- ♦ Goren Farm — 28

Tuesday 17th
- ♦ Goren Farm — 28

Wednesday 18th
- ♦ Goren Farm — 28

Thursday 19th
- ♦ Goren Farm — 28

Friday 20th
- ♦ Goren Farm — 28
- Sidbury Mill — 71
- Southcombe Barn — 74

Saturday 21st
- ♦ Goren Farm — 28
- Harbour Lights — 32
- Heathercombe — 34
- Kentisbeare House — 40
- 🆕 Mowhay — 55
- The Priory — 64

Sunday 22nd
- ♦ Goren Farm — 28
- Harbour Lights — 32
- Heathercombe — 34
- Kia-Ora Farm & Gardens — 41
- 🆕 Mowhay — 55
- The Priory — 64
- Regency House — 65
- Sherwood — 70
- Sidbury Mill — 71
- Upper Gorwell House — 84

Monday 23rd
- ♦ Goren Farm — 28

Tuesday 24th
- ♦ Goren Farm — 28

Wednesday 25th
- ♦ Goren Farm — 28

Thursday 26th
- ♦ Goren Farm — 28

Friday 27th
- ♦ Goren Farm — 28
- Socks Orchard — 72
- Southcombe Barn — 74

Saturday 28th
- Chao Nan — 22
- 2 Middlewood — 52
- Socks Orchard — 72

Sunday 29th
- Chao Nan — 22
- Linden Rise — 46
- 2 Middlewood — 52
- Socks Orchard — 72

July

Saturday 5th
- Bovey Tracey Gardens — 14
- Greatcombe — 29
- 2 Middlewood — 52

Sunday 6th
- Ashley Court — 6
- Bickham House — 11
- Bovey Tracey Gardens — 14
- Greatcombe — 29
- Kia-Ora Farm & Gardens — 41
- 2 Middlewood — 52

Saturday 12th
- Backswood Farm — 9
- Squirrels — 76
- 🆕 Willow Glade Farm — 88

Sunday 13th
- Backswood Farm — 9
- Squirrels — 76
- 🆕 Willow Glade Farm — 88

Friday 18th
- Avenue Cottage — 8
- Musselbrook Cottage Garden — 57

Saturday 19th
- Am Brook Meadow — 3
- 🆕 Larcombe Farmhouse — 43
- 🆕 Mowhay — 55
- Musselbrook Cottage Garden — 57
- Samlingstead — 68

Sunday 20th
- Am Brook Meadow — 3
- Avenue Cottage — 8
- Kia-Ora Farm & Gardens — 41
- 🆕 Larcombe Farmhouse — 43
- Little Ash Bungalow — 47
- 🆕 Mowhay — 55
- Musselbrook Cottage Garden — 57
- Upper Gorwell House — 84

Saturday 26th
- Greatcombe — 29
- 🆕 Journey's End — 39

Sunday 27th
- Bickham House — 11
- Greatcombe — 29
- 🆕 Journey's End — 39
- Whitstone Farm — 87

August

Saturday 2nd
- Brendon Gardens — 17
- Chagford Community Gardens — 20
- 🆕 Mowhay — 55

Sunday 3rd
- Brendon Gardens — 17
- Chagford Community Gardens — 20
- Kia-Ora Farm & Gardens — 41
- 🆕 Mowhay — 55

Saturday 9th
- Stone Farm — 77
- Weston House — 85

Sunday 10th
- Bickham House — 11
- Stone Farm — 77
- Weston House — 85

Sunday 17th
- Barnstaple World Gardens — 10

Friday 22nd
- ♦ Marwood Hill Garden — 50
- Spring Lodge — 75

Sunday 24th
- 32 Allenstyle Drive — 2
- Bickham House — 11
- ♦ Cadhay — 19
- Kia-Ora Farm & Gardens — 41

Monday 25th
- ♦ Cadhay — 19
- Kia-Ora Farm & Gardens — 41

September

Friday 5th
Sutton Mead 79

Saturday 6th
Sutton Mead 79

Sunday 7th
32 Allenstyle Drive 2
Kia-Ora Farm & Gardens 41
Sutton Mead 79

Sunday 14th
Upper Gorwell House 84

Saturday 20th
Little Ash Bungalow 47

Sunday 21st
Kia-Ora Farm & Gardens 41

October

Saturday 18th
Dunley House 25
Regency House 65

Sunday 19th
Dunley House 25
Regency House 65

Sunday 26th
Chevithorne Barton 23
Sherwood 70

Friday 31st
NEW Ashridge Court 7

November

Saturday 1st
NEW Ashridge Court 7

February 2026

Friday 6th
Higher Cherubeer 36

Friday 13th
Higher Cherubeer 36

Saturday 21st
Higher Cherubeer 36

By Arrangement

Arrange a personalised garden visit with your club, or group of friends, on a date to suit you. See individual garden entries for full details.

32 Allenstyle Drive 2
Andrew's Corner 4
Ash Park 5
Avenue Cottage 8
Bickham House 11
Brambly Wood, Haytor Gardens 33
Breach 16
Brendon Gardens 17
Haldon Grange 30
Halscombe Farm 31
Heathercombe 34
Higher Cherubeer 36
Higher Orchard Cottage 37
NEW Journey's End 39
Kia-Ora Farm & Gardens 41
Lee Ford 44
Lewis Cottage 45
Little Ash Bungalow 47
Middle Well 51
The Mount, Delamore 54
NEW Mowhay 55
Old Crebor Farm 58
Old Glebe 59
NEW The Old Rectory 60
NEW 1 Pilton Lawn 61
Regency House 65
Rudd Cottage 67
Samlingstead 68
NEW Sand Farmhouse 69
Sherwood 70
Squirrels 76
Stone Farm 77
Stonelands House 78
Sutton Mead 79
NEW Tamar House 80
Torview 82
NEW Truants Cottage 83
Weston House 85
Whiddon Goyle 86
Whitstone Farm 87

Ermecot House

THE GARDENS

GROUP OPENING

1 ABBOTSKERSWELL GARDENS
Abbotskerswell, TQ12 5PN. *2m SW of Newton Abbot town centre. A381 Newton Abbot/Totnes rd. Sharp L turn from Newton Abbot, R from Totnes. Field parking at Fairfield. Maps & tickets valid for both days avail from 1pm at all gardens & at Church House.* **Sat 24, Sun 25 May (1-5). Combined adm £7.50, chd free. Home-made teas at Church House in the village from 2pm.**

ABBOTSFORD
Wendy & Phil Grierson.

ABBOTSKERSWELL ALLOTMENTS

1 ABBOTSWELL COTTAGES
Jane Taylor.

BRIAR COTTAGE
Peggy & David Munden.

FAIRFIELD
Brian Mackness.

1 FORDE CLOSE
Ann Allen.

NEW 4 LAKELAND
Ali & Dave Peters.

PINE TREES LODGE
Gary & Richard.

THE POTTERY
Beverley & Dougal Dubash.

For 2025 Abbotskerswell offers eight gardens, ranging from small to large, plus the village allotments. The gardens offer a wide range of planting styles and innovative landscaping. Cottage gardens, terracing, wildflower areas, specialist plants and an arboretum. Ideas for every type and size of garden. Visitors are welcome to picnic in the field or arboretum at Fairfield. Tea and cake served in the historic Church House in the centre of the village. Sales of plants, garden produce, jams and chutneys. Disabled access to three gardens. Partial access to most others.

2 32 ALLENSTYLE DRIVE
Yelland, Barnstaple, EX31 3DZ. Steve & Dawn Morgan, 07587 185911, fourhungrycats@gmail.com, www.devonsubtropicalgarden.rocks. *5m W of Barnstaple. From Barnstaple take B3233 towards Instow. Through Bickington & Fremington. L at Yelland sign into Allenstyle Rd. 1st R into Allenstyle Dr. Light blue bungalow. From Bideford go past Instow on B3233.* **Sun 24 Aug, Sun 7 Sept (12-5). Adm £5, chd free. Tea, coffee & cake. Opening with Barnstaple World Gardens on Sun 17 Aug.** Visits also by arrangement 15 Aug to 12 Sept for groups of up to 25.
Our garden is 30m x 15m and is packed full of all our favourite plants. See our collections of bananas, gingers, cannas, colocasias, delicate and scented tropical passion flowers as well as rudbeckias, perennial sunflowers, a wildlife pond and a new large cedar greenhouse. Relax and inhale the heady scents of the garden and rest awhile in the many seating areas.

3 AM BROOK MEADOW
Torbryan, Ipplepen, Newton Abbot, TQ12 5UP. Jennie & Jethro Marles. *5m from Newton Abbot on A381. Leaving A381 at Causeway Cross go through Ipplepen village, heading towards Broadhempston. Stay on Orley Rd for ¾ m. At Poole Cross turn L signed Totnes, then turn 2nd L into field parking.* **Sat 19, Sun 20 July (2-6.30). Adm £6, chd free.**
Country garden developed over past 19 yrs to encourage wildlife. Perennial native wildflower meadows, large ponds with ducks and swans, streams and wild areas covering 10 acres are accessible by gravel and grass pathways. Formal courtyard garden with water features and herbaceous borders and prairie-style planting together with poultry and bees close by. Appeared on Gardeners' World Aug 2024. Wheelchair access to most gravel path areas is good, but grass pathways in larger wildflower meadow are weather dependent.

4 ANDREW'S CORNER
Skaigh Lane, Belstone, EX20 1RD. Robin & Edwina Hill, 01837 840332, edwinarobinhill@outlook.com, www.andrewscorner.garden. *3m E of Okehampton. Signed to Belstone from A30. In village turn L, signed Skaigh. Follow NGS signs. Garden approx ½ m on R. Visitors may be dropped off at house, parking in nearby field.* **Sun 6, Sun 13 Apr, Sun 4, Mon 5, Sun 25, Mon 26 May (2-5). Adm £5, chd free. Home-made teas.** Visits also by arrangement Feb to June for groups of up to 30.
Take a walk on the wild side in this tranquil moorland garden. April openings highlight magnolias, trillium and the lovely erythroniums. Early May the maples, rhododendrons and unusual shrubs provide interest. Late May brings the Snowdrop Tree, Chilean Firebush and the spectacular blue poppies. Wheelchair access difficult when wet.

5 ASH PARK
East Prawle, Kingsbridge, TQ7 2BX. Chris & Cathryn Vanderspar, 07739 108493, cvanderspar@btconnect.com. *Take A379 Kingsbridge to Dartmouth, at Frogmore after pub R to East Prawle, after 1m L, in 1½ m at Cousins Cross bear R (middle of 3 rds). In village head to Prawle Point.* **Sat 14, Sun 15 June (11-5). Adm £6, chd free. Cream teas.** Visits also by arrangement for groups of 10+.
In a stunning location, with 180° view of the sea, Ash Park nestles at the foot of the escarpment, in 3½ acres of sub-tropical gardens, paths to explore, woodland glades, ponds and hidden seating areas. In June, there are spectacular displays of lampranthas, agapanthas, Arum lilies, aeoniums, hostas and echiums, as well as a variety of forms of agaves and cacti.

6 ASHLEY COURT
Ashley, Tiverton, EX16 5PD. Tara Fraser & Nigel Jones, 07768 878015, hello@ashleycourtdevon.co.uk, www.ashleycourtdevon.co.uk. *1m S of Tiverton on the Bickleigh road (A396). Turn off the A396 to Ashley & then immed L. Take the drive to the L of Ashley Court Lodge Cottage (don't go up Ashley Back Lane where the SatNav will direct you).*

Sun 6 Apr, Sun 6 July (12.30-4.30). Adm £6, chd free. Speciality teas inc many delicious vegan recipes & cakes containing fruits & vegetables from the walled kitchen garden.

Ashley Court is a small Regency country house with an historically interesting walled kitchen garden currently undergoing restoration. It is unusually situated in a deep valley and has a frost window and the remains of several glasshouses and cold frames. View the apple loft, root stores, stable buildings, woodland walk and lawns, borders and beautiful mature trees. A walk through discovery and history. The walled garden probably pre-dates the 1805 house as there was previously an older Ashley Court on the other side of the garden. Peculiar features such as a curved garden wall and a frost window make it unusual.

7 NEW ASHRIDGE COURT
North Tawton, EX20 2DH.
Chris & Carolyn Richards,
www.ashridge-court.co.uk. *Just outside North Tawton. From town centre take Market St between Town Hall & chemist past church. Continue for 1½ m, turn L into Ashridge Court. What3words app: truffles.producing. pleasing.* **Sat 17, Sun 18, Wed 21, Thur 22 May, Wed 11, Thur 12 June, Fri 31 Oct, Sat 1 Nov (11-4). Adm £6, chd free. Home-made teas in Ashridge Great Barn. Selection of home baked cakes & hot drinks. Devon cream teas & light lunches.**

Main garden of 6 acres dates from early 1900s, walled garden significantly older. Stunning range of mature conifers, an Arts and Crafts circular garden room featuring Japanese maples. From Ashridge Great Barn steps to woodland walk via tree ferns, newly planted flowering trees and shrubs, Stumpery, Walled garden and Upper arboretum all in various stages of restoration by current owners. Limited mobility parking available. Wheelchair access to top part of garden. Separate parking area for disabled access to teas and WC.

8 AVENUE COTTAGE
Ashprington, Totnes, TQ9 7UT.
Mr Richard Pitts & Mr David Sykes, 01803 732769, richard. pitts@btinternet.com, www.avenuecottage.com.
3m SE of Totnes. A381 Totnes to Kingsbridge for 1m; L for Ashprington, into village then L by pub. Garden ¼ m on R after Sharpham Estate sign. **Fri 9, Sat 10 May, Fri 18, Sun 20 July (11-3.30). Adm £5, chd free. Pre-booking essential, please visit www.ngs. org.uk for information & booking. Visits also by arrangement Apr to Oct for groups of up to 25.**

11 acre woodland valley garden, forming part of the Grade II* Sharpham House Landscape. The garden contains many rare and unusual trees and shrubs with views over the River Dart AONB and Sharpham. Azaleas, hydrangeas and magnolias are a speciality. A spring rises in the garden under a spectacularly large rhododendron feeding two ponds and a small stream running through a meadow with mown paths.

Mowhay

140 DEVON

9 BACKSWOOD FARM
Bickleigh, Tiverton, EX16 8RA. Andrew Hughes, 07860 609609, info@tradingsites.net, www.backswood.co.uk. *2m SE of Tiverton. Take A396 off the A361. Turn L to Butterleigh opp Tesco, L at mini r'about, after 150 yds turn R up Exeter Hill for 2m then 1st R to Bickleigh. After 500 yds turn 1st R into farm entrance.* **Sat 12, Sun 13 July (2-5). Adm £6, chd free. Cream teas.**
Created with the natural environment at its heart, this evolving 2 acre nature garden provides uniquely designed homes for wildlife. Wander through the flower meadow visiting individually designed rooms with many structures, water features and pools. Seating areas afford stunning views towards Exmoor and Dartmoor. Both native and herbaceous plants have been chosen to benefit insect and bird life. Dogs on leads. WC available.

🐕 🛏 ☕

GROUP OPENING

10 BARNSTAPLE WORLD GARDENS
31 Anne Crescent, Little Elche, Barnstaple, EX31 3AF. Gavin Hendry, www.devonsubtropicalgarden.rocks. *32 Allenstyle Dr, from Barnstaple take B3233 towards Instow. Through Bickington & Fremington. L at Yelland sign into Allenstyle Rd. 1st R into Allenstyle Dr. 31 Anne Cres, L off Old Torrington Rd into Philips Ave then follow signs.* **Sun 17 Aug (11-4). Combined adm £5, chd free. Tea, coffee & cake.**

32 ALLENSTYLE DRIVE
Steve & Dawn Morgan.
(See separate entry)

31 ANNE CRESCENT
EX31 3AF. Mr Gavin Hendry.

Explore two amazing spaces in lovely N Devon. 31 Anne Crescent is N Devon's Little Elche, a small urban L-shaped tropical garden complete with wide variety of large palms, agaves, bananas, cacti, tree ferns and delightful pond surrounded by large tree ferns. 32 Allenstyle Drive has a 30 x 15 metre garden packed full of the owners' favourite plants. See huge bananas, cannas, colocasias, delicate and scented tropical passionflowers, rudbeckias, perennial sunflowers, a wildlife pond and a new large cedar greenhouse. Relax and inhale the heady scents of the garden and rest awhile in the many seating areas.

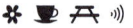

❄ ☕ 🪑 🔊

11 BICKHAM HOUSE
Kenn, Exeter, EX6 7XL. Julia Tremlett, 07715 718040, juliatremlett16@gmail.com. *6m S of Exeter, 1m off A38. Leave A38 at Kennford Services, follow signs to Kenn, 1st R in village, follow lane for ¾ m to end of no through rd. Only use SatNav once you are in the village of Kenn.* **Sun 30 Mar, Sun 13 Apr, Sun 11 May, Sun 1 June, Sun 6, Sun 27 July, Sun 10, Sun 24 Aug (2-5). Adm £6, chd free. Home-made teas. Visits also by arrangement Apr to Aug small coaches only.**
6 acres with lawns, borders, mature trees. Formal parterre with lily pond. 1 acre Walled garden with

Larapinta

DEVON 141

colourful profusion of vegetables and flowers. Palm tree avenue leading to millennium summerhouse. Late summer colour with dahlias, crocosmia, agapanthus etc. Cactus and succulent greenhouse. Pelargonium collection. Lakeside walk. WC, disabled access.

12 ◆ BLACKPOOL GARDENS
Dartmouth, TQ6 0RG. Sir Geoffrey Newman, 01803 771801, beach@blackpoolsands.co.uk, www.blackpoolsands.co.uk. *3m SW of Dartmouth. From Dartmouth follow brown signs to Blackpool Sands on A379. Entry tickets, parking, WCs & refreshments available at Blackpool Sands. Sorry, no dogs permitted.* **For opening times and information, please phone, email or visit garden website.**
Carefully restored C19 subtropical plantsman's garden with collection of mature and newly planted tender and unusual trees, shrubs and carpet of spring flowers. Paths and steps lead gradually uphill and above the Captain's Seat offering fine coastal views. Recent plantings follow the southern hemisphere theme with callistemons, pittosporums, acacias and buddlejas.

13 THE BLUNDELL'S SCHOOL GARDEN
Blundell's Road, Tiverton, EX16 4DN. blundells.org/blundells-community/community-partnerships. *From Tiverton drive up Blundell's Rd to the school & follow direction to parking as signed. What3words app: talked.range.path.* **Fri 16, Sat 17 May (11-5). Adm £5, chd free. Pre-booking essential, please visit www.ngs.org.uk for information & booking. Cream teas.**
The Blundell's Garden, base for our Community Partnerships programme, is run from a lovely wooden cabin which doubles as the Garden Café. Primary Schools and Community groups engage in environmental activities, learning about the garden, wildlife and understanding the world around us. Pupils will show you the wildlife pond, vegetable beds, cut flowers, wildflowers, orchard and apiary. Fairly steep gravel and grass paths.

GROUP OPENING

14 BOVEY TRACEY GARDENS
Bovey Tracey, TQ13 9LZ. *6m N of Newton Abbot. Take A382 to Bovey Tracey. Parking on local roads. Follow the yellow signs and purchase ticket from any garden.* **Sat 5, Sun 6 July (1.30-5.30). Combined adm £6, chd free. Cream teas at 3 Redwoods, next door to No 2.**

GREEN HEDGES
TQ13 9LZ. Alan & Linda Jackson.

2 REDWOODS
TQ13 9YG. Mrs Julia Mooney.

11 ST PETER'S CLOSE
TQ13 9ES. Pauline & Keith Gregory.

NEW SPRINGFIELD
TQ13 9LZ. Helen Griffiths.

Nestling in the Dartmoor foothills, Bovey Tracey offers a wide range of gardens. Colourful 11 St Peter's Close has a mini railway and a watercolours exhibition, while Green Hedges is packed full of interest: colourful borders, shade plants, organic vegetables, greenhouses and a small stream. Springfield just down the road from Green Hedges is full of colour with many pots full of interesting plants. 2 Redwoods has mature trees, a Dartmoor leat, a fernery, a sunny gravel garden and acid loving shrubs. Delicious cream teas will be served next door, at 3 Redwoods. Partial wheelchair access, none at St Peter's Close, Green Hedges or Springfield.

15 BRADFORD TRACY HOUSE
Witheridge, Tiverton, EX16 8QG. Elizabeth Wilkinson. *20 mins from Tiverton. The postcode will get you to the Bradford Tracy Lodge a thatched cottage at the bottom of the drive which has 2 bouncing hares on the top. NGS direction signs from Witheridge & Rackenford.* **Sat 31 May, Sun 1 June (1.30-5). Adm £6, chd free. Tea & home-made cakes served takeaway style to enjoy in the garden or inside.**
A pleasure garden set around a Regency hunting lodge combining flowers with grasses, shrubs and huge trees in a natural and joyful space. It is planted for productivity and sustainability giving harvests of wonderful flowers, fruits, herbs and vegetables (and weeds!). There are beautiful views over the lake,

forest walks, deep blowsy borders, an ancient wisteria and an oriental treehouse garden.

16 BREACH
Shute Road, Kilmington, Axminster, EX13 7ST. Judith Chapman & BJ Lewis, 01297 35159, jachapman16@btinternet.com. *1½m W of Axminster off A35. Turn L off the A35 at the War Memorial, continue up Shute Rd, past farm on R & after 150m, Breach is a short walk along a byway to the L. Parking is on Shute Rd.* **Visits by arrangement May to Oct for groups of 5 to 25. Adm £7, chd free. Tea, coffee & cake.**
Over 3 acres with many mature trees, some unusual trees planted recently, e.g. Hoheria, Cornus mas, Nyssa. Herbaceous borders, shrubberies, vegetable/fruit area. Bog garden using natural spring and 2 ponds attract dragonflies. Disused shale tennis court has orchids and is being developed as wildflower area. Soil mainly acidic and a band of specimen rhododendrons planted 13 yrs ago. Development continues. Partial wheelchair access.

GROUP OPENING

17 BRENDON GARDENS
Brendon, Lynton, EX35 6PU. 01598 741343, lalindevon@yahoo.co.uk. *1m S of A39 N Devon coast rd between Porlock and Lynton.* **Sat 31 May, Sun 1 June, Sat 2, Sun 3 Aug (12-5). Combined adm £6, chd free. Light lunches, home-made cakes, inc gluten free & cream teas. WC. Visits also by arrangement 1 Apr to 1 Sept (Hall Farm & Higher Tippacott Farm only).**

BARN FARM
Andrew & Debra Hodges.

NEW BRENDON BARTON
Nigel & Maria Floyd.

HALL FARM
Karen Wall, 01598 741604, kwall741604@btinternet.com.

HIGHER TIPPACOTT FARM
Angela & Malcolm Percival, 01598 741343, lalindevon@yahoo.co.uk.

Stunning part of Exmoor National Park. Excellent walking along river.

Barn Farm: Stylish courtyard garden on two levels incorporating walls and old stone buildings. Roses, shrubs and other cottage garden flowers and vegetables. Adjoining paddock with copse and young orchard of Devon varieties. Brendon Barton: Garden being developed with a vision and a digger! Big stones and agricultural bygones form the dramatic structure incorporating seating areas, lawn and water, all set against an Exmoor landscape. Hall Farm: C16 longhouse set in 2 acres of tranquil mature gardens, with lake and wild area beyond. Idyllic setting with views. Rare Whitebred Shorthorn cattle. Higher Tippacott Farm: 950ft alt on moor, facing south overlooking its own valley with stream and pond. Interesting planting on many interconnecting levels with lawns. Young fruit trees in meadow. Vegetable patch with sea glimpse. Lovely views along valley and up to high moorland. Plants, books and bric a brac for sale at Higher Tippacott Farm. Display of vintage telephones and toys.

18 ♦ BURROW FARM GARDENS
Dalwood, Axminster, EX13 7ET. Mary & John Benger, www.burrowfarmgardens.co.uk. *3½ m W of Axminster. From A35 turn N at Taunton Xrds then follow brown signs What3words app: guidebook. fetches.fortress.* **For opening times and information, please visit garden website.**
This beautiful 13 acre garden has unusual trees, shrubs and herbaceous plants. Traditional summerhouse looks towards lake and ancient oak woodland with rhododendrons and azaleas. Early spring interest and superb autumn colour. The more formal Millennium garden features a rill. Anniversary garden featuring late summer perennials and grasses. Café, nursery and gift shop with range of garden ironwork. Various events inc spring and summer plant fair and open air theatre held at garden each year. Visit events page on website for more details.

19 ♦ CADHAY
Ottery St Mary, EX11 1QT. Rupert Thistlethwayte, 01404 813511, jayne@cadhay.org.uk, www.cadhay.org.uk. *1m NW of Ottery St Mary. On B3176 between Ottery St Mary & Fairmile. From E exit A30 at Iron Bridge. From W exit A30 at Patteson's Cross, follow brown signs for Cadhay.* **For NGS: Sun 25, Mon 26 May, Sun 24, Mon 25 Aug (2-5). Adm £6, chd free. Cream teas. For other opening times and information, please phone, email or visit garden website.**
Tranquil 2 acre setting for Tudor manor house. 2 medieval fish ponds surrounded by rhododendrons, gunnera, hostas and flag iris. Roses, clematis, lilies and hellebores surround walled water garden. 120ft herbaceous border walk informally planted. Magnificent display of dahlias throughout. Walled kitchen gardens have been turned into allotments and old apple store is now a tearoom. Gravel paths.

20 CHAGFORD COMMUNITY GARDENS
TQ13 8BW. Nicky Scott, wellmoor.org.uk. *What3words app: clinking vegans scarecrow. From Chagford car park walk through play park above car park to gate at the top which takes you to outer allotment gate. Walk along track & the community plot is the 1st one as you enter the site.* **Sat 2, Sun 3 Aug (10-4). Adm £5, chd free. Tea, coffee & cake in adjoining Jubilee Fields where there are picnic tables for people to bring their own picnic.**
This is a community plot consisting of 'starter' beds for people on the waiting list for an allotment as well as a medicinal herbs bed, a culinary herb bed, several fruit trees and two beds for unusual, mainly perennial plants. Lots of native wild flowers around the plot, a pond, two sheds, a composting area and more. We also have people referred from the local health centre. Our shed and decking area is easily accessed by wheelchair from where you can enjoy the view. The gardens themselves are not very accessible.

21 THE CHANTRY
Marshall Close, Tavistock, PL19 9RB. Jan & Ian Gasper. *1m S of Tavistock town centre along Whitchurch Rd. From Plymouth turn off A386 at signs for Whitchurch. Follow Anderton Ln to end, turn L. Marshall Cl 3rd on R. From N(A386) & town follow rd for 1m. Marshall Cl on L. Park Marshall Cl or Whitchurch Rd.* **Sun 18 May (1.30-4.30); Sun 25 May (12.30-4.30). Adm £5, chd free. Home-made teas.**
This is a quiet, modest sized garden, located on the edge of Tavistock. Situated on three levels with two terraces it is set out to make the most of the difficult terrain and maximises space. The many flower beds are filled with perennials, shrubs, ferns and a good collection of shade lovers. In addition we have a patio full of pots, a rill with two small ponds, a fernery and more.

22 CHAO NAN
Forder Lane, Bishopsteignton, Teignmouth, TQ14 9SL. Nicholas & Diane Shaw. *10m N Torquay, 18m S Exeter on the Teign Estuary. From Teignmouth take the A381 past Otter Garden Centre & turn R into Forder Lane. From Exeter take A380, turn L at the Ware Barton Junction onto A381 then L again at Forder Lane junction.* **Sat 28, Sun 29 June (12-5). Adm £5, chd free. Tea, coffee & cake. Picnics welcome on the croquet lawn.**
Chao Nan is a ¾ acre garden full of history and life boasting an impressive collection of trees and shrubs with a large sloping lawn which leads you to the various areas of the garden. An ever evolving space designed primarily for wildlife and year-round interest, highlights inc an ancient Wisteria, large wildlife pond, herbaceous perennial beds and lavender border.

23 CHEVITHORNE BARTON
Chevithorne, Tiverton, EX16 7QB. Head Gardener, chevithornebarton.co.uk. *3m NE of Tiverton. Follow yellow signs from A361 & A396.* **Sun 30 Mar, Sun 27 Apr, Sun 25 May, Sun 26 Oct (1.30-4.30). Adm £6, chd free. Home-made teas.**
Walled garden, summer borders and Robinsonian inspired woodland of rare trees and shrubs. In spring the garden features a large collection of magnolias, camellias, and rhododendrons with grass paths meandering through a sea of bluebells, and grass meadows. Home to National Collection of Quercus (Oaks). Lots of autumn colour.

Truants Cottage

24 ◆ DOCTON MILL
Lymebridge, Hartland, EX39 6EA. Lana & John Borrett, 07507 586144, docton.mill@btconnect.com, www.doctonmill.co.uk. *8m W of Clovelly. Follow brown tourist signs on A39 nr Clovelly.* **For NGS: Sun 8 June (11-5). Adm £7.50, chd free. Cream teas & light lunches available all day. For other opening times and information, please phone, email or visit garden website.**
Situated in a stunning valley location. The garden surrounds the original mill pond and the microclimate created within the wooded valley enables tender species to flourish. Recent planting of herbaceous, stream and summer garden give variety through the season.

🐕 ✤ ☕

25 DUNLEY HOUSE
Bovey Tracey, TQ13 9PW. Mr & Mrs F Gilbert. *2m E of Bovey Tracey on road to Hennock. From A38 going W turn off slip road R towards Chudleigh Knighton on B3344, in village follow yellow signs to Dunley House. From A38 going E turn off on Chudleigh K slip road L and follow signs.* **Sat 31 May, Sun 1 June, Sat 18, Sun 19 Oct (2-5). Adm £6, chd free. Home-made teas.**

Nine acre garden set among mature oaks, sequoiadendrons and a huge liquidambar started from a wilderness in mid eighties. Rhododendrons, camellias and over 40 different magnolias. Arboretum, walled garden with borders and fruit and vegetables, rose garden and new enclosed garden with lily pond. Large pond renovated in 2016 with new plantings. Woodland walk around perimeter of property.

♿ 🐕 ✤ ☕ 🎵

26 EAST WORLINGTON HOUSE
East Worlington, Witheridge, Crediton, EX17 4TS. Barnabas & Campie Hurst-Bannister. *In centre of E Worlington, 2m W of Witheridge. From Witheridge Square R to E Worlington. After 1½ m R at T-junction in Drayford, then L to Worlington. After ½ m L at T-junction. 200 yds on L. Parking nearby, disabled parking at house.* **Sun 23 Feb, Sun 2 Mar (1.30-5). Adm £6, chd free. Cream teas in thatched parish hall next to house.**
Thousands of purple crocuses feature in this 2 acre garden, set in a lovely position with views down the valley to Little Dart river. These spectacular crocuses have spread over many years through the garden and into the neighbouring churchyard. Walks from the garden across the river and into the woods. Dogs on leads please.

♿ 🐕 ☕ 🎵

27 NEW ERMECOT HOUSE
Ermington, Ivybridge, PL21 0LH. Dr Charlotte Grezo. *2m S of Ivybridge & just E of Ermington. Approach from A3121. From E take small lane on R immed after Ermington House Residential Home, from W take small lane on L immed after bridge over River Erme.* **Sat 14, Sun 15 June (12-5). Adm £6, chd free. Tea, coffee & cake.**
3½ acres of gardens and meadows located between the Erme and the Ludbrook. It is managed to encourage wildlife and pollinators, and is opening for the first time. It inc a walled garden planted with roses and herbaceous borders, a newly remodelled vegetable and herb garden, a mature orchard, and river and meadow walks with views over the Ludbrook, which runs through it. A rose covered pergola runs the length of the walled garden. Lovely trees stand in the lawns and along the river bank. No smoking garden. Children to be supervised at all times.

☕ 🎵

Cadhay

28 ♦ GOREN FARM
Broadhayes, Stockland, Honiton, EX14 9EN. Julian Pady, 01404 881335, gorenfarm@hotmail.com, www.goren.co.uk. *6m E of Honiton, 6m W of Axminster. Go to Stockland television mast. Head 400 metres N signed from Broadhayes Cross. Follow NGS signs & brown Goren Meadows signs.* **For NGS: Evening openings Wed 21 May to Fri 27 June (5-9). Adm by donation. Sat 7, Sun 8 June (10-5). Adm £7, chd £3. Cream teas. No refreshments are available for the evening opening; picnics are welcome at any time. For other opening times and information, please phone, email or visit garden website.**
Fifty acres of natural species-rich wildflower meadows. Easy access footpaths. Dozens of varieties of wild flowers and grasses. Thousands of orchids from early June and butterflies in July. Georgian house with stunning views of Blackdown Hills. Late season, when the meadows are setting seed ready to be mown, butterflies, beetles and many other insects are in abundance on the wild flower seed heads. Nature trail with species information signs and picnic tables. Visit the cider museum, walled vegetable garden and greenhouse. Various music events are held throughout the summer. Café open serving cream teas and light refreshments during daytime opening hours. Partial wheelchair access to meadows. Dogs welcome on a lead only, please clean up after your pet.

29 GREATCOMBE
Greatcombe Gardens & Gallery, Holne, TQ13 7SP. Robbie & Sarah Richardson, 07725 314887, sarah@greatcombe.com, www.facebook.com/greatcombegardens. *4m NW Ashburton via Holne Bridge & Holne village. 4m NE Buckfastleigh via Scorriton. Narrow lanes. Large car park adjacent to garden.* **May: Sat 3, Sun 4, Mon 5, Sat 24, Sun 25, Mon 26. July: Sat 5, Sun 6, Sat 26, Sun 27 (1-5). Adm £6, chd free. Home-made teas.**
A hidden gem, offering both inspiration and tranquillity. A wide range of plants and planting schemes add interest around every corner, featuring many flowering shrubs, hardy perennials, herbaceous borders, colourful pots, a stream, arboretum and wildlife pond. Unusual varieties of hydrangeas. 'Enchanting, magical place, a real asset to the NGS, fabulous home-made teas'. Plant nursery, artist's studio. Metal plant supports in all sizes.

30 HALDON GRANGE
Dunchideock, Exeter, EX6 7YE. Ted Phythian, 01392 832349, judithphythian@yahoo.com, youtu.be/G0gluYoWncA. *5m SW of Exeter. From A30 through Ide village to Dunchideock 5m. L to Lord Haldon, Haldon Grange is next L. From A38 (S) turn L on top of Haldon Hill follow Dunchideock signs, R at village centre to Lord Haldon.* **Sat 22, Sat 29, Sun 30 Mar. Sat 5, Sun 6, Sat 12, Sun 13, Sat 19, Sun 20, Mon 21, Sat 26, Sun 27 Apr. Sat 3, Sun 4, Mon 5, Sat 10, Sun 11, Sat 17, Sun 18, Sat 24, Sun 25, Mon 26, Sat 31 May. Sun 1, Sat 7, Sun 8 June (1pm-5pm). Adm £6, chd free. Home-made teas. Our visitors are welcome to bring a picnic.**

Visits also by arrangement 22 Mar to 8 June for groups of 10+. Access for small coach size only.
Peaceful, well established 19 acre garden, parts dating back to 1770s. This hidden gem boasts one of the largest collections of rhododendrons, azaleas, magnolias and camellias. Interspersed with mature and rare trees and complemented by a lake and cascading ponds. 6 acre arboretum, large lilac circle, wisteria pergola with views over Woodbury completes this family run treasure. Plant sale, teas and home bakes (cash only) open at other times. On site car parking. WC available, alcohol wipes and hand gel provided. Strictly no dogs. Wheelchair access to main parts of garden.

31 HALSCOMBE FARM
Halscombe Lane, Ide, Exeter, EX2 9TQ. Prof J Rawlings, jgshayward@tiscali.co.uk. *From Exeter go through Ide to mini r'about take 2nd exit and continue to L turn into Halscombe Lane.* **Visits by arrangement May to Sept. Adm £4, chd free.**
Farmhouse garden created over last 12 yrs. Large collection of old roses and peonies, long and colourful mixed borders, productive fruit cage and vegetable garden all set within a wonderful borrowed landscape.

32 HARBOUR LIGHTS
Horns Cross, Bideford, EX39 5DW. Brian & Faith Butler, harbourlightsgarden.org. *8m W of Bideford, 3m E of Clovelly. On A39 between Bideford & Clovelly, halfway between Hoops Inn & Bucks Cross. There will be a union jack flag & yellow arrow signs at the entrance.* **Sat 21, Sun 22 June (11-5.30). Adm £5, chd free. Cream teas, cakes, light lunches & wine.**
Last year of opening! ½ acre colourful garden with Lundy views. Garden of wit, humour, unusual ideas, installation art, puzzles, volcano and many surprises. Water features, shrubs, grasses in an unusual setting, bonsai and polytunnel, plus masses of colourful plants. You will never have seen a garden like this! Free leaflet. We like our visitors to leave with a smile. Child friendly. A 'must visit' unique and interactive garden with intriguing artwork of various kinds, original plantings and ideas.

GROUP OPENING

33 HAYTOR GARDENS
Haytor, Newton Abbot, TQ13 9XT. *300m from Haytor on road to Ilsington. From Bovey Tracey, turn L at red phone box. After approx 300m Brambly Wood signed on R. Garden 50m. Haytor House next to this turning. Parking 200m further down the road in field on L.* **Sat 17, Sun 18 May (11-5). Combined adm £8, chd free. Home-made teas at both gardens.**

BRAMBLY WOOD
Lindsay & Laurie Davidson, 01364 661474, lindsay.davidson2012@me.com.
Visits also by arrangement 19 May to 30 Sept for groups of 10 to 30.

HAYTOR HOUSE
Judy Gordon Jones & Hilary Townsend.

Haytor Gardens offers 2 very different gardens on the edge of Dartmoor with views across to Torbay and the Teign estuary. The 1 acre garden at Brambly Wood has been developed over the past 40 yrs with packed herbaceous borders, a pond and extensive planting of rhododendrons, azaleas and camellias looking their best in spring with tranquil seating areas throughout the garden. Visitors are also welcome to view the owners' studios showing artisan pottery and textile work. The ¼ acre garden at Haytor House was designed along more classical lines as a project for horticultural students in the 1930s and provides distinctive planting within partitioned areas. An inner walled garden with a folly leads to 3 further distinctive garden 'rooms' with a lily pond, raised beds, mixed herbaceous borders and large shrubs and acers among its many features.

34 HEATHERCOMBE
Manaton, nr Bovey Tracey, TQ13 9XE. Claude & Margaret Pike Woodlands Trust, 01626 354404, gardens@pike.me.uk, www.heathercombe.com. *7m NW of Bovey Tracey. From Bovey Tracey take scenic B3387 to Haytor/Widecombe. 1.7m past Haytor Rocks (before Widecombe Hill) turn R to Hound Tor & Manaton. 1.4m past Hound Tor turn L at Heatree Cross to Heathercombe.* **Sun 23 Mar, Sun 4, Sat 10, Sun 11, Sat 17, Sun 18 May (1.30-5.30). Every Tue to Sun 20 May to 1 June (1.30-5.30). Sat 7, Sun 8, Sat 14, Sun 15, Sat 21, Sun 22 June (11-5.30). Adm £6, chd free. Self service tea & coffee. Pls bring cash. Picnics welcome.** Visits also by arrangement 24 Mar to 31 Oct. Donation to Rowcroft Hospice.
Enjoy our daffodils, widespread bluebells, over 100 varieties of colourful rhododendrons, azaleas and many unusual specimen trees and shrubs, wildflower meadow and cottage garden. Take a leisurely stroll beside streams and ponds and through woodland, 'parkland', gardens and orchard, with many benches and summerhouses where you can sit and enjoy the tranquillity of Heathercombe's natural setting. Disabled reserved parking close to tea room & WC.

35 HIGH GARDEN
Chiverstone Lane, Kenton, Exeter, EX6 8NJ. Chris & Sharon Britton, www.highgardennurserykenton.wordpress.com. *5m S of Exeter on A379 Dawlish Rd. Leaving Kenton towards Exeter, L into Chiverstone Lane, 50yds along lane.* **Sun 1 June (2-5.30). Adm £5, chd free. Home-made teas.**
Stunning garden of over 4 acres. Huge range of trees, shrubs, perennials, grasses, climbers and exotics planted over past 18 yrs. Great use of foliage gives texture and substance as well as offsetting the floral display. 70 metre summer herbaceous border. Over 40 individual mixed beds surrounded by meandering grass walkways. Cut flower and vegetable gardens. Tropical border. Slightly sloping site but the few steps can be avoided.

Our donation to the Army Benevolent Fund supported 700 individuals with front line services and horticultural related grants in 2024.

36 HIGHER CHERUBEER
Dolton, Winkleigh, EX19 8PP. Jo & Tom Hynes, hynesjo@gmail.com. *2m E of Dolton. From the A3124 between Winkleigh & Dolton turn S towards Stafford Moor Fisheries, take 1st R signed Dolton, garden 500m on L.* **Fri 7, Fri 14, Sun 23 Feb (2-5). Adm £6, chd free. Home-made teas. 2026: Fri 6, Fri 13, Sat 21 Feb.** Visits also by arrangement 1 Feb to 23 Feb for groups of 10+.
1¾ acre country garden with gravelled courtyard and paths, raised beds, alpine house, lawns, herbaceous borders, woodland beds with naturalised cyclamen and snowdrops, kitchen garden with large greenhouse and orchard. Winter openings for National Collection of Cyclamen species, hellebores and over 400 snowdrop varieties.

37 HIGHER ORCHARD COTTAGE
Aptor, Marldon, Paignton, TQ3 1SQ. Mrs Jenny Saunders, 01803 551221, jennymsaunders@aol.com, www.facebook.com/HigherOrchardCottage. *1m SW of Marldon. A380 Torquay to Paignton. At Churscombe Cross r'about R for Marldon, L towards Berry Pomeroy, take 2nd R into Farthing Lane. Follow for exactly 1m. Turn R at NGS sign & follow signs for parking.* **Sat 7, Sun 8 June (11-5). Adm £6, chd free. Coffee avail in the morning. Tea & cakes avail from 2pm provided by Marldon Garden Club, if weather permits. Outside seating only.** Visits also by arrangement 30 Apr to 31 Aug for groups of up to 20. due to limited parking.
Two acre garden with generous colourful herbaceous borders, wildlife pond, specimen trees and shrubs, productive vegetable beds. Grass path walks through wildflower meadows in lovely countryside, art and craft installations by local artists and crafters.

38 ◆ HOTEL ENDSLEIGH
Milton Abbot, Tavistock, PL19 0PQ. Olga Polizzi, 01822 870000, hotelendsleigh@thepolizzicollection.com, thepolizzicollection.com/hotel-endsleigh/garden. *7m NW of Tavistock, midway between Tavistock & Launceston. From Tavistock,* take B3362 to Launceston. 7m to Milton Abbot then 1st L, opp school. From Launceston & A30, B3362 to Tavistock. At Milton Abbot turn R opp school. **For NGS: Tue 13 May (11-3). Adm £10, chd free.** For other opening times and information, please phone, email or visit garden website.
Set in 108 acres, Endsleigh was the last garden designed by Humphry Repton in 1814. Today the visitor can enjoy Repton's vision for the gardens with its streams, rills, pools and cascades splashing through valleys of Champion Trees. Closer to the house, a 'cottage orne' style hunting lodge, you will find a 100m herbaceous border, rose arch, yew walk, and Shell House.

39 NEW JOURNEY'S END
Green Lane, Ilsington, Newton Abbot, TQ13 9RB. Brian & Sheree Sedgbeer, 07967 915719, sheree2511@hotmail.co.uk. *½ m from HayTor Dartmoor. From Bovey Tracey take the road towards HayTor, go past Ullacombe Farm Shop. Turn 1st L into Green Lane, 300mts on the L well signed. What3words app: nightcap.fresh.binder.* **Sat 24, Sun 25 May, Sat 26, Sun 27 July (10-5). Adm £5, chd free. Tea, coffee & cake.** Visits also by arrangement 24 May to 26 July.
Journey's End has a 2 acre garden set up for wildlife. We have a Deer Leap, fox and hedgehog feeding stations, 5 seating areas, 3 mixed borders, a large spring fed pond with newts, frogs and lots of dragonflies etc. Two raised beds for herbs and vegetables, a buddleia walkway for butterflies to feast on. Visitors can also enjoy a Wildlife Photographic Exhibition.

40 KENTISBEARE HOUSE
Kentisbeare, Cullompton, EX15 2BR. Nicholas & Sarah Allan. *2m E of M5 J28 (Cullompton). Turn off A373 at Post Cross signed Kentisbeare. After ½ m past cricket field & main drive on R, entrance to car park is through next gate on R.* **Sat 21 June (11-4). Adm £6, chd free. Home-made teas.**
Surrounding the listed former Kentisbeare rectory, the gardens have been redesigned and planted by the present owners in recent years with various planting themes that complement the surrounding countryside. Formal beds, lake walk, kitchen garden and glasshouse, recently established wildflower meadow, orchard. Diverse and interesting collection of trees, shrubs and woodland plants.

41 KIA-ORA FARM & GARDENS
Knowle Lane, Cullompton, EX15 1PZ. Mrs M B Disney, 01884 32347, rosie@kia-orafarm.co.uk. *On W side of Cullompton & 6m SE of Tiverton. M5 J28, through town centre to r'about, 3rd exit R, top of Swallow Way turn L into Knowle Lane, garden beside Cullompton Rugby Club.* **Sun 20, Mon 21 Apr, Sun 4, Mon 5, Sun 18, Sun 25, Mon 26 May, Sun 8, Sun 22 June, Sun 6, Sun 20 July, Sun 3, Sun 24, Mon 25 Aug, Sun 7, Sun 21 Sept (2-5.30). Adm £5, chd free. Home-made teas. Teas, plants & sales not for NGS.** Visits also by arrangement Apr to Oct.
Charming, peaceful 10 acre garden with lawns, lakes and ponds. Water features with swans, ducks and other wildlife. Mature trees, shrubs, rhododendrons, azaleas, heathers, roses, herbaceous borders and rockeries. Interesting garden for all ages and surprises around every corner! To finish off, sit back and enjoy a traditional home-made Devonshire cream tea or choose from a wide selection of cakes.

42 NEW LARAPINTA
Bridgerule, Holsworthy, EX22 7EF. Mr Ian & Mrs Tracy Barker. *Borough Cross. From Holsworthy A3072 approx 5m. L at Redpost to Launceston approx 1.6 m From Launceston B3254 towards Bude. L Marhamchurch/Borough Cross. Follow Yellow signs. What3words app: inventors.releases.boosted* **Sun 11, Sun 25 May (11-4). Adm £5, chd free. Tea, coffee, squash & home-made cakes.**
Our garden is constantly evolving, but the main event is definitely spring when the wisteria bursts into life spanning approx 50 ft dripping with purple flowers and filling the garden with a wonderful scent. It is complemented by colourful borders, a Koi pond, fruit area, small woodland walk and a new Japanese area. We enjoy wonderful views to Bodmin and Widemouth from the top field.

43 NEW LARCOMBE FARMHOUSE
Diptford, Totnes, TQ9 7PD. Jim & Mandy Hanbury. *3m from A38. Turn off at Marley Head between South Brent & Buckfastleigh. Head towards Diptford & Morleigh. From Totnes 4m on Plymouth & Avonwick Rd turn L onto Diptford road.* **Sat 19, Sun 20 July (11-4). Adm £6, chd free. Pre-booking essential, please visit www.ngs.org.uk for information & booking. Tea, coffee & cake.**
A beautiful south facing cottage garden in the rural hamlet of Larcombe. In July expect to see an abundance of traditional cottage florals, roses and hydrangea in an undulating garden of about an acre with a stream running through it. Find some peaceful seating areas and enjoy exploring the features of this tranquil space.

🐕 ☕

44 LEE FORD
Knowle Village, Budleigh Salterton, EX9 7AJ. Mr & Mrs N Lindsay-Fynn, 01395 445894, crescent@leeford.co.uk, www.leeford.co.uk. *3½m E of Exmouth. For SatNav use postcode EX9 6AL.* **Visits by arrangement Apr to Sept for groups of 10 to 26. Adm £7.50, chd free. Discounted entry for 10 or more £7. Morning coffee & biscuits, morning & afternoon teas with selection of cakes or cream teas served in conservatory. Donation to Lindsay-Fynn Trust.**
Extensive, formal and woodland garden, largely developed in 1950s, but recently much extended with mass displays of camellias, rhododendrons and azaleas, inc many rare varieties. Traditional walled garden filled with fruit and vegetables, herb garden, bog garden, hydrangea collection, greenhouses for ornamentals, conservatory with pot plants inc pelargoniums, bougainvilleas and coleus. Direct access to pedestrian route and National Cycle Network Route 2 which follows old railway linking Exmouth to Budleigh Salterton. Woodland and formal garden are an ideal destination for cycle clubs or rambling groups. Formal gardens are lawn with paths. Moderately steep slope to woodland garden on tarmac drive with gravel paths in woodland.

♿ 🐕 🚌 ☕ 🪑

45 LEWIS COTTAGE
Spreyton, nr Crediton, EX17 5AA. Mr & Mrs M Pell and Mr R Orton, 07773 785939, rworton@mac.com, www.lewiscottageplants.co.uk. *5m NE of Spreyton, 8m W of Crediton. From Hillerton X keep stone X to your R. Drive approx 1½m, Lewis Cottage on L, drive down farm track. From Crediton follow A377 N. Turn L at Barnstaple X junction, then 2m from Colebrooke Church.* **Visits by arrangement 19 May to 20 Sept for groups of 12 to 24. Adm £5, chd free. Home-made teas.**
Four acre garden located on SW facing slope in rural mid Devon. Evolved primarily over last 30 yrs, harnessing and working with the natural landscape. Using informal planting and natural formal structures to create a garden that reflects the souls of those who garden in it. It is an incredibly personal space that is a joy to share. Spring camassia cricket pitch, rose garden, large natural dew pond, woodland walks, bog garden, hornbeam rondel, winter garden, hot and cool herbaceous borders, fruit and vegetable garden, outdoor poetry reading room and plant nursery selling plants mostly propagated from the garden.

🐕 ✱ ☕ »)

46 LINDEN RISE
Chapel Lane, Combe Martin, Ilfracombe, EX34 0HJ. Jenny Sheppard. *In Combe Martin High Street turn R, uphill, at old PO onto Chapel Lane, Linden Rise is on R opp Hollands park where parking is available.* **Sun 29 June (2-5). Adm £5, chd free. Tea, coffee & cake.**
In an area of outstanding natural beauty with countryside and sea views, 1½ acre garden of lawns, mature trees and shrubs, pergola, decorative ponds, small orchard and seasonal flower borders. Raffle with 1st prize: weekend in a holiday home. 2nd prize: 2 sessions with a personal trainer. 3rd prize: A bottle of champagne. Art exhibition by local artist. Vintage pre-loved clothes for sale. Wheelchair access to most areas.

♿ ✱ ☕

47 LITTLE ASH BUNGALOW
Fenny Bridges, Honiton, EX14 3BL. Helen & Brian Brown, 07833 247927, helenlittleash@hotmail.com, www.facebook.com/littleashgarden. *3m W of Honiton. Leave A30 at 1st turn off from Honiton 1m, Patteson's Cross from Exeter ½m & follow NGS signs.* **Sun 20 July, Sat 20 Sept (1-5). Adm £5, chd free. Tea, coffee & cake.** Visits also by arrangement May to Sept for groups of 10+. Easy access and parking for coaches.
Country garden of 1½ acres, packed with different and unusual bulbs, herbaceous perennials, trees, and shrubs. Designed for year-round interest, wildlife and owners' pleasure. Naturalistic planting in colour coordinated mixed borders, highlighted by metal sculptures, providing foreground to the view. Natural stream, pond and damp woodland area, mini wildlife meadows and raised gravel/alpine garden. Grass paths.

♿ 🐕 ✱ 🚌 ☕ »)

48 LITTLE DINWORTHY
Bradworthy, Holsworthy, EX22 7QX. Melanie & Simon Osborne, www.LittleDinworthy.co.uk. *3m NW of Bradworthy. In Bradworthy Square, head towards Meddon/Hartland on North Rd. Take 2nd L to Dinworthy at North Moor Cross, & follow yellow NGS signs. The lane entrance to Little Dinworthy will be seen on R.* **Sat 12, Sun 13 Apr, Sat 17, Sun 18 May (11-4.30). Adm £7, chd £2. Home-made teas. Children's woodland trail inc in entry.**
A wildlife garden and lake with young 20 yr old woodland. A developing garden with magnolias, flowering cherries and a variety of different specimen trees. Wild flowers abound encouraging multiple species in the many natural habitats. Around the house, box and yew topiary add a touch of fun and solidity to the profusion of growth. Meadow walks and children's woodland trail. Suitable footwear is recommended due to wet grass and some muddy paths. Dogs welcome on leads in garden and woodland. Tearoom in the stone studio barn with wood burner and WC.

🐕 ✱ ☕ 🪑 »)

In 2024, our donations to Carers Trust meant that 26,081 unpaid carers were supported across the UK.

49 ◆ LUKESLAND
Harford, Ivybridge, PL21 0JF. Mrs R Howell and Mr & Mrs J Howell, 01752 691749, lorna.lukesland@gmail.com, www.lukesland.co.uk. *10m E of Plymouth. Turn off A38 at Ivybridge. 1½m N on Harford rd, E side of Erme valley. Beware of using SatNavs as these can be very misleading.* **For opening times and information, please phone, email or visit garden website.**
24 acres of flowering shrubs, wild flowers and rare trees with pinetum in Dartmoor National Park. Beautiful setting of small valley around Addicombe Brook with lakes, numerous waterfalls and pools. Extensive and impressive collections of camellias, rhododendrons, azaleas and acers; also spectacular *Magnolia campbellii* and huge *Davidia involucrata*. Superb spring and autumn colour. Open Suns, Weds and BH (11-5) 16 March - 8 June and 5 Oct - 16 November. Adm £9, under 16s free. Group discount for parties of 20+. Group tours available by appointment. Children's trail.

🐕 ✿ ☕ 🚌 🍷

50 ◆ MARWOOD HILL GARDEN
Marwood, nr Guineaford, Barnstaple, EX31 4EB. Dr J A Snowdon, 01271 342528, info@marwoodhillgarden.co.uk, www.marwoodhillgarden.co.uk. *4m N of Barnstaple. Signed from A361 & B3230. Look out for brown signs. See website for map & directions. Coach & car park.* **For NGS: Fri 22 Aug (10-4.30). Adm £10, chd £5.50. Garden Tea Room offers light refreshments throughout the day, all home-made or locally sourced.** **For other opening times and information, please phone, email or visit garden website.**
Home to 4 National Plant Heritage collections and numerous Champion trees, these private valley gardens span over 20 acres. Showcasing three stunning lakes, sculptures, rare trees and shrubs, and colourful surprises throughout each season. The gardens, plant nursery and tearooms are a delight. Partial wheelchair access.

♿ 🐕 ✿ ☕ NPC 🍷

51 MIDDLE WELL
Waddeton Road, Stoke Gabriel, Totnes, TQ9 6RL. Neil & Pamela Millward, 01803 782981, neilandpam72@gmail.com. *A385 Totnes towards Paignton. Turn off A385 at Parkers Arms, Collaton St. Mary. After 1m, turn L at Four Cross. Parking at Sandridge Barton Winery.* **Sun 11 May (11-5). Adm £6, chd free. Home-made teas. Visits also by arrangement 1 Mar to 15 Nov. For groups over 20, pls discuss parking before coming.**
Tranquil 2 acre garden plus woodland and streams contain a wealth of interesting plants chosen for colour, form and long season of interest. Many seats from which to enjoy the sound of water. Interesting structural features (rill, summerhouse, pergola, cobbling, slate bridge). Heady mix of perennials, shrubs, bulbs, climbers and specimen trees. Architectural features complemented by striking planting, late colour, vegetable garden. Child friendly. Pls visit www.ngs.org.uk for pop-up openings. Mostly accessible by wheelchair.

♿ ☕ 🍷 🍴

52 2 MIDDLEWOOD
Cockwood, Exeter, EX6 8RN. Cliff & Chris Curd. *1m S of Starcross. A379 from Dawlish, R at Cofton Cross, passing Cofton Holidays. Middlewood ½m on R. A379 from Exeter, turn L at Cockwood Harbour. Turn R & pass The Ship. Park on Church Rd, not in Middlewood.* **Sat 28, Sun 29 June, Sat 5, Sun 6 July (1-5). Adm £6, chd free. Pre-booking essential, please visit www.ngs.org.uk for information & booking. Light refreshments.**
Entered via a courtyard, former market garden on north facing slope. Steep, uneven paths. View over the Exe. Food production and wildlife garden. Self-sufficiency ethos; greenhouse, polytunnel, fruit cage, raised veg beds, wild area, ponds, beehive. Productive fruit bushes and trees inc exotics. Steep access path. Not wheelchair accessible. Called 'inspirational' by visitors. Nearby are 2 well regarded country/harbourside pubs. Cockwood harbour 300 yds. Cofton Country Holidays with superb pool and restaurant open to the public, ½ a mile away.

🐕 ✿ ☕

53 ◆ MOTHECOMBE HOUSE
Mothecombe, Holbeton, Plymouth, PL8 1LA. Mr & Mrs J Mildmay-White, jmw@flete.co.uk, www.flete.co.uk/gardens. *12m E of Plymouth. From A379 between Yealmpton & Modbury turn S for Holbeton. Continue 2m to Mothecombe.* **For NGS: Sun 25 May (11-5). Adm £6, chd free. Home-made teas. For other opening times and information, please email or visit garden website.**
Queen Anne House (not open) with Lutyens additions and terraces set in private estate hamlet. Walled gardens, orchard with spring bulbs and magnolias, camellia walk leading through bluebell woods to streams and pond. Mothecombe Garden is managed for wildlife and pollinators. Bee garden with 250 lavenders in 16 varieties. New project to manage adjacent 6 acre meadow as a traditional wildflower pasture. Sandy beach at bottom of garden, unusual shaped large *Liriodendron tulipifera*. Tea, coffee and cake in the garden. Lunches at The Schoolhouse, Mothecombe village. Gravel paths, two slopes.

♿ 🐕 ☕ 🍷 🔊

54 THE MOUNT, DELAMORE
Cornwood, Ivybridge, PL21 9QP. Mr & Mrs Gavin Dollard, 01752 837605, nicdelamore@gmail.com. *Between Ivybridge & Yelverton. Pls park in car park for Delamore Park Offices not in village. From Ivybridge turn L at Xrds in Cornwood village, keep pub on L, follow wall on R to sharp R bend, turn R.* **Sat 15, Sun 16 Feb (10.30-3.30). Adm £7.50, chd free. Visits also by arrangement 1 Feb to 2 Mar.**
Welcome one of the first signs of spring by wandering through swathes of thousands of snowdrops in this lovely wood. Closer to the village than to Delamore Gardens, paths meander through a sea of these lovely plants, some of which are unique to Delamore and which were sold as posies to Covent Garden market as late as 2002. The Cornwood Inn in the village is now community owned. Main house and garden open for sculpture exhibition every day in May.

🐕 ✿ ☕ 🍴 🔊

55 NEW MOWHAY

Merton, Okehampton, EX20 3DS. Kerry & Neil Littleales, 07727 657246, kerrylittleales@outlook.com, www.facebook.com/makingmowhay. *10 mins S of Great Torrington. Access via the A386. From Torrington or Hatherleigh enter Merton village & follow yellow parking signs. Walk up the hill following yellow signs (approx 5 mins). What3words app: risen.navigate.rural.* **Sat 21, Sun 22 June, Sat 19, Sun 20 July, Sat 2, Sun 3 Aug (10-4). Adm £6, chd free. Home-made teas.** Visits also by arrangement 1 June to 15 Aug for groups of 10+. Adm price of £10 inc a hot/cold drink & home-made cake.
A developing 3 yr old, ¾ acre garden with countryside views featuring ornamental ponds linked by a waterfall. Planted in a broadly cottage style interspersed with some unusual plants. A variety of native/non native trees, a white garden, bonsai collection, roses, recycled structures/ornaments, areas managed for wildlife, a Courtyard garden, and vegetable patch. The garden is mainly laid to grass paths so if wet it will be more difficult for wheelchair users. The garden has gentle slopes and some gravel.

Sand Farmhouse

56 MUSBURY BARTON

Musbury, Axminster, EX13 8BB. Lt Col Anthony Drake. *3m S of Axminster off A358. Turn E into village, follow yellow signs. Garden next to church, parking for 12 cars, otherwise park on road in village.* **Sat 14, Sun 15 June (1-5). Adm £6, chd free. Home-made teas.**
This 6 acre garden surrounds a traditional Devon longhouse. It is planted with much imagination. There are many rare and unusual things to see, inc over 2000 roses. A stream in a steep valley tumbles through the garden. Visit the avenue of horse chestnuts and other interesting trees. There are lots of bridges and steps. Enjoy the many vantage points in this unusual garden with a surprise round every corner.

57 MUSSELBROOK COTTAGE GARDEN

Sheepwash, Beaworthy, EX21 5PE. Richard Coward, 01409 231677, coward.richard@sky.com. *1.3m N of Sheepwash. SatNav may be misleading. A3072 to Highampton. Through Sheepwash. 1.3m on L on track signed Lake Farm. A386 S of Merton take road to Petrockstow. Up hill opp, eventually L. After 350 yds turn R down track signed Lake Farm.* **Fri 18, Sat 19, Sun 20 Apr, Fri 9, Sat 10, Sun 11 May, Fri 13, Sat 14, Sun 15 June, Fri 18, Sat 19, Sun 20 July (11-4.30). Adm £5, chd free.**
One acre naturalistic/wildlife/ plantsman's/sensory garden on sloping site which is autism friendly. Year-round interest with rare and unusual plants. 13 ponds (koi and lilies), stream, Japanese garden, Mediterranean garden, wildflower meadow, massed bulbs. Ericaceous plants inc camellias, magnolias, rhododendrons, acers, hydrangeas. Grasses/bamboo. Clock golf. A mattock and serrated edged spade became essential for digging our rocky soil. Small nursery (inc aquatics, water lilies) can be visited by appointment.

58 OLD CREBOR FARM

Gulworthy, Tavistock, PL19 8HZ. Yvette & Rob Andrewartha, 01822 614355, ynndrwrth@gmail.com. *2½m SW from Tavistock. From Tavistock take the A390 towards Gunnislake. After 2½m turn L marked Buctor & Crebor. Past Buctor Farm next on R.* **Sat 24, Mon 26 May (10.30-4.30). Adm £7, chd free. Pre-booking essential, please visit www.ngs.org.uk for information & booking. Tea, coffee & cake.** Visits also by arrangement 27 May to 20 July for groups of 12+.
Traditional cottage planting around a pretty mid C18 farmhouse with stone walls, streams, bridges, ponds and terracing. Wonderful views of the valley and Dartmoor. Mature wood, orchard, wisteria, vine and walled garden. 3 acres of sloping wildflower meadows with mown paths for a stroll. Lots of spots to rest and enjoy. Supporting biodiversity and coping with climate change a focus.

59 OLD GLEBE
Eggesford, Chulmleigh, EX18 7QU. Joanne Court, 07983 736461, joanne.court0910@gmail.com. *20m NW of Exeter. Turn S off A377 at Eggesford Stn (halfway between Exeter & Barnstaple), cross railway tracks, drive uphill for ¾ m, turn R into bridlepath, drive is on L.* **Sat 17, Sun 18 May (1.30-5). Adm £6, chd free. Home-made teas.** Visits also by arrangement for groups of up to 25.
Seven acre gardens surrounding Georgian rectory. Magnificent display of rhododendrons and azaleas in May. Many interesting mature trees. Walled Long Border and new herbaceous beds. Productive 'no dig' kitchen and cutting garden. 'Messenger' greenhouse (1929) being restored. Small newly planted orchard. Wildflower meadow with mown paths to gazebo and suspension bridge. Series of ponds.

60 THE OLD RECTORY
Ashreigney, Chulmleigh, EX18 7NB. Jill & Gerrit Lemmens, 07482 533593, Jill.leppard@hotmail.co.uk. *Located 100 yds from Bush Corner (Red Post Box) on the road between Ashreigney & Chulmleigh. Take directions from Bush Corner to a public bridleway via a lane; the Old Rectory is the LH fork after 100 yds.* **Sat 31 May, Sun 1 June (11-4). Adm £5, chd free. Tea, coffee & cake.** Visits also by arrangement 1 May to 1 Sept for groups of 8 to 20.
One acre wildlife friendly garden incorporating traditional herbaceous borders with colour themes and seasonal interest, with pond and water features, wildflower meadow, glasshouse, raised vegetable beds; a developing arboretum of recently planted trees, foxglove and fern area and small jungle. Set within tranquil and rural mid Devon with adjoining fields and woodland.

61 1 PILTON LAWN
Pilton, Barnstaple, EX31 4AA. Louise Southworth, 07890 633568, kemp846@gmail.com. *Once in Raleigh Rd, take the 1st L, then immed R. Garden is at the end of this road. Free parking in Raleigh Rd, with some limited parking in parts of Pilton Lawn.* **Visits by arrangement 12 Apr to 19 Oct for groups of up to 20. Strictly no dogs. Cakes,** snacks & drinks.
This modest yet deceptively spacious garden, brings the indoors out, providing a relaxed and chilled vibe. Cornish slab pathways take you around the garden and features inc 'Alice' the boat! Carefully considered planting creates privacy and year-round interest. Enjoy refreshments served from the hand built shack bar and relax in the seating areas amidst the varied range of plants. Wheelchair access will allow the use of the shack bar and socialising area.

62 ♦ PLANT WORLD
St Marychurch Road, Newton Abbot, TQ12 4SE. Ray Brown, 01803 872939, info@plant-world-seeds.com, www.plant-world-gardens.co.uk. *2m SE of Newton Abbot. 1½ m from Penn Inn turn-off on A380. Follow brown tourist signs at end of A380 dual carriageway from Exeter.* **For opening times and information, please phone, email or visit garden website.**
Four acres of landscaped gardens with fabulous views, called Devon's 'Little Outdoor Eden'. Representing 5 continents, they feature an extensive collection of rare and exotic plants from around the world. With attractions for all ages in the gardens. Rare and unusual plant nursery. Attractive viewpoint café and picnic area. Special meal deals for coach parties. Please email for details. Open daily April to end September 9.30am – 430pm.

63 POUNDS
Hemyock, Cullompton, EX15 3QS. Diana Elliott, 07831 870855, shillingscottage@yahoo.co.uk, www.poundsfarm.co.uk. *8m N of Honiton. M5 J26. From ornate village pump, nr pub & church, turn up rd signed Dunkeswell Abbey. Entrance ½ m on R. Park in field. Short walk up to garden on R. Not far from Regency House.* **Fri 18 Apr (1-4). Sat 19 Apr (1-4), open nearby Regency House. Fri 30 May (1-4). Sat 31 May (1-4), open nearby Regency House. Adm £5, chd free. Home-made teas. Teas also at Regency House on Sat 19 Apr & Sat 31 May.**
Cottage garden of lawns, colourful borders and roses, set within low flint walls with distant views. Slate paths lead through an acer grove to a swimming pool, amid scented borders. Beyond lies a traditional ridge and furrow orchard, with a rose hedge, where apple, pear, plum and cherries grow among ornamental trees. Further on, an area of raised beds combine vegetables with flowers for cutting. Some steps, but most of the garden accessible via sloping grass, concrete, slate or gravel paths.

64 THE PRIORY
Priory Road, Abbotskerswell, Newton Abbot, TQ12 5PP. Priory residents. *2m SW of Newton Abbot town centre. A381 Newton Abbot/ Totnes Rd sharp L turn from NA road from Totnes. At mini-r'about in village centre turn L into Priory Rd.* **Sat 21, Sun 22 June (1-5). Adm £7, chd free. Tea, coffee & cake.**
The Priory is a Grade II* listed building, originally a manor house extended in Victorian times as a home for an Augustinian order of nuns, now a retirement complex of 44 apartments and cottages. The grounds extend to approx 5 acres and inc numerous flower borders, a wildflower meadow, an area of woodland with some interesting specimen trees, cottage gardens and lovely views. Small Mediterranean garden and area of individually owned raised beds and greenhouses. Wheelchair access difficult when wet and some slopes.

65 REGENCY HOUSE
Hemyock, EX15 3RQ. Mrs Jenny Parsons, 07772 998982, jenny.parsons@btinternet.com, www.regencyhousehemyock.co.uk. *8m N of Honiton. M5 J26/27. From Catherine Wheel pub & church in Hemyock take Dunkeswell-Honiton Rd. Entrance ½ m on R. Please do not drive on the long grass alongside the drive. Disabled parking (only) at house.* **Sat 19 Apr (2-5), open nearby Pounds. Sun 20 Apr (2-5). Sat 31 May (2-5), open nearby Pounds. Sun 1, Fri 13, Sat 14, Sun 22 June, Sat 18, Sun 19 Oct (2-5). Adm £8, chd free. Home-made teas.** Visits also by arrangement 1 Apr to 30 Oct for groups of 10 to 30. No large coach access. Jenny will accompany groups around the garden.
5 acre plantsman's garden approached across a little ford. Many interesting and unusual trees and shrubs. Visitors can try their hand at identifying plants with the very

DEVON

comprehensive and amusing plant list. Plenty of space to eat your own picnic. Walled vegetable and fruit garden, lake, ponds, bog plantings and sweeping lawns. Horses, Dexter cattle and Jacob sheep. A tranquil space to relax in. Gently sloping gravel paths give wheelchair access to the walled garden, lawns, borders and terrace, where teas are served.

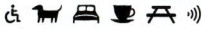

GROUP OPENING

66 ROSEBARN GARDENS
Exeter, EX4 6DY. *Situated in N of the City off Pennsylvania Rd & Rosebarn Lane nr the University. Rosebarn Ave can be reached on the 'P' bus from the City Centre.* **Sat 7, Sun 8 June (1-5). Combined adm £5, chd free. Home-made teas.**

7 ROSEBARN AVENUE
Steve & Sue Bloomfield.

16 ROSEBARN AVENUE
Chris & Jane Read.

25 ROSEBARN AVENUE
Jenny & Mike Phillips.

73 ROSEBARN LANE
Gerry & Lizzy Sones.

Featuring four gardens on a short walking circuit. No. 7 is a traditional 1950's garden with flower borders, pond, wild area and a recently redesigned and planted front garden. No.16 was redesigned in 2022. This landscaped garden features a kitchen garden, pond, summerhouse, herbaceous beds and native trees. No.25 is a typical townhouse garden featuring perennial borders, plant house, potting shed, veg plot and mature apple trees. No.73 has an interesting landscaped front garden and a tranquil mature back garden divided into 'rooms', a large pond and many specimen trees. Partial wheelchair access in one of the gardens.

In 2024 we awarded £232,000 in Community Garden Grants, supporting 89 community garden projects.

---

67 RUDD COTTAGE
Trentishoe, Parracombe, Barnstaple, EX31 4PL. Sally Oxenham & Jonathan Kelway, 01598 763366, sal.skipper2@gmail.com. *Valley 2m W of Hunters Inn, between Combe Martin & Lynmouth. Do not use SatNav. Take road from Rhydda Bank Cross which is 1m W of Hunters Inn, marked 'Unsuitable for Motors 1 Mile Ahead.' Drive 1m to end.* **Visits by arrangement 1 Apr to 10 Oct for groups of up to 15. Short notice can usually be accommodated. No min number. Adm £5, chd free. Tea, coffee & cake.**
In a peaceful Exmoor valley an informal garden blended into the surrounding rural and woodland landscape. 1 acre garden and 8 acres of fields, ponds and streams to explore, and picnic. Spring flowers followed by a succession of flowering trees and shrubs, mature rhododendrons, *Cornus kousa* and perennial plants. 30+ shrub roses. Beautiful setting and always something to see.

68 SAMLINGSTEAD
Near Roadway Corner, Woolacombe, EX34 7HL. Roland & Marion Grzybek, 01271 870886, roland135@msn.com. *1m outside Woolacombe. Stay on A361 all the way to Woolacombe. Passing through town head up Chalacombe Hill, L at T-junction, garden 150metres on L.* **Sat 22 Mar, Sat 19 July (10.30-3.30). Adm £5, chd free. Cream teas in 'The Swallows' a purpose built out-building. Hot sausage rolls (meat & vegetarian), cakes, tea, coffee & soft drinks.** Visits also by arrangement Mar to Sept.
Garden is within 2 mins of N Devon coastline and Woolacombe AONB. 6 distinct areas; cottage garden at front, patio garden to one side, swallows garden at rear, meadow garden, orchard and field (500m walk with newly planted hedgerow). Slightly sloping ground so whilst wheelchair access is available to most parts of garden certain areas may require assistance.

69 NEW SAND FARMHOUSE
Roncombe Lane, Sidbury, Sidmouth, EX10 0QN. Mrs Denise Lyon, 07975 647760, deniselyon@icloud.com, www.greenstudiogardendesign.com. *On the beautiful Roncombe Valley in the E Devon AONB. Recommended approach is from Sidbury Village end. We are 200m past Sand House. From Honiton, your app may take you L at the Hare & Hounds but ignore it & carry on down the hill.* **Visits by arrangement 3 May to 7 Sept for groups of 5+. Parking limited to 6 car spaces. Adm £5, chd free. Home-made teas.**
A wonderful vantage point over a hidden valley, this long, sloping, beautiful $^1/_3$ acre garden has been designed to delight. With long established trees such as *Cedrus deodora* and *Sequoiadendron giganteum* (we think...come and help us decide!) together with many newer trees and lush, varied planting, you might agree with my Dad: 'These borders are better than RHS Wisley!'.

70 SHERWOOD
Newton St Cyres, Exeter, EX5 5BT. Nicola Chambers, 07702 895435, nikkinew2012@yahoo.com, www.facebook.com/SherwoodGardensDevon. *2m SE of Crediton. Off A377 Exeter to Barnstaple road, $^3/_4$ m Crediton side of Newton St Cyres, signed Sherwood, entrance to drive in $1^3/_4$ m. Do not follow SatNav once on lane, don't fork R, just drive straight & keep going.* **Sun 25 May, Sun 22 June, Sun 26 Oct (1-5). Adm £7.50, chd £3. Pre-booking essential, please visit www.ngs.org.uk for information & booking. Cream teas.** Visits also by arrangement 1 Jan to 30 Dec.
23 acres with 2 steep wooded valleys. Wild flowers, spring bulbs, especially daffodils; extensive collections of magnolias, camellias, rhododendrons, azaleas, berberis, heathers, maples, cotoneasters, buddleias, hydrangeas, cornus and epimedium. Collections of magnolias, Knaphill azaleas and berberis. Regret no dogs. Suitable footwear required due to areas of steep terrain.

Journey's End

71 SIDBURY MILL
Burnt Oak, Sidbury, Sidmouth, EX10 0RE. **Helen Munday.** *On the A375 at the southern end of Sidbury village. From Honiton take A375 towards Sidmouth. In Sidbury pass the church on the L & continue for ½ m. Sidbury Mill on L. From Sidmouth take A375 towards Honiton. Sidbury Mill brown signs on R.* **Fri 20, Sun 22 June (11-4). Adm £5, chd free. Tea, coffee, cold drinks, sweet & savoury treats. Seating outside as well as under cover.**
The gardens and grounds of Sidbury Mill extend to 6 acres. As well as diversity of plants and trees, it is a haven for wildlife. The gardens range from a perennial, rose and shrub garden, a greenhouse and vegetable patch, to mature woodland through which the River Sid flows. A 'woodland walk' encompasses many elements of the gardens through which the visitor will appreciate the plants and wildlife. The needs of a water mill are a great influence on the gardens and grounds of Sidbury Mill, inc the river and various leats. The water wheel is an integral part of the back garden. Sidbury Mill is one of the last working water mills in the south-west, milling wheat grown in our nearby field. The garden areas with the floral borders, greenhouse and vegetable gardens are accessible. The woodland walk is mainly flat with grass paths.

72 SOCKS ORCHARD
Smallridge, Axminster, EX13 7JN. **Michael & Hilary Pritchard.** *2m from Axminster. From Axminster on A358 L at Weycroft Mill T-lights. Pass Ridgeway Hotel on L. Continue on lane for ½ m. Park in field opp.* **Fri 27, Sat 28, Sun 29 June (1-5). Adm £5, chd free. Home-made teas.**
1 acre plus plantaholic's garden designed for year-round interest and colour. Many specimen trees, large collection of herbaceous plants, over 200 roses, woodland shrubs, dahlias, small orchard, vegetable patch. Steep bank with trees, shrubs and wild flowers. Viewpoint at top. Alpine troughs and alpine house. Scented leaf pelargonium and succulents collections. Chickens. Wheelchair access to most of garden.

73 SOUTH WOOD FARM
Cotleigh, Honiton, EX14 9HU. **Professor Clive Potter.** *3m NE of Honiton. From Honiton head N on A30, take 1st R past Otter Valley Field Kitchen layby. Follow for 1m. Go straight over Xrds and take first L. Entrance after 1m on R.* **Sat 31 May, Sun 1 June (2-5). Adm £7, chd free. Tea, coffee & cake.**
Designed by renowned Arne Maynard around C17 thatched farmhouse, country garden exemplifying how contemporary design can be integrated into a traditional setting. Herbaceous borders, roses, yew topiary, knot garden, wildflower meadows, wildlife ponds, orchards, lean-to greenhouses and a mouthwatering kitchen garden create an unforgettable sense of place. Gravel pathways, cobbles and steps.

74 SOUTHCOMBE BARN
Widecombe-in-the-Moor, Newton Abbot, TQ13 7TU. **Tom Dixon & Vashti Cassinelli,** info@southcombebarn.com, www.southcombebarn.com. *6m W of Bovey Tracey. B3387 from Bovey Tracey after village church take road SW for 400yds then sharp R signed Southcombe, after 200yds pass C17 farmhouse & park on L.* **Every Fri 6 June to 27 June (11-3). Adm £5, chd free. Home-made teas.**
Southcombe Barn gardens comprises 5 acres of vibrant wildflower meadows and flowering trees with mown grass paths running alongside a gently babbling stream. There is a new apothecary garden on the sheltered hillside with medicinal, dye, culinary, tea plants and herbs and now buzzing with new wildlife. An exciting assortment of fresh apothecary herbal teas will be on offer. Art exhibition open in the gallery.

75 SPRING LODGE
Kenton, Exeter, EX6 8EY. David & Ann Blandford. *Between Lyson & Oxton. Head for Lyson then Oxton.* **Fri 22 Aug (10-4). Adm £5, chd £1. Pre-booking essential, please visit www.ngs.org.uk for information & booking. Teas, coffee, soft drinks, cakes & biscuits.**
Originally part of the Georgian pleasure gardens to Oxton House, the garden at Spring Lodge boasts a hermit's cave, dramatic cliffs and a stream which runs under the house. Built in the quarry of the big house this $\frac{1}{2}$ acre garden is on many levels, with picturesque vistas and lush planting. Pre booking essential due to restricted parking.

76 SQUIRRELS
98 Barton Road, Torquay, TQ2 7NS. Graham & Carol Starkie, 01803 329241, calgra@talktalk.net. *5m S of Newton Abbot. From Newton Abbot take A380 to Torquay. After ASDA store on L turn L at T-lights up Old Woods Hill. 1st L into Barton Rd. Bungalow 200yds on L. Also could turn by B&Q. Parking nearby.* **Sat 12, Sun 13 July (2-5). Adm £5, chd free. Home-made teas. Visits also by arrangement 25 June to 4 Aug. Parking at weekends in trading estate round the corner.**
Plantsman's small town environmental garden, landscaped with small ponds with ducks and 7ft waterfall. Interlinked through abutilons to Moroccan, Japanese, Italianate, Spanish, tropical areas. Specialising in fruit peaches, figs, kiwi. Tender plants inc bananas, tree fern, Brugmansia, many lantanas. Collection of dahlias, abutilons, bougainvillea. Environmental and superclass gold medal winners. 27 hidden rainwater storage tanks. Advice on free electricity from solar panels and solar hot water heating and fruit pruning. Three sculptures, topiary birds and balls. Huge 20ft Torbay palm. 15ft tropical abutilons. New Moroccan and Spanish courtyard with succulents and bougainvillea.

77 STONE FARM
Alverdiscott Rd, Bideford, EX39 4PN. Mr & Mrs Ray Auvray, 01237 421420, rayauvray@icloud.com. *1$\frac{1}{2}$m from Bideford towards Alverdiscott. From Bideford cross river using Old Bridge & turn L onto Barnstaple Rd. 2nd R onto Manteo Way & 1st L at r'about.* **Sat 14, Sun 15 June, Sat 9, Sun 10 Aug (2-5). Adm £5, chd free. Tea, coffee & cake. Visits also by arrangement May to Aug for groups of 10+. We offer a briefing on organic gardening methods and recommended plants.**
Two acre country garden managed by head gardener, Fiona Thompson, with striking herbaceous borders, dry stone terracing, white garden, Japanese themed garden, and "hot" garden. Extensive Soil Association certified organic vegetable gardens with polytunnels and greenhouse and our $\frac{1}{3}$ acre walled garden. Orchard with traditional apple, pear and plum trees. New woodland meadow area and herb garden. Some gravel paths but wheelchair access to whole garden with some help.

78 STONELANDS HOUSE
Stonelands Bridge, Dawlish, EX7 9BL. Mr Kerim Derhalli (Owner) Mr Saul Walker (Head Gardener), 07815 807832, saulwalkerstonelands@outlook.com. *Outskirts of NW Dawlish. From A380 take junction for B3192 & follow signs for Teignmouth, after 2m L at Xrds outside Luscombe Hill, further 2m, main gate on L.* **Visits by arrangement 1 Apr to 27 June for groups of 10 to 20. Tues-Thurs weekdays only. Adm £7, chd free. Tea, coffee & cake. Please book refreshments through Head Gardener, separate payment on the day.**
Beautiful 12 acre pleasure garden surrounding early C19 property designed by John Nash. Many mature specimen trees, shrubs and rhododendrons, large formal lawn, recently landscaped herbaceous beds, vegetable garden, woodland garden, orchard with wildflower meadow and riverside walk. An atmospheric and delightful horticultural secret. Wheelchair access to lower area of gardens. Paths through woodland, meadow and riverside walk may be unsuitable for wheelchairs

79 SUTTON MEAD
Moretonhampstead, TQ13 8PW. Edward & Miranda Allhusen, 01647 440296, miranda@allhusen.co.uk, www.facebook.com/suttonmeadgarden. *$\frac{1}{2}$m N of Moretonhampstead on A382. R at r'about.* **Fri 16, Sat 17, Sun 18 May, Fri 5, Sat 6, Sun 7 Sept (12-5). Adm £6, chd free. Home-made teas. Hot soup & savoury scones. Visits also by arrangement.**
A large garden with splendid views of Dartmoor. Remote yet only a dozen miles from Exeter, Okehampton and Newton Abbot. A constantly colourful garden. May numerous varieties of rhododendron, azalea and late spring bulbs. September hydrangeas, dahlias, agapanthus and much more. Mature orchard, productive vegetable garden, substantial tree planting, croquet lawn. Wander through tranquil woodland. Lawns surround a granite lined pond with a seat at the water's edge. Elsewhere unusual planting, grasses, bog garden, granite walls, rill fed pond, secluded seating and an unusual concrete gothic greenhouse all contribute to a garden of variety that has been developed and constructed over 45 yrs by the current owners. Plants from the garden for sale and teas, cream or otherwise, are a must. Dogs on leads welcome. Partial access, there is a gravel drive.

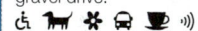

---

70 inpatients and their families are being supported at the newly opened Horatio's Garden Northern Ireland, thanks to National Garden Scheme donations.

154 DEVON

80 NEW TAMAR HOUSE
Bridgerule, Holsworthy, EX22 7EJ. Mr Paul Rutherford, 07711 564072, ozoneeng@aol.com. *11 mins W of Holsworthy. Tamar House is opp the Bridge Inn, Bridgerule. What3words app: somewhere.hotspots.tank.* **Visits by arrangement Apr to Sept for groups of up to 6. Adm £5, chd free. Light refreshments. Japanese cold drinks and snacks.**
This small Japanese style garden inc many Japanese acer palmatum shrubs surrounded by rocks, gravel pathways, bamboo and many other plants indigenous to the Nippon Islands. The garden is divided into rooms which inc a dry garden, water features, a koi pond area, a moss garden, a specimen bonsai area, a Shinto shrine and a raised decking looking out over the Tamar River. The owner of the garden has spent many years in Japan and in 2021 started to build a Zen garden based around wabi sabi which can be defined as "beauty in imperfection" remembering that nothing lasts, nothing is finished, and nothing is perfect.

GROUP OPENING

81 TEIGNMOUTH GARDENS
Lower Coombe Cottage, Coombe Lane, Teignmouth, TQ14 9EX. *½m from Teignmouth town centre. 5m E of Newton Abbot. 11m S of Exeter. Purchase ticket for all gardens at 1st garden visited, a map will be provided showing location of gardens & parking.* **Sat 14, Sun 15 June (1-5). Combined adm £6, chd free. Home-made teas at Lower Coombe Cottage.**

21 GORWAY
Mrs Christine Richman.

26 HAZELDOWN ROAD
Mrs Ann Sadler.

LOWER COOMBE COTTAGE
Tim & Tracy Armstrong.

THE ORANGERY
Teignmouth Town Council.

65 TEIGNMOUTH ROAD
Mr Terry Rogers.

Five gardens, inc the beautifully restored Orangery, are opening in the picturesque coastal town of Teignmouth. A wide range of garden styles and sizes can be explored this year from very small but inspiring manicured gardens to large wildlife havens. Features inc courtyards, greenhouses, pollinator friendly planting, exotic plants, streams and ponds, fruit and vegetable beds and some stunning sea views. Tickets are valid for both days. Partial wheelchair access at some gardens.

82 TORVIEW
44 Highweek Village, Newton Abbot, TQ12 1QQ. Ms Penny Hammond, penny.hammond2@btinternet.com. *On N of Newton Abbot accessed via A38. From Plymouth: A38 to Goodstone, A383 past Hele Park & L onto Mile End Rd. From Exeter: A38 to Drumbridges then A382 past Forches Cross & take next R. Please park in nearby streets.* **Fri 30, Sat 31 May, Sun 1 June (12-5). Adm £6, chd free. Tea, coffee & cake. Visits also by arrangement 1 Apr to 25 Oct for groups of 10 to 20.**
Owned by two semi-retired horticulturists: Mediterranean formal front garden with wisteria clad Georgian house and small alpine house. Rear courtyard with tree ferns, pots/troughs, lean-to 7m conservatory with tender plants and climbers. Steps to 30x20m walled garden - flowers, vegetables and trained fruit. Shade tunnel of woodland plants. Many rare and unusual plants.

83 NEW TRUANTS COTTAGE
Zeal Monachorum, Crediton, EX17 6DF. Jackie Watson, 07979 267009, Jacquelinewatsondevon@gmail.com. *Village between Crediton & Okehampton. From A3072, turn L after church in village centre. Truants on R near bottom of hill. From Bow, just after R turn to Waie Inn, go a few yards up hill, on L. Parking at Waie Inn. Map can be emailed on request.* **Visits by arrangement 5 May to 31 July for groups of up to 8. Adm £5, chd free. Cream teas.**
Listed thatched cottage with pretty garden in village conservation area. ⅓ acre inc variety of roses, colourful mixed herbaceous borders, lawns, wild grasses, wildlife pond with lilies, spring bluebells and range of specimen trees. View of garden 'rooms' from patio. Cream teas in garden or indoors. Limited parking in drive, also at nearby Waie Inn (lunch/dinner available).

84 UPPER GORWELL HOUSE
Goodleigh Rd, Barnstaple, EX32 7JP. Dr J A Marston, www.gorwellhousegarden.co.uk. *¾m E of Barnstaple centre on Bratton Fleming road. Drive entrance between 2 lodges on L coming uphill (Bear St) approx ¾m from Barnstaple centre. Take R fork at end of long drive. New garden entrance to R of house up steep slope.* **Sun 23 Mar, Sun 27 Apr, Sun 25 May, Sun 22 June, Sun 20 July, Sun 14 Sept (2-6). Adm £7.50, chd free. Cream teas. Visitors are welcome to bring their own picnics.**
Created mostly since 1979, this 4 acre garden overlooking the Taw estuary has a benign microclimate which allows many rare and tender plants to grow and thrive, both in the open and in the walled garden. Several strategically placed follies complement the enclosures and vistas within the garden. Mostly wheelchair access but some very steep slopes at first to get into garden.

85 WESTON HOUSE
Boughmore Road, Sidmouth, EX10 8SJ. Anna & Peter Duncan, 07753 818454, duncannab@gmail.com, instagram.com/weston_house_sidmouth. *A3052: At Bowd Inn turn onto A3176 After 1.7m R Broadway (NOT Bickwell Lane) 3rd L Bickwell Valley. Sharp R Boughmore Rd. We're immed L of Faded Yellow Grit Bin. Street Parking only.* **Sat 12, Sun 13 Apr, Sat 17, Sun 18 May, Sat 9, Sun 10 Aug (2-5). Adm £5, chd free. Tea, coffee & cake. Visits also by arrangement 1 Mar to 30 Aug for groups of 10 to 25.**
This stunning garden, covering an acre, is a delightful surprise to visit. It is steeply sloping (lots of steps!) east-facing, providing ever-changing views across the valleys and towards the sea with lots of seating areas. A garden of a plantaholic.

86 WHIDDON GOYLE
Whiddon Down, Okehampton, EX20 2QJ. Mr & Mrs Lethbridge, 07561 440319, cillethbridge@aol.com, quarryflowers.co.uk. *From Whiddon Down, follow signs for Okehampton, take 2nd exit in r'about. Whiddon Goyle is on L, signed.* **Sat 14, Sun 15 June (11-4). Adm £6, chd free. Tea, coffee & cake. Visits also by**

Ashridge Court

arrangement 14 June to 30 Sept. Whiddon Goyle enjoys stunning views over Dartmoor and sits 1000 ft above sea level. Built in 1930s it is cleverly designed to protect its 2 acre garden against the Dartmoor weather. It enjoys many features inc a rockery, croquet lawn, rose garden, herbaceous borders, ponds, a newly developed cut flower garden which supplies seasonal blooms, along with a pair of majestic monkey trees. Access is via a gravelled driveway on a slope.

87 WHITSTONE FARM
Whitstone Lane, Bovey Tracey, TQ13 9NA. Katie & Alan Bunn, 01626 832258, klbbovey@gmail.com. ½m N of Bovey Tracey. From A382 turn L opp golf club, after ⅓m L at swinging sign 'Private road leading to Whitstone'. Follow NGS signs. **Sun 27 Apr, Sun 27 July (2-5). Adm £6,** chd free. Pre-booking essential, please visit www.ngs.org.uk for information & booking. Tea & home-made cakes, gluten free option. Visits also by arrangement 19 Jan to 19 Oct for groups of up to 25. Lane is only accessible by car or mini bus NOT by coach. Donation to Plant Heritage.

Nearly 4 acres of steep hillside garden with stunning views of Haytor and Dartmoor. Snowdrops start in January followed by bluebells throughout the garden. Arboretum planted 45 yrs ago, over 200 trees from all over the world inc magnolias, camellias, acers, alders, betula, davidias and sorbus. Always colour in the garden and wonderful tree bark. Major plantings of rhododendrons and hydrangeas. Late flowering Eucryphias (National Collection). Display of architectural and metal sculptures and ornaments. Partial access to lower terraces for wheelchair users.

88 NEW WILLOW GLADE FARM
Ashwater, Beaworthy, EX21 5DL. Mr K & Mrs M Drowne. *1m off A3079 nr Halwill Junction. From A3072, turn towards Okehampton at Dunsland Cross, onto the A3079. Turn R at Morecombe Cross, in 1m Willow Glade is on R. What3words app: scoots.marinated.detail.* **Sat 12, Sun 13 July (11-4). Adm £5, chd free. Tea, coffee & cake.**
The garden has been in development since 2020, and is divided into 2 main areas. There is a vegetable plot, which uses traditional gardening methods with elements of permaculture and no dig. From here there is a path which takes you through a more naturalised garden with a small woodland walk, pond area, apple orchard and wildflower meadow.

DORSET

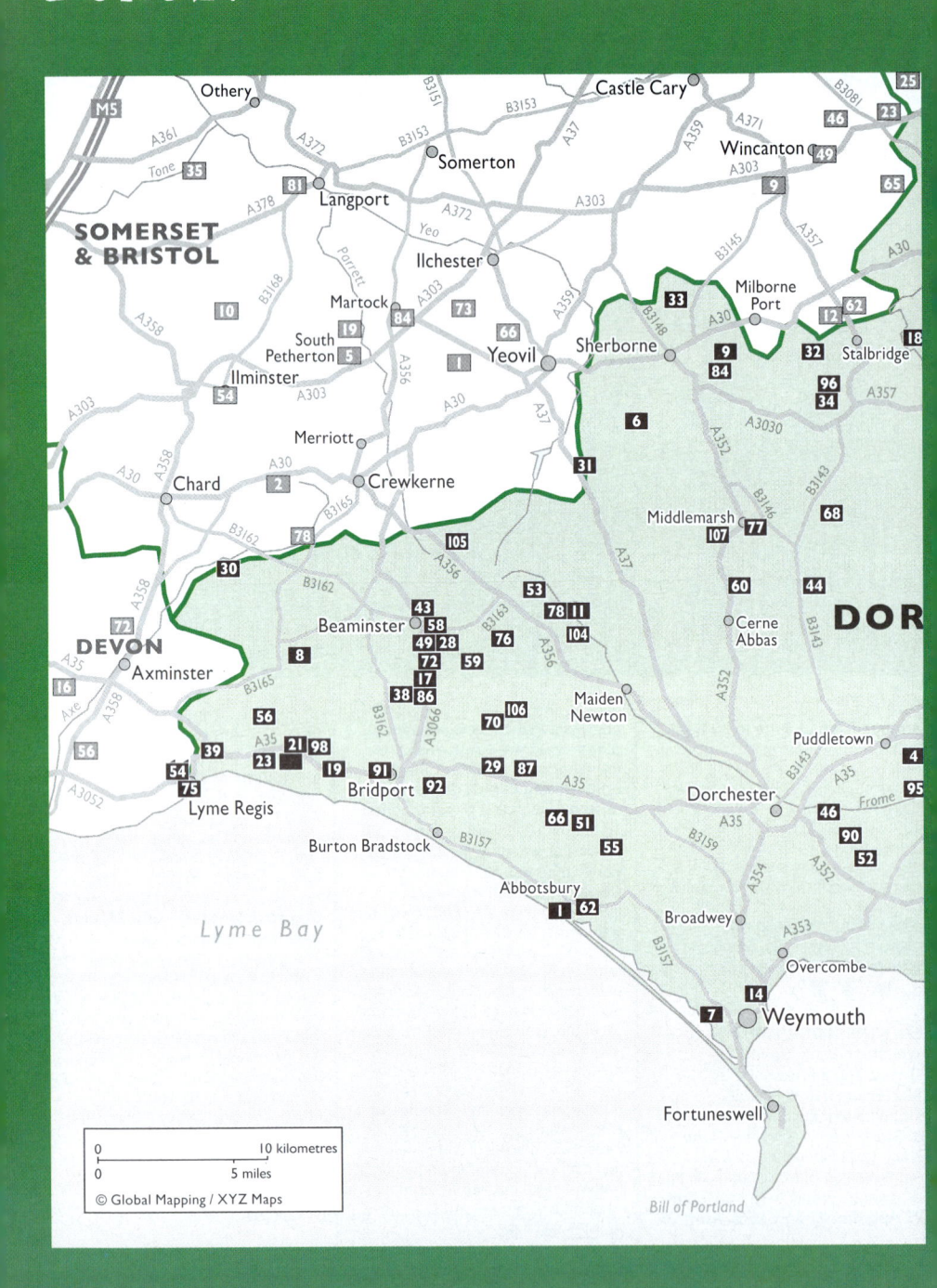

DORSET 157

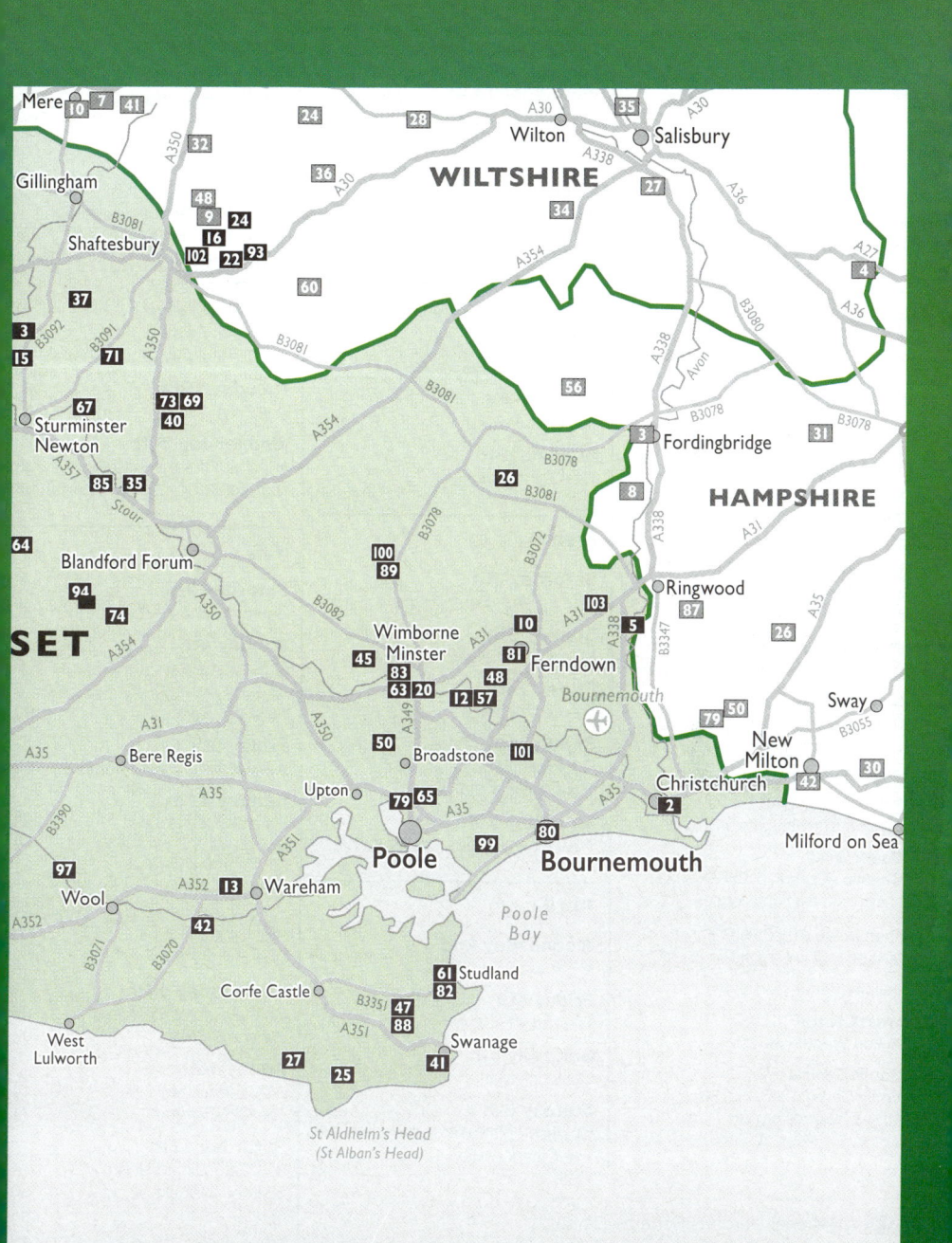

VOLUNTEERS

County Organiser & Social Media
Alison Wright 01935 83652
alison.wright@ngs.org.uk

County Treasurer
Richard Smedley 01202 528286
richard@carter-coley.co.uk

Publicity
Cathy Dalton 07712 139766
cathy.dalton@ngs.org.uk

Booklet Editor
Felicity Perkin 01297 480930
felicity.perkin@ngs.org.uk

Photographer
Christopher Middleton
07771 596458
christophermiddleton@mac.com

Assistant County Organisers

Central East
Joanna Mains 01747 839831
mainsmanor@tiscali.co.uk

North East
Jules Attlee 07837 289964
julesattlee@icloud.com

South East
Mary Angus 01202 872789
mary@gladestock.co.uk

Phil Broomfield 07810 646123
phil.broomfield@ngs.org.uk

North West Central
Suzie Baker 07786 695150
suzie.baker@ngs.org.uk

South East Central
Pip Davidson 07765 404248
pip.davidson@ngs.org.uk

South West
Christine Corson 01308 863923
christine.corson@ngs.org.uk

Trish Neale 01308 863790
trish.neale@ngs.org.uk

Felicity Perkin (see above)

West Central
Alison Wright (see above)

South Central
Emily Cave 01308 482265
emily.cave@ngs.org.uk

@National Gardens Scheme Dorset
@ngsdorset

OPENING DATES

All entries subject to change.
For latest information check
www.ngs.org.uk
Extended openings are shown at the beginning of the month.

Map locator numbers are shown to the right of each garden name.

February

Snowdrop Openings

Friday 7th
The Old Vicarage 71

Friday 14th
The Old Vicarage 71

Sunday 16th
The Old Vicarage 71

March

Saturday 8th
Manor Farm, Hampreston 57

Sunday 9th
Manor Farm, Hampreston 57

Friday 14th
The Old Vicarage 71

Sunday 16th
Frankham Farm 31
The Old Vicarage 71

Thursday 20th
♦ Athelhampton House Gardens 4

April

Wednesday 2nd
♦ Edmondsham House 26

Friday 4th
The Old Vicarage 71

Saturday 5th
Chideock Manor 19

Sunday 6th
Chideock Manor 19
The Old Vicarage 71

Wednesday 9th
♦ Edmondsham House 26

Wednesday 16th
♦ Edmondsham House 26

Monday 21st
♦ Edmondsham House 26

Wednesday 23rd
♦ Edmondsham House 26

Thursday 24th
Slape Manor 86

Saturday 26th
Folly Farm Cottage 29

Sunday 27th
Broomhill 11
Folly Farm Cottage 29
Frankham Farm 31
The Old Rectory, Litton Cheney 66

Tuesday 29th
Horn Park 43

Wednesday 30th
♦ Edmondsham House 26
The Old Rectory, Litton Cheney 66

May

Saturday 3rd
Canford School Arboretum 12

Sunday 4th
Annalal's Gallery 2
22 Avon Avenue 5
Western Gardens 99

Friday 9th
♦ Museum of East Dorset 63

Sunday 11th
Little Benville House 53
Pugin Hall 78
NEW 10 Ryan Close 81
The Secret Garden at Serles House 83
Slape Manor 86
Wincombe Park 102

Wednesday 14th
Oakdale Library Gardens 65
Wincombe Park 102

Friday 16th
24 Carlton Road North 14
The Old Vicarage 71

Saturday 17th
24 Carlton Road North 14
22 Lancaster Drive 50
Myrtle Cottage 64
Well Cottage 98

DORSET 159

Sunday 18th
Bembury Farm 6
24 Carlton Road North 14
22 Lancaster Drive 50
Myrtle Cottage 64
The Old Vicarage 71
The Secret Garden at Serles House 83
Well Cottage 98

Monday 19th
24 Carlton Road North 14

Wednesday 21st
Bembury Farm 6

Friday 23rd
Pipsford Farm 76

Saturday 24th
NEW Karmacations 44
Knitson Old Farmhouse 47
NEW Muddy Patches 62
NEW The Old Vicarage 70
NEW The Stables 88

Sunday 25th
Annalal's Gallery 2
NEW Karmacations 44
Knitson Old Farmhouse 47
NEW Little Fields 54
NEW Muddy Patches 62
The Old Rectory, Pulham 68
NEW The Old Vicarage 70
NEW The Stables 88
Staddlestones 89
White House 100

Monday 26th
Knitson Old Farmhouse 47
NEW The Stables 88
Staddlestones 89
White House 100

Wednesday 28th
Deans Court 20

Thursday 29th
♦ Mapperton House, Gardens & Wildlands 59
The Old Rectory, Pulham 68
Slape Manor 86

Saturday 31st
NEW Grange Cottage 34
Wagtails 96

June

Every Wednesday to Wednesday 18th
East End Farm 24

Sunday 1st
Frankham Farm 31
NEW Grange Cottage 34
Wagtails 96

Wednesday 4th
Chantry Farm 18

Thursday 5th
Bettiscombe Manor 8

Saturday 7th
Philipston House 74
Utopia 95

Sunday 8th
22 Avon Avenue 5
Broomhill 11
The Old School House 69
Penmead Farm 73
Pugin Hall 78
NEW 10 Ryan Close 81
Utopia 95

Tuesday 10th
♦ Holme for Gardens 42

Wednesday 11th
♦ Careys Secret Garden 13
Oakdale Library Gardens 65

Thursday 12th
Eastington Farm 25
Encombe House 27
Farrs 28
The Old School House 69
Penmead Farm 73

Friday 13th
♦ Museum of East Dorset 63

Saturday 14th
Chideock Manor 19
Yew Tree House 107

Sunday 15th
The Chantry 17
Chideock Manor 19
Hanford School 35
Hingsdon 38
Manor Farm, Hampreston 57
Yew Tree House 107

Tuesday 17th
♦ Littlebredy Walled Gardens 55

Thursday 19th
Parnham House 72

Saturday 21st
♦ Athelhampton House Gardens 4
The Hollow, Blandford Forum 40
NEW Stoneleigh 92
Wytherston Farm 106

Sunday 22nd
Annalal's Gallery 2
The Hollow, Blandford Forum 40
NEW Stoneleigh 92
NEW Tulip Tree 93
Western Gardens 99
Wyke Farm 105

Tuesday 24th
Horn Park 43
♦ Littlebredy Walled Gardens 55

Wednesday 25th
Deans Court 20
The Hollow, Blandford Forum 40
Knitson Old Farmhouse 47
NEW The Stables 88

Thursday 26th
Knitson Old Farmhouse 47
NEW The Stables 88

Sunday 29th
Black Shed 9
Pugin Hall 78
Stillpoint Garden & Nursery 91
NEW Wraxall Manor 104

July

Every Wednesday
The Hollow, Swanage 41

Friday 4th
Stafford House 90

Saturday 5th
Lower Abbotts Wootton Farm 56
NEW 8 Manor Gardens 58
NEW Tumblins 94

Sunday 6th
Lower Abbotts Wootton Farm 56
NEW 8 Manor Gardens 58
The Old Rectory, Litton Cheney 66
Slape Manor 86
NEW Tumblins 94

Monday 7th
NEW Tumblins 94

Friday 11th
♦ Museum of East Dorset 63

Saturday 12th
Knowle Cottage 49
NEW 11 School Lane 82

Sunday 13th
22 Avon Avenue 5
Broomhill 11
NEW Dedley Farm 21
♦ Hogchester Farm 39
Knowle Cottage 49
Manor Farm, Hampreston 57
NEW 11 School Lane 82

Thursday 17th
Knitson Old Farmhouse 47
NEW The Stables 88

DORSET

Friday 18th
Knitson Old Farmhouse	47
NEW The Stables	88

Saturday 19th
Hilltop	37

Sunday 20th
Hilltop	37
Langebride House	51
1C Rectory Road	79

Saturday 26th
Glenholme Herbs	33
Hilltop	37
NEW Karmacations	44

Sunday 27th
Annalal's Gallery	2
Black Shed	9
Glenholme Herbs	33
Hilltop	37
NEW Karmacations	44

August

Every Wednesday
The Hollow, Swanage	41

Sunday 3rd
Manor Farm, Hampreston	57
The Old Rectory, Pulham	68

Thursday 7th
Broomhill	11
The Old Rectory, Pulham	68

Saturday 9th
105 Woolsbridge Road	103

Sunday 10th
22 Avon Avenue	5
Hilltop	37
Shillingstone Gardens	85
Stillpoint Garden & Nursery	91
105 Woolsbridge Road	103

Saturday 16th
Brook View Care Home	10

Sunday 17th
Hilltop	37
1C Rectory Road	79

Saturday 23rd
Ardhurst	3
Donhead Hall	22
20 Wicket Road	101

Sunday 24th
Annalal's Gallery	2
Ardhurst	3
Castle Rings	16
20 Wicket Road	101

Monday 25th
20 Wicket Road	101

Saturday 30th
Pugin Hall	78

Sunday 31st
Pugin Hall	78

September

Tuesday 2nd
◆ Knoll Gardens	48

Friday 5th
◆ Bennetts Water Gardens	7

Saturday 6th
NEW Muddy Patches	62

Sunday 7th
22 Avon Avenue	5
Dorset Dahlias	23
Manor Farm, Hampreston	57
NEW Morval	61
NEW Muddy Patches	62

Tuesday 9th
◆ Holme for Gardens	42

Saturday 13th
The Potting Shed	77

Sunday 14th
Annalal's Gallery	2
Pugin Hall	78

Friday 19th
◆ Knoll Gardens	48

Monday 22nd
◆ Athelhampton House Gardens	4

Wednesday 24th
Farrs	28

Thursday 25th
Slape Manor	86

October

Wednesday 1st
◆ Edmondsham House	26

Sunday 5th
Slape Manor	86

Wednesday 8th
◆ Edmondsham House	26

Sunday 12th
Frankham Farm	31

Wednesday 15th
◆ Edmondsham House	26

Wednesday 22nd
◆ Edmondsham House	26

November

Sunday 23rd
Annalal's Gallery	2

December

Sunday 7th
Annalal's Gallery	2

Saturday 20th
◆ Athelhampton House Gardens	4

February 2026

Friday 6th
The Old Vicarage	71

Sunday 8th
The Old Vicarage	71

Sunday 15th
The Old Vicarage	71

By Arrangement

Arrange a personalised garden visit with your club, or group of friends, on a date to suit you. See individual garden entries for full details.

Bembury Farm	6
Broomhill	11
Carraway Barn	15
Chantry Farm	18
Frith House	32
The Hollow, Swanage	41
NEW Karmacations	44
Knowle Cottage	49
Lewell Lodge	52
Manor Farm, Hampreston	57
Myrtle Cottage	64
The Old Rectory, Litton Cheney	66
The Old Rectory, Manston	67
The Old Rectory, Pulham	68
The Old Vicarage	71
1 Pine Walk	75
Pugin Hall	78
Russell-Cotes Art Gallery & Museum	80
Slape Manor	86
South Eggardon House	87
NEW The Stables	88
Staddlestones	89
NEW Tumblins	94
Wagtails	96
Western Gardens	99
White House	100
Yew Tree House	107

Stoneleigh

THE GARDENS

1 ♦ ABBOTSBURY SUBTROPICAL GARDENS
Abbotsbury, Weymouth, DT3 4LA. Ilchester Estates, 01305 871387, info@abbotsbury-tourism.co.uk, www.abbotsburygardens.co.uk. *8m W of Weymouth. From B3157 Weymouth-Bridport, 200yds W of Abbotsbury village.* **For opening times and information, please phone, email or visit garden website.**
30 acres, started in 1760 and considerably extended in C19. Much recent replanting. The maritime microclimate enables this Mediterranean and southern hemisphere garden to grow rare and tender plants. National Collection of Hoherias (flowering Aug in NZ garden). Woodland valley with ponds, stream and hillside walk to view the Jurassic Coast. Open all year except for Christmas week. Partial wheelchair access, some very steep paths and rolled gravel but we have a selected wheelchair route with sections of tarmac hard surface.
♿ 🐕 ✽ 🚗 NPC ☕

2 ANNALAL'S GALLERY
25 Millhams Street, Christchurch, BH23 1DN. Anna & Lal Sims, www.annasims.co.uk. *Town centre. Park in Saxon Square PCP - exit to Millhams St via alley at side of church.* **Sun 4, Sun 25 May, Sun 22 June, Sun 27 July, Sun 24 Aug, Sun 14 Sept, Sun 23 Nov, Sun 7 Dec (2-4). Adm £3.50, chd free.**
Enchanting 180 yr old cottage, home of two Royal Academy artists. 32ft x 12½ ft garden on 3 patio levels. Pencil gate leads to colourful scented Victorian walled garden. Sculptures and paintings hide among the flowers and shrubs. Unusual studio and garden room. Mural of a life-size greyhound makes the cottage easy to find and adds a smile to people's faces.

3 ARDHURST
Nash Lane, Marnhull, Sturminster Newton, DT10 1JZ. Mr & Mrs Ed Highnam. *3m N of Sturminster Newton. From A30 E Stour, B3092 3m to Marnhull, Crown Inn on R. Turn R down Church Hill, follow NGS yellow signs. From Sturminster Newton, 3m into Marnhull, turn L down Church Hill, follow yellow signs. Parking in field indicated.* **Sat 23 Aug (1-5.30). Home-made teas. Sun 24 Aug (1-5.30). Cream teas. Adm £7, chd free.**
The garden has been 8 yrs in the making. A plantsman's garden with deep perennial borders, large netted vegetable area, water harvesting, and all work in progress. A riot of colour with salvias, grasses and hot plants in Aug/Sept. All plants for pollination and year-round interest. Tall grasses and varied fruit trees. Water harvesting made by the owner. New round border of soft planting in 2023. Large netted vegetable area, greenhouse and butternut squash etc scrambling through and up the hedges! Parking in driveway for wheelchair access. Driveway is rough & assistance will be needed. Rest of garden laid to lawn, patio at rear for shade.
♿ ☕

In 2024, we celebrated 40 years of continuous funding for Macmillan Cancer Support equating to more than £19.5 million.

162 DORSET

4 ◆ ATHELHAMPTON HOUSE GARDENS
Athelhampton, Dorchester, DT2 7LG. Giles Keating, 01305 848363, hello@athelhampton.house, www.athelhampton.co.uk. *Between Poole & Dorchester just off the A35. 5m E of Dorchester well signed off A35 trunk road at Puddletown. Easily reached from A31 Ringwood, & A354 Blandford Forum.* **For NGS: Thur 20 Mar, Sat 21 June, Mon 22 Sept (10-5); Sat 20 Dec (10-3.30). Adm £12.50, chd free. Coffee, lunches & afternoon tea are available daily. Adm is for garden only. Tickets to visit the house can be bought on the day.** For other opening times and information, please phone, email or visit garden website.
The award-winning gardens at Athelhampton surround the Tudor manor house and date from 1891. The Great Court with 12 giant yew topiary pyramids is overlooked by two terraced pavilions. This glorious Grade I architectural garden is full of vistas with spectacular planting, ponds with fountains and the River Piddle flowing past. Wheelchair map to guide you around the gardens. There are accessible toilets in the Visitor Centre. Please see our Accessibility Guide on our website.
♿ 🐾 ✱ 🚗 🚌 ☕

5 22 AVON AVENUE
Avon Castle, Ringwood, BH24 2BH. Terry & Dawn Heaver, dawnandterry@yahoo.com. *Past Ringwood from E A31 turn L after garage, L again into Matchams Ln, Avon Castle 1m on L. A31 from W turn R into Boundary Ln, then L into Matchams Ln, Avon Ave ½ m on R.* **Sun 4 May, Sun 8 June, Sun 13 July, Sun 10 Aug, Sun 7 Sept (12-5). Adm £5. Tea, coffee & home-made cakes.**
Japanese themed water garden featuring granite sculptures, ponds, waterfalls, azaleas, rhododendrons, cloud topiary and a collection of goldfish and water lilies. Children must be under parental supervision due to large, deep water pond. No dogs please.
✱ ☕

6 BEMBURY FARM
Bembury Lane, Thornford, Sherborne, DT9 6QF. Sir John & Lady Garnier, 01935 873551, dodie.garnier32@gmail.com. *Bottom of Bembury Lane, N of Thornford village. 6m E of Yeovil, 3m W of Sherborne on Yetminster road. Follow signs in village. Parking in field.* **Sun 18, Wed 21 May (2-6). Adm £8, chd free. Home-made teas.** Visits also by arrangement May to Sept for groups of 10 to 40.
Created and developed since 1996 this peaceful garden has lawns and large herbaceous borders informally planted with interesting perennials around unusual trees, shrubs and roses. Large collection of clematis; also a pretty woodland walk, wildflower corner, lily pond, oak circle, yew hedges with peacock, clipped hornbeam round kitchen garden and plenty of seating to sit and reflect.
♿ 🐾 ✱ ☕ 🔊

7 ◆ BENNETTS WATER GARDENS
Putton Lane, Chickerell, Weymouth, DT3 4AF. James Bennett, 01305 785150, info@bennettswatergardens.com, www.bennettswatergardens.com. *2m W of Weymouth Harbour on the B3157 to Bridport. Follow the brown signs for 'Water Gardens'. From the A35 at Dorchester take the A354 S to Weymouth & Portland, then take the B3157 W towards Chickerell.* **For NGS: Fri 5 Sept (10-4). Adm £10, chd £4. Light refreshments in Café Monet. Home-made lunches, cakes & cream teas.** For other opening times and information, please phone, email or visit garden website. Donation to Plant Heritage.
Bennetts Water Gardens is a main visitor attraction in Dorset. Set over 8 acres the gardens hold the National Plant Collection of Water Lilies with a Claude Monet style Japanese Bridge, Tropical House, Woodland Walks and Museum. Regret no dogs. Partial wheelchair access but during periods of sustained wet weather the gardens are closed to wheelchair users. Pls contact us for further advice.
♿ NPC ☕ ⛺ 🔊

SPECIAL EVENT

8 BETTISCOMBE MANOR
Bettiscombe, Bridport, DT6 5NU. Mr Jasper Conran. *Follow signs for Bettiscombe, park at village hall.* **Thur 5 June (10-5). Adm £60, chd free. Pre-booking essential, please visit www.ngs.org.uk for information & booking. Light refreshments in the village hall. Salmon & cucumber sandwiches, strawberries, pastries, cakes, tea, coffee, champagne & elderflower presse.**
Designer Jasper Conran has given one of England's loveliest smaller houses, Bettiscombe Manor, a garden to match, with orchards, mellow brick enclosures, and broad beds flanking an unforgettable view of the Vale, looking down to the sea. The garden has a magical quality, it is informally planted and flower-filled, reflecting the designer's predilection for constantly evolving and creative planting. A limited number of tickets have been made available for this exclusive special afternoon event, kindly hosted by Jasper's Head Gardener, Midori. It includes a talk on the gardens and how they have evolved to empathetically embrace and work within the surrounding landscape. Midori will also provide a background to how the garden has been created, as well as its ongoing development and provide further detail on what is growing in the garden currently.
☕

9 BLACK SHED
Blackmarsh Farm, Dodds Cross, Sherborne, DT9 4JX. Paul & Helen Stickland, www.blackshed.flowers/blog. *From Sherborne, follow A30 towards Shaftesbury. Black Shed approx 1m E at Blackmarsh Farm, on L, next to The Toy Barn. Large car park shared with The Toy Barn.* **Sun 29 June, Sun 27 July (1-5). Adm £5, chd free. Home-made teas.**
Over 200 colourful and productive flower beds growing a sophisticated selection of cut flowers and foliage to supply florists and the public for weddings, events and occasions throughout the seasons. Traditional garden favourites, delphiniums, larkspur, foxgloves, scabious and dahlias alongside more unusual perennials, foliage plants and grasses, creating a stunning and unique display. A warm welcome and

generous advice on creating your own cut flower garden is offered. Easy access from gravel car park. Wide grass pathways enabling access for wheelchairs. Gently sloping site.

BROOK VIEW CARE HOME
Riverside Road, West Moors, Ferndown, BH22 0LQ. Andy Richards, www.brookviewcare.co.uk. *Go past village shops turn L into Riverside Rd & Brook View Care Home is on the R after 100 metres. There is parking onsite or on nearby roads.* **Sat 16 Aug (11-4). Adm £5, chd free. Tea, coffee & cake. Range of home-made cakes, inc dietary options.** Our colourful and vibrant garden is spread over two main areas, one warm and sunny, the other cooler and shadier. There is a peaceful pond area, games lawn and mixed borders. Walking past our greenhouse leads to further gardens and raised beds, in a courtyard setting. Residents help out with the production of many of our plants, all expertly managed by our gardener.

BROOMHILL
Rampisham, Dorchester, DT2 0PT. David & Carol Parry, 07775 806 875, carol.parry2@btopenworld.com. *11m NW of Dorchester. From Dorchester A37 Yeovil, 9m L Evershot. From Yeovil A37 Dorchester, 7m R Evershot. Follow signs. From Crewkerne A356, 1½m after Rampisham Garage L Rampisham. Follow signs.* **Sun 27 Apr (2-5). Adm £5, chd free. Sun 8 June (12-5). Combined adm with Pugin Hall £10, chd £5. Sun 13 July, Thur 7 Aug (2-5). Adm £5, chd free. Home-made teas.** Visits also by arrangement 5 June to 9 Aug for groups of 8 to 45. A former farmyard transformed into a delightful, tranquil garden set in 2 acres. Clipped box, island beds and borders planted with shrubs, roses, grasses, masses of unusual perennials and choice annuals to give vibrancy and colour into the autumn. Lawns and paths lead to a less formal area with large wildlife pond, meadow, shaded areas, bog garden, late summer border. Orchard and vegetable garden. Gravel entrance, the rest is grass, some gentle slopes.

Dedley Farm

SPECIAL EVENT

12 CANFORD SCHOOL ARBORETUM
Canford Magna, Wimborne, BH21 3AD. Andrew Powell, FLS, MA, MSc. *Pls use the postcode & SatNav. Parking will be signed and there will be further signs directing you to our meeting point.* **Sat 3 May (10-1). Adm £25. Pre-booking essential, please visit www.ngs.org.uk for information & booking. Light refreshments.**
The Arboretum at Canford School has been nationally recognised and has several unusual and rare tree species and two National Collections. A limited number of tickets have been made available for this special one-day event, kindly hosted by Canford School on behalf of The National Garden Scheme. It includes a talk and guided tour with Andrew Powell who is master i/c trees at Canford School. Andrew will share his wealth of botanical knowledge and talk about the history and ongoing developments at the arboretum. His sense of humour and love of the collection is infectious, making this a very entertaining morning amongst this magical and majestic collection of trees.
☕

13 ♦ CAREYS SECRET GARDEN
Wareham, BH20 7PG. *We send the exact location once you have booked a ticket. The garden is within a 3m radius of Wareham, (5 min drive from the train stn). 11m from Poole & 19m from Dorchester.* **For NGS: Wed 11 June (11-3). Adm £8.50, chd free. Pre-booking essential, please phone 07927 132148 or visit www.careyssecretgarden.co.uk for information & booking. Cream teas in the Secret Coffee Shop within the walled garden. For other opening times and information, please phone or visit garden website.**
Behind a 150 yr old wall, situated just outside of Wareham, sits 3 ½ acres in the midst of transformation. Left untouched for more than 40 yrs, this garden is now flourishing again, with a focus on permaculture and rewilding. Awarded Gold in Dorset Tourism's 'Business of the Year' 2021/2022 and Silver in South West Tourism Awards 'New Business of the Year' 2021/2022. Those with mobility issues are welcome to contact us in advance and we can tailor your visit to your needs accordingly.
& ✿ ☕

14 24 CARLTON ROAD NORTH
Weymouth, DT4 7PY. Anne & Rob Tracey. *8m S of Dorchester. A354 from Dorchester, almost opp Rembrandt Hotel R into Carlton Rd North. From Town Centre follow esplanade towards A354 Dorchester, L into Carlton Rd North.* **Fri 16, Sat 17, Sun 18, Mon 19 May (2-5). Adm £4, chd free. Home-made teas.**
Town garden near the sea. Long garden on several levels. Steps and narrow sloping paths lead to beds and borders filled with trees, shrubs and herbaceous plants inc many unusual varieties. A garden which continues to evolve and reflect an interest in texture, shape and colour. Wildlife is encouraged. Raised beds in front garden create a space for vegetable growing.
☕))

15 CARRAWAY BARN
Carraway Lane, Marnhull, Sturminster Newton, DT10 1NJ. Catherine & Mark Turner, 07905 960281, Carrawaybarn.ngs@gmail.com. *From Shaftesbury A30 & B3092. ½ m after The Crown turn R into Carraway Ln. From Sturminster Newton B3092 2.8m turn L into Carraway Ln. Bear R behind 1st house, until in large courtyard.* **Visits by arrangement 2 June to 31 July for groups of 8 to 40.Adm inc home-made teas. Adm £10, chd free.**
Set in 2 acres, around C19 former barn. In recent years, a natural swimming pond, large shrub border, waterfall, late summer borders and pergola have been created. Shady woodland walks, a white border of hydrangeas, hostas and ferns lead to the beautiful established walled garden, where deep borders are planted with roses, peonies, alliums, geraniums and topiary, encircling a water lily pond. Partial wheelchair access; gravelled courtyard and walled garden, gently sloping lawns.
& ☕))

16 CASTLE RINGS
Donhead St Mary, Shaftesbury, SP7 9BZ. Michael Thomas. *2 m N of Shaftesbury. A350 Shaftesbury/ Warminster road, past Wincombe Business Park. 1st R signed Wincombe & Donhead St Mary.* **Sun 24 Aug (2-5). Adm £5, chd free.**
Small, long garden in two parts laid out beside an Iron Age hill fort with

spectacular views. A formal garden with colourful planting and pots is followed by a paved area with steps leading through to a more informal garden. Topiary, roses and clematis on tripods.
))

17 THE CHANTRY
Chantry Street, Netherbury, Bridport, DT6 5NB. Peter Higginson. *1m S of Beaminster, follow signs for Netherbury. Garden is in centre near church.* **Sun 15 June (2-6). Combined adm with Hingsdon £8, chd free. Teas available at Hingsdon.**
Set in the middle of the village and within stone walls and hedges, a 1 acre established traditional garden of lawns, trees, shrubs and colourful mixed borders on a gently sloping site, with a formal pond and some new planting.
🐕 ☕))

18 CHANTRY FARM
Phillips Hill, Marnhull, Sturminster Newton, DT10 1NU. Ivan & Sue Shenkman, 07767 455089, sueshenkman@mac.com. *Between Shaftesbury & Sherborne. From the A30 turn W at East Stour to Marnhull on the B3092. After the Crown pub turn 2nd R onto New St. After 1m at the L bend Chantry Farm is on the R. What3words app: sample.somewhere.send.* **Wed 4 June (1.30-5). Adm £8, chd free. Home-made teas. Visits also by arrangement May to Oct for groups of 10 to 50.**
Chantry Farm offers a series of gardens surrounding the 16C Farmhouse and three renovated barns. Designed by Justin Spink there are colourful long borders, walled gardens, swimming pool area, cutting and vegetable gardens. Espalier fruit trees, pleached hornbeam and weeping pears divide the areas. Fields with mown paths and beautiful views. Seating and wheel chair access.
& 🐕 ☕))

19 CHIDEOCK MANOR
Chideock, Bridport, DT6 6LF. Mr & Mrs Howard Coates, www.chideockmanorgarden.co.uk. *2m W of Bridport on A35. In centre of village turn N at church. The Manor is ¼ m along this road on R.* **Sat 5, Sun 6 Apr, Sat 14, Sun 15 June (2-5). Adm £10, chd free. Home-made teas.**

DORSET

12 acres of formal and informal gardens. Bog garden beside stream and series of ponds. Yew hedges and mature trees. Lime and crab apple walks, herbaceous borders, colourful rose and clematis arches, fernery and nuttery. Walled vegetable garden and orchard. Woodland and lakeside walks. Fine views and much variety. Partial wheelchair access.

20 DEANS COURT
Deans Court Lane, Wimborne Minster, BH21 1EE. Sir William Hanham, 01202 849314, info@deanscourt.org, www.deanscourt.org. *Pedestrian entrance (no parking) is via Deans Court Ln. Vehicle entrance (with parking) is via Poole Rd (BH21 1QF).* **Wed 28 May, Wed 25 June (11-4). Adm £8, chd free. Home-baked cakes & light lunches available in the Café. Donation to Friends of Victoria Hospital, Wimborne.**
13 acres of peaceful, partly wild gardens in ancient monastic setting with mature specimen trees, Saxon fish pond, herb garden and orchard beside River Allen close to town centre. First Soil Association accredited garden, within C18 serpentine walls. The Permaculture system has been introduced here with chemical free produce. For disabled access, please contact us in advance of visiting to help us understand your specific needs and work out the best plan. Follow signs within grounds for disabled parking closer to gardens. Deeper gravel on some paths. See website extended description re access.

21 NEW DEDLEY FARM
Ryall, Bridport, DT6 6EN. Mr & Mrs Giles and Emma O'Bryen. *Off A35, N of Morecombelake, between Whitchurch & Ryall. Take R turn off A35 by Felicity's Farm Shop, cont for 1½m towards Whitchurch. We are on the L. Or from the W, take L fork past Charmouth, through village, past pub, we are 500m up hill on R.* **Sun 13 July (12-5). Adm £5, chd free. Home-made teas.**
Naturalistic garden of about 1 acre surrounds the house, inc gravel garden, wildflower meadow and borders filled with irises, geraniums, herbs, grasses and roses. A tributary of the River Char winds under the bridge to orchard. 11 acres in total, inc woodland path, orchards with fruit and nut trees and larger wildflower meadow. Stunning views of Marshwood Vale and beyond. Dogs welcome on leads. Children's nature trail.

22 DONHEAD HALL
Donhead St Mary, Shaftesbury, SP7 9DS. Paul & Penny Brewer. *4m E of Shaftesbury. A30 towards Shaftesbury. In Ludwell turn R opp brown sign to Tollard Royal. Follow road for ¾m & bear R at T-junction. Donhead Hall 50 yds on L on corner of Watery Lane, cream gates.* **Sat 23 Aug (1-4). Adm £7, chd free. Home-made teas.**
Walled garden overlooking deer park. The house and garden are built into the side of a hill with uninterrupted views to Cranborne Chase. Martin Lane Fox designed the terracing and advised on the landscaping of the gardens which are on 4 different levels. Large mixed borders and specimen trees, kitchen garden with glasshouses.

SPECIAL EVENT

23 DORSET DAHLIAS
Befferlands Farm, Charmouth, Bridport, DT6 6RD. Anna May, 07950 566986, anna@annamayeveryday.co.uk, www.dorsetdahlias.co.uk. *Approach Berne Ln from the A35 by Charmouth. Approx ½m down Berne Ln, Befferlands Farm is on the L. Park at farmyard opp the farm.* **Sun 7 Sept (2-4). Adm £25, chd free. Pre-booking essential, please visit www.ngs.org.uk for information & booking. Tea, coffee & cake.**
Dorset Dahlias started 9 yrs ago at Befferlands Farm and has since overtaken the kitchen garden and a large patch in one of the farm fields. Dahlias are grown in rows and organised by colour, with up to 80 different varieties grown, and around 600 plants, that bloom from late Jul until late Oct. There are multiple colours from whites and baby pinks through to bright corals, oranges and pinks. A limited number of tickets have been made available for this special one-day event, kindly hosted by the owner, Anna May. Park at Farmyard opp Befferlands Farm and meet on the front drive for a talk and guided tour. Regret no dogs or WC.

24 EAST END FARM
Barkers Hill, Semley, Shaftesbury, SP7 9BJ. Celia & Piers Petrie. *From A350 take exit to Semley & continue to church. Take turning next to church towards Tisbury then 1st R to Barkers Hill. Continue along lane (1m) then up hill, East End Farm on R.* **Evening opening every Wed 4 June to 18 June (4-6). Adm £15, chd free. Pre-booking essential, please visit www.ngs.org.uk for information & booking. Wine.**
Exquisite wildflower meadows filled with an abundance of orchids, yellow rattle, grass vetchling, ragged robin, agrimony, meadow cranesbill and various vetches, amongst many other species. The meadows extend just over 3 acres, including wildlife pond and recently planted trees. A flower-filled garden surrounds the house and is informal in style. Wheelchair access to garden only but views from garden to wildflower meadow.

SPECIAL EVENT

25 EASTINGTON FARM
Worth Matravers, Swanage, BH19 3LF. Rachel James. *In Corfe Castle village take the R turn signed Kingston. Take the 2nd R signed Worth Matravers. Eastington Farm is 650 metres on L, long gravel drive & parking at the end of the field.* **Thur 12 June (2-5.30). Combined adm with Encombe House £60, chd free. Pre-booking essential, please visit www.ngs.org.uk for information & booking. Home-made teas at Encombe House. Please arrive promptly at 2pm for the talk on the garden.**
The garden has been created over the last 25 yrs and sits within dry Purbeck stone walls with views to the sea. It is divided into different garden rooms with planting themes, all surrounding the C16/17 house. These inc more formal yew hedge pyramids, lonicera balls and cloud topiary alongside soft floral planting, with an orchard of wild flowers, and a working vegetable garden. The garden owners will give a short talk on the history and development of the gardens on arrival at 2pm. Soft drinks will be provided. Departure at 3.15 for the short drive to Encombe House.

Little Benville House

26 ♦ EDMONDSHAM HOUSE
Edmondsham, Wimborne, BH21 5RE. Mrs Julia Smith, 01725 517207, julia.edmondsham@homeuser.net. 9m NE of Wimborne. 9m W of Ringwood. Between Cranborne & Verwood. Edmondsham off B3081. Wheelchair access and disabled parking at West front door. **For NGS: Every Wed 2 Apr to 30 Apr (2-5). Mon 21 Apr (2-5). Every Wed 1 Oct to 22 Oct (2-5). Adm £4, chd £1. Cash only. Tea, coffee, cake & soft drinks available 3.30pm to 4pm in Edmondsham House on Weds only (excluding 15 Oct).** For other opening times and information, please phone or email. Donation to Prama Care.
Six acres of mature gardens and grounds with trees, rare shrubs, spring bulbs and shaped hedges surrounding C16/C18 house, giving much to explore inc C12 church adjacent to garden. Large Victorian walled garden is productive and managed organically (since 1984) using 'no dig' vegetable beds. Wide herbaceous borders planted for seasonal colour. Traditional potting shed, cob wall, sunken greenhouse. Coaches by appointment only. Some grass and gravel paths.

& ✱ 🚌 ☕

SPECIAL EVENT

27 ENCOMBE HOUSE
Kingston, Corfe Castle, Wareham, BH20 5LW. James & Arabella Gaggero. *From Eastington Farm, L out of drive & follow signs to Corfe. Sharp R on to Kingston Lane, L on Langton road, keep L in Corfe, pass The Scott Arms & church, after 300yds 2nd turning L into Encombe. Follow signs for parking.* **Thur 12 June (3.30-5.30). Combined adm with Eastington Farm £60, chd free. Pre-booking essential, please visit www.ngs.org.uk for information & booking. Home-made teas.**
The historic Encombe House and Estate is nestled within a unique stunning valley in the Purbeck hills. The garden has been extensively redeveloped since 2009, with a modern, sympathetic design for the garden by Tom Stuart-Smith. The main garden to the south of the house inc large sweeping borders filled with grasses and perennials, alongside extensive lawns, lake and deep herbaceous beds. Following your visit to Eastington Farm pls make your way to Encombe for a 3.30 arrival. Meet at the front of the house for an introductory talk on the garden, followed by an opportunity to explore the gardens accompanied by the gardening team. Homemade teas from 4.30pm to 5.30pm at the Temple.

D ☕

SPECIAL EVENT

28 FARRS
3, Whitcombe Rd, Beaminster, DT8 3NB. Mr & Mrs John Makepeace, www.johnmakepeacefurniture.com. *Southern edge of Beaminster. On B3163. Car parking in the Square or Yarn Barton Car Park, or side streets of Beaminster.* **Thur 12 June, Wed 24 Sept (2-4.30). Adm £40. Pre-booking essential, please visit www.ngs.org.uk for information &**

DORSET

booking. Cream teas in the house or garden, weather dependent. Donation to Victoria & Albert Foundation.
Enjoy several distinctive walled gardens, rolling lawns, sculpture and giant topiary around one of Beaminster's historic town houses. John's inspirational grass garden and Jennie's very contrasting garden with an oak fruit cage; a riot of colour. Glasshouse, straw bale studio, geese in orchard. Remarkable trees, planked and seasoning in open sided barn for future furniture commissions. A limited number of tickets have been made available for these two special afternoon openings, hosted by John and Jennie Makepeace. There will be a warm welcome from John at 2pm in the main rooms of the house, with a talk on his furniture design and recent commissions. Jennie will then give a guided walk around the gardens followed by a cream tea. Some gravel paths, alternative wheelchair route through orchard.

29 FOLLY FARM COTTAGE
Spyway Road, Uploders, Bridport, DT6 4PH. Neil & Steph Crabb. Halfway along Spyway Rd inbetween Matravers Uploders & The Spyway Inn Askerswell. On Spyway Rd ½ m on L from Matravers House, Uploders. ½ m on R from The Spyway Inn. **Sat 26, Sun 27 Apr (1-5). Adm £6, chd free. Cream teas, fresh home-made cakes & scones, savoury options, dairy & g/f options, herbal teas, plant base milk alternatives.**
An established garden of approx 1 acre with a contemporary twist. The garden has 4 connecting rooms, a main lawn with borders, ornamental trees and rose bed, a large pond area with mature trees, grasses, golden willow and silver pear which leads on to a natural fruit orchard, tennis court, greenhouse and mixed raised bed. Far-reaching views of Eggardon Hill and the surrounding fields. The majority of the garden can be enjoyed from a wheelchair, there are 3 small steps at the kitchen side entrance of house.

30 ◆ FORDE ABBEY GARDENS
Forde Abbey, Chard, TA20 4LU. Mr & Mrs Julian Kennard, 01460 221290, info@fordeabbey.co.uk, www.fordeabbey.co.uk. *4m SE of Chard. Signed off A30 Chard-Crewkerne & A358 Chard-Axminster. Also from Broadwindsor B3164.* **For opening times and information, please phone, email or visit garden website.**
30 acres of fine shrubs, magnificent specimen trees, ponds, herbaceous borders, rockery, bog garden containing superb collection of Asiatic primulas, Ionic temple, working walled kitchen garden. England's tallest powered fountain. Other features inc crocus lawns, tulip displays and plant fairs. Gardens open for weekends in Feb, daily from 1st Mar - 31st Oct. House from 1st April - 31st Mar, Tues to Fri, Sun and BH Mon but please see our website for updated information. Please ask at reception for best wheelchair route. Wheelchairs available to borrow/hire, advance booking 01460 221699.

31 FRANKHAM FARM
Ryme Intrinseca, Sherborne, DT9 6JT. Susan Ross MBE, 07594 427365, neilandsusanross@gmail.com. *3m S of Yeovil. Just off A37 - turn next to Hamish's farm shop signed to Ryme Intrinseca, go over small bridge and up hill, drive is on L.* **Sun 16 Mar, Sun 27 Apr, Sun 1 June, Sun 12 Oct (12-5). Adm £7, chd free. Light refreshments in our newly converted barn (no steps). BBQ with our own farm produced beef, lamb & pork, vegetarian soup, home-made cakes made by village bakers.**
3½ acre garden, created since 1960 by the late Jo Earle for year-round interest. This large and lovely garden is filled with a wide variety of well grown plants, unusual labelled shrubs and trees. Productive vegetable garden. Clematis and other climbers. Spring bulbs through to autumn colour, particularly oaks. Dogs welcome in selected woodland areas. Ramp avail for the 2 steps to the garden. WCs inc disabled.

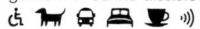

32 FRITH HOUSE
Stalbridge, DT10 2SD. Mr & Mrs Patrick Sclater, 07778 785293, rosalynsclater@frith.farm. *4m E of Sherborne. Between Milborne Port & Stalbridge. From A30 1m, follow sign to Stalbridge. From Stalbridge 2m & turn W by PO.* **Visits by arrangement May & June for groups of 15+. Adm £10, chd free. Home-made teas included in admission.**
Approached down a long drive with fine views, 5 acres of garden around Edwardian house and self-contained hamlet. Range of mature trees, lakes and flower borders. House terrace edged by rose border and featuring Lutyensesque wall fountain and game larder. Well-stocked kitchen gardens. Woodland walks with masses of bluebells in spring. Garden with pretty walks set amidst working farm. Accessible gravel paths.

33 GLENHOLME HERBS
Penmore Road, Sandford Orcas, Sherborne, DT9 4SE. Maxine & Rob Kellaway, www.glenholmeherbs.co.uk. *3m N of Sherborne. Pls see directions on our website & type Glenholme Herbs into Google maps to find us as the postcode will take you to the wrong location.* **Sat 26, Sun 27 July (10-4). Adm £5, chd free. Home-made teas.**
Paths meander through large, colourful beds inspired by Piet Oudolf. Featuring a wide selection of herbs and salvias along with grasses, verbena and echinacea. Planted with wildlife in mind and alive with pollinators. The garden also features a beautiful natural swimming pond. A mixture of grass and firm gravel paths.

34 NEW GRANGE COTTAGE
Golden Hill, Stourton Caundle, DT10 2JP. Pete & Isobel Bull. *6m SE of Sherborne. Park at Manor Farm or close to Grange Cottage.* **Sat 31 May, Sun 1 June (2-5). Combined adm with Wagtails £10, chd free. Home-made teas.**
Grange Cottage is a traditional C18 thatched cottage with an extensive and well-stocked garden. The present owners moved in 3 yrs ago and, as well as maintaining the mature box and yew hedges and topiary, have created many more perennial beds. The garden is particularly attractive in late spring time so do come and visit for our 2025 end of May opening.

35 HANFORD SCHOOL
Child Okeford, Blandford Forum, DT11 8HN. Mrs Hilary Phillips. *From Blandford take A350 to Shaftesbury; 2m after Stourpaine turn L for Hanford. From Shaftesbury take A350 to Poole; after Iwerne Courtney turn R to Hanford. NGS signage from A350 & A257.* **Sun 15 June (1-5). Adm £5, chd free.** Perhaps the only school in England with a working kitchen garden growing quantities of seasonal vegetables, fruit and flowers for the table. The rolling lawns host sports matches, gymnastics, dance and plays while ancient cedars look on. The stable clock chimes on the hour and the chapel presides over it all. Teas in Great Hall (think Hogwarts). What a place to go to school or visit. Several steps/ramp to main house. No wheelchair access to WC.

37 HILLTOP
Woodville, Stour Provost, Gillingham, SP8 5LY. Josse & Brian Emerson, www.hilltopgarden.co.uk. *7m N of Sturminster Newton, 5m W of Shaftesbury. On B3092 turn E at Stour Provost Xrds, signed Woodville. After 1¼m thatched cottage on R. On A30, 4m W of Shaftesbury, turn S opp Kings Arms. 2nd turning on R signed Woodville, 100 yds on L.* **Sat 19, Sun 20, Sat 26, Sun 27 July, Sun 10, Sun 17 Aug (2-6). Adm £4, chd free. Tea, coffee & cake.**
Summer at Hilltop is a gorgeous riot of colour and scent, the old thatched cottage barely visible amongst the flowers. Unusual annuals and perennials grow alongside the traditional and familiar, boldly combining to make a spectacular display, which attracts an abundance of wildlife. Always something new, the unique, gothic garden loo is a great success.

38 HINGSDON
Netherbury, Bridport, DT6 5NQ. Anne Peck. *Between Bridport & Beaminster. 1½m from A3066 or 1m from B3162 signed to Netherbury.* **Sun 15 June (2-6). Combined adm with The Chantry £8, chd free. Home-made teas at Hingsdon only (not at The Chantry).**
Hingsdon is a hilltop garden of about 2 acres with spectacular panoramic views. There are many unusual shrubs, mostly planted within the last 15 yrs, a mixed border of two halves (cool and hot), rose garden and a large kitchen garden. There is also a small arboretum with an idiosyncratic collection of over 90 trees. The main garden is accessible, although sloping, but the arboretum is too steep for wheelchair access. The kitchen garden has steps.

39 ◆ HOGCHESTER FARM
Axminster Road, Charmouth, Bridport, DT6 6BY. Mr Rob Powell, 07714 291846, rob@hogchester.com. *A35 Charmouth Rd, follow dual carriageway and take turning at signs for Hogchester Farm.* **For NGS: Sun 13 July (9-6). Adm £5, chd £2. Coffee shack serving drinks, cream teas & light refreshments.** For other opening times and information, please phone or email.
Hogchester Farm is a collaboration between those seeking connection with nature and themselves through conservation therapy and the arts. The 75 acre old dairy farm has been largely gifted to nature which has helped to preserve the overflowing abundance of natural life. Having worked closely with the Dorset Wildlife Trust, Hogchester Farm has been able to preserve wild meadows and wilding areas which are filled with local flora and fauna inc wild orchids, foxgloves and primroses. The farm offers something for everyone, making a great family day out. There will be a talk on the history of Hogchester wildflower meadows and meadows conservation at 2pm.

40 THE HOLLOW, BLANDFORD FORUM
Tower Hill, Iwerne Minster, Blandford Forum, DT11 8NJ. Sue Le Prevost. *Between Blandford & Shaftesbury. Follow signs on A350 to Iwerne Minster. Turn off at Talbot Inn, cont straight to The Chalk, bear R along Watery Lane for parking in Parish Field on R. 5 min uphill walk to house.* **Sat 21, Sun 22, Wed 25 June (2-5). Adm £4, chd free. Home-made cakes & gluten-free available.**
Hillside cottage garden built on chalk, about ⅓ acre with an interesting variety of plants in borders that line the numerous sloping pathways. Water features for wildlife and well placed seating areas to sit back and enjoy the views. Productive fruit and vegetable garden converted paddock with raised beds and greenhouses. A high maintenance garden which is constantly evolving. Use of different methods to plant steep banks.

41 THE HOLLOW, SWANAGE
25 Newton Road, Swanage, BH19 2EA. Suzanne Nutbeem, 01929 423662, gdnsuzanne@gmail.com. *½m S of Swanage town centre. From town follow signs to Durlston Country Park. At top of hill turn R at red postbox into Bon Accord Rd. 4th turn R into Newton Rd.* **Every Wed 2 July to 27 Aug (2-5). Adm £4, chd free.** Visits also by arrangement 2 July to 27 Aug for groups of up to 50.
Wander in a dramatic sunken former stone quarry, a surprising garden at the top of a hill above the seaside town of Swanage. Stone terraces with many unusual shrubs and grasses form beautiful patterns of colour and foliage attracting butterflies and bees. Pieces of mediaeval London Bridge lurk in the walls. Steps have elegant handrails. WC available. Exceptionally wide range of plants inc cacti and air plants.

42 ◆ HOLME FOR GARDENS
West Holme Farm, Wareham, BH20 6AQ. Simon Goldsack, 01929 554716, simon@holmefg.co.uk, www.holmefg.co.uk. *2m SW Wareham. Easy to find on the B3070 road to Lulworth 2m out of Wareham.* **For NGS: Tue 10 June, Tue 9 Sept (9-5). Adm £8, chd free. Light refreshments in the Orchard Café.** For other opening times and information, please phone, email or visit garden website. Donation to Plant Heritage.
Set within the picturesque Isle of Purbeck, award-winning Holme for Gardens is a family run treasure, with beautifully landscaped gardens, a well-stocked garden centre with friendly knowledgeable staff, gift shop plus our light and airy Orchard Café and conservatory. The 15 acre garden delights the visitor with bold landscape features, colourful borders and achieves a wide diversity of wildlife through floral diversity. Grass paths are kept in good order and soil is well drained so wheelchair access is reasonable except immediately after heavy rain.

43 HORN PARK
Tunnel Rd, Beaminster, DT8 3HB. Mr & Mrs David Ashcroft. 1½ m N of Beaminster. On A3066 from Beaminster, L before tunnel (see signs). **Tue 29 Apr, Tue 24 June (2.30-4.30). Adm £6, chd free. Home-made teas.**
Large plantsman's garden with magnificent views over Dorset countryside towards the sea. Many rare and mature plants and shrubs in terrraced, herbaceous, rock and water gardens. Woodland garden and walks in bluebell woods. Good amount of spring interest with magnolia, rhododendron and bulbs which are followed by roses and herbaceous planting. Wildflower meadow with 164 varieties inc orchids.

44 NEW KARMACATIONS
Bookham Lane, Buckland Newton, Dorchester, DT2 7RP. Mrs Kitty Ebdon-Jacques, 07788 216711, kitty@kittyebdon.com. *Past Buckland Newton village shop on L, after ½ m turn L into Bookham Lane, drive up lane past farm on L, drive down hill past stables, red gates garden entrance on R, park in field opp.* **Sat 24, Sun 25 May, Sat 26, Sun 27 July (12-5). Adm £8, chd £4. Light refreshments. Visits also by arrangement Apr to Sept for groups of 10+.**
'Magical' sums up Karmacations, a brand new Japanese inspired oasis tucked away in the magnificent West Dorset countryside. Our Garden of Tranquility is full of surprises, stories, scenery and sculptures with royal connections. Highlights inc a stunning metal bridge, charming tea house, lucky torii Gate, gilded stepping stones, Buddha Island and ancient meadow. Enchanting installations include a Kominka Pavillion for reflection, sensory waterfall and a restored rickshaw for those who just want to have fun! The garden is accessible to wheelchairs, but some areas of the garden are on a slope or may contain a short gravel pathway.

45 ♦ KINGSTON LACY
Wimborne Minster, BH21 4EA. National Trust, 01202 883402, kingstonlacy@nationaltrust.org.uk, www.nationaltrust.org.uk/kingston-lacy. 2½ m W of Wimborne Minster. On Wimborne-Blandford road B3082. **For opening times and information, please** phone, email or visit garden website.
35 acres of formal garden, incorporating parterre and sunken garden planted with Edwardian schemes during spring and summer. 5 acre kitchen garden and allotments. Victorian fernery containing over 35 varieties. Rose garden, mixed herbaceous borders, vast formal lawns and Japanese garden restored to Henrietta Bankes' creation of 1910. National Collection of Convallaria and *Anemone nemorosa*. Snowdrops, blossom, bluebells, autumn colour and Christmas light display. Deep gravel on some paths but lawns suitable for wheelchairs. Slope to visitor reception and South lawn. Dogs allowed in some areas of woodland.

46 ♦ KINGSTON MAURWARD GARDENS AND ANIMAL PARK
Kingston Maurward, Dorchester, DT2 8PY. Kingston Maurward College, 01305 215003, events@kmc.ac.uk, www.morekmc.com. *1m E of Dorchester off A35. Follow brown Tourist Information signs.* **For opening times and information, please phone, email or visit garden website.**
Stepping into the grounds you will be greeted with 35 impressive acres of formal gardens. During the late spring and summer months, our National Collection of penstemons and salvias display a lustrous rainbow of purples, pinks, blues and whites, leading you on through the ample hedges and stonework balustrades. An added treat is the Elizabethan walled garden, offering a new vision of enchantment. Open early Jan to mid Dec. Hours will vary in winter depending on conditions - check garden website or call before visiting. Partial wheelchair access only, gravel paths, steps and steep slopes. Map provided at entry, highlighting the most suitable routes.

47 KNITSON OLD FARMHOUSE
Corfe Castle, Wareham, BH20 5JB. Rachel Helfer. *Purbeck. Between Corfe Castle & Swanage. Follow the A351 3m E from Corfe Castle. Turn L signed Knitson. After 1m fork R. We are on L after ¼ m.* **Sat 24, Sun 25, Mon 26 May, Wed 25, Thur 26 June, Thur 17, Fri 18 July (12-5). Combined adm with The Stables £8, chd free. Hot & cold drinks, cakes, sweet/savoury pastries, cream teas available.**
Mature cottage garden nestled under chalk downland. Herbaceous borders, rockeries, climbers and shrubs, evolved and designed over 60 yrs for year-round colour. Wildlife friendly, sustainable kitchen garden inc 20+ different fruits for self-sufficiency. Historical stone artefacts, ancient trees and shrubs are part of the integral design. Level lawn for tea but also uneven sloping paths. Plants are selected for drought tolerance and hardiness. 100+ shrubs, both new and some over 100 yrs old. Vegetables year-round sustain a healthy lifestyle. Points of historical interest inc an ancient side-handled quern, Roman padstones, and a C15 farmhouse. Garden is on a slope, main lawn and tea area are level but there are uneven, sloping paths.

SPECIAL EVENT

48 ♦ KNOLL GARDENS
Hampreston, Wimborne, BH21 7ND. Mr Neil Lucas, 01202 873931, enquiries@knollgardens.co.uk, www.knollgardens.co.uk. 2½ m W of Ferndown. Brown tourist signs from all directions, inc from A31. Car park on site. **For NGS: Tue 2 Sept (2-4.30). Adm £25, chd £12.70. Pre-booking essential, please visit www.ngs.org.uk for information & booking. Tea, coffee & cake. Fri 19 Sept (10-5). Adm £8.95, chd £6.95. Self-service refreshment facilities. For other opening times and information, please phone, email or visit garden website.**
A wonderfully calming garden with naturalistic plantings of ornamental grasses interspersed with an array of flowering perennials. Grand specimen trees and beautiful shrubs offer shady spots to take in the open vistas of the prairie style gardens, benefiting both wildlife and environment. On Tues 2nd Sept owner, Neil Lucas, will be offering a guided tour of the gardens (tickets must be pre-booked). The tour will focus on the garden's changing seasonal highlights, from some of the spectacular individual plants to mass plantings of Knoll's acclaimed grasses. Neil will impart something of his knowledge and experience gained during 30 yrs of living and working at Knoll Gardens. Some slopes. Various surfaces inc gravel, paving, grass and bark.

DORSET

Manor Farm, Hampreston

49 KNOWLE COTTAGE
No.1, Shorts Lane, Beaminster, DT8 3BD. Claire & Guy Fender, 07738 042534, claire.fender@live.com. *Nr St Mary's Church. Park in the main square or the main town car park, (disabled parking on-site) & walk down Church Lane & R onto single-track Shorts Lane. Entry is through blue gates after 1st cottage on L.* **Sat 12, Sun 13 July (11.30-4.30). Adm £6, chd free. Tea, coffee & cake.** Visits also by arrangement 1 Apr to 1 Aug for groups of 10 to 20.

Knowle Cottage is a large 1½ acre garden with 35 metre long south facing herbaceous border with year-round colour. Formal rose garden with circular beds interspersed with light floral planting and framed on 3 sides with lavender borders. Small orchard and vegetables in raised beds in adjacent walled area, with whole garden leading to small stream, and bridge to pasture. Plants for sale. Flower beds accessed from level grass, slope not suitable for wheelchairs. Limited outside seating available.

50 22 LANCASTER DRIVE
Broadstone, BH18 9EL. Karen Wiltshire. *2 mins from Broadstone village centre. From B3074 Higher Blandford Rd, take first L onto Springdale Rd, 2nd R onto Springdale Ave, then head straight on to Lancaster Dr, the house will be on the R. Park on Lancaster Dr.* **Sat 17, Sun 18 May (11-5). Adm £5, chd £2.50. Tea, coffee & cake.**

360ft natural woodland garden that is hidden in the heart of Broadstone. Mature oaks and a natural spring make up a magical woodland setting that's left for wildlife to live without disturbance. New acers have been planted in the woodland to add seasonal colour and a new gravel garden closer to the house has water features fed from the natural spring.

51 LANGEBRIDE HOUSE
Long Bredy, DT2 9HU. *8m W of Dorchester. S off A35, midway between Dorchester & Bridport. Well signed. 1st gateway on L in village.* **Sun 20 July (1-5). Adm £6, chd £3. Home-made teas.**

Lovely herbaceous borders surround the house, inc peonies and roses in the summer. An old walled kitchen garden at the back, filled with fruit trees and vegetables. A number of magnificent trees in grounds, underplanted with copper beech, magnolias and hydrangeas. Partial wheelchair access if wet weather.

52 LEWELL LODGE
West Knighton, Dorchester, DT2 8RP. Rose & Charles Joly, 01935 83652, alison.wright@ngs.org.uk. *3m SE of Dorchester. Turn off A35 onto A352 towards Wareham, take West Stafford bypass, turn R for West Knighton at T junction. ¾m turn R up drive after village sign.* **Visits by arrangement Apr to Sept for groups of 10+.**
Elegant 2 acre classic English garden designed by present owners over last 25 yrs, surrounding Gothic Revival house. Double herbaceous borders enclosed by yew hedges with old fashioned roses. Shrub beds edged with box and large pyramidal hornbeam hedge. Crab apple tunnel, box parterre and pleached hornbeam avenue. Large walled garden, many mature trees and woodland walk. Garden is level but parking is on gravel and there are gravel pathways.

53 LITTLE BENVILLE HOUSE
Benville Lane, Corscombe, Dorchester, DT2 0NN. Jo & Gavin Bacon. *2½m (6mins) from Evershot village on Benville Lane. Benville may be approached from A37, via Evershot village. House is on L ½m after Benville Bridge. Alternatively from A356, Dorchester to Crewkerne road, 1m down on R.* **Sun 11 May (12-5). Combined adm with Pugin Hall £10, chd £5. Home-made teas.**
Contemporary garden, with landscape interventions by Harris Bugg Studio within a varied ecological ANOB and historic landscape off Benville Lane, mentioned in Thomas Hardy's Tess. Within the curtilage there are new herbaceous borders, woodland planting, walled vegetable and cutting garden, cloud pruned topiary, ha-ha, ornamental and productive trees and moat which is a listed Ancient Monument. Bring a tennis racquet and appropriate footwear and try the tennis court and enjoy the view.

54 NEW LITTLE FIELDS
Somers Road, Lyme Regis, DT7 3EX. Simon & Lynne Wheatley. *Take the A3052 W towards Seaton/Sidmouth for ½m from the centre of Lyme Regis. Turn R into Somers Rd & Little Fields is on the R after 50 yds through the white gates.* **Sun 25 May (1-5). Adm £5, chd free. Tea, coffee & cake.**
An evolving coastal garden created over the last 6 yrs from a blank canvas with pebble and gravelled connecting areas. The garden entrance is an avenue of cypress trees and lavenders leading into a number of garden rooms, the first of which is an Asian themed tropical garden. The garden wraps around the house featuring ponds, patios, Mediterranean planting, olive trees, loquat trees, a rhododendron hedge and a pergola with sea views. Each area has seating to enjoy the plants and ambience. Regret no dogs.

55 ◆ LITTLEBREDY WALLED GARDENS
Littlebredy, DT2 9HL. The Walled Garden Workshop, 01305 898055, secretary@wgw.org.uk, www.littlebredy.com. *8m W of Dorchester. 10m E of Bridport. 1½m S of A35. NGS days: park on village green then walk 300yds. For the less mobile (and on normal open days) use gardens car park.* **For NGS: Tue 17, Tue 24 June (2-5.30). Adm £6, chd free. Home-made teas.** For other opening times and information, please phone, email or visit garden website.
1 acre walled garden on south facing slopes of Bride River valley. Herbaceous borders, riverside rose walk, lavender beds and potager vegetable and cut flower gardens. Partial wheelchair access, some steep grass slopes. For disabled parking please follow signs to main entrance.

56 LOWER ABBOTTS WOOTTON FARM
Whitchurch Canonicorum, Bridport, DT6 6NL. Clare Trenchard. *6m W of Bridport. Well signed from A35 at Morecombelake (2m) & Bottle Inn at Marshwood on B3165 (1½m). Some disabled off-road parking.* **Evening opening Sat 5 July (5-8). Sun 6 July (12-4). Adm £10. Light refreshments.**
Sculptor owner reflects her creative flair in garden form, shape and colour. Open gravel garden contrasts with main garden consisting of lawns, borders and garden rooms, making a perfect setting for sculptures. The naturally edged pond provides a tranquil moment of calm and tranquillity, but beware of being led down the garden path by the running hares!

57 MANOR FARM, HAMPRESTON
Wimborne, BH21 7LX. Guy & Anne Trehane, 01202 574223, anne.trehane@live.co.uk. *2½m E of Wimborne, 2½m W of Ferndown. From Canford Bottom r'about on A31, take exit B3073 Ham Lane. ½m turn R at Hampreston Xrds. House at bottom of village.* **Sat 8 Mar (10-1); Sun 9 Mar (1-4). Light refreshments. Sun 15 June, Sun 13 July, Sun 3 Aug, Sun 7 Sept (1-5). Home-made teas. Adm £5, chd free. Visits also by arrangement 8 Mar to 7 Sept for groups of 15 to 35.**
Traditional farmhouse garden designed and cared for by 3 generations of the Trehane family through over 100 yrs of farming and gardening at Hampreston. Garden is noted for its herbaceous borders and rose beds within box and yew hedges. Mature shrubbery, water and bog garden. Open for hellebores in March. Excellent plants as usual for sale at openings inc hellebores in March.

Our 2024 donation to The Queen's Nursing institute now helps support over 3,000 Queen's Nurses working in the community in England, Wales, Northern Ireland, the Channel Islands and the Isle of Man.

58 NEW 8 MANOR GARDENS
North Street, Beaminster, DT8 3EE. Nigel & Julie Cowderoy. *7mins walk N. from town square. Walk along North St from the square. Turn 1st R. Garden is at end of close. Public parking in square, public car park & on street parking nearby.* **Sat 5, Sun 6 July (1-5). Adm £5, chd free.**
Beautiful Mediterranean style tranquil, terraced riverside garden, developed over the last few years demonstrating possibilities for harnessing a sloping garden. Various growing zones could provide inspiration for any domestic garden on a south facing slope. Colourful, dense planting with both hardy and exotic plants. Uneven, narrow pathways in some areas.
♨))

SPECIAL EVENT
59 ♦ MAPPERTON HOUSE, GARDENS & WILDLANDS
Mapperton, Beaminster, DT8 3NR. Viscount & Viscountess Hinchingbrooke, 01308 862645, office@mapperton.com, www.mapperton.com. *6m N of Bridport. Off A356/A3066. 2m SE of Beaminster off B3163.* **For NGS: Thur 29 May (10-4). Adm £25, chd free. Pre-booking essential, please visit www.ngs.org.uk for information & booking. Light refreshments in the Coach House cafe (inc in admission price).**
For other opening times and information, please phone, email or visit garden website.
Terraced valley gardens surrounding Tudor/Jacobean manor house. On upper levels, walled croquet lawn, orangery and Italianate formal garden with fountains, topiary and grottoes. Below, C17 summerhouse and fishponds. Lower garden with shrubs and rare trees, leading to woodland and spring gardens. Mapperton is also home to a spectacular rewilding project known as Mapperton Wildlands and a limited number of tickets have been made available for a special 1 day rewilding tour on 29th May. On arrival please meet at the Coach House Café, where you will be joined by Ben Padwick, the ranger at Mapperton. Ben will give an introductory talk and will be your guide throughout your visit. There will be 2 tours, each lasting for 2½ hours covering a distance of 2 miles. Do wear appropriate footwear and bring waterproofs if it is expected to rain. Parts of the tour will take you up steep hills and across uneven ground, which may be challenging for anyone less able. In the gardens there is partial wheelchair access to the lawn and upper levels.

---

60 ♦ MINTERNE GARDEN
Minterne House, Minterne Magna, Dorchester, DT2 7AU. Lord Digby, 01300 341370, enquiries@minterne.co.uk, www.minterne.co.uk. *2m N of Cerne Abbas. On A352 Dorchester-Sherborne road.* **For opening times and information, please phone, email or visit garden website.**
As seen on BBC Gardeners' World and voted one of the 10 prettiest gardens in England by The Times. Famed for their display of historic rhododendrons, azaleas, Japanese cherries and magnolias in April/May when the garden is at its peak. Small lakes, streams and cascades offer new vistas at each turn around the 1m horseshoe shaped gardens covering 23 acres. The season ends with spectacular autumn colour. Snowdrops in Feb. Spring bulbs, blossom and bluebells in April. Easter trails for children. Over 200 acers provide spectacular autumn colour in Sept/Oct, inc Halloween trails for children. Fireworks at end of October.

---

61 NEW MORVAL
Ferry Road, Studland, Swanage, BH19 3AQ. Rohini Finch. *From Swanage & Purbeck direction the garden is 250m beyond the shop on Ferry road. From the Ferry the garden is 250m beyond the Knoll Beach Hotel. Follow yellow NGS signs, car park in field opp.* **Sun 7 Sept (12-5). Adm £8, chd £4. Home-made teas.**
Large 3 acre coastal garden that has recently undergone extensive renovation. Deep, informal, mixed borders surround the front lawn, planted in a contemporary style and containing many unusual plants. The roof garden commands stunning views to long elegant back garden and Studland Bay. Rear garden borders are filled with unusual shrubs and trees giving way to garden heath. Large front and back garden are easily accessible with wheelchairs. Steps to roof garden which is not accessible.

---

62 NEW MUDDY PATCHES
West Street, Abbotsbury, Weymouth, DT3 4JT. P Ellis, www.facebook.com/muddypatchesabbotsbury. *From Bridport take the B3157 coastal road to Abbottsbury. On entering Abbotsbury, Muddy Patches is on West St on the R. What3words app: business.unspoiled.slap.* **Sat 24, Sun 25 May, Sat 6, Sun 7 Sept (10-4). Adm £4, chd £2. Light refreshments.**
A beautiful village garden set in the glorious Dorset countryside with amazing views of the rolling hills and the historic St Catherine's Chapel. Enjoy a stroll around the gardens and see the amazing range of native and tropical plants, explore our wildlife area, visit the fairies in their garden or enjoy a delicious lunch, cake or ice cream. On site free parking available.

---

63 ♦ MUSEUM OF EAST DORSET
23-29 High Street, Wimborne Minster, BH21 1HR. Museum of East Dorset, 01202 882533, info@museumofeastdorset.co.uk, www.museumofeastdorset.co.uk. *Behind the Museum Building, with direct access via Crown Mead by the Library. Wimborne is just off A31. From W take B3078, from E take B3073 towards town centre. From Poole & Bournemouth enter town from S on A341. Although there is no on-site parking there are several public car parks with a 5 min walk of the museum* **For NGS: Evening opening Fri 9 May, Fri 13 June, Fri 11 July (6-8.30). Adm £15, chd free. Pre-booking essential, please visit www.ngs.org.uk for information & booking. Light refreshments in the Museum Tea Room, wine & soft drinks.**
For other opening times and information, please phone, email or visit garden website.
Behind the Museum of East Dorset is a tranquil walled garden tucked away in the centre of Wimborne. Colourful herbaceous borders and heritage orchard trees line the path which stretches 100m down to the mill stream. This year we have 3 evening garden lectures taking place at the Museum from 6pm to 8pm; Abbotsbury Subtropical Gardens presented by David Pearce on Fri 9th May, Sculpture by the Lakes presented by Monique Gudgeon on Fri 13th June and Knoll Gardens

presented by Neil Lucas on Friday 11th July. Wheelchair access through Tea Room entrance via a labelled side door and not the main entrance.
&. ❁ ☕ ⛱

64 MYRTLE COTTAGE
Woolland, Blandford Forum, DT11 0ES. Brian & Lynn Baker, 01258 817432, brian.baker15@ btinternet.com. *7m W of Blandford Forum. Situated at the base of Bulbarrow Hill, pass the church on your L, pass the turning to Ibberton on the R. Myrtle Cottage is on the R after the Elwood Centre.* **Sat 17, Sun 18 May (10-6). Adm £5, chd free. Tea, coffee & cake. Visits also by arrangement 1 Mar to 1 Sept for groups of 10+.**
A small to medium size segmented cottage garden, sympathetic to wildlife with a wildflower meadow and pond, part flower, part fruit and vegetable, a mix for everyone. Interesting hostas in pots and numerous chilli plant varieties grown from seed in the greenhouse.
❁ ☕

65 OAKDALE LIBRARY GARDENS
Wimborne Road, Poole, BH15 3EF. Oakdale Library Gardens Association, www.facebook.com/ Oakdalelibrarygardens. *Corner of Wimborne Rd & Dorchester Rd. Number 25/26 bus towards Canford Heath. Bus stop directly adjacent to Library. Free parking on site.* **Wed 14 May (2-5); Wed 11 June (10-1). Adm by donation. Light refreshments on NGS open days only.**
Award winning gardens comprising of the 'Bookerie' Reading and Rhyme time garden where wildlife is welcomed with bee friendly planting, an insect mansion and pond. Also a Commemorative Garden, a nautical themed garden, herb garden and children's adventure trail. The gardens have been designed and maintained by volunteers. Featured in '111 places in Poole that you shouldn't miss ' by Katherine Bebo. The Bookerie is only open during Library opening hours. Other gardens open at all times. Plant sales on NGS open days. Full wheelchair access in all the gardens except the children's adventure trail.
&. 🐕 ❁ ☕

66 THE OLD RECTORY, LITTON CHENEY
Litton Cheney, Dorchester, DT2 9AH. Richard & Emily Cave, 01308 482266, emilycave@rosacheney.com. *9m W of Dorchester. 1m S of A35, 6m E of Bridport. Park in village and follow signs.* **Sun 27, Wed 30 Apr, Sun 6 July (11-5). Adm £8, chd free. Tea, coffee & cake. Visits also by arrangement 27 Apr to 30 Sept.**
Steep paths lead to beguiling 4 acres of natural woodland with many springs, streams, 2 pools, one a natural swimming pool planted with native plants. Formal front garden, designed by Arne Maynard, with pleached crabtree border, topiary and soft planting inc tulips, peonies, roses and verbascums. Walled garden with informal planting, kitchen garden, orchard & 350 rose bushes for a cut flower business.
🐕 ☕ ⛱ 🔊

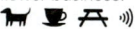

67 THE OLD RECTORY, MANSTON
Manston, Sturminster Newton, DT10 1EX. Andrew & Judith Hussey, 01258 474673, judithhussey@hotmail.com. *6m S of Shaftesbury, 2½m N of Sturminster Newton. From Shaftesbury, take B3091. On reaching Manston go past Plough Inn, L for Child Okeford on R-hand bend. Old Rectory last house on L.* **Visits by arrangement 1 May to 15 Sept for groups of 5 to 40. Adm £8, chd free.**
Beautifully restored 5 acre garden. South facing wall with 120ft herbaceous border edged by old brick path. Enclosed yew hedge flower garden. Wildflower meadow marked with mown paths and young plantation of mixed hardwoods. Well maintained walled Victorian kitchen garden with new picking flower section. Large new greenhouse also installed. Knot garden now well established.
&. ❁ 🚗 ☕ ⛱ 🔊

68 THE OLD RECTORY, PULHAM
Dorchester, DT2 7EA. Mr & Mrs N Elliott, 01258 817595, gilly.elliott@hotmail.com, www. instagram.com/theoldrectory_ pulham. *13m N of Dorchester. 8m SE of Sherborne. On B3143 turn E at Xrds in Pulham. Signed Cannings Court.* **Sun 25, Thur 29 May, Sun 3, Thur 7 Aug (2-5). Adm £9, chd free. Home-made teas. Visits also by arrangement 1 May to 15 Sept for groups of 5 to 50.**
4 acres of formal and informal gardens surrounding C18 rectory with splendid views. Yew pyramid allées and hedges, circular herbaceous borders with late summer colour. Exuberantly planted terrace, purple and white beds. Box parterres, mature trees, pond, sheets of daffodils, tulips, glorious churchyard, ha-ha, pleached hornbeam circle. Enchanting bog garden with stream and islands. 10 acres of woodland walks. Mostly wheelchair accessible.
&. 🐕 ❁ 🚗 ☕ 🔊

69 THE OLD SCHOOL HOUSE
The Street, Sutton Waldron, Blandford Forum, DT11 8NZ. David Milanes. *7m N of Blandford. Turn into Sutton Waldron from A350, continue for 300 yds, 1st house on L in The Street. Entrance past house through gates in wall.* **Sun 8, Thur 12 June (2-6). Adm £5, chd free. Open nearby Penmead Farm. Home-made teas avail at Penmead Farm on 8th June and at Old School House on 12th June.**
Village garden of almost an acre laid out in last 12 yrs with hornbeam hedges creating 'rooms' inc orchard, secret garden and pergola walkway. Raised bed for growing vegetables. Strong framework of existing large trees, beds are mostly planted with roses and herbaceous plants. Pleached hornbeam screen. A designer's garden with interesting semi-tender plants close to the house with benches to sit and relax on. Level lawns.
&. 🐕 ❁ ☕ 🔊

48,000 people affected by cancer were reached by Maggie's centres supported by the National Garden Scheme over the last 12 months.

174 DORSET

Holme For Gardens

70 NEW THE OLD VICARAGE
Powerstock, Bridport, DT6 3TE. Jo Willett & Stuart Rock. *4.7m NE of Bridport. From Bridport or Beaminster follow signs for Powerstock off A3066. Drive into centre of village. Parking up School Hill above church. House is 5 mins walk. What3words app: crunches. fork.sampling.* **Sat 24, Sun 25 May (12-5). Adm £5, chd free. Home-made teas at Old Vicarage Coach House. Tea, coffee, elderflower juice, home-made scones with cream and jam, cakes.**
A classic English garden of 1½ acres with many rooms and several notable trees. Extensively replanted over the past 5 yrs with a variety of herbaceous borders, grasses, a rose terrace and a tulip and dahlia square under a crab apple canopy. It also features a rare 'maiden' ancient mulberry, a 'font garden' (with Victorian font), vegetable garden, pond, orangery, orchard and croquet lawn. Front garden accessible. Gravel path to back.

71 THE OLD VICARAGE
East Orchard, Shaftesbury, SP7 0BA. Miss Tina Wright, 01747 811744, tina_lon@msn.com. *4½ m S of Shaftesbury, 3½ m N of Sturminster Newton. On B3091 between 90° bend & layby with defibrillator red phone box. Parking is on the opp corner towards Hartgrove.* **Fri 7, Fri 14, Sun 16 Feb, Fri 14, Sun 16 Mar, Fri 4, Sun 6 Apr, Fri 16, Sun 18 May (2-5). Adm £5, chd free. Home-made teas in garden but inside if very wet weather. 2026: Fri 6, Sun 8, Sun 15 Feb. Visits also by arrangement 2 Jan to 21 Dec. Adm £6 or £10 to inc refreshments.**
1.7 acre well established garden and a developing wildlife garden of just over an acre, with hundreds of different snowdrops, crocus and many other bulbs and winter flowering shrubs. A stream meanders down to a pond and there are lovely reflections in the swimming pond, the first to be built in Dorset. The wildlife garden has been planted with several unusual trees. Special features inc grotto, old Victorian man pushing his lawn mower (which his owner purchased brand new in 1866). Pond dipping, swing and other children's attractions. Cakes inc gluten free, and vegans are also catered for. Not suitable for wheelchairs if very wet.

SPECIAL EVENT

72 PARNHAM HOUSE
Beaminster, DT8 3LZ. James & Sophie Perkins. *S of Beaminster on the A3066. Enter through main gates on A3066 (look for yellow signs) Parking in car park on R after 250yds.* **Thur 19 June (2-5). Adm £25, chd free. Pre-booking essential, please visit www.ngs.org.uk for information & booking. Home-made teas.**
Parnham House, near Beaminster, is one of the oldest Grade I listed stately homes in Dorset. The beautifully presented spacious gardens surrounding the house have been extensively restored and inc terraced formal gardens, topiary, an avenue of yew tree pinnacles leading to a lake and a walled garden with deeply planted perennial and herbaceous borders. A limited number of tickets have been made available for this special open day. The Head Gardener will give a talk on the history and ongoing recent developments of the garden and grounds, and the gardening team will be on hand throughout the afternoon to answer any questions. Partial wheelchair access, gravel paths and steep grass slopes.

73 PENMEAD FARM
The Street, Sutton Waldron, Blandford Forum, DT11 8PF. Matthew & Claire Cripps. *5½ m S of Shaftesbury. From A350 turn into Sutton Waldron. Drive through the village & entrance is approx ¼ m on R after the road bridge which straddles the stream.* **Sun 8 June (2-6). Home-made teas. Thur 12 June (3-7). Adm £5, chd free. Open nearby The Old School House. Wine & light refreshments from 6pm on Thursday opening.**
Situated on the site of an old brick works the property is bordered by over 30 mature oak trees. The garden comprises a woodland and stream (Fontmell Brook) walk, meadows, substantial vegetable garden, orchard, spring fed pond and small semi walled garden. Being on clay soil roses thrive. Views to Pen Hill and Fontmell Down. Some sloping paths and can be wet under foot. Accessible bar steep slope down to stream and some gravel paths.

74 PHILIPSTON HOUSE
Winterborne Clenston, Blandford Forum, DT11 0NR. Mark & Ana Hudson. *SW of Blandford Forum. 2 km N of Winterborne Whitechurch & 1 km S of Crown Inn in Winterborne Stickland. Park in signed track/field off road, nr Bourne Farm Cottage. Enter garden from field.* **Sat 7 June (2-5). Adm £5, chd free. Cream teas. Pls bring cash for garden entry & refreshments.**
Charming 2 acre garden with lovely views in Winterborne valley. Many unusual trees, rambling roses, wisteria, mixed borders and shrubs. Sculptures, rose parterre, walled garden, swimming pool garden, vegetable garden. Stream with bridge over to wooded shady area with cedarwood pavilion. Orchard with mown paths planted with spring bulbs. Sorry, no WC available. Dogs welcome on leads, pls clear up after them. Wheelchair access is good providing it is dry.

75 1 PINE WALK
Lyme Regis, DT7 3LA. Mrs Erika Savory, erika.savory@btconnect.com. *Pls park in Holmbush Car Park at top of Cobb Rd.* **Visits by arrangement 15 July to 14 Sept for groups of 6 to 20. Pls email to discuss adm & refreshments.**
Unconventional ½ acre, multi level garden above Lyme Bay, adjoining NT's Ware Cliffs. Abundantly planted with an exotic range of shrubs, cannas, gingers and magnificent ferns. Apart from a rose and hydrangea collection, planting reflects owner's love of Southern Africa inc staggering succulents and late summer colour explosion featuring drifts of salvias, dahlias, asters, grasses and rudbeckia.

76 PIPSFORD FARM
Beaminster, DT8 3NT. Charlie & Bee Tuke. *2m SE of Beaminster off B3163, 7m N of Bridport. Postcode & SatNav bring you to the main front drive entrance, clearly signed.* **Fri 23 May (2-5). Adm £10, chd free. Pre-booking essential, please visit www.ngs.org.uk for information & booking. Home-made teas on the front terrace overlooking the garden & valley.**
3 acres of formal and informal gardens. Ponds surrounded by mature specimen trees, acers, hydrangeas, ferns and bamboo. Bog garden, with raised walkway. Walled garden with herbaceous beds, pond, pergola covered in apples and productive beds bordered by *Ilex crenata*. Cut flower area with paths to greenhouses and fruit cage, surrounded by mature yew hedges.

77 THE POTTING SHED
Middlemarsh, Sherborne, DT9 5QN. Andy Cole & Michele Hounsell, www.therapygarden.co.uk. *7m S of Sherborne, 11m N of Dorchester on the A352 in Middlemarsh. 300 yrds S of The Hunters Moon pub.* **Sat 13 Sept (10-4). Adm £5, chd free. Cream teas. Gluten free & vegan scones, freshly picked herbal teas & home-made jams.**
The Potting Shed opened its doors in April 2023. This new 2 acre Wellbeing Nursery, Therapy Garden has been created from scratch to enhance relaxation and tranquillity. The community garden has been planted organically to encourage all forms of wildlife. There is an acre of wildflower meadow, plant nursery and tea garden to explore. It truly is a special place to relax, unwind and be inspired. Partial access, small area of gravel, remainder paved and hard paths plus grass.

The National Garden Scheme donated £281,000 in 2024 to support those looking to work in horticulture as well as those struggling within the industry.

DORSET

78 PUGIN HALL
Rampisham, nr Dorchester, DT2 0PR. Tim & Ali Wright, 01935 83652, alison.wright@ngs.org.uk. *Near centre of village. NW of Dorchester. From Dorchester A37 Yeovil, 9m L Evershot, follow signs. From Crewkerne A356, take 1st L to Rampisham, Pugin Hall is on L after ½ m. Parking at Village Hall.* **Sun 11 May (12-5). Combined adm with Little Benville House £10, chd £5. Sun 8 June (12-5). Combined adm with Broomhill £10, chd £5. Sun 29 June (12-5). Combined adm with Wraxall Manor £10, chd £5. Sat 30, Sun 31 Aug, Sun 14 Sept (12-5). Adm £6, chd £3. Home-made teas.** Visits also by arrangement May to Sept for groups of 10+.
Pugin Hall was once Rampisham Rectory, designed in 1847 by Augustus Pugin, who also helped to design the interior of the Houses of Parliament. A Grade I listed building, it is surrounded by 4½ acres of garden, inc a large front lawn with rhododendrons, a walled garden filled with topiary and soft floral planting, orchard and beyond the River Frome a woodland walk. The walled garden is planted with shrubs, roses, clematis, masses of unusual perennials, and Japanese anemones against a backdrop of espalier fruit trees, box hedging with spirals. Pugin Hall is the only intact Pugin designed building currently in private ownership and is considered to be the most complete example of domestic architecture designed by him. The plan of the house encompasses Pugin's characteristic pinwheel design: an arrangement of rooms whose axis rotate about a central hall and lends itself well to the varying effects of light and shade within.

Our donation to Marie Curie this year equates to 17,496 hours of nursing care or 43 days of care in one of their nine hospices.

79 1C RECTORY ROAD
Poole, BH15 3BH. Dave Hutchings, www.instagram.com/goosesquawks. *5 mins from Poole town centre. The bungalow is behind the main houses on the road down a pedestrian access drive.* **Sun 20 July, Sun 17 Aug (11-4). Adm £5, chd free. Tea, coffee & cake.**
An unusual character house and garden. With a passion for maximalist design the house and garden has been designed and built by the owner over the last 7 yrs. Both garden and house are full of objet d'art spanning centuries, there's curiosities to see in every corner.

80 RUSSELL-COTES ART GALLERY & MUSEUM
East Cliff, Bournemouth, BH1 3AA. Phil Broomfield, 07810 646123, russellcotes@bcpcouncil.gov.uk, www.russellcotes.com. *On Bournemouth's East Cliff Promenade. Next to the Royal Bath Hotel, 2 mins walk from Bournemouth Pier. The closest car park is Bath Road South. Parking also available on the cliff top.* Visits by arrangement Apr to Oct for groups of 6 to 15. Adm £3, chd free.
Enjoy a private garden tour of this sub-tropical garden sited on the cliff top, overlooking the sea, full of a wide variety of plants from around the globe. East Cliff Hall was the home of Sir Merton and Lady Annie Russell-Cotes. The garden was restored allowing for modern access with areas retaining the original 1901 design conceived by the founders, such as the ivy clad grotto and Japanese influence. The Russell-Cotes Café serves a delicious range of light lunches, teas, coffees, and cakes. Some gravel paths and no wheelchair access to terrace.

81 NEW 10 RYAN CLOSE
Ferndown, BH22 9TP. Mrs Jane Norris. *From Tescos in Ferndown, up Church Rd to T-lights. Proceed across Wimborne Rd East into Ameysford Rd, 2nd R into Ryan Close, then immed R into even numbers.* **Sun 11 May, Sun 8 June (2-5). Adm £3.50, chd free. Home-made teas.**
Though a small urban plot, this plantswoman's garden is filled with a remarkable selection of mostly perennial plants, making a vibrant display all year, but especially in early summer. The beds are densely planted to suppress weeds, with alliums and tulips in May followed by salvias in June.

82 NEW 11 SCHOOL LANE
Studland, Swanage, BH19 3AJ. David Kent & Matt Etherington. *Parking at Manor Farm Tearooms, around the corner.* **Sat 12, Sun 13 July (11-4). Adm £5, chd £2.50. Tea, coffee & cake in the garden. Lunches available at Manor Farm Tearooms.**
Coastal cottage garden, close to Old Harry Rocks, located in a quiet leafy lane in the beautiful village of Studland. A varied and established garden, lovingly restored and developed over the last 10 yrs, inc a kitchen garden, areas of lawn surrounded by herbaceous borders, roses and flowering shrubs, old stone pathways, an old bothy, fernery, shrubbery, orchard and small pond.

83 THE SECRET GARDEN AT SERLES HOUSE
47 Victoria Road, Wimborne, BH21 1EN. Chris & Bridget Ryan. *Centre of Wimborne. On B3082 W of town, near hospital, Westfield car park 300yds. Off road parking close by.* **Sun 11, Sun 18 May (1-4.30). Adm £5, chd free. Tea, coffee, cake & sandwiches. Donation to MIND.**
The former home of the late Ian Willis, who lived here for just under 40 yrs. Alan Titchmarsh described this amusingly creative garden as 'one of the best 10 private gardens in Britain'. The ingenious use of unusual plants complements the imaginative treasure trove of garden objets d'art. Wheelchair access to garden only. Narrow steps may prohibit wide wheelchairs.

84 ♦ SHERBORNE CASTLE
New Rd, Sherborne, DT9 5NR. Mr E Wingfield Digby, www.sherbornecastle.com. *½ E of Sherborne. On New Rd B3145. Follow brown signs from A30 & A352.* **For opening times and information, please visit garden website.**
40+ acres. Grade I Capability Brown garden with magnificent vistas across surrounding landscape, inc lake and views to ruined castle. Herbaceous

Wytherston Farm

planting, notable trees, mixed ornamental planting and managed wilderness are linked together with lawn and pathways. Short and long walks available. Partial wheelchair access, gravel paths, steep slopes, steps.

& 🐕 🚗 🪑

GROUP OPENING

85 SHILLINGSTONE GARDENS
Shillingstone, DT11 0SL. Caroline Salt. *4m W of Blandford Forum. The village lies on the A357 between Blandford Forum & Sturminster Newton. Parking at Shillingstone House, additional parking & access to WC at Church Centre.* **Sun 10 Aug (10-4). Combined adm £7, chd free. Home-made teas at Shillingstone Church Centre, Main Rd, Shillingstone DT11 0SW.**

CHERRY COTTAGE
Lal & Gloria Ratnayake.

SHILLINGSTONE HOUSE
Michael & Caroline Salt.

Both gardens are in the centre of this pretty village which lies close to the River Stour with Hambledon Hill as a backdrop. The larger garden has some magnificent trees, traditional borders, old brick walls supporting multiple rambling roses and an old fashioned walled kitchen garden mixing vegetables, fruit and flowers. Nearby a cottage garden packed with exotic plants, Bonsai, pond, fruit and herbs and beds of perenials and annuals. Wheelchair access to Shillingstone House garden only.

& ❀ ☕

In 2024, National Garden Scheme funding for Perennial supported 1,367 people working in horticulture.

178 DORSET

86 SLAPE MANOR
Netherbury, Bridport, DT6 5LH. Paul Mulholland & Tarsha Finney, 07534 676148, info@slapemanor.com. *1m S of Beaminster. Turn W off A3066 to Netherbury. House ½m S of Netherbury on back rd to Bridport signed Waytown.* **Thur 24 Apr, Sun 11, Thur 29 May (1-5). Sun 6 July (1-5), open nearby 8 Manor Gardens. Thur 25 Sept, Sun 5 Oct (1-5). Adm £15, chd free. Tea, coffee & cake. Visits also by arrangement 1 Feb to 1 Dec for groups of 8 to 20.**
River valley garden in a process of transformation. Spacious lawns, wildflower meadows, and primula fringed streams leading down to a lake. Walk over the stream with magnificent hostas, gunneras and horizontal *Cryptomeria japonica* 'Elegans' around the lake. Admire the mature wellingtonias, ancient wisterias, rhododendrons and planting around the house. Kitchen garden renovation underway. Adm price inc optional guided tour (weekdays only). Tours are at 1pm, 2pm, 3pm and 4pm. Max 20 people per tour on a 1st come 1st served basis. Slape Manor is one of the inspirations behind Chelsea 2022 Gold medal winning and Best in Show Garden designed by Urquhart & Hunt with Rewilding Britain. Mostly flat with some sloping paths and steps. Ground is often wet and boggy.

87 SOUTH EGGARDON HOUSE
Askerswell, Dorchester, DT2 9EP. Buffy Sacher, 07920 520280, buffysacher@gmail.com. *From Dorchester on A35 turn R for Askerswell. Through village at T junction. Go straight over. From Bridport on A35 take 1st turning to Askerswell. Pass Spyway Inn on R. Turn next L.* **Visits by arrangement for groups of 8 to 30. Adm £15, chd free. Light refreshments.**
5 acres of formal and informal gardens designed around a 2000 yr old yew tree and lake. Water garden with streams pond and lake. Woodland walk, orchard, wild garden, large herbaceous borders filled with roses and perennials. Ornamental kitchen garden.

88 NEW THE STABLES
Knitson, Corfe Castle, Wareham, BH20 5JB. Rebecca Helfer, beccacharron219@gmail.com. *Follow the A351 3m E from Corfe Castle. Turn L signed Knitson. After 1m fork R. We are on L after ¼m.* **Sat 24, Sun 25, Mon 26 May, Wed 25, Thur 26 June, Thur 17, Fri 18 July (12-5). Combined adm with Knitson Old Farmhouse £8, chd free. Visits also by arrangement Feb to Nov for groups of 10+.**
Much loved garden planted in a contemporary style with deep borders filled with easy care colourful perennials interspersed with shrubs. The garden was established in 2016 on flat compacted sand that had been a horse dressage arena. The aim was to plant a garden full of flowers in a naturalistic style enabling it to fit into the surrounding landscape. There is more to explore than just the garden in front of the house. Working kitchen garden. Pond at the top of the adjoining field and planted trees on the north side of the garden.

89 STADDLESTONES
14 Witchampton Mill, Witchampton, Wimborne, BH21 5DE. Annette & Richard Lockwood, 01258 841405, richardglockwood@yahoo.co.uk. *5m N of Wimborne off B3078. Follow signs through village & park in sports field, 7 mins walk to garden. Limited disabled parking nr garden.* **Sun 25, Mon 26 May (11.30-4.30). Combined adm with White House £10, chd free. Home-made teas at White House. Visits also by arrangement 2 Apr to 2 Oct.**
A beautiful setting for a cottage garden with colour themed borders, pleached limes and hidden gems, leading over a chalk stream to a shady area which has some unusual plants. Plenty of areas just to sit and enjoy the wildlife. Wire bird sculptures by local artist. Wheelchair access to first half of garden.

SPECIAL EVENT

90 STAFFORD HOUSE
West Stafford, Dorchester, DT2 8AD. Lord & Lady Fellowes. *2m E of Dorchester in Frome Valley. Follow signs to West Stafford from the West, 1st house on L before you get to the village, green park railings and gate.* **Fri 4 July (10-12.30). Adm £25, chd free. Pre-booking essential, please visit www.ngs. org.uk for information & booking. Home-made elevenses inc cake & biscuits in a gardening theme.**
The gardens at Stafford House inc a river walk and tree planting in the style of early C19 Picturesque. Humphry Repton prepared landscape proposals for the garden and the designs were later implemented, they were also included in his famous Red Books. A limited number of tickets have been made available for this private morning opening, hosted by Lord and Lady Fellowes. The head gardener, Pip Poulton, will give a talk and guided tour of the gardens and grounds inc ongoing empathetic recent renovations. Special home-made elevenses will be served on the main terrace or underneath the turkey oak tree planted in 1633. There will then be the opportunity to explore the grounds and gardens, finishing at approx 12.30pm.

91 STILLPOINT GARDEN & NURSERY
Sheepwash Barn, Symondsbury, Bridport, DT6 6HH. Charles Chesshire, www.charleschesshire.co.uk. *1m W of Bridport. From A35, head through Symondsbury past Shear Plot on R, down hill & the garden is on R, or from Bridport take Symondsbury Estate road to Mill Lane & the garden is on L.* **Sun 29 June, Sun 10 Aug (1-5). Adm £5, chd free. Home-made teas.**
Set in heavenly Dorset countryside, the ½ garden is composed of an intricate web of gravel paths weaving between deep and colourful borders to create an intimate experience for the extensive collection of new and unusual plants, especially Itoh peonies and hydrangeas. At the heart of the garden is a Japanese styled koshi-kake 'waiting room', surrounded by dwarf pines, grasses and ferns.

DORSET

92 NEW STONELEIGH
Walditch, Bridport, DT6 4LB. Chris & Angela Addis. *A loop road off the A35 immed E of Bridport services Walditch village only. From E on A35, 1m short of Bridport, post points to Walditch on L. From W leave Bridport on A35. Post points to cemetery/Walditch R. Over mini r'about and up hill. Parking adjacent to house.* **Sat 21, Sun 22 June (1.30-5.30). Adm £6, chd free. Home-made teas.**
An amphitheatre is the dramatic backdrop to this garden which is approached via a rockery and opens to terracing, busy borders, undulating lawns and groups of trees. Two ponds are linked by a stream and a raised area enjoys a fish pond with fountain. A bed of ornamental grasses leads the eye to a stone barn. An enclosed vegetable area, greenhouse and fruit cage complete this pretty garden. A large patio for sitting and enjoying refreshments. Most areas of the garden are accessible to wheelchairs although some of the undulations of the lawn could be challenging.

93 NEW TULIP TREE
Donhead St. Mary, Shaftesbury, SP7 9DL. Rodney & Penny Short. *4m E of Shaftesbury. A30 towards Shaftesbury. In Ludwell turn R opp brown sign to Tollard Royal. Follow rd for ¾ m and bear R at T-junction. Bear R at next fork. Pass Chapel on R. Tulip Tree is next L.* **Sun 22 June (2-5). Adm £5, chd free. Home-made teas.**
Two acres of paddock with mown paths behind house and 1acre of garden around house dominated by 120 yr old *Liriodendron tulipifera*, which originates from N America, and the Northofagus trees from S America. Both are unusual plantings for a farmhouse in Dorset. The garden is divided into separate areas by mature hedges and old stone walls. The patio and rose garden are recent additions. Parking is on hard-standing in paddock. Specified disabled parking near the house. Sloping path from top to bottom lawn.

94 NEW TUMBLINS
Bulbarrow Lane, Winterborne Stickland, Blandford Forum, DT11 0ED. John & Claire Scott, 01258 880841, claire@historystore.ltd.uk. *6m W of Blandford Forum. At Blandford Forum follow signs to Brewery. 2nd r'about turn L, 2nd R to Winterborne Stickland. At village turn R for Bulbarrow, then turn L for Bulbarrow. Turn L for Winterborne Houghton.* **Sat 5, Sun 6, Mon 7 July (10-4.30). Adm £5, chd free. Tea, coffee & cake.** Visits also by arrangement 1 May to 1 Oct for groups of up to 20.
3 acre hill top garden with extensive views. Water features, orchards, kitchen garden, mixed borders and unusual trees including, *Wolemia nobolis*, *Ginko biloba* and Monterey pine. Roses and hydrangeas thrive. The garden is accessible for wheelchairs, though sloping & the gravel garden may be difficult.

95 UTOPIA
Tincleton, Dorchester, DT2 8QP. Nick & Sharon Spiller. *4m SE of Dorchester. Take signs to Tincleton from Dorchester, Puddletown. Pick up garden signs in the village.* **Sat 7, Sun 8 June (1-5). Adm £5, chd £4. Light refreshments.**
Approximately ½ acre of secluded, peaceful garden made up of several rooms inspired by different themes. Inspiration is taken from Mediterranean and Italian gardens, woodland space, water gardens. Seating is scattered throughout to enable you to sit and enjoy the different spaces and take advantage of both sun and shade. Parking available within a 10 min walk or park in village.

96 WAGTAILS
Stourton Caundle, Sturminster Newton, DT10 2JW. Sally & Nick Reynolds, Sally.Reynolds@me.com. *6m E of Sherborne. From Sherborne take A3030. At Bishops Caundle, L signed Stourton Caundle. After 1½ m in village on R as descending hill, 5 houses before Trooper Inn. Park at Manor Farm.* **Sat 31 May, Sun 1 June (2-5). Combined adm with Grange Cottage £10, chd free. Home-made teas.** Visits also by arrangement 26 May to 28 Sept for groups of 10 to 50.
Contemporary Arne Maynard inspired garden of almost 3 acres, with wildflower meadows, orchards, kitchen garden and lawns, linked by a sweeping mown pathway, studded with topiary, divided by box, yew and beech hedging. Landscaped and planted over last 10 yrs by current owners, and still work in progress. Wheelchair access over majority of garden and orchards over lawn grade paths. Gentle slopes with grass pathways.

97 ♦ THE WALLED GARDEN
Moreton, Dorchester, DT2 8RH. 01929 405685, info@walledgardenmoreton.co.uk, walledgardenmoreton.co.uk. *In the village of Moreton, near Crossways. Look for the brown signs out on the main road.* **For opening times and information, please phone, email or visit garden website.**
The Walled Garden is a beautiful 5 acre landscaped formal garden in the village of Moreton. The village is close to the historic market town of Dorchester and situated on the River Frome. A wide variety of perennial plants sit in the borders, which have been styled in original Georgian and Victorian designs. Sculpture from various local artists, family area and play park, animal area, and plant shop, plus on site café.

98 WELL COTTAGE
Ryall, Bridport, DT6 6EJ. John & Heather Coley. *Less than 1m N of A35 from Morcombelake. From E: R by farm shop in Morcombelake. Garden 0.9m on R. From W: L entering Morcombelake, immed R by village hall and L on Pitmans Lane to T junc. Turn R, Well Cott on L. Parking on site and nearby.* **Sat 17, Sun 18 May (1-5). £5, chd free. Home-made teas.**
Over an acre of garden brought back to life since 2012. There is now much more light after some trees were taken down and new areas have been cultivated. A number of distinct areas, some quite surprising but most still enjoy wonderful views over Marshwood Vale. Heather's textile art studio will be open to view. Best large garden at Melplash Show 2024.

99 WESTERN GARDENS
24A Western Ave, Branksome Park, Poole, BH13 7AN. Mr Peter Jackson, 01202 708388, pjbranpark@gmail.com. *3m W of Bournemouth. From S end Wessex Way (A338) at gyratory take The Avenue, 2nd exit. At T-lights turn R into Western Rd then at bottom of hill L. At church turn R into Western Ave.* **Sun 4 May, Sun 22 June (2-5). Adm £7, chd free. Home-made teas. Visits also by arrangement 15 Apr to 7 Sept for groups of 15+.**
Created over 40 yrs the garden offers enormous variety with rose, Mediterranean courtyard and woodland gardens, herbaceous borders and cherry tree and camellia walk. Lush foliage and vibrant flowers give year-round colour and interest enhanced by wood sculpture and topiary. 'This secluded and magical 1 acre garden captures the spirit of warmer climes and begs for repeated visits' (Gardening Which?). Plants, home-made jams and chutneys for sale. Wheelchair access to ¾ garden.
& 🐾 ✻ 🚗 ☕ 🔊

100 WHITE HOUSE
Newtown, Witchampton, Wimborne, BH21 5AU. Mr Tim Read, 01258 840438, tim@witchampton.org. *5m N of Wimborne off B3078. Travel through village of Witchampton towards Newtown for 800m. Pass Crichel House's castellated gates on L. White House is a modern house sitting back from road on L after further 300m.* **Sun 25, Mon 26 May (11.30-4.30). Combined adm with Staddlestones £10, chd free. Home-made teas. Visits also by arrangement 1 May to 1 Oct for groups of 8 to 15.**
1½ acre garden set on different levels, with a Mediterranean feel, planted to encourage wildlife and pollinators. Wildflower border, pond surrounded by moisture loving plants, prairie planting of grasses and perennials, orchard. Chainsaw sculptures of birds of prey. Reasonable wheelchair access to all but the top level of the garden.
& ✻ ☕ 🔊

101 20 WICKET ROAD
Kinson, Bournemouth, BH10 5LT. Carron Bowen (& Peter Hellawell). *300 metres SE of Kinson Green. From Kinson Green (The Hub/Library): follow Wimborne Rd (A341) towards Northbourne. Turn R after shops into Kitscroft Rd, R again into Bramley Rd; Wicket Rd is second L. No 20 is on the L.* **Sat 23, Sun 24, Mon 25 Aug (2-5). Adm £5, chd free. Tea, coffee & cake.**
Built around a modern terrace, this small suburban garden (just 18 x 13 metres) sits on an awkward shaped plot, over a bed of clay. Set down from its neighbours, it developed a habit of flooding. But you'd never know. 'Borrow, hint, reveal, distract, attract, conceal' – the design uses every trick in the gardening handbook to create a truly memorable space. Exhibition of the garden's history, some unusual plants, a unique 'quay' (for storing run-off water as part of a hidden drainage system) and an array of small-scale features. Access is via the garage through a narrow doorway (26"). However, once in the garden, paths are wide with step-free route to most areas.
& ✻ ☕

102 WINCOMBE PARK
Shaftesbury, SP7 9AB. John & Phoebe Fortescue, www.wincombepark.com. *2m N of Shaftesbury. A350 Shaftesbury to Warminster, past Wincombe Business Park, 1st R signed Wincombe & Donhead St Mary. ¾ m on R.* **Sun 11, Wed 14 May (2-5). Adm £8, chd free. Home-made teas. Dairy & gluten free options.**
Extensive mature garden with sweeping panoramic views from lawn over parkland to lake and enchanting woods through which you can wander amongst bluebells. Garden is a riot of colour in spring with azaleas, camellias and rhododendrons in flower amongst shrubs and unusual trees. Beautiful walled kitchen garden. Cash payments preferred. Partial wheelchair access only, slopes and gravel paths.
& 🐾 🚗 ☕

103 105 WOOLSBRIDGE ROAD
Ashley Heath, Ringwood, BH24 2LZ. Richard & Lynda Nunn. *A31 W for 2m after Ringwood, R at Woolsbridge Rd r'about. 1m on L. A31 E, L at W'bridge Rd r'bout. Limited parking on drive or use side roads.* **Sat 9, Sun 10 Aug (11-4.30). Adm £4, chd free. Home-made teas.**

Average size back garden with hidden paths meandering through different areas inc architectural jungle exotics, bamboos and bananas, a woodland walkway with rhododendrons, fernery, grass bed, pond and hot gravel bed. Several secluded seating areas, lawn and traditional vegetable patch.
🐾 ☕ 🔊

104 NEW WRAXALL MANOR
Higher Wraxall, Dorchester, DT2 0HP. Mrs Camilla Boileau. *NW of Dorchester. From Dorchester A37 Yeovil, 9m L Evershot, follow signs. From Crewkerne A356, take L to Wraxall, Manor on R after ½ m.* **Sun 29 June (12-5). Combined adm with Pugin Hall £10, chd £5. Home-made teas on terrace overlooking main borders.**
Grade II* listed Manor House built in 1630 with Lutyens extensions in 1905. Large 3 acre elegant garden with deep herbaceous borders planted in a contemporary and naturalistic style. Filled with grasses, verbena, foxgloves, sedum, *stachys byzantina* and asters repeated throughout. Interspersed with yew tree pinnacles and hedging. Kitchen garden, fruit cage and greenhouses. Garden sculptures.
🐾 ☕

SPECIAL EVENT
105 WYKE FARM
Chedington, Beaminster, DT8 3HX. Alex & Robert Appleby, www.wykefarm.com. *Take the turning from the A356, opp The Winyards Gap Inn, away from Chedington, signed to Halstock. Drive 1m down the lane and we are the 1st farm entrance on the L.* **Sun 22 June (1-5.30). Adm £25, chd free. Pre-booking essential, please visit www.ngs.org.uk for information & booking. Home-made teas in the barn by the white courtyard garden.**
The owners of Wyke Farm, Robert and Alex Appleby, are both fanatical about rewilding, environmental conservation and preservation of the natural habitat. They have lived at Wyke Farm for almost 20 yrs and in this time have worked hard to empathically restore the land to inc a substantial wildflower meadow at the front of the house, and a large lake and woodland area. There are herbaceous borders and lawns around the house. There is a rose

garden that leads to the woodland garden, then a more formal courtyard garden that leads through the barn to a kitchen garden. A limited number of tickets have been made available for this special 1 day rewilding event. Meet at the front of the house on the main drive for an introductory talk and guided tour with Ecologist, Tom Brereton, who has supported the Applebys on their work at Wyke Farm. The paths are gravel.

SPECIAL EVENT

106 WYTHERSTON FARM
Powerstock, Bridport, DT6 3TQ. Johnnie & Sophie Boden. *From Mt Pleasant Xrds go down hill for 1m. At very bottom where lane bends to R carry straight on. following sign for Wytherston Farm only. Carry on to end of the drive into a yard. From Powerstock leave village going uphill with church on R. After 1m take 1st turning on R for Wytherston Farm.* **Sat 21 June (9.30-12.30). Adm £25, chd free. Pre-booking essential, please visit www.ngs.org.uk for information & booking. Please meet in the Tithe Barn at 9.30 prompt for light refreshments including tea, coffee, squash and pastries.** Johnnie and Sophie Boden bought Wytherston in 2005. Since then they and their fantastic team have tried to encourage wild flowers in both their garden and in the meadows surrounding the farm, which makes for a breathtaking display. They have also maintained the gardens around the house, which inc deep herbaceous borders, roses and formal topiary structure interspersed with bright floral colour. A limited number of tickets have been made available for this special event, kindly hosted by Johnnie, who will give a talk and guided tour through the wildflower garden and meadows. There is plenty of parking. Dogs are very welcome.

Our donation in 2024 has enabled Parkinson's UK to fund 3 new nursing posts this year directly supporting people with Parkinson's.

107 YEW TREE HOUSE
Hermitage Lane, Hermitage, Dorchester, DT2 7BB. Anna Vines, 07940 513001, anna@annavinesgardens.co.uk, anna@annavinesgardens.co.uk. *7m S of Sherborne. Turn towards Holnest off A352, Dorchester-Sherborne road. Continue 2m to Hermitage. In Hermitage, new build house on N side at the western end of village green.* **Sat 14, Sun 15 June (1-5). Adm £5, chd free. Home-made teas. Visits also by arrangement 31 May to 1 Sept for groups of 5+. Refreshments for groups available by arrangement.** A recently landscaped and planted ½ acre plot, surrounding a new-build eco home. House and garden designed to connect harmoniously and sit naturally within the surrounding rural landscape. The garden comprises a small kitchen garden, orchard, Mediterranean garden, boules court and herbaceous borders, each providing their own ambience. Informal perennial borders enclose terraces around the house. Photographic display in the barn within the garden. Gravel driveway.

Knoll Gardens

ESSEX

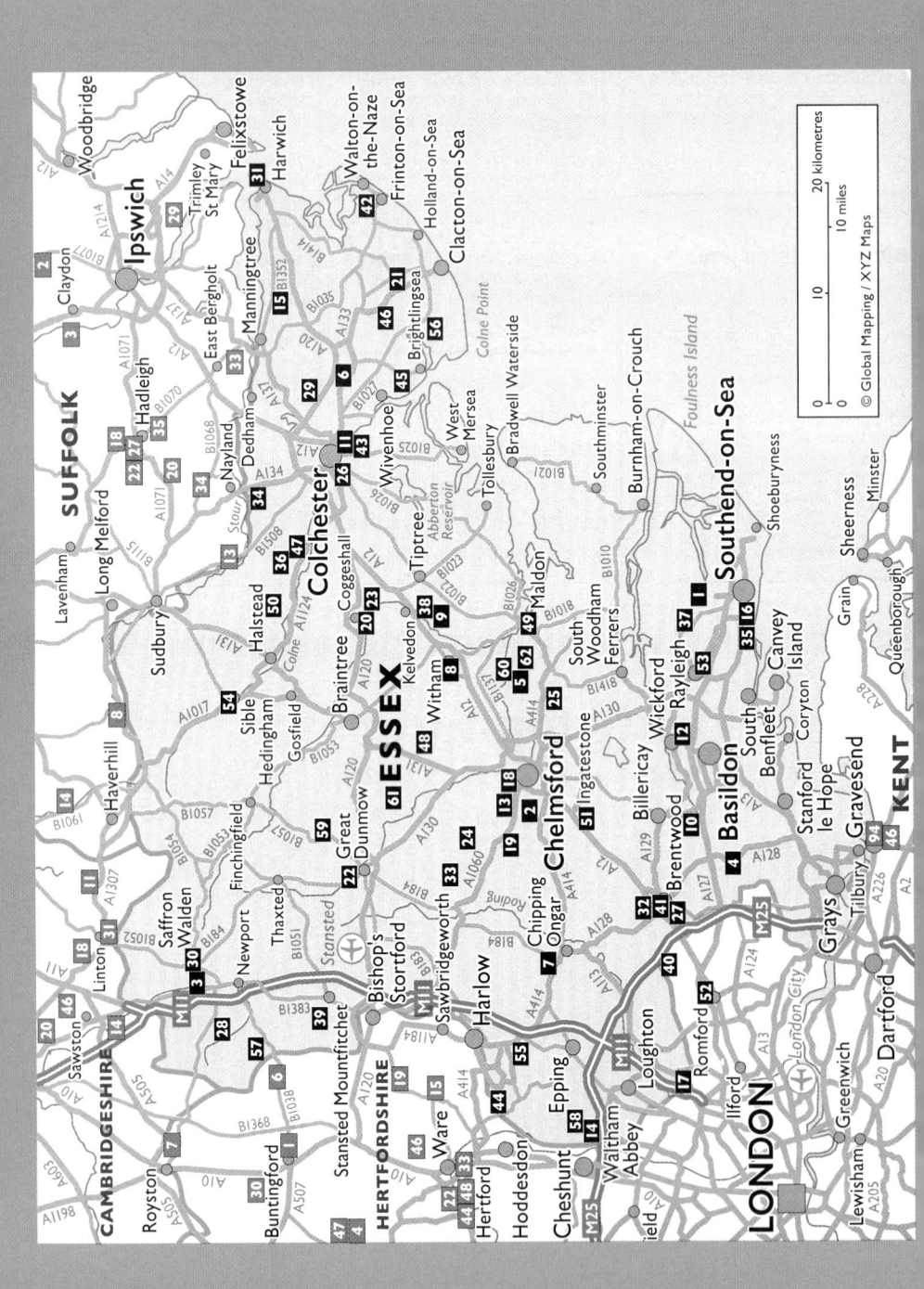

ESSEX

VOLUNTEERS

County Organiser
Victoria Kennedy 07801 039688
victoria.kennedy@ngs.org.uk

County Treasurer
Richard Steers
07392 426490
steers123@aol.com

Publicity & Social Media Co-ordinator
Debbie Thomson
07759 226579
debbie.thomson@ngs.org.uk

By Arrangement Visit Co-ordinator
Alan Gamblin 07720 446797
alan.gamblin@ngs.org.uk

Booklet Co-ordinator
Doug Copeland 07483 839387
doug.copeland@ngs.org.uk

Assistant County Organisers
Tricia Brett 01255 870415
tricia.brett@ngs.org.uk

Avril & Roger Cole-Jones
01245 225726
randacj@gmail.com

Susan Copeland MBE
07534 006179
susan.copeland@ngs.org.uk

Alison Hart
alison.hart@ngs.org.uk

Sharon Holdsworth
07721 528739
sharon.holdsworth@ngs.org.uk

Frances Vincent 07766 707379
frances.vincent@ngs.org.uk

Talks
Richard Wollaston
01245 231428
richard.wollaston@ngs.org.uk

County Photographer
Caroline Cassell 07973 551196
caroline.cassell@ngs.org.uk

◼ @EssexNGS   ✕ @EssexNGS   ⬜ @essexngs

OPENING DATES

All entries subject to change. For latest information check
www.ngs.org.uk

Extended openings are shown at the beginning of the month.

Map locator numbers are shown to the right of each garden name.

February

Snowdrop Openings

Sunday 2nd
◆ Green Island — 29

Saturday 8th
Horkesley Hall — 34

Wednesday 12th
Horkesley Hall — 34

Thursday 13th
Dragons — 19

Wednesday 19th
Dragons — 19

Sunday 23rd
Grove Lodge — 30

March

Saturday 1st
◆ Beth Chatto's Plants & Gardens — 6

Sunday 9th
Anglia Ruskin University Writtle — 2

Sunday 16th
Grove Lodge — 30

Friday 21st
Ulting Wick — 60

April

Every Thursday and Friday
Feeringbury Manor — 23

Sunday 6th
2 Cedar Avenue — 12

Saturday 19th
Ulting Wick — 60

Friday 25th
Ulting Wick — 60

Saturday 26th
Loxley House — 41

Sunday 27th
◆ Green Island — 29
Heyrons — 33

May

Every Thursday and Friday
Feeringbury Manor — 23

Sunday 4th
Furzelea — 25

Wednesday 7th
◆ St Osyth Priory — 56

Sunday 11th
Bassetts — 5
Cannock Mill Cohousing Gardens — 11

Sunday 18th
The Gates — 27
Great Becketts — 28
May Cottage — 42
Oak Farm — 47
1 Whitehouse Cottages — 62

Sunday 25th
Chippins — 15
The Mount — 44
The Old Rectory — 48

June

Every Thursday
Barnards Farm — 4

Every Thursday and Friday
Feeringbury Manor — 23

Sunday 1st
NEW The Chimes, 3-4 Church Street — 14
Furzelea — 25
Jankes House — 36
Silver Birches — 58
Walnut Tree Cottage — 61

Wednesday 4th
Braxted Park Estate — 9

Saturday 7th
Allways — 1
Isabella's Garden — 35
Laurel Cottage — 39

Sunday 8th
Blake Hall — 7
Isabella's Garden — 35
Oak Farm — 47

184 ESSEX

June

Wednesday 11th
8 Dene Court ... 18

Thursday 12th
◆ Audley End House ... 3

Friday 13th
Moynes Farm ... 46

Saturday 14th
Moynes Farm ... 46

Sunday 15th
Grove Lodge ... 30
Over Hall ... 50

Saturday 21st
NEW 1 Brook Cottage ... 10
The Garden Studio ... 26
Great Becketts ... 28

Sunday 22nd
2 Cedar Avenue ... 12
Fudlers Hall ... 24
The Garden Studio ... 26
Peacocks ... 51

Thursday 26th
Oak Farm ... 47

Friday 27th
160 Chignal Road ... 13
8 Dene Court ... 18

Saturday 28th
17 Elm Road ... 21
Moverons ... 45
18 Pettits Boulevard ... 52

Sunday 29th
Barnards Farm ... 4
The Mount ... 44
Moverons ... 45
18 Pettits Boulevard ... 52

In 2024, National Garden Scheme funding for Perennial supported 1,367 people working in horticulture.

The Garden Studio

July

Every Thursday
Barnards Farm 4

Every Thursday and Friday to Friday 25th
Feeringbury Manor 23

Saturday 5th
69 Rundells - The Secret Garden 55

Sunday 6th
Chippins 15
1 Whitehouse Cottages 62

Wednesday 9th
Long House Plants 40

Saturday 12th
NEW 79 Cliffsea Grove 16
30 Queens Road 53

Sunday 13th
NEW 79 Cliffsea Grove 16
The Delves 17
Harwich Gardens 31
The Old Rectory 48
30 Queens Road 53

Wednesday 16th
Ulting Wick 60

Friday 18th
160 Chignal Road 13
8 Dene Court 18

Saturday 19th
160 Chignal Road 13
8 Dene Court 18
Dragons 19
207 Mersea Road 43

Sunday 20th
Furzelea 25
207 Mersea Road 43
Oak Farm 47

Saturday 26th
Isabella's Garden 35

Sunday 27th
Isabella's Garden 35

Tuesday 29th
8 Dene Court 18

August

Every Thursday
Barnards Farm 4

Wednesday 6th
Long House Plants 40

Wednesday 13th
8 Dene Court 18

Friday 15th
Old Timbers 49

Sunday 24th
Laurel Cottage 39

Monday 25th
Ulting Wick 60

Friday 29th
8 Dene Court 18

September

Every Thursday and Friday
Feeringbury Manor 23

Wednesday 3rd
Long House Plants 40

Friday 5th
Ulting Wick 60

Saturday 6th
Loxley House 41
18 Pettits Boulevard 52

Sunday 7th
Barnards Farm 4
Kamala 37
Loxley House 41
18 Pettits Boulevard 52

Sunday 21st
Furzelea 25

October

Every Thursday and Friday to Friday 17th
Feeringbury Manor 23

Wednesday 1st
♦ Beth Chatto's Plants & Gardens 6

Sunday 12th
♦ Green Island 29

Sunday 26th
Elmbridge Mill 22

December

Saturday 6th
Laurel Cottage 39

February 2026

Sunday 8th
♦ Green Island 29

By Arrangement

Arrange a personalised garden visit with your club, or group of friends, on a date to suit you. See individual garden entries for full details.

Bassetts 5
Blunts Hall 8
NEW 1 Brook Cottage 10
2 Cedar Avenue 12
Chippins 15
8 Dene Court 18
Dragons 19
59 East Street 20
Feeringbury Manor 23
Furzelea 25
Great Becketts 28
Grove Lodge 30
262 Hatch Road 32
Heyrons 33
Horkesley Hall 34
Isabella's Garden 35
Kamala 37
Kelvedon Hall 38
May Cottage 42
207 Mersea Road 43
The Mount 44
Moverons 45
Moynes Farm 46
Oak Farm 47
Old Timbers 49
Peacocks 51
Rookwoods 54
69 Rundells - The Secret Garden 55
Sheepcote Green House 57
Silver Birches 58
Snares Hill Cottage 59
Ulting Wick 60

The National Garden Scheme donated over £3.5 million to our nursing and health beneficiaries from money raised at gardens open in 2024.

THE GARDENS

1 ALLWAYS
14 St Andrews Road, Rochford, SS4 1NP. Ms Liz Grant. *Traverse down St Andrews Rd. The blue house can be found 100m on the R.* **Sat 7 June (11-4). Adm £6, chd free. Tea, coffee & cake.**
A cottage style garden of a grade two listed 1930's home. A mature wisteria greets visitors on the front of the cottage. The rear garden has an area of lawn flanked by perennial borders with a viburnum arch leading to an attractive pond with Monet style bridge, pebbled beach area and a mature Indian Bean tree. A new wildlife pond and bog garden has been created in 2022 in the woodland area. After recently discovering some old steps leading down to the diverted River Roach, a new woodland area was opened in 2024.

2 ANGLIA RUSKIN UNIVERSITY WRITTLE
Writtle, CM1 3RR. Anglia Ruskin University Writtle, www.aru.ac.uk. *4m W of Chelmsford. On A414, near Writtle village. Parking available on the main campus (student car park).* **Sun 9 Mar (10-3). Adm £5, chd free. Light refreshments at The Garden Room (main campus).**
Anglia Ruskin University Writtle has 15 acres of informal lawns with naturalised bulbs and wildflowers. Large tree collection, mixed shrubs, herbaceous border, dry/ Mediterranean borders, seasonal bedding and landscaped glasshouses. All gardens have been designed and built by our students studying a wide range of horticultural courses. Wheelchair access: some gravel, however majority of areas accessible to all. Well behaved dogs on lead please.

3 ◆ AUDLEY END HOUSE
Off London Road, Saffron Walden, CB11 4JF. English Heritage. *1m W of Saffron Walden on B1383 (M11 exit 8 or 10).* **For NGS: Evening opening Thur 12 June (5.30-7.30). Adm £20, chd free. Pre-booking essential, please email fundraising@english-heritage.org.uk or visit www.english-heritage.org.uk/visit/places/audley-end-house-and-gardens/events for information & booking. Light refreshments. For other opening times and information, please email or visit garden website.**
Meet our Head Gardener and gardens team for an exclusive evening tour – enjoy sweeping C18 parkland which wraps around C19 formality in the parterre. Explore the enchanting Elysian Garden and the 'Capability' Brown landscape setting for the house, still featuring many of its original trees.

4 BARNARDS FARM
Brentwood Road, West Horndon, CM13 3FY. Bernard & Sylvia Holmes & The Christabella Charitable Trust, 07504 210405, vanessa@barnardsfarm.eu, www.barnardsfarm.eu. *5m S of Brentwood. On A128 1½ m S of A127 Halfway House flyover. From junc continue S on A128 under the railway bridge. Garden on R just past bridge. What3words app: tulip.folds.statue.* **Every Thur 5 June to 28 Aug (11-4.30). Sun 29 June, Sun 7 Sept (1-5.30). Adm £10, chd free. Light refreshments.**
So much to explore! Climb the Belvedere for the wider view and take the train for a woodland adventure. Summer beds and borders, ponds, lakes and streams, walled vegetable plot. 'Japanese garden', sculptures grand and quirky enhance and delight. Barnards Miniature Railway rides (BMR): Separate charges apply. Sunday extras: Bernard's Sculpture tour 2.30pm. Car collection. 1920s Cycle shop. Archery. Model T Ford Rides. Season Tickets cost £40. Aviators welcome (PPO). Picnics welcome. Wheelchair accessible WC. Golf Buggy tours available. An accessible carriage for wheelchair available on the railway. Guide dogs welcome.

5 BASSETTS
Bassetts Lane, Little Baddow, Chelmsford, CM3 4BZ. Mrs Margaret Chalmers, 07940 179572, magschalmers@btinternet.com. *1m down, Tofts Chase becomes Bassetts Ln. Yellow house on L, wooden gates, red brick wall. From Spring Elms Ln go down Bassetts Ln, L at the bottom of the hill. Cont for ¼ m.* **Sun 11 May (10-5). Adm £5, chd free. Visits also by arrangement 4 June to 15 Oct.**
A two acre garden, tennis court, swimming pool surrounding an early C17 house (not open)with plants for year-round interest set on gently sloping ground with lovely distant views of the Essex countryside. Shrub borders and mature ornamental trees, an orchard and two natural ponds. Many places to sit and relax. No refreshments but bring a picnic and enjoy the views. Please check wheelchair access with garden owner.

6 ◆ BETH CHATTO'S PLANTS & GARDENS
Elmstead Market, Colchester, CO7 7DB. Beth Chatto's Plants & Gardens, 01206 822007, customer@bethchatto.co.uk, www.bethchatto.co.uk. *¼ m E of Elmstead Market. On A133 Colchester to Clacton Rd in village of Elmstead Market.* **For NGS: Sat 1 Mar, Wed 1 Oct (10-4). Adm £14.95, chd free. Light refreshments at Chatto's Tearoom inc sandwiches, paninis, soup, salads, cakes, hot & cold beverages. For other opening times and information, please phone, email or visit garden website.**
Internationally famous gardens, inc dry, damp, shade, reservoir and woodland areas. The result of over 60 years of hard work and application of the huge body of plant knowledge possessed by Beth Chatto and her husband Andrew. Visitors cannot fail to be affected by the peace and beauty of the garden. Beth is renowned internationally for her books, her gardens and her influence on the world of gardening and plants. Please visit website for up to date visiting details and pre-booking. Picnic area available in the adjacent field. Disabled WC and parking. Wheelchair access around all of the gardens on gravel or grass.

7 BLAKE HALL
Bobbingworth, CM5 0DG. Mr & Mrs H Capel Cure, www.blakehall.co.uk. *10m W of Chelmsford. Just off A414 between Four Wantz r'about in Ongar & Talbot r'about in N Weald. Signed on A414.* **Sun 8 June (10.30-4). Adm £6, chd free. Tea, coffee & cake in C17 barn.**
25 acres of mature gardens within the historic setting of Blake Hall

(not open). Arboretum with broad variety of specimen and spectacular ancient trees. Lawns overlooking countryside. With its beautiful rose garden, stunning herbaceous border and magnificent rambling roses, June is a wonderful time of the year to visit the gardens at Blake Hall. Some gravel paths.

8 BLUNTS HALL
Blunts Hall Drive, Witham, CM8 1LX.
Alan & Lesley Gamblin, 07720 446797, alan.gamblin@ngs.org.uk, www.bluntshallgarden.co.uk. *Blunts Hall Dr is off of Blunts Hall Rd.* **Visits by arrangement 10 Feb to 15 Aug for groups of 15 to 35. Weekdays only. Adm £10, chd free. Home-made teas. Discuss refreshments when booking.**
Restored three acre Victorian garden. Courtyard garden and terrace leading down to lawns with re-instated parterre surrounded by herbaceous borders. Orchard with old and new fruit trees and vegetable plot. Listed Ancient Monument. Woodland walk around spring-fed pond. Fernery. Steps lead down to front lawns recently planted with a yew avenue. Snowdrops and aconites in early spring. Specimen trees.

9 BRAXTED PARK ESTATE
Braxted Park Road, Great Braxted, Witham, CM8 3EN.
Mr Duncan & Mrs Nicky Clark, www.braxtedpark.com. *A12 N, by-pass Witham. Turn L to Rivenhall & Silver End by pub called the Fox (now closed) At T junc turn R to Gt Braxted & Witham. Follow brown sign to Braxted Pk (NOT Braxted Golf Course). Down drive to Car Park.* **Wed 4 June (10-3.30). Adm £7.50, chd £5. Cream teas in the Orangery. Light lunches and afternoon tea available.**
Idyllic Braxted Park, a prestigious events venue, welcomes gardeners to enjoy its tranquil surroundings. Extensive borders of perennials, shrubs and roses abound. Walled Garden features themed gardens radiating from the central fountain and parasol mulberry trees. Themes inc a Black and White Garden, Italian Garden and English Garden, each containing a wealth of planting inspiration. A native wildflower meadow extends from the house (not open) towards the lake. The Orangery will be open for Ploughmans lunches and of course the obligatory cake, by the slice and to 'take home'. Tea, coffee or a glass of wine available. Head Gardener, Andrea Cooper, will be on hand to answer questions and guided tours for a further donation of £5pp payable upon the day.

10 NEW 1 BROOK COTTAGE
Laindon Common Road, Little Burstead, Billericay, CM12 9TA.
Mr James Slocombe & Dr Benjamin Cooper, 07861 207667, jaslocombe@gmail.com, www.1brookcottage.com. *1m S of Billericay, 1m N of A127/Basildon.* **Sat 21 June (12-4). Adm £7.50, chd free. Cream teas. Cash only for adm and refreshments on the day. Visits also by arrangement. Home-made refreshments available.**
Traditional cottage front and back gardens, with additional curtilage of 3½ acres of secluded meadows and woodland. Gardens combine variety, colours and textures: find a profusion of roses, peonies, lilies, and other classic blooms interspersed with more exotic plants and flowers. Some snowdrops and bluebells appear during the corresponding season. Wander to find an amphitheatre, A-frame 'treehouse', campfire circle, summerhouse and vines. Grounds invite exploration and contemplation; ideal for outdoor book reading, yoga and impromptu performances. Particularly attractive for landscape/nature artists (easels welcome) and picnics.

11 CANNOCK MILL COHOUSING GARDENS
Old Heath Road, Colchester, CO2 8AA. Cannock Mill Cohousing, www.cannockmillcohousing.co.uk. *In SE Colchester. Cannock Mill is easily visible on Old Heath Rd. On road parking. Just over 1m from Colchester city centre. On S1 and S9 bus routes (Scarletts Rd stop).* **Sun 11 May (11-4). Adm £5, chd free. Home-made teas.**
With an emphasis on biodiversity, our two acre sloping site inc both wild and cultivated areas, some private but mostly communal areas, some terraced, some flat, rain gardens, deep green roofs and porous roads as part of a SuDS scheme, grasses - some mown, some not - with flowers, fruit and vegetables all grown for our community meals, as well as a large mill pond and an embryonic bog garden.

12 2 CEDAR AVENUE
Wickford, SS12 9DT. Chris Cheswright & Michael Bodman, 07910 585684, cheswright@blueyonder.co.uk. *Off Nevendon Rd, 5 mins from Wickford High St. From Basildon on A132 turn 1st exit onto Nevendon Rd at BP r'bout, R onto Park Dr, 2nd R Cedar Ave.* **Sun 6 Apr, Sun 22 June (11-4). Adm £6, chd free. Tea, coffee & cake. Home-made cakes and pastries. Visits also by arrangement 7 Apr to 31 July for groups of 10 to 25. When booking a visit please specify if refreshments will be required.**
A large town garden with a dry front garden, pots arranged on a large patio. Plantings of trees, shrubs, grasses and perennials. In spring species tulips, *Narcissus, Camassias* and other spring flowers adorn the garden. Later in the year hostas, carnivorous plants, tropical style plants and a large variety of hardy plants are on display outdoors and in greenhouses. Areas for wildlife and a pond. Access via side of house. The majority of the garden is wheelchair accessible via a flat lawn area, although some paths are uneven.

13 160 CHIGNAL ROAD
Chelmsford, CM1 2JD. Johanna Chapman. *W of Chelmsford take A1060, Roxwell Rd. R at t-lights into Chignal Rd we are on the R in the set of semi-detached bungalows not far past Melbourne Ave.* **Fri 27 June, Fri 18 July (12-4). Sat 19 July (12-4), open nearby Dragons. Combined adm with 8 Dene Court £6, chd free. Tea, coffee & cake.**
A relatively new garden transformed from a rough piece of grass. The five year old garden goes from floral and leafy planting slowly transforming into vegetables and back to the green hues, benefiting from well thought out seating areas to enjoy the garden throughout the seasons. Wisteria covered deck area, summerhouse and a small greenhouse. The garden inc a small pond.

14 THE CHIMES, 3-4 CHURCH STREET
Waltham Abbey, EN9 1DX. **Caroline Moores.** *At M25 junc 26, take the A121 exit to Waltham Abbey/Loughton. Continue on A121 to Church St. House is opp the churchyard of the Abbey Church, on the way into the market square.* **Sun 1 June (12-5). Combined adm with Silver Birches £6, chd free. Refreshments will be provided at Silver Birches.**
A small courtyard partly-walled garden and patio, for a grade II listed house (not open) built in 1537. The garden was created in spring 2022 from a neglected and overgrown plot. It consists of brick-edged raised borders around an area of gravel. Planted with perennials and shrubs. A sanctuary of calm in an urban setting. Most of the garden accessible for wheelchair users.
&

15 CHIPPINS
Heath Road, Bradfield, CO11 2UZ. **Kit & Ceri Leese,** 01255 870730, ceriandkit@gmail.com. *3m E of Manningtree. Take A137 from Manningtree Stn turn L opp garage. Take 1st R towards Clacton. At Radio Mast turn L into Bradfield continue through village. Bungalow opp primary sch on R.* **Sun 25 May, Sun 6 July (11-4). Adm £5, chd free. Home-made teas. Visits also by arrangement 26 May to 1 Aug for groups of 5 to 35.**
Artist's and plantaholics' paradise packed with interest inc hostas in huge pots and a wide range of irises and astrantia. Meandering stream, wildlife pond with gunnera featuring Horace the Huge. Summer is an explosion of colour with daylilies, rambling roses, salvias, cannas and dahlia. An abundance of tubs and hanging baskets in front garden. Studio and press in conservatory with paintings on show. Kit is a landscape artist and printmaker, pictures always on display. Afternoon tea with delicious homemade cakes is also available for small parties (min of 5) on specific days if booked in advance.

16 79 CLIFFSEA GROVE
Leigh-On-Sea, SS9 1NG. **Mr & Mrs J Harding.** *Just off A13, turn R into Cliffsea Grove. Head E towards Southend, turn R off A13, the property is 4 houses up the road on the R. The garden is at the rear of 79 Cliffsea Grove. This is a one way road.* **Sat 12, Sun 13 July (10-5).**

Adm £4, chd free. Home-made teas. Coffee, cake and home-made vegetarian spring rolls.
A compact town garden with many pathways and places to sit and view the packed garden. There are many perennials and mature acers. Discover the pond and a palm grown from seed almost 30 years ago. A collection of original art is also available to view and purchase. Good wheelchair access. Mostly flat garden.
&

17 THE DELVES
37 Turpins Lane, Chigwell, IG8 8AZ. **Fabrice Aru & Martin Thurston.** *Between Woodford & Epping. Chigwell, 2m from N Circular Rd at Woodford. Follow the signs for Chigwell (A113) through Woodford Bridge into Manor Rd & turn L. Bus 275 & W14 go past garden.* **Sun 13 July (11-6). Adm £4, chd free.**
An unexpected hidden, magical, part-walled garden showing how much can be achieved in a small space. An oasis of calm with densely planted rich, lush foliage, tree ferns, hostas, topiary and an abundance of well maintained shrubs complemented by a small pond and three water features designed for year-round interest. This garden is not suitable for visitors with

Fudlers Hall

ESSEX 189

mobility problems as the access has steep steps. Please note that only 10 visitors can be accommodated in the garden at a time.

18 8 DENE COURT
Chignall Road, Chelmsford, CM1 2JQ. Mrs Sheila Chapman, 01245 266156. *W of Chelmsford (Parkway). Take A1060 Roxwell Rd for 1m. Turn R at T-lights into Chignall Rd. Dene Court 3rd exit on R. Parking in Chignall Rd.* **Wed 11 June (12-4). Adm £4, chd free. Fri 27 June, Fri 18 July, Sat 19 July (12-4). Combined adm with 160 Chignal Road £6, chd free. Open nearby Dragons (Sat 19 July). Tue 29 July, Wed 13, Fri 29 Aug (12-4). Adm £4, chd free. Visits also by arrangement 1 June to 12 Sept for groups of 10 to 50.**
Beautifully maintained and designed as a compact garden. Owner is well-known RHS gold medal-winning exhibitor (now retired). Circular lawn, long pergola and walls festooned with roses and climbers. Large selection of unusual clematis. Densely-planted colour coordinated perennials add interest from June to Sept in this immaculate garden.
✤ 🚗

19 DRAGONS
Boyton Cross, Chelmsford, CM1 4LS. Mrs Margot Grice, 01245 248651, margot@snowdragons.co.uk. *3m W of Chelmsford. On A1060. ½ m W of The Hare Pub.* **Thur 13, Wed 19 Feb (11-3). Pre-booking essential, please visit www.ngs.org.uk for information & booking. Sat 19 July (11-4). Open nearby 8 Dene Court. Adm £5, chd free. Visits also by arrangement 3 Feb to 24 Oct for groups of 10+. Refreshments only available for by arrangement visits and Feb opening.**
Galanthus are a passion. A plantswoman's ¾ acre garden, planted to encourage wildlife. Sumptuous colour-themed borders with striking plant combinations, featuring specimen plants, fernery, clematis and grasses. Meandering paths lead to ponds, patio, scree garden and small vegetable garden. Two summerhouses, one overlooking stream and farmland.
🐕 ✤ 🚗 ☕ ⛱

20 59 EAST STREET
Coggeshall, Colchester, CO6 1SJ. Sara Impey and Tom Fenton, 07740 928369, tjhfenton@gmail.com, www.instagram.com/thegardenat59eaststreet/. *12 m W of Colchester, 16m NE of Chelmsford, 2m N of the A12, just off the A120. There is a public car park, free for 2 hours, entered from Stoneham St. 5 mins walk.* **Visits by arrangement 9 June to 15 Sept. Adm £10, chd free.**
Part of an old walled garden, mostly replanted in the last three years, and still developing. A lavender walk with espaliered apples and pears lead to a fountain. Discover a peach cage, greenhouse and box parterre, also a grotto and small Mediterranean garden. Wide range of perennials, shrubs, roses, grasses and bamboo with unusual plants, veg, soft fruit, under an ancient and massive copper beech. Please contact us in advance if you want onsite parking. The paths are all wheelchair accessible and there is an accessible WC.
♿ ✤ ☕ 🔊

21 17 ELM ROAD
Little Clacton, Clacton-on-Sea, CO16 9LP. Stephen Matthews & Martin Picker. *4m from Clacton On Sea. From the A133 at Weeley r'about, take 1st exit B1033. On next r'about take 3rd exit Weeley By Pass B1441. Follow road for >2½ m. Turn R onto Elm Rd. On road parking.* **Sat 28 June (11-4). Adm £4. Tea, coffee & cake.**
A compact country garden beautifully maintained as a modern take on a cottage style garden. Deep borders of herbaceous plants, grasses, roses, ferns, shrubs and trees. Many unusual. An area of succulents and cacti, fruit trees and vegetables. A goldfish pond and aviary with canaries and finches. Set in a village location surrounded by fields.
✤ ☕

22 ELMBRIDGE MILL
Little Easton, Dunmow, CM6 2HZ. Cilla Swan. *N of Great Dunmow, B184.* **Sun 26 Oct (12-4). Adm £5, chd free. Home-made teas.**
This beautiful and tranquil garden last opened for the National Garden Scheme in 2008. A romantic, country garden full of topiary, unusual plants and specimen trees. Elmbridge Mill (not open) with mill stream, one side flowing under the house, and the River Chelmer on the other. Explore

the orchard, productive vegetable garden and walk down to the mill pond. Beautiful autumn colours.
✤ ☕ 🔊

23 FEERINGBURY MANOR
Coggeshall Road, Feering, CO5 9RB. Mr & Mrs Giles Coode-Adams, 01376 561946, seca@btinternet.com. *Between Feering & Coggeshall on Coggeshall Rd, 1m from Feering village.* **Every Thur and Fri 3 Apr to 25 July (10-4). Every Thur and Fri 4 Sept to 17 Oct (10-4). Adm £6, chd free. Visits also by arrangement for groups of up to 30. Donation to Feering Church.**
There is always plenty to see in this peaceful 10 acre garden with two ponds and River Blackwater. Jewelled lawn in early April then spectacular tulips and blossom lead on to a huge number of different and colourful plants, many unusual, culminating in a purple explosion of michaelmas daisies in late Sept. No wheelchair access to arboretum due to steep slope.
♿ 🐕

24 FUDLERS HALL
Fox Road, Mashbury, CM1 4TJ. Mr & Mrs A J Meacock. *7m NW of Chelmsford. Chelmsford take A1060, R into Chignal Rd. ½ m turn L to Chignal St James. Approx 5m, 2nd R into Fox Rd signed Gt Waltham. Fudlers From Gt Waltham. Take Barrack Ln for 3m.* **Sun 22 June (2-5). Adm £6, chd free. Home-made teas.**
Award winning, romantic two acre garden surrounding C17 farmhouse with lovely views. Many long herbaceous borders, ropes and pergolas festooned with rambling, perfumed, old fashioned roses. The entire garden has been designed and planted by the current owners over 45 years and is now a quintessential example of an English country garden. Wonderful views across Chelmer Valley. Two new flower beds, many roses. 500 year old yew tree. Wheelchair access: gravel farmyard and 30ft path to gardens, all of which is level lawn.
♿ 🚗 ☕

In 2024, our donations to Carers Trust meant that 26,081 unpaid carers were supported across the UK.

25 FURZELEA
Bicknacre Road, Danbury, CM3 4JR. Avril & Roger Cole-Jones, 01245 225726, randacj@gmail.com. *4m E of Chelmsford, 4m W of Maldon. S off A414 in Danbury. At village centre S into Mayes Ln. 1st R. Past Cricketers Pub, L on to Bicknacre Rd. Use NT car park on L. Garden 50 m on R, or parking 200 m past on L. Use NT Common paths from back of car park.* **Sun 4 May, Sun 1 June, Sun 20 July, Sun 21 Sept (11-5). Adm £6, chd free. Home-made teas. Gluten free available. Visits also by arrangement 14 Apr to 30 Sept for groups of 15 to 50.**
Country garden of just under an acre designed, planted and maintained by the owners over time to showcase the seasons with colour, scent, and form. Paths lead through archways and box hedging to lawns and flower beds amassed with seasonal planting of shrubs, roses, and herbaceous perennials, bulbs and dahlias. Tulips, salvias and grasses of particular interest along with many unusual plants. Black and White Garden plus exotics add to the visitors interest. Short walk to Danbury Country Park and Lakes and short drive to RHS Hyde Hall Plants and metal plant supports are for sale.

26 THE GARDEN STUDIO
30 Gladwin Road, Colchester, CO2 7HS. Andrea Parsons MSGD & Kevin Looker, www.andreaparsons.co.uk. *1m from Colchester centre. The Garden Studio is easily found with postcode. There is plenty of street parking.* **Sat 21, Sun 22 June (10-5). Adm £5, chd free. Light refreshments. Home-made cakes, teas & cold drinks.**
This beautiful south facing town garden has evolved over the years from family garden to studio garden. A backdrop of large trees in the neighbouring gardens frames the view, beech hedges and clipped yew makes the garden feel more extensive than it is. A stunning artists studio is hidden amongst rich planting, shade and sun loving plants surround focal points and lovely sitting areas.

27 THE GATES
London Road Cemetery, London Road, Brentwood, CM14 4QW. Ms Mary Yiannoullou, www.frontlinepartnership.org. *Enter the Cemetery (opp Tesco Express). Drive to the rear of the cemetery, our garden is on L. Limited parking within but plenty on the surrounding roads.* **Sun 18 May (11-2.30). Adm £4, chd free. Tea, coffee & cake at tea hut with covered outdoor and indoor seating. A selection of home-made cakes and bacon rolls.**
A horticultural project that offers local citizens, inc vulnerable adults, an opportunity to develop new skills within a horticultural setting. Greenhouses and allotments for raising bedding plants, educational workshops and growing fruit and vegetables. Walks through the Woodland Dell and Sensory area. Large variety of plants and produce for sale. Our ethos is reclaim and recycle- everything on site has been sustainably built, modified and planted by the team. The site has many features, inc four large greenhouse used for propagation and the Dingley Dell. Good wheelchair access via slopes and ramps.

28 GREAT BECKETTS
Duddenhoe End Road, Arkesden, Saffron Walden, CB11 4HG. Mr & Mrs John Burnham, 01799 550661. *5m W of Saffron Walden. 10m N of Bishops Stortford. Approx $2/3$ m NW of Arkesden in the direction of Duddenhoe End, near Newland End. Access from S on B1038 via Arkesden village or from N on B1039. 2 or 3m from Audley End Stn.* **Sun 18 May, Sat 21 June (2-6). Adm £6, chd free. Tea, coffee & cake in old timber barn & courtyard. Visits also by arrangement May to Aug for groups of 15 to 50.**
In the middle of arable farm land, surrounding a Tudor house and outbuildings: a garden to explore. Perennials and climbers are the focus. Several perennial borders; courtyard; pergola; arbour; herb garden; dahlia/tulip bed; two ponds; cutting garden; mini-orchard; paths through two established meadows. Newly planted trees and meadows with paths on five additional acres across the road.

29 ♦ GREEN ISLAND
Park Road, Ardleigh, CO7 7SP. Fiona Edmond, 01206 230455, greenislandgardens@gmail.com, www.greenislandgardens.co.uk. *3m NE of Colchester. From Ardleigh village centre, take B1029 towards Great Bromley. Park Rd is 2nd on R after level X-ing. Garden is last on L.* **For NGS: Sun 2 Feb, Sun 27 Apr, Sun 12 Oct (11-4). Adm £10, chd £3. Light lunches, cream teas, cakes, ice creams all available in the tearoom. Picnics welcome in the car park area only. 2026: Sun 8 Feb.** For other opening times and information, please phone, email or visit garden website. Donation to Plant Heritage.
A garden for all seasons, highlights inc bluebells, azaleas, autumn colour, winter *Hamamelis* and snowdrops. A plantsman's paradise. Carved within 20 acre mature woodland are huge island beds, Japanese garden, terrace, gravel, seaside and water gardens, all packed with rare and unusual plants. Flat and easy walking or pushing wheelchairs. Ramps at entrance and tearoom. Disabled parking and WC.

30 GROVE LODGE
3 Chater's Hill, Saffron Walden, CB10 2AB. Chris Shennan, 01799 522271, cds.2022@icloud.com. *Approx 10 mins walk from town centre. Facing the common on E side, about 100 yds from the turf maze. Note: Chater's Hill is one way.* **Sun 23 Feb Sun 16 Mar, Sun 15 June (2-5). Adm £6, chd free. Home-made teas. Visits also by arrangement 2 Jan to 31 Dec. Home-made teas and cake may be offered for larger group sizes.**
A large walled garden close to the town centre with unusually high biodiversity (e.g. 17 species of butterfly recorded) close to the turf maze and Norman castle. Semi-woodland on light free-draining chalk soil allows bulbs, hellebores and winter-flowering shrubs to thrive. Two ponds, topiary and orchard blend some formality with informal areas where wildlife thrives. A profusion of winter aconites, snowdrops, other bulbs and spring blossom. Lots of seating from which to enjoy the garden. Wheelchair access via fairly steep drive leading to terrace from which the garden may be viewed.

GROUP OPENING

31 HARWICH GARDENS
Harwich, CO12 3NH. *Centre of Old Harwich. Car park on Wellington Rd (CO12 3DT) within 50 metres of St Helens Green. Street parking available.* **Sun 13 July (11-4). Combined adm £5, chd free. Light refreshments inc tea, coffee and cake at 8 St Helens Green.**

NEW 38 HARBOUR CRESCENT
Alan and Sue Edgar.

42 KINGS QUAY STREET
Mrs Elizabeth Crame.

QUAYSIDE COURT
Dave Burton.

8 ST HELENS GREEN
Frances Vincent.

All different gardens are within walking distance in the historical town of Harwich with their own special identity. 8 St Helens Green, just 100 metres from the sea, is a small town garden with roses, dahlias, hydrangeas and agapanthus mixed with perennials and many pots. 38 Harbour Crescent is a new garden with an eastern theme. A long narrow garden that gives the impression of a much larger secluded garden. Filled with trees, shrubs, water features and many seating areas. Quayside Court, a community garden, unusually boasts a sunken garden hidden from view at the end of the car park which features a wall mural, pond, vegetable patch, roses and climbers. New additions inc a pergola and greenhouse. 42 Kings Quay Street courtyard garden is behind a Grade II listed house. Raised brick beds incorporate established plants such as a grape vine, David Austin roses, tree peony and a combination of edible and ornamental plants. All feature historical elements or historic views. There will be an art display at 8 St. Helens Green with commission to the National Garden Scheme on any purchases.

32 262 HATCH ROAD
Pilgrims Hatch, Brentwood, CM15 9QR. Mike & Liz Thomas, 01277 220584, mike@astongroup.co.uk. *2m N of Brentwood town centre. After passing the Brentwood Centre on Doddinghurst Rd, turn R into Hatch Rd. 262 is the 4th house on the R.* **Visits by arrangement in July for groups of 20 to 35. All cakes are home-made.**
A formal frontage with lavender. An eclectic rear garden of around an acre divided into 'rooms' with themed borders, several ponds, three greenhouses, fruit and vegetable plots and oriental garden. There is also a secret white garden, spring and summer wildflower meadows, Yin and Yang borders, a folly and an exotic area. There is plenty of seating to enjoy the views and a cup of tea and cake.

Rookwoods

Blake Hall

33 HEYRONS
High Easter, Chelmsford, CM1 4QN. Mr Richard Wollaston, 01245 231428, richard.wollaston@gmail.com. ½ m outside High Easter towards Good Easter. Via High Easter: through village, turn L downhill & ¼ m on R. Via Good Easter: After 2m on L ½ way up hill before the village. Via Leaden Roding: After 2m turn L over bridge. ¼ m on L. **Sun 27 Apr (11-5). Adm £6, chd free. Visits also by arrangement 17 Feb to 30 May for groups of 10 to 30.**
A garden of six parts within and around a C16 restored farmyard. An Essex barn and brick farm buildings surround an intensely planted walled garden. A terraced area with mature trees, pond, herbaceous and shady beds leads up to a rose garden. Beyond is an open area with trees, shrubs and flower beds, grass tennis court, big skies, a small meadow and very fine views over Essex countryside. Wheelchair on gravel driveway can be difficult, but drop off access can be arranged on request.

& ☕ 🪑 »)

34 HORKESLEY HALL
Vinesse Road, Little Horkesley, Colchester, CO6 4DB. Mr & Mrs Johnny Eddis, 07808 599290, horkesleyhall@hotmail.com, www.airbnb.co.uk/rooms/10354093. 6m N of Colchester City Centre. 2m W of A134, 10 mins from A12. On Vinesse Rd, look for the grass triangle with tree in middle, turn into Little Horkesley Church car park. Go to very far end - access is via low double black gates. **Sat 8, Wed 12 Feb (12-4.30). Adm £6, chd free. Light refreshments in St Peter & St Paul's Church. Soups, home-made cakes, bacon rolls and hot drinks. Visits also by arrangement for groups of 8 to 25. We are sorry that we cannot accommodate any visits during July or August.**
Traditional English garden of several acres of romantic garden surrounding classical house overlooking two lakes which are depicted in John Nash paintings. Major 20ft balancing stones sculpture and exceptional trees. We are developing a snowdrop collection and winter walk with an excellent plant stall and teas in the warm church next to the house. Discover 50 varieties of iris from the now disbanded National Collection. Walled garden. This garden inspired the birth of Parasol-UK which is proud to donate a percentage of all parasol sales to the National Garden Scheme. Partial wheelchair access to some areas with easy access to tea area. Some gravel paths and slopes.

& 🐕 ❄ 🚗 🚌 ☕ »)

35 ISABELLA'S GARDEN
42 Theobalds Road, Leigh-on-Sea SS9 2NE. Mrs Elizabeth Isabella Ling-Locke, 01702 714424, ling_locke@yahoo.co.uk. Take A13 towards Southend on Sea. As you pass 'Welcome to Leigh-on-Sea' sign, turn R at T- lights onto Thames Dr then L onto Western Rd. Carry on 0.6m then R onto Theobalds Rd. **Sat 7, Sun 8 June, Sat 26, Sun 27 July (12-4.30). Adm £6, chd free. Cream teas. Wide range of home-made cakes inc gluten free and vegan options. Visits also by arrangement 2 June to 1 Aug for groups of 10 to 30.**
This enchanting town garden is bursting with a profusion of colour from early spring through to the autumn months. Roses, clematis, agapanthus, herbaceous plants, alpines, pots with unusual succulents and cacti fill every corner of this garden. There is a wildlife pond, water features as well as other garden features which are to be found hiding within the shrubbery and throughout the garden. This garden

ESSEX

is situated in Leigh on Sea, and just a five min walk from the cockle sheds of Old Leigh and Leigh railway station. Wheelchair access to the vast majority of the garden, there are steps near to the house.

36 JANKES HOUSE
Jankes Green, Wakes Colne, Colchester, CO6 2AT. Bridget Marshall. *8m NW of Colchester. From A1124 Halstead Rd turn R at Wakes Colne opp village shop to Station Rd. Take 2nd R after stn entrance into Jankes Ln. House signed. Parking on grass verge.* **Sun 1 June (12-4). Adm £5, chd free. Home-made teas.**
A ½ acre traditional English country garden with amazing rural views. Garden has been artistically created by owner. Beautiful mixed borders featuring roses, clematis and architectural shrubs. *Camassia* in wild grass area. Many young specimen trees. Dry garden. Delightful pond and patio area. Vegetable garden and small orchard. Intimate places to sit and relax. Garden owner's artistic cards and home-made preserves for sale. Wheelchair access to whole garden.

37 KAMALA
262 Main Road, Hawkwell, Hockley, SS5 4NW. Karen Mann, 07976 272999, karenmann10@hotmail.com. *3m NE of Rayleigh. From A127 at Rayleigh Weir take B1013 towards Hockley. Garden on L after White Hart Pub & village green.* **Sun 7 Sept (12-5.30). Adm £6, chd free. Tea, coffee & cake. Visits also by arrangement 4 Aug to 6 Sept for groups of 10+. Adm inc refreshments. Discuss refreshments when booking.**
Spectacular herbaceous borders which sing with colour as displays of salvia are surpassed by dahlia drifts. Gingers, *Brugmansia*, various bananas, bamboos and *Canna* add an exotic note. Grasses sway above the blooms, giving movement. Rest in the rose clad pergola while listening to the two Amazon parrots in the aviary. The garden features an RHS accredited dahlia named 'Jake Mann'. Trees and shrubs inc acers, *Catalpa aurea*, *Cercis* 'Forest Pansy' and a large unusual *Sinocalycanthus* (Chinese Allspice) a stunning, rare plant with fantastic flowers.

38 KELVEDON HALL
Kelvedon Hall Lane, Kelvedon, Colchester, CO5 9BN. Mr & Mrs Jack Inglis, 07973 795955, v_inglis@btinternet.com, www.instagram.com/kelvedonhallgarden. *Near Colchester. Take Maldon Rd direction Great Braxted from Kelvedon High St. Go over R Blackwater bridge & bridge over A12. At T-junc turn R onto Kelvedon Rd. Take 1st L, sign for KH, a single gravel road ¾ m.* **Visits by arrangement 20 Mar to 27 June for groups of 20 to 40. Adm £8.50, chd free. Home-made teas in the Courtyard Garden or the Pool Walled Garden - weather permitting. Hot drinks and home-made cakes provided. Please discuss allergies in advance.**
Varied six acre garden surrounding a gorgeous C18 house. A blend of formal and informal spaces interspersed with modern sculpture. Pleached hornbeam and yew and box topiary provide structure. A courtyard walled garden juxtaposes a modern walled pool garden, both providing season long displays. Herbaceous borders offset an abundance of roses around the house. Lily covered ponds with a wet garden.

39 LAUREL COTTAGE
88 The Street, Manuden, CM23 1DS. Stewart and Louise Woskett. *Approx 3m N of Bishop's Stortford. From B/Stort along Rye St. At the Mountbatten Restaurant r'about continue straight to Hazel End Rd. In ½ m turn L to stay on Hazel End Rd. Continue past Yew Tree pub. Gdn is last cottage on R.* **Sat 7 June, Sun 24 Aug (12-4). Tea, coffee & cake. Sat 6 Dec (3.30-7). Adm £5, chd free. Christmas opening: mince pies, Christmas cake, mulled wine & light refreshments.**
A romantic, quintessential cottage garden. Features intimate pathways meandering through borders with an abundance of cottage garden favourites and one or two surprises, rustic charm and an ancient Yew tree. Seating areas to sit and enjoy fragrant borders. Hidden treasures enhance this characterful and quirky garden. Created in just five years from a very neglected plot. Magical and spectacular illuminated Christmas opening. Parking at community centre car park adjacent to cottage and playing field.

40 LONG HOUSE PLANTS
Church Road, Noak Hill, Romford, RM4 1LD. Tim Carter, www.longhouse-plants.co.uk. *3½ m NW of J28, M25. Take A1023 Brentwood. At 1st T-lights, turn L to S Weald. After ⅘ m turn L at T-junc. Travel 1⅗ m & turn L, over M25. ½ m turn R into Church Rd, nursery opp church. Disabled Car Parking.* **Wed 9 July, Wed 6 Aug, Wed 3 Sept (11-4). Adm £7, chd £3. Home-made teas.**
A beautiful garden- yes, but one with a purpose. Long House Plants has been producing homegrown plants for 20 years and here is a chance to see where it all begins. With wide paths and plenty of seats carefully placed to enjoy the plants and views. It has been thoughtfully designed so that the collections of plants look great together through all seasons. Paths are suitable for wheelchairs and mobility scooters. Disabled WC in nursery. Two cobbled areas not suitable.

41 LOXLEY HOUSE
49 Robin Hood Road, Brentwood, CM15 9EL. Robert & Helen Smith. *1m N of Brentwood town centre. On A128 N towards Ongar turn R at mini r'about onto Doddinghurst Rd. Take the 1st road on L into Robin Hood Rd. 2 houses before the bend on L.* **Sat 26 Apr, Sat 6, Sun 7 Sept (11-3). Adm £5, chd free. Tea, coffee & cake.**
On entering the rear garden you will be surprised and delighted by this town garden. A colourful patio with pots and containers. Steps up onto a lawn with circular beds surrounded by hedges, herbaceous borders, trees and climbers. Two water features, one a Japanese theme and another with ferns in a quiet seating area. The garden is planted to offer colour throughout the seasons.

42 MAY COTTAGE
19 Walton Road, Kirby-Le-Soken, Frinton-on-Sea, CO13 0DU. Julie Abbey, 07885 875822, jools.abbey@hotmail.com. *The cottage is the B1034. 2m before Walton on Naze. ¼ m after the Red Lion pub & on the same side as the pub. What3words app: televise.hood.thud.* **Sun 18 May (11-4). Adm £5, chd free. Tea, coffee & cake. Visits also by arrangement 18 May to 31 July.**

194 ESSEX

A quintessential English country garden divided into separate areas with three ponds, a stream and a small waterfall. A wide variety of planting, often grown from cuttings. Follow path down to Bakers Oven, a building over 100 years old. A picket gate leads to a secret garden with a winding path, and an area only planted in 2020 leads to a summerhouse. The garden is full of interesting artefacts.

43 207 MERSEA ROAD
Colchester, CO2 8PN. Kay and Rod, klawrence61@gmail.com. *S part of Colchester. From the town centre drive 2m up Mersea Rd. Garden on the L side of the rd past the cemetery & mini r'about on the B1025.* **Sat 19, Sun 20 July (11-4). Adm £5, chd free. Home-made cakes, tea, coffee & soft drinks also available. Visits also by arrangement for groups of up to 15. Only during school holidays.** The garden is 185ft long divided into sections. There is a decking area with pots leading to a unique fountain made from waste slates. A circular lawn is surrounded by herbaceous perennials, annuals, trees and shrubs with cabin. Behind the cabin are ferns, perennials and beehive. Beyond is a patio with pergola, patio, pond, long raised beds with subtropical planting, vegetable beds, beehive and ducks. Regret, no motorised wheelchairs.

44 THE MOUNT
Epping Road, Roydon, Harlow, CM19 5HT. David & Liz Davison, 07711 231555, david.t.davison@gmail.com. *300 metres W of the junc with the high street. From Harlow, pass the high street on your R. 300 metres you will see yellow signs on R. From the stn, turn R at T-Junc. 300 metres on R.* **Sun 25 May (11-4). Light refreshments. Sun 29 June (11-4). Tea, coffee & cake. Adm £7, chd free. Visits also by arrangement Mar to Aug for groups of 15+.** The garden is set in a total of eight acres. Three acres of formal gardens and five acres woodland planted in 2003. The formal gardens are divided into nine separate areas. The lawns are edged with mixed planting for different seasons from snowdrops, spring bulb displays through the summer plants and shrubs. There are many surprising statues and sculptures throughout the grounds. Fully accessible for wheelchairs and scooter users. There are two steps to WC. Regret no WC access for wheelchair users.

45 MOVERONS
Brightlingsea, CO7 0SB. Lesley & Payne Gunfield, lesleyorrock@me.com, www.moverons.co.uk. *7m SE of Colchester. At old church turn R signed Moverons Farm. Follow lane & garden signs for approx 1m. Some SatNavs take you the wrong side of the river.* **Sat 28, Sun 29 June (10.30-5). Adm £6, chd free. Home-made teas. Visits by arrangement for groups of 10+.** Tranquil four acre garden in touch with its surroundings and stunning estuary views. A wide variety of planting in mixed borders to suit different growing conditions. Large natural ponds, plenty of seating areas, sculptures and barn for rainy day teas. Our reflection pool garden and courtyard have been completely redeveloped. Magnificent trees some over 300 years old give this garden real presence. Sculpture and Art Exhibition. Most of the garden is wheelchair accessible via grass and gravel paths. There are some steps and bark paths.

46 MOYNES FARM
Wick Road, Great Bentley, Colchester, CO7 8RA. Veronica Strucelj and Jim Carr, 07538 604947, verostrucelj@icloud.com. *NE Essex. 9m SE from Colchester towards Clacton on Sea. 2m from Great Bentley, between Aingers Green and Weeley Heath.* **Fri 13, Sat 14 June (12-4). Adm £6, chd free. Home-made teas. Refreshments inc hot and cold drinks and home-made cakes. Visits also by arrangement June to Sept for groups of 10 to 30.** A traditional, large country garden and two acre woodland with walks. Vibrant planting, mature trees, shrubs and perennials. A formal courtyard area with box parterre maze, rose garden, wildlife pond, parkland. Pottery workshop and kiln. For transport enthusiasts a Routemaster London bus and military tanks will be on display.

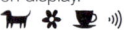

47 OAK FARM
Vernons Road, Wakes Colne, Colchester, CO6 2AH. Ann & Peter Chillingworth, 01206 240230, chillingworthpeter23@gmail.com. *6m NW of Colchester. Vernons Rd off A1124, ½ way between Ford St & Chappel. From Colchester, 3rd R after Ford St; Oak Farm is 200m up on R. From Halstead, 2nd L after Chappel viaduct.* **Sun 18 May, Sun 8, Thur 26 June, Sun 20 July (2-5). Adm £5, chd free. Tea, coffee & cake. Visits also by arrangement 11 May to 28 Sept for groups of up to 25.** Informal farmhouse garden of about an acre on an exposed site. Garden designed to make most of stunning views across Colne Valley to south and west, framed to north by listed house and farmyard. Trees, shrubs, borders, roses and secret garden at best in early and mid summer. Prairie garden, salvias and dahlias come into their own in late summer to early autumn. Wheelchair access to most of the garden although there are steps in places.

48 THE OLD RECTORY
Boreham Road, Great Leighs, Chelmsford, CM3 1PP. Pauline & Neil Leigh-Collyer. *Approx ½m outside the village of Great Leighs. From Boreham village (J19 off A12) turn into Waltham Rd & travel about 5m, Garden on L. From Great Leighs travel on Boreham Rd for ¾m, garden on R.* **Sun 25 May, Sun 13 July (12-4.30). Adm £7.50, chd free. Tea, coffee & cake.** Wander around four acres of mature gardens surrounded by open countryside. Aspects inc herbaceous borders, a delightful courtyard, lake, fountain and sweeping lawns. Wander through arched walkways and discover many specimen trees. Beautiful wisteria climbing along the house. Many seating areas to enjoy alternative vistas. Extensive car parking available on grass off the main road. Picnics allowed. Main areas accessible for wheelchairs. Some areas limited by gravel paths and steps.

49 OLD TIMBERS
53 Church Street, Maldon, CM9 5HW. Margaret McCaskie and Stanley Goulding, 07563 548338, mmccaskie@hotmail.co.uk. *Black timbered building, opp St Mary's church. Public car parking on High St E, Edward Brights Cl, CM9 5RU or*

ESSEX 195

Promenade Park, Park Dr, CM9 5JQ. **Fri 15 Aug (11-4.30). Adm £5, chd free. Light refreshments.** Visits also by arrangement 9 June to 4 July for groups of 8 to 15.

The white shingled spire of St Mary's church, provides historic atmosphere to this weatherboarded house and large walled garden. Raised vegetable garden beds, lawns, wisteria and rose clad pergola, a pond, several colour themed beds and herbaceous border, can all be admired from several seated areas. Pretty summerhouse, a working area with shed, greenhouse and plants for sale. The majority of garden features can be viewed by a wheelchair user.

&

50 OVER HALL
Overhall Hill, Colne Engaine, Colchester, CO6 2HW. Mrs Jane Lambert. *1m E of Colne Engaine. From B1124 Earls Colne to White Colne turn onto Colne Park Rd and continue to Countess Cross. Take L Overhall Hill. Garden on L.* **Sun 15 June (12-4). Adm £5, chd free. Home-made teas.**

A large country house garden surrounding a Georgian house (not open) with sloping gardens down to a large pond and extended countryside views across the Colne Valley. The formal walled garden has an unusual crinkle crankle wall and thatched garden pavilion. Kitchen garden in raised beds and greenhouse. Historic trees and a woodland walk. Garden on a slope so not all areas wheelchair accessible.

&

51 PEACOCKS
Main Road, Margaretting, CM4 9HY. Phil Torr, phil.torr@icloud.com. *Margaretting Village Centre. From Margaretting x-roads go 100yds in the direction of Ingatestone. Entrance gates are on the L, set back from the road. What3words app: visual.global.film.* **Sun 22 June (11-3.30). Adm £5, chd free.** Visits also by arrangement 9 Apr to 7 July for groups of 15+. Donation to St Francis Hospice.

A 10 acre varied garden with many specimen trees and old horticultural buildings. Series of garden rooms; walled paradise garden, Garden of Reconciliation (Moorish fusion), a parterre. Long herbaceous border. Sunken dell and waterfall. Temple of Antheia on the banks of a lily lake. Large areas for wildlife inc woodland walk, nuttery and orchard. Traditionally managed large wildflower meadow and orchard. There are many places to sit with a picnic, we encourage visitors to bring their picnic hampers, whatever size. Display of old Margaretting postcards. Garden sculpture. Most of garden is wheelchair accessible.

&

52 18 PETTITS BOULEVARD
Rise Park, Romford, RM1 4PL. Peter & Lynn Nutley. *From M25 take A12 towards London, turn R at Pettits Ln junc then R again into Pettits Blvd or Romford Stn. 103 or 499 bus to Romford Fire Stn & follow yellow signs.* **Sat 28, Sun 29 June, Sat 6, Sun 7 Sept (1-5). Adm £5, chd free.**

The garden (80ft x 23ft) is on three levels with an ornamental pond, patio area with shrubs and perennials, many in pots. Large eucalyptus tree leads to a woodland themed area with many ferns and hostas. There are agricultural implements and garden ornaments giving a unique and quirky feel to the garden. Tranquil seating areas situated throughout.

&

53 30 QUEENS ROAD
Rayleigh, SS6 8JX. Natasha Gallop, www.instagram.com/gal.inthegarden. *1³⁄₅m from Rayleigh Weir. Head >1m along High Rd, turn R at r'about onto Eastwood Rd, A1015. Continue for 1m then turn L onto Queens Rd.* **Sat 12, Sun 13 July (11.30-4). Adm £5, chd free. Tea, coffee & cake.**

A medium sized family garden with separate zones. The front of the garden features a large decked area for dining and relaxing. The back has a colourful jungle border filled with banana plants and exotic perennials surrounding a hop covered pergola. A cottage garden with roses, shrubs and homegrown annuals. Another seating area sits amongst vibrant planting.

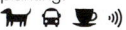

54 ROOKWOODS
Yeldham Road, Sible Hedingham, CO9 3QG. Peter & Sandra Robinson, 07770 957111, sandy1989@btinternet.com, www.rookwoodsgarden.com. *8m NW of Halstead. Entering Sible Hedingham from Haverhill/A1017:* take 1st R after 30mph sign. From the Braintree direction: turn L before the 40mph sign, leaving the village. **Visits by arrangement 14 May to 27 Sept for groups of 10 to 30. Adm £8, chd free. Home-made teas.**

Arriving at the garden there is no need to walk far. You can linger over tea, under a dreamy wisteria canopy while enjoying views across the garden. If a good walk appeals, there is not only the herbaceous borders to walk through, a beautiful meadow leads to an eight acre oak wood and there are grassy paths mown though the rest of the garden shaded by a variety of mature and teenage trees. Wheelchair access over gravel drive.

&

55 69 RUNDELLS - THE SECRET GARDEN
Harlow, CM18 7HD. Mr & Mrs K Naunton, 07981 882448, k_naunton@hotmail.com. *3m from J7 M11. A414 exit T-lights take L exit Southern Way, mini r'about 1st exit Trotters Rd leading into Commonside Rd, after shops on L, 3rd L into Rundells.* **Sat 5 July (2-5). Adm £4, chd free. Tea, coffee & cake.** Visits also by arrangement 1 June to 30 Aug for groups of 6 to 25.

69 Rundells is a very colourful, small town garden packed with a wide variety of shrubs, perennials, herbaceous and bedding plants in over 200 assorted containers. Hard landscaping on different levels has a summerhouse, various seating areas and water features. Various small secluded seating areas. A small fairy garden has been added to give interest for younger visitors. The garden is next to a large allotment and this is open to view with lots of interesting features inc a bee apiary. Honey and other produce for sale (conditions permitting).

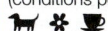

56 ♦ ST OSYTH PRIORY
West Field Lane, St Osyth, Clacton-on-Sea, CO16 8GW. 01206 430160, info@stosythpriory.co.uk, www.stosythpriory.co.uk. *5m from Colchester. W of the village of St Osyth. Best access by car from Mill St into West Field Ln. Parking in The Bury car park.* **For NGS: Wed 7 May (12-4). Adm £6, chd free. Home-made teas in the beautifully restored Darcy House.** For other opening times and information, please phone, email or visit garden website.

St Osyth Priory can trace its history back almost 1,400 years. A Registered Park and Garden County Wildlife Site, featuring historic lakes, woodland, tree lined avenues and ancient reed beds. Magnificent wisteria, Walled Garden, box parterre, Rose Garden, lavender hedging and herbaceous borders. Explore the gardens undergoing restoration. Parts of the Estate are private and some areas may not be accessible to the public. Tractor-trailer tours of the estate at an additional cost.

57 SHEEPCOTE GREEN HOUSE
Sheepcote Green, Clavering, Saffron Walden, CB11 4SJ. Jilly & Ross McNaughton, jillyevans@hotmail.com. *Sheepcote Green. Midway between Clavering & Langley.* **Visits by arrangement May to Sept for groups of 10 to 25. The owner offers wildlife and pond creation & restoration tours. Adm £15, chd free. Tea, coffee & cake.**
An atmospheric old country garden, set in the three acre grounds of a former farmhouse. Herbaceous beds with structure lent by clipped hedging, a sunken vegetable garden housed in a 1930s swimming pool, four ponds (two new and two restored), bug hotels, orchard, laid hedges, woodland and meadow areas. Views of Georgian windmills. Partial wheelchair access due to gravel driveway and uneven paths.

58 SILVER BIRCHES
Quendon Drive, Waltham Abbey, EN9 1LG. Frank & Linda Jewson, 01992 714047, frank.jewson@btconnect.com. *Take M25 J26 to Waltham Abbey. At T-lights by McD turn R to r'about. Take 2nd exit to next r'about. Take 3rd exit (A112) to T-lights. L to Monkswood Ave follow yellow signage.* **Sun 1 June (12-5). Combined adm with The Chimes, 3-4 Church Street £6, chd free. Tea, coffee & cake.** Visits also by arrangement 1 May to 14 Sept for groups of 10 to 25.
The garden boasts three lawns on the two levels. This surprisingly secluded garden has many mixed borders packed with colour. Mature shrubs and trees create a short woodland walk. Crystal clear water flows through a shady area of the garden. Many Chimney Pots for sale of various sizes which add great feature to the garden. There are areas which would not be suitable for wheelchairs.

59 SNARES HILL COTTAGE
Duck End, Stebbing, CM6 3RY. Pete & Liz Stabler, 01371 856565, petestabler@gmail.com. *Between Dunmow & Bardfield. On B1057 from Great Dunmow to Great Bardfield. ½ m after Bran End on L.* **Visits by arrangement Apr to Sept for groups of 6 to 40. Adm £6, chd free. Home-made teas.**
A 'quintessential English garden' - Gardeners' World. Our quirky 1½ acre garden has surprises round every corner and many interesting sculptures. A natural swimming pool is bordered by romantic flower beds, herb garden and Victorian folly. A bog garden borders woods and leads to silver birch copse, beach garden and 'Roman' temple. We have a shepherds hut and numerous water features. There will be classic cars on display.

60 ULTING WICK
Crouchmans Farm Road, Ulting, Maldon, CM9 6QX. Mr & Mrs B Burrough, 07984 614947, philippa.burrough@btinternet.com, www.ultingwickgarden.co.uk. *3m NW of Maldon. Take R turning to Ulting off B1019 as you exit Hatfield Peverel by a green. Garden on R after 2m. SatNav can drop short - carry on.* **Fri 21 Mar (11-4). Adm £7.50. Pre-booking essential, please visit www.ngs.org.uk for information & booking. Light refreshments. Sat 19, Fri 25 Apr, Wed 16 July, Mon 25 Aug, Fri 5 Sept (2-5). Adm £7.50, chd free. Home-made teas. For March opening home-made soup and rolls will be offered as well as cakes.** Visits also by arrangement 3 Feb to 30 Sept for groups of 15 to 50. Parking for a coach. Donation to All Saints Ulting Church.
Listed black barns provide backdrop for vibrant and exuberant planting in eight acres. Snowdrops, narcissus, tulips, flowing innovative spring planting, herbaceous borders, pond, mature weeping willows, kitchen garden, dramatic late summer beds with zingy, tender, exotic plant combinations. Drought tolerant perennial and mini annual wildflower meadows. Woodland. Many plants propagated in-house. Unusual plants for sale. Beautiful walks along the River Chelmer from the garden. Walk and Talk by Head Gardener in February and March. This garden is proud to have provided plants for the National Garden Scheme's Show Garden at Chelsea Flower Show 2024. Some gravel around the house but main areas of interest are accessible for wheelchairs.

61 WALNUT TREE COTTAGE
Cobblers Green, Felsted, Dunmow, CM6 3LX. Mrs Susan Monk. *B1417 brings you into Felsted from both ends of the village then turn into Causeway End Rd. ½ m down the road you will see a yellow sign on your L to turn R into the paddock.* **Sun 1 June (11-4). Adm £6, chd free. Tea, coffee & cake.**
A traditional cottage garden framed by wonderful views over the Essex countryside and planted with well-stocked flower borders and lawns that slope gently down to a natural pond. A productive garden borders the well maintained paddock where chickens and guinea fowl roam. Large patio and other seating areas provide a place to relax and appreciate the garden. There is a path that makes most of the garden wheelchair accessible.

62 1 WHITEHOUSE COTTAGES
Blue Mill Lane, Woodham Walter, CM9 6LR. Mrs Shelley Rand. *In between Maldon & Danbury, short drive from A12. A414 through Danbury. Signs to Woodham Walter, turn L go past The Anchor. Continue through the village. R into Blue Mill Ln. Parking in the top paddock, and a drop-off point near garden.* **Sun 18 May, Sun 6 July (10-3). Adm £5, chd free. Tea, coffee & cake.**
Nestled betwixt farmland in rural Essex, is our small secret garden, that has a wonderful charm to it. Bordered by three acres of paddocks with grazing horses, a little plot of loveliness wraps around our Victorian cottage, roses and grape smother the porch in June. A meandering lawn takes you through beds and borders softly planted with a cottage feel, a haven for wildlife and people alike. Dean Harris, a local artist blacksmith, will have a pop-up forge, making and selling metal garden accessories.

ESSEX 197

Chippins

GLOUCESTERSHIRE

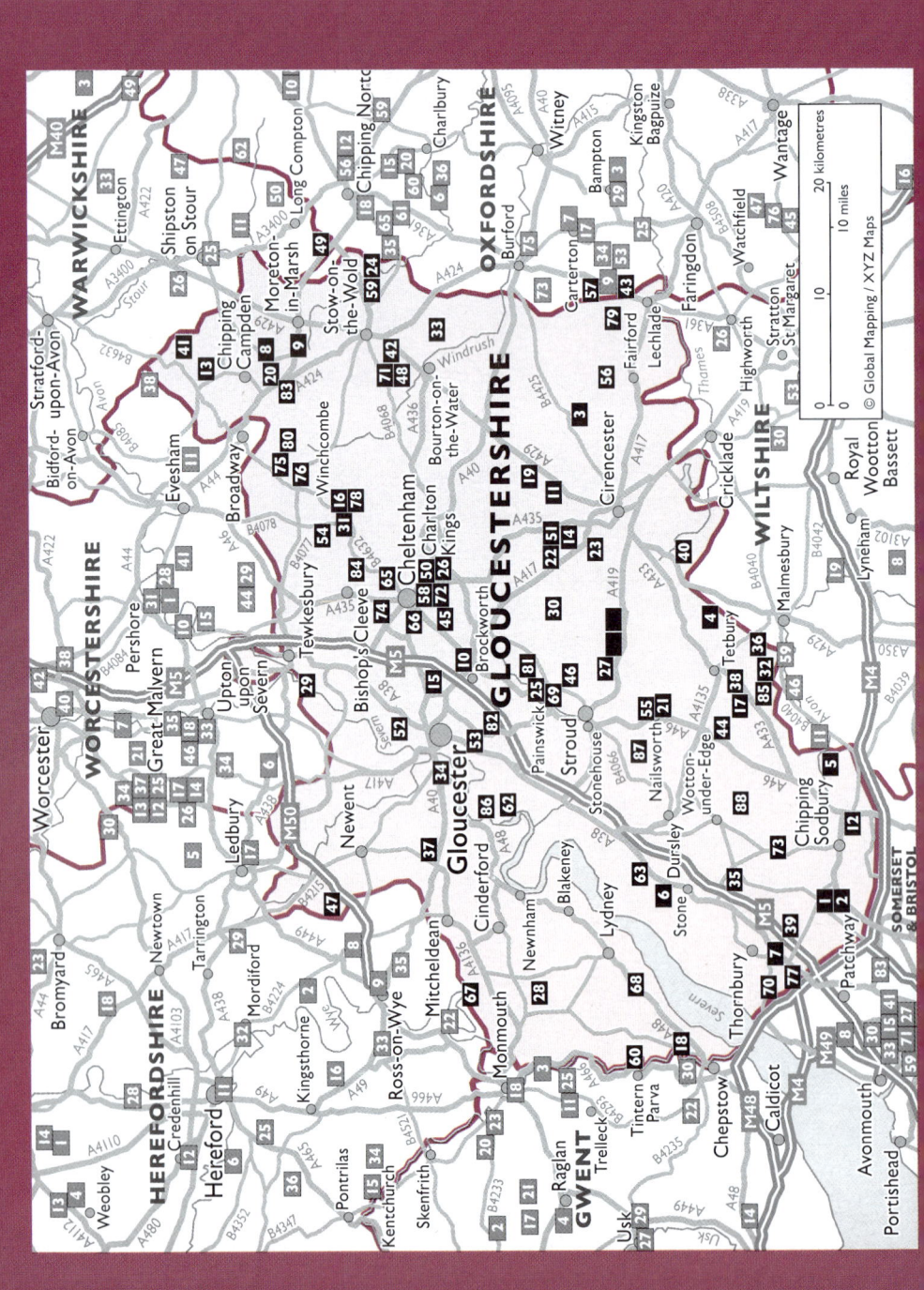

GLOUCESTERSHIRE

VOLUNTEERS

County Organiser
Vanessa Berridge
01242 609535
vanessa.berridge@ngs.org.uk

County Treasurer
Pam Sissons
01242 573942
pam.sissons@ngs.org.uk

Social Media
Mandy Bradshaw
01242 512491
mandy.bradshaw@ngs.org.uk

Publicity
Ruth Chivers
01452 767604
ruth.chivers@ngs.org.uk

Booklet Coordinator
Vanessa Graham 07595 880261
vanessa.graham@ngs.org.uk

By Arrangement Coordinator
Simone Seward 01242 573733
simone.seward@ngs.org.uk

Assistant County Organisers
Yvonne Bennetts 01242 463151
yvonne.bennetts@ngs.org.uk

Jackie Healy 07747 186302
jackie.healy@ngs.org.uk

Ali James 07780 000828
ali.james@ngs.org.uk

Valerie Kent 01993 823294
valerie.kent@ngs.org.uk

Immy Lee 07801 816340
immy.lee@ngs.org.uk

Sally Oates 01285 841320
sally.oates@ngs.org.uk

Jeanette Parker 01454 299699
jeanette_parker@hotmail.co.uk

Rose Parrott 07853 164924
rosemary.parrott@ngs.org.uk

Liz Ramsay 01242 672676
liz.ramsay@ngs.org.uk

@gloucestershirengs
@ngs_gloucestershire

OPENING DATES

All entries subject to change.
For latest information check
www.ngs.org.uk

Map locator numbers are shown to the right of each garden name.

January

Sunday 26th
Home Farm	37
Rock House	70

February

Snowdrop Openings

Sunday 2nd
Campden House	13
Rock House	70

Sunday 9th
1 Birch Drive	7
Home Farm	37
Trench Hill	81

Saturday 15th
Cotswold Farm	22

Sunday 16th
Cotswold Farm	22
Trench Hill	81

March

Sunday 9th
Algars Manor	1
Home Farm	37
Rock House	70

Sunday 16th
Rock House	70
Trench Hill	81

April

Sunday 6th
◆ Highnam Court	34
Home Farm	37

Saturday 12th
Wicks Green Farm	86

Sunday 13th
◆ Upton Wold	83
Wicks Green Farm	86

Monday 14th
◆ Kiftsgate Court	41

Wednesday 16th
Lords of the Manor Hotel	48

Sunday 20th
Trench Hill	81

Monday 21st
Trench Hill	81

Tuesday 22nd
Wortley House	88

Thursday 24th
Kemble House	40

Saturday 26th
NEW Prior's Piece	65

Sunday 27th
Algars Manor	1
Algars Mill	2
Charlton Down House	17
Church Gates	20
The Gate	31
Home Farm	37

May

Sunday 4th
NEW 2 Chapel Hay Close	15
Eastcombe and Bussage Gardens	27
◆ Highnam Court	34
Ramblers	68

Monday 5th
NEW 2 Chapel Hay Close	15
Eastcombe and Bussage Gardens	27
Trench Hill	81

Wednesday 7th
Brockworth Court	10
Daylesford House	24

Saturday 17th
Charingworth Court	16
Stoneleigh Down	77

Sunday 18th
Charingworth Court	16
20 Forsdene Walk	28
Milton Cottage	50
Park House	58
◆ Stanway Fountain & Water Garden	76
Stoneleigh Down	77

Monday 19th
◆ Nature in Art Museum and Art Gallery	52

Thursday 22nd
Richmond Villages Painswick	69

200 GLOUCESTERSHIRE

Saturday 24th
Little Orchard 46

Sunday 25th
Little Orchard 46
Pasture Farm 59
37 Queens Road 66

Monday 26th
Pasture Farm 59
37 Queens Road 66

Wednesday 28th
Downton House 25

Thursday 29th
Downton House 25

Friday 30th
NEW Ashley Manor 4
Hookshouse Pottery 38

Saturday 31st
Cotswold Farm 22
Hookshouse Pottery 38
Tower Close 80

June

Sunday 1st
Cotswold Farm 22
◆ Oxleaze Farm 57
The Patch 60
Rock House 70
Tower Close 80
Tuffley Gardens 82

Wednesday 4th
Trench Hill 81

Friday 6th
Campden House 13
◆ Sudeley Castle Gardens 78

Saturday 7th
Chedworth Gardens 19
Forthampton Court 29

Sunday 8th
Forthampton Court 29
NEW The Glebe House 32
Hodges Barn 36
NEW Ohio 55
Rock House 70
Stanton Village Gardens 75

Monday 9th
NEW The Glebe House 32
Hodges Barn 36

Wednesday 11th
Rockcliffe 71
Trench Hill 81

Friday 13th
Campden House 13
Westaway 84

Saturday 14th
1 Cobden Villas 21
Oak House 54
NEW Pond Cottage 63
Stoneleigh Down 77

Sunday 15th
1 Cobden Villas 21
20 Forsdene Walk 28
NEW Pond Cottage 63
Stoneleigh Down 77

Monday 16th
Badminton House 5
◆ Berkeley Castle 6

Tuesday 17th
Wortley House 88

Wednesday 18th
Lords of the Manor Hotel 48
Trench Hill 81

Friday 20th
Charlton Down House 17

Saturday 21st
Hookshouse Pottery 38
Oak House 54

Sunday 22nd
Blockley Gardens 8
◆ Cerney House Gardens 14
Langford Downs Farm 43
Leckhampton Court Hospice 45
The Old Rectory, Quenington 56

Wednesday 25th
Trench Hill 81

Thursday 26th
Richmond Villages Painswick 69

Saturday 28th
Perrywood House 62
The School Yard 73

Sunday 29th
Kirkham Farm 42
Moor Wood 51
Park House 58
Perrywood House 62

July

Wednesday 2nd
NEW Arlington and Bibury Gardens 3

Thursday 3rd
Charlton Down House 17

Sunday 6th
NEW Arlington and Bibury Gardens 3
NEW 2 Chapel Hay Close 15
Greenfields, Little Rissington 33

Sunday 13th
Trench Hill 81

Thursday 17th
Charlton Down House 17

Friday 18th
Westaway 84

Saturday 19th
The Stables 74

Sunday 20th
Little Orchard Kempley Dymock 47

Thursday 24th
Richmond Villages Painswick 69

Saturday 26th
NEW HMP Leyhill 35

Sunday 27th
NEW 1 Sandy Lane 72

Wednesday 30th
NEW Lasborough Park 44

Thursday 31st
Charlton Down House 17

August

Saturday 2nd
East Court 26
◆ Jekka's Herb Garden & Herbetum 39

Sunday 3rd
◆ Highnam Court 34
◆ Westonbirt School Gardens 85

Monday 4th
◆ Thyme 79

Tuesday 5th
◆ Thyme 79

Wednesday 6th
◆ Thyme 79

Thursday 7th
◆ Thyme 79

Friday 8th
◆ The Garden at Miserden 30
◆ Thyme 79

Monday 11th
◆ Kiftsgate Court 41

Thursday 14th
Charlton Down House 17
Richmond Villages Painswick 69

GLOUCESTERSHIRE 201

Saturday 16th
39 Neven Place — 53

Sunday 17th
◆ Bourton House Garden — 9
The Manor — 49
39 Neven Place — 53
◆ Stanway Fountain & Water Garden — 76

Thursday 21st
Charlton Down House — 17

Sunday 24th
Trench Hill — 81

Monday 25th
Calmsden Manor — 11

Thursday 28th
Charlton Down House — 17

Saturday 30th
Cotswold Farm — 22

Sunday 31st
Cotswold Farm — 22

September

Wednesday 17th
Lords of the Manor Hotel — 48

January 2026

Sunday 25th
Home Farm — 37
Rock House — 70

February 2026

Sunday 1st
Rock House — 70

Sunday 8th
Home Farm — 37
Trench Hill — 81

Saturday 14th
Cotswold Farm — 22

Sunday 15th
Cotswold Farm — 22
Trench Hill — 81

Our donation to the Army Benevolent Fund supported 700 individuals with front line services and horticultural related grants in 2024.

By Arrangement

Arrange a personalised garden visit with your club, or group of friends, on a date to suit you. See individual garden entries for full details.

Awkward Hill Cottage (Arlington and Bibury Gardens) — 3
1 Birch Drive — 7
Brockworth Court — 10
Camers — 12
Charingworth Court — 16
Charlton Down House — 17
Chase End — 18
Daglingworth House — 23
20 Forsdene Walk — 28
The Gate — 31
Kemble House — 40
Little Orchard — 46
Moor Wood — 51
Oak House — 54
The Old Rectory, Quenington — 56
Pasture Farm — 59
The Patch — 60
NEW Pond Cottage — 63
Radnors — 67
Rock House — 70
Stoneleigh Down — 77
Tower Close — 80
Trench Hill — 81
Woodchester Park House — 87

Lasborough Park

THE GARDENS

1 ALGARS MANOR
Station Rd, Iron Acton, BS37 9TB. Mrs B Naish. *9m N of Bristol, 3m W of Yate/Chipping Sodbury. Turn S off Iron Acton bypass B4059, past village green & White Hart pub, 200yds, then over level Xing. No access from Frampton Cotterell via lane; ignore SatNav. Parking at Algars Manor.* **Sun 9 Mar (1-4). Adm £5, chd free. Sun 27 Apr (1-5). Combined adm with Algars Mill £7, chd free. Tea & biscuits in March. Home-made cakes & drinks in April at Algars Manor.**
2 acres of woodland garden beside River Frome, mill stream, native plants mixed with collections of 60 magnolias and 70 camellias, rhododendrons, azaleas, eucalyptus and other unusual trees and shrubs. Daffodils, snowdrops and other early spring flowers.

2 ALGARS MILL
Frampton End Rd, Iron Acton, Bristol, BS37 9TD. Mr & Mrs John Wright. *9m N of Bristol, 3m W of Yate/Chipping Sodbury. (For directions see Algars Manor).* **Sun 27 Apr (1-5). Combined adm with Algars Manor £7, chd free. Home-made cakes & drinks at Algars Manor.**
2 acre woodland garden bisected by River Frome; spring bulbs, shrubs; very early spring feature (Feb-Mar) of wild Newent daffodils. 300-400yr-old mill house (not open) through which millrace still runs.

GROUP OPENING

3 NEW ARLINGTON AND BIBURY GARDENS
Arlington, Arlington, Cirencester, GL7 5ND. Victoria Summerley. *15 mins NE of Cirencester. Pls park at Pudding Hill Barn as no parking at Long Cottage or Awkward H. Access is via country lane leading off the B4425 (the main road through Bibury). 10 min walk between gardens. The lane to Awkward Hill Cottage is steep.* **Wed 2 July (3-7.30); Sun 6 July (10-2.30). Combined adm £12, chd free. Pre-booking essential, please visit www.ngs.org.uk for information & booking. Home-made teas.**

AWKWARD HILL COTTAGE
Mrs Victoria Summerley,
07718 384269,
v.summerley@hotmail.com,
www.awkwardhill.co.uk.
Visits also by arrangement 19 May to 20 July for groups of 10 to 30. Tea and cake inc in adm price.

NEW LONG COTTAGE
Heather & Craig Chapman.

NEW PUDDING HILL BARN
Karen Gray.

Pudding Hill Barn is a large country garden, sloping down to the River Coln, with more formal planting around the house, and meadow and woodland walks. The Trout Hut sits on a vantage point above the river, and there are chickens. Long Cottage is a courtyard cottage garden, crammed with ingenious ideas that make the most of the space. Awkward Hill Cottage is a country garden with a pond, a gravel garden, mixed borders and shade planting.

Awkward Hill Cottage, Arlington and Bibury Gardens

GLOUCESTERSHIRE

4 ASHLEY MANOR NEW
Ashley, Tetbury, GL8 8SX. Mr & Mrs J Lodwick. *Next to the church. From the middle of the village take the lane W toward Larkhill/Long Newnton. The last drive on R is the entrance to the property. What3words app: supple.truck.bombshell.* **Fri 30 May (11-4). Adm £7.50, chd free. Tea, coffee & cake. Ashley Manor pear juice.**
Set in a charming rural hamlet, Grade II* Ashley Manor has the classic elements of a Cotswold garden: stone walls, yew, topiary, ponds, lawns, borders, orchards, paddocks, hedging, fruit and vegetables. The gardens are the result of the incremental work of 3 families of gardeners over 100 yrs. Today you will find nothing is particularly symmetrical and some elements appear oddly placed, having been kept to preserve the evolution. The herbaceous borders are particularly lush in May and June with a multitudes of iris, peonies, alliums and roses. In excessively wet periods we ask that wheelchairs be mindful of the lawns.

5 BADMINTON HOUSE
Badminton, GL9 1DB. Duke & Duchess of Beaufort, www.badmintonestate.co.uk. *4m N of M4 J18. From M4 J18, 1st exit onto A46/Bath Rd. Follow signs to Badminton.* **Mon 16 June (11-4). Adm £10, chd free. Pre-booking essential, please visit www.ngs.org.uk for information & booking. Refreshments will not be available but picnics are welcome. Last entry 3pm.**
Explore the private gardens of the historic Badminton House from the formal beds to the South Garden with its water squares, hedges, beds and borders. Glorious displays of roses and borders of summer colours are combined with herbaceous perennials. The Walled Garden is home to the kitchen garden, providing fruit, vegetables and cut flowers for much of the year. The greenhouse is used for propagation and houses a fine display of pelargoniums. A limited number of tickets have been made available for this special opening by kind permission of the owners, the Duke and Duchess of Beaufort. We regret no dogs are allowed in the private gardens, with the exception of assistance dogs. The majority of the gardens are accessible to wheelchairs. Accessible WCs.

6 ◆ BERKELEY CASTLE
Berkeley, GL13 9PJ. Charles Berkeley, 01453 810303, info@berkeley-castle.com, www.berkeley-castle.com. *Halfway between Bristol & Gloucester, 10mins from J13 &14 of M5. Follow signs to Berkeley from A38 & B4066. Visitor entrance L off Canonbury St, just before town centre.* **For NGS: Mon 16 June (11-5). Adm £8, chd £4. Light refreshments in the Kitchen Garden Restaurant.**
Unique historic garden of a keen plantsman, with far-reaching views across the River Severn. Gardens contain many rare plants which thrive in the warm microclimate against the stone walls of this medieval castle. Woodland, historic trees and stunning terraced borders. The admission price does not inc entrance into the castle.

7 1 BIRCH DRIVE
Alveston, Bristol, BS35 3RQ. Myra Ginns, 07766 021616, m.ginns1@btinternet.com. *14m N of Bristol. Alveston on A38 Bristol to Gloucester. Just before T-lights turn L into David's Lane. At end, L then R onto Wolfridge Ride. Birch Drive 2nd on R.* **Sun 9 Feb (11-3). Adm £6, chd free. Pre-booking essential, please visit www.ngs.org.uk for information & booking. Visits also by arrangement 10 Feb to 22 Feb for groups of up to 10. Inc garden tour by the owner on the differences in snowdrop varieties.**
A garden with particular interest in the spring, having a wide range of bulbs in flower, inc unusual named varieties of anemone, hellebore, hepatica and crocus. The garden's main feature is the snowdrops, collected since 2004. Over a hundred named varieties, flowering between November and March, will interest snowdrop collectors and photographers. 5 main species of snowdrop to view and many varieties collected for differences in shape, markings, colour and name. Ramp to decked area gives a view of the garden and the opportunity to see unusual named snowdrops close up in pots.

GROUP OPENING

8 BLOCKLEY GARDENS
Blockley, Moreton-in-Marsh, GL56 9DB. Rupert & Mandy Williams-Ellis. *3m NW of Moreton-in-Marsh. Just off the A44 Morton-in-Marsh to Evesham road.* **Sun 22 June (1-6). Combined adm £10, chd free. Home-made teas at St George's Hall and The Allotments.**

BLOCKLEY ALLOTMENTS
Blockley and District Allotment Association, blockleyallotments.wixsite.com/blockleyallotments.

CHURCH GATES
Mrs Brenda Salmon.
(See separate entry)

CLAREMONT HOUSE
Linda & Berns Russ.

GARDEN HOUSE
Nick & Ginny Williams-Ellis.

MILL GARDEN HOUSE
Andrew & Celia Goodrick-Clarke.

THE OLD SILK MILL
Mr D Martell.

SNUGBOROUGH MILL
Rupert & Mandy Williams-Ellis.

SOUTHCOT NEW
June Pughe.

WOODRUFF
Paul & Maggie Adams.

This popular historic Cotswold hillside village has a great variety of high quality, well-stocked gardens - large and small, old and new. The delightful spring fed Blockley Brook flows right through the village and some of the gardens, inc former water mills and millponds. From some gardens there are wonderful rural views. Children welcome, but close supervision is essential.

In 2024 we awarded £232,000 in Community Garden Grants, supporting 89 community garden projects.

GLOUCESTERSHIRE

9 ♦ BOURTON HOUSE GARDEN
Bourton-on-the-Hill, GL56 9AE. Mr & Mrs R Quintus, 01386 700754, info@bourtonhouse.com, www.bourtonhouse.com. *2m W of Moreton-in-Marsh on A44.* **For NGS: Sun 17 Aug (10-5). Adm £10, chd free. Light refreshments & home-made cakes in Grade I Listed C16 tithe barn. For other opening times and information, please phone, email or visit garden website.** Award-winning, 3 acre garden featuring imaginative topiary, wide herbaceous borders with many rare, unusual and exotic plants, water features, unique shade house and many creatively planted pots. Fabulous at any time of year, but magnificent in summer months and early autumn. Walk around a 7 acre pasture, with free printed guide to specimen trees available. 70% access for wheelchairs. Disabled WC.
♿ ✿ 🚗 ☕ 🔊

10 BROCKWORTH COURT
Court Road, Brockworth, GL3 4QU. Tim & Bridget Wiltshire, 01452 862938, timwiltshire@hotmail.co.uk. *6m E of Gloucester. 6m W of Cheltenham. Adj St Georges Church on Court Rd. From A46 turn into Mill Lane, turn R, L, R at T junctions. From Ermin St, turn into Ermin Park, then R at r'about then L at next r'about.* **Wed 7 May (2-5). Adm £6, chd free. Tea, coffee & cake. Cash only.** Visits also by arrangement 16 Apr to 7 Oct for groups of 10 to 35. Coach parking.
This intense yet informal tapestry style garden beautifully complements the period manor house which it surrounds. Organic, naturalistic, with informal cottage style planting areas that seamlessly blend together. Natural fish pond, with Monet bridge leading to small island with thatched Fiji house. Kitchen garden once cultivated by monks. Views to Crickley and Coopers Hill. Adjacent Norman church (open). Historic tithe barn, manor house visited by Henry VIII and Anne Boleyn in 1535. Partial wheelchair access.
♿ 🚗 🚌 ☕

11 CALMSDEN MANOR
Calmsden, Cirencester, GL7 5ET. Mr M & Mrs J Tufnell. *5m N of Cirencester. Turn to Calmsden off A429 at The Stump pub. On entering the village Manor gates are straight ahead of you.* **Mon 25 Aug (2.30-6.30). Adm £10, chd free. Tea, coffee & cake.**
With borders originally designed by Mary Keen, Calmsden Manor is a well loved garden. A treat for plant lovers, design enthusiasts, vegetable growers or those simply looking for a lovely day out. Inc herbaceous borders, a small arboretum, wild grass and flower meadow, and a walled garden. The garden moves with the seasons with stunning early season bulbs, summer borders and late season colour.
♿ ✿ ☕ 🔊

12 CAMERS
Badminton Road, Old Sodbury, Bristol, BS37 6RG. Mr & Mrs Michael Denman, 01454 327929, jodenman@btinternet.com, www.camers.org. *2m E of Chipping Sodbury. Entrance in Chapel Lane off A432 at Dog Inn. Enter through the field gate & drive to the top of the fields to park next to the garden.* **Visits by arrangement May to Sept for groups of 20+. Adm £8. Refreshments by arrangement.**
Elizabethan farmhouse (not open) set in 4 acres of constantly developing garden and woodland with spectacular views over Severn Vale. Garden full of surprises, formal and informal areas planted with wide range of species to provide year-round interest. Parterre, topiary, Japanese garden, bog and prairie areas, white and hot gardens, woodland walks. Some steep slopes.
♿ 🐕 ☕ 🔊

13 CAMPDEN HOUSE
Dyer's Lane, Chipping Campden, GL55 6UP. Thomas & Suzanne Smith. *Estate entrance via stone pillars on Dyer's Lane, approx ¼m SW of Chipping Campden. 1¼m drive through woodland and parkland. Do not use Postcode or SatNav. What3words app: vegetable.firebird.trout.* **Sun 2 Feb (10-3); Fri 6, Fri 13 June (10-5). Adm £10, chd £5.**
5 acres featuring mixed borders of plant and colour interest around C17 house and tithe barn (neither open). Set in fine parkland in hidden valley with lakes and ponds. Woodland garden and walks, vegetable garden. Partial wheelchair access. Disabled parking available. Gravel paths, steep slopes.
♿ ☕ 🔊

14 ♦ CERNEY HOUSE GARDENS
North Cerney, Cirencester, GL7 7BX. Mr N W Angus & Dr J Angus, 01285 831300, janet@cerneygardens.com, www.cerneygardens.com. *4m NW of Cirencester. On A435 Cheltenham road turn L opp Bathurst Arms, follow road past church up hill, then go straight towards pillared gates on R (signed Cerney House).* **For NGS: Sun 22 June (10-7). Adm £6, chd £1. Tea, coffee & cake in The Bothy Tearoom. For other opening times and information, please phone, email or visit garden website.**
A romantic English garden for all seasons. There is a secluded Victorian walled garden featuring herbaceous borders overflowing with colour. In the summer the magnificent display of rambling roses comes to life. Enjoy our woodland walk, extended nature trail and new medicinal herb garden. Dogs welcome. Walled garden accessible for electric wheelchairs. Gravel paths and inclines may not suit manual wheelchairs.
♿ 🐕 ✿ 🚗 ☕ 🪑 🔊

15 NEW 2 CHAPEL HAY CLOSE
Churchdown, Gloucester, GL3 2HP. Mrs Shirley Sills. *6m SW of Cheltenham in centre of Churchdown Village. Free parking at Chapel Hay Car Park, Church Rd, GL3 2HS. Height restriction 2m. Entry to garden immed adjacent to car park. No parking or garden entry in Chapel Hay Close.* **Sun 4, Mon 5 May, Sun 6 July (11-5). Adm £4, chd free. Cash only.**
One sixth of an acre plantaholic's garden around 1980s bungalow. Steep garden with terraced borders and retaining walls of stone and timber, mostly planted in last 4 yrs for year-round interest. Steep steps with handrails, paths, patio and structures. Perennials, shrubs, young trees, climbers, tapestry lawn, gravel areas, water features, tiny vegetable plot, greenhouse. Unsuitable for wheelchairs due to many steps. Old Elm Inn pub across road from car park, The Village Cakery, Brookfield Rd open Sundays for cakes & drinks 4 mins walk from garden.
✿

GLOUCESTERSHIRE

16 CHARINGWORTH COURT
Broadway Road, Winchcombe, GL54 5JN. Susan & Richard Wakeford, 07791 353779, susanwakeford@gmail.com, www.charingworthcourtcotswoldsgarden.com. *8m NE of Cheltenham. 400 metres N of Winchcombe town centre on B4632. Limited parking along Broadway Rd. Town car parks in Bull Lane, Chandos St (short stay) and all day parking (£1) in Back Lane. Map on garden website.* **Sat 17, Sun 18 May (11-5.30). Adm £6, chd free. Tea, coffee & cake. Visits also by arrangement 5 May to 20 July for groups of 10 to 25. Owners include a guided tour of the garden & refreshments for group visits.**
Artistically and lovingly created 1½ acre garden surrounding restored Georgian/Tudor house (not open). Relaxed country style with Japanese influences, large pond, sculpture and a walled vegetable/flower garden, all created over 30 yrs from a blank canvas. Mature copper beech trees, Cedar of Lebanon and Wellingtonia; and younger trees replacing an earlier excess of *Cupressus leylandii*. Partial access due to gravel paths which can be challenging but several areas accessible without steps. Pls ring to book disabled parking.
& 🐕 ☕ 🔊

17 CHARLTON DOWN HOUSE
Charlton Down, Tetbury, GL8 8TZ. Neil & Julie Record, cdh.groupbookings@gmail.com. *From Tetbury, take A433 towards Bath for 1½m; turn R (north) just before the Hare & Hounds, then R again after 200yds into Hookshouse Lane. Charlton Down House is 600yds on R.* **Sun 27 Apr (11-5); Fri 20 June, Thur 3, Thur 17, Thur 31 July (1-5). Every Thur 14 Aug to 28 Aug (1-5). Adm £7, chd free. Home-made teas. Cash preferred for refreshments. Visits also by arrangement 1 July to 29 Aug for groups of 20 to 35.**
Extensive country house gardens in 180 acre equestrian estate. Formal terraces, perennial borders, walled topiary garden and large glasshouse. Jubilee copse. Rescue animals. Ample parking. Largely flat terrain; most garden areas accessible.
& 🐕 🚗 ☕ 🔊

18 CHASE END
Tidenham Chase, Chepstow, NP16 7JN. Tim & Penny Wright, pennyjwright63@gmail.com. *On the B4228 between Chepstow & St Briavels. 1st house on R after Boughspring Ln, travelling on the B4228 towards St. Briavels. Parking 2nd entrance on R, through gate into top field. No parking on main road.* **Visits by arrangement 7 June to 21 June for groups of 5 to 25. Tea, coffee & cake.**
4 acre, south facing, sloping site overlooking the Severn, where soil and wildlife are nurtured with organic and no-dig methods. There are 3 acres of mature wildflower meadows, with orchards and a vineyard, and 1 acre of more formal garden with mature herbaceous borders, trees and shrubs (notably roses), 2 ponds with bog gardens, an area of prairie planting and a greenhouse.
❀ ☕ 🔊

GROUP OPENING

19 CHEDWORTH GARDENS
Chedworth, Cheltenham, GL54 4AN. *7m NE of Cirencester. Off Fosseway, A429 between Stow-on-the-Wold (12m) & Cirencester. Follow NGS signs. Follow car parking signs on entering the village.* **Sat 7 June (10-5). Combined adm £10, chd free. Home-made teas. Donation to Chedworth Gardening Club.**

BLISS COTTAGE
GL54 4AN. Ceri Powell & Ajay Shah.

COBBLERS COTTAGE
GL54 4AN. Ceri Powell & Ajay Shah.

KEENS COTTAGE
GL54 4AN. Sue & Steve Bradbury, www.bradburydesigns.co.uk.

THE OXBYRE
GL54 4AN. Adam Wilkie.

Varied collection of country gardens, nestling throughout the mile long Chedworth Valley with tributary of River Coln running below. Stunning views. Featuring lots of ideas to inspire. Other gardens may join the group, please check the website nearer the opening date. Pancake Hill Flowers will be selling plants.
🐕 ❀ 🚗 ☕ 🔊

20 CHURCH GATES
High Street, Blockley, Moreton-in-Marsh, GL56 9ES. Mrs Brenda Salmon. *3m NW of Moreton-in-Marsh. Just off the A44 Morton-in-Marsh to Evesham road.* **Sun 27 Apr (2-6). Adm £4, chd free. Opening with Blockley Gardens on Sun 22 June.**
A well-stocked, plantswoman's garden, in the cottage style, featuring hidden areas of delightful planting. Varied and seasonal herbaceous and mixed borders, with a small lawn and several paved and patio areas, with plenty of design ideas for a smaller space.
🔊

21 1 COBDEN VILLAS
Meadow Bank, Walkley Wood, Nailsworth, GL6 0RT. Sue Ratcliffe. *Parking in Nailsworth town centre with a 10 min walk to Shortwood Rd, L at the Britannia pub onto Horsley Rd; R onto Pike Lane. There is very limited on road parking in Pike Lane/Meadow Bank.* **Sat 14, Sun 15 June (10-4). Adm £5. Light refreshments. Tea, coffee & cold drinks.**
Set into a hillside this organic and wildlife friendly garden is divided into distinct areas. A small mixed woodland area provides separation from the adjacent lane with underplanting of shade loving native and unusual plants. Terraced beds and borders adopt cottage garden planting ethos with extensive ground cover and shrubs. A rill and small pond provides a home for frogs and dragonflies. Regret this garden is not suitable for children.
❀ ☕ 🪑 🔊

---

70 inpatients and their families are being supported at the newly opened Horatio's Garden Northern Ireland, thanks to National Garden Scheme donations.

GLOUCESTERSHIRE

22 COTSWOLD FARM
Duntisbourne Abbots, Cirencester, GL7 7JS. John & Sarah Birchall, www.cotswoldfarmgardens.org.uk. *5m NW of Cirencester off old A417. From Cirencester L signed Duntisbourne Abbots Services, R & R underpass. Drive ahead. From Gloucester L signed Duntisbourne Abbots Services. Pass Services. Drive L.* **Sat 15, Sun 16 Feb (11-3). Light refreshments. Sat 31 May, Sun 1 June, Sat 30, Sun 31 Aug (2-5). Home-made teas. Adm £7.50, chd free. 2026: Sat 14, Sun 15 Feb.** Donation to A Rocha.
This beautiful Arts & Crafts garden overlooks a quiet valley on descending levels with terraces designed by Norman Jewson in the 1930s. Enclosed by Cotswold stone walls and yew hedges, the garden has year-round interest inc a snowdrop collection with over 80 varieties. The terraces, shrub garden, herbaceous borders and bog garden are full of scent and colour from spring to autumn. Rare orchid walks. Picnics welcome.

23 DAGLINGWORTH HOUSE
Daglingworth, Cirencester, GL7 7AG. David & Henrietta Howard, 07970 122122, ettajhoward@gmail.com. *3m N of Cirencester off A417/419. House with blue gate beside church in centre of Daglingworth, at end of No Through Road.* **Visits by arrangement Apr to Sept for groups of 10 to 30. Individuals welcome. Adm £8. Light refreshments.**
Over the last 30 yrs we have created a 3 acre classical garden with a

Pond Cottage

GLOUCESTERSHIRE 207

humorous contemporary twist. There is a grotto, a Temple, a walled garden, woodland, small grass and meadow gardens, and a sunken garden. Pools, a mirror canal, a cascade, topiary shapes, good hedging and sculptures. Pretty village setting next to Saxon Church.

24 DAYLESFORD HOUSE
Daylesford, GL56 0YG. Lord & Lady Bamford. *5m W of Chipping Norton. Off A436 between Stow-on-the-Wold & Chipping Norton. What3words app: greet.kettles. briskly.* **Wed 7 May (1-5). Adm £9, chd free. Tea, coffee & cake. Cash only.**
Magnificent C18 landscape grounds created in 1790 for Warren Hastings, greatly restored and enhanced by present owners under organic regime. Lakeside and woodland walks within natural wildflower meadows. Large formal walled garden, centred around orchid, peach and working glasshouses. Trellised rose garden. Collection of citrus within period orangery. Secret garden, pavilion, formal pools. Very large garden with substantial distances. The owners of Daylesford House have specifically requested that photographs are NOT taken in their garden or grounds. No dogs allowed except guide dogs. Partial wheelchair access.

25 DOWNTON HOUSE
Gloucester St, Painswick, GL6 6QN. Jane Kilpatrick. *4m N of Stroud. Entry to garden is via Hollyhock Lane only. Pls do not park in Lane. Park in Stamages Lane Car Park off A46 below church, or in Churchill Way, 1st L off Gloucester St B4073.* **Wed 28, Thur 29 May (10.30-3.30). Adm £6, chd free. Light refreshments. Afternoon teas in the garden.**
Plant enthusiast and author's walled ⅓ acre garden in heart of historic Painswick. Planted for year-round foliage colour and interest with particular focus on plants that thrive on thin limey soil in a changing climate. Garden features unusual trees, shrubs and peonies associated with owner's interest in plant introductions from China. Exedra Nursery from Painswick Rococo Garden will be selling plants. Steep ramp provides access to path and paved area.

26 EAST COURT
East End Road, Charlton Kings, Cheltenham, GL53 8QN. Ben White. *The garden will be signed off the A40/ East End Rd junction. Parking in the Balcarras School car park, opp the garden (signed).* **Sat 2 Aug (10-4). Adm £10, chd £5. Tea, coffee & cake.**
A garden on 2 levels. The upper around the 1806 house (not open) is traditionally styled with formal beds and lawns and 3 majestic purple beech trees some 200 yrs old. The in-house designed 2½ acre lower garden is in complete contrast. Winding brick paths, swathes of herbaceous plantings towered over by arching Datisca, Miscanthus and Paulownia. An experimental south facing walled area enjoys exciting exotic and unusual tender perennials and annuals. The new pond has attracted a wide range of aquatic wildlife. The garden is always evolving, so visit us and share our excitement. Mostly accessible to wheelchairs. Pls ask for help where needed. WC accessed via a single step.

GROUP OPENING

27 EASTCOMBE AND BUSSAGE GARDENS
Eastcombe, Stroud, GL6 7EB. *3m E of Stroud. Maps/tickets from Eastcombe Village Hall GL67EB, Hawkley Cottage GL67DQ, 20 Farmcote Close GL67EG & Redwood GL68AZ. On street parking only. Tickets valid both days.* **Sun 4, Mon 5 May (1-5.30). Combined adm £8.50, chd free. Tea, coffee & cake at Eastcombe Village Hall (cash only). Ice creams at Hawkley Cottage.**

CADSONBURY
Natalie & Glen Beswetherick.

20 FARMCOTE CLOSE
Ian & Dawn Sim.

21 FARMCOTE CLOSE
Robert & Marion Bryant.

HAMPTON VIEW
Geraldine & Mike Carter.

HAWKLEY COTTAGE
Helen & Gerwin Westendorp.

12 HIDCOTE CLOSE
Mr K Walker.

HIGHLANDS
Helen & Bob Watkinson.

1 JASMINE COTTAGE
Mrs June Gardiner.

NEW LINDENS
John & Ann Cooper.

MOUNT PLEASANT
Mrs G Peyton.

REDWOOD
Heather Collins.

50 STONECOTE RIDGE
Julie & Robin Marsland.

WHITE HOUSE
Jane & Dave Gandy.

WOODVIEW COTTAGE
Julian & Eileen Horn-Smith.

YEW TREE COTTAGE
Andy & Sue Green

Medium and small gardens in a variety of styles and settings within these picturesque hilltop villages, with their spectacular views of the Toadsmoor Valley. In addition, one large garden is located in the bottom of the valley, approachable only on foot as are some of the other gardens in Eastcombe. Full descriptions of each garden and those with wheelchair access can be found on the National Garden Scheme website. Please show any pre-booked tickets at ticket venues where you will be given a trail map. WC at village hall and Hawkley Cottage. Plants for sale at village hall and some gardens.

28 20 FORSDENE WALK
Coalway, Coleford, GL16 7JZ. Pamela Buckland, 01594 837179. *From Coleford take Lydney/Chepstow Rd at T-lights. L after police station ½ m up hill turn L at Xrds then 2nd R (Old Road) straight on at minor Xrds then L into Forsdene Walk.* **Sun 18 May, Sun 15 June (1-5). Adm £4, chd free. Tea, coffee & cake. Cash only. Visits also by arrangement 1 May to 1 Sept for groups of up to 15.**
Corner garden full of design ideas to maximise smaller spaces in interlocking colour themed rooms, some on different levels, packed with perennials and grasses. A shady pergola for ferns and hostas. A small man-made stream. Low maintenance gravelled areas with trees, shrubs and self sown perennials, plus pots in abundance.

208 GLOUCESTERSHIRE

29 FORTHAMPTON COURT
Forthampton, Tewkesbury, GL19 4RD. Alan & Anabel Mackinnon. *W of Tewkesbury. From Tewkesbury A438 to Ledbury. After 2m turn L to Forthampton. At Xrds go L towards Chaceley. Go 1m turn L at Xrds.* **Sat 7, Sun 8 June (12.30-4.30). Adm £7.50, chd free. Home-made teas.**
Charming and varied garden surrounding N Gloucestershire medieval manor house (not open) within sight of Tewkesbury Abbey. Inc borders, lawns, roses and magnificent Victorian vegetable garden. Disabled drop off at entrance, some gravel paths and uneven areas.

&♿ ☕ 🔊

30 ◆ THE GARDEN AT MISERDEN
Miserden, Stroud, GL6 7JA. Mr Nicholas Wills, 01285 821303, hello@miserden.org, www.miserden.org. *6m NW of Cirencester. Leave A417 for Birdlip, drive through Whiteway & follow signs for Miserden.* **For NGS: Fri 8 Aug (10-5). Adm £12, chd free. Light refreshments. For other opening times and information, please phone, email or visit garden website.**
A timeless walled garden designed in the C17 with a wonderful sense of peace and tranquillity. Known for its magnificent mixed borders and Lutyens' Yew Walk and quaint grass steps; there is also an ancient mulberry tree, enchanting arboretum and stunning views across the Golden Valley. Routes around the garden are gravel or grass; there are alternative routes to those that have steps. Disabled WC at the café.

♿ ✿ 🚗 ☕ 🔊

31 THE GATE
80 North Street, Winchcombe, GL54 5PS. Vanessa Berridge & Chris Evans, 01242 609535, vanessa.berridge@gmail.com. *Winchcombe is on B4632 midway between Cheltenham & Broadway. Parking behind Library in Back Lane, 50 yds from The Gate. Entry to garden via Cowl Lane.* **Sun 27 Apr (1-5). Adm £4, chd free. Home-made teas. Visits also by arrangement 28 Apr to 31 July for groups of 5 to 20.**
Compact cottage style garden planted with a colourful display of tulips in spring, and with perennials, annuals and climbers in the walled courtyard of C17 former coaching inn. Also a separate, productive, walled kitchen garden with espaliers and other fruit trees. Wheelchair access to most areas of the garden; other areas are partially visible from negotiable paths.

♿ ✿ ☕ 🔊

32 NEW THE GLEBE HOUSE
Church Lane, Shipton Moyne, Tetbury, GL8 8PW. Mr & Mrs Richard Boggis-Rolfe, glebehouse@gmail.com. *2½ m S of Tetbury. Next to church in Shipton Moyne. What3words app: spoil.prune.snuggle.* **Sun 8, Mon 9 June (12-5). Adm £7.50, chd free. Tea, coffee & cake at both gardens. Tickets to each garden £7.50 at their gates. Open nearby Hodges Barn.**
The gardens and grounds of the former Rectory are about 4 acres. Double herbaceous border, walled kitchen and flower garden, ornamental statuary and water features, swimming pool garden, greenhouses and a paddock with goats, chickens and ponies. Path through the orchard to a copse with a small folly. Walks round the pond and stream to Hodges Barn or to another folly with views of the Church. Gravel and mown paths to each part of the garden and disabled parking in the stable yard by prior arrangement.

♿ 🐐 ☕ 🪑 🔊

33 GREENFIELDS, LITTLE RISSINGTON
Cheltenham, GL54 2NA. Mrs Diana MacKenzie-Charrington. *On Rissington Rd between Bourton-on-the-Water & Little Rissington, opp turn to Grt Rissington (Leasow Lane). SatNav using postcode does not take you to house.* **Sun 6 July (2-5). Adm £6, chd free. Home-made teas.**
The honey coloured Georgian Cotswold stone house sits in 2 acres of garden, created by current owners over last 25 yrs. Lawns are edged with borders full of flowers and flowering bulbs. A small pond and stream overlook fields. Mature apple trees in wild garden, greenhouse in working vegetable garden. Regret no dogs. Partial wheelchair access.

♿ ☕ 🔊

34 ◆ HIGHNAM COURT
Highnam, Gloucester, GL2 8DP. Mr R J Head, www.HighnamCourt.co.uk. *2m W of Gloucester. On A40/A48 junction from Gloucester to Ross or Chepstow. At this r'about take exit at 3 o'clock if coming from Gloucester direction. Do NOT go into Highnam village.* **For NGS: Sun 6 Apr, Sun 4 May, Sun 3 Aug (11-5). Adm £6, chd free. Tea, coffee & cake. For other opening times and information, please visit garden website. Donation to other charities.**
40 acres of Victorian landscaped gardens surrounding magnificent Grade I* listed house (not open), built in 1658 for William Cooke, the son of Sir Robert Cooke, following damage to the original structure in the English Civil War. The gardens were set out by the artist, Thomas Gambier Parry and have been lovingly restored by the current owner, Roger Head. The gardens are home to lakes, shrubberies, a wildflower meadow, multiple rose gardens (5000+ roses), knot gardens, an oriental garden, a newly constructed white garden, a kitchen garden, multiple wood carvings and a listed Pulhamite water garden with grottos and fernery. In the orangery, you can see a selection of rare air plants and carnivorous plants.

🐕 ☕ 🔊

35 NEW HMP LEYHILL
Leyhill, Wotton-Under-Edge, GL12 8BT. Mark Nutley. *1m off the M5 Junction 14, signed. The Gardens are located within HMP Leyhill clearly signed. Pls park in Visitor's Car Park.* **Sat 26 July (10-4). Adm £8. Pre-booking essential, please visit www.ngs.org.uk for information & booking.**
Visitors will be taken on a guided group tour of the gardens. Extensive perennial borders and annual beds lead to an alpine rockery. Meandering via an incline path there are further annual beds, a memorial bed, established trees and extensive lawns. There is a large commercial horticulture section growing salad crops, fruits and vegetables together with a plant nursery. There is a small conservation area with a bug hotel, a pond with waterfall and a tropical area. An important focus for us is to provide a stress-free natural environment that promotes physical and mental health and wellbeing of individuals. Pls note identity documentation will be required and we will contact you prior to your visit. Partial wheelchair access.

♿

36 HODGES BARN

Shipton Moyne, Tetbury, GL8 8PR. Mr & Mrs N Hornby, www.hodgesbarn.com. *3m S of Tetbury. On Malmesbury side of village. What3words app: gashes.crinkled.horn.* **Sun 8, Mon 9 June (12-5). Adm £7.50, chd free. Home-made teas at the Pool House. Tickets to each garden £7.50 at their gates. Open nearby The Glebe House.**

Very unusual C15 dovecote converted into family home. Cotswold stone walls host climbing and rambling roses, clematis, vines, hydrangeas and together with yew, rose and tapestry hedges create formality around house. Mixed shrub and herbaceous borders, shrub roses, water garden, woodland garden planted with cherries and magnolias. Vegetable and picking flower garden.

37 HOME FARM

Newent Lane, Huntley, GL19 3HQ. Mrs T Freeman. *4m S of Newent. On B4216 ½ m off A40 in Huntley travelling towards Newent.* **Sun 26 Jan, Sun 9 Feb, Sun 9 Mar, Sun 6, Sun 27 Apr (11-4). Adm £4.50, chd free. Online booking or cash on the day. 2026: Sun 25 Jan, Sun 8 Feb.**

Set in elevated position with exceptional views. 1m walk through woods and fields to show carpets of spring flowers. Enclosed garden with fern border, sundial and heather bed. White and mixed shrub borders. Stout footwear advisable in winter. Two delightful cafés within a mile.

38 HOOKSHOUSE POTTERY

Hookshouse Lane, Tetbury, GL8 8TZ. Lise & Christopher White, www.hookshousepottery.co.uk. *2½ m SW of Tetbury. Follow signs from A433 at Hare & Hounds Hotel, Westonbirt. Alternatively take A4135 out of Tetbury towards Dursley & follow signs after ½ m on L.* **Fri 30, Sat 31 May, Sat 21 June (1.30-5.30). Adm £6, chd free. Home-made teas.**

Garden offers a combination of long perspectives and intimate corners. Planting inc wide variety of perennials, with emphasis on colour interest throughout the seasons. Herbaceous borders, woodland garden and flower meadow, water garden containing treatment ponds (unfenced) and flowform cascades. Sculptural features. Kitchen garden with raised beds, orchard. Run on organic principles. Pottery showroom with hand thrown woodfired pots inc frost proof garden pots. 'Art in the Garden' will feature a small collection of work by artists working in metal, glass, wood and willow, set in idyllic surroundings. Mostly wheelchair accessible.

Bourton House Garden

39 ♦ JEKKA'S HERB GARDEN & HERBETUM
Shellards Lane, Alveston, Bristol, BS35 3SY. Mrs Jekka McVicar. *7m N of M5 J16 or 6m S from J14 of M5. 1m off A38 signed Itchington. From M5 J16, A38 to Alveston, past church turn R at junction signed Itchington. M5 J14 on A38 turn L after T-lights to Itchington.* **For NGS: Sat 2 Aug (9.30-4). Adm £7.50, chd free. Pre-booking essential, please phone 01454 418878, email sales@jekkas.com or visit www.jekkas.com for information & booking. Our herb inspired café will be serving seasonal herb-based treats, home-made cakes & coffee as well as Jekka's herbal infusions. For other opening times and information, please phone, email or visit garden website.**
Jekka's is home to a living encyclopedia of over 400 different varieties of culinary and medicinal herbs that are displayed in Jekka's Herbetum and Jekka's Herb Garden. Each ticketed session will have either a tour or talk given by Jekka, a member of her team or a Friend of Jekka's. After your tour you can browse their collection, buy herbs, plants and seeds, visit the farm shop or have some tasty treats from Jekka's café. Wheelchair access possible however terrain is rough from car park to Herbetum.

♿ ✿ ☕

40 KEMBLE HOUSE
Kemble, Cirencester, GL7 6AD. Jill Kingston, 07798 830287, kingsjill50@gmail.com. *3m from Cirencester. Approaching Kemble on the A429 from Cirencester, turn L onto School Rd then R onto Church Rd, pass Kemble Church on L. Kemble House is the next house on L.* **Thur 24 Apr (2-5). Adm £7.50, chd free. Visits also by arrangement 6 Mar to 31 May.**
A landscaped garden with many tall lime trees. Herbaceous borders line the lawns. The main one in front of the house is a grass tennis court that was laid in the 1880s. There is a walled garden with many fruit trees and two rose gardens. Two paddocks surround the property with Hebridean sheep. Wheelchair access possible, gravel pathways and some steps.

♿ 🧺 🔊

41 ♦ KIFTSGATE COURT
Chipping Campden, GL55 6LN. Mr & Mrs J G Chambers, 01386 438777, kiftsgate@aol.com, www.kiftsgate.co.uk. *4m NE of Chipping Campden. Opp Hidcote NT Garden.* **For NGS: Mon 14 Apr (2-6); Mon 11 Aug (12-6). Adm £12.50, chd £4. Home-made teas. For other opening times and information, please phone, email or visit garden website.**
Magnificent situation and views, many unusual plants and shrubs, tree peonies, hydrangeas, abutilons, species and old-fashioned roses inc largest rose in England, *Rosa filipes* 'Kiftsgate'.

✿ 🚗 🛏 ☕ 🔊

42 KIRKHAM FARM
Upper Slaughter, Cheltenham, GL54 2JS. Mr & Mrs John Wills. *On road between Lower Slaughter & Lower Swell. Opp farm buildings on roadside. 1½m W of Fosseway A429 & SW of Stow on the Wold.* **Sun 29 June (11-5). Adm £7, chd free. Home-made teas.**
A country garden overlooking lovely views with several mixed borders that always have a succession of colour. Gravel gardens, trees and shrubs and a hidden pool garden, raised beds, cutting beds and a developing wildflower bank give plenty of interest. Teas are served in our beautifully restored stone barn. The majority of the garden is accessible.

♿ 🐕 ✿ ☕ 🔊

43 LANGFORD DOWNS FARM
Langford Downs Farm, nr Lechlade, GL7 3QL. Mr & Mrs Gavin MacEchern, 07778 355115, caroline@macechern.com. *Access from A361 via layby behind copse - 6m from Burford towards Lechlade on the R OR 2m from Lechlade towards Burford on the L (NOT in Langford).* **Sun 22 June (1-5). Adm £7, chd free. Home-made teas. Cash only.**
Cotswold house and good sized garden created in 2009, with extensive tree planting, and mixed tree, shrub and herbaceous borders. Traditional hedges comprising arches and windows and crab apple espalier. Extensive cut flower and vegetable garden, interesting courtyard with raised nursery beds. Cotswold pond with natural spring, bug hotels, magic garden and lots of quirky things to see and find! All areas wheelchair friendly.

♿ ✿ 🚗 ☕

SPECIAL EVENT

44 NEW LASBOROUGH PARK
Lasborough, Tetbury, GL8 8UF. Mr Rausing. *6m W of Tetbury. Continue along the driveway from A46 passing the church, farm & Manor house on L. Keep going along the road passing through the gates, over the cattle grid & drive towards Lasborough.* **Wed 30 July (10-4). Adm £17.50, chd free. Pre-booking essential, please visit www.ngs.org.uk for information & booking. Home-made teas included after the tour.**
12 acre garden inc formal lawns, shrub, roses and herbaceous borders, topiary, woodland garden and parterre garden. The walled garden is designed to display borders, fruit, vegetables and cut flowers. The planting throughout the garden reflects the fruits of a long collaboration between the owner and Tom Stuart-Smith. A limited number of tickets have been made available for 2 guided tours by the Head Gardener, Brian Corr. Brian is former Head of Gardens to the King's Foundation. Each tour will take approx 2 hours and will start at 10am and 2pm.

🅳 ☕

45 LECKHAMPTON COURT HOSPICE
Church Road, Leckhampton, Cheltenham, GL53 0QJ. www.sueryder.org/care-centres/hospices/leckhampton-court-hospice. *2m SW of Cheltenham. From Church Rd take driveway by church signed Sue Ryder Leckhampton Court Hospice & follow parking signs.* **Sun 22 June (11-4). Adm £6, chd free. Tea, coffee & cake. Visitors welcome to picnic on our back lawn (bring your own chairs & picnic blankets).**
Set in Grade II* listed medieval estate, the informal gardens at Leckhampton Court Hospice surround the buildings. Courtyard garden & new feature gardens designed by Peter Dowle, RHS Chelsea gold medal winner. Highlights inc woodland walk around lake, new embankment garden (funded by The National Garden Scheme) and terrace with magnificent views across Cheltenham towards Malvern. Numerous protected mature trees & lawns. Features inc a golden maple tree planted by His Majesty

GLOUCESTERSHIRE

King Charles III to commemorate his 70th birthday, a kitchen garden supplying fresh vegetables for patients and a new bluebell wood (spring only). Wheelchair access in some areas: from back of reception to Sir Charles Irving terrace; woodland walk; main courtyard.

&♿ 🐕 ✻ ☕ 🪑 ♪)

46 LITTLE ORCHARD
Slad, Stroud, GL6 7QD. Rod & Terry Clifford, 07967 253420, terryclifford.tlc@gmail.com. *2m from Stroud, 10 m from Cheltenham. Last property in Slad village, on L before leaving 30mph speed limit travelling from Stroud to Birdlip on B4070. SatNav may not bring you directly to property. Parking on verge opp.* **Sat 24, Sun 25 May (11-5). Adm £5, chd free. Tea, coffee & cake. Cider tasting available. Visits also by arrangement May to Sept for groups of 5 to 30. Talk on evolution of house, garden and Slad Valley Cider.**
One acre garden created from wilderness on a challenging, steeply sloping site using many reclaimed materials, stonework and statuary. Multiple terraces and garden 'rooms' enhanced with different planting styles and water features to complement the natural surroundings. Many seating areas with stunning views. Children's Trail. Cidery offering tastings. Exhibition and sale of local artists' work. Wheelchair access possible to some areas of the garden but challenging due to the severity of slopes and steps. Please phone for further details.

♿ 🐕 ✻ ☕ ♪)

47 LITTLE ORCHARD KEMPLEY DYMOCK
Kempley, Dymock, GL18 2BU. Ros Flook. *7m from Ross-on-Wye, 8m from Ledbury. From Ross M50, J3. L B4221, then R for Kempley. After 2½ m, follow NGS signs for parking & garden. From Ledbury B4126, 5m turn R B4125, 120m turn L onto Kempley Rd. After 2m, follow NGS signs.* **Sun 20 July (1-5). Adm £5, chd free. Tea, coffee & cake.**
4 acre wildlife friendly garden with views borrowed from open countryside. Mature native and specimen trees together with ornamental borders, rose garden and cottage gardens can all be explored from the large connecting lawns. Year-round interest: ponds, productive apple orchard, woodland,

wildflower meadows, ancient horse chestnut. Seasonal floral interest from annual and perennial planting. Limited disabled parking at house. Wheelchair access restricted to garden areas nearest the house, WC not wheelchair accessible.

♿ ☕ ♪)

48 LORDS OF THE MANOR HOTEL
Upper Slaughter, Cheltenham, GL54 2JD. Mike Dron (Head Gardener), 01451 820243, reservations@lordsofthemanor.com, www.lordsofthemanor.com. *2m W of Bourton-on-the-Water. From Fosse way follow signs for the Slaughters from close to Bourton-on-the-Water (toward Stow). From B4077 (Stanway Hill road) coming from Tewkesbury direction, follow signs 2m after Ford village.* **Wed 16 Apr, Wed 18 June, Wed 17 Sept (10-3). Adm £8, chd £5. Light refreshments are available from the hotel, from light lunches to afternoon tea. Pre-booking is essential for afternoon tea.**
Classic Cotswold country garden with a very English blend of semi-formal and informal, merging beautifully with the surrounding landscape. Beautiful walled garden, established wildflower meadow, the River Eye. The herb garden and stunning bog garden were originally designed by Julie Toll around 2012. Wildlife garden, croquet lawn, courtyard and Victorian skating pond. Steps in walled garden & bog garden. Regret that due to the age & layout of the building there are no wheelchair-friendly facilities within the hotel.

♿ 🐕 🛏 ☕ ♪)

49 THE MANOR
Little Compton, GL56 0RZ. Reed Foundation (Charity). *½m from A44 or 2m from A3400. Follow signs to Little Compton, then yellow NGS signs.* **Sun 17 Aug (1-5). Adm £6, chd free. Home-made teas in churchyard next door.**
Arts & Crafts garden surrounding Jacobean manor house. Large plant collection, with deer park, meadow and arboreta. Croquet, golf, and tennis free to play. Children, picnics, and dogs very welcome. Arts and Crafts layout, water features, extensive mixed planting and styles, formal lawns, hedges and topiary, unique enclosed setting, sculptures, deer and sheep. Orchard and flower garden (small part of the

formal gardens) not accessible by wheelchair. Disabled drop-off at entrance.

♿ 🐕 ☕ 🪑 ♪)

50 MILTON COTTAGE
Overbury Street, Charlton Kings, Cheltenham, GL53 8HJ. Jackie Bickell. *Off A40 at Sixways, Charlton Kings. Heading E on A40 Overbury St is on the R just past the pedestrian crossing at Sixways. Heading W, the turning is L just after the Co-op supermarket. Free parking behind Badhams Chemist.* **Sun 18 May (11-5). Adm £4, chd free. Cash only.**
A secluded and attractive walled garden just a short distance from the busy A40 but a tranquil space planted in cottage garden style. Over 40 yrs, the current owners have transformed a sloping site with terracing, brick retaining walls and a wildlife pond. Extensive container planting adds another dimension to the garden. Due to the sloping site and steps, wheelchair access is not possible.

🐕

51 MOOR WOOD
Woodmancote, GL7 7EB. Mr & Mrs Henry Robinson, 07973 688240, henry@moorwoodhouse.co.uk, www.moorwoodroses.co.uk. *3½m NW of Cirencester. Turn L off A435 to Cheltenham at N Cerney, signed Woodmancote 1¼m; entrance in village on L beside lodge with white gates.* **Sun 29 June (2-6). Adm £7.50, chd free. Home-made teas. Visits also by arrangement 15 June to 2 July for groups of 5 to 25.**
Two acres of shrub, orchard and wildflower gardens in beautiful isolated valley setting. Holder of National Collection of Rambler Roses. June 20th to 30th is usually the best time for the roses.

NPC ☕ ♪)

In 2024, we celebrated 40 years of continuous funding for Macmillan Cancer Support equating to more than £19.5 million.

52 ◆ NATURE IN ART MUSEUM AND ART GALLERY

Wallsworth Hall, Sandhurst Lane, Twigworth, Gloucester, GL2 9PA. 01452 731422, enquiries@natureinart.org.uk, www.natureinart.org.uk. *3m N of Gloucester on the A38. SatNav postcode: GL2 9PG. The turning to Nature in Art is opp the Twigworth Co-op. There is a ½m drive to the house.* **For NGS: Mon 19 May (10-5). Adm £6.50, chd free. Tea, coffee & cake in the Hayward coffee shop in the main museum building, next to the garden. Indoor & outdoor seating.**

For other opening times and information, please phone, email or visit garden website.

The Nature in Art garden is an expression of the art found in nature. A haven for wildlife with ponds, a heritage apple orchard, championing old local varieties, and flower beds focusing on native plants and aromatic planting. In May, the cow parsley is a main feature, along with primroses and aquilegia. Insect houses and sculptures nestle in the greenery. Admission gives entry to Garden and Gallery. There will be an exhibition of the work of Rosalind Wise, a painter of gardens, fields and meadows. 2 wheelchairs available to hire, call in advance to book. Majority of garden is wheelchair accessible.

& ✱ ⛟ ☕))

53 39 NEVEN PLACE

Gloucester, GL1 5NF. Mr Chris & Mrs Jenny Brooker. *Approx 3m N of J12 M5. Follow A38 to Bristol Rd, then into Tuffley Ave, Tuffley Cres, Manu Marble Way to Neven Place. Limited on street parking.* **Sat 16, Sun 17 Aug (10.30-4). Adm £3.50, chd free. Cream teas. Cash only.**

A jungle/exotic small scale urban garden featuring tree ferns, palms,

Cotswold Farm

GLOUCESTERSHIRE 213

bamboos, bananas, a rill, raised beds and other interesting features. Limited wheelchair access due to uneven gravel paths and some steps.

54 OAK HOUSE
Greenway Lane, Gretton, Cheltenham, GL54 5ER. Paul & Sue Hughes, 01242 603990, ppphug@gmail.com. *In centre of Gretton. Signed Gretton from B4077, approx 3m from A46 Teddington Hands r'about. Greenway Lane 300 metres R past railway bridge. Parking on main road with short walk to garden.* **Sat 14, Sat 21 June (2-5). Adm £5, chd free. Tea, coffee & cake. Cash only. Visits also by arrangement May to Aug for groups of up to 20.**
One acre secret garden divided into rooms. Gradually developed over the last 30 yrs. Many places to sit and enjoy the scent of honeysuckle, philadelphus and over 50 varieties of roses. Wildflower meadow, gazebo and summerhouse. Formal lily pond and small wildlife pond. Some quirky features. You may even see a fairy.

55 NEW OHIO
Star Hill, Forest Green Nailsworth, Stroud, GL6 0NJ. Tracy Gwyer. *4m S of Stroud. From the centre of Nailsworth go up Spring Hill from the r'about then R into Moffatt Rd (at telephone box). Park in & around the green area & walk down Star Hill to the garden.* **Sun 8 June (12-5). Adm £5, chd free. Tea, coffee & cake.**
Medium sized garden on a slope with far reaching views with 2 wildlife ponds, plus dedicated areas for wildlife. Herbaceous borders packed with colour from perennials, bulbs, grasses, roses and shrubs. Patios with many colourfully planted containers and pots. Plenty of seating areas throughout taking in the fabulous views.

56 THE OLD RECTORY, QUENINGTON
Church Rd, Quenington, Cirencester, GL7 5BN. Mr & Mrs David Abel Smith, 01285 750358, lucyabelsmith@gmail.com, www.queningtonoldrectory.com. *8m NE of Cirencester. Opp St Swithin's Church at bottom of village. Garden well signed once in village.* **Sun 22 June (10-4). Adm £10, chd free. Visits also by arrangement 6 Apr to 31 Aug for groups of up to 15.**
On the banks of the mill race and the River Coln, this is an organic garden of great variety. Mature trees, large vegetable garden, herbaceous borders, shade garden, pool and bog gardens. Homegrown plants for sale. Permanent sculpture collection in the gardens and also home to the bi-annual Quenington Fresh Air Sculpture Show. We have a cosy, country cottage available for rent should you wish to make the most of your visit and spend the night. The majority of the garden is accessible by wheelchair.

57 ◆ OXLEAZE FARM
Between Eastleach & Filkins, Lechlade, GL7 3RB. Mr & Mrs Charles Mann, 07786 918502, chipps@oxleaze.co.uk, www.oxleaze.co.uk. *5m S of Burford, 3m N of Lechlade off A361 to W (signed Barringtons). Take 2nd L then follow signs.* **For NGS: Sun 1 June (11-5). Adm £7, chd free. Coffee, tea & home-made cakes available for NGS opening & visiting groups. For other opening times and information, please phone, email or visit garden website.**
Set among beautiful traditional farm buildings, plantsperson's good sized garden created by owners over 35 yrs. Year-round interest; mixed borders, vegetable potager, decorative fruit cages, pond/bog garden, bees, potting shed, meadow, and topiary for structure when the flowers fade. Garden rooms off central lawn with corners in which to enjoy this organic Cotswold garden. Groups welcome by arrangement. This garden was proud to provide plants for the National Garden Scheme's Show Garden at Chelsea Flower Show 2024. Mostly wheelchair access.

58 PARK HOUSE
Thirlestaine Road, Cheltenham, GL53 7AS. Yoko Mathers. *Off A40 through Cheltenham. Street parking nearby. Enter garden through side gate.* **Sun 18 May, Sun 29 June (2-5). Adm £5, chd free. Cream teas.**
Award-winning ¼ acre rear garden of a Cheltenham Regency town house inc a striking new Japanese 'Karesansui' Garden. Stones and rocks cascade into a gravel pond. Acers, ornamental pine trees and a sheltered 'Machiai' sitting bench complete the scene. Specimen trees are grouped in the lawn. Inviting summerhouse with wisteria walkway. Shrubs and wide herbaceous border frame the garden.

59 PASTURE FARM
Upper Oddington, GL56 0XG. Mrs John LLoyd, 07850 154095, ljmlloyd@yahoo.com. *3m W of Stow-on-the-Wold. Just off A436, midway between Upper & Lower Oddington.* **Sun 25, Mon 26 May (11-5). Adm £7, chd free. Tea, coffee & cake. Visits also by arrangement. Coaches to park at bottom of the drive.**
Informal country garden developed over 40 yrs by current owners. Mixed borders, topiary, orchard and many species of trees. Gravel garden and rambling roses in 'the ruins'. A concrete garden and wildflower area leads to vegetable patch. Large spring-fed pond with ducks. Also bantams, chickens, black Welsh sheep and Kunekune pigs. Public footpath across 2 small fields arrives at C11 church, St Nicholas, with doom paintings, set in ancient woodlands. Truly worth a visit (See Simon Jenkins' Book of Churches). Mostly wheelchair accessible.

60 THE PATCH
Hollywell Lane, Brockweir, Chepstow, NP16 7PJ. Mrs Immy Lee, 07801 816340, immylee1@hotmail.com, www.thepatchbrockweir.com. *6½ m N of Chepstow & 10½ m S of Monmouth, off A466, across Brockweir Bridge. From Monmouth & Chepstow direction follow SatNav to Brockweir Bridge, then yellow signs. From Coleford/ Gloucester direction follow SatNav out of St. Briavels, then yellow signs.* **Sun 1 June (1-5). Adm £5, chd free. Tea, coffee & cake. Visits also by arrangement 1 June to 15 June for groups of 5 to 25. No coaches.**
Rural ¼ acre garden with stunning views across the Wye Valley. The maturing planting of 60+ roses, shrubs, grasses and perennials in a modern English Garden style provides year-round interest. The established borders are linked by meandering grass paths and small seating areas in different parts of the garden. Partial wheelchair access.

62 PERRYWOOD HOUSE
Longney, Gloucester, GL2 3SN. Gill & Mike Farmer. *7m SW of Gloucester, 4m W of Quedgeley. From N, R off B4008 at Tesco r'about. R at 2nd r'about, straight over next 2 & canal then signed. From S, A38 in Moreton Valence L to Epney/Longney, over canal, R at T junction then signed.* **Sat 28, Sun 29 June (11-5). Adm £5, chd free. Home-made teas. Cash only for admission, refreshments & plant sale.**
One acre plant lover's garden in the Severn Vale surrounded by open farmland. Established over 25 yrs ago an informal country garden with mature trees, shrubs, colourful herbaceous borders, a small pond, and planted containers. There are plenty of places to sit and enjoy the garden. Lots of interesting plants for sale. All areas accessible with level lawns and gravel drives. Disabled parking available.

63 NEW POND COTTAGE
Breadstone, Berkeley, GL13 9HG. Nicky Fussell, nickyfussell@aol.com. *8m S of M5 J13; 6m N of M5 J14; 1½ m from A38; 3m NE of Berkeley. After entering Breadstone village from the A38, Pond Cottage is on R immed after Breadstone Care Home, also on the R. What3words app: upgrading. cubic.adhesive.* **Sat 14, Sun 15 June (11.30-4.30). Adm £6, chd free. Home-made cakes (baked by Mimii Makes Cakes) with choice of tea or coffee. Visits also by arrangement 7 Apr to 31 Oct for groups of 6+.**
3 acre plot surrounding a converted former agricultural building comprising 2 acres of informal meadow with naturalised bulbs/wild flowers, old orchard, many mature trees (inc oak, poplar, horse chestnut, sycamore, conifer) a large natural wildlife pond, vegetable plot, rescue hens and 1 acre of formal mixed borders with enclosed courtyard containing Mediterranean plants and herb garden.

65 NEW PRIOR'S PIECE
Mill Street, Prestbury, Cheltenham, GL52 3BQ. Mrs D Taylor. *2m NE of Cheltenham. Take B4632 from Cheltenham to Prestbury or from Winchcombe to Prestbury following signs to Cheltenham.* **Sat 26 Apr (1-5.30). Adm £5, chd free. Tea, coffee & cake.**
Semi-formal garden with lawns & box hedges. Many interesting trees and shrubs inc an enormous magnolia, ginkgos, acers, lilac and Portuguese laurel. In the grounds is an historic dovecote leading to a beautiful part of the garden which is a secluded area of tranquillity. The garden is surrounded by mature trees, historic buildings and views of the church. Wheelchair access possible but may require assistance on the gravel areas. Lunches available in Prestbury at Royal Oak, Kings Arms & The Plough Inn.

66 37 QUEENS ROAD
Cheltenham, GL50 2LX. Geraldine & Richard Pinch. *4 mins walk from Cheltenham Spa train stn. Garden on L as you walk from the stn towards town. Free parking on Queens Rd & Christchurch Rd.* **Sun 25, Mon 26 May (2-5). Adm £4, chd free.**
A wildlife and wildflower-friendly urban garden with many shrubs and climbers. At the front there are shrub borders and a gravel garden. The rear garden slopes upward from the house and is accessed by steps. There are 7 ponds, old fruit trees, a vine-house, raised beds planted with perennials and dwarf shrubs, a wild area and a brickery for alpines. Animal sculpture trail for children. Two cafés 5 mins walk away.

67 RADNORS
Wheatstone Lane, Lydbrook, GL17 9DP. Mrs Mary Wood, 01594 861690/07473 959068, woodmary37@gmail.com. *In the Wye Valley on the edge of the Forest of Dean. From Lydbrook, go down through village towards the River Wye. At the T junction turn L into Stowfield Rd. Wheatstone Ln (300 metres) is 1st turning L after the white cottages. Radnors is at end of lane.* **Visits by arrangement Apr to Oct for groups of up to 20. Adm £5, chd free. Home-made cakes with tea, coffee or fruit juice.**
5 acre hillside woodland garden in AONB on bank above the River Wye. Focus on wildlife with naturalistic planting and weeds, some left for specific insects/birds. It has many paths, a wooded area, wildflower area, flower beds and borders, lawns, stumpery, fernery, vegetable beds and white garden. Of particular interest is the path along a disused railway line, and the summer dahlias.

68 RAMBLERS
Lower Common, Aylburton, Lydney, GL15 6DS. Jane & Leslie Hale. *1½ m W of Lydney. Off A48 Gloucester to Chepstow Rd. From Lydney through Aylburton, out of de-limit turn R signed Aylburton Common, ¾ m along lane.* **Sun 4 May (1.30-5). Adm £5, chd free. Home-made teas. Cash only.**
Peaceful medium sized country garden with informal cottage planting, herbaceous borders and small pond looking through hedge windows onto wildflower meadow and mature apple orchard. Some shade loving plants and topiary. Large productive vegetable garden.

69 RICHMOND VILLAGES PAINSWICK
Stroud Road, Painswick, Stroud, GL6 6UL. Richmond Villages/Bupa. *5m E of Stroud. South of Painswick village on the A46, take R turn into retirement village car park.* **Thur 22 May, Thur 26 June, Thur 24 July, Thur 14 Aug (10-3). Adm £5, chd free. Tea, coffee & cake in Café. Cash only.**
Situated on the southern slopes of Painswick this 4 acre retirement village boasts formal lawns and borders planted for year-round interest. A varied mix of herbaceous and shrubs, with many areas of interest inc a wildflower meadow with fruit trees that combine to attract an abundance of wildlife. The gardens are a blaze of colour. There are gentle slopes in the wildflower meadow and around some areas of the village.

GLOUCESTERSHIRE 215

70 ROCK HOUSE
Elberton, BS35 4AQ. Mr & Mrs John Gunnery, 01454 413225. *10m N of Bristol. From Old Severn Bridge on M48 take B4461 to Alveston. In Elberton, take 1st turning L and then immed R. SatNav starts at top of village, come down hill to Littleton turning on R, R again immediately.* **Sun 26 Jan, Sun 2 Feb, Sun 9, Sun 16 Mar (11-4); Sun 1, Sun 8 June (12-5). Adm £5, chd free. Cash only 2026: Sun 25 Jan, Sun 1 Feb. Visits also by arrangement.** 2 acre garden. Woodland vistas with swathes of snowdrops and carpets of daffodils, some unusual. Spring flowers, cottage garden plants and climbing roses in season. Old yew tree, maturing cedar tree, pond.

❀

71 ROCKCLIFFE
Upper Slaughter, Cheltenham, GL54 2JW. Mr & Mrs Simon Keswick, www.rockcliffegarden.co.uk. *2m from Stow-on-the-Wold. 1½m from Lower Swell on B4068 towards Cheltenham. Leave Stow-on-the-Wold on B4068 through Lower Swell. Continue on B4068 for 1½m. Rockcliffe is well signed on R.* **Wed 11 June (10-5). Adm £8, chd free. Tea, coffee & cake in car park.** Donation to Kate's Home Nursing. Large traditional English garden of 8 acres inc pink garden, white and blue garden, herbaceous borders, rose terrace, large walled kitchen garden and greenhouses. Pathway of topiary birds leading up through orchard to stone dovecote. Regret no dogs. There are 2 wide stone steps through gate, otherwise good wheelchair access.

♿ ❀ ☕ 🪑 🔊

72 NEW 1 SANDY LANE
Charlton Kings, Cheltenham, GL53 9BS. Linda & Geoff Pratt. *A435 Cirencester Rd out of Cheltenham, R at T-lights into Moorend Rd. Sandy Lane ½m on at junction with Greenhills Rd. B bus to & from Cheltenham stops at entrance.* **Sun 27 July (1.30-5.30). Adm £4, chd free. Home-made teas.** ⅓ acre shady garden on dry sandy soil with flowering trees and borders planted within the last 3 yrs. Variety of foliage plants and bulbs for year-round interest. Raised stone beds round the patio with alpines and smaller bulbs. Wisterias and climbers clothe 2 pergolas with seating areas.

☕ 🔊

73 THE SCHOOL YARD
2 High Street, Wickwar, Wotton-Under-Edge, GL12 8NE. Jeanette & Tony Parker. *12m N of Bristol. Between T-lights at N end of High Street. If using SatNav please note High Street Wickwar not High Street Wotton under Edge. Parking in village - please park respectfully and consider our neighbours.* **Sat 28 June (1.30-5). Adm £6, chd free. Tea, coffee & cake in the village hall.** Garden arranged around a former Victorian school. Vegetable plot with sunken garden and large greenhouse. Raised beds edged by espalier and step-over fruit trees. Terraced flower garden with variety of trees and shrubs, rockery, Mediterranean courtyard with ancient yew tree and olive tree. Pond and deep shade garden. Variety of English apples and pear trees.

❀ ☕ 🔊

74 THE STABLES
Hyde Lane, Cheltenham, GL51 9QN. R & Linda Marsh. *10 mins from M5 junction 10. From junction 10 take A4019. At r'about turn L into Kingsditch Lane. Pass under rail bridge into Hyde Lane. Take first L parking opp entrance & parking at playing fields car park & in Swindon Village.* **Sat 19 July (1-5). Adm £6, chd free.** The garden extends to 0.6 acre on the original stables site and is surrounded by fields. Inspired by the work of Piet Oudolf, the garden consists of large perennial beds which merge into the surrounding landscape. The garden has been developed over the last 4 yrs from a bare site and inc a fully grown native hedge which separates the garden from the newly planted 1 acre wildflower meadow.

❀ 🔊

GROUP OPENING

75 STANTON VILLAGE GARDENS
Stanton, nr Broadway, WR12 7NE. Susan Hughes, susanhughes2023@hotmail.com. *3m S of Broadway. Off B4632, between Broadway (3m) & Winchcombe (6m).* **Sun 8 June (1-6). Combined adm £10, chd free. Home-made teas in several gardens around the village.** Donation to Village charities.

A selection of gardens open in this picturesque, unspoilt Cotswold village. Many houses border the street with long gardens hidden behind. Gardens vary from those with colourful herbaceous borders, established trees, shrubs and vegetable gardens to tiny cottage gardens. Some also have attractive natural water features fed by the stream which runs through the village. Church also open. The Mount Inn is open for lunch. An NGS visit not to be missed in this gem of a Cotswold village. Regret gardens not suitable for wheelchair users due to gravel drives.

🐕 ❀ 🚗 ☕ 🔊

76 ♦ STANWAY FOUNTAIN & WATER GARDEN
Stanway, Cheltenham, GL54 5PQ. The Earl of Wemyss & March, 01386 584528, office@stanwayhouse.co.uk, www.stanwayfountain.co.uk. *9m NE of Cheltenham. 1m E of B4632 Cheltenham to Broadway rd on B4077 Toddington to Stow-on-the-Wold rd.* **For NGS: Sun 18 May (2-5); Sun 17 Aug (2.30-5). Adm £7, chd £3. Tea, coffee & cake in Stanway Tearoom. Cash only. For NGS day admission is to garden only.** For other opening times and information, please phone, email or visit garden website. 20 acres of planted landscape in early C18 formal setting. The restored canal, upper pond and fountain have recreated one of the most interesting Baroque water gardens in Britain. Striking C16 manor with gatehouse, tithe barn and church. The garden features Britain's highest fountain at 300ft, and it is the world's highest gravity fountain. It runs at 2.45pm and 4.00pm for 30 mins each time. Partial wheelchair access in garden, some flat areas, able to view fountain and some of garden.

♿ 🐕 🚗 ☕

Our donation to Marie Curie this year equates to 17,496 hours of nursing care or 43 days of care in one of their nine hospices.

77 STONELEIGH DOWN
Upper Tockington Road, Tockington, Bristol, BS32 4LQ. Su & John Mills, 07980 099061, susanlmills@gmail.com. *12m N of Bristol. On LH side of Upper Tockington Rd when travelling from Tockington towards Olveston. Set back from road up gravel drive. Parking in village.* **Sat 17, Sun 18 May, Sat 14, Sun 15 June (12-5). Adm £6, chd free. Home-made teas.** Visits also by arrangement May & June. Refreshments inc in adm for by arrangement groups.
Approaching ⅔ acre, the south facing garden has curved gravel pathways around an S-shaped lawn that connects themed areas: exotic border; summer walk; acers; oriental pond; winter garden; woodland. On a level site, it has been densely planted with trees, shrubs, perennials and bulbs for year-round interest. Plenty of places to sit. Three steps into courtyard.

78 ♦ SUDELEY CASTLE GARDENS
Winchcombe, GL54 5JD. Lady Ashcombe, 01242 604244, enquiries@sudeley.org.uk, www.sudeleycastle.co.uk. *8m NE Cheltenham, 10m from M5 J9. SatNavs use GL54 5LP. Free parking.* **For NGS: Fri 6 June (10-4). Adm £10, chd £5. Light refreshments at The Pavilion & The Castle Coach House serves lunches. Admission is for the garden only.** For other opening times and information, please phone, email or visit garden website.
At Sudeley Castle Gardens you can explore 10 award-winning gardens, including The Queen's Garden, filled with many varieties of roses in the Tudor Parterre fashion. Our gardens reflect the 1000 years of the castle's history with its own unique style and design. Sudeley Castle remains the only private castle in England to have a Queen buried within the grounds - Queen Katherine Parr, the last and surviving wife of King Henry VIII – who lived and died in the castle. A circular route around the gardens is wheelchair accessible although some visitors may require assistance from their companion.

79 ♦ THYME
Southrop Estate, Southrop, Lechlade, GL7 3PW. Caryn Hibbert, 01367 850174, enquiries@thyme.co.uk, www.instagram.com/Thyme.England/. *Pls follow the signs through the village of Southrop towards Lechlade & to our estate drive.* **For NGS: Daily Mon 4 Aug to Fri 8 Aug (11-4). Adm £10, chd free. Tea, coffee & cake. There are 2 restaurants on site that visitors can book, the Ox Barn & The Swan at Southrop.** For other opening times and information, please phone, email or visit garden website.
Situated on the edge of the water meadows, Thyme's carefully managed kitchen gardens ensure abundance from the land while protecting and maintaining the fertile alluvial soil. The garden is productive for much of the year and features a herb garden, cutting gardens and polytunnels to extend the seasons. We grow a large variety of flavoursome and unusual varieties to supply our restaurants. Please note this is a farm environment. Disabled parking is available close to the garden, but some of the pathways are uneven.

80 TOWER CLOSE
Snowshill, Broadway, WR12 7JU. Mr James & Mrs Claire Wright, claireannewright@gmail.com. *2½m SW of Broadway. Parking at Snowshill village car park. 50 metres up the hill from Snowshill Manor car park. Take L fork to the top of the road. Follow signs.* **Sat 31 May, Sun 1 June (11-5). Adm £6, chd free. Home-made teas.** Visits also by arrangement 2 June to 8 June for groups of 10 to 40.
Striking views of the Malvern Hills from this 3 acre Cotswold garden positioned at the top of the charming village of Snowshill. Featured in Country Life in 1928 & 2016, the C17 Grade II listed house is surrounded by terraces of garden rooms. Herbaceous borders, espaliered fruit trees and sunken vegetable garden. Plants tumble down the terraces to a romantic stream, ponds, garden features, orchard and meadow.

81 TRENCH HILL
Sheepscombe, GL6 6TZ. Celia & Dave Hargrave, 01452 814306, celia.hargrave@outlook.com. *1½m E of Painswick between the A46 & Sheepscombe. From Cheltenham A46 take 1st turn signed Sheepscombe, follow for approx 1½m. Or from the Butcher's Arms in Sheepscombe (with it on R) leave village and take lane signed for Cranham.* **Sun 9, Sun 16 Feb (11-4); Sun 16 Mar (11-5); Every Wed 4 June to 25 June (2-6). Sun 13 July, Sun 24 Aug (11-6). Adm £5, chd free. Tea, coffee & cake. Gluten, dairy free & vegan usually available. 2026: Sun 8, Sun 15 Feb.** Visits also by arrangement 10 Feb to 15 Sept for groups of up to 35. Groups using a coach must discuss the size with owners due to narrow lanes.
Approx 3 acres set in a small woodland with panoramic views. Variety of herbaceous and mixed borders, rose garden, tulips, extensive vegetable plots, wildflower areas, plantings of spring bulbs with thousands of snowdrops and hellebores, woodland walk, two small ponds, waterfall and larger conservation pond. Interesting wooden sculptures, many within the garden. Cultivated using organic principles. Children's play area. Mostly wheelchair accessible but some steps and slopes.

GROUP OPENING

82 TUFFLEY GARDENS
Tuffley Lane, Gloucester, GL4 0DT. Martyn & Jenny Parker. *3m S Gloucester. Follow arrows from St. Barnabas r'about. Cash tickets & maps from 24 Tuffley Lane. On road parking.* **Sun 1 June (11-4). Combined adm £5, chd £1. Home-made teas at 389 Stroud Road GL4 0DA. Pls advise of any allergies on ordering. Cash only.**
A number of mature suburban gardens of all sizes and styles. Old favourites plus new openers. Lots of colourful flowers, shrubs, trees, baskets and tubs. Circular route of approx one mile. Close to Robinswood Hill Country Park, 250 acres of open countryside and viewpoint, pleasant walks and way-marked trails. Some gardens have partial wheelchair access.

GLOUCESTERSHIRE 217

83 ◆ UPTON WOLD
Moreton-in-Marsh, GL56 9TR. Mr & Mrs I R S Bond, www.uptonwold.co.uk. 4½m W of Moreton-in-Marsh on A44. From Moreton/Stow ½m past A424 turn R to road into fields then L at mini Xrds. From Evesham 1m past B4081 C/Campden Xrds turn L at end of stone wall to road into fields then as above. **For NGS: Sun 13 Apr (10-5). Adm £15, chd free. Cream teas.** For other opening times and information, please visit garden website.
The Hidden Garden of the Cotswolds, Upton Wold has commanding views, yew hedges, herbaceous walks, vegetable, pond and woodland gardens, and a labyrinth. An abundance of unusual plants, shrubs and trees. National Collections of Juglans and Pterocarya. A garden of interest to any garden and plant lover. Snowdrop walks from 8 Feb to 2 March. Details on website.

84 WESTAWAY
Stockwell Lane, Cleeve Hill, Cheltenham, GL52 3PU. Liz & Ian Ramsay. *5m NW of Cheltenham. Off the B4632 Cheltenham to Winchcombe road at Cleeve Hill. Parking in the lay-bys at the top of Stockwell Ln on B4632. Follow arrows to garden.* **Fri 13 June, Fri 18 July (2-5). Adm £6, chd free. Tea, coffee & cake.**
Hillside 1½ acre garden situated on the Cotswold escarpment with spectacular views. Interesting solutions to the challenges of gardening on a gradient, reflecting the local topography. Mixed shrub and herbaceous borders, bog garden, orchard, small arboretum and several wildflower areas. Landscaping inc extensive terracing with grass banks. Not suitable for visitors with limited mobility.

85 ◆ WESTONBIRT SCHOOL GARDENS
Tetbury, GL8 8QG. Holfords of Westonbirt Trust, 01666 881373, baker@holfordtrust.com, www.holfordtrust.com. *3m SW of Tetbury. Pls enter through main school gates on A433 - some SatNavs will send you via a side entrance where there will be no access - main school gates only please.* **For NGS: Sun 3 Aug 10.30-4.30). Adm £7.50, chd free. Tea, coffee, soft drinks, water & biscuits avail throughout the day.** For other opening times and information, please phone, email or visit garden website.
The former private garden of Robert Holford, founder of Westonbirt Arboretum, the gardens and parkland cover 28 acres. Formal Victorian gardens inc walled Italian garden now restored with early herbaceous borders and exotic border. Rustic walks, lake, statuary and grotto. Rare, exotic trees and shrubs. Beautiful views of Westonbirt House open with guided tours to see fascinating Victorian interior on designated days of the year. Gravelled paths in some areas, grass in others and wheelchair users are limited to downstairs part of the house due to evacuation protocols.

86 WICKS GREEN FARM
Wicks Green, Longney, Gloucester, GL2 3SP. Dianne Evans. *What3words app: broom. almost.messy. From A38 turn into Castle Lane, over Epney Bridge, R to Longney, turn L into Chatter St, follow the lane for 1m. Wicks Green Farm will be signed with parking opp on hardstanding.* **Sat 12, Sun 13 Apr (11-3). Adm £5, chd free. Tea, coffee & cake. Also home-made chutneys & pickles, garden produce. Cash only.**
Set in 1½ acres Wicks Green Farm is surrounded by countryside, has flower borders, vegetable garden, a spring fed pond and orchard; some of the pear trees are very old local varieties. The orchard with apple, pear, and plum trees is beautiful in blossom. The garden is planted for colour year-round. The old bakehouse has been re-purposed for garden entertaining.

87 WOODCHESTER PARK HOUSE
Nympsfield, Stonehouse, GL10 3UN. Robin & Veronica Bidwell, 01453 860213, robin.bidwell@wphouse.com. *Nr Nailsworth. Off the road joining Nailsworth & Nympsfield (Tinkley Ln). Approx 3m from Nailsworth, turn R down next turning after the NT Tinkley Gate.* **Visits by arrangement in July.**
This partially walled garden of approx 3 acres incorporates extensive herbaceous borders, a yew walk, a rose covered belvedere overlooking a large pond, a woodland garden, rose walk, vegetable garden and terrace. Wide variety of plants and settings. Wheelchair access to most parts of the garden but there are steep slopes to be negotiated.

88 WORTLEY HOUSE
Wortley, Wotton-under-Edge, GL12 7QP. Simon & Jessica Dickinson. *On Wortley Rd 1m S of Wotton-under-Edge. Grand entrance on L as you enter Wortley coming from Wotton-Under-Edge.* **Tue 22 Apr, Tue 17 June (2-5). Adm £15, chd free. Pre-booking essential, please visit www.ngs.org.uk for information & booking. Home-made teas inc in admission price.**
A diverse garden of over 20 acres created during the last 30 yrs by the current owners. Inc a walled garden, pleached lime avenues, nut walk, potager, ponds, Italian garden, arbour, shrubberies and wildflower meadows. Strategically placed follies, urns and statues enhance extraordinary vistas. Wheelchair access to most areas, a golf buggy also available.

Our 2024 donation to The Queen's Nursing institute now helps support over 3,000 Queen's Nurses working in the community in England, Wales, Northern Ireland, the Channel Islands and the Isle of Man.

HAMPSHIRE

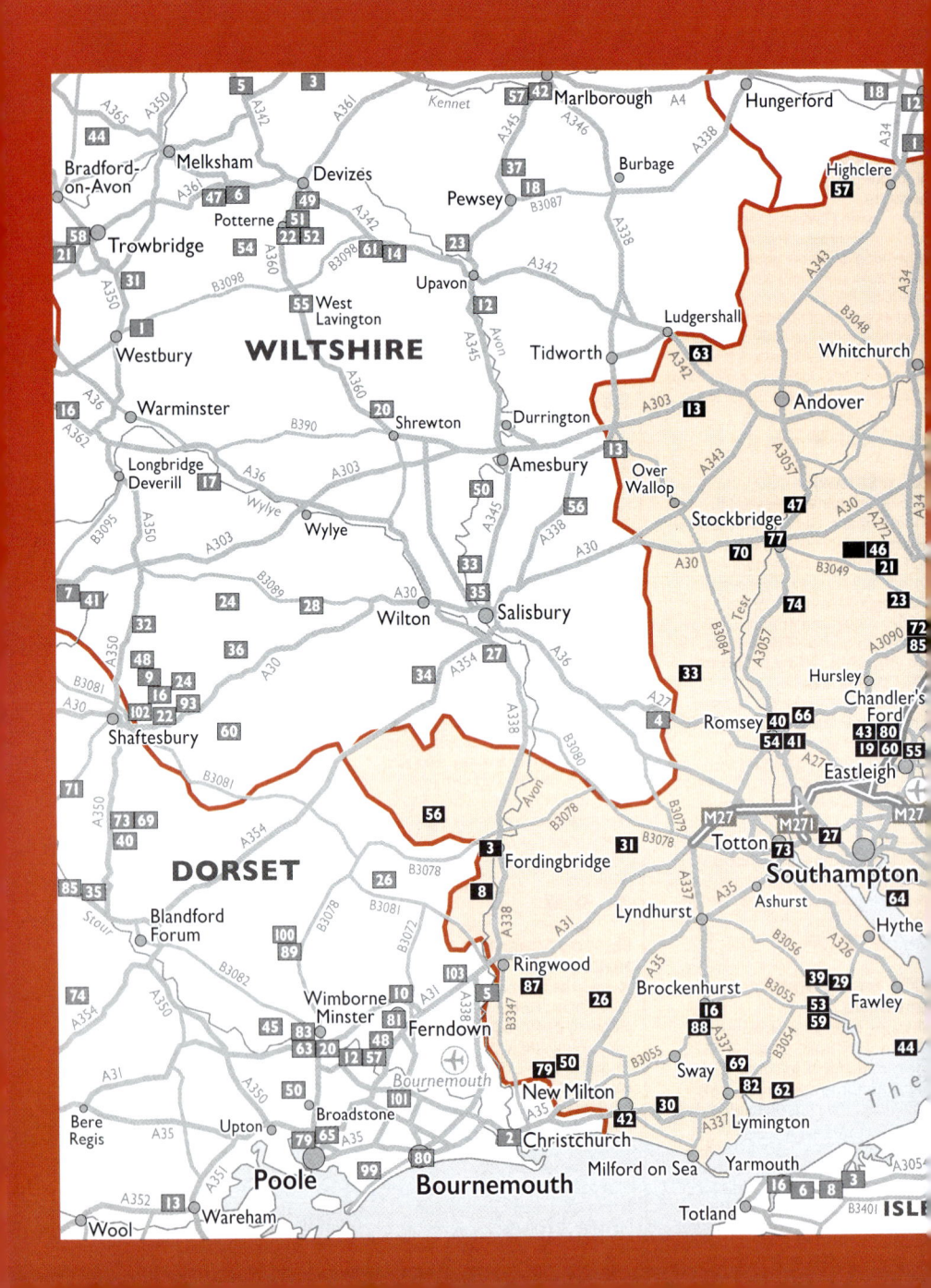

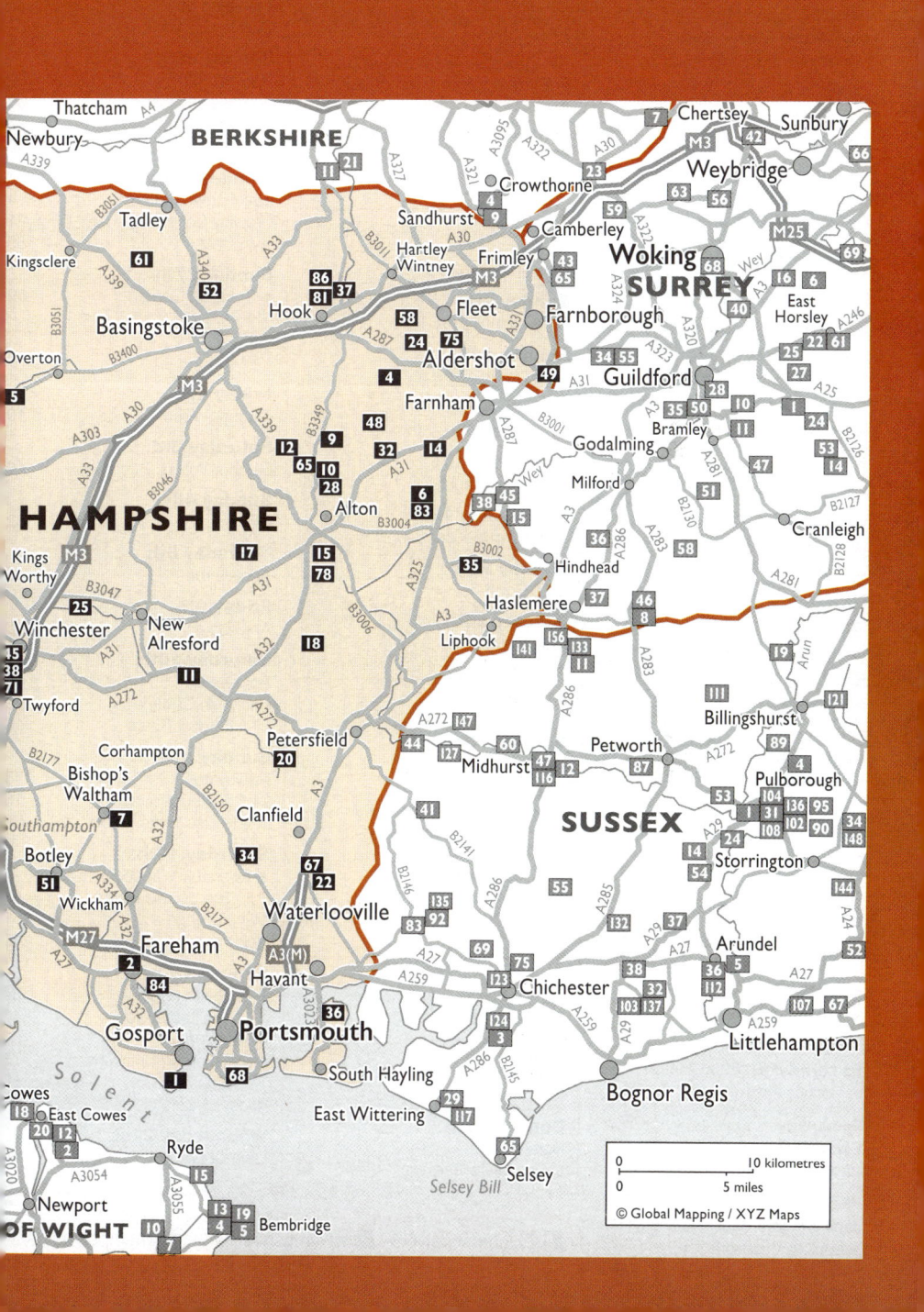

HAMPSHIRE 219

VOLUNTEERS

County Organiser
Mark Porter 07814 958810
markstephenporter@gmail.com

County Treasurer
Fred Fratter 01962 776243
fred@fratter.co.uk

Publicity
Pat Beagley 01256 764772
pat.beagley@ngs.org.uk

Social Media - Facebook
Mary Hayter 07512 639772
mary.hayter@ngs.org.uk

Social Media - Twitter
Louise Moreton 07943 837993
louise.moreton@ngs.org.uk

Booklet Co-ordinator
Mark Porter (as above)

Assistant County Organisers

Kim Donald kd581@aol.com

Victoria Murray 07877 757858
victoria.murray@ngs.org.uk

Central
Sue Cox 01962 732043
suealex13@gmail.com

Central West
Kate Cann 01794 389105
kategcann@gmail.com

East
Linda Smith 01329 833253
linda.ngs@btinternet.com

North
Cynthia Oldale 01420 520438
c.k.oldale@btinternet.com

North East
Lizzie Powell 07799 031044
lizziepowellbroadhatch@gmail.com

North West
Adam Vetere 01635 268267
adam.vetere@ngs.org.uk

South
Barbara Sykes 02380 254521
barandhugh@aol.com

South West
Elizabeth Walker 01590 677415
elizabethwalker13@gmail.com

West
Jane Wingate-Saul 01725 519414
jw-saul@hotmail.com

OPENING DATES

All entries subject to change. For latest information check
www.ngs.org.uk
Map locator numbers are shown to the right of each garden name.

February

Snowdrop Openings

Sunday 9th
Bramdean House 11

Sunday 16th
Little Court 46

Monday 17th
Little Court 46

Tuesday 18th
The Down House 25

Wednesday 19th
The Down House 25

Sunday 23rd
Little Court 46

Monday 24th
Little Court 46

March

Sunday 16th
Bere Mill 5

Tuesday 18th
◆ Chawton House 15

Sunday 30th
Little Court 46

Monday 31st
Little Court 46

April

Sunday 6th
Pylewell Park 62

Saturday 12th
Lord Wandsworth College 48

Sunday 13th
Bere Mill 5
Lepe House Gardens 44

Lord Wandsworth College 48
Old Thatch & The Millennium Barn 58

Friday 18th
Crawley Gardens 21

Sunday 20th
Pylewell Park 62
Southsea Gardens 68
Terstan 77
Twin Oaks 80

Monday 21st
Beechenwood Farm 4
Crawley Gardens 21
Twin Oaks 80

Sunday 27th
◆ Spinners Garden 69

May

Friday 2nd
Bluebell Wood 10

Saturday 3rd
Bluebell Wood 10

Sunday 4th
Walhampton 82

Thursday 8th
Appleyards 3

Friday 9th
Appleyards 3

Saturday 10th
Appleyards 3
Brick Kiln Cottage 12
21 Chestnut Road 16

Sunday 11th
Appleyards 3
21 Chestnut Road 16
The House in the Wood 39

Saturday 17th
◆ Alverstoke Crescent Garden 1
NEW The Laurel House 43
Manor Lodge 51
Twin Oaks 80

Sunday 18th
The Dower House 24
NEW The Laurel House 43
Manor Lodge 51
4 Stannington Crescent 73
Twin Oaks 80
Tylney Hall Hotel 81

Wednesday 21st
Little Court 46

@HampshireNGS @HampshireNGS @hampshirengs

HAMPSHIRE 221

Thursday 22nd
Little Court 46
Old Channel Hill Farmhouse 56

Friday 23rd
NEW The Square House 71

Saturday 24th
4 Stannington Crescent 73
Streamside Trees - Bonsai Experience 75

Sunday 25th
Bridge Cottage 13
Shalden Park House 65
Southsea Gardens 68
NEW The Square House 71

Monday 26th
Beechenwood Farm 4
Bere Mill 5
Bridge Cottage 13

Saturday 31st
Spitfire House 70
Winchester College 85

June

Sunday 1st
◆ The Hospital of St Cross 38
Spitfire House 70
Winchester College 85

Saturday 7th
21 Chestnut Road 16
Froyle Gardens 32
Headley Village Gardens 35
NEW Limberlost 45
NEW The Montagu Arms Hotel 53
Povey's Cottage 61

Sunday 8th
21 Chestnut Road 16
Froyle Gardens 32
Headley Village Gardens 35
NEW Limberlost 45
NEW The Montagu Arms Hotel 53
Old Channel Hill Farmhouse 56
Povey's Cottage 61

Wednesday 11th
Povey's Cottage 61

Thursday 12th
Stockbridge Gardens 74

Friday 13th
Bedenham Park House 63

Saturday 14th
Endhouse 27
Ferns Lodge 30
5 Oakfields 55
Woodend Gardens 87

Sunday 15th
Bramdean House 11
Endhouse 27
Ferns Lodge 30
Fritham Lodge 31
Little Court 46
5 Oakfields 55
Stockbridge Gardens 74
Woodend Gardens 87

Monday 16th
Little Court 46

Saturday 21st
King John's Garden 41
The Nelson Cottage 54
Twin Oaks 80

Sunday 22nd
Broadhatch House 14
King John's Garden 41
The Nelson Cottage 54
NEW Pines Corner Wildlife Garden 60
Terstan 77
The Thatched Cottage 78
Twin Oaks 80
Wicor Primary School Community Garden 84

Monday 23rd
Broadhatch House 14

Tuesday 24th
Broadhatch House 14

Thursday 26th
Mill House 52

Saturday 28th
26 Lower Newport Road 49

Sunday 29th
Kingfishers Care Home 42
Longstock Park Water Garden 47
26 Lower Newport Road 49
Mill House 52
NEW Pines Corner Wildlife Garden 60
Southsea Gardens 68
NEW Stanford House 72
Tylney Hall Hotel 81

July

Saturday 5th
Crawley Gardens 21

Sunday 6th
Crawley Gardens 21
Old Thatch & The Millennium Barn 58

Saturday 12th
Angels Folly 2
NEW Greenview 33

Sunday 13th
Angels Folly 2
NEW Greenview 33
15 Rothschild Close 64
1 Wogsbarne Cottages 86

Monday 14th
1 Wogsbarne Cottages 86

Friday 18th
Fairweather's Nursery 29

Saturday 19th
NEW Bishop's Waltham Gardens 7
Fairweather's Nursery 29
Hook Cross Allotments 37
8 Tucks Close 79

Sunday 20th
NEW Bishop's Waltham Gardens 7
Bleak Hill Nursery & Garden 8
Hook Cross Allotments 37
Terstan 77
8 Tucks Close 79

Monday 21st
Bleak Hill Nursery & Garden 8

Saturday 26th
Angels Folly 2

Sunday 27th
Angels Folly 2

August

Sunday 3rd
The Homestead 36
South View House 67

Saturday 9th
21 Chestnut Road 16
Church House 17
Twin Oaks 80

Sunday 10th
Bleak Hill Nursery & Garden 8
21 Chestnut Road 16
Church House 17
Twin Oaks 80

Monday 11th
Bleak Hill Nursery & Garden 8

Saturday 16th
Wheatley House 83

Sunday 17th
Wheatley House 83

Sunday 24th
The Thatched Cottage 78

Monday 25th
Bere Mill 5
Bleak Hill Nursery & Garden 8
The Thatched Cottage 78

Sunday 31st
Blounce House 9
Woodpeckers Care Home 88

September

Saturday 6th
NEW The Laurel House 43
15 Rothschild Close 64

Sunday 7th
NEW The Laurel House 43
15 Rothschild Close 64
Terstan 77

Sunday 14th
Bramdean House 11

February 2026

Sunday 15th
Little Court 46

Monday 16th
Little Court 46

Sunday 22nd
Little Court 46

Monday 23rd
Little Court 46

By Arrangement

Arrange a personalised garden visit with your club, or group of friends, on a date to suit you. See individual garden entries for full details.

Angels Folly 2
Appleyards 3
Bere Mill 5
Binsted Place 6
Blounce House 9
Brick Kiln Cottage 12
Broadhatch House 14
Church House 17
Colemore House Gardens 18
The Cottage 19
NEW The Court House 20
Crookley Pool 22
The Deane House 23
The Down House 25
Durmast House 26
Endhouse 27
Fairbank 28
Ferns Lodge 30
Frey Elma, Headley Village Gardens 35
Hambledon House 34
The Homestead 36
The Island 40
Lepe House Gardens 44
Little Court 46
Manor Lodge 51
The Old Rectory 57
1 Povey's Cottage 61
15 Rothschild Close 64
Spitfire House 70
Terstan 77
The Thatched Cottage 78
Twin Oaks 80
Wheatley House 83

Limberlost

THE GARDENS

1 ◆ ALVERSTOKE CRESCENT GARDEN
Crescent Road, Gosport, PO12 2DH. Gosport Borough Council, www.alverstokecrescentgarden.co.uk. 1m S of Gosport. From A32 & Gosport follow signs for Stokes Bay. Continue alongside bay to small r'about, turn L into Anglesey Rd. Crescent Garden signed 50yds on R. **For NGS: Sat 17 May (10-4). Adm by donation. Home-made teas.** For other opening times and information, please visit garden website.
Restored Regency ornamental garden designed to enhance fine crescent (Thomas Ellis Owen 1828). Trees, walks and flowers lovingly maintained by community and council partnership. A garden of considerable local historic interest highlighted by impressive restoration and creative planting. Adjacent to St Mark's churchyard, worth seeing together. Heritage, history and horticulture, a fascinating package. Green Flag Award 2024.

2 ANGELS FOLLY
5 Bruce Close, Fareham, PO16 7QJ. Teresa & John Greenwood, 07545 242654, greenwood65@outlook.com, www.facebook.com/angelsfolly. M27 W leave J10 under M27 bridge in the RH-lane, do a U-turn. At 'about, take 3rd exit, across T-lights. 1st R Miller Dr. 2nd R Somervell Dr. 1st R Bruce Cl. **Sat 12, Sun 13, Sat 26, Sun 27 July (10.30-5). Adm £4.50, chd free. Home-made teas.** Visits also by arrangement 12 July to 31 Aug.
The garden has a number of secluded areas each with their own character inc a Mediterranean garden, decking with raised beds and a seating area with a living wall. An arched folly, bench and fish pond leads to a raised planting bed and fireplace adjacent to a summerhouse. There is a wide range of colourful plants, hanging baskets and a lower secluded decked area with a planted gazebo and statue.

3 APPLEYARDS
Bowerwood Road, Fordingbridge, SP6 3BP. Bob & Jean Carr ½ m from Fordingbridge on B3078. After church & houses, 400yds on L as road climbs after bridge. Parking for 8 cars only. No parking on narrow road. **Thur 8, Fri 9, Sat 10, Sun 11 May (12-6). Adm £5, chd free. Pre-booking essential, please phone 01425 657631 or email bob.carr.rtd@gmail.com for information & booking. Tea, coffee & cake.** Visits also by arrangement Apr to June for groups of 10+.
2 acre south facing garden overlooking pasture, restored over last 7 yrs. Sloping lawns and paths though wooded sections with massed daffodils and bluebells in spring. Newly planted rhododendrons in wooded area. Herbaceous beds, two mature rose beds, shrubberies, two wildlife ponds, orchard, sloping rockery beds, soft fruit cages and greenhouse.

4 BEECHENWOOD FARM
Hillside, Odiham, Hook, RG29 1JA. Mr & Mrs M Heber-Percy. 5m SE of Hook. Turn S into King St from Odiham High St. Turn L after cricket ground for Hillside. Take 2nd R after 1½ m, modern house ½ m. **Mon 21 Apr, Mon 26 May (2-5). Adm £5, chd free. Home-made teas.**
Opening for over 40 yrs, this 2 acre garden with many parts. Lawn meandering through woodland with drifts of spring bulbs. Rose pergola with steps, pots with spring bulbs and later aeoniums. Fritillary and cowslip meadow. Walled herb garden with pool and exuberant planting. Orchard inc white garden and hot border. Greenhouse and vegetable garden. Rock garden extending to grasses, ferns and bamboos. Shady walk to belvedere. 8 acre copse of native species with grassed rides. Assistance available with gravel drive and avoidable shallow steps.

5 BERE MILL
London Road, Whitchurch, RG28 7NH. Rupert & Elizabeth Nabarro OBE, 07703 161074, rupertnab@gmail.com, www.beremillfarm.co.uk/garden. 9m E of Andover, 12m N of Winchester. Take B2400 from centre of Whitchurch, turn R at Bere Mill Butchery sign at top of hill (approx ½ m). Visitors with disability or limited mobility park adjacent to Butchery. **Sun 16 Mar, Sun 13 Apr, Mon 26 May, Mon 25 Aug (1-5). Adm £8, chd free. Home-made teas.** Visits also by arrangement 3 Feb to 30 Sept. Fixed charge of £400.
Garden built around early C18 mill on idyllic isolated stretch of the River Test, east of Whitchurch. Gardens have been built incrementally over 30 yrs with extensive bulb planting; herbaceous and Mediterranean borders with magnolia, irises, and tree peonies; summer and autumn borders; a traditional orchard and two small arboretums, one specialising in Japanese shrubs and trees. The garden aims to complement the natural beauty of the site and to incorporate elements of oriental garden design and practice. Unfenced and unguarded rivers and streams. Wheelchair access unless very wet.

6 BINSTED PLACE
River Hill, Binsted Road, Binsted, Alton, GU34 4PQ. Max & Catherine Hadfield, 01420 23146, catherine.hadfield1@icloud.com. At eastern edge of Binsted Village on Binsted Rd. 1m from Jolly Farmer pub in Blacknest. 1½ m from A325. Parking limited, but safe on-road parking outside the property. **Visits by arrangement 24 May to 14 Sept for groups of 15 to 30. No bookings in Aug. Adm £10, chd free. Refreshments inc.**
Binsted Place, a C17 farmhouse with attractive local stone outbuildings, is surrounded by a series of garden rooms covering approx 1½ acres, enclosed by yew hedges and old walls. It is very traditional in style and inc many roses, pergolas, herbaceous borders, lily pond and a productive vegetable garden and orchards. Step free wheelchair access to most of the garden.

In 2024, National Garden Scheme funding for Perennial supported 1,367 people working in horticulture.

GROUP OPENING

7 NEW BISHOP'S WALTHAM GARDENS
Free Street, Bishops Waltham, Southampton, SO32 1EE. *8m S of Winchester. From A32 take B3035 to Bishop's Waltham. Take 2nd L into Free St. Colville Dr is 1st L, where parking is available. Albion Cottage is further along Free St on R after Maypole Green.* **Sat 19, Sun 20 July (1-5). Combined adm £5, chd free. Home-made teas at 9 Colville Drive.**

NEW ALBION COTTAGE
Helen Fuller.

NEW 9 COLVILLE DRIVE
Gill Cooper.

Bishop's Waltham is a medieval market town with a well-preserved High Street. It is the source of the Hamble River and has a ruined medieval palace. Albion Cottage has a courtyard full of planted ceramic pots, a patio and cottage style side garden with a deep fish pond. All paths are made from reclaimed paving. Almost all pots and the greenhouse are preloved. Many plants are from cuttings or seedlings. This tiny garden is wildlife friendly with a profusion of birds and insects. Bishop's Waltham in Bloom, 1st prize for 'Best Display in a Private Residence'. 9 Colville Drive has an illusion of space created in the compact urban garden by a zig-zagging path that reveals shaded spots hidden from the house's view. A stream tumbles from rocks wending its way between two ponds attracting a rich variety of wildlife. The planting scheme highlights the chalky soil with a vivid display of colours from climbing plants, shrubs, dahlias, and begonias. Partial wheelchair access at 9 Colville Drive only.

✿ ☕

8 BLEAK HILL NURSERY & GARDEN
Braemoor, Bleak Hill, Harbridge, Ringwood, BH24 3PX.
Tracy & John Netherway, www.bleakhillplants.co.uk. *2½m S of Fordingbridge. Turn off A338 at Ibsley. Go through Harbridge village to T-junction at top of hill, turn R for ¼m.* **Sun 20 July (2-5); Mon 21 July (11-3); Sun 10 Aug (2-5); Mon 11 Aug (11-3); Mon 25 Aug (2-5). Adm £4, chd free. Home-made teas. No refreshments on 21 July**

& 11 Aug, welcome to bring a picnic. Cash only.
Enjoy this ¾ acre garden, pass through the moongate to reveal the billowing borders contrasting against a seaside scene with painted beach huts and a boat on the gravel. Herbaceous borders complemented by a spectacular tropical border fill the garden with colour wrapping around a pond and small stream. Greenhouses with cacti and sarracenias. Vegetable patch and small wildflower meadow. Small adjacent nursery.

✿ ☕ 🍴

9 BLOUNCE HOUSE
Blounce, South Warnborough, Hook, RG29 1RX. Tom & Gay Bartlam, 07788 911184, tomb@thbartlam.co.uk. *In hamlet of Blounce, 1m S of South Warnborough on B3349 from Odiham to Alton.* **Sun 31 Aug (1-4). Adm £6, chd free. Tea, coffee & cake.** Visits also by arrangement 16 June to 12 Sept for groups of 10 to 30.
A 2 acre garden surrounding a classic Queen Anne house (not open). Mixed planting to give interest from spring to late autumn. Herbaceous borders with a variety of colour themes. In late summer an emphasis on dahlias, salvias and grasses.

♿ ✿ ☕ 🔊

10 BLUEBELL WOOD
Stancombe Lane, Bavins, New Odiham Road, Alton, GU34 5SX. Mrs Jennifer Ospici, www.bavins.co.uk. *On the corner of Stancombe Ln & the B3349, 2½m N of Alton.* **Fri 2, Sat 3 May (11-4). Adm £10, chd free. Light refreshments.**
Unique 100 acre ancient bluebell woodland. If you are a keen walker you will have much to explore on the long meandering paths and rides dotted with secluded seats. The wood is very challenging for those with mobility problems. Refreshments will be served in an original rustic building and inc soups using natural woodland ingredients.

🐕 ☕

11 BRAMDEAN HOUSE
Bramdean, Alresford, SO24 0JU.
Mr & Mrs E Wakefield, garden@bramdeanhouse.com, www.instagram.com/bramdean_house_garden. *4m S of Alresford; 9m E of Winchester; 9m W of Petersfield. In centre of village on A272. Entrance opp sign to the church. Parking is signed across the road from entrance.* **Sun 9 Feb (1.30-3.30); Sun 15 June (1-3.30); Sun 14 Sept (1.30-3.30). Adm £6.50, chd free. Tea, coffee & cake.** Donation to Bramdean Church.
Beautiful 5 acre garden best known for its mirror image herbaceous borders, its 1 acre walled garden, its carpets of spring bulbs, and a large and unusual collection of plants and shrubs giving year-round interest. Features inc fine snowdrops, a large collection of old fashioned sweet peas, an expansive collection of nerines, a boxwood castle and the nation's tallest sunflower 'Giraffe'. Visits also by arrangement for groups of 5+ (non-NGS). The garden is on a slope and mainly grass. Some paths require narrower than standard wheelchair for access. Assistance dogs only.

♿ ✿ ☕ 🔊

12 BRICK KILN COTTAGE
The Avenue, Herriard, nr Alton, RG25 2PR. Barbara Jeremiah & Kay Linnell, 01256 381301, barbara@klca.co.uk. *4m NE of Alton, nr Lasham Gliding Club. A339 Basingstoke to Alton, 7m out of Basingstoke turn L along The Avenue, past Lasham Gliding Club on R, then past Back Ln on L & take next track on L, one field later.* **Sat 10 May (11.30-3). Adm £6, chd free. Home-made teas.** Visits also by arrangement 6 May to 9 May for groups of 10 to 50.
A bluebell woodland garden. The 2 acre garden with a perimeter woodland path inc treehouse, pebble garden, billabong, ferny hollow, bug palace, waterpool, shepherd's hut and a traditional cottage garden filled with herbs. The garden is maintained using eco-friendly methods as a haven for wild animals, butterflies, birds, bees and English bluebells. Children's reading area. Wildlife friendly garden in a former brick works. A haven in the trees. Gallery of textiles.

🐕 ✿ ☕

13 BRIDGE COTTAGE
Amport, Andover, SP11 8AY.
John & Jenny Van de Pette. *3m SW of Andover. Leave the A303 at East Cholderton from E or Thruxton village from W. Follow signs to Amport. Parking in a field by Amport village green.* **Sun 25, Mon 26 May (2-5.30). Adm £6, chd free. Home-made teas.**

This 2 acre garden is a haven for wildlife, developed over 24 yrs by the current owners. A lake is edged with glorious herbaceous borders. A trout stream with water voles and kingfishers. Organic vegetable garden, fruit cage, small mixed orchard and arboretum with unusual trees. Superb plant sale. Treasure hunt for children. Paths in the vegetable garden are not suitable for wheelchairs.

14 BROADHATCH HOUSE
Bentley, Farnham, GU10 5JJ. Bruce & Lizzie Powell, 07799 031044, lizziepowellbroadhatch@gmail.com. *4m NE of Alton. Turn off A31 (Bentley bypass) through village, then L up School Ln. R to Perrylands, after 300yds drive on R.* **Sun 22, Mon 23, Tue 24 June (2-5). Adm £7.50, chd free. Home-made teas. Visits also by arrangement 15 May to 30 June.**

3½ acre garden set in lovely Hampshire countryside with views to Alice Holt. Divided into different areas by yew hedges and walled garden. Focussing on as long a season as possible on heavy clay. Two reflective pools help break up lawn areas; lots of flower borders and beds; mature trees. Working greenhouses and vegetable garden. Wheelchair access with gravel paths and steps in some areas.

15 ♦ CHAWTON HOUSE
Chawton, Alton, GU34 1SJ. Chawton House, 01420 541010, info@chawtonhouse.org, www.chawtonhouse.org. *2m S of Alton. In Chawton village take the Gosport Rd opp Jane Austen House towards St Nicholas Church. Chawton House is at the end of the road on the L. Parking on site & in village.* **For NGS: Tue 18 Mar (10-3). Adm £8, chd £6. Light refreshments.** For other opening times and information, please phone, email or visit garden website.

Daffodils and spring flowering bulbs are scattered through this 15 acre listed English landscape garden. Sweeping lawns, a wilderness, terraces and shrubbery walks surround the Elizabethan manor house. The walled garden designed by Edward Knight inc a rose garden, flower borders, orchard, kitchen garden, and herb garden based on 'A Curious Herbal' (1737-39) by Elizabeth Blackwell. Hot and cold drinks, wine, light lunches, cream teas, home-made cakes and local ice creams available in our tea shed on the main drive and in The Old Kitchen Tearoom at the house.

16 21 CHESTNUT ROAD
Brockenhurst, SO42 7RF. Iain & Mary Hayter, www.21-chestnut-rdgardens.co.uk. *New Forest. Please use village car park a short walk away. Limited parking for those less mobile in road. Leave M27 J2, follow Heavy Lorry Route. Mainline station less than 10 min walk.* **Sat 10, Sun 11 May, Sat 7, Sun 8 June, Sat 9, Sun 10 Aug (11.30-5). Adm £5, chd free. Home-made teas.**

A ⅓ acre in a central village location. Behind the hedge awaits the owner designed garden full of colour, scent and full of inspirational ideas for gardening in sun, shade, wet or dry areas. Experience nature inspired formal, naturalistic, and themed areas with statues, fairies, ponds, and a productive fruit and vegetable area. Paintings, plants and bug boxes usually available for sale (% to NGS).

Pines Corner Wildlife Garden

17 CHURCH HOUSE
Trinity Hill, Medstead, Alton, GU34 5LT. Mr Paul & Mrs Alice Beresford, 01420 562592, pauljames2309@gmail.com. *5m WSW of Alton. From A31 Four Marks follow signs to Medstead for 1½m to village centre, turn R into Church Ln/Trinity Hill. From N on A339, R at Bentworth Xrds & continue via Bentworth to Medstead.* **Sat 9 Aug (2-5.30); Sun 10 Aug (2-5). Adm £8, chd £2. Tea, coffee & cake.** Visits also by arrangement 19 May to 7 Sept for groups of 15+. Contact owners to discuss lunch or evening visit with wine & nibbles.

A colourful 1 acre garden, set within a wide variety of mature trees and shrubs. Long, sweeping, colour themed mixed borders give lots of ideas for planting in sun and shade. Contrasting features and textures throughout the garden are enhanced by interesting sculptures. Espaliered fruit trees, a woodland area, small greenhouse and roses in different settings all contribute to this much loved garden. For further information see Facebook, search Church House Garden Medstead. Wheelchair access via gravel drive to flat lawned garden. No access to some paths and patio.

18 COLEMORE HOUSE GARDENS
Colemore, Alton, GU34 3RX. Mr & Mrs Simon de Zoete, 01420 588202, simondezoete@gmail.com. *4m S of Alton, off A32. Approach from N on A32, turn L into Shell Ln, ¼m S of East Tisted. Go under bridge, keep L until you see Colemore Church. Park on verge of church.* **Visits by arrangement May to July for groups of 10 to 40. Adm £10, chd free. Light refreshments.**

4 acres in lovely unspoilt countryside, featuring rooms containing many unusual plants and different aspects with a spectacular arched rose walk, water rill, mirror pond, herbaceous and shrub borders. Newly designed by David Austin roses, an octagonal garden with 25 different varieties. Explore the interesting arboretum, grass gardens and thatched pavilion. Every yr the owners seek improvement and the introduction of new, interesting and rare plants. We propagate and sell plants, many of which can be found in the garden. Some are unusual and not readily available elsewhere. For private visits, we endeavour to give a conducted tour and try to explain our future plans, rationale and objectives.

19 THE COTTAGE
16 Lakewood Road, Chandler's Ford, Eastleigh, SO53 1ES. Hugh & Barbara Sykes, 02380 254521, barandhugh@aol.com. *Leave M3 J12. At King Rufus on Winchester Rd, turn R into Merdon Ave, then 3rd road on L.* **Visits by arrangement Mar to May for groups of 5+. Adm £5.50, chd free. Home-made teas.**

¾ acre garden. Colourful in spring with azaleas, camellias, trilliums and erythroniums under old oaks and pines. Herbaceous cottage style borders with unusual plants for year-round interest. Bog garden, ponds, kitchen garden. Bantams, bees and birdsong with over 35 bird species noted. Wildlife areas. Garden croquet, natural Easter egg decorating demonstrations and talks about bees can be inc in visits. NGS sundial for opening for 30 yrs. 'A lovely tranquil garden', Anne Swithinbank. Hampshire Wildlife Trust Wildlife Garden Award. Honey from our beehives for sale.

20 NEW THE COURT HOUSE
East Meon, Petersfield, GU32 1NJ. George & Clare Bartlett, 07747 827751, clarebartlett@doctors.org.uk. *5m W of Petersfield. East Meon is signed from A32 in West Meon. Entrance 200yds past church. From A3 at Petersfield take A272 then turn L at Langrish & follow road for 2m. What3words app: pegs.cheaper.presumes.* **Visits by arrangement 20 June to 19 Sept for groups of 10 to 30. Adm £10, chd free. Light refreshments.**

A 2 acre garden, surrounding a medieval manor house (not open), laid out in the 'Arts and Crafts' style with separate areas divided by yew hedges and stone walls. The established herbaceous borders contain some unusual plants providing interest throughout the summer. Steps lead to a lower level with reflecting pool and progressively less formal planting. I acre vineyard.

GROUP OPENING

21 CRAWLEY GARDENS
Crawley, Winchester, SO21 2PR. *5m NW of Winchester. Between B3049 (Winchester - Stockbridge) & A272 (Winchester - Andover). Parking throughout village.* **Fri 18, Mon 21 Apr, Sat 5, Sun 6 July (2-5.30). Combined adm £10, chd free. Home-made teas in the village hall.**

BAY TREE HOUSE
Julia & Charles Whiteaway.

LITTLE COURT
Mrs A R Elkington.
(See separate entry)

PAIGE COTTAGE
Mr & Mrs T W Parker.

Crawley is a pretty period village nestling in chalk downland with thatched houses, C14 church and village pond. The spring and summer gardens provide varied seasonal interest with traditional and contemporary approaches to landscape and planting. Most of the gardens have beautiful country views and other gardens can be seen from the road. Bay Tree House has bulbs, wild flowers, a Mediterranean garden, pleached limes, a rill and contemporary borders of perennials and grasses. Little Court is a 3 acre country garden with carpets of spring bulbs, herbaceous borders and a large meadow. Paige Cottage is a 1 acre traditional English garden surrounding a period thatched cottage (not open) with bulbs and wild flowers in spring and old climbing roses in summer. Plants from the garden for sale at Little Court.

22 CROOKLEY POOL
Blendworth Lane, Horndean, PO8 0AB. Mr & Mrs Simon Privett, 02392 592662, jennyprivett@icloud.com. *5m S of Petersfield, 2m E of Waterlooville, off the A3. From Horndean up Blendworth Ln between bakery & hairdresser. Entrance 200yds before church on L with white railings.* **Visits by arrangement in June for groups of 15 to 30. Tea, coffee & cake.**

Here the plants choose where to grow. Californian tree poppies elbow valerian aside to crowd round the pool. Verbena 'Bampton' obstructs the way to the door. This is a plantsman's garden with borders full of colour and unusual shrubs and tender perennials, salvias thrive in this warm and sheltered garden. Pandorea jasminoides, justicia and ageratum share the greenhouse with the tomatoes. Hellebores bloom under the trees, a 100 yr old wisteria rampages along pergolas, walls and terraces.

&. ✱ 🚗 🍵

23 THE DEANE HOUSE
Sparsholt, Winchester,
SO21 2LR. Mr & Mrs Richard Morse, 07774 863004,
chrissiemorse7@gmail.com.
3½ m NW of Winchester. Off A3049 Stockbridge Rd, onto Woodman Ln, signed Sparsholt. Turn L at cream house on L with green gables & go to top of drive. Plenty of parking. Do not follow SatNav. What3words app: grapevine.sochet.skips. **Visits by arrangement 10 Mar to 11 Sept for groups of 10+. Home-made teas or lunches. Prosecco & canapés for evening visits.**
A beautiful 4 acre rural garden, overlooking Woodman vineyard, nestled on a gentle south facing slope, landscaped to draw the eye from one gentle terraced lawn to another with borders merging into the surrounding countryside and vines. Featuring a good selection of specimen trees, a walled garden, prairie planting and herbaceous borders. Millennium avenue of tulip trees. Water features and sculptures. Tour of Woodman vineyard can be arranged. Sorry, no dogs. Although the garden is on the side of a hill there is always a path to avoid steps.

&. 🚗 🚌 🍵 ᴗ))

24 THE DOWER HOUSE
Church Lane, Dogmersfield, Hook,
RG27 8TA. Anne-Marie & Richard Revell. 3½ m E of Hook. Turn N off A287. For SatNav please use RG27 8SZ. **Sun 18 May (2-4.30). Adm £5, chd free. Home-made teas.**
6 acres inc bluebell wood with large and spectacular collection of rhododendrons, azaleas, magnolias and other flowering trees and shrubs; set in parkland with fine views over 20 acre lake.

🍵 ᴗ))

25 THE DOWN HOUSE
Itchen Abbas, SO21 1AX. Jackie & Mark Porter, 07814 958810,
markstephenporter@gmail.com.
5m E of Winchester on B3047. 5th house on R after the Itchen Abbas village sign, if coming on B3047 from Kings Worthy. 500 metres on L after The Plough pub if coming on B3047 from Alresford. **Tue 18, Wed 19 Feb (1-4). Adm £10, chd free. Pre-booking essential, please visit www.ngs.org.uk for information & booking. Home-made teas inc. Visits also by arrangement in Feb for groups of 10 to 24. Guided tour & home-made teas inc.**
A 2 acre garden laid out in rooms overlooking the Itchen Valley, adjoining the Pilgrim's Way. In winter come and see garden structure, snowdrops, aconites and Crocus tommasinianus, plus borders of dogwoods, willow stems and white birches. Scent from daphnes, and honeysuckle. Pleached hornbeams, rope-lined fountain garden, formal box-edged potager, yew-lined avenue and walks in adjoining meadows.

&. 🍵 ᴗ))

26 DURMAST HOUSE
Bennetts Lane, Burley,
BH24 4AT. Mr & Mrs P E G Daubeney, 01425 402132,
philip@daubeney.co.uk,
www.durmasthouse.co.uk. 5m SE of Ringwood. Off Burley to Lyndhurst road, nr White Buck Hotel, C10 road. **Visits by arrangement 31 Mar to 31 Aug for groups of 10 to 50. Adm £8, chd free.**
Designed by Gertrude Jekyll, Durmast has contrasting hot and cool colour borders, formal rose garden edged with lavender and a long herbaceous border. Many old trees, Victorian rockery and orchard with beautiful spring bulbs. Rare azaleas; Fama, Princeps and Gloria Mundi from Ghent. Features inc rose bowers with rare French roses; Eleanor Berkeley, Psyche and Reine Olga de Wurtemberg. Many old trees inc cedar and Douglas firs. Wheelchair access on stone and gravel paths.

&. 🐎 ✱ 🚗 🚌 🍵 ᴗ))

27 ENDHOUSE
6 Wimpson Gardens,
Southampton, SO16 9ES.
Kevin Liles, 02380 777590,
k.liles1@virginmedia.com. West Southampton. Exit M271 at J1 toward Lordshill. At 2nd r'about, turn R into Romsey Rd towards Shirley. After ½ m turn R at Xrds into Wimpson Ln, 3rd on R Crabwood Rd (additional parking). Wimpson Gardens 4th on R. **Sat 14, Sun 15 June (1.30-4.30). Adm £4, chd free. Home-made teas. Visits also by arrangement 18 May to 27 July for groups of 12 to 20. Morning or afternoon.**
Award-winning urban oasis of linked garden areas inc small secret garden. Best in spring and summer months, but rich year-round plant interest with tree ferns, palms, acers and shrubs. Deep herbaceous borders planted with ferns, roses, grasses, agapanthus and alstroemerias. Significant exhibition of gallery quality sculpture and garden ceramics.

✱ 🍵 ᴗ))

28 FAIRBANK
Old Odiham Road, Alton,
GU34 4BU. Jane & Robin Lees, 01420 86665,
j.lees558@btinternet.com. 1½ m N of Alton. From S, past Sixth Form College, then 1½ m beyond road junction on R. From N, turn L at Golden Pot & then 50yds turn R. Garden 1m on L before road junction. **Visits by arrangement May to Sept for groups of up to 40. Adm £7, chd free. Home-made teas.**
The planting in this large garden reflects our interest in trees, shrubs, fruit and vegetables. A wide variety of herbaceous plants provide colour and are placed in sweeping mixed borders that carry the eye down the long garden to the orchard and beyond. Near the house (not open) there are rose beds and herbaceous borders, as well as a small formal pond. There is a range of acers, ferns and unusual shrubs and 50 different cultivars of fruit, together with a large vegetable garden. Wheelchair access with uneven ground in some areas.

&. 🚗 🍵

29 FAIRWEATHER'S NURSERY
Hilltop, Beaulieu, SO42 7YR.
Patrick Fairweather, 01590 612113,
info@fairweathers.co.uk,
www.fairweathers.co.uk. Hilltop Nursery. 1½ m NE of Beaulieu village on B3054. Please leave plenty of time, the guided tour will start promptly at 11am. **Fri 18, Sat 19 July (11-12.30). Adm £10, chd free. Pre-booking essential, please visit www.ngs.org.uk for information & booking. Tea, coffee & cake.**

Fairweather's hold a specialist collection of over 400 agapanthus grown in pots and display beds, inc AGM award-winning agapanthus trialled by the RHS. Patrick Fairweather will give a guided tour of the nursery at 11am with a demonstration of how to get the best from agapanthus and companion planting. Open nearby Patrick's Patch at Fairweather's Garden Centre, High Street, Beaulieu.

30 FERNS LODGE
Cottagers Lane, Hordle, Lymington, SO41 0FE. Sue Grant, 07860 521501, sue.grant@fernslodge.co.uk, www.fernslodge.co.uk. *Approx 5½m W of Lymington. From Silver St turn into Woodcock Ln, 100 metres to Cottagers Ln, parking in field opp garden. From A337 turn into Everton Rd & drive approx 1½m, Cottagers Ln on R.* **Sat 14, Sun 15 June (2-5.30). Adm £5, chd free. Home-made teas. Visits also by arrangement for groups of 10 to 20 on 24 May, 25 May, 31 May, 1 June, 7 June, 8 June, 21 June, 28 June, 29 June.**
Bustling, 4 acre wildlife garden filled with scent, colour and mature trees inc ½ acre cottage garden around a Victorian lodge, full of sweet peas, foxgloves, clematis, roses, agapanthus and salvia. Brick paths wind through this garden with plentiful seating areas, perfect for a cup of tea. The large garden is in restoration with a Woodpecker greenhouse, tree ferns, masses of new planting and 3D art. New potting shed being built. Wheelchair access to many areas.

31 FRITHAM LODGE
Fritham, SO43 7HH. Sir Chris & Lady Powell. *6m N of Lyndhurst. 3m NW of M27 J1 (Cadnam). Follow signs to Fritham.* **Sun 15 June (2-4). Adm £5, chd free. Home-made teas.**
A walled garden of 1 acre in the heart of the New Forest, set within 18 acres surrounding a house that was originally a Charles I hunting lodge (not open). Herbaceous and blue and white mixed borders, pergolas and ponds. A box hedge enclosed parterre of roses, fruit and vegetables. Visitors will enjoy the ponies, donkeys, sheep and old breed hens on their meadow walk to the woodland and stream.

GROUP OPENING

32 FROYLE GARDENS
Lower Froyle, Froyle, GU34 4LG. www.froyleopengardens.org.uk. *Midway between Alton & Farnham just off the A31. Access to Froyle from A31 between Alton & Farnham at Bentley, or at Hen & Chicken Inn. Park at Recreation Ground in Lower Froyle, GU34 4LG. Map provided. Additional signed parking in Upper Froyle.* **Sat 7, Sun 8 June (1.30-6). Combined adm £10, chd free. Home-made teas in village hall & picnics welcome on the recreation ground in Lower Froyle.**

ALDERSEY HOUSE
Nigel & Julie Southern.

DAY COTTAGE
Nick & Corinna Whines, www.daycottage.co.uk.

2 HIGHWAY COTTAGE
Faith Richards & Gordon Mitchell.

OLD BREWERY HOUSE
Vivienne & John Sexton.

NEW OLD STABLE BARN
Polly & Simon Marshall.

1 TURNPIKE COTTAGES
Ms Pam Walls.

NEW 2 TURNPIKE COTTAGES
Bruce Collinson.

WALBURY
Ernie & Brenda Milam.

WARREN COTTAGE
Gillian & Jonathan Pickering.

WELL LANE CORNER
Mark & Sue Lelliott.

A warm welcome awaits as Froyle Gardens open their gates once again, enabling visitors to enjoy a wide variety of types of garden, all of which have undergone further development since last yr and will be looking splendid. Froyle 'The Village of Saints' has many old and interesting buildings. Our gardens harmonise well with the surrounding landscape and most have spectacular views. The gardens themselves are diverse with rich planting. You will see greenhouses, water features, vegetables, roses, clematis and wildflower meadows. Lots of ideas to take away with you, along with plants to buy and delicious teas served in the village hall. Close by is a playground with a zip wire where children can let off steam.

There is also an exhibition of richly embroidered historic vestments in the Church in Upper Froyle (separate donation). The gardens are well spread out so wear comfortable shoes! No wheelchair access to Day Cottage, Old Stable Barn and 1 Turnpike Cottages, and on request at Warren Cottage. Gravel drive at 2 Highway Cottage.

33 NEW GREENVIEW
Lockerley Green, Lockerley, Romsey, SO51 0JN. Ian Bradford. *What3words app: warms.gave.comment. 7m N of Romsey. A3057 Romsey to Andover road, turn L on B3084 to Awbridge, then Romsey Rd to Lockerley, turn L after railway bridge & follow sign for village shop. Park on village green.* **Sat 12, Sun 13 July (11-5). Adm £5, chd free. Tea, coffee & cake.**
Greenview is a 1½ acre garden with the disused Southampton to Salisbury Canal passing through. A former piggery, now reclaimed with an orchard, vegetable garden with ornate structure, flower borders, gazebo, greenhouse, and a large studio with a path circumventing the gardens large lawns. The gazebo was once sat in by Queen Elizabeth II at the RHS Chelsea Flower Show in 1984. Wheelchair access over concrete paths. Disabled parking on site.

34 HAMBLEDON HOUSE
East Street, Hambledon, PO7 4RX. Capt & Mrs David Hart Dyke, 02392 632380, dianahartdyke@gmail.com. *8m SW of Petersfield, 5m NW of Waterlooville. In village centre, driveway leading to house in East St. Do not go up Speltham Hill even if advised by SatNav.* **Visits by arrangement Apr to Sept for groups of 10 to 30.**
3 acre partly walled plantsman's garden for all seasons. Large borders filled with a wide variety of unusual shrubs and perennials with imaginative plant combinations culminating in a profusion of colour in late summer. Hidden, secluded areas reveal surprise views of garden and village rooftops. A haven of peace, shared with birds, bees and butterflies, unseen or overlooked.

GROUP OPENING

35 HEADLEY VILLAGE GARDENS
All Saints Church Centre, High Street, Headley, GU35 8PW. *From the B3002 turn R into the High St. The car park is opp the church. Please buy ticket in the marquee.* **Sat 7, Sun 8 June (10.30-5). Combined adm £10, chd free. Lunches & teas at All Saints Church Centre. Cream teas at El Rincon & Frey Elma.**

NEW 1 BADGERSWOOD DRIVE
Mr & Mrs D Remington.

NEW BEARS LODGE
Mrs J Mahoney.

CHERRYCROFT
Mr & Mrs R Hall.

NEW 2 CHURCH LANE
Mrs P Tabard.

NEW EL RINCON
Mr & Mrs R Sherburn-Hall.

NEW FIELDFARE HOUSE
Mr & Mrs M Head.

FREY ELMA
Mrs C Leonard, 07791 459068, chrisleo812@hotmail.com. **Visits also by arrangement May to Aug for groups of up to 20.**

NEW 11 GLEBE ROAD
Mr & Mrs I Howard-Duff.

THE HOLLIES
Mr & Mrs R Kemp.

PERRYMEAD
Ms H & Ms A Kempster.

THE TITHE BARN
Mr & Mrs N Goodhew.

Headley offers a huge range of interesting and varied gardens inc meadowland, woodlands, mixed family gardens, sunny borders and shade-loving plants. There is everything one could wish for; courtyards, beautiful mature trees, borders, greenhouses, vegetable gardens, ponds, formal gardens, and a wild cottage garden. The group has a long experience with offering visitors a warm welcome and a great day out.

36 THE HOMESTEAD
Northney Road, Hayling Island, PO11 0NF. Stan & Mary Pike, 02392 464888, jhomestead@aol.com. *3m S of Havant. From A27 Havant & Hayling Island r'about, travel S over Langstone Bridge & turn immed L into Northney Rd. Car park entrance on R after Langstone Hotel.* **Sun 3 Aug (1.30-5). Adm £5, chd free. Home-made teas. Visits also by arrangement July to Sept for groups of 12+.**

1¼ acre garden surrounded by working farmland with views to Butser Hill and boats in Chichester Harbour. Trees, shrubs, colourful herbaceous borders and small walled garden with herbs, vegetables and trained fruit trees. Large pond and woodland walk with shade-loving plants. A quiet and peaceful atmosphere with plenty of seats to enjoy the vistas within the garden and beyond. Extensive range of plants for sale. Wheelchair access with some gravel paths.

37 HOOK CROSS ALLOTMENTS
Reading Road, Hook, RG27 9DB. Hook Allotment Association. *Northern edge of Hook village on B3349, Reading Rd. 900 metres N of A30 r'about. Concealed entrance track is on RHS at foot of hill opp a farm entrance, straight after turns to B & M Fencing & Searle's Ln.* **Sat 19, Sun 20 July (1-5). Adm £5, chd free. Tea, coffee & cake.**

5¼ acre community run allotments overlooking Hook village. More than 100 plots showcasing different vegetables, fruit and flower growing styles. Plot holder demonstrations of how to grow your own. Community orchard, wildflower meadow, beetle banks, wildlife friendly gardening information.

Our donation in 2024 has enabled Parkinson's UK to fund 3 new nursing posts this year directly supporting people with Parkinson's.

38 ♦ THE HOSPITAL OF ST CROSS
St Cross Road, Winchester, SO23 9SD. The Hospital of St Cross & Almshouse of Noble Poverty, 01962 851375, porter@hospitalofstcross.co.uk, www.hospitalofstcross.co.uk. ½m S of Winchester. From city centre take B3335 (Southgate St & St Cross Rd) S. Turn L immed before The Bell Inn. If walking follow riverside path S from Cathedral & College, approx 20 mins. **For NGS: Sun 1 June (2-5). Adm £5, chd free. Light refreshments in the Hundred Men's Hall in the Outer Quadrangle. Open nearby Winchester College.** For other opening times and information, please phone, email or visit garden website.

The Medieval Hospital of St Cross nestles in water meadows beside the River Itchen and is one of England's oldest almshouses. The tranquil, walled Master's Garden, created in the late C17 by Bishop Compton, now contains colourful herbaceous borders, old-fashioned roses, interesting trees and a large fish pond. The plant beds in the Compton Garden were repositioned and replanted in 2023. The Hundred Men's Hall tearoom and the Porter's Lodge gift shop will be open. Wheelchair access, but surfaces are uneven in places.

39 THE HOUSE IN THE WOOD
Beaulieu, SO42 7YN. Victoria Roberts. *New Forest. 8m NE of Lymington. Leaving the entrance to Beaulieu Motor Museum on R (B3056), take next R signed Ipley Cross. Take 2nd gravel drive on RH-bend, approx ½m.* **Sun 11 May (1.30-5). Adm £6, chd free. Cream teas.**

Peaceful 12 acre woodland garden with continuing progress and improvement. Very much a spring garden with tall, glorious mature azaleas and rhododendrons in every shade of pink, orange, red and white, interspersed with acers and other woodland wonders. A magical garden to get lost in with many twisting paths leading downhill to a pond and a more formal layout of lawns around the house (not open). Used in the war to train the Special Operations Executive.

40 THE ISLAND
Greatbridge, Romsey, SO51 0HP. Mr & Mrs Christopher Saunders-Davies, 01794 512100, ssd@littleroundtop.co.uk. *1m N of Romsey on A3057. Entrance at bridge. Follow drive 100yds. Car park on RHS.* **Visits by arrangement June to Aug for groups of 15 to 20. Visits in Aug (am only). Bookings can be made from 1 April to 1 May only. Adm £15, chd free.**
6 acres both sides of the River Test. Fine display of daffodils, tulips, spring flowering trees and summer bedding. The main garden has herbaceous and annual borders, fruit trees, rose pergola, lavender walk and extensive lawns. An arboretum planted in the 1930s by Sir Harold Hillier contains three ponds, shrubs and specimen trees providing interest throughout the yr. No dogs allowed.
&. ☕))

41 KING JOHN'S GARDEN
Romsey, SO51 8BT. Friends of King John's Garden & Test Valley Borough Council, www.facebook.com/KingJohnsGarden. *Central Romsey. Please use Lortemore Place public car park, postcode SO51 8DF.* **Sat 21, Sun 22 June (10.30-4.30). Combined adm with The Nelson Cottage £6, chd free. Tea, coffee & cake.**
Listed C13 house (not open Sunday). Historic community garden planted with plants available before 1700. Small wildflower meadow. Award-winning Victorian garden and north courtyard with water features, fountains and pump. Paved path and fountain courtyard. Sorry, no dogs.
&. ✽ ☕))

42 KINGFISHERS CARE HOME
The Meadows, New Milton, BH25 7FJ. Chris Marsh, www.coltencare.co.uk/kingfishers/your-garden. *New Forest. W on A337 from Lymington to New Milton. L opp fish & chip shop down Southern Rd, 1st R into The Meadows. Park in allocated car parking spaces or on Southern Rd.* **Sun 29 June (11-5). Adm £5, chd free. Home-made teas. Dietary requirements catered for.**
This colourful and vibrant care home garden offers wide winding paths to stroll to its various points of interest; colourful herbaceous borders, a lavender avenue, pergola, greenhouse and vegetable patch and, the recent addition, a fascinating water feature. Residents are very involved in the garden with planning, propagating plants, and building habitats for all our fauna. This easily accessible garden has something for everyone to enjoy.
&. 🐾 ✽ ☕))

43 NEW THE LAUREL HOUSE
4 Beechwood Crescent, Chandler's Ford, Eastleigh, SO53 5PA. Gill Ellaway. *Leave M3 J12, follow signs to Romsey. Follow Hocombe Rd to Xrds. Turn L onto Hursley Rd. Turn 4th R into Beechwood Cres.* **Sat 17, Sun 18 May, Sat 6, Sun 7 Sept (12-5). Adm £5, chd free. Home-made teas & gluten free option.**
An enchanting $^2/_3$ acre, garden designer's garden, developed over 35 yrs has matured into a vibrant tapestry of colour, texture and scent. Woodland walks feature dry-shade plants, while hot beds bloom in late summer. Wildlife thrives with ponds, bird boxes and wood piles. Sustainable practices like composting enrich the soil. This garden offers a tranquil retreat, full of inspiration year-round. Partial wheelchair access. One step to top level of garden and bark paths in woodland area not suitable.
&. ✽ ☕))

44 LEPE HOUSE GARDENS
Lepe, Exbury, Southampton, SO45 1AD. Michael & Emma Page, emma.page@lepe.org.uk, www.lepe.org.uk. *New Forest. $^1/_2$ m from Lepe Country Park, 2m from Exbury Gardens. Entrance to drive through gates on S-side of Lepe Rd. What3words app: belong.nurses.highlight.* **Sun 13 Apr (1-5). Adm £10, chd free. Light refreshments inc.** Visits also by arrangement 16 Apr to 27 June for groups of 15 to 30. Adm £15, chd free inc guided tour.
This 12 acre spring woodland garden was laid out in 1893. An embarkation point for D-Day, the lighthouse in the garden now marks the entrance to the Beaulieu River. Distinct areas inc walled garden with camellias, coastal walk overlooking the Solent, woodland with mature magnolias and rhododendrons, arboretum with drifts of spring bulbs, wildlife ponds plus formal areas with a wishing well.
🐾 ✽ ☕

45 NEW LIMBERLOST
St Giles Hill, Winchester, SO23 0HH. Charles Cole. *$^1/_4$ m E of Winchester. From city centre walk up Magdalen Hill road. Entrance to St Giles Hill is on bend on R after 200yds. Garden is 2nd on R. Nearest parking Chesil St public car park.* **Sat 7, Sun 8 June (2-5). Adm £5, chd free. Home-made teas.**
$^1/_2$ acre garden with views overlooking the city of Winchester. Many interesting features inc Owner-built Monet bridge over pond, bottle wall, a secret garden, peonies and roses, historic religious icons, and lavender ha-ha. Several pleasant seating areas for tea, over twenty apple trees, greenhouse, fruit cages, asparagus bed, water features and pergola.
🐾 ☕))

46 LITTLE COURT
Crawley, Winchester, SO21 2PU. Mrs A R Elkington, 01962 776365, elkslc@btinternet.com. *5m NW of Winchester. Crawley village lies between B3049 (Winchester - Stockbridge) & A272 (Winchester - Andover), 400yds from either pond or church.* **Sun 16, Mon 17, Sun 23, Mon 24 Feb (2-4.30). Adm £5, chd free. Sun 30, Mon 31 Mar, Wed 21, Thur 22 May, Sun 15, Mon 16 June (2-5.30). Adm £6, chd free. Home-made teas in the village hall. Cold drinks in the garden on hot days. 2026: Sun 15, Mon 16, Sun 22, Mon 23 Feb. Opening with Crawley Gardens on Fri 18, Mon 21 Apr, Sat 5, Sun 6 July.** Visits also by arrangement 15 Feb to 15 July.
This sheltered naturalistic garden is one for all seasons, especially memorable in spring. It is mature and exuberant with contrasting areas, inc a traditional walled kitchen garden and free-range bantams. In July there are many butterflies in the wildflower meadow. Rustic seats throughout, good views, and described as 'an oasis of peace and tranquillity.' Sorry, no dogs. Plants grown in this garden for sale.
&. ✽ 🚗 ☕))

47 LONGSTOCK PARK WATER GARDEN
Leckford, Stockbridge, SO20 6EH. Leckford Estate Ltd, part of John Lewis Partnership, www.leckfordestate.co.uk. *4m S of Andover. From Leckford village on A3057 towards Andover, cross*

the river bridge & take 1st turning L signed Longstock. **Sun 29 June (10-3.30). Adm £10, chd £5.**
Famous water garden with extensive collection of aquatic and bog plants set in 7 acres of woodland with rhododendrons and azaleas. A walk through the park leads to National Collections of *Buddleja* and *Clematis viticella*; arboretum and herbaceous border at Longstock Park Nursery. Refreshments at Longstock Park Farm Shop and Nursery (last orders at 3.30pm). Assistance dogs only.

48 LORD WANDSWORTH COLLEGE
Long Sutton, Hook, RG29 1TB. Lord Wandsworth College. *3m S of Odiham. SatNav will take you to the College's main gates. From here our visitor car park is clearly signed.* **Sat 12, Sun 13 Apr (11-3). Adm £4, chd free. Home-made teas.**
Lord Wandsworth College is set in 1200 acres of rolling farmland and wooded valleys. The main college campus is set around formal lawns with mature paper bark maples, cedar trees, cherry trees, and magnolias. The herbaceous borders are planted with an array of tulips, daffodils, and alliums. A South African inspired border runs the full length of the new science centre.

49 26 LOWER NEWPORT ROAD
Aldershot, GU12 4QD. Pete & Angie Myles. *Nr to Aldershot junction of the A331. Parking is normally arranged with the factory opp 'Jondo' & The Salvation Army. Signage in place on the day if available. We are 100 metres away from the McDonalds drive through.* **Sat 28, Sun 29 June (11-4). Adm £3, chd free. Tea, coffee & cake.**
A T-shaped town garden full of ideas, split into four distinct sections; a semi-enclosed patio area with pots and water feature; a free-form lawn with a tree fern, perennials, bulbs and shrubs and over 200 varieties of hosta; secret garden with a 20ft x 6ft raised pond, exotic planting backdrop and African carvings; and a potager garden with vegetables, roses, cannas and plant storage.

50 ♦ MACPENNYS WOODLAND GARDEN & NURSERIES
Burley Road, Bransgore, Christchurch, BH23 8DB. Mr & Mrs T M Lowndes, 01425 672348, office@macpennys.co.uk, www.macpennys.co.uk. *6m SE of Ringwood, 5m NE of Christchurch. From Crown Pub Xrd in Bransgore take Burley Rd, following sign for Thorney Hill & Burley. Entrance ½ m on R.* **For opening times and information, please phone, email or visit garden website.**
4 acre woodland garden originating from worked out gravel pits in the 1950s, offering interest year-round, but particularly in spring and autumn. Attached to a large nursery that offers for sale a wide selection of homegrown trees, shrubs, conifers, perennials, hedging plants, fruit trees and bushes. Tearoom offering locally made cakes, afternoon tea (pre-booking required) and light lunches, using locally sourced produce wherever possible. Nursery closed Christmas through to the New Year. Partial wheelchair access on grass and gravel paths. Can be bumpy with tree roots and, muddy in winter.

The Montagu Arms Hotel

232 HAMPSHIRE

51 MANOR LODGE
Brook Lane, Botley, Southampton, SO30 2ER. Gary & Janine Stone, 07870 189321, manorlodge@globalnet.co.uk. *6m E of Southampton. From A334 to the W of Botley village centre, turn into Brook Ln. Manor Lodge is ½m on the R. Limited disabled parking. Continue past Manor Lodge to parking (signed).* **Sat 17, Sun 18 May (2-5). Adm £5, chd free. Home-made teas.** Visits also by arrangement 19 May to 31 July for groups of 15 to 30. Optional guided tour.

1½ acre garden of an enthusiastic plantswoman. A garden still in evolution with established areas and new projects to give fresh interest each yr. Informal and formal planting, dry/gravel and wet areas, sunny and shady beds, woodland and wildflower meadow walks. There are large established trees and newer specimen shrubs and trees. Planting combinations for year-round interest. Largely flat with hard paving, but some gravel and grass to access all areas.

52 MILL HOUSE
Vyne Road, Sherborne St John, Basingstoke, RG24 9HU. Harry & Devika Clarke. *2m N of Basingstoke. From Basingstoke take the A340 N. 400 metres beyond the hospital, turn R for Sherborne St John. Go through, past a red phone box & 400 metres up a hill. As it crests, on L, take track to Mill House.* **Thur 26, Sun 29 June (2-6). Adm £5, chd free. Home-made teas.**

Set in a private valley, the 3 acres of domestic fruit, vegetables, wild flowers and casual planting are arranged around a power generating watermill. Sustainability and low maintenance lie at its heart, to fit with modern life. Open views, set with mature trees and livestock, give a tranquil sense of space, with moving and static water framed in an undulating landscape. Partial wheelchair access. Park in car park and follow disabled access signs.

53 NEW THE MONTAGU ARMS HOTEL
Palace Lane, Beaulieu, Brockenhurst, SO42 7ZL. Mrs Suzy Bench, 01590 612324, reception@montaguarmshotel.co.uk, montaguarmshotel.co.uk. *What3words app: respects.tightest.*

barman. **Sat 7, Sun 8 June (10-4). Adm £6. Tea, coffee & cake.**
With winding pathways, lush green lawns and vibrant flower beds, our English country garden is a sanctuary for the senses, whatever the season. Visit our productive kitchen garden and greenhouse. Inhale the sweet scent of roses, lilies, sweet peas and honeysuckle that perfume the air as you wander through the garden. Enjoy our many birds as they eagerly hunt for worms in our rich soil.

54 THE NELSON COTTAGE
68 Cherville Street, Romsey, SO51 8FD. Margaret Prosser. *Next to Great Bridge Motors in Romsey. What3words app: pleaser.ranked. palace.* **Sat 21, Sun 22 June (10.30-4.30). Combined adm with King John's Garden £6, chd free.**
Formally one of the many public houses in Romsey. A ½ acre garden with a variety of perennial plants and shrubs, and a wild grass meadow bringing the countryside into the town. Wheelchair access with one step on entry into the garden.

55 5 OAKFIELDS
Allbrook, Eastleigh, SO50 4RP. Martin & Margaret Ward. *7m S of Winchester. M3 J12, follow signs to Eastleigh. 3rd exit at r'about into Woodside Ave, 2nd R into Bosville, 2nd R onto Boyatt Ln, 1st R to Porchester Rise & 1st L into Oakfields.* **Sat 14, Sun 15 June (2-5). Adm £5, chd free. Home-made teas.**

A ⅓ acre garden full of interesting and unusual plants in predominately woodland beds and, rambling roses cascading from birch trees. A pond with rockery, waterfall and flower beds formed from the intermittent winter streams, accommodate moisture loving plants. Colourful mixed herbaceous border and a terrace with architectural plants. Wheelchair access over hard paths and some gravel.

56 OLD CHANNEL HILL FARMHOUSE
North End, Damerham, Fordingbridge, SP6 3HA. Carolyn Andrews & Phil Tandy. *3m W of Fordingbridge. Turn off the A338, go through Fordingbridge & Sandleheath into Damerham & follow the yellow signs. What3words app: chuckling.newly.issued.* **Thur 22 May, Sun 8 June (1-5). Adm £4, chd free. Home-made teas.**
A mature garden divided into different areas of interest; main lawn bounded by perennial borders, wild meadow area, small stumpery, gravel area and a pergola seating area covered in vines and roses. Each area has different styles of planting with mature hedging. Old thatched privy and summerhouse.

57 THE OLD RECTORY
East Woodhay, Newbury, RG20 0AL. David & Victoria Wormsley, 07801 418976, victoria@wormsley.net. *6m SW of Newbury. Turn off A343 between Newbury & Highclere to Woolton Hill. Turn L to East End, continue ¾m beyond East End. Turn R, garden opp St Martin's Church.* **Visits by arrangement 1 May to 24 Oct for groups of 20+. Adm £12, chd free. Tea & home-made cake inc.**
A classic English country garden of about 2 acres surrounding a Regency former rectory (not open). Formal lawns and terrace provide tranquil views over parkland. A large walled garden with topiary and roses, full of interesting herbaceous plants and climbers for successional interest. Also a Mediterranean pool garden, orchard, wildflower meadow and fruit garden. Explore and enjoy.

GROUP OPENING

58 OLD THATCH & THE MILLENNIUM BARN
Sprats Hatch Lane, Winchfield, Hook, RG27 8DD. www.old-thatch.co.uk. *3m W of Fleet. 1½m E of Winchfield Stn, follow NGS signs. Sprats Hatch Ln opp Barley Mow pub. Disabled parking at Old Thatch, other parking in adjacent field if dry. Public car park at Barley Mow slipway ½m away. If weather is wet, check garden website.* **Sun 13 Apr, Sun 6 July (2-6). Combined adm £5, chd free. Tea, coffee & cake. Pimms if hot & mulled wine if cool.**

THE MILLENNIUM BARN
Mr & Mrs G Carter.

OLD THATCH
Jill Ede.

Who could resist visiting Old Thatch, a chocolate box thatched cottage (not open), featured on film and TV, a smallholding with a 5 acre garden and woodland alongside the Basingstoke Canal (unfenced). A succession of spring bulbs, a profusion of wild flowers, perennials and homegrown annuals pollinated by our own bees and fertilised by the donkeys, who await your visit. Over 30 named clematis and rose cultivars. Children enjoy our garden quiz, adults enjoy tea and home-made cakes. Arrive by narrow boat! Trips on 'John Pinkerton' may stop at Old Thatch on NGS days www.basingstoke-canal.org.uk. Also Accessible Boating shuttle from Barley Mow wharf, approx every 45 mins (entrance to garden is an additional charge). Signed parking for Blue Badge holders: please use entrance by the red telephone box. Paved paths and grass slopes give access to the whole garden.

59 ♦ PATRICK'S PATCH
Fairweather's Garden Centre, High Street, Beaulieu, SO42 7YB. Patrick Fairweather, 01590 612307, info@fairweathers.co.uk, www.fairweathers.co.uk. *SE of New Forest at head of Beaulieu River. Leave M27 at J2 & follow signs for Beaulieu Motor Museum. Go up the one-way High St & park in Fairweather's car park on the L.* **For opening times and information, please phone, email or visit garden website.**
Productive fruit and vegetable garden with a full range of vegetables, trained top, soft fruit and herbs. The garden is used as an educational project for primary school children and young people with additional needs. Maintained by volunteers, primary school children and a head gardener. We run the Potting Shed Club, a series of fun educational gardening sessions for children. Open daily. Refreshments available at Steff's Kitchen. Wheelchair access on gravelled site.

60 NEW PINES CORNER WILDLIFE GARDEN
78 Kingsway, Chandler's Ford, Eastleigh, SO53 1FJ. J & S Page. *At M3 J12 follow signs to Chandler's Ford onto Winchester Rd, then 1st R & 2nd L into Kingsway. Entry via side gates on Lake Rd (1st R). What3words app: groups.nodded.snake.* **Sun 22, Sun 29 June (2-5.30). Adm £4, chd free. Tea, coffee & cake.**
¼ acre garden designed for nature with native flowers and shrubs, and maintained for the ecosystem. Meadow and flowering lawn, hedgerows, dragonfly ponds, bee hotels, log piles and a nature reserve in the shape of a garden. It is a garden for those curious about our native nature and wilder gardening. Optional tour and nature corner to show and explain what is here, why and how we garden. Hiltingbury Lakes nearby.

61 1 POVEY'S COTTAGE
Stoney Heath, Baughurst, Tadley, RG26 5SN. Jonathan & Sheila Richards, 01256 850633, smrichards3012@icloud.com, www.facebook.com/onepoveyscottage. *Between villages of Ramsdell & Baughurst, 10 min drive from Basingstoke. Take A339 out of Basingstoke, direction Newbury. Turn R off A339 towards Ramsdell, then 4m to Stoney Heath. Pass under overhead power cables, take next L into unmade road & Povey's is 1st on the R.* **Sat 7, Sun 8, Wed 11 June (1-5). Adm £5, chd free. Home-made teas.** Visits also by arrangement 7 June to 2 Aug for groups of 10 to 30.
Informal herbaceous borders, trees and a small orchard area, two greenhouses, fruit cage, productive vegetable garden, a wildflower meadow area and a small stumpery. Beehives in one corner of the garden and chickens in another corner. A feature of the garden is an unusual natural swimming pond, surrounded by water lilies, frequently visited by diving swallows and dragonflies. Plants and home-made bee pottery for sale. Wheelchair access across flat grassed areas, but no hard pathways.

62 PYLEWELL PARK
South Baddesley, Lymington, SO41 5SJ. Lady Elizabeth Teynham. *Coast road 2m E of Lymington. From Lymington follow signs for Car Ferry to Isle of Wight, continue for 2m to South Baddesley.* **Sun 6, Sun 20 Apr (2-5). Adm £5, chd free.**
A large parkland garden laid out in 1890. Enjoy a walk along the extensive informal grass and moss paths down to the lakes. These are bordered by fine rhododendron, magnolia and azalea trees. Wild daffodils bloom in March and carpets of bluebells in late April and May. The large lakes feature giant gunnera and are home to magnificent swans. Distant views across the Solent to the Isle of Wight. Pylewell House and surrounding garden is private. Glasshouses, swimming pool and other outbuildings are not open to visitors. Lovely day out for families and dogs. Bring your own tea or picnic and wear suitable footwear for muddy areas. Gumboots may be essential in wet conditions.

63 REDENHAM PARK HOUSE
Redenham Park, Andover, SP11 9AQ. Lady Clark. *Approx 1½ m from Weyhill on the A342 Andover to Ludgershall road.* **Fri 13 June (10-1). Adm £6, chd free. Home-made teas at pool house.**
Redenham Park built in 1784. The garden sits behind the house (not open). The formal rose garden is planted with white flowered roses. Steps lead up to the main herbaceous borders, which peak in late summer. A calm green interlude, a gate opens into gardens with espaliered pears, apples, mass of scented roses, shrubs and perennial planting surrounds the swimming pool. A door opens onto a kitchen garden.

64 15 ROTHSCHILD CLOSE
Southampton, SO19 9TE. Steve Campion, 07968 512773, Spcampion10@gmail.com, www.instagram.com/tropical_plant_geezer69. *3m from M27 J8. From M27 J8 follow A3025 towards Woolston. After cemetery r'about L to Weston, next r'about 2nd exit Rothschild Cl.* **Sun 13 July (10-4); Sat 6, Sun 7 Sept (11-4). Adm £4, chd free. Pre-booking essential, please visit www.ngs.org.uk for information & booking. Tea, coffee & cake.** Visits also by arrangement 1 July to 21 Sept for groups of up to 12.
Small, 8 metre x 8 metre, modern city garden incorporating family living with lush tropical foliage. A large range of unusual tropical style plants inc tree ferns, bananas, cannas, gingers and dahlias. The garden has flourished over the last 8 yrs with a tropical oasis with many plants grown from seeds and cuttings. Tropical plant enthusiasts do come to have a cuppa in the jungle! Adjacent to the River Solent and Royal Victoria Country Park.

Little Court

HAMPSHIRE

65 SHALDEN PARK HOUSE
The Avenue, Shalden, Alton, GU34 4DS. Mr & Mrs Michael Campbell. 4½ m NW of Alton. B3349 from Alton or M3 J5 onto B3349. Turn W at Kapadokya Restaurant (formerly The Golden Pot pub) signed Herriard, Lasham, Shalden. Entrance ¼ m on L. Disabled parking on entry. **Sun 25 May (2-5). Adm £5, chd free. Home-made teas.**
Shalden Park House welcomes you to our 4 acre garden to enjoy a stroll through the arboretum, herbaceous borders, rose garden, kitchen garden and wildlife pond. Refreshments will be served from the pool terrace.

66 ♦ SIR HAROLD HILLIER GARDENS
Jermyns Lane, Ampfield, Romsey, SO51 0QA. Hampshire County Council, 01794 369318, info.hilliers@hants.gov.uk, www.hants.gov.uk/hilliergardens. 2m NE of Romsey. Follow brown tourist signs off M3 J11, or off M27 J2, or A3057 Romsey to Andover. **For opening times and information, please phone, email or visit garden website.**
Established by the plantsman Sir Harold Hillier, this 180 acre garden holds a unique collection of 12,000 different hardy plants from across the world. It inc the famous Winter Garden, Magnolia Avenue, Centenary Border, Himalayan Valley, Gurkha Memorial Garden, Magnolia Avenue, spring woodlands, Hydrangea Walk, fabulous autumn colour, 14 National Collections and over 600 champion trees. The Centenary Border is one of the longest double mixed border in the country, a feast from early summer to autumn. Celebrated Winter Garden is one of the largest in Europe. Electric scooters and wheelchairs for hire (please pre-book). Accessible WC and parking. Registered assistance dogs only.

67 SOUTH VIEW HOUSE
60 South Road, Horndean, Waterlooville, PO8 0EP. James & Victoria Greenshields, www.youtube.com/@Southview_House_Exotic_Garden. Between Horndean & Clanfield. From N A3 towards Horndean, R at T-junction to r'about. From S A3, B2149 to Horndean, continue on A3 N to r'about, 1st exit into Downwood Way, 3rd L into South Rd. House is 3rd on R. Park in road. **Sun 3 Aug (1-5). Adm £4, chd free. Tea, coffee & cake.**
A ½ acre site with formal cottage garden to the front and exotic/tropical style garden to the rear. The front inc a large herbaceous border, small woodland garden and formal topiary. The cleverly designed garden to the rear features tropical style planting with many rare palms, bananas, cannas and many unusual plants. Features inc pond, summerhouse, bar and chicken coop. Well worth a visit. Garden is accessed along a gravel drive on a gentle slope.

GROUP OPENING

68 SOUTHSEA GARDENS
Southsea, Portsmouth, PO4 0PR. Ian & Liz Craig, 07415 889648, ian.craig1@mac.com. Parking in Craneswater School, St Ronan's Rd, off Albert Rd. Follow signs from Albert Rd or Canoe Lake on seafront. **Sun 20 Apr, Sun 25 May, Sun 29 June (2-5.30). Combined adm £8, chd free. Home-made teas at 28 St Ronan's Avenue.**

35 GAINS ROAD
Leeann Roots.

67 GAINS ROAD
Lyn & Ian Payne.

NEW 2 KENILWORTH VILLAS
Mr Richard & Mrs Wendy Collins.

28 ST RONAN'S AVENUE
Ian & Liz Craig, www.28stronansavenue.co.uk.

Southsea Gardens expands to four town gardens this year. All are near to the promenade and are examples of what can be done in an urban setting. 35 and 67 Gains Road are small gardens designed and planted with artistic flair by the owners, inc ferns, bamboo and sculpture. The creative gardeners are keen plantspeople and have made the very most of the limited space in both front and rear gardens with planting of an exceptional standard. 28 St Ronan's Avenue is divided into different areas inc a wildflower meadow and pond. Planting is a mixture of traditional and tender plants inc puya, agaves, echeveria, echiums, and tree ferns. Tulips feature in April and alliums in May and June. Recycled items are used to create sculptures. 2 Kenilworth Villas on Kenilworth Road is a new garden to the group: trees have been planted for privacy and as a wind break. Planting is a mixture of herbaceous perennials, climbers, shrubs, spring bulbs, bananas, and dahlias in late summer.

69 ♦ SPINNERS GARDEN
School Lane, Pilley, Lymington, SO41 5QE. Andrew & Vicky Roberts, 07545 432090, info@spinnersgarden.co.uk, www.spinnersgarden.co.uk. New Forest. 1½ m N of Lymington off A337. **For NGS: Sun 27 Apr (1.30-5). Adm £6, chd free. Cream teas. For other opening times and information, please phone, email or visit garden website.**
Peaceful woodland garden overlooking the Lymington valley with many rare and unusual plants. Drifts of trilliums, erythroniums and anemones light up the woodland floor in early spring. The garden continues to be developed with new plants added to the collections and the layout changed to enhance the views over a pond and small arboretum. The house was rebuilt in 2014 to reflect its garden setting. Andy will take groups of 15 on tours of the hillside with its woodland wonders and draw attention to the treats at their feet.

70 SPITFIRE HOUSE
Chattis Hill, Stockbridge, SO20 6JS. Tessa & Clive Redshaw, 07711 547543, tessa@redshaw.co.uk. 2m from Stockbridge. Follow the A30 W from Stockbridge for 2m. Go past the Broughton/Chattis Hill Xrds, do not follow SatNav into Spitfire Ln, take next R to the Wallops & then immed R again to Spitfire House. **Sat 31 May (2-5); Sun 1 June (12-3.30). Adm £5, chd free. Home-made teas on 31 May only. Picnics welcome on 1 June. Visits also by arrangement in June for groups of up to 30.**
A country garden situated high on chalk downland. On the site of a WW11 Spitfire assembly factory with Spitfire tethering rings still visible. This garden has wildlife at its heart and inc fruit and vegetables, a small orchard, wildlife pond, woodland planting and large areas of wildflower meadow. Wander across the downs to be rewarded with extensive views. Wheelchair access with areas of gravel and a slope up to wildflower meadow.

71 NEW THE SQUARE HOUSE
St Cross Road, Winchester, SO23 9RX. **Alison Coulter.** *Southern end of St Cross Rd. From J11 M3, follow signs to Winchester & St Cross. After 2nd r'about on St Cross Rd take 3rd drive on R. Parking in Five Bridges Rd or Park & Ride. Drop off at house for the elderly & disabled only.* **Fri 23, Sun 25 May (1-5). Adm £5, chd free. Home-made teas.** Donation to Christ Church, Winchester. A newly landscaped garden on the edge of Winchester City with beautiful views over the Itchen Valley and St Catherine's Hill. The tiered garden is linked by paved steps and gravel paths, bordered by purple and blue themed planting inc lavender, alliums, geraniums, roses, rosemary and hydrangeas amongst grasses. The lawn leads to a swimming pool, kitchen garden, and children's play area. No wheelchair access to swimming pool area.
& 🐕 ☕ 🔊

72 NEW STANFORD HOUSE
12 St James Lane, Winchester, SO22 4NX. **Mrs Ann Hauser.** *South side of city, leave centre of Winchester by Southgate St. 1st R into St James Ln. Parking 3rd L in Christchurch Rd or over railway bridge on RHS of road.* **Sun 29 June (1-5). Adm £6, chd free. Home-made teas.**
Lovely ¾ acre garden with strong design. Redeveloped since 2003 by architect owners to complement Georgian house, lawned garden, shady woodland and hot garden, with interwoven paths throughout. Long views to the south and east. Koi carp pond, kitchen garden with cutting borders, large greenhouse and Mediterranean outside sitting room. Wide range of hydrangeas, perennials and annuals. Wheelchair access over paved and gravel paths.
& 🐕 ☕

73 4 STANNINGTON CRESCENT
Totton, Southampton, SO40 3QB. **Brian & Julia Graham.** *From M271 at r'about take 2nd exit, continue over causeway then L for Totton. At Totton central r'about take 2nd exit, Salisbury Rd. Stannington Cres 1st L immed after the Memorial car park.* **Sun 18, Sat 24 May (1.30-5). Adm £4, chd free. Home-made teas.**
1930s town house (not open) in 100ft x 50ft plot. A garden of two parts reflecting Brian's passion for nature and Julia's wish for a 'normal' garden. Wildlife area with pond, grasshopper bank and small wild grass meadow. Hedgehog boxes, bat box, numerous bird boxes and bug hotels to encourage wildlife. Mature wisteria, ferns and mixed planting borders.
☕

GROUP OPENING

74 STOCKBRIDGE GARDENS
Stockbridge, SO20 6EX. *9m W of Winchester. On A30, at the junction of A3057 & B3049. All gardens & parking on High St.* **Thur 12, Sun 15 June (1-5). Combined adm £10, chd free.**

FISHMORE HOUSE
Clare & Richard Hills.

THE OLD RECTORY
Robin Colenso & Chrissie Quayle.

SHEPHERDS HOUSE
Kim & Frances Candler.

TROUT COTTAGE
Mrs Sally Milligan.

Four gardens will open this yr in Stockbridge, offering a variety of styles and character. Trout Cottage is a small walled garden, inspiring those with small spaces and little time to achieve tranquillity and beauty. Full of approx 180 plants flowering for almost 10 months of the yr. The Old Rectory has a partially walled garden with formal pond, fountain and planting near the house (not open) with a stream-side walk under trees, newly planted rose garden and a woodland area. Shepherds House on Winton Hill with herbaceous borders, a kitchen garden and a belvedere overlooking the pond. Fishmore House is a 7 yr old garden on a ¾ acre plot. The key elements of design being planting, water and a borrowed landscape. Designed for accessibility incorporating bound gravel paths and no steps. Surrounded by the River Test with seating available to enjoy the views and large, sweeping herbaceous borders. Wheelchair access to all gardens. Gravel path at Shepherds House.
& 🔊

---

75 STREAMSIDE TREES - BONSAI EXPERIENCE
43A Basingbourne Road, Fleet, GU52 6TG. **Julia Griffin.** www.streamsidetrees.co.uk. *Basingbourne Rd, off Reading Rd South (B3013). Opp The Bourne. Roadside parking.* **Sat 24 May (10-2.30). Adm £20, chd free. Pre-booking essential, please visit www.ngs.org.uk for information & booking. Timed slots at 10am & 1pm with guided tour. Tea, coffee & cake inc.**
Something different! Visits start promptly at 10am and 1pm with guided tour around a 140ft garden with stream, azaleas, rhododendrons, camellias, pond and many wildlife habitats. Display of bonsai in development and tree nursery. Then enjoy informal bonsai demonstration from Julia, an enthusiast who also holds 'Create a Bonsai' hands-on experiences. Q&A and refreshments. Trees for sale, payment by cash, PayPal or bank transfer. Assistant dogs only. Please be aware of stream, pond and no fences or gates to road.
& ❀ ☕

77 TERSTAN
Longstock, Stockbridge, SO20 6DW. **Penny Burnfield, paburnfield@gmail.com, www.pennyburnfield.wordpress.com.** *¾ m N of Stockbridge. From Stockbridge (A30) turn N to Longstock at bridge. Garden ¾ m on R.* **Sun 20 Apr, Sun 22 June, Sun 20 July, Sun 7 Sept (2-5). Adm £5, chd free. Home-made teas.** Visits also by arrangement Apr to Sept for groups of 10+.
A garden for all seasons, developed over 55 yrs into a profusely planted, contemporary cottage garden in peaceful surroundings. There is a constantly changing display in pots, starting with tulips and continuing with many unusual plants. Features inc gravel garden, water features, cutting garden, showman's caravan and live music. Wheelchair access with some gravel paths and steps.
& 🐕 ❀ 🚗 ☕ 🔊

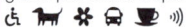

78 THE THATCHED COTTAGE
Church Road, Upper Farringdon, Alton, GU34 3EG. **Mr David & Mrs Cally Horton, 01420 587922, dwhorton@btinternet.com.** *3m S of Alton off A32. From A32, take road to Upper Farringdon. At top of the hill turn L into Church Rd, follow round corner, past Masseys Folly (large red brick building) & we are the 1st house on the R.* **Sun 22 June, Sun 24, Mon 25 Aug (2-5.30). Adm £7, chd free. Home-made teas.**
Visits also by arrangement 1 May

to 1 Sept for groups of 15 to 40. Donation to Cardiac Rehab.
Hidden behind a C16 thatched cottage is an enticing 1½ acre garden. Colourful pots welcome you onto the terrace and four ducks await on the pond. Mature beds burst with cottage garden plants and shrubs. Raised beds are filled with vegetables. Walk through the newly built pergola covered in roses and clematis to a gypsy caravan which sits in a peaceful area of shrub roses and mature specimen trees. Fully accessible by wheelchair after a short gravel drive.

& 🐕 ✻ 🚌 ☕))

79 8 TUCKS CLOSE
Bransgore, Christchurch, BH23 8ND. Bob Sawyer. *5m NE of Christchurch. 3m from Christchurch on A35, turn towards Bransgore at the Cat & Fiddle for 2m past shops & follow yellow signs. From B3347 follow Derritt Ln for 2m then turn R onto Brookside.* **Sat 19, Sun 20 July (11-5). Adm £4, chd free.**
A small garden (12m x 12m) that is full of interest and ideas showing what can be achieved in a small space. The greenhouses contain arisaema, pelargoniums and seasonal plants. Borders have mature trees and shrubs underplanted with perennials, half-hardy plants such as hedychium and annuals add to the overall effect. A gravel area has replaced the lawn making room for a different range of plants. Teas and light lunches available at Macpennys Woodland Garden and Nurseries nearby.

80 TWIN OAKS
13 Oakwood Road, Chandler's Ford, Eastleigh, SO53 1LW. Syd & Sue Hutchinson, 07876 715046, syd@sydh.co.uk, www.facebook.com/twinoaksngs. *Leave M3 J12. Follow signs to Chandlers Ford onto Winchester Rd. After ½m turn R into Hiltingbury Rd. After approx ½m turn L into Oakwood Rd.* **Sun 20, Mon 21 Apr, Sat 17, Sun 18 May, Sat 21, Sun 22 June, Sat 9, Sun 10 Aug (1-5). Adm £5, chd free. Tea, coffee & cake.** Visits also by arrangement 18 Apr to 11 Aug for groups of 10 to 30. 24 hrs notice is required for any changes to booking.
Evolving suburban water garden. Enjoy spring colour from azaleas, rhododendrons and bulbs, then summer colour from perennials, water lilies and tropical plants. A lawn meanders between informal beds and ponds, and bridges lead to a tranquil pergola seating area overlooking a wildlife pond. A rockery is skirted by a stream and a waterfall tumbles into a large lily pond, home to dragonflies. Aviary. Short gravel drive, suitable for mobility scooters and wide tyred wheelchairs leads to step free garden.

& 🐕 ✻ ☕))

81 TYLNEY HALL HOTEL
Ridge Lane, Rotherwick, RG27 9AZ. Elite Hotels, 01256 764881, sales@tylneyhall.com, www.tylneyhall.co.uk. *3m NW of Hook. From M3 J5 via A287 & Newnham, M4 J11 via B3349 & Rotherwick.* **Sun 18 May, Sun 29 June (10-4). Adm £7.50, chd free. Tea, coffee & cake in the Chestnut Suite from 12pm.**
Large garden of 66 acres with extensive woodlands and beautiful vista. Fine avenues of wellingtonias; rhododendrons and azaleas, Italian garden, lakes, large water and rock garden, dry stone walls originally designed with assistance of Gertrude Jekyll. Partial wheelchair access.

& 🐕 ✻ 🚌 🛏 ☕

The Court House

238 HAMPSHIRE

82 WALHAMPTON
Beaulieu Road, Walhampton, Lymington, SO41 5ZG. Walhampton School Trust Ltd. *1m E of Lymington. From Lymington follow signs to Beaulieu (B3054) for 1m & turn R into main entrance at 1st school sign, 200yds after top of hill.* **Sun 4 May (2-6). Adm £6, chd free. Tea, coffee & cake.** Donation to St John's Church, Boldre.
Glorious walks through large C18 landscape garden surrounding magnificent mansion (now a school). Visitors will discover three lakes, serpentine canal, climbable prospect mount, period former banana house and later an orangery, plantsman's glade and Italian terrace by Peto. Drives and colonnade by Mawson, delightful statue of Mercury with his bow and magnificent views to the Isle of Wight. David Hill will give a talk at the Mercury fountain, followed by a guided tour, approx every 70 mins from 2.15pm to about 5.45pm. Wheelchair access with gravel paths and some slopes.

83 WHEATLEY HOUSE
Wheatley Lane, Kingsley, Bordon, GU35 9PA. Susannah Adlington, 01420 23113, adlingtons36@gmail.com. *4m E of Alton, 5m SW of Farnham. Between Binsted & Kingsley. Take A31 to Bentley, follow sign to Bordon. After 2m, R at The Jolly Farmer Pub towards Binsted, 1m L & follow signs to Wheatley.* **Sat 16 Aug (1.30-5.30); Sun 17 Aug (12.30-5). Adm £6, chd free. Home-made teas. Visit website for any changes. Visits also by arrangement for groups of 10 to 30.**
Situated on a rural hilltop with panoramic views over Alice Holt Forest and the South Downs. The owner, being much more of an artist than a plantswoman has had great fun since 1981 creating this 1½ acre garden full of interesting and unusual planting combinations. The sweeping mixed borders and shrubs have spectacular colour throughout the season, particularly in late summer and early autumn. The unusual black, white and red border is very popular with visitors. Plants for sale. Local crafts all in the lovely old barn and a variety of artworks and sculptures for sale in the garden. Wheelchair access with care on lawns, good views of garden and beyond from terrace.

84 WICOR PRIMARY SCHOOL COMMUNITY GARDEN
Portchester, Fareham, PO16 9DL. Louise Moreton, www.wicor.hants.sch.uk. *Halfway between Portsmouth & Fareham on A27. Turn S at Seagull Pub r'about into Cornaway Ln, 1st R into Hatherley Dr. Entrance to school is almost opp. Parking on site, pay at main gate.* **Sun 22 June (12-4). Adm £4, chd free. Home-made teas.**
As shown on BBC Gardeners' World in 2017. Beautiful school gardens tended by pupils, staff and community gardeners. Wander along Darwin's path to see the coastal garden, Jurassic garden, orchard, tropical bed, stumpery, wildlife areas, allotments and apiary, plus one of the few camera obscuras in the south of England. Wheelchair access to all areas over flat ground.

85 WINCHESTER COLLEGE
College Street, Winchester, SO23 9NA. The College, www.instagram.com/winchestercollegeheritage. *Entrance to the College is via the Porters' Lodge on College St, a short walk from Winchester City Centre. There is very limited parking near the College.* **Sat 31 May (11-4). Sun 1 June (11-4), open nearby The Hospital of St Cross. Adm £10, chd free. Tea, coffee & cake in the Warden's Garden.**
The historic gardens of Winchester College inc a traditional college 'quad', a quiet sitting garden for the old College sick house; the tranquil gardens of the College's war memorial, and the Warden's Garden with its herbaceous borders, woodland, and private section of one of the most famous chalk streams in the world.

86 1 WOGSBARNE COTTAGES
Rotherwick, RG27 9BL. Miss S & Mr R Whistler. *2½ m N of Hook. M3 J5, M4 J11, A30 or A33 via B3349.* **Sun 13, Mon 14 July (2-5). Adm £5, chd free. Tea, coffee & cake.**
Small traditional cottage garden with a 'roses around the door' look, much photographed for calendars, jigsaws and magazines. Mixed flower beds and borders. Vegetables grown in abundance. Ornamental pond and alpine garden. Views over open countryside to be enjoyed whilst you take afternoon tea on the lawn. Wheelchair access with some gravel paths.

GROUP OPENING

87 WOODEND GARDENS
Woodend Road, Crow, Ringwood, BH24 3DG. *2½ m to Ringwood. Take the Christchurch Rd (B3347) from Ringwood, after ⅓m turn L onto Moortown Ln (signed Burley), after 1m Woodend Rd is on the L. Last house in road.* **Sat 14, Sun 15 June (11-5). Combined adm £10, chd free. Tea, coffee & cake.**

HOLLYHURST
Mary Reddyhoff.

TROLLS MEAD
Sheila Lister.

Trolls Mead is a 1 acre garden with interest throughout the yr, whether newly planted, in full bloom or left in its natural state with seed heads to create an architectural display or simply for the birds to appreciate. The wooded area and lake is still under construction but all are welcome to explore. The bottom meadow with its mown paths has SSSI status with natural wild flowers inc wild orchids. Hollyhurst is a 2 acre site of mature trees, shrubs and herbaceous perennials, which are generally resistant to deer, has been created on a freely draining acid soil. Ponds and small sculptures augment the vistas.

88 WOODPECKERS CARE HOME
Sway Road, Brockenhurst, SO42 7RX. Chris Marsh. *New Forest. Signed from A337 Lymington to Brockenhurst road. Sway Rd to Brockenhurst centre. L then R past petrol station, then school & Woodpeckers on R.* **Sun 31 Aug (11-5). Adm £5, chd free. Home-made teas.**
Vibrant planting of dahlias, crocosmias and rudbeckias around the residents lounge provides an unusual distraction for both residents and visitors. The courtyard area, small orchard and woodland, all look particularly beautiful in late summer with views through to neighbouring fields of New Forest ponies and deer. Keep a lookout for the disguised bug house, and a wooden chainsaw sculpture.

HAMPSHIRE 239

Fishmore House, Stockbridge Gardens

HEREFORDSHIRE

VOLUNTEERS

County Organiser
Lavinia Sole
07880 550235
lavinia.sole@ngs.org.uk

County Treasurer
Position Vacant

Booklet Coordinator
Chris Meakins
01544 370215
christine.meakins@btinternet.com

Booklet Distribution
Lavinia Sole (As above)

Social Media
Position vacant

Talks
Angela O'Connell
07970 265754
angela.oconnell@icloud.com

Graham O'Connell
07788 239750
graham.oconnell22@gmail.com

Assistant County Organisers
Angela O'Connell
(as above)

Graham O'Connell
(as above)

Penny Usher
01568 611688
pennyusher@btinternet.com

@NGSHerefordshire
@ngsherefordshire

OPENING DATES

All entries subject to change. For latest information check **www.ngs.org.uk**

Extended openings are shown at the beginning of the month.

Map locator numbers are shown to the right of each garden name.

January

Every Thursday from Thursday 23rd
Ivy Croft   14

February

Snowdrop Openings

Every Thursday
Ivy Croft   14

Saturday 15th
Wainfield   33

Sunday 16th
Bury Court Farmhouse   3
Wainfield   33

Friday 21st
◆ The Picton Garden   26

Saturday 22nd
Wainfield   33

Sunday 23rd
Wainfield   33

March

Thursday 6th
Ivy Croft   14

Thursday 13th
◆ The Picton Garden   26

Saturday 15th
◆ Ralph Court Gardens   27

Sunday 16th
Bury Court Farmhouse   3
◆ Ralph Court Gardens   27

Sunday 23rd
Whitfield   36

Monday 24th
◆ Moors Meadow Gardens   20

Wednesday 26th
Ivy Croft   14

Saturday 29th
Coddington Vineyard   5

Sunday 30th
Coddington Vineyard   5

April

Every Wednesday
Ivy Croft   14

Wednesday 2nd
◆ Stockton Bury Gardens   31

Thursday 10th
◆ The Picton Garden   26

Sunday 13th
Lower House Farm   19

Monday 14th
◆ Moors Meadow Gardens   20

Sunday 20th
Bury Court Farmhouse   3

Tuesday 22nd
Aulden Farm   1
Ivy Croft   14

Wednesday 23rd
Aulden Farm   1
Ivy Croft   14

Thursday 24th
Aulden Farm   1
Ivy Croft   14
Lower Hope   18

Saturday 26th
Wainfield   33

Sunday 27th
Wainfield   33

May

Every Wednesday
Ivy Croft   14

Friday 2nd
Coddington Vineyard   5

Sunday 4th
Hillcroft at Dilwyn   13
Lower House Farm   19

Monday 5th
Hillcroft at Dilwyn   13

Thursday 8th
◆ The Picton Garden   26

Friday 16th
◆ Hereford Cathedral Gardens   11

HEREFORDSHIRE

Sunday 18th
Bury Court Farmhouse 3
Eaton Bishop Gardens 6
The Nutshell 22

Monday 19th
◆ Moors Meadow Gardens 20

Tuesday 20th
Lower Hope 18

Sunday 25th
Sheepcote 29
Wainfield 33

Monday 26th
Wainfield 33

Tuesday 27th
Aulden Farm 1
Ivy Croft 14

Wednesday 28th
Aulden Farm 1
Ivy Croft 14

Thursday 29th
Aulden Farm 1
Ivy Croft 14

Saturday 31st
NEW Netherwood Manor 21
The Old Rectory 25

June

Every Wednesday
Ivy Croft 14

Sunday 1st
Brockhampton Cottage 2
Grendon Court 8
NEW Netherwood Manor 21
The Old Rectory 25

Saturday 7th
NEW Netherwood Manor 21
NEW Stone Barn 32

Sunday 8th
Lower House Farm 19
NEW Netherwood Manor 21
NEW Stone Barn 32

Wednesday 11th
◆ The Picton Garden 26

Saturday 14th
Sheepcote 29
NEW Stone Barn 32

Sunday 15th
Bury Court Farmhouse 3
NEW Stone Barn 32
Whitfield 36

Monday 16th
◆ Moors Meadow Gardens 20

Friday 20th
NEW Netherwood Manor 21

Saturday 21st
NEW Netherwood Manor 21

Sunday 22nd
NEW Netherwood Manor 21

Saturday 28th
The Laskett Gardens 16
Wainfield 33
Well House 34

Sunday 29th
Wainfield 33
Well House 34

July

Every Wednesday
Ivy Croft 14

Saturday 5th
NEW Four Winds 7
NEW Greytree Cottage 9
The Laskett Gardens 16
NEW The Old House 24

Sunday 6th
NEW Four Winds 7
NEW Greytree Cottage 9
NEW The Old House 24

Wednesday 9th
◆ The Picton Garden 26

Saturday 12th
◆ Ralph Court Gardens 27

Sunday 13th
◆ Ralph Court Gardens 27

Monday 14th
◆ Moors Meadow Gardens 20

Friday 18th
Coddington Vineyard 5

Sunday 20th
Bury Court Farmhouse 3

Thursday 24th
Kentchurch Court 15

Friday 25th
Kentchurch Court 15

Tuesday 29th
Lower Hope 18

August

Every Wednesday
Ivy Croft 14

Monday 4th
◆ Moors Meadow Gardens 20

Thursday 14th
◆ The Picton Garden 26

Friday 15th
Aulden Farm 1
Ivy Croft 14

Saturday 16th
Aulden Farm 1
Ivy Croft 14

Sunday 17th
Bury Court Farmhouse 3

Saturday 23rd
NEW Ledbury Flower Farmer 17

Sunday 24th
NEW Ledbury Flower Farmer 17

September

Every Wednesday
Ivy Croft 14

Saturday 6th
NEW Herefordshire Growing Point 12

Sunday 7th
NEW Herefordshire Growing Point 12

Sunday 14th
Brockhampton Cottage 2
Bury Court Farmhouse 3
Grendon Court 8

Wednesday 17th
◆ The Picton Garden 26

Saturday 20th
Ivy Croft 14

Sunday 21st
Ivy Croft 14

Saturday 27th
◆ Ralph Court Gardens 27

Sunday 28th
◆ Ralph Court Gardens 27

October

Every Wednesday to Wednesday 8th
Ivy Croft 14

Friday 3rd
Coddington Vineyard 5

Saturday 4th
Coddington Vineyard 5

Sunday 5th
Bury Court Farmhouse 3

Tuesday 14th
◆ The Picton Garden 26

November

Saturday 15th
◆ Ralph Court Gardens 27

Sunday 16th
◆ Ralph Court Gardens 27

February 2026

Sunday 15th
Bury Court Farmhouse 3

By Arrangement

Arrange a personalised garden visit with your club, or group of friends, on a date to suit you. See individual garden entries for full details.

Aulden Farm 1
Bury Court Farmhouse 3
Castle Moat House 4
Coddington Vineyard 5
NEW Hares Orchard 10
Ivy Croft 14
Lower House Farm 19
NEW Old Cottage 23
NEW The Old House 24
The Old Rectory 25
Revilo 28
Shuttifield Cottage 30
NEW Stone Barn 32
Weston Hall 35

Greytree Cottage

THE GARDENS

1 AULDEN FARM
Aulden, Leominster, HR6 0JT. Alun & Jill Whitehead, 01568 720129, web@auldenfarm.co.uk, www.auldenfarm.co.uk. *4m SW of Leominster. From Leominster take Ivington/Upper Hill Rd, ¾m after Ivington church turn R signed Aulden. From A4110 signed Ivington, take 2nd R signed Aulden.* **Tue 22, Wed 23, Thur 24 Apr, Tue 27, Wed 28, Thur 29 May, Fri 15, Sat 16 Aug (11-5). Adm £5, chd free. Home-made teas. Open nearby Ivy Croft. Home-made ice cream also available. Visits also by arrangement 1 Apr to 29 Aug.**
Informal country garden, thankfully never at its Sunday best. Three acres planted with wildlife in mind. Emphasis on structure and form, with a hint of quirkiness, a garden to explore with eclectic planting. Irises thrive around a natural pond, shady beds and open borders, seats abound, feels mature but ever evolving. Our own ice cream and home-burnt cakes available: Lemon Chisel a specialty.

2 BROCKHAMPTON COTTAGE
Brockhampton, HR1 4TQ. Peter Clay & Catherine Connolly. *8m SW of Hereford. 5m N of Ross-on-Wye on B4224. In Brockhampton take road signed to B Court nursing home, pass N Home after ¾m, go down hill & turn L. Car park 500yds downhill on L in orchard.* **Sun 1 June, Sun 14 Sept (11-4). Adm £5, chd free. Open nearby Grendon Court. Picnics welcome by the lake.**
Created from scratch in 1999 by the owner and Tom Stuart-Smith, this beautiful hilltop garden looks south and west over unspoilt countryside. Enjoy a woodland garden, five acre wildflower meadow, a Perry pear orchard and in valley below: lake, stream and arboretum. Extensive borders are planted with drifts of perennials in the modern romantic style. Steep walk from car park. Teas at Grendon Court. Visit Grendon Court (11-4) after your visit to us. This garden is proud to have provided plants for the National Garden Scheme's Show Garden at Chelsea Flower Show 2024.

3 BURY COURT FARMHOUSE
Ford Street, Wigmore, Leominster, HR6 9UP. Margaret & Les Barclay, 01568 770618, l.barclay@zoho.com. *10m from Leominster, 10m from Knighton, 8m from Ludlow. On A4110 from Leominster, at Wigmore turn R just after shop & garage. Garden is on the R. Park on road (disabled in courtyard).* **Sun 16 Feb, Sun 16 Mar, Sun 20 Apr, Sun 18 May, Sun 15 June, Sun 20 July, Sun 17 Aug, Sun 14 Sept, Sun 5 Oct (2-5). Adm £5, chd free. Home-made teas. Gluten and dairy free available. 2026: Sun 15 Feb. Visits also by arrangement 12 Feb to 31 Oct for groups of up to 16.**
¾ acre garden surrounds the 1820's stone farmhouse (not open). The courtyard contains a pond, mixed borders, fruit trees and shrubs, with steps up to a terrace which leads to lawn and vegetable plot. The main garden (semi-walled) is on two levels with mixed borders, greenhouse, pond, mini-orchard, many spring flowers, and wildlife areas. Year-round colour. Mostly accessible for wheelchairs by arrangement.

4 CASTLE MOAT HOUSE
Dilwyn, Hereford, HR4 8HZ. Mr T & Mrs M J Voogd, 07717781662, mjvoogd@outlook.com. *6m W of Leominster. On A44, take exit A4112 to Dilwyn. Garden by the village green.* **Visits by arrangement 1 Mar to 1 Nov for groups of 10 to 30. Tea, coffee & cake. Discuss refreshments when booking.**
A two acre plot consisting of a more formal cottage garden that wraps around the house. The remaining area is a tranquil wild garden with paths to a Medieval Castle Motte, part filled Moat and Medieval Fish and Fowl Ponds. A haven for wildlife and people alike. The garden contains some steep banks and deep water, with limited access to Motte, Moat and Ponds.

5 CODDINGTON VINEYARD
Coddington vineyard, Coddington, HR8 1JJ. Sharon & Peter Maiden, 01531 641817, sgmaiden@yahoo.co.uk, www.coddingtonvineyard.co.uk. *4m NE of Ledbury. From Ledbury to Malvern A449, follow brown signs to Coddington Vineyard HR81JJ.* **Sat 29, Sun 30 Mar, Fri 2 May (11-4).**
Adm £5, chd free. Home-made teas. Evening opening Fri 18 July (6-9). Adm £5. Wine. Fri 3, Sat 4 Oct (11-4). Adm £5, chd free. Home-made teas. Home-made ice cream, cakes & apple juice also available. Visits also by arrangement 2 Feb to 19 Oct for groups of 10+.
Five acres inc two acre vineyard, listed farmhouse, and cider mill. Garden with terraces, wildflower meadow, woodland with massed spring bulbs, large pond with stream garden masses of primula and Hellebores and snowdrops, *Hamamelis and Parottia*. Azaleas followed by roses and perennials. Developing year on year, planting for autumn colour Vineyard with three varieties of grapes. In spring, the gardens are a mass of bulbs. Lots to see all year.

GROUP OPENING

6 EATON BISHOP GARDENS
Martins Croft, Eaton Bishop, HR2 9QD. Dr Tim Coleman. *6m SW of Hereford. Take A465 SW from Hereford. After 3m turn R onto B4349. After 2½m continue onto B4352 for 1m and turn R towards Eaton Bishop. Parking & WC facilities at the Village Hall.* **Sun 18 May (11-4.30). Combined adm £10, chd free. Home-made teas at The White House.**

THE CARPENTERS
Christine Morris.

NEW THE MANOR HOUSE
Mr & Mrs David Stanton.

MARTINS CROFT
Tim & Valerie Coleman.

WHITE HOUSE
Julian and Tanya Hudson.

A delightful group of gardens with much to see. Martins Croft has an area of between ¼ and ⅓ acre and faces south. It is a well planted, semi formal garden. The White House offers three acres of lawns, flower beds and managed woodland with the house located centrally in the garden. The Carpenters is a two acre garden with 25 planted areas inc herbaceous and mixed borders, ditch border, shrubberies, wildlife areas, many trees and pond. Amateur gardener never satisfied, always changing and developing new and existing areas.

Mainly flat with no significant slopes but all paths grass. The Manor House is a walled cottage garden of about ⅓ acre on two levels. There are several mature shrubs and trees, inc a large magnolia. Peonies, alliums, tulips and roses feature strongly in the garden. Part of the lower garden is currently being developed by the owner. Tickets sold at The Manor House. Majority of the gardens are wheelchair accessible although there are some steps.

7 NEW FOUR WINDS
Vowchurch, Hereford, HR2 0RL. Ms Kay Webb. *Going S A465: R turn at Locks Garage (B4348). Kingstone is 4m & turn R at x-roads towards Vowchurch Common (sign dead-end). Hay-on-Wye: E B4348 towards Peterchurch. After 2m, turn L at x-roads.* **Sat 5, Sun 6 July (12-4.30). Combined adm with The Old House £7.50, chd free. Tea, coffee & cake.**
Plantswoman's garden with broad selection of plants. Country-style garden with large herbaceous borders, white border, wildflower meadow, and small vegetable plot. Paddock with fruit cage, unusual apple varieties, newly planted native trees and shrubs, and wildlife pond, plus attractive open-propagation beds for owner's micro-nursery. Plants for sale as part of nursery business. Regret, wheelchair access at The Old House only.

8 GRENDON COURT
Upton Bishop, Ross-on-Wye, HR9 7QP. Mark & Kate Edwards. *3m NE of Ross-on-Wye. M50 J3. Hereford B4224 Moody Cow Pub, 1m open gate on R. From Ross. A40, B449, Xrds R Upton Bishop. 100yds on L by cream cottage.* **Sun 1 June, Sun 14 Sept (11-4). Adm £5, chd free. Home-made teas. Open nearby Brockhampton Cottage. Picnics welcome in car park field.**
A contemporary garden designed by Tom Stuart-Smith. Planted on two levels, a clever collection of mass-planted perennials and grasses of different heights, textures and colour give all year interest. The upper walled garden with a sea of flowering grasses makes a highlight. Wheelchair access possible but some gravel.

9 NEW GREYTREE COTTAGE
Brampton Road, Greytree, Ross-on-Wye, HR9 7HY. Elaine & Simon Leney. *N outskirts of Ross on Wye. From town centre take Greytree Rd into Homs Rd into Greytree. Please park here or in 2nd Ave. Walk to entrance in 1st Ave, HR9 7HX (no parking here). What3words app: enhances.impresses.various.* **Sat 5, Sun 6 July (10-4). Adm £5, chd free. Tea, coffee & cake.**
¾ acre garden with views to the Black Mountains. Gardened with wildlife and nature in mind, inc large pond, wildlife habitats and large bug hotel. Over 120 native trees planted in formal and informal groupings. Traditional sunny and shady herbaceous and prairie borders alongside small container vegetable garden. Large oak gazebo and deck adjacent to pond where refreshments will be served.

10 NEW HARES ORCHARD
Moreton Eye, Leominster, HR6 0DP. Sue Evans & Guy Poulton, 01568 614501, s.evans.gp@btinternet.com. *A49 Ashton turn to Moreton Eye, Luston. Garden is 1m on L. What3words app: betrayed.trapdoor.requested.* **Visits by arrangement May & June for groups of 10 to 20. Adm inc light refreshments. Discuss refreshments when booking. Adm £10, chd free.**
Three acre wildflower meadow with many plant species inc rare orchids. Owner led tour with plant identification. Old tennis court converted to gravel garden with raised vegetable beds and water feature. Explore the large greenhouse and view remnant of Stourport/Leominster canal. Flower beds and pond with candelabra primula and bog plants.

11 ♦ HEREFORD CATHEDRAL GARDENS
Hereford, HR1 2NG. Dean of Hereford Cathedral, 01432 374251, events@herefordcathedral.org, www.herefordcathedral.org/events. *Centre of Hereford, just off the cathedral close. The ticket desk is in the cathedral car park, please approach the desk to sign in with staff.* **For NGS: Fri 16 May (10-3.30). Adm £8, chd free.** For other opening times and information, please phone, email or visit garden website.
Explore the Chapter House garden, Cloister garden, the Canon's garden with plants with ecclesiastical connections and roses, the private Dean's garden with fine trees and an outdoor chapel. These are open session where visitors can explore the gardens at their own pace, with gardeners and guides based within the gardens to share the history of the site. Partial wheelchair access. For more information please visit website or contact the team in advance: events@herefordcathedral.org.

12 NEW HEREFORDSHIRE GROWING POINT
Trenchard Avenue, Credenhill, Hereford, HR4 7DX. Herefordshire Growing Point, www.growingpoint.org.uk. *Look out for signs to Headway Hereford; Our garden is around the back. Volunteers will be here to guide you. Parking at the front and rear of Headway House.* **Sat 6, Sun 7 Sept (10-4). Adm £5, chd free. Tea, coffee & cake.**
A purposefully designed therapy garden, for those living with mental and physical challenges to gain the benefits of therapeutic horticulture. A fully accessible garden featuring a range of mixed plantings, to facilitate activities to promote mental wellbeing. We are excited to display sculptures made by our gardeners under the tuition of potter Miles Johnson. The garden has a sensory area, vegetable garden and a small wildflower area. There is also an outdoor teaching area. Fully wheelchair accessible.

129,032 people were able to access guidance on what to expect when a person is dying through the National Garden Scheme's support for Hospice UK this year.

246 HEREFORDSHIRE

13 HILLCROFT AT DILWYN
Dilwyn, Hereford, HR4 8JF.
Rhonda Wood & Steven Brown.
6m W of Leominster on A44. Turn R opp turning for Dilwyn village. Then immed take L fork and follow lane for 0.3m. Parking in field or farm yard 250yds away. Follow yellow signs. **Sun 4, Mon 5 May (10-4). Adm £5, chd free. Tea, coffee & cake.**
The garden is approximately 1.3 acres with an organic vegetable plot and polytunnel. Main garden has lawn with perennial beds either side containing small shrubs and trees. Paths reveal a wooded area to the rear to containing magnolias, camellias, rhododendrons, eucalyptus and other large trees. Informal and relaxed planting. Visit the on site pottery studio - Steven Brown Ceramics.

14 IVY CROFT
Ivington Green, Leominster,
HR6 0JN. Roger Norman,
01568 720344,
ivycroft@homecall.co.uk,
www.ivycroftgarden.co.uk. 3m SW of Leominster. From Leominster take Ryelands Rd to Ivington. Turn R at church, garden ¾m on R. From A4110 signed Ivington, garden 1¾m on L. **Every Thur 23 Jan to 6 Mar (10-4). Every Wed 26 Mar to 8 Oct (10-4). Tue 22, Wed 23, Thur 24 Apr (11-4). Tue 27, Wed 28, Thur 29 May (11-4). Fri 15, Sat 16 Aug (11-4). Also open Aulden Farm. Sat 20, Sun 21 Sept (11-4). Adm £5, chd free. Home-made teas.**
2026: Every Thur 22 Jan to 5 Mar. Visits also by arrangement.
Now over 25 years old, the garden shows signs of maturity, inc some surprising trees. A very wide range of plants is displayed, blending with countryside and providing habitat for wildlife. The cottage is surrounded by borders, snowdrops, raised beds, trained pear trees and containers giving all year interest. Paths lead to the wider garden inc mixed borders, vegetables framed with espalier apples. Partial wheelchair access.

15 KENTCHURCH COURT
Kentchurch, HR2 0DB.
Mr J Lucas-Scudamore,
www.kentchurchcourt.co.uk.
12m SW of Hereford. From Hereford A465 towards Abergavanny, at Pontrilas turn L signed Kentchurch. After 2m fork L, after Bridge Inn. Garden opp church. **Thur 24 July (11-4). Tea, coffee & cake. Fri 25 July (11-4). Adm £7.50, chd free. Refreshments also at The Bridge Inn, Kentchurch.**
Kentchurch Court is situated close to the Welsh border. Formal garden and traditional vegetable garden redesigned with colour, scent and easy access. Walled garden and herbaceous borders, rhododendrons and wildflower walk. Extensive collection of mature trees and shrubs. Stream with habitat for spawning trout and views into deer park at the heart of the estate. First opened for the NGS in 1927. Wheelchair access over some slopes and shallow gravel.

16 THE LASKETT GARDENS
Laskett Lane, Much Birch,
HR2 8HZ. Perennial,
www.thelaskett.org.uk. Approx 7m from Hereford; 7m from Ross. On A49, midway between Ross-on-Wye & Hereford, turn into Laskett Ln towards Hoarwithy. The drive is approx 350yds on L. **Sat 28 June, Sat 5 July (10.30-4.30). Adm £12, chd free. Tea, coffee & cake.**
The Laskett gardens, created by Sir Roy Strong and Julia Trevelyan Oman, is a living masterpiece, with every flower and sculpture reflecting their love and creativity. In 2021, Sir Roy generously gifted The Laskett to the Perennial charity, supporting horticultural workers with proceeds from visits, purchases, and donations. The garden's uneven surfaces, grassed areas, narrow paths and gravel walkways make many areas unsuitable for wheelchair access.

17 NEW LEDBURY FLOWER FARMER
Gloucester Road, Ledbury,
HR8 2JE. Rozanne Delamore,
07515 773742, rozanne@
theledburyflowerfarmer.co.uk,
www.theledburyflowerfarmer.co.uk.
1m from Ledbury. What3words app: paddocks.bother.blossom. **Sat 23, Sun 24 Aug (11-4). Adm £5, chd free. Tea, coffee & cake.**
A working flower farm specialising in sustainable and seasonal flowers for weddings, funerals, gift bouquets and floral workshops. Come and explore the 450m of outdoor flower farm beds plus 70m of beds undercover in polytunnels. You can see the greenhouses, potting shed and floral studio for a fully immersive and behind the scenes tour. There is also a large garden and tree area to explore. Flowers will be available to purchase. The garden and tree area is quite level on grass. The flower farm has paths wide enough for wheelchairs between the beds but there are some slopes.

18 LOWER HOPE
Lower Hope Estate,
Ullingswick, Hereford,
HR1 3JF. Mrs Sylvia Richards,
www.lowerhopegardens.co.uk. 5m S of Bromyard. A465 N from Hereford, after 6m turn L at Burley Gate onto A417 towards Leominster. After approx 2m take 3rd R to Lower Hope. After ½m garden on L. Disabled parking available. **Thur 24 Apr, Tue 20 May, Tue 29 July (2-5). Adm £7.50, chd £2. Tea, coffee & cake.**
Outstanding five acre garden with wonderful seasonal variations. Impeccable lawns with herbaceous borders, rose gardens, white garden, Mediterranean, Italian and Japanese gardens. Natural streams, man-made waterfalls, bog gardens. Woodland with azaleas and rhododendrons with lime avenue to lake with wildflowers and bulbs. Glasshouses with exotic plants and breeding butterflies. Tickets bought on the gate will be cash only. Wheelchair access to most areas.

19 LOWER HOUSE FARM
Vine Lane, Sutton, Tenbury
Wells, WR15 8RL. Mrs Anne
Durston Smith, 07891 928412,
adskyre@outlook.com,
www.kyre-equestrian.co.uk. 3m SE of Tenbury Wells; 8m NW of Bromyard. From Tenbury take A4214 to Bromyard. After approx 3m turn R into Vine Ln, then R fork to Lower House Farm. **Sun 13 Apr, Sun 4 May, Sun 8 June (11-4). Adm £5, chd free. Home-made teas.** Visits also by arrangement Apr to Sept for groups of 12+.
Award-winning country garden surrounding C16 farmhouse (not open) on working farm. Herbaceous borders, roses, box-parterre, productive kitchen and cutting garden, spring garden, ha-ha allowing wonderful views. Wildlife pond. Walkers and dogs can enjoy numerous footpaths across the farm land. There is spectacular autumn colour and dahlias. Home to Kyre Equestrian Centre with access to safe rides and riding events.

HEREFORDSHIRE

20 ◆ MOORS MEADOW GARDENS
Collington, Bromyard, HR7 4LZ. Ros Bissell, 01885 410318, moorsmeadow@hotmail.co.uk, www.moorsmeadow.co.uk. *4m N of Bromyard, on B4214. ½m up lane follow yellow arrows.* **For NGS: Mon 24 Mar, Mon 14 Apr, Mon 19 May, Mon 16 June, Mon 14 July, Mon 4 Aug (10-5). Adm £8, chd £2.** For other opening times and information, please phone, email or visit garden website.

Multi award winning, inspirational seven acre organic hillside garden with a vast amount of species, many rarely seen; emphasis on working with nature, a wildlife haven. Intriguing features and sculptures, a delight for the garden novice as well as the serious plantsman. Wander through fernery, grass garden, extensive shrubberies, herbaceous beds, meadow, dingle, pools and kitchen garden. Huge range of unusual and rarely seen plants from around the world. Unique home-crafted sculptures.

21 NEW NETHERWOOD MANOR
Stoke Bliss, Tenbury Wells, WR15 8RT. Earl & Countess of Darnley, 01885 410321, bookings@netherwoodestate.co.uk, www.instagram.com/netherwoodestate. *5m N of Bromyard. ½ way between Bromyard & Tenbury Wells on B4214. Signed from road. What3words app: incisions.acrobats.dirt.* **Sat 31 May, Sun 1, Sat 7, Sun 8, Fri 20, Sat 21, Sun 22 June (10-4). Adm £8, chd free. Light refreshments.**

Well established three acre garden centred on medieval dovecote, with historic parkland backdrop. Several distinct areas, each with own interest, inc walled garden with herbaceous borders, 'wilderness' garden, gravel garden and ponds (unfenced). Wide variety of unusual shrubs and trees. Children and dogs on leads very welcome. John Piper art exhibition also present. Excellent restaurant only a mile from the garden recommended for lunch & dinner www.nativerestaurant.co.uk

Four Winds

22 THE NUTSHELL
Goodrich, Ross-on-Wye,
HR9 6HG. Louise Short. *The garden is halfway between Ross on Wye & Monmouth, close to the A40 & the Cross Keys pub.* **Sun 18 May (9-3.30). Adm £5, chd free. Light refreshments. We will be offering bacon rolls before midday. A selection of home-made cakes, tea and coffee is available all day.**
The Nutshell is a cottage garden in approx ½ an acre, created from scratch over the last 25 years. The garden is made up of different areas separated by herbaceous borders and rose arches. There is a lovely selection of plants used inc many peonies and an extensive collection of hostas. The owner has a keen interest in propagation with two polytunnels of plants available to purchase.

23 NEW OLD COTTAGE
Bredenbury, Bromyard, HR7 4TG.
Sue Etherington & Kieran Farrell,
07985 932472, sue.etherington@talktalk.net. *4m W of Bromyard. From Bromyard follow A44 to Leominster. In Bredenbury take R turn signed Edwin Ralph. Continue ⅔m. Turn L down track. Keep L and follow private lane to the bottom.* **Visits by arrangement May to Sept for groups of 8 to 30. Adm £5, chd free. Home-made teas.**
This ⅓ acre tranquil garden sits on a gentle slope surrounded by farmland. Navigated by gravel paths and steps it comprises of herbaceous borders, a summerhouse overlooking a wildlife pond, a small orchard, a pergola, cutting garden, fruit bed, and fernery.

24 NEW THE OLD HOUSE
Vowchurch, Hereford, HR2 0RB.
Mr & Mrs K Waistell,
07733 811284,
kipcarwaistell@hotmail.com.
Behind Vowchurch Parish Church. Pass Vowchurch church on L & cross the bridge. Parking in field on L. Entrance 100yds after bridge. Walk back over bridge to enter churchyard. Cross over to gap in hedge. **Sat 5, Sun 6 July (12-4.30). Combined adm with Four Winds £7.50, chd free. Visits also by arrangement 15 May to 31 July for groups of up to 10.**
Medium-sized riverside garden of a Grade II listed C15 timber-framed house, with a variety of trees, shrubs and borders, and vintage cars to see too. Visit the adjoining unusual parish church, with an exhibition relating to Alice in Wonderland- a former

The Picton Garden

vicar was Lewis Carroll's brother. Teas available at Four Winds garden. Wheelchair access via footpath and drive.

&. ☕ 🪑

25 THE OLD RECTORY
Thruxton, Hereford, HR2 9AX. Mr & Mrs Andrew Hallett, 01981 570401, judy.hallett@gmail.com. *6m SW of Hereford. A465 to Allensmore. At Shell petrol stn take B4348 towards Hay-on-Wye. After 1½m turn L towards Abbey Dore and Cockyard. Turn L opp the church and follow track to car park.* **Sat 31 May, Sun 1 June (11-5). Adm £5, chd free. Tea, coffee & cake. Home-made cake, using produce from the garden.** Visits also by arrangement 16 May to 30 June for groups of 14+. Min charge £70.
Constantly changing plantsman's garden stocked with unusual perennials and shrubs, and Cedric Morris Iris. Woodland borders, gazebo, vegetable parterre and glasshouse. Mown paths meander through rare specimen trees and shrubs to the wildlife pond. This four acre garden, with breathtaking views over Herefordshire countryside has been created since 2007. Many places to sit. Most plants labelled. Wheelchair access over mainly level with some gravel paths.

&. ✽ 🚗 ☕ 🪑))

26 ◆ THE PICTON GARDEN
Old Court Nurseries, Walwyn Road, Colwall, WR13 6QE. Paul, Meriel & Helen Picton, 01684 540416, info@oldcourtnurseries.co.uk, www.autumnasters.co.uk. *3m W of Malvern. On B4218 (Walwyn Rd) N of Colwall Stone. Turn off A449 from Ledbury or Malvern onto the B4218 for Colwall.* **For NGS: Fri 21 Feb, Thur 13 Mar (11-4); Thur 10 Apr, Thur 8 May, Wed 11 June, Wed 9 July, Thur 14 Aug, Wed 17 Sept, Tue 14 Oct (11-5). Adm £5, chd free.** For other opening times and information, please phone, email or visit garden website. Donation to Plant Heritage.
1½ acres west of Malvern Hills. Bulbs and a multitude of woodland plants in spring. Interesting perennials and shrubs in August. In late September and early October colourful borders display the National Plant Collection of Michaelmas daisies, backed by autumn colouring trees and shrubs. Many unusual plants to be seen, inc more than 100 different ferns and over 300 varieties of snowdrop.

🐕 ✽ NPC))

27 ◆ RALPH COURT GARDENS
Edwyn Ralph, Bromyard, Hereford, HR7 4LU. Mr & Mrs Morgan, 01885 483225, ralphcourtgardens@aol.com, www.ralphcourtgardens.co.uk. *1m from Bromyard. From Bromyard follow the Tenbury road for approx 1m. On entering the village of Edwyn Ralph take 1st turning on R towards the church.* **For NGS: Sat 15, Sun 16 Mar, Sat 12, Sun 13 July, Sat 27, Sun 28 Sept, Sat 15, Sun 16 Nov (10-4). Adm £15, chd £10. Light refreshments.** For other opening times and information, please phone, email or visit garden website.
All tickets must be purchased through the garden website or at the gate. 14 amazing gardens set in the grounds of a gothic rectory. A family orientated garden with a twist, incorporating an Italian Piazza, an African Jungle, Dragon Pool, Alice in Wonderland and the elves in their conifer forest and our new section 'The Monet Garden'. These are just a few of the themes within this stunning garden. Overlooking the Malvern Hills 120 seater Licensed Restaurant. Offering a good selection of daily specials, delicious Sunday roasts, afternoon tea and our scrumptious homemade cakes. All areas ramped for wheelchair and pushchair access.

&. ✽ 🚗 ☕

28 REVILO
Wellington, Hereford, HR4 8AZ. Mrs Shirley Edgar, 01432 830189, shirleyskinner@btinternet.com. *6m N of Hereford. On A49 from Hereford turn L into Wellington village, pass church on R. After barn on L, turn L up driveway in front of The Harbour, to furthest bungalow.* **Visits by arrangement 14 Apr to 14 Sept for groups of 10 to 25. Adm £5, chd free. Home-made teas.**
A ⅓ acre flower arranger's garden, surrounding a bungalow. Features inc mixed borders, meadow and woodland areas. Discover the scented garden, late summer bed, graveled herb garden and kitchen garden. Wheelchair access to all central areas of the garden.

&. 🐕 ✽ ☕))

29 SHEEPCOTE
Putley, Ledbury, HR8 2RD. Tim & Julie Beaumont. *5m W of Ledbury. Garden is off the A438 Hereford to Ledbury Rd. Passenger drop off; parking 200 yds.* **Sun 25 May, Sat 14 June (1.30-5). Adm £5, chd free. Light refreshments.**
A ⅓ acre garden taken in hand from 2011 retaining many quality plants, shrubs and trees from earlier gardeners. Topiary holly, box, hawthorn, privet and yew formalise the varied plantings around the croquet lawn and gravel garden. Discover beds with heathers, azaleas, lavender surrounded by herbaceous perennials and bulbs. There are also small ponds and a kitchen garden with raised beds to explore. Art exhibition by Anya Beaumont will be taking place on the day. Anya is a visual artist working across mediums. The physical environment and its influence have been a significant factor in her practice. If any pieces are sold, a percentage will be given as a donation to the National Garden Scheme.

✽ ☕))

30 SHUTTIFIELD COTTAGE
Birchwood, Storridge, Malvern, WR13 5HA. Mr & Mrs David Judge, 01886 884243, judge.shutti@btinternet.com. *15m E of Hereford. Turn L off A4103 at Storridge opp the church to Birchwood. After 1¼m L down tarmac drive signposted to Shuttifield Cottage (150 yards).* **Visits by arrangement 1 Apr to 29 Sept for groups of 10 to 60. Adm £5, chd free. Visitors may bring picnics.**
Superb position and views. Unexpected three acre plantsman's garden, extensive herbaceous borders, many unusual trees, shrubs, perennials, colour themed for all year interest. Anemones, magnolias, bluebells, rhododendrons, azaleas and camelias in the spring. Large old rose garden with many spectacular climbers. Small deer park, and walks in a 20 acre wood containing wildlife ponds and wildflowers.

☕ 🪑

31 ◆ STOCKTON BURY GARDENS
Kimbolton, HR6 0HA. Raymond G Treasure, 07880 712649, twstocktonbury@outlook.com, www.stocktonbury.co.uk. *2m NE of Leominster. From Leominster to Ludlow on A49 turn R onto A4112. Gardens 300yds on R.* **For NGS: Wed 2 Apr (11-4.30). Adm £9, chd £5. Home-made teas in Tithe Barn Café. We offer home-made cakes, coffees, teas, soft drinks, wine, cider and beer. There is also a full menu of seasonal hot and cold lunches available. For other opening times and information, please phone, email or visit garden website.**
Superb, sheltered four acre garden with colour and interest from April until the end of September. Extensive collection of plants, many rare and unusual set amongst Medieval buildings. Features inc pigeon house, tithe barn, grotto, cider press, auricula theatre, Roman hoard, pools, secret garden, garden museum and rill, all surrounded by countryside. Partial wheelchair access. An able bodied companion is advisable for wheelchair users.

&♿ ❋ 🚗 ☕ 🔊

32 NEW STONE BARN
Church Lane, Hampton Bishop, Hereford, HR1 4JY. Mrs Mary-Ann Robinson & Mr Colin Campbell, 01432 870436. *From Hereford take B4224 towards Fownhope for 3m. After Bunch of Carrotts pub take 3rd turning on L. Follow signs to garden and parking.* **Sat 7, Sun 8 June (2-5). Home-made teas. Evening opening Sat 14, Sun 15 June (5-8). Wine. Adm £5, chd free. Visits also by arrangement May to Sept for groups of 8+.**
Developed over 30 years from a farm yard and field with lovely views. Different sections with interesting shrubs, two ponds, a vegetable parterre and flower garden room. A pagoda and orchard with *Magnolia grandiflora, Davidia involucrata* and several varieties of *Cornus*. Mainly flat lawns and gravel paths. Parking in adjacent field where dogs can be walked.

&♿ 🐕 ❋ ☕

33 WAINFIELD
Peterstow, Ross-on-Wye, HR9 6LJ. Nick & Sue Helme. *From the A49 between Ross-on-Wye & Hereford. Take the B4521 to Skenfrith/ Abergavenny. Wainfield is 50yds on R.* **Sat 15, Sun 16, Sat 22, Sun 23 Feb, Sat 26, Sun 27 Apr, Sun 25, Mon 26 May, Sat 28, Sun 29 June (10-4). Adm £5, chd free. Home-made teas.**
Three acre informal, wildlife garden inc rose garden, fruit trees, climbing roses and clematis. Delightful pond with waterfall. Honeysuckle, snowdrops and aconites a plenty. In spring, tulips, bluebells, crocuses and grasses followed by lush summer planting. Fruit walk with naturalised cowslips all set in an open area of interesting, unusual mature trees and sculptures. Wheelchair access via grass and gravel paths.

&♿ ❋ ☕ 🔊

34 WELL HOUSE
Garway Hill, Hereford, HR2 8RT. Mrs Betty Lovering. *12m SW Hereford. A465 from Hereford: turn L at Pontrilas onto B4347. Turn 1st R & immed L signed Orcop & Garway Hill. 3m to Bagwyllydiart then follow signs.* **Sat 28, Sun 29 June (10.30-4.30). Adm £5, chd free. Light refreshments.**
Hillside garden, approx an acre with views over Orcop on Garway Hill. This garden has been created from scratch since 1998 on a steep bank with steps and narrow paths and is ongoing with nature in mind. Herbaceous beds, mature trees, shrubs, wide collection of acers and unusual plants, veg garden, polytunnel, bog garden seating areas, on a working small holding with Dutch Spotted Sheep. Lovely views lots of seating. Secret areas.

❋ ☕

35 WESTON HALL
Weston-under-Penyard, Ross-on-Wye, HR9 7NS. Mr P Aldrich-Blake, 01989 562597, aldrichblake@btinternet.com. *1m E of Ross-on-Wye. On A40 towards Gloucester.* **Visits by arrangement Apr to Sept for groups of 5 to 30. Adm £6, chd free. Light refreshments.**
Six acres surrounding Elizabethan house (not open). Large walled garden with herbaceous borders, vegetables and fruit, overlooked by Millennium folly. Lawns and mature and recently planted trees and shrubs, with many unusual varieties. Orchard, ornamental ponds and lake. Four generations in the family, but still evolving year on year. Wheelchair access to walled garden only.

&♿ ☕

36 WHITFIELD
Wormbridge, HR2 9BA. Mr & Mrs Edward Clive, www.whitfield-hereford.com/gardens. *8m SW of Hereford. The entrance gates are off the A465, Hereford to Abergavenny road, ½m N of Wormbridge. Postcode for SatNav HR2 9DG.* **Sun 23 Mar, Sun 15 June (2-5). Adm £5.50, chd free. Tea, coffee & cake.**
The Whitfield Estate has been a supporter of the National Gardens Scheme for over 50 years with extensive parkland and woodland walks. Our woodland has a grove of coastal redwood trees planted in 1851. Wildflowers, ponds, walled garden, many flowering magnolias (species and hybrids). We also have a wonderful ginkgo tree planted in 1780. Partial access for wheelchair users: some gravel paths and steep slopes. Dogs on leads welcome.

&♿ 🐕 ❋ 🚗 ☕ 🔊

The National Garden Scheme donated £281,000 in 2024 to support those looking to work in horticulture as well as those struggling within the industry.

Weston Hall

HERTFORDSHIRE

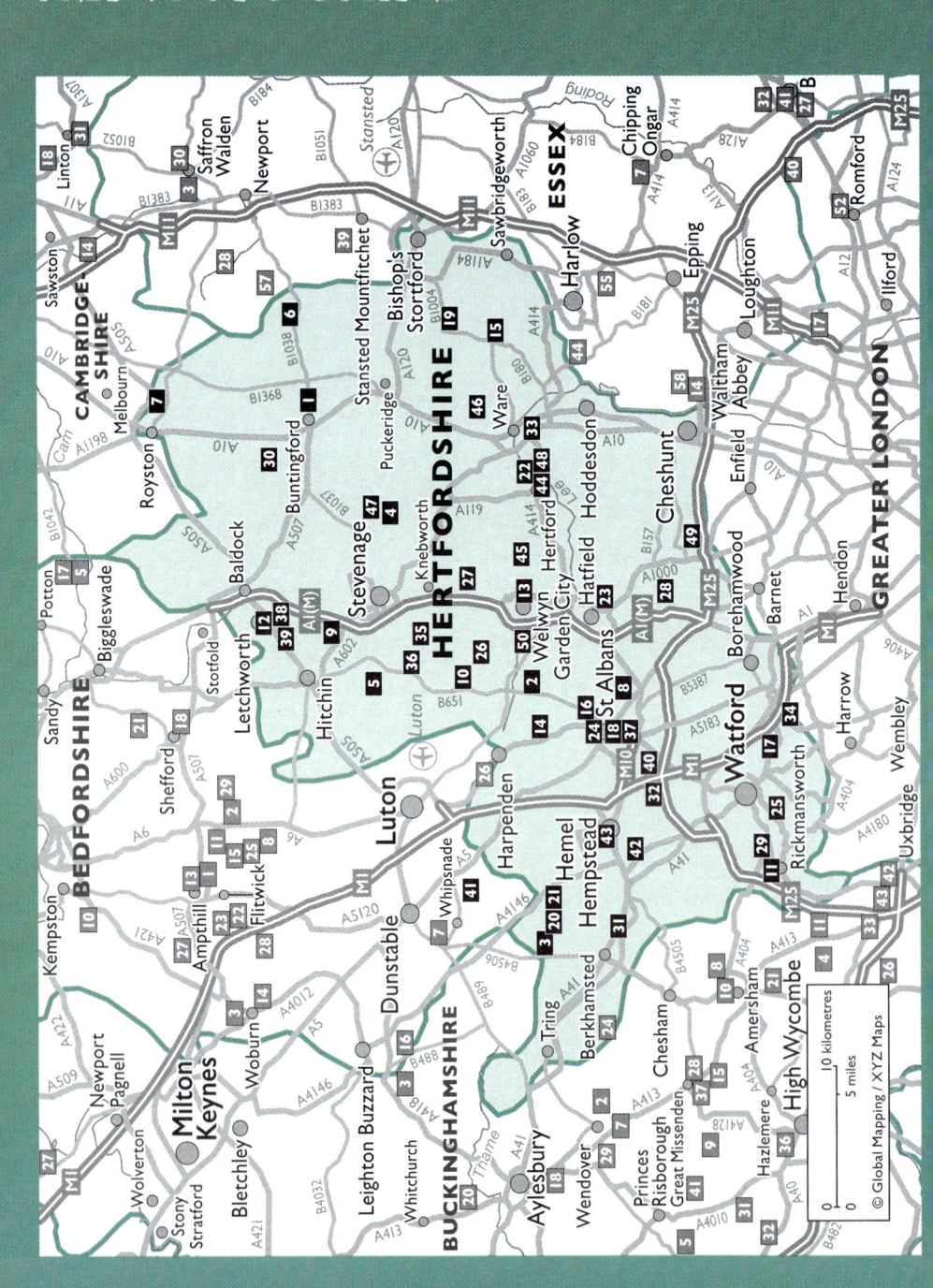

HERTFORDSHIRE 253

VOLUNTEERS

County Organisers
Bella Stuart-Smith 07710 099132
bella.stuart-smith@ngs.org.uk

Kate Stuart-Smith 07551 923217
kate.stuart-smith@ngs.org.uk

County Treasurer
Peter Barrett 01442 393508
peter.barrett@ngs.org.uk

Publicity
Shubha Allard
shubha.allard@ngs.org.uk

Photography
Lucy Standen 07933 261347
lucy.standen@ngs.org.uk

Julie Meakins 07899 985324
meakinsjulie@gmail.com

Photography & Story Telling
Anna Marie Felice 07500 306273
annamarie.felice@gmail.com

Social Media - Facebook
Anastasia Rezanova
anastasia.rezanova@ngs.org.uk

Social Media - Twitter
Mark Lammin 07966 625559
mark.lammin@ngs.org.uk

Radio
Lucy Swift
lucy.swift@ngs.org.uk

Talks
Katy Cheetham
katy.cheetham@ngs.org.uk

Booklet Coordinator
Janie Nicholas 07973 802929
janie.nicholas@ngs.org.uk

New Gardens
Julie Wise 07759 462330
julie.wise@ngs.org.uk

Communications Officer
Lorna Nightinghale 07725 767655
lorna.nightingale@ngs.org.uk

Assistant County Organisers
Parul Bhatt
parul.bhatt@ngs.org.uk

Tessa Birch 07721682481
tessa.birch@ngs.org.uk

Kate de Boinville
kdeboinville@gmail.com

Rebecca Fincham
rebecca.fincham@ngs.org.uk

Jennifer Harmes
jenny.harmes@ngs.org.uk

Kerrie Lloyd-Dawson 07736 442883
kerrie.lloyddawson@ngs.org.uk

Sarah Marsh 07813 083126
sarah.marsh@ngs.org.uk

OPENING DATES

All entries subject to change. For latest information check **www.ngs.org.uk**

Extended openings are shown at the beginning of the month.

Map locator numbers are shown to the right of each garden name.

January

Friday 31st
8 Gosselin Road   22

February

Snowdrop Openings
Saturday 1st
Walkern Hall   47
Sunday 2nd
Walkern Hall   47
Tuesday 4th
◆ Benington Lordship   4
Wednesday 5th
8 Gosselin Road   22
Friday 7th
8 Gosselin Road   22

Sunday 16th
10 Cross Street   12
Serendi   39
Wednesday 19th
10 Cross Street   12
Serendi   39

March

Saturday 22nd
◆ Hatfield House West Garden   23
Walkern Hall   47
Sunday 23rd
Amwell Cottage   2
Walkern Hall   47

April

Sunday 6th
◆ St Paul's Walden Bury   36
Sunday 13th
Alswick Hall   1
Monday 21st
10 Cross Street   12
Sunday 27th
◆ Ashridge House Gardens   3
Pie Corner   32

May

Every day from Saturday 10th to Sunday 18th
42 Falconer Road   17
Sunday 4th
Patchwork   31
Sunday 11th
◆ St Paul's Walden Bury   36
Friday 16th
Rustling End Cottage   35
Saturday 17th
The Manor House, Ayot St Lawrence   26
Rustling End Cottage   35
Sunday 18th
The Manor House, Ayot St Lawrence   26
Saturday 24th
42 Falconer Road   17
Terrace House Garden   44

@HertfordshireNGS   @HertfordshirNGS   @hertsngs

254 HERTFORDSHIRE

Sunday 25th
◆ Benington Lordship 4
42 Falconer Road 17
15 Gade Valley Cottages 21
Morning Light 29
The Pines 33

Monday 26th
43 Mardley Hill 27

Friday 30th
16 Langley Crescent 24

Saturday 31st
16 Langley Crescent 24

June

Sunday 1st
Brambley Hedge 5
Serge Hill Gardens 40
Warrenwood 49

Friday 6th
1 Elia Cottage 15

Sunday 8th
Brent Pelham Hall 6
1 Elia Cottage 15
Gaddesden House 20
◆ St Paul's Walden Bury 36
Serendi 39
NEW Shortgrove Manor Farm 41

Sunday 15th
The Cherry Tree 9
Thundridge Hill House 46

Friday 20th
NEW Walled Garden, 1 Farquhar Street 48

Saturday 21st
Eastmoor Lodge 14

Sunday 22nd
NEW Walled Garden, 1 Farquhar Street 48

Saturday 28th
Sunnyside Rural Trust- Hemel Hempstead 42

Sunday 29th
Gable House 19
St Stephens Avenue Gardens 37
Scudamore 38
9 Tannsfield Drive 43

July

Sunday 6th
15 Gade Valley Cottages 21

Friday 11th
NEW Meadowgate 28

Sunday 13th
NEW Meadowgate 28

Friday 18th
28 Fishpool Street 18

Sunday 20th
Burloes Hall 7
NEW 34 Church Lane 10
49 Ellis Fields 16
28 Fishpool Street 18

Sunday 27th
35 Digswell Road 13
Reveley Lodge 34
Tewin Greens 45

August

Sunday 3rd
12 Longmans Close 25
9 Tannsfield Drive 43

Sunday 17th
Patchwork 31

Wednesday 20th
8 Gosselin Road 22

Saturday 23rd
Terrace House Garden 44

Sunday 31st
St Stephens Avenue Gardens 37

September

Saturday 6th
102 Cambridge Road 8

Sunday 7th
102 Cambridge Road 8
NEW The Old Rectory, Cottered 30

Wednesday 17th
8 Gosselin Road 22

Sunday 28th
The Pines 33

By Arrangement

Arrange a personalised garden visit with your club, or group of friends, on a date to suit you. See individual garden entries for full details.

102 Cambridge Road 8
The Cherry Tree 9
38 The Clump 11
10 Cross Street 12
35 Digswell Road 13
1 Elia Cottage 15
42 Falconer Road 17
12 Longmans Close 25
Morning Light 29
Patchwork 31
Pie Corner 32
Serendi 39
9 Tannsfield Drive 43
Thundridge Hill House 46
Waterend House 50

49 Ellis Fields

48,000 people affected by cancer were reached by Maggie's centres supported by the National Garden Scheme over the last 12 months.

THE GARDENS

1 ALSWICK HALL
Hare Street Road, Buntingford, SG9 0AA. Mike & Annie Johnson, www.alswickhall.com/gardens. *1m from Buntingford on B1038. From the S take A10 to Buntingford, drive into town & take B1038 (after the Co-op) E towards Hare St Village. Alswick Hall is 1m on R.* **Sun 13 Apr (12-4). Adm £8, chd free. Light refreshments. Licensed bar, lunch, teas and home-made cakes.**
Listed Tudor House with five acres of landscaped gardens set in unspoiled farmland. Two well established natural ponds with rockeries. Herbaceous borders, shrubs, woodland walk and wildflower meadow with a fantastic selection of daffodils, tulips, *Camassias* and crown imperials. In 2025, after the April opening, the owners are re-designing the ponds and will not be having a September opening. A plant stall and various trade stands as well as children's face painting. Good access for wheelchair users with lawns and wood chip paths. Slight undulations in places.
&. 🐕 ✿ 🚗 ☕ 🔊

2 AMWELL COTTAGE
Amwell Lane, Wheathampstead, AL4 8EA. Colin & Kate Birss, www.instagram.com/amwellcottage. *½ m S of Wheathampstead. From St Helen's Church, Wheathampstead turn up Brewhouse Hill. At top L fork (Amwell Ln), 300yds down lane, park in field opp.* **Sun 23 Mar (2-5). Adm £5, chd free. Home-made Teas.**
Informal garden of approx 2½ acres around C17 cottage. Large orchard of mature trees, with billows of cow parsley in spring, laid out with paths. Extensive lawns with borders, framed by tall yew hedges and old brick walls. Daffodils early in the year. Many roses in beds, borders and a tunnel. Stone seats with views, woodland pond, greenhouse, vegetable garden with raised beds and fire-pit area. Wheelchair access via gravel drive.
&. 🐕 ✿ ☕ 🔊

3 ♦ ASHRIDGE HOUSE GARDENS
Berkhamsted, HP4 1NS. EF Corporate Education Ltd, 01442 843491, tickets@ashridge.hult.edu, www.ashridgehouse.org.uk. *4m N of Berkhamsted. 1m S of Little Gaddesden. What3words app: fenced.liquid.reverses.* **For NGS: Sun 27 Apr (10-5). Adm £7.50, chd free. Light refreshments at Bakehouse Café. Ashridge House & Bakehouse Cafe only accept payments by card. Dine inside or out in the courtyard, for both light refreshments & substantial meals. For other opening times and information, please phone, email or visit garden website.**
The Grade II* gardens were designed by Humphry Repton, in 1813, and modified by Sir Jeffry Wyatville. The 190 acres inc formal gardens, a large lawn area leading to avenues of trees and arboretum. In May, the highlights of the garden are the azaleas and spring bedding displays. Free garden introduction talks available on the day. Once a monastic site, then home to Henry VIII and his children. One of Repton's finest gardens with influences from the Bridgewater dynasty, comprising colourful formal bedding, a rosary, shrubberies and breathtaking views. NB: Rhododendron Avenue is undergoing major restoration in 2025. The main garden features, cafe and toilets are accessible via wheelchair.
&. 🐕 ✿ 🚗 🛏 ☕ 🔊

4 ♦ BENINGTON LORDSHIP
Stevenage, SG2 7BS. Mr & Mrs R Bott, 01438 869668, garden@beningtonlordship.co.uk, www.beningtonlordship.co.uk. *4m E of Stevenage. In Benington Village, next to church. Signs off A602.* **For NGS: Tue 4 Feb (11-4). Cream teas. Sun 25 May (2-5). Light refreshments. Adm £8, chd £4. In February, refreshments served in onsite tearoom. In May, refreshments in parish hall adjacent to garden. For other opening times and information, please phone, email or visit garden website.**
A seven acre site with ruin of C12 Norman keep and C19 neo Norman folly. Highlights inc spectacular snowdrops and spring bulbs; formal rose garden; walled kitchen garden with vegetables, bantams, and wildflower meadow; orchard with perennial meadow; lake; unspoilt panoramic views over surrounding parkland. Recent replanting of main border with plants resistant to climate change and wildlife friendly. Unspoilt parkland views. Walled garden. Naturalistic planting. Large pond. The garden is on a slope and paths are uneven. There is only partial wheelchair access. Accessible WC available in parish hall.
&. 🚗 ☕ 🔊

5 BRAMBLEY HEDGE
1 Chequers Lane, Preston, Hitchin, SG4 7TX. Lynda & Steve Woodward. *3m S of Hitchin. From A602, Three Moorhens r'about take exit to Gosmore, pass through Gosmore and continue for about 2m into Preston. Chequers Ln is 1st on R, by white fence.* **Sun 1 June (1-5.30). Adm £4, chd free. Home-made teas.**
Brambley Hedge covers an area of approx ¼ acre. The front garden is mainly set to shrubs and small trees. The rear garden is sections or 'rooms' planted in a cottage style, with around 40 varieties of roses, popular and some less common perennials. There is also a vegetable plot and numerous pots for annuals. The owner is a keen amateur wood turner and some of his work will be on show. The paths are mainly flat and level, some may be slightly narrow.
&. 🐕 ✿ ☕ 🔊

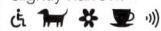

6 BRENT PELHAM HALL
Brent Pelham, Buntingford, SG9 0HF. Alex & Mike Carrell. *Brent Pelham. From Buntingford take the B1038 E for 5m. From Clavering take the B1038 W for 3m.* **Sun 8 June (1-4). Adm £8, chd free. Tea, coffee & cake in the Estate Office.**
Surrounding a beautiful Grade I listed property, the gardens consist of 12 acres of formal gardens, redesigned in 2007 by the renowned landscaper Kim Wilkie. With two walled gardens, a potager, walled kitchen garden, greenhouses, orchard and a new double herbaceous border, there is lots to discover. The further 14 acres of parkland boast lakes and wildflower meadows. Access by wheelchair to most areas of the garden, inc paths of paving, gravel and grass.
&. ✿ ☕ 🔊

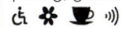

256 HERTFORDSHIRE

7 BURLOES HALL
Newmarket Road, Royston, SG8 9NE. Lady Newman, www.burloeshallweddings.co.uk. *1m N of Royston. From M11/A505 turn L on Newmarket Rd. 200yds 1st turning on L Burloes Hall or B1329 from Barley to Royston, turning on L signed Burloes Farm.* **Sun 20 July (11-5). Adm £6, chd free. Tea, coffee & cake.**
The garden was designed and created in the 1900's. Extensive planting by Gill Chamberlain of Garden Rescue Limited from 2007 to the present day. Formal gardens with deep colourful mixed herbaceous borders. Bountiful Nepeta and white roses. Handsome beech trees and mature yew hedges with extensive lawns.

8 102 CAMBRIDGE ROAD
St Albans, AL1 5LG. Anastasia & Keith, arezanova@gmail.com. *Nr Ashley Rd end of Cambridge Rd in The Camp neighbourhood on E side of city. S of A1057 (Hatfield Rd). Take the A1057 from A1(M) J3. Take A1081 from M25 J22.* **Sat 6, Sun 7 Sept (1-6). Adm £5, chd free. Tea, coffee & cake.** Visits also by arrangement 1 July to 17 Oct for groups of 10 to 25. Donation to Alzheimer's Research UK.
Contemporary space sympathetically redesigned in 2017 to keep many of the existing plants, trees and shrubs from a 1930s semi's garden. Modern take on the classic garden in two halves: ornamental and vegetable. All-year interest gabion borders packed with perennials and annuals, central bed featuring a pond and a mature Japanese maple. All vegetables, annuals, and some perennials, grown from seed. 'Count the Frog' activity for children and young-at-heart. Dogs and photography welcome.

9 THE CHERRY TREE
Stevenage Road, Little Wymondley, Hitchin, SG4 7HY. Patrick Woollard & Jane Woollard, 07952 655613, cherrywy@btinternet.com. *½m W of J8 off A1M. Follow sign to Little Wymondley; under railway bridge & house is R at central island flower bed opp Bucks Head Pub. Parking in adjacent roads.* **Sun 15 June (11-5). Adm £5, chd free. Tea, coffee & cake.** Visits also by arrangement Apr to July for groups of 5 to 30.
The garden has been recently updated. This is a colourful space on several levels containing shrubs, trees and climbers enabling the garden to be viewed from different aspects. Much of the planting, inc exotics of which many are perfumed, is in containers that are re-sited in various positions throughout the seasons. A heated greenhouse and summerhouse maintain tender plants in winter.

10 NEW 34 CHURCH LANE
Kimpton, Hitchin, SG4 8RR. Mary Turner. *3m N of Wheathampstead. From B651, Hitchin Rd, take 1st turning on L, signposted cricket club. Parking at end of track.* **Sun 20 July (2-5.30). Adm £5, chd free. Tea, coffee & cake.**
Surrounded by the pretty village greens of Kimpton, next to a meadow, this small, newly planted cottage style garden has already attracted an abundance of wildlife, particularly butterflies, bees and insects. Facing south west, the garden is packed with a huge variety of hardy perennials. The planting is tolerant of dry conditions.

11 38 THE CLUMP
Rickmansworth, WD3 4BQ. Rupert & Fiona Wheeler, 01923 776858, rupert_wheeler@sky.com. *1m W of Rickmansworth. From M25 J18, drive towards Rickmansworth for about 350yds. Turn R into The Clump. No. 38 is about 350yds on the R.* **Visits by arrangement May to Sept for groups of 5 to 20. Adm £7, chd free. Light refreshments.**
A plantsman's garden containing unusual trees and shrubs on the edge of a wood. The shrubs and trees in the middle garden surround a pond and create an air of relaxing tranquillity. The rear garden is the setting for modern sculptures. There is also a collection of cacti.

12 10 CROSS STREET
Letchworth Garden City, SG6 4UD. Renata & Colin Hume, 01462 678430, renata@cyclamengardens.com, www.cyclamengardens.com. *Nr town centre. From A1(M) J9 signed Letchworth, across 2 r'abouts, R at 3rd, across next 3 r'abouts L into Nevells Rd, 1st R into Cross St.* **Sun 16, Wed 19 Feb (1-4.30). Combined adm with Serendi £8,** chd free. **Mon 21 Apr (1-5). Adm £5, chd free. Tea, coffee & cake.** Visits also by arrangement 3 Feb to 31 July.
A garden with mature fruit trees is planted for interest throughout the year. The structure of the garden evolved around three circles - two grass lawns and a wildlife pond. Mixed borders connect the different levels of the garden.

13 35 DIGSWELL ROAD
Welwyn Garden City, AL8 7PB. Adrian & Clare de Baat, 01707 324074, adrian.debaat@ntlworld.com, www.adriansgarden.org. *½m N of Welwyn Garden City centre. From the Campus r'about in city centre take N exit just past Campus West into Digswell Rd. Over the White Bridge, 200yds on L.* **Sun 27 July (2-5.30). Adm £5, chd free. Home-made teas.** Visits also by arrangement July to Oct for groups of 10 to 20. Adm inc refreshments.
Town garden of around a ⅓ acre with naturalistic planting inspired by the Dutch garden designer, Piet Oudolf. The garden has perennial borders plus a small meadow packed with herbaceous plants and grasses. The contemporary planting gives way to the exotic, inc a succulent bed and under mature trees, a lush jungle garden inc bamboos, bananas, palms and tree ferns. Daisy Roots Nursery will be selling plants. Grass paths and gentle slopes to all areas of the garden.

14 EASTMOOR LODGE
East Common, Harpenden, AL5 1DA. Ekaterina and Julian Gilbert, www.egilbertgardens.com. *1m S of Harpenden, turn L onto Limbrick Rd. After 400 yds, turn R onto East Common Rd. After 100 yds turn L. The house is the 3rd on the L. For parking use the car park opp Bamville Cricket club.* **Sat 21 June (11-4). Adm £7, chd free. Tea, coffee & cake.**
Beautiful modern garden of ½ acre featuring an extensive collection of David Austin roses. Various perennials, dwarf azaleas, rhododendrons and beautiful hydrangeas, within a woodland setting of giant redwood and other conifer trees.

1 ELIA COTTAGE
Nether Street, Widford, Ware, SG12 8TH. **Margaret & Hugh O'Reilly, 01279 843324, hughoreilly56@yahoo.co.uk.** *B1004 from Ware towards Much Hadham. Travel down dip towards Much Hadham, at Xroad take R into Nether St. 8m W of Bishop's Stortford on B1004 through Much Hadham at Widford sign turn L. B180 from Stanstead Abbots.* **Fri 6, Sun 8 June (1-5.30). Adm £5, chd free. Light refreshments. Visits also by arrangement 10 Feb to 31 Aug.**
A ⅓ acre romantic garden. Snowdrops, hellebores and crocus welcome visitors in spring. Followed in June by clematis and roses. Pond, cascade water features, stream with Monet-style bridge. Plenty of seats, two summerhouses. Steep nature of garden and uneven paths means there is no wheelchair access. New ½ acre nature meadow opposite. Fairy Hunt for children and solve the Riddle of the Stones.

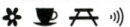

49 ELLIS FIELDS
St Albans, AL3 6BG. **K Blain.** *Situated at the far end of Ellis Fields.* **Sun 20 July (12.30-5). Adm £5, chd free. Tea, coffee & cake. Cream teas also available.**
A small tranquil urban garden, with both front and back gardens for viewing. Different structural evergreen plants and seasonal planting. There are lots of bee and bird friendly summer flowers, and copious numbers of hydrangeas. Painted wooden arches and pathways lead you to raised decked seating areas to enjoy the plants. Wheelchair access via a side gate. The garden should be mostly accessible to all. There are two short steps to slightly higher levels.

42 FALCONER ROAD
Bushey, Watford, WD23 3AD. **Mrs Suzette Fuller, 07714 294170, suzettesdesign@btconnect.com.** *M1 J5 follow signs for Bushey. From London A40 via Stanmore towards Watford. From Watford via Bushey Arches, through to Bushey High St, turn L into Falconer Rd, opp St James church.* **Daily Sat 10 May to Sun 18 May (12-6). Sat 24, Sun 25 May (12-6). Adm £6, chd free. Light refreshments. Visits also by arrangement May to Aug for groups of 10 to 15.**
Enchanting, magical and unusual Victorian style space. Bird cages and chimney pots feature, plus a walk through conservatory with many plants.

28 FISHPOOL STREET
St Albans, AL3 4RT. **Jenny & Antony Jay, www.instagram.com/jenjay.fishpool.** *No. 28 is at the Cathedral end of Fishpool St. Entrance to the garden is through the Lower Red Lion car park.* **Evening opening Fri 18 July (6-8). Wine. Sun 20 July (2-5). Home-made teas. Adm £7, chd free.**
This secret garden, in the vicinity of St. Albans cathedral, highlights a C17 Tripe House set amongst box and yew topiary. Gravel paths lead through a rose garden to a circular lawn surrounded by abundant hot perennials and shrubs and then onto a tranquil woodland retreat. Plants for sale.

Ashridge House Gardens

258 HERTFORDSHIRE

19 GABLE HOUSE
Church Lane, Much Hadham, SG10 6DH. Tessa & Keith Birch. *Follow signs to the church. Continue around the R bend & past several white cottages. Gable House driveway is immed on R. Please park in the High St.* **Sun 29 June (12-4). Adm £5, chd free. Home-made teas.**
Enjoy this colourful and walled village garden of just under an acre. Surrounding the house on three sides, the design is both formal and naturalistic, with structural clipped evergreens and sweeping abundant herbaceous borders. The planting displays an emphasis on strong colour and varied texture. Features inc a woodland walk, a wildlife pond and a cutting garden. Matched funding of all sales goes to Brain Tumour Research. Level garden with easy wheelchair access.
&

20 GADDESDEN HOUSE
Nettleden Road, Little Gaddesden, Berkhamsted, HP4 1PP. Jilly & David Scriven. *3½ m N of Berkhamsted. SW of Little Gaddesden village on Nettleden Rd. Look for NGS signs for the gate and off road parking in field. What3words app: winemaker.maps.wake.* **Sun 8 June (12-5). Adm £6, chd free. Home-made teas.**
10 acre garden with lovely views onto the NT Golden Valley. Variety of established wildflower meadows, 30m mixed border planted with bulbs, grasses, 'prairie' plants, perennials, unusual annuals, shrubs and topiarised holly trees, kitchen garden with raised beds and bay topiary, an orchard, rhododendrons, interesting trees and woodland paths. Lots to see and places to wander through. All grass pathways, some uneven. Garden mainly flat with some slightly sloping paths. Woodland & back field meadows on steep hill.
&

21 15 GADE VALLEY COTTAGES
Dagnall Road, Great Gaddesden, Hemel Hempstead, HP1 3BW. Bryan Trueman. *3m N of Hemel Hempstead. Follow B440 N from Hemel Hempstead. Through Water End. Go past turning for Great Gaddesden on L. Park in village hall car park on R. Gade Valley Cottages on R (short walk).* **Sun 25 May, Sun 6 July (1.30-5). Adm £5, chd free.**

Tea, coffee & cake.
Medium sized sloping rural garden. Patio, lawn, borders and pond. Paths lead through a woodland area emerging by wildlife pond and sunny border. A choice of seating offers views across the beautiful Gade Valley or quiet shady contemplation with sounds of rustling bamboos and bubbling water. Many acers, hostas and ferns in shady areas. *Hemerocallis*, iris, *Crocosmia* and *Phlox* found in sun.

22 8 GOSSELIN ROAD
Bengeo, Hertford, SG14 3LG. Annie Godfrey & Steve Machin, www.daisyroots.com. *Take B158 from Hertford signed to Bengeo. Gosselin Rd 2nd R after White Lion Pub.* **Fri 31 Jan (1-4). Adm £5. Wed 5 Feb (1-4). Adm £5, chd free. Fri 7 Feb (1-4); Wed 20 Aug, Wed 17 Sept (12-4). Adm £5.**
Daisy Roots nursery garden acts as trial ground and show case for perennials and ornamental grasses grown there. Over 250 varieties of snowdrop in February, deep borders packed with perennials and grasses later in the year. Small front garden with lots of foliage interest. Regret, no dogs.

23 ♦ HATFIELD HOUSE WEST GARDEN
Hatfield, AL9 5HX. The Marquess of Salisbury, 01707 287010, r.ravera@hatfield-house.co.uk, www.hatfield-house.co.uk. *Pedestrian entrance to Hatfield Park is opp Hatfield train stn. From here you can obtain directions to the gardens. Free parking is available.* **For NGS: Sat 22 Mar (11-3). Adm £14, chd £7. For other opening times and information, please phone, email or visit garden website. Donation to a charity to be nominated by Lady Salisbury.**
Visitors can enjoy the spring bulbs in the lime walk, sundial garden and view the famous Old Palace garden, childhood home of Queen Elizabeth I. The adjoining woodland garden is at its best in spring with masses of naturalised daffodils and bluebells. Beautifully designed gifts, jewellery, toys and much more can be found in the Stable Yard shops. Visitors can also enjoy relaxing at the Coach House Kitchen Restaurant which serves a variety of delicious foods throughout the day. There is a good

route for wheelchairs around the West Garden and a plan can be picked up at the garden kiosk.
&

24 16 LANGLEY CRESCENT
St Albans, AL3 5RS. Jonathan Redmayne. *½ m S of St Albans city centre. J21a M25, follow B4630. At mini-r'about by King Harry Pub turn L. At big r'about turn R along A4147, then R at mini-r'about. Langley Cres is 2nd L.* **Evening opening Fri 30 May (5-8). Wine. Sat 31 May (2.30-5.30). Home-made teas. Adm £5, chd free.**
A compact walled garden set on a slope with a wide range of unusual herbaceous perennials, shrubs and trees, both edible and ornamental, and a gentle ambience. The rear garden is divided into two parts; the lower section comprises extensive herbaceous beds inc a collection of *Phlomis* and leads to a secluded area for quiet contemplation beside a wildlife pond surrounded by rambling roses. Fruit trees, herbaceous borders for pollinators, glasshouse and plant propagation also feature. Access by wheelchair to most areas of the garden, inc paved paths, grass and brick terrace beside pond. Garden is on a slope.
&

25 12 LONGMANS CLOSE
Byewaters, Watford, WD18 8WP. Mark Lammin, 07966 625559, mark.lammin@ngs.org.uk, www.instagram.com/hertstinytropicalgarden. *Leave M25 J18 (A404) & follow Rickmansworth/Croxley Green then A412 to Watford. Follow signs for Watford & Croxley Business Parks & then NGS signs. Parking on neighbouring roads.* **Sun 3 Aug (12-6). Adm £4.50, chd free. Tea, coffee & cake. Visits also by arrangement 1 July to 1 Sept for groups of up to 10.**
Hertfordshire's Tiny Tropical Garden. See how dazzling colour, scent, lush tropical foliage, trickling water and clever use of pots in a densely planted small garden can transport you to the tropics. Stately bananas and canna rub shoulders with delicate lily and roses amongst a large variety of begonia, hibiscus, ferns and houseplants in a tropical theme more often associated with warmer climes. Beautiful walks along the Grand Union Canal and on the Croxley Boundary Walk (signposted). Croxley Common Moor is a very short level stroll away

Meadowgate

with acres of open moor land, woods and river.

26 THE MANOR HOUSE, AYOT ST LAWRENCE
Welwyn, AL6 9BP. *4m W of Welwyn. 20 mins J4 A1M. Take B653 Wheathampstead. Turn into Codicote Rd follow signs to Shaws Corner. Parking in field, short walk to garden. A disabled drop-off point is available at the end of the drive.* **Sat 17, Sun 18 May (11-5). Adm £8, chd free. Home-made teas. Home-made cakes, scones, coffee and cold drinks available.**
A six acre garden set in mature landscape around Elizabethan Manor House (not open). A one acre walled garden inc glasshouses, fruit and vegetables, double herbaceous borders, rose and herb beds. Herbaceous perennial island beds, topiary specimens. Parterre and temple pond garden surround the house. Gates and water features by Arc Angel. Garden designed by Julie Toll. Produce for sale. The drop off point is 5 min walk from the garden. There are steps in part of the garden but the majority of the garden is suited to wheelchair access.

27 43 MARDLEY HILL
Welwyn, AL6 0TT. Kerrie Lloyd Dawson & Pete Stevens, www.agardenlessordinary. blogspot.co.uk. *5m N of Welwyn Garden City. On B197 between Welwyn & Woolmer Green, on crest of Mardley Hill by bus stop. Please consider our neighbours and other road users when parking.* **Mon 26 May (12-5). Adm £5, chd free. Home-made teas.**
An unexpected garden created by plantaholics and packed with unusual plants. Focus on foliage and long season of interest. Various areas: alpine bed; sunny border; deep shade; white-stemmed birches and woodland planting; naturalistic stream, pond and bog; chicken house and potted vegetables; potted exotics. Seating areas on different levels. This garden is proud to have provided plants for the National Garden Scheme's Show Garden at Chelsea Flower Show 2024.

The National Garden Scheme donated over £3.5 million to our nursing and health beneficiaries from money raised at gardens open in 2024.

28 NEW MEADOWGATE
36 Bluebridge Road, Brookmans Park, Hatfield, AL9 7SA. Alison Anscombe. *4m S of Hatfield, 3½m N of M25 J23. From Hatfield 2⅕m S on A1000, turn R onto Dixons Hill Rd, L onto Station Rd, L over Rlwy bridge onto Bluebridge Rd. From M25 J23 1⅘m N on Swanland Rd, R onto Warrengate Rd, R onto Hawkshead Ln.* **Evening opening Fri 11 July (6-8). Wine. Sun 13 July (1.30-5). Home-made teas. Adm £5, chd free. Coffee and a selection of home-made cakes.**
A garden designer's own medium size garden enclosed by mature beech hedging. Patio borders feature roses, lavender, *Achillea* and colourful pots, also hydrangeas, *Brunnera* and *Sarcococca*. Steps flanked by topiary yew to lawn. Island beds full of grasses and colourful perennials, with the emphasis on colour, form, texture and movement. A relaxing patio at the back features a pond and more planting.

✽ ☕))

29 MORNING LIGHT
7 Armitage Close, Loudwater, Rickmansworth, WD3 4HL. Roger & Patt Trigg, 01923 774293, roger@triggmail.org.uk. *From M25 J18 take A404 towards Rickmansworth, after ¾m turn L into Loudwater Ln, follow bends, then turn R at T-junc & R again into Armitage Close. Limited parking for cars.* **Sun 25 May (12-5). Adm £5, chd free. Tea, coffee and biscuits, on a self-service basis. Visits also by arrangement 1 Apr to 14 Sept for groups of up to 20.**
The May opening features a major plant sale with our early summer garden display in evidence. A south facing plantsman's garden, densely planted with hardy and tender perennials and shrubs in a shady environment. *Astilbes* and phlox feature along with island beds, a pond, chipped wood paths. Tall perennials can be viewed from the raised deck. Large conservatory stocked with sub-tropicals.

✽ ☕))

30 NEW THE OLD RECTORY, COTTERED
The Old Rectory, Cottered, Nr Buntingford, SG9 9QP. Debbie Taussig. *Between Baldock and Buntingford on the A507. On the A507 in the centre of Cottered. Garden is on the L travelling from Buntingford. After the Bull pub and opp the recreation ground.* **Sun 7 Sept (11.30-5.30). Adm £7, chd free. Tea, coffee & cake.**
This five acre garden is a garden of many parts and surrounds the house, a former rectory. Discover our herbaceous garden, rose garden, and an ornamental kitchen and cutting garden. Wander through a perennial meadow, winter garden, bog garden and woodland. There are formal lavender beds and an orchard with wildflowers. Explore the lake with an island and two further ponds.

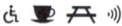

& ☕ ⛱))

31 PATCHWORK
22 Hall Park Gate, Berkhamsted, HP4 2NJ. Jean & Peter Block, 01442 864731, patchwork2@btinternet.com. *3m W of Hemel Hempstead. Entering E side of Berkhamsted on A4251, turn L 200yds after 40mph sign.* **Sun 4 May, Sun 17 Aug (2-5). Adm £5, chd free. Light refreshments. Visits also by arrangement Apr to Sept for groups of 5 to 20. Adm £7, chd free.**
¼ acre garden with lots of year-round colour, interest and perfume, particularly on opening days. Sloping site containing rockeries, two small ponds, herbaceous borders, island beds with bulbs in spring and dahlias in summer, roses, fuchsias, hostas, begonias, patio pots and tubs galore - all set against a background of trees and shrubs of varying colours. Seating and cover from the elements.

🐾 ✽ ☕

32 PIE CORNER
Millhouse Lane, Bedmond, Abbots Langley, WD5 0SG. Bella & Jeremy Stuart-Smith, 07710 099132, piebella1@gmail.com, www.instagram.com/piecornergarden. *Near Watford, Hemel Hempstead & St Albans. Head to the centre of Bedmond. Millhouse Ln is opp the shops. Entry is 50m down Millhouse Ln. Parking in field. Alternative parking in village, a short walk away.* **Sun 27 Apr (2-5). Adm £6, chd free. Home-made teas. Visits also**

Gaddesden House

by arrangement 12 May to 14 Sept for groups of 15+.
A garden designed to complement the modern classical house. Formal borders near the house, pond, views across a large lawn, punctuated with wildflowers to the valley beyond. More informal shrub plantings with bulbs edge the woodland. A dry gravel garden leads through more meadow planting to the vegetable garden. Enjoy blossom, tulips, wild garlic, bluebells and young rhododendron in late spring. Early spring bulbs inc masses of snowdrops and daffodils followed by lovely shrubs, perennials and wild roses. Robust wheelchairs can access most areas on grass or gravel paths except the formal pond where there are steps. There are some steep grassy slopes.
& 💐 ☕ »))

33 THE PINES
58 Hoe Lane, Ware, SG12 9NZ. Peter Laing. Approx ½ m S of Ware centre. At S (top) end of Hoe Ln, close to Hertford Rugby Club (car parking) and opp Pinewood Sch. Look for prominent white gateposts with lions. **Sun 25 May, Sun 28 Sept (2-5.30). Adm £5, chd free.**
Plantsman's garden with many unusual plants, created by present owner over 30 years. An acre, on an east to west axis so much shade, sandy soil over chalk but can grow ericaceous plants. Front garden formal with fountain. Main garden mature trees, herbaceous borders and island beds. Features inc gravel garden, pergola and obelisk with moss rose "William Lobb". Among many specimen trees, the rare Kashmir cypress. Wheelchair access unless recent heavy rain.
& ☕ »))

34 REVELEY LODGE
88 Elstree Road, Bushey Heath, WD23 4GL. Reveley Lodge Trust, www.reveleylodge.org. 3m SE of Watford & 2m N of Stanmore. From A41 take A411 to Bushey & Harrow. At mini r'about take 2nd exit into Elstree Rd. Garden ½ m on L. **Sun 27 July (1-5). Adm £6, chd free. Light refreshments.**
2½ acre gardens surrounding a Grade II listed Victorian house. Restored 50 ft conservatory with a large collection of cacti and succulents. Kitchen and cut flower garden and beehives. Rose garden planted with old roses. Themed borders featuring a range of medicinal, scented and tropical plants. Live music and refreshments. Stalls offering plants, vintage items and local arts and crafts for sale. Partial wheelchair access.
& 💐 ❀ ☕ »))

35 RUSTLING END COTTAGE
Rustling End, Codicote, SG4 8TD. Julie & Tim Wise, www.instagram.com/juliewise2018. 1m N of Codicote. From B656 turn L into 'Houses Ln' then R to Rustling End. House 2nd on L. **Evening opening Fri 16, Sat 17 May (5-8). Adm £6, chd free. Wine.**
Meander through our wildflower meadow to a cottage garden with contemporary planting. Behind lumpy hedges explore a garden managed for wildlife. Natural planting provides an environment for birds, small mammals and insects. Our terrace features drought tolerant low maintenance plants. A flowery mead surrounds the formal pond and an abundant floral vegetable garden provides produce for the summer. Hens in residence. www.rustlingend.com.
❀ ☕ »))

36 ♦ ST PAUL'S WALDEN BURY
Whitwell, Hitchin, SG4 8BP. The Bowes Lyon family, stpaulswalden@gmail.com, www.stpaulswaldenbury.co.uk. 5m S of Hitchin. On B651; ½ m N of Whitwell village. From London leave A1(M) J6 for Welwyn (not Welwyn Garden City). Pick up signs to Codicote, then Whitwell. **For NGS: Sun 6 Apr, Sun 11 May, Sun 8 June (2-6). Adm £8, chd free. Home-made teas. For other opening times and information, please email or visit garden website. Donation to St Paul's Walden Charity.**
Spectacular formal woodland garden, Grade I listed, laid out 1720, covering over 50 acres. Long rides lined with beech hedges lead to temples, statues, lake and a terraced theatre. Seasonal displays of daffodils, camelias, irises, magnolias, rhododendrons, lilies. Wildflowers encouraged - cowslips, bluebells. This was the childhood home of the late Queen Mother. Children welcome. Dogs on leads. Lake, temples, classical statues. Good wheelchair access to part of the garden.
& 💐 🚗 ☕ 🪑 »))

GROUP OPENING

37 ST STEPHENS AVENUE GARDENS
St Albans, AL3 4AD. Heather Osborne, Carol and Roger Harlow, www.instagram.com/heather.osborne20. 1m S of St Albans City Centre. From A414 take A5183 Watling St. At mini r'about by St Stephens Church/King Harry Pub take B4630 Watford Rd. St Stephens Ave is 1st R. **Sun 29 June, Sun 31 Aug (2.30-5.30). Combined adm £7, chd free. Home-made teas.**

20 ST STEPHENS AVENUE
Heather Osborne.

30 ST STEPHENS AVENUE
Carol & Roger Harlow.

Only five doors apart, these two town gardens have been developed in totally different but equally inspiring ways - from an innovative drought tolerant front garden full of achilleas, eryngiums and self seeding perennials, to paths winding through plant packed borders with specimen trees, flowering shrubs and climbers in a series of 'rooms'. Our June opening at no 20 features roses, clematis and geraniums; in August, dahlias, asters, salvias and late season perennials come to the fore. Seasonal patio containers, hostas, wildlife pond, seating in sun and shade, home-made cakes and teas served in the conservatory, WC. The gravelled front at no 30 leads round to a sunken garden used as an outdoor kitchen to enjoy the fruits of a productive allotment. Clipped box, beech and hornbeam in the back garden provide a cool backdrop for the strong colours of the double herbaceous borders. A gate beneath an apple arch frames the view to the park beyond. Plants for sale at June opening only.
❀ ☕ »))

In 2024, our donations to Carers Trust meant that 26,081 unpaid carers were supported across the UK.

38 SCUDAMORE
1 Baldock Road, Letchworth Garden City, SG6 3LB. Michael & Sheryl Hann. *Opp Spring Rd, between Muddy Ln & Letchworth Ln. J9 A1M. Follow directions to Letchworth. Turn L to Hitchin A505. After 1m House on L after Muddy Ln. Parking in Muddy Ln & Spring Rd.* **Sun 29 June (11-5). Adm £7, chd free. Tea, coffee & cake.**

½ acre garden surrounding early C17 cottages that were converted and extended in 1920s to form current house. Garden of mature trees, many mixed herbaceous borders with shrubs, wildflowers, pond, wet bed, wilder garden and orchard/vegetable area. Arbour, geodesic dome and many sculptures add interest to this garden of both unusual and traditional planting.

39 SERENDI
22 Hitchin Road, Letchworth Garden City, SG6 3LT. Valerie, 07548 776809, valerie.aitken22@gmail.com, www.instagram.com/serendigarden. *1m from city centre. A1M J9 signed Letchworth on A505. At 2nd r'about take 1st exit Hitchin A505. Straight over T-lights. Garden 1m on R.* **Sun 16, Wed 19 Feb (1-4.30). Combined adm with 10 Cross Street £8, chd free. Sun 8 June (11-5). Adm £5, chd free. Home-made teas.** Visits also by arrangement Apr to Oct for groups of 10 to 25.

Massed snowdrops and other spring bulbs. Many different areas within a well designed garden: silver birch grove, a 'dribble of stones', rill, contemporary knot garden, gravel area with alliums. Later in the year an abundance of roses climbing five pillars, perennials, grasses and dahlias. A greenhouse for over wintering, a Griffin glasshouse with, *Tibochina, Aeoniums, Pelargoniums* and more. Wheelchair access via gravel entrance, driveway and paths.

GROUP OPENING

40 SERGE HILL GARDENS
Serge Hill Lane, Bedmond, WD5 0RT. www.tomstuartsmith.co.uk. *½ m E of Bedmond. Go to Bedmond & take Serge Hill Ln, where you will be directed past the lodge & down the drive. Parking is in a large field.* **Sun 1 June (1-5). Combined adm £15, chd free. Pre-booking essential, please visit www.ngs.org.uk for information & booking. Home-made teas.**

THE BARN
Sue & Tom Stuart-Smith, www.tomstuartsmith.co.uk/our-work/toms-garden.

THE PLANT LIBRARY
Tom & Sue Stuart-Smith, www.sergehillproject.co.uk.

SERGE HILL
Kate Stuart-Smith, www.instagram.com/katestuartsmith.

Three large country gardens a short walk from each other. Tom and Sue Stuart-Smith's garden at The Barn has an enclosed courtyard with tanks of water, herbaceous perennials and shrubs tolerant of generally dry conditions. To the north there are views over the five acre wildflower meadow. The West Garden is a series of different gardens overflowing with bulbs, herbaceous perennials, and shrubs. There is also an exotic prairie planted from seed in 2011. The Plant Library is a collection of over 1000 herbaceous plants first planted in 2021. Next door at Serge Hill, there is a lovely walled garden with a large Foster and Pearson greenhouse, orderly rows of vegetables, and disorderly self-seeded annuals and perennials. The walls are crowded with climbers and shrubs. From here you emerge to a meadow, a mixed border and a wonderful view over the ha-ha to the park and woods beyond. Follow the gardens on Instagram: @tomstuartsmith @suestuartsmith @katestuartsmith @tomstuartsmithstudio.

41 NEW SHORTGROVE MANOR FARM
Dovehouse Lane, Kensworth, Dunstable, LU6 2PQ. Helen & David Barlow. *Between Kensworth and Whipsnade. If using SatNav, please do not follow the postcode. Entrance is on Buckwood Ln. What3words app: jeeps.best.legal.* **Sun 8 June (11-4). Adm £7, chd free. Tea, coffee & cake.**

A 6½ acre garden set in mature landscape around a Grade II listed C15 Farmhouse. Formal gardens inc a sunken garden with pond, rose-covered pergola, terraces, fountain, Orangery and topiary specimens. There is also a wild area and derelict orchard. Shortgrove Manor Farm is home to The National Citrus Collection. The citrus are on display outside during the summer months.

NPC

42 SUNNYSIDE RURAL TRUST - HEMEL HEMPSTEAD
Two Waters Road, Hemel Hempstead, HP3 9BY. Sunnyside Rural Trust Charity, www.sunnysideruraltrust.org.uk. *5mins from the A41, Hemel Hempstead exit. The entrance & car park to Sunnyside - Hemel Hempstead are found off the Two Waters Rd, behind the K2 restaurant accessed by the road to its L.* **Sat 28 June (10-4). Adm £5, chd free. Tea, coffee & cake at the Sunnyside Up Cafe and Farmshop.**

Sunnyside - Hemel Hempstead is the base for the charity's Green Flag awarded plant nursery. We work with people with learning disabilities to grow peat-free perennial and annual bedding for domestic and commercial clients. Arit Anderson's peat-free Hampton Court show garden features on site, alongside an orchard, Tranquillity Garden, Market Garden and our Sunnyside Up cafe and farmshop. A select range of perennial plants, veg seedlings and herb plants will be available for sale as well as homemade chutneys and jams from their own produce. Assisted wheelchair access where there are woodland and grass paths.

43 9 TANNSFIELD DRIVE
Hemel Hempstead, HP2 5LG. Peter & Gaynor Barrett, 01442 393508, peteslittlepatch@virginmedia.com, www.peteslittlepatch.co.uk. *Approx. 1m NE of Hemel Hempstead town centre & 2m W of J8 on M1. From M1 J8, cross r'about to A414 to Hemel Hempstead. Under footbridge, cross r'about then 1st R across dual c'way to Leverstock Green Rd. On to High St Green. L into Ellingham Rd then follow signs.* **Sun 29 June, Sun 3 Aug (1.30-4.30). Adm £4, chd free. Home-made teas.** Visits also by arrangement 30 June to 10 Aug for groups of 10 to 15. Adm £8 inc tea, coffee and cake.

A town garden to surprise. Dense planting together with the ever-present sound of water, create an intimate and welcoming oasis of calm.

Narrow paths divide, leading visitors on a voyage of discovery of the garden's many features. The owners regularly experiment with the planting scheme which ensures the 'look' of the garden changes from year to year. Dense planting together with simple water features, stone statues, metal sculptures, wall art and mirrors can be seen throughout the garden. As a time and cost saving experiment all hanging baskets are planted with hardy perennials most of which are normally used for ground cover.

44 TERRACE HOUSE GARDEN
35 Fanshawe Street, Bengeo, Hertford, SG14 3AT. Peter Freeland & Rosie Freeland, www.instagram.com/peter_freeland_gardens. *1m from Hertford town centre. Please park on nearby Elton Rd & not Fanshawe St due to limited parking.* **Sat 24 May (11-5); Sat 23 Aug (12-6). Adm £5, chd free.** Terraced garden with stunning views across the Beane Valley. Seven levels featuring beautiful front garden in May plus rockery, secluded pond, wisteria tunnel and orchard with wildflowers. August highlights inc late summer perennials and ornamental grasses. Some steep steps with railings.

45 TEWIN GREENS
Hertford Rd, Welwyn, AL6 0JB. Lloyd Harrison, www.tewingreens.co.uk. *Set within the grounds of Tewinbury Farm. Head to the main entrance then follow signs to the main car park.* **Sun 27 July (11-3). Adm £5, chd free. Tea, coffee & cake.** Tewin Greens is a market garden set within the beautiful grounds of Tewinbury Farm. We grow seasonal vegetables, fruit and flowers using no chemicals, minimum till and organic principles for the local community as well as providing fresh produce to the chefs at Tewinbury as well as other local establishments. www.instagram.com/tewingreens.

46 THUNDRIDGE HILL HOUSE
Cold Christmas Lane, Ware, SG12 0UE. Christopher & Susie Melluish, 01920 462500, c.melluish@btopenworld.com. *2m NE of Ware. ¾m from Maltons off the A10 down Cold Christmas Ln, crossing the bypass.* **Sun 15 June (2-5.30). Adm £5, chd free. Home-made teas. Visits also by arrangement for groups of 15 to 50.** Well established garden of approx 2½ acres; good variety of plants, shrubs and roses, attractive hedges. Visitors often ask for the unusual yellow only bed, 'A most popular garden to visit'. Wonderful views in and out of the garden especially down to the Rib Valley to Youngsbury and the ruined Tower of St Mary and All Hallows church. Youngsbury was visited briefly by Lancelot Capability Brown. Dogs on leads welcome. A level garden with paved, gravel and grass areas.

47 WALKERN HALL
Walkern, Stevenage, SG2 7JA. Mrs Kate de Boinville. *4m E of Stevenage. Turn L at War Memorial as you leave Walkern, heading S for Benington (immed after small bridge). Garden 1m up hill on R.* **Sat 1, Sun 2 Feb, Sat 22, Sun 23 Mar (12-4). Adm £6, chd free. Home-made teas. Warming home-made soup, tea, coffee and cakes.** Walkern Hall is essentially a winter woodland garden. Set in eight acres, the carpet of snowdrops and aconites is a constant source of wonder in Jan-Feb. This medieval hunting park is known more for its established trees such as the tulip trees and a magnificent London plane tree which dominates the garden. Following on in March and April is a stunning display of daffodils and other spring bulbs. There is wheelchair access but quite a lot of gravel and a cobbled courtyard. No disabled WC.

48 NEW WALLED GARDEN, 1 FARQUHAR STREET
Bengeo, Hertford, SG14 3BN. Stacey and Carrick Lambert, www.instagram.com/littlebirden. *½m from Hertford Town Centre in the conservation area of Bengeo. Continue out of town up Port Hill and take the 1st L into Cross Rd. Turn L at the end and along to our house.* **Evening opening Fri 20 June (6-8.30). Wine. Sun 22 June (12-5). Tea, coffee & cake. Adm £5, chd free. Wine, soft drinks and nibbles provided on the Friday evening opening. Refreshments will be provided by Isabel Hospice on the Sunday opening.** A passionate plant persons town garden set within Victorian walls, incorporating full curvaceous borders of select herbaceous and woody plants which surround an ever decreasing central lawned area. Many plants are homegrown within the greenhouse with wildlife in mind and adorn the borders year-round whilst the mature trees surrounding the garden, welcome many birds. Wheelchair access via gravel paths.

49 WARRENWOOD
39 Firs Wood Close, Potters Bar, EN6 4BY. Val & Peter Mackie. *Potters Bar, High St (A1000) fork R towards Cuffley, along the Causeway. Immed before the T-lights, R down Coopers Ln Rd. ½m on L Firs Wood Close.* **Sun 1 June (11-5). Adm £6, chd free. Tea, coffee & cake.** Situated within Northaw Park, a three acre garden made up of a woodland area, a field inc a wildflower meadow and a more formal ½ acre around the house. Raised vegetable beds and Victorian greenhouse. Choice of seating areas inc a breeze house, sunken fire pit area and colourful patio benches under the pergola covered with wisteria. Tranquil views up to Northaw village. Good wheelchair access.

50 WATEREND HOUSE
Waterend Lane, Wheathampstead, St Albans, AL4 8EP. Mr & Mrs J Nall-Cain, 07736 880810, sj@nallcain.com, www.instagram.com/waterendhousegarden. *2m E of Wheathampstead. Approx 10 mins from J4 of A1M. Take B653 to Wheathampstead, past Crooked Chimney Pub, after ½m turn R into Waterend Ln. Cross river, house is immed on R.* **Visits by arrangement 10 Feb to 20 Oct for groups of 20 to 25. A personalised tour of the garden awaits you. Adm £12. Home-made teas. Adm inc refreshments.** A hidden garden of four acres sets off an elegant Jacobean Manor House (not open). Steep grass slopes and fine views of glorious countryside. Large quantities of spring bulbs, formal flint-walled garden. Roses, peonies and irises in the summer. Formal beds and lots of colour throughout the year. Mature specimen trees, ponds, formal vegetable garden and chickens. A meditation garden surrounded by a gallery of hornbeam. Take a peak at a row of elephants. A woodland path lined with hellebores. Hilly garden. Wheelchair access to lower gardens only.

ISLE OF WIGHT

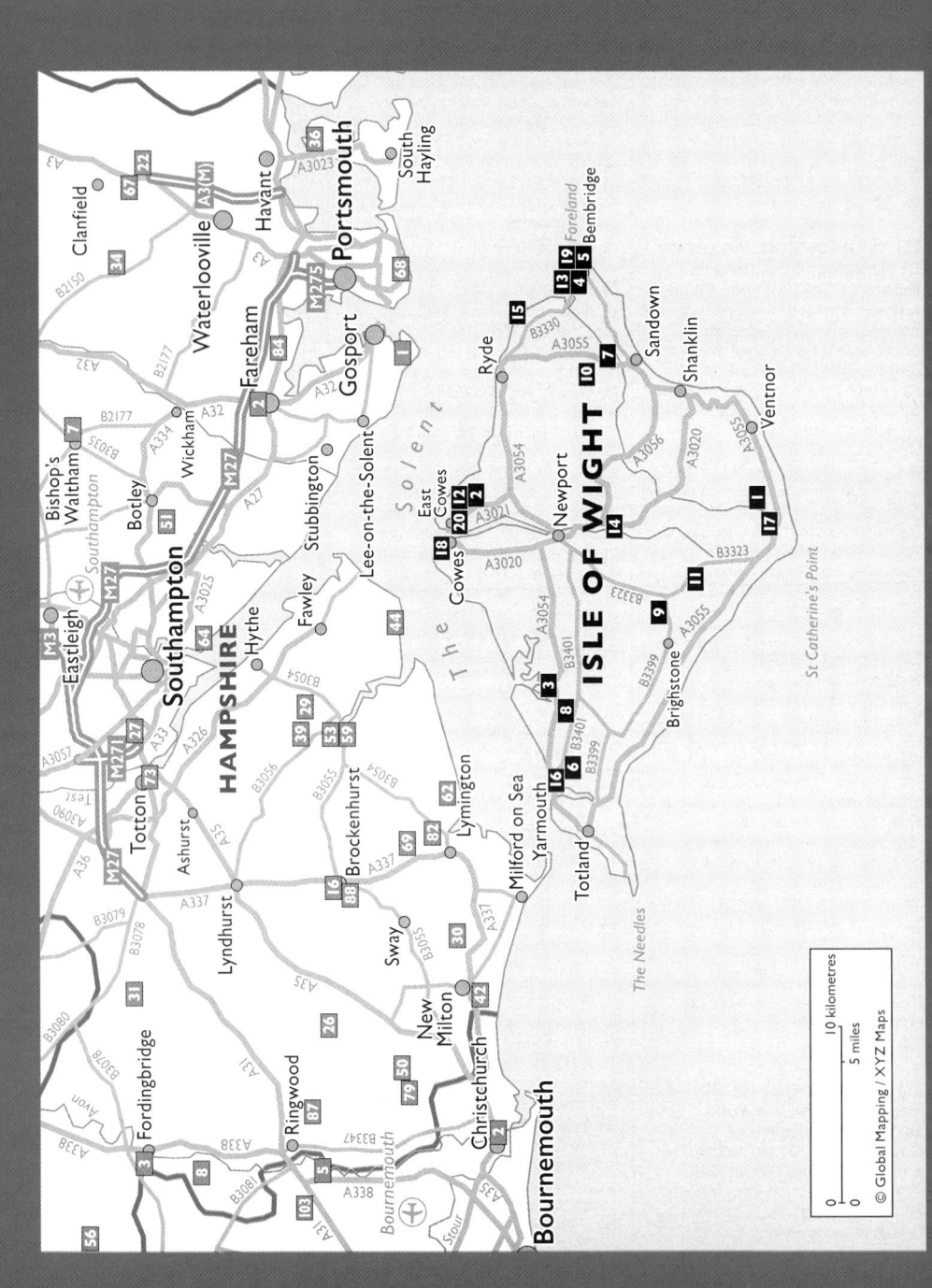

ISLE OF WIGHT

VOLUNTEERS

County Organiser
Jane Bland 01983 874592
jane.bland@ngs.org.uk

County Treasurer
Sally Parker 01983 612495
sally.parker@ngs.org.uk

Booklet Co-ordinator
Jane Bland (as above)

Booklet Advertising
Joanna Truman 01983 873822
joanna_truman@btinternet.com

Assistant County Organisers
Sally Parker
(as above)

Joanna Truman
(as above)

@iow_ngs

OPENING DATES

All entries subject to change. For latest information check
www.ngs.org.uk
Map locator numbers are shown to the right of each garden name.

May

Saturday 10th
NEW Pump Lane Cottage 13

Sunday 18th
Goldings 6
Thorley Manor 16

Sunday 25th
Northcourt Manor Gardens 9

June

Saturday 7th
Rookley Gardens 14

Sunday 8th
Morton Manor 7
Rookley Gardens 14

Saturday 14th
Darts 4
The Old Rectory 11
Yew Tree Lodge 19

Sunday 15th
◆ Nunwell House 10

Saturday 21st
Ashknowle House 1

Sunday 22nd
Ashknowle House 1
Salterns Cottage 15

Saturday 28th
Tillington Villa 17

Sunday 29th
Tillington Villa 17

July

Sunday 6th
NEW Barton Manor 2

Sunday 27th
Dove Cottage 5

August

Saturday 2nd
1 Union Road 18

Sunday 24th
Morton Manor 7

September

Tuesday 16th
◆ Osborne House 12

Thursday 18th
1 Union Road 18

By Arrangement

Arrange a personalised garden visit with your club, or group of friends, on a date to suit you. See individual garden entries for full details.

Crab Cottage 3
Morton Manor 7
Ningwood Manor 8
Northcourt Manor Gardens 9
1 Union Road 18
163 York Avenue 20

Nunwell House

THE GARDENS

1 ASHKNOWLE HOUSE
Ashknowle Lane, Whitwell, Ventnor, PO38 2PP. Mr & Mrs K Fradgley. *4m W of Ventnor. Take the Whitwell Rd from Ventnor or Godshill. Turn into unmade lane next to Old Rectory, ignore the no motor vehicles sign. Field parking. Disabled parking at house.* **Sat 21, Sun 22 June (12-4). Adm £5, chd free. Home-made teas.**
The mature garden of this Victorian house (not open) has great diversity inc woodland walks, water features, colourful beds and borders. The large, well maintained kitchen garden is highly productive and boasts a wide range of fruit and vegetables grown in cages, tunnels, glasshouses and raised beds. Diversely planted and highly productive orchard inc protected cropping of strawberries, peaches and apricots. Propagation areas for trees, shrubs and crops.

2 NEW BARTON MANOR
Barton Estate, East Cowes, PO32 6LB. Dawn Haig-Thomas. *5 min drive from East Cowes. Enter the property from the Whippingham Rd (A3021). Two gate lodges punctuate the top of the drive. Continue along the tree-lined drive & turn R into the car park field.* **Sun 6 July (12-4). Adm £8, chd free. Home-made teas.**
The garden provides a setting for Barton Manor, a Grade II listed building (not open). The main significance of the garden is its historic association with the Royal family and the influence of both Prince Albert and King Edward VII on the garden design. Features inc a large pond with boat house, herbaceous borders, specimen trees, cork oak plantation, walled garden and a yew tree maze.

3 CRAB COTTAGE
Mill Road, Shalfleet, PO30 4NE. Mr & Mrs Scott, 07768 065756, susch11@icloud.com. *4½ m E of Yarmouth. At New Inn, Shalfleet, turn into Mill Rd. Continue 400yds to end of metalled road, drive onto unmade road through NT gates. After 100yds pass Crab Cottage on L. Park opp on grass.* **Visits by arrangement. Adm £5, chd free. Home-made teas.**

1¼ acres on gravelly soil. Part glorious views across croquet lawn over Newtown Creek and Solent, leading through wildflower meadow to hidden water lily pond, secluded lawn and woodland walk. Part walled garden protected from westerlies with mixed borders, leading to terraced sunken garden with ornamental pool and pavilion, planted with exotics, tender shrubs and herbaceous perennials. Wheelchair access over gravel and uneven grass paths.

4 DARTS
Darts Lane, Bembridge, PO35 5YH. Joanna Truman. *Up the hill from Bembridge Harbour, turn L after the Co-op down Love Ln & take 1st L. The house is painted grey.* **Sat 14 June (12.30-5). Combined adm with Yew Tree Lodge £7, chd free.**
Classic walled garden with roses, climbers, shrubs, two large raised vegetable beds and running water feature. Access to garden via two raised steps and three steps up to top garden.

5 DOVE COTTAGE
Swains Lane, Bembridge, PO35 5ST. Mr James & Mrs Alex Hearn. *Head E on Lane End Rd, passing Lane End Court Shops on L. Take 3rd turning on L onto Swains Ln. Dove Cottage is on R.* **Sun 27 July (12-4). Adm £6, chd free.**
An enclosed garden with lawn and woodland area. A central path leads through the woodland setting which has mature variegated shrubs and perennials, leading to the swimming pool area and tennis court.

6 GOLDINGS
Thorley Street, Thorley, Yarmouth, PO41 0SN. John & Dee Sichel. *E of Yarmouth. Follow directions for Thorley from Yarmouth/Newport road or from Wilmingham Ln. Then follow NGS signs. Parking shared with Thorley Manor.* **Sun 18 May (2-5). Combined adm with Thorley Manor £5, chd free. Home-made teas at Thorley Manor.**
A country garden with many focuses of interest. A newly planted orchard already producing cider apples in large amounts. A small, but productive vegetable garden and a well maintained lawn with shrub borders and roses. A microclimate

has been created by the adjustment of levels to create a series of terraced areas for planting.

7 MORTON MANOR
Morton Manor Road, Brading, Sandown, PO36 0EP. Mr & Mrs G Godliman, 07768 605900, patricia.godliman@yahoo.co.uk. *Off A3055, 5m S of Ryde, just out of Brading. At Yarbridge T-lights turn into The Mall. Take next L into Morton Manor Rd.* **Sun 8 June, Sun 24 Aug (11-4). Adm £5, chd free. Home-made teas. Visits also by arrangement Apr to Oct.**
A colourful garden of great plant variety. Mature trees inc many acers with a wide variety of leaf colour. Early in the season a display of rhododendrons, azaleas and camellias and later many perenials, hydrangeas and hibiscus. Ponds, sweeping lawns, roses set on a sunny terrace and much more to see in this extensive garden surrounding a picturesque C16 manor house (not open). Wheelchair access over gravel driveway.

8 NINGWOOD MANOR
Station Road, Ningwood, nr Newport, PO30 4NJ. Nicholas & Claire Oulton, 07738 737482, claireoulton@gmail.com. *Nr Shalfleet. From Newport, turn L opp the Horse & Groom Pub. Ningwood Manor is 300-400yds on the L. Please use 2nd set of gates.* **Visits by arrangement 12 May to 31 Aug for groups of up to 30. Light refreshments.**
A 3 acre, landscaped country garden divided into several areas: a walled courtyard, croquet lawn, white garden and kitchen garden. They flow into each other, each with their own gentle colour schemes; the exception to this is the croquet lawn garden which is a riot of colour, mixing oranges, reds, yellows and pinks. Much new planting has taken place over the last few yrs. The owners have several new projects underway, so the garden is a work in progress. Features inc a vegetable garden with raised beds and a small summerhouse, part of which is alleged to be Georgian.

Yew Tree Lodge

9 NORTHCOURT MANOR GARDENS
Main Road, Shorwell, Newport, PO30 3JG. **Mr & Mrs J Harrison, 01983 740415, john@northcourt.info, www.northcourt.info.** *4m SW of Newport. On entering Shorwell from Newport, entrance at bottom of hill on R. If entering from other directions head through village in direction of Newport. Garden on the L, on bend after passing the church.* **Sun 25 May (12-5). Adm £7, chd free. Home-made teas.** Visits also by arrangement 15 Mar to 10 Nov for groups of 5 to 40. Group visit with talk by owner, teas & tour £14.
15 acre garden surrounding large C17 manor house (not open). Boardwalk along jungle garden. Stream and bog garden. A large variety of plants enjoying the different microclimates. Large collection of camellias and magnolias. Woodland walks. Tree collection. Salvias and subtropical plantings for autumn drama. Productive 1 acre walled kitchen garden. Numerous shrub roses. Formal parterre. Picturesque wooded valley around the house. Bathhouse and snail mount leading to terraces. A plantsman' garden.

10 ◆ NUNWELL HOUSE
Coach Lane, Brading, PO36 0JQ. **Mr & Mrs S Bonsey, info@nunwellhouse.co.uk, www.nunwellhouse.co.uk.** *3m S of Ryde. Signed off A3055 as you arrive at Brading from Ryde & turn into Coach Ln.* **For NGS: Sun 15 June (1-4.30). Adm £5, chd free. Home-made teas.** For other opening times and information, please email or visit garden website.
6 acres of tranquil and beautifully set formal and shrub gardens. Exceptional Solent views over historic parkland and Brading Haven from the terraces. Small arboretum and herbaceous borders. House developed over 5 centuries and full of architectural interest.

11 THE OLD RECTORY
Kingston Road, Kingston, PO38 2JZ. **Derek & Louise Ness, www.instagram.com/louise_ness1.** *8m S of Newport. Entering Shorwell from Carisbrooke, take L turn at mini-r'about towards Chale (B3399). Follow road, house 2nd on L, after Kingston sign. Park in adjacent field.* **Sat 14 June (2-5). Adm £5, chd free. Home-made teas.**
Romantic country garden surrounding the late Georgian Rectory (not open). Areas of interest inc the walled kitchen garden, orchard, formal and wildlife ponds, a wonderfully scented collection of old and English roses and three perennial wildflower meadows.

Osborne House

12 ◆ OSBORNE HOUSE
York Avenue, East Cowes,
PO32 6JY. English Heritage. *1m SE of East Cowes. For SatNav use postcode PO32 6JT.* **For NGS: Evening opening Tue 16 Sept (5.30-7.30). Adm £20, chd free. Pre-booking essential, please email fundraising@english-heritage.org.uk or visit www.english-heritage.org.uk/visit/places/osborne/events for information & booking. Light refreshments.** For other opening times and information, please email or visit garden website.
A garden fit for a Queen: Explore the family home of Queen Victoria and Prince Albert on the Isle of Wight with an exclusive evening tour by our Head Gardener and expert gardens team. Wander amongst the ornate terraces and the spectacular bedding displays, the productive Victorian walled garden, all set within the historic wider parkland featuring trees planted by Prince Albert.
&. 🍵

In 2024 we awarded £232,000 in Community Garden Grants, supporting 89 community garden projects.

13 NEW PUMP LANE COTTAGE
Pump Lane, Bembridge,
PO35 5NG. Lady Annabel Fairfax. *From St Helens, pass the harbour on your L, Pump Ln is diagonally opp The Pilot Boat Inn. Signed, short walk to the garden.* **Sat 10 May (12-4). Adm £6, chd free. Home-made teas.**
The garden was originally designed by Peter Coates, it is on two levels, the lower garden is circular and it was the kitchen garden to the neighbours house, West Cliff House. It still has a few fruit trees but has changed a lot over the yrs with new planting and ideas working with Garden Designer, Virginia von Celsing.
🍵

GROUP OPENING

14 ROOKLEY GARDENS
Rookley, Newport, PO30 3BJ.
4m S of Newport. From the main Newport to Sandown road, take turning for Rookley at Blackwater. **Sat 7, Sun 8 June (12.30-5). Combined adm £6, chd free. Home-made teas at Oakdene.**

OAKDENE
Mr Tim Marshall.
OLD SCHOOL COTTAGE
Mr Nigel Palmer.
THE OLD STABLES
Mrs Susan Waldron.

A varied group of gardens diverse in size, design and interest. Set within the area of Rookley Village, these gardens are in a well kept and lively village. Features inc grassy pathways with colourful borders and places to rest, to beautiful designs displaying a riot of colour, shape and form, plus fruit and vegetables, wild flowers and bees.

15 SALTERNS COTTAGE
Salterns Road, Seaview, PO34 5AH. Susan & Noël Dobbs, 01983 612132, sk.dobbs@icloud.com. *E of Ryde. Enter Seaview from W via Springvale, Salterns Rd links the Duver Rd with Bluett Ave.* **Sun 22 June (12.30-5). Adm £5, chd free. Light refreshments.**
A glasshouse, a potager, exotic borders and fruit trees are some of the many attractions in this 40 metre x 10 metre plot. Salterns Cottage is a listed building built in 1640 and was bought in 1927 by Noël's grandmother Florence, married to Bram Stoker the author of Dracula. The garden was created by Susan in 2005 when she sold her school. Flooding and sandy soil poses a constant challenge to the planting. The greenhouse and potager all raised to cope with floods. Visitors welcome to see garden renovation in progress.

16 THORLEY MANOR
Thorley, Yarmouth, PO41 0SJ. Mr & Mrs Blest. *1m E of Yarmouth. From Bouldnor take Wilmingham Ln, house ½m on L.* **Sun 18 May (2-5). Combined adm with Goldings £5, chd free. Home-made teas.**
Mature informal gardens of over 3 acres surrounding manor house (not open). Garden set out in a number of walled rooms, perennial and colourful self-seeding borders, shrub borders, lawns, large old trees and an unusual island lawn, all seamlessly blending into the surrounding farmland. The delightful cottage garden of Goldings is open, a short walk away.

17 TILLINGTON VILLA
Pan Lane, Niton, PO38 2BT. Paul & Catherine Miller, 01983 730108. *Coming from Blackgang into Niton, turn L at the lych gate of the parish church. Tillington Villa is the 5th house on the R.* **Sat 28, Sun 29 June (12.30-4). Adm £6, chd free. Home-made teas.**
A small garden with mixed borders, a vegetable patch, native trees and fruit trees. There is a wildlife pond and wildlife friendly planting. The patio adjoins a former barn and stable, with a southwest facing conservatory built on. The emphasis is on perennials and shrubs in informal combinations. Wheelchair access over sloping drive and wide path to the back door. One shallow step within the garden.

18 1 UNION ROAD
Cowes, PO31 7TW. Mr & Mrs B Hicks, georgeous1@gmail.com. *Old Town. Take the Cowes Rd (A3020) as far as Northwood T-lights (by the car garage). Bear L & follow signs for Northwood House. Parking at Northwood House, PO31 8AZ, then 3 min walk.* **Sat 2 Aug (11-5). Adm £6, chd free. Home-made teas. Evening opening Thur 18 Sept (6-9). Adm £8, chd free. Wine. Visits also by arrangement 7 Apr to 22 Sept for groups of 5 to 50.**
A south facing town garden with views of the Solent and plenty of sea air. Planting is tropical and takes full advantage of the many hours of sunshine. A combination of unusual plants from drier, arid environments, with lush planting in the zones towards the bottom of the garden. Specimen trees and beautiful walled garden area. A pond featuring wildlife and Mediterranean planting. Working area of the garden features grapevines and olive, apple, fig, citrus and walnut trees. A living agapanthus wall and finally, a herb wall within the outdoor kitchen. Garden designed by Helen Elks-Smith in 2019. Refreshments made from our garden and allotment produce.

19 YEW TREE LODGE
Love Lane, Bembridge, PO35 5NH. Jane Bland, 01983 874592. *On the Bembridge circular one-way system, take 1st L after Co-op into Love Ln. Darts is on the L, Yew Tree Lodge is facing you when Love Ln turns sharply to the R.* **Sat 14 June (12.30-5). Combined adm with Darts £7, chd free. Home-made teas.**
Yew Tree Lodge is flanked by mature oak trees and well established gardens, its main axis being north south. It is divided into separate areas which take into account available natural light and soil type. I have been gardening here for over10 yrs, during this time the garden has altered a great deal. As well as flowering plants there is a vegetable garden, fruit cages and a cool greenhouse. Wheelchair access over paved path connecting the front and back gardens and paved access to decking area.

20 163 YORK AVENUE
East Cowes, PO32 6BD. Mr Roy Dorland, 07768 107779, roydorland@hotmail.co.uk. *Approach East Cowes through Whippingham by the A3021. Pass Barton Manor on R & continue past Osborne House on R. York Ave on L. Ample roadside parking on LHS.* **Visits by arrangement 15 May to 27 July for groups of 10 to 20. Home-made teas.**
Situated near Osborne House, this large colourful garden is packed with unusual hardy perennials and many lovely trees and shrubs. On the terrace is a large date palm, and beyond the main garden there are tropical plants and ferns. You then pass through a gate into a small meadow. There are plenty of seats with tables throughout this relaxing garden.

ISLE OF WIGHT 269

KENT

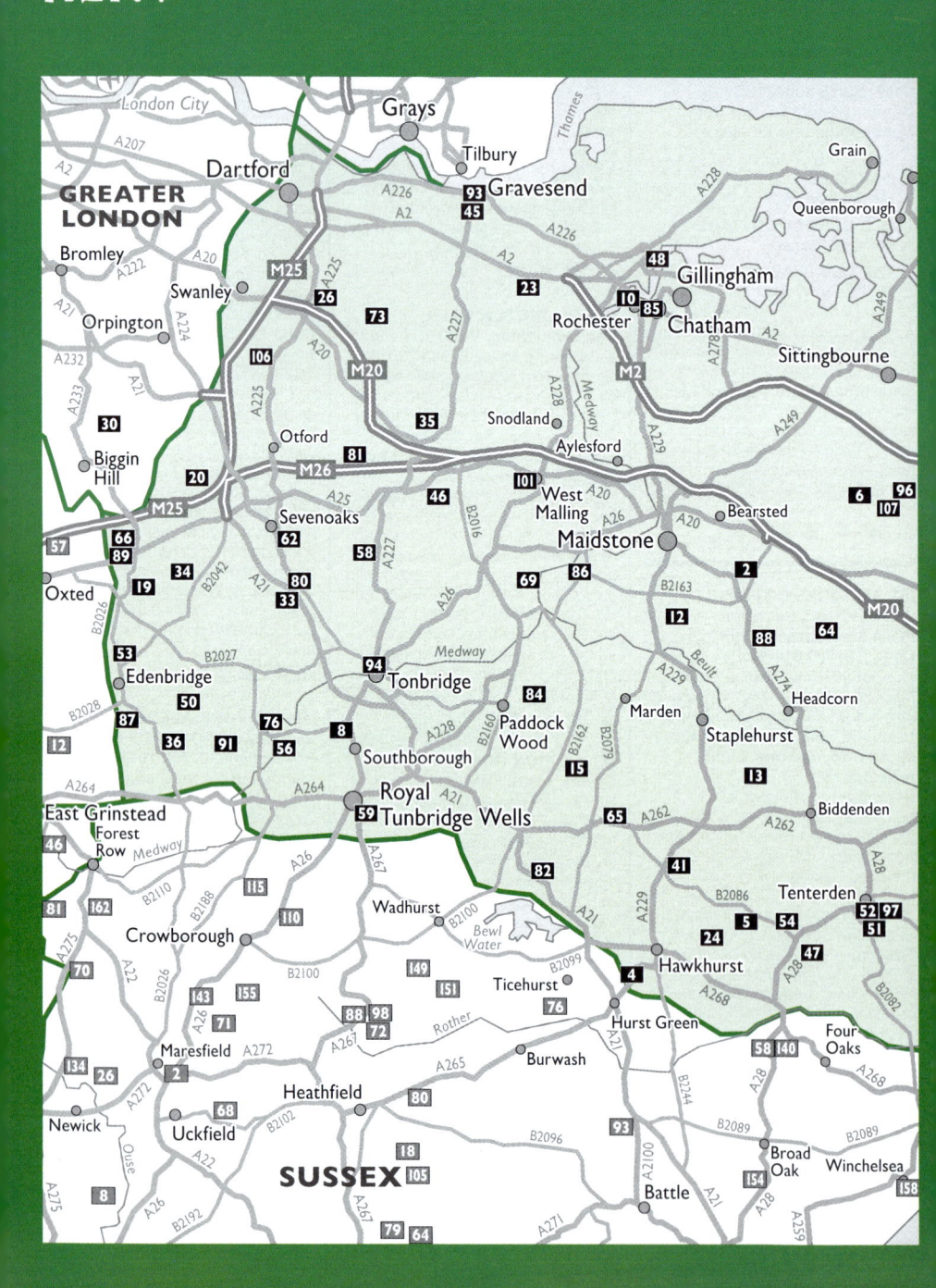

KENT

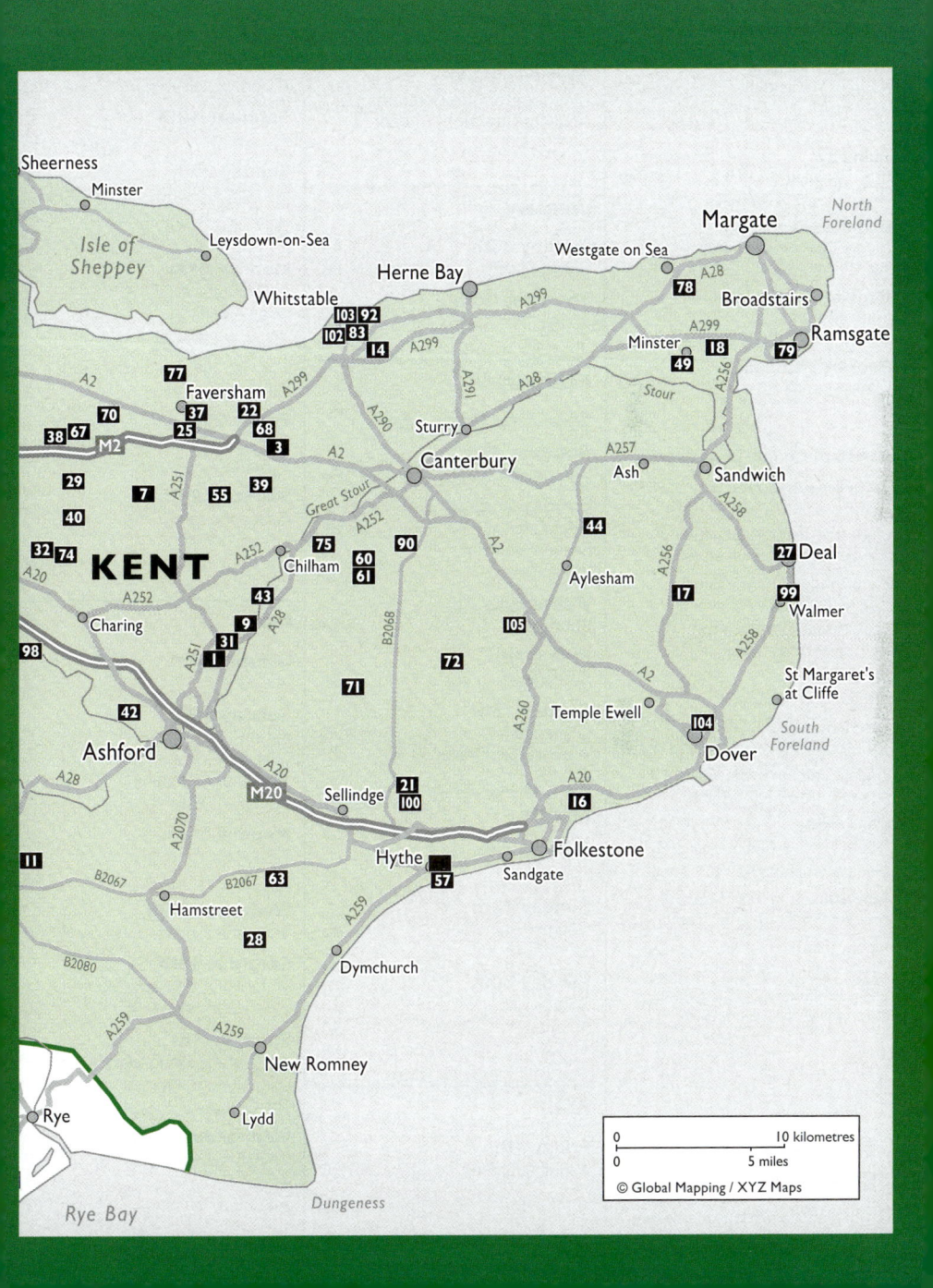

VOLUNTEERS

County Organiser
Nicola Denoon Duncan
01233 758600
nicola.denoonduncan@ngs.org.uk

County Treasurer
Andrew McClintock
01732 838605
andrew.mcclintock@ngs.org.uk

Publicity
Susie Challen
susie.challen@ngs.org.uk

Booklet Advertising
Nicola Denoon Duncan
(see above)

Booklet Co-ordinator
Ingrid Morgan
ingrid@morganhitchcock.co.uk

Booklet Distribution
Diana Morrish
07831 432528
diana.morrish@ngs.org.uk

Assistant County Organisers

Jacqueline Anthony 01892 518829
jacquelineanthony7@gmail.com

Clare Barham 01580 241386
clarebarham@holepark.com

Pam Bridges 07999 525516
pam.bridges@ngs.org.uk

Mary Bruce 01795 531124
mary.bruce@ngs.org.uk

Andy Garland
andy.garland@bbc.co.uk

Sue Harris 07582 718658
sue.harris@powell-cottonmuseum.org

Virginia Latham 01303 862881
virginia.latham@ngs.org.uk

Sian Lewis
sian.lewis@ngs.org.uk

Diana Morrish (as above)

Jane Streatfeild 01342 850362
janestreatfeild@btinternet.com

Nicola Talbot 01342 850526
nicola@falcornhurst.co.uk

Philip Whitaker 07771 765215
philip.whitaker@ngs.org.uk

@KentNGS
@NGSKent
@nationalgardenschemekent

OPENING DATES

All entries subject to change.
For latest information check
www.ngs.org.uk

Map locator numbers are shown to the right of each garden name.

January

Sunday 26th
Spring Platt   88

Thursday 30th
Spring Platt   88

February

Snowdrop Openings

Saturday 1st
Knowle Hill Farm   64

Sunday 2nd
Copton Ash   25
Knowle Hill Farm   64
Spring Platt   88

Wednesday 5th
Spring Platt   88

Friday 7th
Spring Platt   88

Sunday 16th
Copton Ash   25
◆ Doddington Place   29

March

Sunday 16th
Haven   49

Sunday 23rd
Godmersham Park   43
Stonewall Park   91

Sunday 30th
Copton Ash   25
◆ Great Comp Garden   46
◆ Mount Ephraim Gardens   68

April

Friday 4th
◆ Ightham Mote   58

Sunday 6th
Balmoral Cottage   5
◆ Doddington Place   29
Nettlestead Place   69

Sunday 13th
Bilting House   9
◆ Boldshaves   11
◆ Doddington Place   29

Saturday 19th
◆ Godinton House & Gardens   42

Sunday 20th
Balmoral Cottage   5
Copton Ash   25
Haven   49

Monday 21st
◆ Cobham Hall   23
Copton Ash   25

Thursday 24th
Oak Cottage and Swallowfields
    Nursery   71

Friday 25th
Oak Cottage and Swallowfields
    Nursery   71

Saturday 26th
Bishopscourt   10
1 Fox Cottages   39
The Knoll Farm   63

May

Saturday 3rd
Avalon   3

Sunday 4th
Avalon   3
Balmoral Cottage   5
1 Brickwall Cottages   13
Stonewall Park   91

Monday 5th
1 Brickwall Cottages   13
Haven   49

Wednesday 7th
◆ Riverhill Himalayan Gardens   80

Saturday 10th
◆ Godinton House & Gardens   42
NEW Hurst House   56

Sunday 11th
◆ Boughton Monchelsea Place   12
NEW Hurst House   56
The Orangery   75

Wednesday 14th
Great Maytham Hall   47
◆ Hole Park   54
◆ Scotney Castle   82

272 KENT

KENT

Friday 16th
◆ Squerryes Court 89

Saturday 17th
Little Gables 66

Sunday 18th
Bilting House 9
Ladham House 65
Little Gables 66
Whitstable Joy Lane Gardens 102

Thursday 22nd
◆ Goodnestone Park Gardens 44

Friday 23rd
Oak Cottage and Swallowfields Nursery 71

Saturday 24th
NEW Kenfield House 61
Oak Cottage and Swallowfields Nursery 71

Sunday 25th
Copton Ash 25
NEW Kenfield House 61
Old Bladbean Stud 72

Monday 26th
Copton Ash 25
Eagleswood 32
Falconhurst 36
Haven 49

Thursday 29th
◆ Down House 30

Saturday 31st
Windy Ridge 104

June

Sunday 1st
◆ Belmont 7
West Malling Early Summer Gardens 101

Thursday 5th
NEW Brookfield 14

Saturday 7th
Avalon 3
Bishopscourt 10
Churchfield 21
Court Lodge 26
Ivy Chimneys 59
Little Gables 66
West Court Lodge 100

Sunday 8th
Avalon 3
Churchfield 21
Downs Court 31
Godmersham Park 43
Haven 49

Little Gables 66
Nettlestead Place 69
Old Bladbean Stud 72
Tankerton Gardens 92
West Court Lodge 100

Monday 9th
Norton Court 70

Tuesday 10th
Norton Court 70

Wednesday 11th
Great Maytham Hall 47
◆ Hole Park 54
The Old Rectory, Otterden 74

Thursday 12th
◆ Mount Ephraim Gardens 68
The Old Rectory, Otterden 74

Friday 13th
◆ Godinton House & Gardens 42

Saturday 14th
95 High Street 51
99 High Street 52
NEW 4 Southview Cottages 87

Sunday 15th
Downs Court 31
95 High Street 51
99 High Street 52
The Silk House 84
Whitstable Town Gardens 103
◆ The World Garden at Lullingstone Castle 106

Wednesday 18th
Pheasant Barn 77
◆ Riverhill Himalayan Gardens 80

Thursday 19th
Pheasant Barn 77

Saturday 21st
NEW 1 Barnfield Cottages 6
69 Capel Street 16
Pheasant Barn 77

Sunday 22nd
Arnold Yoke 2
NEW 1 Barnfield Cottages 6
Downs Court 31
Old Bladbean Stud 72
Pheasant Barn 77
St Clere 81
Smiths Hall 86

Wednesday 25th
◆ Hever Castle & Gardens 50

Saturday 28th
NEW Finch's 38
Sir John Hawkins Hospital 85

Sunday 29th
Bidborough Gardens 8
Deal Town Gardens 27
NEW Faversham Open Gardens 37
Haven 49
Sir John Hawkins Hospital 85
Torry Hill 96
Yokes Court 107

Monday 30th
Pheasant Barn 77

July

Tuesday 1st
Pheasant Barn 77
NEW ◆ Walmer Castle 99

Friday 4th
Hoppickers East 55
Pheasant Barn 77

Saturday 5th
Avalon 3
NEW Hythe Gardens 57
Lynsted Community Kitchen Garden 67
Pheasant Barn 77

Sunday 6th
Avalon 3
Chevening 20
Gravesend Garden for Wildlife 45
NEW Hythe Gardens 57
Old Bladbean Stud 72
Pheasant Barn 77
Thames House 93

Wednesday 9th
◆ Knole 62
Tonbridge School 94

Saturday 12th
Chapel Farmhouse 17
Hammond Place 48
Stable House 90

Sunday 13th
Chapel Farmhouse 17
Hammond Place 48
Haven 49
Stable House 90

Wednesday 16th
Falconhurst 36

Friday 18th
Hoppickers East 55

Saturday 19th
NEW 1 Barnfield Cottages 6
2 Highfields Road 53
NEW 4 Southview Cottages 87

Sunday 20th
NEW	1 Barnfield Cottages	6
◆	Boughton Monchelsea Place	12
NEW	1 Elses Cottages	33
	Goddards Green	41
	Old Bladbean Stud	72
◆	Quex Gardens	78

Saturday 26th
1 Fox Cottages	39
Knowle Hill Farm	64
The Orangery	75

Sunday 27th
Knowle Hill Farm	64
The Orangery	75

August

Friday 1st
Hoppickers East	55

Saturday 2nd
	Avalon	3
NEW	The Woodman	105

Sunday 3rd
	Avalon	3
NEW	The Woodman	105

Sunday 10th
Chapel House Estate	18
Haven	49

Friday 15th
Hoppickers East	55

Saturday 16th
NEW	1 Barnfield Cottages	6

Sunday 17th
NEW	1 Barnfield Cottages	6

Sunday 24th
The Silk House	84

Monday 25th
Haven	49
Ivy Chimneys	59

September

Wednesday 3rd
◆	Emmetts Garden	34

Sunday 7th
	The Copper House	24
NEW	Hurst House	56

Wednesday 10th
◆	Chartwell	19

Friday 12th
◆	Goodnestone Park Gardens	44

Sunday 14th
Ramsgate Gardens	79

Wednesday 17th
◆	Penshurst Place & Gardens	76

Friday 19th
◆	Godinton House & Gardens	42

Sunday 21st
Haven	49

Thursday 25th
◆	Mount Ephraim Gardens	68

Sunday 28th
◆	Doddington Place	29

October

Sunday 5th
	Balmoral Cottage	5
◆	Hole Park	54

Sunday 12th
Haven	49

Sunday 26th
◆	Great Comp Garden	46

November

Sunday 9th
Haven	49

January 2026

Saturday 31st
Copton Ash	25

February 2026

Sunday 15th
Copton Ash	25

By Arrangement

Arrange a personalised garden visit with your club, or group of friends, on a date to suit you. See individual garden entries for full details.

NEW	Applecote	1
	Arnold Yoke	2
	Avalon	3
	Badgers	4
NEW	1 Barnfield Cottages	6
	Bilting House	9
	Boundes End, Bidborough Gardens	8
	1 Brickwall Cottages	13
	Cacketts Farmhouse	15
	Churchfield	21
	The Coach House	22
	The Copper House	24
	Copton Ash	25
	Court Lodge	26
	Dean House	28
	Downs Court	31
	Eagleswood	32
	Fairseat Manor	35
	Frith Old Farmhouse	40
	Goddards Green	41
	Gravesend Garden for Wildlife	45
	Haven	49
	2 Highfields Road	53
	Kenfield Hall	60
	The Knoll Farm	63
	Knowle Hill Farm	64
	The Old Rectory, Fawkham	73
	The Old Rectory, Otterden	74
	Pheasant Barn	77
	45 Seymour Avenue	83
	The Silk House	84
NEW	4 Southview Cottages	87
	Thames House	93
	Townland	97
	Tram Hatch	98
	West Court Lodge	100

Our 2024 donation to The Queen's Nursing institute now helps support over 3,000 Queen's Nurses working in the community in England, Wales, Northern Ireland, the Channel Islands and the Isle of Man.

Kenfield House

THE GARDENS

1 NEW APPLECOTE

Pilgrims Way, Boughton Aluph, Ashford, TN25 4EX. Jenny and Angus Fraser, 07778 881346, jennyafraser@btinternet.com. *3m N of Ashford. At corner of Boughton Aluph village green take Pilgrims Way for 500 metres and turn 1st L into Brewhouse Ln. 2nd entrance on R 200 metres up lane.* **Visits by arrangement 5 May to 19 June for groups of up to 15. Adm £10, chd free. Tea, coffee & cake inc in adm price.**

A romantic garden created from an old chalk pit and farmyard. There are three distinct areas, a gravel garden, middle garden of mixed planting beds connected by a rose arch to a wilder natural area. The garden abounds with topiary, roses, flowering shrubs and perennials suited to the very dry soil. The garden is steeply banked on two sides with paths to explore for the more adventurous.

2 ARNOLD YOKE

Back Street, Leeds, Maidstone, ME17 1TF. Richard & Patricia Stileman, 07968 787950, richstileman@btinternet.com. *5m E of Maidstone. From M20 J8 take A20 Lenham R to B2163 to Leeds. Through Leeds R into Horseshoes Ln, 1st R into Back St. House ¾ m on L. From A274 follow B2163 to Langley L into Horseshoes Ln 1st R Back St.* **Sun 22 June (2-7). Adm £6, chd free. Home made teas from 2pm; wine and other drinks from 5pm. Visits also by arrangement 10 May to 14 Sept for groups of 10 to 24.**

12 yrs in the making, this one acre garden bordering a C15 Hall House features extensive yew and box hedging, a paradise garden with water feature, a rock garden and many mixed borders. Water featuring in paradise garden. Extensive planting of small trees of special interest. Borders planted to offer interest from March to October. Wheelchair access from the car park and around most parts of the garden.

3 AVALON

57 Stoney Road, Dunkirk, ME13 9TN. Mrs Croll, avalongarden8@gmail.com. *4m E of Faversham, 5m W of Canterbury, 2½ m E of J7 M2. M2 J7 or A2 E of Faversham take A299, 1st L, Staplestreet, then L, R past Mt Ephraim, turn L, R. From A2 Canterbury, turn off Dunkirk, bottom hill turn R, Staplestreet then R, R. Park in side roads.* **Sat 3, Sun 4 May, Sat 7, Sun 8 June, Sat 5, Sun 6 July, Sat 2, Sun 3 Aug (11-4.30). Adm £7, chd free. Refreshments on request. Visits also by arrangement May to Aug for groups of 5 to 30.**

½ acre edge of woodland garden, for all seasons, on north west slope, something round every corner, views of surrounding countryside. Collections of roses, hostas and ferns plus rhododendrons, shrubs, trees, vegetables, fruit, unusual plants and flowers. Planted by feeling, making it a reflective space and plant lovers' garden. Plenty of seating for taking in the garden and resting from lots of steps. Wide variety of plants and planting zones. Friendly chickens. Borrowed countryside landscape and views across Thames estuary.

4 BADGERS
Bokes Farm, Horns Hill, Hawkhurst, Cranbrook, TN18 4XG. Bronwyn Cowdery, 01580 754178, cowderyfamily@btinternet.com. *On the border of Kent & E Sussex. In centre of Hawkhurst, follow A229 in the direction of Hurst Green. Pass 'The Wealden Advertiser'. At sharp L bend turn R up Horns Hill. Drive slowly up Horns Hill.* **Visits by arrangement 26 Aug to 19 Sept for groups of 8 to 25. Adm £5, chd free. Home-made teas.**
The garden comes into its own from end of August, when the Tropical Garden is in full growth. There is also a walled Italian style garden, small Japanese area and woodland with ponds and a waterfall. The Tropical Garden has a wide variety of Palms, Bananas, Gingers, Eucomis and Dahlias and has a network of paths threading through for you to explore and immerse yourself in the Tropics.

5 BALMORAL COTTAGE
The Green, Benenden, Cranbrook, TN17 4DL. Charlotte Molesworth. *Few 100 yds down unmade track to W of St George's Church, Benenden.* **Sun 6, Sun 20 Apr, Sun 4 May, Sun 5 Oct (12-5). Adm £7, chd £2.**
An owner created and maintained garden now 40 yrs mature. Varied, romantic and extensive topiary form the backbone for mixed borders. Vegetable garden, organically managed. Particular attention to the needs of nesting birds and small mammals behind this artistic plantswoman's garden a rare and unusual quality. No hot borders or dazzling dahlias here.

6 NEW 1 BARNFIELD COTTAGES
The Street, Wormshill, Sittingbourne, ME9 0TU. Mr Ian Bond-Webster, 07982 659718, ibondwebster@gmail.com. *Between Maidstone and Sittingbourne on North downs. Top Hollingbourne Hill turn R, at the next Xrds turn L. From A2 at Sittingbourne, Highsted Rd, then Highsted Valley, R fork up Bottom Pond Rd. 2 m to Wormshill, follow signs.* **Sat 21, Sun 22 June, Sat 19, Sun 20 July, Sat 16, Sun 17 Aug (1-5). Adm £5, chd free. Tea, coffee & cake. Visits also by arrangement 31 May to 30 Sept for groups of up to 20.**

A medium-size 4 yr old garden divided into two areas. The main area consists of herbaceous borders and island beds, planted with unusual perennials and grasses, both tender and hardy to give year-round colour and interest. The second area is chiefly devoted to vegetables and fruit with flowering shrubs to provide interest. Fully wheelchair accessible.

7 ♦ BELMONT
Belmont Park, Throwley, Faversham, ME13 0HH. Harris (Belmont) Charity, 01795 890202, administrator@belmont-house.org, www.belmont-house.org. *4½ m SW of Faversham. A251 Faversham-Ashford. At Badlesmere, brown tourist signs to Belmont.* **For NGS: Sun 1 June (11-4). Adm £7, chd free.** For other opening times and information, please phone, email or visit garden website.
Belmont House is surrounded by large formal lawns that are landscaped with fine specimen trees, a pinetum and a walled garden containing long borders, wisteria and large rose border. Across the drive there is a second walled kitchen garden, restored in 2001 to a design by Arabella Lennox-Boyd inc vegetable and herbaceous borders, hop arbours and walls trained with a variety of fruit.

GROUP OPENING

8 BIDBOROUGH GARDENS
Bidborough, Tunbridge Wells, TN4 0XB. Carole & Mike Marks. *3m N of Tunbridge Wells, between Tonbridge & Tunbridge Wells W off A26. Take B2176 Bidborough Ridge signed to Penshurst. Take 1st L into Darnley Dr, then 1st R into St Lawrence Ave. (Boundes End, 2 St Lawrence Ave).* **Sun 29 June (12-5). Combined adm £10, chd free. Home-made teas at Boundes End inc gluten & dairy free options.** Donation to Hospice in the Weald.

BOUNDES END
Carole & Mike Marks, 01892 542233, carole.marks@btinternet.com, www.boundesendgarden.co.uk. **Visits also by arrangement 15 June to 31 Aug for groups of up to 25.**

NEW 12 BOUNDS OAK WAY
Mrs Sue Martin.

NEW 7 BROOKHURST GARDENS
Mr Mark & Mrs Melanie Mason.

4 THE CRESCENT
Mrs Ann Tyler.

8 DOWER HOUSE CRESCENT
Judy & Bill Liddall.

SHEERDROP
Mr John Perry.

The Bidborough gardens (collect garden list from Boundes End, 2 St Lawrence Avenue) are in a small village at the heart of which are The Kentish Hare pub (book in advance), the church, village store and primary school. Partial wheelchair access, some gardens have steps.

9 BILTING HOUSE
nr Ashford, TN25 4HA. Mr John Erle-Drax, 07764 580011, johnerledrax@gmail.com. *A28, 5m E from Ashford, 9m S from Canterbury. Wye 1½ m.* **Sun 13 Apr, Sun 18 May (1.30-5.30). Adm £8, chd free. Home-made teas. Visits also by arrangement April to July for groups of 10+.**
Six acre garden with ha-ha set in beautiful part of Stour Valley. Wide variety of rhododendrons, azaleas and ornamental shrubs. Woodland walk with spring bulbs. Mature arboretum with recent planting of specimen trees. Rose garden and herbaceous borders.

10 BISHOPSCOURT
24 St Margaret's Street, Rochester, ME1 1TS. *Central Rochester, nr castle & cathedral. On St Margaret's St at junction with Vines Ln.* **Sat 26 Apr, Sat 7 June (11-2). Adm £6, chd free. Tea, coffee & cake.**
Bishopscourt has been home to the Bishops of Rochester since 1920. The 1½ acre walled garden has been continuously developed for over a decade and provides a secluded oasis. The garden comprises of lawns, meadow, mature trees, hedging, rose garden, gravel garden, mixed herbaceous borders, glasshouse, vegetable garden and a raised 'lookout' offering views of the castle and the river.

KENT

11 ◆ BOLDSHAVES
Woodchurch, nr Ashford, TN26 3RA. Mr & Mrs Peregrine Massey, 01233 860283, masseypd@hotmail.co.uk, www.boldshaves.co.uk. *Between Woodchurch & High Halden off Redbrook St. From centre of Woodchurch, with church on L & Bonny Cravat/Six Bells pubs on R, 2nd L down Susan's Hill, then 1st R after ½ m before L after a few 100 yrds to Boldshaves. Straight on past oast on L.* **For NGS: Sun 13 Apr (2-6). Adm £10, chd free. Home-made teas in the Cliff Tea House (weather permitting), otherwise in the Barn.** For other opening times and information, please phone, email or visit garden website. Donation to Childhood First.

7 acre garden developed over past 30 yrs, partly terraced, south facing, with wide range of ornamental trees and shrubs, walled garden, Italian garden, Diamond Jubilee garden, Camellia Dell, herbaceous borders (inc flame bed, red borders and rainbow border), vegetable garden, bluebell walks in April, woodland and ponds; wildlife haven renowned for nightingales and butterflies. Home of the Wealden Literary Festival. Grass paths & slope.

&. ❀ 🚗 ☕

12 ◆ BOUGHTON MONCHELSEA PLACE
Church Hill, Boughton Monchelsea, Maidstone, ME17 4BU. Mr & Mrs Dominic Kendrick, 01622 743120, mk@boughtonplace.co.uk, www.boughtonplace.co.uk. *4m SE of Maidstone. For SatNav use ME17 4HP. What3words app: couch.blocks.picked. From Maidstone follow A229 S for 3½ m to T-lights at Linton Xrds, turn L onto B2163, house 1m on R or take J8 off M20 & follow Leeds Castle signs to B2163, house 5½ m on L.* **For NGS: Sun 11 May (2-5.30). Tea, coffee & cake. Sun 20 July (2-5.30). Adm £5, chd £1. Cash payment only.** For other opening times and information, please phone, email or visit garden website.

150 acre estate mainly park and woodland, spectacular views over own deer park and the Weald. Grade I manor house (not open). Courtyard herb garden, intimate walled gardens, box hedges, herbaceous borders, orchard. Planting is romantic rather than manicured. Terrace with panoramic views, bluebell woods, wisteria tunnel, David Austin roses, traditional greenhouse and kitchen garden. Visit St. Peter's Church next door to see the huge stained glass Millennium Window designed by renowned local artist Graham Clark and the tranquil rose garden overlooking the deer park of Boughton Place. Steep steps and narrow paths make the garden unsuitable for wheelchairs and disabled visitors.

❀ 🚗 ☕

Hurst House

In 2024, we celebrated 40 years of continuous funding for Macmillan Cancer Support equating to more than £19.5 million.

KENT

3 1 BRICKWALL COTTAGES
Frittenden, Cranbrook, TN17 2DH. Mrs Sue Martin, 01580 852425, suemartin41@icloud.com, www.geumcollection.co.uk. 6m NW of Tenterden. E of A229 between Cranbrook & Staplehurst & W of A274 between Biddenden & Headcorn. Park in village & walk along footpath opp school. **Sun 4, Mon 5 May (2-5.30). Adm £6, chd free. Home-made teas.** Visits also by arrangement 26 Apr to 31 May for groups of up to 30. Donation to Plant Heritage.
The garden is a secluded oasis in the centre of the village. It is filled with a wide range of plants, inc many trees, shrubs, perennials and over 100 geums which make up the National Collection. In an effort to attract more wildlife some areas of grass have been left unmown, and a new butterfly and moth 'meadow' was created during lockdown to replace the main nursery area. Some paths are narrow and wheelchairs may not be able to reach far end of garden.

4 NEW BROOKFIELD
127 South Street, Whitstable, CT5 3EL. Penny Stefani. Whitstable. Past Tesco to T-junc. Turn R into South St. Last house on the R before farm. **Thur 5 June (10.30-4.30). Adm £5, chd free. Tea, coffee & cake.**
Established mature garden created and tended for 40 yrs. Lawns, mature and young trees, rose beds a large feature, and a woodland glade situated on the Crab and Winkle line which used to pass through the garden. Three ponds, shrubs, beds planted with pollinators in mind.

5 CACKETTS FARMHOUSE
Haymans Hill, Horsmonden, TN12 8BX. Mr & Mrs Lance Morrish, 07831 432528, diana.morrish@hotmail.co.uk. Take B2162 from Horsmonden towards Marden. 1st R into Haymans Hill, 200yds 1st L, drive immed to R of Little Cacketts/H Engineering. **Visits by arrangement 26 May to 26 July for groups of 10+. Adm £10 inc tea, coffee and cake.**
1½ acre garden surrounding C17 farmhouse (not open). Walled garden, bog garden and ponds, woodland garden with unusual plants, bug hotel. Four acre hayfield with self planted wildflowers, an extra three acres of wildflowers newly planted this year. Small area in the main garden with many orchids.

6 69 CAPEL STREET
Capel-Le-Ferne, Folkestone, CT18 7LY. John & Jenny Carter. Between Dover and Folkestone. B2011 from Folkestone to Dover. Past Battle of Britain Memorial on R & then 1st L into Capel St. 69 is 400yds on L. **Sat 21 June (10-4). Adm £5, chd free. Home-made teas.**
A contemporary urban cottage garden. A clever use of traditional and modern planting providing colour throughout the seasons. A rectangular garden where straight lines have been diffused by angles and planting. Space is provided for vegetables for self sufficiency. A quiet location occasionally amplified by a passing Spitfire. Walking distance to the famous Battle of Britain Memorial and pleasant walks along the White Cliffs of Dover. Garden access for wheelchairs achieved via the garage.

7 CHAPEL FARMHOUSE
Lower Street, Tilmanstone, Deal, CT14 0HY. Nigel Watts and Tanuja Pandit. 4m N of Dover. Exit A256 at Tilmanstone r'about then immed R to Dover Rd. Garden is 100 yds down Chapel Rd on the L past the Plough and Harrow. Limited parking on Chapel Rd, more on Dover Rd. **Sat 12, Sun 13 July (12-6). Adm £5, chd free.**
Recently established small garden designed by Kristina Clode on three sides of a semi-detached listed farmhouse. It is divided into a number of separate spaces inc a courtyard style front garden, a Japanese style garden with pond, a formal lawn area, deep herbaceous borders, a meadow with fruit trees and a formal vegetable garden. Emphasis on sustainability and friendliness to wildlife. Wheelchair access via rear gate. Front garden and adjacent pond area can be viewed from other parts of garden.

8 CHAPEL HOUSE ESTATE
Thorne Hill, Ramsgate, CT12 5DS. Chapel House Estate, www.chapelhouseestate.co.uk. 3m W of Ramsgate. From Canterbury take A253 towards Ramsgate, from Sandwich take A256 towards Ramsgate. At Sevenscore r'about take slip road turn R, Cottington Rd, follow Chapel House Estate signs. **Sun 10 Aug (1-5). Adm £6, chd free. Tea, coffee & cake in the Thorne Barn. The No 9 Restaurant will be open, please book through www.chapelhouseestate.co.uk/no-9-restaurant.**
Discover the serene beauty of Chapel House Estate Garden, a hidden gem blending traditional charm with modern elegance. Stroll through beautifully manicured lawns, vibrant flower beds, and peaceful water features, all set against a backdrop of historic architecture. It is a tranquil retreat that delights the senses, offering inspiration for garden lovers of all ages. 35 acre estate, with Arts and Craft style gardens, a wild apple orchard and C13 Chapel House. Helipad just off the Orchard. Uneven paving and steps may cause difficulties.

9 ♦ CHARTWELL
Mapleton Road, Westerham, TN16 1PS. National Trust, 01732 868381, chartwell@nationaltrust.org.uk, www.nationaltrust.org.uk/chartwell. 4m N of Edenbridge, 2m S of Westerham. Fork L off B2026 after 1½ m. **For NGS: Wed 10 Sept (10-5). Adm £10, chd £5.** For other opening times and information, please phone, email or visit garden website.
Informal gardens on hillside with glorious views over Weald of Kent. Water features and lakes together with red brick wall built by Sir Winston Churchill, former owner of Chartwell. Lady Churchill's rose garden. Avenue of golden roses runs down the centre of a must see productive kitchen garden. Hard paths to Lady Churchill's rose garden and the terrace. Some steep slopes and steps.

20 CHEVENING
nr Sevenoaks, TN14 6HG. The Board of Trustees of the Chevening Estate, www.cheveninggardens.com. 4m NW of Sevenoaks. Turn N off A25 to Sundridge T-lights on to B2211; at Chevening Xrds 1½ m turn L. **Sun 6 July (2-5). Adm £12, chd £1. Local ice cream, picnic area.**
The pleasure grounds of the Earls Stanhope at Chevening House are today characterised by lawns and wooded walks around an ornamental

lake. First laid out between 1690 and 1720 in the French formal style, in the 1770s a more informal English design was introduced. In the early C19 lawns, parterres and a maze were established, a lake was created from the ornamental canal and basin, and many specimen trees were planted to shade woodland walks. Expert-guided group tours of the park and gardens can sometimes be arranged with the Estate Office when the house is unoccupied. Gentle slopes, gravel paths throughout.

21 CHURCHFIELD
Pilgrims Way, Postling, Hythe, CT21 4EY. **Chris & Nikki Clark**, 01303 863558, coulclark@hotmail.com. *2m NW of Hythe. From M20 J11 turn S onto A20. 1st L after ½m on bend take road signed Lyminge. 1st L into Postling.* **Sat 7, Sun 8 June (12-5). Combined adm with West Lodge £10, chd free. Tea, coffee & cake in the Postling Village Hall.** Visits also by arrangement 1 Mar to 1 Oct for groups of up to 40.
At the base of the Downs, springs rising in this garden form the source of the East Stour. Two large ponds are home to wildfowl and fish and the banks have been planted with drifts of primula, large leaved herbaceous bamboo and ferns. The rest of the five acre garden is a Kent cobnut platt and vegetable garden, large grass areas and naturally planted borders and woodland. Postling Church open for visitors. Footpaths onto the North Downs with extensive views. Areas around water may be slippery. Children must be carefully supervised.

22 THE COACH HOUSE
Kemsdale Road, Hernhill, Faversham, ME13 9JP. **Alison & Philip West**, 07801 824867, alison.west@kemsdale.plus.com. *3m E of Faversham. At J7 of M2 take A299, signed Margate. After 600 metres take 1st exit signed Hernhill, take 1st L over dual carriageway to T-junc, turn R & follow yellow NGS signs.* **Visits by arrangement May to Sept. Adm £7, chd free. Cream teas or tea, coffee & cake available by prior arrangement at £5pp.**
The ¾ acre garden has views over surrounding fruit-producing farmland.

Sloping terraced site and island beds with year-round interest, a pond room, herbaceous borders containing bulbs, shrubs, perennials and a tropical bed. The different areas are connected by flowing curved paths. Unusual planting on light sandy soil where wildlife is encouraged. Some garden accessible to wheelchairs but some slopes. Seating available in all areas.

23 ◆ COBHAM HALL
Brewers Road, Cobham, DA12 3BL. **Commercial Manager: Louis Glynn-Williams**, www.cobhamhall.com. *3m W of Rochester, 8m E of M25 J2. Entrance drive is off Brewers Rd, 50 metres E from Cobham/Shorne A2 junc. Closest train stn: Sole St (2.8m) or Ebbsfleet International (6.8m).* **For NGS: Mon 21 Apr (2-5). Adm £5, chd free. Cream teas in the Gilt Hall.** For other opening times and information, please visit garden website.
Landscaped for the 4th Earl of Darnley by Humphrey Repton, the gardens inc extensive tree planting, The Gothic Dairy, The Pump House and some of the classical garden buildings are also being renovated for all our visitors. The grounds yield many delights for the lover of nature, especially in spring, when the gardens and woods are resplendent with daffodils, narcissi and a myriad of rare bulbs. Film location for the TV series 'The Crown'. Gravel and slab paths throughout the gardens. Land uneven with many slopes. Stairs and steps in Main Hall. Please call in advance for assistance.

24 THE COPPER HOUSE
Hinksden Road, Benenden, Cranbrook, TN17 4LE. **Eleanor Cochrane**, 07710 614962, eleanor.cochrane@btinternet.com. *Located close to Hinksden Dairy.* **Sun 7 Sept (11-4). Adm £6, chd free. Tea, coffee & cake.** Visits also by arrangement 19 May to 15 Sept for groups of 10+. Adm £7.50.
The Copper House garden is a modern flower garden planted to provide continuous interest and colour throughout the season. Mixed planting of annuals, perennials, bulbs and shrubs. Small wildflower meadow and orchard. Three small ponds to encourage wildlife. Recently renovated woodland ponds.

25 COPTON ASH
105 Ashford Road, Faversham, ME13 8XW. **Drs Tim & Gillian Ingram**, 01795 535919, coptonash@yahoo.co.uk, www.coptonash.co.uk. *½ m S of A2. On A251 Faversham to Ashford road. Opp E bound J6 with M2. Parking possible beyond Aldi in Tettenhall Way. A251 single yellow lines are Mon to Fri restrictions, so available at weekends.* **Sun 2 Feb (12-4). Sun 16 Feb (12-4), open nearby Doddington Place. Sun 30 Mar (12-5), open nearby Mount Ephraim Gardens. Sun 20, Mon 21 Apr (12-5). Sun 25 May (12-5), open nearby Kenfield House. Mon 26 May (12-5). Adm £5, chd free. Home-made teas. 2026: Sat 31 Jan, Sun 15 Feb.** Visits also by arrangement 3 Feb to 30 June for groups of up to 30.
Garden grown out of a love and fascination with plants. Contains wide collection inc many rarities and newly introduced species raised from wild seed. Special interest in woodland flowers, snowdrops and hellebores with flowering trees and shrubs of spring. Refreshed Mediterranean plantings to adapt to a warming climate. Raised beds with choice alpines and bulbs. Alpine and dryland plant nursery. Gravel drive, shallow step by house and some narrow grass paths.

26 COURT LODGE
Horton Road, Horton Kirby, Dartford, DA4 9BN. **Louise Cannon and Tristan Ward**, 07957 183290, louisecannon@btinternet.com. *9m N of Sevenoaks, 5m S of Dartford. In Horton Kirby village off Horton Rd: white gates, next to St Mary's Church. Please look out for parking and entrance signs. Farningham Rd nearest railway stn (15-20 min walk).* **Sat 7 June (2-5.30). Adm £8, chd free.** Visits also by arrangement 5 May to 31 July for groups of 20 to 30.
Beautifully situated on the River Darenth, beyond the old farmyard and C18 dovecote, are gardens evolved over 4 generations. Mature trees and an elegant lawn lead down to the river. Behind old yew hedges lie a secluded white garden, kitchen garden, a renovated rose walk, and bee loving mixed borders. There is a walled Italian Garden and also a wild bank to meander through. Well behaved dogs on leads allowed.

1 Elses Cottages

GROUP OPENING

27 DEAL TOWN GARDENS
Deal, CT14 6EB. *Deal Town centre. Signs from all town car parks. Maps & tickets at the 1st garden you go to.* **Sun 29 June (10-4). Combined adm £5, chd free.**

61 COLLEGE ROAD
Andrew Tucker.

4 GEORGE ALLEY
Lyn Freeman & Barry Popple.

14 SUTHERLAND ROAD
Joan Bull.

88 WEST STREET
Lyn & Peter Buller.

NEW **160 WEST STREET**
Helen Charlton.

Start from any town car park (signs from here). 88 West Street: A non water cottage garden with perennials, shrubs, clematis and roses and shade garden. 4 George Alley: A pretty alley leads to a secret garden with courtyard, leading to a vibrant cottage garden with summerhouse. 14 ~~Rd:~~ Three small gardens ~~~~ for all year interest and support for wildlife. 61 College Rd: Small garden filled with colour and a profusion of plants. 160 West St: Tiny corner plot. Drought tolerant planting, green roofed bike shelter, metal and wood sculptures.

28 DEAN HOUSE
Newchurch, Romney Marsh, TN29 0DL. Jaqui Bamford, 07480 150684, jaquibamford@gmail.com. *Between the village of Newchurch & New Romney. Bilsington Xrds SE towards New Romney. 2.9m to S bend. Garden R after bend. New Romney leave A259 NE on St Marys Rd. 3.7m. Garden on L.* **Visits by arrangement 9 June to 7 Sept. Adm £5, chd free. Tea, coffee & cake.**

A garden created over 25 yrs, from an old farmyard, featuring mature trees, shady areas, wildlife pond, secluded seating areas, sun-drenched gravel beds and herbaceous borders designed for pollinators. Extensive views across Romney Marsh. Visitors can explore further land to which the garden leads to see a rewilding project in its infancy. Large collection of cacti and succulents. Photos of the garden and surrounding area in different seasons are on display throughout the garden. Prints can be made up to order. Wheelchair must be operable on flat gravel and grass areas. Stepping stone paths and some seating will not be accessible.

29 ♦ DODDINGTON PLACE
Church Lane, Doddington, Sittingbourne, ME9 0BB. Mr & Mrs Richard Oldfield, 07596 090849, enquiries@ doddingtonplacegardens.co.uk, www.doddingtonplacegardens. co.uk. *6m SE of Sittingbourne. From A20 turn N opp Lenham or from A2 turn S at Teynham or Ospringe (Faversham), all 4m.* **For NGS: Sun 16 Feb (11-4); Sun 6, Sun 13 Apr, Sun 28 Sept (11-5). Adm £12, chd £3. Light refreshments.** For other opening times and information, please phone, email or visit garden website.

10 acre garden, wide views; trees and cloud clipped yew hedges; woodland garden with azaleas and rhododendrons; Edwardian rock garden; formal garden with mixed borders. A flint and brick late C20

gothic folly; a disused pinnacle from the southeast tower of Rochester Cathedral at the end of the Wellington Walk and the translucent tower newly installed above the sunk garden. Snowdrops in February. This garden proudly provided plants for the National Garden Scheme's Show Garden at Chelsea Flower Show in 2024. Wheelchair access possible to majority of gardens except rock garden.

30 ◆ DOWN HOUSE
Luxted Road, Downe, BR6 7JT. English Heritage. *Luxted Rd, Downe. Off A21or A233. Down House is within ULEZ. Visit TFL's website to check if vehicle meets the emission requirements. If not, charges may apply.* **For NGS: Evening opening Thur 29 May (5.30-7.30). Adm £20, chd free. Pre-booking essential, please email fundraising@english-heritage.org.uk or visit www.english-heritage.org.uk/visit/places/home-of-charles-darwin-down-house/events for information & booking. Light refreshments.** For other opening times and information, please email or visit garden website.
Join us for an exclusive evening with our Head Gardener and expert gardens team. Discover Charles Darwin's 'living laboratory' at Down House, the family home where he developed many of his ground-breaking ideas on evolution and natural selection. Tread the same paths as Darwin along the sandwalk and marvel at the collection of carnivorous plants in the glasshouses. All-terrain wheelchairs available for loan.

31 DOWNS COURT
Church Lane, Boughton Aluph, Ashford, TN25 4EU. Mr Bay Green, 07984 558945, bay@baygee.com. *4m NE of Ashford. From A28 Ashford or Canterbury, after Wye Xrds take next turn NW to Boughton Aluph Church signed Church Ln. Fork R at pillar box, garden only drive on R. Park in field. Disabled parking in drive.* **Sun 8, Sun 15, Sun 22 June (2-5). Adm £8, chd free.** Visits also by arrangement 24 May to 6 July.
3 acre downland garden on alkaline soil with fine trees, mature yew and box hedges, mixed borders. Shrub roses and rose arch pathway, small parterre. Sweeping lawns and lovely views over surrounding countryside.

32 EAGLESWOOD
Slade Road, Warren Street, Lenham, ME17 2EG. Mike & Edith Darvill, 01622 858702, mike.darvill@btinternet.com. *Approx 12m E of Maidstone. E on A20 nr Lenham, L into Hubbards Hill for approx 1m then 2nd L into Slade Rd. Garden 150yds on R. Coaches permitted by prior arrangement.* **Mon 26 May (11-5). Adm £5, chd free. Tea, coffee & cake.** Visits also by arrangement Mar to Nov for groups of 5 to 50. Not open from June to September. Donation to Demelza House Hospice.
2 acre plant enthusiasts' garden. Wide range of trees and shrubs (many unusual), herbaceous material and woodland plants grown to give year-round interest.

33 NEW 1 ELSES COTTAGES
Morleys Road, Weald, Sevenoaks, TN14 6QR. Amanda and Stuart Miles. *2m S of Sevenoaks. Take exit from A21 at Morleys r'about to S'oaks Weald onto Morleys Rd. Just past the restaurant on R you will see parking signs.* **Sun 20 July (12-5). Adm £5, chd £2. Tea, coffee & cake.**
Our garden is about the location and experience rather than the planting. Created from scratch over the last 30+ yrs, the garden inc a large pond, kitchen garden, wildflowers and fun, quirky elements. A good selection of hostas and plenty of places to sit, relax and enjoy the atmosphere.

34 ◆ EMMETTS GARDEN
Ide Hill, Sevenoaks, TN14 6BA. National Trust, 01732 751507, emmetts@nationaltrust.org.uk, www.nationaltrust.org.uk/emmetts-garden. *5m SW of Sevenoaks. 1½m S of A25 on Sundridge-Ide Hill Rd. 1½m N of Ide Hill off B2042.* **For NGS: Wed 3 Sept (10-5). Adm £10, chd £5.** For other opening times and information, please phone, email or visit garden website.
5 acre hillside garden, with the highest tree top in Kent, noted for its fine collection of rare trees and flowering shrubs. The garden is particularly fine in spring, while a rose garden, rock garden and extensive planting of acers for autumn colour extend the interest throughout the season. Hard paths to the Old Stables for light refreshments and WC. Some steep slopes. Volunteer driven buggy available for lifts up steepest hill.

35 FAIRSEAT MANOR
Vigo Road, Fairseat, Sevenoaks, TN15 7LU. Robert and Anne-Marie Nelson, 01732 822256, anne.marie.nelson@btinternet.com. *Fairseat Village. Opp the pond in Fairseat.* **Visits by arrangement 3 Feb to 14 Mar for groups of up to 15. Adm £7, chd free. Light refreshments.**
2 acre mature garden on top of the North Downs. Extensive spring bulbs with many varieties of snowdrops, Rose and perennial borders, sunken garden with pond, and meadows. All accessible, with one step to sunken pond garden. Wheelchair access through the garage and shed, with no steps to much of the garden.

36 FALCONHURST
Cowden Pound Road, Markbeech, Edenbridge, TN8 5NR. Mr & Mrs Charles Talbot, www.falconhurst.co.uk. *3m SE of Edenbridge. B2026 at Queens Arms pub turn E to Markbeech. 2nd drive on R before Markbeech village.* **Mon 26 May (11-5); Wed 16 July (10-4). Adm £8.50, chd free. Home-made teas.**
Country garden with fabulous views devised and cared for by the same family for 170 yrs. Deep mixed borders with old roses, peonies, shrubs and a wide variety of herbaceous and annual plants, ruin garden, walled garden, cutting garden, interesting mature trees and shrubs, kitchen garden, woodland areas. Opening on 16 July will inc access to Stone 25, a contemporary stone sculpture exhibition. The majority of the garden is accessible. Disabled parking by the house.

Our donation to Marie Curie this year equates to 17,496 hours of nursing care or 43 days of care in one of their nine hospices.

GROUP OPENING

37 NEW FAVERSHAM OPEN GARDENS
Market Place, Faversham, ME13 7AG. www.instagram.com/favershamopengardens. *Central Faversham and surrounding area. Pre-book tickets online or purchase tickets on the day from Market Place, Faversham ME13 7AG.* **Sun 29 June (10-5). Combined adm £7, chd free. Some gardens offer refreshments (details in ticket/handbook) and cafes and pubs are open in Faversham.**
Faversham Open Gardens & Garden Market Day is a community-led event showcasing over 25 small and larger town gardens. Don't miss the Garden Market selling plants and other gardening items. Enjoy the contrasts between the different gardens, from plant lovers' plots to 'outdoor rooms', family spaces, tiny courtyards, allotments, wildlife-friendly gardens, community projects and more. Those opening their gardens may not always be expert gardeners but they all love their gardens enough to share them for the day. Faversham's historic architecture makes this a special day out - it is famous for its pubs and cafes. Access to all gardens is only by ticket/handbook listing all the gardens and their addresses. Buy from the Faversham Open Gardens stall in Market Place from 10am. Tickets bought through the NGS website must be shown at the stall in exchange for an entry ticket/handbook. The Garden Market runs from 10am-4pm in the historic Market Place and features a large number of garden-related stalls and leading nurseries selling plants, local pottery, gardenalia, garden books and more. Some gardens are accessible by wheelchair, details can be found in the ticket handbook.

38 NEW FINCH'S
Kingsdown, Sittingbourne, ME9 0RA. Leonie and Nick Britcher, www.instagram.com/leonie_in_the_garden. *4m SE of Sittingbourne, 6m W of Faversham. Entry and parking for the garden will be via a gate into our field on Ludgate Ln. What3words app: visa.gains.candle.* **Sat 28 June (11-4). Adm £6, chd free. Tea, coffee & cake.**
Gardening for wildlife in the North Kent Downs. The garden at Finch's was redesigned by the current owners when they purchased the property in 2021. Areas to explore inc formal garden, kitchen garden, nuttery, wildlife pond and 1½ acre woodland planted in 2021.

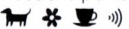

39 1 FOX COTTAGES
Fox Lane, Oversland, Faversham, ME13 9PG. Rachel & Andrew Stead. *4m SE of Faversham. Opp Foxhill Stud, 1 Fox Cottages is the house with dragons on the roof. Oversland is 1 m to the W of Selling & close to Selling train stn.* **Sat 26 Apr, Sat 26 July (12-4). Adm £5, chd free. Tea, coffee & cake.**
Organic cottage garden with relaxed planting style used in borders; multiple fruit trees and apple arches with beautiful Spring blossom, a meadow in summer and wildlife pond with dead hedge. Productive vegetable/cut flower garden with most grown from seed. Produce own compost. Certainly not a perfect garden but one that feeds us and brings us much joy. Far-reaching views from the top of the garden.

40 FRITH OLD FARMHOUSE
Frith Road, Otterden, Faversham, ME13 0DD. Drs Gillian & Peter Regan, 01795 890556, peter.regan@cantab.net. *½ m off Lenham to Faversham Rd. From A20 E of Lenham follow signs Eastling. After 4m L into Frith Rd. From A2 in Faversham turn S (Brogdale Rd); cont 7m (thro' Eastling), R into Frith Rd. Limited parking.* **Visits by arrangement Mar to Sept for groups of up to 30. Adm £7.50, chd free. Tea, coffee & cake.**
An eclectic collection of plants growing together as if in the wild, developed over nearly 50 yrs. Several hundred interesting (and some very unusual) plants. Trees and shrubs chosen for year-round appeal. Special interest in bulbs and woodland plants. Visitor comments - 'one of the best we have seen, natural and full of treasures', 'a plethora of plants', 'inspirational', 'a hidden gem'. Altered habitat areas to increase the range of plants grown. Areas for wildlife. Unusual trees and shrubs, some rare outside Botanic Gardens.

41 GODDARDS GREEN
Angley Road, Cranbrook, TN17 3LR. John & Linde Wotton, 07768 500552, jpwotton@gmail.com, www.goddardsgreengarden.com. *½ m SW of Cranbrook. On W of Angley Rd. (A229) at junction with High St, opp War Memorial.* **Sun 20 July (12-4). Adm £6, chd free. Home-made teas. Prior notice needed of dietary restrictions. Visits also by arrangement Apr to Sept for groups of 10 to 50. No visits in August. Refreshments £4 per person.**
Gardens of about 7 acres, surrounding beautiful 500+yr old clothier's hall (not open), laid out in 1920s and redesigned since 1992 to combine traditional and modern planting schemes. fountain and rill, water garden, fern garden, mixed borders of bulbs, perennials, shrubs, trees and exotics; birch grove, grass border, pond, kitchen garden, meadows, arboretum and mature orchard; 2 wild acres. Some slopes and steps, but most areas (though not the toilets) are wheelchair accessible. Disabled parking is reserved near the house.

42 ◆ GODINTON HOUSE & GARDENS
Godinton Lane, Ashford, TN23 3BP. The Godinton House Preservation Trust, 01233 643854, info@godintonhouse.co.uk, www.godintonhouse.co.uk. *1½ m W of Ashford. M20 J9 to Ashford. Take A20 towards Charing & Lenham, then follow brown tourist signs.* **For NGS: Sat 19 Apr, Sat 10 May, Fri 13 June, Fri 19 Sept (12.30-5.30). Adm £10.50, chd £2.50. Cream teas. Ticket office serves takeaway refreshments, please check garden website for tearoom opening times. For other opening times and information, please phone, email or visit garden website.**
Predominantly Sir Reginald Blomfield's design of 1896, the 12 acres of tranquil gardens surrounding Godinton House are enclosed by a vast yew hedge and showcase features added by different owners over time. The gardens inc terraced lawns, herbaceous borders, a rose garden, ponds, large walled garden, a wild garden and the Italian garden and glasshouses. Partial wheelchair access to ground floor of house and most of gardens.

Kenfield Hall

43 GODMERSHAM PARK
Godmersham, CT4 7DT. Mrs Fiona Sunley. *5m NE of Ashford. Off A28, midway between Canterbury & Ashford.* **Sun 23 Mar, Sun 8 June (1-5). Adm £8, chd free. Home-made teas in the Orangery.**
24 acres of restored wilderness and formal gardens set around C18 mansion (not open). Topiary, rose garden, herbaceous borders, walled kitchen garden and recently restored Italian and swimming pool gardens. Superb daffodils in spring and roses in June. Historical association with Jane Austen. Also visit the Heritage Centre. Deep gravel paths.

44 ♦ GOODNESTONE PARK GARDENS
Wingham, Canterbury, CT3 1PL. Julian Fitzwalter, 01304 840107, office@goodnestonepark.co.uk, www.goodnestonepark.co.uk. *6m SE of Canterbury. Village lies S of B2046 from A2 to Wingham. Brown tourist signs off B2046. Use CT3 1PJ for SatNav.* **For NGS: Thur 22 May, Fri 12 Sept (9-5). Adm £9, chd £3.50. Light refreshments at The Old Dairy Cafe. Café tel: 01304 695098. For other opening times and information, please phone, email or visit garden website.**
One of Kent's outstanding gardens and the favourite of many visitors. 14 acres with views over parkland. Something special year-round, from snowdrops and spring bulbs to the famous walled gardens. Outstanding trees and woodland garden with cornus collection and hydrangeas later. Two arboreta and a contemporary gravel garden.

45 GRAVESEND GARDEN FOR WILDLIFE
68 South Hill Road, Windmill Hill, Gravesend, DA12 1JZ. Judith Hathrill, 07810 550991, judith.hathrill@live.com. *On Windmill Hill. From A2 take A227 towards Gravesend. At T-lights with Cross Ln turn R then L at next T-lights, following yellow NGS signs. Park in Sandy Bank Rd or Rouge Ln.* **Sun 6 July (2-5). Adm £5, chd free. Tea, coffee & cake. Visits also by arrangement June & July for groups of up to 16. Adm charge given on enquiry to inc teas unless not required.**
This small cottage garden combines native wildflowers, perennials, annuals, herbs, shrubs and grasses to attract and sustain wildlife throughout the year. Container grown vegetables, 3 ponds and a wildflower-studded lawn with seating for teas. Photographic display in summerhouse. Information and leaflets about gardening for wildlife always available.

46 ♦ GREAT COMP GARDEN
Comp Lane, Platt, nr Borough Green, Sevenoaks, TN15 8QS. Great Comp, 01732 885094, office@greatcompgarden.co.uk, www.greatcompgarden.co.uk. *7m E of Sevenoaks. 2m from Borough Green Station. Accessible from M20 & M26 motorways. A20 at Wrotham Heath, take Seven Mile Ln, B2016; at 1st Xrds turn R; garden on L ½ m.* **For NGS: Sun 30 Mar, Sun 26 Oct (10-5). Adm £10, chd £3.50. For other opening times and information, please phone, email or visit garden website.**
Skillfully designed 7 acre garden of exceptional beauty. Spacious setting with maintained lawns and paths lead visitors through plantsman's collection of trees, shrubs, heathers and herbaceous plants. Early C17 house (not open). Magnolias, hellebores and snowflakes (leucojum), hamamellis and winter flowering heathers are a great feature in the spring. A great variety of perennials in summer inc salvias, dahlias and crocosmias. Tearoom open daily for morning coffee, home-made lunches and cream teas. Most of garden accessible to wheelchair users. Disabled WC.

47 GREAT MAYTHAM HALL
Maytham Road, Rolvenden, Tenterden, TN17 4NE. The Sunley Group. *3m from Tenterden. Maytham Rd off A28 at Rolvenden Church, ½ m from village on R. Designated parking for visitors.* **Wed 14 May, Wed 11 June (12.30-3.30). Adm £8, chd free.**
Lutyens designed gardens famous for having inspired Frances Hodgson Burnett to write The Secret Garden (pre Lutyens). Parkland, woodland with bluebells. Walled garden with herbaceous beds and rose pergola. Pond garden with mixed shrubbery and herbaceous borders. Interesting specimen trees. Large lawned area, rose terrace with far-reaching views.

48 HAMMOND PLACE
High Street, Upnor, Rochester, ME2 4XG. Paul & Helle Dorrington. *3m NE of Strood or at A2. J1 take A289 twds Grain at r'about follow signs to Gillingham. After 2nd r'about take 1st L following signs to Upnor & Upnor Castle. Park in free car park & continue by foot to the High St.* **Sat 12, Sun 13 July (11-4). Adm £7, chd free. Tea, coffee & cake.**
A small garden in a historically interesting village growing an eclectic mix of flowers, fruit and vegetables around a Scandinavian style house. Features inc greenhouse, pond and a Sauna Hut.

49 HAVEN
22 Station Road, Minster, Ramsgate, CT12 4BZ. Robin Roose-Beresford, 01843 822594, robin.roose@hotmail.co.uk. *1 m E of Manston. Off A299 Ramsgate Rd, take Minster exit from Manston r'bout, straight road, R fork at church is Station Rd.* **Sun 16 Mar, Sun 20 Apr, Mon 5, Mon 26 May, Sun 8, Sun 29 June, Sun 13 July, Sun 10, Mon 25 Aug, Sun 21 Sept, Sun 12 Oct, Sun 9 Nov (10-4). Adm £5, chd free. Visits also by arrangement 2 Mar to 16 Nov for groups of up to 20. Free local parking available.**
Award winning 300ft garden, designed in the Glade style, similar to Forest gardening but more open and with use of many exotic and unusual trees, shrubs and perennials from all over the world and with wildlife in mind. Devised and maintained by the owner, densely planted in a natural style with stepping stone paths. Two ponds (one for wildlife, one for fish with water lilies plants inc tree ferns and bamboos and year-round colour. Features inc a tree fern grove. There are many Palms, Bamboos and exotic trees. Refreshments available locally.

50 ♦ HEVER CASTLE & GARDENS
Edenbridge, TN8 7NG. Hever Castle Ltd, 01732 865224, info@hevercastle.co.uk, www.hevercastle.co.uk. *3m SE of Edenbridge. Between Sevenoaks & East Grinstead off B2026. Signed from J5 & J6 of M25, A21, A264.* **For NGS: Wed 25 June (10.30- 4.30). Please check garden website for 2025 admission prices.** For other opening times and information, please phone, email or visit garden website.
Romantic double-moated castle, the childhood home of Anne Boleyn, set in 150 acres of formal and natural landscape. Topiary, Tudor herb garden, magnificent Italian garden with classical statuary, sculpture and fountains. 38 acre lake, yew and water mazes. Summer is a wonderful time to view the gardens as over 5,000 roses create a kaleidoscope of colour. Partial wheelchair access.

51 95 HIGH STREET
Tenterden, TN30 6LB. Judy & Chris Older. *Enter via Bridewell Car Park. Parking Free on Sundays. Drive to far end, venue on R.* **Sat 14, Sun 15 June (12-5). Combined adm with 99 High Street £6, chd free.**
Small town house garden divided into 3 rooms. Has developed since June 2021 from a blank canvas, now well-stocked with perennials and summer flowers to capacity. Colourful and traditional. Plenty of seating. Two small steps.

52 99 HIGH STREET
Tenterden, TN30 6LB. Mrs Veryan Rahr. *9½ m SW of Ashford. Entrance via far end of Bridewell Ln Car Park. Entrance through No. 95 High Street garden.* **Sat 14, Sun 15 June (12-5). Combined adm with 95 High Street £6, chd free.**
Narrow garden with long brick path and 'rooms', seating areas, mainly shaded with interesting planting over 25 yrs. A few small steps.

53 2 HIGHFIELDS ROAD
Edenbridge, TN8 6JN. Auralucia Brook, auraluciabrook@hotmail.com. *Marlpit Hill / Edenbridge. From the main road B2026, turn into Swan Ln. Turn into Highfields Rd. 2nd house on the L.* **Sat 19 July (11-5). Combined adm with 4 Southview Cottages £8. Tea, coffee & cake at 4 Southview Cottages. Visits also by arrangement July & Aug for groups of up to 12.**
The garden is a multi-season, in the hope of attracting wildlife, birds, amphibians, and, of course, humans. A large collection of plants, upcycled pots, abundant ornaments. It has won 1st and 2nd prizes in the last few years in the local district. Enjoy the sounds, scents, textures, secrecy, relaxation, and diversity in a very small space and an unusual, unique garden.

54 ♦ HOLE PARK
Benenden Road, Rolvenden, Cranbrook, TN17 4JB. Mr & Mrs Edward Barham, 01580 241344, info@holepark.com, www.holepark.com. *4m SW of Tenterden. Midway between Rolvenden & Benenden on B2086. Follow brown tourist signs from Rolvenden. What3words app: sized. sticking.bypasses.* **For NGS: Wed 14 May, Wed 11 June, Sun 5 Oct (11-5.30). Adm £12.50, chd £2.50. Light refreshments. Picnics only in picnic site & car park please.** For other opening times and information, please phone, email or visit garden website.
Hole Park is proud to stand amongst the group of gardens which first opened in 1927 soon after it was laid out by my great-grandfather. Our 15 acre garden is surrounded by parkland and contains fine yew hedges, large lawns with specimen trees, walled gardens, pools and mixed borders combined with bulbs, rhododendrons and azaleas. Massed bluebells in woodland walk, standard wisterias, orchids in flower meadow and glorious autumn colours make this a garden for all seasons. Redesigned and newly planted walled garden with oval path and deep herbaceous beds a particular feature. Wheelchairs are available for loan and may be reserved. Please email info@ holepark.com.

55 HOPPICKERS EAST
Hogbens Hill, Selling, Faversham, ME13 9QZ. **Katherine Pickering.** *Signs from HogbensHill. From A251 signed Selling 1m, then NGS signs.* **Fri 4, Fri 18 July, Fri 1, Fri 15 Aug (11-4). Adm £5, chd free.**
A new garden, started in autumn 2020 on the edge of a field. No dig principles. Emphasis on plants for pollinators and other insects. New this year removed rose border and replaced with dahlias and mixed planting. Flat grass paths.

56 NEW HURST HOUSE
Poundsbridge Lane, Penshurst, Tonbridge, TN11 8AG. AJ Lampitt, www.instagram.com/ajarchard_walledgarden. *Penshurst. A21 S, exit onto A26 to Bidborough. Cont for 0.8m, turn R onto B2176. Cont for 2.7m then turn L onto Poundsbridge Ln. Take 1st R onto single track lane. What3words app: windmills.magical.strongly.* **Sat 10, Sun 11 May, Sun 7 Sept (10-4.30). Adm £10, chd free. Tea, coffee & cake.**
A Victorian walled garden under restoration since 2021, with restored 1902 Thomas Messenger vinery and glasshouse, a beautiful formal garden with far reaching views, filled with perennials, roses and other unusual plants, an orchard and ponds. The wildflower meadow is an ongoing project and a native woodland was planted in 2022 with a Woodland Trust grant. Features inc natural swimming pond, formal rose garden, secluded Mediterranean garden, rockery and woodland walk. Wheelchair access inside the walled garden.

GROUP OPENING

57 NEW HYTHE GARDENS
Hythe, CT21 5UF. *Two on hillside above Hythe town and one near the sea. Transport required to visit all 3 gardens. Topgallant: 5 North Rd, CT21 5UF. Lisbon Cottage: 56 Park Rd, CT21 6EU. 20 Spanton Crescent: CT21 4SF.* **Sat 5, Sun 6 July (1.30-5.30). Combined adm £8, chd free. Home-made teas at Topgallant.**

NEW LISBON COTTAGE
Heidi Bailey.

NEW 20 SPANTON CRESCENT
Nikki Griffith, www.nikkigriffithart.co.uk.

TOPGALLANT
Mary Sampson.

Three very different gardens: on the hillside, Spanton Crescent is open and sunny and packed with flowers. Topgallant is green and shady, and will be doing teas. A terraced hillside garden with sea views. Lisbon Cottage is a smaller designer garden nearer the sea. The three gardens give an insight to seaside gardening.

58 ♦ IGHTHAM MOTE
Mote Road, Ivy Hatch, Sevenoaks, TN15 0NT. National Trust, 01732 810378, ighthammote@nationaltrust.org.uk, www.nationaltrust.org.uk/ightham-mote. *Nr Ivy Hatch: 6m E of Sevenoaks; 6m N of Tonbridge; 4m SW of Borough Green. E from Sevenoaks on A25 follow brown sign R along Coach Road. W from Borough Green on A25 follow brown sign L along Coach Rd. N from Tonbridge on A227 follow brown sign L along High Cross Rd.* **For NGS: Fri 4 Apr (10-5). Adm £16, chd £8. Light refreshments served in The Mote Café. Visitors are welcome to bring a picnic. For other opening times and information, please phone, email or visit garden website.**
Lovely 14 acre garden surrounding a picturesque medieval moated manor house c1320, open for NGS since 1927. Herbaceous borders, lawns, C18 cascade, fountain pools, courtyards, cutting garden and newly reinstated walled garden provide formal interest; while the informal lakes, stream, pleasure grounds, stumpery/fernery, dell and orchard complete the sense of charm and tranquillity. Please check NT website for access details (map available). Assistance dogs only in garden.

59 IVY CHIMNEYS
28 Mount Sion, Tunbridge Wells, TN1 1TW. **Laurence & Christine Smith.** *At the end of Tunbridge Wells High St, with Pizza Express on the corner, turn L up Mount Sion. Ivy Chimneys is a red brick Queen Anne house at the top of the hill on the R.* **Sat 7 June (11-5); Mon 25 Aug (1-5). Adm £5, chd free.**
Town centre garden with herbaceous borders and masses of roses set on three levels of lawns, all enclosed in an old walled garden. Large veg/cutting garden and herb garden. Additional August opening will appeal to dahlia lovers. The property is Queen Anne and one of the oldest houses in Tunbridge Wells. Car Parking in public car parks near the Pantiles. High Street cafes and restaurants nearby.

60 KENFIELD HALL
Kenfield, Petham, Canterbury, CT4 5RN. **Barnaby & Camilla Swire,** kenfieldhallgarden@gmail.com. *Petham nr Canterbury. Continue along Kenfield Rd, down the hill & up the other side. Pass the farm & look out for signs.* **Visits by arrangement 5 May to 30 Sept. Adm £10, chd free.**
An evolving, 8 acre, organic garden set in a peaceful AONB with fantastic views of the surrounding landscape. The site inc an historic arboretum, an C18 formal sunken garden as well as a Japanese garden incorporating a naturally managed pool with diverse wildlife. There are also herbaceous beds, spring bulbs, a wildflower meadow, glasshouses and vegetable garden with cut flowers.

61 NEW KENFIELD HOUSE
Kenfield, Petham, Canterbury, CT4 5RN. **Rorke and Sarah Henderson.** *Located outside of Petham village in the same lane as Kenfield Hall. Opp a large oast house and adjacent to a thatched house.* **Sat 24 May (11-4). Sun 25 May (11-4), open nearby Copton Ash. Adm £7.50, chd free. Home-made teas.**
In an AONB, this 3½ acre garden has many areas varying from a white garden and a wild garden with an orchard and unusual trees, to a spiral lawn. There are several flowering borders of perennials and shrubs and wild flowers abound in several unmown areas. The influence of Marian Boswell can be seen in the design and planting plan when she recreated this garden in 2012.

KENT 285

Ightham Mote

62 ♦ KNOLE
National Trust Knole, Sevenoaks, TN15 0RP. Lord Robert Sackville-West, 01732 462100, knole@nationaltrust.org.uk, www.nationaltrust.org.uk/knole. *1½ m SE of Sevenoaks. Leave M25 at J5 (A21). Park entrance S of Sevenoaks town centre off A225 Tonbridge Rd (opp St Nicholas Church). For SatNav use TN13 1HX. Additional parking charges apply.* **For NGS: Wed 9 July (11-4). Adm £5, chd £2.50. For other opening times and information, please phone, email or visit garden website.**
Lord Sackville's private garden at Knole is a magical space, featuring sprawling lawns, a walled garden, an untamed wilderness area and a medieval orchard. Follow signage on site for the entrance to the garden. Doors will open to reveal the secluded lawns of the 26 acre garden and stunning views of the house. Last entry at 3.30pm and closes at 4pm. Please book in advance using Knole's website. Refreshments are available in the Brewhouse Café. Bookshop and shop in Green Court. Food and drink, inc picnics are not allowed in Lord Sackville's private garden. Wheelchair access via the bookshop. Some paths may be difficult for manual wheelchair users. Assistance dogs are allowed in the garden.
& ☕

63 THE KNOLL FARM
Giggers Green Road, Aldington, Ashford, TN25 7BY. Lord & Lady Aldington, ca@aldingtonlow.com. *Above the Royal Military Canal on the Aldington Dymchurch road. The postcode leads to Goldenhurst, the drive entrance is opp & further down hill.* **Sat 26 Apr (11-4). Adm £10, chd free. Visits also by arrangement 1 Mar to 1 July.** Donation to Bonnington Church.
10 acres of woodland garden with over 130 camellias, acer japonica, and a growing collection of specimen pines and oaks; bluebell wood; formal elements; flock of Jacob Sheep around lake; far reaching views across Romney Marsh. Paths throughout but the whole garden is on a slope and clay can be slippery.
& 🐑 ✳ 🪑 ♫

64 KNOWLE HILL FARM
Ulcombe, Maidstone, ME17 1ES. The Hon Andrew & Mrs Cairns, 07860 177101, elizabeth@knowlehillfarm.co.uk, www.knowlehillfarmgarden.co.uk. *7m SE of Maidstone. From M20 J8 follow A20 towards Lenham for 2m. Turn R to Ulcombe. After 1½ m, L at Xrds, after ½ m 2nd R into Windmill Hill. Past Pepper Box Pub, ½ m 1st L to Knowle Hill.* **Sat 1, Sun 2 Feb (11-3). Light refreshments. Sat 26, Sun 27 July (2-5). Home-made teas. Adm £6, chd free. Visits also by arrangement Feb to Sept for groups of up to 25.**
2 acre garden created over nearly 40 yrs on south facing slope below the Greensand Ridge. Spectacular

views. Snowdrops and hellebores, many tender plants, china roses, agapanthus, salvias and grasses flourish on light soil. Box hedges and topiary lend structure. Lavender ribbons hum with bees. Pool enclosed in small walled white garden. Spring bulbs followed by cowslips flower early in the grass. Access only for 35 seater coaches. Some steep slopes.

65 LADHAM HOUSE
Ladham Road, Goudhurst, TN17 1DB. Paul and Jill Thompson. *8m E of Tunbridge Wells. On NE of Goudhurst, off A262. Through village towards Cranbrook, turn L at The Goudhurst Inn. 2nd R into Ladham Rd, main gates approx 500yds on L.* **Sun 18 May (2-5). Adm £7, chd free. Tea, coffee & cake.**
10 acres of garden with many interesting plants, trees and shrubs, inc rhododendrons, camellias, azaleas and magnolias. A beautiful rose garden, arboretum, an Edwardian sunken rockery, ponds, a vegetable garden and a woodland walk. There is also a spectacular 60 metre twin border designed by Chelsea Flower Show Gold Medal winner, Jo Thompson. Small Classic Car Display.

66 LITTLE GABLES
Holcombe Close, Westerham, TN16 1HA. Mrs Elizabeth James. *Centre of Westerham. Off E side of London Rd A233, 200yds from The Green. Please park in public car park. No parking available at house.* **Sat 17, Sun 18 May, Sat 7, Sun 8 June (1.30-4.30). Adm £5, chd free. Home-made teas.**
½ acre plant lover's garden extensively planted with a wide range of trees, shrubs, perennials etc, inc many rare varieties in the middle of Westerham. Collection of climbing and bush roses. Bog garden. Large greenhouse.

67 LYNSTED COMMUNITY KITCHEN GARDEN
Lynsted Park, Lynsted, Sittingbourne, ME9 0JH. Mrs V R Ross Russell, www.lynstedkitchengarden.com. *15min drive from Faversham or Sittingbourne. Nearest Train - Teynham stn. Postcode ME9 0JH brings you to the start Lynsted Park's drive, please follow signs from there. Lynsted Community Kitchen Garden is on google maps.* **Sat 5 July (11-4). Adm £6, chd free. Home-made teas. Open nearby Pheasant Barn.**
½ acre community garden set up and run by local people, who grow organic fruit and vegetables together, sharing all aspects of sowing, growing and harvesting. Use the 'No Dig' approach with soil health, sustainable water management and composting being key elements. We keep bees and are working hard to improve the biodiversity of the garden. Lynsted Community Kitchen Garden is set in a 7 acre field that is largely left wild but with small areas mown that can be used to sit down and picnic. The garden is sited in a field and in wet ground conditions, we would not advise wheelchairs.

68 ♦ MOUNT EPHRAIM GARDENS
Hernhill, Faversham, ME13 9TX. Mr & Mrs Dawes, 01227 751496, info@mountephraimgardens.co.uk, www.mountephraimgardens.co.uk. *3m E of Faversham. From end of M2, then A299 take slip road 1st L to Hernhill, signed to gardens.* **For NGS: Sun 30 Mar, Thur 12 June, Thur 25 Sept (11-4). Adm £10, chd £4. Home-made teas in West Wing Tea Room..** For other opening times and information, please phone, email or visit garden website.
Mount Ephraim is a privately-owned family home set in 10 acres of terraced Edwardian gardens with stunning views over the Kent countryside. Highlights inc a Japanese rock and water garden, arboretum, unusual topiary and a spectacular grass maze plus many mature trees, shrubs and spring bulbs. Partial wheelchair access; top part manageable, but steep slope. Disabled WC. Full access to tea room.

69 NETTLESTEAD PLACE
Nettlestead, Maidstone, ME18 5HA. Mr & Mrs Roy Tucker, www.nettlestead-place.co.uk. *6 m W/SW of Maidstone. S off A26 onto B2015 then 1m on L, Nettlestead Court Farm after Nettlestead Church.* **Sun 6 Apr, Sun 8 June (1.30-4.30). Adm £10, chd free. Home-made teas.**

C13 manor house in 10 acre plantsman's garden. Large formal rose garden. Large herbaceous garden of island beds with rose and clematis walkway leading to a recently planted garden of succulents. Fine collection of trees and shrubs; sunken pond garden, maze of thuja, terraces, bamboos, camellias, glen garden, acer and daffodil lawns. Young pinetum adjacent to garden. Sculptures featured throughout. Beautiful countryside views. Gravel and grass paths. Most of garden accessible (but not sunken pond garden). Large steep bank and lower area accessible with some difficulty.

70 NORTON COURT
Teynham, Sittingbourne, ME9 9JU. Tim & Sophia Steel. *Off A2 between Teynham & Faversham. L off A2 at Esso garage into Norton Ln; next L into Provender Ln; L signed Church for car park.* **Mon 9, Tue 10 June (2-5). Adm £10, chd free. Home-made teas inc in adm price.**
10 acre garden within parkland setting. Mature trees, topiary, wide lawns and clipped yew hedges. Orchard with mown paths through wildflowers. Walled garden with mixed borders and climbing roses. Pine tree walk. Formal box and lavender parterre. Treehouse in the Sequoia. Church open, adjacent to garden. Flat ground except for 2 steps where ramp is provided.

71 OAK COTTAGE AND SWALLOWFIELDS NURSERY
Elmsted, Ashford, TN25 5JT. Martin & Rachael Castle. *6m NW of Hythe. From Stone St (B2068) turn W opp the Stelling Minnis turning. Follow signs to Elmsted. Turn L at Elmsted village sign. Limited parking at house, further parking at Church (7min walk).* **Thur 24, Fri 25 Apr, Fri 23, Sat 24 May (11-4). Adm £6, chd free. Home-made teas.**
Get off the beaten track and discover this beautiful ½ acre cottage garden in the heart of the Kent countryside. This plantsman's garden is filled with unusual and interesting perennials. Curving lawns framed by abundantly planted borders. There is a small specialist nursery packed with herbaceous perennials. Greenhouses containing species pelargonium and Salvia collections.

72 OLD BLADBEAN STUD
Bladbean, Canterbury, CT4 6NA. Carol Bruce, www.oldbladbeanstud.co.uk. *6m S of Canterbury. From B2068, follow signs into Stelling Minnis, turn R onto Bossingham Rd, then follow yellow NGS signs through single track lanes.* **Sun 25 May, Sun 8, Sun 22 June, Sun 6, Sun 20 July (2-6). Adm £6, chd free. Cream teas.** Romantic walled rose garden with 90+ old fashioned rose varieties, tranquil yellow and white garden, square garden with a tapestry of self sowing perennials and Victorian style greenhouse, 300ft long colour schemed symmetrical double borders and an organic fruit garden. Maintained entirely by the owner, the gardens were designed to be managed as an ornamental ecosystem. Voted 2023 Winner of the Nation's Favourite Garden in the south east by readers of The English Garden Magazine.

73 THE OLD RECTORY, FAWKHAM
Valley Road, Fawkham, Longfield, DA3 8LX. Karin & Christopher Proudfoot, 01474 707513, keproudfoot@gmail.com. *1m S of Fawkham. Midway between A2 & A20, on Valley Rd 1½m N of Fawkham Green, 0.3m S of Fawkham church, opp sign for Gay Dawn Farm/ Corinthian Sports Club. Parking on drive only. Not suitable for coaches.* **Visits by arrangement in Feb for groups of up to 20. Small numbers welcome but may be combined to make up a larger group. Adm £6, chd free. Home-made teas.** 1½ acres with impressive display of long-established naturalised snowdrops and winter aconites; collection of over 130 named snowdrops. Garden developed around the snowdrops over 40 yrs, inc hellebores, pulmonarias and other early bulbs and flowers, with foliage perennials, shrubs and trees, also natural woodland. Gentle slope, gravel drive, some narrow paths.

74 THE OLD RECTORY, OTTERDEN
Bunce Court Road, Faversham, ME13 0BY. Mrs Gry Iverslien, 07734 538272, gry@iverslien.com. *North Downs. Postcode takes you to Bunce Ct. We are 600 yds further on just past Cold Harbour Ln.* **Wed 11, Thur 12 June (10-4). Adm £10,** chd free. Pre-booking essential, please visit www.ngs.org.uk for information & booking. Tea, coffee & cake inc in adm price. Visits also by arrangement 20 Mar to 30 Sept for groups of 15 to 30. 4 acre woodland garden with numerous large Rhododendrons and Camellias, mass of spring bulbs with a formal rose garden, cutting garden and large hydrangea beds throughout the garden. The garden also has a large wildlife pond and a variety of trees of interest, pots of tulips and narcissus in the spring accompanied with lots of spring flowering plants.

75 THE ORANGERY
Mystole, Chartham, Canterbury, CT4 7DB. Rex Stickland & Anne Prasse. *5m SW of Canterbury. Turn off A28 to Shalmsford St. In 1½m at Xrds turn R downhill. Continue & ignore drive on L (Mystole House only). At sharp R bend in 600yds turn L into drive.* **Sun 11 May, Sat 26, Sun 27 July (1-5). Adm £7, chd free. Home-made teas.** 1½ acre gardens around C18 orangery, now a house (not open). Magnificent extensive herbaceous border and impressive ancient wisteria. Large walled garden with a wide variety of shrubs, mixed borders and unusual specimen trees. Water features and intriguing collection of modern sculptures in natural surroundings. Splendid views from the terrace over ha-ha to the lovely Chartham Downs. Ramps to garden.

76 ♦ PENSHURST PLACE & GARDENS
Penshurst, TN11 8DG. Lord & Lady De L'Isle, 01892 870307, contactus@penshurstplace.com, www.penshurstplace.com. *6m NW of Tunbridge Wells. SW of Tonbridge on B2176, signed from A26 N of Tunbridge Wells.* **For NGS: Wed 17 Sept (10-5). Adm £14, chd £8.50. Light refreshments at The Porcupine Pantry.** For other opening times and information, please phone, email or visit garden website. 11 acres of garden dating back to C14. The garden is divided into a series of rooms by over a mile of yew hedge. Profusion of spring bulbs, formal rose garden and famous peony border. Woodland trail and arboretum. Year-round interest. Toy museum. Some paths not paved and uneven in places; own assistance will be required. 2 wheelchairs available for hire.

77 PHEASANT BARN
Church Road, Oare, ME13 0QB. Paul & Su Vaight, 07843 739301, suvaight46@gmail.com. *2m NW of Faversham. Entering Oare from Faversham, turn R at Three Mariners pub towards Harty Ferry. Garden 400yds on R, before church. Parking on roadside.* **Wed 18, Thur 19, Sat 21, Sun 22, Mon 30 June, Tue 1, Fri 4, Sat 5, Sun 6 July (11-4). Adm £7, chd free. Pre-booking essential, please visit www.ngs.org.uk for information & booking.** Visits also by arrangement 24 May to 15 July for groups of up to 20. Series of smallish gardens around award-winning converted farm buildings in beautiful situation overlooking Oare Creek. Main garden is nectar rich planting in formal design with a contemporary twist inspired by local landscape. Also vegetable garden, dry garden, water features, mowed paths in wildflower meadow, fruit trees, late summer perennial beds and grass labyrinth. Kent Wildlife Trust Oare Marshes Bird Reserve within 1m. Two village inns serving lunches/ dinners, booking recommended. Cafe by the Creek.

78 ♦ QUEX GARDENS
Quex Park, Birchington, CT7 0BH. Powell-Cotton Museum, 01843 842168, enquiries@powell-cottonmuseum.org, www.powell-cottonmuseum.org. *3m W of Margate. Follow signs for Quex Park on approach from A299 then A28 towards Margate, turn R into B2048 Park Ln. Quex Park is on L.* **For NGS: Sun 20 July (10-4). Adm £5, chd £4. Light refreshments in Felicity's Café & Quex Barn.** For other opening times and information, please phone, email or visit garden website. 10 acres of woodland and gardens with fine specimen trees unusual on Thanet, spring bulbs, wisteria, shrub borders, old figs and mulberries, herbaceous borders. Victorian walled garden with cucumber house, long glasshouses, cactus house, fruiting trees. Peacocks, dovecote, chickens, bees, woodland walk, wildlife pond, children's maze, croquet lawn, picnic grove, lawns and fountains. Head Gardener and team will be available on the day for a chat to answer

questions. Concession tickets can be purchased at the door. Garden almost entirely flat with tarmac paths. Sunken garden has sloping lawns to the central pond.

& ✿ 🚗 ☕))

GROUP OPENING

79 RAMSGATE GARDENS
Ramsgate, CT11 9PX. Anne-Marie Nixey. *Enter Ramsgate on A299, continue on A255. At r'about take 2nd exit London Rd. Continue for less than 1m to the r'about and turn L onto Grange Rd or straight ahead down West Cliff Rd.* **Sun 14 Sept (12-5). Combined adm £5, chd free. Tea, coffee & cake.**

104 GRANGE ROAD
Anne-Marie Nixey.

6 VALE SQUARE
Stephen Davies.

10 VALE SQUARE
Mr Graham & Mrs Alyson Brett.

51 VALE SQUARE
Bindi Holding.

Evolving gardens in the beautiful, yet windy, coastal town of Ramsgate showing different sized plots and how to make unique gardens out of them. Varied planting from traditional roses and bedding plants to a range of vegetables and fruit trees, as well as use of recycled and sustainable materials and incorporating traditional family areas. Vale Square Gardens highlight what can be achieved in front gardens too.

& ✿ ☕))

80 ◆ RIVERHILL HIMALAYAN GARDENS
Riverhill, Sevenoaks, TN15 0RR. The Rogers Family, 01732 459777, info@riverhillgardens.co.uk, www.riverhillgardens.co.uk. *2m S of Sevenoaks on A225. Leave A21 at A225 & follow signs for Riverhill Himalayan Gardens.* **For NGS: Wed 7 May, Wed 18 June (10-5). Adm £13, chd £7.50. Light refreshments at our Cafe, Malabar.** For other opening times and information, please phone, email or visit garden website.
Beautiful hillside garden, privately owned by the Rogers family since 1840. Spectacular rhododendrons, azaleas and fine specimen trees. Edwardian Rock Garden with extensive fern collection, Rose Walk and Walled Garden with sculptural terracing. Bluebell walks. Extensive views across the Weald of Kent. Hedge maze, adventure playground and den building. Café serves speciality coffee, light lunches and cakes. Plant sales and quirky shed shop selling beautiful gifts and original garden ornaments. Disabled parking. Easy access to café, shop and tea terrace. Accessible WC.

& 🐕 ✿ 🚗 ☕ 🍽

81 ST CLERE
Kemsing, Sevenoaks, TN15 6NL. Mr Simon & Mrs Eliza Ecclestone, www.stclere.co.uk. *6m NE of Sevenoaks. 1m E of Seal on A25, turn L signed Heaverham. In Heaverham turn R signed Wrotham. In 75yds straight ahead marked Private Rd; 1st L to house. Main entrance What3words app: trail.inner.valid.* **Sun 22 June (2-5). Adm £7.50, chd free. Home-made teas in the Garden Room. Tea and cake provided by local primary school.**
4 acre garden, full of interest. Formal terraces surrounding C17 mansion (not open), with beautiful views of the Kent countryside. Herbaceous and shrub borders, productive kitchen and herb gardens, lawns and rare trees. Some gravel paths and small steps. Assistance dogs only.

& 🚗 ☕))

82 ◆ SCOTNEY CASTLE
Lamberhurst, TN3 8JN. National Trust, 01892 893820, scotneycastle@nationaltrust.org.uk, www.nationaltrust.org.uk/scotneycastle. *6m SE of Tunbridge Wells. On A21 London - Hastings, brown tourist signs. Bus: (Mon to Fri) 256 Tunbridge Wells to Wadhurst Autocar service via Lamberhurst alight Lamberhurst Green.* **For NGS: Wed 14 May (10-5). Adm £17, chd £8.50. Light refreshments in the Courtyard tearoom.** For other opening times and information, please phone, email or visit garden website.
The medieval moated Old Scotney Castle lies in a peaceful wooded valley on the Kent/Sussex border. In the 1830s its owner, Edward Hussey III, set about building a new house, partially demolishing the Old Castle to create a romantic ruin, the centrepiece of his visionary landscape. Manual wheelchairs and individual mobility scooters are available to borrow. Booking recommended for mobility scooters by calling 01892 893820.

& 🐕 ✿ 🚗 ☕ 🍽

83 45 SEYMOUR AVENUE
Whitstable, CT5 1SA. Kevin Tooher, 07962 972882, sirplantalot@outlook.com. *Near the centre of Whitstable town & 400yds from Whitstable stn. Take Thanet Way off A299 towards Whitstable. 2nd r'about, L into Millstrood Rd, bottom of hill R into Old Bridge Rd, Station car park on L & Seymour Ave on R.* **Visits by arrangement May to Oct (not August). Weekends only May & June. Tea & cake extra by arrangement. Adm £5, chd free.**
Larger than usual town centre garden - about $\frac{1}{4}$ acre with wide range of unusual plants grown on heavy wet clay with lots of exotics growing in containers, troughs and pots. Main driveway gravel but mostly wheelchair accessible over chip bark paths in the garden itself.

& 🐕 ✿ ☕))

84 THE SILK HOUSE
Lucks Lane, Rhoden Green, nr Paddock Wood, Tunbridge Wells, TN12 6PA. Mrs S Barnwell, 07463 897435, info@silkhousedining.com, www.silkhousedining.com. *Rhoden Green. Silk House is $\frac{1}{2}$m from Queen St on sharp bend. Look out for blue sign. Also approached from Maidstone Rd. Parking at house or in lane when full.* **Sun 15 June, Sun 24 Aug (11-4). Adm £10, chd £4. Tea, coffee & cake in the Japanese garden, usually served from the tea house. Visits also by arrangement May to Aug for groups of 10+.**
Highly regarded, calming 2 acre Japanese garden with koi ponds, statuary, spectacular maples, cherries, giant bamboos, bonsai, cloud pruned niwaki, pines, zen garden and tea house. Small woodland walk, kitchen garden for Silk House Dining restaurant, dry garden and apiary. Created entirely by owners. Bonsai classes and garden design talks available for groups. Many say this is the best private Japanese garden in the South East. Looks good year-round. Picnics welcome for an additional charitable donation of £10. Restaurant available for separate bookings. Wheelchair users please tell us on arrival if you need help. Some steps, banks, bridges, ponds & gravel, but mostly flat and accessible.

& ✿ ☕

85 SIR JOHN HAWKINS HOSPITAL
High Street, Chatham, ME4 4EW. www.hawkinshospital.org.uk. *On the N side of Chatham High St, on the border between Rochester & Chatham. Leave A2 at J1 & follow signs to Rochester. Pass Rochester Stn & turn L at main junc T-lights, travelling E towards Chatham.* **Sat 28, Sun 29 June (11-5). Adm £3, chd free. Farm House teas and light refreshments served all day.**
Built on the site of Kettle Hard - part of Bishop Gundulph's Hospital of St Bartholomew, the Almshouse is a square of Georgian houses dating from the 1790s. A delightful small secluded garden overlooks the River Medway, full of vibrant and colourful planting. A lawn with cottage style borders leads to the riverside and a miniature gnome village captivates small children. Disabled access via stairlift, wheelchair to be carried separately.

86 SMITHS HALL
Lower Road, West Farleigh, ME15 0PE. Mr and Mrs S Norman. *3m W of Maidstone. A26 towards Tonbridge, turn L into Teston Ln B2163. At T-junc turn R onto Lower Rd B2010. Opp Tickled Trout pub.* **Sun 22 June (11-5). Adm £5, chd free. Home-made teas.** Donation to Heart of Kent Hospice.
Delightful 3 acre gardens surrounding a beautiful 1719 Queen Anne House (not open). Lose yourself in numerous themed rooms: sunken garden, four colour deep herbaceous borders, many roses (300) in formal rose garden and elsewhere, irises and peonies plus woodland walk. Some gravel paths.

87 NEW 4 SOUTHVIEW COTTAGES
Marsh Green Road, Marsh Green, Edenbridge, TN8 5QG. Deon Swanepoel and David Paddon, 07940 782819, swanpad@live.co.uk. *B2028 between Edenbridge and Dormansland. From Edenbridge, take B2026 S towards Hartfield, then turn R onto B2028 towards Dormansland. 0.6 m to garden. Turn R and park by the church.* **Sat 14 June (11-5). Adm £5. Sat 19 July (11-5). Combined adm with 2 Highfields Road £8. Tea, coffee & cake. Confectionery also available for sale.**

Visits also by arrangement May to Sept for groups of 5 to 10.
A compact 'secret' garden of multiple spaces. Entrance courtyard with a green wall, glass conservatory, rear terrace catching the sun, central circular seating area, shaded tropical areas, and working space, divided by a zig-zagging freestanding espaliered beech hedge that frames the path that draws you through the garden and opens up to the different spaces. We have created a localised microclimate supporting tropical planting.

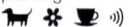

88 SPRING PLATT
Boyton Court Road, Sutton Valence, Maidstone, ME17 3BY. Mr & Mrs John Millen, 01622 843383, j.millen@talktalk.net, www.kentsnowdrops.com. *5m SE of Maidstone. From A274 nr Sutton Valence follow yellow NGS signs What3words app: angry.steers. reseller.* **Sun 26, Thur 30 Jan, Sun 2, Wed 5, Fri 7 Feb (10.30-3). Adm £5, chd free. Pre-booking essential, please phone 01622 843383, email j.millen@talktalk. net or visit www.kentsnowdrops. com for information & booking. Light refreshments.**
1 acre garden with panoramic views of the Weald. Major reconstruction taking place but still have approx 500 different varieties of snowdrops in raised sleeper beds but many more now planted in grass around the garden with spring flowers in borders. Large vegetable garden, 4 greenhouses, natural spring fed water feature and a croquet lawn. Citrus fruit trees now in large Alpine House. Garden on a steep slope and many steps.

89 ♦ SQUERRYES COURT
Squerryes, Westerham, TN16 1SJ. Henry Warde, www.squerryes.co.uk. *½m W of Westerham. Signed from A25.* **For NGS: Fri 16 May (11-5). Adm £8, chd free. Tea, coffee & cake. For other opening times and information, please visit garden website.**
15 acres of garden, lake and woodland surrounding beautiful C17 manor house (not open). Lovely throughout the seasons from the spring bulbs to later-flowering borders. Cenotaph commemorating General Wolfe. C18 dovecote. Lawns, yew hedges, ancient trees, parterres, azaleas and roses.

90 STABLE HOUSE
Street End, Canterbury, CT4 7AN. Charlie & Lucy Markes. *2m S of Canterbury, off B2068. 1st R after Bridge Rd if coming from Canterbury, 400m after Granville pub on the L if coming towards Canterbury.* **Sat 12, Sun 13 July (10-2). Adm £5, chd free. Tea, coffee & cake.**
5 acre mature wildflower meadow with winding mown paths adjoining 2 acres of relaxed, informal interlinked gardens. These surround converted Edwardian stable block in lovely setting with views across vineyards towards the North Downs. Gravel garden, vegetable garden and walkthrough garden room beneath clocktower. Disabled parking by arrangement close to garden. Not all areas wheelchair accessible.

91 STONEWALL PARK
Chiddingstone Hoath, nr Edenbridge, TN8 7DG. Mr & Mrs Fleming. *4m SE of Edenbridge. Via B2026. Halfway between Markbeech & Penshurst. Plenty of parking which will be signed.* **Sun 23 Mar, Sun 4 May (2-5). Adm £7, chd free. Home-made teas.** Donation to MSA & St Mary's Church, Chiddingstone.
Vast amounts of C19 self-seeded daffodils which lead down to a romantic woodland garden in an historic setting, featuring species such as rhododendrons, magnolias and azaleas. In May, bluebells take over the daffodils in abundance. Winding, mossy paths lead you to a range of interesting trees, sandstone outcrops and lakes. Please wear boots and bring walking sticks as the paths can be slippery and muddy during the spring months. The paths are quite steep so care is needed going down towards the lakes.

GROUP OPENING

92 TANKERTON GARDENS
Tankerton, CT5 1NS. *1 m E of Whitstable.* All five are in central Tankerton. No more than 15min walk between gardens. **Sun 8 June (10-5). Combined adm £7, chd free.**

- **NEW** **61 GRAYSTONE ROAD**
Ms Lisa Chapman.
- **NEW** **25 OAKWOOD DRIVE**
Ms Joanna Janicka.
- **NEW** **16 PARK AVENUE**
Ms Luise Shepherdson.
- **96 QUEENS ROAD**
Ms Wendy Cunningham.
- **50 SUMMERFIELD AVENUE**
Janet Maxwell.

A group of diverse gardens inc an artists gravel garden, an exotic jungle garden, plantswoman's garden, flowers, raised beds, sheds, chickens and vegetables. Close to cafes and WC facilities.

✿ ⁾⁾

93 THAMES HOUSE
29 Royal Pier Road, Gravesend, DA12 2BD. Dr Daniel Curran, 07753 605407. *Gravesend Heritage Quarter. Last house on L along Royal Pier Rd, past the Clarendon Hotel, and up a short set of steps from the pavement.* **Sun 6 July (12-5). Adm £5, chd free. Tea, coffee & cake.** Visits also by arrangement May to Sept for groups of 10 to 20.

Three different outdoor spaces connected by steps. The main terrace, with views over the Thames River, and the small western terrace with fish pond, are classically planted to sit harmoniously with the listed building which dominates these areas. The third and largest space is our main garden, a modern styled walled garden with lawn, mixed borders, fruit trees and contemporary seating areas. Regency period building on the waterfront.

✿ ☕ ⁾⁾

94 TONBRIDGE SCHOOL
High Street, Tonbridge, TN9 1JP. The Governors. *Maps & guides available for visitors. At N end of Tonbridge High St. Parking signed off London Rd (B245 Tonbridge-Hildenborough) in the Tonbridge Sports Centre car park.* **Wed 9 July (9.30-3.30). Adm £7, chd free. Cream teas at Orchard Centre Restaurant. Gluten Free scones available.**

In front of and behind Tonbridge School you will find five gardens that you can visit. These are: The Boars Head, The Garden of Remembrance, Smythe Library Garden, Skinners Library Garden, and the Barton Science Centre Garden. We hope the Chapel will be open for visits. Cream teas available for purchase. Head Gardener guided tours throughout the day. Toilets on site. All gardens can be accessed by wheelchair. Please note that Skinners Library path is uneven. Easy access to the Orchard Centre Restaurant.

♿ ✿ 🚗 ☕ 🧺 ⁾⁾

Court Lodge

96 TORRY HILL
Frinsted/Milstead, Sittingbourne, ME9 0SP. Miranda & Arthur Leigh Pemberton. *5m S of Sittingbourne. M20 J8, A20, B2163 (Hollingbourne). R at Xrds (Ringlestone Rd). Frinsted-Doddington, NGS signs. M2 J5, A249 (Maidstone), 1st L (Bredgar), L (Bredgar), R at War Memorial, 1st L (Milstead), NGS signs.* **Sun 29 June (1-5). Combined adm with Yokes Court £10, chd free. Tea, coffee & cake. Picnics welcome in garden. Donation to St. Dunstan's Church, Frinsted.**
Spectacular views across the Medway and Thames estuaries frame these C19 landscaped gardens and mid-C20 formal walled gardens. There are specimen trees, wildflower meadows, a rose garden, herbaceous borders and a walled kitchen garden. Some shallow steps. No wheelchair access to rose garden due to very uneven surface but can be viewed from pathway.

& ✿ ☕ 🍴 »))

97 TOWNLAND
Six Fields Path, Tenterden, TN30 6EX. Alan & Lindy Bates, 01580 764505, alanandlindybates@yahoo.co.uk. *Just off Tenterden High St. Park in Bridewell Ln car park (Sunday free). From centre of Tenterden High St, walk down Jackson's Ln next to Webbs Ironmongers. Follow lane to end (400m). Phone for disabled parking.* **Visits by arrangement June to Aug for groups of 8 to 20. Adm £6, chd free. Tea, coffee & cake.**
A redesigned 0.7 acre family garden in a unique position. Mixed borders, with a wide range of shrubs, flowers and grasses providing a riot of colour throughout the year. A gravel garden, rose arbour and fruit and vegetable areas complete the experience. Wheelchair accessible from the paved roadway outside (Fuggle Dr).

& ✿ ☕

98 TRAM HATCH
Barnfield Road, Charing Heath, Ashford, TN27 0BN. Mrs P Scrivens, 07835 758388, Info@tramhatch.com, www.tramhatch.com. *10m NW of Ashford. A20 towards Pluckley, over motorway then 1st R to Barnfield. At end, turn L past Barnfield, Tram Hatch ahead.* **Visits by arrangement 7 Apr to 14 Sept for groups of 10 to 30. Adm £5, chd free. Tea, coffee & cake.**

Meander your way off the beaten track to a mature 3 acre garden changing through the seasons. You will enjoy a garden laid out in rooms. Large selection of trees, vegetable, rose and gravel gardens, colourful containers. River Stour and the Angel of the South enhance your visit. Please come and enjoy, then relax in our lovely garden room for tea. Great River Stour plus other water features. Large variety of trees. Large vegetable garden. The garden is totally flat, apart from a very small area which can be viewed from the lane.

& ✿ ☕

99 NEW ♦ WALMER CASTLE
Kingsdown Road, Walmer, Deal, CT14 7LJ. English Heritage. *On coast S of Walmer, on A258; J13 of M20 or from M2 to Deal.* **For NGS: Evening opening Tue 1 July (5.30-7.30). Adm £20, chd free. Pre-booking essential, please email fundraising@english-heritage.org.uk or visit www.english-heritage.org.uk/visit/places/walmer-castle-and-gardens/events for information & booking. Light refreshments. For other opening times and information, please email or visit garden website.**
With a backdrop of undulating cloud yew hedge, the double borders at Walmer Castle are full of colour throughout the summer months. Alongside our expert gardens team, explore the herbaceous borders in the Broadwalk Garden, and marvel at The Kitchen Garden which has grown produce for the castle for nearly 300 yrs.

☕

100 WEST COURT LODGE
Postling Court, The Street, Postling, nr Hythe, CT21 4EX. Mr & Mrs John Pattrick, 07814 419638, pattrickmalliet@gmail.com. *2m NW of Hythe. From M20 J11 turn S onto A20. Immed 1st L. After ½ m on bend take road signed Lyminge. 1st L into Postling.* **Sat 7 June (12-5); Sun 8 June (1-5). Combined adm with Churchfield £10, chd free. Tea, coffee & cake in Postling village hall.** Visits also by **arrangement 1 Mar to 1 Oct.**
South facing one acre walled garden at the foot of the North Downs, designed in two parts: main lawn with large sunny borders and a romantic woodland glade planted with shadow loving plants and spring bulbs, small wildlife pond. Lovely C11 church will

be open next to the gardens.

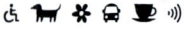

& ✿ ✿ 🚗 ☕ »))

GROUP OPENING

101 WEST MALLING EARLY SUMMER GARDENS
West Malling, ME19 6LW. *On A20, nr J4 of M20. Park (Ryarsh Ln & Stn) in West Malling. Please start your visit either at Brome House or Went House. Parking available at New Barns Cottages. A map of the locations will be provided.* **Sun 1 June (12-5). Combined adm £9, chd free. Home-made teas at New Barns Cottages.**

ABBEY BREWERY COTTAGE
Dr David & Mrs Lynda Nunn.

BROME HOUSE
John Pfeil & Shirley Briggs.

NEW BARNS COTTAGES
Mr & Mrs Anthony Drake.

NEW 26 OFFHAM ROAD
Mr & Mrs Mary and David Herrington.

TOWN HILL COTTAGE
Mr & Mrs P Cosier Veronica and Peter.

WENT HOUSE
Alan & Mary Gibbins.

West Malling is an attractive small market town with some fine buildings. Enjoy six lovely gardens that are entirely different from each other and cannot be seen from the road. Brome House and Went House have large gardens with specimen trees, old roses, mixed borders, attractive kitchen gardens and garden features inc a coach house, Roman temple, fountain and parterre. Town Hill Cottage is a walled town garden with mature and interesting planting. Abbey Brewery Cottage is a recent jewel-like example of garden restoration and development. 26 Offham Road is a charming, closely planted, small town garden. New Barns Cottages is an extensive cottage and woodland garden threequarters of a mile from West Malling High Street, in iconic Kent countryside. Numerous cameos, viewing platform, photos of the garden's evolution. Wheelchair access to Brome House and Went House only.

✿ ☕ »))

GROUP OPENING

102 WHITSTABLE JOY LANE GARDENS
Whitstable, CT5 4LT. www.facebook.com/whitstableopengardens. *Off A299, or A290. Down Borstal Hill, L by garage into Joy Ln. Tickets and map from 19 Joy Lane.* **Sun 18 May (10-4). Combined adm £7, chd free. Light refreshments.**
Enjoy a day visiting a dozen or so eclectic gardens along Joy Lane and neighbourhood by the sea. From Arts & Crafts villas to mid century bungalows, some productive, others wildlife friendly, large or compact, we garden on heavy clay, are prone to northerly winds and hope to inspire those new to gardening with our ingenuity and style. To find out more: visit Whitstable Gardens on Facebook. Plant stalls at 19 Joy Lane.

GROUP OPENING

103 WHITSTABLE TOWN GARDENS
Whitstable, CT5 1DD. www.facebook.com/whitstableopengardens. *Tickets & map at: Stream Walk (CT5 1HJ), Umbrella Centre (CT5 1DD) & The Guinea 31 Island Wall (CT5 1EW).* **Sun 15 June (10-5). Combined adm £7, chd free. Café offering light refreshments at Whitstable Umbrella Centre.**
From fishermen's yards to formal gardens, the residents of Whitstable are making the most of the mild climate. Enjoy contemporary gardens, seaside gardens, rose gardens, gravel gardens, designers' gardens and wildlife friendly plots, both large and small. We hope to encourage those new to gardening with our ingenuity and style, rather than rolling acres. To find out more see Whitstable Gardens on Facebook. Refreshments at Stream Walk Community Garden and Whitstable Umbrella Centre. NGS plant sale at The Guinea No 31 Island Wall.

104 WINDY RIDGE
Dover Road, Guston, Dover, CT15 5EH. Canon David & Mrs Marianne Slater. *1m N of Dover. From Dover Castle take Guston Rd next to Coach Park follow for ¾ m, Windy Ridge on L side. Please use Car Park on opp side, signposted.* **Sat 31 May (1-5). Adm £6, chd free. Home-made teas.**
Well established series of separate areas in ⅓ acre plot developed since 2008. Shrubs, herbaceous borders, lawns, pergola with wisteria, trees in pots, productive raised beds, soft and top fruit. Self sufficient in water (in most years) due to extensive rain harvesting, gravity fed to vegetable area. Paths mostly smooth but narrow in places with some low steps to some seating areas.

105 NEW THE WOODMAN
Derringstone Hill, Barham, Canterbury, CT4 6QD. Carolyn Hunt. *5 m S of Canterbury. Situated at S end of Barham on RHS of up slope Derringstone Hill, 50 metres past Derringstone St. What3words app: short.lampost.debate.* **Sat 2, Sun 3 Aug (10.30-5). Adm £7, chd free.**
Two adjoining gardens, single entry. The Woodman garden has been completely restructured since 2019. Both gardens have sloping grounds with a range of colourful borders using perennials, roses, dahlias, hydrangeas and evergreens, wildlife ponds, water features, established trees and vegetable garden. Nestled in the Elham Valley, the gardens benefit from beautiful views across the valley. Wheelchair access to The Woodman garden only. No wheelchair access to Woodman Cottage garden.

106 ◆ THE WORLD GARDEN AT LULLINGSTONE CASTLE
Eynsford, DA4 0JA. Mrs Guy Hart Dyke, 01322 862114, info@lullingstonecastle.co.uk, www.lullingstonecastle.co.uk. *1m from Eynsford. Over Ford Bridge in Eynsford Village. Follow signs to Roman Villa. Keep Roman Villa immed on R then follow Private Rd to Gatehouse.* **For NGS: Sun 15 June (11-5). Adm £10, chd £5. Light refreshments.** For other opening times and information, please phone, email or visit garden website.
The World Garden is located within the two acre, C18 Walled Garden in the stunning grounds of Lullingstone Castle, where heritage meets cutting-edge horticulture. The garden is laid out in the shape of a miniature map of the world. Thousands of species are represented, all planted out in their respective beds. The World Garden Nursery offers a host of horticultural and homegrown delights, to reflect the unusual and varied planting of the garden. There is also the opportunity on your visit to purchase the new World Garden puzzle showcasing our 'Hot & Spiky' cactus house. Wheelchairs available upon request.

107 YOKES COURT
Coal Pit Lane, Frinsted, Sittingbourne, ME9 0ST. John & Kate Leigh Pemberton. *2.4m from Doddington. Old Lenham Rd to Hollingbourne. 1st R at Torry Hill Chestnut Fencing, then 1st L to Torry Hill. 1st L into Coal Pit Ln.* **Sun 29 June (1-5). Combined adm with Torry Hill £10, chd free. Tea, coffee & cake at Torry Hill House.**
3 acre garden surrounded by countryside. Hedges and herbaceous borders set in open lawns. Rose beds. New prairie planting. Serpentine walkway through wildflowers. Walled vegetable garden.

---

70 inpatients and their families are being supported at the newly opened Horatio's Garden Northern Ireland, thanks to National Garden Scheme donations.

LANCASHIRE
Merseyside, Greater Manchester

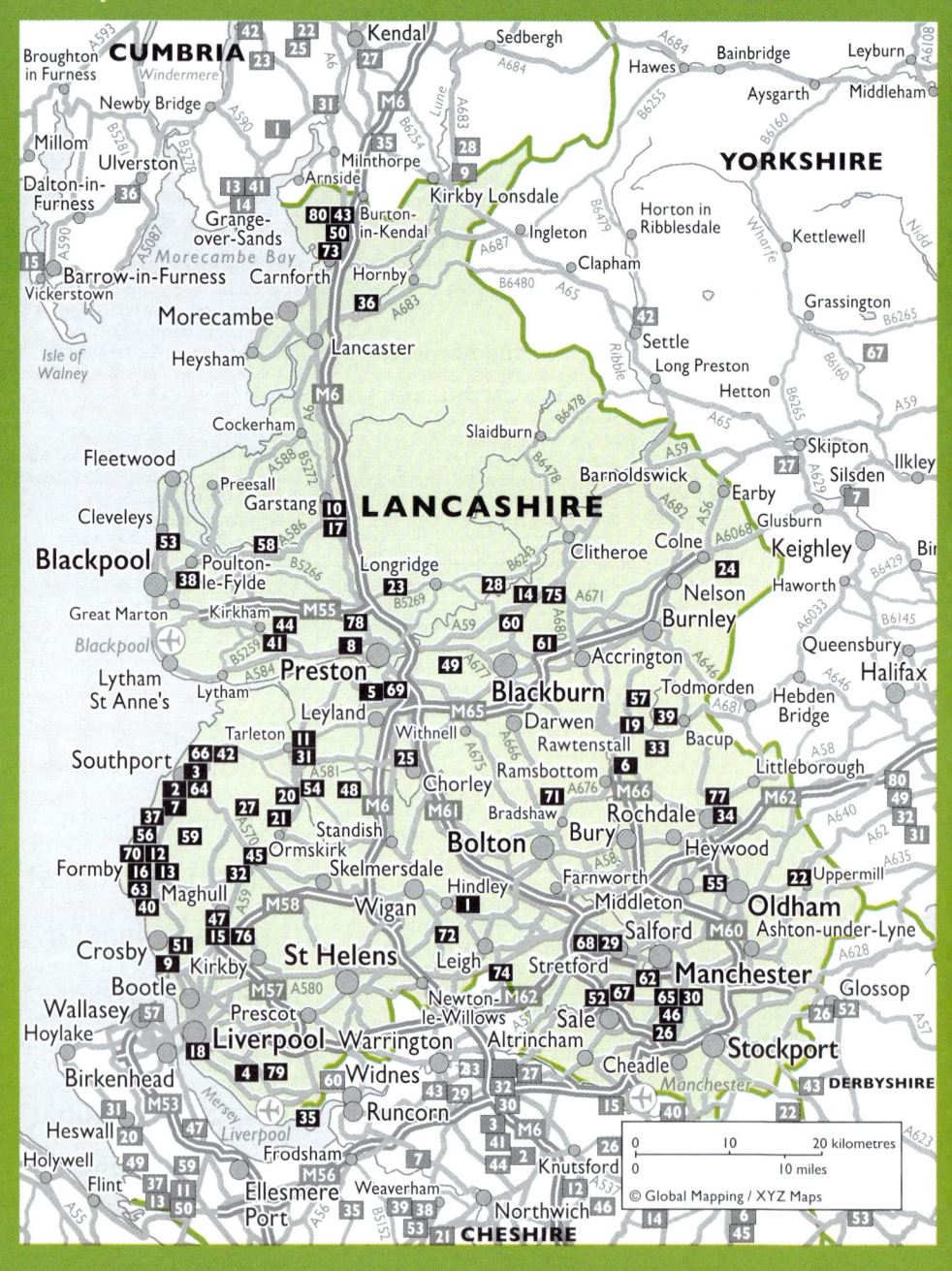

VOLUNTEERS

County Organiser
Marian & Brian Jones
01695 574628
marianandbrian.jones@ngs.org.uk

County Treasurer
Peter Curl
01704 893713
peter.curl@ngs.org.uk

Publicity
Christine Ruth
07740 438994
caruthchris@aol.com

Social Media
John Spendlove
07746 378194
john.spendlove@ngs.org.uk

Tony Shepherd
07834 452180
tony.shepherd@ngs.org.uk

Booklet Co-ordinator
Brian Jones
(see above)

Booklet Distribution
Claire Spendlove
01524 727770
claire@lavenderandlime.co.uk

Visits by Arrangement
Marian Jones
(see above)

Talks
Maureen Sawyer & Sue Beacon
077092 43986
sbeacon303@gmail.com

Photographer
Norman Rigby
01704 840329
norman.rigby@ngs.org.uk

Assistant County Organisers
Sue Beacon 077092 43986
sbeacon303@gmail.com

Laura Carstensen 07784 221919
laura@carstensen.co.uk

Karen Clough 07703 636196
karen.clough@ngs.org.uk

Sandra Curl 01704 893713
peter.curl@btinternet.com

Assistant County Organisers cont'd
Margaret & Geoff Fletcher
01704 567742
margaret.fletcher@ngs.org.uk

Margaret Richardson 07867 848218
marg254@btinternet.com

Claire & John Spendlove
(see left)

Carolyn Waite 07437 527599
carolyn.waite@ngs.org.uk

OPENING DATES

All entries subject to change.
For latest information check
www.ngs.org.uk
Map locator numbers are
shown to the right of each
garden name.

February

Snowdrop Openings

Sunday 9th
Weeping Ash Garden 74
Sunday 16th
Weeping Ash Garden 74

April

Sunday 6th
Derian House Children's
  Hospice 25
33 Pershore Grove 56
Saturday 12th
Dale House Gardens 23
Sunday 13th
Dale House Gardens 23

May

Saturday 10th
NEW 3 Tower End 70
Sunday 11th
NEW 3 Tower End 70
Saturday 17th
Halton Park House 36

Sunday 18th
Halton Park House 36
NEW 12 Willow Hey 76
Woolton Village Gardens 79
Sunday 25th
Bretherton Gardens 11
Kington Cottage 44
Saturday 31st
Dent Hall 24
NEW Greenacres 33
The Hawes 37
Mill Barn 49

June

Sunday 1st
Dent Hall 24
Mill Barn 49
Saturday 7th
136 Buckingham Road 15
31 Cousins Lane 20
Hale Village Gardens 35
Mill Barn 49
Oaklands 54
NEW 101 Woodplumpton Road 78
Sunday 8th
Ainsdale & Birkdale Gardens 2
136 Buckingham Road 15
31 Cousins Lane 20
Didsbury Village Gardens 26
Hale Village Gardens 35
Hightown Gardens 40
Maggie's, Manchester 46
Mill Barn 49
Oaklands 54
Wednesday 11th
NEW HMP Kirkham 41
Saturday 14th
Calder House Lane Gardens 17
Dale House Gardens 23
Ellesmere Park Gardens 29
Sunday 15th
Bretherton Gardens 11
Calder House Lane Gardens 17
79 Crabtree Lane 21
Dale House Gardens 23
NEW St Wilfrid's Community
Garden 62
Wednesday 18th
NEW HMP Kirkham 41
Saturday 21st
◆ Turton Tower Kitchen Garden 71
Warton Gardens 73

@NGSLancs   @NGSLancs   @NGSLancs

LANCASHIRE

Sunday 22nd
NEW 40 Acreswood Avenue	1
Arevinti	6
Canning and Toxteth Gardens	18
Dutton Hall	28
Warton Gardens	73

Saturday 28th
Whalley and District Gardens	75

Sunday 29th
16 Beach Lawn	9
Glynwood House	31
Kington Cottage	44
18 Moor Drive	51
Whalley and District Gardens	75

July

Saturday 5th
Fallowfield & Ladybarn Gardens	30

Sunday 6th
Fallowfield & Ladybarn Gardens	30
Gorse Hill Nature Reserve	32
72 Ludlow Drive	45

Saturday 12th
5 Crib Lane	22
NEW 204 Norbreck Road	53

Sunday 13th
NEW Allerton & Grassendale Gardens	4
33 Brewery Lane	12
5 Crib Lane	22
Maghull Station	47
NEW Mawdesley Gardens	48
Moss Park Allotments	52
NEW 204 Norbreck Road	53
NEW Sandywood Cottage	63

Saturday 19th
NEW 18 Highcross Hill	38
Higher Bridge Clough House	39
85 Ribchester Road	60

Sunday 20th
23 Ashton Road	7
Bretherton Gardens	11
79 Crabtree Lane	21
Drummersdale Crossing Cottage	27
NEW 18 Highcross Hill	38
Higher Bridge Clough House	39
85 Ribchester Road	60
14 Saxon Road	64
Southlands	67
280 Warrington Road	72

Saturday 26th
2 Brookside	14
NEW Civic Pride, Rossendale	19
NEW The Quaker Meeting House	57

Sunday 27th
3 Alexander Mews	3
30 Bonds Lane	10
2 Brookside	14
NEW Civic Pride, Rossendale	19
Glynwood House	31
The Growth Project	34
46 Holmdale Avenue	42
Kington Cottage	44
NEW The Quaker Meeting House	57
The Shakespearean Garden, Platt Fields Park	65
32 Wood Hey Grove	77

August

Saturday 2nd
Ambledene, Moss Lane	5

Sunday 3rd
NEW Holmere Lodge	43
Oldham Gardens	55
NEW Shellfield Gardens	66
Weeping Ash Garden	74
NEW 55 Yealand Road	80

Sunday 10th
Weeping Ash Garden	74

Saturday 16th
28 Stafford Road	68

Saturday 30th
Rainbag Cottage	59
Rishton Tropical Garden	61

Sunday 31st
NEW Allerton & Grassendale Gardens	4
Rainbag Cottage	59
Rishton Tropical Garden	61

September

Saturday 6th
Ashton Walled Community Gardens	8
NEW Quakers Rest	58
28 Stafford Road	68

Sunday 7th
NEW Quakers Rest	58

October

Saturday 4th
NEW Monastery of Our Lady of Hyning	50

Sunday 5th
NEW Monastery of Our Lady of Hyning	50

By Arrangement

Arrange a personalised garden visit with your club, or group of friends, on a date to suit you. See individual garden entries for full details.

Ambledene, Moss Lane	5
Arevinti	6
Ashton Walled Community Gardens	8
Bridge Inn Community Farm	13
4 Buttermere Close	16
Calder House Lane Gardens	17
79 Crabtree Lane	21
Dale House Gardens	23
The Growth Project	34
3 Harrock View, Mawdesley Gardens	48
Hazel Cottage, Bretherton Gardens	11
Kington Cottage	44
Mill Barn	49
Moss Park Allotments	52
33 Pershore Grove	56
14 Saxon Road	64
Southlands	67
28 Stafford Road	68
87 Todd Lane North	69
NEW 101 Woodplumpton Road	78

129,032 people were able to access guidance on what to expect when a person is dying through the National Garden Scheme's support for Hospice UK this year.

THE GARDENS

1 NEW 40 ACRESWOOD AVENUE
Hindley Green, Wigan, WN2 4NJ. Angie Barker. *4m E of Wigan. Take A577 from Wigan to Manchester, L at Victoria Hotel, at T-junction R & 1st L.* **Sun 22 June (11-4). Adm £5, chd free. Home-made teas.**
This relatively small garden in the middle of a modern housing estate, has been created from scratch over the last 18 yrs. It uses planting to create privacy in an overlooked space with a mix of contemporary and cottage garden styles. It features a contemporary courtyard area, a small vegetable plot, cottage garden borders and a decked area with formal pond. The garden reached the final six in Gardeners' World's Garden of the Year competition 2024.
&

GROUP OPENING

2 AINSDALE & BIRKDALE GARDENS
14 Saxon Road, Southport, PR8 2AX. Mrs Margaret Fletcher. *1-4m S of Southport. Gardens signed from A565 & A5247.* **Sun 8 June (11-5). Combined adm £6, chd free. Tea, coffee & cake at all gardens.**

12 SAXON ROAD
PR8 2AX. Karen & Douglas Traynor.

14 SAXON ROAD
Margaret & Geoff Fletcher.
(See separate entry)

45 STOURTON ROAD
PR8 3PL. Pat & Bill Armstrong.

A group formed to showcase some of the beautiful gardens to visit around the Victorian seaside town of Southport. They range in size and design from a walled garden featuring tender perennials, a mature tranquil ever evolving garden, a flower arrangers garden of infinite detail and surprises. Gardens illustrate successful growing of shrubs and perennials in sandy soils. Not all gardens are wheelchair friendly due to narrow paths or gravel.
&

3 3 ALEXANDER MEWS
Queens Road, Southport, PR9 9JH. Ian Whitaker. *½ m N of Southport. M6 J26 join M58 for Liverpool, M58 J3 A570 to Ormskirk & then Southport. Turn R onto A565 over r'about 2nd exit 2nd R onto Alexandra Rd. Garden is at the next junction.* **Sun 27 July (11-5). Combined adm with 46 Holmdale Avenue £5, chd free. Home-made teas.**
Large corner plot with deep colourful cottage style beds transformed from an area totally covered in slate. A small wildlife pond that overflows into a bog garden. 2 pergolas with climbing roses, honeysuckle and jasmine. Small enclosed seating area, another seating area in sunny position. Summerhouse and plans for a large water feature.
&

GROUP OPENING

4 NEW ALLERTON & GRASSENDALE GARDENS
Mather Avenue, Liverpool, L18 7HB. Barbara Peers. *3m S from end of M62. On the R of Mather Ave heading out of town: on the same side as Tesco and 800 metres beyond.* **Sun 13 July (11-4). Combined adm £5, chd free. Sun 31 Aug (11-4). Combined adm £4, chd free. Light refreshments at 146 Mather Avenue.**

33 GREENHILL ROAD
L18 6JJ. Tony Rose.
Open on all dates

NEW 5 HIGHGROVE PARK
L19 9EQ. Deborah & John Vivis.
Open on Sun 13 July

146 MATHER AVENUE
L18 7HB. Barbara Peers.
Open on all dates

Three very distinctive Liverpool gardens, one full of rare exotics, cacti, bamboo and tropical plants with a pond and stream running through. A small tree fringed town garden with a wildlife pond and a fish pond, borders packed full of wildflowers and perennials in shades of blues and pinks all grown in home-made compost. Joining them is a new garden well-stocked with shrubs and perennials interspersed with ornamental features and seating.

5 AMBLEDENE, MOSS LANE
Penwortham, Preston, PR1 9TX. Teressa Ryan, 07887 334481, Teressaryan@live.co.uk. *From Leyland Rd, into Bee Lane, turn R onto Moss Ln. Ambledene is the white house on the R at the end of the single track lane. Parking in field opp the house. What3words app: ready.worms.scouts.* **Sat 2 Aug (10.30-5). Adm £4, chd free. Home-made bakes & biscuits with a choice of hot & cold beverages. Visits also by arrangement 4 Aug to 5 Sept.**
There are gardens to both the front and back of the house with views over fields. Some mature trees create woodland like areas and there are also areas in full sun with planting to suit each aspect. A large patio at the back has gazebos and seating. Other features inc a slate bed with fountain, pond, greenhouse and containers for alpines, vegetables, herbs etc. Planting style is naturalistic. The garden is flat with some areas covered in gravel.
&

6 AREVINTI
1 School Court, Ramsbottom, Bury, BL0 0SD. Lavinia Tod, 01706 822474, arevintgarden@gmail.com. *4m N of Bury. Exit at J1 turn R onto A56 signed Ramsbottom continue straight until yellow signs.* **Sun 22 June (11-5). Adm £4, chd free. Tea, coffee & cake. Visits also by arrangement 2 May to 2 Oct for groups of 6 to 22. We offer lunch to pre booked groups. Max 22 so if wet we can move indoors.**
The garden is enhanced by views of the West Pennine moors. The front and side gardens are of oriental style, with topiary, ferns and bamboo. There are water features, stone dragons, and a terracotta warrior. The teahouse includes a miniature railway. The main garden has a fish pond and clematis covered pergola. The church yard garden has herbaceous borders and wildlife pond. Talk on the history of the area by the garden owner at 1pm. History walk at 2pm - please meet at the Porrits Tomb in the churchyard. Fairy House and children's Quiz.

23 ASHTON ROAD
Hillside, Southport, PR8 4QE. John & Jennifer Mawdsley. *2m S of Southport. signed from A565 & A5267.* **Sun 20 July (11-5). Combined adm with 14 Saxon Road £5, chd free. Tea, coffee & cake at 14 Saxon Rd.**
A lawn in the front garden is surrounded by a new collection of ferns plus alpine plants and perennials. A well established long back garden with circular lawn and pergola hides a water feature, vegetable plot, greenhouses, fruit cage and runner bean arch.

ASHTON WALLED COMMUNITY GARDENS
Pedders Lane, Ashton-on-Ribble, Preston, PR2 1HL. Let's Grow Preston, 07535 836364, letsgrowpreston@gmail.com, www.letsgrowpreston.org. *W of Preston. From M6 J30 head towards Preston turn R onto Blackpool Rd, continue for 3½ m, turn L onto Pedders Lane & next R onto the park. Entrance to walled garden is 50 metres on L.* **Sat 6 Sept (10-3). Adm £5, chd free. Tea, coffee & cake. Vegan & gluten free options. Visits also by arrangement Apr to Nov for groups of up to 20. Includes a talk about the garden & biodiversity**
Formal raised beds within a walled garden, a peace garden and an edible garden. The formal part of the garden uses plants predominantly from just 3 families, rose, geranium and aster. It is punctuated by grasses and has been designed to demonstrate how diverse and varied plants can be from just the one family. Practical demonstrations and talking tour about the work that Let's Grow Preston does within the PR postcode inc improving mental and physical wellbeing and working with the 41 food hubs of Preston. Flat ground with ramps where necessary to enable access for all. Disabled WC.

Our donation to the Army Benevolent Fund supported 700 individuals with front line services and horticultural related grants in 2024.

16 BEACH LAWN
Waterloo, Liverpool, L22 8QA. Ms Claire Curtis Thomas. *What3words app: novel.given.simple. Access on foot from end of Beach Lawn & Harbord Rd. No 53 Bus stops nearby.* **Sun 29 June (11-4). Combined adm with 18 Moor Drive £5, chd free. Tea, coffee & cake at 15 Beach Lawn.**
Originally this coastal garden was little more than a 30m long, 7m wide and 1m tall sand dune. Now, some 10 yrs later the garden is full of colour for 8 months of the year. There are quiet immersive places to sit and always something beautiful to catch the eye. Despite many failures everything in this garden has been grown by the owner who will be happy to answer any questions. The public sculpture installation Another Place by Anthony Gormley, is less than 10 mins walk from the garden. Crosby Coastal Park is a very short walk away and is a designated Site of Local Biological interest, Sefton Coast Special Area of Conservation and a Special Protection Area. The garden has wide paths built for wheelchair users for most of the garden.

48 Blundell Road, Hightown Gardens

LANCASHIRE 299

10 30 BONDS LANE
Garstang, Preston, PR3 1ZB. Mr Alan & Mrs Liz Pearson. ½ m S of Garstang town centre. From the South follow the B6430 N from the A6 (signed Garstang). From the North follow the B6430 S through the town & follow the signs for Preston. Parking adjacent to the property. **Sun 27 July (10.30-5). Adm £5, chd free. Tea, coffee & cake.**

A 90 yr old garden, which has been in the hands of the current owners for 30 yrs. To the front are formal lawns and beds of annuals with topiary and a side bed of perennials and gatepost features To the rear are 3 lawned areas with one now being left as meadow and orchard. A varied planting throughout with a lot of hostas, a year-round garden with many features, seating and vistas. A steep gradient to the drive otherwise mainly accessible.

GROUP OPENING

11 BRETHERTON GARDENS
Bretherton, Leyland, PR26 9AD. 8m SW of Preston. Between Southport & Preston, from A59, take B5247 towards Chorley for 1m. Gardens signed from South Rd (B5247) & North Rd (B5248). Maps & tickets at all gardens. **Sun 25 May, Sun 15 June, Sun 20 July (12-5). Combined adm £6, chd free. Home-made teas at Bretherton Congregational Church from 12 noon on all dates. Light lunches on 20 July.**

HAZEL COTTAGE
PR26 9AN. John & Kris Jolley, 01772 600896, jolley@johnjolley.plus.com. Visits also by arrangement 13 Apr to 19 Oct for groups of up to 30.

◆ HAZELWOOD
PR26 9AY. Jacqueline Iddon & Thompson Dagnall, 01772 601433, jacquelineiddon@gmail.com, www.jacquelineiddon.co.uk.

LANESIDE, 10 BAMFORDS FOLD
PR26 9AL. Robert & Ann Alty.

OWL BARN
PR26 9AD. Richard & Barbara Farbon.

PALATINE, 6 BAMFORDS FOLD
PR26 9AL. Alison Ryan.

A group of contrasting gardens spaced across an attractive award winning village with a conservation area. Hazelwood is a 1½ acre plant lover's paradise with herbaceous and mixed borders, kitchen and cutting garden, alpine house, sculpture gallery, pond and plant nursery. At the sculpture gallery there are usually demonstrations at 2pm. Hazel Cottage's former Victorian orchard plot has evolved into a series of themed spaces while the adjoining land has a natural pond, meadow and developing native woodland. Owl Barn has herbaceous borders filled with cottage garden and hardy plants, a productive kitchen garden with fruit, vegetables and cut flowers. There are two ponds with water features and secluded seating areas. Palatine is a garden of 3 contrasting spaces started in 2019 around a modern bungalow to attract wildlife and give year-round interest. In the same cul-de-sac Laneside is still a work in progress, the garden is on 3 sides of the bungalow, with mature shrubs and trees, a rose garden, perennials and a small fruit growing area. Also an inherited Woodland Walk which is a current project. Home-made preserves for sale. Full wheelchair access at Palatine, the majority of Hazelwood is accessible, other gardens have narrow paths or gravel limiting accessibility.

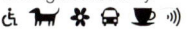

12 33 BREWERY LANE
Formby, Liverpool, L37 7DY. Sue & Dave Hughes. 7m S of Southport. S on Formby by-pass A565 past RAF Woodvale. R at r'about to Southport Rd, R to Green Ln continues to Massams Ln, first R into West Ln continues to Brewery Ln. **Sun 13 July (11-4). Combined adm with Sandywood Cottage £5, chd free. Home-made teas.**

We started planting up the garden in 2015 with perennials, shrubs and climbers. There are colour themed raised beds with lawns and a paved terrace. Seating throughout the garden. Productive area with raised beds of vegetables and cut flowers raised from seed in the greenhouse.

13 BRIDGE INN COMMUNITY FARM
Moss Side, Formby, Liverpool, L37 0AF. 01704 830303, bridgeinnfarm@talktalk.net, www.bridgeinncommunityfarm.co.uk. 7m S of Southport. From Formby bypass A565, L onto Moss Side. **Visits by arrangement 1 May to 30 Aug. Adm £5, chd free.**
Bridge Inn Community Farm was established in 2010 in response to a community need. Our farm sits on a beautiful 4 acre smallholding with views looking out over the countryside. We provide a quality service of training in a real life work environment and experience in horticulture, conservation and animal welfare.

14 2 BROOKSIDE
Old Langho, Blackburn, BB6 8AP. Mr Peter Lumsden. 3m W of Whalley. Leave A59 at Northcote Manor, onto Northcote Lane. At the bottom, after 1m, turn R at T-junction, and 2 Brookside is on L. **Sat 26, Sun 27 July (11-4). Adm £4, chd free. Light refreshments.**
A recently created rural cottage garden, designed to support birds and other wildlife, and in particular, providing year-round flowers for foraging bees and butterflies. Features inc 3 beehives, pond, raised beds for vegetables, cordon fruit trees, perennial flower beds, quirky sculptures, water features, and an enclosed patio with variety of plants in pots. Seating areas located throughout.

15 136 BUCKINGHAM ROAD
Maghull, L31 7DR. Debbie & Mark Jackson. 7m N of Liverpool. End M57/M58, take A59 towards Ormskirk. Turn L after Aldi onto Liverpool Rd Sth, cont' on past Meadows pub, 3rd R into Sandringham Rd, L into Buckingham Rd. **Sat 7, Sun 8 June (12-5). Adm £4, chd free. Home-made teas.**
Donation to Queenscourt Hospice.
A suburban garden brimming with cottage garden plants and colour. A border dedicated to shade loving plants and another to herbaceous perennials. The garden features a wisteria covered pergola, rose bed, apple trees, acers and much more. A small pond, water feature and planters add interest to this relaxing garden.

4 BUTTERMERE CLOSE
Formby, Liverpool,
L37 2YB. Marilyn & Alan
Tippett, 07794 491141,
metippett@gmail.com. *Off
Ennerdale Rd, Formby. Pls park on
Ennerdale Rd if possible.* **Visits by arrangement May to Aug.**
A corner garden made in the last 7 yrs on shallow, sandy soil. The garden is a mixture of shrubs and perennials, many of the plants being of special interest and adapted to a coastal site with poor soil. There is a small pond for wildlife (newts, frogs and dragonflies), several seating areas and a new gravel garden is being established. A working artist's studio may also be open to visit.

GROUP OPENING

CALDER HOUSE LANE GARDENS
Calder House Lane, Bowgreave, Preston, PR3 1ZE. Mrs Margaret Richardson, 07867 848218, marg254@btinternet.com. *1m S of Garstang. From J32, A6, turn R on to B6340 1m. From J33 follow A6 for 7m, turn L onto Cock Robin Lane, Catterall turn L at the end, B6340. ½m turn R into Calder House Lane.* **Sat 14 June (11-5); Sun 15 June (12-5). Combined adm £7, chd free. Tea, coffee & cake at the Friends Meeting House, adjacent to the gardens. Visits also by arrangement 15 June to 31 Aug for groups of 8 to 30.**

CALDER COACH HOUSE
Mr & Mrs J Deninson.

1 CALDER HOUSE COTTAGE
Paul Hafren & Gaynor Gee.

2 CALDER HOUSE COTTAGE
Phil & Sarah Schofield.

3 CALDER HOUSE COTTAGE
Margaret & Mick Richardson.

The gardens range from a small satellite to a large (relatively new) garden featuring over 100 hosta varieties. They are mainly cottage gardens in style, each having its own features and interest. The small front gardens have all been made to 3 very different designs. No 1 has a satellite garden at the top of the track, a small but beautiful use of the space, making a tranquil haven. No 2's garden is divided into 3 rooms, a cottage garden, a secluded seating area and finally a greenhouse with vegetables and fruit. A newly built garden room adds to this lovely garden. No 3 has the largest garden, planted with perennials, trees, roses, hostas (over 100 varieties mainly in pots) and shrubs with a separate fruit and cut flower garden and greenhouse. Plus a gravel area with seating and a pond. Coach House has a cobbled frontage, with patio and large lawn to the rear. The new owners have plans for a pond and chicken run amongst other ideas. The Friends Meeting House is a beautiful setting for teas.

GROUP OPENING

CANNING AND TOXTETH GARDENS
27 Canning Street, Liverpool, L8 7NN. *No 86 bus runs every 12 mins from city centre. Ask for bus stop Back Canning St.* **Sun 22 June (1-5). Combined adm £6, chd free. Light refreshments.**

27 CANNING STREET
L8 7NN. Mrs Waltraud Boxall.

EL JARDIN DE LA NUESTRA SENORA
L8 7NL. R.C. Archdiocese of Liverpool.

GRANBY BACK ALLEY GARDEN
L8 2UW.

GRANBY WINTER GARDEN
L8 2UW. Granby Four Streets CLT, www.granby4streetsclt.co.uk.

GRAPES COMMUNITY FOOD GARDEN
L8 1XE. Squash Liverpool, admin@squashliverpool.co.uk.

PAKISTAN ASSOCIATION LIVERPOOL WELLBEING GARDEN
L8 2TF. Pakistan Association Liverpool.

A wide range of city gardens from the grandeur of the Georgian terraces, to the restored Toxteth Victorian streets. They now inc Granby Winter Garden and an innovative back alley garden recently featured on Gardeners' World. The winter garden was created out of two derelict houses, in an area being beautifully regenerated thanks to the efforts of the local residents. They join a well planted private garden behind one of Liverpool's grand Georgian terrace houses, and the unusual classically designed Spanish garden of St Philip Neri church. El Jardin de la Nuestra Senora was created on a bomb site after WW2. The church's exquisite Byzantine interior, designed by PS Gilby, will also be open. In contrast to the Georgian Quarter classicism are the vibrant Grapes Community Food Garden and Squash cafe garden in Windsor Street, plus the Wellbeing garden of the Liverpool Pakistan Association. It is a fascinating group, all within the historic heart of Liverpool, with many architecturally important buildings. These inc Liverpool's Anglican cathedral, the largest cathedral and religious building in Europe.

CIVIC PRIDE, ROSSENDALE
Queen's Square, Rawtenstall, Rossendale, BB4 6QU. Janet Allcock, www.civic-pride.org.uk. *The starting point is Sparrow Park, between the Library & the Church BB4 6QU. Maps will be provided & volunteers from Civic Pride Rossendale will be available to help and advise visitors. Limited time parking at supermarkets.* **Sat 26, Sun 27 July (1-5). Adm £5, chd free. Tea, coffee & cake at Sparrow Park. We have seating in our gardens and lawns for picnics.**
Rawtenstall in Bloom is made up of over 10 gardens following a lovely route around the town, offering a wide variety of planting styles to enjoy, inc a small private front garden. We have won many top awards, inc RHS Britain in Bloom, national competitions and Green Flag Award, reflecting the work of our volunteers, who ensure our gardens are of a very high standard. Pls allow 1hr to walk around the route. Special features inc flower train in the roundabout, rockery at Sparrow Park, peaceful Old Fold Garden, Boots' Boulevard, barrier baskets and planters. Most gardens are accessible, taking care with busy roads. Shorter, easier routes will be available for less able people.

55 Yealand Road

20 31 COUSINS LANE
Ardilea 31 Cousins Lane, Rufford, Ormskirk, L40 1TN. Brenda & Roy Caslake. *From M6 J27, follow signs for Parbold then Rufford. Turn L onto the A59. Turn R at Hesketh Arms pub. 4th turn on L.* **Sat 7, Sun 8 June (10-4). Combined adm with Oaklands £5, chd free. Home-made teas at Oaklands on Saturday & Rufford Cricket Club (adjacent to 31 Cousins Lane) on Sunday.**
A cottage garden with mixed borders running round 3 sides of the house. Discrete corners punctuated with open view of the village cricket ground. Planting and ponds encourage wildlife whilst secluded corners allow one to enjoy the tranquil atmosphere of a country garden. A glass of prosecco and delicious home-made cakes can be enjoyed on the Sunday at the cricket club.

21 79 CRABTREE LANE
Burscough, L40 0RW. Sandra & Peter Curl, 01704 893713, peter.curl@btinternet.com, www.youtube.com/watch?v=CW7S8nB_iX8. *3m NE of Ormskirk. A59 Preston - Liverpool Rd. From N before bridge R into Redcat Lane signed for Martin Mere. From S over 2nd bridge L into Redcat Lane after ¾m L into Crabtree Lane.* **Sun 15 June, Sun 20 July (11-4). Adm £5, chd free. Home-made teas. Visits also by arrangement 1 May to 17 Aug. Includes introductory talk on how the garden developed.**
¾ acre year-round plantsperson's garden with many rare and unusual plants. Herbaceous borders and island beds, pond, rockery, rose garden, and autumn hot bed. Many stone features built with reclaimed materials. Shrubs and rhododendrons, Koi pond and waterfall, hosta and fern walk. Gravel garden with Mediterranean plants. Patio surrounded by shrubs and raised alpine bed. Trees give areas for shade loving plants. Many beds replanted recently. Many stone buildings and features. Flat grass paths.

22 5 CRIB LANE
Dobcross, Oldham, OL3 5AF. Helen Campbell. *5m E of Oldham. From Dobcross head towards Delph on Platt La. Crib La opp Dobcross Band Club. Limited parking for disabled visitors only up steep lane. All other visitors to park in the village.* **Sat 12, Sun 13 July (1-4). Adm £3.50, chd free. Home-made teas.**
A challenging garden as on a high terraced hillside on tip site. Visited by deer, hares and the odd cow! One elderly gardener. An example of an ordinary family Pennine garden. Of additional interest are wildlife ponds, wildflower areas, a polytunnel, four beehives with 250,000 bees, an art gallery and garden sculptures. Areas re thought annually, dug up and changed. Local honey, cards and art work for sale.

23 DALE HOUSE GARDENS

off Church Lane, Goosnargh, Preston, PR3 2BE. **Caroline & Tom Luke**, 01772 862464, tomlukebudgerigars@hotmail.com. *2½ m E of Broughton. M6 J32 signed Garstang Broughton, T-lights R at Whittingham Lane, 2½m to Whittingham. At PO turn L into Church Lane. Garden between nos 17 & 19.* **Sat 12, Sun 13 Apr, Sat 14, Sun 15 June (10-4). Adm £3.50, chd free. Home-made teas.** Visits also by arrangement Apr to June for groups of 10 to 50. Donation to St Francis School, Goosnargh.

½ acre tastefully landscaped gardens comprising limestone rockeries, well-stocked herbaceous borders, raised alpine beds with many new plants, well-stocked koi pond, lawn areas, greenhouse and polytunnel, patio areas, specialising in alpines, rare shrubs and trees, large display of unusual spring bulbs. Secret Garden and year-round interest. Constantly evolving planting schemes. Large indoor budgerigar aviary with 300+ budgies. Gravel path, lawn areas.

24 DENT HALL

Colne Road, Trawden, Colne, BB8 8NX. **Chris Whitaker-Webb & Joanne Smith.** *10 min from end of M65. Turn L at end of M65. Follow A6068 for 2m; just after 3rd r'about turn R down B6250. After 1½m, in front of church, turn R, signed Carry Bridge. Keep R, follow road up hill, garden on R after 300yds.* **Sat 31 May, Sun 1 June (12-5). Adm £4.50, chd free. Tea, coffee & cake.**

Nestled in the oldest part of Trawden villlage and rolling Lancashire countryside, this mature and evolving country garden surrounds a 400 yr old grade II listed property (not open); featuring a parterre, lawns, herbaceous borders, shrubbery, wildlife pond with bridge to seating area and a hidden summerhouse in a woodland area. Plentiful seating throughout. Some uneven paths and gradients.

Anderton Mill Cottage, Mawdesley Gardens

LANCASHIRE

25 DERIAN HOUSE CHILDREN'S HOSPICE
Chancery Road, Chorley, PR7 1DH. www.derianhouse.co.uk. *2m from Chorley town centre. From B5252 pass Chorley Hospital on L, at r'about 1st exit to Chancery Lane. Hospice on L after 0.4 m. Parking around the building & on the road. SatNav directions not always accurate.* **Sun 6 Apr (10-4.30). Adm £3, chd free. Light refreshments.** The Chorley-based children's hospice provides respite and end-of-life care to more than 400 children and young people from across the North West and South Cumbria. The gardens at the hospice help to create an atmosphere of relaxation, tranquillity and joy. Distinct areas inc the seaside garden, the sensory garden, the memorial garden and the Smile Park adventure playground. Family activities. Home-made cakes and plant sale. Gardens and refreshments area are wheelchair friendly, accessible parking and WC facilities also available.

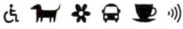

GROUP OPENING

26 DIDSBURY VILLAGE GARDENS
Tickets from 68 Brooklawn Drive M20 3GZ or any garden, Didsbury, Manchester, M20 3GZ. *5m S of city centre. From M60 J5 follow signs to Northenden. Turn R at T-lights onto Barlow Moor Rd to Didsbury. From M56 follow A34 to Didsbury.* **Sun 8 June (12-5). Combined adm £6, chd free. Home made teas at 68 Brooklawn Drive.**

68 BROOKLAWN DRIVE
M20 3GZ. Anne & Jim Britt, www.annebrittdesign.com.

3 THE DRIVE
M20 6HZ. Peter Clare & Sarah Keedy, www.peterclaregardendesign.co.uk.

40 PARRS WOOD AVENUE
M20 5ND. Tom Johnson.

38 WILLOUGHBY AVENUE
M20 6AS. Simon Hickey.

We have 4 very beautiful and individual gardens to visit in the attractive suburb of Didsbury. There is so much to see and inspire in these gardens, from our traditional cottage gardens complete with a new wrought iron verandah with alliums, roses, clematis and topiary, to the soft lines of a very natural wildlife friendly garden buzzing with wildlife. If you have shady conditions you could learn so much from one of the best shady gardens that you'll find in a suburban setting and many tips on creating beautiful planterly privacy in a previously overlooked setting. Our gardens offer a diverse range of water features and inspirational stylish wildlife friendly planting ideas - all within our relatively small garden spaces which are a feast to the eye and full of detail to imitate at home. Wheelchair access to some gardens.

27 DRUMMERSDALE CROSSING COTTAGE
Wholesome Lane, Scarisbrick, Ormskirk, L40 9SW. Mrs Janet & Mr Mike Hinton. *500 yds SE of Bescar Ln Railway Stn. There is no parking at the garden. Postcode will take you to parking in adjacent meadow. Follow yellow signs from Drummersdale Lane. What3words app: wedge.flock.blemishes. OS Grid SD 399 144.* **Sun 20 July (11-5). Adm £4, chd free. Home-made cakes, cream teas inc vegan options.**
Beautiful ½ acre country garden with open views to adjacent farmland. Colour themed beds with herbaceous perennials set within lawned area. Various trees and shrubs. Wildlife ponds, summerhouse with viewing window overlooking beehives. Shaded areas with ferns and hostas. Polytunnel with a variety of fruit, vegetables and vine. Meadow, orchard and woodland walks. Vegetable patch and wildflower areas are under development.

28 DUTTON HALL
Gallows Lane, Ribchester, PR3 3XX. Mr & Mrs A H Penny, www.duttonhall.co.uk. *2m NE of Ribchester. Signed from B6243 & B6245 Directions on website also. What3words app: copying.botanists. mostly.* **Sun 22 June (1-5). Adm £7.50, chd free. Home-made teas. Donation to Plant Heritage.**
An increasing range of unusual trees and shrubs have been added to the existing collection of old fashioned roses, inc rare and unusual varieties and Plant Heritage National Collection of Pemberton Hybrid Musk roses. Formal garden at front with backdrop of C17 house (not open). Analemmatic Sundial, pond, meadow areas all with extensive views over Ribble valley. Wildlife trail. Plant Heritage plant stall with unusual varieties for sale.

GROUP OPENING

29 ELLESMERE PARK GARDENS
35 Ellesmere Road, Eccles, Manchester, M30 9FE. Enid Noronha. *4m S from central Manchester. At M602 junction turn L onto Gilda Brook Rd, then R onto Half Edge Ln. Follow round to Monton Rd & turn R onto Stafford Rd. At the top turn L onto Ellesmere Rd then R x2 for 11 Westminster Rd.* **Sat 14 June (11.30-4). Combined adm £7, chd free. Cakes, coffee & tea at 35 Ellesmere Rd, hot dogs at 20 Stafford Rd and tea & biscuits at 11 Westminster Rd.**

35 ELLESMERE ROAD
M30 9FE. Enid Noronha.

20 STAFFORD ROAD
M30 9HW. Mrs Paula Gibson.

11 WESTMINSTER ROAD
M30 9HF. George & Lynne Meakin.

The group consists of 3 diverse suburban gardens in adjoining streets in Eccles. 35 Ellesmere Road is a cottage style garden with walkways, palisade, greenhouse and raised beds with vegetables and herbs. Lawns with box hedges. Mature fruit and other trees. At 11 Westminster Road there is a pretty front garden with topiary chickens, well-stocked with perennials, mature trees, and box hedging. The garden is divided by a trellis and rose arch which separates the flower beds and lawn from the fruit growing area, and there are a large number of fuchsias grown in pots. Finally at 20 Stafford Road the garden features mature trees and shrubs alongside many recent additions. An ongoing project involves upcycling items the garden owners find interesting that others have discarded. The owners like to put bold colours and statements in wherever they can to enable colour year-round. Some areas with only partial access.

GROUP OPENING

30 FALLOWFIELD & LADYBARN GARDENS
27 Clifton Avenue, Manchester, M14 6UD. Mrs Kattie Kincaid. *Trail runs from M14 6NF to M14 6RN. Approaching Fallowfield from Withington on Wilmslow Rd, turn R into Whiteoak Rd after the Shell garage and you can park on the streets around there.* **Sat 5, Sun 6 July (11-4.30). Combined adm £6, chd free. Refreshments & WC at Tatton Villa, 3 Brook Road.**

NEW 6 AMHERST ROAD
M14 6UQ. Mr Tom Harle.

1 BESFORD CLOSE
M14 6NF. Mr Matthew Baddeley.

6 CLIFTON AVENUE
M14 6UB. Mrs Lesley Bowers.

27 CLIFTON AVENUE
M14 6UD. Mrs Kattie Kincaid.

NEW THE COACH HOUSE, 1(A) DERBY ROAD
M14 6UN. Ms Liz Bayliffe-Smith.

NEW LADYBARN COMMUNITY GARDEN, LADYBARN COMMUNITY HUB
M14 6RN.
www.instagram.com/ladybarn_hub.

TATTON VILLA, 3 BROOK ROAD
M14 6UJ. Sian Astley,
www.instagram.com/makeitmoregeous.

Fallowfield and Ladybarn suburbs grew rapidly from the mid C19. The oldest house on the trail belongs to a coach house built in 1863 and evokes an era when the area was still semi rural, the newest is a smart modern town house built for a bustling suburb. Wending your way round you will discover many sources of inspiration; an established walled garden, wildlife ponds, pergolas and gazebos, shade loving nature areas, stunning mixed and herbaceous borders and some wonderfully creative outdoor entertaining spaces where you can sit and enjoy afternoon tea. In addition to 2 new gardens, there is also a community garden with edibles, ornamentals and a wildflower meadow area. Along a large part of the trail you will pass some beautiful tree bases cared for by local residents and this year we will be creating a riddle trail along our route to amuse and entertain you. Most of the gardens on this trail have easy wheelchair access and are on flat terrain.

31 GLYNWOOD HOUSE
Eyes Lane, Bretherton, Leyland, PR26 9AS. Terry & Sue Riding. *Once in Bretherton, turn onto Eyes Lane by the War Memorial. After 50yds take the R fork, after100yds follow the road around to the L. Glynwood House is a further 200yds on the L.* **Sun 29 June, Sun 27 July (11-5). Adm £4, chd free. Home-made teas.**
Set in a peaceful rural location with spectacular views. Highlights of this ¾ acre garden inc colour themed mixed borders with rare and unusual plants, wildlife pond with cascade water feature and meandering paths through a woodland shaded area. A patio garden, surrounded by a large pergola, features a kinetic sycamore seed sculpture. Access available to most of the garden apart from paths in the woodland walk area.

32 GORSE HILL NATURE RESERVE
Holly Lane, Aughton, Ormskirk, L39 7HB. Jonathan Atkins (Reserve Manager), www.gorsehillnaturereserve.co.uk. *1½ m S of Ormskirk. A59 from L'pool past Royal Oak pub take 1st L Gaw Hill Lane turn R Holly Lane. From Preston follow A59 across T-lights at A570 J & at r'about. After Xing lights turn R Gaw Hill Lane turn R Holly Lane.* **Sun 6 July (11-4). Combined adm with 72 Ludlow Drive £5, chd free. Tea, coffee & cake. Our Gorse Hill Heritage Orchard apple juice is also available.**
In summer our wildflower hay meadow is brimming with a wide variety of wild flowers and grasses and offers spectacular views across the Lancashire Plain. The wildlife pond is patrolled by dragonflies and damselflies and the air is full of butterflies and bees. Mown grassy paths take you through the meadow to enable close views of the flowers and insects. The adjacent woodland walk is also open.

33 NEW GREENACRES
Cowpe Road, Rossendale, BB4 7AE. Mr & Mrs Graham Chown. *Head N on A681, turn L Cowpe Rd, ½ m R at Community Hall, up lane ¼ m. What3words app: laptop.ultra.switch.* **Sat 31 May (10-4). Adm £5, chd free. Tea, coffee & cake.**
A rural 2 acre garden set on a hillside, with a variety of trees, a large range of unusual conifers, shrubs and perennial beds. A bog garden which hosts a variety of plants, the most impressive being Gunnera. We have a large collection of primulas, mainly candelabras. A quiet location with a meandering woodland path through wild garlic.

34 THE GROWTH PROJECT
Kellett Street Allotments, Kellett St, Rochdale, OL16 2JU. Karen Hayday, 07464 546962, k.hayday@hourglass.org.uk, www.facebook.com/Hourglass.org.uk. *From A627 M. R A58 L Entwistle Rd then R Kellett St.* **Sun 27 July (11.30-3). Adm £4, chd free. Home-made teas. Visits also by arrangement 3 July to 2 Oct (Thursdays only) Donation to The Growth Project.**
The project covers over an acre inc a huge variety of organic veg, wildlife pond, insect hotels, formal flower and Japanese garden, potager, cut flower and woodland garden. See the mock Elizabethan strawbale build, the witch's hat, and railway station. Stroll down the pergola walk to the secret annual wildflower meadow, orchard and theatre. The new attractions this year are the development of the Japanese garden and the 'witch's hat'. Home-made tea and lunch on the lawn, produce, jams and flowers for sale. Regret no disabled WC, ground can be uneven.

In 2024, National Garden Scheme funding for Perennial supported 1,367 people working in horticulture.

GROUP OPENING

35 HALE VILLAGE GARDENS
2 Pheasant Field, Hale Village, Liverpool, L24 5SD. Roger & Tania Craine. *6m S of M62 J6. Take A5300, A562 towards L'pool, then A561 and then L for Hale. From S L'pool head for the airport then L sign for Hale. The 82A bus from Widnes/Runcorn to L'pool has village stops.* **Sat 7, Sun 8 June (1-5). Combined adm £5, chd free. Home-made teas at 2 Pheasant Field & at 33 Hale Rd.**

66 CHURCH ROAD
L24 4BA. Liz Kelly-Hines & David Hines.

2 PHEASANT FIELD
L24 5SD. Roger & Tania Craine.

WHITECROFT, 33 HALE ROAD
L24 5RB. Donna & Bob Richards.

The delightful village of Hale is set in rural South Merseyside between Widnes and Liverpool Airport. It is home to the cottage, sculpture and grave of the famous giant known as the Childe of Hale. Three gardens of various sizes have been developed by their present owners. There are 2 gardens (a large skilfully landscaped one and a beautiful contemporary one) to the west of the village and a delightful garden in Church Rd to the east of the village.

36 HALTON PARK HOUSE
Halton Park, Halton, Lancaster, LA2 6PD. Mr & Mrs Duncan Bowring. *7min drive from both J34 & 35 M6. On Park Lane, approx 1½ m from Halton or Caton. Park Lane accessed either from Low Rd or High Rd out of Halton. From Low Rd turn into Park Lane through pillars over cattle grid.* **Sat 17, Sun 18 May (11-4). Adm £6, chd free. BBQ over lunch time. Home-made cakes & cream teas.**
Approx 6 acres of garden, with gravel paths leading through large mixed herbaceous borders, terraces, orchard with developing wildflower meadow and terraced vegetable beds. Wildlife pond and woodland walk in dell area, extensive lawns, large greenhouse and herb garden. Plenty of places to sit and rest to enjoy the view. Gravel paths (some sloping) give access to viewing points over the majority of the garden. Hard standing around the house.

37 THE HAWES
Sandringham Road, Ainsdale, Southport, PR8 2NZ. Niall & Joan Roy. *5m S of Southport. From A565, at r'about turn R into Station Rd through Ainsdale Village. Take 1st R after level crossing and drive to far end of Sandringham Rd.* **Sat 31 May (11-4). Adm £5, chd free. Light refreshments.**
A 6 acre woodland garden plus numerous lawns and borders with stunning summer colour as well as several water features. The formal garden is designed with an arts and crafts theme. A long woodland walk leads you through rhododendron and pinewoods where you may glance shy red squirrels. The garden has several wilding areas.

38 NEW 18 HIGHCROSS HILL
Poulton-le-Fylde, FY6 8BT. Simon & Julie Clark. *3m W of Blackpool Tower. No parking on Highcross Hill pls follow parking signs. M55 J3 A585/A586 to Poulton. At 4th T-lights turn L onto Hardhorn Rd. R onto Longhouse Lane then L onto Highcross Rd. Garden on L off Staining Old Rd. What3words app: holds.entry.tuned.* **Sat 19, Sun 20 July (11-4). Adm £4, chd free. Tea, coffee & cake.**
Relaxed garden on a sloping plot accessed via 10 steps. Planted to encourage wildlife. Colour-themed herbaceous perennials; alliums, geraniums, verbena and penstemon. Trees inc fig, apple and plum. Vegetable beds and gravel borders. Live music at 2pm. Art sale.

39 HIGHER BRIDGE CLOUGH HOUSE
Coal Pit Lane, Rossendale, BB4 9SB. Karen Clough, Cloughinbloom.co.uk. *4m from Rawtenstall. Take A681 into Waterfoot. Turn L onto the B6238. Approx ½ m turn R onto Shawclough Rd. Follow the road up until you reach the yellow signs.* **Sat 19, Sun 20 July (12-6). Adm £5, chd free. Tea, coffee & cake.**
Nestled within Rossendale farmland in an exposed site the garden is split by a meandering stream. There are raised mixed borders with shrubs and perennials enclosed with loose planting of shrubs and water loving plants around the stream. A local farmer once told me 'you won't grow 'owt up 'ere...' so the challenge is on. In 2024 we opened our flower farm 'Clough in Bloom'. The Rossendale area provides some excellent walking and rambling sites. Rawtenstall has the famous East Lancashire railway, which is worth a visit.

GROUP OPENING

40 HIGHTOWN GARDENS
Mark Road, Hightown, Liverpool, L38 0BG. Barbara Jones. *11m N of Liverpool & 11m S of Southport. M57/58 Join A5758 Brooms Cross at r'about 2nd exit A565. At lights L onto B5193/Orrell Hill Lane. Turn R Moss Lane. Turn L onto Alt Rd, then R (over bridge) Kerslake Way & follow NGS signs at r'about.* **Sun 8 June (1-5). Combined adm £6. Tea, coffee & cake at 7 Mark Rd.**

11 BLUNDELL AVENUE
L38 9ED. Karen Rimmer.

NEW 48 BLUNDELL ROAD
L38 9EQ. Nina & Colin Mitchell-Price.

75 BLUNDELL ROAD
L38 9EF. Shirley & Phil Roberts.

NEW 7 MARK ROAD
L38 0BG. Barbara & Derek Jones.

NEW WEST BANK, SCHOOL ROAD
L38 0BN. Barbara MacArthur.

A welcoming group of five gardens in the village of Hightown. Visit a plantswoman's quirky garden full of surprises, a recently-built, contemporary garden with pond feature, an organic garden with a Mediterranean planting theme, a wildlife, organic garden with pergola, pond and literary-themed areas and a small garden with a modern touch that's full of colour. There is wheelchair access to one garden in Blundell Rd, West Bank in School Rd and the Mark Rd garden.

306 LANCASHIRE

41 NEW HMP KIRKHAM
Freckleton Road, Kirkham, Preston, PR4 2RN. Diane Clare. *The prison is located off the A583 (Freckleton Rd). Visitors should park at the farm shop which is 1st R as you turn off Freckleton Rd for the prison. Overspill parking also avail in general visitor car park.* **Wed 11, Wed 18 June (10-12). Adm £10. Pre-booking essential, please visit www.ngs.org.uk for information & booking. Light refreshments at the farm shop near the entrance.**
The prison has 150 acres of farm and grounds maintained by prisoners learning horticultural and agricultural skills. The site has gardens with herbaceous borders, lawns, heritage orchard, allotments, greenhouses, wildflower meadow, wellness garden, wildlife and fish ponds and extensive woodland. You will be accompanied by the farm managers who will give a guided tour of the farm and grounds. Produce, inc fruit, veg, plants and meat from rare breeds, are sold through the farm shop. Pls note identity documentation will be required and we will contact you prior to your visit.

42 46 HOLMDALE AVENUE
Southport, PR9 8PS. Ms June Slater. *3½ m N of Southport. By car signed from A565 or by bus no 49 or X2 to Preston New Rd, alight at the Mormon church, into North Rd, take 1st L to Holmdale Ave.* **Sun 27 July (10-4). Combined adm with 3 Alexander Mews £5, chd free. Cream teas.**
A small and pretty garden filled with love for a peaceful experience. Borders filled with shrubs and plants in season. The lawn area incorporates a small pond, greenhouse and leads to a beach garden. In the autumn season hops flourish into fruition, these are a passion of the owner who comes from a hop picking family. The front garden is flagged from a central display with an abundance of flowering tubs.

43 NEW HOLMERE LODGE
Dykes Lane, Yealand Conyers, Carnforth, LA5 9SN. Mr & Mrs L Hornby. *From Carnforth heading N, follow A6 towards Milnthorpe passing through 3 r'abouts until reaching Holmere Hall on L. Turn sharp L here onto Dykes Lane. Holmere Lodge is the 3rd gate on R.*

Sun 3 Aug (11-5). Combined adm with 55 Yealand Road £5, chd free. Tea, coffee & cake.
Three distinct garden areas. A managed wildlife area of prairie planting, wildflowers and trees, a formal courtyard with seasonal planting and structured shrubs featuring stone floor artwork and a glasshouse and a 'secret' semi walled garden with geometric topiary.

44 KINGTON COTTAGE
Kirkham Road, Treales, Preston, PR4 3SD. Mrs Linda Kidd, 01772 683005. *M55 J3. Take A585 to Kirkham, exit Preston St, L into Carr Lane to Treales village. Cottage on L.* **Sun 25 May, Sun 29 June, Sun 27 July (10-5). Adm £4, chd free. Home-made teas. Visits also by arrangement 1 May to 1 Sept for groups of 8 to 30. Escorted tours by garden owner.**
Nestling in the beautiful village of Treales this generously sized Japanese garden has many authentic and unique Japanese features, alongside its 2 ponds linked by a stream. The stroll garden leads down to the tea house garden. The planting and the meandering pathways blend together to create a tranquil meditative garden in which to relax. New additions complete four Japanese garden styles. Wheelchair access to some areas, uneven paths.

45 72 LUDLOW DRIVE
Ormskirk, L39 1LF. Marian & Brian Jones. *½ m W of Ormskirk on A570. From M58 J3 follow A570 to Ormskirk town centre. Continue on A570 towards Southport. At A570 junction with A59 cross T-lights after ½ m turn R at Spar garage onto Heskin Lane then 1st R Ludlow Drive.* **Sun 6 July (11-4). Combined adm with Gorse Hill Nature Reserve £5, chd free. Tea, coffee & cake. Gluten free & vegan cake also provided.**
A town garden overflowing with a wide variety of bee friendly planting. It inc a gravel garden, jewel garden, shady textured borders and a sunny raised bed with perennials, roses and clematis. A large Victorian style glasshouse has a collection of pelargonium, succulents, aeoniums and cacti. There is also a pond, and many alpine troughs. Wheelchair access to front and rear garden.

46 MAGGIE'S, MANCHESTER
Kinnaird Road, Manchester, M20 4QL. Laura Birch, www.maggies.org/our-centres/maggies-manchester. *At the end of Kinnaird Rd which is off Wilmslow Rd opp the Christie Hospital.* **Sun 8 June (12-4). Adm £5, chd free. Light refreshments.**
The architecture of Maggie's Manchester, designed by world-renowned architect Lord Foster, is complemented by gardens designed by Dan Pearson, Best in Show winner at Chelsea Flower Show. Combining a rich mix of spaces, inc the working glasshouse and vegetable garden, the garden provides a place for both activity and contemplation. The colours and sensory experience of nature becomes part of the Centre through micro gardens and internal courtyards, which relate to the different spaces within the building. Wheelchair access to most of the garden from the front entrance.

47 MAGHULL STATION
Station Road, Maghull, Liverpool, L31 3DE. Merseyrail. *7 m N of Liverpool. Follow A59 into Maghull turning R at 2nd set of T-lights (opp Maghull Town Hall) Follow road over canal bridge & station is approx ½ m.* **Sun 13 July (11-4.30). Adm £4, chd free. Coffee bar on site serving light refreshments hot & cold.**
Filled with colourful herbaceous plants, shrubs, rockery, hanging baskets, troughs and large planters tumbling with a wide variety of bedding plants - a wonderful sight for commuters arriving in Maghull plus a hidden surprise garden. Winners of RHS North West In Bloom Best Station in 2021 and the Best in Britain in the World Cup of Stations competition 2024. Our Hornby train made from waste products sits in its own beautifully planted cottage garden. Hidden pathways with their own secrets. Disabled parking spaces available.

GROUP OPENING

48 NEW MAWDESLEY GARDENS
Bentley Lane, Mawdesley, Ormskirk, L40 3AD. Jill & Mark Brindle. *10 mins from M6 J27. From M6 J27 take 1st exit, past*

Crow Orchard petrol station. Turn R onto Moss Ln. After ¾ m turn R onto Courage Low Ln. Turn L onto Bentley Lane. Garden is on R after Ridley Lane. **Sun 13 July (11-5). Combined adm £5, chd free. Tea, coffee & cake at 10 Anderton's Mill & Harrock View.**

NEW ANDERTON MILL COTTAGE
L40 3AD. Jill & Mark Brindle.

NEW 10 ANDERTON'S MILL
L40 3TW. Heather & Alan Beezley.

NEW FERNDALE
L40 2RA. Bob & Margaret Mercer.

3 HARROCK VIEW
PR7 5PZ. Tony & Janet Trafford, 07809 656388, tony.trafford@norlec.com. **Visits also by arrangement 20 July to 31 Aug for groups of 10 to 30. Sundays only.**

A group of 4 gardens in and around Mawdesley, a pretty rural village between Chorley and Ormskirk. Each garden has something different to offer, from cottage gardens, shaded areas, carnivorous plants, handcrafted metalworks, colourful container plantings, idyllic views of neighbouring countryside, exotic planting and even animal sculptures. Of course there are home-made cakes and refreshments to be had along the way! Most gardens are partially accessible to wheelchair users.

49 MILL BARN
Goosefoot Close, Samlesbury, Preston, PR5 0SS. Chris Mortimer, 07742 924124, chris@millbarn.net. 6m E of Preston. From M6 J31 2½ m on A59/A677 B/burn. Turn S. Nabs Head Ln, then Goosefoot Ln. **Sat 31 May, Sun 1, Sat 7, Sun 8 June (11.30-5). Adm £5, chd free. Home-made teas. Picnics welcome. Visits also by arrangement 3 May to 31 Aug for groups of up to 30.**

The unique and quirky garden at Mill Barn is a delight, or rather a series of delights. Along the River Darwin, through the tiny secret grotto, past the suspension bridge and view of the fairytale tower, visitors can stroll past folly, sculptures, lily pond, and lawns, enjoy the naturally planted flower beds, then enter the secret garden and through it the pathways of the wooded hillside beyond. A garden developed on the site of old mills gives a fascinating layout which evolves at many levels. The garden jungle provides a smorgasbord of flowers to attract insects throughout the season. Children enjoy the garden very much. Partial wheelchair access.

50 NEW MONASTERY OF OUR LADY OF HYNING
Warton, Carnforth, LA5 9SE. Sr Stella, www.bernardine.org/hyning-hospitality. *Between Warton & Yealand Conyers, Carnforth. From M6 J35, take A6070 W then A6 N ½ m, turn L Borwick Lane follow to end 1m, turn R & proceed for ½ m. Our Lady of Hyning on R down long private drive. What3words app: greet.wordplay.obeyed.* **Sat 4, Sun 5 Oct (12-4). Adm £5, chd free. Light refreshments.**

The gardens and grounds extend to over 10 acres with tranquil glades, veteran trees, productive greenhouses and vegetable plot. Views over the countryside will take your breath away. In the late 1940's Ralph Hancock designed garden rooms, terraces and features for the owner, Lord Peel. Elements of his design remain but the 6 gardeners of his time are something we can only dream about!

Greenacres

51 18 MOOR DRIVE
Crosby, Liverpool, L23 2UP. Mrs Vicki Hall, vickihallhome@gmail.com. *12m S of Southport & 7m N of Liverpool close to Crosby village. A565 from Southport. Formby bypass becomes Southport Rd. Continues onto Moor Ln. Turn into Moor Drive, turn R at junction, then R into cul-de-sac. House on L at the bottom of the cul-de-sac.* **Sun 29 June (11-4). Combined adm with 16 Beach Lawn £5, chd free. Tea, coffee & cake.**
Wonderfully planted, picturesque urban garden with numerous trees, shrubs and climbers developed over several years. Emphasis on encouraging wildlife and organic gardening practices. Lawned areas, mixed perennial planting, small vegetable garden with crop rotation. Greenhouse. Ornamental and wildlife ponds. Seating areas surrounded by scented climbers and roses. Several frogs and a tortoise live here. Crosby beach is a short drive away where it is possible to visit the art installation 'Another Place' by renowned sculptor Anthony Gormley. Good access to front garden, seating areas & most of rear garden. Some uneven pebble paths around greenhouse area.

52 MOSS PARK ALLOTMENTS
Lesley Road, Stretford, Manchester, M32 9EE. Peter Bazley, 07738 761220, peterdb56@hotmail.co.uk. *3m SW of Manchester. From M60 J7 (Manchester), A56 (Manchester), A5181 Barton Rd, L onto B5213 Urmston Lane, ½m L onto Lesley Rd signed Stretford Cricket Club. Parking at 2nd gate.* **Sun 13 July (11-4). Adm £5, chd free. Gorgeous array of home-made cakes.** Visits also by arrangement 2 June to 1 Oct.
Moss Park is a stunning, award winning allotment site in Stretford, Manchester. Wide grass paths flanked by pretty flower borders give way to a large variety of well-tended plots bursting with ideas to try at home, from insect hotels to unusual fruits and vegetables. Take tea and cake on the lawn outside the quirky society clubhouse that looks like a beamed country pub. WC facilities. Partial wheelchair access but most plots can be viewed from grass runways.

53 NEW 204 NORBRECK ROAD
Thornton-Cleveleys, FY5 1RE. Mrs Nicola & Mr David Barnett. *5m N of Blackpool. Short drive from the M55. J3 towards Fleetwood. Follow A585 to Norcross r'about. At Norcross take 2nd exit to Warren Dr. Follow Warren Dr to Norbreck Rd. Parking on road. What3words app: zebra.truly.heads.* **Sat 12, Sun 13 July (10-4). Adm £4, chd free. Self service tea, coffee cake & biscuits.**
A colourful garden with deep planted borders of mixed perennial planting, bedding, shrubs and trees. Lots of containers and pots. Interesting use of recycled items as planters. Large Hosta collection in pots and planted out. Plenty of seating areas. Two small frog ponds. There are 2 small steps down in to the garden. Accessible to top paved area with views down the garden.

54 OAKLANDS
Flash Lane, Rufford, Ormskirk, L40 1SW. Mr John & Mrs Jane Hoban. *Pls park in the village hall car park which is situated on the L at the end of Flash Lane.* **Sat 7, Sun 8 June (10-4). Combined adm with 31 Cousins Lane £5, chd free. Home-made teas at Oaklands on Saturday & Rufford Cricket Club (adjacent to 31 Cousins Lane) on Sunday.**
Oaklands is a beautiful tranquil woodland garden full of mature trees, acers, camellias and rhododendrons. We have over the years created pathways and seating areas flanked with ferns and hostas. The garden also has several water features and large areas of lawn. Most areas of our garden are wheelchair accessible but most of the pathways are through the woodlands so it can be quite uneven.

GROUP OPENING

55 OLDHAM GARDENS
Lark Rise 515 Burnley Lane, Chadderton, Oldham, OL9 0BW. Wendy & Ian Connor. *Green Ln leave M60 J22 towards Manchester.1st exit L (Hollins Rd). In 1m turn R into Garden Suburb. Lark Rise leave A627(M) at J1 Elk Mill R'about taking Middleton exit. House is ½m on L. Maggie's is in Royal Oldham Hospital grounds next to A&E. Maps at all gardens.* **Sun 3 Aug (12-5). Combined adm £6, chd free. Tea, coffee & cake.**

76 GREEN LANE
OL8 3BA. Susan & John Clegg.
LARK RISE
OL9 0BW. Wendy & Ian Connor.
MAGGIE'S, OLDHAM
OL1 2JH. Maggie's Centres, www.maggies.org/oldham.

3 gardens less than 3m from Oldham town centre, all different in style. 76 Green Lane is entered through a wooden pergola past a cutting garden. Steps lead through a rose arch onto a path past 2 greenhouses down to another cutting patch. The garden consists of large mature trees and borders containing many cottage garden favourites inc roses, clematis, sweet peas and foxgloves. Lark Rise is a ½ acre suburban garden with borders surrounding the garden planted with perennials, shrubs and small decorative trees. Its features inc an apple archway leading to a box parterre with a decorative ironwork water feature. There is a beehive in a wild area at the bottom of the garden. Maggie's Oldham is a one storey building supported over its garden by steel legs. The building 'floats' aloft like a drop curtain to the scene creating a picture window effect. The garden flows below the building into a walled and secluded woodland sanctuary. Designed by Rupert Muldoon, it has featured on Gardeners' World. Wheelchair access at Lark Rise. Limited views of the garden at Maggie's from the Maggie's Centre building.

56 33 PERSHORE GROVE
Ainsdale, Southport, PR8 2SY. Mr Francis Proctor, 07866 667066, francisandbarbara33@gmail.com. *4.9 m S of Southport. Disabled parking on the garden driveway. Other parking pls use Westminster Drive.* **Sun 6 Apr (11-5). Adm £5, chd free. Tea, coffee & cake.** Visits also by arrangement 18 May to 19 Oct.
Small garden, inc a bridge, romantic ruin and man made caves with many entertaining features, 30 years in the construction. Use of recycled building materials. Entrance to caves may not be suitable for those with mobility issues.

LANCASHIRE 309

57 NEW THE QUAKER MEETING HOUSE
Co Operation Street, Crawshawbooth, Rossendale, BB4 8AG. Mr Philip Whitehead, www.crawshawboothquakers.org.uk. *2m N of Rawtenstall, off the A682. Turn L at zebra crossing from Rawtenstall. Enter walled garden opp Masons Arms pub.* **Sat 26 July (11-5); Sun 27 July (1-5). Adm £3, chd free. Tea, coffee & cake.**
Our walled garden is situated at a Quaker C18 2* listed Meeting House and burial ground. The garden, which has manicured lawns and borders with two benches, reflects an atmosphere of peace and tranquillity with a colourful display of plants, shrubs and trees. An accessible WC is available at the left side of the building beneath the cottage.

58 NEW QUAKERS REST
Blackpool Old Road, Little Eccleston, Preston, PR3 0YQ. Mr Stephen Ralphs. *Between Poulton-le-Fylde & Churchtown just off A586. M6 J32 follow A6 N for 7m, L A586, signed Blackpool & Fleetwood, 5m R onto Blackpool Old Rd. From W A586, turn L onto Blackpool Old Rd.* **Sat 6, Sun 7 Sept (10-4). Adm £4, chd free. Tea, coffee & cake.**
Quakers Rest was built in the early 1700s and was the original Quaker Meeting House for the Preston area. The garden area to the front and rear was a burial ground. In 2017 the house was renovated and work started on the gardens which had become overgrown. Summerhouse, BBQ patio area, lawns, statues and mixed beds.

59 RAINBAG COTTAGE
Carr Moss Lane, Halsall, Ormskirk, L39 8RZ. Sue & Mick Beacon. *8m NW of Ormskirk. What3words app: doll.talkative.hamsters. A570 from Ormskirk to Southport after 4m, L into Gorsuch Lane A5147. After 1½m pass church R into Carr Moss Ln which becomes single track, house sign on L after 2m.* **Sat 30, Sun 31 Aug (10.30-4). Adm £5, chd free. Home-made teas.**
A magical ½ acre garden in a rural setting with open views to the surrounding countryside. Oriental themed stroll garden with wildlife ponds and moongate. Herbaceous borders and woodland walk. Raised beds with vegetables and cut flowers. Small flower meadow, fruit trees, greenhouse, wormery and bug pad. Various seating areas. Fairies, a scarecrow and an angel live here. Secret garden under development.

60 85 RIBCHESTER ROAD
Clayton Le Dale, Blackburn, BB1 9HT. Mrs Elizabeth Seed. *1m N of Blackburn. From Preston/Clitheroe take B6245 off A59 for ¾m and from B/burn take A666, turn L on B6245 for ½m. Garden opp St Peters Church, Salesbury. Parking at Salesbury School, Lovely Hall Ln, ¼m.* **Sat 19, Sun 20 July (12-4). Adm £3, chd free. Home-made teas.**
Small suburban garden with herbaceous borders inc a mix of perennials, shrubs, roses, climbers and grasses. Decorative ironwork arches and pergola complement the planting. Two raised ponds with water features, fruit trees, a small vegetable area and greenhouse complete the garden. New for 2025 is a wildlife pond. Seating available and home-made cakes. Some uneven paths and steps.

61 RISHTON TROPICAL GARDEN
52 Tomlinson Place, Rishton, Blackburn, BB1 4AZ. Mr Tez Donnelly, www.facebook.com/LancsTropicalGarden. *Junction 7 M65, then Clitheroe exit on the r'about, then turn L to Rishton. Turn R into Parker St, then L into Wheatfield St. Pls note there is no parking at the address.* **Sat 30, Sun 31 Aug (12-4). Adm £4, chd free. Light refreshments. Delicious home-made cakes.**
A tropical style new build garden around 3 sides of the house. With lots of unusual lush exotic style plants, such as bananas, palm trees, cannas, gingers, tree ferns and a massive tetrapanax. New plants and beds added for 2025. Many of the unusual plants available for sale. The garden is located next to the Leeds Liverpool canal.

62 NEW ST WILFRID'S COMMUNITY GARDEN
Royce Road, Manchester, M15 5BJ. Jackie Garvey, www.firmstart.co.uk. *From Stretford Rd (A5067) turn R into Chorlton Rd then R into Royce Rd. From Princess Rd turn. L into Old Birley St, follow onto Royce Rd; from Mancunian Way take A506 at Cambridge St Junction, follow road round to R (as it becomes Cavendish St) then Stretford Rd. What3words app: brain.slip.models.* **Sun 15 June (10-3). Adm £5, chd free. Tea, coffee & cake. On-site vegan bakery will provide refreshments.**
The Community Garden is a hidden gem tucked away in the car park of St Wilfrid's Enterprise Centre, a vibrant and tranquil retreat. The garden's design is a beautiful mosaic of varied plantings, with a strong emphasis on colour. Winding pathways lead visitors through an array of flower beds towards the former Grade II listed St Wilfrid's Church, designed by renowned architect AW Pugin (1842). Many of the local community were married or christened in this Pugin-designed church which visitors can explore at the opening (many original features remain). Small on site car park and street parking nearby.

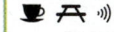

63 NEW SANDYWOOD COTTAGE
Andrews Lane, Formby, Liverpool, L37 2EP. Julie Turton. *9m S of Southport. Take A565 towards Liverpool on Formby bypass filling station 3rd exit to Ryeground Ln. At r'about take 1st exit to Church Rd. 1st exit at next r'about, 2nd exit at next on Raven Meols Ln. Signs here.* **Sun 13 July (11-4). Combined adm with 33 Brewery Lane £5, chd free. Home-made teas.**
A large garden with 2 lawned areas, for many years a children's playground. 30 years in the making and mainly planted by my late father. In his memory I am learning to look after it. We recently created a new patio area covered in roses and other climbers and over the winter there are plans to create raised beds.

64 14 SAXON ROAD
Birkdale, Southport, PR8 2AX. Margaret & Geoff Fletcher, 01704 567742, margaret.fletcher@ngs.org.uk. *1m S of Southport. Garden signed from A565 Southport to Liverpool Rd.* **Sun 20 July (11-5). Combined adm with 23 Ashton Road £5, chd free. Tea, coffee & cake. Opening with Ainsdale & Birkdale Gardens on Sun 8 June. Visits also by arrangement May to Aug for groups of 10 to 50.**
A mature walled garden surrounding a Victorian house with formal and informal planting mainly cottage garden style, accessed by bark and gravel paths. Bee friendly planting with constantly changing island beds and herbaceous borders. Newly planted echiums for 2025.

✻ 🚗 ☕

65 THE SHAKESPEAREAN GARDEN, PLATT FIELDS PARK
Manchester, M14 6LA. Manchester City Council, www.facebook.com/ShakespeareanGarden. *The garden is situated off Wilmslow Rd, down Mabfield Rd. There is a car park in the park nr the Mabfield Rd entrance; if that is full people can park on the streets near the park entrance.* **Sun 27 July (11.30-5.30). Adm £5, chd free. Tea, coffee & cake. WC at the Lakeside Centre nr the car park, approx 5-10 mins walk from the garden.**
The concept of a Shakespearean Garden was first developed in Victorian England with the idea of creating a garden with some, or all, of the trees and flowers mentioned in the Bard's works. With strong links to the suffrage movement and Edwardian society our garden opened in 1922 and was rescued from near obscurity by volunteers 4 yrs ago. There is an Elizabethan style parterre and a human sunclock. At our summer Open Day there will be information boards around the garden and a lovely nature trail inc various forms of hibernacula hidden amongst the banks. We list our annual Xmas event details on our FB page in Nov. There are 2 entrances into the garden; one down steps, but the entrance on the E side is sloped. There are wide paths inside the garden.

♿ ✻ ☕ 🔊

GROUP OPENING

66 NEW SHELLFIELD GARDENS
Shellfield Road, Southport, PR9 9UP. Mr Robert Jones. *3m N Southport Town Centre. What3words app: llur.rounds.fend. A565 to Preston. Cambridge Rd. At Junction with Marshside Rd T-lights L onto Marshside Rd, 3rd L Shellfield Rd. White Cottages opp Methodist Chapel on corner of Kirkham Rd.* **Sun 3 Aug (11-5). Combined adm £5, chd free. Tea, coffee & cake.**

NEW 72 SHELLFIELD ROAD
Mrs Anne Goatcher.

NEW 74 SHELLFIELD ROAD
Mr Robert Jones.

NEW 76 SHELLFIELD ROAD
Rick & Linda Thorne.

12 Willow Hey

Three adjacent C19 'Shrimpers' Cottages' which existed before the establishment of Shellfield Road, opposite what became the lifeboat station. The sea is now some distance away! 3 different front gardens for Bluebell, Rainbow and Anbil cottages provide no clue to the rear gardens, again all are very different; 2 are established over 20 yrs, one in the last 2 yrs, yet all provide interest and inspiration in showing how similar sized plots can be landscaped and utilised. One of the 3 rear gardens is accessible and has been designed to allow full access to all areas, there is access to the other 2 if accompanied.

67 SOUTHLANDS
12 Sandy Lane, Stretford, M32 9DA. Maureen Sawyer & Duncan Watmough, 0161 283 9425, moe@southlands12.com, www.southlands12.com. *3m S of Manchester. Sandy Lane (B5213) is situated off A5181 (A56) ¼ m from M60 J7.* **Sun 20 July (12-5.30). Adm £5, chd free. Tea, coffee & cake. Cake-away service (take a slice of your favourite cake home).** Visits also by arrangement 2 June to 31 Aug. Seating arrangements restricted to 25.
This beautiful and unique multi-award winning artist's garden inc a Mediterranean, ornamental and tranquil woodland garden. Stunning herbaceous borders and an organic kitchen potager with large greenhouse add to its continued appeal. Fabulous container plantings throughout. Described as 'Wonderful to walk through' 'Absolutely stunning' and 'an English garden at its very best'. Artist's work on display.

68 28 STAFFORD ROAD
Ellesmere Park, Monton, Manchester, M30 9HW. Tracey & Tony, 07834 452180, shepsurf@gmail.com, www.instagram.com/monton_garden/7tseNHyl. *M602 Eccles exit, take the 1st exit then at the lights, turn L. Follow the road for 1m heading towards Monton, go over small r'about, next R is Stafford Rd.* **Sat 16 Aug (10-4); Sat 6 Sept (12.30-4.30). Adm £5, chd free. Tea, coffee & cake.** Visits also by arrangement 1 May to 15 Oct for groups of up to 20.
A large garden in Manchester with borders full of woodland jungle plants. Mature bamboos, inc a magnificent *Borinda papyrifera*, large palm trees and a collection of rare, hardy plants from around the world inc a number of hardy Schefflera plants. Search for Tony's YouTube channel at "montongarden". There is a small gravel area over which a wheelchair will have to pass.

69 87 TODD LANE NORTH
Lostock Hall, Preston, PR5 5UP. Sue & Steve Green, 07948 710075, steveandsuegreen87@outlook.com. *3m S of Preston. From J29 off the M6, Preston, follow signs to Lostock Hall along London Way, at r'about 1st exit onto Brownedge Rd, L at T-lights, Todd Lane. Entrance is through the front gate. Street parking.* **Visits by arrangement 1 Apr to 7 Sept. Adm £5, chd free. Tea, coffee & cake.**
The front and side gardens have a number of raised beds, a large Buddha and relaxation pod. The main garden at the rear of the property takes you through a number of 'garden rooms' inc a cut flower section, an orchard, a large lawned garden with a number of stone features, summerhouse, greenhouse, a ying-yang woodland, and a child's play area. In 2025 we hope to have added a wildlife pond. Most parts of the garden are on level ground. The front garden has steps but this can also be accessed via an adjacent sloping drive.

70 NEW 3 TOWER END
Victoria Road, Formby, Liverpool, L37 1LP. Phil & Sue Allison. *6m S of Southport off A565 Formby by pass. At r'about 3rd exit to Ryeground Ln. Follow NGS signs to Victoria Rd cul-de-sac. Blue badge holders can park on yellow lines. Otherwise park on Harrington Rd Estate on L.* **Sat 10, Sun 11 May (11-5). Adm £6.50, chd free. Tea, coffee & cake.**
Created by former owners of Lady Green Garden Centre, nearly an acre of vistas and walkways in a pine woodland setting off the NT Nature Reserve. Different styles of garden incorporating many water and stone features, folly, topiary, fernery, rock and gravel garden. Japanese style area. Patios with seating. Large variety of trees, shrubs, rhododendrons, wisteria, acers and conifers, all linked by paths, steps and lawns.

71 ◆ TURTON TOWER KITCHEN GARDEN
Tower Drive, Turton, Bolton, BL7 0HG. Nancy Walsh, nancy.walsh@hotmail.co.uk, www.turtontower-kitchengarden.co.uk. *1½ m from Edgworth. Turton Tower is signed off the B6391 between Bolton & Edgworth.* **For NGS: Sat 21 June (10.30-4). Adm £4, chd free.**
The garden is set in the historic Turton Tower grounds and was originally the kitchen garden in Victorian times. A group of volunteers have restored and created the garden over the last 15 yrs. The garden today consists of raised vegetable beds and soft fruit areas but most of the garden is divided into smaller feature gardens. Turton Tower's history is reflected in its Tudor and Victorian beds. More contemporary gardens are The White Garden and Japanese Garden. There are also 2 long herbaceous borders with a large variety of perennials. We have an interesting variety of ferns and shade loving plants in our stumperies. Our new garden is a wildlife garden and pond surrounding the ruined Bothy funded by a grant from the NGS. Plants, cards and jam will be for sale. The paths are wheelchair friendly but in some places are moderately sloped.

72 280 WARRINGTON ROAD
The Land, Abram, Wigan, WN2 5RJ. Andy & Paula Prescott. *2m S of Wigan. Pls park at Uberrima Village Club, opp house. Look out for yellow signs.* **Sun 20 July (11-4). Adm £4, chd free. Tea, coffee & cake.**
The garden is about ¾ of an acre of back land behind our property. Our little haven has been transformed into a garden from overgrown land with brambles, nettles and self seeding trees. It now has colourful borders, both shade and full sun, trees, shrubs, a large pond with fish and visiting ducks. We are self taught gardeners and still learning, with a love for saving plants and being outdoors. Pond, summerhouse, potting shed, greenhouse.

LANCASHIRE

GROUP OPENING

73 WARTON GARDENS
Warton, LA5 9NT. www.facebook.com/6WartonGardensNGS. *3m J35 M6, 1m N of Carnforth. 4 gardens on Main St span approx ½ m, 1 garden is just off Main St in Church Hill Ave.* **Sat 21, Sun 22 June (11-5). Combined adm £6, chd free. Home-made teas at 9 Main Street & 111 Main Street.**

2 CHURCH HILL AVENUE
LA5 9NU. Mr & Mrs J Street.

9 MAIN STREET
LA5 9NR. Mrs Sarah Baldwin.

80 MAIN STREET
LA5 9PG. Mrs Yvonne Miller.

107 MAIN STREET
LA5 9PJ. Becky Hindley, www.erdabotanicals.co.uk.

111 MAIN STREET
LA5 9PJ. Mr & Mrs J Spendlove.

The 5 gardens are spread across the village and offer a wide variety of planting and design ideas. They comprise a flower picking garden, a plantsman's garden with unusual herbaceous planting, trees and productive vegetable/soft fruit section, a large garden with a series of rooms each with a different atmosphere, a garden with the epitome of country style and a recently created garden designed to encourage pollinators. Families are encouraged and we will be offering children's activities at some gardens. Warton is the birthplace of the medieval ancestors of George Washington. The ruins of the Old Rectory (English Heritage) is the oldest surviving building in the village. Ascent of Warton Crag (AONB) provides panoramic views across Morecambe Bay to the Lakeland hills beyond.

74 WEEPING ASH GARDEN
Bents Garden & Home, Warrington Road, Glazebury, WA3 5NS. John Bent, www.bents.co.uk. *15m W of Manchester. Next to Bents Garden & Home, just off the A580 East Lancs Rd at Greyhound r'about nr Leigh. Follow brown 'Garden Centre' signs.* **Sun 9, Sun 16 Feb, Sun 3, Sun 10 Aug (10-4). Adm by donation.**
Created by retired nurseryman and photographer John Bent, Weeping Ash is a garden of year-round interest with a beautiful display of early snowdrops. Broad sweeps of colour lend elegance to this stunning garden which is much larger than it initially seems with hidden paths and wooded areas creating a sense of natural growth. Bents Garden & Home offers a choice of dining destinations inc The Fresh Approach Restaurant, Caffe nel Verde and a number of al fresco dining options as well as an extensive homegrown plant collection.

GROUP OPENING

75 WHALLEY AND DISTRICT GARDENS
Whalley, Clitheroe, BB7 9TN. *4m S of Clitheroe. From M6 J31 take A59 to Clitheroe. Whalley signed from A59. What3words app: miles.scarecrow.photo.* **Sat 28, Sun 29 June (10.30-4). Combined adm £6, chd free. Light refreshments at Whalley Methodist Church, English Martyrs Church, St Mary & All Saints Church. Picnics permitted in the Abbey Grounds.**

NEW THE ALLOTMENTS
BB7 9SY. Miss Judith Davies.

ENGLISH MARTYRS' CHURCH
BB7 9TN. Alison Butler.

THE HOLLIES
BB7 9AA. Mrs Linzee Greenhalgh.

NEW 5 PAINTER CRESCENT
BB7 9XN. Laura Hodkinson.

ST MARY AND ALL SAINTS CHURCH
BB7 9SY. Miss Judith Davies, www.whalleypc.org.uk.

WHALLEY ABBEY
BB7 9SS. Reverend Anna Walker, 01254 828400, bookings@whalleyabbey.org, www.whalleyabbey.org.

Whalley and District Gardens inc 2 small private gardens, a few minutes' journey from the town centre, which also offers a peaceful community garden at its hub. The Hollies, has colourful borders framing a pond with interesting perennial planting and seating areas. The small, terraced garden at 5 Painter Crescent, sits at the top of a hill, with panoramic views across surrounding countryside. The garden of the English Martyrs' Church has magnificent mature trees, glorious, fragrance filled borders and sweeping lawns. St Mary & All Saints has C10 stone crosses, old stone paths and grassed areas. Whalley Abbey offers a tranquil garden on the banks of the River Calder and photographic opportunities amid historic surroundings. The 4 allotments feature planting with a nod to the history of their surroundings as well as food grown for use in community projects; they sit opposite the Primary School's Forest Garden area, where the young pupils learn about nature and the environment.

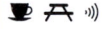

76 NEW 12 WILLOW HEY
Maghull, Liverpool, L31 3DL. Dr Mike & Mrs Di Pearson. *From A59, aim for Maghull Railway Stn & cross the level Xing. Willow Hey is 1st on R & our house is at the 1st corner with a bright yellow door. Limited parking on road.* **Sun 18 May (11-4). Adm £5, chd free. Light refreshments. Cafe at nearby Maghull station.**
Developed over 40 yrs the garden is ⅔ of an acre with many interesting features and a wide range of plants shrubs and over 60 different trees, inc many unusual and rare specimens. Features inc a beautiful limestone water feature, alpine beds, an orchard and canal bank. Designed for year-round colour, in May expect wisteria, *Buddleia alternifolia*, cornus, azaleas, rhododendrons and more. Most areas can be accessed with care and a sturdy 'pusher'.

77 32 WOOD HEY GROVE
Syke, Rochdale, OL12 9UA. Mr Graham & Mrs Janine Bullas. *Around 2m N of Rochdale town centre. Follow the A671 (Whitworth Rd) out of Rochdale towards Burnley & turn R at the 2nd r'about (Fieldhouse Ln) At the next junction turn L & Wood Hey Grove will be 1m on L.* **Sun 27 July (11-4). Adm £4, chd free. Tea, coffee & cake.**
The garden was Graham's retirement landscape project and continues to evolve 13 yrs on. The planting only really started when Janine also retired 5 yrs ago and the garden is now taking shape. The hard landscaping is a mix of complex curves over 4 levels with paved patios, hardwood decking, lawns, trees and herbaceous borders complementing the overall scheme. We plan to offer home-made bread and craft items for sale. The

LANCASHIRE

Monastery of Our Lady of Hyning

steps within the garden would prevent access to the whole plot but most of the garden is visible due to the slope of the garden.

78 NEW 101 WOODPLUMPTON ROAD
Fulwood, Preston, PR2 3LF. Mr Andy Gaskill, 07708 111245, Andygas101@gmail.com, Fulwoodbonsai.co.uk. *Situated on Woodplumpton Rd approx ½ m N from the Lane Ends junction on Blackpool Rd, 200yds S from junction with Cadley Causeway.* **Sat 7 June (11-4). Adm £5, chd free. Tea, coffee & cake. Visits also by arrangement May to Sept for groups of up to 20.**
A west facing garden that is mainly used to house numerous bonsai trees, hydrangeas and hostas. The garden is viewed from the raised patio area, then accessed via stone steps, over a bridge spanning a 4 metre Koi carp pond. Other features inc a lawn, seating area and, at the rear of the garden, a secret garden with a bar. Home-made ceramics are dotted around the garden, many housing bonsai trees.

GROUP OPENING

79 WOOLTON VILLAGE GARDENS
Hillside Drive, Woolton, Liverpool, L25 5NR. *6m SE of Liverpool city centre. Gardens are best accessed by car or bus (75, 78, 81, 89). Nearest train: Hunts Cross (1.7m) Parking is easiest on Hillside Drive.* **Sun 18 May (12-5). Combined adm £5, chd free. Tea, coffee & cake.**

GREEN RIDGES, RUNNYMEDE CLOSE
L25 5JU. Sarah & Michael Beresford.

23 HILLSIDE DRIVE
L25 5NR. Bruce & Fiona Pennie.

15 LYNTON GREEN
L25 6JB. Gill & Danny O'Donoghue, www.instagram.com/thegardeninbloomuk.

MERRICK, 4 HILLSIDE DRIVE
L25 5NS. Kerry & Tony Marson.

Four suburban gardens located in the beautiful historic village of Woolton featuring C17 buildings that act as a backdrop to the public space plant displays maintained by Woolton in Bloom, for whom the gardens also open. The gardens feature herbaceous borders, water features, tropical plants, greenhouses, kitchen garden, and garden sculptures.

80 NEW 55 YEALAND ROAD
Yealand Conyers, Carnforth, LA5 9SJ. Mrs Christine Morgan. *10m N of Lancaster. J35 M6. Take A6070 Carnforth. 2nd exit at r'about A6 N signed Milnthorpe. 1st exit next r'about, under railway bridge. Rose Acre Lane is 3rd road on L. Garden signed from end of road.* **Sun 3 Aug (11-5). Combined adm with Holmere Lodge £5, chd free. Refreshments available at Holmere Lodge.**
On an East/West slope, surrounded by limestone walls and native hedging. A ½ acre plot with productive fruit and vegetable area, gravel paths with steps take you through large herbaceous borders planted to attract butterflies and bees, wildlife pond and meadow with wonderful views. Parking has kindly been agreed in the New Inn car park which is directly across the road from the garden.

LEICESTERSHIRE & RUTLAND

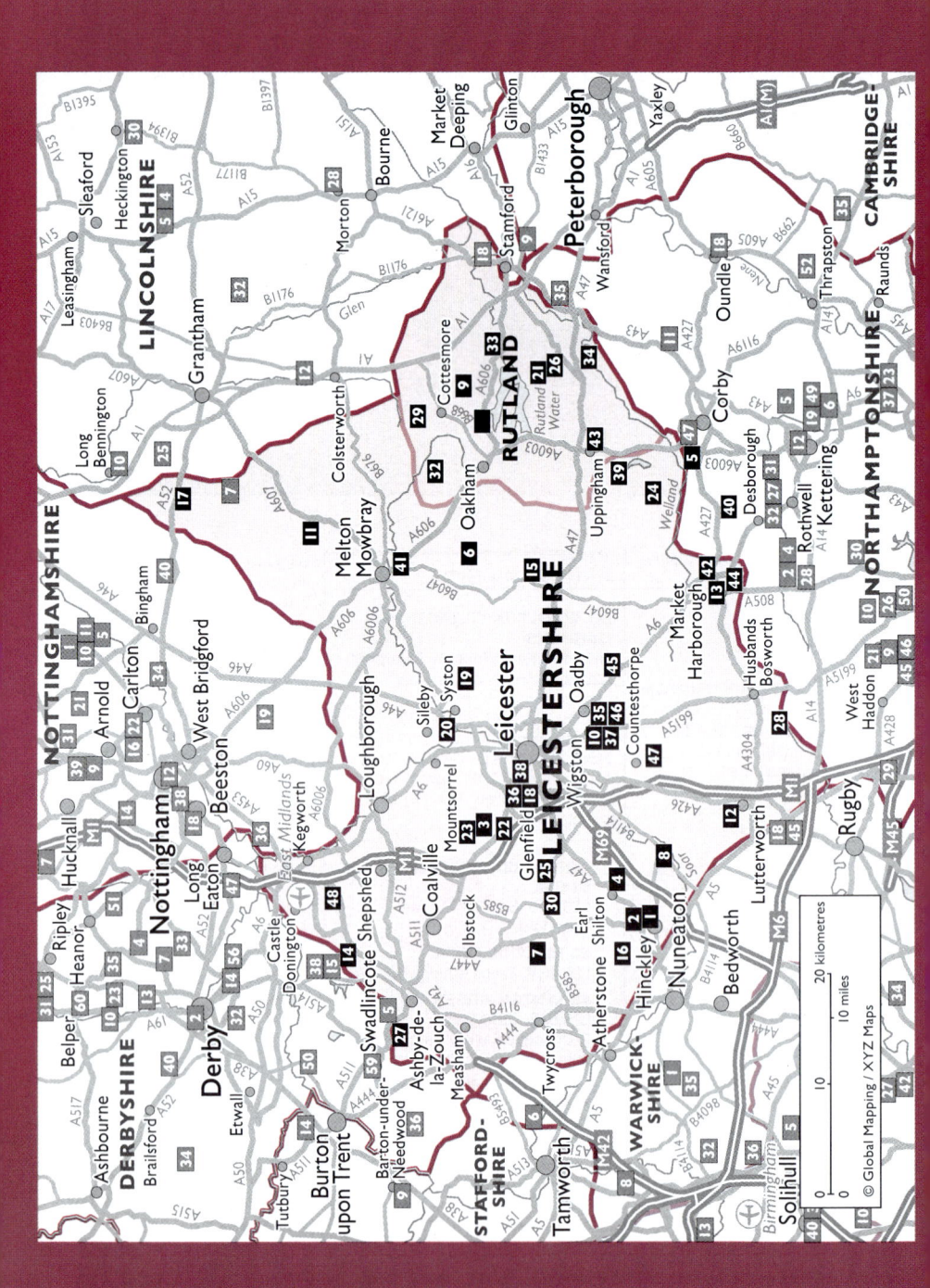

LEICESTERSHIRE & RUTLAND

VOLUNTEERS

Leicestershire
County Organiser
Pamela Shave 01858 575481
pamela.shave@ngs.org.uk

County Treasurer
Martin Shave 01455 556633
martin.shave@ngs.org.uk

Publicity
Carol Bartlett 01616 261053
carol@dekbe.plus.com

Booklet Co-ordinator (Leicestershire & Rutland)
Carole Troake 07580 500261
carole.troake@ngs.org.uk

Social Media
Zoe Lewin 07810 800 007
zoe.lewin@ngs.org.uk

Photographer
Rosie Furniss 07837 793321
rosie.furniss@ngs.org.uk

Talks
Karen Gimson 07930 246974
k.gimson@btinternet.com

John Fraser 07502 015663
jmf9216@gmail.com

Group Visit Co-ordinator
Judith Boston 07740 945332
judith.boston@ngs.org.uk

Assistant County Organisers
Emma Clanfield 01162 478819
emma.clanfield@ngs.org.uk

Gill Hadland 01162 592170
gillhadland1@gmail.com

Janet Rowe 01162 597339
janetnandrew@btinternet.com

Rutland
County Organisers
Sally Killick 07799 064565
sally.killick@ngs.org.uk

Lucy Hurst 07958 534778
lucy.hurst@ngs.org.uk

County Treasurer
Sandra Blaza 01572 770588
sandra.blaza@ngs.org.uk

Publicity
Lucy Hurst (see above)

Social Media
Sally Killick (see above)

Assistant County Organiser
Nicola Oakey 07516 663358
nicola.oakey@ngs.org.uk

OPENING DATES

All entries subject to change.
For latest information check
www.ngs.org.uk

Extended openings are shown at the beginning of the month.

Map locator numbers are shown to the right of each garden name.

February
Snowdrop Openings
Sunday 9th
The Acers 1

Sunday 16th
Oak Cottage 27

Saturday 22nd
Hedgehog Hall 15
Westview 45

Sunday 23rd
Hedgehog Hall 15
Tresillian House 41
Westview 45

April
Sunday 6th
Oak Cottage 27

Sunday 13th
Tresillian House 41

Sunday 27th
Westbrooke House 44

May
Sunday 4th
NEW Tudor House 42

Saturday 10th
NEW Manor House 20

Sunday 11th
Burrough Hall 6
NEW Manor House 20

Saturday 17th
Goadby Marwood Hall 11
8 Hinckley Road 16

Sunday 18th
8 Hinckley Road 16
The Old Vicarage, Whissendine 32

Saturday 24th
Westview 45

Sunday 25th
Westbrooke House 44

Monday 26th
2 Manor Farm Mews 19
Westview 45

June
Every Wednesday
Stoke Albany House 40

Sunday 1st
Carlton Gardens 7
Redhill Lodge 34
St Wolstan's House 35

Saturday 7th
28 Gladstone Street 10

Sunday 8th
28 Gladstone Street 10
Manton Gardens 21

Thursday 12th
Nevill Holt Hall 24

Friday 13th
Nevill Holt Hall 24

Saturday 14th
Nevill Holt Hall 24
The Old Rectory 30

Sunday 15th
Dairy Cottage 8
Nevill Holt Hall 24
The Old Rectory 30
Uppingham Gardens 43

Friday 20th
Brickfield House 5

Saturday 21st
The Secret Garden at Wigston Framework Knitters Museum 37
The Secret Garden, Glenfield Hospital 38

 @NGSLeicestershire   @rutlandngs
 @LeicsNGS   @RutlandNGS
 @leicestershire_ngs   @rutlandngs

LEICESTERSHIRE & RUTLAND

Sunday 22nd
Exton Hall 9
The Secret Garden at Wigston
 Framework Knitters Museum 37

Saturday 28th
Oak Tree House 28

Sunday 29th
Oak Tree House 28
Tresillian House 41

July

Every Wednesday
Stoke Albany House 40

Saturday 5th
Wigston Gardens 46

Sunday 6th
NEW Stockerston Hall 39
Wigston Gardens 46
Willoughby Gardens 47

Friday 11th
The Old Hall 29

Sunday 13th
Green Wicket Farm 12
NEW North Luffenham Hall 26

Wednesday 16th
Green Wicket Farm 12

Saturday 19th
8 Hinckley Road 16
The Secret Garden, Glenfield
 Hospital 38

Sunday 20th
12 Hastings Close 14
8 Hinckley Road 16

Sunday 27th
Prebendal House 33

August

Every Sunday
Honeytrees Tropical Garden 17

**Every day from Saturday
2nd to Sunday 10th**
221 Markfield Road 22

Saturday 2nd
182 Ashby Road 2

Sunday 3rd
182 Ashby Road 2

Saturday 9th
NEW 2 Ilmington Close 18
NEW 8 Saintbury Road 36

Sunday 10th
NEW 2 Ilmington Close 18
NEW 8 Saintbury Road 36
15 The Woodcroft 48

Sunday 31st
Tresillian House 41

September

Saturday 20th
St Wolstan's House 35

Saturday 27th
The New Barn 25

Sunday 28th
The New Barn 25

October

Sunday 5th
Hammond Arboretum 13

Sunday 26th
Tresillian House 41

February 2026

Sunday 22nd
Tresillian House 41

By Arrangement

Arrange a personalised garden visit with your club, or group of friends, on a date to suit you. See individual garden entries for full details.

The Acers 1
Bank Cottage 3
Barracca 4
Brickfield House 5
Farmway, Willoughby Gardens 47
Goadby Marwood Hall 11
Green Wicket Farm 12
Honeytrees Tropical Garden 17
221 Markfield Road 22
Mountain Ash 23
The New Barn 25
Stoke Albany House 40
Tresillian House 41
Westview 45
15 The Woodcroft 48

2 Ilmington Close

… LEICESTERSHIRE & RUTLAND

THE GARDENS

1 THE ACERS
10 The Rills, Hinckley, LE10 1NA. Mr Dave Baggott, 01455 617237, davebaggott18@hotmail.com. *10 mins from J1 of M69. Off B4668 out of Hinckley. Turn into Dean Rd then 1st R into The Rills. Last house on the R.* **Sun 9 Feb (10-4). Adm £5, chd free. Tea, coffee & cake.** Visits also by arrangement.
Medium sized garden, with a Japanese theme inc a zen garden, Japanese tea house, koi pond, more than 20 different varieties of acers, many choice alpines, trilliums, cyclamen, erythroniums, cornus, hamamelis and dwarf conifers. Approximately 200 different varieties of snowdrops in spring. Large greenhouse.

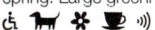

2 182 ASHBY ROAD
Hinckley, LE10 1SW. Ms Lynda Blower. *Hinckley is SW Leics nr to the border with Warks, with access off the M69 or A5. From Hinckley town centre on the B4667 on R 400yds before the A47/A447 jnc. Parking on road nearby.* **Sat 2, Sun 3 Aug (11-4). Adm £3.50, chd free. Tea, coffee & cake.**
120ft cottage style garden packed with lots of colourful perennials and annuals. Many pots and containers full of cannas, agapanthus, banana plants and dahlias. A small pond and bog garden planting. A garden room and plenty of comfortable seating to sit and view different aspects of the garden. Many salvage collectables cited around the garden which provide further interest.

3 BANK COTTAGE
90 Main Street, Newtown Linford, Leicester, LE6 0AF. Jan Croft, 07429 159910/01530 244865, gardening91@icloud.com. *6m NW Leicester. 2½m from M1 J22. From Leicester via Anstey, Bank cottage is on the L after Markfield Ln, just before a public footpath sign. If coming via Warren Hill Bank Cottage is on the R just after public footpath sign.* **Visits by arrangement in Apr for groups of up to 23. Adm £3, chd free. Home-made teas or bring your own picnic to eat by the river. Celebration parties can be accommodated.**
Traditional cottage garden set on different levels leading down to the River Lin. Providing colour all year-round but at its prettiest in spring. Aconites, snowdrops, blue and white bells, primroses, alliums, aquilegia, poppies, geraniums, roses, honeysuckle, philadelphus, acers, wisteria, perennial sweet pea, perennial sunflowers and some fruit trees. A small pond full of wildlife.

4 BARRACCA
Ivydene Close, Earl Shilton, LE9 7NR. Mr John & Mrs Sue Osborn, 01455 842609, susan.osborn1@btinternet.com. *10m W of Leicester. From A47 after entering Earl Shilton, Ivydene Cl is 4th on L from Leicester side of A47.* **Visits by arrangement 15 Feb to 19 July for groups of up to 45. Adm £10, chd free. Tea, coffee & cake inc in adm price.**
1 acre garden with lots of different areas, silver birch walk, wildlife pond with seating, apple tree garden, Mediterranean planted area and lawns surrounded with herbaceous plants and shrubs. Patio area with climbing roses and wisteria. There is also a utility garden with greenhouses, vegetables in beds, herbs and perennial flower beds, lawn and fruit cage. Part of the old gardens owned by the Cotton family who used to open approx 9 acres to the public in the 1920's. Partial wheelchair access.

5 BRICKFIELD HOUSE
Rockingham Road, Cottingham, Market Harborough, LE16 8XS. Simon & Nicki Harker, 07775 672403, nickiharker@gmail.com. *SatNav will take you into Cottingham Village but garden is ½m from Cottingham on Rockingham Rd/B670 towards Rockingham.* **Fri 20 June (12-4). Adm £5, chd free. Tea, coffee & cake.** Visits also by arrangement 9 June to 27 June.
Lovely views overlooking the Welland Valley, this 2 acre garden has been developed from a sloping brickyard rubbish plot over 37 yrs. There is a kitchen garden, orchard, herbaceous borders filled with roses, perennials and shrubs, paths and many pots, filled with succulents, herbs and colourful annuals.

6 BURROUGH HALL
Somerby Road, Burrough on the Hill, Melton Mowbray, LE14 2QZ. Richard & Alice Cunningham. *Close to B6047. 10 mins from A606. 20 mins from Melton Mowbray.* **Sun 11 May (2-5). Adm £5, chd free. Tea, coffee & cake.**
Burrough Hall was built in 1867 as a classic Leicestershire hunting lodge. The garden, framed by mature trees and shrubs, was extensively redesigned by garden designer George Carter in 2007. The garden continues to develop. This family garden designed for all generations to enjoy is surrounded by magnificent views across High Leicestershire. In addition to the garden there will be a small collection of vintage and classic cars on display. Gravel paths and lawn.

GROUP OPENING

7 CARLTON GARDENS
64, Main Street, Carlton, Nuneaton, CV13 0EZ. Mr and Mrs Boston. *2m N of Market Bosworth & 5m S of Ibstock. All the gardens are on or close to Main St. There is plenty of on-street parking.* **Sun 1 June (10.30-4.30). Combined adm £6, chd free. Tea, coffee & cake in St Andrew's Parish Church, Main Street, Carlton.**

BUMBLE COT
Murray & Pat Lockwood.

DROVERS BARN NEW
Mr Steve & Mrs Julia Martin.

HILLSDON
Veronica & John Storer.

HOME FARM HOUSE
Mr & Mrs C J Peat.

64 MAIN STREET
Paul & Judith Boston.

WOODMILL
Tom & Liz Alun-Jones.

Six very different and interesting gardens displaying a variety of styles and a range of early summer flowers. Bumble Cot is a small courtyard style garden, 64, Main Street is planted to encourage wildlife with views to open countryside with a variety of trees. Woodmill is a recently redeveloped garden with areas planted in both traditional and modern styles. Drovers Barn is a large country garden with beautiful views of the surrounding landscape and Home Farm is an informal, family garden with a beautiful spring woodland of 1½ acres, planted in 2000. All of the gardens are partially wheelchair accessible, although some have gravel paths. Inaccessible areas will be clearly labelled.

8 DAIRY COTTAGE
15 Sharnford Road, Sapcote, LE9 4JN. Mrs Norah Robinson-Smith. *9m SW of Leicester. Sharnford Rd joins Leicester Rd in Sapcote to B4114 Coventry Rd. Follow NGS signs.* **Sun 15 June (11-4). Adm £5, chd free. Home-made teas.**
Peaceful garden with places to sit and enjoy the old cottage setting. The garden is over ½ an acre which inc a walled cottage garden, stumpery, potager, fernery and woodland walk. The planting consists of many unusual shrubs and trees and over 90 clematis, climbing roses and colourful herbaceous borders. An ideal garden for plant collectors. Featured in Garden News and Garden Answers. May need to access over a gravel drive.

9 EXTON HALL
Cottesmore Road, Exton, LE15 8AN. Viscount & Viscountess Campden, www.extonpark.co.uk. *Exton. 5m E of Oakham. 8m from Stamford off A1 (A606 turning).* **Sun 22 June (2-5). Adm £5, chd free. Home-made teas.**
Extensive park, lawns, specimen trees and shrubs, lake, private chapel and C19 house (not open). Pinetum, woodland walks, lakes, ruins, dovecote and formal herbaceous garden. Whilst there is wheelchair access, areas of the garden are accessible along grass or gravel paths which, weather dependent, may make access difficult.

10 28 GLADSTONE STREET
Wigston Magna, LE18 1AE. Chris & Janet Huscroft. *4m S of Leicester. Off Wigston by-pass (A5199) follow signs off McDonalds r'about.* **Sat 7, Sun 8 June (11-5). Adm £3.50, chd free. Home-made teas. Opening with Wigston Gardens on Sat 5, Sun 6 July.**
The mature 70'x15' town garden is divided into rooms and bisected by a pond with a bridge. It is brimming with unusual hardy perennials, inc collections of ferns and hostas. David Austin roses chosen for their scent feature throughout, inc a 30' rose arch. A shade house with unusual hardy plants and a Hosta Theatre. Regular changes to planting. Wigston Framework Knitters Museum and Secret garden nearby - open Sunday afternoons. Parts of the garden can be viewed, narrow paths and step limit full access.

11 GOADBY MARWOOD HALL
Goadby Marwood, Melton Mowbray, LE14 4LN. Mr & Mrs Westropp, 01664 464202, vwestropp@gmail.com. *6m NE of Melton Mowbray. Adjacent to the church. Plenty of parking.* **Sat 17 May (10.30-5). Adm £6, chd free. Light refreshments in village hall. Visits also by arrangement Apr to Oct.**
Redesigned in 2000 by the owner based on C18 plans. A chain of five lakes (covering 10 acres) and several ironstone walled gardens all interconnected. Lakeside woodland walk. Planting for year-round interest. Landscaper trained under plantswoman Rosemary Verey at Barnsley House. Beautiful C13 church open. Gravel paths and lawns.

12 GREEN WICKET FARM
Ullesthorpe Road, Bitteswell, Lutterworth, LE17 4LR. Mrs Anna Smith, 01455 552646, greenfarmbitt@hotmail.com. *2m NW of Lutterworth J20 M1. From Lutterworth follow signs through Bitteswell towards Ullesthorpe. Garden situated behind Bitteswell Cricket Club. Use this as a landmark rather than relying on SatNav.* **Sun 13, Wed 16 July (2-5). Adm £5, chd free. Light refreshments. Visits also by arrangement in July for groups of up to 25.**
A fairly formal garden on an exposed site surrounded by open fields. Mature trees enclosing the many varied plants chosen to give all round year interest. Many unusual hardy plants grown along side good reliable old favourites present a range of colour themed borders. Grass and gravel paths allow access to the whole garden. Disabled parking areas.

13 HAMMOND ARBORETUM
Burnmill Road, Market Harborough, LE16 7JG. The Robert Smyth Academy, www.hammondarboretum.org.uk. *15m S of Leicester on A6. From High St, follow signs to The Robert Smyth Academy via Bowden Ln to Burnmill Rd. Park in 1st entrance on L.* **Sun 5 Oct (2-4.30). Adm £7, chd free. Home-made teas.**
A site of just under 2½ acres containing an unusual collection of trees and shrubs, many from Francis Hammond's original planting dating from 1913 to 1936 whilst headmaster of the school. Species from America, China and Japan with malus and philadelphus walks and a moat. Proud owners of three champion trees identified by national specialist and 37 which are the best in Leicestershire. Walk plans available.

14 12 HASTINGS CLOSE
Breedon-on-the-Hill, Derby, DE73 8BN. Mr & Mrs P Winship. *5m N from Ashby de la Zouch. Follow NGS signs in the Village. Parking around the Village Green. Please do not park in the close due to limited parking.* **Sun 20 July (1-4.30). Adm £3.50, chd free. Tea, coffee & cake.**
A medium sized prairie garden, organically managed and planted in the Piet Oudolf style. Also many roses and a wide range of perennials. A small 'white' back garden with box hedging and more colourful style perennial borders.

15 HEDGEHOG HALL
3 Loddington Road, Tilton on the Hill, LE7 9DE. Janet & Andrew Rowe. *8m W of Oakham. 2m N of A47 on B6047 between Melton & Market Harborough. Follow yellow NGS signs in Tilton towards Loddington. Disabled parking on road outside the White House 20 yds past our entrance.* **Sat 22, Sun 23 Feb (11-4). Adm £5, chd free. Light refreshments in St Peters Church, Tilton. Open nearby Westview.**
½ acre organically managed plant lover's garden. Beautiful shade and woodland areas, with a large collection of approximately 350 different snowdrops. All set on our north facing terraces along with many unusual hellebores, trilliums, euphorbias, ferns, cyclamen, pulmonaria and many rare bulbs.

Many highly perfumed winter flowering shrubs inc daphne, viburnum, sarcococca and hamamelis. Regret, no wheelchair access to terraced borders.

16 8 HINCKLEY ROAD
Stoke Golding, Nuneaton, CV13 6DU. **John & Stephanie Fraser.** *3m NW of Hinckley. Approach from any direction into village then follow NGS signs. Please park roadside with due consideration to other residents properties.* **Sat 17, Sun 18 May, Sat 19, Sun 20 July (12-4). Adm £4, chd free. Tea, coffee & cake.**
A small SSW garden with water features to add interest to the colourful and some unusual perennials inc climbers to supplement the trees and shrubs in May and July.

Garden established and recently re-established by current owner to provide seating for a variety of views of the garden. Many perennials in the garden are represented in the plants for sale. Wheelchair access to garden room patio which provides a view of the lower part of the garden.

17 HONEYTREES TROPICAL GARDEN
85 Grantham Road, Bottesford, NG13 0EG. **Julia Madgwick & Mike Ford,** 01949 842120, Julia_madgwick@hotmail.com, www.facebook.com/HoneytreesTropicalGarden. *6 m NW of Grantham. 7m E of Bingham on A52. Turn into village. Garden is on L on slip road behind hedge going out of village towards Grantham. Parking on grass opposite property.* **Every Sun 3 Aug to 31 Aug (11-4). Adm £5, chd free. Tea, coffee & cake.** Visits also by arrangement July & Aug for groups of 10+.
Tropical and exotic with a hint of jungle! Raised borders with different themes from lush foliage to arid cacti. Exotic planting as you enter the garden gives way on a gentle incline to surprises, inc glasshouses dedicated to various climatic zones interspersed with more exotic planting, ponds and a stream. Representation of over 20 yrs plant hunting. Treehouse and viewing platform to view tree ferns from above whilst being among the canopy of the trees. Fernery new for 2025. There are some steps and ramps. Gravel and bark in certain areas but wheelchair access to most parts of the garden.

Tudor House

18 NEW **2 ILMINGTON CLOSE**
Glenfield, Leicester, LE3 8BF. Mr
Chris Ensell, www.instagram.
com/thejunglelookuk. *Glenfield,
Leicester. Please do not use on
street parking. Arrangements have
been made for visitors to use the
rear car park at Morrisons (0.3m
away / 7min walk). What3words app:
voices.marker.view.* **Sat 9, Sun 10
Aug (11-4). Combined adm with 8
Saintbury Road £6, chd free.**
Tropical style garden featuring various
exotic planting with pops of floral
colour. Various rare and unusual
plants set within a 35m x 10m family
garden. Featuring bananas, gingers,
palms and other exotic oddities.
❀

19 2 MANOR FARM MEWS
Main Street, Queniborough,
Leicester, LE7 3EA. Mrs Jo Dolan.
*7½m NE of Leicester. Off A46 follow
signs for Queniborough. Entrance
opp St Mary's Church on Main St.*
No parking in Manor Farm Mews.
**Mon 26 May (11-4). Adm £5, chd
free. Light refreshments.**
A modern, contemporary formal
garden of approx ¼ acre that rises
gently up a shallow slope. Large
overflowing borders filled with a
variety of bird, bee and butterfly
friendly planting, surround formal
lawns, topiary, hedging and shady
retreats inc a small woodland and a
summerhouse. There are collections
of roses, salvias, agapanthus and a
wide variety of year-round bulbs.
♿ ☕ 🔊

20 NEW **MANOR HOUSE**
70 Main Street, Cossington,
Leicester, LE7 4UW. Harry
Longman & Alison Armstrong.
*Soar Valley, between Leicester and
Loughborough. Take Platts Ln on
S approach to Cossington (NOT
from house on Main St). Gateway
on N side of lane 400m from Syston
Rd. Turn at: What3words app:
pampering.progress.challenge.* **Sat
10, Sun 11 May (11-5). Adm £6,
chd free. Home-made teas.**
Entering from the field,
rhododendrons under a great oak
welcome you to Lovers' Walk,
drawing you past feathery acers to
the main lawn, where to the scent
of azalea you take in a treescape of
scale. Pendent limes, pines, birches
and cedars feature, above them all a
great copper beech. Move on to the
mixed borders where roses, cistus
and iris will delight you among the
dozens of species planted. Space to
walk and take in huge trees. Mixed
borders for the plant enthusiast,
encouraging wildlife of all sizes. Huge
swings for kids of all ages. Easily
accessible by cycle route 6 and
Leicestershire Round footpath. The
ground from the car park and around
the garden is flat, but mainly grass, so
is fine for wheelchairs in dry weather
but may be soft if wet.
♿ ❀ ☕ 🔊

Stockerston Hall

GROUP OPENING

21 MANTON GARDENS
Oakham, LE15 8SR. *3m N of Uppingham & 3m S of Oakham. Manton is on S shore of Rutland Water ¼m off A6003. Please park carefully in village.* **Sun 8 June (1-5). Combined adm £7, chd free. Home-made teas in Village Hall.**

22 LYNDON ROAD
Chris & Val Carroll.

NEW MANOR BARN
Mrs Jenny Jones.

MANTON LODGE
Emma Burnaby-Atkins, 01572 737258, info@mantonlodge.co.uk, www.mantonlodge.co.uk.

3 ST MARY'S ROAD
Ruth Blinch.

SHAPINSAY
Tony & Jane Bews.

5 gardens in small village on south shore of Rutland Water. 22 Lyndon Road: A beautiful combination of cottage garden and unusual plants in overflowing borders, hanging baskets and decorative pots. Manton Lodge: Steeply sloping garden with wonderful views and colourful beds of shrubs, roses and perennials, with ornamental pond and terrace. Shapinsay: ⅔ acre garden with mature trees and framed views, perennial borders, island shrub borders and stream linking numerous ponds. Manor Barn: Converted barn with distinct areas, abundantly planted sunken courtyard with well. 3 St. Mary's Road: Tiny cottage garden wrapped around pretty brick cottage.

22 221 MARKFIELD ROAD
Groby, Leicester, LE6 0FT. Jackie Manship, 01530 249363, jackiemanship@btinternet.com. *From M1 J22 take A50 towards Leicester. In approx 3m at the T-lights junc with Lena Dr turn L. Parking available along this road, no parking on A50.* **Daily Sat 2 Aug to Sun 10 Aug (10-4). Adm £5, chd free. Light refreshments. Visits also by arrangement 21 July to 31 July for groups of 20+.**
A south facing plot of land nestled between the village of Groby and Markfield approx 1 acre in size. The hidden treasures are deceptive from the front of the property which sits on one of the main trunk roads out of Leicester. Packed with interest and created over the last 20 yrs from a dishevelled overgrown plot you will be presented with a garden full of delight.

23 MOUNTAIN ASH
140 Ulverscroft Lane, Newtown Linford, LE6 0AJ. Mike & Liz Newcombe, 01530 242178, mjnew12@gmail.com. *7m SW of Loughborough, 7m NW of Leicester, 1m NW of Newtown Linford. Head ½m N along Main St towards Sharpley Hill, fork L into Ulverscroft Ln & Mountain Ash, is about ½m along on the L. Parking is along the opp verge.* **Visits by arrangement 15 Apr to 31 July for groups of 15 to 50. Adm £10, chd free. Tea, coffee & cake inc in adm price.**
2 acre garden with stunning views across Charnwood countryside. Near the house are patios, lawns, water feature, flower and shrub beds, fruit trees, soft fruit cage, greenhouses and vegetable plots. Lawns slope down to gravel garden, large wildlife pond and small areas of woodland with walks through many species of trees. Over 50 garden statues and ornaments. Many places to sit and relax. Dogs on leads welcome.

24 NEVILL HOLT HALL
Drayton Road, Nevill Holt, Market Harborough, LE16 8EG. Mr David Ross, nevillholtfestival.com. *5m NE of Market Haborough. Signed off B664 at Medbourne.* **Thur 12, Fri 13, Sat 14, Sun 15 June (12-9). Adm £10, chd free. Tea, coffee & cake in restaurant marquee. BBQ during festival performances. Adm £6 after 6pm. Donation to another charity.**
Nevill Holt Hall dates from the C13. Spacious and well proportioned, 10 acres of gardens are designed by Chelsea gold medal winner Rupert Golby. Highlights inc 3 distinctive walled gardens and generous herbaceous borders showing off an ancient Cedar of Lebanon. Nevill Holt Festival is a month long programme of exceptional events featuring world class musicians, performers, and speakers. Full details of the festival programme will be announced in January on www.nevillholtopera.co.uk - where tickets will be available for purchase. Walk-up tickets will also be available for purchase on the day of your visit subject to availability.

25 THE NEW BARN
Newbold Road, Desford, Leicester, LE9 9GS. A Nichols & R Pullin, 07949 082501, anthonyrnichols@rocketmail.com. *8m from J21 M1 & 12m from J22 M1.* **Sat 27, Sun 28 Sept (11-4). Adm £5, chd free. Tea, coffee & cake. Visits also by arrangement. Donation to Plant Heritage.**
A large, sloping ¾ acre garden with wonderful views. Enter via a side gate and follow a narrow path opening up into what feels like a secret garden, different levels and spaces add to this illusion enabling you to admire the planting and views. This is a well established plantsman's garden with many unusual plants, inc a collection of asters and Benton irises. National Collection of Geranium Phaeum cultivars.

26 NEW NORTH LUFFENHAM HALL
Church Street, North Luffenham, Oakham, LE15 8JR. Roger & Mary Canham. *5m from Stamford A1, 2m from A47 Morcott. In the heart of the village next to the church.* **Sun 13 July (1-5). Adm £6, chd free. Home-made teas.**
6 acres inc topiary formal gardens around a C16 hall, a sunken pond, an octagonal pond under a beech tree, and nature pond flow from one to the next. North of the house are 3 glasshouses, fruit trees, and a vegetable patch. A pergola with 5 beehives is nearby. 40 acre rewilding area created in 2022 is rich in native flora and fauna. The water garden, designed by Russel Paige in 1928, has been restored, revealing stone walls, pathways, and a spring-fed stream. Gillian Durno's studio situated in The Hall grounds will be open, selling cards, prints, and paintings. 20% of sales on the day will be donated to the NGS.

Our donation in 2024 has enabled Parkinson's UK to fund 3 new nursing posts this year directly supporting people with Parkinson's.

27 OAK COTTAGE
Well Lane, Blackfordby, Swadlincote, DE11 8AG. Colin & Jenny Carr. *Blackfordby, just over 1m from (& between) Ashby-de-la-Zouch or Swadlincote. From Ashby-de-la-Zouch take Moira Rd, turn R on Blackfordby Ln. As you enter Blackfordby, turn L to Butt Ln & quickly R to Strawberry Ln. Park then it is a 2 min walk to Well Ln entrance.* **Sun 16 Feb, Sun 6 Apr (10-4). Adm £5, chd free. Tea, coffee & cake.**
½ acre garden set around Blackfordby's 'hidden' listed thatched cottage, which itself is more than 300 years old. 3.4 acres of paddocks, front and rear gardens to explore with extensive displays of snowdrops (inc a named collection) as well as hellebores throughout. Later in spring the display changes to Snakes Heads and mature magnolias. The lower paddock has been planted with 450 native trees as part of the National Forest Freewoods scheme, with a drainage pond created at its base. The central swathe is being developed with wildflowers. At the top of the rear garden there is a chicken run, old and new orchards and a peach house.

28 OAK TREE HOUSE
North Road, South Kilworth, LE17 6DU. Pam & Martin Shave. *15m S of Leicester. From M1 J20, take A4304 towards Market Harborough. At North Kilworth turn R, signed South Kilworth. Garden on L after approx 1m.* **Sat 28 June (11-5); Sun 29 June (11-2). Adm £5, chd free. Tea, coffee & cake.**
⅔ acre beautiful country garden full of colour, formal design, softened by cottage style planting. Modern sculptures. Large herbaceous borders, vegetable plots, pond, greenhouse, shady area, colour-themed borders. Extensive collections in over 300 pots, home to everything from alpines to trees. Trees with attractive bark. Many clematis and roses. Dramatic arched pergola. Constantly changing garden. Access to patio and greenhouse via steps.

29 THE OLD HALL
Main Street, Market Overton, LE15 7PL. Mr & Mrs Timothy Hart. *6m N of Oakham; 5m from A1 via Thistleton. 10m E from Melton Mowbray.* **Evening opening Fri 11 July (5.30-8.30). Adm £10, chd free. Pre-booking essential, please visit www.ngs.org.uk for information & booking. Hambleton Bakery savouries inc; wine and soft drinks for sale.**
Set on a southerly ridge. Stone walls and yew hedges divide the garden into enclosed areas with herbaceous borders, shrubs, long walks and young and mature trees. There are interesting plants flowering most of the time. In 2020 a Japanese Tea House was added at the bottom of the garden. Partial wheelchair access. Gravel and mown paths. Return to house is steep. It is, however, possible to just sit on the terrace.

30 THE OLD RECTORY
Main Street, Newbold Verdon, Leicester, LE9 9NN. Gianni and Kate De Fraja, www.flic.kr/s/aHBqjBuEsk. *10m W of Leicester. On the village Main St, just before the turning for the church. Bus stop 'Old White Swan' on lines 153.* **Sat 14 June (11-6.30); Sun 15 June (10-4). Adm £5.50, chd free. Tea, coffee & cake.**
The garden surrounds the Georgian Old Rectory. It contains many species of trees, ranging in age from centuries-old to very young saplings. In June the roses are at their best, we have new hydrangeas. Hostas and the woods around the gravel paths are good throughout the season. We have a large (15m diameter) new circular bed, where we removed the rhododendron ponticum. The garden is accessed via a gravel drive. Wheelchair access is possible with some attention.

32 THE OLD VICARAGE, WHISSENDINE
2 Station Road, Whissendine, LE15 7HG. Prof Peter & Dr Sarah Furness, www.rutlandlordlieutenant.org/garden. *Up hill from St Andrew's church, 1st L in Station Rd.* **Sun 18 May (2-5). Adm £6, chd free. Home-made teas in St Andrew's Church, Whissendine (next door).**
⅔ acre garden, terrace with topiary, formal fountain courtyard and raised beds backed by gothic orangery. Herbaceous borders surround main lawn, hidden white walk. Wisteria tunnel to raised vegetable beds and large ornate greenhouse, beehives, Gothic hen house plus rare breed hens. Features inc pebble mosaics and woodwork. The gravel drive is hard work for wheelchair users. Some areas are accessible only by steps.

33 PREBENDAL HOUSE
Crocket Lane, Empingham, LE15 8PW. Matthew & Rebecca Eatough. *5m E of Oakham. Facing the church on Church St, through large gates on H.* **Sun 27 July (1.30-5). Adm £7, chd free. Home-made teas.**
A garden reimagined. The garden has undergone a total redesign and transformation. Drawing on and incorporating elements of an early and long forgotten design of the garden. Areas and aspects have been developed to inc more herbaceous borders, a white garden, entirely new beds and structure in the C18 walled garden. Mostly wheelchair friendly over gravel.

34 REDHILL LODGE
Seaton Road, Barrowden, Oakham, LE15 8EN. Richard & Susan Moffitt, www.m360design.co.uk. *1m from village of Barrowden along Seaton Rd.* **Sun 1 June (12-5.30). Adm £6, chd free. Light refreshments.**
A bold contemporary garden on varying levels. The formal structure inc landform and water in the form of a modern rill and a natural swimming pond. Planting is colourful and varied. The prairie style garden is naturalistic and vibrant especially in autumn. Features inc turf amphitheatre and modern sculpture.

35 ST WOLSTAN'S HOUSE
Church Nook, Wigston Magna, LE18 3RA. Mr Kevin De-Voy & Mr Stephen Walker. *On corner of Church Nook & Bull Head St opp St Wistan's church. No parking at garden. Public car parks, all within 5 min walk on Frederick St, Junction Rd & Paddock St.* **Sun 1 June (11-5). Home-made teas. Evening opening Sat 20 Sept (6.30-9). Light refreshments. Adm £5, chd free.**
Approx ½ acre divided into garden rooms with formal and informal planting plus specimen trees. Inc formal white garden, rose garden, sunken Italian garden, rose and wisteria pergola and laburnum arch,

Edwardian conservatory, terracotta garden and well garden with raised beds. Sept opening to view garden lit up at night.

36 NEW **8 SAINTBURY ROAD**
Glenfield, Leicester, LE3 8EL. Martin and Rosie Furniss. *3m NW of Leicester. Off Faire Rd which is opp County Hall on the A50. 2m from A50 and A46 interchange.* **Sat 9, Sun 10 Aug (11-4). Combined adm with 2 Ilmington Close £6, chd free. Tea, coffee & cake.**

Colourful, medium sized town garden crammed with plants and flowers. Planting focuses on texture, contrast and colour. Deep borders edge an oval lawn filled with shrubs, perennials, cannas, dahlias, hostas and climbers. A rear area, accessed through an arch has vegetable boxes, a greenhouse and flower nooks. Surrounding a patio water feature are container plants with a tropical feel.

48,000 people affected by cancer were reached by Maggie's centres supported by the National Garden Scheme over the last 12 months.

Oak Tree House

37 THE SECRET GARDEN AT WIGSTON FRAMEWORK KNITTERS MUSEUM
42-44 Bushloe End, Wigston, LE18 2BA. Wigston Framework Knitters Museum, www.wigstonframeworkknitters.org.uk. *4m S of Leicester. On A5199 Wigston bypass, follow yellow signs to Paddock St public car park. yellow signs onto Long St to All Saints Church turn R onto Bushloe End, Museum on R.* **Sat 21, Sun 22 June (11-5). Adm £3.50, chd free. Home-made teas.**
Victorian walled garden approx 70'x80' with traditional cottage garden planting, referred to as higgledy-piggledy because of the random planting. Managed by a group of volunteers with much replanting over the past few years. Garden located in the grounds of a historic museum, (an extra charge applies). A unique garden in the centre of Wigston which still retains an air of peace and tranquillity. Cobbled area before garden, gravel paths through main parts of the garden.
& ✿ ☕

38 THE SECRET GARDEN, GLENFIELD HOSPITAL
Groby Road, Leicester, LE3 9QP. Karen James. *Upon arrival to the Glenfield Hospital, please follow the blue directional signage.* **Sat 21 June, Sat 19 July (10.30-3). Adm £3.50, chd free. Light refreshments in the Secret Garden cafe.**
Set within the grounds of the Glenfield Hospital, the Secret Garden is 1 acre in size, hidden behind the walls of a Victorian Walled garden which has been lovingly designed and restored for the benefit of all those who visit it and in consideration of the rich history and heritage of the garden and the wider Leicester Frith site. All main pathways are wheelchair accessible.
& 🐕 ✿ 🚗 ☕ 🪑 »)

39 NEW STOCKERSTON HALL
Stockerston, Uppingham, LE15 9JD. Henry & Catherine Nicholson. *2m SW of Uppingham. From B664, in centre of village take lane to St Peter's Church. Parking will be signed at top of lane.* **Sun 6 July (2-5). Adm £6, chd free. Home-made teas.**
Stockerston Hall was built on site of an earlier house in 1797. The garden has been quietly reimagined over the past 12 yrs to inc the extended landscape and views towards the Eyebrook Reservoir and woods. The partly walled garden has formal herbaceous borders, an orchard and cutting garden. Courtyard with herbs and high summer colour. Beautiful C13 church open. Gravel paths and lawns.
& ☕ 🪑 »)

40 STOKE ALBANY HOUSE
Desborough Road, Stoke Albany, Market Harborough, LE16 8PT. Mr & Mrs A M Vinton, 01858 535227, del.jones7@googlemail.com, www.stokealbanyhouse.co.uk. *4m E of Market Harborough. Via A427 to Corby, turn to Stoke Albany, R at the White Horse (B669) garden ½ m on the L.* **Every Wed 4 June to 30 July (2-4.30). Adm £6, chd free. Visits also by arrangement 4 June to 30 July. Preferably weds afternoons. Donation to Marie Curie Cancer Care.**
4 acre country house garden; fine trees and shrubs with wide herbaceous borders and sweeping striped lawn. Good display of bulbs in spring, roses June and July. Walled grey garden; nepeta walk arched with roses, parterre with box and roses. Mediterranean garden. Heated greenhouse, potager with topiary, water feature garden and sculptures.
& 🐕 ✿ 🚗 🪑

41 TRESILLIAN HOUSE
67 Dalby Road, Melton Mowbray, LE13 0BQ. Mrs Alison Blythe, 01664 481997, alisonblythe@tresillianhouse.com, www.tresillianhouse.com. *½ m S of Melton Mowbray centre. Situated on B6047 Dalby Rd, S of Melton town centre. (Melton to Gt Dalby/ Market Harborough rd). Parking on site.* **Sun 23 Feb, Sun 13 Apr, Sun 29 June, Sun 31 Aug, Sun 26 Oct (11-4). Adm £5.50, chd free. Light refreshments inc cream teas, ploughmans' lunches, soup in winter, stew & dumplings in February & October. 2026: Sun 22 Feb. Visits also by arrangement 1 Apr to 1 Oct for groups of up to 30.**
¾ acre garden re-established by current owner. Beautiful blue cedar trees, specimen tulip tree. Variety of trees, plants and bushes reinstated. Original bog garden and natural pond. Koi pond; glass garden room holds exhibitions and recitals. Vegetable plot. Cowslips and bulbs in springtime. Wide variety of unusual plants, trees and shrubs. Quiet and tranquil oasis. Small Art Exhibition by local artists. The natural pond has been replanted by pond specialists, Wild Water Ponds. Hot food served in February. Relax in June and August with ploughman's lunches or cream tea listening to live traditional jazz. Keep warm in October with stew and dumplings or soup. Slate paths, steep in places but manageable.
& 🐕 ✿ 🚗 🏠 ☕ »)

42 NEW TUDOR HOUSE
Manor Road, Great Bowden, Market Harborough, LE16 7HE. Tim and Liz Blades. *1m from Market Harborough train stn. From A6 r'about, take exit for Great Bowden. Cont for ½ m. Turn R at xrds onto Main St. Cont on Main St, past the Red Lion pub, then turn R onto Manor Rd. Garden is 90 yds on L.* **Sun 4 May (11-5). Adm £5, chd free. Tea, coffee & cake.**
One acre family garden featuring woodland, lawns, greenhouse, pond, fire pit, sculptures and the owners' impulse plant purchases. Three trees were felled in 2024 and there is a race to rejuvenate this area to incorporate a new vegetable patch and fruit cage before the garden opens. Witness the battle with dry shade and perennial weeds and find out if the vegetable patch is ready for action.
☕ »)

GROUP OPENING

43 UPPINGHAM GARDENS
Uppingham, Oakham, LE15. *Uppingham town centre. Close to Oakham, Corby & Rutland Water. Maps available in Church Hall in Market Square.* **Sun 15 June (1-5). Combined adm £7, chd free. Home-made teas in Church Hall (next to Market Square).**

HILLSIDE
Mr & Mrs Lawrence Fenelon.

NEW 1 PIG LANE
Tony & Clare Wilks.

Two contrasting gardens opening in the historic market town of Uppingham. Hillside is a 1 acre south facing garden with terraces, patio, new rose planting, orchard, vegetable garden, woodland walk and spring fed pond. 1 Pig Lane is a newly constructed garden in the centre of the town with raised borders containing herbaceous plants, perennials, annuals and ornamental trees. Wheelchair access is available at Hillside but garden is on steep slope in parts, 1 Pig Lane has gravel paths.

44 WESTBROOKE HOUSE
52 Scotland Road, Little Bowden, Market Harborough, LE16 8AX. Bryan & Joanne Drew. ½m S Market Harborough. From Northampton Rd follow NGS arrows & park in public car park or on nearby roads - not on the road directly opp the entrance. No parking at property. **Sun 27 Apr, Sun 25 May (10-4.30). Adm £6, chd free. Cream teas.**
Westbrooke House is a late Victorian property built in 1887. The gardens comprise 6 acres in total and are approached through a tree lined driveway of mature limes and giant redwoods. Key features are walled flower garden, walled kitchen garden, fernery, lower garden, wildlife pond, spring garden, lawns, woodland paths and a meadow with a wildflower area, ha-ha and hornbeam avenue.

45 WESTVIEW
1 St Thomas's Road, Great Glen, Leicester, LE8 9EH. Gill & John Hadland, 01162 592170, gillhadland1@gmail.com. *7m S of Leicester. Take either r'about from A6 into village centre then follow NGS signs. Please park in Oaks Rd.* **Sat 22, Sun 23 Feb (11-4), open nearby Hedgehog Hall. Sat 24, Mon 26 May (11-4). Adm £3.50, chd free. Home-made teas. Home-made soup & rolls served at the Feb openings. Visits also by arrangement Feb to Sept for groups of up to 20.**
Organically managed small walled cottage garden with year-round interest. Rare and unusual plants, many grown from seed. Formal box parterre, courtyard garden, alpines, herbaceous borders, woodland areas with unusual ferns, small wildlife pond, greenhouse, vegetables, fruit and herbs. Collection of Snowdrops. Recycled materials used to make quirky garden ornaments and water feature. Restored Victorian outhouse functions as a garden office and houses a collection of old garden tools and ephemera.

GROUP OPENING

46 WIGSTON GARDENS
Wigston, LE18 3LF. Zoe Lewin. *Just S of Leicester off A5199.* **Sat 5, Sun 6 July (11-5). Combined adm £6, chd free. Home-made teas at Little Dale Wildlife Garden and 28 Gladstone St.**

28 GLADSTONE STREET
Chris & Janet Huscroft.
(See separate entry)

2A HOMESTEAD DRIVE
Mrs Sheila Bolton.

LITTLE DALE WILDLIFE GARDEN
Zoe Lewin & Neil Garner, www.facebook.com/zoesopengarden.

'VALLENVINA' 6 ABINGTON CLOSE
Mr Steve Hunt.

Wigston Gardens consists of 4 relatively small gardens all within a 2 mile radius of each other. There is something different to see at each garden from traditional to a taste of the unusual via wildflowers, interesting artifacts, upcycling, and prairie style planting. You will need to travel by car to visit all of the gardens in the group or it will make for quite a long walk and you'll need your comfy shoes.

GROUP OPENING

47 WILLOUGHBY GARDENS
Willoughby Waterleys, LE8 6UD. *9m S of Leicester. From A426 heading N turn R at Dunton Bassett lights. Follow signs to Willoughby. From Blaby follow signs to Countesthorpe. 2m S to Willoughby.* **Sun 6 July (11-5). Combined adm £6, chd free. Tea, coffee & cake in the Village Hall.**

FARMWAY
Eileen Spencer, 07795 058582, eileenfarmway9@msn.com.
Visits also by arrangement 30 June to 20 Aug for groups of up to 25. Any day. Evening visits welcome.

HIGH MEADOW
Phil & Eva Day.

JOHN'S WOOD
John & Jill Harris.

3 ORCHARD ROAD
Diane Brearley.

3 YEW TREE CLOSE
Emma Clanfield.

Willoughby Waterleys lies in the South Leicestershire countryside. 5 gardens will be open. John's Wood is a 1½ acre nature reserve planted to encourage wildlife. Farmway is a plant lovers garden with many unusual plants in colour themed borders. 3 Orchard Road is a small south facing garden packed with interesting features. High Meadow has been evolving over 15 yrs. Inc mixed planting and ornamental vegetable garden. 3 Yew Tree Close is a wrap around garden that naturally creates a series of rooms with cottage garden style borders.

48 15 THE WOODCROFT
Diseworth, Derby, DE74 2QT. Nick Hollick, 07736 672585, nicknollick@me.com. *The Woodcroft is off The Green, parking on The Woodcroft.* **Sun 10 Aug (11-4). Adm £4, chd free. Home-made teas. Visits also by arrangement 1 Feb to 28 Sept for groups of 6+. February opening for snowdrops.**
⅓ acre garden developed by the owner over 45 yrs with mature choice trees and shrubs, old and modern shrub roses, fern garden, wildlife garden, drifts of snowdrops and colour themed mixed herbaceous borders. Gazebo overlooking large wildlife pond, seating throughout the garden. Three steps from the upper terrace to the main garden accessible with wheelchair.

The National Garden Scheme donated £281,000 in 2024 to support those looking to work in horticulture as well as those struggling within the industry.

LINCOLNSHIRE

VOLUNTEERS

County Organisers
Lesley Wykes
01673 860356
lesley.wykes@ngs.org.uk

County Treasurer
Kate Richardson
07496 550516
kate.richardson@ngs.org.uk

Social Media
Diane Puncheon
01427 800008
diane.puncheon@ngs.org.uk

Publicity
Tricia Elliott
01427 788517
t.elliott575@gmail.com

Booklet Co-Ordinator
Linda Dawes
07854 661155
linda.dawes@ngs.org.uk

Talks Co-ordinator
Neil Timm
01472 398092
neilfernnursery@gmail.com

Assistant County Organisers
Karen Bourne
07860 504047
karen@karenwrightpr.com

Heather Charles
07496 329471
heather.charles@ngs.org.uk

Sylvia Ravenhall
01507 526014
sylvan@btinternet.com

@LincolnshireNGS
@LincsNGS

OPENING DATES

All entries subject to change.
For latest information check
www.ngs.org.uk
Extended openings are shown at the beginning of each month.
Map locator numbers are shown to the right of each garden name.

February
Snowdrop Opening
Sunday 23rd
Woodlands   35

April
Saturday 5th
◆ Burghley House Private South Gardens   9
Sunday 6th
◆ Burghley House Private South Gardens   9
Friday 18th
◆ Easton Walled Gardens   12
Sunday 20th
Ashfield House   3
Woodlands   35

May
Thursday 1st
NEW The Ash   2
Saturday 3rd
23 Accommodation Road   1
Sunday 4th
23 Accommodation Road   1
NEW The Ash   2
Dunholme Lodge   11
66 Spilsby Road   31
Monday 5th
23 Accommodation Road   1
Saturday 10th
NEW ◆ Belvoir Castle   7
Sunday 11th
Woodlands   35
Saturday 17th
Willoughby Road Allotments   34

Sunday 18th
The Old Vicarage   26
Old White House   27
Saturday 31st
The Old Stables   25

June
Sunday 1st
Firs Farm   14
23 Linden Walk   20
Manor Farm   22
The Old Stables   25
Tuesday 3rd
23 Linden Walk   20
Saturday 7th
3 Stone Lane   32
Sunday 8th
3 Stone Lane   32
Sunday 15th
Shangrila   30
Woodlands   35
Saturday 21st
Home Farm   18
Sunday 22nd
NEW 49 Church Street   10
The Fern Nursery and Bowling Club   13
Hackthorn Hall   17
Home Farm   18
Thursday 26th
NEW The Ash   2
Sunday 29th
NEW The Ash   2
Dunholme Lodge   11

July
Sunday 6th
2 Mill Cottage   24
Saturday 12th
Aswarby House   4
Aswarby Park   5
Sunday 13th
NEW 49 Church Street   10
Sunday 20th
Walnut Tree Cottage   33
Yew Tree Farm   36
Thursday 24th
NEW The Ash   2
Sunday 27th
NEW The Ash   2
◆ Gunby Hall and Gardens   16

August

Every Thursday and Sunday
The Secret Garden of Louth   29

Sunday 3rd
Fydell House   15

Sunday 10th
The Fern Nursery and Bowling Club   13

Sunday 17th
Woodlands   35

Saturday 23rd
NEW Boston Exotic Garden   8
Willoughby Road Allotments   34

September

Saturday 20th
Inley Drove Farm   19

Sunday 21st
Inley Drove Farm   19
Woodlands   35

By Arrangement

Arrange a personalised garden visit with your club, or group of friends, on a date to suit you. See individual garden entries for full details.

Ashfield House   3
NEW Battleford Hall   6
NEW Boston Exotic Garden   8
NEW 49 Church Street   10
Firs Farm   14
Fydell House   15
Home Farm   18
Inley Drove Farm   19
23 Linden Walk   20
Ludney House Farm   21
Marigold Cottage   23
The Old Stables   25
The Old Vicarage   26
The Plant Lover's Garden   28
The Secret Garden of Louth   29
Walnut Tree Cottage   33
Woodlands   35

Battleford Hall

THE GARDENS

1 23 ACCOMMODATION ROAD
Horncastle, LN9 5AS. Mr & Mrs D Chapman. *From turning off Lincoln Rd A158, onto Accommodation Rd we are situated approx 600yds on R.* **Sat 3, Sun 4, Mon 5 May (11-4). Adm £3.50, chd free.**
A medium sized garden to wander around and discover different plants; A range of tall and dwarf bearded iris, Auricula theatres showing off lovely doubles and there are also a range of fruit trees and bushes. Sitting in the garden, which is designed to have small rooms showing off flowers, you can relax and take it all in. Talk to the owners and discover garden plaques throughout. Plants to purchase finishes an enjoyable experience. Partial wheelchair access to decking area.

& 🐕 ❀

2 NEW THE ASH
Main Road, Covenham St. Bartholomew, Louth, LN11 0PF. Mrs Angela & Mr Mervyn Aylett. *N of Louth. From A16 go E on Pear Tree Ln. At the x-roads turn R to Covenham St. Bartholomew. Continue into the village, garden is on the R. What3words app: rides. bronze.circulate.* **Thur 1, Sun 4 May, Thur 26, Sun 29 June, Thur 24, Sun 27 July (10-3). Adm £5, chd free.**
What is now the garden was a field when we moved here in 2021. Work commenced in the October and today the garden is full of shrubs, trees, cutting garden and vegetable patch. This, along with the pond, has brought a great amount wildlife to the garden and is a constant source of joy. The development of the garden has been totally based on no dig principals, which has proved a great success.

🐕 ❀ D ☕)))

3 ASHFIELD HOUSE
Lincoln Road, Branston, Lincoln, LN4 1NS. John & Judi Tinsley, 07977 505682, john@tinsleyfarms.co.uk. *3m S of Lincoln on B1188. N outskirts of Branston on the B1188 Lincoln Rd. Signed 'Tinsley Farms - Ashfield'. Nr bus stop, follow signs down drive.* **Sun 20 Apr (11-4). Adm £6, chd free. Light refreshments.** Visits also by arrangement Apr to Oct.
Discover 140 flowering cherries and 30 magnolias. Many thousands of spring bulbs, sweeping lawns and lake. Beautiful naturally landscaped garden with some superb mature trees as well as a fascinating arboretum. One of the best flowering cherry displays in the area. Fairly level garden. Wheelchair access via grass paths.

& 🐕 ❀ ☕)))

4 ASWARBY HOUSE
Aswarby, Sleaford, NG34 8SE. Penny & James Herdman. *Past church on R of road. 300yds from the gates of Aswarby Park. Plenty of parking available on the roadside.* **Sat 12 July (2-5). Combined adm with Aswarby Park £10, chd free. Home-made teas in Aswarby Park.**
Garden of one acre planted six years ago in the grounds of a handsome C18 house and coachhouse. It has a partial walled garden, wildflower meadow surrounded by ornamental grasses and a 30 metre long herbaceous border. With two box parterres, and woodland shrubs, it has stunning views over ancient ridge and furrow grassland. This garden would complement your visit to Aswarby Park.

& ❀ ☕

5 ASWARBY PARK
Aswarby, Sleaford, NG34 8SD. Mr & Mrs George Playne, www.aswarbyestate.co.uk. *5m S of Sleaford on A15. Take signs to Aswarby. Entrance is straight ahead by church through black gates.* **Sat 12 July (2-5). Combined adm with Aswarby House £10, chd free. Home-made teas and cakes.**
Formal and woodland garden in a parkland setting of approximately 20 acres. Yew trees form a backdrop to borders and lawns surrounding the house, formally a converted stable block. The walled garden incorporating a greenhouse with a Muscat grapevine which is over 300 years old. Other attractions inc a unique Rosewalk, a cutting garden created in 2022 and a wildflower bed in 2023. Partial wheelchair access on gravel paths and drives.

& ❀ ☕)))

6 NEW BATTLEFORD HALL
Bensgate Road, Fleet, Holbeach, Spalding, PE12 8NL. Mr John Holmes, 01406 423794, john.holmesfcis@yahoo.co.uk. *Approx 3m E from Holbeach. Access via main gates from Bensgate (formerly Proudfoot Ln). A former old rectory found next to St. Mary Magdalene Church.* **Visits by arrangement 19 Apr to 27 Apr for groups of up to 40. Discuss refreshments when booking. Adm £5, chd free.**
'A new garden on old bones'. A sea of wild garlic under a canopy of mature trees, comprising of *Ginkgo Biloba*, mulberry, london plane and Cedar of Lebanon plus others. A Victorian garden with a formal arrangement of hedging with rose and bluebell parterres alongside colourful borders and a Herbalist walled garden. A pavilion houses more tender plants. Wheelchair access to most of the garden. Some uneven surfaces and steps.

& 🐕 ❀ 🚗 ☕

7 NEW ♦ BELVOIR CASTLE
Belvoir, Grantham, NG32 1PE. The Duke & Duchess of Rutland, 01476 871001, reception@belvoircastle.com, www.belvoircastle.com. *9m W of Grantham. Follow brown heritage signs for Belvoir Castle on A52, A1, A607.* **For NGS: Sat 10 May (9-5). Adm £10, chd £6.** For other opening times and information, please phone, email or visit garden website.
The striking Regency castle sits proudly overlooking the beautiful Vale of Belvoir and is surrounded by Capability Brown landscape. The plans to the ten hectares of pleasure gardens originally designed by Harold Peto have only recently been rediscovered with all the classic hallmarks of the designer. The roses in the garden today are the design of Emma, the current Duchess of Rutland. Flat shoes essential and steep climb to Castle. Aviary Tearoom serving a range of home-cooked lunches and afternoon teas. Bistro cafe and farm shop selling a range of fresh produce available at Belvoir's Retail Village. Adventure playground and nature walks through the Capability Brown designed parkland. Historic Castle tours available. Only rose garden accessible by wheelchair. Steep slopes and steps in places.

& 🚗 ☕ 🪑

LINCOLNSHIRE 329

330 LINCOLNSHIRE

8 NEW BOSTON EXOTIC GARDEN
40 Allington Garden, Boston, PE21 9DW. Nigel Smith, 07932 626266, bostonexoticgarden@gmail.com. *1m NE of Boston town centre. From Boston take A16 towards Spilsby. Take 3rd L into Hospital Ln then 2nd R into Linden Way. 1st L is Allington Garden. What3words app: hatch. awake.magic.* **Sat 23 Aug (11-4). Adm £4, chd free. Tea, coffee & cake. Open nearby Willoughby Road Allotments.** Visits also by arrangement 26 July to 31 Aug for groups of up to 20. Adm inc refreshments.

Built from a blank canvas since 2017, this 42m x 12m garden has been transformed into an exotic garden full of interesting tropical plants with huge lush foliage. Various forms of banana plants, *Canna* and *Brugmansia*. Many of the plants are tender so need protection over winter. Various paths to explore. Small wildlife pond. There are two steps up to main lawn from large patio area. A ramp will be available. There are a few narrow paths.

9 ◆ BURGHLEY HOUSE PRIVATE SOUTH GARDENS
Stamford, PE9 3JY. Burghley House Preservation Trust, 01780 752451, burghley@burghley.co.uk, www.burghley.co.uk. *1m E of Stamford. From Stamford follow signs to Burghley via B1443.* **For NGS: Sat 5, Sun 6 Apr (10-4). Adm £10, chd £8.50. Pre-booking essential, please visit www.ngs.org.uk for information & booking. Light refreshments in The Orangery Restaurant, Garden Café, Potting Shed and Muddy Mole.** For other opening times and information, please phone, email or visit garden website.

The Private South Gardens at Burghley House will open for the NGS with spectacular spring bulbs in a park like setting with magnificent trees. Relish the opportunity to enjoy Capability Brown's famous lake and summerhouse. Entry via Garden Kiosks. Adm charge is a special pre-book price only via NGS website. Visitors paying at the gate on the day will be charged a Gardens ticket price. Wheelchair access via gravel paths.

10 NEW 49 CHURCH STREET
Long Bennington, Newark, NG23 5ES. Di Ablewhite, 01400 282130, di.ablewhite@btinternet.com, www.withamsidehouse.com. *Equidistant between Grantham and Newark, just off the A1. Enter Church St opp the sch. Garden is halfway down on the L. 2 large brick pillars at the top of the drive. What3words app: mini.waistcoat.delighted.* **Sun 22 June, Sun 13 July (1.30-4.30). Adm £5, chd free. Tea, coffee & cake.** Visits also by arrangement 1 July to 8 Aug for groups of up to 25.

A beautiful riverside garden with fabulous open views. We have mature trees, topiary, borders and several relaxing seating areas in different styles. The house and garden are also used as a photoshoot location. Fairly wheelchair friendly, but some gravel areas and low steps.

11 DUNHOLME LODGE
Dunholme, Lincoln, LN2 3QA. Hugh & Lesley Wykes. *4m NE of Lincoln. Turn off A46 towards Welton at the r'about. After ½ m turn L up long private road. Garden at top.* **Sun 4 May, Sun 29 June (11-5). Adm £5.50, chd free. Home-made teas.**

A five acre garden with mature trees, spring bulbs and ferns, shrubs, roses, natural pond, wildflower walk, orchard and vegetable garden. Young arboretum. RAF Dunholme Lodge Museum and War Memorial within the grounds. Craft stalls. Ukulele Band. Vintage vehicles. Most areas wheelchair accessible but some loose stone and gravel.

12 ◆ EASTON WALLED GARDENS
Easton, NG33 5AP. Sir Fred & Lady Cholmeley, 01476 530063, info@eastonwalledgardens.co.uk, www.visiteaston.co.uk. *7m S of Grantham. 1m from A1, off B6403.* **For NGS: Fri 18 Apr (11-4). Adm £11, chd £5.** For other opening times and information, please phone, email or visit garden website.

A 400 year old, restored 12 acre garden set in the heart of Lincolnshire. Home to snowdrops, sweet peas, roses and meadows. The River Witham meanders through the gardens, teeming with wildlife. Other garden highlights inc a yew tunnel, turf maze and cut flower gardens. The Applestore Tearoom and Coffee Room offers hot and cold drinks, light savoury snacks, homemade cakes. Regret no wheelchair access to lower gardens but tearoom, shop, upper gardens and facilities are all accessible.

13 THE FERN NURSERY AND BOWLING CLUB
Grimsby Road, Binbrook, Market Rasen, LN8 6DH. Neil Timm, www.fernnursery.co.uk. *On B1203 from Market Rasen. On the Grimsby rd from Binbrook Square, 400m.* **Sun 22 June, Sun 10 Aug (11-4). Adm £4, chd free. Tea, coffee & cake in the bowling pavilion. Refreshments are provided by Binbrook Bowling Club.**

The garden has been designed as a wildlife garden with a number of features of interest to both visitors and wildlife, helped by having a natural stream running through the garden, which supplies water to a pond and water features. Visitors can also enjoy rock features, acid beds, and a sheltered winter garden with a sundial at its centre. From which a path leads to a small wood with the main fern collection. In addition there is a semi formal herb garden and bowling green, where they will often see a game being played, large shrubs, a bank of drought tolerant plants and herbaceous perennials, while steps, seats, a gazebo, and bridge. Partial wheelchairs access, gravel paths.

14 FIRS FARM
Hoop Lane, Langton-by-Wragby, Market Rasen, LN8 5QB. Jean and Malcolm Clarke, 01673 857887. *2m SE of Wragby. Approx 2m from Wragby on A158, turn R on sharp bend into Hoop Ln. Continue for approx 1m. Turn R at yellow signs into car park.* **Sun 1 June (10-4). Adm £5, chd free. Home-made teas.** Visits also by arrangement 16 June to 31 Aug for groups of 10 to 30.

Discover this medium sized garden with herbaceous borders featuring dahlias. There is a pond, large vegetable patch and a wooded area with beautiful woodland walks. The perimeter walk is 1m and suitable for well behaved dogs on leads. Chambers Farm Wood is approx ½ m away. Its one of Lincolnshire's ancient limewoods, important for wildlife. Much of Hoop Lane is a roadside nature reserve. Some rough ground through the wood.

&. ⚑ ✻ ☕ ⛱

15 FYDELL HOUSE
South Square, Boston, PE21 6HU.
Boston Preservation Trust,
01205 351520,
info@fydellhouse.org.uk. *Central Boston down South St. Through the Market Sq, past Boots. One way street by Guildhall. There are 3 car parks within 200 yds of the house. Disabled parking in council car park opp the house.* **Sun 3 Aug (10-4). Adm £4, chd free. Visits also by arrangement.**
Within three original red brick walls a formal garden was been created in 1995. Yew buttresses, arbours and four parterres use Dutch themes. The borders contain herbaceous plants and shrubs. The north facing border holds shade loving plants. There is a mulberry and walnut tree. The astrolabe was installed in 1997. A Victorian rockery is built from slag from ironworks in Boston. Walled garden Astrolabe Parterres formal borders topiary of box and yew. Wheelchair access is along the south alleyway from the front to the back garden.

&. ✻ ☕))

16 ♦ GUNBY HALL AND GARDENS
Spilsby, PE23 5SS.
National Trust, 01754 892998,
nigel.hodges@nationaltrust.org.uk,
www.nationaltrust.org.uk/gunby-hall. *2½ m NW of Burgh-le-Marsh. 7m W of Skegness. On A158. Signed off Gunby r'about.* **For NGS: Sun 27 July (10-4). Adm £8.50, chd £4.25. Tea, coffee & cake in the Gunby tearoom.** For other opening times and information, please phone, email or visit garden website.
Eight acres of formal and walled gardens. Old roses, herbaceous borders, herb garden and kitchen garden with fruit trees and vegetables. Greenhouses, carp pond and sweeping lawns. Tennyson's Haunt of Ancient Peace. Enjoy a sweet treat from the tearoom, or visit one of many craft and trade stalls in the courtyard. Adm inc entry to the House - Adult £14, Child £7. Wheelchair access in gardens and with Gunby's dedicated wheelchair on ground floor of house. There are steps into the house.

&. ⚑ ✻ ☕ ⛱))

17 HACKTHORN HALL
Hackthorn, Lincoln, LN2 3PQ.
Mr & Mrs William Cracroft-Eley,
www.hackthorn.com. *6m N of Lincoln. Follow signs to Hackthorn. Approx 1m off A15 N of Lincoln.* **Sun 22 June (1-5). Adm £5, chd free. Tea, coffee & cake at Hackthorn Village Hall.**
Formal and woodland garden, productive and ornamental walled gardens surrounding Hackthorn Hall and church extending to approx 15 acres. Parts of the formal gardens designed by Bunny Guinness. The walled garden boasts a magnificent Black Hamburg vine, believed to be second in size to the vine at Hampton Court. Partial wheelchair access. There are some gravel and grass paths.

&. ⚑ ✻ ☕

Boston Exotic Garden

49 Church Street

18 HOME FARM
Little Casterton Road, Ryhall, Stamford, PE9 4HA. Steve & Karen Bourne, 07860 504047, karen@karenwrightpr.com. 1½ m N of Stamford. Just off the A6121 Stamford to Bourne Rd. 1½ m N of Stamford. At mini-r'about turn towards Little Casterton & Tolethorpe Hall. Car park 50 yards on the L. **Sat 21, Sun 22 June (11-4). Adm £5, chd free. Tea, coffee & cake.** Visits also by arrangement 9 June to 27 June for groups of 15 to 40. More than 100 roses, inc many old English fragrant varieties, lavender avenue and striking display of delphiniums. Mediterranean border and new 'hot and more' border adapted to drier conditions. Wildflower meadow where rare butterflies have been spotted, woodland walk, fruit cage and vegetable garden make up the 9 acre site. Large terrace over looking the garden with far-reaching views. Most areas accessible by wheelchair.

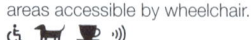

19 INLEY DROVE FARM
Inley Drove, Sutton St James, Spalding, PE12 0LX. Francis & Maisie Pryor, 01406 540088, maisietaylor7@gmail.com, www.pryorfrancis.wordpress.com. 5m S of Holbeach. Just off road from Sutton St James to Sutton St Edmund. 2m S of Sutton St James. Look for yellow NGS signs on double bend. **Sat 20, Sun 21 Sept (11-5). Adm £6, chd free. Home-made teas.** Visits also by arrangement June & July for groups of 10 to 30. Garden developed over 27 years for colour, scent and wildlife (inc butterflies, moths and dragonflies). Three acres of predominantly flower gardens with formal and informal areas, all framed by hornbeam hedges. Wide variety of traditional and unusual plants, shrubs and trees (inc Black Poplars), meadow, vegetable garden and orchard. Walks through seven acre wood. Good wheelchair access. Some gravel and a few steps but mostly flat, firm turf. Steps to WC.

20 23 LINDEN WALK
Louth, LN11 9HT. Darren & Jane Cunningham, janecunningham0707@gmail.com. ½ m S from Louth town centre. Free car park at Louth Cattle Market, LN11 9HF. Entrance is on Linden Walk between Boars Head Pub and pedestrian x-ing close to petrol stn. Garden is a 3 min walk S on Linden Walk. **Sun 1 June (1-4); Tue 3 June (11-2). Adm £5, chd free. Tea, coffee & cake. Gluten free option available.** Visits also by arrangement 6 May to 31 May for groups of 5 to 15. This garden was created seven years ago from bare earth by the current owners, retaining just a few of the original specimen trees. The front garden is laid out in formal Victorian style. The enclosed rear garden is on two levels with lawn areas and a water feature bordered by Victorian brick walls and herbaceous perennial borders. There are seating areas throughout to enjoy your tea and cakes.

21 LUDNEY HOUSE FARM
Ludney, Louth, LN11 7JU. Jayne Bullas, 07733 018710, jayne@theoldgatehouse.com. Between Grainthorpe & Conisholme we are on the main road. There is a paddock for parking. **Visits by arrangement 8 May to 31 July for groups of 10 to 30. Adm £8, chd free. Cakes inc in adm.**

LINCOLNSHIRE

A beautiful large garden lovingly developed over the last 20 years with several areas of formal and informal planting inc a pond which attracts a wonderful variety of wildlife. There is an excellent mix of trees, shrubs, perennials, rose garden and wildflower area. There are plenty of seats positioned around to sit and enjoy a cuppa and piece of cake. Wheelchair access to most of garden.

22 MANOR FARM
Horkstow Road, South Ferriby, Barton-upon-Humber, DN18 6HS. Geoff & Angela Wells. *3m W of Barton-Upon-Humber. On A1077 bear L in South Ferriby onto B1204. Turn R opp Village Hall. What3words app: airtime.printer.encloses.* **Sun 1 June (11-4.30). Adm £6, chd free. Home-made teas.**

A formal garden with many seating areas which is much praised by visitors. Set within approx two acres with mature shrubberies, herbaceous borders, gravel garden and pergola walk. Roses and white garden and fernery. Many old trees with preservation orders. Wildlife pond set within a paddock, also on the day a Classic Car display and various stalls.

23 MARIGOLD COTTAGE
Hotchin Road, Sutton-on-Sea, LN12 2NP. Stephanie Lee & John Raby, 07362 419721, marigoldlee@icloud.com, www.rabylee.uk/marigold. *16m N of Skegness on A52. 7m E of Alford on A1111. 3m S of Mablethorpe on A52. Turn off A52 on High St at Cornerhouse Cafe. Follow road past playing field on R. Road turns away from the dunes. House 2nd on L.* **Visits by arrangement 1 May to 1 Sept for groups of 10 to 30. Adm inc home-made teas. Adm £7, chd free.**

Slide open the Japanese gate to find secret shaded paths. You will be taken aback by the abundance of planting combinations. There are pergolas covered in climbers, raised beds, a large kitchen garden and everywhere places to rest and absorb the ambience. Stephanie is always on hand to share her love of gardening and expertise. Not forgetting, substantial plant sales propagated from the garden. Most of garden is wheelchair accessible along flat, paved paths.

24 2 MILL COTTAGE
Barkwith Road, South Willingham, Market Rasen, LN8 6NN. Mrs Jo Deaton & Mr Andrew Deaton. *5m E of Wragby. On A157 turn R at pub in East Barkwith then immed L to S Willingham. Cottage 1m on L.* **Sun 6 July (11-4). Adm £5, chd free. Home-made teas. Home-made cakes and savouries also available.**

A garden of several defined spaces, packed with interesting features, unusual plants and well placed seating areas and extended borrowed views, created by garden designer Jo. Renovated windmill engine shed and themed summerhouses, working well, local rock used in the front. Clipped box, alpines, roses. Greenhouses, herbs and raised vegetable beds. Living Sofa, two outdoor BBQ areas. Log and bottle wall. Partial wheelchair access. Gravel at far end of garden. Steps down to main greenhouse.

25 THE OLD STABLES
The Green, Allington, Grantham, NG32 2EA. Jacqueline Fisher, 07544 397183, jgcontralto@gmail.com. *The Village Green, next to Welby Arms. Allington is signposted from A52 at Sedgbrook and from A1 at Downtown.* **Sat 31 May, Sun 1 June (11-4). Adm £4, chd free. Tea, coffee & cake. Visits also by arrangement 1 May to 15 Sept for groups of up to 20.**

Small cottage style garden with courtyard featuring large pots and raised beds. Flowering shrubs and trees within colourful mixed borders and island beds which inc perennials, roses and bulbs. Sit in our raised summerhouse or on the deck area with its lavender hedge and take in the garden. Many scented leaved pelargoniums are raised in the greenhouse, as are annuals for the low dry stone walled border. C12 church of The Holy Trinity nearby. Disabled parking in driveway and partial wheelchair access to garden.

26 THE OLD VICARAGE
Low Road, Holbeach Hurn, PE12 8JN. Mrs Liz Dixon-Spain, lizdixonspain@gmail.com. *2m NE of Holbeach. Turn off A17 N to Holbeach Hurn. 1st R at war memorial into Low Rd. Old Vicarage is on R approx 400yds. Parking in grass paddock.* **Sun 18 May (1-5).**
Combined adm with Old White House £7.50, chd free. Home-made teas at Old White House. Visits also by arrangement 15 Mar to 28 Sept for groups of 5 to 30.

A two acre garden with 150 year old tulip, plane and beech trees: borders of shrubs, roses, herbaceous plants. Shrub roses and herb garden in old paddock area, surrounded by informal areas with pond and bog garden, wildflowers, grasses and bulbs. Small fruit and vegetable gardens. Flower and grass meadow. Kids love exploring winding paths through the wilder areas. Garden is managed environmentally. Wheelchair access via gravel drive. Some hard paths but mostly grass.

27 OLD WHITE HOUSE
Baileys Lane, Holbeach Hurn, PE12 8JP. Mrs A Worth. *2m N of Holbeach. Turn off A17 N to Holbeach Hurn, follow signs to village, cont through, turn R after Rose & Crown pub at Baileys Ln.* **Sun 18 May (1-5). Combined adm with The Old Vicarage £7.50, chd free. Home-made teas. Home-made cake.**

A mature garden of 1½ acres featuring herbaceous borders, roses, patterned garden, herb garden and walled kitchen garden. Large catalpa, tulip tree that flowers, ginko and other specimen trees. Wheelchair access to all areas.

The National Garden Scheme donated over £3.5 million to our nursing and health beneficiaries from money raised at gardens open in 2024.

334 LINCOLNSHIRE

28 THE PLANT LOVER'S GARDEN
Bourne, PE10 0XF.
Danny & Sophie, 07850 239393, plantloversgarden@outlook.com. *2m N of Bourne off the A15. Situated on the edge of S Lincolnshire, bordering Cambridgeshire & Rutland.* **Visits by arrangement Apr to Aug for groups of up to 40. Adm £6.50, chd free. Light refreshments available by prior arrangement only.**
Make an arrangement to visit the Plant Lovers Garden for a friendly welcome and informative visit. Be inspired by a garden packed with plants showcasing colour, form, texture, various planting combinations and conditions. Elements of garden design and structures throughout. With a guided tour inc to tell the stories behind the design and planting. Large variety of plants for sale. Most areas accessible for wheelchair users.
& ✿ ☕))

29 THE SECRET GARDEN OF LOUTH
68 Watts Lane, Louth, LN11 9DG.
Jenny & Rodger Grasham ½ m S of Louth town centre. For SatNav & to avoid gate on Watts Ln, use postcode LN11 9DJ - Mount Pleasant Ave, leads straight to our house. **Every Thur and Sun 3 Aug to 31 Aug (11-4). Adm £4, chd free. Pre-booking essential, please phone 07977 318145, email sallysing@hotmail.co.uk or visit www.facebook.com/thesecretgardenoflouth for information & booking. Tea, coffee & cake.** Visits also by arrangement 3 Aug to 31 Aug for groups of 10 to 30. Not guided tours, visitors explore, we're on hand for questions.
Blank canvas of ⅕ acre in early 90s. Developed into lush, colourful, exotic plant packed haven. A whole new world on entering from street. Exotic borders, raised exotic island, long hot border, ponds, stumpery. Intimate seating areas along garden's journey. Can children find where the frogs are hiding? Butterflies and bees but how many different types? Feed the fish, find Cedric the spider, Simon the snake, Colin the Crocodile and more. Main areas wheelchair accessible with care. Narrow paths. Not suitable for mobility scooters.
& ✿ ☕

30 SHANGRILA
Little Hale Road, Great Hale, Sleaford, NG34 9LH. Marilyn Cooke & John Knight. *On B1394 between Heckington & Helpringham.* **Sun 15 June (11-5). Adm £4.50, chd free. Home-made teas.**
Approx. three acre garden with sweeping lawns, long herbaceous borders and colour themed island beds. Discover the hosta collection, and relax in the seating area by the lavender beds. Features also inc topiary, acer collection and a Japanese garden. Wheelchair access to all areas.
& ✿ ☕

31 66 SPILSBY ROAD
Boston, PE21 9NS. Rosemary & Adrian Isaac. *From Boston town take A16 towards Spilsby. On L after Trinity Church. Parking on Spilsby Rd.* **Sun 4 May (11-4). Adm £5, chd free. Tea, coffee & cake.**
1⅓ acre with mature trees, moat, Venetian Folly, summerhouse and orangery, lawns and herbaceous borders. Children's Tudor garden house, gatehouse and courtyard. Wide paths suitable for wheelchairs.
& ✿ ☕

32 3 STONE LANE
Rutland House, 3 Stone Lane, Little Humby, NG33 4HX. Paul & Marijka Hance. *7m from Grantham. Proceed along A52 follow signs to Ropsley. At Ropsley proceed along Humby Rd. After 1m, turn R & proceed uphill into Little Humby. Follow signage on village green. Garden is located at rear of property. Park around village green.* **Sat 7, Sun 8 June (11-4). Adm £5, chd free. Tea, coffee & cake.**
Our family garden is approx. ⅔ acre and slopes gently downwards from the terrace towards the valley. It has been created over the last 16 years from a simple lawn to encompass a wide range of herbaceous plants, shrubs and climbing roses. We also have an orchard and wildlife pond.
🐕 ✿ ☕))

33 WALNUT TREE COTTAGE
6 Hall Lane, Welbourn, Lincoln, LN5 0NN. Nina & Malcolm McBeath, 01400 279027. *Approx 11m S of Lincoln, 12m N of Grantham on A607. From Newark A17 then A607. On A607 from Lincoln turn R into Hall Ln by Welbourn Hall Nursing Home. From Leadenham take L after Nursing Home. Garden is 3rd gate on L. Please Park at Village Hall, Beck St.* **Sun 20 July (12-6). Adm £5, chd free. Tea, coffee & cake at Welbourn Village Hall.** Visits also by arrangement 1 May to 15 Sept.
A peaceful ½ acre garden full of interesting perennials planted in long, curved and colour themed borders. Winding paths surrounded by shrubs and climbing roses provide varied vistas and secluded seating areas. Many old varieties of roses feature throughout, with spectacular displays in June of Paul's Himalayan Musk, and Adelaide d'Orleans climbing through trees. Plant stall by John Cullen's Gardens. Artisan honey and bee products for sale. Garden tools by Tinker and Fix. Welbourn Forge dating from 1864 and still in full working order (open 12-6pm), with the fire lit and Friends of the Forge on hand to answer questions. Wheelchair access over gravel drive. Some steps and narrow paths at the rear.
& 🐕 ✿ ☕

34 WILLOUGHBY ROAD ALLOTMENTS
Willoughby Road, Boston, PE21 9HN. Willoughby Road Allotments Association, www.willoughbyroadallotments.com. *Entrance is adjacent to 109 Willoughby Rd. Street parking only.* **Sat 17 May (11.30-3.30), Sat 23 Aug (11.30-3.30), open nearby Boston Exotic Garden. Adm £4, chd free. Light refreshments.**
Set in five acres the allotments comprise 60 plots growing fine vegetables, fruit, flowers and herbs. There is a small orchard and wildflower area and a community space adjacent. Grass paths run along the site. Artwork created by Bex Simon situated on site. A small cafe is now open to the public on site. We work with schools, social proscribing and community groups. Small orchard and wildflower beds. Community area with kitchen and disabled WC. Large polytunnel with raised beds inside and out. Accessible for all abilities. The allotments are completely wheelchair accessible and good for mobility scooters.
& 🐕 ✿ ☕

35 WOODLANDS

Peppin Lane, Fotherby, Louth, LN11 0UW. Ann & Bob Armstrong, 01507 603586, annbobarmstrong@btinternet.com, www.woodlandsplants.co.uk. *2m N of Louth off A16 signed Fotherby. Please park on R verge opp allotments & walk approx 350 yds to garden. If full, please park considerately in the village. No parking at garden.* **Sun 23 Feb, Sun 20 Apr, Sun 11 May, Sun 15 June, Sun 17 Aug, Sun 21 Sept (10.30-3.30). Adm £5, chd free. Home-made teas. For our February opening we are offering home-made soup to warm visitors, in addition to home-made teas.** Visits also by arrangement Apr to Sept.

Renowned for its rich planting of shaded beds, but plenty to interest sun lovers too, especially salvias. A good selection available in the RHS listed nursery. The new crevice garden is developing nicely and once again we are holding a winter opening featuring drifts of snowdrops and aconites amongst winter flowering shrubs and a small, but expanding collection of named snowdrops. Award winning professional artist's studio open to visitors. Specialist collection of *Codonopsis* with Plant Heritage status. Wheelchair access possible with care. Some parking at the house for those with limited mobility.

36 YEW TREE FARM

Westhorpe Road, Gosberton, Spalding, PE11 4EP. Robert & Claire Bailey-Scott. *Enter the village of Gosberton. Turn into Westhorpe Rd, opp The Bell Inn, cont for approx. 1½ m. Property is 3rd on R after bridge.* **Sun 20 July (11-4.30). Adm £6, chd free. Home-made teas.**
A lovely country garden, 1½ acres. Large herbaceous and mixed borders surround well kept lawns. Wildlife pond with two bog gardens, woodland garden, shaded borders containing many unusual plants. Stunning reflective pool surrounded by ornamental grasses. Orchard, wildflower meadow, beehives and vegetable plot.

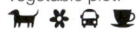

3 Stone Lane

LONDON

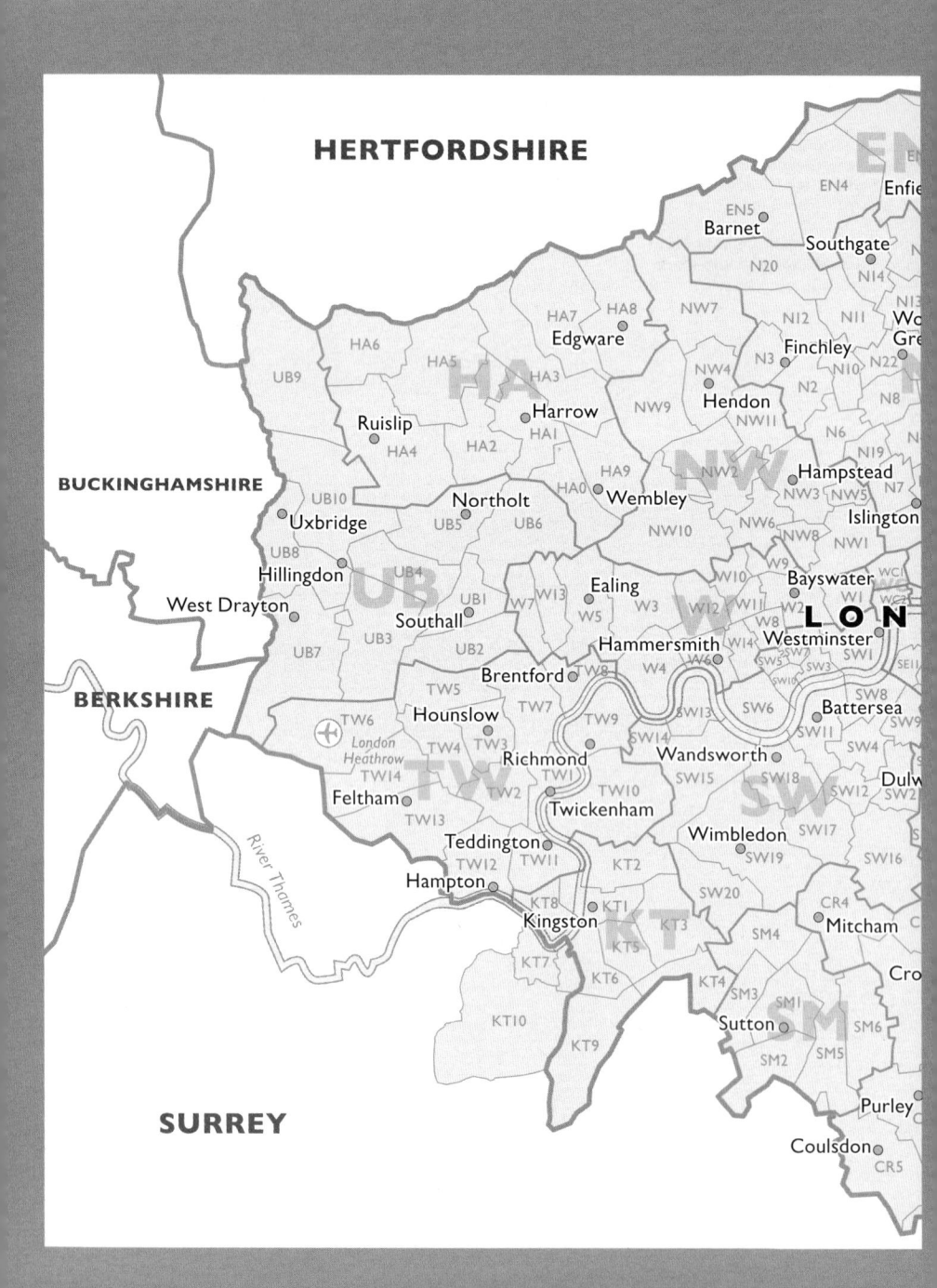

LONDON

LONDON

VOLUNTEERS

County Organiser
Penny Snell
01932 864532
pennysnellflowers@btinternet.com

County Treasurer
Marion Smart
marion.smart@ngs.org.uk

Publicity
Sonya Pinto
07779 609715
sonya.pinto@ngs.org.uk

Booklet Co-ordinator
Sue Phipps
07771 767196
sue@suephipps.com

Booklet Distributor
Joey Clover
joey.clover@ngs.org.uk

Social Media
Sonya Whaley
07941 010005
sonya.whaley@ngs.org.uk

Assistant County Organisers

Central London
Eveline Carn
07831 136069
evelinecbcarn@icloud.com

Croydon & outer S London
Christine Murray & Nicola Dooley
07889 888204
christineandnicola.gardens@gmail.com

Dulwich & surrounding area
Clive Pankhurst
07941 536934
alternative.ramblings@gmail.com

E London
Teresa Farnham
07761 476651
farnhamz@yahoo.co.uk

Finchley & Barnet
Debra & Tim Craighead
07415 166617
dcraighead@icloud.com

Hackney
Philip Lightowlers
020 8533 0052
plighto@gmail.com

Hampstead
Joan Arnold
07850 764543
joan.arnold40@gmail.com

Islington
Vanessa Easlea
020 7700 7335
vanessa.easlea@ngs.org.uk

Northwood, Pinner, Ruislip & Harrow
Brenda White
020 8863 5877
brenda.white@ngs.org.uk

NW London
Susan Bennett & Earl Hyde
020 8883 8540
suebearlh@yahoo.co.uk

Outer NW London
James Duncan Mattoon
07504 565612

Outer W London & Clapham
Sarah Corvi
07803 111968
sarah.corvi@ngs.org.uk

SE London
Janine Wookey
07711 279636
j.wookey@btinternet.com

SW London
Joey Clover (as above)

W London, Barnes & Chiswick
Siobhan McCammon
07952 889866
siobhan.mccammon@gmail.com

@LondonNGS
@LondonNGS
@londonngs

36 Park Village East

LONDON GARDENS LISTED BY POSTCODE

Inner London Postcodes

E and EC London
Spitalfields Gardens, E1
69 Antill Road, E3
22 Betoyne Avenue, E4
26 College Gardens, E4
Lower Clapton Gardens, E5
42 Latimer Road, E7
84 Lavender Grove, E8
London Fields Gardens, E8
St Joseph's Hospice, E8
37 Harold Road, E11
Wanstead Gardens, E11
Aldersbrook Gardens, E12
51 Tweedmouth Road, E13
12 Western Road, E13
84 Higham Street, E17
28a Worcester Road, E17
83 Cowslip Road, E18
85 Cowslip Road, E18
68 Derby Road, E18
Amwell Gardens, EC1
The Inner and Middle Temple Gardens, EC4

N and NW London
Arlington Square Gardens, N1
Barnsbury Group, N1
De Beauvoir Gardens, N1
57 Huntingdon Street, N1
King Henry's Walk Garden, N1
5 Northampton Park, N1
19 St Peter's Street, N1
6 Thornhill Road, N1
7 Deansway, N2
12 Lauradale Road, N2
24 Twyford Avenue, N2
4 Atterbury Road, N4
32 Highbury Place, N5
Olden Community Garden, N5
33 Hampstead Lane, N6
10 Furlong Road, N7
11 Park Avenue North, N8
Mona's Garden, N10

Princes Avenue Gardens, N10
5 St Regis Close, N10
25 Springfield Avenue, N10
Golf Course Allotments, N11
Holtwhites Bakery & Deli, N13
2 Conway Road, N14
70 Farleigh Road, N16
15 Norcott Road, N16
21 Gospatrick Road, N17
36 Ashley Road, N19
21 Oakleigh Park South, N20
10 York Road, N21
Ally Pally Allotments, N22
Railway Cottages, N22
2 Camden Mews, NW1
36 Park Village East, NW1
Royal College of Physicians, Garden of Medicinal Plants, NW1
Candlewood House Care Home, NW2
16 Purley Avenue, NW2
93 Tanfield Avenue, NW2
1A Primrose Gardens, NW3
The Mysteries of Light Rosary Garden, NW5
50 Deanscroft Avenue, NW9
25 Asmuns Hill, NW11
48 Erskine Hill, NW11
92 Hampstead Way, NW11
100 Hampstead Way, NW11

SE and SW London
Garden Barge Square at Tower Bridge Moorings, SE1
The Garden Museum, SE1
Lambeth Palace, SE1
71 Coldharbour Lane, SE5
24 Grove Park, SE5
16 Sears Street, SE5
30 Urlwin Street, SE5
41 Southbrook Road, SE12
Choumert Square, SE15
Court Lane Group, SE21
103 & 105 Dulwich Village, SE21
19 Lovelace Road, SE21
38 Lovelace Road, SE21
4 Piermont Green, SE22
86 Underhill Road, SE22
86A Underhill Road, SE22
58 Cranston Road, SE23
27 Horniman Drive, SE23
39 Wood Vale, SE23

5 Burbage Road, SE24
73 Fawnbrake Avenue, SE24
28 Ferndene Road, SE24
South London Botanical Institute, SE24
Stoney Hill House, SE26
Cadogan Place South Garden, SW1
Eccleston Square, SW1
Spencer House, SW1
62 Brixton Water Lane, SW2
51 The Chase, SW4
52 The Chase, SW4
Royal Trinity Hospice, SW4
35 Turret Grove, SW4
152a Victoria Rise, SW4
25 Stirling Road, SW9
Roehampton Garden Society Allotments, SW15
31 Ryecroft Road, SW16
61 Arthur Road, SW19
123 South Park Road, SW19
40 Bronson Road, SW20
35 Burstow Road, SW20
11 Ernle Road, SW20
Paddock Allotments & Leisure Gardens, SW20

W and WC London
Rooftopvegplot, W1
Warren Mews, W1
Hyde Park Estate Gardens, W2
118b Avenue Road, W3
29 Heathfield Road, W3
41 Mill Hill Road, W3
65 Mill Hill Road, W3
Zen Garden at Japanese Buddhist Centre, W3
Chiswick Mall Gardens, W4
Maggie's West London, W6
27 St Peters Square, W6
1 York Close, W7
Edwardes Square, W8
57 St Quintin Avenue, W10
Arundel & Elgin Gardens, W11
Arundel & Ladbroke Gardens, W11
4 Wharton Street, WC1X

Outer London postcodes

37 Crescent Road, BR3
20 Hazelmere Road, BR5
Tudeley House, BR7
59 Ashburton Avenue, CR0
MHA The Wilderness, CR9
Theobald's Farmhouse, EN2
West Lodge Park, EN4
190 Barnet Road, EN5
3 Old Fold Close, EN5
3 King Edward Road, EN8
9 Trafalgar Terrace, HA1
42 Risingholme Road, HA3
31 Arlington Drive, HA4
4 Manningtree Road, HA4
Long Cottage, HA5
Frith Lodge, HA6
Horatio's Garden, HA7
53 Lady Aylesford Avenue, HA7
26 Hillcroft Crescent, HA9
19 Rokeby Gardens, IG8
7 Woodbines Avenue, KT1
The Watergardens, KT2
Hampton Court Palace, KT8
5 Pemberton Road, KT8
Stud Nursery Community Garden, KT8
61 Wolsey Road, KT8
40 Ember Lane, KT10
9 Imber Park Road, KT10
The Bungalows, RM6
12 Cedar Avenue, RM14
Maggie's at The Royal Marsden, SM2
100 Colne Road, TW2
Sussex Cottage, TW3
116 Whitton Road, TW3
Kew Green Gardens, TW9
119 Mortlake Road, TW9
31 West Park Road, TW9
Cairn Cottage, TW10
Ormeley Lodge, TW10
Petersham House, TW10
93 Clarence Road, TW11
26 Teddington Park Road, TW11
Hampton House, TW12
16 Links View Road, TW12
106 Station Road, TW12
9 Warwick Close, TW12
70 Wensleydale Road, TW12
Church Gardens, UB9
61 The Courtway, WD19

OPENING DATES

All entries subject to change. For latest information check
www.ngs.org.uk

April

Sunday 6th
Edwardes Square, W8
🆕 Olden Community Garden, N5
Royal Trinity Hospice, SW4

Thursday 10th
♦ Hampton Court Palace, KT8

Sunday 13th
🆕 Hampton House, TW12
Petersham House, TW10
9 Warwick Close, TW12
39 Wood Vale, SE23

Wednesday 16th
39 Wood Vale, SE23

Sunday 20th
84 Lavender Grove, E8

Friday 25th
Maggie's at The Royal Marsden, SM2

Sunday 27th
51 The Chase, SW4
🆕 52 The Chase, SW4
Horatio's Garden, HA7
South London Botanical Institute, SE24
🆕 Wanstead Gardens, E11
The Watergardens, KT2

Tuesday 29th
51 The Chase, SW4

May

Sunday 4th
Garden Barge Square at Tower Bridge Moorings, SE1
42 Risingholme Road, HA3
5 St Regis Close, N10

Monday 5th
King Henry's Walk Garden, N1

Sunday 11th
Arundel & Ladbroke Gardens, W11
7 Deansway, N2
Eccleston Square, SW1
Royal Trinity Hospice, SW4
27 St Peters Square, W6

Saturday 17th
11 Ernle Road, SW20

Sunday 18th
Amwell Gardens, EC1
Arundel & Elgin Gardens, W11
190 Barnet Road, EN5
🆕 71 Coldharbour Lane, SE5
40 Ember Lane, KT10
11 Ernle Road, SW20
9 Imber Park Road, KT10
Kew Green Gardens, TW9
MHA The Wilderness, CR9
Princes Avenue Gardens, N10
🆕 16 Purley Avenue, NW2
Stoney Hill House, SE26
West Lodge Park, EN4

Monday 19th
♦ The Garden Museum, SE1
Lambeth Palace, SE1

Thursday 22nd
57 Huntingdon Street, N1

Saturday 24th
Cadogan Place South Garden, SW1
16 Links View Road, TW12

Sunday 25th
Aldersbrook Gardens, E12
36 Ashley Road, N19
Kew Green Gardens, TW9
16 Links View Road, TW12
Lower Clapton Gardens, E5
19 St Peter's Street, N1
12 Western Road, E13

Monday 26th
36 Ashley Road, N19
🆕 35 Burstow Road, SW20

Thursday 29th
57 Huntingdon Street, N1

Friday 30th
Chiswick Mall Gardens, W4

Saturday 31st
🆕 59 Ashburton Avenue, CR0
🆕 St Joseph's Hospice, E8

June

Sunday 1st
31 Arlington Drive, HA4
2 Camden Mews, NW1
Chiswick Mall Gardens, W4
Choumert Square, SE15
De Beauvoir Gardens, N1
10 Furlong Road, N7
92 Hampstead Way, NW11
100 Hampstead Way, NW11
Maggie's West London, W6
21 Oakleigh Park South, N20
Theobald's Farmhouse, EN2
61 Wolsey Road, KT8

Wednesday 4th
The Inner and Middle Temple Gardens, EC4

Saturday 7th
Hyde Park Estate Gardens, W2
41 Southbrook Road, SE12
Spitalfields Gardens, E1
70 Wensleydale Road, TW12
Zen Garden at Japanese Buddhist Centre, W3

Sunday 8th
Barnsbury Group, N1
51 The Chase, SW4
🆕 52 The Chase, SW4
68 Derby Road, E18
20 Hazelmere Road, BR5
27 Horniman Drive, SE23
London Fields Gardens, E8

36 Park Village East, NW1
Royal Trinity Hospice, SW4
41 Southbrook Road, SE12
25 Springfield Avenue, N10
Tudeley House, BR7
152a Victoria Rise, SW4
70 Wensleydale Road, TW12
7 Woodbines Avenue, KT1
Zen Garden at Japanese Buddhist Centre, W3

Saturday 14th
The Mysteries of Light Rosary Garden, NW5

Sunday 15th
🆕 25 Asmuns Hill, NW11
26 College Gardens, E4
28 Ferndene Road, SE24
37 Harold Road, E11
32 Highbury Place, N5
4 Wharton Street, WC1X

Saturday 21st
Paddock Allotments & Leisure Gardens, SW20
Roehampton Garden Society Allotments, SW15
6 Thornhill Road, N1

Sunday 22nd
Ally Pally Allotments, N22
61 Arthur Road, SW19
🆕 Cairn Cottage, TW10
♦ Church Gardens, UB9
37 Crescent Road, BR3
103 & 105 Dulwich Village, SE21
🆕 33 Hampstead Lane, N6
🆕 Long Cottage, HA5
38 Lovelace Road, SE21
🆕 19 Lovelace Road, SE21
Ormeley Lodge, TW10
31 Ryecroft Road, SW16
123 South Park Road, SW19
Warren Mews, W1

Sunday 29th
Arlington Square Gardens, N1
Court Lane Group, SE21
70 Farleigh Road, N16

LONDON 341

July

Saturday 5th
26 Hillcroft Crescent, HA9
Rooftopvegplot, W1

Sunday 6th
69 Antill Road, E3
118b Avenue Road, W3
NEW 12 Cedar Avenue, RM14
83 Cowslip Road, E18
NEW 85 Cowslip Road, E18
NEW 73 Fawnbrake Avenue, SE24
NEW 29 Heathfield Road, W3
84 Higham Street, E17
26 Hillcroft Crescent, HA9
NEW 119 Mortlake Road, TW9
NEW 3 Old Fold Close, EN5
Railway Cottages, N22
Rooftopvegplot, W1
57 St Quintin Avenue, W10
Sussex Cottage, TW3
NEW 26 Teddington Park Road, TW11
31 West Park Road, TW9
116 Whitton Road, TW3

Monday 7th
Royal College of Physicians, Garden of Medicinal Plants, NW1

Thursday 10th
◆ Hampton Court Palace, KT8

Friday 11th
NEW Candlewood House Care Home, NW2

Saturday 12th
4 Atterbury Road, N4
5 Northampton Park, N1

Sunday 13th
NEW 93 Clarence Road, TW11
5 Pemberton Road, KT8

NEW Stud Nursery Community Garden, KT8

Saturday 19th
NEW 50 Deanscroft Avenue, NW9
NEW Frith Lodge, HA6
106 Station Road, TW12
NEW 25 Stirling Road, SW9

Sunday 20th
NEW Frith Lodge, HA6
42 Latimer Road, E7
11 Park Avenue North, N8
57 St Quintin Avenue, W10
NEW 16 Sears Street, SE5
106 Station Road, TW12
93 Tanfield Avenue, NW2
35 Turret Grove, SW4
24 Twyford Avenue, N2
30 Urlwin Street, SE5

Sunday 27th
100 Colne Road, TW2
58 Cranston Road, SE23

August

Saturday 2nd
The Bungalows, RM6
53 Lady Aylesford Avenue, HA7

Sunday 3rd
The Bungalows, RM6
5 St Regis Close, N10

Sunday 10th
NEW Candlewood House Care Home, NW2
NEW 3 King Edward Road, EN8
4 Manningtree Road, HA4
51 Tweedmouth Road, E13

Friday 15th
41 Mill Hill Road, W3
65 Mill Hill Road, W3

Saturday 16th
The Bungalows, RM6
1 York Close, W7

Sunday 17th
The Bungalows, RM6
51 The Chase, SW4
NEW 52 The Chase, SW4
4 Piermont Green, SE22
86 Underhill Road, SE22

NEW 86A Underhill Road, SE22
9 Warwick Close, TW12
1 York Close, W7

Saturday 23rd
NEW 22 Betoyne Avenue, E4

Sunday 24th
NEW 61 The Courtway, WD19

Saturday 30th
The Bungalows, RM6
2 Conway Road, N14

Sunday 31st
The Bungalows, RM6
42 Risingholme Road, HA3

September

Saturday 6th
NEW 25 Stirling Road, SW9
9 Trafalgar Terrace, HA1

Sunday 7th
NEW Candlewood House Care Home, NW2
Golf Course Allotments, N11
24 Grove Park, SE5
12 Lauradale Road, N2

Sunday 14th
NEW 40 Bronson Road, SW20
Royal Trinity Hospice, SW4

Saturday 20th
1A Primrose Gardens, NW3

Sunday 21st
1A Primrose Gardens, NW3

October

Sunday 26th
The Watergardens, KT2
West Lodge Park, EN4

By Arrangement

Arrange a personalised garden visit with your club, or group of friends, on a date to suit you. See individual garden entries for full details.

8 Almack Road, Lower Clapton Gardens, E5
36 Ashley Road, N19
118b Avenue Road, W3
190 Barnet Road, EN5
62 Brixton Water Lane, SW2
5 Burbage Road, SE24
NEW Candlewood House Care Home, NW2
51 The Chase, SW4
100 Colne Road, TW2
7 Deansway, N2
40 Ember Lane, KT10
11 Ernle Road, SW20
48 Erskine Hill, NW11
21 Gospatrick Road, N17
NEW 33 Hampstead Lane, N6
NEW Hampton House, TW12
26 Hillcroft Crescent, HA9
57 Huntingdon Street, N1
9 Imber Park Road, KT10
NEW 3 King Edward Road, EN8
12 Lauradale Road, N2
84 Lavender Grove, E8
NEW Long Cottage, HA5
41 Mill Hill Road, W3
65 Mill Hill Road, W3
Mona's Garden, N10
The Mysteries of Light Rosary Garden, NW5
15 Norcott Road, N16
21 Oakleigh Park South, N20
1A Primrose Gardens, NW3
27 St Peters Square, W6
57 St Quintin Avenue, W10
5 St Regis Close, N10
93 Tanfield Avenue, NW2
Tudeley House, BR7
24 Twyford Avenue, N2
152a Victoria Rise, SW4
9 Warwick Close, TW12
West Lodge Park, EN4
4 Wharton Street, WC1X
28a Worcester Road, E17

NEW Holtwhites Bakery & Deli, N13
NEW 19 Rokeby Gardens, IG8
5 St Regis Close, N10
10 York Road, N21

THE GARDENS

GROUP OPENING
ALDERSBROOK GARDENS, E12
Wanstead, E12 5ES. *Empress Ave is a turning off Aldersbrook Rd. Bus 101 from Manor Park or Wanstead stns. From Manor Park stn take the 3rd R off Aldersbrook Rd. From Wanstead, drive past St Gabriel's Church, take 6th turning on L.* **Sun 25 May (1-5). Combined adm £5, chd free. Tea, coffee & cake at 16 Wanstead Park Avenue.**

19 BELGRAVE ROAD
Gill Usher.

39 DOVER ROAD
Brenda Keer.

NEW 16 WANSTEAD PARK AVENUE
Mrs Ruth Seager.

Three town gardens situated in the Aldersbrook Estate between Wanstead Park and Wanstead Flats. 19 Belgrave Road is a diverse garden. Eclectic and bursting at the seams with trees and plants. Gill is a ceramicist who uses the plants in her garden studio. 39 Dover Road has a surviving Edwardian layout with mature trees (inc a female *Ginkgo biloba*) and shrubs. 16 Wanstead Park Avenue is a cottage garden with mixed planting irrigated by a grey water system.

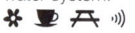

ALLY PALLY ALLOTMENTS, N22
Alexandra Palace Way, N22 7BB. Peter Campbell. *Entry gate in fence, nr footpath to Springfield Ave & Alexandra Palace Garden Centre, follow NGS signs. Bus W3 to Alexandra Palace Garden Centre. Parking nearby in Duke's Ave, N10. Blue Badge holder parking in The Grove. No parking onsite.* **Sun 22 June (1-4.30). Adm £5, chd free. Home-made teas.**
Situated on a south facing hillside alongside Alexandra Park, this 140 plot allotment site has the feel of an urban village with spectacular views towards central London and, on a clear day, the North Downs. Its diverse community of gardeners grow fruit, vegetables and flowers with an emphasis on promoting biodiversity.

Clearly marked trails will enable you to explore the site and meet plotholders. Plants, produce and used tools on sale. Pre-booking preferred or please bring cash on the day for admission. Card reader available for teas and produce.

GROUP OPENING
AMWELL GARDENS, EC1
South Islington, EC1R 1YE. *Tube: Angel, 5 min walk. Buses: 19, 38 to Rosebery Ave; 30, 73 to Pentonville Rd.* **Sun 18 May (2.30-6). Combined adm £7.50, chd free. Home-made teas.**

LLOYD SQUARE
Lloyd Square Garden Committee.

NEW RIVER HEAD
NRH Residents.

The Amwell Gardens group is in a secluded corner of Georgian Clerkenwell. Contrasting gardens of Lloyd Square, a mature space with drifting borders in the centre of the Lloyd Baker Estate and the nearby gardens surrounding the historic New River Head, where a stylish fountain and pergola have replaced the outer pond, which distributed fresh water to London.

---

69 ANTILL ROAD, E3
Bow, E3 5BT. Mr William Dowden. *Short walk from Mile End tube or buses 277, 339, 425 & D6 on Grove Rd.* **Sun 6 July (1-7). Adm £5, chd free. Tea.**
A tropically inspired garden with a range of trees and shrubs. The garden is divided into rooms which show off the elegance of hydrangeas and roses and the lushness of palms, yews and acers. There are several water features and an elegant gazebo. A tranquil place in which to relax with friends and family.

---

31 ARLINGTON DRIVE, HA4
Ruislip, HA4 7RJ. John & Yasuko O'Gorman. *Tube: Ruislip, then bus H13 to Arlington Dr (opp Millar & Carter), or 15 min walk up Bury St). Please note: No parking on Arlington Dr. Ample parking on roads south of Arlington Dr.* **Sun 1 June (2-5). Adm £5, chd free. Home-made teas.**

Cottage garden at heart with a wonderful oriental influence. Traditional cottage garden favourites have been combined with Japanese plants, a reflection of Yasuko's passion for plants and trees of her native Japan. Acers, tree peonies, rhododendrons and flowering cherries underplanted with hostas, ferns, hellebores and perennials create a lush exotic scheme, with emphasis on structure and texture.

GROUP OPENING
ARLINGTON SQUARE GARDENS, N1
N1 7DP. *South Islington. Off New North Rd via Arlington Ave or Linton St. Buses: 21, 76, 141. 15 min walk from Angel tube. LTNs operate in this area. Free parking on Sundays.* **Sun 29 June (2-5.30). Combined adm £10, chd free.**

4 ARLINGTON AVENUE
Helen Nowicka.

15 ARLINGTON AVENUE
Armin Eiber & Richard Armit.

26 ARLINGTON AVENUE
Thomas Blaikie, www.instagram.com/thomas_blaikie.

21 ARLINGTON SQUARE
Alison Rice.

25 ARLINGTON SQUARE
Michael Foley.

30 ARLINGTON SQUARE
James & Maria Hewson.

5 REES STREET
Gordon McArthur & Paul Thompson-McArthur.

Seven early Victorian terraced houses with similar sized small gardens and conditions but with very different garden styles. From a garden designer's exotic contemporary space to an organic wildlife haven, there should be something for all gardeners, whether green-fingered or complete beginners: exotic and unusual plants, gorgeous flowers, lawn paths, hard landscaping, composting, rewilding, thrifty up-cycling, fruit, vegetables, herbs, beehives and a wildlife pond. These gardens reflect the diverse tastes and interests of friends who got to know each other through community gardening, helping transform and maintain Arlington Square from a drab and rundown space to an award-winning beautiful

11 Park Avenue North

and plant-rich public garden which, like the seven private gardens, offers a calm oasis just minutes from the bustle of the City of London. Entrance to all the gardens involves steps. The only step-free exception is Arlington Square public garden.

🛋 ⬤))

61 ARTHUR ROAD, SW19
Wimbledon, SW19 7DN. Daniela McBride. *5 mins from St Mary's Church. Tube: Wimbledon Park, then 8 min walk. Train: Wimbledon, 18 min walk.* **Sun 22 June (2-6). Adm £5, chd free. Home-made teas. Open nearby 123 South Park Road.**
This steeply, sloping garden comprises woodland walks filled with flowering shrubs and ferns. In early summer the focus is the many roses grown around the garden, alongside colourful perennials and a productive herb garden. Partial wheelchair access to top lawn and terrace only, steep slopes elsewhere.

🛋 ✹ ☕ ⬤))

ARUNDEL & ELGIN GARDENS, W11
Kensington Park Road, Notting Hill, W11 2JD. Residents of Arundel Gardens & Elgin Crescent, www.instagram.com/arundelelgin. *Entrance opp 174 Kensington Park Rd. Nearest tube within walking distance: Ladbroke Grove (5 mins), Notting Hill Gate (15 mins), Holland Park (15 mins). Buses: 52, 452, 23, 228 all stop opp garden entrance.* **Sun 18 May (2-6). Adm £5, chd free. Home-made teas.**
A friendly and informal garden square. One of the best preserved gardens of the Ladbroke Estate with mature and rare trees, plants and shrubs laid out according to the original Victorian design of 1862. The larger garden inc a topiary hedge, a rare mulberry tree, a pergola and benches from which vistas can be enjoyed. The central hedged garden is an oasis of tranquillity with extensive and colourful herbaceous borders. All looked after by Gardener, Paul Walsh. Play areas for young children.

🛋 ✹ ☕ ⬤))

ARUNDEL & LADBROKE GARDENS, W11
Kensington Park Road, Notting Hill, W11 2PT. Arundel & Ladbroke Gardens Committee, www.arundelladbrokegardens.co.uk. *Entrance on Kensington Park Rd, between Ladbroke & Arundel Gardens. Tube: Notting Hill Gate or Ladbroke Grove. Buses: 23, 52, 228, 452. Alight at stop for Portobello Market/Arundel Gardens.* **Sun 11 May (2-6). Adm £5, chd free.**
This private communal garden is one of the few that retains its attractive mid-Victorian design of lawns and winding paths. A woodland garden at its peak in spring with rhododendrons, flowering dogwoods, early roses, bulbs, ferns and rare exotics. Picnics welcome and local bakeries and food shops nearby. Playground for small children. Wheelchair access with a few steps and gravel paths to negotiate.

🛋 ✹ ⬤))

NEW **59 ASHBURTON AVENUE, CR0**
Croydon, CR0 7JG. Paul Cooper & Neil Miller. *South London. What3words app: ground.manliness.badly.* **Sat 31 May (1-4.30). Adm £6, chd free. Tea, coffee & cake.**
Stroll around a ⅓ acre enclosed suburban garden, whilst enjoying imaginative planting in flowing borders. Explore a mixture of cottage garden and hardy tropical plants, and be surprised by some rarities you might not expect to see growing outdoors in the UK. Good selection of hedychiums, pelargoniums, heliotropes, agave/mangaves and proposed National Dispersed Collection of Ajuga. Features inc a wildlife pond, beehives, a 12' x 8' greenhouse, herb garden, and several seating areas. Level wheelchair access to main garden.

🛋 ✹ ☕

36 ASHLEY ROAD, N19
Crouch Hill, N19 3AF. Alan Swann & Ahmed Farooqui, swann.alan@googlemail.com, www.instagram.com/space36garden. *Between Stroud Green & Crouch End. Tube: Archway or Finsbury Park. Overground: Crouch Hill. Buses: 210 or 41 from Archway to Hornsey Rise. W7 from Finsbury Park to Heathville Rd. Car: Free parking in Ashley Rd at weekends.* **Sun 25, Mon 26 May (2-6). Adm £5, chd free. Home-made teas.** Visits also by arrangement May to Aug for groups of up to 40. Optional talk on the development of the garden.
A lush town garden rich in textures, colour and forms. At its best in late spring as Japanese maple cultivars display great variety of shape and colour whilst ferns unfurl fresh, vibrant fronds over a tumbling stream, and wisteria and clematis burst into flower on the balcony and pergola. A number of microhabitats inc fern walls, bog garden, stream and ponds, rockeries, alpine and shade plantings. Young ferns and plants propagated from the garden for sale. Pop-up café with a variety of cakes, biscuits, gluten free and vegan options, and traditional home-brewed ginger beer. Seating areas around the garden.

♿ ✿ ☕ 🔊

NEW 25 ASMUNS HILL, NW11
Golders Green, NW11 6ES. Lorraine Wilder. *North West London. Tube: Golders Green then buses 82, 102, 460 to Temple Fortune, then 2 mins walk along Hampstead Way. Asmuns Hill 2nd on L.* **Sun 15 June (1.30-5.30). Adm £7, chd free. Home-made teas.**
Set in the historic Artisans' Quarter of Hampstead Garden Suburb, this ½ acre garden is, to quote Alys Fowler 'a charming and inspiring take on the rural idyll'. Three distinct areas, a formal area filled with colour and a rose arbour, a vegetable plot, and a secret orchard with a wildflower area, log piles, rose dragon structure, walnut and hazel trees.

♿ ✿ ☕ 🔊

4 ATTERBURY ROAD, N4
Harringay, N4 1SF. Clare & Raj Panjwani. *Harringay Ladder. Closest stns: Harringay overground, Manor House tube. Buses 29, 141, 341 to Green Ln, then walk.* **Sat 12 July (2-6). Adm £5, chd free. Cream teas.**
Four yrs ago, this garden underwent a complete transformation. Once a traditional suburban lawn and border garden, the owners turned it into a lush oasis for practical outdoor living. At its heart lies a serene pond, encircled by a walkway that guides you through banana palms, kiwis, figs, grapevines, and apricots. An ash deck, oak bench cooking area, and self-built greenhouse complete the space.

☕ 🔊

118B AVENUE ROAD, W3
Acton, W3 8QG. Gareth Sinclair, 07713 020002, garethsinclair65@yahoo.com. *Go to block 118, look R & go through gates to arrive at 118b. 10 mins walk from Acton Town tube stn or South Acton overground stn.* **Sun 6 July (2-6). Combined adm with 29 Heathfield Road £7, chd free. Tea, coffee & cake.** Visits also by arrangement 3 May to 12 Oct for groups of up to 20.
Acquired just before lockdown and built on builders' rubble (150 tons of which had to be removed) the garden is maturing nicely. Its purpose is to encourage wildlife with its planting and design. Beehive, wormery, stumpery, ponds, orchard, and much more.

✿ 🚗 ☕ 🔊

190 BARNET ROAD, EN5
The Upcycled Garden, Arkley, Barnet, EN5 3LF. Hilde Wainstein, 07949 764007, hildewainstein@hotmail.co.uk. *1m S of A1, 2m N of High Barnet tube stn. Garden located on corner of A411 Barnet Rd & Meadowbanks cul-de-sac. Nearest tube: High Barnet, then 107 bus, Glebe Ln stop. Ample unrestricted roadside parking. NB Do not park half on pavement.* **Sun 18 May (2-5.30). Adm £5, chd free. Home-made teas & gluten free options.** Visits also by arrangement 19 May to 7 Sept for groups of up to 25.
Walled garden, 90ft x 36ft with a modern design and year-round interest. Handmade copper pipe trellis divides space into contrasting areas. Herbaceous planting and bulbs drift around trees, shrubs and pond. Kitchen garden with soft fruit and vegetables. Upcycled containers, recycled objects, and home-made sculptures. Gravel garden areas that are never watered. Garden continues evolving as planted areas are expanded. Organic. Home-made jams and plants for sale, all propagated from the garden.
Wheelchair access with single steps within garden.

♿ ✿ ☕ 🔊

GROUP OPENING

BARNSBURY GROUP, N1
N1 1BX. *Barnsbury N1. Tube: King's Cross, Caledonian Rd or Angel. Train: Caledonian Rd & Barnsbury. Buses: 17, 91, 259 to Caledonian Rd. Buses: 4, 19, 30, 38, 43 to St Mary's Church, Upper St, for Lonsdale Sq.* **Sun 8 June (2-6). Combined adm £12, chd free. Home-made teas at 57 Huntingdon Street. Individual garden £4 each.**

♦ **BARNSBURY WOOD**
London Borough of Islington, ecologycentre@islington.gov.uk.

57 HUNTINGDON STREET
Julian Williams.
(See separate entry)

2 LONSDALE SQUARE
Jenny Kingsley.

36 THORNHILL SQUARE
Anna & Christopher McKane.

Discover four contrasting spaces in Barnsbury's Georgian squares. 57 Huntingdon Street is a secluded garden with birches, ferns, perennials, grasses and container ponds to encourage wildlife. 36 Thornhill Square, a 120ft garden with a country atmosphere, is filled with scented roses, clematis, specimen trees, perennials and a wildlife pond. Bonsai and planters surround the patio. 2 Lonsdale Square is a charming small cobblestoned garden with herbaceous beds and apple trees, structured with euonymus and yew hedges. Climbing roses and star jasmine add delicious scent; planters overflow with lavender and pansies. Barnsbury Wood is London's smallest nature reserve, a hidden gem and one of Islington's few sites of semi-mature woodland, a tranquil oasis of wild flowers and massive trees minutes from Caledonian Road. Wildlife information available. The gardens reveal what can be achieved with the right plants in the right conditions, surmounting difficulties of dry walls and shade. 36 Thornhill Square won Gold Award, Best Hidden Gem, Islington In Bloom 2024. Unusual plants for sale at 36 Thornhill Square.

✿ ☕ 🔊

22 BETOYNE AVENUE, E4
Chingford, E4 9SG. **Rebecca & Tim Rowden-Birch.** *From Winston Churchill statue r'about turn L onto Chingford Ln/A1009. Turn L onto Betoyne Ave. Chingford Ln has speed limit of 20 mph.* **Sat 23 Aug (3-5). Adm £4, chd free. Tea, coffee & cake.**
Rewilded garden using agroforestry principles on the edges of Epping Forest. Modern arbours and terracing, pollinator friendly borders, productive vegetable garden, tropical wildlife pond and a forest garden leading down to the River Ching. Borrowed landscape from beautiful mature broadleaf trees. A tranquil haven on a 1950s street in Highams Park.

62 BRIXTON WATER LANE, SW2
Brixton, SW2 1QB. **Daisy Garnett & Nicholas Pearson,** 07764 614080, dgarnett@mac.com. *Tube: Brixton. Train: Herne Hill, both 10 mins. Buses: 3, 37, 196 or 2, 415, 432 along Tulse Hill.* **Visits by arrangement May, June & Sept for groups of 6 to 12.**
Country garden with exuberant borders of soft colours, a productive greenhouse and a mass of pots on the terrace. Plenty of spring and summer interest from magnolias, roses, peonies and other perennials and, in September, dahlias and various annuals.

NEW 40 BRONSON ROAD, SW20
West Wimbledon, SW20 8DY. **Sara Faulkner.** *7 min walk from Wimbledon Chase stn; 13 min walk from Raynes Park stn. Free on street parking at weekends.* **Sun 14 Sept (12-5). Adm £5, chd free. Pre-booking essential, please visit www.ngs.org.uk for information & booking. Light refreshments.**
This very small prize-winning garden, winner of BBC Gardeners' World Garden of the Year 2024, 'Judges' Choice', approx 60 square metres, designed for year-round interest. There are three distinct areas filled with perennials, shrubs and climbers, pollinator-friendly flowers and vintage or reclaimed furniture and pots. The summerhouse is a repurposed cabin and makes a lovely lounge and art studio. There is a canopy of small trees, mainly fruit trees, creating privacy and shelter for the seating areas.

THE BUNGALOWS, RM6
2 Kenneth Road, Romford, RM6 6QR. **John Seaman.** *Close to Chadwell Heath stn if arriving by train.* **Sat 2, Sun 3, Sat 16, Sun 17, Sat 30, Sun 31 Aug (10-5). Adm £4, chd free. Tea.**
A new garden featuring a wide range of exotic style planting, inc canna, ginger, and bananas amongst many other plants. Rich in colour, shape, and form, with several ponds with frogs. This evolving garden has no grass, replaced with wood chips, and is filled with good ideas for small gardens.

5 BURBAGE ROAD, SE24
Herne Hill, SE24 9HJ. **Crawford & Rosemary Lindsay,** 020 7274 5610, rl@rosemarylindsay.com, www.rosemarylindsay.com. *Nr junction with Half Moon Ln. Herne Hill & N Dulwich train stns, 5 min walk. Buses: 3, 37, 40, 68, 196, 468.* **Visits by arrangement 15 Mar to 21 Sept. Light refreshments. Payment by cash, cheque or BACS.**
The garden of a member of The Society of Botanical Artists and regular writer for Hortus journal. 150ft x 40ft with large and varied range of plants, many unusual. Herbaceous borders for sun and shade, climbing plants, pots, terraces and lawns. Immaculate topiary. Gravel areas to reduce watering. All the box has been removed because of attack by blight and moth, and replaced with suitable alternatives to give a similar look. A garden that delights from spring through to summer.

NEW 35 BURSTOW ROAD, SW20
Wimbledon, SW20 8ST. **Martin & Primavera Moretti.** *Wimbledon/Raynes Park. 15 min walk from Wimbledon tube. 15 min bus, plus 5 min walk from South Wimbledon. Limited free parking on Burstow Rd.* **Mon 26 May (10-4). Adm £4, chd free. Tea, coffee & cake inc gluten free options.**
A small suburban garden packed with herbaceous perennials and seasonal bedding displays. Features inc an ornamental fish pond, a small wildlife pond and herb garden. A good example of what can be achieved in a small space with a bit of love and attention.

CADOGAN PLACE SOUTH GARDEN, SW1
93 Sloane Street, Knightsbridge, SW1X 9RX. **The Cadogan Estate,** www.cadogan.co.uk. *Directly opp Cadogan House, 93 Sloane St, SW1X 9PD.* **Sat 24 May (10-4). Adm £5, chd free.**
Many surprises, unusual trees and shrubs are hidden behind the railings of this large London square. The first square to be developed by architect Henry Holland for Lord Cadogan at the end of C18, it was then called the London Botanic Garden. Mulberry trees planted for silk production at end of C17. Cherry trees, wisteria pergola and bulbs are outstanding in spring. Beautiful 300 yr old black mulberry tree (originally planted to produce silk, but incorrect variety!). Area of drought resistant, pollinator plants. This was once the home of the Royal Botanic Garden. Now featuring a bug hotel, children's playground and four wildlife ponds.

NEW CAIRN COTTAGE, TW10
Upper Ham Road, Richmond, TW10 5LA. **Rachel Lipscomb.** *At the end of driveway next to Hand & Flower pub, opp Ham Common. No. 65 bus from Richmond to Kingston every 6 mins. 400yds from bus stop on Ham Parade. Parking on Ham Common.* **Sun 22 June (3-6). Adm £4, chd free. Open nearby Ormeley Lodge.**
Around Cairn Cottage is a hidden garden with magnificent magnolia and robinias underplanted with interesting shrubs and roses. There are many herbaceous perennials and stunning hydrangea 'Annabelle' in a contemporary setting.

2 CAMDEN MEWS, NW1
Camden Town, NW1 9DB. **Annabel & Beverley Rowe.** *Arriving by bus, take 29 or 253 to Murray St. Go N for a couple of mins & turn R on Murray St. Take 1st R on Camden Mews & you will see the yellow signs.* **Sun 1 June (3-6). Adm £5, chd free. Light refreshments.**
Twenty yrs ago, two long gardens were turned into one. This resulted in a good sized garden, unusually broad for London and very secluded. Established trees, shrubs and flower beds break up the space so you don't see it all at once. A pool with good marginal planting. Wheelchair access over paved paths. No steps or narrow spaces.

LONDON

NEW CANDLEWOOD HOUSE CARE HOME, NW2
Bentley Drive, Cricklewood, NW2 2TD. Jan Guerin, 020 3893 2929, bdm@candlewoodhouse.co.uk, www.tlccare.co.uk/homes/candlewood-house. *Located nr Child's Hill Library on Cricklewood Ln with access via Bentley Dr. Look for the green and orange flag post at the entrance. Bus routes 245, 460 & 113 stop outside the home.* **Fri 11 July, Sun 10 Aug, Sun 7 Sept (1.30-5.30). Adm £5, chd free. Tea, coffee, cakes & sandwiches. Adm inc a cup of tea.** Visits also by arrangement 7 Mar to 30 Sept for groups of up to 30.

Our care home features a beautiful, accessible central courtyard garden designed for residents, families, and visitors. With ample seating, bird feeders, and a greenhouse project underway, the garden showcases tall sunflowers, tomatoes, ferns, camellias, grasses, hostas, and a serene pond. Enjoy a visit with tea and cakes, and friendly company beneath our cercis trees and vibrant Japanese anemones. Our garden has full wheelchair access.

NEW 12 CEDAR AVENUE, RM14
Upminster, RM14 2LW. Joan & Chris Allen. *Tube: Upminster Bridge. Rail: From A124 Hall Ln down to T-lights turn R, take 2nd L into Bridge Ave, R at South View Dr, then L into Cedar Ave.* **Sun 6 July (1-5). Adm £5, chd free. Tea, coffee & cake.**

An enchanting garden, approx 140ft x 40ft, full of colour, inc specimen trees, shrubs, and water features. Planted small rooms with secluded seating areas, a fun summerhouse, and a fish pond. There is lots of interest throughout. Classical music played by Grandson who is a composer at the Royal College of Music.

51 THE CHASE, SW4
SW4 0NP. Mr Charles Rutherfoord & Mr Rupert Tyler, 07841 418399, charles@charlesrutherfoord.net, www.charlesrutherfoord.net. *Off Clapham Common Northside. Tube: Clapham Common. Buses: 137, 452, 77, 87, 345, 37.* **Sun 27 Apr (12-5). Combined adm with 52 The Chase £8.50, chd free. Evening opening Tue 29 Apr (5.30-8). Adm £5, chd free. Sun 8 June, Sun 17 Aug (12-5). Combined adm with 52 The Chase £8.50, chd free. Entry to one garden: Adult £5, chd free. Light refreshments. Open nearby Royal Trinity Hospice & 152a Victoria Rise on 8 June only.** Visits also by arrangement 21 Apr to 12 Oct for groups of 10 to 30.

Charles, past Chairman of Society of Garden Designers, and Rupert, Chairman of NGS, have created the garden over 40 yrs. Spectacular in spring when 2500 tulips bloom among camellias, irises and tree peonies. Scented front garden. Rupert's geodetic dome shelters seedlings, succulents and the subtropical. Roses, brugmansia, hibiscus and dahlias later in the season. New vegetable garden added in 2023.

NEW 52 THE CHASE, SW4
Clapham, SW4 0NH. *Off Clapham Common Northside. Tube: Clapham Common. Buses: 137, 452, 77, 87, 345, 37.* **Sun 27 Apr, Sun 8 June, Sun 17 Aug (12-5). Combined adm with 51 The Chase £8.50, chd free. Entry to one garden: Adult £5, chd free. Light refreshments at 51 The Chase. Open nearby Royal Trinity Hospice & 152a Victoria Rise on 8 June only.**

52 The Chase is a newly created garden which inc existing and established planting. Garden designer Charles Rutherfoord worked closely with the owners to make a space of calm and quiet reflection as well as for entertaining. Old climbing roses and well established camellias fuse with acers and hydrangeas. A stunning cascade links the terraced beds of tree ferns, hostas, and Musa. Darley stone and Gault brick paviours add to the sense of sanctuary and harmony. Not suitable for those unsteady on their feet.

GROUP OPENING

CHISWICK MALL GARDENS, W4
Chiswick Mall, Chiswick, W4 2PF. *By car: Hogarth r'about turn down Church St or A4 (W), turn L to Eyot Gardens. Tube: Stamford Brook or Turnham Green, walk under A4 to river. Buses: 110, 190, 267, H91.* **Evening opening Fri 30 May (6-8). Combined adm £12.50, chd free. Wine at Miller's Court on 30 May only. Sun 1 June (1-5). Combined adm £15, chd free.**

CEDAR HOUSE
Stephanie & Philippe Camu.
Open on all dates

FIELD HOUSE
Rupert King,
www.fieldhousegarden.co.uk.
Open on all dates

LONGMEADOW
Charlotte Fraser.
Open on Sun 1 June

MILLER'S COURT
Miller's Court Tenants Ltd.
Open on all dates

THE OLD VICARAGE
Eleanor Fein.
Open on Sun 1 June

ST JOHN'S
George Spalton KC & Jemma Spalton.
Open on Sun 1 June

ST PETERS WHARF
Barbara Brown.
Open on all dates

SWAN HOUSE
Mr & Mrs George Nissen.
Open on all dates

Gardens on or near the Thames in historic Old Chiswick. You will visit a riverside garden in an artist's community, several large walled gardens, and a communal garden on the riverbank with well-planted borders and lovely views. Field House will feature in Gardeners' World magazine (May 2025).

CHOUMERT SQUARE, SE15
Off Choumert Grove, Peckham, SE15 4RE. The Residents. *Close to Choumert Grove car park. Off Choumert Grove. Trains from London Victoria, London Bridge, London Blackfriars, Clapham Junction to Peckham Rye; buses 12, 36, 37, 63, 78, 171, 312, 345. Choumert Grove car park free on Sundays.* **Sun 1 June (1-6). Adm £5, chd free. Savoury items, home-made teas & Pimms.** Donation to St Christopher's Hospice.

About 46 mini cottage gardens with maxi planting in a Shangri-la situation that the media has described as a floral canyon leading to a small communal secret garden. The day is primarily about gardens and sharing with others our residents' love of this little corner of the inner city, but it is also renowned for its demonstrable community spirit and a variety of stalls and attractions. Wheelchair access;

one tiny step to raised paved area in the communal garden.

♦ **CHURCH GARDENS, UB9**
Church Hill, Harefield, Uxbridge, UB9 6DU. **Patrick & Kay McHugh,** 01895 823539, churchgardensharefield@gmail.com, www.churchgardens.co.uk. *From Harefield village, continue for ¼ m down Church Hill. From A40 Uxbridge junction, follow signs to Harefield. Turn off Church Hill towards St Mary's Church.* **For NGS: Sun 22 June (11-5). Adm £7, chd £4. Pre-booking preferred, please visit www.churchgardens.co.uk for information & booking. Light refreshments. For other opening times and information, please phone, email or visit garden website.** Harefield's own secret garden. C17 Renaissance walled gardens on the outskirts of Harefield inc a geometrically designed organic kitchen garden, 60 metre long herbaceous borders, fruit cage, alpines, herb garden, vine mount and an orchard with large wildlife pond, forest garden and rare arcaded wall, dating back to the early 1600s. Unique opportunity to view ongoing restoration project. Lunches between 12-3pm and a selection of home-made cakes and drinks available throughout the day.

🆕 **93 CLARENCE ROAD, TW11**
Teddington, TW11 0BN. **Kate Brittin.** *10 min walk from Teddington stn. Limited parking in street.* **Sun 13 July (12-4). Adm £6, chd free. Home-made teas.**
The owner of this garden is a plant enthusiast and passionate about wildlife. Connected by pathways and a central lawn are a kitchen garden with vegetable beds, soft fruit, espalier apples and pears; a gravel courtyard garden with a potting shed and greenhouse; a formal natural swimming pond and summerhouse; herbaceous borders and a small fernery; chickens and bees; and a veranda and conservatory.

🆕 **71 COLDHARBOUR LANE, SE5**
SE5 9NS. **Mr Joshua May,** www.instagram.com/theurban_gardener. *Close to both Denmark Hill & Loughborough Junction train stns.* **Sun 18 May (11-3). Adm £4, chd free. Tea, coffee & cake.**

A front garden designed to brighten up a neighbouring bus stop and small (7 x 5 metre) cottage back garden planted for bees and butterflies. Featuring rambling, climbing and shrub roses and a variety of other native and exotic plants. Aiming for continuous flowers from winter Scillonian narcissi to autumn dahlias.

26 COLLEGE GARDENS, E4
Chingford, E4 7LG. **Lynnette Parvez.** *2m from Walthamstow. 15 min walk from Chingford train stn. Bus 97 from Walthamstow Central tube stn, alight at College Gardens, then short walk downhill.* **Sun 15 June (2-5). Adm £4, chd free.**
Large suburban garden, approx ⅔ acre. Sun terrace leads to established borders and a variety of climbing roses. Beyond this, wildlife pond and lawn, small woodland walk with spring plants and wildlife. A further area to the end with raised vegetable beds.

100 COLNE ROAD, TW2
Twickenham, TW2 6QE. **Karen Grosch,** 020 8893 3660, info@whettonandgrosch.co.uk, www.instagram.com/karensroofgarden. *5 min walk from Twickenham Green. 12 min walk from Twickenham or Strawberry Hill train stn. Bus 406, H22 from Richmond train & tube stn, alight Twickenham Green, then short walk. By road, turn off Staines Rd coming from M25/M3 & A416.* **Sun 27 July (11-6). Adm £7. Pre-booking essential, please visit www.ngs.org.uk for information & booking. Light refreshments. Visits also by arrangement 15 June to 3 Aug for groups of 5 to 6. Contact owner for larger groups as weight limitations apply.**
Enchanting first floor roof garden above 1850s workers cottage with converted 1950s studios, and artist workshops to the rear. Access via wide spiral staircase to sheltered garden 9 x 8 metres, intensively planted and fully containerised. Trees, shrubs, climbers, subtle annual perennial plant combinations and new 7 x 10 metre rear extensive roof area with biodiverse mix of sedums and wild flowers. Not suitable for those who are unsteady on their feet.

2 CONWAY ROAD, N14
Southgate, N14 7BA. **Eileen Hulse.** *Nr Palmer's Green & Southgate. Buses: 121 & W6 from Palmers Green or Southgate to Broomfield Park stop. Walk up Aldermans Hill, R into Ulleswater Rd, 1st L into Conway Rd. What3words app: fame.pens.slurs.* **Sat 30 Aug (2-5.30). Adm £5, chd free. Tea, coffee & home-made cake.**
A passion nurtured from childhood for growing unusual plants has culminated in two contrasting gardens. The original, calming with lawn, pond and greenhouse, complements the adjoining Mediterranean terraced rooms with pergolas clothed in exotic climbers, vegetable beds and cordon fruit. Tumbling achocha, figs, datura and *Rosa banksiae* mingle creating a horticultural adventure. Unusual plant varieties from many realms, inc tomatoes.

GROUP OPENING

COURT LANE GROUP, SE21
SE21 7EA. *SE London. Buses: P4, 12, 40, 176, 185 to Dulwich Library 37. Train stn: North Dulwich, then 12 min walk. Ample free parking in Court Ln.* **Sun 29 June (2-5.30). Combined adm £10, chd free. Tea & cakes at 122 Court Lane. Light refreshments at 164 Court Lane.**

122 COURT LANE
Jean & Charles Cary-Elwes.

164 COURT LANE
James & Katie Dawes.

No. 164 was recently redesigned to create a more personal and intimate space with several specific zones. A modern terrace and seating area leads onto a lawn with abundant borders and a beautiful mature oak. A rose arch leads to the vegetable beds and greenhouse. No. 122 has a countryside feel, backing onto Dulwich Park with colourful herbaceous borders and unusual plants. Live jazz on the terrace, a children's trail, plant sale and a wormery demonstration at No.122.

NEW **61 THE COURTWAY, WD19**
Carpenders Park, Watford,
WD19 5DP. Carol White. *Between Carpenders Park & Bushey. On Oxhey Ln (A4008), turn into By the Wood & turn L into Greenfield Ave at junction. The Courtway is the 2nd turn on the R. On street parking.* **Sun 24 Aug (2-5). Adm £5, chd free. Tea, coffee & cake.**
A very productive and well organised vegetable garden featuring raised beds and a greenhouse, as well as herbaceous beds with a mix of perennials, annuals, shrubs, and relaxed planting to encourage pollinators. The garden has a patio with raised beds and areas of lawn.
✿ ☕ 🔊

83 COWSLIP ROAD, E18
South Woodford, E18 1JN. Fiona Grant. *5 min walk from Central line tube. Close to exit for A406.* **Sun 6 July (2-6). Combined adm with 85 Cowslip Road £6, chd free. Home-made teas.**
80ft long wildlife friendly garden, on two levels at rear of Victorian semi. Patio has a selection of containers with a step down to the lawn past a pond full of wildlife. Flowerbeds stuffed with an eclectic mix of perennials. Ample seating on patio and overspill seating in delightful adjacent garden. Wheelchair access via side of house to patio. Steps down to main garden.
♿ 🐕 ✿ ☕ 🔊

NEW **85 COWSLIP ROAD, E18**
South Woodford, E18 1JN.
Hayley Kyle. *5 min walk from South Woodford tube stn (Central line). Parking on street.* **Sun 6 July (2-6). Combined adm with 83 Cowslip Road £6, chd free. BBQ & chilled drinks.**
Family friendly garden with spacious patio and decking area, and a variety of colourful perennials in established flowerbeds. I love to just try and see what grows, encouraged and guided by my wonderful neighbour, and that's why I'm opening with her!
♿ 🐕 ☕ 🔊

58 CRANSTON ROAD, SE23
Forest Hill, SE23 2HB. Mr Sam Jarvis & Mr Andres Sampedro. *12 min walk from nearest train stns Forest Hill or Honor Oak. Nearest bus stops: Stanstead Rd/Colfe Rd (185, 122), Kilmorie Rd (185, 171) or Brockley Rise/Cranston Rd (122, 171).*

Sun 27 July (12-5). Adm £4, chd free. Teas, cakes, tortilla & sangria.
An exotic style plant lover's garden features a modern landscaped path and carefully curated subtropical planting. Vivid evergreens inc palms, cordyline, loquat and cycad provide structure and year-round interest. Tree ferns, bananas and tetrapanax add to the striking foliage, while cannas, dahlias and agapanthus provide vibrant pops of colour against the black painted boundaries.
✿ ☕ 🔊

37 CRESCENT ROAD, BR3
Beckenham, BR3 6NF. Myra & Tim Bright. *15 min walk from Beckenham Junction stn. Bus route 227 from Shortlands stn. Street parking in adjacent roads.* **Sun 22 June (2-5). Adm £4, chd free. Home-made teas.**
A romantic garden. In spring tulips abound amongst euphorbias and forget-me-nots. In summer, an abundance of geraniums, foxgloves and allium fill the front borders. Go past the potting shed and under the vine arch to arrive in the garden filled with herbaceous plants, roses, and clematis, a magnet for bees and butterflies. Gravel paths lead to secret corners with seating.
✿ ☕ 🔊

GROUP OPENING

DE BEAUVOIR GARDENS, N1
100 Downham Road, Hackney, N1 5BE. *Tube stns: Highbury & Islington, then 30 bus; Angel, then 38, 56 or 73 bus; Bank, then 21, 76 or 141 bus. 10 min walk from Dalston Junction train stn. Street parking. LTNs operate in this area.* **Sun 1 June (2-6). Combined adm £12, chd free. Home-made teas at 100 Downham Road.**

100 DOWNHAM ROAD
Ms Cecilia Darker.

64 LAWFORD ROAD

1 NORTHCHURCH TERRACE
Joan Ward.

21 NORTHCHURCH TERRACE
Nancy Korman.

NEW **42 OAKLEY ROAD**
Mrs Moira Taylor.

10 UFTON GROVE
Ms Lynn Brooks.

Six gardens to explore in De Beauvoir, a leafy enclave of Victorian villas near

to Islington and Dalston. The area boasts some of Hackney's keenest gardeners and a thriving garden club. New this yr is 42 Oakley Road which features a sunken lawn surrounded by mature shrubs and trees inc New Zealand lancewoods. No. 1 Northchurch Terrace is tiny, packed with a diverse range of potted shrubs, ferns and flowers. 21 Northchurch Terrace is a walled garden with a formal pond and deep borders which have recently been replanted. 10 Ufton Grove is a contemporary professionally designed town garden with an abundance of water features, carp pond and interesting sculptures. 100 Downham Road features two green roofs, a pond with a miniature Giverny-style bridge and cosy seating areas giving different viewpoints. 64 Lawford Road is a small cottage style garden with old-fashioned roses, espaliered apples and scented plants.
✿ ☕ 🔊

NEW **50 DEANSCROFT AVENUE, NW9**
The Hyde, NW9 8EN. Kunvar Jesani. *North West London. Nearest stn Wembley Park & bus number 83 to Deanscroft Ave, followed by a 5 min walk. Use public transport if there is a fixture at Wembley to avoid difficulty parking.* **Sat 19 July (1-5). Adm £5, chd free. Light refreshments.**
A character filled garden created and transformed since 2020. It combines tropical plants with shrubs, hints of Indian heritage and plenty of places to sit and relax with paths to take you on a secret journey through the garden. Tree ferns and exotic plants bring colour to this beautiful oasis with bananas, palms, schefflera and albizia. Enjoy Indian tea and traditional snacks and cakes. No steps to see main garden. Two small steps to view the top of the garden.
♿ ✿ ☕ 🔊

7 DEANSWAY, N2
East Finchley, N2 0NF. Joan Arnold & Tom Heinersdorff, 07850 764543, joan.arnold40@gmail.com. *Hampstead Garden Suburb. From East Finchley tube stn take exit along the Causeway to East End Rd, then L down Deansway. From Bishops Ave, head N up Deansway towards East End Rd, close to the top. Bus 143 to Abbots Gardens.* **Sun 11 May (12.30-5.30). Adm £5, chd free.**

Home-made teas. Visits also by arrangement 17 Mar to 31 July for groups of 5 to 30. Tea, coffee & cake (daytime) or wine & nibbles (evening). A garden of stories, statues, shapes and structures surrounded by trees and hedges. Bird friendly, cottage style with scented roses, clematis, mature shrubs, a weeping mulberry and abundant planting. Containers, spring bulbs and grapevine provide year-round colour. Secret, shady and wild woodland area with ferns and a tiny water feature. Cakes, gluten free cakes and plants for sale (cash or card). Wheelchair access through side passage to patio. Assistance may be required with three shallow steps to the lawn and main garden.

♿ ✿ ☕))

68 DERBY ROAD, E18
South Woodford, E18 2PS. Mrs Michelle Greene. *Nearest tube: South Woodford (Central line). Buses: 20 & 179 to Chelmsford Rd. Close to Epping Forest & the Waterworks r'about.* **Sun 8 June (1-5). Adm £4, chd free. Tea, coffee & cake.** Old fashioned summer garden with two ponds, one for wildlife and one for goldfish. Tiny orchard, vegetable beds and rockery. Highlights inc American pokeweed and Himalayan honeysuckle. Many unusual plants with small plants for sale.

✿ ☕))

GROUP OPENING

103 & 105 DULWICH VILLAGE, SE21
SE21 7BJ. *Train: North Dulwich or West Dulwich then 10-15 min walk. Tube: Brixton then P4 bus, alight Dulwich Picture Gallery stop. Street parking.* **Sun 22 June (2-5). Combined adm £10, chd free. Home-made teas at 103 Dulwich Village (adm inc tea, coffee & soft drink).** Donation to Link Age Southwark.

103 DULWICH VILLAGE
Mr & Mrs N Annesley.

105 DULWICH VILLAGE
Mr & Mrs A Rutherford.

Two adjoining Georgian houses with large gardens, 3 mins walk from Dulwich Picture Gallery (well worth a visit) and Dulwich Park. 103 Dulwich Village is a country-style garden in London, featuring a long herbaceous border against a fine old wall, a large lawn, a pond with native fish, roses, and fruit and vegetable gardens, all immaculately kept. 105 Dulwich Village is a haven for wildlife. A very pretty flower garden with a number of unusual plants, and others grown for insects. Featuring old-fashioned roses, lawns and shrubbery, a formal fish pond, and wildlife water garden. Teas with home-made cakes on the lawn at No. 103. Amazing collection of plants for sale from both gardens (cash preferred). Please bring your own bags for plants.

✿ ☕))

ECCLESTON SQUARE, SW1
Pimlico, SW1V 1NP. The Residents of Eccleston Square, www.ecclestonsquaregardens.com. *Off Belgrave Rd, nr Victoria stn. Parking allowed on Sundays.* **Sun 11 May (2-5). Adm £5, chd free. Home-made teas.**
Planned and developed by Thomas Cubitt in the 1830s, the 3 acre garden square is subdivided into sections with noteworthy collections of roses, camellias, ferns and tree peonies. The garden holds the National Collection of Ceanothus comprising over 70 species and cultivars, some of which are now rare. Notable important additions of unusual and tender plants are being grown and tested.

♿ ✿ NPC ☕))

52 The Chase

© Maciek Groman

EDWARDES SQUARE, W8
South Edwardes Square,
Kensington, W8 6HL. Edwardes
Square Garden Committee, www.
edwardes-square-garden.co.uk.
*Tube: Kensington High St & Earls Court.
Buses: 9, 10, 27, 28, 31, 49 & 74 to
Odeon Cinema. Entrance in South
Edwardes Square.* **Sun 6 Apr (12-5).
Adm £6, chd £3. Tea, coffee & cake.**
One of London's prettiest secluded
garden squares. 3½ acres laid
out differently from other squares
with serpentine paths by Agostino
Agliothe, an Italian artist and
decorator who lived at No.15 from
1814-1820. This quiet oasis is a
wonderful mixture of rolling lawns,
mature trees and imaginative planting.
Children's play area. WC. Near
Holland Park, only a 5 min walk.
Wheelchair access through main
gate, South Edwardes Square.
& ☕))

40 EMBER LANE, KT10
Esher, KT10 8EP. Sarah &
Franck Corvi, 07803 111968,
sarah.corvi@ngs.org.uk. *½ m from
centre of Esher. From the A307, turn
into Station Rd which becomes Ember
Ln.* **Sun 18 May (1-5). Combined
adm with 9 Imber Park Road £7,
chd free. Home-made teas. Visits
also by arrangement 8 June to 28
Sept for groups of 8 to 20.**
A contemporary family garden
designed and maintained by the
owners with distinct areas for outdoor
living. A 70ft east facing plot where
the lawn has been mostly removed to
make space for the owner's love of
plants and several ornamental trees
which provide privacy.
✿ ☕))

11 ERNLE ROAD, SW20
Wimbledon, SW20 0HH. Theresa-
Mary Morton, 07484 868786,
Theresammorton@aol.com. *200yds
from Crooked Billet pub on Woodhayes
Rd. Exit A3 at A238 to Wimbledon,
turning L at Copse Hill. Train:
Wimbledon or Raynes Park. Tube:
Wimbledon. Bus: 200 to High Cedar
Dr, 200yds walk.* **Sat 17 May (2.30-6).
Adm £5, chd free. Home-made
teas. Evening opening Sun 18 May
(5-7.30). Adm £8, chd free. Wine.
Visits also by arrangement 7 Apr to
25 May. Evening welcome.**
Established suburban garden of ⅓
acre on sandy acid soil, spatially
organised into separate sections;
oak pergola framing the main vista,
woodland garden, yew circle,

water lily pond, trees and shrubs.
Wheelchair access with beaten gravel
paths and one step to main garden.
& ☕))

48 ERSKINE HILL, NW11
Hampstead Garden Suburb,
NW11 6HG. Marjorie Harris,
020 8455 6507, marjorieharris@
btinternet.com. *1m from Golders
Green. Nr A406 & A1. Tube: Golders
Green. H2 Hail & Ride bus from
Golders Green to garden, or 13, 102
or 460 buses to Temple Fortune (10
min walk). Free street parking.* **Visits
by arrangement 5 May to 31 Aug
for groups of 5 to 28. Adm £10,
chd free. Tea, coffee & cake inc.**
Colourful but restful bird and bee-
friendly organic and pesticide free
cottage garden, wrapped around
1909 Arts and Crafts artisan's cottage
in Hampstead Garden Suburb. Wide
sunny borders stuffed with perennials,
roses and clematis rampaging up
through structures, shrubs and trees.
Climber wrapped pergola, container
vegetable plot, and greenhouse. Nest
box, bee-friendly plants and quirky
water feature. Pre-book dairy-free
or gluten free cake and soya milk.
Wheelchair access to terrace. Narrow
paths. Single step from gate with
ramp available. Handrail and step to
lawn. No wheelchair access to WC.
& 🚗 ☕

70 FARLEIGH ROAD, N16
Stoke Newington, N16 7TQ. Mr
Graham Hollick. *Short walk from
junction of Stoke Newington High St
& Amhurst Rd. LTNs operate in this
area.* **Sun 29 June (10-6). Adm £4,
chd free. Home-made teas.**
A diverse garden in a Victorian terrace
with an eclectic mix of plants, many
in vintage pots reflecting the owner's
interests. A small courtyard leads onto
a patio surrounded by pots followed
by a lawn flanked by curving borders.
At the rear is a paved area with raised
beds containing vegetables.
✿ ☕))

**NEW 73 FAWNBRAKE AVENUE,
SE24**
Herne Hill, SE24 0BE. Alan Oliver
& Jorge Sanchez. *10 min walk from
Herne Hill stn via Milkwood Rd &
Gubyon Ave. By bus: 68 or 468 (alight
at Hollingbourne Rd & walk down
Kestrel Ave); 3 or 37 (alight at Herne
Hill stn).* **Sun 6 July (1-6). Adm £5,
chd free. Tea, coffee & cake.**
The garden of art and music lovers.

Jorge Sanchez (a professional artist)
and Alan Oliver. Art and music provide
much of the inspiration for this small,
plant packed garden which erupts
into a riot of colour along its winding
paths in summer. Features inc a
wildlife pond, a small patio almost
hidden by lush planting, a twisted
willow, *Salix contorta*, and a collection
of small acers.
✿ ☕))

28 FERNDENE ROAD, SE24
Herne Hill, SE24 0AB. Mr David &
Mrs Lynn Whyte, www.instagram.
com/dsw_garden. *Buses 68, 468,
42, a 5 min walk from Denmark Hill.
Train stns: Herne Hill, Denmark Hill,
Loughborough Junction, all 15 min
walk. House overlooks Ruskin Park.
Free parking.* **Sun 15 June (1.30-
5.30). Adm £4.50, chd free. Tea,
coffee & cake.**
It is all about structure and careful
planting in this dramatically sloping
south south east facing garden,
30 x 18 metres. A lively blend of
perennials and shrubs shows definite
Kiwi influences. The kitchen garden
with raised beds and soft fruits is
wonderfully secluded. Lower-level
planting has a coastal feel. Upper-level
has a hot colour border. Borrowed
views of mature trees and big
skies set it off. The garden studio/
summerhouse was constructed from
sustainably sourced materials, and has
a rubble roof to attenuate water runoff.
Recycling and re-use of materials.
✿ ☕))

NEW FRITH LODGE, HA6
Sandy Lane, Northwood, HA6 3ES.
Mr & Mrs Doig. *From Watford Rd,
head along Sandy Ln in the direction
of Seven Acres. The garden is around
300 metres along on the R. Entrance
gate located at What3words app:
film.audio.beside.* **Sat 19, Sun 20
July (2-5). Adm £5, chd free. Tea,
coffee & cake.**
Garden of approx 1 acre at the former
gate lodge of Eastbury Park Estate
(now Northwood HQ). Dominated by
mature oak trees, the current owners
have sought to cut back overgrowing
ponticum and laurel to establish a
diverse garden with year-round interest.
The garden has extensive lawns, some
sloping with alternative access to lower
areas. The garden uses block planting
to great effect. No step access to main
patio and a graded ramp to the lower
part of garden. Limited Blue Badge
parking on the main drive.
& ☕))

10 FURLONG ROAD, N7

N7 8LS. Gavin & Nicola Ralston. *Close to Highbury & Islington tube stn. Tube & Train: Highbury & Islington, 3 min walk along Holloway Rd, 2nd L. Furlong Rd runs between Holloway Rd & Liverpool Rd. Buses on Holloway Rd: 21,43, 263, 393; other buses 4, 19, 30.* **Sun 1 June (1-4.30). Adm £5, chd free. Home-made teas.**
A green oasis in the heart of a densely populated area, 10 Furlong Road is an open, sunny garden of considerable size for its urban location. Its owners extensively remodelled the garden in 2019, building on a foundation of trees, shrubs and roses, adding herbaceous planting, seating, winding brick path, pergola, raised vegetable bed and wildflower circle. Plenty of seating dotted around the garden.

GARDEN BARGE SQUARE AT TOWER BRIDGE MOORINGS, SE1

31 Mill Street, SE1 2AX. Mr Nick Lacey. *5 min walk from Tower Bridge. Mill St off Jamaica Rd, between London Bridge & Bermondsey stns, Tower Hill also nearby. Buses: 47, 188, 381, RV1.* **Sun 4 May (2-5). Adm £5, chd free. Home-made teas.**
Series of seven floating barge gardens connected by walkways and bridges. Gardens have an eclectic range of plants for year-round seasonal interest. Marine environment: suitable shoes and care needed. Small children must be closely supervised.

♦ THE GARDEN MUSEUM, SE1

5 Lambeth Palace Road, SE1 7LB. The Garden Museum, 020 7401 8865, info@gardenmuseum.org.uk, www.gardenmuseum.org.uk. *Lambeth side of Lambeth Bridge. Tube: Lambeth North, Vauxhall, Waterloo. Buses: 507 Red Arrow from Victoria or Waterloo stns, also 3, 77, 344, C10.* **For NGS: Evening opening Mon 19 May (5.30-8). Adm £7, chd free. Open nearby Lambeth Palace.** For other opening times and information, please phone, email or visit garden website.
At the heart of The Garden Museum is our courtyard garden, designed by Dan Pearson as an 'Eden' of rare plants inspired by John Tradescant's journeys as a plant collector. Taking advantage of the sheltered, warm space, Dan has created a green retreat in response to the bronze and glass architecture, conjuring up a calm, reflective atmosphere. Visitors will also see a permanent display of paintings, tools, ephemera and historic artefacts; a glimpse into the uniquely British love affair with gardens. Garden tours with Head Gardener at 6pm and 7pm. Adm covers access to museum and garden. The museum and garden are accessible for wheelchairs.

GOLF COURSE ALLOTMENTS, N11

Winton Avenue, N11 2AR. GCAA Haringey, www.golfcourseallotments.co.uk. *Junction of Winton Ave & Blake Rd. Tube: Bounds Green. Buses: 102, 184, 299 to Sunshine Garden Centre, Durnsford Rd. Through park to Bidwell Gardens. Straight on up Winton Ave. New LTN on Blake Rd, beware cameras. No parking on site.* **Sun 7 Sept (1-4.30). Adm £5, chd free. Home-made teas & light lunches (cash only).**
Large, long established allotment with over 200 plots, some organic. Maintained by culturally diverse community, growing a wide variety of fruit, vegetables and flowers, enjoyed by bees. Picturesque corners, quirky sheds, tours of best plots. Admire prize-winning exhibits at Autumn Show. Plot 147, a jewel not to be missed! A visit feels like a holiday in the countryside. Healthy, fresh allotment produce, chutneys, jams and honey for sale (cash only). Wheelchair access to main paths only. Gravel and uneven surfaces. WC inc disabled.

21 GOSPATRICK ROAD, N17

Tottenham, N17 7EH. Matthew Bradby, 07985 169471, mattbradby@hotmail.com. *London Zone 3. Tube: Turnpike Ln or Wood Green stns. Train: Bruce Grove stn. Bus routes: 144, 217, 231, 444 to Gospatrick Rd, or 123, 243 to Waltheof Ave, or 318 to Gt Cambridge Rd.* **Visits by arrangement Mar to July. Ideal for groups with an interest in the Arts and Crafts era and horticulture. Light refreshments.**
Located in Tower Gardens Arts and Crafts Estate, diverse 40 metre plot with contrasting areas. A large weeping willow provides shade over fan palms, camellias, ferns and climbers. Fruit and herb garden with Japanese banana, grapevine, olive, bay and loquat trees. Greenhouse and two ponds. A very tranquil and welcoming garden following organic principles.

24 GROVE PARK, SE5

Camberwell, SE5 8LH. Clive Pankhurst, www.alternative-planting.blogspot.com. *Chadwick Rd end of Grove Park. Peckham Rye or Denmark Hill stns, both 10 min walk. Good street parking.* **Sun 7 Sept (11-4.30). Adm £5, chd free. Home-made teas.**
An inspiring exotic jungle of lush, big leafed plants and Southeast Asian influences transport you to the tropics. Huge hidden garden created from derelict land that had been the bottom halves of two neighbouring gardens gives the wow factor and unexpected size. Lawn and lots of hidden corners give spaces to sit and enjoy. Renowned for delicious home-made cake and plant sale.

NEW 33 HAMPSTEAD LANE, N6

Highgate, N6 4RT. Michelle Berriedale-Johnson, michelle@salonmusic.co.uk, walksonhampsteadheath.co.uk. *8 min walk from Highgate going W down Hampstead Ln towards Kenwood. On bus routes 210 & 310. $1/3$ m W down Hampstead Ln just before you reach Bishopswood Rd/Highgate School playing fields, or just past playing fields & Bishopswood Rd if going E.* **Sun 22 June (12-6). Adm £5, chd free. Tea, coffee & cake. Adm inc a cup of tea.** Visits also by arrangement May to Aug for groups of 5 to 10.
New, lush south facing walled garden bounded by Hampstead Heath with mature trees, no-mow lawn, and shady patios under a mirrored trellis. Features inc a herbaceous border, fern garden, hot dry banks and a pond. A wild area with compost and wood store can be seen under the apple tree. In development, a 'growing garden' for SEND children with raised vegetable beds, fruit bushes, trees, and a fire pit. The group working on the 'growing garden' will be on site to explain the project and its progress. Two steps up to the entrance patio, but accessible with a ramp.

92 HAMPSTEAD WAY, NW11
Hampstead Garden Suburb, NW11 7XY. **Ann & Tom Lissauer.** *In square set back on Hampstead Way, between Finchley Rd & Meadway. 15 min walk from Golders Green stn. Buses 13,102 & 460 on Finchley Rd, stop at Temple Fortune Ln & walk down Hampstead Way to the square.* **Sun 1 June (1.30-5). Combined adm with 100 Hampstead Way £10, chd free. Home-made teas.** An informal garden, interesting year-round, combining wildlife friendly planting with a passion for plants. Different areas provide a variety of habitats. These inc a wildlife pond and, where there used to be lawns, there are now meadows with mown paths and wild flowers. Shaded and sunny beds offer opportunities to grow a wide range of interesting plants.

100 HAMPSTEAD WAY, NW11
Hampstead Garden Suburb, NW11 7XY. **S & J Fogel.** *North West London. In square set back on Hampstead Way, between Finchley Rd & Meadway. Buses 13,102 &* 460 *on Finchley Rd, getting off at Temple Fortune Ln & walk down Hampstead Way to the square. Golders Green tube.* **Sun 1 June (1.30-5). Combined adm with 92 Hampstead Way £10, chd free.** Corner cottage garden with a variety of viewing perspectives and featuring sculpture and planting in recycled objects (pallets, sinks, dustbins, mattress on wheels, wine boxes, poles, chimneys). The garden comprises a number of rooms inc a formal parterre, wooded area, walkway, small meadow and formal lawn.

SPECIAL EVENT

◆ **HAMPTON COURT PALACE, KT8**
East Molesey, KT8 9AU. Historic Royal Palaces, www.hrp.org.uk. *Follow brown tourist signs on all major routes. Junction of A308 with A309 at foot of Hampton Court Bridge. Traffic is heavy around Hampton Court. Please leave plenty of time, the tour will start promptly at 6pm & will not be able to wait.* **For NGS: Evening opening Thur 10 Apr, Thur 10 July (6-8). Pre-booking essential, please visit www.ngs.org.uk for information & booking. Adm £18, chd free. Wine.** **For other opening times and information, please visit garden website. Donation to Historic Royal Palaces.**
Take the opportunity to join special National Garden Scheme private tours after the wonderful historic gardens have closed to the public. Spring walk during the tulip festival and July walk to enjoy the summer bedding in the remarkable gardens of Hampton Court Palace. Wheelchair access over some unbound gravel paths.

NEW HAMPTON HOUSE, TW12
90 High Street, Hampton, TW12 2SW. Mrs Gillie Hamshere, 07810 463826, 138wpj@gmail.com. *⅓ m from Hampton Open Air Pool. N.B. Not Hampton Hill.* **Sun 13 Apr (12-5). Adm £6, chd free. Tea, coffee & cake. Open nearby 9 Warwick Close.** Visits also by arrangement 14 Apr to 11 May for groups of 6 to 10.

Arundel & Elgin Gardens

LONDON 353

Step off the High Street into this secluded garden of half an acre that stretches from an elegant Queen Anne house (not open) to its border with Bushy Park. A long herbaceous border, large lawn and well established trees inc a pair of 200 yr old yew, as well as mulberry and cherry trees. A wonderful vista from the terrace enjoys the borrowed landscape of Bushy Park. Several dog themed garden statutory. Tulips and hyacinths feature heavily in spring to reflect their popularity during the Queen Anne period.

37 HAROLD ROAD, E11
Leytonstone, E11 4QX. Dr Matthew Jones Chesters. *Tube: Leytonstone, exit L subway, 5 min walk. Train: Leytonstone High Road, 5 min walk. Buses: 257 & W14. Parking at stn or limited on street.* **Sun 15 June (1-5). Adm £5, chd free. Home-made teas.**
50ft x 60ft pretty corner garden arranged around seven fruit trees. Fragrant climbers, woodland plants and shade-tolerant fruit along north wall. Fastigiate trees protect raised vegetable beds and rockery. Long lawn bordered by roses and perennials on one side, prairie plants on the other. Patio with raised pond, palms and rhubarb. Planting designed to produce fruit, fragrance and lovely memories. Garden map with planting plans inc. Adm inc tea and fruit drinks. Home-made cakes, muffins and preserves for sale.

20 HAZELMERE ROAD, BR5
Petts Wood, Orpington, BR5 1PB. Victoria & Matthew Stephens. *A 10 min walk from Petts Wood stn (22 mins direct from London Bridge / 35 mins from London Victoria). Free on street parking. Adjacent to Petts Wood NT woodland (free).* **Sun 8 June (2.30-5.30). Adm £5, chd free. Home-made teas.**
A recently designed contemporary garden which was part built by the owners and features perennial planting with a mix of trees, blending into the borrowed landscape. Gravel pathways from the generous terrace lead you on a journey through the planting with a secret garden over the brook that runs through the garden. Clipped hedging and contemporary features punctuate the planting and pathways.

NEW 29 HEATHFIELD ROAD, W3
Acton, W3 8EH. Alister Thorpe & Lucy Kirkpatrick, www.instagram.com/alistergthorpe. *5 min walk from Acton Town tube stn. 15 mins walk from South Acton overground stn.* **Sun 6 July (2-6). Combined adm with 118b Avenue Road £7, chd free.**
A small but enchanting woodland garden that surrounds an Arts and Crafts house. Designed and planted in February 2023 by designer Stefano Marinaz. The garden has two small seating areas joined by a long meandering slate chip path. Many interesting and unusual woodland plants. Accent pots, water feature, and man shed.

84 HIGHAM STREET, E17
Walthamstow, E17 6DA. Paula Siqueira & Andrew Durham. *15 min walk from Blackhorse tube stn.* **Sun 6 July (2-6). Adm £4, chd free. Tea, coffee & cake.**
A low-maintenance garden that will take you on a journey through a wildlife friendly oasis into a small woodland hideaway. The large rainwater pond provides a great contrast to draught tolerant perennial flowers, ornamental grasses, trees and shrubs, all planted with a naturalistic style under a thick layer of gravel mulch. An olive tree set against a 4 metre ivy wall provides a strong focal point. There will be QR codes where visitors can read more about the plants, the inner workings of the pond rainwater collection and natural filtration, and also take a look at the garden before-and-after photos.

32 HIGHBURY PLACE, N5
Islington, N5 1QP. Michael & Caroline Kuhn. *Highbury Fields. Tube & Train: Highbury & Islington. Buses: 4, 19, 30, 43, 271, 393 to Highbury Corner. 3 min walk up Highbury Place which is opp stn.* **Sun 15 June (2.30-5.30). Adm £5, chd free. Home-made teas.**
An 80ft garden behind a C18 terrace house (not open). An upper York stone terrace leads to a larger terrace surrounded by overfilled beds of cottage garden style planting. Further steps lead to a lawn by a rill and a lower terrace. A willow tree dominates the garden; amelanchiers, fruit trees and dwarf acers, winter flowering cherry, lemon trees and magnolia.

26 HILLCROFT CRESCENT, HA9
Wembley Park, HA9 8EE. Gary & Suha Holmyard, 07773 691331, garyh@lawyer.com. *½ m from Wembley Park stn. If held on Wembley event day, we can provide free parking permits. Turn R out of Wembley Park stn walking down Wembley Park Dr, turn L into Manor Dr, Hillcroft Cres is 2nd on R.* **Sat 5, Sun 6 July (11-5). Adm £5, chd free. Home-made teas. Visits also by arrangement 2 June to 20 July for groups of 5 to 25. Ten day advanced notice required.**
Small cottage front garden with arched entrance with cloud tree, wisteria, yucca, canna, hydrangeas, roses and lilies. Rear garden approx 70 x 80ft with summerhouse, arbours and water features. Planting inc 'pagoda fig tree', apple, pear, olive, banana and soft fruit. Ten different flower beds each holding its own particular interest with feature plants, unusual shrubs, and exotics. Plenty of seating around the garden. Wheelchair access through side gate via driveway.

NEW HOLTWHITES BAKERY & DELI, N13
66 Aldermans Hill, N13 4PP. Kate Smith. *North London. A few mins walk from Palmers Green stn (National Rail). Turn R out of the stn & you will find us on the corner of Aldermans Hill & Grovelands Rd, opp Broomfield Park.* **Sun 29 June (1.30-5.30). Adm £3.50, chd free. Tea, coffee & cake. Open nearby 10 York Road.**
Our walled, courtyard garden was designed by Julia of The English Potted Plant Co, and opened in the spring of 2023 with an exuberant burst of colour to welcome our customers and a host of pollinators. The garden reflects our ethos of sharing food and space with the wider community; edible herbs and flowers are used in the café, and the planting is evolving with sustainable practices. All profits from refreshment sales will be donated to the NGS. Visitors are encouraged to explore historic Broomfield Park, directly opposite the garden with its lakes, wildlife, orchard, conservatory and magnificent views. Wheelchair access to the lower level of the courtyard garden, café and WC.

HORATIO'S GARDEN, HA7
Royal National Orthopaedic
Hospital, Brockley Hill, Stanmore,
HA7 4LP. Horatio's Garden,
www.horatiosgarden.org.uk. *Public
transport from Stanmore tube stn
to the hospital. There is also a taxi
rank outside the stn. Parking in the
main car park (10 min walk). Disabled
parking available.* **Sun 27 Apr (2-5).
Adm £5, chd free. Tea, coffee &
cake. Vegan & gluten free options.**
Opened in September 2020, Horatio's
Garden London & South East located
at the Royal National Orthopaedic
Hospital, Stanmore is designed
by Tom Stuart-Smith. The garden
is on one level with smooth paths
throughout ensuring that it is easily
accessible to patients in beds and
wheelchairs. The essential design
features inc a social space, private
areas for patients to seek solitude or
share with a family member or friend,
the calming sound of flowing water, a
garden room and a greenhouse. May
is the perfect time to see the carpet
of tulips and other bulbs. The Head
Gardener Ashley Edwards will be on
hand to answer any plant questions
and give guided tours of this unique
sanctuary. The whole site is designed
for wheelchairs. The route from the
car park is an uphill walk of approx
5-10 mins.

♿ ❋ 🅳 ☕ 🔊

27 HORNIMAN DRIVE, SE23
Forest Hill, SE23 3BJ. Rose
Agnew. *On top of the hill behind the
Horniman Museum. The garden can
be reached by walking or driving up
Horniman Dr or Westwood Park, turn
R into Horniman Dr.* **Sun 8 June (1-
5.30). Adm £4.50, chd free. Light
refreshments.**
A garden full of colour, inc mini-
meadow, jewels among much
loved purple leaved plants in a
contemporary setting. A low trellis
with Minarette apple trees and
rambler roses allows wonderful far-
reaching views across to the North
Downs. Lower down, a cut flower
and vegetable plot with seating,
a greenhouse, and compost bins
extend this peaceful haven for insects
and humans alike. Plants for sale.

❋ ☕

57 HUNTINGDON STREET, N1
Barnsbury, Islington, N1 1BX.
Julian Williams, 07759 053001,
julianandroman@me.com. *Train:
Caledonian Rd & Barnsbury. Tube:
Kings Cross, Highbury & Islington or*
*Caledonian Rd. Buses: Caledonian
Rd 17, 91, 259, 274; Hemingford Rd
153 from Angel.* **Evening opening
Thur 22, Thur 29 May (6-8). Adm
£5, chd free. Wine. Opening with
Barnsbury Group on Sun 8 June.
Visits also by arrangement May to
July for groups of up to 6.**
A secluded woodland garden room
below an ash canopy and framed
by timber palisade supporting
roses, hydrangea and clematis. An
understorey of silver birch and hazel
provides the setting for shade loving
ferns, perennials and grasses. New
for 2025: Reclaimed brick and stone
pathways offset the informal planting
and lead to a tranquil central space
with bench seating in steel and
oak, and two container ponds to
encourage wildlife.

☕ 🔊

GROUP OPENING

**HYDE PARK ESTATE GARDENS,
W2**
Kendal Street, W2 2AN. Church
Commissioners for England,
www.hydeparkestate.com. *The
Hyde Park Estate is bordered
by Sussex Gardens, Bayswater
Rd & Edgware Rd. Nearest tube
stns: Marble Arch, Paddington &
Edgware Rd.* **Sat 7 June (10.30-
4). Combined adm £8, chd free.
Pre-booking essential, please visit
www.ngs.org.uk for information &
booking.**

CONISTON COURT

DEVONPORT

**GLOUCESTER SQUARE
GARDEN**
gloucestersquare.org.

OXFORD SQUARE GARDEN

THE QUADRANGLE

REFLECTIONS 2020

THE WATER GARDENS

Unique opportunity to visit seven
Central London gardens usually only
seen by residents. These gardens
only open to the public for the NGS.
Each garden planted sympathetically
to reflect the surroundings and to
support biodiversity. The gardens
on the Hyde Park Estate are owned
and managed by the Church
Commissioners for England and play
a key part in the environmental and
ecological strategy on the Hyde Park
Estate. The estate covers 90 acres of
which 12½% is 'green', not only with
the garden spaces but by installing
planters on unused paved areas,
green roofs on new developments
and olive trees throughout Connaught
Village. We are delighted to inc
Gloucester Square garden as part
of the opening with the kind co-
operation of the Garden Committee.
Wheelchair access to most gardens.
There are some steps to the upper
levels of The Water Gardens.

♿ 🐾 ☕

9 IMBER PARK ROAD, KT10
Esher, KT10 8JB. Jane & John
McNicholas, 07867 318655,
jane_mcnicholas@hotmail.com.
*½m from centre of Esher. From the
A307, turn into Station Rd which
becomes Ember Ln. Go past Esher
train stn on R. Take 3rd road on R into
Imber Park Rd.* **Sun 18 May (1-5).
Combined adm with 40 Ember
Lane £7, chd free. Home-made
teas. Visits also by arrangement
8 June to 28 Sept for groups of 8
to 20.**
An established cottage style garden,
always evolving, designed and
maintained by the owners who
are passionate about gardening
and collecting plants. The garden
is south facing with well-stocked,
large, colourful herbaceous
borders containing a wide variety of
perennials, evergreen and deciduous
shrubs, a winding lawn area and a
small garden retreat.

❋ ☕ 🔊

SPECIAL EVENT

**THE INNER AND MIDDLE
TEMPLE GARDENS, EC4**
Crown Office Row, Inner Temple,
EC4Y 7HL. The Honourable
Societies of the Inner & Middle
Temples, www.innertemple.org.
uk/www.middletemple.org.uk.
*Entrance: Main Garden Gate on
Crown Office Row, access via Tudor
St Gate or Middle Temple Ln Gate.
Please note the tour starts promptly
at 11.30am.* **Wed 4 June (11.30-3).
Adm £55. Pre-booking essential,
please visit www.ngs.org.uk for
information & booking. Adm inc
conducted tour of the gardens by
Head Gardeners & light lunch in
Middle Temple Hall.**
Inner Temple Garden is a haven of

tranquillity and beauty with sweeping lawns, unusual trees and charming woodland areas. The well known herbaceous border shows off inspiring plant combinations from early spring through to autumn. The award-winning gardens of Middle Temple are comprised of a series of courtyards and a main garden which extends from the Medieval Hall to the Embankment. Please note this event is not suitable for children. Please email hello@ngs.org.uk in advance of any dietary requirements and if wheelchair access is required.

& 🍵

GROUP OPENING

KEW GREEN GARDENS, TW9
Kew, TW9 3AH. *NW side of Kew Green. Tube: Kew Gardens. Train stn: Kew Bridge. Buses: 65, 110. Entrance via riverside.* **Sun 18 May (2-5). Combined adm £8, chd free. Evening opening Sun 25 May (6-8). Combined adm £10, chd free. Teas in St Anne's Church (18 May). Wine (25 May).**

69 KEW GREEN
John & Virginia Godfrey.

71 KEW GREEN
Mr & Mrs Jan Pethick.

73 KEW GREEN
Sir Donald & Lady Elizabeth Insall.

The long gardens run for 100yds from the back of historic houses on Kew Green down to the Thames towpath. Together they cover nearly 1 acre, and in addition to the style and structures of the individual gardens they can be seen as one large space, exceptional in London. The borders between the gardens are mostly relatively low and the trees and large shrubs in each contribute to viewing the whole, while roses and clematis climb between gardens giving colour to two adjacent gardens at the same time.

🍵))

NEW 3 KING EDWARD ROAD, EN8
Waltham Cross, EN8 7HZ. Bryan Hewitt, bryan.hewitt@me.com. *Waltham Cross, nr Enfield via Bullsmoor Ln. 7 min walk from Waltham Cross train stn. 10 mins from M25 J25 by car. Look for big yellow arrows on the day.* **Sun 10 Aug (1-5.30). Adm £4, chd free. Light refreshments. Pre-booking preferred or cash only on the day.** Visits also by arrangement 1 June to 15 Oct for groups of 10 to 15. Ideal for visitors with a special interest in tropical plants.
A small courtyard garden transformed into an 'urban jungle' with many exotic trees and shrubs. Author of 'The Crocus King', Bryan drew inspiration from working at nearby E A Bowles Garden at Myddelton House, as gardener and historian for 34 yrs. Walls are clad with a collection of vintage advertising signs. Statuary and architectural salvage lurk in shady alleys. Every corner tells a story. Horticultural advice can be sought.

✻ 🍵

KING HENRY'S WALK GARDEN, N1
11c King Henry's Walk, N1 4NX. Friends of King Henry's Walk Garden, www.khwgarden.org.uk. *Buses: 30, 38, 56, 141. Behind adventure playground on KHW, off Balls Pond Rd.* **Mon 5 May (2-4.30). Adm £4.50, chd free. Home-made teas.** Donation to Friends of KHW Garden.
Vibrant ornamental planting welcomes the visitor to this hidden oasis leading into a verdant community garden with secluded woodland area, beehives, wildlife pond, wall trained fruit trees, and plots used by local residents to grow their own fruit and vegetables. Live music. Disabled access WC.

& ✻ 🍵))

53 LADY AYLESFORD AVENUE, HA7
Stanmore, HA7 4FG. Jadon. *About 15 min walk from Stanmore stn, off Uxbridge Rd, close to St John Church. H12, 340 & 324 bus stops are 5 min walk from garden. Limited free parking nearby.* **Sat 2 Aug (12-5). Adm £5. Home-made teas.**
A compact tropical fusion garden developed over the past 7 yrs. The garden is set in a development of the Battle of Britain, RAF base. This delightful gem of a corner garden with water features and a stunning display of plants and flowers, shows what can be achieved, even in a small space. Colours and textures blend effortlessly to create a harmonious space with exceptional attention to detail.

✻ 🍵))

LAMBETH PALACE, SE1
Lambeth Palace Road, SE1 7JU. The Church Commissioners, www.archbishopofcanterbury.org. *Entrance via Main Gatehouse (Morton's Tower) facing Lambeth Bridge. Stn: Waterloo. Tube: Westminster, Vauxhall all 10 min walk. Buses: 3, C10, 77, 344.* **Evening opening Mon 19 May (5-8). Adm £7, chd free. Wine. Open nearby The Garden Museum.**
Lambeth Palace has one of the oldest and largest private gardens in London. It has been occupied by Archbishops of Canterbury since 1197. Formal courtyard boasts historic White Marseilles fig planted in 1556. Parkland style garden features mature trees, woodland and native planting. There is a formal rose terrace, summer gravel border, scented chapel garden and active beehives. Please note: Gates will open at 5pm, last entry is 7pm and garden closes at 8pm. Garden Tours will be available. Wheelchair access with ramped path to rose terrace. Disabled WC.

& 🐕 ✻ 🍵 🪑))

42 LATIMER ROAD, E7
Forest Gate, E7 0LQ. Janet Daniels. *8 mins walk from Forest Gate or Wanstead Park stns. From Forest Gate cross to Sebert Rd, then 3rd road on L.* **Sun 20 July (11-4). Adm £4, chd free. Tea, coffee & cake.**
Passionate plant collector's garden in two separate areas. First (90ft x 15ft) has an abundance of baskets, climbers, shrubs, fruit trees and ponds. Step down to large secret garden (70ft x 30ft) containing exuberant borders, wildlife pond with gunnera and walnut tree. Unusual and exotic plants and other quirky features. Wildlife friendly. Plants for sale.

✻ 🚗 🍵 🪑))

12 LAURADALE ROAD, N2
N2 9LU. David & Mary Gilbert, drgilbertprivate@gmail.com, www.davidgilbertart.com/garden. *Muswell Hill / East Finchley. 300 metres from 102 & 234 bus stops. 500 metres from 43 & 134 bus stops. 10 min walk from East Finchley tube stn. Look out for NGS signs.* **Sun 7 Sept (1-6). Adm £5, chd free. Tea, coffee & cake.** Visits also by arrangement.
Exotic, huge, featuring tropical and Mediterranean zone plants, now very much maturing and extended

with recent developments. Dramatic, architectural planting inc bananas, large tree ferns, and rare palms weave along curving stone paths, culminating in a paradise garden. A modern take on the rockery embeds glacial boulders amid dry zone plants inc many succulents. Sculptures by artist owner.

☕ ⬤))

84 LAVENDER GROVE, E8
Hackney, E8 3LS. Anne Pauleau, 07930 550414, a.pauleau@hotmail.co.uk. *Walk from Haggerston or London Fields train stns. The nearest bus stop is the 394 in Lansdowne Dr, just round the corner. LTNs operate in this area.* **Sun 20 Apr (2-5). Adm £4, chd free. Cream teas. Opening with London Fields Gardens on Sun 8 June. Visits also by arrangement for groups of 6 to 18.**
Courtyard garden with tropical backdrop of bamboos and palms, foil to clipped shrubs leading to wilder area. The cottage garden with mingling roses, lilies, alliums, grasses, clematis, poppies, star jasmine and jasmine. A very highly scented garden with rampant ramblers and billowing vegetation enchanting all senses. Tulips and daffodils herald spring. Fiery crocosmias and dahlias trumpet late summer. Children's quiz offered with prize on completion.

🐕 ❀ ☕ ⬤))

16 LINKS VIEW ROAD, TW12
Hampton Hill, TW12 1LA. Guy & Virginia Lewis. *South West London, nr Richmond & Kingston upon Thames. 5 min walk from Fulwell stn. On 281, 267, 285 & R70 bus routes.* **Sat 24, Sun 25 May (2.30-4.30). Adm £5, chd free. Home-made teas.**
A surprising garden featuring acers, hostas and fern collection, and other unusual shade loving plants. Many climbing roses, clematis and herbaceous border, and pots of exotic plants. Rockery and folly with shell grotto and waterfall to small pond and bog garden. Lawn and formal pond. Wild area with chickens and summerhouse. Greenhouse with succulent collection. A veranda with pelargonium collection. One very friendly dog. Plants for sale inc many succulents and greenhouse/ conservatory plants, species pelargoniums and a variety of plectranthus. Wheelchair access with assistance.

♿ 🐕 ❀ ☕ ⬤))

GROUP OPENING

LONDON FIELDS GARDENS, E8
Hackney, E8 3JW. *London Fields. LTNs operate in this area. 7 min walk from 149, 242, 243 bus stop, Middleton Rd. 10 mins from 30, 38, 55 stops on Dalston Ln. 7 mins from Haggerston train stn or 10 min walk through London Fields from Mare St buses.* **Sun 8 June (2-6). Combined adm £10, chd free.**

84 LAVENDER GROVE
Anne Pauleau.
(See separate entry)

36 MALVERN ROAD
Kath Harris.

53 MAPLEDENE ROAD
Tigger Cullinan.

55 MAPLEDENE ROAD
Amanda & Tony Mott.

84 MIDDLETON ROAD
Penny Fowler.

92 MIDDLETON ROAD
Mr Richard & Dr Louise Jarrett.

A fascinating and very diverse collection of gardens in London Fields within easy walking distance of each other. At 84 Lavender Grove there are twin south facing gardens, a courtyard with a tropical backdrop, and a highly scented, romantic cottage garden. At 36 Malvern Road you will find a little gem of rills and mirrors and forest pansy trees. 92 Middleton Road is elegant and serene with a circular theme inc roses, acers and examples of stone lettering. At 84 Middleton Road lies an unusually large secret garden where you can wander down meandering woodland paths and forget you are in London. The other two are north facing with much the same space but totally different styles. 53 Mapledene Road is an established plantaholic's garden in five sections with not a spare unplanted inch. 55 Mapledene Road has a Moorish-inspired terrace leading

Stud Nursery Community Garden

to a wildlife garden with plants chosen to attract birds, bees and butterflies. A fabulous afternoon to see six such contrasting gardens. ☕))

NEW LONG COTTAGE, HA5
54 High View, Pinner, HA5 3PB. David & Prue Ruback, 07775 643055. *15 min walk from Pinner tube stn (Met line). High View runs between West End Ln & Cuckoo Hill.* **Sun 22 June (2-5.30). Adm £5, chd free. Tea, coffee & cake.** Visits also by arrangement for groups of up to 6.
Large colourful suburban garden enclosed by trees and varieties of bamboo. Lawned with raised beds and several tranquil seating areas providing alternative vistas. Patio with range of potted plants giving a spectrum of colour. Planting inc a variety of shrubs, rose garden, clematis and perennials all designed to show colour, leaf design and texture for all seasons. Access by side entrance. One shallow step, remainder of garden easily accessible. ♿ ☕))

NEW 19 LOVELACE ROAD, SE21
SE21 8JY. Dilys Gane. *Short walk from Tulse Hill & West Dulwich stns.* **Sun 22 June (11.30-5). Combined adm with 38 Lovelace Road £8, chd free. Light refreshments.**
Discover this artist's garden, a tranquil south facing space where art and nature unite. Enjoy a mosaic of junipers, euonymus, and hebes at the front and explore wide borders with a rose arch, rose and blackberry hedging and bee-friendly flowers at the back. A pond teems with wildlife, and there is a veranda growing tomatoes, cucumbers, and lemons. ✤ ☕))

38 LOVELACE ROAD, SE21
Dulwich, SE21 8JX. José & Deepti Ramos Turnes. *Trains from Victoria to West Dulwich stn (12 mins) or London Bridge/Blackfriars to Tulse Hill stn (18 mins). Buses: 2, 3 & 68, then a short 10 min walk.* **Sun 22 June (11.30-5). Combined adm with 19 Lovelace Road £8, chd free. Light refreshments.**
This charming garden welcomes you with an elegant all-white front, while the back has the illusion of endless space. Curving borders overflow with a mix of roses, delphiniums, foxgloves and unusual plants for sun and shade, complemented by a tranquil, hosta-

lined stream. Mature Japanese acers, a Holm oak, and fruit trees provide structure and colour, adding depth to this hidden oasis. A lovely selection of delicious home-made cakes and savoury snacks will be available alongside tea, coffee and soft drinks. ☕))

GROUP OPENING

LOWER CLAPTON GARDENS, E5
Lower Clapton, E5 0RL. *12 min walk from Hackney Central, Hackney Downs or Homerton stns. Buses 38, 55, 106, 242, 253, 254 or 425, alight Lower Clapton Rd or Powerscroft Rd. Street parking.* **Sun 25 May (2-5). Combined adm £7, chd free. Home-made teas at 77 Rushmore Road.**

8 ALMACK ROAD
Philip Lightowlers, 07910 850276, plighto@gmail.com.
Visits also by arrangement 12 Apr to 31 Aug for groups of up to 20.

10 ALMACK ROAD
Mr Ben Myhill.

75 MAYOLA ROAD
Ms Christine Taylor.

77 RUSHMORE ROAD
Penny Edwards.

Lower Clapton is an area of mid-Victorian terraces sloping down to the River Lea. These gardens reflect their owner's tastes and interests. 10 Almack Road is a long garden with architectural plants like trachycarpus palms and cordylines, a large pond and much Yorkstone and London brick. Next door at No. 8 is a similar space but divided into two rooms, one cool and peaceful the other with hot colours, succulents and greenhouse. 77 Rushmore Road has a fruit and vegetable garden and wildlife pond. 75 Mayola Road has a woodland walk and Caribbean style shed.
✤ ☕))

MAGGIE'S AT THE ROYAL MARSDEN, SM2
17 Cotswold Road, Sutton, SM2 5NG. Maggie's at The Royal Marsden, www.maggies.org/royalmarsden. *Maggie's is on corner of Cotswold Rd via the staff entrance to The Royal Marsden Hospital. Belmont train stn, 10 min walk uphill. Buses: 80, 420, 820 & S1. Parking in pay & display patient car park.*

Fri 25 Apr (1-5). Adm £4, chd free. Tea, coffee & home-made cake.
The garden surrounding the centre is designed by the world-famous Dutch Landscape Architect Piet Oudolf, who envisioned a dynamic landscape. The garden is divided into four interconnected zones. Piet has carefully chosen the plants according to how much sun each zone receives. We have the shaded, woodland, spring and summer zones, creating a powerful experience for the eyes. Wheelchair access over raised paths.
♿ 🐕 ✤ ☕))

MAGGIE'S WEST LONDON, W6
Charing Cross Hospital, Fulham Palace Road, Hammersmith, W6 8RF. Maggie's West London, www.instagram.com/maggies.west.london. *Follow Fulham Palace Rd from Hammersmith stn towards Charing Cross Hospital. The centre is on the corner of the hospital grounds of St Dunstan's Rd, and is painted tomato-orange.* **Sun 1 June (10-1). Adm £5, chd free. Tea, coffee & cake.**
The garden at Maggie's West London was designed by Dan Pearson OBE in 2008. It is now a well established space offering therapy and peace to those affected by cancer each yr. The gardens surround the vivid orange walls of the centre. The path leading to the centre meanders through scented beds and mature trees. Visitors have access to various courtyards with a wonderful array of flora, grapevines and even a mature pink silk mimosa. Maggie's West London won the RIBA Stirling Prize for the best building designed by a British architect when first built. Wheelchair access to ground floor gardens and courtyards. Roof gardens not accessible.
♿ 🐕 ☕))

4 MANNINGTREE ROAD, HA4
Ruislip, HA4 0ES. Costas Lambropoulos & Roberto Haddon. *Manningtree Rd is just off Victoria Rd, 10-15 min walk from South Ruislip tube stn.* **Sun 10 Aug (2-6). Adm £5, chd free. Tea, coffee & cake.**
Compact garden with an exotic feel that combines hardy architectural plants with more tender ones. A feeling of a small oasis inc plants like *Musa basjoo*, *Ensete ventricosum* 'Montbeliardii' and a tree fern. Potted Mediterranean plants on the patio inc a fig tree, jasmines and two olive trees. Cakes, savouries, home-made jams and biscuits for sale.
✤ ☕))

MHA THE WILDERNESS, CR9
Hall Grange Care Home, 17 Shirley Church Road, Croydon, CR9 5AL. Methodist Homes, www.mha.org.uk/get-involved/the-wilderness. *2m E of Croydon. Situated behind MHA Hall Grange Care Home. The garden is accessed via a green gate to the R of care home & car park (for residents only). Street parking nearby. Buses: 466 & 130, plus 5 min walk.* **Sun 18 May (12-5). Adm £5, chd free. Hot & cold drinks, home-made cakes & vegan options.**
MHA The Wilderness is a reformed heritage garden first created by Rev William Wilks, Vicar of Shirley and former secretary of the Royal Horticulture Society, between 1904 and 1923. In spring/early summer there are mature rhododendrons planted by Wilks, azaleas and Shirley poppies (bred by Wilks). At 2pm Lucy James, Head Gardener, will give a tour of the garden inc its history and development. Accessible path circles the entire garden, though on a slight incline.

41 MILL HILL ROAD, W3
Acton, W3 8JE. Marcia Hurst, marcia.hurst@sudbury-house.co.uk. *Tube: Acton Town, cross zebra crossing on to Gunnersbury Ln, 2nd R to Mill Hill Rd.* **Evening opening Fri 15 Aug (6-8). Combined adm with 65 Mill Hill Road £7, chd free. Wine.** Visits also by arrangement May to Sept for groups of 5 to 15.
Surprisingly secluded original garden with varied selection of plants, borders, topiary, lavender hedge and large lawn. Adjoining sunny new garden from 2019 with meadow, pond and gravel garden. Ample seating. Good selection of plants growing in the garden are for sale in pots with planting and growing advice from the knowledgeable plantaholic owner.

65 MILL HILL ROAD, W3
Acton, W3 8JF. Anna Dargavel, 07802 241965, annadargavel@mac.com. *Tube: Acton Town, turn R, Mill Hill Rd 2nd R off Gunnersbury Ln.* **Evening opening Fri 15 Aug (6-8). Combined adm with 41 Mill Hill Road £7, chd free. Wine at 41 Mill Hill Rd.** Visits also by arrangement May to Sept for groups of 5 to 15.
Garden designer's garden. A secluded and tranquil space, paved with changes of level and borders. Sunny areas, topiary, a greenhouse and interesting planting combine to provide a wildlife haven. A pond and organic principles are used to promote a green environment and give a stylish walk to a studio at the end of the garden.

MONA'S GARDEN, N10
33 Wood Vale, Muswell Hill, N10 3DJ. Mona Abboud, 07913 775634, monaabboud@hotmail.com, www.monasgarden.co.uk. *Tube: Highgate, 10 min walk. Buses: W3, W7 to top of Park Rd.* **Visits by arrangement May to Sept for groups of 5 to 20. Adm £5, chd free. Light refreshments. Donation to Plant Heritage.**
This award-winning garden has just got bigger! An adjacent 600 square metre of wasteland is transformed into a sustainable mini prairie and more exotic and woodland planting. The garden hosts the National Collection of Corokia along with many other unusual Australasian and Mediterranean plants complemented by thriving perennials and grasses. Emphasis on structure, texture, foliage and distinctive pruning.

NEW 119 MORTLAKE ROAD, TW9
Richmond, TW9 4AW. Karen Penney. *Kew. What3words app: drop.bravo.charm. Nearest tube/overground stn: Kew Gardens. Bus route R68. Parking in West Park Ave (free on Sundays) or Kew Retail Park car park (max 4 hrs).* **Sun 6 July (2-5.30). Adm £5, chd free. Tea, coffee & cake.**
Thoughtful combinations of form and colour create a stunning summer themed and packed with a wide range of perennials. A lush 'fernarium' gives way to pastel cottage planting. The garden's sunny side boasts a riot of colour with an impressive 'hot' border. With something new around every corner, this garden shows the potential of an ordinary-sized town garden. Pollinator and butterfly friendly.

THE MYSTERIES OF LIGHT ROSARY GARDEN, NW5
St Dominic's Priory (the Rosary Shrine), Southampton Road, Kentish Town, NW5 4LB. Raffaella Morini on behalf of the Church & Priory, 07778 526434, garden@raffaellamorini.com, rosaryshrine.co.uk/rosary-shrine/visit-the-shrine/garden. *Entrance to the garden is from Alan Cheales Way on the RHS of the church, next to the school.* **Sat 14 June (1-5). Adm £5, chd free. Tea, coffee & cake.** Visits also by arrangement May to Sept.
A walled garden behind the Priory Church of Our Lady of the Rosary and St Dominic, commissioned by the Dominican Friars as a representing and meditative space representing the 'Mysteries of Light' of the Holy Rosary. The sandstone path marks out a Rosary with black granite beads, surrounded by flowers traditionally associated with the Virgin Mary: roses, lilies, iris, periwinkle, and columbine. The garden is fully accessible with stone path and wheelchair friendly gravel path.

15 NORCOTT ROAD, N16
Stoke Newington, N16 7BJ. Amanda & John Welch, 020 8806 5723, amandashetlandwelch@gmail.com. *Buses: 67, 73, 76, 106, 149, 243, 393, 476, 488. Clapton & Rectory Road train stns. LTNs operate in this area.* **Visits by arrangement 13 Jan to 1 Dec.**
Large walled garden developed over 45 yrs by the present owners with pond, aged fruit trees and an abundance of herbaceous plants. After 32 yrs we've decided to change from the 'one big open day' to 'come when you choose' (by arrangement). Our garden is always ready for visitors! We have plenty of room for people to sit, relax and enjoy their tea.

5 NORTHAMPTON PARK, N1
N1 2PP. Andrew Bernhardt & Anne Brogan. *Backing on to St Paul's Shrubbery, Islington. 5 min walk from Canonbury train stn, 10 mins from Highbury & Islington tube (Victoria line). Buses: 73, 30, 56, 341, 476.* **Sat 12 July (1.30-6). Adm £5, chd free. Wine, prosecco & strawberries.**
A total transformation: this once neglected south facing, walled garden (1840s), has for three decades become an open garden regular. Closed in 2024 for a complete

redesign our intention is to use a blend of traditional and tropical planting to better capture the colour, sunlight and space. With many outcomes as yet uncertain we hope you will visit to share our trepidation and excitement.

21 OAKLEIGH PARK SOUTH, N20
N20 9JS. Carol & Robin Tullo, 07909 901731/07930 480707, robin.tullo@btinternet.com. *Totteridge & Whetstone tube stn (Northern line), 15 min walk or 251 bus. Oakleigh Park train stn, 10 min walk. Also buses 34 & 125 from High Rd. Plenty of street parking.* **Sun 1 June (2-6). Adm £5, chd free. Home-made teas.** Visits also by arrangement 5 Apr to 29 June for groups of 10 to 25.
A mature 200ft garden framed by a magnificent 100 yr old ash tree. Path leads to a pond area fed by a natural spring within landscaped terraced paving. Beyond is a herb and vegetable area, orchard with bulbs and wild flowers and the working part of the garden. A mix of sunny borders, pond marginals and woodland shade areas with lots of seating. Level wheelchair access to terrace and lawn. Path to pond area, but raised levels beyond.

NEW 3 OLD FOLD CLOSE, EN5
Barnet, EN5 4QL. Amanda Magill. *1m S of M25 J24 in Hadley Highstone. Follow signs for Old Fold Manor Golf Course. Note: Entrance to garden only from Old Fold Ln, opp Hadley Common. Bus: 234, 326, 384 to Barnet High St (10 min walk). Train: Great Northern to Hadley Wood stn or Tube: High Barnet stn, Northern line (20 min walk).* **Sun 6 July (2-5.30). Adm £5, chd free. Tea, coffee & cake.**
A foliage centred garden with weaving caramel-coloured paths and featuring bronze coloured metal art installations throughout. Beth Chatto inspired dry beds dominate the top part of the garden with a shrub surrounded woodland zone in the centre and a grassy mound, rockery and Japanese themed area closest to the back gate which opens out to an extensive rockery in the garage area. Hadley Common 1 min walk for picnics.

NEW OLDEN COMMUNITY GARDEN, N5
Whistler Street (opp No. 22), N5 1NH. London Borough of Islington, www.oldengarden.org. *Islington. Walk from Highbury & Islington, Arsenal or Holloway Rd tube stn, or Drayton Park train stn. Or from bus stops in Holloway Rd. Along Drayton Park to Whistler St.* **Sun 6 Apr (2-5). Adm £5, chd free. Home-made teas.**
A 2 acre secret oasis of biodiversity on a railway embankment. Spring bulbs and blossom flourish. A lawn, herbaceous garden, wildflower meadow, wildlife pond and 1 acre woodland delight visitors. We have an orchard, vegetable beds and new butterfly garden. We compost green waste, use harvested water and build dead hedges. Visitors enjoy walks in the woodland and tea on the patio or in the garden house. Wheelchair access to all areas of top terrace. Accessible WC.

ORMELEY LODGE, TW10
Ham Gate Avenue, Richmond, TW10 5HB. Lady Annabel Goldsmith. *From Richmond Park exit at Ham Gate into Ham Gate Ave, 1st house on R. From Richmond A307 after 1½ m, past New Inn on R. At T-lights turn L into Ham Gate Ave.* **Sun 22 June (3-6). Adm £5, chd free. Tea. Open nearby Cairn Cottage.**
Large walled garden in delightful rural setting on Ham Common. Wide herbaceous borders and box hedges. Walk through to orchard with wild flowers. Vegetable garden, knot garden, aviary and chickens. Trellised tennis court with roses and climbers. A number of historic stone family dog memorials. Dogs not permitted.

PADDOCK ALLOTMENTS & LEISURE GARDENS, SW20
51 Heath Drive, Raynes Park, SW20 9BE. Paddock Horticultural Society. *Buses 57, 131, 200 to Raynes Park stn, then 10 min walk or bus 163. Bus 152 to Bushey Rd, 7 min walk. Bus 413, 5 min walk from Cannon Hill Ln. Street parking.* **Sat 21 June (12-5). Adm £4, chd free. Light refreshments.**
An allotment site not to be missed, over 150 plots set in 5½ acres. Our tenants come from diverse communities growing a wide range of flowers, fruit and vegetables. Some plots are purely organic, others resemble English country gardens. Winner of London in Bloom Best Allotment on four occasions. Plants and produce for sale. Ploughman's lunch available. Wheelchair access over mainly level paved and grass paths.

11 PARK AVENUE NORTH, N8
Crouch End, N8 7RU. Steven Buckley & Liz Roberts. *Between Crouch End & Muswell Hill. Buses: 144, W3, W7. Tube: Finsbury Park or Turnpike Lane. Train: Hornsey or Alexandra Palace.* **Sun 20 July (11.30-5.30). Adm £5, chd free. Pre-booking essential, please visit www.ngs.org.uk for information & booking. Home-made teas.**
An award-winning exotic garden, subject of a major feature in the RHS The Garden magazine, July 2024. Much developed recently. Dramatic foliage, spiky and lush, dominates, with the focus on palms, cycads, aloes, agaves, dioons, dasylirions, aeoniums, tree ferns, nolinas, bamboos, yuccas, bananas, cacti, puyas and succulents. Trees inc orange, peach, *Cussonia spicata* and Szechuan pepper.

36 PARK VILLAGE EAST, NW1
Camden Town, NW1 7PZ. Christy Rogers. *Tube: Mornington Cres or Camden Town, 7 mins. Opp railway, just S of Mornington St bridge. Free parking on Sundays.* **Sun 8 June (2-6). Adm £6, chd free. Home-made teas.**
A large peaceful garden behind a sympathetically modernised John Nash house. Relandscaped in 2014, retaining the original mature sycamores and adding hornbeam hedges dividing a woodland area and orchard from a central large lawn, mixed herbaceous border and rose bank now with a newly planted seating area. Children enjoy an artificial grass slide. Musical entertainment provided by young musicians. Wheelchair access via grass ramp down from driveway to main garden (steeper than wheelchair regulations).

5 PEMBERTON ROAD, KT8
East Molesey, KT8 9LG. Armi Maddison. *Please enter the garden down the side path to R of house.* **Sun 13 July (2-5). Adm £5, chd free. Tea, coffee & cake.**
An artist's sheltered and secluded gravel garden, designed alongside our new build in 2015. Many grasses, pink, blue and white planting with occasional pops of bright colour, a galvanised drinking trough with bulrushes and water lilies, a large mature central acer tree, combine with several seating areas to extend the living space into this fabulous outdoor room.

PETERSHAM HOUSE, TW10
Petersham Road, Petersham, Richmond, TW10 7AA.
Francesco & Gael Boglione, www.petershamnurseries.com. *Stn: Richmond, bus 65 to Dysart. Entry to garden off Petersham Rd, through Petersham Nurseries. Parking very limited on Church Ln.* **Sun 13 Apr (11-3). Adm £7.50, chd free.**
Broad lawn with large topiary and generously planted herbaceous borders. Adjoins Petersham Nurseries with extensive plant sales, shop and café serving lunch, tea and cake (pre-booking advised).

4 PIERMONT GREEN, SE22
East Dulwich, SE22 0LP. Janine Wookey. *Triangle of green, facing Peckham Rye at the Honor Oak Rd end. Stns: Peckham Rye & Honor Oak. Buses: 63 & 363 (pass the door) & 12. No parking on green, but free parking on side streets nearby.* **Sun 17 Aug (1.30-4.30). Adm £5, chd free. Home-made teas. Open nearby 86 Underhill Road.**
This L-shaped garden partly enclosed by a Victorian wall has an old fashioned woodland feel with spreading mulberry and viburnum trees overlooked by ginkgo and purple elder. Global warming lets a banana grove flourish with fig, lemon, pear and apricot. A low maintenance gravel area offers aeoniums, and towering pretty mallow, and *Althaea cannabina*. By the house bright pots give a Mediterranean feel. An attractive pebble mosaic under the mulberry tree. Wheelchair access with a couple of front steps to negotiate.

1A PRIMROSE GARDENS, NW3
Hampstead, NW3 4UJ. Debra & Tim Craighead, dcraighead@me.com. *Belsize Park. Convenient from Belsize & Chalk Farm tube stns (5 mins) or Swiss Cottage (12 mins). Also, buses 1, 268 & C11. Free parking on Sundays.* **Evening opening Sat 20 Sept (4-6). Adm £10. Wine. Sun 21 Sept (2.30-5.30). Adm £5, chd free. Home-made teas. Visits also by arrangement 26 May to 30 Sept for groups of 10 to 35.**
Hidden oasis in the heart of Belsize Park, cool and relaxing. Planted with various microclimates for surrounding buildings, walls, and desire for privacy. Mirrors help create sense of intrigue. Densely planted for texture and revolving seasonality; tree ferns, foxglove, clematis, ferns, salvias and lillies. A restricted colour palette of white, purple and pops of orange/ russet throughout the yr. Bird friendly with a sedum rooftop attracting bees and butterflies.

GROUP OPENING

PRINCES AVENUE GARDENS, N10
Muswell Hill, N10 3LS. *Buses: 43 & 134 from Highgate tube stn; also W7, 102, 144, 234, 299. Princes Ave opp M&S in Muswell Hill Broadway & The Village Green pub in Fortis Green Rd.* **Sun 18 May (12-6). Combined adm £6, chd free. Home-made teas. Gluten free & vegan options.**

17 PRINCES AVENUE
Patsy Bailey & John Rance.

NEW 28 PRINCES AVENUE
Lucinda Oppenheimer.

In a beautiful Edwardian avenue in the heart of Muswell Hill Conservation Area, there are two peaceful traditional gardens off the bustling Broadway, for relaxing and entertaining. The gardens are very different. No. 17 is south facing, but shaded by large surrounding trees inc a ginkgo. The garden features a superb hosta and fern display. No. 28, opp, is north facing; mature trees, shrubs, and beautifully planted mixed borders give a feeling of calm with acers, fruit trees and a rose arch; a trampoline lurks in a secret corner. Live music at 17 Princes Avenue by the Secret Life Sax Quartet at 3pm and 4pm. Small step at No. 17, help available on request.

NEW 16 PURLEY AVENUE, NW2
Cricklewood, NW2 1SJ. Mr & Mrs Mansi. *Between Cricklewood Ln & The Vale. Nr bus stops 460, 102, 113 & C11. Golders Green tube; Cricklewood & Brent Cross Town Thames Link.* **Sun 18 May (2-6). Adm £5, chd free. Tea, coffee & cake.**
This vibrant garden blends lush established plants with tropical and Mediterranean varieties. An apple tree and silver birch offer shade, while a small wildlife pond invites nature in. A raised shady border is filled with ferns and hostas. Fragrant jasmine and roses greet visitors in the garden. Mosaic sculptures add artistic flair, making this garden a private, peaceful retreat, full of life.

GROUP OPENING

RAILWAY COTTAGES, N22
2 Dorset Road, N22 7SL. *Nr Alexandra Palace. Tube: Wood Green, 10 min walk. Train: Alexandra Palace, 3 mins. Buses: W3, 184, 3 mins. Free parking in local streets on Sundays.* **Sun 6 July (2-5.30). Combined adm £5, chd free. Home-made teas at 2 Dorset Road.**

2 DORSET ROAD
Jane Stevens.

4 DORSET ROAD
Mark Longworth.

14 DORSET ROAD
Cathy Brogan.

22 DORSET ROAD
Mike & Noreen Ainger.

24A DORSET ROAD
Eddie & Jane Wessman.

A row of historical railway cottages, tucked away from the bustle of Wood Green nr Alexandra Palace, takes the visitor back in time. The tranquil country style garden at 2 Dorset Road flanks three sides of the house. Clipped hedges contrast with climbing roses, clematis, honeysuckle, abutilon, grasses and ferns. Trees inc mulberry, quince, fig, apple and a mature willow creating an interesting shady corner with a pond. There is an emphasis on scented flowers that attract bees and butterflies and the traditional medicinal plants found in cottage gardens. No. 4 is a pretty secluded garden (accessed through the rear of No. 2) and sets off the sculptor owners figurative and abstract work. There are three front gardens open for view. No. 14 is an informal, organic, bee-friendly garden, planted with fragrant and useful herbs, flowers and shrubs. No. 22 is nurtured by the grandson of the original railway worker occupant. A lovely place to sit and relax and enjoy the varied planting. No. 24a reverts to the potager style cottage garden with raised beds overflowing with vegetables and flowers. A large green beside Dorset Road is perfect for a picnic. Popular plant sale.

42 RISINGHOLME ROAD, HA3
Harrow, HA3 7ER. Brenda White. *Wealdstone/Harrow Weald. Buses: 258, 340,182,140 Salvatorian College/St Joseph's Catholic Church, Wealdstone. Tube/train: Harrow & Wealdstone stn (10 min walk or bus). Road opp the Salvatorian College.* **Sun 4 May, Sun 31 Aug (2-5). Adm £5, chd free. Tea, coffee & cake.** A stunning, paved 120ft long garden packed with plants, divided into different themed areas inc a raised bed vegetable garden, a large aviary, beehive and summerhouse. A shady garden that makes the most of every space!

ROEHAMPTON GARDEN SOCIETY ALLOTMENTS, SW15
18A The Pleasance, Putney, SW15 5HF. Roehampton Garden Society, www.roehamptonallotments.co.uk. *Bus: 430 to Gibbon Walk stop then 2 min walk. 337 coming from the E, Dover House Rd stop; from the W, Gipsy Lane stop, then 8 min walk. Train: Putney Mainline. Street parking.* **Sat 21 June (2-5). Adm £4, chd free. Home-made teas.**
Our two allotments sites were established in the 1920s, set within the Dover House Estate, a Conservation area in a garden suburb environment. The Pleasance site has 90 plots, cultivated by a diverse community. The opening inc our annual Summer Show, a lovely celebration where prize-winning flowers, fruit and vegetables are exhibited then auctioned at 4.30pm. Fresh produce and plants for sale. Cake competition too!

NEW 19 ROKEBY GARDENS, IG8
Woodford Green, IG8 9HT. Pauline Gunn. *From Churchill statue, Woodford Green, take 1st L turn Forest Approach to Xrds, straight across on Forest Approach, at top of hill L into Rokeby Gardens. Please park on one side of the road.* **Sun 29 June (2-5). Adm £4. Tea, coffee, soft drinks & home-made cakes.**
Calming, colourful town garden (75ft x 25ft) with Koi pond and raised bed with north facing border. Convivial seating areas provide different views of the garden when entertaining. Cottage planting with perpetual flowering roses purchased from RHS flower shows inc fuchsia, brunnera, hosta, primula, and phlox. Pots of roses and fruit provide seasonal interest.

St Joseph's Hospice

ROOFTOPVEGPLOT, W1
122 Great Titchfield Street, W1W 6ST. Miss Wendy Shillam, 07597 438666, coffeeinthesquare@Me.com, www.rooftopvegplot.com. *Westminster. Located on the 5th floor, flat roof of a private house. Ring the doorbell marked Shillam & Smith to be let into the building.* **Sat 5, Sun 6 July (11-5). Adm £6, chd free. Pre-booking essential, please visit www.ngs.org.uk for information & booking. Home-made teas.**
A nutritional garden with views across London, where fruit and vegetables grow amongst complementary flowers in six inches of soil, in raised beds on a flat roof. Trellis and greenhouse tomatoes. This is a tiny garden, so tours are restricted to six visitors. Home-made cakes, and growing and nutritional tips from Wendy Shillam, a clinical nutritionist and health writer with an extensive knowledge of green nutrition.

ROYAL COLLEGE OF PHYSICIANS, GARDEN OF MEDICINAL PLANTS, NW1
11 St Andrews Place, Regents Park, NW1 4LE. Royal College of Physicians of London, garden.rcplondon.ac.uk. *Tubes: Great Portland St & Regent's Park. Garden is one block N of stn exits, on Outer Circle opp SE corner of Regent's Park. There is no access via Peto Place.* **Mon 7 July (11-4). Adm £6, chd free. Tea, coffee & cake.**
We have almost 1000 different plants connected with the role of plants in medicine today and in the past. These inc plants named after physicians, plants which make modern medicines and those with long standing traditional uses. There are plants used in medical traditions from all the continents of the world and plants from the College's own Pharmacopoeia of 1618. Guided tours will be offered throughout the day by physicians explaining the uses of the plants, their histories and other stories. Books about the plants in the medicinal garden will be on sale alongside free leaflets. All the plants are labelled with their botanical names. Entry to the garden is at far end of St Andrews Place. Accessible paths around the garden. Some slopes. Wheelchair lift for WC. No parking on site.

ROYAL TRINITY HOSPICE, SW4
30 Clapham Common North Side, SW4 0RN. Royal Trinity Hospice, www.royaltrinityhospice.london/our-gardens. *1⅓m from Clapham Junction. 8 min walk from Clapham Common tube. Buses: 35, 37, 345,137, 249 & 322 (137 stops outside).* **Sun 6 Apr, Sun 11 May, Sun 8 June, Sun 14 Sept (11-4). Adm £4, chd free. Light refreshments. Open nearby 51 The Chase, 52 The Chase & 152A Victoria Rise on 8 June only.**
Our front gardens feature wisteria, shrubs and trees. The rear landscaped gardens have lawns with herbaceous borders either side of a path that leads to the Koi pond. Plenty of year-round colour from annuals, perennials, roses and shrubs. We have added more perennials and shrubs with autumn colours. We use our large glasshouse to grow plants and vegetables from seed. Interesting sculpture by George Rickey called Four Open Squares Horizontal Tapered in the pond. Wheelchair access via ramps and pathways.

31 RYECROFT ROAD, SW16
Streatham, SW16 3EW. Chrissy Silver, www.instagram.com/chrissysgarden2024. *Nr Crown Point. Mainline: Streatham & West Norwood stns. Buses: 68, 196, 249, 417, & 468 all to Crown Point.* **Sun 22 June (12-6). Adm £5.50, chd free. Tea, coffee & cake. Prosecco.**
Large, sunny garden with an open aspect and far-reaching views towards the North Downs from a roof terrace. Herbaceous border around a large lawn, cut flower bed, small woodland area, and a rockery with Mediterranean planting. Old-fashioned roses both front and back. Lovely old Yorkstone and slate paths help to divide the garden into smaller, cosier areas.

NEW ST JOSEPH'S HOSPICE, E8
Mare Street, Hackney, E8 4SA. St Joseph's Hospice, www.stjh.org.uk/about-us/our-gardens. *South end of Mare St, nr Broadway Market. South of King Edward's Rd. Buses 254, 106, 388, 26. Use King Edward's Rd bus stop coming S from Hackney Central & Victoria Park Rd bus stop coming N from Bethnal Green (Central line).* **Sat 31 May (10-4.30). Adm £3, chd free. Light refreshments.**
The formal gardens at St Joseph's Hospice are a healing space. Made up of seven distinct garden spaces, each with secluded seating, intended to promote important end of life conversations with friends and family. When you visit at the end of May, you will find an abundance of roses in full bloom as the impressive wisteria fades away. Wheelchair access to gardens, although there are some slopes. Wheelchair accessible WC.

27 ST PETERS SQUARE, W6
British Grove, W6 9NW. Oliver & Gabrielle Leigh Wood, 07810 677478, oliverleighwood@hotmail.com. *Tube to Stamford Brook, exit stn & turn S down Goldhawk Rd. At T-lights continue ahead into British Grove. Entrance to garden at 50 British Grove, 100yds on L.* **Sun 11 May (2-6). Adm £8, chd free. Home-made teas. Visits also by arrangement 1 May to 1 June.**
This long, secret space, is a plantsman's eclectic semi-tamed wilderness. Created over the last 12 yrs it contains lots of camellias, magnolias and fruit trees. Much of the hard landscaping is from skips and the whole garden is full of other people's unconsidered trifles of fancy inc a folly and summerhouse.

19 ST PETER'S STREET, N1
Islington, N1 8JD. Adrian Gunning. *Angel, Islington. Tube: Angel. Bus: Islington Green.* **Sun 25 May (3-6). Adm £5, chd free.**
A charming, secluded town garden featuring climbing roses, trees, shrubs, climbers, a pond, a patio with containers, and a gazebo with a trompe l'oeil mural.

57 ST QUINTIN AVENUE, W10
W10 6NZ. Mr H Groffman, 020 8969 8292. *Less than 1m from Ladbroke Grove or White City tube stn. Buses: 7, 70, 220 all to North Pole Rd.* **Sun 6, Sun 20 July (2-5.30). Adm £5, chd free. Home-made teas. Visits also by arrangement July to Sept.**
Award-winning 30 x 40ft garden with a diverse selection of plants inc shrubs for foliage effects. Patio with colour themed bedding. Focal points

throughout. Clever use of mirrors and plant associations. New look front garden, new rear patio layout and new plantings for 2025 with a good selection of climbers and wall shrubs. This year's special display commemorates the 80th Anniversary of VE and VJ Day.

❀ ☕

5 ST REGIS CLOSE, N10
Alexandra Park Road, Muswell Hill, N10 2DE. Mrs S Bennett & Mr E Hyde, 020 8883 8540, suebearlh@yahoo.co.uk. *2nd L in Alexandra Park Rd coming from Colney Hatch Ln. 102 & 299 bus from Bounds Green tube to St Andrew's Church or 102 from East Finchley. Buses 43 & 143 stop in Colney Hatch Ln. Short walk. Follow NGS signs. Parking on side roads inc coaches.* **Sun 4 May, Sun 29 June, Sun 3 Aug (2-6.30). Adm £5, chd free. Home-made teas. Herbal teas & gluten free option. Purchase ticket in advance or cash preferred on the day.** Visits also by arrangement 20 Apr to 15 Oct for groups of 10+. Short talk on history of the garden.
Cornucopia of sensual delights. Artist's garden famous for architectural features and delicious cakes. Baroque temple, pagodas, Raku tiled mirrored wall conceals plant nursery. American Gothic shed overlooks Liberace terrace and stairway to heaven. Maureen Lipman's favourite garden; combines colour, humour, trompe l'oeil with wildlife friendly ponds, waterfalls, weeping willow, lawns and abundant planting. A unique experience awaits! Unusual architectural features inc Oriental tea house overlooking carp pond. Mega plant sale and open studio with ceramics and cards (cash only). Wheelchair access not suitable for everyone, please check with owners for details.

♿ 🐕 ❀ 🚗 ☕ 🎵

NEW 16 SEARS STREET, SE5
SE5 7JL. Jonathan Gregson, www.backyardbotanics.co.uk. *5 min walk from Bowyer Place stop N (Camberwell Rd) for buses from Elephant & Castle, or Wyndham Rd bus stop from Denmark Hill. TfL cycle hire docking station on corner of Camberwell Rd/Albany Rd.* **Sun 20 July (11-4.30). Adm £5, chd free. Tea, coffee & cake.**
Described as a 'backyard botanic garden', this small city garden crams in plants from more than 200 plant families, making it one of the more botanically diverse in London. Created by a plant addict, it has spaces dedicated to different regions of the world. Bananas, monkey puzzle trees and ferns native to the rainforests of Borneo, jostle for space with traditional roses, lilies and foxgloves.

❀ ☕ 🎵

SOUTH LONDON BOTANICAL INSTITUTE, SE24
323 Norwood Road, SE24 9AQ. South London Botanical Institute, www.slbi.org.uk. *Mainline: Tulse Hill. Buses: 2, 415, 68, 196, 322 & 468 all from Brixton.* **Sun 27 Apr (2-5). Adm by donation. Light refreshments.** Donation to South London Botanical Institute.
London's smallest botanical garden. Spring highlights inc unusual bulbs, ferns, flowering trees and early roses. Wild flowers flourish beside medicinal herbs. Scented, native and woodland plants are featured, growing among rare trees and shrubs. There is a small dye plant bed and a collection of succulents in our greenhouse.

❀ ☕ 🎵

123 SOUTH PARK ROAD, SW19
Wimbledon, SW19 8RX. Susan Adcock. *Mainline & tube: Wimbledon, 10 mins; South Wimbledon tube, 5 mins. Buses: 57, 93, 131, 219 along High St. Entrance in Bridges Rd (next to Church Hall), off South Park Rd.* **Sun 22 June (2-6). Adm £4, chd free. Home-made cake & cordial. Open nearby 61 Arthur Road.**
This small, romantic L-shaped garden has a high treetop deck overlooking a woodland area with a second deck below and small hut. Paving from the garden room with pots and seating, several small water containers, a fish pond and a secluded courtyard with raised beds for flowers and herbs, as well as a discreet hot tub. Lots of ideas for giving a small space atmosphere and interest.

☕ 🎵

41 SOUTHBROOK ROAD, SE12
Lee, SE12 8LJ. Barbara Polanski. *Southbrook Rd is situated off A205 S Circular, off Burnt Ash Rd. Train: Lee & Hither Green, both 10 min walk. Bus: P273, 202. Please enter via side access & look out for the yellow balloons!* **Sat 7, Sun 8 June (2-5.30). Adm £5, chd free. Home-made teas.**
Developed over 15 yrs, this garden has a formal layout with wide mixed herbaceous borders full of colour, surrounded by mature trees, framing sunny lawns, an immaculate central box parterre and an Indian pergola. Ancient pear trees festooned in June with large clouds of white Kiftsgate and Rambling Rector roses. Discover fish and damselflies in two lily ponds. Orangery, gazebo and wall fountain. Many sheltered places to sit and relax. Enjoy refreshments in a small classical garden building with interior wall paintings, almost hidden by roses climbing way up into the trees. Side access for standard wheelchairs. Gravel driveway and one step.

♿ ☕ 🎵

♦ **SPENCER HOUSE, SW1**
27 St James' Place, Westminster, SW1A 1NR. RIT Capital Partners, www.spencerhouse.co.uk. *From Green Park tube stn, exit on S side, walk down Queen's Walk, turn L through narrow alleyway. Turn R & Spencer House will be in front of you.* **For opening times and information, please visit garden website.**
Originally designed in the C18 by Henry Holland, the garden was among the grandest in the West End. Restored in 1990 under the Chairmanship of Lord Rothschild, the garden now evokes its original layout with planting suggested by early C19 nursery lists and supplemented with native wild flowers for biodiversity.

GROUP OPENING

SPITALFIELDS GARDENS, E1
E1 6QE. *Nr Spitalfields Market. 10 min walk from Liverpool Street stn, Aldgate East tube, Shoreditch High Street overground.* **Sat 7 June (10-4). Combined adm £20, chd free. Home-made teas at The Rectory (2 Fournier Street) & 29 Fournier Street.**

30 CALVIN STREET, FLAT 1
Susan Young.

29 FOURNIER STREET
Juliette Larthe.

THE RECTORY, 2 FOURNIER STREET
Jack McCausland.

37 SPITAL SQUARE
Society for the Protection of Ancient Buildings.

21 WILKES STREET
Rupert Wheeler.

Discover a unique selection of secluded gardens in Spitalfields, just a stone's throw from the buzz of Spitalfields Market. The feel of a country garden behind the Church offering fabulous teas and music, a contemporary architectural walled garden behind a C18 weaver's house, another courtyard garden behind one of the fine French Huguenot houses of the C17, a small paved garden unconstrained by its high boundary walls and another undaunted by the shade of the surrounding tall buildings. Each garden has adapted to its particular urban space with vertical and horizontal beds, inspired planting, pots, statuary and architectural artefacts.

25 SPRINGFIELD AVENUE, N10
Muswell Hill, N10 3SU. Heather Hampson & Nigel Ragg, www.facebook.com/hampsonragg. *Centre of Muswell Hill. From main r'about in Muswell Hill, down Muswell Hill towards Crouch End. Springfield Ave 1st on L. No. 25 is opp the steps to Grosvenor Gardens.* **Sun 8 June (2-6). Adm £5, chd free. Homemade teas.**
Be pleasantly surprised by this city garden! Magical, packed with colour, fragrance, rambling roses and quirky ideas to stimulate conversation and imagination. A visual delight with three terraces, each with an individual atmosphere that lead to the summerhouse with a backdrop of mature trees. Plenty of spots to sit and enjoy scrumptious tea and cakes. Good plant sale. The summerhouse is somewhere to rest and view the owner's art works for sale in aid of the NGS. Please note this is a steep garden, on different levels with uneven steps.

106 STATION ROAD, TW12
Hampton, TW12 2AS. Diane Kermack. *From Hampton stn, turn L along Station Rd, past St Theodore's Church, opp the green. Access to garden via the garden gate on the adjacent side road Station Cl.* **Sat 19, Sun 20 July (11-5). Adm £5, chd free. Tea, coffee & cake.**
An apiary garden with six busy hives which will be of special interest to beekeepers. The garden has six distinct rooms to cater for children, animals, vegetable growing and leisure. Bushy front garden with vegetable plot and perimeter flower bed. Walk through past swimming pool, greenhouses, seating and many pots. Informal back garden featuring beehives, pond, chickens and informal flower beds.

NEW 25 STIRLING ROAD, SW9
Stockwell, SW9 9EF. Francis O'Kane. *Equidistant from Clapham North & Stockwell tube stns. Free parking on Saturdays on Stirling Rd.* **Sat 19 July (10.30-5.30). Adm £6, chd free. Sat 6 Sept (10.30-5.30). Adm £6. Pre-booking essential, please visit www.ngs.org.uk for information & booking. Homemade teas.**
A small but perfectly formed tropical oasis set in South London in this south west facing plot. In what has evolved over a number of yrs from English country garden style to a more exotic paradise, it still retains many elements of a woodland forest with a variety of ferns hidden in its nooks and crannies. Visitors will be drawn to an array of large lush green foliage and bright, bold flowers in this jungle style garden. Water feature and seated area.

Long Cottage

STONEY HILL HOUSE, SE26
Rock Hill, Sydenham, SE26 6SW.
Cinzia & Adam Greaves. *Off Sydenham Hill. Nearest train stns: Sydenham, Gipsy Hill or Sydenham Hill. Buses: To Crystal Palace, 202 or 363 along Sydenham Hill. House at end of cul-de-sac on L coming from Sydenham Hill.* **Sun 18 May (2-6). Adm £7, chd free. Home-made teas. Prosecco.**
Garden and woodland of approx 1 acre providing a secluded secret green oasis in the city. Paths meander through mature rhododendron, oak, yew and holly trees, offset by pieces of contemporary sculpture. The garden is on a slope and a number of viewpoints set at different heights provide varied perspectives. The planting in the top part of the garden is fluid and flows seamlessly into the woodland. Swings and woodland treehouse for entertainment of children and adults alike! Dogs welcome if kept on a lead. Wheelchair access to the main lawn is via a series of about ten shallow steps and the grassy slope alongside the steps.

NEW STUD NURSERY COMMUNITY GARDEN, KT8
Home Park (Kingston Gate entrance), Hampton Court Road, Kingston Upon Thames, KT8 9DB. balancesupport.org.uk/horticultural-services. *Within Home Park, Hampton Court Palace. Enter from gate next to The Old Kings Head Pub (located on Hampton Court Rd, KT1 4AE). To entrance, What3words app: look.sketch.custom.* **Sun 13 July (11-3). Adm £5, chd free. Home-made teas.**
Stud Nursery is a community garden for adults with learning disabilities. We support around 40 clients each week to get involved with gardening, growing vegetables and propagating plants. Our Edwardian walled garden of nearly 1 acre is a wonderful resource, with three glasshouses, two polytunnels, several raised beds, vegetable garden, wildlife habitat, and chickens.

SUSSEX COTTAGE, TW3
128 Whitton Road, Hounslow, TW3 2EP. John Meinke. *Hounslow stn, 5 min walk. Bus 281 passes outside. Unrestricted parking on local roads.* **Sun 6 July (1-5). Combined adm with 116 Whitton Road £8, chd free. Home-made teas.**

A surprising garden with a number of unique features, many of which date back to the 1920s. The garden is on several levels, and features a stone bridge, pond and air raid shelter. There are many well established trees which gives the garden a woodland feel. Traditional planting inc roses, lavender, peonies, acanthus and philadelphus.

93 TANFIELD AVENUE, NW2
Dudden Hill, NW2 7SB. Mr James Duncan Mattoon, 07504 565612. *Nr Dollis Hill, Willesden & Wembley. Nearest stn: Neasden (Jubilee line), then 10 min walk; or various bus routes to Neasden Parade or Tanfield Ave.* **Sun 20 July (2-6). Adm £5, chd free. Home-made teas.** Visits also by arrangement June to Sept for groups of 5 to 15.
Intensely exotic Mediterranean and subtropical paradise garden! Sunny deck with implausible planting and panoramic views of Harrow and Wembley, plunges into incredibly exotic, densely planted oasis of delight, with two further seating areas engulfed by flowers, such as, acacia, abutilon, eryngium, hedychium, plumbago, salvias and hundreds more in vigorous competition! Birds and bees love it! Previous garden was Tropical Kensal Rise (Doyle Gardens), featured on BBC2 Open Gardens and in Sunday Telegraph. This garden featured in Garden Week and Garden Answers magazine. Steep steps down to main garden.

NEW 26 TEDDINGTON PARK ROAD, TW11
Teddington, TW11 8ND. Fiona & Roy Trosh. *South West London, between Twickenham & Kingston. 10 min walk from Teddington stn & town centre, 15 min walk from Strawberry Hill stn. 33 & R68 bus routes. Very limited parking locally.* **Sun 6 July (12-5). Adm £4, chd free. Pre-booking essential, please visit www.ngs.org.uk for information & booking. Light refreshments.**
Suburban garden, approx 60ft in length, partially redesigned by RHS Chelsea Gold Medal winning designer Tom Massey who we asked to come up with a design to replace our lawn whilst keeping existing mature borders. The garden inc a stream and pond, stepping stones instead of paths, relaxed and informal planting

and a stunning tree support for a leaning willow tree, incorporating a swing.

THEOBALD'S FARMHOUSE, EN2
Burnt Farm Ride, Crews Hill, Enfield, EN2 9DY. Alison Green, theobaldsfarmhousegarden.com. *N Enfield, $\frac{1}{4}$ inside M25 J24 or J25. Under $\frac{1}{2}$ m from Crews Hill stn. From Crews Hill stn, down the hill (Cattlegate Rd) to sharp bend (Jollye's), then turn L into Burnt Farm Ride, from Enfield turn R on the bend. Garden 200yds along road on R.* **Sun 1 June (1-5.30). Adm £20, chd free. Pre-booking essential, please visit www.ngs.org.uk for information & booking. Timed slots at 1pm, 2.30pm & 4pm. Tea, coffee, cakes & gluten free option on covered terrace.**
Award-winning, 2 acre organic Arts and Crafts garden created by designer owner Alison Green. The garden and its 1650s farmhouse now have 14 distinct gardens with colour themed garden rooms and borders, knot gardens, spiral land form, topiary, water gardens and wildflower meadow, woodlands and a vegetable garden. Colour themed design, exotics and unusual annuals and biennials for all year interest. During the afternoon Alison will do a short talk on the garden. Visits also by arrangement (non-NGS), please email alison.g.green@talk21.com.

6 THORNHILL ROAD, N1
Islington, N1 1HW. Janis Higgie. *Barnsbury. Tube: Angel or Highbury & Islington. Train: Caledonian & Barnsbury. Bus: to Liverpool Rd.* **Sat 21 June (11-5). Adm £4, chd free. Tea, coffee & cake.**
150ft Islington garden, designed and planted over the last 30 yrs. This fully accessible family garden draws inspiration from the owner's antipodean roots. A brick path leads visitors past lawns, raised beds, a water feature, a fire bowl, and a creative mix of plants from around the world, inc kowhai and hoheria trees, along with many shade-tolerant plants. This garden has a lot, even the kitchen sink! Completely wheelchair friendly.

9 TRAFALGAR TERRACE, HA1
Harrow, HA1 3EU. George Reeve, www.instagram.com/thehillsjunglegarden. *Harrow-on-the-Hill stn; 10 min walk via Churchfields & path to Trafalgar Terrace. Free roadside parking on West St; L onto Nelson Rd to end, L to 9 Trafalgar Terrace following NGS signs.* **Sat 6 Sept (1-5). Adm £5, chd free. Pre-booking essential, please visit www.ngs.org.uk for information & booking. Tea, coffee & cake.**
Small jungle and tropical themed garden with big leaf plants down to small succulents. The garden is a tranquil space with running water and views up to Harrow's famous St Mary's Church. Overall winner of the 2023 Andrew Bishop Trophy for Harrow On The Hill's 'Hill in Flower' awards. We look forward to welcoming you to our piece of paradise.

TUDELEY HOUSE, BR7
Royal Parade, Chislehurst, BR7 6NW. Mrs Bernadette & Mr Colin Katchoff, 07786 854943, katchoff@hotmail.com. *1m from the A20 at J3 of M25. 20 min walk from Chislehurst stn. Buses 61, 160, 161,162, 269 & 273 to Chislehurst War Memorial. Limited parking in side roads.* **Sun 8 June (11-5). Adm £5, chd free. Tea, coffee & cake.** Visits also by arrangement 28 June to 5 Oct for groups of 6 to 12.
The layout of this Victorian town house garden has remained as shown in the original architect's plans of 1896. The current owners have recently restored the house; employing Jo Thompson, an RHS Chelsea Gold winner, to bring the garden up to date, whilst remaining sympathetic to a Victorian era town garden. Phase one and two, of three sections being restored, is completed. The garden is 95% flat. Some older paths (25% of garden) are narrow, so may be difficult for large mobility scooters.

35 TURRET GROVE, SW4
Clapham Old Town, SW4 0ES. Wayne Amiel, www.turretgrove.com. *Off Rectory Grove. 10 min walk from Clapham Common tube & Wandsworth Rd Mainline. Buses: 87, 137.* **Sun 20 July (10-5). Adm £5.50, chd free. Home-made teas.**
As featured on BBC2 Gardeners' World, 2018, this north facing garden shows what can be achieved in a small space (8 metres x 20 metres). The owner, who makes no secret of disregarding the rule book, describes this visual feast of intoxicating colours as Clapham meets Jamaica. This is gardening at its most exuberant, where bananas, bamboos, tree ferns and fire bright plants flourish beside the traditional. Children very welcome.

51 TWEEDMOUTH ROAD, E13
Plaistow, E13 9HT. Cary Rajinder Sawhney MBE. *10 mins walk from Plaistow District line & Hammersmith & City line stn. From Stratford stn, 15 mins by bus (262, 473) to Balaam St stop. Parking free on Sundays.* **Sun 10 Aug (2-4.30). Adm £4, chd free. Teas, coffees, soft drinks & home-made cakes.**
Hidden away in the East End of London a micro tropical garden with formal Islamic garden design accents. Asian influences inc Indian vegetables grown for foliage. Tall plantains meld with black mulberry, loquat, various types of palms and lilies, and many other species in this secret 10 metre x 4 metre plot. Also inc a canal-style pond which is home to Koi Carp and terrapins. No WC access.

24 TWYFORD AVENUE, N2
N2 9NJ. Rachel Lindsay & Jeremy Pratt, 07930 632902, jeremypr@blueyonder.co.uk. *Twyford Ave runs parallel to Fortis Green, between East Finchley & Muswell Hill. Tube: Northern line to East Finchley. Buses: 102, 143, 234, 263 to East Finchley. Buses 43, 134, 144, 234 to Muswell Hill. Buses: 102 & 234 stop at end of road. Garden signed from Fortis Green.* **Sun 20 July (2-6). Adm £5, chd free. Home-made teas.** Visits also by arrangement 1 June to 10 Oct for groups of up to 20.
A very sunny, 120ft south facing garden, planted for colour. Featuring brick-edged borders and many containers packed with traditional herbaceous and perennial cottage garden plants and shrubs. There's a shady area at the rear, an experimental gravel area that is never watered, and some uneven ground. The garden also inc a water feature, a greenhouse, and many areas to sit and think, chat or doze. Local honey and bee products for sale.

86 UNDERHILL ROAD, SE22
East Dulwich, SE22 0QU. Claire & Rob Goldie. *Between Langton Rise & Melford Rd. Stn: Forest Hill. Buses: P13, 363, 63, 176, 185 & P4.* **Sun 17 Aug (2-6). Combined adm with 86A Underhill Road £9, chd free. Home-made teas. Open nearby 4 Piermont Green.**
A generous family garden packed with surprises around every corner. Opening in August shows the garden off in its more jungle appearance with hot and spicy tones from the cannas and chocolate sunflowers to the hot pinks of salvias and *Houttuynia cordata*. Lots of variegated foliage to sparkle in the sunshine and the rain, pittosporum, cornus and vinca major. The garden is near The Horniman Garden which is free and within walking distance or a short bus ride. Plants for sale at 86A Underhill Road.

NEW 86A UNDERHILL ROAD, SE22
East Dulwich, SE22 0QU. Tony Edwards. *Between Langton Rise & Melford Rd. Stn: Forest Hill. Buses: P13, 363, 63, 176, 185 & P4.* **Sun 17 Aug (2-5). Combined adm with 86 Underhill Road £9, chd free. Home-made teas at 86 Underhill Road. Open nearby 4 Piermont Green.**
An evolving garden that is changing as our child grows up and our dog calms down. It is split into five parts: a deck nearest the house, a lawn with borders, a seating area under the shade of a large acer, a play area that adults are reclaiming, and a functional section with raised beds, a greenhouse, and a shed. Mature trees and bushes surround the garden, providing a sense of privacy. The garden is near The Horniman Garden which is free and within walking distance or a short bus ride.

30 URLWIN STREET, SE5
Camberwell, SE5 0NF. Mrs Judith Gregory. *Close to junction of Albany Rd & Camberwell Rd. From bus stop Urlwin St, a continuation of Albany Rd, 5 min walk. Nearest tube is Elephant & Castle, 15 min walk. Access to garden is via private road, Horsman St.* **Sun 20 July (2-5). Adm £5, chd free. Home-made teas.**
Lovingly created out of a wilderness over 16 yrs, this immaculate garden reflects the elegance of the Georgian house (not open), in a quiet street off

busy Camberwell. Structure is key and unusual trees and shrubs are kept well shaped. Water lilies thrive in a goldfish pond with Golden Orfe and Shubunkin. An unexpected gate leads to a deeply planted gravel garden. Don't miss the trompe l'oieil corner.
✿ ☕))

152A VICTORIA RISE, SW4
Clapham, SW4 0NW. Benn Storey, bennstorey@gmail.com, www.instagram.com/thenorthsouthgarden/. *South West London. Entry via basement flat. Closest tube Clapham Common. Bus 77, 87, 137, 156, 345, 452.* **Sun 8 June (12-5). Adm £4.50, chd free. Tea, coffee & cake. Open nearby 51 The Chase, 52 The Chase & Royal Trinity Hospice. Visits also by arrangement Apr to July for groups of 5 to 15.**
Featured on Gardeners' World in August 2024, this terraced garden is 21 metres long by 8 metres wide. Planting ranges from the lush greens of the courtyard to the frothy, insect friendly plants of the main level, to the espalier fruit trees and vegetables of the productive levels. A copper beech hedge hides a secluded arbour seat and fire pit at the top of the plot, hidden from surrounding neighbours.
☕))

GROUP OPENING

NEW WANSTEAD GARDENS, E11
Wanstead, E11 2RS. *From Voluntary Pl turn L into Greenstone Mews, then follow the cul-de-sac round to the R to access 17 Greenstone Mews. Go through the garage & rear garden gates of No. 28 & 32 Voluntary Pl.* **Sun 27 Apr (2-5). Combined adm £5. Home-made teas at 28 Voluntary Place.**

17 GREENSTONE MEWS, E11
Mrs T Farnham.
NEW 28 VOLUNTARY PLACE
Georgia Ward-Dyer.
NEW 32 VOLUNTARY PLACE
Derek Kelly.

Combined admission to three small town gardens, all very different in design and concept. 17 Greenstone Mews is planted with evergreen clothed fences with a raised bed and border of perennials, vegetables, and fruit. The bog garden houses newts and is overhung by a mature strawberry tree with a 'Graham Thomas' honeysuckle climber attached. 28 Voluntary Place is packed tight with a vegetable bed, mini greenhouse, mixed planting of herbs and flowers, all framed by two magnificent magnolias. 32 Voluntary Place is a newly designed, one yr old garden, already showing exuberantly planted low maintenance flowerbeds, along with generous entertaining space.
☕))

WARREN MEWS, W1
Fitzrovia, W1T 5NQ. Rebecca Hossack. *2 mins from Warren Street tube stn. Entrance to garden on Warren St, W1T 5NQ.* **Sun 22 June (12-4). Adm by donation. Tea, coffee & cake.**
Tucked away behind bustling Tottenham Court Road is the enchanting garden of Warren Mews. On first glance, it is impossible to tell that the plants in this verdant garden have no access to the earth. Warren Mews is a place where pots of paradise flowers, window boxes bursting with geraniums and containers of olive trees rule the street. Eclectic container planting with an Australian influence. The Rebecca Hossack Art Gallery is a 5 min walk away. The Mews is fully accessible and entirely cobbled.
♿ 🐕 ☕))

9 WARWICK CLOSE, TW12
Hampton, TW12 2TY. Chris Churchman, 07756 318781, cc@cquester.co.uk. *2m W of Twickenham, 2m N of Hampton Court, overlooking Bushy Park. 100 metres from Hampton Open Air Swimming Pool.* **Sun 13 Apr (12-5). Light refreshments. Open nearby Hampton House. Sun 17 Aug (10.30-5). Tea, coffee & cake. Adm £4, chd free. Visits also by arrangement 30 May to 31 July for groups of 7 to 25.**
A small suburban garden in South West London divided into four distinct spaces. Front garden with espaliered American lime trees, featuring roses, lavender and stipa. Shade garden with rare ferns and herbaceous. Formal rear garden with canal water feature, rectangular lawn with prairie style planting crossed with subtropical species. Roof top allotment on garage (the garotment).
♿ ☕))

THE WATERGARDENS, KT2
Warren Road, Kingston-upon-Thames, KT2 7LF. The Residents' Association. *1m E of Kingston. From Kingston take A308 (Kingston Hill) towards London; after approx ½ m turn R into Warren Rd. No. 57 bus along Coombe Lane West, alight at Warren Rd. Roadside parking only.* **Sun 27 Apr, Sun 26 Oct (1-4.30). Adm £5, chd free.**
Japanese themed landscaped garden originally part of Coombe Wood Nursery, planted by the Veitch family in the 1860s. Approx 9 acres with ponds, streams and waterfalls. Many rare trees, which in spring and autumn provide stunning colour. For the tree lover this is a must-see garden. Gardens attractive to wildlife. Major renovation and restoration have taken place over the past yrs, revealing a hitherto lost lake and waterfall. Restoration works ongoing. Unsuitable for those unsteady on their feet.
))

70 WENSLEYDALE ROAD, TW12
Hampton, TW12 2LX. Mr Steve Pickering. *9 min walk from Hampton stn. From Hampton stn, turn L onto Station Rd towards the village green. L over the railway bridge. R onto Wensleydale Rd. Keep L at large traffic island.* **Sat 7, Sun 8 June (1-5). Adm £4, chd free. Visitors are welcome to bring their own light refreshments.**
Small traditional garden in classic layout with greenhouse, summerhouse, pergolas, patio and rockery with an emphasis on year-round colour. Many evergreen shrubs and perennials. Wisteria over pergola flowers in spring. David Austin Desdemona rose repeat flowering on the patio. Greenhouse containing succulents and many flowering plants. All created by the amateur gardener owners. Wheelchair access only to one section of rear garden, nearest the house.
♿ ✿

Our donation to the Army Benevolent Fund supported 700 individuals with front line services and horticultural related grants in 2024.

WEST LODGE PARK, EN4
Cockfosters Road, Hadley Wood, EN4 0PY. Beales Hotels, 020 8216 3904, janegray@bealeshotels.co.uk, www.bealeshotels.co.uk/westlodgepark. *1m S of Potters Bar. On A111. J24 from M25 signed Cockfosters.* **Sun 18 May (2-5); Sun 26 Oct (1-4). Adm £7.50, chd free. Light refreshments. Pre-booking preferred or cash only on the day.** Visits also by arrangement Apr to Oct.
Open for the NGS for over 40 yrs, the 35 acre Beale Arboretum consists of over 800 varieties of trees and shrubs inc National Collections of hornbeam cultivars *Carpinus betulus*, Indian bean tree *Catalpa bignonioid*, and swamp cypress *Taxodium distichum*. Network of paths through good selection of conifers, oaks, maples and mountain ash, all specimens labelled. Stunning collection within the M25. Guided tours available. Breakfasts, morning coffee and biscuits, afternoon tea, restaurant lunches, light lunches, and dinner, all served in the hotel. Please see website for details.

&♿ 🐕 🚗 NPC 🛏 ☕

31 WEST PARK ROAD, TW9
Kew, Richmond, TW9 4DA. Anna Anderson. *Close to the E side of Kew Gardens stn. From Richmond bound exit from Kew Gardens stn, West Park Rd is straight ahead & No.31 is the 2nd house on the LHS.* **Sun 6 July (2-6). Adm £4, chd free.**
Modern botanical garden with an oriental twist. Emphasis on foliage and an eclectic mix of unusual plants, a reflecting pool and willow screens. Shady beds, mature trees and a private paved dining area with dappled light and shade.

🎵

12 WESTERN ROAD, E13
Plaistow, E13 9JF. Elaine Fieldhouse. *Nearest stn: Upton Park, 3 min walk. Buses: 58, 104, 330, 376. No parking restrictions on Sundays.* **Sun 25 May (1-5). Adm £4, chd free. Tea, coffee & cake. Gluten free & vegan options.**
Urban oasis, 85ft garden designed and planted by owners. Relying heavily on evergreen, ferns, foliage and herbaceous planting. Rear of garden leads directly onto a 110ft allotment with half allotment adjoining it; part allotment, part extension of the garden featuring topiary, medlar

tree, mulberry tree, two ponds, small fruit trees, raised beds and small iris collection.

✿ ☕ 🎵

4 WHARTON STREET, WC1X
Bloomsbury, WC1X 9PX. Barbara Holliman, 07733 485324, jugglingsheep@hotmail.co.uk. *Off Kings Cross Rd. Short walk from Kings Cross (10 mins), Angel & Farringdon tube (15 mins). Buses 19, 38, & 341 to Rosebery Ave or 73 to Claremont Sq stop on Pentonville Rd.* **Sun 15 June (2-5.30). Adm £4.50, chd free. Light refreshments.** Visits also by arrangement 12 May to 7 Sept for groups of up to 5.
Tiny award-winning 16ft x 26ft north facing town garden is five minutes' walk from Kings Cross. The garden is on two levels; lower ground has a shade patio with camellia, ferns and fatsia, then steps lead up to the main garden which is gravelled with seating areas, and contains borders and potted plants for structure and year-round interest. Planting inc exotics, evergreens, herbaceous, climbers, wild flowers, plants to attract birds and butterflies, and plants for shade and sun.

☕ 🎵

116 WHITTON ROAD, TW3
Hounslow, TW3 2EP. Colin Powe. *5 mins from Twickenham Rugby Ground. Hounslow stn, 5 min walk. 281 bus passes outside. Unrestricted parking on local roads.* **Sun 6 July (1-5). Combined adm with Sussex Cottage £8, chd free. Home-made teas at Sussex Cottage.**
A small, romantic, traditional garden inspired by Edwardian country gardens. Approx 85ft long with a manicured and striped lawn. Planting inc peonies, myrtle, clematis, old roses, fennel, lavender, and crab apples. The lawn is cut using a Ransomes Ajax (one on display at The Garden Museum). Hazel features at the end of the garden and was planted in 1900 (the house is called Hazeldene).

☕ 🎵

61 WOLSEY ROAD, KT8
East Molesey, KT8 9EW. Jan & Ken Heath. *Less than 10 min walk from Hampton Court Palace & stn, very easy to find.* **Sun 1 June (2-6). Adm £6, chd free. Tea, coffee & cake.**
Romantic, secluded and peaceful garden of two halves designed and maintained by the owners. Part is

shaded by a large copper beech tree with woodland planting and fernery, the second is reached through a beech arch with cottage garden planting, pond and wooden obelisks covered with roses. Beautiful octagonal gazebo overlooks pond, plus an oak framed summerhouse designed and built by the owners. Extensive seating throughout the garden to sit quietly and enjoy your tea and cake.

&♿ 🚗 ☕ 🎵

39 WOOD VALE, SE23
Forest Hill, SE23 3DS. Nigel Crawley. *Entrance through Thistle Gates, 48 Melford Rd. Train stns: Forest Hill & Honor Oak Park. Victoria stn to West Dulwich, then P4. Buses: 363 Elephant & Castle to Wood Vale/Melford Rd; 176, 185 & 197 to Lordship Ln/Wood Vale.* **Sun 13 Apr (1-5). Cream teas. Evening opening Wed 16 Apr (5-7). Wine. Adm £5, chd free.**
Diverse garden dominated by a gigantic perry pear forming part of one of the East Dulwich orchards. View our displays of aricula and pulsatilla. The emphasis in the garden is on its inhabitants; white comfrey and pear blossom keeps the bees busy in the spring. There are clumps of narcissi around the old apple tree and pots of hyacinths, fritillary, early tulips and sempornium and other succulents. Surprising green oasis in Forest Hill. Close to Sydenham Woods, Horniman Gardens and Camberwell Old Cemetery. Level wheelchair access, but rough terrain in the lane.

&♿ ✿ ☕ 🎵

7 WOODBINES AVENUE, KT1
Kingston-upon-Thames, KT1 2AZ. Mr Tony Sharples & Mr Paul Cuthbert. *5 mins from Kingston town centre. Take K2, K3, 71 or 281 bus. From Surbiton, walk or bus stop outside Waitrose & exit bus at Kingston University stop. From Kingston, walk or K2, K3, 71 or 281 bus from Eden St (opp Heals).* **Sun 8 June (11-5). Adm £5, chd free. Tea, coffee & cake.**
We have created a winding path through our 70ft garden with trees, evergreen structure, perennial flowers and grasses. Wide herbaceous borders, an ancient grapevine, a box hedge topiary garden, silver birches, and a hot summer terrace provide contrast.

🐕 🚗 ☕ 🎵

28A WORCESTER ROAD, E17
Walthamstow, E17 5QR. Mark & Emma Luggie, 07970 920019, pipinleshrew@hotmail.com. *12 min walk from Blackhorse Road tube stn. Just off Blackhorse Ln. On street parking.* **Visits by arrangement July to Sept for groups of up to 15. Small groups welcome, just get in touch. Adm £4, chd free. Light refreshments.**
A typical London terraced back garden, turned into a lush oasis of foliage. Rare and exotic mixed with more usual plants create a calming retreat in the midst of the city. Varying leaf textures and forms intermix to create a garden with year-round visual interest. A small rill leads from the patio to the pond seating area. Picnics welcome, however we have a hungry Beagle, who loves food!

1 YORK CLOSE, W7
Hanwell, W7 3JB. Tony Hulme & Eddy Fergusson. *By road only, entrance to York Cl via Church Rd. Nearest stn Hanwell train stn. Buses E3, 195, 207.* **Sat 16, Sun 17 Aug (2-6). Adm £5, chd free.**
Tiny, quirky, prize-winning garden extensively planted with an eclectic mix inc hosta collection, and many unusual and tropical plants. Plantaholics paradise. Many surprises in this unique and very personal garden.

10 YORK ROAD, N21
N21 2JL. Androulla & Harry Tsappas. *Winchmore Hill. Buses: 329 & W8 bus routes.* **Sun 29 June (2-6). Adm £4, chd free. Tea, coffee & cake. Open nearby Holtwhites Bakery & Deli.**
This suburban garden is full of country perennials canopied with beautiful trees such as Indian bean, olive and acer trees, and has a pretty, dainty look inspired by country cottages. There is a large pond with Koi fish which is surrounded by luscious grasses and a rockery. The garden inc a wood choppers' enclave, and an array of wildlife such as frogs, butterflies and bees.

ZEN GARDEN AT JAPANESE BUDDHIST CENTRE, W3
Three Wheels, 55 Carbery Avenue, Acton, W3 9AB. London Shogyoji Trust, www.threewheels.org.uk/zen-garden. *Tube: Acton Town, 5 min walk. 200yds off A406.* **Sat 7, Sun 8 June (2-5). Adm £4, chd free. Matcha tea £4.**
Pure Japanese Zen garden (so no flowers) with 12 large and small rocks of various colours and textures, set in islands of moss and surrounded by a sea of grey granite gravel raked in a stylised wave pattern. Garden surrounded by trees and bushes outside a cob wall. Oak framed wattle and daub shelter with Norfolk reed thatched roof. Talk on the Zen garden. Buddha Room open to public.

In 2024, our donations to Carers Trust meant that 26,081 unpaid carers were supported across the UK.

29 Heathfield Road

NORFOLK

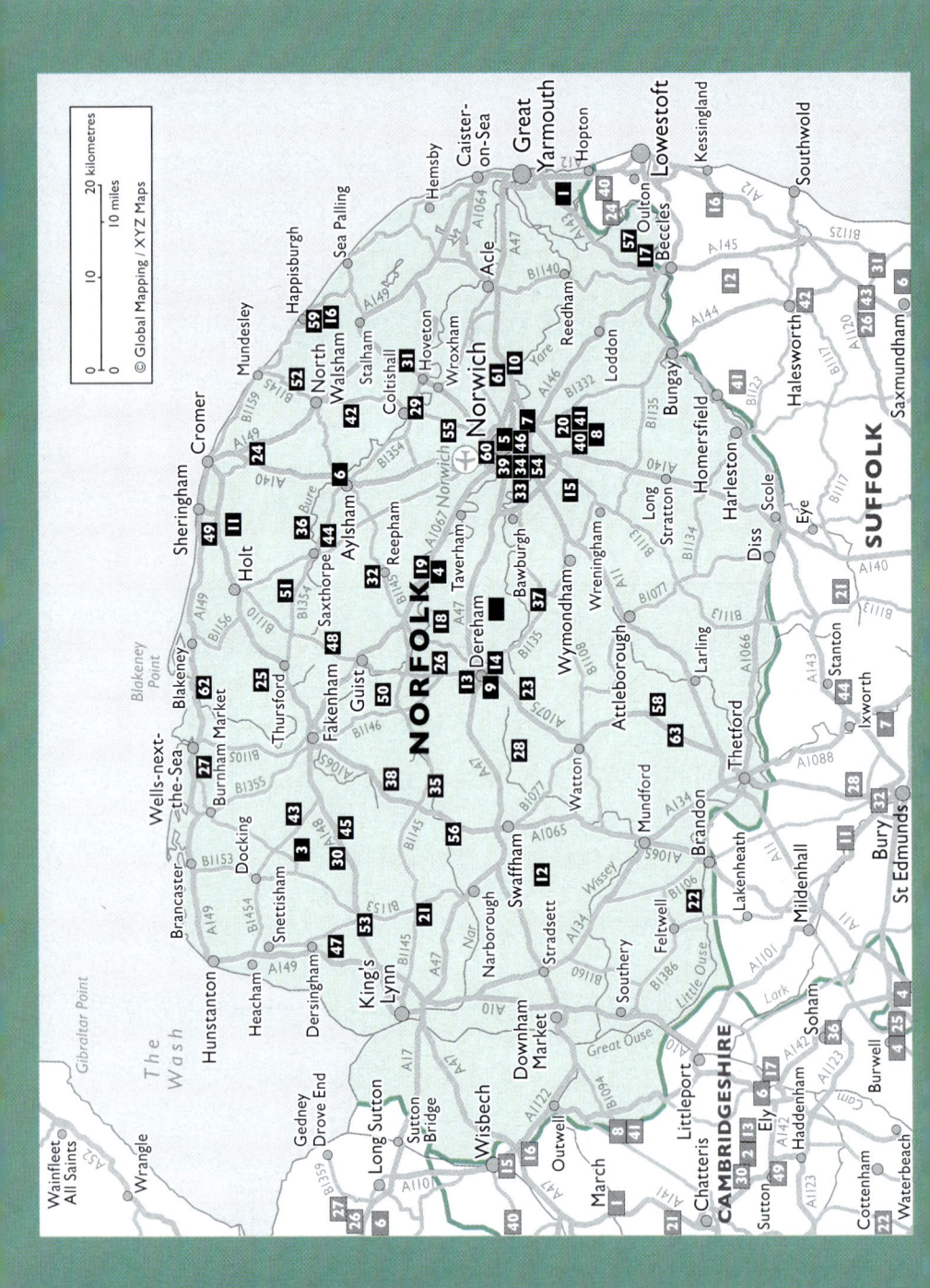

VOLUNTEERS

County Organiser
Julia Stafford Allen 01760 755334
julia.staffordallen@ngs.org.uk

Graham Watts 01362 690065
graham.watts@ngs.org.uk

County Treasurer
Andrew Stephens OBE
07595 939769
andrew.stephens@ngs.org.uk

Publicity
Julia Stafford Allen 07778 169775
julia.staffordallen@ngs.org.uk

Social Media
Kenny Higgs 07791 429052
kenny.higgs@ngs.org.uk

Photographer
Simon Smith 01362 860530
simon.smith@ngs.org.uk

Booklet Co-ordinator
Juliet Collier 07986 607170
juliet.collier@ngs.org.uk

New Gardens Organiser
Fiona Black 01692 650247
fiona.black@ngs.org.uk

Group Talks & Visits
Graham Watts
(as above)

Assistant County Organisers
Jenny Clarke 01508 550261
jenny.clarke@ngs.org.uk

Nick Collier 07733 108443
nick.collier@ngs.org.uk

Gill Cook 07841 569003
gill.cook@ngs.org.uk

Sue Guest 01362 858317
guest63@btinternet.com

Sue Roe 01603 455917
sueroe8@icloud.com

Retty Wace 07876 648543
retty.wace@ngs.org.uk

@ngsnorfolk
@norfolkngs

OPENING DATES

All entries subject to change.
For latest information check
www.ngs.org.uk
Map locator numbers are shown to the right of each garden name.

January

Friday 31st
Chestnut Farm 11

February

Snowdrop Openings

Sunday 9th
Lexham Hall 35

Saturday 15th
Horstead House 29

Sunday 16th
Lexham Hall 35

Sunday 23rd
Bagthorpe Hall 3
Chestnut Farm 11

March

Saturday 15th
◆ East Ruston Old Vicarage 16

Saturday 22nd
Gayton Hall 21

Sunday 23rd
◆ Mannington Estate 36

April

Saturday 5th
NEW The Elms 17

Sunday 13th
Holme Hale Hall 28

Sunday 20th
Wretham Lodge 63

Monday 21st
Wretham Lodge 63

May

Wednesday 7th
◆ Stody Lodge 51

Saturday 10th
Sheringham Hall 49

Sunday 18th
Bracondale Gardens 7
Manor Farm, Coston 37

Saturday 24th
NEW Greenacres Farmhouse 22

Sunday 25th
◆ Hoveton Hall Gardens 31
NEW 20 Le Strange Close 33
NEW 9 Le Strange Close 34
Lexham Hall 35
Warborough House 62

Friday 30th
Silverstone Farm 50

June

Sunday 1st
Oulton Hall 44

Saturday 7th
Elsing Hall Gardens 18

Sunday 8th
Blickling Lodge 6
Ferndale 20
High House Gardens 23
The Rudhams 45

Saturday 14th
47 Norwich Road 40
51 Norwich Road 41

Sunday 15th
Manor House Farm, Wellingham 38
47 Norwich Road 40
51 Norwich Road 41

Saturday 21st
Swafield Hall 52

Sunday 22nd
Broadway Farm 9
Holme Hale Hall 28
The Old Rectory, Syderstone 43
Swafield Hall 52
Three Eaton Gardens 54

Friday 27th
Old Manor Farmhouse 42

Saturday 28th
Old Manor Farmhouse 42

Sunday 29th
Kerdiston Manor 32
Old Manor Farmhouse 42
The Norfolk Hospice, Tapping House 53
Tyger Barn 57

July

Sunday 6th
Bishop's House | 5

Wednesday 16th
Lexham Hall | 35
The Walled Garden, Little Plumstead | 61

Sunday 20th
North Lodge | 39
🆕 St Stephen's Square Gardens | 46

Sunday 27th
Charnwood | 10
Dale Farm | 13
Ferndale | 20
North Lodge | 39
61 Trafford Way | 55

August

Sunday 3rd
Brick Kiln House | 8
33 Waldemar Avenue | 60

Sunday 10th
Beck House | 4
Severals Grange | 48

Sunday 24th
Acre Meadow | 1
Cobweb Cottage | 12
🆕 84 Fakenham Road | 19

Monday 25th
Acre Meadow | 1

Sunday 31st
33 Waldemar Avenue | 60

September

Saturday 6th
Vicarage House | 58

Sunday 7th
Vicarage House | 58

Sunday 14th
High House Gardens | 23

October

Saturday 11th
◆ Hindringham Hall | 25

Saturday 18th
◆ East Ruston Old Vicarage | 16

Saturday 25th
East Carleton Manor | 15

By Arrangement

Arrange a personalised garden visit with your club, or group of friends, on a date to suit you. See individual garden entries for full details.

Acre Meadow | 1
Blickling Lodge | 6
Brick Kiln House | 8
Broadway Farm | 9
Chestnut Farm | 11
Cobweb Cottage | 12
Dale Farm | 13
Dunbheagan | 14
Highview House | 24
Hoe Hall | 26
Holme Hale Hall | 28
Horstead House | 29
Old Manor Farmhouse | 42
Severals Grange | 48
Tudor Lodgings | 56
Vicarage House | 58
Walcott House | 59
33 Waldemar Avenue | 60
Wretham Lodge | 63

Dragonfly Cottage, Rudhams

East Carleton Manor

THE GARDENS

1 ACRE MEADOW
New Road, Bradwell,
Great Yarmouth, NR31 9DU.
Mr Keith Knights, 07476 197568,
kk.acremeadow@gmail.com,
www.acremeadow.co.uk. *Between
Bradwell & Belton in arable
surroundings. At Bradwell r'about
on A143 take Belton/ Burgh Castle
turn (New Road). Entrance 400yds
on R. Please use NR31 9JW for
SatNav. What3words app: verge.
tasks.dynamics.* **Sun 24, Mon 25
Aug (10-4). Adm £5, chd free. Pre-
booking essential, please visit
www.ngs.org.uk for information
& booking. Tea, coffee & cake.
Visits also by arrangement Aug &
Sept for groups of 6+.**
Dramatic, intensely planted mix of
exotic and other late season plants,
complementary and contrasting
combinations of foliage and flowers
and lots of late season colour. Alive
with insects on sunny days. Planting
inc *Brugmansia*, dahlias, tall grasses,
herbaceous perennials, *Aeoniums*,
and lots of cannas. Separate areas inc
tea garden, traditional conservatory
and wildlife pond. Disabled access
good throughout. No mobility scooters
allowed in main garden.

3 BAGTHORPE HALL
Bagthorpe, Bircham, King's Lynn,
PE31 6QY. Mr & Mrs D Morton.
*3½m N of East Rudham, off A148.
Take turn opp The Crown in East
Rudham. Look for white gates in
trees, slightly set back from road.*
**Sun 23 Feb (11-4). Adm £6, chd
free. Home-made teas.**
A delightful circular walk which
meanders through a stunning display
of snowdrops naturally carpeting a
woodland floor, and then returning
through a walled garden.

4 BECK HOUSE
Lyng Easthaugh Road, Weston
Longville, Norwich, NR9 5LP.
Chris & Wendy Fitch. *11m NW
of Norwich, near Lenwade (Gt
Witchingham). From either A47 at
Honingham or A1067 at Lenwade,
turn onto the B1535. Follow this road
until you reach Lyng Easthaugh Rd.
Follow until you reach Beck House.*
**Sun 10 Aug (10.30-4.30). Adm £5,
chd free. Home-made teas.**
A ¾ acre garden surrounded by
open countryside, tirelessly updated
over the past four years by the
current owners. Bordered by shallow
streams, feeding a large natural
pond with Japanese inspired plants.
There are Mediterranean borders,
woodland walkway, flower garden,
yew hedge, kitchen garden, patio
areas with seating and lots of vertical
interest with pergolas and specimen
trees. Garden is fairly level and mainly
grassed with gravel area at entrance.

5 BISHOP'S HOUSE
Bishopgate, Norwich, NR3 1SB. The Bishop of Norwich, www.dioceseofnorwich.org/gardens. *Located in the city centre near the Law Courts & The Adam & Eve Pub. Parking available at town centre car parks inc one by the Adam & Eve pub.* **Sun 6 July (1-4.30). Adm £5, chd free. Tea, coffee & cake.**
A four acre walled garden dating back to the C12. Extensive lawns with specimen trees. Borders with many rare and unusual shrubs. Spectacular herbaceous borders flanked by yew hedges. Rose beds underplanted with hostas. A meadow labyrinth, organic kitchen garden, herb garden and bamboo walk. Popular plant sales. Wheelchair access over gravel paths and some slopes.

6 BLICKLING LODGE
Blickling, Norwich, NR11 6PS. Michael & Henrietta Lindsell, nicky@lindsell.co.uk. ½ m N of Aylsham. *Leave Aylsham on Old Cromer Rd towards Ingworth, over hump back bridge & house is on your R.* **Sun 8 June (12-5). Adm £6, chd free. Home-made teas.** Visits also by arrangement 8 June to 26 Sept for groups of 10 to 40.
Georgian house (not open) set in 17 acres of parkland inc cricket pitch, mixed borders, walled kitchen garden, yew garden, woodland and water garden.

GROUP OPENING

7 BRACONDALE GARDENS
Norwich, NR1 2BB. Mr Andrew Sankey. *Park at County Hall. Walk up Bracondale take 1st L for 14 Conesford Dr & 1 Woodside Cottages. Return to Bracondale, turn L up the hill, Southgate House is off Southgate Ln on R.* **Sun 18 May (10.30-4.30). Combined adm £9, chd free. Home-made teas at Southgate House. Tickets for all three gardens sold at Southgate House.**

14 CONESFORD DRIVE
Mr Andrew Sankey.

SOUTHGATE HOUSE
Mr Matthew Williams.

1 WOODSIDE COTTAGES
Mr Wayne Waith.

A warm welcome awaits you at these three attractive compact town gardens a short walk apart and each with a different character. 1 Woodside Cottages: A very pretty, small cottage garden packed with colourful plants both ornamental and edible and even the resident chickens are decorative. Fruit trees and vegetables grow side by side with perennial and annual flowers and a small pond supports a multitude of frogs each spring. 14 Conesford Drive: Lush planting of fruit, vegetables and flowers greet you at the side of this 1960s modernist house leading to a densely planted cottage garden of carefully selected perennials and climbers. Southgate House: The former Harbour Master's house. The garden is about an acre, half of which is formed on a steep escarpment. Garden rooms with ornamental beds and interesting plants. Woodland hillside walks.

8 BRICK KILN HOUSE
Priory Lane, Shotesham, Norwich, NR15 1UJ. Jim & Jenny Clarke, 07748 655815, jennyclarke985@gmail.com. *6m S of Norwich. From Shotesham All Saints church Priory Ln is 200m on R on Saxlingham Rd.* **Sun 3 Aug (10-4). Adm £6, chd free. Home-made teas.** Visits also by arrangement July to Sept for groups of up to 35.
Two acre country garden with a large terrace, lawns and colourful herbaceous borders. There is a contemporary designed pergola garden, sculptures and a stream running through a diversely planted wood. Easy access for wheelchair users.

9 BROADWAY FARM
The Broadway, Scarning, Dereham, NR19 2LQ. Michael & Corinne Steward, 07881 691899, corinneasteward@gmail.com. *16m W of Norwich. 12m E of Swaffham. From A47 W take a R into Fen Rd, opp Drayton Hall Ln. From A47 E take L into Fen Rd, then immed L at T-junc, immed R into The Broadway.* **Sun 22 June (11-5). Adm £5, chd free. Home-made teas.** Visits also by arrangement June & July for groups of 10 to 40.
A ½ acre cottage garden surrounding a C14 clapboard farmhouse. Colourful herbaceous borders with a wide range of perennial and woody plants and a well planted pond, providing habitat for wildlife. A plantswoman's garden. From the back of the garden is flat and onto grass lawn.

10 CHARNWOOD
7 Postwick Lane, Brundall, Norwich, NR13 5RD. Vicci and Martin Hine. *5m E of Norwich. From A47 take Brundall exit. Proceed along Cucumber Ln to T-junc and turn R onto Postwick Ln. Charnwood is on the L.* **Sun 27 July (10-4). Adm £5, chd free. Home-made teas.**
A summer garden which has been evolving over the last three years. It has mixed and herbaceous borders, standards and topiary, a small vegetable garden, a wildlife garden with a pond inc a greenhouse, terrace and pots. Its southerly aspect overlooks the Yare valley.

11 CHESTNUT FARM
Church Road, West Beckham, Holt, NR25 6NX. Mr & Mrs John McNeil Wilson, 01263 822241, judywilson100@gmail.com. *2½ m S of Sheringham. From A148 opp Sheringham Park entrance. Take the road signed 'By way To West Beckham', about ¾ m to the garden by village sign. N.B. SatNav will take you to the pub.* **Fri 31 Jan (11-4). Pre-booking essential, please visit www.ngs.org.uk for information & booking. Sun 23 Feb (11-4). Adm £5, chd free. Light refreshments inc gluten free options.** Visits also by arrangement 26 Jan to 28 Sept for groups of 6 to 40.
Mature three acre garden developed over 60 years with collections of many rare and unusual plants. Aconites, 100+ varieties of snowdrops, drifts of crocus with seasonal flowering shrubs. Later, wood anemones, fritillary meadow, wildflower walk, pond, small arboretum and colourful herbaceous borders. In May the handkerchief tree, cercis, camassias and early roses. Always something new. Wheelchair access is tricky if wet.

12 COBWEB COTTAGE
51 Shingham, Beachamwell, Swaffham, PE37 8AY. Sue Bunting, 01366 328428, susannahbunting@btinternet.com. *5m from Swaffham. Shingham is next to Beachamwell. The cottage is 1st on L after the Shingham village sign.* **Sun 24 Aug (10.30-4.30). Adm £5, chd free. Tea, coffee & cake.** Visits also by arrangement 5 Apr to 4 Oct for groups of up to 40.
A small cottage garden on the edge of the village with mixed borders, a sunken greenhouse, pergola, and a wildlife pond. There is also a large productive ornamental kitchen garden with bees, chickens, treehouse, prairie planting and fruit cage.

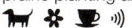

13 DALE FARM
Sandy Lane, Dereham, NR19 2EA. Graham & Sally Watts, 01362 690065, grahamwatts@dsl.pipex.com. *16m W of Norwich. 12m E of Swaffham. From A47 take B1146 signed to Fakenham, turn R at T-junc, ½m turn L into Sandy Ln (before pelican Xing).* **Sun 27 July (10.30-5). Adm £6, chd free. Home-made teas.** Visits also by arrangement June & July for groups of 15 to 50.
A two acre plant lovers' garden with a large spring-fed pond. Over 1000 plant varieties in exuberantly planted borders with sculptures. Also, gravel, vegetable, nature and waterside gardens. Collection of 150 hydrangeas. Some grass paths and gravel drive. Wide choice of plants for sale.

14 DUNBHEAGAN
Dereham Road, Westfield, NR19 1QF. Jean & John Walton, 01362 696163, jandjwalton@btinternet.com. *2m S of Dereham. From Dereham turn L off A1075 into Westfield Rd by the Vauxhall garage/Premier food store. Straight ahead by Xrds into lane which becomes Dereham Rd. Garden on L.* **Visits by arrangement 26 June to 31 July for groups of 20+. Discuss refreshments when booking. Adm £7, chd free. Home-made teas.**
Relax and enjoy the garden where the rare and unusual rub shoulders with the more recognisable plants in densely planted beds and borders in this ever-changing plantsman's garden. Lots of paths to explore. A riot of colour all summer. Lots of seating. Wheelchair access via gravel driveway.

15 EAST CARLETON MANOR
Rectory Road, East Carleton, Norwich, NR14 8JY. Clive Chapman. *4m S of Norwich. Entrance is at the junc of Scott's Hill and Rectory Rd in East Carleton.* **Sat 25 Oct (10-4). Adm £10, chd free. Pre-booking essential, please visit www.ngs.org.uk for information & booking.**
A 10 acre garden designed and planted in the 1960's for autumn colour, with many interesting trees and shrubs. There is a summerhouse, with a knot garden, a walled garden with a hydrangea border, a moongate and Italian garden. Water circulates through smaller ponds into a lake with water lilies. Wheelchair access along slightly uneven gravel paths. Some areas have steps.

16 ◆ EAST RUSTON OLD VICARAGE
East Ruston, Norwich, NR12 9HN. Alan Gray & Graham Robeson, 01692 650432, office@eastrustonoldvicarage.co.uk, www.eastrustonoldvicarage.co.uk. *3m N of Stalham. Turn off A149 onto B1159 signed Bacton, Happisburgh. After 2m turn R 200yds N of East Ruston Church (ignore sign to East Ruston).* **For NGS: Sat 15 Mar, Sat 18 Oct (12-5.30). Adm £14.50, chd £2. Light refreshments in the restaurant.** For other opening times and information, please phone, email or visit garden website.
Large garden with traditional borders and modern landscapes. Discover our various types of gardens inc walled, rose and exotic gardens, topiary and box parterres. We have water features, Mediterranean garden, fruit cage and containers to die for in spring and summer. Cornfield and meadows, vegetable and cutting gardens, parkland and heritage orchard, in all 32 acres. Rare and unusual plants abound.

17 NEW THE ELMS
Elms Road, Toft Monks, Beccles, NR34 0EJ. Mr & Mrs Andrew Freeland, www.elmsbarnweddings.co.uk. *Follow grey signs off A143 to 'Elms Barn'. Past the pond, L to main house. Follow signs for wedding traffic to the car park.* **Sat 5 Apr (10-4). Adm £6, chd free. Pre-booking essential, please visit www.ngs.org.uk for information & booking. Tea, coffee & cake in our Marquee.**
Gardens are set around a beautiful moated Queen Anne house. Extensive spring bulbs, herbaceous borders, formal rose garden, ponds, arboretum and year round interest.

18 ELSING HALL GARDENS
Elsing Hall, Hall Road, Elsing, NR20 3DX. Patrick Lines & Han Yang Yap, www.elsinghall.com. *6km NW of Dereham. From A47 take the N Tuddenham exit. From A1067 take the turning to Elsing opp the Bawdeswell Garden Centre.* **Sat 7 June (10-4). Adm £6, chd free. Tea, coffee & cake. Picnics allowed in the car park.**
C15 fortified manor house (not open) with working moat. 10 acre gardens and 10 acre park surrounding the house. Significant collection of old roses, walled garden, formal garden, marginal planting, ginkgo avenue, viewing mound, moongate, interesting pinetum and terraced garden. NB: Very limited WC facilities available.

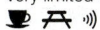

19 NEW 84 FAKENHAM ROAD
Great Witchingham, Norwich, NR9 5AE. Trevor King. *On the B1067 at Lenwade heading to Fakenham. Look for the Chip Shop on L. The garden is opp, by the bus shelter. Please park in the Chip Shop forecourt.* **Sun 24 Aug (10-4.30). Adm £5, chd free. Pre-booking essential, please visit www.ngs.org.uk for information & booking. Light refreshments.**
This is a garden for keen plant enthusiasts, especially if you've an interest in exotics. Boundaries disappear behind dense planting, and narrow paths lead you round the garden. Space is at a premium. Even so, you will also see exotic pigeons, pheasants and parakeets among the plants. The owner is a firm believer in reuse and recycle and many of the garden structures reflect this ethos.

20 FERNDALE
14, Poringland Road, Upper Stoke Holy Cross, Norwich, NR14 8NL. Dr Alan & Mrs Sheila Sissons.
4m S of Norwich. From Norwich or Poringland on B1332, take Stoke Rd at Railway Tavern r'about. Ferndale is 0.7m on L. Parking on road. **Sun 8 June, Sun 27 July (11-4). Adm £4, chd free. Light refreshments.**
⅓ acre garden, paved area with seating surrounded by borders of shrubs and flowers. A pond with water feature. In a second area is more seating plus apple trees, soft fruit, vegetable plot, greenhouse, herb bed. Shingled area with water feature, rose arbour, semi-circular wall planted with flowers. If dry, there will be an accordionist playing French music, plants for sale and a craft stall. Wheelchair access via 1 metre wide passageway.
♿ ✿ ☕

21 GAYTON HALL
Gayton, King's Lynn, PE32 1PL. David and Katherine Marsham.
6m E of King's Lynn. Off the B1145. At village sign take 2nd exit off Back St to entrance. **Sat 22 Mar (11-4). Adm £6, chd free. Tea, coffee & cake.**
This rambling semi-wild garden, has over two miles of paths which meander through lawn, streams, bridges and woodland. Primulas, astilbes, hostas, *Lysichiton* and gunnera grow along the water's edge. There is a good display of spring bulbs and a variety of unusual trees and shrubs, many labelled, have been planted over the years. Wheelchair access to most areas via gravel and grass paths.
♿ 🐕 ☕ 🔊

22 NEW GREENACRES FARMHOUSE
Nursery Lane, Hockwold, Thetford, IP26 4ND. Reverend Ray and Mrs Victoria Burman. *Drive along Main St, Hockwold-cum-Wilton and turn into Nursery Ln, follow NGS Yellow Signs to car park further down Nursery Ln.* **Sat 24 May (11-4). Adm £5, chd free. Tea, coffee & cake.**
A very pretty traditional cottage garden on the edge of the village. With mature trees, this garden, adjacent to C18 farmhouse is crammed with colour, roses, shrubs, flowers, pond and gravel dry garden, with beehives. Wheelchair access but some gravel and small steps so will require help. Parking in meadow short walk from garden. Local honey for sale.
♿ ☕ 🔊

23 HIGH HOUSE GARDENS
Blackmoor Row, Shipdham, Thetford, IP25 7PU. Sue & Fred Nickerson. *6m SW of Dereham. Take the airfield or Cranworth Rd off A1075 in Shipdham. Blackmoor Row is signed.* **Sun 8 June, Sun 14 Sept (12-5). Adm £6, chd free. Home-made teas.**
Three acre plantsman's garden developed and maintained by the current owners, over the last 40 years. Garden consists of colour themed herbaceous borders with an extensive range of perennials, box edged rose and shrub borders, woodland garden, pond and bog area, orchard and small arboretum. Plus large vegetable garden. Wheelchair access via gravel paths.
♿ ✿ ☕

24 HIGHVIEW HOUSE
Norwich Road, Roughton, Norwich, NR11 8NA. Graham & Sarah Last, 07976 066896, grahamrc.last@gmail.com. *Located on A140, approx ½ m N of Roughton. Village mini r'abouts on R after layby. What3words app: warriors.town.shielding.* **Visits by arrangement July to Oct for groups of 20 to 80. Tea & cake inc in adm. Adm £12, chd free.**
Two acre garden designed and maintained by the current owners over the last 20 years. Large range of perennial plants, bulbs and shrubs. More than 200 salvia varieties feature through the planting of over 12,000 plants to encourage wildlife. Acer trees, interesting garden structures, water feature. Home of the National Collection on *Salvia microphylla cvs.* and relatives. Wheelchair access: park on the main driveway with path. Some slopes will need to be accommodated.
♿ ✿ NPC ☕

25 ♦ HINDRINGHAM HALL
Blacksmiths Lane, Hindringham, NR21 0QA. Mr & Mrs Charles Tucker, 01328 878226, hindhall@btinternet.com, www.hindringhamhall.org. *7m from Holt/ Fakenham/ Wells. Turn off A148 at Crawfish Pub towards Hindringham. Drive 2m. Enter village of Hindringham. Turn L into Blacksmiths Ln after village hall. For* **NGS: Sat 11 Oct (10-4). Adm £10, chd free. Light refreshments inc hot soup and sausage rolls as well as tea, coffee and cakes. For other opening times and information, please phone, email or visit garden website.**
Listed Medieval moat and fishponds surrounding the Grade II* Tudor Hall. Discover the working walled vegetable garden and Victorian nut walk. Wander along formal beds, bog and stream gardens. Something of interest throughout the year, continuing well into autumn. History and horticulture combine in this special place. Wheelchair access via gravel paths.
♿ ✿ 🚗 🛏 ☕ 🔊

26 HOE HALL
Hall Road, Hoe, Dereham, NR20 4BD. Mr & Mrs James Keith, 01362 693169, vrkeith@hoehall.co.uk. *The garden is situated next to Hoe church.* **Visits by arrangement 15 May to 30 June. Adm £10, chd free. Light refreshments.**
The main visual is a walled garden featuring a long white wisteria walk. This is set in the grounds of a Georgian rectory surrounded by parkland. The garden was redesigned in 1990 to incorporate climbers and herbaceous plants, with box parterres replacing the kitchen garden. There are espaliered fruit trees, and an old swimming pool with water lilies. Seating area and WC available in the walled garden.
♿ 🚗 ☕

27 ♦ HOLKHAM HALL GARDEN
Holkham Hall, Wells-next-the-Sea, NR23 1AB. Holkham Estate, 01328 713111, info@holkham.co.uk, www.holkham.co.uk. *Drive through the main visitor entrance to main Holkham Park car park. On arrival, you will be greeted by the team. Once parked you can wander down to the Walled Garden, located to the W of the Hall.* **For opening times and information, please phone, email or visit garden website.**
Stepping through the Venetian gates, visitors can explore Holkham's enchanting Walled Garden dating back to the late 1700s. There is a spectacular stand of Georgian and Victorian glasshouses and vineries, a formal ornamental garden, established vineyard, working kitchen garden and cutting garden with

The Elms

its beautiful array of blooms to be discovered. Entry and car parking charges apply. Wheelchair access via gravel paths. Two mobility scooters available.

28 HOLME HALE HALL
Holme Hale, Swaffham, Thetford, IP25 7ED. Mr & Mrs Simon Broke, 01760 440328, simon.broke@hotmail.co.uk, www.instagram.com/holmehalehallgarden. *2m S of Necton off A47. 1m E of Holme Hale village on Bradenham Rd.* **Sun 13 Apr, Sun 22 June (12-4). Adm £8, chd free. Refreshments served all day. Visits also by arrangement Apr to Sept.** Walled kitchen garden designed by Arne Maynard and replanted in 2016-17. Soft palette of herbaceous plants inc some unusual varieties which provide a long season of interest. Greenhouse, vegetables, trained fruits, roses and topiary. 280 year old wisteria. Wildlife friendly with wildflower meadow and renovated island pond. Historic buildings with a dry garden formed from crushed concrete and rubble. Wheelchair access to most areas.

29 HORSTEAD HOUSE
Mill Road, Horstead, Norwich, NR12 7AU. Mr & Mrs Matthew Fleming, 07771 655637, horsteadsnowdrops@gmail.com. *6m NE of Norwich on North Walsham Rd, B1150. Down Mill Rd opp the Recruiting Sergeant pub.* **Sat 15 Feb (11-4). Adm £6, chd free. Tea, coffee & cake. Visits also by arrangement 8 Feb to 21 Feb.** Stunning display of beautiful snowdrops carpet the woodland setting with winter flowering shrubs. Another beautiful feature is the dogwoods growing on a small island in the River Bure, which flows through the garden. There is also a small walled garden. Wheelchair access to main snowdrop area.

30 ♦ HOUGHTON HALL WALLED GARDEN
Bircham Road, Houghton, King's Lynn, PE31 6TY. The Cholmondeley Gardens Trust, 01485 528569, info@houghtonhall.com, www.houghtonhall.com. *11m W of Fakenham. 13m E of King's Lynn. Signed from A148.* **For opening times and information, please phone, email or visit garden website.** The award-winning, five acre walled garden, beautifully divided into different areas designed by the Bannermans, inc a kitchen garden with espalier fruit trees, glasshouses, a Mediterranean garden, rose parterre, wisteria pergola and a spectacular double-sided herbaceous border. Many antique statues, fountains and contemporary sculptures. Gravel and grass paths. Electric buggies available in the walled garden.

31 ♦ HOVETON HALL GARDENS
Hoveton Hall Estate, Hoveton, Norwich, NR12 8RJ. Mr Harry & Mrs Rachel Buxton, 01603 784297, office@hovetonhallestate.co.uk, www.hovetonhallestate.co.uk. *8m N of Norwich. 1m N of Wroxham Bridge. Off A1151 Stalham Rd. Follow brown tourist signs.* **For NGS: Sun 25 May (10.30-5). Adm £10, chd £5. For other opening times and information, please phone, email or visit garden website.** Explore the 15 acre gardens and woodlands taking you through the seasons. Mature walled herbaceous and kitchen gardens. Informal woodlands and lakeside walks. Nature spy activity trail for our younger visitors. A varied events programme runs throughout the season. Light lunches and afternoon tea from our on site Garden Kitchen Cafe. Picnics are allowed for garden patrons only. The gardens are accessible to wheelchair users.
& ❀ 🚗 🪑 ☕ 🪑 ♪))

32 KERDISTON MANOR
Kerdiston, Norwich, NR10 4RY. Philip & Mararette Hollis. *1m from Reepham. Turn at Bawdswell garden centre towards Reepham. After 3⅗ m turn L Smugglers Rd leaving Reepham surgery on L. Take L into Kerdiston Rd 1½ m house on R.* **Sun 29 June (11-5). Adm £6, chd free. Home-made teas.**
A two acre tranquil garden surrounding Manor House (not open) that has been developed by the owners for over 30 years. Mature trees, colourful herbaceous borders, dell garden, potager style vegetable plot, pond, a 15 acre wild meadow walk and wonderful thatched C18 barn. Wheelchair access to teas and terrace overlooking garden.
& 🐕 ❀ ☕ ♪))

33 NEW 9 LE STRANGE CLOSE
Norwich, NR2 3PN. Alan Hunter. *On entering Le Strange Cl turn R at the T-junc & walk to the end of the close. No 9 is straight ahead. On-street parking available on Sundays.* **Sun 25 May (10.30-4.30). Combined adm with 20 Le Strange Close £7, chd free.** Enclosed by mature trees and yet still full of light, this garden is a tranquil oasis. Dwarf heritage apples, irises, mulberry and highly scented roses contrast with low maintenance borders for dry loving plants and pots of succulents. Wheelchair access via gravel drive. Garden on one level.
&

34 NEW 20 LE STRANGE CLOSE
Norwich, NR2 3PW. Rajul Shah, www.instagram.com/rajulshahgardendesign. *Le Strange Close is off Christchurch Rd. On-street parking available on Sundays.* **Sun 25 May (10.30-4.30). Combined adm with 6 Le Strange Close £7, chd free. Home-made teas.**
A city garden that is plant-filled and wildlife-friendly, with unusual materials and structures. The front garden is a mini allotment with crab apple arches framing the path. Designed and planted by the owner, garden designer, Rajul Shah. Access to back garden is possible via driveway and paved path. A very gentle slope leads to the rear. The front path has one step.
& 🅿 ☕

35 LEXHAM HALL
nr Litcham, PE32 2QJ. Mr & Mrs Neil Foster, www.lexhamestate.co.uk. *6m N of Swaffham off B1145. 2m W of Litcham.* **Sun 9, Sun 16 Feb (11-4). Adm £6, chd free. Sun 25 May, Wed 16 July (11-5). Adm £8, chd free. Light refreshments.** Donation to East Lexham Church (Feb only).
Parkland with lake and river walks surround C17 Hall (not open). Formal garden with terraces, roses and mixed borders. Traditional working kitchen garden with crinkle-crankle wall. Year-round interest; woods and borders carpeted with snowdrops in February, rhododendrons, azaleas, camellias and magnolias in the three acre woodland garden in May, and July sees the walled garden borders at their peak.
🐕 ❀ 🚗 ☕ 🪑 ♪))

36 ♦ MANNINGTON ESTATE
Mannington, Norwich, NR11 7BB. Lady Walpole, 01263 584175, admin@walpoleestate.co.uk, www.manningtonestate.co.uk. *18m NW of Norwich. 2m N of Saxthorpe via B1149 towards Holt. At Saxthorpe/Corpusty follow signs to Mannington.* **For NGS: Sun 23 Mar (11-4). Adm £8, chd free. Light refreshments in the Garden Tearooms. Home-made locally sourced food with home-made teas. For other opening times and information, please phone, email or visit garden website.**
Explore 20 acres of gardens which feature shrubs, lake and trees, period garden and sensory garden. Extensive countryside walks and trails from the garden. There is also a moated manor house and Saxon church with C19 follies. We have wildflowers and birds a plenty. Wheelchair access via gravel paths. One steep slope.
& 🐕 ❀ 🚗 ☕ ♪))

37 MANOR FARM, COSTON
Coston Lane, Coston, Wymondham, NR9 4DT. Mr & Mrs J D Hambro. *10m W of Norwich. Off B1108 Norwich-Watton Rd. Take B1135 to Dereham at Kimberley. After 300yds sharp L bend, go straight over to Coston Ln. Garden on L. What3words app: onions.croak.springing.* **Sun 18 May (12-5). Adm £6, chd free. Light refreshments.**
Wonderful five acre country garden set in larger estate. Several small garden rooms with both formal and informal planting. Climbing roses, walled kitchen garden, white, grass and late summer themes, classic herbaceous and shrub borders, box parterres and large areas of wildflowers. Many interesting trees and collection of sculptures dotted round the garden. Good wheelchair access. Some gravel paths and steps that may be difficult to access.
& 🐕 ❀ 🚗 ☕ 🪑

38 MANOR HOUSE FARM, WELLINGHAM
Fakenham, King's Lynn, PE32 2TH. Robin & Elisabeth Ellis, 01328 838227, libbyelliswellingham@gmail.com, www.manor-house-farm.co.uk. *½ m off A1065. 7m W from Fakenham & 8m E. Swaffham.* **Sun 15 June (11-5). Adm £7, chd free. Home-made teas.**
Charming four acre country garden surrounds an attractive farmhouse. Formal quadrants, 'hot spot' of grasses and gravel, small arboretum, pleached lime walk, vegetable parterre and rose tunnel. Unusual walled 'Taj' garden with old-fashioned roses, tree peonies, lilies and formal pond. A variety of herbaceous plants. Small herd of Formosan Sika deer.
🐕 ❀ ☕ 🪑

39 NORTH LODGE
51 Bowthorpe Road, Norwich, NR2 3TN. Bruce Bentley & Peter Wilson. *1½ m W of Norwich City*

Centre. Turn into Bowthorpe Rd off Dereham Rd, garden 150m on L. By bus: 21, 22, 23, & 24 from city centre, Old Catton, Heartsease, Thorpe & most of W Norwich. Parking available outside & room for bikes. **Sun 20, Sun 27 July (11-5). Adm £5, chd free. Home-made teas. Gluten-free and vegan cakes available.**
Magical town garden surrounding Victorian Gothic Cemetery Lodge. Strong structure and vistas inc a classical temple, oriental water gardens, formal ponds linked with winding pathways with a surprise around every corner. Original 25m-deep well. Predominantly herbaceous planting. Carnivorous and succulent collection in hand-built conservatory. Wheelchair access possible but difficult. Sloping gravel drive followed by steep, narrow ramp.
&. ✿ 🍵 »)

40 47 NORWICH ROAD
Stoke Holy Cross, Norwich, NR14 8AB. **Anna & Alistair Lipp.** *Heading S through Stoke Holy Cross on Norwich Rd. Garden on R down private drive. Parking at sports ground car park on L of Long Ln, 500 yds to garden.* **Sat 14, Sun 15 June (11-5). Combined adm with 51 Norwich Road £6, chd free. Home-made teas.**
Medium sized, west facing garden developed over 25 years with views over Tas Valley and water meadows. Vine and rose covered pergola, gravel beds, terrace with raised beds and shading magnolias, large greenhouse with exotic plants. Small wildflower meadow and informal pond. Majority of garden accessible for wheelchair users.
&. ✿ 🍵 »)

41 51 NORWICH ROAD
Stoke Holy Cross, Norwich, NR14 8AB. **Mrs Vivian Carrington.** *5m S of Norwich. Heading S through Stoke Holy Cross on Norwich Rd, garden on R down private drive. No parking at property. Parking at sports ground car park on L of Long Ln, 500 yds to garden.* **Sat 14, Sun 15 June (11-5). Combined adm with 47 Norwich Road £6, chd free. Home-made teas at 47 Norwich Road.**
The garden has a variety of perennials, roses and annuals at the front with an asparagus bed and vegetables to the side and rear. There are cold frames and a small greenhouse. Behind the house there are further flower beds and a small lawn. Wheelchair access at the front and rear of garden.
&. ✿ 🍵 »)

42 OLD MANOR FARMHOUSE
The Hill, Swanton Abbott, Norwich, NR10 5EA. **Drs Paul and Sian Everden,** 07768 376621, info@hostebarn.com, www.hostebarn.com. *N Norfolk Coast. From Swanton Abbott, take Long Common Ln until you see the car park sign on The Hill. The garden is 100m along the lane. What3words app: brimmed.lift.middle.* **Fri 27 June (1-5); Sat 28, Sun 29 June (9-5). Adm £6, chd free. Tea, coffee & cake. Visits also by arrangement Apr to Aug.**
Originally a field surrounding a derelict C17 listed Farmhouse (not open). Winning the 1991 Graham Allen Conservation Award, the garden structure, sympathetic to the Dutch style of the house was laid down. Open knot garden of box surrounded by pleached hornbeam, pollarded plane trees, beech and yew hedges divide areas and flank walks, herbaceous borders and lawns, clematis and rose walk to potager and paddock.
🐕 🚗 🏠 🍵 🪑 »)

43 THE OLD RECTORY, SYDERSTONE
Creake Road, Syderstone, King's Lynn, PE31 8SF. **Mr & Mrs Tom White.** *Off B1454, 8m W of Fakenham. Access from Creake Rd, or side gate opp Village Hall on The St.* **Sun 22 June (11-5). Adm £5, chd free. Home-made teas.**
Charming Old Rectory garden designed in 1999 by Arne Maynard. There are lawns, box, hornbeam, yew and beach hedging to view. Discover our pleached crab apple trees, wisteria and climbing roses. We also have a parterre of English shrub roses, herbaceous beds, a shrubbery and an orchard to explore.
&. 🍵

44 OULTON HALL
Oulton, Aylsham, NR11 6NU. **Bolton Agnew.** *4m NW of Aylsham. From Aylsham: take B1354. After 4m turn L for Oulton Chapel. Hall ½ m on R. From B1149 (Norwich/Holt Rd): take B1354, next R, Hall ½ m on R.* **Sun 1 June (1.30-5). Adm £6, chd free. Home-made teas.**
C18 manor house (not open) and clocktower set in six acre garden with lake and woodland walks. Chelsea designer's own garden-herbaceous, Italian, bog, water, wild, verdant, sunken and parterre gardens all flowing from one tempting vista to another. Developed over 25 years with emphasis on structure, height and texture, with a lot of recent replanting in the contemporary manner.
&. 🐕 ✿ 🍵 »)

GROUP OPENING

45 THE RUDHAMS
East & West Rudham, PE31 8TD. **Mrs Amanda McCallum.** *6m W of Fakenham straddling A148. Car Parking at The Rudhams Village Hall, Wensum Farmhouse, W Rudham & Rudham House, E Rudham.* **Sun 8 June (11-5). Combined adm £10, chd free. Light refreshments in the Rudhams Village Hall, PE31 8GN.**

NEW DRAGONFLY COTTAGE
Mr & Mrs N Akers.

WENSUM FARMHOUSE
The Earl and Countess of Romney.

WENSUM HOUSE
Mr & Mrs A Dessent.

THE WHITE COTTAGE
Mr & Mrs I McCallum.

East and West Rudham are adjoining villages surrounded by countryside with Anglo Saxon origins. Easily accessible from Kings Lynn and Fakenham, The Crown pub sits on the village green with a coffee shop and deli close by. There are large playing fields and a jolly playground. The four gardens are very varied in history, design and planting providing inspiration and enjoyment for visitors. C18 Dragonfly Cottage has a ½ acre plot with lawned areas, mature trees and colourful herbaceous borders, two small ponds, wildflower areas and small vegetable/cutting garden. Georgian Wensum House has associations with the Royal family and has a two acre established garden with large herbaceous borders, rose arches, statuary and small meandering stream. Wensum Farmhouse also sits on two acres with a walled cottage style garden and adjoining wild meadow with ponds and meandering paths. Close by, The White Cottage is a young naturalistic, colourful, cottage garden and courtyard.
🐕 ✿ 🍵 🪑 »)

GROUP OPENING

46 NEW **ST STEPHENS SQUARE GARDENS**
St Stephens Square, Norwich, NR1 3SS. **Margaret Hope.** *Norwich City Centre. St Stephens Square is off St Stephen's r'about by The Champion pub In Norwich City Centre. Paid parking if needed in Chantry Place or NCP next to the bus stn.* **Sun 20 July (11-4.30). Combined adm £6, chd free. Tea, coffee & cake.**

NEW **3 ST STEPHENS SQUARE**

NEW **11A ST STEPHENS SQUARE**

NEW **15 ST STEPHENS SQUARE**

NEW **35 ST STEPHENS SQUARE**

NEW **37 ST STEPHENS SQUARE**

NEW **39 ST STEPHENS SQUARE**

A group of six city centre front gardens and a vibrant community garden. Starting at the top of the square the community garden is in full sun and boasts colour throughout the year. As you move along the street of Georgian houses you go from sun loving plants in the sunny gardens of 3, 11A and 15 to shade loving plants in gardens 35, 37 and 39 at the end of the street. Each garden has its own individual and unique charm. All six gardens face onto the street and pavement with level access into each garden.

In 2024 we awarded £232,000 in Community Garden Grants, supporting 89 community garden projects.

47 ♦ **SANDRINGHAM GARDENS**
Sandringham Estate, Sandringham, PE35 6EH. **His Majesty The King,** 01485 522283, sally.porter@sandringhamestate.co.uk, www.sandringhamestate.co.uk. *Sandringham is 6m NE of King's Lynn. Signposted from the A148 Fakenham Rd and the A149 Hunstanton Rd. The Royal Park's postcode for SatNav is PE35 6AB.* **For opening times and information, please phone, email or visit garden website.**
Set in 25 hectares (60 acres) and enjoyed by the British Royal Family and their guests when in residence, the more formal gardens are open from April - October. The grounds have been developed in turn by each Monarch since 1863 when King Edward VII and Queen Alexandra purchased the Estate. Topiary Garden, Cottage Garden and Historic Trees, and a new Maze. Gravel paths are not deep, some long distances. Please contact us or visit the website for an Accessibility Guide.

Blickling Lodge

48 SEVERALS GRANGE
Holt Road B1110, Wood Norton, NR20 5BL. Jane Lister, 01362 684206, hoecroft@hotmail.co.uk. *8m S of Holt, 6m E of Fakenham. 2m N of Guist on L of B1110. Guist is 5m SE of Fakenham on A1067 Norwich Rd.* **Sun 10 Aug (1-5). Adm £6, chd free. Home-made teas.** Visits also by arrangement May to Sept. For other opening times and information please phone or email.
The gardens surrounding Severals Grange are a perfect example of how colour, shape and form can be created by the use of foliage plants, from large shrubs to small alpines. Movement and lightness are achieved by interspersing these plants with a wide range of ornamental grasses, which are at their best in late summer. Splashes of additional colour are provided by a variety of herbaceous plants. Wheelchair access via some gravel paths but help can be provided.
& 🐕 ✽ 🚗 🚻 ☕

49 SHERINGHAM HALL
Upper Sheringham, Sheringham, NR26 8TB. *5m W of Cromer, 6m E of Holt. Turn off A148 to Upper Sheringham, past NT car park. Follow NGS signs, L into Park Rd. Ignore 'Private, No Entry' signs. Continue over cattle grids to hall and parking.* **Sat 10 May (1-5). Adm £8, chd free. Pre-booking essential, please visit www.ngs.org.uk for information & booking. Light refreshments.**
An opportunity to visit this wonderful garden. Designed by Repton, the park is open regularly, the hall and walled garden are private. Kitchen garden redesigned by Arabella Lennox-Boyd with restored glasshouses and cold frames. Replanted orchards, hornbeam temple, new herbaceous borders, parterres and a white garden. Wildflower meadow between hot and cool borders in the east and restored Repton pleasure grounds in the west. Repton's walks have been reopened.
☕

50 SILVERSTONE FARM
North Elmham, Dereham, NR20 5EX. George Carter, 01362 668130, george@georgecartergardens.co.uk, www.georgecartergardens.co.uk. *Nearer to Gateley than N Elmham. From N Elmham church head N to Guist. Take 1st L onto Great Heath Rd. L at T-junc. Take 1st R signed Gateley, Silverstone Farm is 1st drive on L by a wood.* **Evening opening Fri 30 May (6-8). Adm £7, chd free. Wine.**
Garden belonging to George Carter described by the Sunday Times as 'one of the 10 best garden designers in Britain'. 1830s farmyard and formal gardens in two acres. Inspired by C17 formal gardens, the site consists of a series of interconnecting rooms with framed views and vistas designed in a simple palette of evergreens and deciduous trees and shrubs such as available in that period. Books by the owner for sale with a new book 'A Garden Pattern Book' (working title) will be published 2025. Level site, mostly wheelchair accessible.
& 🐕 🚗 🚻 ☕

51 ♦ STODY LODGE
Melton Constable, NR24 2ER. Mr & Mrs Charles MacNicol, 01263 860572, enquiries@stodyestate.co.uk. *16m NW of Norwich, 3m S of Holt. Off B1354. Signed from Melton Constable on Holt Rd. For SatNav NR24 2ER. Gardens signed as you approach.* **For NGS: Wed 7 May (1-5). Adm £9, chd free. Home-made teas. Refreshments provided by selected local and national charities.** For other opening times and information, please phone or email.
Spectacular gardens with one of the largest concentrations of rhododendrons and azaleas in East Anglia. Created in the 1920s, the gardens also feature magnolias, camellias, a variety of ornamental and specimen trees, late daffodils and bluebells. Expansive lawns and magnificent yew hedges. Woodland walks and four acre water garden filled with over 2,000 vividly-coloured azalea mollis. Wheelchair access to most areas of the garden. Some gravel paths with uneven ground.
& 🐕 🚗

52 SWAFIELD HALL
Knapton Road, Swafield, North Walsham, NR28 0RP. Tim Payne & Boris Konoshenko, www.swafieldhall.co.uk. *Swafield Hall is approx ½m along Knapton Rd from its start in the village of Swafield. Disabled parking is available at the Hall. There is a paddock nearby for general parking.* **Sat 21, Sun 22 June (10-5). Adm £6, chd free. Tea, coffee & cake.**
C16 Manor House with Georgian additions (not open) set within four acres of gardens inc a parterre and various rooms inc a summer garden, orchard, cutting garden, pear tunnel, secret oriental garden (with nine flower beds based on a Persian carpet), the Apollo Promenade of theatrical serpentine hedging, a duck pond and woodland walk. Garden is wheelchair accessible.
& 🐕 ✽ ☕ 🚻

53 THE NORFOLK HOSPICE, TAPPING HOUSE
Wheatfields, Hillington, King's Lynn, PE31 6BH. www.norfolkhospice.org.uk. *Wheatfields is in Hillington off Station Rd, B1153. From the A148, take the turning into Station Rd, B1153 towards Grimston. Wheatfields is 1st turning on the R. The Hospice is located straight ahead at the end of the road.* **Sun 29 June (10-2). Adm £4.50, chd free. Light refreshments.**
The Hospice garden has been created and maintained by a team of volunteers. The site was purpose built and formally opened in 2016. The gardens are still being developed but many areas are well established and provide a peaceful and tranquil backdrop to patients, visitors and staff alike. Set in grounds of approx two acres there is a variety of cottage garden plants, perennials and shrubs. There is a vegetable plot, the produce of which is used by the kitchen team and wildlife area with pond. Full wheelchair access means that our garden space is available for all to enjoy.
& 🐕 ✽ ☕

70 inpatients and their families are being supported at the newly opened Horatio's Garden Northern Ireland, thanks to National Garden Scheme donations.

GROUP OPENING

54 THREE EATON GARDENS
15 Waverley Road, Norwich,
NR4 6SG. *Branksome Rd is off Newmarket Rd near the Daniels Rd r'about. Waverley Rd intersects halfway. Coach House Court is off Unthank Rd a short walk from the other 2 gardens. All are 1m from City Centre.* **Sun 22 June (10.30-4.30). Combined adm £7, chd free. Home-made teas at 19 Branksome Rd.**

19 BRANKSOME ROAD
Sue & Chris Pike.

4 COACH HOUSE COURT
Jackie Floyd.

15 WAVERLEY ROAD
Sue & Clive Lloyd.

Three town gardens 15 minutes from the City Centre. 19 Branksome Road has been designed with quite formal shaped lawns and terraces to fit around the house and make sunny seating areas. There are clipped yews, an oak pergola and swing seat to provide structure, while the planting is a relaxed mixture of perennials, shrubs and trees. A traditional vegetable plot with fruit cage and greenhouse is a small but important part of the garden. 15 Waverley Road has a long town garden that's pretending it is in the country. Divided into three section, it is packed with herbaceous perennials, roses, native plants and a large (and growing) collection of Pelargoniums. Although it is in the city, it still manages to look natural. It is gardened with a streak of wildness. Coach House Court is a tranquil and secluded courtyard garden with abundant trees, shrubs inc roses, climbers, perennials and container plants that gives all year interest. A nature pond attracts lots of birds and insects. All three gardens have water features designed and made by the owners.

55 61 TRAFFORD WAY
Spixworth, Norwich, NR10 3QL.
Mr & Mrs Colin Ryall. *Please park in Spixworth Community car park on Crosswick Ln.* **Sun 27 July (10-5). Adm £4, chd free. Home-made teas.**
Small garden showing what can be achieved with careful planting and the use of pleached hornbeam trees. Gravel garden with flower beds and pot plants. Colourful herbaceous borders with roses.

56 TUDOR LODGINGS
Pales Green, Castle Acre, King's Lynn, PE32 2AN. Gus & Julia Stafford Allen, 01760 755334, julia.staffordallen@ngs.org.uk. *4m N of Swaffham off A1065. Parking in field below the house. Disabled access via Pales Green.* **Visits by arrangement June & July for groups of up to 25. Home-made teas.**
The two acre garden fronts a C15 flint house (not open), and incorporates part of the Norman earthworks. A variety of planting in mixed borders, abstract topiary, and a C18 dovecote. Ornamental grasses, hot border and cutting garden with a productive fruit cage. Natural wild area with a shepherd's hut and informal pond inhabited by ducks and poultry. Newly planted orchard with beehive. Some areas are accessible. Disabled WC.

57 TYGER BARN
Wood Lane, Aldeby, Beccles,
NR34 0DA. Julianne Fernandez, www.chasing-arcadia.com. *Approx 1m from Toft Monks. From A143 towards Great Yarmouth: at Toft Monks turn R into Post Office Lane opp White Lion Pub. After ¼m turn L into Wood Ln. After ½m Tyger Barn is 2nd house on L.* **Sun 29 June (12-4). Adm £5, chd free. Tea, coffee & cake.**
Tyger Barn is a modern country garden started in 2007. Discover extensive perennial borders and cloud pruned hedges. Explore a secret cottage garden, wildflower meadow and wildlife pond. A traditional hay meadow and ancient woodland provide a beautiful setting. Garden is mainly level, but is divided by a shingle drive which wheelchairs may find difficult to cross.

58 VICARAGE HOUSE
Vicarage Road, Great Hockham, Thetford, IP24 1PE. Richard and Katie Darby, 07976 814450, info@vicaragehousenorfolk.com, www.vicaragehousenorfolk.com. *7m NE of Thetford, 6m S of Watton. L off A11,onto A1075 towards Watton. R into Great Hockham, L at* village green and L into Vicarage Rd. Penultimate house on R. **Sat 6 Sept (10-4); Sun 7 Sept (11-4). Adm £5, chd free. Tea, coffee & cake.**
Visits also by arrangement 1 June to 1 Oct for groups of 5 to 20.
Six acres with walled garden, gravel garden, sunken garden, cutting garden and small arboretum. Further cottage style long borders around house and pool house. Pool House garden with box-edged beds and fruit trees. Avenue of yew drums with trained white hornbeam. Semi-circle of yew. Garden has developed over the last 35 years.

59 WALCOTT HOUSE
Walcott Green, Walcott,
Norwich, NR12 0NU. Nick & Juliet Collier, 07986 607170, julietcollier1@gmail.com. *3m N of Stalham. Off the Stalham to Walcott Rd (B1159).* **Visits by arrangement in July for groups of 10 to 30. Adm £10, chd free. Light refreshments.**
A 12 acre site with over an acre of formal gardens based on model C19 Norfolk farm buildings. Woodland and damp gardens, arboretum, vistas with tree lined avenues, woodland walks. Wheelchair access, small single steps to negotiate when moving between gardens in the yards.

60 33 WALDEMAR AVENUE
Hellesdon, Norwich, NR6 6TB.
Sonja Gaffer & Alan Beal,
07798 522380,
sonja.gaffer@ntlworld.com, www.facebook.com/Hellesdontropicalgarden. *Near Norwich Airport. Waldemar Ave is situated approx 400 yds off Norwich ring road towards Cromer, on A140.* **Sun 3, Sun 31 Aug (10-5). Adm £5, chd free. Tea, coffee & cake. Sausage rolls also available. Visits also by arrangement 4 Aug to 30 Sept.**
A surprising and large suburban garden of many parts with an exciting mix of exotic and tropical plants combined with unusual perennials. A quirky palm-thatched Tiki hut is an eye catching feature. There is a wonderful treehouse draped in plants. You can sit by the pond which is brimming with wildlife and rare plants. A large collection of succulents will be on show and there will be plants to buy. This garden is about big leaves and foliage textures and colours. A wildlife pond snuggles beneath the

61 THE WALLED GARDEN, LITTLE PLUMSTEAD
Old Hall Road, Little Plumstead, Norwich, NR13 5FA. Little Plumstead Walled Garden Community Shop & Cafe, www.thewalledgardenshop.co.uk. *On arriving in Little Plumstead follow signs to The Walled Garden.* **Evening opening Wed 16 July (6-8). Adm £10, chd free. Pre-booking essential, please visit www.ngs.org.uk for information & booking. Light refreshments in the cafe.** Richard Hobbs will be taking two guided walks around the recently restored Victorian walled garden with heritage apples and pears on beautifully restored brick walls. There are cutting beds, herbaceous and shrub areas together with a Victorian style glasshouse. There is a newly planted alpine area, a stumpery a big leaves. Good wheelchair access. Surfaces are mostly of lawn and concrete and are on one level.

& 🐕 ✻ ☕

62 WARBOROUGH HOUSE
2 Wells Road, Stiffkey, NR23 1QH. Mr & Mrs J Morgan. *13m N of Fakenham, 4m E of Wells-Next-The-Sea. Parking is available onsite & is signed at garden entrance (A149). Coasthopper bus stops outside garden. Do not park on the main road as this causes congestion.* **Sun 25 May (1-5). Adm £6, chd free. Home-made teas.**
A seven acre garden on a steep chalk slope, surrounding C19 house (not open) with views across the Stiffkey valley and to the coast. Woodland, formal terraces, shrub borders, lawns, wildflower areas and walled garden create a garden of contrasts. Garden slopes steeply in parts. Paths are gravel, bark chip or grass. Disabled parking allows access to garden nearest the house and teas.

& ✻ ☕))

63 WRETHAM LODGE
East Wretham, IP24 1RL. Mr Gordon Alexander & Mr Ian Salter, 01953 498997, grdalexander@btinternet.com. *6m NE of Thetford. A11 E from Thetford, L up A1075, L by village sign, R at Xroads then bear L.* **Sun 20, Mon 21 Apr (11-5). Adm £7, chd free. Home-made teas at local church. Visits also by arrangement Apr to Sept for groups of 10 to 30.**
A 10 acre garden surrounding former Georgian rectory (not open). In spring masses of species tulips, hellebores, fritillaries, daffodils and narcissi; bluebell walk and small woodland walk. Topiary pyramids and yew hedging lead to double herbaceous borders. Shrub borders and rose beds (home of the Wretham Rose). Traditionally maintained walled garden with fruit, vegetables and perennials.

& 🐕 ☕))

Holkham Hall Garden

COUNTY DURHAM, NORTHUMBERLAND & TYNE AND WEAR

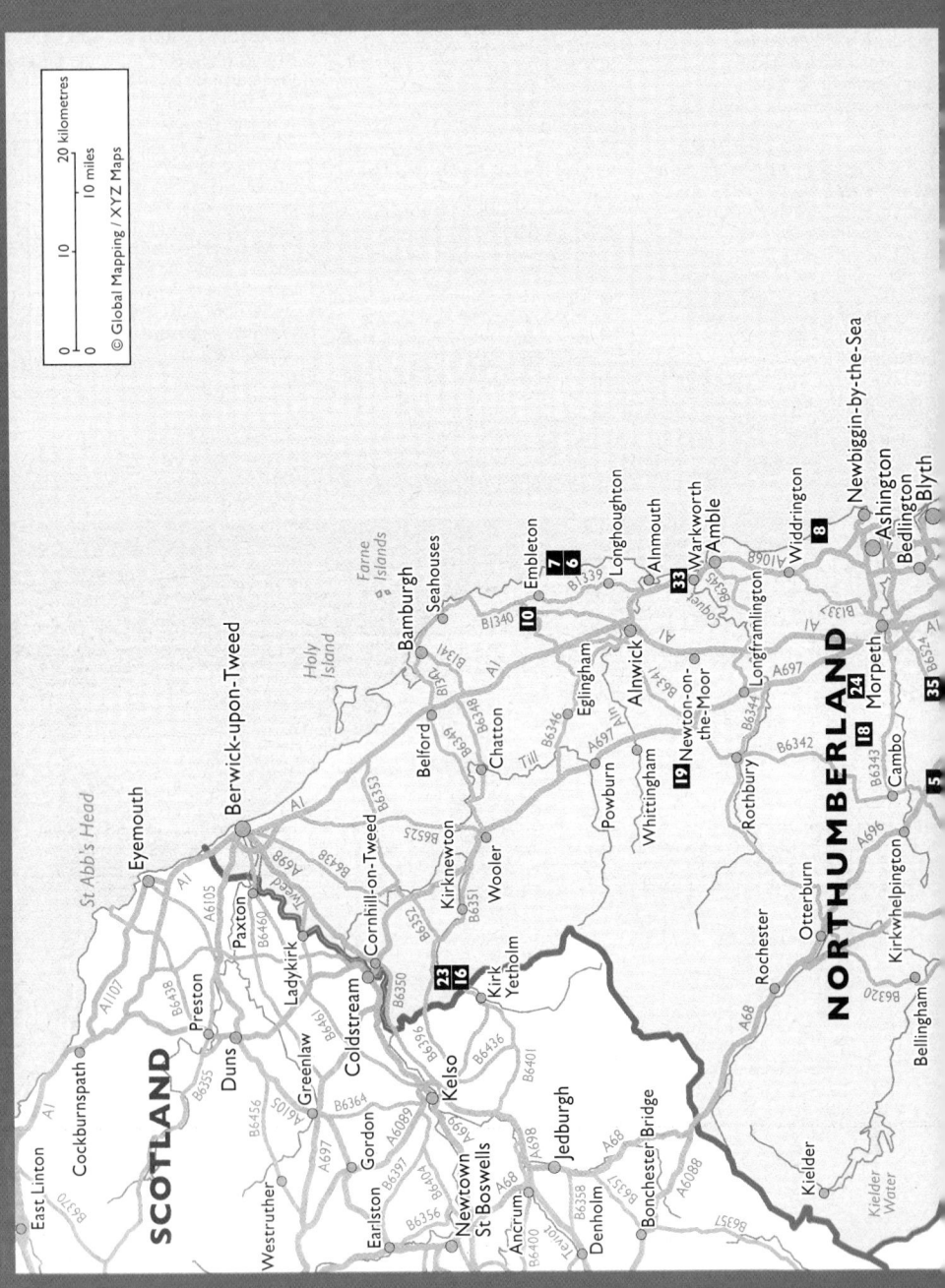

COUNTY DURHAM, NORTHUMBERLAND & TYNE AND WEAR 385

VOLUNTEERS

County Durham

County Organiser
Aileen Little
01325 356691
aileen.little@ngs.org.uk

County Treasurer
Monica Spencer
01325 286215
monica.spencer@ngs.org.uk

Publicity
Margaret Stamper
01325 488911
margaretstamper@tiscali.co.uk

Booklet Co-ordinator
Sue Walker
07849 451079
walker.sdl@gmail.com

Assistant County Organisers
Iain Anderson
01325 778146
iain.anderson@ngs.org.uk

Sarah Garbutt
sarah.garbutt@ngs.org.uk

Helen Jackson
helen.jackson@ngs.org.uk

Gill Naisby
01325 381324
gillnaisby@gmail.com

Margaret Stamper (see above)

Sue Walker (see above)

@gardensopenforcharity
@NGSNorthumberl1
@ngsnorthumber
@ngscountydurham

Northumberland & Tyne and Wear County Organiser & Booklet Coordinator
Maxine Eaton 077154 60038
maxine.eaton@ngs.org.uk

County Treasurer
David Oakley 07941 077594
david.oakley@ngs.org.uk

Publicity, Talks Co-ordinator & Social Media
Liz Reid 01914 165981
liz.reid@ngs.org.uk

Assistant County Organisers
Maureen Kesteven 01914 135937
maureen.kesteven@ngs.org.uk

Natasha McEwen 07917 754155
natashamcewengd@aol.co.uk

Liz Reid (see above)

Susie White 07941 077594
susie@susie-white.co.uk

David Young 01434 600699
david.young@ngs.org.uk

OPENING DATES

All entries subject to change.
For latest information check
www.ngs.org.uk
Map locator numbers are shown to the right of each garden name.

February
Sunday 23rd
Lorbottle Hall   19

April
Saturday 5th
Shortridge Hall   33

May
Saturday 17th
♦ Whalton Manor Gardens   35

Sunday 18th
NEW High Trees   14

Sunday 25th
Blagdon   4

June
Sunday 1st
Ferndene House   11

Saturday 7th
NEW ♦ Shieldfield Art Works   32

Sunday 8th
Lambshield   17
Oliver Ford Garden   27

Tuesday 10th
♦ Belsay Hall, Castle & Gardens   2

Friday 13th
Hidden Gardens of Croft Road   13

Saturday 14th
Walworth Gardens   34

Sunday 15th
Halton Castle   12
Hidden Gardens of Croft Road   13
Kirky Cottage   16
♦ Mindrum House Garden   23

Saturday 21st
NEW 1 Chapel Row   6
NEW 2 Chapel Row   7

Sunday 22nd
Longwitton Hall   18
Marie Curie Hospice   21
Willow Burn Hospice   36

Saturday 28th
Capheaton Hall   5
Fallodon Hall   10
Wolsingham Village Gardens   37

Sunday 29th
Capheaton Hall   5

July
Sunday 6th
NEW 13 Durham Road   9
Netherwitton Village Gardens   24
Old Quarrington Gardens   26
St Margaret's Allotments,
     Churchyard & Centre   30
Secret Gardens of Langholm
     Crescent   31

Saturday 12th
Maggie's   20

Sunday 13th
Bichfield Tower   3
♦ Cresswell Pele Tower Walled
     Garden   8

Sunday 27th
St Cuthbert's Hospice 29

August

Saturday 2nd
Middleton Hall Retirement
  Village 22

Sunday 3rd
◆ Cresswell Pele Tower Walled
  Garden 8

By Arrangement

Arrange a personalised garden visit with your club, or group of friends, on a date to suit you. See individual garden entries for full details.

The Beacon 1
Fallodon Hall 10
Ferndene House 11
NEW High Trees 14
Hill House 15

Old Quarrington Gardens 26
Ravensford Farm 28
Secret Gardens of Langholm
  Crescent 31
Woodlands 38

Our donation to Marie Curie this year equates to 17,496 hours of nursing care or 43 days of care in one of their nine hospices.

Halton Castle

THE GARDENS

1 THE BEACON
10 Crabtree Road, Stocksfield, NE43 7NX. Derek & Patricia Hodgson OBE, 07765 862374, patandderek@btinternet.com. *12m W of Newcastle. From A69 follow signs into village. Stn & cricket ground on L. Turn R into Cadehill Rd then 1st R into Crabtree Rd (cul-de-sac) Park on Cadehill. Train to Stocksfield or Bus 10, 10A/10B.* **Visits by arrangement for groups of 5+. Adm £7, chd free. Cream teas £6pp and/or Piano recitals and comedy £4pp (in aid of the NSPCC).**
This garden illustrates how to create a cottage garden on a steep site with loads of interest at different levels. Planted with acers, roses and a variety of cottage plants and formal plants. Water runs gently through it and there are tranquil places to sit and talk or just reflect. Stunning colour and plant combinations. Wildlife friendly with numerous birds, frogs, newts and hedgehogs. Haven for butterflies and bees. Owner available for entertaining group talks.

2 ◆ BELSAY HALL, CASTLE & GARDENS
Belsay, nr Morpeth, NE20 0DX. English Heritage. *Off A696 at Belsay village. Follow the brown signs. SatNav NE20 0DU. Bus X75 Belsay Express from Newcastle.* **For NGS: Evening opening Tue 10 June (5.30-7.30). Adm £20, chd free. Pre-booking essential, please email fundraising@english-heritage.org.uk or visit www.english-heritage.org.uk/visit/places/belsay-hall-castle-and-gardens/events for information & booking. Light refreshments. For other opening times and information, please email or visit garden website.**
Explore a rare surviving picturesque garden with our expert gardening team. Follow the paths into the Quarry garden, whose rocky walls offer shelter to a vast range of exotics all hidden within the Northumberland countryside, and enjoy beautifully planted borders designed by Dan Pearson.

3 BICHFIELD TOWER
Belsay, Newcastle Upon Tyne, NE20 0JP. Lesley & Stewart Manners, 07511 439606, lesleymanners@gmail.com. *Private road off B6309, 4m N of Stamfordham & SW of Belsay village.* **Sun 13 July (1-4). Adm £8, chd free.**
A 6 acre mature garden set around a Medieval Pele Tower. There is an impressive stone water feature, large trout lake, mature woodland, pear orchard, and 2 walled gardens. Extensive herbaceous borders, prairie borders and contemporary grass borders.

4 BLAGDON
Seaton Burn, NE13 6DE. Viscount Ridley, www.blagdonestate.co.uk. *5m S of Morpeth on A1. 8m N of Newcastle on A1, N on B1318, L at r'about (Holiday Inn) & follow signs to Blagdon. Entrance to parking area signed. Bus No.44.* **Sun 25 May (1-4). Adm £8, chd free. Home-made teas.**
Unique 27 acre garden encompassing formal garden with Lutyens designed 'canal', Lutyens structures and walled kitchen garden. Valley with stream and various follies, quarry garden and woodland walks. Masses of daffodils in spring. Large numbers of ornamental trees and shrubs planted over many generations. National Collections of Acer, Alnus and Sorbus. Partial wheelchair access.

5 CAPHEATON HALL
Capheaton, Newcastle Upon Tyne, NE19 2AB. William & Eliza Browne-Swinburne, 01913 758152, estateoffice@capheatonhall.co.uk, www.capheatonhall.co.uk. *Off A696 24 m N of Newcastle. From S turn L off A696 onto Silver Hill Rd signed Capheaton. From N, past Wallington/Kirkharle junction, turn R. Bus X74 then 1.3m walk. What3words app: guardian.blueberry.traps.* **Sat 28, Sun 29 June (10-4). Adm £10, chd free. Tea, coffee & cake.**
Set in parkland, Capheaton Hall has magnificent views over the Northumberland countryside. Formal ponds sit south of the house which has C19 conservatory and a walk to a Georgian folly of a chapel. The outstanding feature is the very productive walled kitchen garden, mixing colourful vegetables, espaliered fruit with annual and perennial flowering borders. Victorian glasshouse and conservatory. Pre-booking recommended.

6 NEW 1 CHAPEL ROW
Craster, Alnwick, NE66 3TU. Mike & June Drage. *8 m NE from Alnwick. Park in the Pay and Display parking at village entrance. Walk to harbour, turn L on Dunstanburgh Rd. Look for NGS sign on LHS before Castle field. No parking within village.* **Sat 21 June (11-4). Combined adm with 2 Chapel Row £5, chd free. Pub and cafes in the village.**
In the picturesque fishing village of Craster, with sea views, sits a row of cottages and former fishermen's allotments. The gardens show what can be achieved in a windy seaside setting. Number 1 features 2 ponds, colour themed borders framed by stone walls, and a small orchard. Another section has prairie style planting, a gravel garden and vegetable beds.

7 NEW 2 CHAPEL ROW
Craster, Alnwick, NE66 3TU. Sue Chapman. *8 m NE from Alnwick. For directions, see 1 Chapel Row* **Sat 21 June (11-4). Combined adm with 1 Chapel Row £5, chd free. Pub and cafes in the village.**
The garden has borders planted with shrubs, bee friendly perennials, abundant roses and vegetable beds. It also has a wild garden area with a small pond, seasonal flowers and vegetable beds. In sight of Dunstanburgh Castle.

129,032 people were able to access guidance on what to expect when a person is dying through the National Garden Scheme's support for Hospice UK this year.

High Trees

❖ CRESSWELL PELE TOWER WALLED GARDEN
Cresswell Road, Cresswell, Morpeth, NE61 5LE. Mr Steve Lowe, www.cresswellpeletower.org.uk. *10 m E of Morpeth. W of Cresswell Pele Tower, accessed through double gate. No parking on the village green. Public parking on seafront nearby. Arriva Bus1 Blyth to Amble.* **For NGS: Sun 13 July, Sun 3 Aug (2-4). Adm £5, chd free. Light refreshments. For other opening times and information, please visit garden website.**
A newly restored C18 walled garden which was part of Cresswell Hall kitchen gardens, abandoned in the 1930's when the main house was demolished. With a grant from Heritage Lottery in 2022, the garden has been restored to inc borders, orchard, gazebo, wildlife pond and greenhouse. Work to increase plantings is underway. The garden is managed by volunteers. Features inc Medieval Orchard and cordoned fruit, raised beds for food growing, diverse floral borders, fern border, re-enactments, interpretation History book in print and beehives. Short slope on lightly gravelled path initially, then level paths to Tower and Garden, which is fully accessible.

NEW 13 DURHAM ROAD
East Herrington, Sunderland, SR3 3NR. Mr & Mrs A C Winfield. *3 m SW of Sunderland. 700yds from A19/A690 junc, direction Sunderland, considerate parking in side streets or designated at St Chad's 200yds (signposted). Drop off possible. Bus from Newcastle and Durham.* **Sun 6 July (1.30-4.30). Adm £6, chd free. Light refreshments.**
A very interesting, well established, suburban garden, just under an acre, which has been in the same family for over 70 yrs. Mature trees, mixed herbaceous and perennial borders, roses, and vegetable garden. A hidden gem which is an inspiration for gardeners. Access is from a busy road. Various levels but paths provide wheelchair access - steep paths.

10 FALLODON HALL
Alnwick, NE66 3HF. Mark and Lucia Bridgeman, 07765 296197, luciabridgeman@gmail.com, www.bruntoncottages.co.uk. *5m N of Alnwick, 2m off A1. From the A1 turn R onto the B6347 signed Christon Bank & Seahouses. Turn into the Fallodon gates after exactly 2m, at Xrds. Follow drive for 1m.* **Sat 28 June (2-5). Adm £8, chd free. Visits also by arrangement 15 May to 30 Sept for groups of 5 to 25.**
Part of Northumberland's history. Extensive, well established garden, with a hot greenhouse beside the bog garden. The late C17 kitchen garden walls surround cutting and vegetable borders and the fruit greenhouse. Natasha McEwen replanted the sunken garden (from 1898) and her redesigned 30 metres border was planted in 2019. Woodlands, pond and arboretum with over 10 acres to explore. Grave of Sir Edward Grey, Foreign Secretary during WW1, famous ornithologist and fly fisherman, is in the woods near the pond and arboretum. The walls of the kitchen garden contain a fireplace built to heat the fruit trees of the Salkeld family, renowned for their gardening expertise in the C17. Partial wheelchair access.

11 FERNDENE HOUSE
2 Holburn Lane Court, Holburn Lane, Ryton, NE40 3PN. Maureen Kesteven, 01914 135937, maureen.kesteven@ngs.org.uk, www.facebook.com/northeastgardenopenforcharity. *In Ryton Old Village, 8m W of Gateshead. Off B6317, on Holburn Ln. Park on street or in Co-op car park on High St, cross rd through Ferndene Park following yellow signs. Bus 10 10A/10B.* **Sun 1 June (12.30-4). Adm £6, chd free. Home-made teas. Pizza & prosecco. Visits also by arrangement 21 Apr to 4 Aug for groups of 10+.**
¾ acre garden surrounded by trees. Informal areas of herbaceous perennials, formal box bordered area, wildlife pond, gravel and bog gardens (with boardwalk). Willow work. Early interest - hellebores, snowdrops, daffodils, bluebells and tulips. Summer interest from wide range of flowering perennials. 1½ acre mixed broadleaf wood with beck running through. Driveway, from which main borders can be seen, is wheelchair accessible but phone if assistance required.

& 🐕 ❋ 🍵 •))

12 HALTON CASTLE
Corbridge, NE45 5PH. Hugh & Anna Blackett. *2m N of Corbridge turn E off the A68 onto the B6318 (Military Rd) towards Newcastle. Turn R onto drive through stone pillars after ¼ m. Or train to Hexham then Bus 74 (Matfen).* **Sun 15 June (11.30-4.30). Adm £6, chd free. Home-made teas. Light lunches and cream teas from 12pm.**
The terraced garden has stunning views over the Tyne Valley. Massive beech hedges give protection for herbaceous borders, lawns and shrubs. A box parterre is filled with fruit, vegetables and picking flowers. Paths lead through a wildflower meadow garden. The Castle (not open) is a C14 Pele tower with Jacobean manor house attached beside a charming chapel with Norman origins. Limited wheelchair access.

& 🐕 ❋ 🍵 •))

GROUP OPENING

13 HIDDEN GARDENS OF CROFT ROAD
Croft Road, Darlington, DL2 2SD. Jo & Ian Fearnley. *2m S of Darlington on A167. ¾ m S from A167/A66 r'about between Darlington & Croft. What3words app: makeovers.kettles.caravans.* **Fri 13, Sun 15 June (1-5). Combined adm £6, chd free. Home-made teas at Oxney Flatts Farm.**

NAGS HEAD FARM
Jo & Ian Fearnley.

NEW COTTAGE
Jane & John Brown.

OXNEY FLATTS FARM
Carol & Chris Pratt.

Three very different and interesting gardens, well named as 'Hidden Gardens' as they are not visible from the road. Nags Head Farm has a wonderful rill running alongside a sloping garden with a variety of plants leading to a quiet, peaceful courtyard. There is a large vegetable garden in which stands a magnificent glasshouse with vines. A woodland walk leads to a polytunnel, view point and wildflower meadow. Oxney Flatts has well-stocked herbaceous borders and a wildlife pond. New Cottage garden has established flower beds inc herbaceous plants, shrubs and roses. There is also a productive fruit and vegetable garden. A newly created wildlife pond area inc a rockery and seating. Aycliffe Bee Keepers Association will have a stall in the garden of Nags Head Farm. There will be information about bees and bee keeping plus a small display hive where you can safely view bees in action. Honey will be on sale, subject to availability, and 10% of proceeds will be donated to NGS. Partial wheelchair access, grassy and mostly flat. Some areas of gravel. Dogs on a lead welcome.

& 🐕 ❋ 🍵 •))

14 NEW HIGH TREES
South Park, Hexham, NE46 1BT. John and Sheila Richards, 078113 67902, hightreesgarden@btinternet.com. *½ m S of Hexham town centre (train and bus stations and Wentworth car park). Take B6306 S, fork L at 500 yards. No parking at garden. Park in National*

Park Office car park on L or on the street beyond South Park which is 400 yds on L. Garden entrance 1st on L down lane. **Sun 18 May (1-5). Adm £5, chd free. Visits also by arrangement 15 Feb to 20 July for groups of 8 to 30.**
Specialist ½ acre plantsman's garden, with unusual plants; alpines; shrubs, small trees, woodland plants, herbaceous. Many grown from Alpine Garden Society seed; some new introductions. Much botanical interest- small rock gardens, troughs, tiny meadow, magnolias, rhododendrons, Himalayan poppies. Terrace: sun loving plants, annuals. Wildlife-friendly.

•))

15 HILL HOUSE
Haydon Bridge, Hexham, NE47 6HL. John and Mary Milford, 07850 464509, jmilford749@btinternet.com. *1½ m NW of Haydon Bridge. Satnav will bring visitors to the car park. Preferred route via Haydon Village, not lane from the A69 at Lipwood.* **Visits by arrangement 5 June to 4 Sept for groups of 15 to 50. While refreshments are not provided, visitors are welcome to bring a picnic. Adm £8, chd free.**
Unusual double Walled Garden, generously planted in Cottage Garden style. Circle of box hedges, yew square and topiary; aquiegia and lupins in early June and dahlias, roscoeas and annuals in early September provide much colour. The old orchard, with wildflowers, gives access to a mown walk through a sheep grazed meadow to a woodland area, affording good views across South Tyne valley.

❋ 🪑

16 KIRKY COTTAGE
12 Mindrum Farm Cottages, Mindrum, TD12 4QN. Mrs Ginny Fairfax, 01890 850246, ginny@mindrumgarden.co.uk, www.mindrumestate.co.uk/kirky-garden. *6m SW of Coldstream. 9m NW of Wooler on B6352. 4m N of Yetholm village.* **Sun 15 June (12-5). Combined adm with Mindrum House Garden £10, chd free. Home-made teas at Mindrum House Garden.**
Ginny Fairfax has created Kirky Cottage Garden in the beautiful Bowmont valley surrounded and protected by the Border Hills. A gravel garden in cottage garden style, old

COUNTY DURHAM, NORTHUMBERLAND & TYNE AND WEAR 391

roses, violas and others jostle with favourites from Mindrum. A lovely, abundant garden and, with Ginny's new and creative ideas, ever evolving. All plants propagated from garden.

17 LAMBSHIELD
Hexham, NE46 1SF. David Young. *2m S of Hexham. Take the B6306 from Hexham. After 1.6m turn R at chevron sign. Lambshield drive is 2nd on L after 0.6m.* **Sun 8 June (12.30-4.30). Adm £7, chd free. Home-made teas.**

3½ acre country garden begun in 2010 with strong structure and exciting plant combinations. Distinct areas and styles with formal herbaceous, grasses, contemporary planting, cottage garden, pool and orchard. Cloud hedging, pleached trees, and topiary combine with colourful and exuberant planting. Modern sculpture. Oak building and fencing by local craftsmen. Woodland garden. Mostly level ground but gravel paths not suitable for most wheelchairs.

18 LONGWITTON HALL
Longwitton, Morpeth, NE61 4JJ. Michael & Louise Spriggs. *2m N of Hartburn off B6343. Bus X14,15,16,18 or train to Morpeth then taxi. Entrance at E end of Longwitton village.* **Sun 22 June (12-4). Adm £8, chd free.**

6 acre historic site with glorious views to the south. Sheltered, mature garden, with specimen trees and acers, redeveloped with new borders. Circular rose garden, crescent shaped pool surrounded by foliage plants, 'standing stone' feature and a rhododendron and azalea glade leading to newly planted tunnel and cherry circle. Tree peonies and yew walk.

19 LORBOTTLE HALL
Whittingham, Alnwick, NE66 4TD. Ms Kate Donaghy. *What3words app: promises.struggle.variously. From Whittingham, 1½ m beyond Callaly, on L. From Rothbury, 4½ m. From Thropton, on the road to Whittingham, on R.* **Sun 23 Feb (12-4). Adm £8, chd free. Light refreshments.**

Garden and woodlands set in 20 acres with beautiful vistas, lovingly transformed over the last 8 yrs from considerable neglect. A Walled Garden contains wisteria arches, wild flowers and a long mixed border richly planted with shrubs, roses and herbaceous perennials. The wood has masses of snowdrops, woodland/shade loving plants and meandering paths leading to the large meadow. The lawns around the house, the walled and the pond gardens can be accessed by wheelchair users.

20 MAGGIE'S
Melville Grove, Newcastle Upon Tyne, NE7 7NU. www.maggies.org/our-centres/maggies-newcastle. *Driving into the grounds of the Freeman Hospital, Maggie's opp entrance to Northern Centre for Cancer Care. Nearest parking the Freeman Hospital multi-storey. Bus X63, 37 and 38.* **Sat 12 July (1-4). Adm by donation. Light refreshments.**

The garden (recently enlarged), by Chelsea medal winner, Sarah Price, is a sheltered sun trap. Banked wildflower beds and multiple planters, with seasonal displays, at ground level, plus two roof gardens. This gives a choice of outside spaces for visitors to enjoy. Copper beech, cherry blossom, crocus, bulbs, wildflowers and herbs give a colourful seasonal planting palette. A tranquil oasis. Gardener available to give a brief explanation of the garden and its design. Partial wheelchair access, gravel in the garden and roof garden, but the main section can be accessed.

21 MARIE CURIE HOSPICE
Marie Curie Drive, Newcastle Upon Tyne, NE4 6SS. www.mariecurie.org.uk/help/hospice-care/hospices/newcastle/about. *In W Newcastle just off Elswick Rd. At bottom of housing estate. Turning is between MA Brothers & Dallas Carpets. Bus numbers 30 and 31.* **Sun 22 June (2-4.30). Adm by donation. Light refreshments in garden Café.**

The landscaped garden of the purpose-built Marie Curie Hospice overlooks the Tyne and Gateshead and offers a beautiful, tranquil place for patients and visitors to sit and chat. Rooms open onto a patio garden with gazebo and fountain. There are climbing roses, evergreens and herbaceous perennials. The garden is well maintained by volunteers. Come and see the work NGS funding helps make possible. The Hospice and gardens are wheelchair accessible.

22 MIDDLETON HALL RETIREMENT VILLAGE
Middleton St George, Darlington, DL2 1HA. Middleton Hall Retirement Village, www.middletonhallretirementvillage.co.uk. *From A67 D'ton/Yarm, turn at 2nd r'about signed to Middleton St George. Turn L at the mini r'about & immed R after the railway bridge, signed Low Middleton. Main entrance is ¼ m on L.* **Sat 2 Aug (11-4). Adm £5, chd free. Light refreshments.**

Main features are natural woodland and parkland walks within the 45 acre estate. There is a Japanese themed garden, and a Mediterranean garden alongside wetland, ponds, a bird hide, fernery, a ceramic garden and allotments. There is also a Putting Green and Golf course. For more information please visit our website. All wheelchair accessible and linked by a series of woodland walks.

23 ♦ MINDRUM HOUSE GARDEN
Mindrum, TD12 4QN. Mr & Mrs T Fairfax, 01890 850634, info@mindrumpartnership.com, www.mindrumestate.com. *6m SW of Coldstream, 9m NW of Wooler. Off B6352. Disabled parking close to house. Parking is available at both gardens.* **For NGS: Sun 15 June (12-5). Combined adm with Kirky Cottage £10, chd free. Home-made teas at Mindrum House. Plant Stall at Kirky Cottage. For other opening times and information, please phone, email or visit garden website.**

A magical combination of old-fashioned roses, hardy perennials and wildlife gardens in a natural setting. Lawns surround the house with borders of climbing roses, mature shrubs and trees throughout. Mindrum House's more extensive gardens inc a rose garden, limestone rock garden (steep slope), fish ponds with terraced walk, and woodland walk with mature pines.

GROUP OPENING

24 NETHERWITTON VILLAGE GARDENS
Netherwitton, Morpeth, NE61 4NN. www.facebook.com/Netherwittonvh. *5m W of Morpeth. The gardens are spread throughout this small village. Parking in the village at Netherwitton Hall.* **Sun 6 July (12-5). Combined adm £15, chd free. Home-made teas at Netherwitton Village Hall on the village green.**
Netherwitton is a hidden gem nestling in the Font Valley west of Morpeth. The gardens of this picturesque village are very private and rarely open to the public (Last open 2015).There is a variety of gardens ranging from small back gardens, to colourful cottage gardens, to larger rural gardens. Most gardens are within the village, but some are within a mile of the village. Not all gardens are accessible for wheelchairs. This is a real community event, raising money for the NGS and the village hall. Most of the gardens are accessible for wheelchairs but some have steps.

& ✿ ☕))

25 ♦ NGS BUZZING GARDEN
Saltwell Park, East Park Road, Gateshead, NE9 5AX. Gateshead Council, maureen.kesteven@ngs.org.uk, www.gateshead.gov.uk/article/11548/Growing-Gateshead-The-Buzzing-Garden. *Between Pets' Corner & Saltwell Towers from E Park Rd/car park in Joicey Rd. In 55 acre Saltwell Park, 'The People's Park'. Bus number 53 or 54.* **For opening times and information, please email or visit garden website.**
Unique collaboration between the National Garden Scheme North East, Trädgårdsresan, Region Västra Götaland and Gateshead Council. Opened 2019, it was funded by sponsorship and is a tribute to the importance of international friendship. The Swedish design reflects the landscape of West Sweden, with coast, meadow and woodland areas. Many of the plant species grow wild in Sweden, providing a welcoming vision for visitors and a feast for pollinators. Donate at https://www.justgiving.com/ngs. Refreshments at Saltwell Towers Café; and Prism Cafe, Almond Pavilion. Wide tarmac path around the garden and mown grass paths through the meadow, but much of the garden is loose gravel.

& 🐕 🚗

GROUP OPENING

26 OLD QUARRINGTON GARDENS
The Stables, Old Quarrington, Durham, DH6 5NN. John Little, 07967 267864, johndlittle10@gmail.com, www.facebook.com/thestablesOQ. *1m from J61 of A1(M). All vehicle access from Crow Trees Ln, Bowburn. SatNav may be misleading.* **Sun 6 July (10-5). Combined adm £6, chd free. Home-made teas at The Stables - also picnics and WC. Visits also by arrangement 1 May to 4 Oct for groups of 12+. By arrangement entry and refreshments £10 per person.**

ORCHARD COTTAGE
Chrissy and Steve Skinner.

ROSE COTTAGE
Mr Richard Cowen.

THE STABLES
John & Claire Little, www.facebook.com/thestablesOQ.

Three very distinct gardens in the hamlet of Old Quarrington. The Stables is a large family garden full of hidden surprises and extensive views. The main garden is about an acre inc gravel garden, orchard, play area, lawn and woodland gardens. There is a further 4 acres to explore which inc wildlife ponds, woodlands, meadows, hens, ducks and alpacas. The main garden at Rose Cottage is planted with wildlife friendly flowers and a pond that attracts 2 species of newts. To the rear there is a Mediterranean area and a woodland garden with stream beyond. Orchard Cottage has a strong focus on self sufficiency, re use and recycling, with a large vegetable plot growing a wide range of interesting edibles. Plant sales at The Stables.

& 🐕 ✿ ☕ 🪑))

27 OLIVER FORD GARDEN
Longedge Lane, Rowley, Consett, DH8 9HG. Bob & Bev Tridgett, www.gardensanctuaries.co.uk. *5m NW of Lanchester. Signed from A68 in Rowley. From Lanchester take road towards Sately. Garden will be signed as you pass Woodlea Manor.* **Sun 8 June (1-5). Adm £5, chd free. Tea, coffee & cake.**
A peaceful, contemplative 3 acre garden developed and planted by the owner and BBC Gardener of the Year as a space for quiet reflection. Arboretum specialising in bark, stream, wildlife pond and bog garden. Semi-shaded Japanese maple and dwarf rhododendron garden. Rock garden and scree bed. Insect nectar area, orchard and 1½ acre meadow. David Austin rose bed. Terrace and ornamental herb garden. The garden is managed to maximise wildlife and there are a number of sculptures around the garden.

🐕 ☕

28 RAVENSFORD FARM
Hamsterley, Bishop Auckland, DL13 3NH. Jonathan & Caroline Peacock, 01388 488305, caroline@ravensfordfarm.co.uk. *7m W of Bishop Auckland. From A68 between Witton-le-Wear & Toft Hill, turn W to Hamsterley. Our postcode will bring you here, but we are the older farm set back from the road, not the similarly named one on the roadside.* **Visits by arrangement Mar to Oct. Adm £5, chd free. Tea, coffee & cake on request.**
In 1984 Ravensford Farm was a ruin in a field full of weeds, with one tree. Today it is surrounded by a richly varied garden, a wood, two ponds, orchard, rhododendron dell and extensive flower beds. This is a garden of year-round interest and variety. The focus is on hardy plants that survive in all conditions, and on colour in all seasons. Unusual shrubs and trees, and working towards a national collection of Osmanthus. Some gravel, so assistance will be needed for wheelchairs. Assistance dogs only, please.

& ☕

In 2024, we celebrated 40 years of continuous funding for Macmillan Cancer Support equating to more than £19.5 million.

The Stables, Old Quarrington Gardens

29 ST CUTHBERT'S HOSPICE
Park House Road, Durham, DH1 3QF. St Cuthbert's Hospice, www.stcuthbertshospice.com. *1m SW of Durham City on A167. Turn into Park House Rd, the hospice is on L after the Merryoaks Community Hub building and play park. Parking available.* **Sun 27 July (10-4). Adm £5, chd free. Tea, coffee & cake. Café open 10am-4pm for light refreshment (cash or card).**
5 acres of mature gardens surround the Hospice. In development since 1988, the gardens are cared for by volunteers inc a Victorian-style greenhouse and large vegetable, fruit and cut flower area. Lawns surround smaller scale specialist planting, and areas for patients and visitors to relax. Woodland area with walks, sensory garden, and an 'In Memory' garden with stream. Winner of the 2024 Northumbria In Bloom in the Care/Residential Homes, Hospices & Day Centres category. Almost all areas are accessible for wheelchairs.

30 ST MARGARET'S ALLOTMENTS, CHURCHYARD & CENTRE
Margery Lane, Durham City, DH1 4QU. St Margaret's Allotments Association, www.stmargaretsallotments.com. *Close to Durham City Centre, S side; limited free on-street parking; car parks in city centre. From A1(M), take A690 to City Centre/Crook; straight ahead at T-lights after 4th r'about. From A167, turn R along A690, and R at next T-lights. 10mins walk from bus /rail stn.* **Sun 6 July (11-5). Adm £5, chd free. Light refreshments at Old School Cafe in St Margaret's Centre, adjacent to allotments.**
Almost 100 allotments against the spectacular backdrop of Durham Cathedral, with the chance to speak to gardeners, many using organic methods. Six acre churchyard, rich in nature and history, with 500 gravestones and also Commonwealth war graves. Norman church open to visitors. St Margaret's centre open to showcase its work for mental health and wellbeing. There will be self-guided tours, a scarecrow competition, musical programme and talks. Wildlife activities, crafts and trails for children. History and archaeology. Crafts will also be on sale.

GROUP OPENING

31 SECRET GARDENS OF LANGHOLM CRESCENT
Langholm Crescent, Darlington, DL3 7ST. Barbara-Anne Johnson, 07773 417169, x07baj@gmail.com. *Town centre. All on street parking in the surrounding streets.* **Sun 6 July (11.30-5). Combined adm £6, chd free. Tea, coffee & cake at The Cottage, 20 Langholm Crescent.** Visits also by arrangement.

The Cottage Garden at 20 Langholm Crescent is a mature garden but new to the present owner. It is evolving, hidden from public view, has large lawns, borders, mature trees, small pond, rose garden and more. The gardens behind the Langholm Terrace houses are individually delightful, with each making creative use of the limited space available.

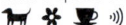

32 NEW ◆ SHIELDFIELD ART WORKS
1 Clarence Street, Newcastle Upon Tyne, NE2 1YH. www.saw-newcastle.org/shieldfield-grows. *What3words app: indeed.frogs.known. 1m E of Newcastle city centre. SatNav will take visitors to car park. Metro to Manors or Bus No.22.* **For NGS: Sat 7 June (11-3). Adm £4, chd free. Tea, coffee & cake. Refreshments proceeds to SAW.** For other opening times and information, please visit garden website.

An urban community garden promoting sustainable food production, fair land usage and flourishing community. Enjoy exploring the vegetable garden, mown labyrinth, bustling wildflower and fruit tree banks, children's sensory play space, pergola, rotating art poster gallery and the famous chair made from a bath. Garden on one level with different surfaces inc paved areas, grass and a hoggin path. Level access to/from the car park and building.

33 SHORTRIDGE HALL
Warkworth, Morpeth, NE65 0WJ. Rachael & Mike Wyllie. *N of Warkworth off A1068. Garden about 1½ m from Warkworth. Please note: Parking along a narrow roadside verge, considerate parking please. Bus X18 direction Berwick.* **Sat 5 Apr (11-3). Adm £8, chd free. Light refreshments.**

3½ acre garden based on a design by well-known landscape designer, Adam Frost. The garden surrounds a Victorian Hall. Year-round interest, inc wildflower meadows, a woodland garden, herbaceous and mixed shrub borders, mixed rose garden and ornamental ponds. A small walled garden houses the greenhouse and a cutting garden. There are significant, but young hedges. Lots of bulbs planted for a good spring display. Massed daffodils.

Cresswell Pele Tower Walled Garden

GROUP OPENING

34 WALWORTH GARDENS
Walworth, Darlington, DL2 2LY. Iain & Margaret Anderson. *Approx 5m W of Darlington on A68 or ½m E of Piercebridge on A67. Follow brown signs to Walworth Castle Hotel. Just up the hill from the Castle entrance, follow NGS yellow signs down private track. Tickets & teas at Quarry End.* **Sat 14 June (11-4). Combined adm £6.50, chd free. Home-made teas at Quarry End.**

THE ARCHES
Stephen & Becky Street-Howard.

CASTLE BARN
Joe & Sheila Storey.

THE DOVECOTE
Tony & Ruth Lamb.

QUARRY END
Iain & Margaret Anderson.

Quarry End is a 1½ acre woodland garden developed over 20 yrs on the site of an ancient quarry. The garden offers a wide variety of mature trees, shrubs, perennials, a fernery and potager. There is a reclaimed quarry woodland, an C18 ice house and lovely views over South Durham. The Dovecote has three themes. An English cottage garden featuring espalier fruit trees, and heavily scented tea roses. A Japanese garden with a moongate drawing you through to specimen acer trees and a small Zen garden overlooking a Koi pond. The vegetable plot is wrapped round with a Grade II listed vented wall and has great space saving ideas. Castle Barn gardens are now well established with fruit trees, raised beds and colourful borders. Recent additions inc a herb garden and grape vines and a new patio area. The Arches' expansive garden comprises an orchard, a large vegetable garden, a wild swimming pond, an ornamental garden and an arboretum. There will be plants for sale at Quarry End. Some areas of the Quarry End garden are not accessible for wheelchairs but most is grassy and flat.

& 🐾 ✤ ☕ »))

35 ♦ WHALTON MANOR GARDENS
Whalton, Morpeth, NE61 3UT. Mr T R P S Norton, 07881 938080, pn@whaltonmanor.com, www.whaltonmanor.co.uk. *5m W of Morpeth. On the B6524, at E end of the village (signed). Public transport - Bus/train to Morpeth then taxi.* **For NGS: Sat 17 May (11-4). Adm £9, chd free. Tea, coffee & cake in the Game Larder.** For other opening times and information, please phone, email or visit garden website.
The historic Whalton Manor, altered by Sir Edwin Lutyens in 1908, is surrounded by 3 acres of magnificent walled gardens, designed by Lutyens with the help of Gertrude Jekyll. The gardens, developed by the Norton family since the 1920s inc extensive herbaceous borders, spring bulbs, 30 yd peony border, rose garden, listed summerhouses, pergolas and walls festooned with rambling roses and clematis. Partial wheelchair access to main area but otherwise stone steps and gravel paths.

& ✤ 🚗 🚌 ☕ »))

36 WILLOW BURN HOSPICE
Howden Bank, Lanchester, DH7 0BF. Rachel Quince, www.willowburnhospice.org.uk. *Located in the Maiden View estate. Turn into the Maiden View Estate from the main road. Then take the 2nd L once inside the estate and drive down to car park.* **Sun 22 June (10-3). Adm £3, chd free. Light refreshments in the Willows Café, inc a selection of baked goods available.**
With a mix of both natural and cultivated areas, this beautiful garden is the setting for outstanding views from the hospice across the Derwent Valley. The gardens are maintained and cared for by volunteers and inc wildflowers, shrubs, perennials, and a large wooded area, as well as memorials and dedications for loved ones. The Willows Café is open throughout the duration of the open day. There are lawn games and 'The Potting Shed' plant and gift shop. Pathways give access to view all the areas of the garden.

& 🐾 ✤ ☕ 🪑 »))

GROUP OPENING

37 WOLSINGHAM VILLAGE GARDENS
Wolsingham, Bishop Auckland, DL13 3AY. Janette Kelly. *Gardens are spread throughout the village. Parking is available in village centre & at the recreation field. Start at 9 West End which is a narrow lane, opp Italian restaurant.* **Sat 28 June (1-5). Combined adm £6, chd free. Tea, coffee & cake at St Anne's community centre in the recreation field.**
Enjoy a group of 5 gardens and a collection of allotments. The gardens vary in style from a rose garden to a contemporary to historic, as one is the site of an old mill, another a dye house.

🐾 ✤ ☕ »))

38 WOODLANDS
Peareth Hall Road, Springwell Village, Gateshead, NE9 7NT. Liz Reid, 07719 875750, liz.reid@ngs.org.uk, www.facebook.com/visitgarden. *3½m N Washington Galleries. 4m S Gateshead town centre. On B1288 turn opp Guide Post pub (NE9 7RR) onto Peareth Hall Rd. Continue for ½m passing 2 bus stops on L. 3rd drive on L past Highbury Ave. Bus 56 Newcastle – Sunderland. Stop Heugh Hill* **Visits by arrangement 10 June to 31 July for groups of 10 to 30. Adm £8, chd free. Home-made teas. Beer & wine also available.**
Mature garden on a site of approx 1/7 of an acre - quirky, with tropical themed planting and Caribbean inspired bar. Also an area of cottage garden planting. A fun garden with colour year-round, interesting plants, informal beds and borders and pond area. Tropical themed garden with display of mature tree ferns and palms. wildlife pond and water feature as well as significant area of well established cottage style planting.

✤ ☕

48,000 people affected by cancer were reached by Maggie's centres supported by the National Garden Scheme over the last 12 months.

NORTHAMPTONSHIRE

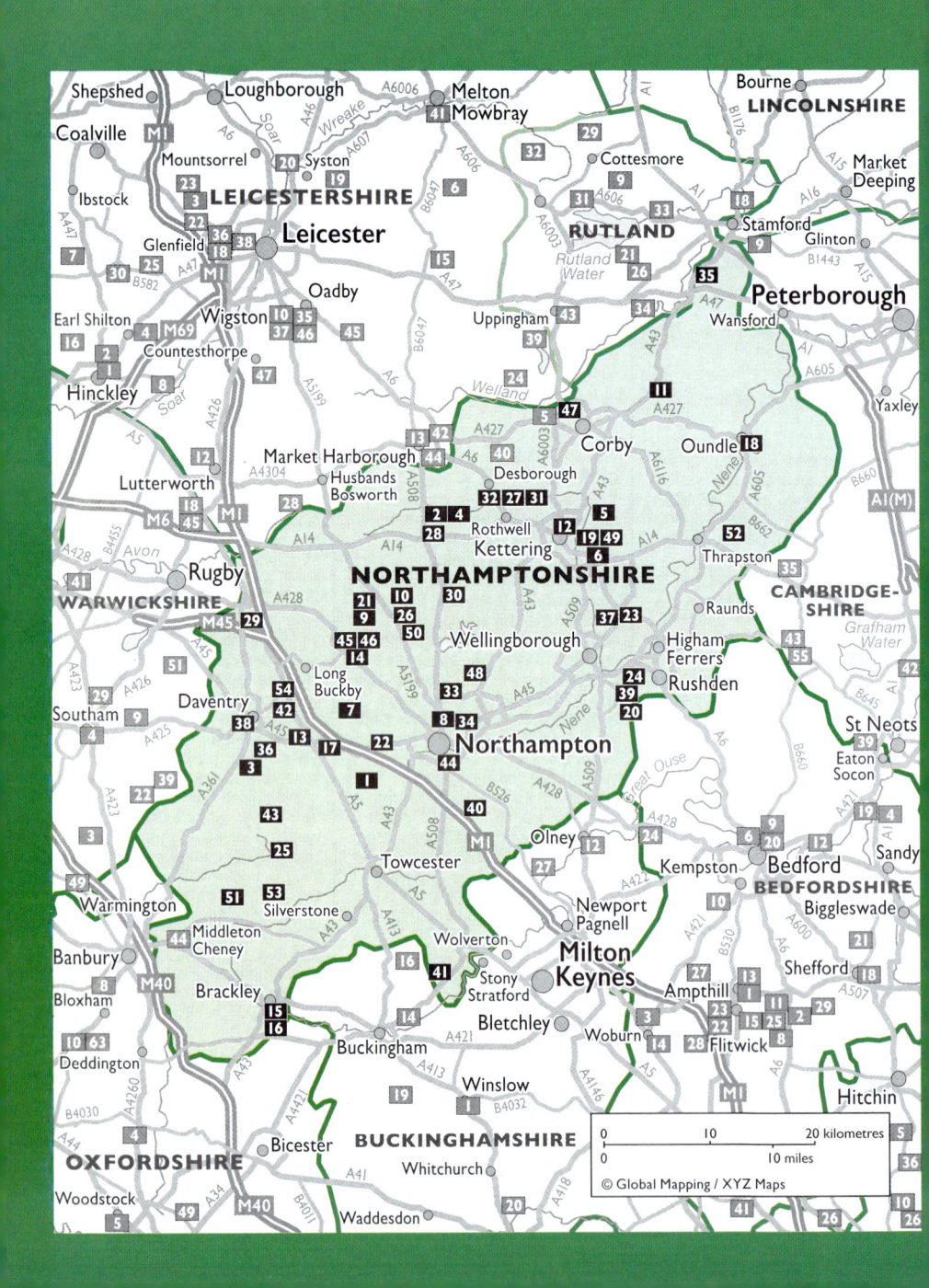

VOLUNTEERS

County Organisers
David Abbott
01933 680363
david.abbott@ngs.org.uk

Gay Webster
01604 740203
gay.webster@ngs.org.uk

County Treasurer
David Abbott (as above)

Publicity
David Abbott (as above)

Photographer
Snowy Ellson
07508 218320
snowyellson@googlemail.com

Booklet Coordinator
William Portch
01536 522169
william.portch@ngs.org.uk

Talks
Elaine & William Portch
01536 522169
elaine@ngs.org.uk

Assistant County Organisers
Amanda Bell
01327 860651
amanda.bell@ngs.org.uk

Belinda Fletcher
07758 845717
fletcher.belinda@googlemail.com

Philippa Heumann
01327 860142
pmheumann@gmail.com

Tom Higginson
01327 349434
tom.higginson@ngs.org.uk

Elaine & William Portch
(as above)

@Northants Ngs
@NorthantsNGS
@northantsngs

OPENING DATES

All entries subject to change.
For latest information check
www.ngs.org.uk
Map locator numbers are
shown to the right of each
garden name.

February
Snowdrop Openings
Sunday 9th
Bosworth House 4
The Old Vicarage 42
Friday 14th
136 High Street 24
Saturday 15th
136 High Street 24
Sunday 16th
◆ Boughton House 5
136 High Street 24
NEW 17 Lynton Avenue 33

March
Sunday 23rd
Woodcote Villa 54

April
Sunday 6th
The Old Vicarage 42
Sunday 13th
Flore Gardens 17
Sunday 27th
Briarwood 6
◆ Cottesbrooke Hall Gardens 10
◆ Deene Park 11
◆ Holdenby House & Gardens 26
Rosi's Taverna 49

May
Sunday 4th
Guilsborough Gardens 21
136 High Street 24
Newnham Gardens 36
Friday 9th
Ravensthorpe Nursery 46
Saturday 10th
◆ Evenley Wood Garden 16
Ravensthorpe Nursery 46

Sunday 11th
Ravensthorpe Nursery 46
Sunday 18th
Badby Gardens 3
NEW The Bringtons 7
Dene Lodge 12
Sunday 25th
NEW Lynton Avenue Gardens 34
Oaklea 39
Monday 26th
East Haddon Gardens 14

June
Sunday 1st
83 Main Road 35
Old Rectory, Quinton 40
Saturday 7th
The Old Rectory, Wicken 41
Sunday 8th
Evenley Gardens 15
Foxtail Lilly 18
Harpole Gardens 22
Hostellarie 27
◆ Kelmarsh Hall & Gardens 28
14 Leys Avenue 31
16 Leys Avenue 32
Spratton Gardens 50
Friday 13th
Ravensthorpe Nursery 46
Saturday 14th
Ravensthorpe Nursery 46
Sunday 15th
Ravensthorpe Gardens 45
NEW Weston Gardens 53
Saturday 21st
Flore Gardens 17
Sunday 22nd
Flore Gardens 17
Rosearie-de-la-Nymph 48
Tuesday 24th
◆ Rockingham Castle 47
Sunday 29th
Arthingworth Open Gardens 2
Dodford Gardens 13
Kilsby Gardens 29
Rosearie-de-la-Nymph 48
Sulgrave Gardens 51

July
Friday 11th
Ravensthorpe Nursery 46

Saturday 12th
Ravensthorpe Nursery 46
Sunday 13th
Ravensthorpe Nursery 46
Sunday 20th
C2C Grows - Community
   Allotment Garden 8
Woodcote Villa 54
Saturday 26th
◆ Lamport Hall 30
Sunday 27th
The Green Patch 19
Nonsuch 37

August
Sunday 3rd
136 High Street 24
3 Pilgrims Place 44
Sunday 10th
Highfields 25
3 Pilgrims Place 44

Sunday 31st
3 Pilgrims Place 44
Woodcote Villa 54

September
Saturday 13th
◆ Coton Manor Garden 9

October
Sunday 12th
◆ Boughton House 5

February 2026
Friday 13th
136 High Street 24
Saturday 14th
136 High Street 24
Sunday 15th
136 High Street 24

By Arrangement

Arrange a personalised garden visit with your club, or group of friends, on a date to suit you. See individual garden entries for full details.

16 Ace Lane 1
Bosworth House 4
Briarwood 6
Dene Lodge 12
Foxtail Lilly 18
NEW 26 The Green, Evenley
   Gardens 15
Greywalls 20
67-69 High Street 23
136 High Street 24
Hostellarie 27
83 Main Road 35
19 Manor Close, Harpole
   Gardens 22
North Farm 38
The Old Rectory, Wicken 41
Old West Farm 43
3 Pilgrims Place 44
Ravensthorpe Nursery 46
Titchmarsh House 52
Woodcote Villa 54

26 The Green, Evenley Gardens

THE GARDENS

■ 16 ACE LANE
Bugbrooke, Northampton, NN7 3PQ. Steve & Kate, 01280 860811, kate@qdl.co.uk, www.katewhitearchitects.co.uk/portfolio/our-garden. Located 1m E of the A5, 3m S of M1 J16. Parking at church car park nearby, SatNav for parking NN7 3RG. **Visits by arrangement Apr to Sept for groups of 10 to 30. Adm £5, chd free. Light refreshments on request (additional charge).** Over the last 14 yrs we have evolved our enclosed garden from what was previously extensively laid to lawn with traditional borders, to a varied characterful garden structured by hedges, paths and herbaceous borders. Topiary, creative planting and water features give emphasis and contrast with the lavender rill, pyramid and globe gardens. The lawn has gradually disappeared!
& •))

GROUP OPENING

❷ ARTHINGWORTH OPEN GARDENS
Arthingworth, nr Market Harborough, LE16 8LA. *6m S of Market Harborough. From Market Harborough via A508, after 4m take L to Arthingworth. From Northampton, A508 turn R just after Kelmarsh. Park cars in Arthingworth village & tickets for sale in the village hall.* **Sun 29 June (1.30-6). Combined adm £7, chd free. Home-made teas at Bosworth House & village hall.**
Arthingworth features a Grade II* listed St Andrew's Church, a friendly pub, and a scenic setting by the River Ise, which you can cross via a small bridge. The village offers a variety of open gardens, ranging from small to park-like. Visitors are welcome to explore eight gardens, inc hidden ones and Bosworth House, which has taken 25 yrs to develop. St Andrew's Church will be open. The village is also next to the national cycle path. Wheelchair access to some gardens.
& ❈ ☕

GROUP OPENING

❸ BADBY GARDENS
Badby, Daventry, NN11 3AR. *3m S of Daventry on E-side of A361.* **Sun 18 May (1-5). Combined adm £6, chd free. Home-made teas in St Mary's Church.**

THE GLEBE
Linda Clow.

SHAKESPEARES COTTAGE
Jocelyn Hartland-Swann & Pen Keyte.

SOUTHVIEW COTTAGE
Alan & Karen Brown.

SPRINGFIELD HOUSE
Chris & Linda Lofts.

Delightful hilly village with attractive old houses of golden coloured Hornton stone, set around a C14 church and two village greens (no through traffic). There are four gardens of differing sizes and styles; a wisteria-clad thatched cottage with a sloping garden and modern sculptures; an elevated garden with views over the village and beyond; a new garden with a comparatively modern house that will develop over the next few yrs as the owner continues working with it; a garden which has been remodelled over the last 2 yrs with lawns, herbaceous beds, a pond, and a small vegetable and soft fruit area. We look forward to welcoming you to our lovely village!
❈ ☕ •))

❹ BOSWORTH HOUSE
Oxendon Road, Arthingworth, nr Market Harborough, LE16 8LA. Mr & Mrs C E Irving-Swift, 01858 525202, cirvingswift@gmail.com. *When in Oxendon Rd, take the little lane with no name, 2nd to the R.* **Sun 9 Feb (1-4). Adm £6, chd free. Tea, coffee & cake. Visits also by arrangement May to July for groups of 10 to 20. Rose tour: £12, focusing on pruning & planting roses.**
For 25 yrs, the Bosworth House garden has matured, like us. Yet, we still joyfully welcome snowdrops, aconites, and fritillaries. In February, you can share this wonder with us in a small part of our sleeping garden, awaiting spring. In 2024, we made our first mulberry jam, tried making medlar and quince jelly, and harvested grapes, along with the first trimming of our stunning Wellingtonia. Partial wheelchair access.
& 🚗 ☕

❺ ♦ BOUGHTON HOUSE
Geddington, Kettering, NN14 1BJ. Duke of Buccleuch & Queensberry, KT. *3m NE of Kettering. From A14, 2m along A43 Kettering to Stamford, turn R into Geddington, house entrance 1½ m on R. What3words app: crispier. sensible.maps.* **For NGS: Sun 16 Feb, Sun 12 Oct (1-4). Adm £8, chd £4. Pre-booking essential, please phone 01536 515731, email info@boughtonhouse.co.uk or visit www.boughtonhouse. co.uk for information & booking. Light refreshments. For other opening times and information, please phone, email or visit garden website.**
The Northamptonshire home of the Duke of Buccleuch. The garden opening inc opportunities to see the historic walled garden and herbaceous border, and the sensory and wildlife gardens. The wilderness woodland will open for visitors to view the spring flowers or the autumn colours. As a special treat the garden originally created by Sir David Scott (cousin of the Duke of Buccleuch) will also be open. Designated disabled parking. Gravel around house, please see our accessibility document for further information.
& ❈ 🚗 ☕

Our 2024 donation to The Queen's Nursing institute now helps support over 3,000 Queen's Nurses working in the community in England, Wales, Northern Ireland, the Channel Islands and the Isle of Man.

BRIARWOOD
4 Poplars Farm Road, Barton Seagrave, Kettering, NN15 5AF.
William & Elaine Portch,
01536 522169, elaine@ngs.org.uk, www.briarwoodgarden.com. 1½ m SE of Kettering town centre. J10 off A14 turn onto Barton Rd (A6) towards Wicksteed Park. R into Warkton Ln, after 200 metres R into Poplars Farm Rd. **Sun 27 Apr (10-4). Combined adm with Rosi's Taverna £6.50, chd free. Light lunches & refreshments.** Visits also by arrangement 21 Apr to 31 July for groups of 10 to 30. Adm inc home-made teas.

A garden for all seasons with quirky original sculptures and many faces. Firstly, a south aspect lawn and borders containing bulbs, shrubs, roses and rare trees with year-round interest; hedging, palms, climbers, a wildlife, fish and lily pond, terrace with potted bulbs and unusual plants in odd containers. Secondly, a secret garden with garden room, small orchard, raised bed potager and greenhouse. Good use of recycled and repurposed materials throughout the garden, inc a unique self-build garden cabin, sculpture and planters.

For further info see Instagram @elaineportch.

GROUP OPENING

THE BRINGTONS
Little and Great Brington, NN7 4HS. *6m N of Northampton & 5m S of Rugby, just off M1 J16 or J18. What3words app: lectured. decorate.worker. Signed parking on Folly Ln in Little Brington & on the cricket pitch, Back Ln, in Great Brington. Tickets for sale & map for all gardens available at ticket booth in Little Brington & at Folly House in Great Brington.* **Sun 18 May (10.30-4.30). Combined adm £10, chd free. Tea, coffee & cake.**

ASHFIELD HOUSE
Alastair & Debbie Smith.

1 FERMOY COURT
Hilary & Chris Moore.

FOLLY HOUSE
Sarah & Joe Sacarello.

MANOR COTTAGE
Derek & Carol Bull.

MANOR FARM HOUSE
Rob Shardlow.

6 PINE COURT
Stephan Beeusaert.

14 PINE COURT
Chris & Judy Peck.

2 THE POUND
Mrs Sue Saunders.

RIDLEY LODGE
Richard & Anne Wright.

ROCHE COTTAGE
Malcolm & Susan Uttley.

ROSE COTTAGE
David Green & Elaine MacKenzie.

THE STABLES
Mrs J George.

STONECROFT
Peter & Jenny Holman.

SUNDERLAND HOUSE
Mrs Margaret Rubython.

THE WICK
Ray & Sandy Crossan.

A collection of gardens opening across Little and Great Brington. Eight gardens will open in Little Brington and seven gardens will open in Great Brington. Some large and formal and others smaller but of no less interest.

3 Pilgrims Place

All set in rolling countryside and two of the most attractive villages in the county. Two lovely pubs serving great food, the Althorp Coaching Inn in Great Brington and The Saracens Head in Little Brington, best to book ahead!

8 C2C GROWS - COMMUNITY ALLOTMENT GARDEN
Kingsthorpe Park Allotments, off Tollgate Close, Northampton, NN2 6RP. www.c2csocialaction.com/c2cgrows. *Off Mill Ln, towards Kingsthorpe. On arrival into Tollgate Cl, bear L at the T-junction & drive along to a free car park. Cross over the grass in the park following a line of wooden bollards up to the metal allotment gate.* **Sun 20 July (12-4). Adm £4, chd free. Pre-booking essential, please visit www.ngs.org.uk for information & booking. Tea, coffee & cake.**
C2C Grows is a community allotment project run by the charity C2C Social Action. The project offers social and therapeutic horticultural sessions for women referred to the project who may be experiencing poor health and social disadvantage. The project takes place on a triple sized allotment with several polytunnels, a greenhouse, fruit cages, raised beds and a peaceful wildlife area with pond. Artwork displayed. Allotment site is next to Thornton Park. Accessible, but contact garden on 07885 685731 for further details.

9 ♦ COTON MANOR GARDEN
Coton, Northampton, NN6 8RQ. Mr & Mrs Ian Pasley-Tyler, 01604 740219, pasleytyler@cotonmanor.co.uk, www.cotonmanor.co.uk. *10m N of Northampton, 11m SE of Rugby. From A428 & A5199 follow tourist signs.* **For NGS: Sat 13 Sept (11.30-5). Adm £10, chd £3.50. Light refreshments & home-made teas at Stableyard Café.** For other opening times and information, please phone, email or visit garden website.
10 acre garden set in peaceful countryside with old yew and holly hedges and extensive herbaceous borders, containing many unusual plants. One of Britain's finest throughout the season, the garden is at its most magnificent in September and is an inspiration as to what can

be achieved in late summer. Adjacent specialist nursery with over 1000 plant varieties propagated from the garden. This garden was proud to provide plants for the National Garden Scheme's Show Garden at Chelsea Flower Show 2024. Partial wheelchair access as some paths are narrow and the site is on a slope.

10 ♦ COTTESBROOKE HALL GARDENS
Cottesbrooke, Northampton, NN6 8PF. Mr & Mrs A R Macdonald-Buchanan, 01604 505808, welcome@cottesbrooke.co.uk, www.cottesbrooke.co.uk. *Cottesbrooke Hall is 3m off A14, J1. Follow brown signs S towards Northampton & in Creaton turn L onto Violet Ln. What3words app: expand.allow.curly.* **For NGS: Sun 27 Apr (2-5.30). Adm £14, chd £5. Chd 12 yrs old and under free. Home-made teas. Please visit www.cottesbrooke.co.uk to pre-book tickets.** For other opening times and information, please phone, email or visit garden website. Donation to All Saints Church, Cottesbrooke.
Award-winning gardens by Geoffrey Jellicoe, Dame Sylvia Crowe, and more recently Arne Maynard and Angel Collins. Formal gardens and terraces surround Queen Anne house with extensive vistas onto the lake and C18 parkland containing many mature trees. Wild and woodland gardens, a short distance from the formal areas, are exceptional in spring. Partial wheelchair access as paths are grass, stone and gravel, please call ahead to discuss. Access map identifies best route.

11 ♦ DEENE PARK
Deene, Corby, NN17 3EW. Mr Robert & Mrs Charlotte Brudenell, 01780 450278, admin@deenepark.com, www.deenepark.com. *6m N of Corby. Deene Park is located 12m SW of Stamford off the A43. Use postcode NN17 3EG for Porters Lodge entrance & follow blue estate signs. What3words app: sings.waistcoat.irony.* **For NGS: Sun 27 Apr (12-4). Adm £10, chd free. Tea, coffee & cake in the Old Kitchen Tea Room.** For other opening times and information, please phone, email or visit garden website.

Tranquil garden set in beautiful rolling parkland. Features inc box hedge parterre with teapot topiary designed by David Hicks echoing the C16 decoration on the porch stonework, long mixed borders, old-fashioned roses, Tudor courtyard, the White Garden and Golden Garden, and Victorian summerhouse. Lake and waterside walks with rare mature trees in a natural garden. Wheelchair access to main features of the garden with grass, gravel, and stone pathways.

12 DENE LODGE
257 Rockingham Road, Kettering, NN16 9JE. Mr & Mrs R Pooley, 01536 481012, denelodge@btinternet.com. *N of Kettering town centre on A6003. From J7 of A14 take A43 towards Stamford, at next r'about take A6003 to town centre, then over r'about. Entrance opp Cotswold Ave. No parking on Rockingham Rd, road side parking by The Beeswing pub.* **Sun 18 May (11-5). Adm £5, chd free. Home-made teas with gluten free option & cream teas.** Visits also by arrangement 6 May to 28 Sept for groups of 10 to 30.
An established garden sloping downward from east to west with many trees, shrubs, roses, perennials and bulbs. Small pond, terrace with wisteria covered pergola leads past the rock garden to the lower patio, a larger pond with pergola, decking, climbing roses, jasmine and clematis. A further lawn leads through an arch to the vegetable garden with fruit trees and soft fruit, bushes and climbers. Wheelchair access over concrete, paved patios and paths.

Our donation in 2024 has enabled Parkinson's UK to fund 3 new nursing posts this year directly supporting people with Parkinson's.

NORTHAMPTONSHIRE

GROUP OPENING
13 DODFORD GARDENS
Dodford House, Dodford, Northampton, NN7 4SX. Paul & Stephanie Russell. *Off the A5 or A45, nr Weedon. The garden of Dodford House is located at the lower end of the village on a no through road.* **Sun 29 June (11-4). Combined adm £7.50, chd free. Home-made teas.**

DODFORD HOUSE
Paul & Stephanie Russell.

NEW **MAGIC MUSHROOM HOUSE**
Amanda Robinson,
www.magic-mushroom.biz.

RUSHBROOKE
Michele & Simon Langhorn.

Dodford is a charming small village in a very peaceful location. This new and evolving group, based around the beautiful 1½ acre garden at Dodford House which inc productive kitchen and cut flower garden, rose walkway, long borders, formal lawns and topiary, and a box parterre. There will be several gardens open on the day of contrasting types and styles, please visit www.ngs.org.uk for information closer to the open day. There is something to delight everyone in this group from children, who be able to meet the lovely alpacas and join in with the duck run on the stream that runs through the village, to adults exploring the lovely gardens. For 2025 we will also be welcoming a community choir who will be singing in the grounds of Dodford House.
✿ ☕ »))

In 2024, National Garden Scheme funding for Perennial supported 1,367 people working in horticulture.

GROUP OPENING
14 EAST HADDON GARDENS
East Haddon, Northampton, NN6 8BT. *A few hundred yds off the A428 (signed) between M1 J18 (8m) & Northampton (8m). On-road parking. Strictly no parking in Priestwell Court, St Andrews Rd or on the properties.* **Mon 26 May (1-5). Combined adm £7, chd free. Tea, coffee & cake at St Mary's Church.**

BRAEBURN HOUSE
Judy Darby.

NEW **FOLLY COTTAGE**
Hazel Warburton.

◆ **HADDONSTONE, THE JUBLIEE GARDENS**
Haddonstone Ltd, 01604 770711, info@haddonstone.co.uk, www.haddonstone.com/en-gb/visit-haddonstone.

LIMETREES
Barry & Sally Hennessey.

9 PRIESTWELL COURT
Emma Forbes.

SADDLER'S COTTAGE
Val Longley.

THARFIELD
Julia Farnsworth.

TOWER COTTAGE
John Benson.

The pretty village of East Haddon dates back to the Norman invasion. The oldest surviving building is St Mary's, a C12 church. The village has many thatched cottages built in the local honey-coloured ironstone. Other features inc a thatched village pump and fire station which used to house a hand drawn pump and is now used as the bus shelter. The gardens opening this yr are a mixture of small, mature and family gardens with some having beautiful views across rolling hills. They are bursting with rare and unusual plants, various shrubs, climbers, roses and perennials, borders galore, vegetable beds, espaliered fruit trees, and woodland areas. Tickets and refreshments will be available at the church and plants propagated from the gardens and raised from seed will be on sale inc some rarities at Limetrees. The village is less than 10 mins from Coton Manor Gardens. Partial wheelchair access at Tower Cottage and access to some gardens via gravel drives.
♿ ✿ ☕ »))

GROUP OPENING
15 EVENLEY GARDENS
Evenley, Brackley, NN13 5SG. *1m S of Brackley, off the A43. Gardens situated around the village green & in Church Ln. Follow signs around the village. Tickets available at each garden, to cover entry to all gardens.* **Sun 8 June (2-5.30). Combined adm £7, chd free. Home-made teas in St George's Church (2.30-5pm).**

FINCH COTTAGE
Cathy & Chris Ellis.

NEW **FINDON BELL**
Heather & Brian Howells.

NEW **26 THE GREEN**
Christine Scaysbrook, 07934 911830, www.instagram.com/gggardengirl. Visits also by arrangement in June. Wednesdays only, 5-8pm.

NEW **29 THE GREEN**
Ms Dale Cornes.

38 THE GREEN
Anna & Matt Brown.

Evenley is a charming village with a central village green surrounded by many period houses (not open), an excellent village shop and The Red Lion pub which offers first class food and a warm welcome. Evenley gardens are a mix of established gardens and those being developed over the past 5 yrs. They all have mixed borders with established shrubs and trees. There are also orchards and vegetable gardens in some.
☕ »))

16 ◆ EVENLEY WOOD GARDEN
Evenley, Brackley, NN13 5SH. Whiteley Family, 07788 207428, info@evenleywoodgarden.co.uk, www.evenleywoodgarden.co.uk. *1m outside Brackley. Turn off at Evenley r'about on A43 & follow signs within the village to the garden which is situated off the Evenley & Mixbury road.* **For NGS: Sat 10 May (10-4). Adm £9.50, chd £2. Tea, coffee & cake.** For other opening times and information, please phone, email or visit garden website.
Set among the beautiful Northamptonshire countryside, our unique 60 acre private woodland garden has a large and notable collection of plants, trees, and shrubs.

As May ushers in warmer weather, around 100 magnolias put on a magnificent display, complemented by azaleas and rhododendrons. The garden fills with delightful sights and scents. In previous yrs, we have let some of our areas grow wilder, leaving the grass longer and allowing wild flowers to bloom, which helps support our insect and bird population. Enjoy nature unfolding by taking a leisurely stroll through the garden, relaxing on one of our many benches, or simply soaking up the peaceful atmosphere. Morning tea or coffee, lunch with a glass of wine and home-made cakes available in the café. Please take care as all paths are grass or woodchip.

GROUP OPENING

17 FLORE GARDENS
Flore, Northampton, NN7 4LS. *Situated between the towns of Daventry & Northampton. 2m from J16 of the M1.* **Sun 13 Apr (2-6). Combined adm £7, chd free. Sat 21 June (11-6); Sun 22 June (11-5). Combined adm £10, chd free. Home-made teas in Chapel School Room (Apr). Morning coffee & teas in Church & light lunches & teas in Chapel School Room (June).** Donation to All Saints Church & United Reform Church, Flore (June).

THE CROFT
John & Dorothy Boast.
Open on all dates

THE GARDEN HOUSE
Gary & Julie Moinet.
Open on Sat 21, Sun 22 June

25 LARBOURNE PARK ROAD
Jaqui Hoyle & Julian Hendon.
Open on Sat 21, Sun 22 June

THE OLD BAKERY
John Amos & Karl Jones.
Open on all dates

PRIVATE GARDEN OF BLISS LANE NURSERY
Christine & Geoffrey Littlewood.
Open on all dates

ROCK SPRINGS
Tom Higginson & David Foster.
Open on all dates

RUSSELL HOUSE
Peter Pickering & Stephen George, 01327 341734,
peterandstephen@btinternet.com.
Open on all dates

64 SUTTON STREET
Heather & Andy Anderson.
Open on Sun 13 Apr

6 THORNTON CLOSE
William & Lesley Craghill.
Open on Sun 13 Apr

THREE CORNERS
Marg & Fabian Blamires.
Open on Sat 21, Sun 22 June

1 YEW TREE GARDENS
Mr & Mrs Martin Millard.
Open on all dates

Flore gardens have been open since 1963 as part of the Flore Flower Festival. The partnership with the NGS started in 1992 with openings every yr since. Flore is an attractive village with views over the Upper Nene Valley. We have a varied mix of gardens, large and small. They have all been developed by friendly, enthusiastic and welcoming owners who are in their gardens when open. Our gardens range from the traditional to the eccentric providing year-round interest. Some have been established over many yrs and others have been developed more recently. There are greenhouses, gazebos, summerhouses, water features and seating opportunities to rest while enjoying the gardens. The village Flower Festival is our main event on the same two days as the June opening and garden tickets will be valid for both days. Partial wheelchair access to most gardens, some assistance may be required.

18 FOXTAIL LILLY
41 South Road, Oundle, PE8 4BP. Tracey Mathieson, 01832 274593, foxtaillilly41@gmail.com. *1m from Oundle town centre. From A605 at Barnwell Xrds take Barnwell Rd, 1st R to South Rd.* **Sun 8 June (11-4). Adm £4.50, chd free. Tea & cakes.** Visits also by arrangement May to July for groups of 10 to 50.
A cottage garden where perennials and grasses are grouped creatively together amongst gravel paths, complementing one another to create a natural look. Some unusual plants and quirky oddities create a different and colourful informal garden. Lots of flowers for cutting and a gift shop in the barn. New meadow pasture turned into new cutting garden.

19 THE GREEN PATCH
Valley Walk, Kettering, NN16 0LU. www.greenpatch.org.uk. *NE of Kettering town centre. Signed from A4300 Stamford Rd, on the junction of Valley Walk & Margaret Rd.* **Sun 27 July (10-3). Adm £5, chd free. Tea, coffee, biscuits & cake.**
The Green Patch is a 2½ acre, Green Flag award-winning community garden, nestled in the heart of England. We have hens, ducks, beehives, ponds, children's play area, orchard and so much more. We rely on our wonderful volunteers to make our friendly and magical garden the warm and welcoming place it is. Run by the environmental charity Groundwork Northamptonshire. Vegetable seedlings, herbs, and apple trees for sale. Bring a blanket for a picnic. Wheelchair access and disabled WC.

20 GREYWALLS
Farndish, nr Wellingborough, NN29 7HJ. Mrs P M Anderson, 01933 353495, greywalls@dbshoes.co.uk. *2½ m SE of Wellingborough. A609 from Wellingborough, B570 to Irchester, turn to Farndish by cenotaph. House adjacent to church.* **Visits by arrangement May to Sept for groups of 10+. Adm £5, chd free. Tea.**
Greywalls is an old vicarage set in 2 acres of relaxed country gardens planted for year-round interest. Featuring mature specimen trees, an impressive Banksia rose, three large ponds, many stone features, wildflower meadow and a Highgrove inspired stumpery. The borders feature unusual plants and there is an outside aviary. Strictly no dogs.

The National Garden Scheme donated £281,000 in 2024 to support those looking to work in horticulture as well as those struggling within the industry.

GROUP OPENING

21 GUILSBOROUGH GARDENS
Guilsborough, NN6 8PT. www.instagram.com/gardenatfouracres. 10m NW of Northampton. 10m E of Rugby. Between A5199 & A428. J1 off A14. Parking in field on Cold Ashby Rd NN6 8QN. Please park in car park to avoid congestion in the village centre. If wet, ticket sales in village hall. **Sun 4 May (2-6). Combined adm £8, chd free. Home-made teas in the village hall.**

NEW BORSDANE HOUSE
John & Victoria Hall.

NEW BRAMSTEAD HOUSE
Mrs Aubyn De Lisle.

FOUR ACRES
Mark & Gay Webster.

THE GATE HOUSE
Mike & Sarah Edwards.

HOLLY COTTAGE
Mr Mark & Mrs Beverley Brennan.

NEW IVY HOUSE
Alistair & Diana Herschell.

THE OLD HOUSE
Vanessa Berry.

THE OLD VICARAGE
John & Christine Benbow.

ROSE COTTAGE
Mr Ian & Mrs Amanda Miller.

Enjoy a warm welcome in this village with its very attractive rural setting of rolling hills and reservoirs. We have a group of contrasting gardens for you to visit, with several new gardens recently added inc a 1⅓ acre garden undergoing a complete rebirth. Most of us grow fruit and vegetables in various settings such as a walled kitchen garden and raised beds in cottage gardens. We aim for spring flowers in abundance from bulbs (badgers permitting), shrubs and blossom. No wheelchair access at Holly Cottage, Rose Cottage or The Gate House.

ප 🐕 🚗 ☕ 🔊

GROUP OPENING

22 HARPOLE GARDENS
Harpole, NN7 4BX. On A45, 4m W of Northampton towards Weedon. Turn R at The Turnpike Hotel into Harpole. Village maps given to all visitors. **Sun 8 June (1-6). Combined adm £7, chd free.**

BRYTTEN COLLIER HOUSE
Heather & Darren Jennings.

CEDAR COTTAGE
Spencer & Joanne Hannam.

THE CLOSE
Michael Orton-Jones.

KINGSLEY HOUSE
Gregory Hearne & Caroline Fisermanis.

NEW 1 LARKHALL LANE
Helen & Peter Fish.

19 MANOR CLOSE
Caroline & Eamonn Kemshed, 01604 830512, carolinekemshed@live.co.uk. Visits also by arrangement 9 June to 15 June.

THE OLD DAIRY
David & Di Ballard.

Harpole is an attractive village nestling at the foot of Harpole Hills with many houses built of local sandstone. Visit us and delight in a wide variety of gardens of all shapes, sizes and content. You will see luxuriant lawns, mixed borders with plants for sun and shade, mature trees, shrubs, herbs, alpines, water features and tropical planting. We have interesting and quirky artifacts dotted around, garden structures and plenty of seating for the weary.

🐕 ☕

23 67-69 HIGH STREET
Finedon, NN9 5JN. Mary & Stuart Hendry, 01933 680414, sh_archt@hotmail.com. 6m SE Kettering. On A6. **Visits by arrangement Feb to Sept. Adm £3.50, chd free. Soup & roll inc for Feb visits. Other times tea, coffee & biscuits, or cream teas for 10 or more.**
⅓ acre rear garden of C17 cottage (not open). Early spring garden with snowdrops and hellebores, summer and autumn mixed borders, many obelisks and containers, kitchen garden, herb bed, rambling roses and at least 60 different hostas. All giving varied interest from Feb through to Oct. Large selection of home-raised plants for sale (all proceeds to NGS).

🐕 🐾 🚗 ☕

24 136 HIGH STREET
Irchester, NN29 7AB. Ade & Jane Parker, jane692@btinternet.com. 200yds past the church on the bend as you leave the village going towards the A45. Please park on

High St. Disabled parking only in driveway. **Fri 14, Sat 15, Sun 16 Feb (11-3). Tea, coffee & cake. Sun 4 May, Sun 3 Aug (11-4). Light refreshments. Adm £5, chd free. 2026: Fri 13, Sat 14, Sun 15 Feb. Visits also by arrangement 10 Feb to 10 Aug.**
Large garden developed by the current owners over the past 20 yrs. Various different planting habitats inc areas designed for shade, sun, and pollinator-friendly sites. Wildlife pond attracting large range of birds, insects and other creatures into the garden. Alpine houses, planted stone sinks and raised beds. Seasonally planted tubs add bold summer colour. Wildflower meadow. WC available. Wheelchair access mainly over grass with some gravel pathways.

ප 🐾 🚗 🚐 ☕ 🔊

25 HIGHFIELDS
Adstone, Towcester, NN12 8DS. Rachel Halvorsen. 7m W of Towcester. The village of Adstone is midway between Banbury & Northampton, about 15m from each. **Sun 10 Aug (2-5.30). Adm £7, chd free. Cream teas.**
Two sheltered, mixed courtyard gardens with vibrant colours. A granite path winds between the lawn borders, leading to a formal walled garden with a central aquaglobe. There's also a plantsman's garden with a collection of succulents. Enjoy cream teas on the patio overlooking panoramic views with ha-ha and miles of unbroken countryside, a lake, and 100 acre Plumpton Wood. Walk down to lake across a couple of fields to see wildlife, beds, and water lilies. Wheelchair access with a few single steps.

ප 🐾 🐕 ☕

26 ♦ HOLDENBY HOUSE & GARDENS
Holdenby House, Holdenby, Northampton, NN6 8DJ. Mr & Mrs James Lowther, 01604 770074, office@holdenby.com, www.holdenby.com. 7m NW of Northampton. Off A5199 or A428 between East Haddon & Spratton. **For NGS: Sun 27 Apr (11-4). Adm £9, chd £5. Adm subject to change. Home-made teas & light refreshments. For other opening times and information, please phone, email or visit garden website.**
Holdenby has a historic Grade I listed garden. The inner garden

inc Rosemary Verey's renowned Elizabethan Garden and Rupert Golby's Pond Garden and long borders. There is also a delightful walled kitchen garden. Away from the formal gardens, the terraces of the original Elizabethan Garden are still visible, one of the best preserved examples of their kind. Accessible, but contact garden for further details. Assistance dogs only.

27 HOSTELLARIE
78 Breakleys Road, Desborough, NN14 2PT. **Stella Freeman, 01536 760124, stelstan78@outlook.com.** *6m N of Kettering. 5m S of Market Harborough. From church & war memorial turn R into Dunkirk Ave, then 3rd R. From cemetery L into Dunkirk Ave, then 4th L.* **Sun 8 June (2-5). Combined adm with 14 Leys Avenue & 16 Leys Avenue £5, chd free. Home-made teas & a gluten-free option. Visits also by arrangement 1 June to 27 July for groups of 10 to 25.**
Hostellarie is a long town garden divided into rooms. Lawns and grass paths lead you through varied colour borders, ponds and water features. Courtyard garden shaded by an old clematis has over 40 different hostas, there are even more mature specimen hostas in the north facing bed and other shady spots. Roses, clematis, cottage and gravel borders, and a welcoming relaxing atmosphere.

28 ◆ KELMARSH HALL & GARDENS
Main Road, Kelmarsh, Northampton, NN6 9LY. **The Kelmarsh Trust, 01604 686543, marketing@kelmarsh.com, www.kelmarsh.com.** *Kelmarsh is 5m S of Market Harborough & 11m N of Northampton. From A14, exit J2 & head N towards Market Harborough on the A508.* **For NGS: Sun 8 June (10-4). Adm £8, chd £4.50. Light lunches, cream teas & cakes in Sweet Pea's Tearoom. For other opening times and information, please phone, email or visit garden website.**
Kelmarsh Hall is an elegant Palladian house set in glorious Northamptonshire countryside with highly regarded gardens, which are the work of Nancy Lancaster, Norah Lindsay and Geoffrey Jellicoe. Hidden gems inc an orangery, sunken garden,

long border, rose gardens and, at the heart of it all, a historic walled garden. Highlights throughout the seasons inc fritillaries, tulips, roses and dahlias. Beautiful interiors brought together by Nancy Lancaster in the 1930s, in a Palladian style hall designed by James Gibbs. The recently restored laundry and servants' quarters in the hall are open to the public, providing visitors the incredible opportunity to experience life 'below stairs'. This garden provided plants for the National Garden Scheme's Show Garden at Chelsea Flower Show 2024. Blue Badge disabled parking close to the Visitor Centre entrance. Paths are loose gravel, wheelchair users advised to bring a companion.

GROUP OPENING

29 KILSBY GARDENS
Middle Street, Kilsby, Rugby, CV23 8XT. *5m SE of Rugby. 6m N of Daventry on A361.* **Sun 29 June (1-5.30). Combined adm £7, chd free. Home-made teas at Kilsby Village Hall (1-5).**
Kilsby's name has long been associated with Stephenson's famous railway tunnel and an early skirmish in the Civil War. The houses and gardens of the village offer a mixture of sizes and styles, which reflect its development through time. A selection of gardens will be open, visit www.ngs.org.uk in the spring for information. Expect a warm welcome and delicious teas.

30 ◆ LAMPORT HALL
Lamport, Northampton, NN6 9HD. **Lamport Hall Preservation Trust, 01604 686272, house@lamporthall.co.uk, www.lamporthall.co.uk.** *For SatNav please use postcode NN6 9EZ. Exit J2 of the A14. Entry through the gate flanked by swans on the A508. What3words app: miracles. unusual.botanists.* **For NGS: Sat 26 July (10-4). Adm £8, chd £4. Light refreshments in The Stables Café. For other opening times and information, please phone, email or visit garden website.**
Home of the Isham family for over 400 yrs, the extensive herbaceous borders complement the Elizabethan bowling lawns, together with topiary from the 1700s. The 2 acre walled garden is full of colour, with 250 rows of perennials. Another highlight is the famous Lamport rockery, among the earliest in England, which was extensively refurbished in 2024. Wheelchair access on gravel paths within the gardens.

31 14 LEYS AVENUE
Desborough, Kettering, NN14 2PY. **Dave & Linda Pascan.** *6m N of Kettering, 5m S of Market Harborough. From St Giles Church (with spire) in Desborough & War Memorial turn into Dunkirk Ave & 5th R into Leys Ave.* **Sun 8 June (2-5). Combined adm with 16 Leys Avenue & Hostellarie £5, chd free. Tea at 16 Leys Avenue.**
Town garden with patio, two lawns bordered by curved pathway and a rockery with 'lion's head' waterfall feature. Mature trees give structure to herbaceous borders planted with flowering shrubs, lupins, clematis, primulas and more. Brick pillars and climbing plants provide the entrance through to a small orchard, greenhouse and log cabin.

32 16 LEYS AVENUE
Desborough, NN14 2PY. **Keith & Beryl Norman.** *6m N of Kettering. 5m S of Market Harborough. From church & War Memorial turn R into Dunkirk Ave & 5th R into Leys Ave.* **Sun 8 June (2-5). Combined adm with 14 Leys Avenue & Hostellarie £5, chd free. Tea.**
A town garden with two water features, plus a stream and a pond flanked by a 12ft clinker-built boat. There are six raised beds and an area of sweet peas. A patio lined with acers has two steps down to a gravel garden with paved paths. Mature trees and acers give the garden year-round structure and interest. Wheelchair access down two steps from patio to main garden.

The National Garden Scheme donated over £3.5 million to our nursing and health beneficiaries from money raised at gardens open in 2024.

NORTHAMPTONSHIRE

33 NEW 17 LYNTON AVENUE
Lynton Avenue, Northampton, NN2 8LX. Stuart & Anita Smart. *Off the A508, Lynton Ave is opp The Whitehills pub.* **Sun 16 Feb (1-3). Adm £4, chd free. Opening with Lynton Avenue Gardens on Sun 25 May.**
A plantsman's garden with an eclectic range of unusual plants and water features in a constant state of flux. The latest project is a new pond. The Feb opening features over 70 varieties of snowdrops. Stuart's favourites inc Wendy's Gold, Green Tip and Green Tears. There will also be hellebores, crocus and other winter delights.

GROUP OPENING

34 NEW LYNTON AVENUE GARDENS
Northampton, NN2 8LX. *Off the A508, Lynton Ave is opp The Whitehills pub.* **Sun 25 May (1-3). Combined adm £5, chd free. Tea, coffee & cake at 18 Lynton Avenue.**

NEW 2 LYNTON AVENUE
Josie Cuccia.

NEW 10 LYNTON AVENUE
Paul & Jenny Beeden.

NEW 17 LYNTON AVENUE
Stuart & Anita Smart.
(See separate entry)

NEW 18 LYNTON AVENUE
Sianne Castle.

A group of varied gardens in a suburban, but surprisingly green, setting. Some of the gardens are on steeply sloping sites, which present their own challenges. Two gardens are owned by horticultural professionals, so this is the place to come for expert advice on making the most of the size of garden that most of us have.

35 83 MAIN ROAD
Collyweston, Stamford, PE9 3PQ. Rosemary & Robert Fromm, 07597 684816, rrfromm@msn.com. *On A43, $3\frac{1}{2}$ m SW of Stamford. 1m from A43/A47 r'about. Three doors from The Collyweston Slater pub.* **Sun 1 June (1-5). Adm £5, chd free. Home-made teas on the patio with seating. Visits also by** arrangement Mar to Oct for groups of 5 to 10. Optional tour of garden for groups, weather permitting.
Wildlife friendly garden with many small trees, bushes and perennials. We aim to have something flowering every month of the yr, to support insect life. Gravel paths and stone steps give access to the sloping site which is just under a $\frac{1}{4}$ acre. The garden is in the process of being made even more wildlife friendly, with many more plants being added to feed bees, moths and butterflies. Plants for sale.

GROUP OPENING

36 NEWNHAM GARDENS
Newnham, Daventry, NN11 3HF. *2m S of Daventry on B4037 between the A361 & A45. Continue to the centre of the village & follow signs for the car park, just off the main village green.* **Sun 4 May (11-5). Combined adm £6, chd free. Light refreshments in village hall.**

1 CHURCH STREET
Joan & Harry Ferguson.

THE COTTAGE
Jacqueline Minor, www.instagram.com/ newnhamngs.

HILLTOP
Mercy Messenger.

STONE HOUSE
Pat & David Bannerman.

WREN COTTAGE
Mr & Mrs Judith Dorkins.

You are so welcome to Newnham. Five plant-lovers' gardens all set in our beautiful old village nestled in the unspoilt Northamptonshire Uplands. The gardens, from large to small, are packed with spring colour, horticultural delights, lots of inspiration and lovely views. There is something to delight everyone. Spend the day with us enjoying the gardens, buying at our ever-popular plant sale, strolling around the village lanes and visiting our C14 church. Treat yourself to a tasty light lunch and delicious cakes and refreshments in the village hall (several times!). We look forward to seeing you. The old village is hilly in parts. Most gardens are, at least, partially accessible for wheelchairs but may have steps or narrow paths.

37 NONSUCH
11 Mackworth Drive, Finedon, Wellingborough, NN9 5NL. Carrie Whitworth. *Off Wellingborough Rd (A510) onto Bell Hill, then to Church Hill, 2nd L after church, entrance on the L as you enter Mackworth Dr.* **Sun 27 July (1-5). Adm £4, chd free. Drinks, cakes & biscuits.**
$\frac{1}{3}$ acre country garden within a conservation boundary stone wall. Mature trees, enhanced by many rare and unusual shrubs and perennial plants. A garden for all seasons with several seating areas. Wheelchair access on a level site with paved and gravel paths.

38 NORTH FARM
Daventry, NN11 3TF. Mr & Mrs Tim Coleridge, timothycoleridge@gmail.com. *Little Preston. $\frac{3}{4}$ m E of Preston Capes. Located down no through lane opp Old West Farm. What3words app: modifies.lung.herbs.* **Visits by arrangement May & June for groups of up to 25. Combined adm with Old West Farm £7, chd free. Home-made teas at Old West Farm.**
Rural farmhouse garden with roses and borders maintained by owners. Outstanding view towards Fawsley and High Wood. Wheelchair access over grass.

39 OAKLEA
84 Wollaston Road, Irchester, NN29 7DF. Mr Keith Wilson & Mrs Nicola Wilson-Brown. *3m SE of Wellingborough. Leave Wellingborough via A509 heading towards Wollaston, turn L at r'about onto B570 signed Irchester Country Park. Continue to end of road, turn L at r'about into Wollaston Rd.* **Sun 25 May (12-5). Adm £4, chd free. Tea, coffee & cake.**
An interesting and deceptive garden featuring courtyard area with succulents, seasonal pots, troughs and baskets. Borders well-stocked with shrubs and herbaceous perennials together with climbing plants and roses giving colour throughout the growing season. Two lawned areas, a pond planted with plants and stocked with fish and frogs. Several seating areas and a vegetable garden with potting shed. Wheelchair access over level garden.

The Old Rectory, Wicken

40 OLD RECTORY, QUINTON
Preston Deanery Road, Quinton, Northampton, NN7 2ED.
Alan Kennedy & Emma Wise, www.garden4good.co.uk. *M1 J15, 1m from Wootton towards Salcey Forest. House is next to the church. On-road parking in village. Please note parking on village green is prohibited.* **Sun 1 June (10-4). Adm £10, chd free. Pre-booking essential, please visit www.ngs. org.uk for information & booking. Light refreshments. Entry times at 10am, 12pm & 2pm. Hot drinks & cake (all day). Lunches to pre-order via garden website (11am-2pm).**
A contemporary 3 acre rectory garden designed by multi-award-winning designer, Anoushka Feiler. Taking the Old Rectory's C18 history and its religious setting as a key starting point, the main garden at the back of the house has been divided into six parts; a kitchen garden, glasshouse and flower garden, a woodland menagerie, a pleasure garden, a park and an orchard. Elements of C18 design such as formal structures, parterres, topiary, long walks, occasional seating areas and traditional craft work have been introduced, but with a distinctly C21 twist through the inclusion of living walls, modern materials and features, new planting methods and abstract installations. Pop-up shop selling plants, garden produce, local honey, home-made bread and organic gifts. Wheelchair access with gravel paths.

41 THE OLD RECTORY, WICKEN
Cross Tree Road, Wicken, Milton Keynes, MK19 6BX. **Mr & Mrs William Francklin,** 07967 155589, celinafrancklin@gmail.com. *The entrance is on the corner of Cross Tree Rd & Leckhampstead Rd. Please follow signs in village. Roadside parking only. What3words app: hills. ending.continued.* **Sat 7 June (2-5). Adm £7, chd free. Home-made teas.** Visits also by arrangement 12 May to 30 June for groups of 12 to 20. Adm inc refreshments.
A sunken walled garden, designed and planted in 2002 with a parterre, step-over fruit trees and roses. There is also a bank of camassias, a wall of wisteria and a quince avenue. The village church will also be open on the day to visit.

42 THE OLD VICARAGE
Daventry Road, Norton, Daventry, NN11 2ND. **Barry & Andrea Coleman.** *Norton is approx 2m E of Daventry, 11m W of Northampton. From Daventry follow signs to Norton for 1m. On A5 N from Weedon follow road for 3m, take L turn signed Norton. On A5 S take R at Xrds signed Norton, 6m from Kilsby. Garden is R of All Saints Church.* **Sun 9 Feb (11-2); Sun 6 Apr (1-5). Adm £5, chd free. Soup & bread in Feb (inc in adm). Home-made teas in orangery (Apr).**
The vicarage garden was once the centre of village life. Fifty yrs on, garden life is different with unexpected trees, bulbs, shrubs, perennials bursting out year-round with birdlife, wildlife and life in general. A warm welcome awaits both at the winter opening and in April. The interesting and beautiful C14 Church of All Saints will be open to visitors.

43 OLD WEST FARM

Little Preston, Daventry, NN11 3TF. Mr & Mrs G Hoare, caghoare@gmail.com. *7m SW Daventry, 8m W Towcester, 13m NE Banbury. ¾m E of Preston Capes on road to Maidford. Last house on R in Little Preston with white flagpole. Beware, the postcode applies to all houses in Little Preston. Off road parking.* **Visits by arrangement May & June for groups of up to 25. Combined adm with North Farm £7, chd free. Home-made teas.**

Large rural garden lovingly developed over the past 43 yrs on a very exposed site, planted with hedges and shelter for wildlife and birds. Roses, shrubs and borders aiming for year-round interest. Particularly attractive in May and June. A peaceful place to sit and listen to birdsong. Home-made teas served on the terrace (weather permitting). Partial wheelchair access over grass.

& ❋ ☕))

44 3 PILGRIMS PLACE

Delapre, Northampton, NN4 8NX. Joe & Linda Pemberton, 07572 158883, joeppemberton@gmail.com, www.facebook.com/joeandlindastropicalwatergarden. *1½m from Northampton town centre. From the r'about at Mere Way/A45 junction, exit onto A508 toward Delapre. After ½m turn L onto Queen Eleanor Rd & immed L into Pilgrims Pl.* **Sun 3, Sun 10, Sun 31 Aug (11-6). Adm £5, chd free. Pre-booking essential, please visit www.ngs.org.uk for information & booking. Tea, coffee & cake.** Visits also by arrangement Mar to Oct.

Escape the town and visit a small tropical rainforest in a water garden oasis. A wonderful example of what is possible in an urban space, featuring a pond, waterfalls, curved bridge, fire pit and many more surprises. The jungle feel is enhanced by large-leaved plants under-planted with ferns, hostas, mosses and bright pops of colour. Plenty of ideas and plants to take home. Additional refreshments are available at the cafes of the historical building and grounds of Delapre Abbey, a half-mile walk or drive away.

❋ ☕))

GROUP OPENING

45 RAVENSTHORPE GARDENS

Ravensthorpe, NN6 8ES. *7m NW of Northampton. Please start & purchase tickets at Ravensthorpe Nursery which is the 1st property on the L when entering the village from the A428 via Long Ln. What3words app: edits.dispensed.shifting.* **Sun 15 June (1.30-5.30). Combined adm £7.50, chd free. Tea, coffee & cake in village hall.**

5 CHURCH GARDENS
Mr & Mrs Glyn Lewis.

CORNERSTONE
Lorna Jones.

MANOR VIEW
Viv & David Rees.

QUIETWAYS
Russ Barringer.

RAVENSTHORPE NURSERY
Mr & Mrs Richard Wiseman.
(See separate entry)

TREETOPS
Ros Smith.

Attractive village in Northamptonshire uplands near to Ravensthorpe reservoir and Top Ardles Wood, Woodland Trust which have bird watching and picnic opportunities. Established and developing gardens set in beautiful countryside displaying a wide range of plants, many available from the nursery that now only opens on NGS open days. Offering inspirational planting, quiet contemplation, beautiful views, water features and gardens encouraging wildlife. N.B. Not all gardens welcome dogs. Disabled WC in village hall.

& ❋ ☕))

Deene Park

NORTHAMPTONSHIRE 409

46 RAVENSTHORPE NURSERY
6 East Haddon Road,
Ravensthorpe, NN6 8ES. Mr & Mrs
Richard Wiseman, 01604 770548,
ravensthorpenursery@hotmail.
com. *7m NW of Northampton. 1st
property on L approaching from
A428 via Long Ln.* **Fri 9, Sat 10,
Sun 11 May, Fri 13, Sat 14 June,
Fri 11, Sat 12, Sun 13 July (11-5).
Adm £6, chd free. Tea, coffee &
cake. Opening with Ravensthorpe
Gardens on Sun 15 June.** Visits
also by arrangement 13 May to
3 Oct.
Over an acre of garden wrapped
around the old nursery with beautiful
views. Planted with many unusual
shrubs and herbaceous perennials
over the last 30+ yrs to reflect the
wide range of plants produced. Plants
for sale. Wheelchair access with
gradual slope to garden and nursery.

♿ 🐾 ☕ 🔊

47 ♦ ROCKINGHAM CASTLE
Rockingham Castle Estate,
Rockingham, Market Harborough,
LE16 8TH. 01536 770240,
estateoffice@rockinghamcastle.
com, www.rockinghamcastle.com.
*1m N of Corby. Off the A6003, 1m N
of Corby; 24m from Peterborough,
Northampton & Leicester; 30 mins
from the A1 & the M1 & 10 mins
from the A14 at Kettering.* **For NGS:
Tue 24 June (11-4). Adm £9, chd
£3. Home-made teas in Walker's
House Tearoom.** For other
opening times and information,
please phone, email or visit garden
website.
Rockingham Castle was built on the
orders of William the Conqueror and
offers a spectacular view over the
Welland Valley. The original Motte
and Bailey design still influences
the sweeping formal gardens you
see today. These inc a wealth of
roses from hybrid teas to climbers
covering every wall and features five
key areas covering 13 acres, they are
the terrace, the cross, rose garden,
jewel borders and the dramatic
wild garden. Lunches, cream teas,
home-made cakes, coffee and wine
in Walker's House Tearoom. Tickets
can be booked online in advance
through garden website or purchased
on arrival at the ticket office. Disabled
parking. Ramps provided. Accessible
WC.

♿ 🐾 ☕ 🚗 🍽 🔊

48 ROSEARIE-DE-LA-NYMPH
55 The Grove, Moulton,
Northampton, NN3 7UE. Peter
Hughes, Mary Morris, Irene Kay,
Steven & Netta Hughes & Jeremy
Stanton. *N of Northampton town.
Turn off A43 at small r'about to
Overstone Rd. Follow NGS signs in
village. The garden is on the Holcot
Rd out of Moulton.* **Sun 22, Sun 29
June (11-5). Adm £5, chd free.
Home-made teas.**
We have been developing this
romantic garden for about 20 yrs
and now have over 1800 roses inc
English, French and Italian varieties.
Many unusual water features and
specimen trees. Ferns inc tree ferns
over 8ft high. Roses, scramblers
and ramblers climb into trees, over
arbours and arches. Collection of
140 Japanese maples. Mostly flat
wheelchair access via a standard
width doorway.

♿ 🐾 ☕

49 ROSI'S TAVERNA
20 St Francis Close, Barton
Seagrave, Kettering, NN15 5DT.
Rosi & David Labrum, www.
instagram.com/rosistaverna.
*Approx 2m from J10 of the A14.
Head towards Barton Seagrave,
going through 3 sets of T-lights. At
the 4th set turn R onto Warkton Ln.
At the r'about turn L & take the next
2 R turns into St Francis Cl.* **Sun 27
Apr (10-4). Combined adm with
Briarwood £6.50, chd free. Tea,
coffee & cake at Briarwood.**
An established medium south
facing town garden. Kitchen garden
intermingles with flowers, shrubs,
plenty of fruit trees, soft fruits and
vegetables in raised beds. Cacti
and succulents are in the new
greenhouse. A new archway is under
construction. A bog garden and a
pyramid water feature. A unique
taverna with mosaic flooring offers
perfect shelter from sun, wind and
drizzle.

☕ 🔊

GROUP OPENING

50 SPRATTON GARDENS
Smith Street, Spratton, NN6 8HP.
*6½m NNW of Northampton. Parking
in Spratton Hall School car park,
please follow yellow NGS signs from
outskirts of village from A5199 or
Brixworth Rd.* **Sun 8 June (11-5).
Combined adm £7, chd free.
Home-made teas.**

THE COTTAGE
Mrs Judith Elliott.

28 GORSE ROAD
Lee Miller.

11 HIGH STREET
Philip & Frances Roseblade.

MULBERRY COTTAGE
Kerry Herd.

OLD HOUSE FARM
Susie Marchant.

NEW THE SHEILING
Jane & William Marshall.

STONE HOUSE
John Forbear.

VALE VIEW
John Hunt.

As well as attractive cottage gardens
alongside old Northampton stone
houses, Spratton also has unusual
gardens. These inc those showing
good use of a small area, those
dedicated to encouraging wildlife with
views of the surrounding countryside,
renovated gardens and those with
new planting. You will also find a
courtyard garden, a gravel garden
with sculpture, and mature gardens
with fruit trees and herbaceous
borders. Refreshments in the Norman
St Andrew's Church. The King's Head
Pub will be open, lunch reservations
recommended. Full or partial
wheelchair access to most gardens,
but some do have gravel and steps.

♿ 🐾 ☕ 🚗 🍽 🔊

*Our donation
to the Army
Benevolent Fund
supported 700
individuals with
front line services
and horticultural
related grants
in 2024.*

GROUP OPENING

51 SULGRAVE GARDENS
Banbury, OX17 2RP. *8m NE of Banbury. Just off B4525 Banbury to Northampton road, 7m from J11, off M40. Car parking available in village.* **Sun 29 June (2-6). Combined adm £7, chd free.**

NEW BENTLEYS FARM BUNGALOW
Kym & Tony Keatley.

NEW CHAPMANS CLOSE
Hywel & Ingram Lloyd.

THE CHESTNUTS
Mrs Mel Kirkpatrick.

EAGLE HOUSE
Sue & Andrew Dixon.

MILL HOLLOW BARN
David & Judith Thompson.

RECTORY FARM
Charles & Joanna Smyth-Osbourne, 01295 760261, sosbournejm@gmail.com.

NEW THE THATCHED HOUSE
Pamela & Colin Wagman.

THE WATERMILL
Mr & Mrs Frost.

WOOTTON HOUSE
Zoe & Richard McCrow.

Sulgrave is a small historic village with nine gardens opening, and teas and plants for sale. There is something for everyone, from perfectly trimmed bonsai to large oaks. Rectory Farm has lovely views, a rill, well, and planted arbours. Mill Hollow Barn, a large garden with lakes, streams, ponds and many rare and interesting trees, shrubs and perennials. The Watermill, a contemporary garden designed by James Alexander-Sinclair, set around a C16 watermill and mill pond. A quirky garden at Wootton House with a good selection of rare and interesting plants. The Chesnuts, a small garden, but with huge interest, where every plant tells a story. Four new gardens opening this yr. Bentleys Farm Bungalow has some exotic plants and an extensive bonsai collection. The Thatched House demonstrates substantial new planting in an established 1 acre garden, inc a stumpery. Chapmans Close is a developing garden under new ownership and Eagle House is a beautiful, traditional garden. An award-winning community owned and run village shop will be open.

52 TITCHMARSH HOUSE
Chapel Street, Titchmarsh, NN14 3DA. Sir Ewan & Lady Harper, 01832 732439, ewan@ewanh.co.uk, www.titchmarsh-house.uk. *2m N of Thrapston. 6m S of Oundle. Exit A14 at junction signed A605, Titchmarsh signed as turning E towards Oundle & Peterborough.* **Visits by arrangement Apr to June for groups of 10+. Refreshments available.**
The gardens are spread over 4½ acres with formal and wild areas, a hedged quiet garden, and inc collections of naturalised bulbs, irises, peonies, magnolias, shrub roses, cherries, malus and a number of rare trees, expanded and planted by the existing owners over the past 55 yrs. Plant stall with proceeds to NGS. Wheelchair access to most of the garden without using steps. No dogs.

GROUP OPENING

53 NEW WESTON GARDENS
Weston, Towcester, NN12 8PU. *7m W of Towcester, 7m N of Brackley. Turn off A43 at Towcester towards Abthorpe & Wappenham, then turn R in Wappenham to Weedon Lois & onwards to Weston. Gardens within walking distance, follow NGS signs. Parking along main road.* **Sun 15 June (1.30-5). Combined adm £6, chd free. Tea, coffee & cake in the Baptist Chapel, High Street.**

4 HELMDON ROAD
Mrs S Wilde, www.wilde.enterprises.

MIDDLETON HOUSE
Mark & Donna Cooper.

POST COTTAGE
Jane Kellar.

RIDGEWAY COTTAGE
Jonathan & Elizabeth Carpenter.

Come and discover the village of Weston with gardens from large and formal to small and intimate. Features inc wonderful herbaceous borders, fruit and vegetable gardens, cutting edge modern design and traditional cottage garden planting. 4 Helmdon Road is a mature and structural garden using local stone and stainless steel to create a modern twist on a traditional garden. Middleton House is a gently terraced garden designed by James Alexander-Sinclair with beautifully planted beds and vegetable area, and productive greenhouse. Post Cottage is a quiet peaceful garden which has been designed to give colour and interest throughout the seasons. Ridgeway Cottage garden is surrounded by a stone wall with borders, beds, and semi-mature trees. Plant sale at Middleton House.

54 WOODCOTE VILLA
Old Watling Street, Long Buckby Wharf, Long Buckby, Northampton, NN6 7EW. Sue & Geoff Woodward, geoff.and.sue@btinternet.com. *2m NE of Daventry, just off A5. From M1 J16, take Flore by-pass, turn R at A5 r'about for approx 3m. From Daventry follow Long Buckby signs but turn L at A5 Xrds. From M1 J18 signed Kilsby, follow A5 S for approx 6m.* **Sun 23 Mar (11.30-4); Sun 20 July, Sun 31 Aug (11-4.30). Adm £4, chd free. Home-made teas. Gluten free option. Visits also by arrangement 24 Mar to 24 Aug for groups of 15 to 35. Morning, afternoon or evening visits possible.**
In a much admired location, this stunning canalside garden has a large variety of plants, styles, structures and unusual bygones. Bulbs and hellebores abound in March, colourful planting in July/September, many pots, all set against a backdrop of trees and shrubs in themed areas. Places to sit and watch the narrowboats and wildlife. Plants for sale (cash only). Sorry, no WC. Wheelchair access via ramp at entrance to garden.

In 2024, our donations to Carers Trust meant that 26,081 unpaid carers were supported across the UK.

Foxtail Lilly

NOTTINGHAMSHIRE

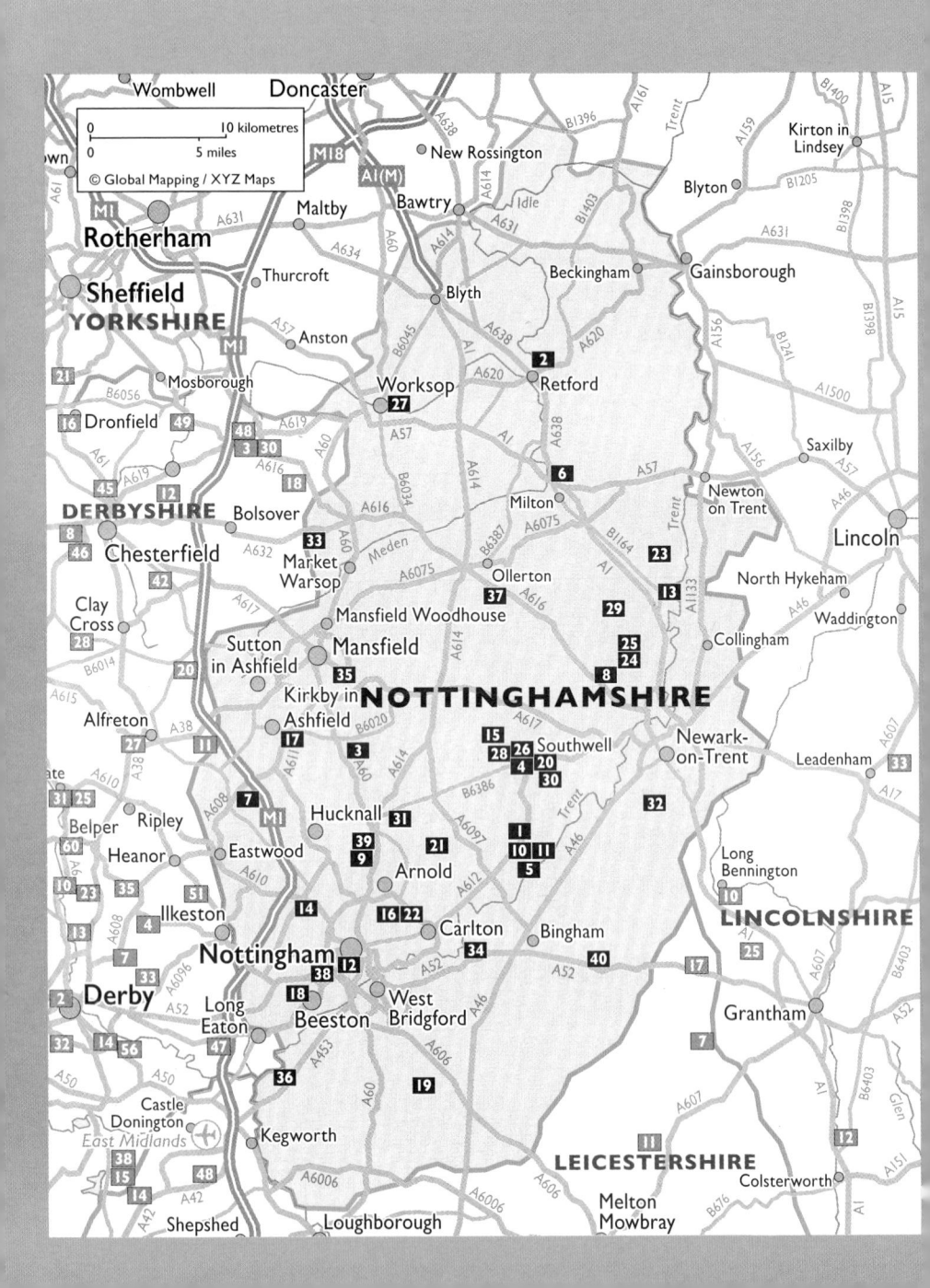

NOTTINGHAMSHIRE 413

VOLUNTEERS

County Organiser
Andrew Young
01623 863327
andrew.young@ngs.org.uk

County Treasurer
Nicola Cressey
01159 655132
nicola.cressey@gmail.com

Publicity
Julie Davison
01302 719668
julie.davison@ngs.org.uk

Social Media
Malcolm Turner
01159 222831
malcolm.turner14@btinternet.com

Booklet Co-ordinator
Martyn Faulconbridge
01949 850942
mjfaulconbridge@gmail.com,

Assistant County Organisers
Ian Brownhill & Michael Hirschl
07970 126318
ian.brownhill@ngs.org.uk

Beverley Perks
01636 812181
perks.family@talk21.com

Mary Thomas
01509 672056
nursery@piecemealplants.co.uk

@National Garden Scheme Nottinghamshire

@ngs_nottinghamshire

OPENING DATES

All entries subject to change. For latest information check
www.ngs.org.uk
Map locator numbers are shown to the right of each garden name.

January

Friday 31st
1 Highfield Road   14

February

Snowdrop Openings
Sunday 2nd
1 Highfield Road   14
Sunday 9th
Norwood Park   26
Sunday 16th
Church Farm   6

April

Saturday 19th
Oasis Community Gardens   27
Sunday 20th
♦ Felley Priory   7
Saturday 26th
Capability Barn   5
Sunday 27th
Capability Barn   5

May

Sunday 4th
160 Southwell Road West   35
Sunday 11th
38 Main Street   21
Saturday 17th
NEW Hall Farmhouse   11
Sunday 18th
NEW Hall Farmhouse   11
10 Harlaxton Drive   12
6 Hope Street   18
♦ Norwell Nurseries   25
Saturday 24th
The Old Vicarage   28

Sunday 25th
NEW Brook Cottage   4
NEW Mapperley Gardens   22
The Poplars   32

June

Sunday 1st
Capability Barn   5
NEW 78 Hilton Road   16
Keyworth Gardens   19
Saturday 14th
Park Farm   30
Sunday 15th
Hollinside   17
Patchings Art Centre   31
Thrumpton Hall   36
Thursday 19th
Rhubarb Farm   33
Saturday 21st
Hill's Farm   15
The Old Vicarage   28
Sunday 22nd
10 Harlaxton Drive   12
Ossington House   29
Saturday 28th
Glebe Steading   10
Sunday 29th
Glebe Steading   10
Norwell Gardens   24

July

Wednesday 2nd
Norwell Gardens   24
Sunday 6th
Normanton Hall   23
NEW Whatton Gardens   40
Sunday 13th
Gaunts Hill   9
Thursday 17th
Rhubarb Farm   33
Sunday 20th
5a High Street   13
The Old Vicarage   28
Saturday 26th
Floral Media   8
Sunday 27th
Oasis Community Gardens   27

August

Sunday 3rd
NEW 5 Bourne Drive — 3

Sunday 10th
University Park Gardens — 38

Saturday 16th
NEW Allington — 1

Sunday 17th
NEW Allington — 1
The Poplars — 32

Thursday 21st
Rhubarb Farm — 33

Sunday 24th
The Old Vicarage — 28

Monday 25th
NEW Whatton Gardens — 40

September

Sunday 7th
NEW Brook Cottage — 4
NEW 20 Kirklington Road — 20

October

Sunday 5th
◆ Norwell Nurseries — 25

By Arrangement

Arrange a personalised garden visit with your club, or group of friends, on a date to suit you. See individual garden entries for full details.

Bolham Manor — 2
NEW 5 Bourne Drive — 3
5 Burton Lane, Whatton Gardens — 40
Cedarwood, Whatton Gardens — 40
NEW The Cottage, Whatton Gardens — 40
Gaunts Hill — 9
10 Harlaxton Drive — 12
1 Highfield Road — 14
Home Farm House, 17 Main Street, Keyworth Gardens — 19
6 Hope Street — 18
Oasis Community Gardens — 27
The Old Vicarage — 28
Park Farm — 30
Patchings Art Centre — 31
The Poplars — 32
Riseholme, 125 Shelford Road — 34
Rose Cottage, Keyworth Gardens — 19
160 Southwell Road West — 35
Tithe Barn — 37
Waxwings & Goldcrest — 39

Allington

THE GARDENS

1 NEW **ALLINGTON**
Gonalston, Nottingham,
NG14 7JA. Mrs Catharine Bailey,
www.hortusbaileyana.co.uk. *NE of Lowdham. From Lowdham, take A612 to Southwell and take 2nd L into the village, then follow the NGS signs for Parking. As directed from there with NGS signage.* **Sat 16, Sun 17 Aug (2-5). Adm £5, chd free. Tea, coffee & cake.**
An invitation to visit my tranquil front garden leading onto a Rose Garden reminiscent of Victorian times. The colour theories of Gertrude Jekyll are brought to life in the Long Border and you can taste ripe Mulberries in the knot garden. The productive side of the garden inc a potager, a small orchard and a decorative greenhouse.

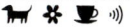

2 BOLHAM MANOR
Bolham Way, Bolham, Retford,
DN22 9JG. Pam & Butch
Barnsdale, 07790 896022,
pamandbutch@hotmail.co.uk. *1m from Retford. A620 Gainsborough Rd from Retford, turn L onto Tiln Ln, signed 'A620 avoiding low bridge'. At sharp R bend, take road to Tiln then L Bolham Way.* **Visits by arrangement 11 Feb to 21 Sept for groups of up to 30. Adm £5, chd free. Tea, coffee & cake.**
This 3 acre mature garden provides year-round interest. In February, swathes of snowdrops greet you, followed by daffodils and other spring bulbs. Topiary features and sculptures guide you through the different areas of the garden, with its mixed planted terraces and herbaceous borders, ponds, orchard and wildflower areas. Partial wheelchair access to parts of garden.

3 NEW **5 BOURNE DRIVE**
Ravenshead, Nottingham,
NG15 9FN. Nick and Jayne
Allen, 07540 919581,
nickcopperB1@aol.com. *2 m from Newstead Abbey. Situated in the middle of Ravenshead, 7 m from Mansfield and 7 m from Nottingham.* **Sun 3 Aug (11-5). Adm £4, chd free.** Visits also by arrangement 14 July to 5 Sept for groups of 5 to 10.
Very colourful garden with several aspects, two ponds an allotment and leisure area and outdoor dining experience. Well-stocked with a multitude of plants and trees Several seating areas to capture the day's sunlight.

4 NEW **BROOK COTTAGE**
41 Church Street, Southwell,
NG25 0HQ. Mr Alastair Murray. *In Southwell 200 metres E of The Minster. What3words app: lemmings. octagonal.offline.* **Sun 25 May, Sun 7 Sept (1-5). Adm £5, chd free. Home-made teas.**
An atypical cottage garden within Southwell, walking distance of Southwell Minster. Climbing roses, wisteria, clematis adorn the front of the cottage/adjacent garage. The back/sides of the garden are hidden by a clothed arbour and birch trees - will surprise visitors with wildflower meadow/perennial planting to give autumn colour. Mostly propagated by the owner. Working area on view. Wheelchairs will be able to access the majority of the garden across the lawn.

5 CAPABILITY BARN
Gonalston Lane, Hoveringham,
NG14 7JH. Malcolm & Wendy
Fisher, www.capabilitybarn.com. *8m NE of Nottingham. A612 from Nottingham through Lowdham. Take 1st R into Gonalston Ln. Garden is 1m on L.* **Sat 26, Sun 27 May, Sun 1 June (11-4.30). Adm £5, chd free. Home-made teas. 25% donation to NGS from refreshment income.**
Imaginatively planted large country garden with something new each year. April brings displays of daffodils, hyacinths and tulips along with erythroniums, brunneras and primulas. Wisteria, magnolia, rhodos and apple blossom greet May/June. Established trees, shrubs and shady paths give a charming country setting. Large vegetable/fruit gardens with orchard and flower meadow completes the picture.

6 CHURCH FARM
Church Lane, West Drayton,
Retford, DN22 8EB. Robert &
Isabel Adam. *5m S of Retford. A1 exit Markham Moor. A638 Retford 500 yds signed West Drayton, turn R, into Church Ln, 1st R past church. Ample parking in farm yard.* **Sun 16 Feb (10.30-4). Adm £5, chd free. Light refreshments. Served from 11.30am.**
Essentially a spring garden with a woodland area carpeted with snowdrops, aconites and cyclamen which have seeded also into the adjoining churchyard. Approx 180 named snowdrops flourish in island beds, along with hellebores and daffodils. Natural planting contrasts with elegant topiary.

7 ♦ **FELLEY PRIORY**
Underwood, NG16 5FJ. The
Brudenell Family, 01773 810230,
michelle@felleypriory.co.uk,
www.felleypriory.co.uk. *8m SW of Mansfield. Off A608 ½ m W M1 J27.* **For NGS: Sun 20 Apr (10-4). Adm £7.50, chd free. Light refreshments.** For other opening times and information, please phone, email or visit garden website.
Garden for all seasons with yew hedges and topiary, snowdrops, hellebores, herbaceous borders and rose garden. There are pergolas, a white garden, small arboretum and borders filled with unusual trees, shrubs, plants and bulbs. The grass edged pond is planted with primulas, bamboo, iris, roses and eucomis. Bluebell woodland walk. Orchard with extremely rare daffodils.

8 FLORAL MEDIA
Norwell Road, Caunton, Newark,
NG23 6AQ. Mr & Mrs Steve
Routledge, 07811 399113,
info@floralmedia.co.uk,
www.floralmedia.co.uk. *Take Norwell Rd from Caunton. Approx ½ m from Caunton on L.* **Sat 26 July (10-4). Adm £5, chd free. Tea, coffee & cake.**
A beautifully maintained country garden. Beds overflowing with a variety of roses, shrubs and flowers. A gravel/oriental garden, cutting gardens, vegetable beds, Flower Farm supplying British grown stems to florists/farm shops. Long sweeping borders surrounding the main lawn leading to the wildflower meadows where you will find an interesting garden retreat. A horticulturalist's haven. Often live music in the garden from a local folk group of musicians. A good range of plants available for sale. Full wheelchair access inc disabled WC.

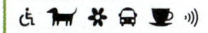

GAUNTS HILL
Bestwood Lodge, Arnold,
NG5 8NF. Nigel & Penny
Lymn Rose, 07778 028010,
penny@lymn.co.uk. *5m N of Nottingham. Take Bestwood Lodge Dr up to the Bestwood Lodge Hotel, then turn R & continue until you see a sign saying vehicle access to stables only. Then turn R down the drive through the gates.* **Sun 13 July (11-3). Adm £5, chd free. Tea, coffee & cake. Visits also by arrangement.**
An historic Victorian kitchen garden with listed brick walls. Featuring roses, dahlias, a tropical border and a small orchard. Features also inc original Victorian circular pond, French fountain, two gazebos and a large greenhouse. Some gravel paths and lawns. There are some steps but these can be avoided.

GLEBE STEADING
Gonalston, Nottingham,
NG14 7JA. Smita and Craig Jobling. *Gonalston. 1st R off A612 from Southwell into village, 1st house on R. Green outbuildings and barn conversion. Signs on Gate post and by roadside turn off.* **Sat 28, Sun 29 June (2-5). Adm £5, chd free. Home-made teas.**
Welcome to a garden designed around a small pool, with full brightly coloured borders and plants reminiscent of the owners childhood in Kenya, mingled with grasses for a looser feel. Flowering perennials attract pollinators and are left standing tall. A hillside of 35 trees with coppice/orchard and small kitchen garden. A small stream runs down the slope with a botanical medicinal border. Small natural pool with a summerhouse.

NEW HALL FARMHOUSE
Gonalston, Nottingham,
NG14 7JA. Helen Pusey. *From Southwell A612 take 1st R sign for Gonalston, Garden 500yds on R or from Nottingham take A612 L into Gonalston at Xrds. Follow road round L bend, take R after the postbox, Garden 100yds on L.* **Sat 17, Sun 18 May (1-5). Adm £5, chd free. Tea, coffee & cake.**
Recently acquired established Cottage Garden with 3 distinct areas. The month of May brings a riot of colour including wisteria, rhododendron, iris, allium, roses, ceanothus, bluebells and a range of spring bulbs. There are herbaceous borders and mature trees inc paulownia tomentosa, magnolia, ancient yew and varieties of apple. An historic pond is being re-developed to attract wildlife. Wheelchair access to two areas with ramp available for third.

The Poplars

NOTTINGHAMSHIRE 417

12 10 HARLAXTON DRIVE
Lenton, Nottingham, NG7 1JA. Jan Brazier, 07968 420046, jan-28b@hotmail.com, www.instagram.com/citygarden_oasis. *W of Nottingham city centre. From Nottingham centre, follow Derby Rd signs (A52), past St Barnabas Cathedral & just after Canning Circus, take 3rd L. From M1 J25, take A52 Nottingham & after 7m, 5th R after Savoy cinema.* **Sun 18 May, Sun 22 June (11.30-4.30). Adm £5, chd free. Home-made teas.** Visits also by arrangement 11 May to 31 Aug for groups of 15+.
City centre oasis, a short walk from the centre of Nottingham. Garden presented on three levels, separated by steep steps with handrails. The top terrace overlooks a large koi pond surrounded by bog plants, marginals and herbaceous perennials. Seating areas on second terrace under mature beech trees. On third level, a summerhouse as well as a small pond and densely-planted borders. Free on-street parking.

13 5A HIGH STREET
Sutton-on-Trent, NG23 6QA. Kathryn & Ian Saunders. *6m N of Newark. Leave A1 at Sutton on Trent, follow Sutton signs. L at Xrds. 1st R turn (approx 1m) onto Main St. 2nd L onto High St. Garden 50 yds on R. Park on road.* **Sun 20 July (1-4). Adm £5, chd free. Tea, coffee & cake.**
Vistas lead past a gravel planting area to tropical areas and vibrant herbaceous beds. Ponds run through the plot, leading to woodland walks and a dedicated fernery (180+ varieties, with magnificent tree ferns). Topiary links all the different planting areas to great effect. There are different planting areas and ideas around every corner. Paintings for sale.

14 1 HIGHFIELD ROAD
Nuthall, Nottingham, NG16 1BQ. Richard & Sue Bold, 07866 696752, sue.bold1@gmail.com. *4 mins from J26 of the M1 - 4m NW of Nottingham City. From J26 of the M1 take the A610 towards Notts. R lane at r'about, take turn-off to Horsendale. Follow road to Woodland Dr, then 2nd R is Highfield Rd.* **Fri 31 Jan, Sun 2 Feb (10-4). Adm £5, chd free.** Light refreshments inc tea, coffee, fruit teas and squash. Bacon rolls, sausage rolls, a variety of home-made cakes will be available inc a gluten free option. Visits also by arrangement 27 Jan to 21 Feb for groups of 10 to 20. Weekdays only.
Visit in Feb to see the collection of 700+ snowdrop varieties, with 300 varieties in the garden and many more in show benches. The spring garden has lots of colour with many rare and unusual plants - miniature narcissus, acers, aconites and hellebores A good selection of unusual pots and garden ornaments. Many snowdrop varieties and other plants available for sale.

15 HILL'S FARM
Edingley, NG22 8BU. John & Margaret Hill. *1 m drive or walk W. Hill's Farm wildflower meadow - a short drive of ½ m towards Edingley from Old Vicarage & turn R at brow of the hill as signed - tarmac farmyard for parking. Adm tickets at Old Vicarage.* **Sat 21 June (1-4.30). Combined adm with The Old Vicarage £6, chd free.** Home-made teas at The Old Vicarage in Halam (next door village).
Created with passion to produce a delightful walk - 6 acres of Nottinghamshire hay meadow carpeted with colourful wildflowers - ragged robin, yellow rattle, pyramidal orchids. 40+ acres of this mixed organic farm were taken out of arable production 2006 to create traditional hay meadows - hay taken in July is fed to the native beef shorthorn cattle. See some of the cows in adjoining fields. This is a meadow visible from the farm path. Mown through the meadow for walking and admiring. Sturdy shoes suggested as can be uneven route. Talk from John Hill for his organic passion.

16 NEW 78 HILTON ROAD
Nottingham, NG3 6AP. Julie Pinches. *What3words app: silk.lamps.lion. From Nottingham turn R at the junc of B684 Woodborough Rd onto Porchester Rd then 3rd L to Hilton Rd. No.78 is located 300yrds on R.* **Sun 1 June (10.30-5.30). Adm £4, chd free. Tea, coffee & cake.**
This contemporary garden, is set in the leafy suburb of Mapperley, on the edge of the City of Nottingham. The style of the garden echoes the clean lines of our 1960's mid-century house which is built in a split-level design. It has a series of angular raised beds with white retaining walls of various heights softened by the planting with is now very established since we started the garden in 2012.

17 HOLLINSIDE
252 Diamond Avenue, Kirkby-in-Ashfield, Nottingham, NG17 7NA. Sue & Bob Chalkley. *1m E of Kirkby in Ashfield at the Xrds of the A611 & B6020. Please park away from the busy junction.* **Sun 15 June (1-5). Adm £4, chd free. Tea, coffee & cake.**
A formal front garden with terraced lawns and mixed borders lead to a shadier area with ferns, camellias, clematis, hydrangeas and other flowering shrubs. The rear garden has mixed borders with many roses, a wildlife pond, a wildflower meadow and a Victorian style greenhouse. There are topiary box and yews and formal hedges surrounding the garden and several secluded places to sit. Majority of garden is suitable for wheelchairs. Disabled parking near house by prior arrangement.

18 6 HOPE STREET
Beeston, Nottingham, NG9 1DR. Elaine Liquorish, 01159 223239, eliquorish@outlook.com. *3 m S of Nottingham. From M1 J25, A52 for Nottingham. After 2 r'abouts, turn R for Beeston at The Nurseryman (B6006). Beyond hill, turn R into Bramcote Dr. 3rd turn on L into Bramcote Rd, then immed R into Hope St.* **Sun 18 May (1.30-5). Adm £4, chd free. Cream teas inc gluten and dairy free cakes.** Visits also by arrangement 10 May to 9 Aug for groups of 5 to 20.
A small garden packed with a wide variety of plants providing flower and foliage colour year-round. Collections of alpines, bulbs, mini, small and medium size hostas (60+), ferns, grasses, carnivorous plants, succulents, perennials, shrubs and trees. A pond and a greenhouse with subtropical plants. Troughs and pots. Home-made crafts. Shallow step into garden, into greenhouse and at rear. No wheelchair access to plant sales area or the back garden.

GROUP OPENING

19 KEYWORTH GARDENS
Keyworth, Nottingham, NG12 5AA. Graham Tinsley. *Keyworth, between the A60 & A606 7m S of Nottingham. Home Farm is near the church, Rose Cottage is at 81 Nottingham Rd NG12 5GS & 2 High View Ave NG12 5EL is off Nicker Hill. There is about a 15 min walk between each garden. Maps available in each garden.* **Sun 1 June (12-5). Combined adm £6, chd free. Home-made teas at Home Farm and Rose Cottage.**

NEW 2 HIGH VIEW AVENUE
Erika and Trevor Lax.

HOME FARM HOUSE, 17 MAIN STREET
Graham & Pippa Tinsley, 07780 672196, Graham_Tinsley@yahoo.co.uk, www.homefarmgarden.wordpress.com.
Visits also by arrangement May to Sept for groups of up to 25.

ROSE COTTAGE
Richard & Julie Fowkes, 01159 376489, richardfowkes@yahoo.co.uk.
Visits also by arrangement 5 May to 31 July for groups of 8 to 35.

2 High View Ave: Almost ⅓ of an acre, cottage style, set mainly to lawn with several mixed borders which contain a variety of herbaceous perennials, roses and bulbs. There are fruit bushes, a wildflower area, pond and small woodland of snowdrops and bluebells. Seating dotted around give views of the different areas. Home Farm: Large garden behind old farm near village centre which is defined by its trees. The old garden is divided by laurel, beech and yew hedges explore it to find the orchard, the old cart shed pergola, 'Green Man' pond, rose garden and mixed borders. Further on, it merges into an ornamental wilderness with turf mound and ponds. Rose Cottage: Densely-planted with colourful wildlife-friendly plants. Many features and different zones add unique interest. A wildlife stream meanders down between several ponds and bog areas. Art studio open with paintings and art cards designed by Julie on sale. Plants for sale by local nurseryman. At Home Farm, interesting and unusual perennials for sale by Piecemeal Plants (nursery@piecemealplants.co.uk).
❀ ☕ 🔊

20 NEW 20 KIRKLINGTON ROAD
Southwell, NG25 0AY. Mr & Mrs George and Margaret Sharman. *9m W of Newark-on-Trent. Limited parking on Kirklington Rd. Car parks in Southwell are a 10 min walk away at most.* **Sun 7 Sept (12-5). Adm £5, chd free. Tea, coffee & cake.**
Developed over recent years, while incorporating some existing mature fruit trees, this garden contains a wide variety of mainly ornamental varieties of flowers and shrubs. These are intended and planned to provide a year-round display of vibrant colour for the observer from different viewing points. Lovingly tended by skilful owners, the garden is described as "beautiful" by all who see it. A number of seating areas and hard surfaces are incorporated for leisurely enjoyment of the wildlife-friendly environment.
☕

21 38 MAIN STREET
Woodborough, Nottingham, NG14 6EA. Martin Taylor & Deborah Bliss. *About 8m NE of Nottingham centre. Turn off Mapperley Plains Rd at sign for Woodborough. Alternatively, follow signs to Woodborough off A6054 (Epperstone bypass). Property is between Park Ave & Bank Hill.* **Sun 11 May (1-5). Adm £5, chd free. Tea, coffee & cake. £4 for cake and drink.**
Started as a lawn at the front and back with 125 junipers and one rosebush. Now a varied ⅓ acre. Bamboo fenced Asian species area with traditional outdoor wood fired Ofuro bath, herbaceous border, raised species rhododendron bed, vegetables, greenhouse, pond area and art studio and terrace. The art studio will be open.
❀ ☕

GROUP OPENING

22 NEW MAPPERLEY GARDENS
147 Kenrick Road, Nottingham, NG3 6EY. Mr Alex Purdon, www.instagram.com/small_english_garden. *Please park with consideration for residents. Additional parking is available at Mapperley Day Nursery on Westdale Ln NG3 6ES.* **Sun 25 May (10-4). Combined adm £5, chd free. Light refreshments.**

NEW 15 ASHWORTH CRESCENT
The Manterfields.

NEW 147 KENRICK ROAD
Mr Alex Purdon.

NEW 13 NORTHCLIFFE AVENUE
Carol Wilby.

NEW 30 NORTHCLIFFE AVENUE
Sallie Cooper.

NEW 46 NORTHCLIFFE AVENUE
Lesley Ings.

We have 5 gardens (in total) that are open for the first time on Kenrick Road, Northcliffe Avenue and Ashworth Crescent. They show achievable ideas and projects for the average amateur gardener with a small plot. Garden owners will be on hand to discuss how they have developed their garden and a range of homegrown plants and home-made cakes will be available in support of the NGS. Additional parking is available at Mapperley Day Nursery on Westdale Lane. We hope for this event to grow annually, so if you live nearby and would like to get involved in the future, please speak to one of the garden owners.
❀ ☕ 🔊

23 NORMANTON HALL
South Street, Normanton-on-Trent, NG23 6RQ. His Honour John & Mrs Machin. *3m SE of Tuxford. Leave A1 at Sutton Carlton/Normanton-on-Trent jnc. Turn L onto B1164 in Carlton. In Sutton-on-Trent turn R at Normanton sign. Go through Grassthorpe, turn L at Normanton sign.* **Sun 6 July (1-6). Adm £5, chd free.**
3 acres with mature oak, lime beech and yew and recently planted trees. New plantings of bulbs, rhododendrons and a camellia walk. Arboretum planted with unusual, mainly hardwood trees which are between three and twelve yrs old. Also specimen oaks and beech. New planting of wood anemones. Recently established parkland. Award winning woodland. Picnics welcome on the swimming pool lawn. All surfaces level from car park.
♿ ❀ ☕ 🪑

GROUP OPENING

24 NORWELL GARDENS
Newark, NG23 6JX. *6m N of Newark. Halfway between Newark & Southwell. Off A1 at Cromwell turning, take Norwell Rd at bus shelter. Or off A616 take Caunton turn. Field parking on 29th at Foxhall Close (opp pub) if dry.* **Sun 29 June (1-5). Evening opening Wed 2 July (6-8.30). Combined adm £6.50, chd free. Home-made teas in Village Hall (29 June) and Norwell Nurseries (2 July).**

ASH HOUSE
Mrs Fiona Mountford.

CHERRY TREE HOUSE
Simon & Caroline Wyatt.

FAUNA FOLLIES
Lorraine & Roy Pilgrim.

NORWELL ALLOTMENTS / PARISH GARDENS
Norwell Parish Council.

♦ **NORWELL NURSERIES**
Andrew & Helen Ward.
(See separate entry)

PINFOLD COTTAGE
Mrs Pat Foulds.

ROSE COTTAGE
Mr Iain & Mrs Ann Gibson.

This is the 29th year that Norwell has opened a range of different, very appealing gardens all making superb use of the beautiful backdrop of a quintessentially English countryside village. Inc a garden and nursery of national renown. To top it all there are a plethora of breathtaking village gardens showing the diversity that is achieved under the umbrella of a cottage garden description. The beautiful medieval church and its peaceful churchyard with grass labyrinth will be open for quiet contemplation.
♿ ❋ 🚗 ☕

25 ♦ NORWELL NURSERIES
Woodhouse Road, Norwell, NG23 6JX. Andrew & Helen Ward, 01636 636317, wardha@aol.com, www.norwellnurseries.co.uk. *6m N of Newark halfway between Newark & Southwell. Off A1 at Cromwell turning, take road to Norwell at bus stop. Or from A616 take Caunton turn.* **For NGS: Sun 18 May, Sun 5 Oct (2-5). Adm £4.50, chd free. Home-made teas. Opening with Norwell Gardens on Sun 29 June, Wed 2 July.** For other opening times and information, please phone, email or visit garden website.
Jewel box of over 3,000 different, beautiful and unusual plants sumptuously set out in a 1 acre plantsman's garden inc shady garden with woodland gems, cottage garden borders, alpine and scree areas. Pond with opulently planted margins. Extensive herbaceous borders and effervescent colour themed beds. Sand beds showcase Mediterranean, North American and alpine plants. Nationally renowned nursery open with over 1,500 different rare plants for sale. Autumn opening features UK's largest collection of hardy chrysanthemums for sale and the National Collection of Hardy Chrysanthemums. New borders inc the National Collection of Astrantias. Innovative sand beds. Grass paths, no wheelchair access to woodland paths.
♿ ❋ 🚗 NPC ☕

26 NORWOOD PARK
Halam Road, Southwell, NG25 0PF. Sir John Starkey, 01636 302099, events@norwoodpark.co.uk, www.norwoodpark.co.uk. *NW edge of Southwell. From Southwell follow brown signs to Norwood Park.* **Sun 9 Feb (10-3). Adm £8, chd free. Light refreshments at Norwood Park Golf Club.**
The grounds of Norwood Park date back to medieval times when they were part of a series of deer parks. A new garden on the south front of the C18 house was created in 2021 to showcase plants for all seasons. To the west a lime avenue lined with snowdrops and daffodils leads on to Mrs. Delaney's Path to the ornamental temple.
♿ 🐕 ❋ 🚗 🚌 ☕ 🔊

27 OASIS COMMUNITY GARDENS
2a Longfellow Drive, Kilton Estate, Worksop, S81 0DE. Steve Williams, 07795 194957, Stevemark126@hotmail.com, www.oasiscommunitycentre.org. *Nottinghamshire. From Kilton Hill (leading to the Worksop hospital), take 1st exit to R (up hill) onto Kilton Cres, then 1st exit on R Longfellow Dr. Car Park off Dickens Rd (1st R).* **Sat 19 Apr, Sun 27 July (10-3). Adm by donation. Tea, coffee & cake in Oasis Garden Cafe.** Visits also by arrangement Mar to Oct for groups of up to 30.
Oasis Gardens is a community project transformed from abandoned field to an award winning garden. Managed by volunteers the gardens boast over 30 project areas and hosts many community events. Take a look in the Cactus Kingdom, the Liquorice Garden, the Aviaries, Pre-school play village, Wildlife Wonderland and the wonderful variety of trees, plants, seasonal flowers and shrubs. The Oasis Gardens hosts the first Liquorice Garden in Worksop for 100 yrs. The site hosts the 'Flowers for Life' project which is a therapeutic gardening project growing and selling cut flowers and floristry. There is disabled access from Longfellow Dr. From the town end there is a driveway after the 1st fence on the right next to house No.2.
♿ ❋ ☕ 🔊

28 THE OLD VICARAGE
Halam Hill, Halam, NG22 8AX. Mrs Beverley Perks, 01636 812181, perks.family@talk21.com. *1m W of Southwell, 1st house on L as entering Halam village. Please park diagonally into beech hedge on verge with speed interactive sign or in village. Entry at top gate. Probable building works bottom entrance.* **Sat 24 May (1-4.30). Adm £5, chd free. Home-made teas. Sat 21 June (1-4.30). Combined adm with Hill's Farm £6, chd free. Home-made teas. Sun 20 July (1-4.30). Adm £5, chd free. Home-made teas. Sun 24 Aug (1-4.30). Adm £5, chd free. Tea, coffee & cake.** Visits also by arrangement 2 June to 22 Aug for groups of 10 to 35. Adm inc refreshments and guided tours by gardener/owner.
An artful eye for design/texture/colour/love of unusual plants/trees makes this a welcoming gem to visit. One time playground for 4 children, this 2 acre organic hillside garden has matured over 28 yrs into a much admired, popular, landscape garden with beautiful views. New bottom garden planting/design. Pond attracts diverse wildlife to complement plantings. Beautiful C12 Church open only a short walk into the village or across field through attractively planted churchyard - rare C14 stained glass window. Top entrance gravel drive. Undulating levels as on a hillside. Plenty of help available.
♿ 🐕 ❋ 🚗 ☕ 🔊

29 OSSINGTON HOUSE
Moorhouse Road, Ossington, Newark, NG23 6LD. Georgina Denison. *10m N of Newark, 2m off A1. From A1 N take exit marked Carlton, Sutton-on-Trent, Weston etc. At T-junc turn L to Kneesall. Drive 2 m to Ossington. Roadside parking on Main St and Moorhouse Rd.* **Sun 22 June (2-5). Adm £6, chd free. Home-made teas in The Hut, Ossington.**
Vicarage garden redesigned in 1960 and again in 2014. Chestnuts, lawns, formal beds, woodland walk, poolside planting, orchard. Terraces, yews, grasses. Ferns, herbaceous perennials, roses and kitchen garden. Disabled parking available in drive to Ossington House.

&. 🐐 ❋ ☕ 🍺

30 PARK FARM
Crink Lane, Southwell, NG25 0TJ. Ian & Vanessa Johnston, 01636 812195, v.johnston100@gmail.com. *1m SE of Southwell. From Southwell town centre go down Church St, turn R on to Fiskerton Rd & 200yds up hill turn R into Crink Ln. Park Farm is on 2nd bend.* **Sat 14 June (1-4.30). Adm £5, chd free. Tea, coffee & cake.** Visits also by arrangement 21 Apr to 12 July for groups of up to 30. Guided tours (min10 visitors) £1 extra.
3 acre garden noted for its extensive variety of trees, shrubs and perennials, many rare or unusual. Long luxuriant herbaceous borders, rose arches, alpine/scree garden, large wildlife pond and area of woodland and acid loving plants. Spectacular views of the Minster across a wildflower meadow and ha-ha.

&. 🐐 ❋ ☕ 🍺

31 PATCHINGS ART CENTRE
Oxton Road, Calverton, Nottingham, NG14 6NU. Pat and Chas Wood, 01159 653479, Chas@patchingsartcentre.co.uk, www.patchingsartcentre.co.uk. *N of Nottingham city take A614 towards Ollerton. Turn R on to B6386 towards Calverton & Oxton. Patchings is on L before turning to Calverton. Brown tourist directional signs.* **Sun 15 June (10.30-3.30). Adm £4, chd free. Light refreshments at Patchings Café.** Visits also by arrangement June to Aug. Arranged group visits of 10 plus will inc a brief visual presentation.

Patchings is set in 50 acres with a visitor centre and galleries - a haven for artists and a tranquil setting of countryside and garden walks for visitors. Watch artists at work and enjoy the exhibition of 140 selected works from the annual international competition organised with The Artist and Leisure Painter magazines, alongside 70 winning entries from new Young Persons section. The Patchings Artists' Trail - a walk through art history, famous paintings presented in glass takes visitors through the centuries. The winning entries of the 2025 TALP Open Competition - 210 works on show in three galleries. Grass and compacted gravel paths with some undulations and uphill sections accessible to wheelchairs with help. Please enquire for assistance.

&. 🐐 ☕ 🍺 🔊

32 THE POPLARS
Cotham Lane, Hawton, Newark, NG24 3RL. Ian Brownhill & Michael Hirschl, 07970 126318, ian@staghill.co.uk. *Hawton village is approx 2m S of Newark-on-Trent. House is 2nd turning on the L past All Saint's church in Hawton village. Parking in All Saints' church car park.* **Sun 25 May, Sun 17 Aug (2-5). Adm £5, chd free. Tea, coffee & cake.** Visits also by arrangement 2 June to 12 Sept for groups of 10 to 25.
1.2 acre garden extensively remodelled and replanted by its current owners. The garden wraps around an early Georgian farmhouse (not open). Explore a number of distinct areas inc a formal garden planted with ornamental grasses and white-flowering plants, Mediterranean-style gravel patio and contemporary cottage garden. Each area planned for interest throughout the year including masses of spring bulbs. The garden is wheelchair accessible (driveways, lawned areas) apart from the gravel patio.

&. 🐐 ❋ 🍺 🔊

33 RHUBARB FARM
Hardwick Street, Langwith, nr Mansfield, NG20 9DR. Rhubarb Farm, www.rhubarbfarm.co.uk. *On NW border of Nottinghamshire in village of Nether Langwith. From A632 in Langwith, by bridge (single file traffic) turn up steep Devonshire Dr. Take 2nd L into Hardwick St. Rhubarb Farm at end. Parking to R of gates.* **Thur 19 June, Thur 17**

July, Thur 21 Aug (10.30-3). Adm £3, chd free. Tea, coffee & cake in our on-site café, made by Rhubarb Farm volunteers.
This 2 acre horticultural social enterprise provides training and volunteering opportunities to 60 ex-offenders, drug and alcohol misusers, older people, school students, people with mental and physical ill health and learning disabilities. Eight polytunnels, 100 hens, pigs, donkey and a Shetland pony. Forest school barn, willow dome and arch, large Keder polytunnel (bubblewrap walls), flower borders, Farm shop, pond, raised beds, comfrey bed and comfrey fertiliser factory, junk sculpture, Heath Robinson Feature. Chance to meet and chat with volunteers and staff. Main path suitable for wheelchairs but bumpy. Not all site accessible. Cafe & composting toilet wheelchair-accessible.

&. ❋ 🐐 ☕ 🍺 🔊

34 RISEHOLME, 125 SHELFORD ROAD
Radcliffe on Trent, NG12 1AZ. John & Elaine Walker, 01159 119867, elaine.walker10@hotmail.co.uk. *4m E of Nottingham. From A52 follow signs to Radcliffe. In village centre take turning for Shelford (by Co-op). Approx ¾ m on L.* Visits by arrangement June & July for groups of 15 to 50. Discuss refreshments with garden owner when booking. Adm £9, chd free. Tea, coffee & cake.
Imaginative and inspirational is how the garden has been described by visitors. A huge variety of perennials, grasses, shrubs and trees combined with an eye for colour and design. Jungle area with exotic lush planting contrasts with tender perennials particularly salvias thriving in raised beds and in gravel garden with stream. Unique and interesting objects complement planting. Artwork, fairies and dragons feature in the garden.

🐐 ❋ 🍺 ☕

Our donation to Marie Curie this year equates to 17,496 hours of nursing care or 43 days of care in one of their nine hospices.

147 Kenrick Road, Mapperley Gardens

In 2024 we awarded £232,000 in Community Garden Grants, supporting 89 community garden projects.

35 160 SOUTHWELL ROAD WEST

Mansfield, NG18 4HB. Barrie & Lynne Jackson, 01623 750466, landbjackson@gmail.com. *Approx half way between Mansfield & Rainworth on A1691. From A60 towards Mansfield, turn R at T-lights up Berry Hill Ln. At the T-junc turn L. We are on the service road on the L. No parking on the service road.* **Sun 4 May (1-4.30). Adm £4, chd free. Tea, coffee & cake.** Visits also by arrangement 28 Apr to 31 May for groups of 10+. Please coordinate with the owner regarding parking arrangements.

The $\frac{1}{3}$ acre garden was started from scratch in spring 2018. We have a range of growing environments inc a woodland garden, a border designed to cope with sun, large island beds, a vegetable garden and a wide range of climbers growing up a variety of structures. Our particular interests are Agapanthus, woodland plants inc Trillium, plus fruit and vegetables. A sloping site which is accessible with assistance. Some grass paths.

Tithe Barn

NOTTINGHAMSHIRE

36 THRUMPTON HALL
Thrumpton, NG11 0AX. Miranda Seymour, www.thrumptonhall.com. *7m S of Nottingham. M1 J24 take A453 towards Nottingham. Turn L to Thrumpton village & cont to Thrumpton Hall.* **Sun 15 June (11-4). Adm £6, chd free.**
2 acres inc lawns, rare trees, flower borders, rose garden, and box-bordered sunken herb garden, all enclosed by C18 ha-ha and encircling a Jacobean house. Garden is surrounded by C18 landscaped park bordered by a river. Rare opportunity to visit Jacobean mansion, Thrumpton Hall (separate admission).

37 TITHE BARN
Potter Lane, Wellow, Newark, NG22 0EB. Andrew & Carrie Young, 01623 863327, andrew.young@ngs.org.uk. *12 m NW of Newark on A616 about 1m SE from Ollerton on A616. Potter Ln is 1st L after the 30mph limit from Newark or 50yd past Maypole hotel on R from Ollerton, Tithe Barn is the long drive on R after churchyard and Lodge Farm Bungalow.* **Visits by arrangement 1 May to 6 July for groups of 15+. Adm £5, chd free. Home-made teas.**
The grass-lined approach to this garden between yew hedges sets the tone to the wide sweeps of lawn and generous terrace. Herbaceous beds, irises, roses and rambling roses scrambling into fruit trees. The mature planting of shrubs and weeping trees enhances this pretty barn conversion on the edge of the Wellow Dyke. Woodland garden along the edge of Wellow Dyke open. Patio not accessible by wheelchair without assistance. Woodland path not wheelchair accessible.

In 2024, we celebrated 40 years of continuous funding for Macmillan Cancer Support equating to more than £19.5 million.

38 UNIVERSITY PARK GARDENS
Nottingham, NG7 2RD. University of Nottingham, www.nottingham.ac.uk/estates/grounds. *Approx 4m SW of Nottingham city centre & opp Queens Medical Centre. Purchase adm tickets online or on arrival in the Millennium Garden (in centre of campus), signed from N & W entrances to University Park & within internal road network.* **Sun 10 Aug (11.30-3). Adm £5, chd free. Light refreshments in Pavilion Café in the Lakeside Arts Centre. Also light refreshments adjacent to Millennium Garden in Monica Partridge Building (& WC facilities).**
University Park has many beautiful gardens inc the award-winning Millennium Garden with its dazzling flower gardens, timed fountains and turf maze. Also the huge Lenton Firs rock garden, and the Jekyll garden. For the NGS, the Walled Garden is also open and alive with exotic plantings. In total, 300 acres of landscape and gardens. Newly-added in 2024 is a Memorial Woodland Walk. Picnic area, café, walking tours, information desk, workshop, accessible minibus within the campus takes visitors to feature gardens. Car parking next to the Millennium Garden where tickets and plants are for sale. Some gravel paths and steep slopes.

39 WAXWINGS & GOLDCREST
Lamins Lane, Bestwood Village, Nottingham, NG6 8WS. Rob & Jill Carlyle, 07495 934449, jill.carlyle@outlook.com, www.sustainablegarden.blogspot.com. *Nottingham. A60 N of Redhill r'about. Take Lamins Ln. Single track road, limited visibility & passing places. The properties are 1m along the lane on L.* **Visits by arrangement 7 July to 20 July for groups of 20 to 40. Adm £8, chd free. Home-made teas.**
Two architect-designed eco-homes within six acres of stunning, tranquil gardens developed with biodiversity in mind including meadows, orchard, woodland and vegetable gardens. Mature trees, lawns, ponds and stumpery. Home to a rich diversity of pollinators, birds and habitats. A haven for humans and wildlife.

GROUP OPENING

40 NEW WHATTON GARDENS
Whatton, Nottingham, NG13 9EQ. *3 m E of Bingham. Cedarwood and 5 Burton Ln: Follow signs to Whatton from A52. Gardens are around the corner from local church. The Cottage: Within 100 metres of Whatton Church.* **Sun 6 July, Mon 25 Aug (11-4). Combined adm £7, chd free. Tea, coffee & cake at 5 Burton Lane inc options for special dietary requirements.**

5 BURTON LANE
Ms Faulconbridge, 01949 850942, jpfaulconbridge@hotmail.co.uk, www.ayearinthegardenblog.wordpress.com.
Visits also by arrangement 26 May to 13 Sept for groups of up to 30.

CEDARWOOD
Louise Bateman, 01949 850227, louise.bateman@hotmail.co.uk.
Visits also by arrangement 5 July to 26 Sept for groups of 10+.

NEW THE COTTAGE
Toni Aplin, 07484 744183, tim.aplin@btinternet.com.
Visits also by arrangement 6 July to 25 Aug for groups of 10 to 25.

5 Burton Lane: Organic cottage style garden which is productive, highly decorative and wildlife friendly. It is full of colour and scent from spring to autumn. Several distinct areas inc fruit and vegetables. Large beds filled with over 600 varieties of plants with paths you can wander and get close. Also features seating, gravel garden, pond, shade planting, pergola with grapevine, wildflower lawn. Cedarwood: A 1,240m² plantswoman's garden developed over the last 20 yrs. Planted for year-round colour. Plants are chosen for their attractiveness to wildlife as well as people. It inc various mixed borders, a pond, alpine crevice garden and woodland planting. Additionally there is a newly replanted matrix style grass bed. Many species of bees live here due to the variety of habitats and flower type. The Cottage: Walled cottage garden with generous herbaceous borders, vine covered pergola, herb area, patios, vegetable patch, rose arbour, a plant lovers paradise. By arrangement visits also available, please contact group coordinator, Ms Faulconbridge (01949 850942, jpfaulconbridge@hotmail.co.uk) to discuss.

OXFORDSHIRE

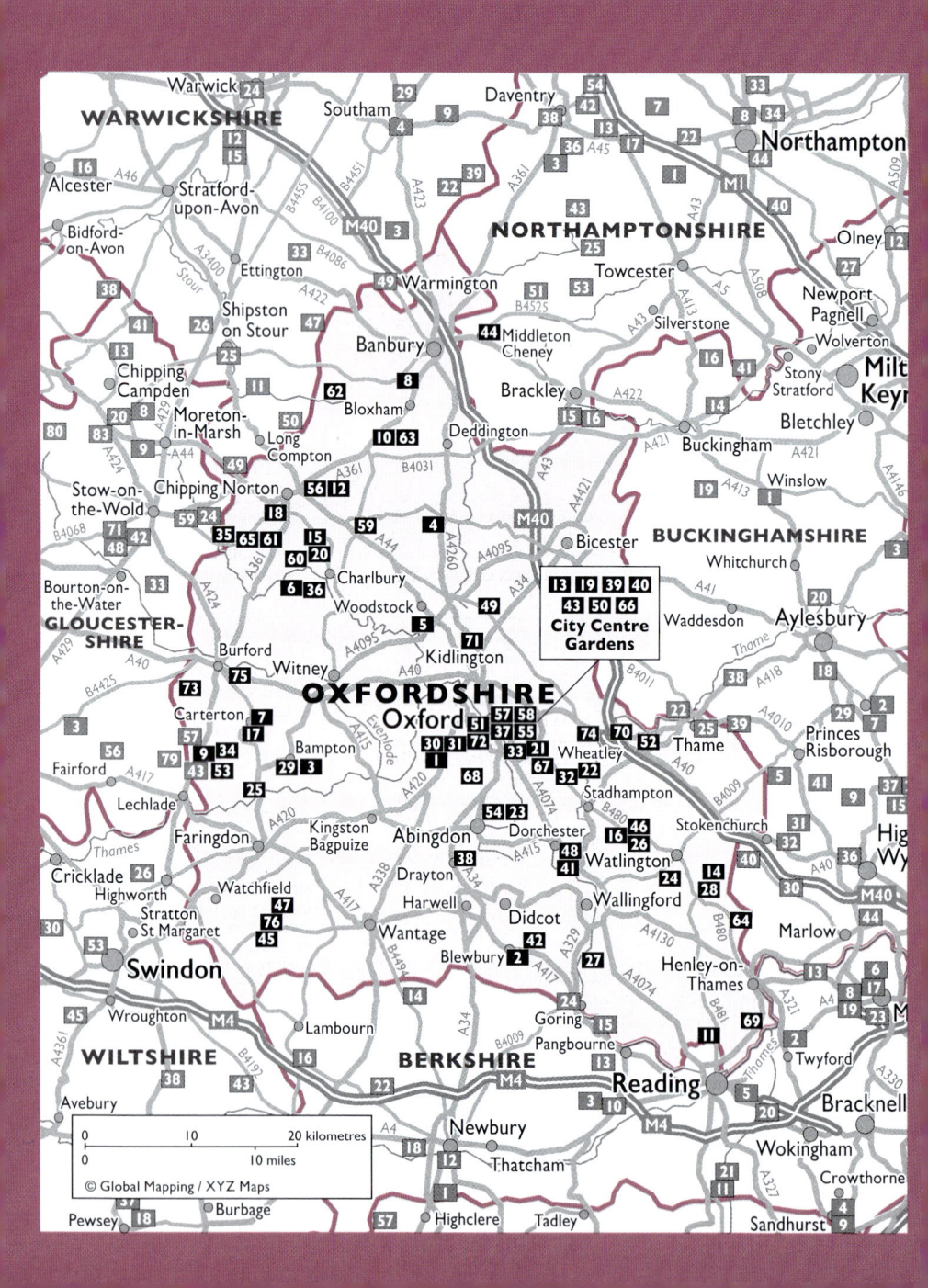

VOLUNTEERS

County Organiser
Marina Hamilton-Baillie
01367 710486
marina.hamilton-baillie@ngs.org.uk

Treasurer
Tom Hamilton-Baillie
01367 710486
tom.hamilton-baillie@ngs.org.uk

Talks Co-Ordinator
Priscilla Frost 01608 811818
info@oxconf.co.uk

Dr David Edwards
07973 129473
david.edwards@ngs.org.uk

Social Media- Instagram
Dr Jill Edwards 07971 201352
jill.edwards@ngs.org.uk

Social Media & Marketing
John Fleming 01865 739327
john@octon.scot

Assistant County Organisers
Lynn Baldwin 01608 642754
elynnbaldwin@gmail.com

Dr David Edwards (as above)

Dr Jill Edwards (as above)

Sarah Fernback 07500 009313
sarah.fernback@ngs.org.uk

Penny Guy 01865 862000
penny.theavon@virginmedia.com

Michael & Pat Hougham
01865 890020
gmec@outlook.com

Lyn Sanders
01865 739486
sandersc4@hotmail.com

Paul Youngson 07946 273902
paulyoungson48@gmail.com

@NGSOxfordshire
@ngs_oxfordshire
@ngs_oxfordshire

OPENING DATES

All entries subject to change.
For latest information check
www.ngs.org.uk

Map locator numbers are
shown to the right of each
garden name.

February

Snowdrop Openings

Sunday 9th
6 High Street 30

March

Tuesday 11th
◆ Waterperry Gardens 70

Saturday 22nd
Claridges Barn 15

Sunday 23rd
Claridges Barn 15

April

Sunday 6th
Ashbrook House 2
Sarsden Glebe 61

Sunday 13th
Corpus Christi College 19
Magdalen College 40

Monday 21st
Kencot Gardens 34

Saturday 26th
Claridges Barn 15
50 Plantation Road 55

Sunday 27th
◆ Broughton Grange 8
Claridges Barn 15
38 Leckford Road 37
50 Plantation Road 55

May

Friday 2nd
Midsummer House 45

Sunday 4th
Bolters Farm 6
Kings Cottage 36

Monday 5th
Bolters Farm 6
Kings Cottage 36

Friday 9th
NEW 61 Cornish Road 18

Saturday 10th
◆ Blenheim Palace 5

Sunday 11th
The Manor Garden 42

Sunday 18th
Broughton Poggs & Filkins Gardens 9
NEW 29 Corbett Road 17
Lime Close 38

Wednesday 21st
Kingham Lodge 35

Sunday 25th
Barton Abbey 4
The Priory, Charlbury 56

Friday 30th
NEW 61 Cornish Road 18

June

Sunday 1st
NEW Archangel House 1
19 High Street 31

Friday 6th
Midsummer House 45

Sunday 8th
Failford 23
Friars Court 25
6 High Street 30
Iffley Gardens 33
Middleton Cheney Gardens 44
Mill House Garden 47
116 Oxford Road 54
Tythe Barn 67
West Oxford Gardens 72

Thursday 12th
◆ Stonor Park 64

Friday 13th
Claridges Barn 15
NEW 61 Cornish Road 18
Sandys House 60

Saturday 14th
NEW Christmas Common Gardens 14
Claridges Barn 15
Sandys House 60

Sunday 15th
◆ Broughton Grange 8
9 Rawlinson Road 57
11 Rawlinson Road 58
Wheatley Manor 74

OXFORDSHIRE 425

OXFORDSHIRE

Monday 16th
New College, The Warden's
Garden   50

Thursday 19th
Dean Manor   20

Saturday 21st
Stow Cottage Arboretum &
Garden   65

Sunday 22nd
Brize Norton Gardens   7
Chalkhouse Green Farm   11
NEW 29 Corbett Road   17
Sibford Gardens   62

Friday 27th
NEW 61 Cornish Road   18

Sunday 29th
Green and Gorgeous   27
26 Manor Farm Road   41
6 Monks Close   48

July

Friday 4th
Midsummer House   45
Woolstone Mill House   76

Friday 11th
NEW 61 Cornish Road   18

Sunday 13th
Whitehill Farm   75

Sunday 20th
Merton College Oxford Fellows'
Garden   43
NEW North Hinksey Gardens   51
Upper Bolney House   69

Friday 25th
NEW 61 Cornish Road   18

Sunday 27th
◆ Broughton Grange   8

August

Friday 1st
Midsummer House   45

Sunday 3rd
NEW Lincoln College   39
Trinity College   66

Friday 15th
NEW 61 Cornish Road   18

Saturday 16th
Aston Pottery   3

Sunday 17th
Aston Pottery   3

Sunday 24th
Bolters Farm   6
Kings Cottage   36

Monday 25th
Bolters Farm   6
Kings Cottage   36

September

Friday 5th
NEW 61 Cornish Road   18
Midsummer House   45

Saturday 6th
Christ Church Masters,
Pococke & Cathedral Gardens   13

Sunday 7th
Ashbrook House   2
Ham Court   29

Tuesday 16th
◆ Waterperry Gardens   70

Sunday 21st
50 Plantation Road   55

October

Friday 3rd
Midsummer House   45

Sunday 26th
Lime Close   38

By Arrangement

Arrange a personalised garden visit with your club, or group of friends, on a date to suit you. See individual garden entries for full details.

Bolters Farm   6
Bush House   10
Carter's Yard, Sibford Gardens   62
Chivel Farm   12
Claridges Barn   15
NEW Copper Corners   16
NEW 61 Cornish Road   18
Dean Manor   20
103 Dene Road   21
Denton House   22
Failford   23
Foxington   24
The Grange   26
Greenfield Farm   28
Home Close, Garsington   32
Kings Cottage   36
Lime Close   38
Mill Barn   46
The Old Rectory, Albury   52
The Old School   53
116 Oxford Road   54
Rectory Farmhouse   59
South Newington House   63
Uplands   68
Wayside   71
Westwell Manor   73
Whitehill Farm   75

Lincoln College

THE GARDENS

1 NEW **ARCHANGEL HOUSE**
Abingdon Road, Cumnor, Oxford,
OX2 9QN. Sasha Bond. *Coming off the A420, R then R again, up the hill, then L into Cumnor. Follow the road until church on L. Large house opp church. Black gates.* **Sun 1 June (12-5). Combined adm with 19 High Street £5, chd free. Tea.**
Coming through the gate, admire beautiful hanging wisteria floating above. Further on, to the left a paved area bears bright pots and a rusty Japanese maple. Straight ahead, a wildflower section. To the right, a large lawn with colourful herbaceous borders. Highlights inc a ruddy, smoke bush, golden Choisya and pretty lined geraniums. In the front garden, cherish the bright purple lavender.
☕ 🔊

2 ASHBROOK HOUSE
Westbrook Street, Blewbury,
OX11 9QA. Mr & Mrs S A Barrett. *4m SE of Didcot. Turn off A417 in Blewbury into Westbrook St. 1st house on R. Follow yellow signs for parking in Boham's Rd at W entrance to the village.* **Sun 6 Apr, Sun 7 Sept (2-5.30). Adm £5, chd free. Tea, coffee & cake.**
The garden where Kenneth Grahame read Wind in the Willows to local children and where he took inspiration for his description of the oak doors to Badger's House. Come and see, you may catch a glimpse of Toad and friends in this 3½ acre chalk and water garden, in a beautiful spring line village. In spring the banks are a mass of daffodils and in late summer the borders are full of unusual plants.
♿ 🐕 ☕ 🔊

3 ASTON POTTERY
Bampton Road, Aston, Bampton,
OX18 2BT. Mr Stephen Baughan,
www.astonpottery.co.uk. *4m S of Witney. On the B4449 between Bampton & Standlake.* **Sat 16 Aug (10-5); Sun 17 Aug (10.30-5). Adm £5, chd free.**
6 stunning borders set around Aston Pottery. 72 metre double hornbeam border full of riotous perennials. 80 metre long hot bank of alstroemeria, salvias, echinacea and kniphofia. Quadruple dahlia border with over 600 dahlias, grasses and asters. Tropical garden with bananas, cannas and ricinus. Finally, 80 metres of 120 different annuals planted in four giant successive waves of over 6000 plants. The gardens are fully accessible for wheelchair users. Please note that the paths consist of a mixture of paving, tarmac and grass.
♿ ✿ ☕

4 BARTON ABBEY
Steeple Barton, OX25 4QS. Mr & Mrs P Fleming. *8m E of Chipping Norton. On B4030, ½m from junc of A4260 & B4030.* **Sun 25 May (2-5). Adm £5, chd free. Tea.**
15 acre garden with views from house (not open) across sweeping lawns and picturesque lake. Walled garden with colourful herbaceous borders, separated by established yew hedges and espalier fruit, contrasts with more informal woodland garden paths with vistas of specimen trees and meadows. Working glasshouses and fine display of fruit and vegetables.
♿ 🐕 ✿ ☕ 🪑

5 ♦ **BLENHEIM PALACE**
Woodstock, OX20 1UL. His Grace the Duke of Marlborough, 01993 810530, customerservice@blenheimpalace.com,
www.blenheimpalace.com. *8 m N of Oxford. The S7 bus runs every 30 mins from Oxford Stn to Blenheim Palace. The S3 runs hourly from Chipping Norton and Charlbury to Blenheim Palace. For bus times visit www.stagecoachbus.com.* **For NGS: Sat 10 May (10-5.30). Adm £8, chd £6. For other opening times and information, please phone, email or visit garden website.**
Created over the centuries by esteemed garden designers such as Henry Wise and Achille Duchêne, our Formal Gardens reflect a journey through the styles of the ages. Explore the majestic Water Terraces, the Duke's Private Italian Garden, the tranquil Secret Garden, the Churchill Memorial Garden, and the beautifully delicate Rose Garden. Admire Vanbrugh's Grand Bridge, the focal point of over 2,000 acres of landscaped parkland. Ride the miniature train to the Walled Garden where you will find the Marlborough Maze, Butterfly House, and Blenheim Palace Adventure Play. Wheelchair access with some gravel paths, uneven terrain and slopes. Dogs permitted on short leads in the Parkland and East Courtyard only.
♿ 🚗 ☕ 🪑 🔊

6 BOLTERS FARM
Pudlicote Lane, Chilson, Chipping Norton, OX7 3HU. Robert & Mandy Cooper, 07778 476517,
art@amandacooper.co.uk,
www.instagram.com/amandacooper684. *Centre of Chilson village. On arrival in the hamlet of Chilson, heading N, we are the last in an old row of cottages on R. Please drive past & park considerately on the L in the lane. Limited parking, car sharing recommended.* **Sun 4, Mon 5 May, Sun 24, Mon 25 Aug (1-5). Combined adm with Kings Cottage £8, chd free. Tea, coffee & cake inc gluten free options.** Visits also by arrangement May & June for groups of 10+. Adm inc tea and cake. Donation to Hands Up Foundation.
A cherished old cottage garden restored over the last 17 yrs. Tumbly moss covered walls and sloping lawns down to a stream with natural planting and quirky characterful moments. Running water, weeping willows, sloping lawns, wild area, some unusual planting and an enormous sense of peace.
🐕 ☕ 🔊

Our 2024 donation to The Queen's Nursing institute now helps support over 3,000 Queen's Nurses working in the community in England, Wales, Northern Ireland, the Channel Islands and the Isle of Man.

OXFORDSHIRE 427

GROUP OPENING

7 BRIZE NORTON GARDENS
Brize Norton, OX18 3LY.
www.bncommunity.org/ngs. *3m SW of Witney. Brize Norton Village, S of A40, between Witney & Burford. Parking at Elderbank Hall. Coaches welcome with plenty of parking nearby. Tickets & maps available at Elderbank Hall & at each garden.* **Sun 22 June (1-6). Combined adm £7.50, chd free. Tea, coffee & cake in Elderbank Village Hall.**

BARNSTABLE HOUSE
Mr & Mrs P Butcher.

17 CHICHESTER PLACE
Mr & Mrs D Howard.

CLUMBER
Mr & Mrs S Hawkins.

2 ELM GROVE
Rod and Sonja Coles.

MILLSTONE
Bev & Phil Tyrell.

PAINSWICK HOUSE
Mr & Mrs T Gush.

ROSE COTTAGE
Brenda & Brian Trott.

95 STATION ROAD
Mr & Mrs P A Timms.

STONE COTTAGE
Mr & Mrs K Humphris.

Doomsday village on the edge of the Cotswold's offering a number of gardens open for your enjoyment. You can see a wide variety of planting inc ornamental trees and grasses, herbaceous borders, traditional fruit and vegetable gardens. Features inc a Mediterranean style patio, courtyard garden, water features; plus gardens where you can just sit, relax and enjoy the day. Plants for sale at individual gardens. A Flower Festival will take place in the Brize Norton St Britius Church. Partial wheelchair access to some gardens.

8 ♦ BROUGHTON GRANGE
Wykham Lane, Broughton, Banbury, OX15 5DS. S Hester, 07791 747371, enquiries@broughtongrange.com, www.broughtongrange.com. *¼ m out of village. From Banbury take B4035 to Broughton. Turn L at Saye & Sele Arms Pub up Wykham Ln (one way). Follow road out of village for ¼ m. Entrance on R.* **For NGS: Sun 27 Apr, Sun 15 June, Sun 27 July (10-5). Adm £12, chd free. Tea.** For other opening times and information, please phone, email or visit garden website.

An impressive 25 acres of gardens and light woodland in an attractive Oxfordshire setting. The centrepiece is a large terraced walled garden created by Tom Stuart-Smith in 2001. Vision has been used to blend the gardens into the countryside. Good early displays of bulbs followed by outstanding herbaceous planting in summer. Formal and informal areas combine to make this a special site inc newly laid arboretum with many ongoing projects.

GROUP OPENING

9 BROUGHTON POGGS & FILKINS GARDENS
Filkins, nr Lechlade, GL7 3JH. www.filkins.org.uk. *3m N of Lechlade. 5m S of Burford. Just off A361 between Burford & Lechlade on the B4477.* **Sun 18 May (2-6). Combined adm £10, chd free. Home-made teas at Filkins Village Hall.**

ANSTRUTHER
Nicky & Stephen Evans.

BROUGHTON POGGS MILL
Charlie & Avril Payne.

THE CORN BARN
Ms Alexis Thompson.

THE FIELD HOUSE
Peter & Sheila Gray.

FILKINS ALLOTMENTS
Filkins Allotments.

FILKINS HALL
LITTLE PEACOCKS
Colvin & Moggridge.
MERCHANTS COTTAGE
Paul & Corina Floyd.
MUFFITIES
PEACOCK FARMHOUSE
Pauline & Peter Care.
PIGEON COTTAGE
Lynne Savege.
PIP COTTAGE
G B Woodin.
TAYLOR COTTAGE
Mrs Ronnie Bailey.

13 gardens and flourishing allotments in these beautiful and vibrant Cotswold stone twin villages. Scale and character vary from the grand landscape setting of Filkins Hall, to the small but action packed Pigeon Cottage, Taylor Cottage, Muffities and Corn Barn. Broughton Poggs Mill has a rushing mill stream with an exciting bridge; Pip Cottage combines topiary, box hedges and a fine rural view. In these and the other equally exciting and varied gardens horticultural interest abounds. Features inc Swinford Museum of Cotswolds tools and artefacts, and Cotswold Woollen Weavers and Saxon church will be open. Many gardens have gravel driveways, but most are suitable for wheelchair access. Most gardens welcome dogs on leads.

10 BUSH HOUSE
Wigginton Road, South Newington, Banbury, OX15 4JR. Mr John Ainley, 07503 361050, rojoainley@btinternet.com. *In S Newington on A361 from Banbury to Chipping Norton, take 1st R to Wigginton, Bush House 1st house on the L in Wigginton Rd.* **Visits by arrangement Mar to Oct. Adm inc Bush House and South Newington House with refreshments. Adm £12, chd free. Tea, coffee & cake at South Newington House.**
Set in eight acres, over 13 years, a two acre garden has emerged. Herbaceous borders partner dual level ponds and stream. The terrace leads to a walled parterre framed by roses and wisteria. The 'wildflower meadow' (sown 2021) orchard is screened by rose and vine covered wrought iron trellis. Kitchen gardens, greenhouses and fruit cage provide organically grown produce. Stream and interconnecting ponds. Walled parterre and knot garden. 1000 native broadleaved trees planted 2006, 2011 and 2014. Gravel drive, a few small steps, and two gentle grass slopes on either side of the garden.

11 CHALKHOUSE GREEN FARM
Chalkhouse Green, Kidmore End, Reading, RG4 9AL. Mr J Hall, www.chgfarm.com. *2m N of Reading, 5m SW of Henley-on-Thames. Situated between A4074 & B481. From Kidmore End take Chalkhouse Green Rd. Follow yellow signs.* **Sun 22 June (2-6). Adm £4, chd free.**
One acre garden and open traditional farmstead. Herbaceous borders, herb garden, shrubs, old fashioned roses, trees inc medlar, quince and mulberries, walled ornamental kitchen garden and cherry orchard. Rare breed farm animals inc British White cattle, Suffolk Punch horses, donkeys, geese, chickens, ducks and turkeys. Features inc plant and jam stall, donkey rides, grass tennis court, trailer rides, farm trail, WWII bomb shelter, heavy horse and bee display. Partial wheelchair access.

12 CHIVEL FARM
Heythrop, OX7 5TR. John & Rosalind Sword, 01608 683227, rosalind.sword@btinternet.com. *4m E of Chipping Norton. Off A361 or A44. Parking at Chivel Farm.* **Visits by arrangement Feb to Sept for groups of 10+.**
Beautifully designed country garden with extensive views, designed for continuous interest that is always evolving. Colour schemed borders with many unusual trees, shrubs and herbaceous plants. Small formal white garden and a conservatory.

13 CHRIST CHURCH MASTERS, POCOCKE & CATHEDRAL GARDENS
St Aldate's, Oxford, OX1 1DP. Christ Church, www.chch.ox.ac.uk/visit/gardens. *5 mins walk from Oxford city centre. Entry from St Aldate's through the Memorial Gardens, into Christ Church Meadow, then turn L into Masters' Garden gate after main visitor entrance. No parking available.* **Sat 6 Sept (10-4). Adm £8, chd free.**
3 walled gardens, not normally open to visitors, with herbaceous, shrub, Mediterranean and tropical borders. Inc the magnificent 'Jabberwocky' Tree, an Oriental Plane planted in the mid 1600s, as well as other links to Alice in Wonderland, St Frideswide and Harry Potter. Wheelchair access over gravel paths.

GROUP OPENING

14 NEW CHRISTMAS COMMON GARDENS
Christmas Common, OX49 5HW. *9½ m W of High Wycombe. From Watlington: coming from Oxford M40 to J6. Turn R & go to Watlington. Turn L up Hill Rd to top. Turn R after 50yds, turn L into field to park.* **Sat 14 June (1-6). Combined adm £8, chd free. Home-made teas at Priors Grove Cottage.**

MEADOW COTTAGE
Mrs Zelda Kent-Lemon.
NEW THE OLD CHURCH HALL
Judy Jordan.
NEW PRIORS GROVE COTTAGE
Sue Yerburgh.

Sitting at one of the highest points of the Chilterns AONB, visitors to this picturesque area can explore 3 distinct gardens, each offering their own charm and character. Priors Grove Cottage: Over ½ an acre and bordered by woodland, this 6 yr old garden is focussed around a large wildlife pond and waterfall. Koi Carp are separated from the surrounding wildlife by an island with planting. A formal lily pond can be found on the terrace. A mixture of shrubs and herbaceous plants ensure vibrant displays throughout the year. Meadow Cottage: Enchanting 1¾ acre garden adjoins ancient woodlands and inc a wildflower garden, tranquil pond, fruit trees, and a variety of shrubs. The garden has indigenous trees and features a historic C17 barn (not open). The Old Church Hall: This charming cottage garden embraces a relaxed and informal style, allowing many self-seeded varieties to flourish naturally. Colourful and interesting herbaceous beds flank the lawn path, which leads around the garden. Partial wheelchair access over gravel driveways and lawns.

15 CLARIDGES BARN
Charlbury Road, Chipping Norton, OX7 5XG. Drs David & Jill Edwards, 07973 129473, drdavidedwards@hotmail.co.uk. *3m SE of Chipping Norton. Take B4026 from Chipping Norton to Charlbury after 3 m turn R to Dean, we are 200 metres on the R. Please park on the verge.* **Sat 22, Sun 23 Mar, Sat 26, Sun 27 Apr (11-5). Adm £5, chd free. Fri 13, Sat 14 June (11-5). Combined adm with Sandys House £7, chd free. Light refreshments inc coffee & light lunches. Wine is available for evening openings. Visits also by arrangement Mar to Sept.**
3½ acres of family garden, wood and meadow hewn from a barley field on limestone brash. Situated on top of the Cotswolds, it is open to all weathers, but rewarding views and dog walking opportunities on hand. Large vegetable, fruit and cutting garden, wildlife pond and five cedar greenhouses, all loved by rabbits, deer and squirrel. Herbaceous borders and woodland gardens with gravel and flagged paths, divided by stone walls. Claridges Barn dates back to the 1600s, the cottage 1860s, converted about 35 yrs ago. Plants for sale. Mainly level site with flagstone and gravel paths, flat lawns and some uneven steps. The gravel driveway can be hard work for wheelchair users.

&♿ 🐾 ✻ 🚗 ☕ 🔊

16 NEW COPPER CORNERS
Mill Lane, Chalgrove, Oxford, OX44 7SL. Mrs Fiona Giles, 07960 992798, fiona.giles@hotmail.co.uk. *12m E of Oxford, 4m W of Watlington off B480. Copper Corners in Mill Ln W Chalgrove, 400 yds from The Lamb PH. RHS after white bridge railings behind red hedge. Park on property.* **Visits by arrangement June to Sept for groups of 5 to 25. Adm £5, chd free. Tea, coffee & cake.**
A three acre wildlife friendly informal family garden backing onto farmland with the mill brook forming one boundary. Large front garden - mostly lawn with large mixed, all-season border in front of house and mature native trees. Back garden of mixed borders and mature fruit trees. Paddock with mature native trees, inc magnificent aspens and enclosed vegetable garden. Access to main garden - all on one level but all grass.

&♿ ☕

17 NEW 29 CORBETT ROAD
Carterton, OX18 3LG. Mr & Mrs Alina and John Curtis. *SW edge of Carterton off Alvescot Rd. Corbett Rd is located ½ m along on the L of Alvescot Rd from the town centre Xrds.* **Sun 18 May, Sun 22 June (12-4). Adm £3.50, chd free. Tea, coffee & cake.**
Mixed variety garden on the edge of Carterton, with lawns, specimen trees, flower borders, raised vegetable beds, mixed hedging, gravel and grass surfaces, with a large patio. On 3 stepped levels with a variety of self seeded and mixed meadow plants to encourage wildlife. The front lawn is of wildflowers and meadow grasses, inc cyclamen, primulas and an occasional wild orchid.

☕

18 NEW 61 CORNISH ROAD
Chipping Norton, OX7 5JX. Matthias Gentet, darcydante@gmail.com. *Towards Churchill on the B4450, take last L before leaving Chipping Norton. Go up on Hailey Rd then 1st R turn into Cornish Rd then down 500 metres. Garden is on the RHS.* **Fri 9, Fri 30 May, Fri 13, Fri 27 June, Fri 11, Fri 25 July, Fri 15 Aug, Fri 5 Sept (10-3). Adm £4, chd free. Pre-booking essential, please visit www.ngs.org.uk for information & booking. Visits also by arrangement 9 May to 5 Sept for groups of up to 10.**
Small residential garden created from scratch, consisting of shrubs, herbaceous/perennials and rose beds and borders with over 60 roses (shrubs, standards and climbers), wisteria, soft fruits and fruit trees, raised beds, all of which with the aim of accommodating as many varieties of plants as possible; composting bins and a lean-to greenhouse.

☕ 🔊

19 CORPUS CHRISTI COLLEGE
Merton Street, Oxford, OX1 4JF. Domestic Bursar, www.ccc.ox.ac.uk/about-corpus/corpus-garden. *Just off Oxford High St. Entrance from Merton St.* **Sun 13 Apr (10-4). Adm £5, chd free. Home-made teas in the Old Lodgings.**
Said by some to have inspired Lewis Carroll, the gates of Corpus conceal winding passageways linking several distinctive quads filled with historical and botanical curiosities like pelican sundials, Kings' gates and "fossil trees". At the rear of the college sits the main garden with its huge copper beech, old town walls, and views over Christ Church and its meadows. Features inc Pelican Sundial, King Charles Gate and the City walls. Wheelchair access with one slope in the garden.

&♿ ☕ 🔊

20 DEAN MANOR
Dean, Chipping Norton, OX7 3LD. Mr & Mrs Johnny Hornby, 07786 110561, pippa.hornby@gmail.com. *In Dean, 3 m SE of Chipping Norton. Leaving Chipping Norton follow the B4026 for 2 m. At the sharp bend, take the 2nd turning to the R to Dean (there is no road sign). Follow the lane for 1 m, Dean Manor is R at the next junction.* **Thur 19 June (11-5). Adm £9, chd free. Home-made teas inc ice cream teas. Visits also by arrangement.**
The gardens at Dean Manor cover approx six acres. Stone walls are home to an abundant and varied selection of climbing/rambling roses, clematis and hydrangeas. The formal gardens inc complex yew hedging and herbaceous borders, kitchen and cutting garden, areas of wildflower meadow, an orchard and water gardens make up areas around the house. A spectacular new kitchen and cutting garden designed by Frances Rasch complete with new large glasshouse is currently in development, offering the opportunity to witness the beginnings of a major new chapter in the garden's rich history.

&♿ ✻ ☕ 🔊

21 103 DENE ROAD
Headington, Oxford, OX3 7EQ. Steve & Mary Woolliams, 07778 617616, stevewoolliams@gmail.com. *S Headington, nr Nuffield. Dene Rd accessed from The Slade from the N, or from Hollow Way from the S. Both access roads are B4495.* **Garden on sharp bend. Visits by arrangement 12 Apr to 14 Sept for groups of up to 12. Adm £4, chd free. Tea, coffee & cake.**
A surprising eco-friendly garden with borrowed view over the Lye Valley Nature Reserve. Lawns, a wildflower meadow, pond and large kitchen garden are inc in a gently sloping 60ft x 120ft site. Fruit trees, soft fruit and mixed borders of shrubs, hardy perennials, grasses and bulbs, designed for seasonal colour. This garden has been noted for its wealth of wildlife inc a variety of birds,

butterflies and other insects such as the rare Brown Hairstreak butterfly, the rare Currant Clearwing moth and the Grizzled Skipper.

22 DENTON HOUSE
Denton, Oxford, OX44 9JF. Mr & Mrs Luke, 01865 874440, waveneyluke28@gmail.com. *Nr Oxford. In a valley between Garsington & Cuddesdon.* **Visits by arrangement Feb to Oct for groups of up to 30. Adm £6, chd free. Home-made teas.**
Large walled garden surrounds a Georgian mansion (not open) with shaded areas, walks, topiary and many interesting mature trees, large lawns, herbaceous borders and rose beds. The windows in the wall were taken in 1864 from Brasenose College Chapel and Library. Wild garden and a further walled fruit garden. separate access for wheelchairs without steps.

23 FAILFORD
118 Oxford Road, Abingdon, OX14 2AG. Miss R Aylward, 01235 523925, aylwardsdooz@hotmail.co.uk. *North Abingdon. Entrance is via 116 Oxford Rd. No. 118 is on L of Oxford Rd after Picklers Hill when coming from Abingdon Town, or on R when approaching from the A34 Abingdon N.* **Sun 8 June (11-4). Combined adm with 116 Oxford Road £6, chd free. Home-made teas.** Visits also by arrangement in June for groups of 10 to 30.
This town garden is an extension of the home divided into rooms both formal and informal. It changes every year. Features inc walkways through shaded areas, arches, a beach, grasses, fernery, roses, topiaries, acers, hostas and heucheras.
Be inspired by the wide variety of planting, many unusual and quirky features, all within an area 570sq ft.

24 FOXINGTON
Britwell Salome, Watlington, OX49 5LG. Mrs Mary Roadnight, 01491 612418, mary@foxington.co.uk. *1 m from Watlington. On B4009 at Red Lion Pub take turning to Britwell Hill. After 350yds turn into drive on L.* **Visits by arrangement 26 Apr to 22 June for groups of 10 to 30. Adm £11, chd free. Home-made teas inc in adm price. Special dietary options by prior request.**
Stunning views to the Chiltern Hills provide a wonderful setting for this impressive garden remodelled in 2009. Patio, heather and gravel gardens enjoy this view, whilst the back and vegetable gardens are more enclosed. A very large apple tree blew down in the spring of 2022 and has been replaced by a summerhouse. This has resulted in a major revision of the planting. There is an orchard and a flock of white doves. Well behaved dogs are welcome but they must be kept on a lead at all times as there are many wild animals in the garden. Wildflower meadow, wood and neighbouring fields. Wheelchair access throughout the garden on level paths with no steps.

Priors Grove Cottage, Christmas Common Gardens

25 FRIARS COURT
Clanfield, OX18 2SU. Charles Willmer, www.friarscourt.com. *4m N of Faringdon. On A4095 Faringdon to Witney road. ½ m S of Clanfield. What3words app: burst.courts.from.* **Sun 8 June (2-5). Adm £4, chd free. Cream teas.**
Over three acres of formal and informal gardens with flower beds, borders and specimen trees, lie within the remaining arms of a C16 moat which partially surrounds the large C17 Cotswold stone house. Bridges span the moat with water-lily-filled ponds to the front whilst beyond the gardens is a woodland walk. A museum about Friars Court is located in the old Coach House. A level path goes around part of the gardens. The museum is accessed over gravel.
& 🐎 ☕ 🔊

26 THE GRANGE
1 Berrick Road, Chalgrove, OX44 7RQ. Mrs Vicky Farren, 01865 400883, vickyfarren@mac.com, www.thegrangegardener.com. *12m E of Oxford & 4m from Watlington, off B480. The entrance to The Grange is at the grass triangle between Berrick Rd & Monument Rd, by the pedestrian crossing. GPS is not reliable in the final 200yds.* **Visits by arrangement 1 June to 27 Oct for groups of 10 to 35. Adm £8, chd free. Home made teas can be separately arranged.**
11 acres of gardens inc herbaceous borders and a large expanse of prairie with many grasses and a wildflower meadow. There is a lake with bridges and a planted island, a dry river bed and a labyrinth. A brook runs through the garden with a further pond, arboretum, old orchard and partly walled vegetable garden. Partial wheelchair access on many grass paths.
& 🐎 🚗 ☕

27 GREEN AND GORGEOUS
Little Stoke, Wallingford, OX10 6AX. Rachel Siegfried, www.greenandgorgeousflowers.co.uk. *3m S of Wallingford. Off B4009 between N & S Stoke, follow single track road down to farm.* **Sun 29 June (1-5). Adm £6, chd free. Tea, coffee & cake.**
6 acre working flower farm next to River Thames. Cut flowers (many unusual varieties) in large plots and polytunnels, planted with combination of annuals, bulbs, perennials, roses and shrubs, plus some herbs, vegetables and fruit to feed the workers! Flowers selected for scent, novelty, nostalgia, weather tolerance and naturalistic style. Hourly floristry demonstrations, cut flowers, lots of plants for sale and craft stalls. Wheelchair access on short grass paths, with large concrete areas.
& 🐎 ❄ ☕

28 GREENFIELD FARM
Christmas Common, nr Watlington, OX49 5HG. Andrew & Jane Ingram, 01491 612434, andrew@andrewbingram.com. *4m from J5 M40, 7m from Henley. J5 M40, A40 towards Oxford for ½ m, turn L signed Christmas Common. ¾ m past Fox & Hounds Pub, turn L at Tree Barn sign.* **Visits by arrangement 5 May to 14 Sept for groups of 5 to 30. Adm £5, chd free.**
10 acre wildflower meadow surrounded by woodland, established 28 yrs ago under the Countryside Stewardship Scheme. Traditional Chiltern chalkland meadow in beautiful peaceful setting with 100 species of perennial wildflowers, grasses and ten species of orchids. ½ mile walk from parking area to meadow. Opportunity to return via typical Chiltern beechwood.
🐎 🚗

29 HAM COURT
Ham Court Farm, Weald, Bampton, OX18 2HG. Matthew Rice. *Drive through the village towards Clanfield. The drive is on the R, exactly opp Weald St.* **Sun 7 Sept (11-4). Adm £7.50, chd free. Home-made teas.**
Several acres of garden, orchard and paddock surround the last gatehouse fragment of the medieval Bampton Castle, partially moated with walled kitchen garden, a productive greenhouse and farmyard with a variety of farm animals. This project begun by Emma Bridgewater and Matthew Rice is 12 yrs old so now 'bearing fruit' but will always be in a state of permanent change. Delicious teas and vintage tractors.
& ☕

30 6 HIGH STREET
Cumnor, Oxford, OX2 9PE. Dr Dianne & Prof Keith Gull. *4m from central Oxford. Exit to Cumnor from the A420. In centre of village opp Post Office. Parking at back of Post Office.* **Sun 9 Feb (2-5); Sun 8 June (2-6). Adm £3, chd free.**
Front, side and rear garden of a thatched cottage. Front is partly gravelled and side courtyard has many pots. Rear garden overlooks meadows with old apple trees underplanted with ferns, wildlife pond, unusual plants, many with black or bronze foliage, planted in drifts and repeated throughout the garden. Planting has mild Japanese influence; rounded, clipped shapes interspersed with verticals. There are two pubs in the village serving food; The Bear & Ragged Staff and The Vine, the former has accommodation. Wheelchair access to garden via gravel drive.
& 🐎 ❄ 🚗 🔊

31 19 HIGH STREET
Cumnor, Oxford, OX2 9PE. Janet Cross. *5½ m W of Oxford. A34 onto A420 heading W. Take exit onto B4017. Follow signs for Cumnor. Take 2nd exit at r'about and garden is 100 metres on L.* **Sun 1 June (12-5). Combined adm with Archangel House £5, chd free.**
Sun and shade: a courtyard garden with paths and gravel beds. The shade loving trees and plants with their varying foliage give a special brand of colour. A pergola and pots add to the architectural features of the design and ornamental benches provide seating to enjoy this unusual garden.
🔊

32 HOME CLOSE, GARSINGTON
29 Southend, Garsington, OX44 9DH. Mrs M Waud & Dr P Giangrande, 01865 361394, m.waud@btinternet.com. *3m SE of Oxford. N of B480, opp Garsington Manor.* **Visits by arrangement May to Sept. Adm £6, chd free. Refreshments can be made available upon request.**
Two acre garden with listed house (not open), listed granary and one acre mixed tree plantation. Unusual trees and shrubs planted for year-round effect. Terraces, stone walls and hedges divide the garden and the planting, which inc topiary, reflects a Mediterranean interest. Vegetable garden, orchard and woodland garden. Countryside views to the south of the garden.
🚗 ☕

GROUP OPENING

33 IFFLEY GARDENS
Iffley, Oxford, OX4 4EF. *2m S of Oxford. Within Oxford's ring road, off A4158 Iffley road, from Magdalen Bridge to Littlemore r'about, to Iffley village. Map provided at each garden.* **Sun 8 June (2-6). Combined adm £6, chd free. Tea, coffee & cake in Church Hall and 25 Abberbury Road.**

17 ABBERBURY ROAD
Mrs Julie Steele.

50 CHURCH WAY
William and Sarah Beaver.

6 FITZHERBERT CLOSE
Eunice Martin.

NEW MANOR HOUSE
Mr Sam Webster & Mr Thomas Hale.

THE PRIORY
Nanda Pirie.

4A TREE LANE
Pemma & Nick Spencer-Chapman.

Secluded old village with renowned Norman church. Visit several gardens ranging in variety and style. Mixed family gardens with shady borders and vegetables. Varied planting throughout the gardens inc herbaceous borders, shade loving plants, roses, fine specimen trees and plants in terracing. Features inc a small Japanese garden. Plant sales at several gardens. Wheelchair access to some gardens.

&. ✿ ☕))

GROUP OPENING

34 KENCOT GARDENS
Kencot, Lechlade, GL7 3QT. *5m NE of Lechlade. E of A361 between Burford & Lechlade.* **Mon 21 Apr (2-6). Combined adm £6, chd free. Tea, coffee & cake at village hall.**

THE ALLOTMENTS
Amelia Carter Charity.

BELHAM HAYES
Mr Joseph Jones.

IVY NOOK
Gill & Wally Cox.

MANOR FARM
Henry & Kate Fyson.

NEW QUENTON HOUSE
Henny and Rupert Haworth-Booth.

WELL HOUSE
Janet & Richard Wheeler.

The 2025 group consists of 5 gardens and allotments. The Allotments: Tended by 9 people, growing a variety of vegetables, flowers and fruit. Belham Hayes: Mature cottage garden, mixed herbaceous borders, 2 old fruit trees, vegetables. Emphasis on scent and colour coordination. Manor Farm: 2 acre walled garden Grade II C17 house (not open) with bulbs, wood anemones, fritillaries, mature orchards, pleached limewalk, clipped 130 yr old yew balls, revolving summerhouse. A greenhouse with ancient Black Hamburg vine. Well House: ⅓ acre garden, mature trees, hedges, miniature woodland glade, brook with waterfall. Spring bulbs, rockeries. ⅓ acre garden, 2 old apple trees, old well, herbaceous beds. Rear garden newly planted with perennial borders and bulbs pots of seasonal flowers. Ivy Nook: Medium sized garden, mixed borders with spring bulbs, vegetable garden, greenhouse, small pond and magnolia tree. Quenton House: Vegetable garden with yew hedging. The rear of the property is a mixture of herbaceous borders, shaded areas and wildflower areas. Wheelchair access to The Allotments, difficult due to step entrance and narrow paths. Other gardens maybe difficult due to gravel and uneven paths.

&. 🐕 🚗 ☕))

35 KINGHAM LODGE
West End, Kingham, Chipping Norton, OX7 6YL. Christopher Stockwell, 01608 658226, info@sculptureatkinghamlodge.com, www.sculptureatkinghamlodge.com. *Kingham Village. From Kingham Village, West St turns into West End at tree in middle of road, bear R & you will see black gates for Kingham Lodge immed on L. Follow signs for parking. Do not park on street.* **Wed 21 May (10.30-5). Adm £8, chd free. Pre-booking essential, please phone 01608 658226, email info@sculptureatkinghamlodge.com or visit www.sculptureatkinghamlodge.com for information & booking. Cream teas.**

Many ericaceous plants not normally seen in the Cotswolds grow on 6 acres of garden, planted over 3 decades. Big display of rhododendron, laburnum arch and azaleas. Formal 150 metre border, backed with trellis, shaded walks with multi-layered planting, an informal quarry pond, formal mirror pond, pergola, parterre and unique Islamic garden with rills and fountains. Sculpture show from 16-26 May 2025. Disabled parking on gravel at entrance and level access to all areas of the garden.

&. 🐕 🛏 ☕))

36 KINGS COTTAGE
Pudlicote Lane, Chilson, Chipping Norton, OX7 3HU. Mr Michael Anderson, 07771 861928, michaelfanderson66@outlook.com. *S end of Chilson village. Entering Chilson from the S, off the B4437 Charlbury to Burford road, 1st house on the L. Please drive past & park considerately in centre of village.* **Sun 4, Mon 5 May, Sun 24, Mon 25 Aug (1-5). Combined adm with Bolters Farm £8, chd free. Tea, coffee & cake inc gluten free options. Visits also by arrangement May & June for groups of 10+. Adm inc refreshments.**

An old row of cottages with mature trees, yew hedging, orchard and perennial and seasonal beds. Over the last nine years a new design and planting scheme has been started to reduce the areas of lawn, bring in planting to complement the house (not open) and setting, introduce new borders and encourage wildlife. Partial wheelchair access via gravel drive and grass paths. Moderate slopes, grass and some sections of garden only accessible via steps.

&. 🐕 ✿ ☕))

In 2024, National Garden Scheme funding for Perennial supported 1,367 people working in horticulture.

37 38 LECKFORD ROAD
Oxford, OX2 6HY. Dinah Adams. *Central Oxford. N on Woodstock Rd take 3rd L. Coming into Oxford on Woodstock Rd, 1st R after Farndon Rd. Some 2 hr parking nearby.* **Sun 27 Apr (2-5). Combined adm with 50 Plantation Road £8, chd free. Tea, coffee & cake.**
Behind the rather severe façade of a Victorian town house (not open) is a very protected long walled garden with mature trees. The planting reflects the varied levels of shade and inc rare and unusual plants. The trees in the front garden deserve attention. The back garden is divided into 3 distinct parts, each with a very different character. Amongst other things there is a hornbeam roof.

38 LIME CLOSE
35 Henleys Lane, Drayton, Abingdon, OX14 4HU.
M C de Laubarede, mail@mclgardendesign.com, www.mclgardendesign.com. *2m S of Abingdon. Henleys Ln is off main road through Drayton. When visiting Lime Cl, please respect local residents & park considerately.* **Sun 18 May (2-5.30); Sun 26 Oct (2-5). Adm £5, chd free. Home-made teas.** Visits also by arrangement 15 Jan to 15 Nov for groups of 10+. Donation to International Dendrology Society.
Five acre plantsman's garden with rare trees, shrubs, roses and bulbs. Mixed borders, raised beds, pergola, topiary and shade borders. Herb garden by Rosemary Verey. C16 house (not open). Cottage garden by MCL Garden Design, planted for colour, an iris garden with 100 varieties. Winter bulbs. Arboretum with rare exotic trees and shrubs from Asia and America and new field planted by continents. The garden is flat and mostly grass with gravel drive and paths.

39 NEW LINCOLN COLLEGE
Turl Street, Oxford, OX1 3DR. *100 metres N on Turl St from High St or 120 metres S on Turl St from Broad St.* **Sun 3 Aug (11-3). Adm £6, chd free. Open nearby Trinity College.**
Lincoln is one of the University of Oxford's oldest colleges, founded in 1427. The gardens offer formal lawns, mixed borders in traditional and contemporary styles, container displays, climbing plants and mature trees. The gardens are laid out in the classic quadrangle style, where each passageway leads into a different 'room', creating a uniquely varied horticultural and architectural experience.

40 MAGDALEN COLLEGE
Oxford, OX1 4AU. Magdalen College, www.magd.ox.ac.uk. *Oxford. Entrance in High St.* **Sun 13 Apr (10-7). Adm £9.50, chd £8.50. Light refreshments in the Old Kitchen Bar.**
60 acres inc deer park, college lawns, numerous trees 150-200 yrs old; notable herbaceous and shrub plantings. Magdalen meadow where purple and white snake's head fritillaries can be found is surrounded by Addison's Walk, a tree lined circuit by the River Cherwell developed since the late C18. Ancient herd of 60 deer.

Archangel House

41 26 MANOR FARM ROAD
Dorchester-on-Thames, Wallingford, OX10 7HZ. David & Judy Parker. *8m SSE of Oxford. Off A4074, signed from village centre. Parking at Bridge Meadow, at SE end of the bridge. Parking in the drive for disabled visitors only.* **Sun 29 June (2-5). Combined adm with 6 Monks Close £5, chd free. Home-made teas in the tearoom at Abbey Guesthouse.**
Originally part of a larger, old garden, this one slopes down to the River Thame with a lovely view of Dorchester Abbey. Close to the house (not open) there are formal gardens, a vegetable garden and greenhouse. Between the yew hedge and the river are apple trees, old and new, underplanted with spring bulbs, and on the river bank, over by the wall, there is a variegated Turkey oak tree. On the driveway there is space for several cars for disabled visitors and visitors with wheelchairs. Access for wheelchairs to all parts of garden.

& ☕

42 THE MANOR GARDEN
The Manor House, Berry Lane, Blewbury, OX11 9QJ. *4m SE of Didcot. In the middle of the Berry Ln. Black metal grid gates. Parking at the village hall (2 min walk). 3 disabled parking spaces by the house.* **Sun 11 May (11-5). Adm £5, chd free. Tea, coffee & cake in the barn and courtyard. Provided by the local WI.**
100% organic 10 acre garden with the owners striving to make it as wildlife friendly as possible. Natural springs from chalk Downs flow through the village and converge in the grounds. The large lake, with 2 islands, has trout and is favoured by various birds. Great attention to detail has gone into visual sight lines that lead the eye through each aspect of the garden. The main lawn leads down to the moat, with views through to sunken dial garden surrounded by hornbeam 'cloistered' hedge. Moat, lake, streams, dial garden, wild beehives, wildlife supporting initiatives, organic gardening, formal and wild gardens.

& 🚗 ☕ 🔊

43 MERTON COLLEGE OXFORD FELLOWS' GARDEN
Merton Street, Oxford, OX1 4JD. Merton College, 01865 276310, www.facebook.com/ MertonGardens. *Merton St runs parallel to High St about halfway down.* **Sun 20 July (10-5). Adm £8, chd free.**
Ancient mulberry, said to have associations with James I. Specimen trees, long mixed border, recently established herbaceous bed. View of Christ Church meadow.

& 🔊

GROUP OPENING

44 MIDDLETON CHENEY GARDENS
Middleton Cheney, Banbury, OX17 2ST. *3m E of Banbury. Parking on Main Rd between primary school & library (OX17 2PD) for access to Upper & Lower Middleton. Open garden maps available at the library.* **Sun 8 June (1-6). Combined adm £8, chd free. Home-made teas at Peartree House.**

NEW **5 CENTENARY ROAD**
Kim Woodlock.

CROFT HOUSE
Richard & Sandy Walmsley.

19 GLOVERS LANE
Michael Donohoe & Jane Rixon.

LEXTON HOUSE
Matthew & Diane Tims.

38 MIDWAY
Margaret & David Finch.

PEARTREE HOUSE
Roger & Barbara Charlesworth.

POPLARS FARMHOUSE
Ruth & Martin Edwards.

2A RECTORY LANE
Debbie Evans.

Large village with C13 church (open) with renowned pre-Raphaelite stained glass. Eight open gardens with a variety of sizes, styles and maturity. Of the smaller gardens, one modern garden contrasts formal features with colour-filled borders and exotic plants, another with flowing curves feels restrained and serene. A mature small front and back garden is planted profusely with a feel of an intimate haven. A new-build garden provides a peaceful setting whilst inc many features - rockery, topiary, pond with waterfall, borders. A stately garden inc a formal terrace surrounded by hedges and fig trees with steps down to secluded lower space and small vegetable garden. A large garden has colourful cottage planting and vegetable garden. Another has an air of mystery with hidden corners and an extensive water feature weaving its way throughout the garden. A family garden with mature mixed planting inc a secret garden.

& 🐕 ❀ ☕

45 MIDSUMMER HOUSE
Woolstone, Faringdon, SN7 7QL. Penny Spink. *7m W & 7m S of Faringdon. Woolstone is a small village off B4507, below Uffington White Horse Hill. Take road towards Uffington from the White Horse Pub.* **Fri 2 May, Fri 6 June (2-5). Fri 4 July (2-5), open nearby Woolstone Mill House. Fri 1 Aug, Fri 5 Sept, Fri 3 Oct (2-5). Adm £5, chd free. Home-made teas.**
Midsummer Garden was designed by Justin Spink for his parents, Anthony and Penny Spink, in 2015. In 2018 Mike and Ann Collins continued designing and planting the garden. Over the road there is a newly planted arboretum and nature reserve established 2019. Rare and unusual plants. Picnics welcome in the field opp. Wheelchair access over short gravel drive at entrance.

& ❀ 🚗 ☕ 🔊

46 MILL BARN
25 Mill Lane, Chalgrove, OX44 7SL. Pat Hougham, 01865 890020, Gmec@outlook.com. *12m E of Oxford. Chalgrove is 4m from Watlington off B480. Mill Barn is in Mill Ln, W of Chalgrove, 300yds S of Lamb Pub.* **Visits by arrangement May to Sept. Adm £4, chd free. Cream teas.**
Mill Barn is an informal cottage garden set in a millstream landscape. It has 12 herbaceous borders with displays of flowers throughout the seasons that inc a variety of roses. A pergola covered in grape vines and roses lead to a vegetable plot surrounded by a cordon of fruit trees. A variety of fruit trees throughout the garden inc mulberry, medlar and quince.

& 🐕 ☕

47 MILL HOUSE GARDEN
Fernham Road, Uffington, Faringdon, SN7 7RD. Rupert & Julia Lycett Green. Turn into Fernham Rd by the Tom Brown Museum. After 100 metres, turn into the private road marked 'Grounds Farm', Mill House is the 1st open gate on L. **Sun 8 June** (11.30-5). Adm £5, chd free. Light refreshments inc tea, lemonade and cakes.
Wonderful setting overlooking the Uffington White Horse and wide views of the Downs. 1 acre garden divided into seasonal rooms connecting around the house. A walled garden leads into a lawned room of box-edged beds and follows into a spring garden and out to a wild growing bank and a rill following the course of the old mill race. Lastly, a vegetable garden with roses and cutting beds. Wheelchair access to central garden and then sloping grass paths to top garden. Exit possible through top stable yard.

48 6 MONKS CLOSE
Dorchester-on-Thames, Wallingford, OX10 7JA. Leif & Petronella Rasmussen. *8m SSE of Oxford. Off A4074 signed from village centre. Parking at Bridge Meadow at SE end of Dorchester Bridge. Follow signs down Manor Farm Rd to Monks Cl.* **Sun 29 June** (2-5). Combined adm with 26 Manor Farm Road £5, chd free.
At 6 Monks Close a small spring-fed stream and sloping lawn, surrounded by naturalistic planting, runs down to a monastic fish pond. Bridges over this deep pond lead to the River Thame with steep banks. Children should be accompanied.

The National Garden Scheme donated £281,000 in 2024 to support those looking to work in horticulture as well as those struggling within the industry.

SPECIAL EVENT

50 NEW COLLEGE, THE WARDEN'S GARDEN
Holywell Street, Oxford, OX1 3BN. www.new.ox.ac.uk. *No parking available. Garden entrance from New College Lane, off Catte St.* **Mon 16 June (3-6.30). Adm £50.** Pre-booking essential, please visit www.ngs.org.uk for information & booking. Light refreshments.
This special event takes place in the Warden's private garden which isn't open to members of the public; It is an Oxford secret. The event will begin with Tea in the Warden's garden followed by a short lecture on New College. After this, visitors are given a private tour of the College and garden from The Warden, Miles Young. The College gardens, which have been developed and curated for by a distinguished series of Garden Fellows over the generations, most recently by Robin Lane-Fox. A highlight of the garden is the long herbaceous border, set against the medieval City wall.

GROUP OPENING

51 NEW NORTH HINKSEY GARDENS
North Hinksey Lane, Oxford, OX2 0LX. *Gardens are on North Hinksey Ln and on Halliday Ln. From Botley Rd at McDonalds, near A34 junc turn into N Hinksey Ln. Halliday Ln (pvt road no parking) is on R after cemetery. Parking at Botley WI Hall (OX2 0LT) or on street further S on N Hinksey Ln.* **Sun 20 July (2-5.30). Combined adm £6, chd free.** Home-made teas at 3 Halliday Lane.

3 HALLIDAY LANE
John and Viccy Fleming.

4 HALLIDAY LANE
Mr Nathaniel Ward.

NEW 50-52 NORTH HINKSEY LANE
John & Mary Lines.

Each of this group of 3 town gardens is different. Two are relatively new:3 Halliday Lane is intensively planted with a crevice garden with alpines at the front. 4 Halliday Lane is a family garden with both formally planted beds and a meadow area. Opening for the first time is 50/52 North Hinksey Lane. This has a more open aspect with colourful beds set on a sloping site.

52 THE OLD RECTORY, ALBURY
Albury, Thame, OX9 2LP. Mr & Mrs J Nowell-Smith, 01844 339650, Moonowellsmith@gmail.com. *Off A418 Wheatley to Thame road, 5 m from Thame. From Tiddington, turn R onto single track road before 50mph signs.* Visits by arrangement for groups of up to 30. Adm £5, chd free. Tea, coffee & cake.
5 acres of extensive herbaceous borders, rose avenue, woodland and lake walk, kitchen and cutting gardens. Surrounded by orchards and the glebe land with some beautiful mature trees with close access to Fernhill Wood, famous for bluebells. There is extensive planting of snowdrops and early bulbs, followed by perpetual roses, and continual herbaceous and annual planting. Sculptures by Andy Goldsworth and Tom Stogdon.

53 THE OLD SCHOOL
Langford, GL7 3LF. David Freeman, 01367 860283, davidg. freeman@btinternet.com. *Opp the Bell Inn at Langford. 1 m from A361.* Visits by arrangement for groups of 5 to 15. Adm £12, chd £6. Teas, coffee or glass of wine or soft drink.
Small formal garden designed in 1973 by the late Sir Hardy Amies KCVO, with advice from Rosemary Verey and Alvilde Lees-Milne. Inc collection of old roses *Rosa de Rescht, Ferdinand Pichard, Rosa Mundi, Etoile de Holland*. Former home of the late Sir Hardy Amies KCVO, dressmaker to her late Majesty Queen Elizabeth II. Here he designed a highly structured walled garden in the former village playground.

54 116 OXFORD ROAD
Abingdon, OX14 2AG. Mr & Mrs P Aylward, 01235 523925, aylwardsdooz@hotmail.co.uk. *North Abingdon. On R if coming from A34 N Abingdon exit, or on L after the Picklers Hill turn if approaching from Abingdon town centre.* **Sun 8 June (11-4). Combined adm with**

OXFORDSHIRE 437

Failford £6, chd free. Home-made teas. Visits also by arrangement in June for groups of 10 to 30.
This town garden brings alive the imagination of its creators. It will inspire both the enthusiast and the beginner. Use of recycled materials, lots of colour and architectural plants. A folly and greenhouse is just one of many quirky features. Raised beds, rockeries, specimen plants, beds of roses and hostas. Pushes the boundaries of conventional gardening. There is something for everyone.

55 50 PLANTATION ROAD
Oxford, OX2 6JE. Philippa Scoones. *Central Oxford. N on Woodstock Rd take 2nd L. Coming into Oxford on Woodstock Rd turn R after Leckford Rd. Best to park on Leckford Rd. No disabled parking near house.* **Sat 26 Apr (2-5). Adm £4, chd free. Home-made teas. Sun 27 Apr (2-5). Combined adm with 38 Leckford Road £8, chd free. Tea, coffee & cake. Sun 21 Sept (2-5). Adm £4, chd free. Home-made teas.**
Surprisingly spacious city garden designed in specific sections. North facing front garden, side alley filled with shade loving climbers. South facing rear garden with hundreds of tulips in spring, salvias, tithonias and dahlias in autumn, unusual trees inc Mount Etna Broom, conservatory, terraced area and secluded water garden with water feature, woodland plants and alpines. Good design ideas for small town garden and 100s of pots that add to the overall atmosphere.

56 THE PRIORY, CHARLBURY
Church Lane, Charlbury, OX7 3PX. Dr D El Kabir & Colleagues. *6m SE of Chipping Norton. Large Cotswold village on B4022 Witney-Enstone Rd, near St Mary's Church.* **Sun 25 May (2-5). Adm £6, chd free.**
1½ acre of formal terraced topiary gardens with Italianate features. Foliage colour schemes, shrubs, parterres with fragrant plants, old roses, water features, sculpture and inscriptions aim to produce a poetic, wistful atmosphere. Formal vegetable and herb garden. Arboretum of over three acres borders the River Evenlode and inc wildlife garden and pond. Partial wheelchair access.

57 9 RAWLINSON ROAD
Oxford, OX2 6UE. Ramnique Lall. *¾m N of Oxford City Centre. Rawlinson Rd runs between Banbury & Woodstock roads midway between Oxford City Centre & Summertown shops.* **Sun 15 June (1-5.30). Combined adm with 11 Rawlinson Road £8, chd free.**
Townhouse garden with structured disarray of roses. Terrace of stone inlaid with brick and enclosed by Chinese fretwork balustrade, chunky brick and oak pergola covered with roses, wisteria and clematis; potted topiary. Until autumn the garden is delightfully replete with aconites, lobelias, phloxes, daisies and meandering clematis.

58 11 RAWLINSON ROAD
Oxford, OX2 6UE. Emma Chamberlain. *Central N Oxford. Halfway between Central Oxford & Summertown, off Banbury Rd.* **Sun 15 June (1-5.30). Combined adm with 9 Rawlinson Road £8, chd free. Tea.**
A south facing 120ft walled Victorian town garden created from scratch since 2010. Interesting mix of herbaceous and shrubs with particular interest in late tulips, and unusual plants. Great emphasis on colour and succession planting with paths running through the beds. Constantly changing as owner is restless. Some sculptures. There are wide paths through the garden and it is level.

59 RECTORY FARMHOUSE
Church Enstone, Chipping Norton, OX7 4NN. Andrew Hornung & Sally Coles, 01608 677374, giussanese@yahoo.co.uk. *N from Oxford on the A44. Turn R in Enstone to Church Enstone. Parking is on the Little Tew Rd by the church. Proceed through the churchyard, turn R and down the hill. Entrance on unmade road behind The Crown Inn.* **Visits by arrangement 6 June to 7 July for groups of 6+. Adm £5, chd free. Tea, coffee & cake.**
A large and very varied garden with a rich mix of formal and informal planting inc fruit trees, soft fruit and vegetable garden. About 100 varieties of rose, particularly climbers; many unusual, some rare plants. The garden inc many different settings, ranging from gravel areas to fruit trees and pondside plantings. More recently developed areas alongside well established plantings. Garden slopes - assistance will be required for wheelchair user.

60 SANDYS HOUSE
Bull Hill, Chadlington, Chipping Norton, OX7 3ND. Jane Bell. *Centre of Chadlington village accessible via A361 (Burford-Chipping Norton) or A44 (Oxford). At Xrds turn down Bull Hill & enter garden on L through wooden gates. Parking on surrounding streets but not at property.* **Fri 13, Sat 14 June (11-5). Combined adm with Claridges Barn £7, chd free. Teas, coffees and light lunches available at Claridges Barn.**
Bulbs, perennials and shrubs create a colourful mix in this informal cottage-style garden to the rear of the former Sandys Arms pub. There is a strong emphasis on wildlife-friendly planting, and a series of small ponds and wildflower area encourage bio-diversity. The garden inc a mature summer-flowering Magnolia Grandiflora against the house and tender annuals are displayed in the main greenhouse. Partial access for wheelchair users down the driveway. Please note that there are steps to the main lawn area and terrace.

61 SARSDEN GLEBE
Churchill, Chipping Norton, OX7 6PH. Mr & Mrs Rupert Ponsonby. *Situated between Sarsden and Churchill. Sarsden Glebe is ¼ m S of Churchill on the road to Sarsden. Turn in to the drive by a small lodge.* **Sun 6 Apr (12.30-5). Adm £7.50, chd free. Home-made teas.**
A rectory garden and park laid out by Humphry Repton and his son George. Terraced formal garden; wild garden with spring bulbs and mature oaks; and walled kitchen garden. Wild garden with a sea of blue and white anemone blanda interspersed with fritillaries and daffodils in spring. Most of the garden can be accessed in a wheelchair.

GROUP OPENING

62 SIBFORD GARDENS
Sibford Ferris, OX15 5RE. *7m W of Banbury. Near the Warwickshire border, S of B4035, in centre of Sibford Ferris village at T-junc & additional gardens near the Xrds & Wykham Arms Pub in Sibford Gower. Parking in both villages.* **Sun 22 June (2-6). Combined adm £7, chd free. Home-made teas at Sibford Gower Village Hall (opp the church).**

CARTER'S YARD
Sue & Malcolm Bannister, 01295 780265, sebannister@gmail.com.
Visits also by arrangement May to Sept.

COPPERS
Mr Andrew & Mrs Chris Tindsley.

GOWERS CLOSE
Philip Hilton.

HOME CLOSE, SIBFORD FERRIS
Graham & Carolyn White, www.instagram.com/homeclosegardens.

SHRUBBERY COTTAGE
Nic Durrant.

Two charming small villages of Sibford Gower and Sibford Ferris, off the beaten track with thatched stone cottages. 5 contrasting gardens comprising a truly traditional plants woman's cottage garden, a private garden of a renowned landscape architect an Artists garden with planting designed to inspire her works and a beautiful country garden using the natural gradient to divide the garden into different zones that draw your eye and encourage you to explore and the gardens, and lastly the gardens of an early C20 Arts and Crafts house. A fantastic collection bursting with bloom, structural intrigue, interesting planting and some rather unusual plants. Some wheelchair access to Coppers, Home Close and Shrubbery Cottage.

🐕 ✿ ☕ 🔊

63 SOUTH NEWINGTON HOUSE
South Newington, OX15 4JW. Mr & Mrs David Swan, 07711 720135, claire_ainley@hotmail.com. *6m SW of Banbury. South Newington is between Banbury & Chipping Norton. Take Barford Rd off A361, 1st L after 100yds in between oak bollards. For SatNav use OX15 4JL.* Visits by arrangement Mar to Oct. Adm covers visits to South Newington House and Bush House plus refreshments. **Adm £12, chd free. Tea, coffee & cake.**
A tree lined drive leads to a garden of interest. Herbaceous borders designed for year-round colour. Organic kitchen garden with established beds, rotation and companion planting. Orchard of fruit trees with a pond for wildlife and hydration for the hives. Walled parterre planted for seasonal colour. A family garden, designed to blend seamlessly into the environment; a warm welcome awaits you. Some gravel paths, otherwise full wheelchair access.

♿ 🚗 ☕

64 ♦ STONOR PARK
Stonor, Henley-on-Thames, RG9 6HF. Lord and Lady Camoys, 01491 638587, administrator@stonor.com, www.stonor.com. *4 m from Henley on Thames. Located between the M4 (J8/J9) & the M40 (J6) on the B480 Henley-on-Thames to Watlington road. If approaching Stonor on the M40 from the E, please exit at J6 only.* **For NGS: Thur 12 June (10.30-4.30). Adm £8, chd free.** For other opening times and information, please phone, email or visit garden website.
Nestled within a hidden valley and ancient deer park, you will find the gardens at Stonor, which date back to Medieval times. Visitors love the serenity of our C17 walled, Italianate Pleasure Garden and Old Kitchen Garden beyond. In the four acre walled gardens you'll find a 400ft long herbaceous border, topiary, ancient yews, ponds with water lilies, and beautiful park land views. Medieval Walled Garden 400 ft -long herbaceous border Huge Rosa 'Kiftsgate' which hangs from a vast yew Stunning parkland views Shrubbery.

🚗 ☕ 🔊

65 STOW COTTAGE ARBORETUM & GARDEN
Junction Road, Churchill, Chipping Norton, OX7 6NP. Tom Heywood-Lonsdale, www.stowcott.co.uk. *2½ m SW of Chipping Norton, off the B4450. Parking: use postcode OX7 6NP & parking will be sign posted from William Smith Cl.* **Sat 21 June (2-5.30). Adm £5, chd free. Tea, coffee & cake.**
The arboretum and garden cover approx 15 acres with extensive views towards Stow-the-Wold and beyond. The arboretum began in 2009 and has been extensively developed over the years. There is an array of 650 different trees, particularly oaks as well as sorbus and limes and many magnolias, dogwoods, walnuts, birches and liquidambars. The arboretum began in 2009 and has been extensively developed over the years. There is an array of 500 trees inc different oaks, sorbus and limes as well as many magnolias, dogwoods, walnuts, birches and liquidambars.

🐕 ☕ 🔊

66 TRINITY COLLEGE
Broad Street, Oxford, OX1 3BH. Kate Burtonwood, Head Gardener, www.trinity.ox.ac.uk. *Central Oxford. Entrance in Broad St (Opp Turl St) Purchase tickets from Trinity College, Broad St, OX1 3BH.* **Sun 3 Aug (11-3). Adm £8, chd free. Cream teas in Trinity's historic Dining Hall. Open nearby Lincoln College. Cafes on Broad Street, 50 metres from the college.**
Historic, listed Oxford College gardens, on a site dating back to C13. Open again after several years of restoration work, with a new 120 metre border by garden designer Chris Beardshaw and other new areas by Head Gardener Kate Burtonwood. The park-like front quadrangle has mature specimen trees inc Catalpa and Cedrus. Formal courtyards house seasonal pot displays. New planting areas were created in the Woodland and Library Quad in 2021 following extensive redevelopment of college buildings. The private walled gardens - the President's Garden and Fellows' Garden - will be open for viewing. Please note that this opening is cashless payments only. Restored gardens and dining hall. A focus on sustainable plantings. Most of site is accessible for wheelchair users. Some uneven paths and gravel at points. Accessible facilities are provided.

♿ ☕ 🔊

67 TYTHE BARN
Guydens Hamlet, Oxford Road Garsington, Oxford, OX44 9AZ. Claire and Dave Parker. *Beyond the Oxford ring road to the E, after Unipart, at the edge of Garsington. Parking is available in the Unipart Car park, about 150 metres from the house. OX4 2PG. Disabled parking, and passenger drop off at Tythe Barn*

itself (OX44 9AZ). **Sun 8 June (1.30-5). Adm £5, chd free. Home-made teas inc local honey and home-made preserves for sale.**
½ acre garden, designed by RHS Chelsea award winner Sarah Naybour. Bee friendly planting in the formal garden leads to woodland area. Oak pergola with roses overlooks the wildlife pond with orchard. Raised vegetable beds behind a mature beech hedge with vintage doorway. 2½ acre wildflower meadow with apiary. Children's wildlife quiz available. Garden is flat and designed to be accessible to wheelchairs. Disabled parking adjacent to the house.

68 UPLANDS
Old Boars Hill, Oxford, OX1 5JF. Lyn Sanders, 01865 739486, sandersc4@hotmail.com. *3m S of Oxford. From S ring road towards A34 at r'about follow signs to Wootton & Boars Hill. Up Hinksey Hill take R fork. 1m R into Berkley Rd. Follow road around 2 bends, garden opp 3rd bend. Parking in lane.* **Visits by arrangement 12 Apr to 5 Oct for groups of up to 30. Adm £6, chd free. Home-made teas.**
A hidden ½ acre garden with borrowed views and colour throughout the year. The long sloping lawn leads to a sunny formal garden. There is a wildlife pond inhabited by great crested and smooth newts in spring and damselflies and dragonflies later, plus an extensive range of perennial plants, spring bulbs, roses, dahlias, Michaelmas daisies and clematis. Wheelchair access with some steps that can be avoided by using the sloping lawns.

69 UPPER BOLNEY HOUSE
Upper Bolney Road, Harpsden, Henley-on-Thames, RG9 4AQ. Anna and Richard Wilson. *2m S of Henley on Thames, between Shiplake and Harpsden. Upper Bolney Rd can be accessed from Woodlands Rd. Only use the postcode in Google Maps.* **Sun 20 July (11-4). Adm £7, chd £3. Home-made teas inc cakes and hot & cold drinks.**
The four acre garden has been extensively developed over the last 15 yrs. There are lawns with herbaceous borders. Terraces around the house inc planted areas and yew topiary. Various interesting areas lie beyond; a rose garden, wildflower meadow, rhododendron bed, tropical area, Victorian style stumpery, kitchen garden and greenhouse. Some garden statuary and several sitting areas and benches.

26 Manor Farm Road

The Manor Garden

OXFORDSHIRE 441

70 ♦ WATERPERRY GARDENS
Waterperry, Wheatley, OX33 1JZ.
The School of Philosophy and
Economic Science, 01844 339254,
office@waterperrygardens.co.uk,
www.waterperrygardens.co.uk.
7½ m from Oxford city centre.
From E M40 J8, from N M40 J8a.
Follow brown tourist signs. For
SatNav please use OX33 1LA. **For
NGS: Tue 11 Mar (10-5). Adm £9,
chd free. Tue 16 Sept (10-5.30).
Adm £12.50, chd free. Light
refreshments in the teashop
(10-5).** For other opening times and
information, please phone, email or
visit garden website.
Eight acres of beautifully landscaped
ornamental gardens featuring a
spectacular 200ft herbaceous
border. Established as a School of
Horticulture for Ladies by Beatrix
Havergal in 1932, it is now also home
to a quality plant centre, garden
shop, art gallery, gift barn, museum,
teashop and Saxon Church. Newly
redesigned walled garden, river
walk, statues and pear orchard.
Riverside walk may be inaccessible to
wheelchair users if very wet.
&. ❋ 🚗 NPC 🍵 ♪))

71 WAYSIDE
82 Banbury Road, Kidlington,
OX5 2BX. Margaret & Alistair
Urquhart, 01865 460180,
alistairurquhart@ntlworld.com. *5m
N of Oxford. On R of A4260 travelling
N through Kidlington.* **Visits by
arrangement June to Aug for groups
of up to 25. Adm £4, chd free.**
¼ acre garden shaded by mature
trees. Mixed border with some rare
and unusual plants and shrubs. A
climber clothed pergola leads past
a dry gravel garden to the woodland
garden with an extensive collection of
hardy ferns. Conservatory and large
fern house with a collection of unusual
species of tree ferns and tender
exotics. Partial wheelchair access.
&. ❋ 🍵

*48,000 people affected
by cancer were reached
by Maggie's centres
supported by the National
Garden Scheme over the
last 12 months.*

GROUP OPENING

72 WEST OXFORD GARDENS
Cumnor Hill, Oxford, OX2 9HH.
*Take Botley interchange off A34
from N or S. Follow signs for Oxford
& then turn R at Botley T-lights opp
McDonalds & follow NGS yellow
signs. Street parking.* **Sun 8 June
(1-5). Combined adm £7, chd free.
Home-made teas at 10 Eynsham
Road.**

10 EYNSHAM ROAD
Jon Harker.

NEW **7 THE GARTH**
Mrs Silvana Losito.

26 HURST RISE ROAD
Mrs Sylvie Thorn.

86 HURST RISE ROAD
Ms P Guy & Mr L Harris.

New for 2025: 7 The Garth - a
medium sized mature natural town
garden with a mix of flower beds,
trees, shrubs, vegetables and
meadow flowers. 26 Hurst Rise Road
- a beautiful contemporary garden
created by the owners. Shrubs and
bee friendly herbaceous borders and
sculptures. 86 Hurst Rise Road - a
small garden abounding in perennials,
roses, small trees and shrubs
displayed at different levels around a
circular lawn and path with sculptural
features. 10 Eynsham Road a New
Zealander's take on an English-style
garden inc many rose varieties, white
garden, herbaceous borders and
pond. Pebble path at 86 Hurst Rise
Road, gravel driveways at 26 Hurst
Rise Road & 7 The Garth with narrow
pathway down one side.
&. ❋ 🍵 ♪))

73 WESTWELL MANOR
Westwell, nr Burford, OX18 4JT.
Mr Thomas Gibson, 02074 998572,
agnese@tgfineart.com. *2m SW
of Burford. From A40 Burford-
Cheltenham, turn L ½ m after
Burford r'about signed Westwell.
After 1½ m at T-junc, turn R &
Manor is 2nd house on L.* **Visits by
arrangement Apr to Aug. Donation
to Aspire.**
Seven acres surrounding old
Cotswold manor house (not open)
with knot garden, potager, shrub
roses, herbaceous borders, topiary,
earth works, moonlight garden,
auricula ladder, rills and water garden.
❋ 🍵

74 WHEATLEY MANOR
26 High Street, Wheatley,
OX33 1XX. Mark and Juliet Byford.
5 m E of Oxford. Off A40. **Sun 15
June (2-6). Adm £5, chd free. Tea,
coffee & cake.**
1½ acre garden of Elizabethan
manor house (not open). Formal
box walk with herbaceous borders;
many mature and unusual trees, herb
garden and secret garden, lily pond
in cottage garden with roses, orchard
with Medlar and ancient Mulberry
trees and a shrubbery with old roses.
A romantic oasis in this busy village.
🐕 🍵 ♪))

75 WHITEHILL FARM
Widford, Burford, OX18 4DT. Mr &
Mrs Paul Youngson, 01993 822894,
paulyoungson48@gmail.com. *1m E
of Burford and 100 metres N of A40.
From A40 take road signed Widford.
Turn R at bottom of hill, 1st house
on R with ample car parking.* **Sun
13 July (1-5). Adm £5, chd free.
Tea, coffee & cake.** Visits also
by arrangement June to Sept for
groups of 10+.
Two acres of hillside gardens and
woodland with spectacular views
overlooking Burford and Windrush
valley. Informal plantsman's garden
built up by the owners over 25 yrs.
Herbaceous and shrub borders,
ponds and bog area, old fashioned
roses, ground cover, ornamental
grasses, bamboos and hardy
geraniums. Wildflower meadow with
specimen trees. Features inc large
cascade water feature, pretty tea
patio and wonderful Cotswold views.
🐕 ❋ 🚗 🍵 🪑 ♪))

76 WOOLSTONE MILL HOUSE
Woolstone, Faringdon, SN7 7QL.
Mr & Mrs Justin Spink. *7m W
of Wantage. 7m S of Faringdon.
Woolstone is a small village off
B4507, below Uffington White Horse
Hill.* **Fri 4 July (2-5). Adm £5, chd
free. Open nearby Midsummer
House.**
Redesigned by new owner, garden
designer Justin Spink in 2020, this
1½ acre garden has large mixed
perennial beds, and small gravel,
cutting, kitchen and bog gardens.
Topiary, medlars and old fashioned
roses. Treehouse with spectacular
views to Uffington White Horse and
White Horse Hill. C18 millhouse and
barn (not open). Partial wheelchair
access.
&. 🚗 🍵 ♪))

SHROPSHIRE

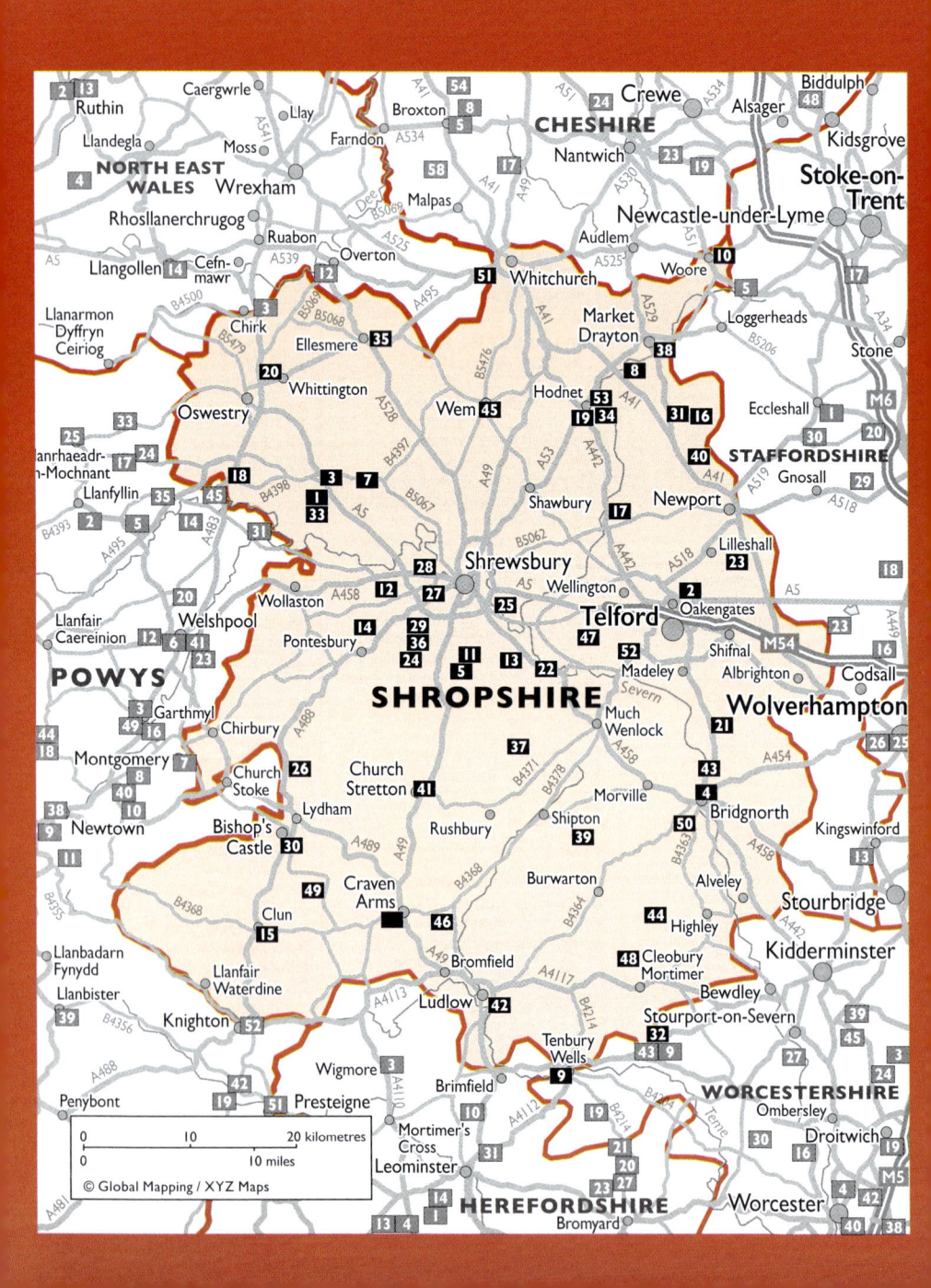

… SHROPSHIRE 443

VOLUNTEERS

County Organiser
Andy Chatting
07546 560615
andy.chatting@ngs.org.uk

Treasurer
Elaine Jones 01588 650323
elaine.jones@ngs.org.uk

Volunteers Co-ordinator
Sheila Jones 01743 244108
smaryjones@icloud.com

Publicity
Douglas Wood 07704 683095
douglas.woods@ngs.org.uk

Facebook/Twitter
Vicky Kirk 01743 821429
vicky.kirk@ngs.org.uk

Instagram
John Butcher 07817 443837
butchinoz@hotmail.com

Booklet Co-ordinator
Martin Clifford-Jones
07506 140434
martin.jones@ngs.org.uk

Assistant County Organisers
Fiona Chancellor
01952 507675
fiona.chancellor@ngs.org.uk

Stella Clifford-Jones
01630 639746
stellaandmartin@ngs.org.uk

Jane Wood 01691 839564
jane.liz.wood@gmail.com

Angela Woolrich
angelawoolrich@hotmail.co.uk

@Shropshire NGS
@shropshirengs

OPENING DATES

All entries subject to change.
For latest information check
www.ngs.org.uk
Map locator numbers are shown to the right of each garden name.

April

Saturday 5th
Upper Farm Garden 47
Sunday 6th
Upper Farm Garden 47
Saturday 12th
Cherry Tree Arboretum 10
Wednesday 16th
◆ Goldstone Hall Gardens 16
Saturday 26th
Stottesdon Village Open Gardens 44
Sunday 27th
Westwood House 50
Wednesday 30th
Hundred House Hotel 21

May

Sunday 4th
The Bramleys 5
Court Acre 11
Longner Hall 25
Ruthall Manor 39
Monday 5th
Ruthall Manor 39
Wednesday 7th
Neen View 32
Sunday 11th
The Ferns 15
Longden Manor 24
Oteley 35
Riverside 38
Wednesday 14th
Neen View 32
Saturday 17th
Cherry Tree Arboretum 10
The Leasowes, Cound 22
Sunday 18th
Brownhill House 7

NEW Buntingsdale Park Gardens 8
Stanley Hall Gardens 43
Tuesday 20th
Brownhill House 7
Saturday 24th
◆ Burford House Gardens 9
The Paddock 36
Ruthall Manor 39
Sunday 25th
◆ Burford House Gardens 9
Ruthall Manor 39
◆ Walcot Hall 49
Monday 26th
◆ Walcot Hall 49
Saturday 31st
Beaufort 2
Upper Farm Garden 47

June

Sunday 1st
Beaufort 2
Eaton Mascott Hall 13
Upper Farm Garden 47
Friday 6th
Lilleshall Home Farm 23
Saturday 7th
Horatio's Garden 20
Windy Ridge 52
Sunday 8th
Windy Ridge 52
Wednesday 11th
◆ Goldstone Hall Gardens 16
Hundred House Hotel 21
Sunday 15th
Preen Manor 37
Saturday 21st
Grooms Cottage 17
Ruthall Manor 39
The Secret Gardens at Steventon Terrace 42
Sunday 22nd
NEW Brooches House 6
Grooms Cottage 17
Ruthall Manor 39
Tuesday 24th
Brownhill House 7
Saturday 28th
1 Scotsmansfield 41
Sunday 29th
Edge Villa 14
Riverside 38
Sambrook Manor 40

July

Sunday 6th
◆ Hodnet Hall Gardens 19
Upper Marshes 48

Wednesday 9th
◆ Goldstone Hall Gardens 16

Thursday 10th
Appledore 1
Offcot 33

Friday 11th
Appledore 1
Offcot 33

Saturday 12th
Appledore 1
Offcot 33

Sunday 13th
Appledore 1
1 Mount Pleasant Cottages 31
Offcot 33

Wednesday 16th
Hundred House Hotel 21

Saturday 19th
Ruthall Manor 39

Sunday 20th
Grooms Cottage 17
Ruthall Manor 39
Sunningdale 45

Saturday 26th
Lower Brookshill 26
Upper Farm Garden 47

Sunday 27th
Lower Brookshill 26
Upper Farm Garden 47

August

Every day from Saturday 2nd to Sunday 17th
Gwynt Newydd 18

Sunday 3rd
Moat Hall 29

Sunday 10th
NEW Buntingsdale Park Gardens 8
The Ferns 15

Wednesday 13th
◆ Goldstone Hall Gardens 16

September

Wednesday 3rd
◆ Wollerton Old Hall 53

Wednesday 10th
◆ Goldstone Hall Gardens 16

Saturday 13th
Upper Farm Garden 47

Sunday 14th
Upper Farm Garden 47

October

Saturday 4th
Cherry Tree Arboretum 10

Friday 10th
Appledore 1
Offcot 33

Saturday 11th
Appledore 1
◆ Burford House Gardens 9
Offcot 33

Sunday 12th
Appledore 1
◆ Burford House Gardens 9
Offcot 33

By Arrangement

Arrange a personalised garden visit with your club, or group of friends, on a date to suit you. See individual garden entries for full details.

Bramble Cottage 3
48 Bramble Ridge 4
Brownhill House 7
Cruckfield House 12
Eaton Mascott Hall 13
The Ferns 15
Grooms Cottage 17
Gwynt Newydd 18
Hundred House Hotel 21
The Leasowes, Cound 22
107 Meadowbout Way 27
Merton 28
Moat Hall 29
17 Mortimer Road, Buntingsdale Park Gardens 8
The Mount 30
The Old Rectory, Hodnet 34
Riverside 38
Ruthall Manor 39
Sambrook Manor 40
Sunningdale 45
Tower House 46
Upper Farm Garden 47
NEW The White House 51

Cherry Tree Arboretum

THE GARDENS

1 APPLEDORE
Kynaston, Kinnerley, Oswestry, SY10 8EF. Lionel Parker. *Just off A5 on Wolfshead r'about (at Oswestry end of Nesscliffe bypass) towards Knockin. Follow NGS signs from this road.* **Thur 10, Fri 11, Sat 12, Sun 13 July, Fri 10, Sat 11, Sun 12 Oct (10-5). Combined adm with Offcot £7. Tea, coffee & cake.**
Appledore adjoins neighbouring garden Offcot. It has gone through extensive changes and is managed by Tom Pountney from Offcot. Both gardens are opening together this year so that visitors can see a developing 'edible garden' with six large beds for a wide range of fruit and vegetables, all grown organically. To encourage pollinators, the garden also has a wildlife pond and a small wildflower meadow.

2 BEAUFORT
Coppice Drive, Moss Road, Wrockwardine Wood, Telford, TF2 7BP. Mike King, www.carnivorousplants.uk.com. *Approx 2m N from Telford town centre. From Asda Donnington, turn L at lights on Moss Rd, ⅓m, turn L into Coppice Drive. 4th Bungalow on L with solar panels.* **Sat 31 May, Sun 1 June (1-5). Adm £5, chd free. Tea, coffee & cake. Donation to Plant Heritage.**
If carnivorous plants are your thing, then come and visit our National Collection of *Sarracenia* (pitcher plants); also over 100 different Venus flytrap clones *(Dionaea muscipula)*, Sundews *(Drosera)* and Butterworts*(Pinguicula)* - over 6000 plants in total. Large greenhouses at Telford's first carbon negative house; a great place to visit - kids will love it. Regret, greenhouses are not wheelchair accessible.

3 BRAMBLE COTTAGE
Shotatton, Ruyton XI Towns, Shrewsbury, SY4 1JG. Brigette and Adam Wilson, 07739 182315, brigette.wilson14@gmail.com, www.instagram.com/our.english.topiarygarden. *1m W of Ruyton Village towards Shotatton.* **Visits by arrangement May to Oct. Adm by donation.**
Bramble Cottage is a topiary garden created and maintained by us for 27 years. We have box parterres, a formal rose garden and yew topiary. It is a ¾ of an acre site in rural Shropshire with lots of box balls and new topiary in development. In addition, we have yew, box and beech hedges and all things topiary.

4 48 BRAMBLE RIDGE
Bridgnorth, WV16 4SQ. Heather, 07572 706706, heatherfran48@gmail.com. *From Bridgnorth N on B4373 signed Broseley. 1st on R Stanley Ln, 1st R Bramble Ridge. From Broseley S on B4373, nr Bridgnorth turn L into Stanley Ln, 1st R Bramble Ridge.* **Visits by arrangement Apr to Sept for groups of up to 20. Adm £5, chd free.**
Steep cottage style garden with many steps; part wild, part cultivated, terraced in places and overlooking the Severn Valley with views to High Rock and Queens Parlour. The garden features shrubs, perennials, wildlife pond, summerhouse and, in the wilderness area, wildflowers, fruit trees and a sandstone outcrop. I love my garden very much and am looking forward to sharing it with other people.

5 THE BRAMLEYS
Condover, Shrewsbury, SY5 7BH. Toby & Julie Shaw. *3m S of Shrewsbury. Through Condover towards Dorrington. Pass village hall follow road round, cross the bridge, in approx 100 metres there is a drive on L. Parking limited, please park at school & walk down to garden.* **Sun 4 May (11-5). Combined adm with Court Acre £6, chd free. Home-made teas.**
A large country garden extending to two acres with a variety of trees and shrubs, herbaceous borders and a woodland with the Cound Brook flowing through. A courtyard oasis welcomes you as you enter the garden with far-reaching views over open countryside. Wheelchair access around most of the garden, although not for the woodland area.

6 NEW BROOCHES HOUSE
Park Lane, Craven Arms, SY7 9AB. Anthony & Julia Wood. *1m out of Craven Arms. From Craven Arms take B4368 towards Clun, as you leave the town turn L to Rowton, go under Railway Bridge & you will see a turning on your R. Follow signs up grass track to parking.* **Sun 22 June (12-5). Adm £5, chd free. Tea, coffee & cake.**
The house and gardens have been created by the present owners over 40 years. A traditional layout with mixed herbaceous borders, rose beds, lawns and terraces with beautiful views towards the Stretton Hills. Further five acres recently acquired with kitchen and soft fruit sections, wildlife pools, and large areas of wildflower meadows with grassland walks. Majority of the gardens can be accessed by wheelchairs but some gravel paths.

7 BROWNHILL HOUSE
Ruyton XI Towns, SY4 1LR. Roger & Yoland Brown, 01939 261121, brownhill@eleventowns.co.uk, www.eleventowns.co.uk. *9m NW of Shrewsbury on B4397. On the B4397 in the village of Ruyton XI Towns.* **Sun 18, Tue 20 May, Tue 24 June (10-5). Adm £5, chd free. Home-made teas. Visits also by arrangement 19 Apr to 13 July.**
A unique two acre hillside garden with many steps and levels bordering River Perry. Visitors can enjoy a wide variety of plants and styles from formal terraces to woodland paths. The Good Garden Guide said 'It has to be seen to be believed'. The lower areas are for the sure-footed while the upper levels with a large kitchen garden and glasshouses have many places to sit and enjoy the views. Kit cars on show.

The National Garden Scheme donated £281,000 in 2024 to support those looking to work in horticulture as well as those struggling within the industry.

GROUP OPENING

8 NEW **BUNTINGSDALE PARK GARDENS**
Buntingsdale, Market Drayton, TF9 2EP. Stella and Martin Clifford-Jones. *Access only via Tern Hill A41. N on A41. Enter Tern Hill take 1st R onto Hedley Way, or going S turn L onto Hedley Way after Nationwide Caravans sales. What3words app: undivided.orbited.apprehend.* **Sun 18 May, Sun 10 Aug (2-5). Combined adm £6, chd free. Tea, coffee & cake at 17 Mortimer Rd.**

17 MORTIMER ROAD
Martin & Stella Clifford-Jones, 07484 327979, pomona_scj@hotmail.com.
Open on all dates
Visits also by arrangement 12 Apr to 26 Oct. Disabled visitors are welcome to arrange private visits for easier access.

NEW **18 MORTIMER ROAD**
Michael and Christine Simpson.
Open on Sun 18 May

NEW **10 OTTLEY WAY**
Jean and Steve Carter.
Open on Sun 10 Aug

Buntingsdale Park is a hidden gem comprised of former RAF officers' houses built during World War II. Three very different gardens (two on each date) will open this year with features inc an orchard, vegetable plots, meadow, ponds and roses, plus rare and interesting plants inc orchids. There is an emphasis on encouraging wildlife through the planting of native species, habitat provision and avoidance of chemicals. Parking, WC, plant sale and refreshments are available at 17 Mortimer Road where there are a dozen different seating areas from which to choose. Wheelchair access to most areas of the gardens with one small step between some areas.
&

9 ♦ **BURFORD HOUSE GARDENS**
Burford House, Burford, Tenbury Wells, WR15 8HQ. British Garden Centres, 01584 810777, pbenson@britishgardencentres.com, www.britishgardencentres.com/burford-house-garden-centre. *1m W of Tenbury Wells on A456. Follow signs for Burford House Garden Centre off the A456 and the A49 at Wooferton.*
For NGS: Sat 24, Sun 25 May, Sat 11, Sun 12 Oct (10-4). Adm £5, chd free. Tea, coffee & cake in Burford House. Cafe open nearby on site for breakfast, lunch & teas. For other opening times and information, please phone, email or visit garden website.
The garden is being restored by the Garden Angels (volunteers) under the leadership of the newly appointed Head Gardener. Four acres of sweeping lawns bordered by the River Teme, and serpentine borders, set in the beautiful Teme Valley, around an elegant Georgian House (open for teas). Designed by the late, great plantsman, John Treasure and featuring over 100 varieties of clematis in addition to a myriad of plants in wonderful combinations and colours. Garden centre offers a comprehensive range of plants, gifts and outdoor leisure. Well behaved dogs on lead welcomed.

10 CHERRY TREE ARBORETUM
Cherry Tree Lane, Woore, CW3 9SR. John & Liz Ravenscroft, www.cherrytreearboretum.org. *½ m N of Woore on the Nantwich Rd. Off the A51 Nantwich Rd in Woore (just N of the village centre). Signs directing you along Cherry Tree Ln to its end.* **Sat 12 Apr, Sat 17 May, Sat 4 Oct (10.30-4). Adm £10, chd free. Light refreshments.**
Created in 2006 on 50 acres of unspoilt, pastureland scattered with mature oaks by John and Liz Ravenscroft. Located on a hilly area overlooking the Cheshire plain with views to the Pennines in the north, the Peckforton Hills to the northwest and the Breiddons to the southwest. It is a showcase of specimen trees with magnolias, peonies, dahlias, lilacs, deciduous azaleas and North American oaks. April is an avenue of white Magnolias in many varieties. The earliest of the cherries will also be opening. A series of trails and paths run between meadows and native wildflowers in the arboretum. Many of the trees are rare and unusual. It also contains 19 of England's Champion Trees.

11 COURT ACRE
Condover, Shrewsbury, SY5 7AA. Ian and Michelle Roberts. *3m S of Shrewsbury. Heading S into the centre of Condover. Post Office on R. Drive on L virtually opp Post Office. Parking limited. Please park at sch and walk to garden.* **Sun 4 May (11-5). Combined adm with The Bramleys £6, chd free.**
The garden is about an acre in size comprising four different areas. A gravelled driveway leads to lawned areas and mixed borders containing a variety of shrubs and herbaceous plants. There are steps approaching the swimming pool which is surrounded by a paved patio area. There is a small orchard of mainly apple trees. The garden also has several patio and seating areas and a variety of mature trees. Most of the garden is wheelchair accessible.
&

12 CRUCKFIELD HOUSE
Shoothill, Ford, SY5 9NR. Geoffrey Cobley, 01743 850222, geoffcobley541@btinternet.com. *5m W of Shrewsbury. A458 from Shrewsbury, turn L towards Shoothill.* **Visits by arrangement 2 June to 31 July for groups of 10+. Adm £10, chd free. Tea & cakes only available to larger groups.**
An artist's romantic three acre garden, formally designed, informally and intensively planted with a great variety of unusual herbaceous plants. Nick's garden, with many species' trees, shrubs and wildflower meadow, surrounds a lake with bog and moisture-loving plants. Ornamental kitchen garden. Rose and peony walk. Courtyard fountain garden, large shrubbery and extensive clematis collection. Extensive topiary, and lily pond.

13 EATON MASCOTT HALL
Eaton Mascott, Cross Houses, Shrewsbury, SY5 6HG. Mr W. Blum Gentilomo, 01743 761541, pjgyldard@aol.com. *7m S of Shrewsbury. On A458 2nd R past Cross Houses, thereafter follow signs.* **Sun 1 June (10-4.30). Adm £5, chd free. Tea, coffee & cake.**
Visits also by arrangement 1 May to 14 Sept.
A six acre garden consisting of 1½ acre walled garden with extensive rose collection. Emphasis on symmetry with pergolas, water features and cross views. Bamboo walk and acer collection, specimen trees. 4½ acre woodland garden with walks and glimpses of parkland and surrounding countryside, plus ferns, azaleas and rhododendrons. Wheelchair access possible if accompanied by helper.

Goldstone Hall Gardens

14 EDGE VILLA
Edge, nr Yockleton, Shrewsbury, SY5 9PY. Mr & Mrs C Williams. *6m SW of Shrewsbury. From A5 take either A488 signed to Bishops Castle or B4386 to Montgomery for approx 6m then follow NGS signs.* **Sun 29 June (2-5). Adm £5, chd free. Home-made teas.**
Two acres nestling in south Shropshire hills. Self-sufficient vegetable plot. Chickens in orchard, foxes permitting. Large herbaceous borders. Dewpond surrounded by purple elder, irises, candelabra primulas and dieramas. Large selection of fragrant roses. Wendy house for children. Plant and book sales in aid of National Garden Scheme charities. Wheelchair access via some gravel paths.

15 THE FERNS
Newport Street, Clun, SY7 8JZ. Andrew Dobbin, 01588 640064, andrew.clun@outlook.com. *Enter Clun from Craven Arms. Take 2nd R signed into Ford St. At T-junc turn R for parking in the Memorial Hall car park (100 yds). Retrace steps to T-junc. The Ferns is on L.* **Sun 11 May, Sun 10 Aug (12-5). Adm £5, chd free. Visits also by arrangement Jan to Sept for groups of up to 20.**
A formal village garden of ¾ acre, approached via a drive lined with crab apple and pear trees. On the right is the autumn garden, giving fine views of the surrounding hills. From the front courtyard garden a path leads through double herbaceous borders full of late summer colour, to further rooms, of yew, beech and box. There is also a rear courtyard with tender exotics. Lily pond and statuary.

16 ♦ GOLDSTONE HALL GARDENS
Goldstone, Market Drayton, TF9 2NA. John Cushing, 01630 661202, enquiries@goldstonehall.com, www.goldstonehall.com. *5m N of Newport on A41. From Shrewsbury A53, R for A41 Hinstock & follow brown signs & yellow NGS signs What3Words app: stirs.describes. mute.* **For NGS: Wed 16 Apr, Wed 11 June, Wed 9 July, Wed 13 Aug, Wed 10 Sept (11-5). Adm £8.50, chd free. Tea, coffee & cake. Hotel restaurant open for lunches. Pre-bookings only. For other opening times and information, please phone, email or visit garden website.**
Five acres with highly productive beautiful kitchen garden. Unusual vegetables and fruits - alpine strawberries, heritage tomatoes, salad, chillies, brassicas. Roses in Walled Garden from May; double herbaceous in front of old English garden wall at its best July and August; sedums and roses stunning in September. Extensive kitchen garden, living box sign, colourful herbaceous borders, unusual plants and extensive well maintained lawns. Winner of the prestigious Good Hotel Guide's Editor's Choice Award for Gardens. Majority of garden can be accessed on gravel and lawns.

17 GROOMS COTTAGE
Waters Upton, Telford, TF6 6NP. Joanne & Andi Butler, 07484 236893, groomscottagegarden@gmail.com, www.instagram.com/groomscottagegarden. *No parking at the property due to restricted access. Parking available on the verge opp the church or in the village hall car park.* **Sat 21, Sun 22 June, Sun 20 July (10-5). Adm £6, chd free. Tea, coffee & cake.** Visits also by arrangement 19 June to 31 July for groups of up to 40.
A cottage garden around ½ an acre in size comprising mixed herbaceous borders and an abundance of English roses. Highlights inc home-made water features, raised beds and pergolas, oriental garden, hosta garden, alpine and herb beds and a productive fruit and vegetable garden and greenhouse. Many established trees and shrubs, unusual plants and shady plant areas. Travel inspired garden set out as different garden rooms. Some gravel areas not accessible for wheelchair users.

& ✿ ☕))

18 GWYNT NEWYDD
3 Penygarreg Rise, Pant, Oswestry, SY10 8JR. Douglas and Jane Wood, 07967 283721, douglas.woods@ngs.org.uk. *5m S of Oswestry. A483 S from Oswestry towards Welshpool. Follow signs when in Pant Village, turning opp shop.* **Daily Sat 2 Aug to Sun 17 Aug (10-7). Adm £5, chd free. Tea, coffee & cake.** Visits also by arrangement 2 Aug to 17 Aug for groups of up to 20.
Average size garden to the side and rear of detached bungalow in a quiet close. Acer trees, borders with mixed herbaceous perennials, cannas, hostas, ferns, phlox, greenhouse with succulents. Small area with raised vegetable beds, fruit trees and ornamental trees.

✿ ☕

19 ◆ HODNET HALL GARDENS
Hodnet, Market Drayton, TF9 3NN. Sir Algernon & The Hon Lady Heber-Percy, 01630 685786, secretary@hodnethall.com, www.hodnethallgardens.org. *5½m SW of Market Drayton. 12m NE Shrewsbury. At junc of A53 & A442. Tickets available to purchase online or on the gate on the day. What3words app: footpath.shortens.challenge.* **For NGS: Sun 6 July (11-5). Adm £10. Light refreshments in the Garden Restaurant.** For other opening times and information, please phone, email or visit garden website.
The 60+ acres of Hodnet Hall Gardens are amongst the finest in the country. There has been a park and gardens at Hodnet for many hundreds of years. Magnificent forest trees, ornamental shrubs and flowers planted to give interest and colour from early spring to late autumn. Woodland walks alongside pools and lakes, home to abundant wildlife. Productive walled kitchen garden and historic dovecot. Maps are available to show access for our less mobile visitors.

& 🐕 🚌 NPC ☕))

20 HORATIO'S GARDEN
The Robert Jones & Agnes Hunt Orthopaedic Hospital, Gobowen, Oswestry, SY10 7AG. Horatio's Garden, www.horatiosgarden.org.uk. *From A5 follow signs to Orthopaedic Hospital and park in Visitor Car Park (pay & display). Follow yellow NGS signs along Twmpath Ln to entrance gate.* **Sat 7 June (12-4). Adm £7, chd free. Tea, coffee & cake.**
Beautifully designed by Bunny Guinness and delightfully planted, Horatio's Garden Midlands opened to great acclaim in September 2019. Partly funded by the National Garden Scheme, the garden offers a stunning sanctuary for patients, their loved ones and NHS staff spending time in the Midland Centre for Spinal Injuries. Featuring social spaces and sheltered areas, raised beds, beautiful planting, garden room, glasshouse and a serpentine rill, this is a horticultural and therapeutic delight like no other. Very good wheelchair access throughout.

& ✿ ☕))

Oteley

SHROPSHIRE 449

21 HUNDRED HOUSE HOTEL
Bridgnorth Road, Norton, Telford, TF11 9EE. Henry Phillips, 01952 580240, reservations@hundredhouse.co.uk, www.hundredhouse.co.uk. *10 mins from Ironbridge, Shropshire. Situated on the A442 in the village of Norton. Midway between Bridgnorth & Telford.* **Wed 30 Apr, Wed 11 June, Wed 16 July (11-4). Adm £5, chd free. Coffee, cakes and three menus on offer in our restaurant. Please see our website for details. Visits also by arrangement for groups of 10 to 50.**
An acre of gardens crafted over 35+ years, complete with sculptures, stonework and working herb and kitchen garden. From March onwards, you will find over 5000 bulb flowers inc tulips, hyacinths, daffodils, alliums, blossoming trees and dancing pond flowers. Summer brings a variety of flowers, inc David Austin roses, giant agapanthus, dahlias, clary, foxgloves, fuchsias and arum lilies. Please see website for restaurant booking and information.

22 THE LEASOWES, COUND
Cound, Shrewsbury, SY5 6AF. Robert & Tricia Bland, 07802 667636, rjbbland1@outlook.com. *7m SE of Shrewsbury. On the A458 SE of Shrewsbury, 500m to the E of the Riverside Inn adjoining Oakleys, the lawnmower business.* **Sat 17 May (10-4.30). Adm £7, chd free. Tea, coffee & cake. Visits also by arrangement Apr to Oct for groups of 15 to 25. Donation to International Dendrology Society.**
Within the super structure of mature larches and interconnected ponds, a wide range of rhododendrons and azaleas have been planted as well as shade appreciating trees and shrubs over 10 acres. A large offering of roses of all descriptions provide colour throughout the formal gardens.

23 LILLESHALL HOME FARM
The Incline, Lilleshall, Newport, TF10 9AP. Connie Sansom. *Follow signs for Lilleshall National Sports Centre. Our entrance is off the sports centre drive, which will be signposted.* **Fri 6 June (10-4). Adm £5, chd free. Tea, coffee & cake.**
A beautiful country farmhouse garden with far-reaching views across the Shropshire countryside. The garden is split into several areas for you to explore inc formal herbaceous borders with rose beds, a tennis court lined with hydrangeas, pergola and more. Discover our croquet lawn, pond, orchard, greenhouse and veg patch. The farm is also home to horses, sheep, chickens, a goat and two pigs. There will be a small plant sale. There is a wheelchair accessible route around the garden, over areas of grass and gravel.

24 LONGDEN MANOR
Plealey, SY5 0XL. Karen Lovegrove. *From Shrewsbury take C150 Longden Rd. On entering Longden Village, opp The Tankerville Arms & Village Shop on L, turn R into Manor Ln.* **Sun 11 May (10-4). Adm £5, chd free. Tea, coffee & cake.**
Large estate garden with lots of character and interest: woodland walks and grass paths; humongous topiary; wide variety of specimen trees; rhododendrons and azaleas; wildflowers; restored water garden; panoramic vistas of surrounding countryside; holly garden. A great place for all the family to visit. Topiary trail for children inc giraffe, pelican, otter, kingfisher, shark, gorilla and a goose.

25 LONGNER HALL
Atcham, Shrewsbury, SY4 4TG. Mr & Mrs R L Burton, www.longner.co.uk. *4m SE of Shrewsbury. From M54 follow A5 to Shrewsbury, then B4380 to Atcham. From Atcham take Uffington Rd, entrance ¼ m on L. What3Words app: brilliant.overtime.plugged.* **Sun 4 May (2-5). Adm £6, chd free. Home-made teas.**
A long drive approach through parkland designed by Humphry Repton. Walks lined with golden yew through extensive lawns, with views over the Severn Valley. Borders containing roses and herbaceous shrubs, also an ancient yew wood. Enclosed one acre walled garden open to National Garden Scheme visitors. Mixed planting, garden buildings, tower and game larder. Short woodland walk around old moat pond which is not suitable for wheelchairs.

26 LOWER BROOKSHILL
Nind, nr Lydham, SY5 0JW. Patricia & Robin Oldfield, 01588 650137, robin.oldfield@live.com. *3m N of Lydham on A488. Take signed turn to Nind & after ½ m sharp L & follow narrow road for another ¾ m.* **Sat 26, Sun 27 July (1-6). Adm £6, chd free. Cream teas.**
Ten acres of hillside garden and woods at 950ft within the AONB. Begun in 2010 from a derelict and overgrown site, cultivated areas now rub shoulders with the natural landscape using fine borrowed views over and down a valley. Inc brook side walks, a 'pocket' park, four ponds (inc a Monet lily pond), mixed borders and lawns, cottage garden and wildflowers. Lovely picnic spots. Cash only at gate.

27 107 MEADOWBOUT WAY
Bowbrook, Shrewsbury, SY5 8QB. Sue and Mark Smith, 07736 837427, sue1706@outlook.com. *2m S of Shrewsbury. On the estate follow Squinter Pip Way until you see Meadowbout Way on R. You will see the NGS sign at the end of the straight section.* **Visits by arrangement 12 July to 24 Aug. Adm £6, chd free. Tea, coffee & cake.**
Our oasis is a small town garden completed in a tropical style. There are several examples of plants native to other shores but which are happy in the space we have created. With over 200 plants inc tree ferns, bananas, palm trees and cottage garden plants arranged around a variety of seating areas, our visitors have a perpetual sense of being on holiday. Direct access to the garden via a side gate.

Our donation in 2024 has enabled Parkinson's UK to fund 3 new nursing posts this year directly supporting people with Parkinson's.

28 MERTON
Shepherds Lane, Bicton, Shrewsbury, SY3 8BT. David & Jessica Pannett, 01743 850773, jessicapannett@hotmail.co.uk. *3m W of Shrewsbury. Follow B4380 from Shrewsbury past Shelton for 1m. Shepherd's Ln turn L garden signed on R. Or from A5 bypass at Churncote r'about, turn towards Shrewsbury, 2nd turn L is Shepherds Ln.* **Visits by arrangement 1 June to 28 Sept for groups of up to 25. Adm £5, chd free.**
Mature ½ acre botanical garden with a rich collection of trees and shrubs inc unusual conifers from around the world. Hardy perennial borders with seasonal flowers and grasses plus an award winning collection of hosta varieties in a woodland setting. Outstanding gunneras in a waterside setting with moisture loving plants. Wheelchair access over level paths and lawns.

29 MOAT HALL
Annscroft, Shrewsbury, SY5 8AZ. Martin & Helen Davies, 01743 860216, helenatthefarm@hotmail.co.uk. *3m S of Shrewsbury. Take the Longden road from Shrewsbury to Hook a Gate. Our lane is 2nd on R after Hook a Gate & before Annscroft. Single track lane with passing places for ½ m.* **Sun 3 Aug (1-5). Adm £6, chd free. Home-made teas. Visits also by arrangement 1 Mar to 28 Sept.**
An acre garden around an old farmhouse within a dry moat. Well organised and extensive kitchen garden, fruit garden and orchard for self-sufficiency. Colourful herbaceous borders; stumpery; raised cut flower borders; ⅔ acre pond nearby with oak gazebo; many interesting stone items inc troughs, cheese weights, staddle stones some uncovered in the garden. Plenty of seating areas on the lawns for enjoying the garden. Wheelchair access: mostly lawn with one grass and one concrete ramp; kitchen garden has 2' wide paved paths. Paved path to the pond and gazebo.

30 THE MOUNT
Bull Lane, Bishops Castle, SY9 5DA. Heather Willis, 07779 314609, adamheather@btopenworld.com. *Off A488 Shrewsbury to Knighton Rd. At top of the town, 130 metres up Bull Ln on R. No parking at property. Free parking in Bishops Castle.* **Visits by arrangement Apr to Sept. Tea, coffee & cake.**
An acre of garden that has evolved over 24 years, with four lawns, a rose bed in the middle of the drive with pink and white English roses, and herbaceous and mixed shrub borders. There are roses planted throughout the garden and in the spring daffodils and tulips abound. Two large beech trees frame the garden with a view that sweeps down the valley over fields and then up to the Long Mynd. Wheelchair access easy to most parts of the garden, but not to WC.

31 1 MOUNT PLEASANT COTTAGES
Lockley Wood, Market Drayton, TF9 2LS. Chris & Clive Brown. *Lockley Wood, near Hinstock. From Newport turn off A41 at Hinstock. Follow A529. At x-roads in Lockley Wood turn L. Garden 1st property on R. From Market Drayton, A529 towards Newport. In Lockley Wood turn R at x-roads.* **Sun 13 July (2-5). Adm £5, chd free. Tea, coffee & cake.**
The garden extends to ⅕ acre, situated in a rural location. The main garden comprises a long border and island beds with cottage style planting, all colour themed to flow throughout the seasons. Box and yew punctuate the planting. Other features inc a fish pond and productive vegetable plot. The back garden is planted predominantly with shade tolerant plants.

32 NEEN VIEW
Neen Sollars, Cleobury Mortimer, DY14 9AB. Ian & Chris Ferguson. *3m from Cleobury Mortimer. From A456 past Mamble, turn R at Neen Sollars, follow lane to Live & Let Live for parking. From Cleobury take the Tenbury Rd, turn L & L again then up the hill to Neen View gardens.* **Wed 7, Wed 14 May (12-5). Adm £5, chd free. Regret, cash only.**
A woodland garden with stunning panoramic views of the Clee Hills and Teme Valley. Mature trees inc: azaleas, camellias and rhododendrons. Wildlife ponds and wildflower meadow. There are plenty of seats to enjoy the views. Walking around you will find a ruined bothy and Japanese stream garden.

33 OFFCOT
Kynaston, Kinnerley, SY10 8EF. Tom Pountney. *Just off A5 on Wolfshead r'about (Oswestry end of Nesscliffe bypass) towards Knockin. Then take the 1st L towards Kinnerley. Follow NGS signs from this road.* **Thur 10, Fri 11, Sat 12, Sun 13 July, Fri 10, Sat 11, Sun 12 Oct (10-5). Combined adm with Appledore £7. Tea, coffee & cake.**
A cottage garden with lots of winding pathways leading to different focal points. The garden is packed with a wide range of evergreen and deciduous trees and shrubs and underplanted with herbaceous perennials. There is a natural looking pond with a running stream feeding into it. A haven for wildlife. So many different areas to see and enjoy inc the garden bar.

34 THE OLD RECTORY, HODNET
Hearne Lane, Hodnet, Market Drayton, TF9 3NG. Sarah Riley, 01630 685671, rileys55@icloud.com. *¼ m NW of the village of Hodnet. SatNav takes you to the end of Hearne Ln. Bear L, on the single track road, up the hill towards the trees.* **Visits by arrangement 15 Feb to 9 Sept for groups of up to 25. Adm £6, chd free. Tea, coffee & cake.**
Set amidst farmland, 3½ acres of gardens, created over 45 years by John and Elizabeth Ravenscroft, surrounding the Grade II listed old rectory. Formal gardens, a walled garden, man-made stream, large pool with stepping stones, lawns and wilder wooded areas. Collections of azaleas, magnolias, peonies. New owners (5 years) are enjoying editing and developing the garden.

35 OTELEY
Ellesmere, SY12 0PB. Mainwaring Family, www.oteley.com. *1m SE of Ellesmere. Entrance out of Ellesmere past Mere, opp Convent nr to A528/495 junc.* **Sun 11 May (10-4). Adm £8, chd free. Light refreshments.**
Explore 10 acres running down to The Mere with stunning views. Walled kitchen garden, architectural features, many old interesting trees. Rhododendrons, azaleas, woodland walk and views across Mere to Ellesmere. First opened in 1927 when the National Garden Scheme started.

36 THE PADDOCK
Annscroft, Shrewsbury, SY5 8AN. Ian Ross. *On road from Annscroft to Hanwood/Plealey. 200 yds from the Xrds. Parking is at The Farriers, SY5 8AN.* **Sat 24 May (11-5). Adm £6. Tea, coffee & cake.**
A mini arboretum in which 70 trees - some of which are rare. The collection inc 12 different acers and a cluster of six *Gingko bilobas*. A waterfall cascades through three levels. As the new owner since 2001, I see myself as the custodian of an impressive small garden. Wheelchair access to most of the garden.

37 PREEN MANOR
Church Preen, SY6 7LQ. Mr & Mrs J Tanner, 07971 955609, katytanner@msn.com. *6m W of Much Wenlock; For SatNav, please use SY6 7LF. From A458 turn off at Harley and follow signs to Kenley & Church Preen. From B4371 Much Wenlock to Church Stretton Rd, go via Hughley to Church Preen. What3words app: roving.irrigated. text.* **Sun 15 June (2-5). Adm £6, chd free. Tea, coffee & cake.**
Fine historical and architectural six acre garden on site of Cluniac priory and former Norman Shaw mansion. Compartmentalised with large variety of garden rooms, inc kitchen parterre and fernery. Formal terraces with fine yew and hornbeam hedges have panoramic views over parkland to Wenlock Edge. Dell, woodland walks and specimen trees.

38 RIVERSIDE
Berrisford Road, Market Drayton, TF9 1JH. Eric and Susan Harrison, 01630 655678, riversidegardensuk@yahoo.co.uk. *Market Drayton. Enter Market Drayton on Newcastle Rd & turn into Great Hales St. Then take L into Berrisford Rd.* **Sun 11 May, Sun 29 June (2-5). Adm £5, chd free. Tea, coffee & cake. Visits also by arrangement 1 May to 30 July for groups of 15 to 40.**
The garden is ¾ acre, with different planting areas. We have hydrangeas, hostas, woodland walk, hot garden and herbaceous borders with white garden with loggia. Plus an old and large wisteria and a very old climbing rose. Gravel drive but mainly level paths.

39 RUTHALL MANOR
Ditton Priors, Bridgnorth, WV16 6TN. Mr & Mrs G T Clarke, 01746 712608, clrk608@btinternet.com. *7m SW of Bridgnorth. At Ditton Priors Church take road signed Bridgnorth, then 2nd L. Garden 1m.* **Sun 4, Mon 5, Sat 24, Sun 25 May, Sat 21, Sun 22 June, Sat 19, Sun 20 July (12.30-5.30). Adm £7, chd free. Home-made teas. Visits also by arrangement.**
Offset by a mature collection of specimen trees, the garden is divided into intimate sections, carefully linked by winding paths. The front lawn flanked by striking borders, extends to a gravel, art garden and ha-ha. Clematis and roses scramble through an eclectic collection of wrought-iron work, unique pottery and secluded seating. Designed and planted by present owners since 1960. A stunning horse pond with primulas, iris and bog plants. Jigsaw puzzle sale. Wheelchair access to most areas of garden.

40 SAMBROOK MANOR
Sambrook, TF10 8AL. Mrs E Mitchell, 01952 550256. *Between Newport & Tern Hill, 1m off A41.* **Sun 29 June (12-5). Adm £5, chd free. Home-made teas. Visits also by arrangement for groups of 10+.**
Deep, colourful, well-planted borders offset by sweeping lawns surrounding an early C18 manor house (not open). Wide ranging herbaceous planting with plenty of roses to enjoy; the arboretum below the garden, with views across the river, has been further extended with new trees. The waterfall and Japanese garden are now linked by a pretty rill. Lovely garden to visit for all the family. Wheelchair access to most areas. Woodland area may be difficult.

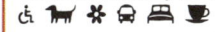

SHROPSHIRE

41 1 SCOTSMANSFIELD
Burway Road, Church Stretton, SY6 6DP. Peter Vickers & Hilary Taylor. *Scotsmansfield is on L, c.200m up Burway Rd (quite steep). Approach Church Stretton from A49. At Sandford Rd/ High St jct, turn R & then L, up Burway Rd. No parking. Easthope Rd car park (near Co-op) available SY6 6BL. Shuttle bus running from here.* **Sat 28 June (11-5). Adm £6, chd free. Tea, coffee & cake.**
Terraced garden of ¾ acre, renewed over a decade after long neglect. Attached to E wing of 'Scotsmansfield' (not open), built 1908. Celebration of favourite plants, with colour, shape, texture, scent, light, shade and plentiful wildlife. Trees, fernery, lily pond, mixed borders, yew hedges, lavish roses. Areas of tranquillity and intimacy, occasions of drama and long views of surrounding woods and hills. Partial access via steep gravelled paths to some areas. Wheelchair users will need support from an assistant.
&

GROUP OPENING

42 THE SECRET GARDENS AT STEVENTON TERRACE
Steventon Terrace, Steventon New Road, Ludlow, SY8 1JZ. Kevin & Carolyn Wood. *Gardens are located behind row of terraced cottages. Easily accessible from A49; on-street parking; Park & Ride stops outside the garden.* **Sat 21 June (12-4). Combined adm £5, chd free. Tea, coffee & cake. Ice cream also available.**
Discover some very secret gardens hidden behind a row of Victorian terraced cottages in Ludlow. A ½ acre south facing garden that has been developed over 30 years. It has been divided into different sections which inc a rose garden, herbaceous borders, koi fish, chickens, polytunnel and greenhouse and a Mediterranean garden.
&

43 STANLEY HALL GARDENS
Bridgnorth, WV16 4SP. Mr & Mrs M J Thompson. *½m N of Bridgnorth. Leave Bridgnorth by N gate B4373; turn R at Stanley Ln. Pass Golf Course Club House on L & turn L at Lodge.* **Sun 18 May (2-5.30). Adm £5, chd free. Home-made teas.**

Regency and later landscaped garden with rhododendrons, woodland walks, fish ponds and fine trees in parkland setting. Dower House (Mr and Mrs C Wells): four acres of specimen trees, contemporary sculpture and walled vegetable garden South Lodge (Mr Tim Warren): Hillside cottage garden. Wheelchair access to the main gardens.
&

GROUP OPENING

44 STOTTESDON VILLAGE OPEN GARDENS
Stottesdon, DY14 8TZ. www.facebook.com/StottesdonandDistrictOpenGardens. *S Shropshire near Cleobury Mortimer (A4117/B4363). 30m W of B'ham (M5/42), 15m E of Ludlow (A49/4117) & 10m S of Bridgnorth (A458/442) Stottesdon is between Clee Hill & the Severn Valley. NGS Signed from B4363.* **Sat 26 Apr (12-5). Combined adm £7.50, chd free. Light refreshments in the Parish Church.**
Located in unspoilt countryside below the Clee Hills, up to eight gardens and the heritage church in Stottesdon village are open to visitors. Several places have stunning views. Some gardens feature spaces for outdoor living. Many are traditional or more modern 'cottage gardens', containing fruit, vegetables and livestock. There are contrasting vegetable gardens inc one devoted to permaculture principles. Take teas, home-made cake and refreshments in the Norman church; guided tours of the historic building and its heritage treasures available. Lunches available at The Fighting Cocks Inn - call to book 01746 718270 (advised). Most gardens have some wheelchair access. Gardens not suitable for wheelchair access will be listed on our garden guide and map.
&

45 SUNNINGDALE
9 Mill Street, Wem, SY4 5ED. Mrs Susan Griffiths, 07760 663730, sue.griffiths@btinternet.com. *Town centre. Wem is on B5476. Parking in car park at Barnard St. Garden is opp the purple house below the church. Some on-street parking on High St. Coaches can drop off at the main gate.* **Sun 20 July (11-3.30). Adm £4, chd free. Tea, coffee & cake. Visits also by arrangement**

Mar to Oct for groups of 6 to 52. Discuss refreshments when booking.
A ½ acre town garden. Wildlife haven for a variety of birds inc nesting gold crests. A profusion of excellent nectar rich plants means that butterflies and other pollinators are in abundance. Interesting plantings with carefully collected rare plants and unusual annuals means there is always something new to see. Large perennial borders, with exotic climbers, designed as an all year-round garden. Discover the Koi pond and natural stone waterfall rockery. There are antique and modern sculptures. Gravel garden and beautiful seating areas many of which are under cover. Sound break yew walkway. Wheelchair access the garden is on the level but with several steps mostly around the pond area; paths are mainly gravel or flags; flat lawn.
&

46 TOWER HOUSE
Bache, Craven Arms, SY7 9LN. Lady Spicer, 01584 861692, nicspicer@yahoo.com. *6m NW of Ludlow. B4365: Ludlow to Much Wenlock. Turn L after 3m (Bache, Burley), garden at top of hill after 1½m. B4368: Craven Arms to Bridgnorth. 2m R at Xrds. L after 200yds. 1m fork L. garden after 200yds.* **Visits by arrangement Mar to June. Adm £6, chd free.**
A folly built in 1838 with a two acre garden created by the present owner over 50 years. On a perfect site with views over the Corvedale, with veg, herbaceous borders, a small parterre and pond. Wheelchair access challenging in the wood.
&

47 UPPER FARM GARDEN
Rushton, Telford, TF6 5AG. Pete & Paul Turpin-Ottley, 07515 352538, upperfarm@icloud.com. *3m from M54 J7 Wellington. Exit 7 M54 take Little Wenlock/Wrekin turn. In 1m at bollards R for Uppington. In 2m at junc, turn L for Eaton Constantine. In ½m R for Charlton Hill. See NGS signs on your L for Garden & Parking.* **Sat 5, Sun 6 Apr, Sat 31 May, Sun 1 June, Sat 26, Sun 27 July, Sat 13, Sun 14 Sept (11-4). Adm £6. Tea, coffee & cake. Visits also by arrangement 7 Apr to 14 Sept for groups of 10 to 40.**
Farmhouse Garden with views of the Wrekin and the Stretton Hills.

Comprising several garden 'rooms' connected by gravelled walkways interspersed with ample seating opportunities. Unusual features inc a raised scree terrace, a rose pergola and bed with 40 varieties of English shrub roses, a two sided herbaceous walk, an elevated viewing deck, a cactus house and self-sufficient allotment beds.

✿ ☕))

48 UPPER MARSHES
Catherton Common, Hopton Wafers, nr Cleobury Mortimer, DY14 0JJ. Jo & Chris Bargman. *3m NW of Cleobury Mortimer. From A4117 follow signs to Catherton. Property is on common land 100yds at end of track.* **Sun 6 July (12-5). Adm £5, chd free. Home-made teas.**
Commoner's stone cottage and three acre small holding. 800' high. Garden has been developed to complement its unique location on edge of Catherton common with herbaceous borders, vegetable plot, rose garden. New Mediterranean garden, spring fed wildlife pond and wildflower meadow. Plenty of seats to stop and take in the tranquillity. Optional circular walk across Wildlife Trust common to SSI field.

✿ ☕

49 ♦ WALCOT HALL
Lydbury North, SY7 8AZ. Mr & Mrs C R W Parish, 01588 680570, enquiries@walcothall.com, www.walcothall.com. *4m SE of Bishop's Castle. B4385 Craven Arms to Bishop's Castle, turn L by The Powis Arms in Lydbury North.* **For NGS: Sun 25, Mon 26 May (1.30-5). Adm £5, chd free. Home-made teas in the Ballroom.** For other opening times and information, please phone, email or visit garden website.
Arboretum planted by Lord Clive of India's son, Edward in1800. Cascades of rhododendrons and azaleas amongst specimen trees and pools. Fine views of Sir William Chambers' Clock Towers, with lake and hills beyond. Walled kitchen garden, dovecote, meat safe, ice house and mile-long lakes. Russian wooden church, grotto and fountain, tin chapel. Relaxed borders and rare shrubs. Lakeside replanted and water garden at western end re-established.

🐕 ✿ 🚗 🏛 ☕))

50 WESTWOOD HOUSE
Oldbury, Bridgnorth, WV16 5LP. Hugh & Carolyn Trevor-Jones. *Take the Ludlow Rd (B4364) out of Bridgnorth. Past the Punch Bowl Inn, turn 1st L, Westwood House signed on R.* **Sun 27 Apr (2-5). Adm £6, chd free. Home-made teas.**
A country garden, well designed and planted around the house, particularly known for its tulips and use of colour. Sweeping lawns offset by deeply planted mixed borders; pool garden and lawn tennis court; kitchen and cutting garden, with everything designed to attract wildlife for organic growth. Far-reaching views of this delightful corner of the county and woodland walks to enjoy. Reasonable wheelchair access but there are gravel paths and some steps.

♿ 🐕 ✿ ☕ 🪑))

51 NEW THE WHITE HOUSE
Redbrook Maelor, Whitchurch, SY13 3AD. Claire and James Hennie, 07795 573205, clairehennie1@gmail.com. *2m W of Whitchurch. From Chester: Take A41 towards Whitchurch, (from Shrewsbury take A49 towards Whitchurch, then A41). At McDonalds r'about take A525 towards Wrexham. Garden approx 2m on L.* **Visits by arrangement 3 May to 28 Sept for groups of up to 12. Adm £10, chd free inc light refreshments.** Situated on a busy A-road with limited parking. Car share if possible.
Created over the past 18 years by current owners from open sloping lawn, into garden 'rooms'. ⅕ acre garden on the site of a former smithy dating back to the 1700's. Cottage garden: roses, perennials, evergreen shrubs. Vegetable garden: raised beds, asparagus border, central pergola, pretty potting shed. Yew garden: topiary, 'castle wall' hedge. Front garden parterre and water features.

🐕 ☕

52 WINDY RIDGE
Church Lane, Little Wenlock, TF6 5BB. George & Fiona Chancellor. *2m S of Wellington. Follow signs for Little Wenlock from N (J7, M54) or E (off A5223 at Horsehay). Parking signed. Do not rely on SatNav.* **Sat 7, Sun 8 June (12-5). Adm £7, chd free. Home-made teas.**

Universally admired for its structure, inspirational planting and balance of texture, form and all-season colour, the garden more than lives up to its award-winning record. Developed over 39 years, 'open plan' garden rooms display over 1000 species (mostly labelled) in a range of colour-themed planting styles, beautifully set off by well-tended lawns, plenty of water and fascinating sculpture. Wheelchair access via some gravel paths but help available.

♿ 🚗 ☕))

53 ♦ WOLLERTON OLD HALL
Wollerton, Market Drayton, TF9 3NA. Lesley & John Jenkins, 01630 685760, info@wollertonoldhallgarden.com, www.wollertonoldhallgarden.com. *4m SW of Market Drayton. On A53 between Hodnet & A53-A41 junc. Follow brown signs.* **For NGS: Wed 3 Sept (11-5). Adm £9.50, chd free. Light lunches available from 12.00; afternoon tea and cream teas from 14.00.** For other opening times and information, please phone, email or visit garden website.
Four acre garden created around C16 house (not open). Formal structure creates variety of gardens each with own colour theme and character. Planting is mainly of perennials many in their late summer- early autumn hues, particularly the asters. Ongoing lectures by gardening personalities, designers and technical experts. Mondays (not B/Hols)Tuesdays and Wednesdays reserved for garden club visits. Winter Workshops. Partial wheelchair access.

♿ ✿ 🚗 ☕))

---

70 inpatients and their families are being supported at the newly opened Horatio's Garden Northern Ireland, thanks to National Garden Scheme donations.

SHROPSHIRE 453

SOMERSET & BRISTOL

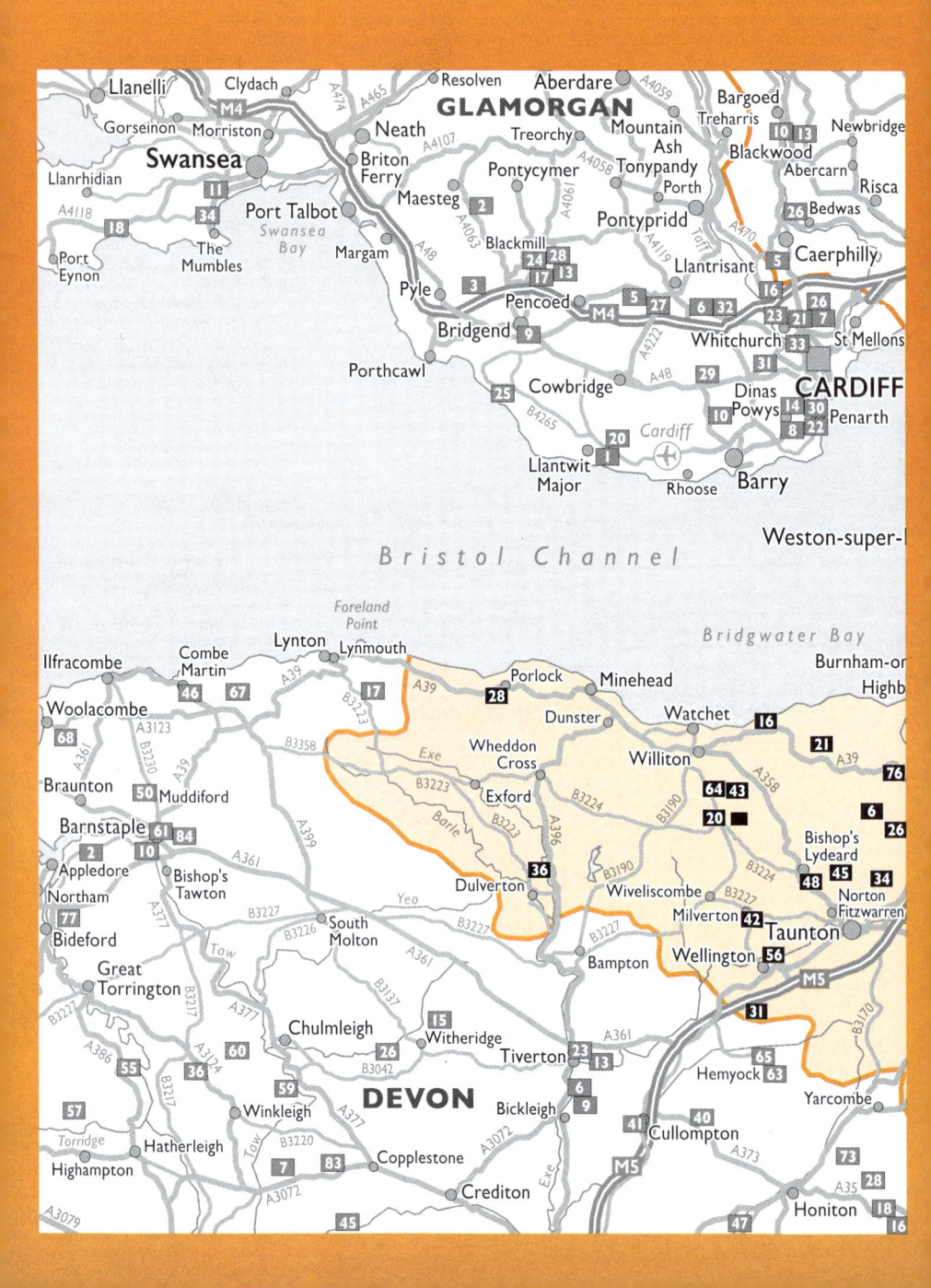

SOMERSET & BRISTOL

SOMERSET VOLUNTEERS

County Organiser
Laura Howard 01460 282911
laura.howard@ngs.org.uk

County Treasurer
Jill Wardle 07702 274492
jill.wardle@ngs.org.uk

Publicity
Roger Peacock
roger.peacock@ngs.org.uk

Social Media
Janet Jones 01749 850509
janet.jones@ngs.org.uk

Lisa Prior 07773 440147
lisa.prior@ngs.org.uk

Presentations
Dave & Prue Moon
01373 473381
davidmoon202@btinternet.com

Booklet Co-ordinator
John Simmons 07855 944049
john.simmons@ngs.org.uk

Booklet Distributor
Laura Howard (see above)

Assistant County Organisers
Jo Beaumont 07534 777278
jo.beaumont@ngs.org.uk

Marsha Casely 07854 882616
marsha.casely@ngs.org.uk

Patricia Davies-Gilbert
01823 412187
pdaviesgilbert@gmail.com

Alyson Holland 07729 059382
alyson.holland@btinternet.com

Janet Jones (as above)

Sue Lewis 07885 369280
sue.lewis@ngs.org.uk

Judith Stanford 01761 233045
judith.stanford@ngs.org.uk

@nationalgardenschemesomerset
@SomersetNGS
@ngs_bristol_s_glos_somerset

BRISTOL AREA VOLUNTEERS

County Organiser
Roxanne Ismail 07966 474966,
roxanne.ismail@ngs.org.uk

County Treasurer
Harsha Parmar 07889 201185
harsha.parmar@ngs.org.uk

Publicity
Position vacant

Social Media
Harsha Parmar (see above)

Booklet Co-ordinator
John Simmons 07855 944049
john.simmons@ngs.org.uk

Booklet Distributor
Simon Cruickshank 07415 183624,
simon.cruickshank@ngs.org.uk

Assistant County Organisers
John Burgess
07795 466513
jb@chh.org.uk

Irene Randow
01275 857208
irene.randow@sky.com

Karl Suchy 07873 588540
karl.suchy@icloud.com

OPENING DATES

All entries subject to change.
For latest information check
www.ngs.org.uk
Map locator numbers are shown to the right of each garden name.

February

Snowdrop Openings

Wednesday 5th
Elworthy Cottage 20
Friday 14th
♦ East Lambrook Manor Gardens 19
Elworthy Cottage 20
Tuesday 25th
Elworthy Cottage 20

March

Sunday 2nd
Greystones 29
Wednesday 5th
♦ Hestercombe Gardens 34
Saturday 15th
Forest Lodge 23
Lower Shalford Farm 46

April

Thursday 10th
♦ The Yeo Valley Organic Garden at Holt Farm 82
Sunday 13th
Elworthy Cottage 20
Fairfield 21
Watcombe 77
Tuesday 15th
♦ Greencombe Gardens 28
Wednesday 16th
Caisson Gardens 11
Saturday 19th
Skool Beanz Children's Allotment 66
Tuesday 22nd
Elworthy Cottage 20

SOMERSET & BRISTOL

Saturday 26th
◆ East Lambrook Manor
  Gardens 19
◆ The Walled Gardens of
  Cannington 76

Sunday 27th
4 Haytor Park 33
Lucombe House 47
◆ The Walled Gardens of
  Cannington 76

May

Saturday 3rd
Hillcrest 35

Sunday 4th
Hillcrest 35
Little Yarford Farmhouse 45

Monday 5th
Little Yarford Farmhouse 45

Saturday 10th
New Wood House, 19 The
  Beacon 54

Sunday 11th
◆ Milton Lodge 52
Wayford Manor 78

Thursday 15th
Barford House 6

Saturday 17th
◆ East Lambrook Manor
  Gardens 19

Sunday 18th
Court House 16
Stoke Bishop Gardens 71
Watcombe 77
The Yews 83

Saturday 24th
Forest Lodge 23
Lower Shalford Farm 46
The Manor 49

Sunday 25th
The Manor 49

Monday 26th
Elworthy Cottage 20

Saturday 31st
NEW Little Bucklers 44
◆ Stoberry Garden 70

June

Sunday 1st
NEW Little Bucklers 44
Mellowstones 51
◆ Stoberry Garden 70

Tuesday 3rd
NEW The Pony 60

Wednesday 4th
◆ Hestercombe Gardens 34
Mathlin Cottage 50

Saturday 7th
Badgworth Court Barn 4
Hanham Court 32
Westbrook House 80

Sunday 8th
Badgworth Court Barn 4
Coleford House 14
Greystones 29
Hanham Court 32
Lydeard House 48
Mathlin Cottage 50
◆ Milton Lodge 52
Penny Brohn UK 59

Tuesday 10th
Pennard House 58

Thursday 12th
◆ Kilver Court Gardens 40
Watcombe 77

Saturday 14th
Batcombe House 7
NEW 87 Hallen Road 30
Japanese Garden Bristol 38
NEW Shanks House 65
Tintinhull Gardens 73

Sunday 15th
Frome Gardens 25
NEW 87 Hallen Road 30
Tintinhull Gardens 73

Thursday 19th
◆ Special Plants 68

Friday 20th
Cherry Bolberry Farm 12
NEW Rose Cottage 62

Saturday 21st
Cherry Bolberry Farm 12
NEW 84 Fenshurst Gardens 22
John's Corner 39
The Old Rectory, Doynton 57
The Rib 61
NEW Rose Cottage 62
Standerwick Court 69

Sunday 22nd
Crete Hill House 17
John's Corner 39
Nynehead Court 56

Tuesday 24th
Elworthy Cottage 20

Sunday 29th
Court House 16

NEW Frogbury 24
NEW Kingsland 42

July

Sunday 6th
Doynton House 18
◆ Milton Lodge 52
◆ University of Bristol Botanic
  Garden 74
Yews Farm 84

Tuesday 8th
Elworthy Cottage 20

Saturday 12th
Babbs Farm 3

Sunday 13th
Babbs Farm 3

Monday 14th
◆ Berwick Lodge 8

Tuesday 15th
◆ Greencombe Gardens 28

Thursday 17th
◆ Special Plants 68

Saturday 19th
Goathurst Gardens 26
NEW Shanks House 65
Wick Gardens 81

Sunday 20th
Goathurst Gardens 26
Stowey Gardens 72
Wick Gardens 81

Saturday 26th
Babbs Farm 3

Sunday 27th
Babbs Farm 3
Elworthy Cottage 20
Hangeridge Farmhouse 31

August

Tuesday 5th
Elworthy Cottage 20

Tuesday 12th
NEW The Pony 60

Saturday 16th
NEW 30 Great Brockeridge 27

Sunday 17th
NEW 30 Great Brockeridge 27

Thursday 21st
◆ Special Plants 68

Saturday 23rd
NEW 30 Kingsholm Road 41
Westbrook House 80

SOMERSET & BRISTOL

Monday 25th
Elworthy Cottage 20

September

Saturday 6th
Batcombe House 7
Skool Beanz Children's Allotment 66

Sunday 7th
Yews Farm 84

Thursday 11th
◆ Kilver Court Gardens 40

Saturday 13th
South Kelding 67

Thursday 18th
◆ Special Plants 68

Saturday 20th
◆ The Walled Gardens of Cannington 76

Sunday 21st
◆ The Walled Gardens of Cannington 76

October

Thursday 16th
◆ Special Plants 68

By Arrangement

Arrange a personalised garden visit with your club, or group of friends, on a date to suit you. See individual garden entries for full details.

Abbey Farm 1
Avalon 2
Barcroft Hall 5
Batcombe House 7
Blackmore House 9
Bradon Farm 10
Cherry Bolberry Farm 12
Coldharbour Cottage 13
81 Coombe Lane 15
Doynton House 18
Elworthy Cottage 20
Hangeridge Farmhouse 31
4 Haytor Park 33
Hillcrest 35
Hollam House 36
Honeyhurst Farm 37
NEW Kingsland 42
Knoll Cottage 43
Little Yarford Farmhouse 45
Lucombe House 47
165 Newbridge Hill 55
Pennard House 58
Penny Brohn UK 59
Rose Cottage, East Harptree 63
NEW Rose Cottage, Henstridge 62
Rowdon 64
South Kelding 67
Valley Spring 75
Watcombe 77
Wellfield Barn 79
Westbrook House 80

Doynton House

THE GARDENS

1 ABBEY FARM
Montacute, TA15 6UA. Elizabeth McFarlane, 01935 823556, abbey.farm64@gmail.com. *4m from Yeovil. Follow A3088, take slip rd to Montacute, turn L at T-junction into village. Turn R between church & King's Arms (no through rd).* **Visits by arrangement 2 June to 30 June for groups of 15 to 30. Adm £9, chd free. Home-made teas. Details on request.**
A country house garden and wider historic landscape setting the scene for the Cluniac Priory gatehouse. Old ham stone walls together with a strong green structure gently restrain the exuberant planting. Towards the top of the garden a small arboretum has been planted with a view looking down on the ancient pastures.

2 AVALON
Moor Lane, Higher Chillington, Ilminster, TA19 0PT. Dee & Tony Brook, 07506 688191, dee1jones@hotmail.com. *Just off the A30 between Crewkerne & Chard. From A30 take turning signed to Chillington opp Swandown Lodges. Take 2nd L down Coley Ln & 1st L Moor Ln. Avalon is the large pink house. Parking limited, so please car share if possible.* **Visits by arrangement 2 June to 1 Aug for groups of up to 40. Adm £5, chd £2. Home-made teas. Gluten & dairy free cakes available if requested in advance.**
Secluded hillside garden with wonderful views as far as Wales. The lower garden has large herbaceous borders, a sizeable wildlife pond and 2 greenhouses filled with RSA succulents. The middle garden has mixed borders, wild spotted orchids on the lawn, allotment area and a small orchard. The upper garden has a spring fed watercourse with ponds, and many terraces with different planting schemes. Partial wheelchair access across lower lawns & side paths. Steep slope & gravel paths. Wheelchairs will require to be pushed & attended at all times.

3 BABBS FARM
Westhill Lane, Bason Bridge, Highbridge, TA9 4RF. Sue & Richard O'Brien. *1½ m E of Highbridge, 1½ m SSE of M5 exit 22. Turn into Westhill Ln off B3141 (Church Rd), 100yds S of where it joins B3139 (Wells-Highbridge road).* **Sat 12, Sun 13, Sat 26, Sun 27 July (2-5). Adm £8, chd free. Tea, coffee & cake.**
A 1½ acre plantsman's garden on Somerset Levels, gradually created out of fields surrounding old farmhouse over last 30 yrs and still being developed. Trees, shrubs and herbaceous perennials have been planted with an eye for form, foliage and shape in big flowing borders. The garden now consists of several interconnected areas, to suit a range of plants with diverse requirements. Plants for sale if circumstances allow. Many unusual Salvias, especially in late summer. A garden with a restful atmosphere and attractive vistas.

4 BADGWORTH COURT BARN
Notting Hill Way, Stone Allerton, Axbridge, BS26 2NQ. Trish & Jeremy Gibson, www.instagram.com/theoldbarngardeners. *4m SW of Axbridge. Turn off A38 in Lower Weare, signed Wedmore, Weare. Continue 1m, past rd on R (Badgworth Arena). Continue 100 metres to 'No Footway for 600 yds' sign. Garden & car park will be signed.* **Sat 7, Sun 8 June (2-5.30). Adm £6, chd free. Home-made teas.**
In this 1 acre plot around old stone barn buildings, a small orchard leads to a part-walled garden with perennial meadow areas and multi-stemmed trees. Gently curving beds are flanked by a more formal oak pergola walk. The planting is a relaxed contemporary mix. In the atmospheric courtyard, planting is more established and leads to an innovative, colourful sand garden in front of the barns. Main garden is level and accessible. Courtyard and drive areas are loose stone chippings and can be difficult for some wheelchairs. No accessible WC.

5 BARCROFT HALL
North Street, South Petherton, TA13 5DA. Richard & Tracey Killen, 07702 128483, richard.killen02@gmail.com. *N side of S Petherton. From A303 drive to centre of S Petherton, through village, R at fork with Methodist Church into North St (St James St), R into Barcroft Ln, follow signs.* **Visits by arrangement 3 Feb to 30 Sept for groups of 10 to 30. Adm £7.50, chd free. Tea, coffee & cake.**
A lovely 10 acre garden with glorious views over the surrounding countryside. The garden has many features of interest inc formal planting, water and wildlife areas, a kitchen garden and greenhouse, soft fruits and large orchard. Over 1000 trees all set within the extensive lawns and 7 lakes and ponds. Seating areas throughout the gardens and on the beautiful terraces. There is some disabled parking by the main house plus drop off. Some gravel paths and slopes may only be accessible by motorised mobility vehicles.

6 BARFORD HOUSE
Spaxton, Bridgwater, TA5 1AG. Donald & Bee Rice. *4½ m W of Bridgwater. Midway between Enmore & Spaxton.* **Thur 15 May (2-5). Adm £7, chd free. Home-made teas.**
Secluded walled garden contains wide borders, kitchen garden beds, shrubs and fruits trees. Lawns lead to a 6 acre woodland garden of camellias, rhododendrons, azaleas and magnolias. Stream-side gardens feature candelabra primulas, ferns, foxgloves and lily-of-the-valley among veteran pines and oaks, and some rarer trees. Partial wheelchair access. Some areas of woodland garden inaccessible.

129,032 people were able to access guidance on what to expect when a person is dying through the National Garden Scheme's support for Hospice UK this year.

7 BATCOMBE HOUSE
Gold Hill, Batcombe, Shepton Mallet, BA4 6HF. Libby Russell, 0207 931 9996, libby@mazzullorussell.com, www.mazzullorussell.com. *In centre of Batcombe, 3m from Bruton. Parking between Batcombe House & church at centre of village will be clearly marked.* **Sat 14 June (12-5.30); Sat 6 Sept (2-5). Adm £8, chd free. Home-made teas.** Visits also by arrangement 19 May to 19 Sept for groups of 15+. Tea, coffee and a private guided tour available to groups over 15 . Plantswoman's and designer's garden of two parts – one a riot of colour through kitchen terraces, potager leading to wildflower orchard; the other a calm contemporary amphitheatre with large herbaceous borders and interesting trees and shrubs. Always changing. Dogs are welcome on a lead. On 14th June Somerset Hardy Plant Society are holding a Plant Fair with many top nurseries selling interesting plants.

8 ♦ BERWICK LODGE
Berwick Drive, Bristol, BS10 7TD. Sarah Arikan, 01179 581590, info@berwicklodge.co.uk, www.berwicklodge.co.uk. *Leave M5 at J17. A4018 towards Bristol West. 2nd exit on r'about, straight on at mini r'about. At next r'about by Old Crow pub do 360° turn back down A4018, follow sign saying Berwick Lodge off to L.* **For NGS: Mon 14 July (11-2). Adm £5, chd free. Cream teas.** For other opening times and information, please phone, email or visit garden website.
Berwick Lodge, named Bristol's hidden gem by its customers, is an independent hotel with beautiful gardens on the outskirts of Bristol. Built in 1890, this Victorian Arts & Crafts property is set within 18 acres, of which 4 acres are accessible and offer a peaceful garden for use by its visitors. The gardens enjoy pretty views across to Wales, and continue to evolve. Created by Head Gardener Robert Dunster, an ex Royal gardener who worked for Prince Charles at Highgrove, it features an elegant water fountain, Victorian summerhouse, orchard, wildflower meadow, beehives, pond, plus a thriving house martin colony.

9 BLACKMORE HOUSE
Holton Street, Holton, Wincanton, BA9 8AN. Mrs Lisa Prior, 07773 440147, lisa.prior@ngs.org.uk, www.instagram.com/lisaprior. *Just off A303 from W - Holton turn off, from E - Wincanton turn off. In the centre of Holton village, round the corner from The Old Inn. 2 doors to the E of Holton Village Hall, Limited street parking. What3words app: batches.drum.superbly.* **Visits by arrangement 27 Jan to 28 Feb for groups of 5 to 20. Tea, coffee & cake inc in adm price, served inside the house. Adm £7, chd free.**
A hidden terraced cottage garden with dry stone walls and gravel paths, designed for year-round interest complementing the Georgian listed house. Wide borders packed full of perennials and self-seeded surprises. In winter there are 2 intensely scented 10ft daphnes, sarcocca, hellebores popping up everywhere, a few snowdrops and early daffodils all inviting you outside while most gardens sleep.

10 BRADON FARM
Isle Abbotts, Taunton, TA3 6RX. Mr & Mrs Thomas Jones, deborahjstanley@hotmail.com. *Take turning to Ilton off A358. Bradon Farm is 1½m out of Ilton on Bradon Lane.* **Visits by arrangement for groups of 10+. Adm £8, chd free. Home-made teas.**
Classic formal garden demonstrating the effective use of structure with parterre, knot garden, pleached lime walk, formal pond, herbaceous borders, orchard and wildflower planting.

11 CAISSON GARDENS
Caisson House, Combe Hay, Bath, BA2 7EF. Amanda & Phil Honey, info@caissongardens.com, www.caissongardens.com. *3m S of Bath. Take A367 from centre of Bath towards Radstock, at 2nd r'about take 1st exit, follow signs to Combe Hay. 1st L after Wheatsheaf pub, marked No Through Rd. Entrance 1st on R.* **Wed 16 Apr (10-4). Adm £13.50, chd free. Pre-booking essential, please visit www.ngs.org.uk for information & booking. Tea, coffee & cake.**
This is a wonderfully eclectic and romantic garden set in the most beautiful English countryside around a Georgian house built in 1815. It is a mix of herbaceous borders, topiaries, ponds and rills, a walled garden with fruit trees, greenhouses, flower and vegetable beds.There are wildflower meadows surrounding the garden and the disused Somerset Coal Canal runs through the property. Great variety of species and biodiversity, inc native orchids, kitchen walled garden, ponds and rills.

12 CHERRY BOLBERRY FARM
Furge Lane, Henstridge, BA8 0RN. Mrs Jenny Raymond, 01963 362177, cherrybolberryfarm@tiscali.co.uk. *6m E of Sherborne. In centre of Henstridge, R at small Xrds signed Furge Ln. Continue straight up lane, over 2 cattle grids, garden at top of lane on R.* **Fri 20, Sat 21 June (2-5). Combined adm with Rose Cottage £8, chd free. Home-made teas.** Visits also by arrangement 16 June to 29 June for groups of 10 to 20. The booking can be a combined visit with Rose Cottage.
Designed and maintained by the owner, this 50 yr-old award winning 1 acre garden has been planted for year-round interest with wildlife in mind. Colour themed island beds, shrub and herbaceous borders, unusual perennials, shrubs, old roses and an area of specimen trees. Lots of hidden areas, brilliant for hide and seek! Vegetable and flower cutting garden, greenhouses, nature ponds. Wonderful extensive views. Garden surrounded by our dairy farm which has been in the family for over 100 yrs.

13 COLDHARBOUR COTTAGE
Radford Hill, Radford, Radstock, BA3 2XU. Ms Amanda Cranston, amanda.cranston@yahoo.co.uk. *In Radford between Bath & Frome. Pls ask for directions when booking. Regret the garden is unsuitable for children.* **Visits by arrangement 2 June to 25 July for groups of up to 10. Gardening Club members & interested gardeners very welcome. Adm £10. Tea & coffee. Regret no WC facilities.**
Bath In Bloom Award Winner 2024. Idyllic rural cottage garden set in peaceful countryside. Sublime mix of thoughtful planting, natural areas reflect historical and modern heritage of this secluded acre. Natural hedges

Little Bucklers

with uninterrupted fields form the backdrop to the gentle calm of the design. Glorious spring flowers give way to peonies, lavender and formal rose garden. Romantic arches with climbing roses, clematis, box hedges. Deep herbaceous borders, hidden natural areas frame the lawns, home to old fruit trees. Productive kitchen and cut flower garden adds practicality to this quiet, sensitive space. Wheelchair access to grassed areas weather dependent. Some narrow and uneven paths and areas.

&

14 COLEFORD HOUSE
Underhill, Coleford, Radstock, BA3 5LU. Mr James Alexandroff. *5m from Frome. Coleford House is opp Kings Head pub in Lower Coleford with black wrought iron gates just before bridge over river. Parking in field 100 metres away.*

Sun 8 June (10.30-5). Adm £6, chd free. Tea, coffee & cake.
The River Mells flows through this picturesque garden with large lawns, wildflower planting, ornamental pond, woodland, substantial herbaceous borders, walled garden, arboretum/orchard, kitchen garden, vegetable garden, bat house and orangery. Most of garden is wheelchair friendly.

&

15 81 COOMBE LANE
Stoke Bishop, Bristol, BS9 2AT. Karl Suchy, 07873 588540, karl.suchy@icloud.com. *4m from Bristol city centre. J17 of M5, then follow A4018, direction Bristol for approx 2m. Turn R onto Canford Lane A4162. After 0.8m turn L onto Coombe Lane. Destination on R.* **Visits by arrangement 14 Apr to 1 Aug for groups of 10 to 40. Adm £9, chd free. Tea, coffee & cake.**

Hidden Victorian walled garden. Substantial mixed borders contain traditional and contemporary planting. Large lawns, numerous seating areas, summerhouse and French inspired patio with coppiced lime trees. Parterre and large raised Koi pond surrounded by bananas and tree ferns. Access to parterre and Koi pond might be difficult for wheelchair due to narrow gravel path, main part of garden is accessible.

&

In 2024, our donations to Carers Trust meant that 26,081 unpaid carers were supported across the UK.

16 COURT HOUSE
East Quantoxhead, TA5 1EJ. Mr & Mrs Hugh Luttrell. *12m W of Bridgwater. Off A39, house at end of village past duck pond. Enter by Frog St (Bridgwater/Kilve side from A39). Car park £1 in aid of church.* **Sun 18 May, Sun 29 June (2-5). Adm £7, chd free. Home-made teas.** Lovely 5 acre garden, trees, shrubs (many rare and tender), herbaceous and 3 acre woodland garden with spring interest and late summer borders. Views to sea and Quantocks. Gravel, stone and some mown grass paths.

17 CRETE HILL HOUSE
Cote House Lane, Durdham Down, Bristol, BS9 3UW. John Burgess. *2m N of Bristol city centre, 3m S J16 M5. A4018 Westbury Rd from city centre, L at White Tree r'about, R into Cote Rd, continue into Cote House Lane across the Downs. 2nd house on L. Parking on street.* **Sun 22 June (1-5). Adm £5, chd free. Home-made teas.**

C18 house in hidden corner of Bristol. Mainly SW facing garden, 80'x40', with shaped lawn, heavily planted traditional mixed borders - shrub, rose, clematis and herbaceous. Pergola with climbers, terrace with pond, several seating areas. Shady walled garden. Roof terrace (44 steps) with extensive views. Some of the seating areas and roof terrace not accessible by wheelchair. Whole garden can be viewed.

18 DOYNTON HOUSE
Bury Lane, Doynton, Bristol, BS30 5SR. Frances & Matthew Lindsey-Clark, franceslc11@gmail.com. *5m S of M4 J18, 6m N of Bath, 8m E of Bristol. Doynton is NE of Wick (turn off A420 opp Bath Rd) & SW of Dyrham (signed from A46). Doynton House is at S end of Doynton village, opp Culleysgate/Horsepool Lane. Park in signed field.* **Sun 6 July (2-6). Adm £7.50, chd free. Home-made teas.** Visits also by arrangement Apr to Sept for groups of up to 30.

A variety of garden areas separated by old walls and hedges. Mixed borders, lawns, wall planting, parterre, rill garden, walled vegetable garden, cottage beds, pool garden, dry gardens, peach house and greenhouse. Bees, chickens and meadow. Annual bed planned for 2025. We can recommend our local pub, the Cross House, just a short stroll across our parking field. Paths are of hoggin, stone and gravel. The grade of the gravel makes it a hard push in places, but all areas are just about wheelchair accessible.

19 ♦ EAST LAMBROOK MANOR GARDENS
Silver Street, East Lambrook, TA13 5HH. Mike Werkmeister, 01460 240328, enquiries@eastlambrook.com, www.eastlambrook.com. *2m N of South Petherton. Follow brown tourist signs from A303 South Petherton r'about or B3165 Xrds with lights N of Martock. What3words*

Forest Lodge

app: motivations.minivans.
earmarked. **For NGS: Fri 14 Feb, Sat 26 Apr, Sat 17 May (10-5). Adm £7, chd free. Tea, coffee & cake. For other opening times and information, please phone, email or visit garden website.**
The quintessential English cottage garden created by C20 gardening legend Margery Fish. Plantsman's paradise with contemporary and old-fashioned plants grown in a relaxed and informal manner to create a remarkable garden of great beauty and charm. With noted collections of snowdrops, hellebores and geraniums and the excellent specialist Margery Fish Plant Nursery. Partial wheelchair access. Margery Fish's 1956 first book 'We Made A Garden' was republished June 2024.

🐕 ♿ 🚌 ☕ 🔊

20 ELWORTHY COTTAGE
Elworthy, Taunton, TA4 3PX. Mike & Jenny Spiller, 01984 656427, mike@elworthy-cottage.co.uk, www.elworthy-cottage.co.uk. *12m NW of Taunton. On B3188 between Wiveliscombe & Watchet. What3words app: hazelnuts.stormy. sprinter.* **Wed 5, Fri 14, Tue 25 Feb, Sun 13, Tue 22 Apr, Mon 26 May, Tue 24 June, Tue 8, Sun 27 July, Tue 5, Mon 25 Aug (11-4.30). Adm £5, chd free. Home-made teas. Visits also by arrangement Feb to Sept.**
One acre plantsman's garden in tranquil setting. Island beds, scented plants, unusual perennials and ornamental trees and shrubs provide year-round interest. In spring, pulmonarias, hellebores and more than 350 varieties of snowdrops. Planted to encourage birds, bees and butterflies. Lots of birdsong, wildflower areas and developing wildflower meadow, decorative vegetable garden, living willow screen. Seats for visitors to enjoy views of the surrounding countryside. Garden attached to plantsman's nursery, open at the same time.

🐕 ♿ 🚌 ☕ 🔊

21 FAIRFIELD
Stogursey, Bridgwater, TA5 1PU. Lady Acland Hood Gass. *7m E of Williton. 11m W of Bridgwater. From A39 Bridgwater to Minehead road turn N. Garden 1½m W of Stogursey on Stringston road. No coaches.* **Sun 13 Apr (2-4.30). Adm £7, chd free. Tea, coffee & cake.**
Woodland garden with many interesting bulbs inc naturalised anemones, fritillaria with roses, shrubs and fine trees. Paved maze. Views of Quantocks. The ground is flat and should be accessible, around half the paths are grass so may be more difficult when wet.

♿ 🐕 ☕ 🔊

22 NEW 84 FENSHURST GARDENS
Long Ashton, Bristol, BS41 9AR. Mrs Hazel Mallett, www.instagram.com/hazelgardening. *From the main road through Long Ashton (Weston Rd) turn onto Lampton Rd, then R (straight ahead) onto Fenshurst Gardens. No 84 is opp Bradville Gardens.* **Sat 21 June (12-4.30). Adm £5, chd free. Home-made teas.**
A semi-urban garden, 100ft from the road to the back on the Festival Way NCN cycle path. A cottage garden with metal art work, lawn, patio, roses, raised beds for vegetables sown in our greenhouse as well as climbers, fruit trees and soft fruit. The terraced front garden has one of our container ponds and a self-made bin store with green roof. We maximise recycling with composts and water butts. We have steps and a slope to the main garden and a path plus lawn to acccess the rear of the garden.

♿ 🐕 ✿ 🚌 ☕ 🔊

23 FOREST LODGE
Pen Selwood, BA9 8LL. James & Lucy Nelson, forestlodgegardens.co.uk. *1½m N of A303, 3m E of Wincanton. Leave A303 at B3081 (Wincanton to Gillingham road), up hill to Pen Selwood, L towards church. ½m, garden on L - low curved wall and yellow NGS signs.* **Sat 15 Mar (10-3); Sat 24 May (10-4). Combined adm with Lower Shalford Farm £10, chd free. Home-made teas. Lavender blue famous carrot cake, brownies & flapjacks. Donation to Well Wessex group of Mental Health charities in Somerset.**
3 acre mature garden with beautiful lake, full of bulbs and flowering trees. Many camellias and rhododendrons from March till May. Lovely views towards Blackmore Vale. Part formal with pleached hornbeam allée and rill, part water garden. Wonderful roses in June. Unusual spring flowering trees such as paulownia, *Davidia involucrata* and many beautiful cornus. Interesting garden sculpture. Good plant interest year-round due to acidic greensand soil (hamamelis, Daphne, magnolia, lovely rhododendrons, camellias and flowering trees in the spring) and south west facing slope. Beautiful in all seasons and good structure which underpins the planting. Wheelchair access to front garden only, however much of garden viewable from there.

♿ 🐕 ✿ 🚌 ☕ 🪑 🔊

24 NEW FROGBURY
Upper Vobster, Radstock, BA3 5SA. Matthew & Penny Bennett. *5m W of Frome, ½m from Mells. At Xrds follow signpost to Upper Vobster and further signs to field parking on L after 200yds.* **Sun 29 June (2-5.30). Adm £6.50, chd free. Tea, coffee & cake.**
An undiscovered pretty south facing exposed garden, sloping gently, with views across the Mells Brook valley. Yew, lime, box and beech hedges give structure and some protection from winds, colourful beds with mixed perennials, annuals and roses. Patio area with formal pond, water lilies, two summerhouses, croquet lawn, greenhouse and vegetable beds. Seating spots throughout the garden. Partial wheelchair access, mainly grass either flat or gently sloping. Some steep slopes and steps plus gravel driveway and path may be difficult to navigate.

♿ ✿ ☕ 🪑 🔊

The National Garden Scheme donated over £3.5 million to our nursing and health beneficiaries from money raised at gardens open in 2024.

GROUP OPENING

25 FROME GARDENS
9 Catherston Close, Frome, BA11 4HR. **Dave & Prue Moon.** *15m S of Bath. Town Centre W towards Shepton Mallet (A361). R at Sainsbury's r'about, follow lane for ½ m. L into Critchill Rd. Over Xrds, 1st L Catherston Close.* **Sun 15 June (12-5). Combined adm £8, chd free. Tea, coffee & cake at Highclere. Cash payment for admission & refreshments (card payments at 9 Catherston Close only).**

9 CATHERSTON CLOSE
BA11 4HR. Dave & Prue Moon.

HIGHCLERE
BA11 4DS. Mrs Sally Gregory.

61 NUNNEY ROAD
BA11 4LA. Mrs Caroline Toll.

NEW THE RETREAT
BA11 5JU. Dinah Bardgett.

1 TUCKER CLOSE
BA11 5LS. Bev Revie & Tim Cutting.

Five contrasting and exciting secret town gardens with unusual and interesting styles of design and planting complementing each other. 4 are returning gardens; Highclere, a large garden, created by the owner's parents, flower borders are a riot of colour combine with a mix of trees, shrubs, climbers and vegetables. 9 Catherston Close is where the unexpected awaits the visitor. The garden grew to ⅓ acre, with colour themed shrub, herbaceous borders and much more. 61 Nunney Rd, a well-cared for garden, has been re designed from 2020 by a new owner who considers herself an untidy planter as she falls for plants and then finds the right place for them! Finally, 1 Tucker Close, a small walled town garden of unusual design planted by the owners with wildlife in mind. Its borders are set with decking and slate rather than grass. New for 2025 is The Retreat, a large garden with mature trees, a pond, grasses and rockeries, and a small allotment with wild woodland area, inc bees. Shallow steps & a gravel path at Catherston Close, small step onto lawn at Nunney Road, and gravel paths at The Retreat.

GROUP OPENING

26 GOATHURST GARDENS
Goathurst, Bridgwater, TA5 2DF. *4m SW of Bridgwater, 2½ m W of N Petherton. Parking available at Halswell House & near the Temple of Pan. Disabled parking only at the Temple of Pan.* **Sat 19, Sun 20 July (2-5). Combined adm £7.50, chd free. Tea, coffee & cake.**

HALSWELL HOUSE
Mrs Oksana Kadatskaya.

THE TEMPLE OF PAN
Peter Strivens & Tessa Shaw.

Two gardens in the picturesque village of Goathurst on the edge of the Quantock Hills linked by a common history. The gardens at Halswell Park are a history of garden design in England, with a knot garden created to reflect an original C16 design, a walled garden and Georgian pleasure gardens with follies, bridges and ponds. The garden of the Temple of Pan surrounds an C18 baroque folly built as part of Halswell Park's Georgian pleasure gardens, now with herbaceous borders, lawns, ponds and woodland gardens. Halswell knot gardens has wheelchair access to most areas. Some but not all of the gardens at The Temple of Pan are wheelchair accessible.

27 NEW 30 GREAT BROCKERIDGE
Westbury on Trym, Bristol, BS9 3TZ. **Albina & Robert Nobbs.** *Approx 3½ m NW of Bristol City centre. Parking on residential streets. Access either from Westbury Rd or Reedley Rd.* **Sat 16, Sun 17 Aug (1-5). Adm £5, chd free. Home-made teas.**
A suburban garden with south facing front garden having views across the BS9 area of Bristol and beyond. Three levels slope down to the road via 37 steps with eclectic planting from arid to hardy tropical. The patio around the house has potted plants and raised beds. The rear garden is relatively level with a mature oak tree, Japanese acers, fruit trees, shrubs, perennials, a small bog garden, pond and a vegetable plot. Houseplants are displayed in and around our small greenhouse. Various repurposed items are dotted around the garden.

28 ♦ GREENCOMBE GARDENS
Porlock, Minehead, TA24 8NU. Greencombe Garden Trust, 01643 862363, info@greencombe.org, www.greencombe.org. *W of Porlock below the wooded slopes of Exmoor. Take A39 to west end of Porlock & turn onto B3225 to Porlock Weir. Drive ½ m, turn L at Greencombe Gardens sign. Go up drive; parking signed.* **For NGS: Tue 15 Apr, Tue 15 July (2-6). Adm £7, chd £1. Cream teas.** For other opening times and information, please phone, email or visit garden website. Donation to Plant Heritage.
Organic woodland garden of international renown, Greencombe stretches along a sheltered hillside and offers outstanding views over Porlock Bay. Moss-covered paths meander through a collection of ornamental plants that flourish beneath a canopy of oaks, hollies, conifers and chestnuts. Camellias, rhododendrons, azaleas, lilies, roses, clematis, and hydrangeas blossom among 4 National Collections. Champion English Holly tree (*Ilex aquifolium*), one of the largest and oldest in the UK. Giant rhododendrons species and exceptionally large camellias. A millennium chapel hides in the mossy banks of the wood. A moon arch leads into a walled garden.

29 GREYSTONES
Hollybush Lane, Bristol, BS9 1JB. **Mrs Pam Townsend.** *2m N of Bristol city centre, close to Durdham Down, backing onto the Botanic Garden. A4018 Westbury Rd, L at White Tree r'about, L into Saville Rd, Hollybush Lane 2nd on R. Narrow lane, parking limited, recommended to park in Saville Rd.* **Sun 2 Mar, Sun 8 June (11-4). Adm £4.50, chd free. Light lunches & home made teas.**
Peaceful garden with places to sit and enjoy a quiet corner of Bristol. Interesting courtyard, raised beds, large variety of conifers and shrubs leads to secluded garden of contrasts - sunny beds with olive tree and brightly coloured flowers to shady spots, with acers, hostas and ferns. Snowdrops, hellebores, spring bulbs, naturalised daffodils. Small orchard, espaliered pears. Paved footpath provides level access to all areas.

Barcroft Hall

30 NEW 87 HALLEN ROAD
Henbury, Bristol, BS10 7RA.
Andrew Hockey & Janet Hunt.
½m from Blaise Castle Estate, nr Bristol/S Glos border. From Henbury to Hallen (Avonmouth Way becomes Hallen Rd), semi-detached on L (opp end of school field) before Windmill Lane. What3words app: late.clown.into. Park on side roads, not main road. **Sat 14, Sun 15 June (2-5). Adm £4, chd free. Pre-booking essential, please visit www.ngs.org.uk for information & booking. Tea, coffee & cake.**
125 foot plantaholic's garden divided into different beds with unusual plants giving year-round interest. Almost 1000 different types inc many hardy geraniums, heucheras, ferns, grasses, alpines and geums, plus several pots, troughs, 2 small ponds and an old Bramley apple tree. Some steps and uneven paths. Unsuitable for wheelchairs.
☕

31 HANGERIDGE FARMHOUSE
Wrangway, Wellington,
TA21 9QG. Mr & Mrs R E Chave & Mrs J Dobson, 07896 134920, treborchaver1978@gmail.com. *2m S of Wellington. Off A38 Wellington bypass signed Wrangway. 1st L towards Wellington monument,* over motorway bridge 1st R. **Sun 27 July (2-5). Adm £4, chd free. Home-made teas. Visits also by arrangement May to Aug for groups of 10 to 30.**
Nestled between the Blackdown & Quantock hills, sits this stunning 1 acre plantsman's garden. Rural countryside surrounds the garden, and with a cottage feel you will find a plethora of different plants to suit all tastes, island beds with unusual perennials, shrubs, old roses and specimen trees. There is somewhere for all to just sit back and relax, and let the tranquillity infiltrate your senses.
♿ 🐕 ☕

32 HANHAM COURT
Ferry Road, Hanham Abbots,
BS15 3NT. Hanham Court Gardens, connie@hanhamcourtgardens.com, www.hanhamcourtgardens.com. *5m E of Bristol centre, 9m W of Bath centre. E-A431 from Bath, via Willsbridge, L at mini r'about, Court Farm Rd 1m. Entrance sharp L bend. W-A420 from Bristol. A431,1m. R at mini r'about Memorial Rd 1m. Entrance on Court Farm Rd sharp R bend.* **Sat 7, Sun 8 June (11-4.30). Adm £8, chd free. Home-made teas.**
Hanham Court Gardens is a deeply romantic and enchanting idyll. Hidden in a rural bowl, the gardens contain a rich mix of bold formal topiary and blowsy planting, with water, woodland, orchard, meadow and kitchen gardens. The emphasis is on scent, structure and romance, all set amid a remarkable cluster of manorial buildings between Bath and Bristol.
✿ 🐕 🎵

33 4 HAYTOR PARK
Bristol, BS9 2LR. Mr & Mrs
C J Prior, 07779 203626, p.l.prior@gmail.com. *3m NW of Bristol city centre. From A4162 Inner Ring Rd take turning into Coombe Bridge Ave, Haytor Park is 1st on L. Please no parking in Haytor Park.* **Sun 27 Apr (1-5). Adm £4, chd free. Open nearby Lucombe House. Opening with Stoke Bishop Gardens on Sun 18 May. Visits also by arrangement 28 Apr to 28 Sept for groups of 10 to 30.**
A very personal haven of gorgeous plants and secret spaces. Discover a wildlife pond, green roof and so many pots. Many paths and quirky screens add an air of mystery. Sit awhile on numerous benches to see plants at many levels and for every season. You may spot dragons everywhere!
✿ 🐕 🎵

Westbrook House

SPECIAL EVENT

34 ♦ **HESTERCOMBE GARDENS**
Cheddon Fitzpaine, Taunton, TA2 8LG. Hestercombe Gardens Trust, 01823 413923, info@hestercombe.com, www.hestercombe.com. *3m N of Taunton, less than 6m from J25 of M5. Follow brown daisy signs. SatNav postcode TA2 8LQ.* **For NGS: Wed 5 Mar (10-3.30). Adm £15.30, chd £7.65. Light refreshments. Evening opening Wed 4 June (6-8). Adm £20, chd free. Pre-booking essential, please visit www.ngs.org.uk for information & booking. Discount/ prepaid vouchers not valid on the National Garden Scheme charity day.** For other opening times and information, please phone, email or visit garden website.
Magnificent Georgian landscape garden designed by artist Coplestone Warre Bampfylde, a contemporary of Gainsborough and Henry Hoare of Stourhead. Victorian terrace and shrubbery and an exquisite example of a Lutyens/Jeykll designed formal garden. Enjoy 50 acres of woodland walks, temples, terraces,

pergolas, lakes and cascades. A limited number of tickets have been made available for a private tour of the gardens on the evening of the 4th June. Please arrive promptly at 6pm for a glass of wine, and an introductory talk by Head Gardener, Claire Greenslade, after which there will be the opportunity to explore the gardens, accompanied by Claire. This will be a unique experience to wander the gardens in the early evening when the garden is closed to other visitors. Restaurant and café, restored watermill and barn, contemporary art gallery. Gravel paths, steep slopes, steps. An all-access route is shown on the guide map, & visitors can pre-book an all-terrain tramper vehicle (5 Mar only).
♿ 🐕 ✿ 🚗 ☕ 🪑 🔊

35 HILLCREST
Curload, Stoke St Gregory, Taunton, TA3 6JA. Charles & Charlotte Sundquist, 01823 490852, chazfix@gmail.com. *At top of Curload. From A358 take A378, L to & through North Curry, L ½m after Willows & Wetlands centre. Hillcrest on R (parking directions). From A361 turn S at Burrowbridge Xrds. Then 1st R follow NGS signs.*

Sat 3, Sun 4 May (12-5). Adm £5, chd free. Tea, coffee & cake. Visits also by arrangement Apr to June for groups of 5 to 30.
Boasting stunning views of the Somerset Levels, Burrow Mump and Glastonbury Tor this 6 acre garden offers plenty of interest, inc a standing stone. Enjoy woodland walks, varied borders, flowering meadow and several ponds. There are greenhouses, orchards, a new produce garden and newly built large gravel garden. Garden is mostly level with gentle sloping paths down through meadow. Cash only for refreshments and plants. Gravel around refreshment area.
♿ 🐕 ✿ ☕ 🪑 🔊

In 2024 we awarded £232,000 in Community Garden Grants, supporting 89 community garden projects.

© Heather Edwards

36 HOLLAM HOUSE
Dulverton, TA22 9JH. Annie Prebensen, 01398 323445, annie@hollam.co.uk. *From Dulverton Bridge, go straight & bear R at the chemist. At the garage, Hollam Ln is the 2nd L turning immed after the garage, it is between a cottage & music shop.* **Visits by arrangement 22 Apr to 4 July. Adm £7, chd free. Tea, coffee & cake.** Extending over 5 acres, this sloping Exmoor garden inc ponds, a water garden, woodland planting, borders and meadow areas. There are magnificent mature trees and old rhododendrons. Spring highlights are the thousands of tulips and other bulbs as well as flowering shrubs and trees; magnolia, cornus and viburnum among others. Not suitable for those of limited mobility or small children. No dogs.

37 HONEYHURST FARM
Honeyhurst Lane, Rodney Stoke, Cheddar, BS27 3UJ. Don & Kathy Longhurst, 01749 870322, donlonghurst@btinternet.com, www.ciderbarrelcottage.co.uk. *4m E of Cheddar. From Wells (A371) turn into Rodney Stoke signed Wedmore. Pass church on L & continue for almost 1m. Car park signed. From Cheddar (A371) turn R signed Wedmore, through Draycott to car park.* **Visits by arrangement 1 May to 21 Sept for groups of 10 to 40. Home-made teas avail for additional charge. Adm £5, chd free.** ⅔ acre part walled rural garden with babbling brook and 4 acre traditional cider orchard, with views. Specimen hollies, copper beech, paulownia, yew and poplar. Pergolas, arbour and numerous seats. Mixed informal shrub and perennial beds with many unusual plants. Many pots planted with shrubs, hardy and half-hardy perennials. Level, grass and some shingle.

38 JAPANESE GARDEN BRISTOL
13 Glenarm Walk, Brislington, Bristol, BS4 4LS. Martin Fitton, www.japanesegardenbristol.com. *A4 Bristol to Bath. A4 Brislington, at Texaco Garage at bottom of Bristol Hill turn into School Rd & immed R into Church Parade. Car park 1st turn on R or proceed to Glenarm Walk.* **Sat 14 June (12-5). Adm £6,** chd £2. Pre-booking essential, please visit www.ngs.org.uk for information & booking. Home-made teas.
As you walk through the gate you will be welcomed by Japanese Koi. Then take a step to another level to the relaxing Japanese garden room and tea house surrounded by acers and cloud trees. Walk past Buddha corner into the Bonsai and Zen water feature area. Continue to a Japanese courtyard through a gate to a peaceful Japanese tea garden. There you will find seating to enjoy the serene atmosphere. Please note steps to different levels means the garden is unsuitable for disabled access.

39 JOHN'S CORNER
2 Fitzgerald Road, Bedminster, Bristol, BS3 5DD. John Hodge. *3m from city centre. South Bristol, off St. John's Lane, Totterdown end. 1st house on R entrance at side of house. On number 91 bus route. Parking in residential street.* **Sat 21, Sun 22 June (12-5). Adm £5, chd free. Tea, coffee & cake.**
Unusual and interesting city garden with a mixture of exciting plants and features. Ponds, ferns and much more. Eden project style greenhouse with collection of cacti. Not all areas accessible by wheelchair.

40 ◆ KILVER COURT GARDENS
Kilver Street, Shepton Mallet, BA4 5NF. The Showering Family, 01749 705279, enquiries@kilvercourt.co.uk, www.kilvercourt.com. *30 mins drive from Bristol & Bath on the A37. Opp Showerings factory on Kilver St. Disabled parking in lower car park.* **For NGS: Thur 12 June, Thur 11 Sept (10-4). Adm £7.50, chd free. Discount/Prepaid vouchers not valid on the above NGS open days. For other opening times and information, please phone, email or visit garden website.**
Visitors can wander by the millpond, explore the formal and informal gardens and enjoy a replica of the splendid Chelsea Flower Show Gold Medal winning rockery where a gushing recirculated stream flows from pool to pool and waterfalls into the lake. All this set against the stunning backdrop of Charlton Viaduct with the 100m herbaceous flower border beyond. Seek out the famous Babycham whilst here! Please note, on site payment is card only. Some slopes, rockery not accessible for wheelchairs but can be viewed from garden.

41 NEW 30 KINGSHOLM ROAD
Southmead, Bristol, BS10 5LH. Ms Emma Nelder, www.instagram.com/second_bassoon. *North Bristol. Turning is at the Bear & Rugged Staff T-lights on Southmead Rd. Pedestrian access avail from Kendon Drive & Kelston Rd. Kingsholm Rd is a no-through road for cars.* **Sat 23 Aug (1-5). Adm £3.50, chd free. Pre-booking essential, please visit www.ngs.org.uk for information & booking. Tea, coffee & cake.**
170ft urban garden developed over the last 4 yrs and divided into ornamental and productive areas. Herbaceous border, cutting beds, greenhouse, pond, and water features, along with a productive kitchen garden and resident flock of hens. Collections of pelargoniums, citrus trees, succulents, hostas, and dahlias.

42 NEW KINGSLAND
North Street, Milverton, Taunton, TA4 1LG. Mrs Mary-Anne Robb, 07563 367644. *Entering Milverton pass the sawmill & turn R into North St. From Wellington, go past the village shop & turn L, up the hill, turn R into North St.* **Sun 29 June (11-5). Adm £7.50, chd £3. Home-made teas in the side garden, supplied by the village church between 2 & 5pm. Visits also by arrangement 1 June to 28 Sept.**
A plantsman's walled village garden of approx 1 acre that was gutted in 2021 and started from scratch - large trees brought in from Holland gave it immediate structure. The garden is laid out in 3 sections with many unusual plants. Herbaceous borders, sunken gravel garden and a mound with grasses and spring bulbs. A garden continuously changing for lovers of structure and experimentation. Partial access as several areas cannot be reached by wheelchairs, due to gravel paths etc.

43 KNOLL COTTAGE
Stogumber, Taunton, TA4 3TN. Elaine & John Leech, 01984 656689, john@Leech45.com, www.knoll-cottage.co.uk. *3m SE of Williton. From A358 follow signs to Stogumber. After 2½ m, at T-junction, turn R towards Williton. After ⅓ m turn R up narrow lane. Knoll Cottage on L after 100yds.* **Visits by arrangement June to Sept for groups of up to 20. Adm £5, chd free. Home-made teas.**
Four acre garden started from fields in 1998. Extensive mixed beds with shrubs, perennials and annuals. Over 80 different roses, and many salvias and dahlias later in the season. Small arboretum area inc many different cornus, rowans, hawthorns, oaks and birches. Pond, large vegetable and fruit areas.

44 NEW LITTLE BUCKLERS
Brockley Hall, Brockley Lane, Brockley, Bristol, BS48 3AZ. Carol & Peter Parfrey. *10m S of Bristol. Little Bucklers is in the grounds of Brockley Hall, just off the A370 Bristol to Weston-Super-Mare road at the bottom of Brockley Coombe. What3words app: perfumed. trombone.chip.* **Sat 31 May (1-5); Sun 1 June (1-5.30). Adm £5, chd free. Home-made cakes inc gluten free & vegan.**
¾ acre garden with countryside views. The garden has been developed gradually over the last 40 yrs. Mixed colour themed borders, herbaceous perennials, gravel gardens, 2 small ponds, path leading to small woodland area and onward to vegetable plot and greenhouse. Mature trees and lots of seating areas make the garden a delight to work and be in. The garden is mainly flat. Easy access to the front garden and rear patio. Access to the rear garden via 2 shallow steps.

45 LITTLE YARFORD FARMHOUSE
Kingston St Mary, Taunton, TA2 8AN. Mrs D Bradley, 01823 451350, dilly.bradley@gmail.com. *1½ m W of Hestercombe, 3½ m N of Taunton. From Taunton on Kingston St Mary road. At 30mph sign turn L at Parsonage Ln. Continue 1¼ m W, to Yarford sign. Continue 400yds. Turn R up concrete road.* **Sun 4 May (2-5). Cream teas. Mon 5 May (11-3).**

Light refreshments. Adm £7, chd free. Visits also by arrangement Apr to Oct. Guided tours limited to 10/12 participants at any one time. Refreshments.
Unusual 5 acre garden embracing C17 house (not open) Natural pond and 90ft water lily pond. A plantsman's garden notable for the aesthetics of its planting especially its 300+ rare and unusual tree cultivars: the best collection of broad leaf and conifer specimens in Western Somerset (link to full list can be found under Extended Description on NGS website); those trees not available to Bampfylde Warre at Hestercombe in C18. There will be a brief guided tree tour at 2.30 and 3.30pm. An exercise in landscaping, contrast planting and creating views both within the garden and without to the vale and the Quantock Hills. Mostly wheelchair access.

46 LOWER SHALFORD FARM
Shalford Lane, Charlton Musgrove, Wincanton, BA9 8HE. Mr & Mrs David Posnett. *Lower Shalford is 2m NE of Wincanton. Leave A303 at Wincanton go N on B3081 towards Bruton. Just beyond Otter Garden Centre turn R Shalford Lane, garden is ½ m on L. Parking opp house.* **Sat 15 Mar (10-3); Sat 24 May (10-4). Combined adm with Forest Lodge £10, chd free. Tea, coffee & cake.**
Fairly large open garden with extensive lawns and wooded surroundings with drifts of daffodils in spring. Small winterbourne stream running through with several stone bridges. Walled rose/parterre garden, hedged herbaceous garden, mature wisterias in all their glory and several ornamental ponds.

47 LUCOMBE HOUSE
12 Druid Stoke Ave, Stoke Bishop, Bristol, BS9 1DD. Malcolm Ravenscroft, 01179 682494, famrave@gmail.com. *4m NW of Bristol centre. At top of Druid Hill. Turn in Druid Stoke Ave. Garden on R 300m from junction.* **Sun 27 Apr (1-5). Adm £4, chd free. Home-made teas. Open nearby 4 Haytor Park. Teas & home-made cakes provided by local scout group. Visits also by arrangement Apr to Sept for groups of up to 30. Please give 3-4 weeks notice of arranged visit.**

For tree lovers of all ages! As well as a 260 yr old Lucombe Oak - one of the most significant trees in the UK - there are over 30 mature English trees planted to create an urban woodland. A tree trail leaflet identifying all significant trees will be available and a woodland path provides a behind the scenes look at the garden. Trio of recorder players will entertain visitors. Rough paths in woodland area, 2 steps to patio.

48 LYDEARD HOUSE
West Street, Bishops Lydeard, Taunton, TA4 3AU. Mrs Vaun Wilkins. *5m NW of Taunton. A358 Taunton to Minehead, do not take 1st 3 R turnings to Bishops Lydeard but 4th signed to Cedar Falls. Follow signs to Lydeard House.* **Sun 8 June (2-5). Adm £6, chd free. Tea, coffee & cake.**
4 acre garden with C18 origins and many later additions. Sweeping lawns, lake overhung with willows, canal running parallel to Victorian rose-covered pergola, along with box parterre, chinoiserie-style garden, recent temple folly and walled vegetable garden plus wonderful mature trees. Plants for sale. Children must be supervised because of very deep water. Deep gravel paths and steps may cause difficulty for wheelchairs but most features are accessible by lawn and parking will be available.

49 THE MANOR
South Street, Wincanton, BA9 9DL. Anna Hughes. *On the R of South St on the one-way system in central Wincanton, opp Our Lady's Primary School. Parking on the High St or in the Memorial Hall car park. The garden is also known as 'The Dogs'.* **Sat 24, Sun 25 May (10-5). Adm £7, chd free. Tea, coffee & cake.**
Hidden and unexpected large walled garden in town centre around seventeenth-century manor house. Developed by the current owners over the last 25 yrs. Yew hedges provide good structure and divide the garden into distinct areas. Formal pond garden. Vegetable garden with box edging. Orchard. Tiny 'lockdown' garden created in 2020. A small number of parking places by the house for disabled use. Wheelchair access is available to the main upper part of the garden.

SOMERSET & BRISTOL 469

50 MATHLIN COTTAGE
School Road, Wrington, Bristol, BS40 5NB. Sally & Tony Harden. 10m SW of Bristol. Midway between A38 at Redhill or Lower Langford & A370 at Congresbury. **Wed 4, Sun 8 June (2-4.30). Adm £5, chd free. Home-made teas.**
A cottage garden accessed by numerous shallow steps with wonderful views of the Mendip hills. Enjoy the front garden border with pergola and walkway before entering the back, more cottage style space full of bee/butterfly friendly plants. There is a small pond, greenhouse with tomatoes, cucumbers and chilies alongside a salad/soft fruit plot. Plenty of seating and places to relax as well as a large specimen of Paul's Himalayan Musk over a walkway to enjoy.

51 MELLOWSTONES
Staples Hill, Freshford, Bath, BA2 7WL. Mrs Jackie Kennedy. 5m S of Bath. A36 Bath/Warminster rd. Take exit to Freshford; past pub over bridge up Staples Hill to top. Mellowstones is on the R. Parking at Downside Nurseries, 1st L after property (a 15 min walk). **Sun 1 June (11-4). Adm £6, chd free. Home-made cakes & teas.**
Developed over the last 5 yrs, this 1 acre south facing hillside terraced garden is set in woodland, with wonderful views across the Frome valley. The upper level has cottage garden plants and yew hedges, a quarry kitchen and a grass path through wildflowers to the summerhouse. The Mediterranean terrace has olive trees, a gravel planting area with stepping stones across a corten steel pond. The lower terrace is a formal garden leading to a grass path which extends through the sloping wildflower orchard. Woodland and valley walks. Short distance from the canal.

52 ♦ MILTON LODGE
Old Bristol Road, Wells, BA5 3AQ. Simon Tudway Quilter, 01749 679341, www.miltonlodgegardens.co.uk. ½m N of Wells. From A39 Bristol-Wells, turn N up Old Bristol Rd; car park 1st gate on L signed. **For NGS: Sun 11 May, Sun 8 June, Sun 6 July (2-5). Adm £5, chd free. Home-made teas. (cash only). Children 14 & under free entry to garden.** Discount/membership/prepaid vouchers not accepted on our 3 National Garden Scheme charity days. **For other opening times and information, please phone or visit garden website.**
This garden is a must for garden lovers, well worth a visit. Land transformed into architectural terraces capitalising on views of Wells Cathedral and Vale of Avalon. A Grade II terraced garden restored to its former glory by the owner's parents, who moved here in 1960, replacing the orchard with a collection of ornamental trees, specimen trees and yew hedges. A serene, relaxing atmosphere within the garden succeeds the ravages of two World Wars. Cross over Old Bristol Rd to our 7 acre woodland garden, 'The Combe', open on NGS days, a natural peaceful contrast to the formal garden of Milton Lodge. Cash only for teas, card machine or cash for admission.

53 ♦ MODEL FARM
Perry Green, Wembdon, Bridgwater, TA5 2BA. Dave & Roz Young, 01278 429953, dave@modelfarm.com, www.modelfarm.com. 4m from J23 of M5. Follow Brown signs from r'about on A39 2m W of Bridgwater. **For opening times and information, please phone, email or visit garden website.**
Four acres of flat gardens to south of Victorian country house. Created from a field in last 15 yrs and still being developed. A dozen large mixed flower beds planted in cottage garden style with wildlife in mind. Wooded areas, mixed orchard, lawns, wildflower meadows and wildlife ponds. Plenty of seating throughout the gardens which are open on weekdays in term time from Easter.

54 NEW WOOD HOUSE, 19 THE BEACON
Ilminster, TA19 9AH. Mr & Mrs Julian Gibbs. ½m from Ilminster Market Place. Northern outskirts of Ilminster on B3168 (Curry Rivel road), on W side of road. **Sat 10 May (2-5.30). Adm £5, chd free. Tea, coffee & cake.**
Building on an existing design of terraces, paths and some fine mature trees, the garden has been extensively restored over 9 yrs, replanting with several unusual species, inc wild-collected acers, oaks and malus. Formal areas close to the house, with long views, and steep winding paths on both sides leading through unexpected incidents to the bottom of the garden and an orchard.

55 165 NEWBRIDGE HILL
Bath, BA1 3PX. Helen Hughesdon, 07793 085267, thefragrantlife@hotmail.com. On the western fringes of Bath (A431), 100m on L after Apsley Rd. Several bus routes go to Newbridge Hill. **Visits by arrangement 1 May to 26 July for groups of 10 to 16. Parking available for a minibus or coach drop off. Cream tea included. Adm £10, chd free.**
A south facing garden on the edge of the city with unusual and exotic plants, vegetable garden, small wildlife pond, greenhouse, treehouse and swing, fabulous views and a sunny terrace overlooking the garden where cream teas are served.

56 NYNEHEAD COURT
Nynehead, Wellington, TA21 0BN. Nynehead Care Ltd, 01823 662481, admin@nyneheadcourt.co.uk, www.nyneheadcourt.co.uk. 1½m N of Wellington. M5 J26 B3187 towards Wellington. R at Lidl r'about marked Nynehead & Poole, follow lane for 1m, take Milverton turning at fork, turning into Chipley Rd. **Sun 22 June (2-4.30). Adm £5, chd free. Light refreshments in Orangery. Tea, coffee, squash, cake & biscuits available.**
Nynehead Court was the home of the Sandford family from 1590-1902. The 14 acres of gardens are noted for specimen trees, and there will be a garden tour with the Head Gardener at 2pm (pls wear suitable footwear). Nynehead is now a private residential care home. The garden combines Victorian formality with natural style promoting wildlife further into the parkland in a managed grassland Park. A Historic England garden of national importance, Nynehead won a landscape heritage award in 2007 from Taunton Deane Borough Council. Partial wheelchair access: cobbled yards, gentle slopes, chipped paths, liable to puddle during or after rain.

57 THE OLD RECTORY, DOYNTON
18 Toghill Lane, Doynton, Bristol, BS30 5SY. Edwina & Clive Humby, www.tumblr.com/doyntongardens. *At heart of village of Doynton, between Bath & Bristol. Parking in Bury Lane, just after junction with Horsepool Lane. Car parking is signed. Parking is restricted to designated areas.* **Sat 21 June (11-5). Adm £6, chd free. Cream teas.** Doynton's Grade II listed Georgian Rectory's walled garden and extended 15 acre estate. Renovated over 12 yrs, it sits within AONB. Garden has diversity of modern and traditional elements, fused to create an atmospheric series of garden rooms. Large landscaped kitchen garden with canal, vegetable plots, fruit cages and treehouse. Bees and a woodland area are also features for a longer stroll.

58 PENNARD HOUSE
East Pennard, Shepton Mallet, BA4 6TP. Martin Dearden, 07802 243569, martin@pennardcottage.co.uk. *5m S of Shepton Mallet on A37. 1m W of A37 Turn R at the top of the hill, or L if coming from the south.* **Tue 10 June (12-5). Adm £6, chd free. Light lunches, teas, coffee & cakes. Visits also by arrangement May to Sept for groups of 10 to 30.** Two delightful separate gardens, both with extensive lawns, mature trees, rose beds, rustic topiary, a Victorian spring fed swimming pool and ponds. Garden layout dates from 1835 when the Napier family enlarged the main house and acquired the house next door. Next door, Pennard Plants, will also open for plant purchasing. On offer is a selection of edible plants, fruit trees, herbs and seeds. The gardens are on a slope, but accessible with assistance.

59 PENNY BROHN UK
Chapel Pill Lane, Pill, BS20 0HH. Penny Brohn UK, 0303 3000118, fundraising@pennybrohn.org.uk, www.pennybrohn.org.uk. *4m W of Bristol. Off A369 Clifton Suspension Bridge to M5 (J19 Gordano Services). Follow signs to Penny Brohn UK & to Pill/Ham Green (5 mins).* **Sun 8 June (10-4). Adm £6, chd free. Jacket potato lunches, hot & cold drinks, home-made cakes. Visits also by arrangement** 1 Feb to 1 Dec for groups of 5 to 30. 3½ acre tranquil garden surrounds Georgian mansion with many mature trees, wildflower meadow, flower garden and cedar summerhouse. Fine views from historic gazebo overlooking the River Avon. Courtyard gardens with water features. Garden is maintained by volunteers and plays an active role in the charity's personalised cancer care approach. Plants, teas, music and plenty of space to enjoy a picnic. Tours of centre to find out more about the work of Penny Brohn UK. Some gravel and grass paths.

60 NEW THE PONY
Moorledge Road, Newtown, Chew Magna, Bristol, BS40 8TQ. Josh & Holly Eggleton, theponychewvalley.co.uk. *2m E of Chew Magna. Turn off the A386 onto Moorledge Rd between Stanton Wick & Bishop Sutton. Or if coming through Chew Magna, turn off High St onto Tunbridge Rd which then becomes Moorledge Rd.* **Tue 3 June, Tue 12 Aug (10-3). Adm £7, chd free. Tea, coffee & cake.** Designed by RHS Chelsea Garden Show designer Jon Wheatley and his daughter Lizzy, the garden embraces the gentle slopes of the Chew Valley. Planted with an eye to the often changing weather patterns that move through the valley, the pub garden offers year-round interest and edible delights to serve the pub. The 'no dig' kitchen garden is in the adjoining field. Features inc fabulous views, unusual vegetables and polytunnel growing. There are gravelled paths in the main garden and grassed paths in the kitchen garden. The garden is sloped. Accessible toilets available.

61 THE RIB
St Andrew Street, Wells, BA5 2UR. Paul Dickinson & David Morgan-Hewitt. *Wells City Centre, adjacent to east end of Wells Cathedral & opp Vicars Close. There is absolutely no parking at or very near this city garden. Visitors should use one of the 5 public car parks and enjoy the 10-15 minutes stroll through the city to The Rib.* **Sat 21 June (12-5). Adm £6, chd free.**
The Rib is one of the few houses in England that can boast a cathedral and a sacred well in its garden. Whilst the garden is compact, it delivers a unique architectural and historical punch. Long established trees, interesting shrubs and more recently planted mixed borders frame the view in the main garden. Ancient walled orchard and traditionally planted cottage garden. Lunch, tea and WC facilities available in the nearby Bishop's Palace, Wells marketplace or Wells Cathedral. Slightly bumpy but short gravel drive and uneven path to main rear garden. 2-3 steps up to orchard and cottage gardens. Grass areas uneven in places.

62 NEW ROSE COTTAGE
Church Street, Henstridge, Templecombe, BA8 0QE. Carol Perrett, 01963 363338, carolperrett5@outlook.com. *6m E of Sherborne just off the A30. At T-lights turn into Henstridge, take 2nd R into Church St.* **Fri 20, Sat 21 June (2-5). Combined adm with Cherry Bolberry Farm £8, chd free. Visits also by arrangement 16 June to 29 June for groups of 10 to 20. The booking can be a combined visit with Cherry Bolberry Farm.**
¼ acre plantswoman's cottage garden on the site of the former village millpond, exuberantly planted to create a romantic atmosphere with emphasis on scent, colour, form and texture creating a wildlife haven. The garden is enthusiastically maintained by the owner on three levels, with a bog garden on the lower level, planted with bold waterside architectural perennials.

63 ROSE COTTAGE
Smithams Hill, East Harptree, Bristol, BS40 6BY. Bev & Jenny Cruse, 01761 221627, bandjcruse@gmail.com. *5m N of Wells, 15m S of Bristol. From B3114 turn into High St in EH. L at Clock Tower & immed R into Middle St, up hill for 1m. From B3134 take EH road opp Castle of Comfort, continue 1½ m. Off road car parking on R.* **Visits by arrangement in Apr for groups of up to 30. (excluding Sundays &the weekend of 17th-21st April). Adm £5.50, chd free. Home-made teas.**
Organically gardened and planted to encourage wildlife. Bordered by a stream and mixed hedges, our acre of hillside cottage garden is carpeted with seasonal bulbs, primroses and hellebores and magnolias add to the

spring colour. Plenty of seating areas to enjoy the panoramic views over Chew Valley. Full of spring colour.

64 ROWDON
Monksilver, Taunton, TA4 4JD. **Mr & Mrs David Gliddon, 07787 154522, gliddonrowdon@gmail.com.** *From Stogumber take road to Monksilver. After 1m, take the drive on R down to farm buildings. From Monksilver take directions to Stogumber 1m take the drive down to farm.* **Visits by arrangement Mar to Oct for groups of up to 30. Refreshments can be provided on request. Adm £7.50, chd free.**
This is an old farmhouse surrounded by farmland with beautiful views of the Quantocks beyond. Parts of the garden are still being constructed. There are formal and informal areas herbaceous borders and a walled kitchen garden. The arboretum borders a 5 acre lake with abundant wildlife. There are steps and boggy areas. Not suitable for wheelchairs. Regret no dogs.

65 NEW SHANKS HOUSE
Long Lane, Cucklington, Wincanton, BA9 9QL. **Mr Stephen Herrington, Head Gardener.** *Just on the outskirts of Cucklington village, 5m from Wincanton & 4m from Gillingham. Parking is on the L as you enter the estate.* **Sat 14 June, Sat 19 July (10-4). Adm £8, chd free. Tea, coffee & cake.**
Beautiful 5 acre formal gardens set in 100 acres of parkland and wildflower meadows. The gardens were originally designed by Tom Stuart-Smith. The gardens are a collection of rooms with a walled garden, cut flowers, vegetable garden, bulb meadows, large pot displays and a glasshouse. A long lime avenue and apple orchards surround the elegant house which sits in the middle of the gardens.

66 SKOOL BEANZ CHILDREN'S ALLOTMENT
Little Sammons Allotments, Chilthorne Domer, BA22 8RB. **South Somerset County Council, www.skoolbeanzcic.com.** *The garden is situated between Villa Verde Restaurant & the village school adjacent to Tintinhull rd. Parking is a short walk at The Rec just off Main Street.* **Sat 19 Apr, Sat 6 Sept (12-5). Adm £3, chd free. Home-made tea & cakes.**
Skool Beanz is a children's gardening club run from their very own award winning No-Dig children's allotment which has a huge dahila bed, vegetable area, fruit trees, rainwater collecting station, 'Muddy Buddy' compost heap, quiet wildlife garden with tiny pond, secret den, polytunnel, upcycled sculptures and plenty of seating. Lara contributed to Charles Dowding's No-Dig Children's Gardening Book sharing tips she has learnt from Skool Beanz on teaching the joys of gardening to children.

67 SOUTH KELDING
Brewery Hill, Upton Cheyney, Bristol, BS30 6LY. **Barry & Wendy Smale, 07463 920222, wendy.smale@yahoo.com.** *Halfway between Bristol & Bath. Upton Cheyney lies ½ m up Brewery Hill off A431 just outside Bitton. Detailed directions & parking arrangements given prior to visit. Restricted access means pre-booking essential.* **Sat 13 Sept (10.30-4). Adm £12, chd free. Pre-booking essential, please visit www.ngs.org.uk for information & booking. Adm inc refreshments & tour. Visits also by arrangement 3 Mar to 24 Oct for groups of up to 30.**
7 acre hillside garden offering panoramic views from its upper levels, with herbaceous and shrub beds, prairie-style scree beds, orchard, native copses and small, labelled arboretum grouped by continents. Large wildlife pond, boundary stream and wooded area featuring shade and moisture-loving plants. Due to slopes and uneven terrain this garden is unsuitable for disabled access.

68 ♦ SPECIAL PLANTS
Greenway Lane, Cold Ashton, Chippenham, SN14 8LA. **Derry Watkins, 01225 891686, derry@specialplants.net, www.specialplants.net.** *6m N of Bath. From Bath on A46, turn L into Greenways Lane just before r'about with A420.* **For NGS: Thur 19 June, Thur 17 July, Thur 21 Aug, Thur 18 Sept, Thur 16 Oct (10.30-5). Adm £7, chd free. Home-made teas.** For other opening times and information, please phone, email or visit garden website.
Architect-designed ¾ acre hillside garden with stunning views. Started autumn 1996. Exotic plants. Gravel gardens for borderline hardy plants. Black and white (purple and silver) garden. Vegetable garden and orchard. Hot border. Lemon and lime bank. Annual, biennial and tender plants for late summer colour. Spring fed ponds. Bog garden. Woodland walk. Allium alley. Free list of plants in garden.

69 STANDERWICK COURT
Standerwick, Frome, BA11 2PP. **Mr Guy Monson & Lady Rose Monson.** *3m from Frome, 12m from Bath to Beckington. Follow A36 to Beckington r'about. Take turning to White Row Farm Shop. Follow lane in front of farm shop to end, pass gatehouse, entrance to garden on L, through black gates, parking signed.* **Sat 21 June (11-4). Adm £7.50, chd free. Home-made teas at the back of the house in the courtyard, or if wet in The Woolhouse.**
A hidden gem near the Somerset/Wilts border. With far-reaching views over the White Horse and Cley Hill lies a stunning Queen Anne House nestled in 76 acres of parkland. Ha-ha and woodland partially surround the formal gardens recently redesigned by Mark Lutyens and Catherine Fitzgerald to include an Italian inspired terrace, walled garden with tiki hut, tennis court, greenhouse and pool garden. Over the past 7 yrs the surrounding grounds have developed into a mix of contemporary cottage garden, formal hedging and lawns throughout. Do take an enjoyable stroll up the lime avenue to the folly, where deer, hares, rabbits and squirrels gather. Pls supervise children at all times. Dogs on leads.

70 ♦ STOBERRY GARDEN
Stoberry Park, Wells, BA5 3LD. **Frances & Tim Young**, 01749 672906, stay@stoberry-park.co.uk, www.stoberryparkgarden.co.uk. ½ m N of Wells. From Bristol - Wells on A39, L into College Rd & immed L through Stoberry Park, signed. **For NGS: Sat 31 May, Sun 1 June (10.30-4). Adm £6, chd free. Light refreshments. Discount/ prepaid vouchers not valid on NGS charity days.** For other opening times and information, please phone, email or visit garden website.

With breathtaking views over Wells Cathedral, this 5 acre family garden is planted sympathetically within its landscape providing stunning combinations of vistas accented with wildlife ponds and water features. In comparison the 1½ acre walled garden is full of interesting planting. Colour and interest for every season; spring bulbs, irises, salvias, newly planted wildflower area, new modern rockery. Interesting sculpture artistically integrated in the garden. Gardening is great fun, the exciting reality is that everyone's opinions of the way a garden should look, differ!

GROUP OPENING

71 STOKE BISHOP GARDENS
Stoke Bishop, Bristol, BS9 1DD. All gardens are within the BS9 postal code area of Bristol. 1 Sunnyside & Oak Lodge are within a 5 min walk of each other. Haytor Park is a 20 min walk away or very short drive. **Sun 18 May (1-5). Combined adm £7.50, chd free. Tea, coffee & cake at Oak Lodge.**

4 HAYTOR PARK
Mr & Mrs C J Prior.
(See separate entry)

NEW OAK LODGE, 44 STOKE HILL
BS9 1EX. Jo Pople.

1 SUNNYSIDE
BS9 1BQ. Mrs Magda Goss.

Three very different gardens all within ½ m of each other. 4 Haytor Park has been lovingly created over 35 yrs. Wildlife in abundance with a pond and insect friendly plants. A totally peaceful haven in spite of being in a city suburb. Plenty of places to sit awhile and reflect, while spotting myriad plants for all seasons. Many arches lead to secret places, quirky features inc a bicycle wheel trellis. Oak Lodge is a country garden in an urban setting. On entering, the garden reveals its ½ acre size within a Georgian stone wall. It has herbaceous borders, hedging, mixed beds, privet trees, courtyard with potted plants, tennis court and lawns. A weeping silver birch provides a focal point whilst a shepherd's hut offers a quiet retreat. Sunnyside is an artist's C17 cottage in the heart of Stoke Bishop with part walled, cottage style front garden. Garden sculptures dominated by large magnolia, perennials, roses and spring bulbs. Courtyard garden with open studio at rear.

GROUP OPENING

72 STOWEY GARDENS
Stowey, Bishop Sutton, Bristol, BS39 5TL. 10m W of Bath. Stowey Village on A368 between Bishop Sutton & Chelwood. From Chelwood r'about take A368 to Weston-s-Mare. At Stowey Xrds turn R to car park, 150yds down lane, ample off road parking opp Dormers. Limited disabled parking at each garden which will be signed. **Sun 20 July (2-6). Combined adm £7, chd free. Home-made teas at Stowey Mead (cash only for refreshments & plants).**

DORMERS
Mr & Mrs G Nicol.

♦ MANOR FARM
Richard Baines & Alison Fawcett, 01275 332297.

STOWEY MEAD
Mr Victor Pritchard.

These gardens continue to attract visitors from near and far, and offer a broad spectrum of interest, styles and developments each year. The visitor's senses are aroused by the sights, scents and wide diversity of the gardens in this tiny, ancient village. There are abundant collections of mature trees and shrubs and ample seating within tranquil areas of the gardens, often with glorious views. Visitors enjoy the flower-packed borders and pots, roses, topiary, hydrangeas, exotic garden, many unusual trees and shrubs, orchards, vegetables, ponds, specialist sweet peas, lawns and a ha-ha. There is something of interest for everyone, all within a few minutes walk of the car park at Dormers. Plant sales at Dormers. Teas at Stowey Mead. Well behaved dogs on short leads welcome. Wheelchair access restricted in places, many grassed areas in each garden.

GROUP OPENING

73 TINTINHULL GARDENS
68 Queen Street, Tintinhull, Yeovil, BA22 8PQ. **Felicity Down**. Turn off A303 towards Tintinhull. Follow garden signs & park at village hall BA22 8PY where tickets can be purchased. **Sat 14, Sun 15 June (12-5). Combined adm £8, chd free. Tea, coffee & cake at village hall.**

3 CHURCH STREET
Derek & Anita Mills.

28 CHURCH STREET
Geoff & Jo Fisher.

FRANCIS HOUSE
Steve & Sue Creaney.

11 HEAD STREET
Dave & Sue Shorey.

THE OLD DAIRY HOUSE
Geoff & Sarah Stone.

NEW 47 QUEEN STREET
Ros Bassnett.

68 QUEEN STREET
Alan & Felicity Down.

SOUTH VIEW
Patrick & Ruth Sullivan.

NEW 7 VICARAGE STREET
Tracey Hughes.

WALTERS FARM
Ed & Anette Lorch.

These 10 beautiful gardens set in the conservation village of Tintinhull offer a full range of plants, many to encourage bees and butterflies. From enclosed courtyards to large country house landscapes, there is something for everyone. Roses climbing up hamstone walls and billowing over borders will encourage visitors to explore these well cared for gardens. As you wander through the village, some gardens are visible from the road. Scrumptious teas can be enjoyed in the Village Hall.

74 ♦ UNIVERSITY OF BRISTOL BOTANIC GARDEN

Stoke Park Road, Stoke Bishop, Bristol, BS9 1JG. 01174 282041, botanic-gardens@bristol.ac.uk, botanic-garden.bristol.ac.uk. Located in Stoke Bishop ¼ m W of Durdham Downs & 1m from city centre. After crossing the Downs to Stoke Hill, Stoke Park Rd is 1st on R. **For NGS: Sun 6 July (10-5). Adm £9, chd free. Tea, coffee & cake. Light refreshments provided by local deli.** For other opening times and information, please phone, email or visit garden website. Donation to University of Bristol Botanic Garden. Exciting and contemporary Botanic Garden with dramatic collections illustrating plant evolution on land, Mediterranean flora, rare native and useful plants (inc European and Chinese Medicinal herbs). New Guangzhou Garden, winner of Chelsea gold medal and coveted 'Best in Show' in 2021, now rebuilt and open. Glasshouses home to Amazon water lily, tropical fruit, exotic plants, orchids, cacti and unique sacred lotus. The Guangzhou Garden features a Chinese plant collection with many unusual and unique plants. Wheelchair available to borrow from Welcome Lodge on request. Wheelchair friendly primary route through garden inc glasshouses, accessible WCs.

75 VALLEY SPRING

Southstoke Road, Bath, BA2 5SP. Liz Bloor, 07741 001833, liz_bloor@hotmail.com. *2m S of Bath. The entrance to Valley Spring is on Southstoke Rd. It is a clearly signed single track road. We have very limited parking & turning, pls park on Southstoke Rd & walk down.* **Visits by arrangement 10 May to 19 Sept for groups of 10 to 30. Home-made teas.**
Mid-Century modernist house with extensive views over Horsecombe Valley south of Bath looking over 5 acres of garden, meadow and woodland. The garden has been created over the last 8 yrs to complement distant views, capture spring water that runs through the property and create distinct areas of interest. A new woodland was planted in 2020 and a series of winter beds are being developed.

76 ♦ THE WALLED GARDENS OF CANNINGTON

Church Street, Cannington, TA5 2HA. Bridgwater College, 01278 655042, walledgardens@btc.ac.uk, www.btc.ac.uk/the-college/open-to-the-public/the-walled-gardens-of-cannington. *Part of Bridgwater & Taunton College Cannington Campus, 3m NW of Bridgwater. On A39 Bridgwater-Minehead road, at 1st r'about in Cannington 2nd exit, through village. War memorial, 1st L into Church St then 1st L.* **For NGS: Sat 26, Sun 27 Apr, Sat 20, Sun 21 Sept (10-4). Adm £7, chd free.** For other opening times and information, please phone, email or visit garden website.
Within the grounds of a medieval priory, the Walled Gardens of Cannington are a gem waiting to be discovered! Classic and contemporary features inc hot herbaceous border, blue garden, sub-tropical walk and Victorian style fernery, amongst others. Botanical glasshouse where arid, sub-tropical and tropical plants can be seen. Tearoom, plant nursery, gift shop, also events throughout the year. Gravel paths.

Halswell House, Goathurst Gardens

77 WATCOMBE
92 Church Road, Winscombe, BS25 1BP. Peter & Ann Owen, 01934 842666, peterowen449@btinternet.com. *12m SW of Bristol, 3m N of Axbridge. 100 yds after yellow signs on A38 turn L, (from S), or R (from N) into Winscombe Hill. After 1m reach The Square. Watcombe is on L after 150yds.* **Sun 13 Apr, Sun 18 May, Thur 12 June (2-5). Adm £5, chd free. Tea, coffee & cake. Gluten-free available. Visits also by arrangement 14 Apr to 27 June for groups of 10+.** ¾ acre mature Edwardian garden with colour-themed, informally planted herbaceous borders. Strong framework separating several different areas; pergola with varied wisteria, unusual topiary, box hedging, lime walk, pleached hornbeams, cordon fruit trees, 2 small formal ponds and growing collection of clematis. Many unusual trees and shrubs. Small vegetable plot. Some steps but most areas accessible by wheelchair with minimal assistance.

78 WAYFORD MANOR
Wayford, Crewkerne, TA18 8QG. *Wayford Manor. 3m SW of Crewkerne. Turn N off B3165 at Clapton, signed Wayford or S off A30 Chard to Crewkerne road, signed Wayford.* **Sun 11 May (2-5). Adm £6, chd £3. Tea, coffee & cake.** The mainly Elizabethan manor (not open) mentioned in C17 for its 'fair and pleasant' garden was redesigned by Harold Peto in 1902. Formal terraces with yew hedges and topiary have fine views over W Dorset. Steps down between spring-fed ponds past mature and new plantings of magnolia, rhododendron, maples, cornus and, in season, spring bulbs, cyclamen and giant echium. Primula candelabra, arum lily and gunnera around lower ponds.

Abbey Farm

79 WELLFIELD BARN
Walcombe Lane, Wells, BA5 3AG. Virginia Nasmyth, 01749 675129. ½m N of Wells. From A39 Bristol to Wells road turn R at 30 mph sign into the narrow Walcombe Lane. Entrance at 1st cottage on R, parking signed. **Visits by arrangement June & July for groups of 10+. Adm £5.50, chd free. Please bring your own picnic.**
Our garden is a haven for wildlife. 28 yrs ago, a once bustling concrete farmyard grew into a tranquil ½ acre garden. Planned, created and still evolving today to provide enjoyment of colour and form for year-round enjoyment. Structured design integrates house, lawn and garden with the landscape. Wonderful views, ha-ha, specimen trees, mixed borders, hydrangea bed, hardy geraniums and roses. Formal sunken garden, grass walks with interesting young and semi-mature trees for each season. Now tranquillity, sheep as neighbours, perfect peace. Our collection of hardy geraniums was featured on BBC Gardeners' World with Carol Klein. Moderate slopes in places, an abundance of grass with some gravel paths.

80 WESTBROOK HOUSE
West Bradley, BA6 8LS. Keith Anderson & David Mendel, 01458 850604, andersonmendel@aol.com, www.instagram.com/keithbfanderson. 4m E of Glastonbury; 8m W of Castle Cary. From A361 at W Pennard follow signs to W Bradley (2m). From A37 at Wraxall Hill follow signs to W Bradley (2m). **Sat 7 June, Sat 23 Aug (11-5). Adm £6, chd free. Visits also by arrangement 1 May to 6 Sept for groups of 10+. Donation to West Bradley Church.**
Layout and planting began in 2003 by a garden designer and a painter. 4 acres comprising 3 distinct gardens around house with exuberant mixed herbaceous and shrub borders leading to a meadow and orchard with wildflowers, masses of spring bulbs, species roses and lilacs.

GROUP OPENING

81 WICK GARDENS
Wick, Langport, TA10 0NL. Mrs Penny Horne. *Nr Langport. From Langport to Curry Rivel take R turn at Hurds Hill ¾m Wick Farm on L before sharp bend. Or from Burrow Bridge follow road to Langport.* **Sat 19 July (12-5); Sun 20 July (12-4). Combined adm £10, chd free. Tea, coffee & cake.**

PERHAM HOUSE
Chloe Stickland, www.instagram.com/gatheringswallows.

THE STUDIO HOUSE
Andy Waller.

WICK FARM
Mrs Penny Horne, www.awakeningsatwick.com.

WICK MANOR
Rachel Spencer, www.instagram.com/rachel.spencer.somerset.

Four gardens in close proximity with structure yet informality, lovely planting and much colour Three gardens on old sites and one modern converted from a concrete farmyard. All worth exploring in this delightful village.

82 ♦ THE YEO VALLEY ORGANIC GARDEN AT HOLT FARM
Bath Road, Blagdon, BS40 7SQ. Mr & Mrs Tim Mead, 01761 462798, visit@yeovalleyfarms.co.uk, www.yeovalley.co.uk. *12m S of Bristol. Off A368. Entrance approx ½m outside Blagdon towards Bath, on L, then follow garden signs past dairy.* **For NGS: Thur 10 Apr (10-5). Adm £8, chd free. Tea, coffee & cake.** For other opening times and information, please phone, email or visit garden website.
One of only a handful of ornamental gardens that is Soil Association accredited, 6½ acres of contemporary planting, quirky sculptures, bulbs in their thousands, purple palace, glorious meadow and posh vegetable patch. Great views, green ideas. Events, workshops and exhibitions held throughout the year - see website for further details. Level access to café. Around garden there are some grass paths and some uneven bark and gravel paths. Accessibility map available at ticket office.

83 THE YEWS
Harry Stoke Road, Stoke Gifford, Bristol, BS34 8QH. Dr Barbara Laue & Dr Chris Payne. *From A38/Filton, take A4174 ring road to M32. L turn at Sainsbury R'about. Straight across next R'about. After 200 yds, sharp R turn into Harry Stoke Rd. Parking in paddock.* **Sun 18 May (2-5). Adm £5, chd free. Home-made teas.**
Approx 1 acre, developed by present owners since 1987. Part of the old hamlet of Harry Stoke. Formal area with pond, gazebo, herbaceous borders, clipped box and yew, 300 yr old yew trees, wedding cake tree, magnolias, eucalyptus, Indian bean trees, ginkgoes. Vegetable garden, greenhouse, orchard and meadow. Spring bulbs and blossom. Six bin compost system and 'dead hedge'. Many topiary pieces, yew topiary 'Anubis' on top of hedge by the gate.

84 YEWS FARM
East Street, Martock, TA12 6NF. Louise & Fergus Dowding, www.instagram.com/dowdinglouise. *Turn off main road, Church St, at Market House/visitor's centre, onto East St, go past White Hart & PO on R. Yews Farm 150 yds on R, opp Foldhill Lane. Turn around if you get to Nag's Head.* **Sun 6 July, Sun 7 Sept (1.30-5). Adm £8, chd free. Home-made teas.**
Theatrical planting in large south facing walled garden, plants selected for height, form, leaf and texture. Prolific box topiary. Low maintenance perennials. High maintenance pots. Vegetables and cut flowers grown together. Self seeding hugely encouraged. Working organic kitchen garden. Greenhouses bursting with summer vegetables. Organic orchard with heritage varieties and active cider barn. Hens.

In 2024, we celebrated 40 years of continuous funding for Macmillan Cancer Support equating to more than £19.5 million.

STAFFORDSHIRE
Birmingham & West Midlands

STAFFORDSHIRE, BIRMINGHAM & WEST MIDLANDS

VOLUNTEERS

County Organiser
Anita & David Wright
01889 441049
davidandanita@ngs.org.uk

County Treasurer
Brian Bailey
01902 424867
brian.bailey@ngs.org.uk

Publicity
Ruth & Clive Plant
07591 886925
ruthandcliveplant@ngs.org.uk

Booklet Co-ordinator
Ruth Plant
07591 886925
ruthandcliveplant@ngs.org.uk

Assistant County Organisers
Fiona Horwath
07908 918181
fiona.horwath@ngs.org.uk

Alison & Peter Jordan
01785 660819
alisonandpeterjordan@ngs.org.uk

Ken & Joy Sutton
07791 041189
kenandjoysutton@ngs.org.uk

f @ National Garden Scheme Staffordshire

OPENING DATES

All entries subject to change. For latest information check www.ngs.org.uk

Map locator numbers are shown to the right of each garden name.

January

Friday 31st
'John's Garden' at Ashwood Nurseries 13

February

Snowdrop Opening

Sunday 16th
5 East View Cottages 6

March

Sunday 23rd
Millennium Garden 15

April

Sunday 20th
'John's Garden' at Ashwood Nurseries 13

May

Monday 5th
Westview 27

Sunday 11th
NEW 115 Dartmouth Ave 4

Thursday 15th
23 St Johns Road 21

Friday 16th
23 St Johns Road 21

Sunday 18th
NEW 115 Dartmouth Ave 4
Millennium Garden 15
10 Paget Rise 19

Tuesday 20th
The Secret Garden 22

Sunday 25th
The Old Dairy House 17

Monday 26th
The Old Dairy House 17

Saturday 31st
Springfield Cottage 23

June

Sunday 1st
12 Waterdale 25
19 Waterdale 26

Friday 6th
The Secret Garden 22

Saturday 7th
14 Longbow Close 14

Sunday 8th
Ashcroft 1
The Bungalow, Wood Farm 2
33 Gorway Road 8
Izaak Walton Farm 12
The Pintles 20

Saturday 14th
Yew Trees 30

Sunday 15th
Monarchs Way 16
Yew Trees 30

Wednesday 18th
5 East View Cottages 6

Thursday 19th
23 St Johns Road 21

Friday 20th
23 St Johns Road 21
Yarlet House 28

Sunday 22nd
5 East View Cottages 6

Friday 27th
The Secret Garden 22

Saturday 28th
Fifty Shades of Green 7

Sunday 29th
NEW 115 Dartmouth Ave 4
Fifty Shades of Green 7
The Old Mission 18
12 Waterdale 25
19 Waterdale 26
Westview 27

July

Every Thursday to Thursday 17th
Yew Tree Cottage 29

Sunday 6th
Grafton Cottage 9
76 Station Street 24

STAFFORDSHIRE, BIRMINGHAM & WEST MIDLANDS

Saturday 12th
Yew Trees 30

Sunday 13th
Cheadle Allotments 3
Yew Trees 30

Thursday 17th
Grafton Cottage 9

Saturday 19th
Springfield Cottage 23

Sunday 20th
The Bungalow, Wood Farm 2
Grafton Cottage 9
Yew Tree Cottage 29

Sunday 27th
Westview 27

August

Sunday 3rd
Grafton Cottage 9

Saturday 9th
Yew Trees 30

Sunday 10th
Yew Trees 30

Saturday 23rd
Fifty Shades of Green 7

Sunday 24th
Fifty Shades of Green 7

Monday 25th
Fifty Shades of Green 7

October

Sunday 19th
♦ Dorothy Clive Garden 5

February 2026

Sunday 15th
5 East View Cottages 6

By Arrangement

Arrange a personalised garden visit with your club, or group of friends, on a date to suit you. See individual garden entries for full details.

5 East View Cottages 6
Fifty Shades of Green 7
33 Gorway Road 8
Grafton Cottage 9
22 Greenfield Road 10
Hamilton House 11
Monarchs Way 16
The Old Dairy House 17
The Pintles 20
23 St Johns Road 21
19 Waterdale 26
Yew Tree Cottage 29
Yew Trees 30

Fifty Shades of Green

THE GARDENS

1 ASHCROFT
1 Stafford Road, Eccleshall, ST21 6JP. Gillian Bertram. *7 m W of Stafford. M6 J14 Take A5013 to Eccleshall. Ashcroft is 100 metres before junc with A518.* **Sun 8 June (2-5). Adm £3.50, chd free. Tea, coffee & cake.**
Tranquillity descends as you enter this one acre wildlife friendly garden. Pass the pond into a covered courtyard. Rooms flow seamlessly around the Edwardian house. Sunken herb bed, treillage, Victorian style greenhouse with raised beds. A topiary peacock struts in the gravel bed. In the woodland area a goblin lurks in the steps of the ruin. Look for the stone carvings and stained glass sculpture. Wheelchair access to most of garden.
&. ❀ ☕

2 THE BUNGALOW, WOOD FARM
Great Gate, Nr Tean, Stoke-on-Trent, ST10 4HF. Mrs Dorothy Hurst. *Arrive in Great Gate & follow yellow signs.* **Sun 8 June, Sun 20 July (11-5). Adm £5, chd free. Light refreshments inc gluten free & dairy free cakes.**
Unique 1 acre country cottage garden with stunning views of the Weaver Hills surrounded by farm land. The garden inc a Thai theme underground temple with water feature, a relaxing Japanese area, also an area with a New Zealand and Mediterranean vibe, all with varied planting. As you wander around you will find plenty of quiet and tranquil seating. It is an experience that will lift your spirits. Most areas are wheelchair accessible with some assistance.
&. ❀ ☕

3 CHEADLE ALLOTMENTS
Delphouse Road, Cheadle, Stoke-on-Trent, ST10 2NN. Cheadle Allotment Association. *On the A521 1m to W of Cheadle town centre.* **Sun 13 July (1-5). Adm £5, chd free. Cream teas.**
The allotments, which were opened in 2015, are located on the western edge of Cheadle. There are 29 plots growing a variety of vegetables, fruits and flowers. A new addition in 2019 was a community area, with an adjacent wildlife area. A small orchard is currently being developed.
&. 🐾 ☕

4 NEW 115 DARTMOUTH AVE
Cannock, WS11 1EQ. June and Ian Clayton. *½ m from Cannock town centre. From A5 at Longford Island turn onto A4601 to Cannock. At next island take 1st exit- Longford Rd bearing L. Take next R Dartmouth Ave. Garden on R 200yds. What3words app: sleep.pokers.zealous.* **Sun 11, Sun 18 May, Sun 29 June (11.30-4). Adm £3.50, chd free. Tea, coffee & cake.**
Under ⅓ acre, this garden surrounds the bungalow. The front and back garden are full of herbaceous perennials, grasses, bulbs, ferns and shrubs, inc hosta, iris, allium, dierama and much more. With stand alone plants - cardoon, helenium, giant rudbeckia, scabious and sea kale. Sit in the beech hut or under the grapevine in the greenhouse. Admire the acers, cercis and snowdrop tree.
❀ ☕

5 ♦ DOROTHY CLIVE GARDEN
Willoughbridge, Market Drayton, TF9 4EU. Willoughbridge Garden Trust, 01630 647237, info@dorothyclivegarden.co.uk, www.dorothyclivegarden.co.uk. *3m SE of Bridgemere Garden World. From M6 J15 take A53 W, then A51 N. Midway between Nantwich & Stone, near Woore.* **For NGS: Sun 19 Oct (10-4). Adm £13, chd £2. Light refreshments in the tearooms. Afternoon tea can be pre-booked. For other opening times and information, please phone, email or visit garden website.**
12 informal acres, inc superb woodland garden, alpine scree, gravel garden, fine collection of trees and spectacular flower borders. Renowned in May when woodland quarry is brilliant with rhododendrons. Waterfall and woodland planting. Laburnum Arch in June. Creative planting has produced stunning summer borders. Large Glasshouse. Spectacular autumn colour. Much to see, whatever the season. The Dorothy Clive Tearooms will be open throughout the weekend during winter for refreshments, lunch and afternoon tea. Open all week in summer. Plant sales, gift room, picnic area and children's activities for a wide age range. Wheelchairs (inc electric) are available to book through garden website. Disabled parking is available. WC on both upper and lower carparks.
&. 🐾 ❀ 🚗 ☕ 🔊

6 5 EAST VIEW COTTAGES
School Lane, Shuttington, nr Tamworth, B79 0DX. Cathy Lyon-Green, 01827 892244, cathyatcorrabhan@hotmail.com, www.ramblinginthegarden.wordpress.com. *2m NE of Tamworth. From Tamworth, Amington Rd or Ashby Rd to Shuttington. From M42 J11, B5493 for Seckington & Tamworth. Pink house nr top of School Ln. Parking signed, overspill at Wolferstan Arms.* **Sun 16 Feb (12-4), Wed 18 June (12-4), Sun 22 June (1-5). Adm £4, chd free. Tea, coffee & cake. 2026: Sun 15 Feb. Visits also by arrangement in Feb and June for groups of 15 to 30. Refreshments by arrangement at additional cost.**
Deceptive, quirky plantlover's garden, full of surprises and always something new. Informally planted themed borders, cutting beds, woodland and woodland edge, stream, water features, sitooterie, folly, greenhouses and many artefacts. Roses, clematis, perennials, potted hostas. Snowdrops and witch hazels in Feb. Seating areas for contemplation and enjoying home-made cake. 'Wonderful hour's wander'.
🐾 ❀ ☕

7 FIFTY SHADES OF GREEN
20 Bevan Close, Shelfield, Walsall, WS4 1AB. Annmarie & Andrew Swift, 07963 041402, annmarie.1963@hotmail.co.uk, www.facebook.com/50SOGTheSwifts. *M6 J10 take A454 to Walsall for 1.6m, L at Lichfield St for ⅓ m, L onto A461 Lichfield Rd for 2m, at Co-op T-lights turn L onto Mill Rd then follow yellow signs. Parking limited, some in Broad Ln.* **Sat 28 June (10-4); Sun 29 June (10-5); Sat 23 Aug (10-4); Sun 24 Aug (10-5). Evening opening Mon 25 Aug (4-9). Adm £3.50, chd free. Tea, coffee & cake. Visits also by arrangement 1 May to 26 Oct.**
Our award winning garden took many years to create and landscape. Distinctive areas inc 2 ponds, stream, stone waterfalls, unique water features, places to sit, watch and relax. Wildlife encouraged and welcomed. Planting style is varied inc architectural plants, unusual foliage and textures, over 70 trees and plant collections. Calm garden full of surprises, intrigue and discovery. As well as our fixed openings, we have a 'one off' special illuminated evening on Mon 25 Aug (4-9). Refreshments will inc hot sausage or veggie rolls as well as hot drinks and cake.
❀ ☕ 🔊

8 33 GORWAY ROAD
Walsall, WS1 3BE. Gillian Brooks, 07972 615501, Brooks.gillian@gmail.com. *M6 J9 turn N onto Bescot Rd, at r'about take Wallows L (A4148), in 2m at r'about, 1st exit Birmingham Rd, L to Jesson Rd, L to Gorway Rd.* **Sun 8 June (11-3.30). Adm £3.50, chd free. Home-made teas. Visits also by arrangement 2 May to 30 June.** Cottage style Edwardian house garden. Late spring bulbs and roses. Willow tunnel, pond and rockery. Garden viewing is over flat grass and paths. Wheelchair access through garage.
&♿ 🍵 🎵

9 GRAFTON COTTAGE
Bar Lane, Barton-under-Needwood, DE13 8AL. Margaret & Peter Hargreaves, 01283 713639, marpeter1@btinternet.com. *6m N of Lichfield. Leave A38 for Catholme S of Barton, follow sign to Barton Green, L at Royal Oak, ¼ m.* **Sun 6, Thur 17, Sun 20 July, Sun 3 Aug (12.30-4.30). Adm £5, chd free. Cream teas. Visits also by arrangement 20 June to 20 Aug. Min group adm £100 if less than 20 visitors. Donation to Alzheimer's Research UK.** Described as 'Absolutely stunning'. Viticella clematis and roses cover the trellis. Hollyhocks adorn the front of cottage. Many dahlias, salvias and unusual perennials. Colour themed borders with scent, amphitheatre, stream, parterre and more has attracted visitors for over 30 yrs. Oak outdoor seating area overlooking borders brimming with colour and vegetable plot. An extension to the cottage garden in 2024, providing numerous seats around the garden, which has views over surrounding countryside. It now has an extended bed with hot colours, additional clematis and a vegetable garden. Wheelchair access around garage to oak outdoor seating area.
♿ 🎵 🚻 🍵

10 22 GREENFIELD ROAD
Stafford, ST17 0PU. Alison & Peter Jordan, 01785 660819, alisonandpeterjordan@ngs.org.uk. *3m S of Stafford. Follow the A34 out of Stafford towards Cannock. 2nd L onto Overhill Rd.1st R into Greenfield Rd.* **Visits by arrangement 25 May to 6 July for groups of 6 to 25. Cream teas.** Suburban garden, working towards year round interest. In spring bulbs and stunning azaleas and rhododendrons. June onwards perennials and grasses. A garden that shows being diagnosed with Parkinson's needn't stop you creating a peaceful place to sit and enjoy. You might be able to catch a glimpse of Pete's model railway running. Flat garden but with some gravelled areas.
♿ 🐕 🎵 🍵

11 HAMILTON HOUSE
Roman Grange, 3 Roman Road, Little Aston Park, Sutton Coldfield, B74 3GA. Philip & Diana Berry, 07785 997508, ptdr@btinternet.com, www.hamiltonhousegarden.co.uk. *3m N of Sutton Coldfield. Follow A454 (Walsall Rd) & enter Roman Rd, Little Aston Park. Roman Grange is 1st L after church but enter Roman Grange via pedestrian gate. Limited parking on Roman Rd. Car sharing preferable.* **Visits by arrangement 17 Feb to 29 Sept for groups of 10 to 25. Adm £10, chd free. Light refreshments inc in adm price.** ½ acre north-facing English woodland garden in a tranquil setting, making the most of challenging shade, providing a haven for birds and other wildlife. Large pond with a stone bridge, pergolas, water features, box garden with a variety of roses. Interesting collection of rhododendrons, clematis, hostas, ferns, old English roses and stunning artworks in the garden.
🍵 🎵

12 IZAAK WALTON FARM
Cresswell Lane, Cresswell, Stoke-on-Trent, ST11 9RE. Mr Mark & Mrs Veronica Swinnerton. *Entrance off Cresswell Old Ln, 100 metres from railway Xing.* **Sun 8 June (11-4). Adm £4, chd free. Light refreshments inc home-made cakes.** The garden has lots of small interesting areas. Flower borders, gravel gardens, shaded areas, vegetables and fruit trees, beautiful bug hotel made from a wine rack and oak pagoda. Water fountain and small greenhouse with cacti. Interesting children's den, lawn and gravel paths and small grass meadow. Plenty of seating to enjoy tea and cakes.
♿ 🐕 🍵

13 'JOHN'S GARDEN' AT ASHWOOD NURSERIES
Ashwood Lower Lane, Ashwood, nr Kingswinford, DY6 0AE. John Massey, www.ashwoodnurseries.com. *9m S of Wolverhampton. 1m past Wall Heath on A449 turn R to Ashwood along Doctor's Ln. At T-junc turn L. Garden entrance off main car park at Ashwood Nurseries.* **Fri 31 Jan, Sun 20 Apr (10-4). Adm £8, chd free.** A stunning private garden adjacent to Ashwood Nurseries, it has a huge plant collection and many innovative design features in a beautiful canal-side setting. There are informal beds, woodland dells, a stunning rock garden, unique ruin garden, an *Anemone pavonina* meadow and wildlife garden. Fine displays of snowdrops, spring bulbs, spring-flowering plants and a notable collection of Malus. Tearoom, garden centre and gift shop at adjacent Ashwood Nurseries. Coaches are welcome by appointment only. Disabled access difficult if very wet. Sorry no disabled access to the wildlife garden.
♿ 🎵 NPC 🍵 🎵

14 14 LONGBOW CLOSE
Stretton, Burton upon Trent, DE13 0XY. Debbie & Gavin Richards. *3m NW of Burton upon Trent in the village of Stretton. From A38 turn off at A5121 (Burton N) Follow signs to Stretton turning into Claymills Rd, then L to Church Rd, R into Bridge St & R into Athelstan Way. Please park on Athelstan Way.* **Sat 7 June (11-4). Adm £4, chd free. Home-made teas.** A plantwoman's garden with exotic evergreens, gorgeous smelling roses, a flower-filled sunny patio where refreshments can be enjoyed and a welcoming front garden. Its design features planting of herbaceous perennials, climbers and evergreen trees with a mauve, pink and purple colour theme. There is good level access to most of the garden with one shallow step.
🎵 🍵 🎵

15 MILLENNIUM GARDEN
London Road, Lichfield, WS14 9RB. Carol Cooper. *1m S of Lichfield. Off A38 along A5206 towards Lichfield ¼ m past A38 island towards Lichfield. Park in field on L. Yellow signs on field post.* **Sun 23 Mar, Sun 18 May (1-5). Adm £4, chd free. Tea, coffee & cake.** Two acre garden with mixed spring bulbs in the woodland garden. In May

the laburnum walk and wisteria arch are in full bloom in this English country garden. Designed with a naturalistic edge and with the environment in mind. A relaxed approach creates a garden of quiet sanctuary with the millennium bridge sitting comfortably, with surroundings of lush planting and mature trees. Well-stocked borders give shots of colour to lift the spirit and the air fills with the scent of wisterias and climbing roses. A stress free environment awaits you at the Millennium Garden. Park in field then follow the footpath round garden. Some uneven surfaces.

&

16 MONARCHS WAY
Park Lane, Coven, Wolverhampton, WV9 5BQ. Eileen & Bill Johnson, 07785 934085, snappy_eileen@hotmail.com, www.monarchsway-garden.co.uk. *Near Chillington Hall, Brewood. From Port Ln (main road between Codsall & Brewood) turn E onto Park Ln. Monarchs Way is on the sharp bend on Park Ln. Limited parking, (further parking is available at other end of Park Ln).* **Sun 15 June (11-4). Adm £6, chd free. Cream teas for an additional charge. Visits also by arrangement 1 May to 24 Aug for groups of 6 to 16. Car parking limited to six cars or one minibus .**

The owners bought a 1¾ acre bare, treeless blank canvas in 2010 with grass around 3ft high! Since then they have designed a Tudor folly and jungle hut, built a pergola, excavated a lily pond with bog garden, created a cottage garden, orchard and vegetable garden. They have planted hundreds of conifer, evergreen, fruit and flowering trees, roses, hydrangeas, perennials and designed numerous flower beds. Rare and interesting trees, shrubs and borders, sub tropical border, cottage garden, grass beds, vegetable garden, seasonal colour, pond, bog garden, waterfall. The garden has been designed planted and maintained over the past twelve years from a bare paddock. Wheelchair access is easy for most of the garden, on arrival request side gate for access. Minibuses can be accepted.

&

17 THE OLD DAIRY HOUSE
Trentham Park, Stoke-on-Trent, ST4 8AE. Philip & Michelle Moore, 07779 158394, olddairyhouse@hotmail.com. *S edge of Stoke-on-Trent. Next to Trentham Gardens. Off Whitmore Rd. Please follow NGS signs or signs for Trentham Park Golf Club. Parking in church car park.* **Sun 25 May (1.30-5). Home-made teas. Mon 26 May (1-5.30). Adm £4.50, chd free. Visits also by arrangement 3 May to 15 June for groups of 12+.**

Grade II listed house which originally formed part of the Trentham Estate forms backdrop to this 2 acre garden in parkland setting. Shaded area for rhododendrons, azaleas and expanding hosta and fern collection. Mature trees, 'cottage garden', long borders and stumpery. Narrow brick paths in vegetable plot. Large courtyard area for teas. Wheelchair access - some gravel paths but lawns are an option.

& ✱ ☕))

18 THE OLD MISSION
Bickford Road, Whiston, Penkridge, ST19 5QH. Mr Jason & Mrs Laura Beet. *Postcode accurate for SatNav.* **Sun 29 June (10.30-6). Adm £5, chd free. Tea, coffee & cake.**

The old Mission is situated amongst farmland in the small hamlet of Whiston. The one acre garden boasts an ancient giant oak, many shrub and flower borders, statues, carvings and other artistic ornaments. An amazing swimming pool with seating and an outdoor kitchen completes the scene. There are many shrub and climbing roses plus an orchard, kitchen garden and soft fruit cages.

&

33 Gorway Road

10 PAGET RISE
Paget Rise, Abbots Bromley, Rugeley, WS15 3EF. Mr Arthur Tindle. *4m W of Rugeley 6m S of Uttoxeter & 12m N of Lichfield. From Rugeley: B5013 E. At T-junc turn R on B5014. From Uttoxeter take the B5013 S then B5014. From Lichfield take A515 N then turn L on B5234. In Abbots Bromley follow NGS yellow signs.* **Sun 18 May (11-4). Adm £3, chd free. Tea, coffee & cake.**
This medium sized split level garden has a strong Japanese influence. Rhododendrons and a wide range of flowering shrubs. Many bonsai-style Acer trees in shallow bowls occupy a central gravel area with stepping stones. The rear of the garden has a woodland feel with a fairy dell under the pine tree. A gem of a garden. Arthur hopes visitors will be inspired with ideas to use in their own garden. Arthur is a watercolour artist and will be displaying a selection of his paintings for sale.

20 THE PINTLES
18 Newport Road, Great Bridgeford, Stafford, ST18 9PR. Peter & Leslie Longstaff, 01785 282582, peter.longstaff@ngs.org.uk. *About 2 m from M6 J14. From J14 M6 take A5013 towards Eccleshall, in Great Bridgeford turn L onto B5405 after 600 metres turn L onto Great Bridgeford Village Hall car park. The Pintles is opp the hall main doors.* **Sun 8 June (1-5). Adm £3.50, chd free. Home-made teas inc gluten free & reduced sugar options.** Visits also by arrangement 10 June to 29 June for groups of 15 to 30. Parking available for small coaches.
Located in the village of Great Bridgeford this traditional semi-detached house has a medium sized wildlife friendly garden designed to appeal to many interests. There are two greenhouses, 100s of cacti and succulents, vegetable and fruit plot, wildlife pond, weather station and hidden woodland shady garden. Plenty of outside seating to enjoy the home-made cakes and refreshments. Steps or small ramp into main garden.

21 23 ST JOHNS ROAD
Rowley Park, Stafford, ST17 9AS. Colin & Fiona Horwath, 07908 918181, fiona_horwath@yahoo.co.uk. *½ m S of Stafford Town Centre. Just a few mins from J13 M6, towards Stafford. After approx 2m on the A449, turn L into St John's Rd after bus-stop.* **Thur 15 May (2-5). Tea, coffee & cake. Evening opening Fri 16 May (6-9). Wine. Thur 19 June (2-5). Tea, coffee & cake. Evening opening Fri 20 June (6-9). Wine. Adm £5, chd free.** Visits also by arrangement 14 May to 18 June for groups of 20 to 50. Min group adm £100 if less than 20 visitors.
Pass through the black and white gate of this Victorian house into a part-walled gardener's haven. Bulbs, alpines and shady woodlanders in spring and masses of unusual herbaceous plants and climbers. Numerous Japanese maples. Many spots to sit in sun or shade. Steps and gravel in places. Gardener is keen Hardy Plant Society member and sows far too many seeds, so always something good for sale. The outdoor kitchen and revolving summerhouse are great for refreshments. Plenty of places to sit and enjoy your tea, coffee and home-made cake.

22 THE SECRET GARDEN
3 Banktop Cottages, Little Haywood, ST18 0UL. Derek Higgott & David Aston. *5m SE of Stafford. A51 from Rugeley or Weston signed Little Haywood A513 Stafford Coley Ln, Back Ln R into Coley Gr. Entrance 50 metres on L.* **Tue 20 May, Fri 6, Fri 27 June (11-4). Adm £5, chd free. Tea, coffee & cake.**
Wander past other gardens and through the evergreen arch to a fantasy for the eyes and soul. Stunning garden approx ½ acre, created over the last 30+yrs. Strong colour theme of trees and shrubs, underplanted with perennials and 1000 bulbs. Laced with clematis, roses and a laburnum tunnel. Other features inc water and a warm bothy for inclement days.

The Old Mission

STAFFORDSHIRE, BIRMINGHAM & WEST MIDLANDS 483

23 SPRINGFIELD COTTAGE
Kiddemore Green Road, Bishops Wood, Stafford, ST19 9AA. Mrs Rachel Glover. *A5 to Telford from Gailey Island. Turn L at sign for Boscobel House. Follow Ivetsey Bank Rd to Bishop's Wood. Turn 1st L Old Coach Road past church 2nd white cottage on L.* **Sat 31 May, Sat 19 July (11-3). Adm £4, chd free. Tea, coffee & cake inc vegan options.**
5 yr old designed and landscaped plant enthusiasts cottage garden with unusual planting in areas, a tropical area inc gunnera, canna, hedychium and palms, a rose garden, a herb garden and an established vegetable garden with large greenhouse. Fantastic views of the south Staffordshire countryside from all sides of the garden. Disabled parking for two cars, flat garden area and WC facilities.

24 76 STATION STREET
Cheslyn Hay, Walsall, WS6 7EE. Mr Paul Husselbee. *Located on B4156. Limited on road parking.* **Sun 6 July (12-5). Adm £4, chd free. Tea, coffee & cake.**
40 yrs of gardening on this site has produced a hosta filled courtyard which leads to a Mediterranean patio, steps down to small area with folly, formal gardens area with stream, gated courtyard then finally find the secret garden. A quirky garden with a surprise round every corner.

25 12 WATERDALE
Compton, Wolverhampton, WV3 9DY. Colin & Clair Bennett. *1½ m W of Wolverhampton city centre. From Wolverhampton Ring Rd take A454 towards Bridgnorth for 1m. Waterdale is on the L off A454 Compton Rd West.* **Sun 1, Sun 29 June (11-4.30). Combined adm with 19 Waterdale £6, chd free.**
A riot of colour welcomes visitors to this quintessentially English garden. The wide central circular bed and side borders overflow with classic summer flowers, inc the tall spires of delphiniums, lupins, irises, campanula, poppies and roses. Clematis tumble over the edge of the decked terrace, where visitors can sit among pots of begonias and geraniums to admire the view over the garden.

26 19 WATERDALE
Compton, Wolverhampton, WV3 9DY. Anne & Brian Bailey, 01902 424867, m.bailey1234@btinternet.com. *1½ m W of Wolverhampton city centre. From Wolverhampton Ring Rd take A454 towards Bridgnorth for 1m. Waterdale is on L off A454 Compton Rd West.* **Sun 1, Sun 29 June (11-4.30). Combined adm with 12 Waterdale £6, chd free. Home-made teas.** Visits also by arrangement 4 June to 15 Aug for groups of 10 to 35.
A romantic garden of surprises, which gradually reveals itself on a journey through deep, lush planting, full of unusual plants. From the sunny, flower filled terrace, a ruined folly emerges from a luxuriant fernery and leads into an oriental garden, complete with tea house. Towering bamboos hide the way to the gothic summerhouse and mysterious shell grotto.

27 WESTVIEW
Straight Mile, Calf Heath, Wolverhampton, WV10 7DW. David & Mary. *3 m E of Cannock. Leave A5 on to Four Crosses Ln. Go under M6 motorway, garden is ¼ m on L.* **Mon 5 May, Sun 29 June, Sun 27 July (10.30-4). Adm £4, chd free.**
Walking into the garden you are greeted by borders of mainly perennial plants. As you continue through you move to a Japanese themed area with a large collection of bonsai trees. Learn about how to prepare bonsai plants from David as you relax and practice your zen with tea and cake with Mary.

28 YARLET HOUSE
Yarlet, Stafford, ST18 9SD. Mr & Mrs Nikolas Tarling. *2m S of Stone. Take A34 from Stone towards Stafford, turn L into Yarlet School & L again into car park.* **Fri 20 June (10-1). Adm £4, chd free. Tea, coffee & cake. Donation to Staffordshire Wildlife Trust.**
Four acre garden with extensive lawns, walks, lengthy herbaceous borders and traditional Victorian box hedge. Peaceful Japanese water garden with fountain and rare lilies. Sweeping views from south walk across Trent Valley to Sandon. Victorian School Chapel and War Memorial. Garden chessboard and boules pitch. Yarlet School Art Display. Gravel paths.

29 YEW TREE COTTAGE
Podmores Corner, Long Lane, White Cross, Haughton, ST18 9JR. Clive & Ruth Plant, 07591 886925, pottyplantz@aol.com. *4m W of Stafford. Take A518 W Haughton, turn R Station Rd (signed Ranton) 1m, then turn R at Xrds ¼ m on R.* **Every Thur 3 July to 17 July (11-4). Sun 20 July (2-5). Adm £5, chd free. Tea, coffee & cake.** Visits also by arrangement 4 July to 27 July. Donation to Plant Heritage.
Hardy Plant Society member's garden brimming with unusual plants. Year-round interest inc meconopsis, trillium and other shade lovers. ½ acre inc gravel, borders, vegetable and plant sales. National Collection Dierama (Angels Fishing Rods) featured on BBC Gardeners' World, flowering first half July. Covered vinery for tea if weather is unkind, seats in the garden for sunny days. A series of different areas and interests. Cottage garden, shade garden, and a working vegetable garden. A garden for plantaholics. Find us on facebook at 'Dierama Species in Staffordshire'. Partial wheelchair access, grass and paved paths, some narrow and some gravel.

30 YEW TREES
Whitley Eaves, Eccleshall, Stafford, ST21 6HR. Mrs Teresa Hancock, 07973 432077, hancockteresa@gmail.com. *7m from J14 M6. Situated on A519 between Eccleshall (2.2m) & Woodseaves, (1m). Traffic cones & signs will highlight the entrance.* **Sat 14, Sun 15 June, Sat 12, Sun 13 July, Sat 9, Sun 10 Aug (10-4). Adm £4, chd free. Pre-booking essential, please visit www.ngs. org.uk for information & booking. Tea, coffee & cake.** Visits also by arrangement 1 June to 1 Sept.
One acre garden divided into rooms by mature hedging, shrubs and trees enjoying views over the surrounding countryside. Large patio area with containers and seating. Other features inc pond, topiary, vegetable plot, hen run and wildlife area - always adding lots of new features, and lots of new plants. During June and July there are 8 acres of natural wildflower meadow to enjoy before it is cut for hay. Most of the garden can be accessed by wheelchair or mobility scooter, help is always on hand for anyone who may need it.

SUFFOLK

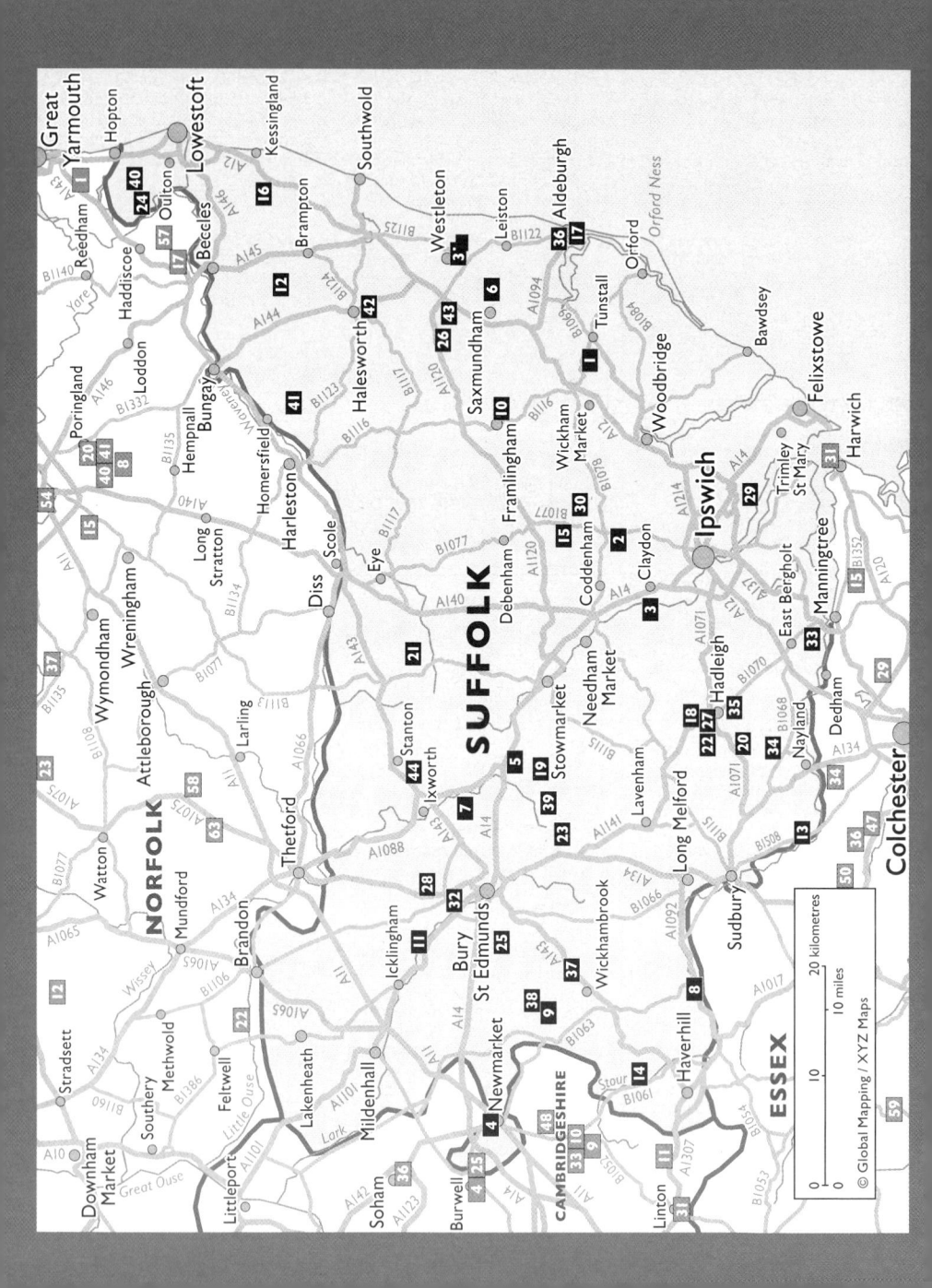

SUFFOLK

VOLUNTEERS

County Organiser
Jenny Reeve
01638 715289
jenny.reeve@ngs.org.uk

County Treasurer
Julian Cusack
01728 649060
julian.cusack@ngs.org.uk

Publicity
Jenny Reeve
(as above)

Social Media
Barbara Segall
01787 312046
barbara.segall@ngs.org.uk

Booklet Co-ordinator
Michael Cole
07899 991307
michael.cole@ngs.org.uk

Assistant County Organisers
John Ball
07770 378373
jb204@hotmail.co.uk

Michael Cole
(as above)

Barbara Segall
(as above)

Peter Simpson
01787 249845
peter.simpson@ngs.org.uk

@SuffolkNGS
@SuffolkNGS
@suffolkngs

OPENING DATES

All entries subject to change.
For latest information check
www.ngs.org.uk
Map locator numbers are shown to the right of each garden name.

February

Snowdrop Openings

Sunday 9th
◆ Blakenham Woodland Garden   3

Sunday 16th
Gable House   12

Sunday 23rd
Great Thurlow Hall   14

April

Sunday 6th
Great Thurlow Hall   14
◆ The Place for Plants, East Bergholt Place Garden   33

Sunday 13th
◆ Blakenham Woodland Garden   3

Sunday 27th
◆ The Place for Plants, East Bergholt Place Garden   33

May

Sunday 4th
◆ Fullers Mill Garden   11

Sunday 11th
2 Holmwood Cottages   20

Saturday 24th
◆ Wyken Hall   44

Sunday 25th
Bridges   5
NEW Manor House Farm   24
NEW St Francis Cottage   38
◆ Wyken Hall   44

Monday 26th
NEW Rookery Farm   37

June

Sunday 1st
Great Bevills   13
2 Holmwood Cottages   20
Wenhaston Grange   42

Friday 6th
Helmingham Hall   15

Saturday 7th
Holm House   19

Sunday 8th
Ashe Park   1
Great Thurlow Hall   14
Moat House   25
Oakley Cottage   26

Saturday 14th
Lillesley Barn   22
Old Gardens   27

Sunday 15th
Berghersh Place   2
Hillside   18
5 Parklands Green   32

Sunday 22nd
Brampton Manor Care Home   4

Sunday 29th
Otley Hall   30
Squires Barn   41

July

Wednesday 2nd
◆ The Red House   36

Sunday 13th
Paget House   31

Sunday 20th
NEW Clare Gardens   8
Heron House   17

August

Wednesday 6th
◆ The Red House   36

Saturday 9th
Ivy Chimneys   21

Sunday 10th
Ivy Chimneys   21

Sunday 24th
Bridges   5
Henstead Exotic Garden   16

September

Tuesday 2nd
◆ Somerleyton Hall Gardens   40

Sunday 14th
NEW Wolsey Farmhouse   43

Sunday 28th
2 Holmwood Cottages   20

October

Sunday 5th
◆ Fullers Mill Garden   11
◆ The Place for Plants, East Bergholt Place Garden   33

By Arrangement

Arrange a personalised garden visit with your club, or group of friends, on a date to suit you. See individual garden entries for full details.

Ashe Park	1
By the Crossways	6
Church Cottage	7
Dip-on-the-Hill	9
28 Double Street	10
Heron House	17
2 Holmwood Cottages	20
Lillesley Barn	22
The Lodge	23
Moat House	25
Old Gardens	27
The Old Rectory, Ingham	28
The Old Rectory, Nacton	29
Paget House	31
5 Parklands Green	32
Polstead Mill	34
NEW 18 Raven Way	35
Smallwood Farmhouse	39

Our donation to Marie Curie this year equates to 17,496 hours of nursing care or 43 days of care in one of their nine hospices.

Rookery Farm

THE GARDENS

1 ASHE PARK
Ivy Lodge Road, Campsea Ashe, Woodbridge, IP13 0QB.
Mr Richard Keeling, 01728 746983.
Using the postcode in SatNav will bring you to the entrance to Ashe Park on Ivy Lodge Rd. Drive through entrance signed Ashe Park, past the gate cottage on L & follow signs to car park. **Sun 8 June (10.30-4.30). Adm £8, chd free.** Visits also by arrangement.
An old 12 acre garden comprised of different areas; a large yew hedge, ancient cedars of Lebanon, canal and other water features. Walled garden and wild areas. Garden planted in ruins of old house. Partial wheelchair access, some gravel paths and steps.
&

2 BERGHERSH PLACE
Witnesham, Ipswich, IP6 9EZ.
Mr & Mrs T C Parkes. *N of Witnesham village, B1077 double bends. Farm entrance, concrete drive, approx 1m S of Ashbocking Xrds. Entrance on sharp bend so please drive slowly. Turn in between North Lodge & Berghersh House.* **Sun 15 June (12-5). Adm £5, chd free. Light refreshments. Gluten-free cakes available.**
Peaceful walled and hedged gardens surround elegant Regency house (not open) among fields with a pretty view of the Fynn Valley. Circular walk with mature native trees, a mound, three ponds, bog area and orchard paddock. Informal family garden with shrub and perennial beds. Many varieties of roses, some trained on to old farm buildings. Garden created over last 30 years by current owner. Parking for elderly and disabled available. Most areas are accessible, but paths are thick grass, so difficult to push manual wheelchairs.
&

3 ♦ BLAKENHAM WOODLAND GARDEN
Little Blakenham, Ipswich, IP8 4LZ. M Blakenham, info@blakenhamfarms.com, www.blakenhamwoodlandgarden.org.uk. *4m NW of Ipswich. Follow signs at Little Blakenham, 1m off B1113.* **For NGS: Sun 9 Feb, Sun 13 Apr (10-4). Adm £5, chd £3. Tea, coffee & cake.** For other opening times and information, please email or visit garden website.
Beautiful six acre woodland garden with variety of rare trees and shrubs, Chinese rocks and a landscape spiral form. Lovely in spring with snowdrops, daffodils and camellias followed by magnolias and bluebells. Woodland Garden open from 1 March to 28 June. On NGS openings: Suffolk Punch Horses, Tosier Artisan Chocolate Stall, Cafe.

4 BRAMPTON MANOR CARE HOME
Fordham Road, Newmarket, CB8 7AQ. Mr Carl Roberts, www.boutiquecarehomes.co.uk/care-homes-suffolk/brampton-manor. *1m S of J37 on A14 or ½ m N of Newmarket High St.* **Sun 22 June (1.30-4). Adm £4, chd free. Tea, coffee & cake.**
Brampton Manor Care Home's gardens are focused on health and wellbeing of residents living with dementia and residential care needs. With sweeping accessible pathway and a variety of interesting horticultural features the garden inc mature trees, a resident run allotment, beautiful lawn, bedding plants and raised planters. The gardens are lovingly maintained by residents and the team. On our open day we will be hosting a community event with a variety of activities and entertainment to enjoy. Fully accessible garden with step free access throughout Brampton Manor.
&

5 BRIDGES
The Street, Woolpit, Bury St Edmunds, IP30 9SA. Mr Stanley Bates & Mr Michael Elles. *From A14 take slip road to Woolpit, follow signs to centre of village. Road curves to R. Bridges is on L & covered in Wisteria, opp Co-op.* **Sun 25 May, Sun 24 Aug (11-5). Adm £5, chd free. Home-made teas.**
C15 Grade II terraced house in the centre of a C12 Suffolk village with walled garden to the rear of the property. Additional land was acquired 20 years ago, and this garden was developed into formal and informal planting. The main formal feature is the Shakespeare Garden featuring the bust of Shakespeare, and the 'Umbrello' a recently constructed pavillion in an Italianate design. Usually a Wind Quintet playing in the main garden.

6 BY THE CROSSWAYS
Kelsale, Saxmundham, IP17 2PL.
Mr & Mrs William Kendall, miranda@bythecrossways.co.uk. *2m NE of Saxmundham, just off Clayhills Rd. ½ m N of town centre, turn R to Theberton on Clayhills Rd. After 1½ m, 1st L to Kelsale, turn L immed after white cottage.* **Visits by arrangement in Sept for groups of 5 to 10. Adm by donation.**
A three acre wildlife garden designed as a garden within a working organic farm where wilderness areas lie next to productive beds. Large semi-walled vegetable and cutting garden and a spectacular crinkle-crankle wall. Extensive perennial planting, grasses and wild and uneven areas. The garden is mostly flat, with paved or gravel pathways around the main house, a few low steps and extensive grass paths and lawns.
&

7 CHURCH COTTAGE
Church Lane, Troston, Bury St Edmunds, IP31 1EX. Graeme & Marysa Norris, 07855 284816, marysanorris@gmail.com. *5m NE of Bury St Edmunds. From the A143 turn at the Bunbury Arms, signed Troston & Gt Livermere. Follow the rd through Gt Livermere, signed to Troston.* **Visits by arrangement 19 May to 29 June for groups of up to 30. Adm inc refreshments. Discuss when booking . Adm £8. Tea, coffee & cake.**
A ¾ acre garden, of several different themes. A yew allee, mixed borders inc grasses, roses and perennials, an informal pond and a 'New Wave Perennial' open border. Also a small area of woodland plants, trees and shrubs, a gravel garden and a productive kitchen garden with raised beds, inc one for alpine plants and two greenhouses. Church Cottage is opposite St Mary's Church, famous for its medieval wall paintings. There is an excellent pub in the village. The Bull is friendly and has a well regarded restaurant.

In 2024, National Garden Scheme funding for Perennial supported 1,367 people working in horticulture.

GROUP OPENING

8 NEW CLARE GARDENS
Cliftons, Nethergate Street, Clare, CO10 8NP. *On the outskirts of Clare, a small rural town. Follow road signs.* **Sun 20 July (11.30-4.30). Combined adm £10, chd free. Home-made teas at Cliftons. Cake and scones also available.**

NEW CLIFTONS
Mr Chris Allan and Mrs Antonia Brandes.

RIVERSIDE HOUSE
Mr & Mrs A C W Bone, www.clare-bulbs.co.uk/garden.

NEW STOUR HOUSE
Mr & Mrs Robert Eyre.

A group of three adjacent gardens in Clare offering a wide variety of garden styles from a sculpture park with follies, ponds, an orchard and jungle planting leading down to the River Stour, to a former prize winning cottage garden with manicured lawns and a bridge over the Stour and finally a more formal garden with beds, lawns, a vegetable and fruit garden, topiary and a tudor style physic garden. All three gardens are in an historic setting and feature beautiful mature trees. Wheelchair access at Cliftons but not at Stour House or Riverside House.

9 DIP-ON-THE-HILL
Ousden, Newmarket, CB8 8TW. Geoffrey & Christine Ingham, 07947 309900, gki1000@cam.ac.uk. *5m E of Newmarket; 7m W of Bury St Edmunds. From Newmarket: 1m from junc of B1063 & B1085. From Bury St Edmunds follow signs for Hargrave. Parking at village hall. Follow yellow NGS sign at the end of the lane.* **Visits by arrangement for groups of up to 15. Adm £6, chd free. Tea, coffee & cake.**
Approx an acre in a dip on a south facing hill based on a wide range of architectural/sculptural evergreen trees, shrubs and groundcover: pines; grove of *Phillyrea latifolia*; 'cloud pruned' hedges; palms; large bamboo; ferns; range of *Kniphofia* and *Croscosmia*. Visitors may wish to make an appointment when visiting gardens nearby.

10 28 DOUBLE STREET
Framlingham, IP13 9BN. Mr & Mrs David Clark, 01728 720161, clarkdn@btinternet.com. *250 yds from Market Hill (main square) Framlingham opp Church Entrance. Leave square from top L into Church St. Double St is 100yds on R. Car parking in main square & near to Framlingham Castle.* **Visits by arrangement June to Sept for groups of up to 25. Adm £5, chd free. Tea, coffee & cake.**
A town garden featuring roses together with a wide range of perennials and shrubs. Conservatory, greenhouse, gazebo, summerhouse and terrace full of containers all add interest to the garden. Good views of Framlingham's rooftops. Wheelchair access via fine shingle drive with two ramps.

11 ♦ FULLERS MILL GARDEN
West Stow, IP28 6HD. Perennial, 01284 728888, fullersmillgarden@perennial.org.uk, www.fullersmill.org.uk. *6m NW of Bury St Edmunds. Turn off the A1101 (Bury to Mildenhall Rd) signposted West Stow Anglo Saxon Village. Continue for 1½ m and the entrance is clearly marked. Follow yellow signs on all major routes.* **For NGS: Sun 4 May, Sun 5 Oct (11-5). Adm £10, chd free. Tea, coffee & cake.** For other opening times and information, please phone, email or visit garden website.
An enchanting and tranquil seven acre creation on the banks of the River Lark. It combines a beautiful light dappled woodland with a plantsman's collection of unusual shrubs, perennials, lilies and marginal plants. It is a garden of truly year-round interest. Tour our garden, and be inspired by our cards, gifts, bulbs and plants. Some uneven surfaces, grassed areas, proximity to water and sloping ground limit disabled access to some areas.

12 GABLE HOUSE
Halesworth Road, Redisham, Beccles, NR34 8NE. Brenda Foster. *5m S of Beccles. Signed from A144 Bungay/Halesworth Rd.* **Sun 16 Feb (11-4). Adm £5, chd free. Light refreshments inc soup, tea and cakes.**
We have a large collection of snowdrops, cyclamen, hellebores and other flowering plants for our opening in February for you the discover. Many bulbs and plants will be for sale. The greenhouses contain rare bulbs and tender plants. We have a wide range of unusual trees, shrubs, perennials and bulbs collected over the last 50 years. The main garden is wheelchair accessible.

13 GREAT BEVILLS
Sudbury Road, Bures, CO8 5JW. Mr & Mrs G T C Probert. *4m S of Sudbury. N of Bures on the Sudbury Rd (B1508).* **Sun 1 June (2-5). Adm £5, chd free. Home-made teas.**
Overlooking the Stour Valley the gardens surrounding an Elizabethan manor house (not open) are formal and Italianate with Irish yews and mature specimen trees. Terraces, borders, ponds and woodland walks. A short drive away from Great Bevills visitors may wish to also see the C13 St Stephen's Chapel with wonderful views of the Old Bures Dragon recently re-created by the owner. Woodland walks give lovely views over the Stour Valley. There is also a recently created wildflower meadow with mown paths. Wheelchair access via gravel paths.

14 GREAT THURLOW HALL
Great Thurlow, Haverhill, CB9 7LF. Mr & Mrs George Vestey. *12m S of Bury St Edmunds, 4m N of Haverhill. Great Thurlow village on B1061 from Newmarket; 3½ m N of junc with A143 Haverhill/Bury St Edmunds rd.* **Sun 23 Feb (1-4). Home-made teas in the church. Sun 6 Apr, Sun 8 June (2-5). Tea, coffee & cake in the church. Adm £7, chd free.**
13 acres of beautiful gardens set around the River Stour, Masses of snowdrops in late winter are followed by daffodils and blossom around the riverside walk in spring. Herbaceous borders, rose garden and extensive shrub borders come alive with colour from late spring onwards, there is also a large walled kitchen garden and arboretum. Also open is the Curwen Print Study Centre, Art Studios and Gallery, located adjacent to Great Thurlow Hall will also be open to all garden visitors. Artists will be demonstrating fine art printmaking skills. Many paths are gravel and there is some uneven terrain that may make access more difficult for some.

Cliftons, Clare Gardens

15 HELMINGHAM HALL
Helmingham, Stowmarket, IP14 6EF. Helmingham Events, www.helmingham.com. *From A14 take J51 onto A140. Take 1st R onto Needham Rd (B1078). After 1½ m, turn L onto Church Rd then R onto High St. R turn on Stonewall Hill towards Gosbeck. At end of Gosbeck Rd, turn L. Garden on L.* **Fri 6 June (10-5). Adm £9, chd £4.50.**
It is hard to exaggerate the effect this beautiful park, with red deer and spectacular moated Hall in mellow patterned red brick with its famous gardens will have on the visitor. The whole combines to give an extraordinary impression of beauty and tranquillity. A classic parterre flanked by hybrid musk roses lies before a stunning walled kitchen garden with exquisite herbaceous borders and beds of vegetables interspersed by tunnels of sweet peas, runner beans and gourds. On the other side lies a herb and knot garden behind which is a rose garden of unsurpassable beauty.

16 HENSTEAD EXOTIC GARDEN
Church Road, Henstead, Beccles, NR34 7LD. Andrew Brogan, www.hensteadexoticgarden.co.uk. *Equal distance between Beccles, Southwold & Lowestoft approx 5m. 1m from A12 turning after Wrentham (signed Henstead) very close to B1127.* **Sun 24 Aug (11-4). Adm £6, chd free. Tea, coffee & cake. Home-made cheese scones and sausage rolls.**
A two acre exotic garden featuring 100 large palms, 20+ bananas and giant bamboo, some of biggest in the UK. Streams, 20ft tiered walkway leading to Thai style wooden covered pavilion. Mediterranean and jungle plants around three large ponds with fish. Unique garden buildings, waterfalls, rock walkways, different levels and a Victorian grotto. Wheelchair access to parts of garden.

17 HERON HOUSE
Priors Hill Road, Aldeburgh, IP15 5EP. Mr & Mrs Jonathan Hale, 07968 906715, jonathanrhhale@aol.com. *At the SE junc of Priors Hill Rd & Park Rd. Last house on Priors Hill Rd on S side, at the junc where it rejoins Park Rd. Please note, entrance to Park Rd from SE is generally closed at weekends.* **Sun 20 July (2-5). Adm £5, chd free. Tea.** Visits also by arrangement 7 Apr to 30 Sept.
Two acres with superb views over the North Sea, River Alde and marshes. Unusual trees, herbaceous beds, shrubs and ponds with a waterfall in large rock garden, and a stream and bog garden. Some half hardy plants in the coastal microclimate. Partial wheelchair access.

Church Cottage

© Rosalind Simon

18 HILLSIDE
Union Hill, Semer, Ipswich, IP7 6HN. Mr & Mrs Neil Mordey. *2½ m N of Hadleigh. Head NW on B1070. Turn R onto Calais St & continue to Aldham MI Hl. Turn L onto A1071 & after 500 metres turn R onto Stone St. Follow for 1½ m. Car park through field gate.* **Sun 15 June (11-4). Adm £5, chd free. Light refreshments.**
This garden, in its historic setting of 10½ acres, has sweeping lawns running down to a spring fed pond. The formal garden has island beds of mixed planting for a long season of interest. The wild area of meadow has been landscaped with extensive tree planting to complement the existing woodland. There is also a small walled kitchen garden and raised beds in the stable yard. Most areas are wheelchair accessible. Kitchen garden access over deep gravel drive.

&

19 HOLM HOUSE
Garden House Lane, Drinkstone, Bury St Edmunds, IP30 9FJ. Mrs Rebecca Shelley. *7m SE of Bury St Edmunds. Coming from the E, exit A14 at J47. From W J46. Follow signs to Drinkstone, then Drinkstone Green. Turn into Rattlesden Rd & look for Garden House Ln on L. 1st house on L.* **Sat 7 June (10.30-4.30). Adm £8, chd free. Home-made teas.**
Approx 10 acres inc orchard and lawns with mature trees and clipped holm oaks; formal garden with topiary, parterre and mixed borders; rose garden; woodland walk with hellebores, camellias, rhododendrons and bulbs; lake set in wildflower meadow; cut-flower garden with greenhouse; large kitchen garden with impressive greenhouse; Mediterranean courtyard with mature olive tree.

20 2 HOLMWOOD COTTAGES
Bower House Tye, Polstead, Colchester, CO6 5BZ. Neil Bradfield, 07887 516054, scuddingclouds2@gmail.com. *3m W of Hadleigh. Just off A1071, Hadleigh to Sudbury Rd, (ignore Polstead signs). At The Brewers Arms, turn off A1071 into Bower House Tye. Cottage 100yds along this road.* **Sun 11 May, Sun 1 June, Sun 28 Sept (11-5). Adm £5, chd free.** Visits also by arrangement 6 Apr to 31 Oct for groups of 5 to 35. Not opening July and August. Donation to Plant Heritage.
Plantsman's garden with many unusual plants. Hot, sunny borders and areas of dappled shade planted to explore flower colour, foliage, texture, form, autumn interest and design principles. Rich variety of perennials, grasses, species and shrub roses, ferns and woodland plants, matrix and gravel planting. Also summerhouse, several seats and a part of the National Collection Engleheart Narcissus. No refreshments served, but visitors welcome to bring their own tea, cakes, sandwiches etc to enjoy in the garden. Tables and chairs available. Wheelchair access along narrow paths and slightly uneven ground. Please note: there are two steps.

& NPC

21 IVY CHIMNEYS
Gislingham, IP23 8JT. Iris & Alan Stanley. *A pale pink house in Mill St, ¼ m from the village hall. Gislingham is 4m W of Eye; 3m W of A140; 9m N of Stowmarket and 8m S of Diss.* **Sat 9, Sun 10 Aug (11-4.30). Adm £5, chd free. Tea, coffee & cake. Savouries, gluten free cake, cordials and fruit teas also available.**
A garden planted for year-round interest and late summer colour. Ornamental trees, topiary, exotic border and fish pond set in an area of Japanese style; wisteria draped pergola supports a productive vine. A custom built planter fills a difficult corner and a large terrace gives views over the whole garden. Discover a secluded ornamental vegetable garden at the side of the house. Wheelchair access via low step to flat lawn.

&

SUFFOLK 491

22 LILLESLEY BARN
The Street, Kersey, Ipswich, IP7 6ED. Mr Karl & Mrs Bridget Allen, 07939 866873, bridgetinkerseybarn@gmail.com, www.instagram.com/bridgets. garden.in.suffolk. *In village of Kersey, 2m NW Hadleigh. Driveway is 200m above 'The Bell' pub. Lillesley Barn is situated behind 'The Ancient Houses'. Parking is on street.* **Sat 14 June (10-5). Combined adm with Old Gardens £6, chd £3. Tea, coffee & cake.** Visits also by arrangement May to Sept for groups of up to 40. Evening visits with wine may be arranged.
Dry gravel garden (inspired by the Beth Chatto Garden) inc variety of Mediterranean plants, ornamental grasses and herbs. Large herbaceous borders, pleached hornbeam hedge, rose arbours and small orchard. The garden contains various species of trees inc birch, amelanchier and willow in less than an acre of garden bordered on two sides by fields. Large collection of David Austin Roses.
✿ ☕ ⸫

23 THE LODGE
Bury Road, Bradfield St Clare, Bury St Edmunds, IP30 0ED. Christian & Alice Ward-Thomas, 07768 347595, alice.baring@btinternet.com, www.instagram.com/alicewardthomas. *4m S of Bury St Edmunds. From N: turn L up Water Ln off A134, at Xrds, turn R & go exactly 1m on R. From S: turn R up Ixer Ln, R at T-junc, ½ m on R. Before post box on R & next door to Lodge Farm.* **Visits by arrangement 1 Apr to 19 Oct. Discuss refreshments when booking.**
From extensive spring bulbs to late summer perennials this large country garden set in parkland is constantly changing throughout the year, and there's usually plenty to see inc Beth Chatto inspired gravel garden and large naturalistic perennial garden flowering May to October. Discover herbaceous borders, a courtyard, roses, vegetable garden and meadows which lead to a sedum hedge and young orchard. Wheelchair access over uneven ground - please contact for more information.
♿ 🚗 ☕ 🧺

24 NEW MANOR HOUSE FARM
St Olaves Road, Herringfleet, Lowestoft, NR32 5QS. Mr Tommaso Del Buono. *Manor Farm sits next to the Somerleyton Estate Office and is accessed through a farm gate next to a very large brick and flint thatched barn.* **Sun 25 May (10.30-5.30). Adm £6.50, chd free. Tea, coffee & cake.**
Surrounding a Grade II listed 1655 house with a distinctive Dutch Gable, the garden at Manor Farm is being redeveloped by its landscape designer owner since 2020. Existing elements inc a Medieval wall. Tall Taxus hedges have been retained and incorporated within a framework that notably inc a new courtyard at the front, vegetable and cut flower gardens and more naturalistic areas. Separately listed medieval brick and flint walled garden, bee orchids in the wildflower meadow.
♿ 🐕 D ☕ ⸫

25 MOAT HOUSE
Little Saxham, Bury St Edmunds, IP29 5LE. Mr & Mrs Richard Mason, 01284 810941, suzannem207@gmail.com. *2m SW of Bury St Edmunds. A14 J42: leave r'about towards Westley. Through Westley village at Xroads. R towards Barrow/Saxham. After 1.3m turn L down track and follow signs. Garden is ½ m from church.* **Sun 8 June (1-5). Adm £6, chd free. Home-made teas. All refreshments are home-made.** Visits also by arrangement May to July for groups of 20+. Ample parking for a coach, plenty of parking for cars.
Set in a two acre historic and partially moated site. This tranquil, mature garden has been developed over 20 years. Bordered by mature trees the garden has various sections inc a sunken garden, rose and clematis arbours, herbaceous borders with hydrangeas and alliums, small arboretum. A Hartley Botanic greenhouse erected and parterre have been created. Secluded and peaceful setting and wonderful fencing. Each year the owners enjoy new garden projects.
♿ 🐕 ✿ 🚗 ☕

26 OAKLEY COTTAGE
Chapel Street, Peasenhall, Saxmundham, IP17 2JD. Mr Robin Brooks. *Centre of Peasenhall Village. On the A1120 in the centre of the village of Peasenhall, next door to the Weavers Tearooms.* **Sun 8 June (12-4.30). Adm £5, chd free. Tea, coffee & cake.**
This little cottage garden is divided into five small areas- a formal-ish courtyard with *Lonicera nitida* instead of box, two lawns, a vegetable plot, lots of soft fruit and an apprentice rose garden. Persicaria, hardy geraniums, honesty, gaura, foxgloves, monardas in the borders. Pergolas and associated climbers. Mostly flat with a few low steps, but grass and gravel to be negotiated.
♿ ☕ ⸫

27 OLD GARDENS
The Street, Kersey, Ipswich, IP7 6ED. Mr & Mrs David Anderson, 01473 828044, davidmander15@gmail.com. *10m W of Ipswich. Up hill, approx 100m from The Bell Inn Pub. On the same side of the road.* **Sat 14 June (10-5). Combined adm with Lillesley Barn £6, chd £3. Tea, coffee & cake at Lillesley Barn.** Visits also by arrangement May to Sept for groups of up to 40.
Entered from The Street, a natural garden with wildflowers under a copper beech tree. To the rear, a formal garden designed by Cherry Sandford with a sculpture by David Harbour.
✿ ☕ ⸫

28 THE OLD RECTORY, INGHAM
Ingham, Bury St Edmunds, IP31 1NQ. Mr J & Mrs E Hargreaves, InghamOldRectory@gmail.com. *5m N of Bury St Edmunds & A14. Parking signed, close to Ingham church.* **Visits by arrangement 1 Apr to 10 Aug for groups of 10+. Variety of home-made teas, cakes and scones.**
Lovely setting of large formal gardens around Grade II listed Georgian rectory. Lawns, parterre, large wisteria, alliums, roses, dahlias and lavender. Mini-arboretum of mature trees inc weeping willows, wellingtonia and small orchard. We're building a vibrant display of colours in insect-friendly beds. Talk about history of house (not open) and gardens on offer for groups. Child friendly. All areas wheelchair accessible through 1m wide gate (surfaces are gravel, York stone slabs and grass).
♿ ☕

29 THE OLD RECTORY, NACTON
Nacton, IP10 0HY. Tizy and James Wellesley Wesley, 01473 659673, tizyww@gmail.com. *3m from Ipswich close to N side of the Orwell Estuary. Located on road to Nacton from the 1st A14 turn off after Orwell bridge going SE. Parking on Church Rd, by the church, opp Old Rectory driveway.* **Visits by arrangement 1 Apr to 24 Oct. Excluding August. Discuss refreshments when booking.**
Just under two acres of garden divided into areas for different seasons: mature trees and herbaceous borders, ample spring bulbs and blossom. Light soil so many self sown flowers. Damp area with emphasis on foliage (rheum, darmera, rodgersia, hydrangea). Still a work in progress after 35 years. We're looking at how to bring in more butterflies and deal with very dry conditions in most of the garden. We are redeveloping our damp garden to incorporate a stream (diverting from elsewhere with aid of pump) and rearranging all the planting in that area. Most areas are wheelchair accessible, however grassy slopes and levels.

30 OTLEY HALL
Hall Lane, Otley, Ipswich, IP6 9PA. Steve Southgate, www.otleyhall.co.uk. *Take Chapel Rd past the Otley village Post Office. After 250 yds take 1st L onto Hall Ln.* **Sun 29 June (10-4). Adm £5.50, chd free. Light refreshments at Marthas Barn Cafe (please reserve). Coffee and tea in the garden, also a stocked bar.**
The 10 acres of both formal and informal gardens at Otley Hall are managed with an eye to nature. There are stew ponds and woodland to explore. The garden features three Elizabethan Garden recreations by Sylvia Landsberg. Marthas Barn Cafe has varied recipes using fresh seasonal produce. Booking in advance advised.

31 PAGET HOUSE
Back Road, Middleton, Saxmundham, IP17 3NY. Julian & Fiona Cusack, 01728 649060, julian.cusack@btinternet.com. *3m from RSPB Minsmere. From A12 at Yoxford take B1122 towards Leiston. Turn L after 1.2m at Middleton Moor. After 1m enter Middleton & drive straight ahead into Back Rd. Turn 1st R on Fletchers Ln for car park.* **Sun 13 July (11-5). Adm £6, chd free. Light refreshments. Visits also by arrangement May to Aug for groups of 5 to 40. Guided tours available. Discuss refreshments when booking.**
The 1½ acre garden is designed to be wildlife friendly with wild areas meeting formal planting. There is an orchard and a vegetable plot to explore. Walk through areas of woodland and see laid hedges and a pond supporting amphibians and dragonflies. There is also an abstract garden sculpture by local artist Paul Richardson. We are making changes designed to increase our resilience to drought. We have recorded over 40 bird species each year and a good showing of butterflies, dragonflies and wildflowers inc orchids. Wheelchair access: gravel drive and mown paths. Parking on drive by prior arrangement.

32 5 PARKLANDS GREEN
Fornham St Genevieve, Bury St Edmunds, IP28 6UH. Mrs Jane Newton, newton.jane@talktalk.net. *2m NW of Bury St Edmunds off B1106. Plenty of parking on the green.* **Sun 15 June (11-4). Adm £5, chd free. Tea, coffee & cake. Visits also by arrangement Apr to Sept for groups of up to 50.**
1½ acres of gardens developed since the 1980s for all year interest. There are mature and unusual trees and shrubs and riotous herbaceous borders. Explore the maze of paths to find four informal ponds, a treehouse, the sunken garden, greenhouses and woodland walks.

33 ♦ THE PLACE FOR PLANTS, EAST BERGHOLT PLACE GARDEN
East Bergholt, CO7 6UP. Mr & Mrs Rupert Eley, 01206 299224, sales@placeforplants.co.uk, www.placeforplants.co.uk. *2m E of A12, 7m S of Ipswich. On B1070 towards Manningtree, 2m E of A12. Situated on the edge of E Bergholt.* **For NGS: Sun 6, Sun 27 Apr (2-5); Sun 5 Oct (1-5). Adm £9, chd free. Home-made teas. For other opening times and information, please phone, email or visit garden website.**
A 20 acre woodland garden originally laid out at the turn of the last century by the present owner's great grandfather. Full of many fine trees and shrubs, many seldom seen in East Anglia. A fine collection of camellias, magnolias and rhododendrons, topiary, and the National Collection of deciduous Euonymus. Partial wheelchair access in dry conditions. Advisable to call before visiting.

34 POLSTEAD MILL
Mill Lane, Polstead, Colchester, CO6 5AB. Mrs Lucinda Bartlett, 07711 720418, lucyofleisure@hotmail.com, www.instagram.com/polsteadmill. *Between Stoke by Nayland & Polstead on the River Box. From Stoke by Nayland take road to Polstead. Mill Ln is 1st on L & garden is 1st on R.* **Visits by arrangement for groups of 10 to 50. Adm £7, chd free. Cream teas. Range of refreshments available, discuss when booking.**
The garden has been developed since 2002, it has formal and informal areas, a wildflower meadow and a large productive kitchen garden. The River Box runs through the garden and there is a mill pond, which gives opportunity for damp gardening, while the rest of the garden is arid and is planted to minimise the need for watering. Partial wheelchair access.

35 NEW 18 RAVEN WAY
Hadleigh, Ipswich, IP7 5AX. Mrs Angela Wild, 01473 790141, wild123@talktalk.net. *From A12 take junc 31 to A1070. Follow signs for Hadleigh Town Centre. From High St continue onto Benton St. Raven Way 2nd L off Benton St. What3words app: grow.fulfilled.cove.* **Visits by arrangement Apr to July for groups of 5 to 16. Not open 1st to 31st May inclusive. Adm £5, chd free. Tea, coffee & cake.**
A ¼ acre garden, renovated and restyled five years ago. Large herbaceous beds, mature trees, ferns, roses, hostas, pond, plus greenhouse and small vegetable area. Mature trees inc a stunning 58 year old acer and spinney of silver birch trees. Various seating areas overlooking Hadleigh Water Meadows.

36 ◆ THE RED HOUSE
Golf Lane, Aldeburgh, IP15 5PZ. Britten Pears Arts, 01728 451700, info@brittenpearsarts.org, www.brittenpearsarts.org/visit-us/the-red-house. *Top of Aldeburgh, approx. 1m from the sea. From A12, take A1094 to Aldeburgh. Follow the brown sign directing you towards the r'about, take 1st exit: B1122 Leiston Rd. Golf Ln is 2nd L, follow sign to 'The Red House'.* **For NGS: Wed 2 July, Wed 6 Aug (10.30-3.30). Adm £5, chd free. Light refreshments.** For other opening times and information, please phone, email or visit garden website.

The former home of the renowned British composer Benjamin Britten and partner, the tenor Peter Pears. The five acre garden provides an atmospheric setting for the house they shared and contain many plants loved by the couple. Mixed herbaceous borders, kitchen garden, meadows, contemporary planting and mature trees. The Red House inc the collections left by Britten and Pears and the archive holds an extraordinary wealth of material documenting their lives. The garden offers a peaceful setting to this beautiful corner of Suffolk. For museum opening times, see website. Wheelchair access: brick, concrete, gravel paths and grass. Some areas are uneven. Wheelchair available on request.

♿ 🐕 ☕

37 NEW ROOKERY FARM
Depden, Bury St Edmunds, IP29 4BU. Tim Freathy and Mark Leadbetter. *7m SW of Bury St Edmunds. Rookery Farm is directly on the A143. Use car park for Depden Care Farm (not open to the public). Rookery Farm Garden is next door. What3words app: shuffle.sprouts.skidding.* **Mon 26 May (10.30-4.30). Adm £5, chd free. Tea, coffee & cake. Wide selection of home-made cakes, bakes and biscuits.**

There is always plenty to see in this spectacular plantsman's garden with two ponds - one more formal than the other, rockery, dry garden, white garden, jungle area as well as lawns and herbaceous borders.

☕ 🔊

48,000 people affected by cancer were reached by Maggie's centres supported by the National Garden Scheme over the last 12 months.

Manor House Farm

38 NEW ST FRANCIS COTTAGE
Dunstall Green, Dalham, Newmarket, CB8 8TZ. Trevor & Francine Wilkins-Smith. *6m W of Bury St Edmunds. Exit A14 at Barrow/Cavenham. Head into Barrow & turn R to Denham. Continue for 4m. Turn L into Dunstall Green Rd and follow yellow signs to drive on R. What3words app: saga.afternoon.juggle.* **Sun 25 May (11-5). Adm £5, chd free. Tea, coffee & cake.**
The C17 thatched cottage is surrounded by a variety of garden 'rooms', which inc a natural pond with marginal planting, wildflower meadow with yellow rattle, cowslips and primroses. There is also a vegetable garden and greenhouse, shaded 'all green' terrace, raised seating terrace with rambling roses and nepeta. The garden inc hardy perennials, overflowing pots and a stunning Rambling Rector.

39 SMALLWOOD FARMHOUSE
Smallwood Green, Bradfield St George, Bury St Edmunds, IP30 0AJ. Mr & Mrs P Doe, 01449 736127, philipdoe142@btinternet.com. *S of A14, E of A134 on Bradfield St George to Felsham Rd. Disregard sign to Smallwood Green & follow the NGS yellow signage.* **Visits by arrangement for groups of up to 20. Please discuss refreshments when booking.**
The garden is a combination of traditional cottage planting and contemporary styles. At its heart, a C16 farmhouse provides the backdrop to a number of old English roses, a profusion of clematis and honeysuckle, and a variety of perennials. There are two natural ponds, a Mediterranean garden and productive kitchen garden, whilst paths meander through an area of ancient meadow. Partially wheelchair accessible, although not suitable in damp or wet weather.

40 ♦ SOMERLEYTON HALL GARDENS
Somerleyton, NR32 5QQ. Lord Somerleyton, www.somerleyton.co.uk. *5m NW of Lowestoft. From Norwich take the B1074, 7m SE of Great Yarmouth (A143). Coaches should follow signs to the rear W gate entrance.* **For NGS: Tue 2 Sept (11-4). Adm £10.95, chd free. Tea, coffee & cake. For other opening times and information, please visit garden website.**
Beautiful gardens of 12 acres contain a wide variety of magnificent specimen trees, shrubs, borders and plants providing colour and interest throughout the year. Sweeping lawns and formal gardens combine with majestic statuary and original Victorian ornamentation. Highlights inc the Paxton glasshouses, pergola, walled garden and yew hedge maze. House and gardens remodelled in 1840s by Sir Morton Peto. House created in Anglo-Italian style with lavish architectural features. Most areas of the gardens are wheelchair accessible. Path surfaces are gravel, stone and can be difficult in places.

41 SQUIRES BARN
St Cross South Elmham, Harleston, IP20 0PA. Stephen & Ann Mulligan. *6m W of Halesworth, 6m E of Harleston & 7m S of Bungay. On New Rd between St Cross & St James. Parking in field opp. Yellow signs from A143 and other local roads.* **Sun 29 June (11-4). Adm £5, chd free. Tea, coffee & cake inc gluten free, vegan options and ice creams.**
A garden of three acres with views over surrounding countryside. Raised vegetable beds, an orchard, greenhouse and fruit cage. There is also a large ornamental pond with water lilies, fish and waterfall. A wildflower mound, island beds of mixed planting and a range of mature and younger trees. A recent addition is a swimming pool area. Plant stall, art exhibition and a brass band will play at the opening. The garden is largely grass with some slight slopes. Seating is available across the garden. One single flight of steps can be bypassed.

42 WENHASTON GRANGE
Wenhaston, Halesworth, IP19 9HJ. Mr & Mrs Bill Barlow. *S of Halesworth. Turn SW from A144 between Bramfield & Halesworth. Take the single track road (signed Walpole 2). Wenhaston Grange is approx ½ m, at the bottom of the hill on L.* **Sun 1 June (11-4). Adm £5, chd free. Light refreshments inc home-made teas.**

Over three acres of varied gardens on a long established site which has been extensively landscaped and enhanced over the last 20 years. Long herbaceous borders, old established trees and a series of garden rooms created by beech hedges. Levels and sight lines have been carefully planned. The vegetable garden is now coming on nicely and there is also a wildflower meadow and woodland garden.

43 NEW WOLSEY FARMHOUSE
Hog Hill Lane, Yoxford, Saxmundham, IP17 3JF. Mrs Marion Anthony. *Im out of Yoxford. In the village, turn into Strickland Manor Hill & continue to the fork in the road. Take the L fork and continue to Wolsey Farm House. What3words app: workroom.cattle.swanky.* **Sun 14 Sept (11-4). Adm £6, chd free. Tea, coffee & cake.**
A large country garden with recently created wildflower meadow and prairie garden. Discover an established walled garden with shrub borders and rose beds surrounded by box hedging. Explore an orchard, a pond planted with marginal plants for wildlife and a moat with two bridges. The pond and moat are unfenced - children take care. Well behaved dogs on leads are welcome. The garden is generally level with areas of mown grass. There are some steps close to the house. The WC is not adapted for wheelchairs.

44 ♦ WYKEN HALL
Stanton, IP31 2DW. Sir Kenneth & Lady Carlisle, 01359 250262, shop@wykenvineyards.co.uk, www.wykenvineyards.co.uk. *9m NE of Bury St Edmunds. Along A143. Follow signs to Wyken Vineyards on A143 between Ixworth & Stanton.* **For NGS: Sat 24, Sun 25 May (10-5). Adm £6, chd free. For other opening times and information, please phone, email or visit garden website.**
Four acres around the old manor. The gardens inc knot and herb gardens, old-fashioned rose garden, kitchen and wild garden, nuttery, pond, gazebo and maze; herbaceous borders and old orchard. Enjoy a woodland walk and visit the vineyard nearby. Restaurant (booking 01359 250287), shop and vineyard.

Stour House, Clare Gardens

SURREY

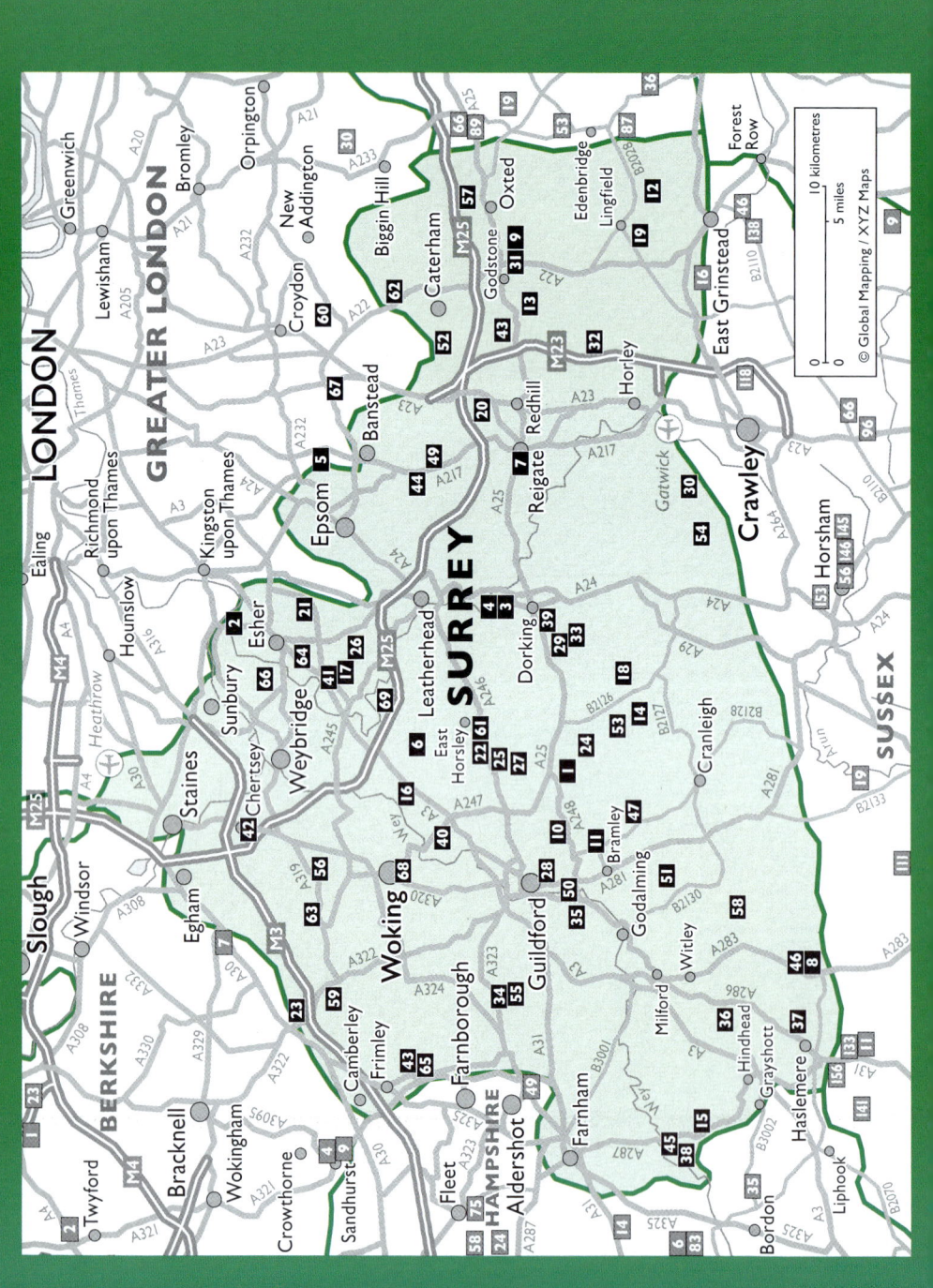

VOLUNTEERS

County Organiser
Clare Bevan
07956 307546
clare.bevan@ngs.org.uk

County Treasurer
Nigel Brandon
020 8643 8686
nbrandon@ngs.org.uk

Booklet Co-ordinator
Annabel Alford-Warren
01483 203330
annabel.alford-warren@ngs.org.uk

Booklet Distributor
Jānis Raubiška 07478 025188
janis.raubiska@ngs.org.uk

Publicity
Sarah Wilson
07932 445868
sarah.wilson@ngs.org.uk

Social Media
Annette Warren
07790 045354
annette.warren@ngs.org.uk

Assistant County Organisers
Jane Allison 07790 476394
jane.allison@ngs.org.uk

Margaret Arnott 01372 842459
margaret.arnott@ngs.org.uk

Jan Brandon 020 8643 8686
janmbrandon@outlook.com

Angela Gilchrist 01306 884613
ar.gilchrist@btinternet.com

Susie Gent 07831 585501
susanjmgent@gmail.com

Di Grose 01883 742983
di.grose@btinternet.com

Annie Keighley 01252 838660
annie.keighley12@btinternet.com

Jānis Raubiška (as above)

Kate Smith 07788 746719
kate.smith@ngs.org.uk

Kerry Tucker 07876 216056
kerry.tucker@ngs.org.uk

 @surreyngs
 @SurreyNGS
 @surreyngs

OPENING DATES

All entries subject to change.
For latest information check
www.ngs.org.uk
Extended openings are shown at the beginning of the month.
Map locator numbers are shown to the right of each garden name.

January

Thursday 9th
Timber Hill 56
Thursday 23rd
Timber Hill 56
Thursday 30th
Timber Hill 56

February

Snowdrop Openings
Sunday 9th
◆ Gatton Park 20
Thursday 13th
Timber Hill 56
Sunday 16th
Shieling 49
Thursday 20th
Timber Hill 56
Thursday 27th
Timber Hill 56

March

Wednesday 5th
Timber Hill 56
Thursday 13th
Timber Hill 56
Sunday 16th
Albury Park 1
Thursday 20th
Timber Hill 56
Thursday 27th
Timber Hill 56
Monday 31st
◆ Vann 58

April

Every Sunday from Sunday 13th
Coverwood Lakes 14
Every day to Sunday 6th
◆ Vann 58
Wednesday 2nd
Timber Hill 56
Thursday 10th
Timber Hill 56
Saturday 12th
11 West Hill 60
Sunday 13th
Moleshill House 41
11 West Hill 60
Wednesday 16th
◆ Dunsborough Park 16
Thursday 17th
Timber Hill 56
Sunday 20th
Shieling 49
Monday 21st
NEW Waterer's Garden 59
Thursday 24th
Timber Hill 56
Sunday 27th
◆ Hatchlands Park 25

May

Thursday 1st
Crosswater Farm 15
Friday 2nd
Crosswater Farm 15
Saturday 3rd
Crosswater Farm 15
Sunday 4th
Coverwood Lakes 14
The Garth Pleasure Grounds .. 19
West Horsley Place 61
Monday 5th
Fairmile Common Gardens 17
Wednesday 7th
Timber Hill 56
Thursday 8th
Crosswater Farm 15
Friday 9th
Chauffeur's Flat 9
Crosswater Farm 15

SURREY 497

498 SURREY

Saturday 10th
Chauffeur's Flat 9
Crosswater Farm 15

Sunday 11th
Chauffeur's Flat 9
The Garth Pleasure Grounds 19
Westways Farm 63

Wednesday 14th
Claridge House 12
Timber Hill 56

Thursday 15th
Claridge House 12
Crosswater Farm 15

Friday 16th
Claridge House 12
Crosswater Farm 15
Leigh Place 31
◆ Ramster 46

Saturday 17th
Crosswater Farm 15
Hall Grove School 23
Leigh Place 31

Sunday 18th
NEW Chaleshurst 8
NEW Feldemore Corner 18
The Manor House 37
Slades Farm 51
The Therapy Garden 55

Saturday 24th
Monks Lantern 42

Sunday 25th
15 The Avenue 5
Chilworth Manor 10
◆ Titsey Place Gardens 57
57 Westhall Road 62

Monday 26th
57 Westhall Road 62

Friday 30th
Little Orchards 32

June

Sunday 1st
Little Orchards 32

Sunday 8th
The Old Rectory 44
Shooting Star Children's
   Hospices, Christopher's 50

Saturday 14th
The Old Vicarage 45

Sunday 15th
◆ Loseley Park 35
Milton Way House 39
The Old Vicarage 45
Wildwood 65

Thursday 19th
Lower House 36
Timber Hill 56

Friday 20th
Ashleigh Grange 4

Sunday 22nd
Ashleigh Grange 4
NEW Highmount 28
Lower House 36

Sunday 29th
Logmore Place 33
◆ Titsey Place Gardens 57
NEW 63 Wolsey Drive 66
Wrens' Nest Cottage 69

July

Saturday 5th
NEW Longer End Cottage 34

Sunday 6th
High Clandon Estate Vineyard 27
Ichi-Coo Park 30

Saturday 12th
NEW 16 Arnison Road 2

Saturday 19th
Bridge End Cottage 6
The White House 64

Sunday 20th
21 Glenavon Close 21
The White House 64

Sunday 27th
Grace & Flavour Community
   Garden 22
◆ Titsey Place Gardens 57

August

Sunday 10th
Shieling 49

Sunday 24th
Woodpeckers 68

Saturday 30th
NEW Mill House 38

Sunday 31st
NEW Mill House 38
◆ Titsey Place Gardens 57
Woodpeckers 68

September

Friday 5th
Little Orchards 32

Sunday 7th
Hill Farm 29
Little Orchards 32
West Horsley Place 61

Sunday 21st
The Therapy Garden 55

Saturday 27th
Hall Grove School 23

October

Sunday 5th
Albury Park 1

Thursday 16th
Timber Hill 56

Sunday 19th
Coverwood Lakes 14

Thursday 30th
Timber Hill 56

November

Wednesday 5th
Timber Hill 56

By Arrangement

Arrange a personalised garden visit with your club, or group of friends, on a date to suit you. See individual garden entries for full details.

Ashcombe 3
Ashleigh Grange 4
15 The Avenue 5
Bridge End Cottage 6
Caxton House 7
2 Chinthurst Lodge 11
Coldharbour House 13
Coverwood Lakes 14
Crosswater Farm 15
Harry Edwards Healing Sanctuary 24
Heathside 26
Leigh Place 31
Lower House 36
Mole End 40
Moleshill House 41
Monks Lantern 42
The Nutrition Garden 43
The Old Vicarage 45
Shamley Wood Estate 47
41 Shelvers Way 48
Shieling 49
South Wind 52
Spurfold 53
Tanhouse Farm 54
Westways Farm 63
The White House 64
48 Woodmansterne Lane 67
Woodpeckers 68
Wrens' Nest Cottage 69

THE GARDENS

1 ALBURY PARK
Albury, GU5 9BH. Trustees of Albury Estate. *5m SE of Guildford. From A25 take A248 towards Albury for ¼ m, then up New Rd, entrance to Albury Park immed on L.* **Sun 16 Mar, Sun 5 Oct (2-5). Adm £6, chd free. Home-made teas.**
14 acre pleasure grounds laid out in 1670s by John Evelyn for Henry Howard, later 6th Duke of Norfolk. ¼ m of terraces, fine collection of trees, lake and river. Wheelchair access over gravel path and slight slope.
&. ♨ »))

2 NEW 16 ARNISON ROAD
East Molesey, KT8 9JJ. Georgy Evans & Matthew Hill. *Nr Hampton Court Palace. 10 min walk from Hampton Court Train Stn. Buses from Richmond & Kingston. Limited parking locally but some at Hampton Court Palace, Hampton Court Green & station (charges apply).* **Sat 12 July (11-4). Adm £5. Tea, coffee & cake.**
This plant-lovers' town garden has colour and interest year-round. Paved walkways between densely planted and varied beds lead up a gentle slope through three connected areas, ending in vegetable beds and a Victorian-style greenhouse. Four seating/dining areas. The front garden has a similar planting scheme and is intended to give as much pleasure from the pavement as from the house. Gravel drive and access to step free garden via side gate.
&. ✿ D ♨ »))

3 ASHCOMBE
Chapel Lane, Westhumble, Dorking, RH5 6AY. Vivienne & David Murch, 01306 743062, murch@ashcombe.org. *2m N of Dorking. From A24 at Boxhill/Burford Bridge follow signs to Westhumble. Through village & take L drive by ruined chapel (1m from A24). Limited on site parking for up to 10 cars.* **Visits by arrangement 2 June to 1 Aug for groups of 10+. Tea, coffee & cake. Wine for eve visits.**
Rose lovers, 1⅓ acre wildlife friendly, sloping garden on chalk and flint. Enclosed ⅓ acre cottage garden with borders of roses, delphiniums and clematis. Amphibian pond. Secluded decking and patio area with colourful acers and views to Boxhill. Gravel bed of salvia and day lilies. House surrounded by banked flower beds and lawn leading to meadow and bee and butterfly garden.
🐕 ✿ ☕

4 ASHLEIGH GRANGE
Off Chapel Lane, Westhumble, RH5 6AY. Angela & Clive Gilchrist, 01306 884613, ar.gilchrist@btinternet.com. *2m N of Dorking. From A24 at Boxhill/Burford Bridge follow signs to Westhumble. Sorry, no access for coaches.* **Evening opening Fri 20 June (5.30-8). Adm £10, chd free. Wine. Sun 22 June (2-5). Adm £5, chd free. Home-made teas. Visits also by arrangement 21 May to 20 July.**
Plantswoman's country garden on 3½ acre sloping chalk site in charming rural setting with delightful views. Many areas of interest inc rockery with water feature, raised ericaceous bed, prairie style bank, foliage plants, woodland walk, fernery and folly. Large mixed herbaceous and shrub borders planted for dry alkaline soil and widespread interest.
&. 🐕 ✿ ☕

5 15 THE AVENUE
Cheam, Sutton, SM2 7QA. Jan & Nigel Brandon, 020 8643 8686, janmbrandon@outlook.com. *1m SW of Sutton. By car: exit A217 onto Northey Av, 2nd R into The Ave. By train: 10 min walk from Cheam Stn. By bus: use 470. Not in ULEZ.* **Sun 25 May (1-5). Adm £5, chd free. Home-made teas. Visits also by arrangement 31 May to 6 July for groups of 10 to 50.**
A contemporary garden designed by RHS Chelsea Gold Medal Winner, Marcus Barnett. Four levels divided into rooms by beech hedging and columns: formal entertaining area, contemporary outdoor room, lawn and wildflower meadow. Over 100 hostas hug the house. Silver birch, cloud pruned box, ferns, grasses, tall bearded irises, and contemporary sculptures. Partial wheelchair access; terraced with steps. Sloping path provides view of whole garden.
&. ☕ ♨ »))

6 BRIDGE END COTTAGE
Ockham Lane, Ockham, GU23 6NR. Clare & Peter Bevan, 07956 307546, clare.bevan@ngs.org.uk, bridgeendcottage.co.uk. *Nr RHS Garden Wisley. At Wisley r'about turn L onto B2039 to Ockham/Horsley. After ½ m turn L into Ockham Ln. House ½ m on R. From Cobham go to Blackswan Xrds.* **Sat 19 July (11-4). Adm £7, chd free. Tea, coffee & cake in the garden room. Visits also by arrangement 19 May to 21 July for groups of 5 to 25.**
2 acre country garden with different areas of interest inc perennial borders, mature trees, pond and streams, fruit trees, greenhouse and a colourful vegetable patch. An adjacent 2 acre field was sown with perennial wildflower seed 10 yrs ago and should be at its best in July. This garden has evolved over 20 yrs according to the owners' preferences and you can feel the pleasure it gives.
🐕 ✿ 🚗 ☕ 🪑 »))

7 CAXTON HOUSE
67 West Street, Reigate, RH2 9DA. Bob Bushby, 07836 201740, bob.bushby@sky.com. *On A25 towards Dorking, approx ¼ m W of Reigate. Parking on road or past Black Horse on Flanchford Rd.* **Visits by arrangement Apr to Sept for groups of 10 to 40. Adm £10, chd free. Tea, coffee & cake.**
Lovely large spring garden with arboretum, two well-stocked ponds, large collection of hellebores and spring flowers. Pots planted with colourful displays, plants. Small Gothic folly built by owner. Herbaceous borders with grasses, perennials and spring bulbs, parterre, bed with wild daffodils and prairie style planting in summer, and new wildflower garden in arboretum. Wheelchair access to most parts of the garden. Dogs on leads please.
&. 🐕 ✿ 🚗 ☕

Our donation to the Army Benevolent Fund supported 700 individuals with front line services and horticultural related grants in 2024.

8 NEW CHALESHURST
Petworth Road, Chiddingfold, Godalming, GU8 4ST. David & Louisa Henriques. *2m S of Chiddingfold, approx 400yds S of The Mulberry Inn, on opp side of the road. At the bottom of Cripple Crutch Hill.* **Sun 18 May (10-5). Adm £7, chd free. Tea, coffee & cake.** Mature trees and extensive lawns with flower beds created and planted by the owners. This garden offers a feeling of open space and tranquillity with pockets of interest to be explored and discovered inc an ornamental pond and fountain, a small stumpery, an insect hotel, and a woodland walk with bluebells in spring. The jewel in the crown is the large renovated Victorian glasshouse in which refreshments will be served. Wheelchair access over grass (weather permitting).
&

9 CHAUFFEUR'S FLAT
Tandridge Lane, Tandridge, RH8 9NJ. Mr & Mrs Richins. *2m E of Godstone. 2m W of Oxted. Turn off A25 at r'about for Tandridge. Take 2nd drive on L past church. Follow arrows to circular courtyard. Do not use Jackass Ln even if your SatNav tells you to do so.* **Fri 9, Sat 10, Sun 11 May (10-5). Adm £5, chd free. Home-made teas. Cash only on the day.** Enter a 1½ acre tapestry of magical secret gardens with magnificent views. Touching the senses, all sure footed visitors may explore the many surprises on this constantly evolving, exuberant escape from reality. Imaginative use of recycled materials creates an inspired variety of ideas, while wild and specimen plants reveal an ecological haven.

10 CHILWORTH MANOR
Halfpenny Lane, Chilworth, Guildford, GU4 8NN. Mia & Graham Wrigley, www.chilworthmanorsurrey.com. *3½ m SE of Guildford. From centre of Chilworth village turn into Blacksmith Ln. 1st drive on R on Halfpenny Ln.* **Sun 25 May (11-5). Adm £7.50, chd free. Pre-booking essential, please visit www.ngs.org.uk for information & booking. Tea, coffee & cake. Chilworth Manor Vineyard sparkling & rose wine for sale by the glass & bottle.** The grounds of the C17 Chilworth Manor create a wonderful tapestry, a jewel of an C18 terraced walled garden, topiary, herbaceous borders, sculptures, mature trees and stew ponds that date back a 1000 yrs. A fabulous, peaceful garden for all the family to wander and explore or just to relax and enjoy! Perhaps our many visitors describe it best, 'Magical', 'a sheer delight', 'elegant and tranquil', 'a little piece of heaven', 'spiffing!'. Garden or tree talk at 12.15pm, 1.15pm and 3.15pm. Sorry, dogs are not allowed.

11 2 CHINTHURST LODGE
Wonersh Common, Wonersh, Guildford, GU5 0PR. Mr & Mrs M R Goodridge, 01483 535108, michaelgoodridge@ymail.com. *4m S of Guildford. From A281 at Shalford turn E onto B2128 towards Wonersh. Just after Waverley sign, before village, garden on R, via stable entrance opp Little Tangley. No parking for coaches on site.* **Visits by arrangement 11 May to 20 July for groups of 12 to 40. Adm £10, chd free. Home-made teas.**
1 acre enthusiast's atmospheric and tranquil garden divided into rooms with year-round interest. Herbaceous borders, dramatic white garden, specimen trees and shrubs, gravel garden with water feature, small kitchen garden, fruit cage, two wells, ornamental ponds, herb parterre and Millennium rose, iris and hollyhock garden. Wheelchair access with some avoidable gravel paths.

12 CLARIDGE HOUSE
Dormans Road, Dormansland, Lingfield, RH7 6QH. Meredith Wood, 01342 832150, welcome@claridgehouse.org.uk, www.claridgehouse.org.uk. *1m from Lingfield Stn. From Racecourse Rd, veer R onto Dormans Rd, & follow yellow signs. Claridge House is clearly signed.* **Wed 14, Thur 15, Fri 16 May (10.30-3). Adm £5, chd free.**
An established 2 acre woodland garden with a variety of specimen trees and a woodland walk. Two wildflower meadows as well as more formal beds, with many benches to stop for a minute and enjoy. We are as sustainable as possible, using compost created from the Retreat food waste and no pesticides to support nature. We have beehives, bats, hedgehogs and butterflies. Our natural pond has dragonflies, mayflies and newts. Children must be accompanied and supervised. Dogs on leads only. Partial wheelchair access on paths to the formal garden.

13 COLDHARBOUR HOUSE
Coldharbour Lane, Bletchingley, Redhill, RH1 4NA. Mr Tony Elias, 01883 742685, eliastony@hotmail.com. *Coldharbour Ln, off Rabies Heath Rd, ½ m from A25 at Bletchingley & 1m from Tilburstow Hill Rd. Parking at the house for up to 20 cars.* **Visits by arrangement Apr to Oct for groups of 10+. Adm £10, chd free. Coffee or tea & a slice of something sweet inc.**
This 1½ acre garden offers breathtaking views to the South Downs. Originally planted in the 1920s, it has since been adapted and enhanced. Several mature trees and shrubs inc a copper beech, a Canadian maple, magnolias, azaleas, rhododendrons, camellias, wisterias, *Berberis* 'Georgei', *Vitex agnus-castus*, fuchsias, hibiscus, potentillas, mahonias, a fig tree and a walnut tree.

14 COVERWOOD LAKES
Peaslake Road, Ewhurst, GU6 7NT. The Metson Family, 01306 731101, farm@coverwoodlakes.co.uk, www.coverwoodlakes.co.uk. *7m SW of Dorking. From A25 follow signs for Peaslake; garden ½ m beyond Peaslake on Ewhurst Rd.* **Every Sun 13 Apr to 4 May (11-5). Sun 19 Oct (11-5). Adm £7.50, chd free. Light refreshments. Visits also by arrangement 14 Apr to 30 Sept for groups of 20+.**
14 acre landscaped garden in stunning position high in the Surrey Hills with four lakes and bog garden. Extensive rhododendrons, azaleas and fine trees. 3½ acre lakeside arboretum. Marked trail through the 180 acre working farm with Hereford cows and calves, sheep and horses, extensive views of the surrounding hills. Light refreshments inc home produced beef and lamb burgers, gourmet coffee and home-made cakes from the Fillet & Bean Café (outdoor mobile kitchen). Sorry, dogs are not allowed.

Longer End Cottage

15 CROSSWATER FARM
Crosswater Lane, Churt, Farnham, GU10 2JN. David & Susanna Millais, 07771 558397, crosswaterfarmoffice@gmail.com. *6m S of Farnham, 6m NW of Haslemere. From A287 turn E into Jumps Rd, ½m N of Churt village centre. After ¼m turn acute L into Crosswater Ln & follow signs for Millais Nurseries, Crosswater Farm.* **Thur 1, Fri 2, Sat 3, Thur 8, Fri 9, Sat 10, Thur 15, Fri 16, Sat 17 May (11-4). Adm £6, chd free. Visits also by arrangement 24 Apr to 31 May for groups of 10 to 25.** Idyllic 5 acre woodland garden. Plantsman's collection of rhododendrons and azaleas inc rare species collected in the Himalayas and hybrids raised by the family. Everything from alpine dwarfs to architectural large leaved trees. Ponds, stream and companion plantings inc sorbus, magnolias and Japanese acers, and many recent new plantings. A specialist collection of rhododendrons and azaleas. Grass paths may be difficult for wheelchairs after rain.

16 ◆ DUNSBOROUGH PARK
Ripley, GU23 6AL. Baron & Baroness Sweerts de Landas Wyborgh. *6m NE of Guildford. For SatNav use GU23 6BZ. Entrance via Newark Ln, Ripley, through Tudor-style gatehouses & courtyard up drive. Car park signed.* **For NGS: Wed 16 Apr (9.30-3.30). Entry between 9.30-10am & 1-1.30pm only. Adm £9, chd free. Pre-booking essential, please visit www.dunsboroughpark.com for information & booking. For queries only, please email events@dunsboroughpark.com. Charity teas for sale.** For other opening times and information, please phone, email or visit garden website.
6 acre garden redesigned by Penelope Hobhouse and Rupert Golby. Garden rooms, lush herbaceous borders, standard wisteria, 70ft ginkgo hedge, potager and 300 yr old mulberry tree. Rose Walk, Italian Garden and Water Garden with folly bridge. April Tulip Festival: Formal borders. Colourful informal display in meadow. Wheelchair access over gravel paths and grass, cobbled over folly bridge.

GROUP OPENING

17 FAIRMILE COMMON GARDENS
Portsmouth Road, Cobham, KT11 1BG. *2m NE of Cobham. On A307 Esher to Cobham Rd next to free car park by A3 bridge, at entrance to Waterford Cl.* **Mon 5 May (2-5). Combined adm £12, chd free. Tea, coffee & cake at Fairmile Lea.**

23 FAIRACRES
Miranda Filkins.

FAIRMILE LEA
Steven Kay.

MOLESHILL HOUSE
Penny Snell.
(See separate entry)

Three contrasting gardens inc many mature specimen trees. One with new water feature surrounding oak room (not open), vegetables and potager. Another large garden with a castle folly alongside a new and extensive natural pond, sanctuary garden, triffid bed and wilderness mound. The third, a romantic, naturalistic garden on the wild side, much photographed and published. Plants for sale at Moleshill House.
✿ ☕))

18 NEW FELDEMORE CORNER
Pasturewood Road, Holmbury St Mary, Dorking, RH5 6LQ. Mr Richard & Mrs Sally Frost. *Between Dorking and Shere, 1¾m S of A25. From A25 at Wotton turn into Hollow Ln. After 1⅓m turn R into Pasturewood Rd. Feldemore Corner is on the R after ½m. From S on entering Holmbury turn R into Pasturewood Rd.* **Sun 18 May (11-5). Adm £5, chd free. Tea, coffee & cake.**
A 4 acre woodland garden that started in the 1870s and has been added to since, particularly in the last 40 yrs. A wide range of rhododendrons and azaleas, beech trees and Douglas Firs.
✿ ☕))

19 THE GARTH PLEASURE GROUNDS
The Garth, Newchapel Road, Lingfield, RH7 6BJ. Mr Sherlock & Mrs Stanley, hello@thegarth.info, www.thegarth.info. *Western edge of Lingfield. From A22 take B2028 by the Mormon Temple to Lingfield. The Garth is on the L after 1½m, opp Barge Tiles. Parking: Gun Pit Rd in Lingfield & limited space for disabled at Barge Tiles.* **Sun 4, Sun 11 May (1-5). Adm £10, chd free. Tea, coffee & cake.**
Mature 9 acre Pleasure Grounds created by Walter Godfrey in 1919, present an idyllic setting surrounding the former parish workhouse refurbished in Edwardian style. The formal gardens, enchanting nuttery, a spinney with many mature trees and a pond attract wildlife. Wonderful bluebells in spring. The woodland gardens and beautiful borders are full of colour and fragrance for year-round pleasure. Many areas of interest and large specimen plants inc ancient oak. Picnics are welcome. Wheelchair access to most areas of the garden.
♿ 🐕 ✿ 🛏 ☕ 🪑))

20 ♦ GATTON PARK
Reigate, RH2 0TW. Royal Alexandra & Albert School. *3m NE of Reigate. Entrance off Rocky Ln at main gate of Royal Alexandra & Albert School.* **For NGS: Sun 9 Feb (12-5). Adm £8, chd free. Pre-booking preferred, please visit www.gattonpark.co.uk, email events@gatton-park.org.uk or phone 01737 649068 for information & booking. Light refreshments.** For other opening times and information, please phone, email or visit garden website.

Mill House

Historic 260 acre estate in the Surrey Hills AONB. Capability Brown parkland with ancient oaks. Discover the Japanese garden, Victorian parterre and breathtaking views over the lake. Seasonal highlights inc displays of snowdrops and aconites in February. Ongoing restoration projects by the Gatton Trust. Bird hide open to see herons nesting. Free guided tours. A selection of hot and cold drinks, cakes and snacks. Plants for winter interest for sale. Adm: Adults £6 pre-book tickets (£8 on the day).

21 21 GLENAVON CLOSE
Claygate, Esher, KT10 0HP. Selina & Simon Botham. *2m SE of Esher. From A3 S exit Esher, R at T-lights. Continue straight through Claygate village, bear R at 2 mini r'abouts. Past church & rec. Turn L at bollards into Causeway. At end straight over to Glenavon Cl.* **Sun 20 July (2-6). Adm £6, chd free. Home-made teas.**
An oasis of plants, natural sculptures and water features created for year-round interest by RHS award-winning garden designer, Selina Botham. The garden, as featured on BBC Gardeners' World, showcases how to design an awkward shaped plot to create a space that can be enjoyed by wildlife and people alike. The garden features an outdoor bath, a pond, water features and a river of naturalistic planting. Free tours by the designer start at 2pm and 3pm alongside a display of design work in her garden studio.

22 GRACE & FLAVOUR COMMUNITY GARDEN
Ripley Lane, West Horsley, Leatherhead, KT24 6JW. Grace & Flavour CIC, www.graceandflavour.org. *Approx halfway between Guildford & Leatherhead, just off the A246. At r'about on A246 in West Horsley, turn L (signed West Horsley & Ripley) into The Street. Follow road for ⅓ m. Turn L into Ripley Ln. Garden is ⅓ m on L. Entrance via Dene Place BUPA Nursing Home.* **Sun 27 July (12-4). Adm £5, chd free. Tea, coffee & cake.**
Grace & Flavour is a community kitchen garden and 28 allotments. In 2009 it took over a derelict 3 acre walled garden and orchard, part of NT's Hatchlands Estate. It features vegetable beds, soft fruit cages, polytunnels, fruit tree avenue with lavender borders, cut flower beds, wildlife area and pond. It is free of chemicals and pesticides, and has a no dig policy. Wheelchair access to main paths, but not the uneven side paths.

23 HALL GROVE SCHOOL
London Road (A30), Bagshot, GU19 5HZ. Mr & Mrs Graham. *6m SW of Egham. M3 J3, follow A322 for 1m until sign for Sunningdale A30. 1m E of Bagshot, opp Longacres Garden Centre. Entrance at footbridge. Ample car parking.* **Sat 17 May, Sat 27 Sept (2-5). Adm £5, chd free. Home-made teas.**
Formerly a small Georgian country estate, now a co-educational preparatory school. Grade II listed house (not open). Mature parkland with specimen trees. Historical features inc ice house and a recently restored walled kitchen garden with flower borders, fruit and children's vegetable plots. There is also a lake, woodland walks, rhododendrons, azaleas and acers. Live music at 3pm.

24 HARRY EDWARDS HEALING SANCTUARY
Hook Lane, Burrows Lea, Shere, Guildford, GU5 9QG. The Harry Edwards Foundation, 01483 202054, info@he-foundation.org, he-foundation.org. *Close to Shere & Gomshall. From the A25 take the turning to Shere village & drive through the village. Cross over the railway bridge & turn L into Hook Ln. The Sanctuary is on the R & clearly signed.* **Visits by arrangement 10 May to 11 Oct for groups of 10 to 25. Adm £7, chd free.**
The Harry Edwards Foundation offers holistic therapies and healing gardens. Everyone is welcome to come and explore the grounds, take part in various wellbeing activities, or simply enjoy coffee.

25 ◆ HATCHLANDS PARK
East Clandon, Guildford, GU4 7RT. National Trust, 01483 222482, hatchlands@nationaltrust.org.uk, www.nationaltrust.org.uk/hatchlands-park. *4m E of Guildford. Follow brown signs to Hatchlands Park (NT).* **For NGS: Sun 27 Apr (10-5). Adm £12, chd £6. Adm charges subject to change.** For other opening times and information, please phone, email or visit garden website.
Garden and park designed by Repton in 1800. Follow one of the park walks to the stunning bluebell wood in spring (2½ km round walk over rough and sometimes muddy ground). Partial wheelchair access to parkland with rough and undulating terrain, tracks and cobbled courtyard. Mobility scooter booking essential.

26 HEATHSIDE
10 Links Green Way, Cobham, KT11 2QH. Miss Margaret Arnott & Mr Terry Bartholomew, 07927 136308, margaret.arnott@ngs.org.uk. *1½ m E of Cobham. Through Cobham A245, 4th L after Esso garage into Fairmile Ln. Straight on into Water Ln. Links Green Way 3rd turning on L.* **Visits by arrangement. Morning coffee, afternoon tea, or wine & canapés.**
Terraced plants persons garden, designed for year-round interest. Gorgeous planting all set off by harmonious landscaping. Many urns and pots give seasonal displays. Several water features add tranquil sound. Stunning colour combinations excite. Dahlias and begonias a favourite. Beautiful Griffin Glasshouse housing the exotic. Many inspirational ideas. Situated 5 miles from RHS Garden Wisley.

Our donation in 2024 has enabled Parkinson's UK to fund 3 new nursing posts this year directly supporting people with Parkinson's.

SURREY 503

27 HIGH CLANDON ESTATE VINEYARD
High Clandon, East Clandon, GU4 7RP. Sibylla & Bruce Tindale, www.highclandon.co.uk. *A3/Wisley junction, L for Ockham/Horsley for 2m to A246. R for Guildford for 2m, then 100yds past landmark Hatchlands NT, turn L into Blakes Ln, straight uphill through gates High Clandon to vineyard entrance. Extensive parking in our woodland area.* **Sun 6 July (11-4.30). Adm £7.50, chd free. Pre-booking preferred. Cream teas & home-made cakes. Gold awarded English sparkling wine for sale by the glass & bottle.**
Multi-gold award-winning English sparkling wine vineyard featuring gardens, a 2 acre wildflower meadow home to rare butterflies, water features, a Japanese garden, a truffière, an apiary, and sculptures. Set in 12 acres of beautiful Surrey Hills AONB, with sweeping vistas and panoramic views to London. Twice winner Cellar Door of the Year. Exhibition of over 180 works of art and sculptures on show. During this season, the main wildlife pond often attracts wild Mallard ducks and their ducklings. Access is good; all garden paths are lawns on firm ground based on hard chalky substrate.
& 🐕 ☕))

28 NEW HIGHMOUNT
12 Fort Road, Guildford, GU1 3TD. Mr William & Mrs Anne Whitley. *Within ½ m of central Guildford. What3words app: seated.store. income. For SatNav please use GU1 3TD.* **Sun 22 June (12-5). Adm £5, chd free. Home-made teas.**
Part of an original Gertrude Jekyll garden with much of the original hard landscaping. There is still some of her original planting with huge box hedges and a vine going over a pergola. The garden is on the side of a very steep hill with steep brick steps that has evolved over the yrs with herbaceous borders and a wilding area.
✽ ☕))

29 HILL FARM
Logmore Lane, Westcott, Dorking, RH4 3JY. Helen Thomas. *1m W of Dorking. Parking on Westcott Heath just past church. Entry to garden opp. What3words app: putty.ballots. arrive.* **Sun 7 Sept (11-4.30). Adm £5, chd free. Tea, coffee & cake.**
1¾ acre set in the magnificent Surrey Hills landscape. The garden has a wealth of different natural habitats to encourage wildlife, and planting areas which come alive through the different seasons. Features inc a wildlife pond, woodland walk, a tapestry of heathers, glorious late summer grasses and perennials, wildflower meadow, a vegetable and cut flower garden with greenhouse. A garden to be enjoyed by all. Everyone welcome. Sloping garden; most areas are accessible for wheelchair users but may require assistance. Most paths are grass so care needed if very wet.
& 🐕 ✽ D ☕))

30 ICHI-COO PARK
Russ Hill Farm, Russ Hill, Charlwood, RH6 0EL. Robin Redmile-Gordon, ichicoopark.com. *5m E of Gatwick Airport. From A23 N from Gatwick, or A23 S from Horley, or A217 S from Reigate, arrive at Longbridge r'about. Take exit heading E, signed Charlwood. Stay on road all the way.* **Sun 6 July (11-5). Adm £20, chd free. Teas, coffee, cake, wine & beer.**
Ichi-Coo Park is unlike any garden you've ever visited. With 16 acres, allow a minimum of two hours, if you don't dally. Glorious shapes and shades of green, painted onto the natural background of the Sussex Weald. It is an eclectic collection of plants, trees and water, spaces, forms and vistas, habitats and sanctuaries. A place for reflection, for relaxation, oh and a plane spotter's dream! With assistance, there are ample level routes but be aware we are on a 1:10 hill. If you descend to the bottom we have to get you back up!
& 🐕 ☕ 🍴))

31 LEIGH PLACE
Leigh Place Lane, Godstone, RH9 8BN. Mike & Liz McGhee, 01883 743320. *Take B2236 Eastbourne Rd from Godstone village. Parking for a max of 8 cars each hour.* **Fri 16, Sat 17 May (10-4). Adm £5, chd free. Pre-booking essential, please visit www.ngs.org.uk for information & booking. Cream teas.**
Visits also by arrangement Mar to Oct for groups of 10+.
Leigh Place garden has 25 acres on greensand. Part of the Godstone Ponds with SSSI with lakeside paths, walled garden inc cutting garden, orchard and vegetable quadrant with greenhouses. Beehives and large rock garden. Features inc Edwardian apple arch and historic wisteria. The walled garden has Breedon gravel paths suitable for wheelchairs and pushchairs. Well behaved dogs welcome on leads.
& 🐕 ✽ ☕))

32 LITTLE ORCHARDS
Prince Of Wales Road, Outwood, Redhill, RH1 5QU. Nic Howard, www.instagram.com/nichoward. *A few hundred metres N of The Dog & Duck pub.* **Fri 30 May, Sun 1 June, Fri 5, Sun 7 Sept (12-4). Adm £6, chd £3. Tea, coffee & cake.**
A magical, artistic, plantsman's paradise planted for year-round interest using a tapestry of foliage as well as flower interest. The garden is arranged as a series of connected areas that flow between two properties, the old gardener's cottage, and the old stables. Often compared to a mini Petersham Nursery by our visitors; we have a gift shop selling garden paraphernalia and a lovely café area.
🐕 ✽ 🚗 D ☕))

33 LOGMORE PLACE
Logmore Lane, Westcott, Dorking, RH4 3JN. Jane Clarke. *In between Westcott & Coldharbour. From A25 past the church, turn L into Logmore Ln & Logmore Place is approx ½ m on the R next to Florents Farm. Off road parking in sloping field. Disabled parking in front of house only.* **Sun 29 June (12-4). Adm £7.50, chd free. Tea, coffee & cake.**
Established trees, rhododendrons and yew hedges create a framework for the far-reaching views of the Surrey Hills. Small Japanese garden, walled flower garden, orchard, plus two formal lawns featuring Piet Oudolf inspired beds. Walks on the estate inc field tracks, lake with bridges, quiet ancient woodland and stunning views to Ranmore from the trig point. Wheelchair access to terrace and views only. Gravel paths, steps and sloping grass paths to rest of site.
& 🐕 ☕))

34 NEW LONGER END COTTAGE

Normandy Common Lane, Normandy, Guildford, GU3 2AP. Mrs Caroline Lenton. *4m W of Guildford on A323. At War Memorial Xrds in Normandy turn into Hunts Hill Rd, then 1st R into Normandy Common Ln. Longer End Cottage is 3rd property on L. Parking at Hunts Hill Rd car parks. Limited parking along lane.* **Sat 5 July (10-5). Adm £5, chd free. Pre-booking essential, please visit www.ngs.org.uk for information & booking. Tea, coffee & cake.**

A 1½ acre garden, previously opened in 2004 for 9 yrs. It has changed considerably since then, due to remodelling by the current garden designer owner. Divided into rooms surrounding a historic cottage, features inc mixed borders, meadows, a wildlife pond, gravel planting, grass borders and an exotic area. Designed to maximise colour, variety, resilience and value to wildlife. Lunches available in Normandy Village Shop and Café nearby.

35 ♦ LOSELEY PARK

Guildford, GU3 1HS. Mr & Mrs A G More-Molyneux, 01483 304440/01483 405112, pa@loseleypark.co.uk, www.loseleypark.co.uk. *4m SW of Guildford. For SatNav please use GU3 1HS, Stakescorner Ln.* **For NGS: Sun 15 June (10.30-4). Adm by donation. Tea, coffee & cake in the tea hut in the White Garden.** For other opening times and information, please phone, email or visit garden website.

Delightful 2½ acre walled garden. Award-winning rose garden (over 1000 bushes, mainly old fashioned varieties), extensive herb garden, fruit and flower garden, white garden with fountain and spectacular organic vegetable garden. Magnificent vine walk, herbaceous borders, moat walk, ancient wisteria and mulberry trees.

16 Arnison Road

© Toby Hornby-Patterson

36 LOWER HOUSE
Lower House Road, Bowlhead Green, Godalming, GU8 6NW. Georgina Harvey, 07710 797698, georgina@gharvey.co.uk. *1m from A3 Thursley/Bowlhead Green junction. A3 leave at Thursley/Bowlhead Green junction. Follow NGS signs. A286 leave at Brook. Follow Bowlhead Green & NGS signs for approx 2m. Parking at property.* **Thur 19 June (10.30-5); Sun 22 June (1-5). Adm £7, chd free. Home-made teas.** Visits also by arrangement May & June for groups of 20 to 35. Garden tour with Head Gardener, Mart Veerus.
Gertrude Jekyll's 1916 plans resonate throughout the garden but recent horticultural practices like top-worked Amelanchier and grafted Cobnuts reflect continuing skills. Two topiary areas highlight traditional Buxus and white roses, against a climate change response of drought resistant, pest and disease-free species. Over 300 roses, historic and modern, grow throughout even into the kitchen garden. Plants for sale. Alternative routes to avoid steps for wheelchair users and some narrow paths.
& ⛫ ✿ ☕))

37 THE MANOR HOUSE
Three Gates Lane, Haslemere, GU27 2ES. Mr & Mrs Gerard Ralfe. *NE of Haslemere. From Haslemere centre take A286 towards Milford. Turn R after museum into Three Gates Ln. At T-Junction turn R into Holdfast Ln. Car park on R.* **Sun 18 May (10-5). Adm £8, chd free. Tea, coffee & cake.**
Described by Country Life as 'The Hanging Gardens of Haslemere', the well established Manor House gardens are tucked away in a valley of the Surrey Hills. Set in 6 acres, it was one of Surrey's inaugural NGS gardens with fine views, an impressive show of azaleas, wisteria, beautiful trees underplanted with bulbs, enchanting water gardens and a magnificent rose garden.
☕))

70 inpatients and their families are being supported at the newly opened Horatio's Garden Northern Ireland, thanks to National Garden Scheme donations.

38 NEW MILL HOUSE
Mill Lane, Frensham, Farnham, GU10 3EE. Roger & Kate Holmes. *Signed parking off Pitt Ln.* **Sat 30, Sun 31 Aug (2-6). Adm £6. Tea, coffee & cake.**
Set in a stunning Surrey valley, the 2 acre riverside garden surrounds a historic mill and offers formal borders and lawns, a walled rose garden and vegetable garden. Bridges lead to a woodland riverside walk, orchard and a further 6 acre meadow. The historic mill has been transformed for sustainability, with a hydroelectric system powered by an Archimedes screw. Wheelchair access with shallow steps and gravel paths, assistance maybe required.
& ☕))

39 MILTON WAY HOUSE
Guildford Road, Westcott, Dorking, RH4 3PZ. Ingrid Andree Wiltens. *2m E of Dorking. Access to & from the site is from the A25. The lane is assisted by CCTV to provide visibility around a blind corner. On exit L turns only are recommended. Parking is limited.* **Sun 15 June (11-4.30). Adm £5.50, chd free. Pre-booking essential, please visit www.ngs.org.uk for information & booking. Timed slots at 11am, 1pm or 3pm. Home-made teas.**
Set in the beautiful Surrey Hills on a sloping site surrounded by mature trees. A small country garden, just shy of an acre, with a lush and green walled garden and a social area where teas will be available. There is also a vegetable garden, woodland area and informal/wildflower lawn surrounded by mixed borders of perennials, grasses and shrubs.
⛫ ☕))

40 MOLE END
10 Farm Lane, Send, Woking, GU23 7AT. Mrs Pat Hutchings, 07810 461144, farm.lane@btinternet.com. *Pass Send Recreation Ground on Sandy Ln, turn L into Farm Ln.* Visits by arrangement 11 Aug to 15 Sept for groups of 5 to 15. Adm £5, chd free. Tea, coffee & cake.
A tranquil and meditative garden with architectural/jungle planting style that comes to its best in late summer. Lush, bold foliage, striking contrasts and showy specimen plants reflect the owner's love for the unusual. Lots of little quirky creatures are hidden around two ponds in a playful way for visitors to discover.
☕))

41 MOLESHILL HOUSE
The Fairmile, Cobham, KT11 1BG. Penny Snell, pennysnellflowers@btinternet.com, www.pennysnellflowers.co.uk. *2m NE of Cobham. On A307 Esher to Cobham Rd next to free car park by A3 bridge, at entrance to Waterford Cl.* **Sun 13 Apr (2-5). Adm £5, chd free. Light refreshments. Opening with Fairmile Common Gardens on Mon 5 May.** Visits also by arrangement 13 Apr to 31 Aug.
Romantic disarray. Naturalistic garden on the wild side featuring many mature and interesting trees. Short woodland path leads from dovecote to beehive. Informal planting contrasts with formal topiary, box and garlanded cisterns. Colourful courtyard, conservatory, pond with fountain, white beam avenue, circular gravel garden, gipsy caravan garden, green wall and stumpery. Espaliered crab apples. Garden 5 mins from Claremont Landscape Garden, Painshill Park and RHS Garden Wisley.
✿ 🚗 ☕))

42 MONKS LANTERN
Ruxbury Road, Chertsey, KT16 9NH. Mr & Mrs J Granell, 01932 569578, janicegranell@hotmail.com. *1m NW from Chertsey. M25 J11, signed A320/Woking. At r'about take 2nd exit A320/Staines, then straight over next r'about. L onto Holloway Hill, R Hardwick Ln. $\frac{1}{2}$m, R over motorway bridge, on Almners then Ruxbury Rd.* **Sat 24 May (2-5.30). Adm £5, chd free. Tea, coffee & cake. Wine.** Visits also by arrangement 9 June to 8 Sept for groups of up to 30.
A delightful garden with borders arranged with colour in mind; silvers and white, olive trees blend together with nicotiana and senecio. A weeping silver birch leads to the oranges and yellows of a tropical bed with large bottle brush, hardy palms and *Fatsia japonica*. Large rockery and an informal pond. There is a display of hostas, *Cytisus battandieri* and a selection of grasses in an island bed. Aviary with canaries. Workshop with a display of handmade guitars, wine and refreshments. Wheelchairs welcome; two reserved parking spaces at entrance to garden as gravel drive is not easy.
& ⛫ ✿ ☕ 🪑))

43 THE NUTRITION GARDEN
156A Frimley Green Road, Frimley Green, Camberley, GU16 6NA. Dr Trevor George RNutr, 07914 911410, t-george@hotmail.co.uk. *2m (5 mins) from J4 of the M3. From M3, follow signs for A331 towards Farnborough, then follow signs to Frimley Green (B3411). The house is down a long drive with telegraph poles at each end, almost opp the recreation ground.* **Visits by arrangement 28 June to 7 Sept for groups of up to 20. Adm £5, chd free.**
A garden designed by a registered nutritionist to produce and display a wide variety of edible plants inc fruits, vegetables, herbs, and plants for infusions. There are trees, shrubs, tubers, perennials and annual plants. Over 100 types of edible plants and over 200 varieties are grown throughout the yr. These inc unusual food plants, plus heritage and unusual coloured varieties. Tea, coffee, light refreshments and infusions from plants growing in the garden available. Wheelchair access on paved paths around fruit and vegetable beds. Other areas are step free, but around uneven grass lawn.

& ❋ ☕ ♫)

44 THE OLD RECTORY
Sandy Lane, Brewer Street, Bletchingley, RH1 4QW. Mr & Mrs A Procter. *Top of village nr The Red Lion pub, turn R into Little Common Ln, then R at Cross Rd into Sandy Ln. Parking nr house, disabled parking in courtyard.* **Sun 8 June (11-4). Adm £5, chd free. Home-made teas.**
Georgian Manor House (not open). Quintessential Italianate topiary garden, statuary, box parterres, courtyard with columns, water features and antique terracotta pots. Much of the 4 acre garden is the subject of ongoing reclamation inc the ancient moat and woodland with fine specimen trees and one of the largest tulip trees in the country. New sunken water garden and tropical garden. Wheelchair access with gravel paths.

& ☕ ♫)

45 THE OLD VICARAGE
The Street, Frensham, Farnham, GU10 3DU. Kate & David Smith, 07788 746719, smithkrdr@me.com, www.instagram.com/katesmithgardendesign. *3m S of Farnham, 4m N of Hindhead. Turn off A287 Farnham to Hindhead road at small village green at St Mary's School. Travel along The Street for ½ m, the Old Vicarage is on the* RHS, *next to St Mary's Church.* **Sat 14 June (10.30-2.30); Sun 15 June (2-5.30). Adm £6, chd free. Home-made teas.** Visits also by arrangement 1 June to 1 July for groups of 15+.
12 acres of garden surrounding the Old Vicarage in Frensham. The garden consists of 2 acres of herbaceous borders and lawns adjacent to the house. Steep slopes lead to the less formal grounds with large pond and the River Wey. Mown paths cut through the water meadows and small woodland.

☕ 🏛 ♫)

46 ♦ RAMSTER
Chiddingfold, GU8 4SN. Mrs Rosie Glaister, 01428 654167, office@ramsterhall.com, www.ramsterevents.com. *12m S of Guildford. Ramster is on A283, 1½m S of Chiddingfold. Enter via large iron gates, signed from the main road. Ample free car parking. What3words app: coast.unto.immediate.* **For NGS: Fri 16 May (10-5). Adm £10, chd £3. Light refreshments.** For other opening times and information, please phone, email or visit garden website.
A stunning, mature woodland garden set in 25 acres, famous for its rhododendron and azalea collection, and its carpets of bluebells in spring. Explore the bog garden with its stepping stones, or relax in the tranquil enclosed tennis court garden. Ramster has been opening for the NGS since the beginning in 1927 and we are very proud to still be supporting them. The tea house by the entrance to the garden is open every day while the garden is open, serving locally roasted coffee, delicious cakes and fresh sandwiches, home-made quiches and soup. Sculpture Exhibition runs in May. Wheelchair access to the tea house and some paths in the garden.

& 🐕 ❋ 🚗 ☕ ♫)

47 SHAMLEY WOOD ESTATE
Woodhill Lane, Shamley Green, Guildford, GU5 0SP. Mrs Claire Merriman, 07595 693132, claire@merriman.co.uk. *5m (15 mins) S of Guildford in village of Shamley Green. Entrance is approx ¼ m up Woodhill Ln from centre of Shamley Green.* **Visits by arrangement 3 Mar to 21 Nov for groups of 10+. Adm £9, chd free. Teas with gluten free options.**
A relative newcomer, this garden is worth visiting just for the setting! Sitting high on the North Downs, the garden enjoys beautiful views of the South Downs and is approached through a 10 acre deer park. Set within approx 3 acres, there is a large pond and established rose garden. More recent additions inc fire pits, vegetable patch, stream, tropical pergola and terraced wildflower lawn. Wheelchair access to most of garden. Step to access ground level WC.

& 🐕 🚗 📅 ☕ ♫)

48 41 SHELVERS WAY
Tadworth, KT20 5QJ. Keith & Elizabeth Lewis, 01737 210707, kandelewis@ntlworld.com. *6m S of Sutton off A217. 1st turning on R after Burgh Heath T-lights heading S on A217. 400yds down Shelvers Way on L.* **Visits by arrangement 1 Apr to 30 Aug for groups of 5+. Adm £10, chd free. Tea, coffee & cake.**
In spring a myriad of small bulbs, specialist daffodils and an assortment of many pots of tulips. In May azaleas and *Iris sibirica*. Choice perennials follow together with annuals to ensure colour until Sept. Plenty of seating plus a large conservatory to seat fourteen. A garden for all seasons.

❋ 🚗 ☕

49 SHIELING
The Warren, Kingswood, Tadworth, KT20 6PQ. Drs Sarah & Robin Wilson, 07932 445868, sarahwilson@doctors.org.uk. *Kingswood Warren Estate. Off A217, gated entrance just before church on S-bound side of dual carriageway after Tadworth r'about. ¾ m walk from station. Parking on The Warren or by church on A217.* **Sun 16 Feb, Sun 20 Apr (11-3); Sun 10 Aug (12-4). Adm £5, chd free. Tea, coffee & cake.** Visits also by arrangement 17 Feb to 19 Apr for groups of 10 to 30.
1 acre garden restored to its original 1920s design. Formal front garden with island beds and shrub borders. Unusual large rock garden and mixed borders with collection of bothy slug free hostas and uncommon woodland perennials and acid loving plants, a new shrub border and a stumpery. Lots for children to do with play area, Wendy house and amazing treehouse. Plant list provided for visitors. Wheelchair access over resin drive, grass and paths. Some narrow paths in back garden.

& 🐕 ❋ 📅 ☕ 🏛 ♫)

Chaleshurst

50 SHOOTING STAR CHILDREN'S HOSPICES, CHRISTOPHER'S
Old Portsmouth Road, Artington, Guildford, GU3 1LP. Lucy Hooper. *Situated next to Artington Park & Ride. Christopher's signage shown at entrance. Take 1st exit at the r'about if coming from Guildford or 3rd exit at the r'about if coming from Peasmarsh.* **Sun 8 June (12-4). Adm £5, chd free. Tea, coffee & cake.**
The gardens at the Guildford Hospice are enjoyed by families year-round, having been specifically designed with the needs of children in mind, from adapted play equipment and sensory trails to tranquil open areas for remembrance and reflection. They are maintained by a dedicated team of volunteer gardeners. Accessible pathway running throughout the garden. Accessible WC on site.

51 SLADES FARM
Thorncombe Street, Bramley, Guildford, GU5 0LT. Edward & Lulu Hutley. *Take the A281 to Bramley, at the r'about turn in to Snowdenham Ln; Slades Farm is 2½ m. Follow NGS signs.* **Sun 18 May (12-5). Adm £8, chd free. Tea, coffee & cake.**
Slades Farm gardens are predominantly a woodland garden with an abundance of azaleas, camellias, rhododendrons, and gunnera glades. There are many different species of trees, home to a variety of birds and wildlife. Bridges cross beautiful lakes and streams, but please take care as the ground can be uneven and please ensure children are supervised.

52 SOUTH WIND
23 Doctors Lane, Chaldon, Caterham, CR3 5AE. Mrs Catherine Jones, opengardenchaldon@gmail.com. *2½ m W of Caterham. Head W on Rook Ln past Surrey National Golf Club. After 1m turn R onto Doctors Ln. Limited parking on Doctors Ln. Alternative parking on Leazes Ave.* **Visits by arrangement 25 June to 7 Aug for groups of 10 to 35. Adm £5, chd free. Home-made teas.**
Delightful 1⅓ acre peaceful haven with a cottage garden feel. A 'multi-roomed' garden to maintain constant interest. Surefooted visitors can meander along gravel paths to the mixed herbaceous borders, vegetable beds and orchard. The oak gazebo with fire pit is a perfect place to sit whilst listening to the birds in the woodland. Sorry, no dogs.

53 SPURFOLD
Radnor Road, Peaslake, Guildford, GU5 9SZ. Mr & Mrs A Barnes, 01306 730196, spurfold@btinternet.com. *8m SE of Guildford. A25 to Shere then through to Peaslake. Pass village stores & L up Radnor Rd.* **Visits by arrangement 6 May to 20 June for groups of 15 to 30. Home-made teas or evening wine & nibbles.**
2½ acres, large herbaceous and shrub borders, formal pond with Cambodian Buddha head, sunken gravel garden with topiary box and water feature, terraces, beautiful lawns, mature rhododendrons, azaleas, woodland paths, and gazebos. Garden contains a collection of Indian elephants and other objets d'art. Topiary garden and formal lawn area.

54 TANHOUSE FARM
Rusper Road, Newdigate, RH5 5BX. Mrs N Fries, 01306 631334. *8m S of Dorking. On A24 turn L at r'about at Beare Green. R at T-junction in Newdigate, 1st farm on R approx $^2/_3$m. Signed Tanhouse Farm Shop.* **Visits by arrangement June to Sept. Adm £5, chd free.**
Country garden created by owners since 1987. 1 acre of charming rambling gardens surrounding a C16 house (not open). Herbaceous borders and stream with ducks and geese. Orchard with wild garden, and plentiful seats and benches to stop for contemplation.
& ☕

55 THE THERAPY GARDEN
Manor Fruit Farm, Glaziers Lane, Normandy, Guildford, GU3 2DT. The Therapy Garden General Manager, www.thetherapygarden.org. *SW of Guildford. Take A323 travelling from Guildford towards Aldershot, turn L into Glaziers Ln in centre of Normandy village, opp War Memorial. The Therapy Garden is 200yds on L.* **Sun 18 May, Sun 21 Sept (10-4). Adm £5, chd free. Teas, coffee & home-made cakes. BBQ & light lunches.**
The Therapy Garden is a horticulture and education charity that uses gardening to have a positive and significant impact on the lives of people facing challenges in life. In our beautiful and tranquil 2 acre garden we work to change lives for the better and we do this by creating a safe place to enjoy the power of gardening and to connect with nature. We are a working garden full of innovation with an on site shop selling plants and produce. There will be a selection of fun family garden related activities to take part in. Wheelchair access over paved pathways throughout most of garden, many with substantial handrails.
& 🐕 ✽ 🚗 ☕))

56 TIMBER HILL
Chertsey Road, Chobham, GU24 8JF. Nick & Lavinia Sealy, 01932 873875/07747 024695, lavinia@chobham.net, www.timberhillgarden.com. *A319 E of Chobham, & nr Woking, Chertsey, Sunningdale & Camberley. 2m from J11 M25, but avoid J10 intersection with A3 Wisley until June 2025. 1$^1/_3$m from Ottershaw* r'about, 2$^1/_3$m from Chobham on side of A319, 400yds from Fairoaks airport. Lookout for large yellow sign! **Thur 9, Thur 23, Thur 30 Jan, Thur 13, Thur 20, Thur 27 Feb, Wed 5, Thur 13, Thur 20, Thur 27 Mar, Wed 2, Thur 10, Thur 17, Thur 24 Apr, Wed 7, Wed 14 May, Thur 19 June, Thur 16, Thur 30 Oct, Wed 5 Nov (11.30-2.30). Adm £7, chd £1. Pre-booking essential, please visit www.ngs.org.uk for information & booking. Tea, coffee & home-made cake in The Barn.**
Welcome to 16 acres of informal garden, park and woodland; enticing views to Surrey Hills from the hill. Enjoy winter and spring walks, through witch-hazel and winter honeysuckle, crocus and snowdrops, daffodils/narcissi and spring flowers, then gorgeous bluebells and azaleas and fleeting cherry blossom. Large camellia collection in woodland from Oct/Nov, and Jan/Feb, climax in Mar/Apr. Additional dates planned in June, Oct and Nov. For further information, please telephone, email or visit garden website. No wheelchair access to the wood when ground is soft/wet unless electric-powered.
& 🐕 ☕

57 ◆ TITSEY PLACE GARDENS
Pitchfont Lodge, Water Lane, Titsey, Oxted, RH8 0SA. The Trustees of the Titsey Foundation, 07889 052461, office@titsey.org, www.titsey.org. *3m N of Oxted. A25 between Oxted & Westerham. Follow brown heritage signs to Titsey Estate from A25 at Limpsfield or see website for directions. Please enter via Water Ln & the Pitchfont car park (not Titsey Hill).* **For NGS: Sun 25 May, Sun 29 June, Sun 27 July, Sun 31 Aug (1-5). Adm £7.50, chd £2. Light refreshments.** For other opening times and information, please phone, email or visit garden website.
One of the largest surviving historic estates in Surrey. Magnificent ancestral home and gardens of the Gresham family since 1534. Walled kitchen garden and Golden Jubilee rose garden. Etruscan summerhouse adjoining picturesque lakes and fountain bed. 15 acres of formal and informal gardens. Titsey is in the English landscaped garden style. Pedigree herd of Sussex Cattle roam the park. Walks through the estate woodlands are open year-round. Tearoom serving home-made cakes and selling local produce from 12-5pm. Last admission to gardens at 4pm. Guide dogs only.
🚗 ☕))

58 ◆ VANN
Hambledon, Godalming, GU8 4EF. Caroe Family, www.vanngarden.co.uk. *6m S of Godalming. A283 to Lane End, Hambledon. Follow yellow Vann signs for 2m. Please park in the field as signed, not in road.* **For NGS: Daily Mon 31 Mar to Sat 5 Apr (10-4). No refreshments Mon-Sat. Sun 6 Apr (12-4). Tea, coffee & cake on Sun 6 Apr (cash only). Adm £10, chd free. Pre-booking essential, please visit www.ngs.org.uk for information & booking.** For other opening times and information, please visit garden website.
5 acre, 2* English Heritage registered garden surrounding house dating back to 1542 with Arts and Crafts additions by W D Caröe inc a Bargate stone pergola. At the front, brick paved original cottage garden; to the rear a lake, yew walk with rill and Gertrude Jekyll water garden. Snowdrops and hellebores, spring bulbs, and spectacular fritillaria. Island beds, crinkle crankle wall, orchard with wild flowers. Vegetable garden. Also open for by arrangement visits for individuals or groups (not for NGS).
🚗

59 NEW WATERER'S GARDEN
43 Ambleside Road, Lightwater, GU18 5TA. Alison & Trevor Millard. *In the village of Lightwater in NW Surrey. Enter Lightwater via the A322, head to the r'about with estate agent on the corner. Waterer's Garden is 200 metres on the LHS of Ambleside Rd.* **Mon 21 Apr (12-5). Adm £5, chd free. Pre-booking essential, please visit www.ngs.org.uk for information & booking. Home-made teas.**
A $^1/_3$ acre plot within the village of Lightwater, hidden away behind the house built for George Waterer and his family in 1931. Garden designed and laid out in the 1930s by the Waterer family, who were nursery owners and now own Crocus. Restored and gardened by Trevor & Alison Millard since 1997.
☕))

60 11 WEST HILL
Sanderstead, CR2 0SB. Rachel & Edward Parsons. *M25 J6, A22, 3m r'about 4th exit to Succombs Hill, R to Westhall Rd, at r'about 2nd exit to Limpsfield Rd, r'about 2nd exit on Sanderstead Hill 1m, sharp R to West Hill. Please park on West Hill.* **Sat 12, Sun 13 Apr (2-5). Adm £5, chd free. Home-made teas. Donation to Croydon Animal Samaritans.**
A hidden gem tucked away. A beautiful country cottage style garden set in ½ acre, designed by Sam Aldridge of Eden Restored. The garden flows through pathways, lawn, vegetable and play areas. Flower beds showcase outstanding tulips, and informal seating areas throughout the garden allows you to absorb the wonderful garden, whilst observing our ex battery chickens and rescue rabbits!

61 WEST HORSLEY PLACE
Epsom Road, West Horsley, Leatherhead, KT24 6AN. West Horsley Place Trust, www.westhorsleyplace.org. *5m E of Guildford. West Horsley Place is off the A246 between Guildford & Leatherhead. A 10 min drive from the A3/M25 intersection. Leave the A3 at J10.* **Sun 4 May, Sun 7 Sept (10-4). Adm £10, chd free. Light refreshments in the Place Farm Barn courtyard.**
West Horsley Place is set within a 380 acre estate. The garden adjacent to the Manor House dates back to the C15 and is approx 5 acres, completely surrounded by a wall over 300 yrs old. It has an ancient orchard, rose garden, interestingly striped formal lawns, an historic box hedge, many herbaceous borders, a magnificent white wisteria over 60ft tall and many wildflower areas. Recently opened new sensory garden in formerly neglected paddock. Accessible via a step-free route. Unpaved and the predominant surface is turf. Accessible ground floor WC suitable for wheelchair users.

62 57 WESTHALL ROAD
Warlingham, CR6 9BG. Rob & Wendy Baston. *3m N of M25. M25, J6, A22 London, at Whyteleafe r'about, take 3rd R, under railway bridge, turn immed R into Westhall Rd.* **Sun 25, Mon 26 May (2-5).**

Adm £5, chd free. Home-made teas. Donation to Warlingham Methodist Church.
Reward for the sure footed, many steps to three levels! Mature kiwi and grape vines. Mixed borders, and raised vegetable beds. Bay, cork oak and yew topiaries. Amphitheatre of potted plants on lower steps. Stunning views of Caterham and Whyteleafe from top garden. Olive tree floating on a circular pond of white and pink flowers. Flint walls, vegetable borders, summerhouse, apple tree with child swing, and gravel garden.

63 WESTWAYS FARM
Gracious Pond Road, Chobham, GU24 8HH. Paul & Nicky Biddle, 01276 856163, nicolabiddle@rocketmail.com. *4m N of Woking. From Chobham Church proceed over r'about towards Sunningdale, 1st Xrds R into Red Lion Rd to junction with Mincing Ln. Ample parking, also for coaches.* **Sun 11 May (10.30-5). Adm £8, chd free. Home-made teas. Visits also by arrangement 21 Apr to 6 June for groups of 10 to 50.**
6 acre garden surrounded by woodlands planted in 1930s with mature and some rare rhododendrons, azaleas, camellias and magnolias, underplanted with bluebells, lilies and dogwood. Extensive lawns and sunken pond garden. Working stables and sand school. Lovely Queen Anne House (not open) covered with listed *Magnolia grandiflora*. Victorian design glasshouse. New planting round garden room. This is our 25th year of opening for the National Garden Scheme so a cause for celebration!

64 THE WHITE HOUSE
21 West End Lane, West End, Esher, KT10 8LB. Lady Peteranne Hunt & Mr David John, peajaya@btinternet.com. *Heading from Esher to Cobham on the old Portsmouth Rd take the 1st turning on the R into Hawkshill Way, at T-junction turn R.* **Sat 19, Sun 20 July (11-4). Adm £6, chd free. Light refreshments. Visits also by arrangement 1 June to 30 July for groups of 8 to 15. Wine & canapés for private visits.**
Our garden is on three levels centred on a lovely mature oak tree. There

are peaceful spots to rest and contemplate the vibrant planting, an unusual water feature, various sculptures, lots of colour and a variety of grasses and shrubs. A very peaceful and serene garden. We live in a delightful village with a duck pond and cricket on the green on Sundays. Wheelchair access on patio only. Dogs on leads only.

65 WILDWOOD
34 The Hatches, Frimley Green, Camberley, GU16 6HE. Annie & Richard Keighley. *3m S of Camberley. M3 J4 follow A325 to Frimley Centre, towards Frimley Green for 1m. Turn R by the green, R into The Hatches for on-street parking. 10 min walk from Farnborough North train stn.* **Sun 15 June (11-5). Adm £5, chd free. Pre-booking essential, please visit www.ngs.org.uk for information & booking. Tea, coffee & cake.**
Discover hidden surprises in this romantic cottage garden with tumbling roses, topiary and scented *Magnolia grandiflora*. Enjoy a sensory haven of sun and shade with wildlife pond, hidden dell, fernery and sheltered loggia. Cutting garden with topiary birds, raised beds, vegetables, fruit trees and potting shed patio. Celebrating 20 yrs of gardening at Wildwood, there will be birthday cake! Display of garden paintings.

66 NEW 63 WOLSEY DRIVE
Walton-on-Thames, KT12 3BB. Carl & Pamela Fisher. *1m from Walton on Thames centre. Wolsey Dr is off Rydens Rd (accessed from Tudor Dr), take L from Tudor Dr & follow road for approx 500 metres. No. 63 is located on LHS. On-street parking. Nearest stns: Hersham & Walton on Thames.* **Sun 29 June (11-5). Adm £5, chd free. Tea, coffee & cake.**
Our decision was always to attract pollinators and wildlife to our garden. Over the last 10 yrs, we have transformed the space using our horticultural and design backgrounds, evolving the garden bit by bit. Large planting beds, gravel paths and a raised bridge through the centre lead to the pergola at the end. Scented plants and a colour palette of purple, orange, white and green envelop you.

67 48 WOODMANSTERNE LANE
Wallington, SM6 0SW. Joanne & Graham Winn, 07985 213179, info@joannewinngardendesign.co.uk. 2½m NE of Banstead. From A217 head E on A2022 for 2½m, turn L onto Woodmansterne Ln. Plenty of parking along the road. Do not park on grass verges (traffic wardens). What3words app: during.plates.closes. **Visits by arrangement 24 May to 21 Sept for groups of 6 to 24. Tea & home-made cakes inc for afternoon visits. Wine for evening visits.** Approx ⅓ acre. Part of former smallholding, converted by garden designer Joanne Winn and husband Graham. Built around the original orchard's fruit trees, the bold, curvy design is softened by a sumptuous palette of perennials and grasses. Pop into the kitchen garden, relax on the pond's deck amongst darting dragonflies, take a peek into the shepherd's hut and enjoy tea and cakes near the chickens. Partial wheelchair access; some gravel and narrow paths, raised deck and boardwalk.

68 WOODPECKERS
Poplar Grove, Woking, GU22 7SD. Mr Janis Raubiška, 07478 025188, janis@grandiflorus.co.uk, www.instagram.com/grandiflorus.co.uk. Next to Woking Leisure Centre. Please use Woking Leisure Centre car park (GU22 9BA) & follow signs for garden entrance. Coach parking available. **Sun 24, Sun 31 Aug (12-4). Adm £6, chd free. Cream teas. Visits also by arrangement for groups of 8 to 35 on Mon 25 Aug & Mon 1 Sept at 10am, 1pm & 3pm.** A journey through a horticultural designer's own garden where plants take centre stage in succession, providing year-round colour and interest. Three rooms, each with a different planting style and purpose: vibrant colours in the jewel's amphitheatre, leafy textures and pastels in the social room, glasshouse and grow your own productive area. Created in 2022, the garden has sustainability at its heart. Slight slope by the entrance gate, assistance will be provided.

69 WRENS' NEST COTTAGE
Ockham Lane, Cobham, KT11 1PG. Mrs Patty Robertson & Mr Fil Towers, 07957 495934, pattyrobertson45@gmail.com. 1½m from Cobham High St. At Wisley r'about turn L onto B2039 to Ockham/Horsley. After ½m turn L into Ockham Ln. House 2m on R. From Cobham go to Downside Bridge Rd, turn R into Chilbrook Rd then turn R. Garden on R. **Sun 29 June (11-5). Adm £5, chd free. Tea, coffee & cake. Visits also by arrangement 1 Apr to 25 July for groups of 6 to 15.** 1½ acre country garden with island beds of perennials and ancient bluebell wood. Wildlife friendly with a butterfly corner, a stream running the length of the garden, and many beautiful mature trees. Front garden with many pots and courtyard. Sunny sitting areas to enjoy a cup of tea and a slice of cake. 2 miles from RHS Garden Wisley. Wheelchair access to most of garden.

63 Wolsey Drive

SUSSEX

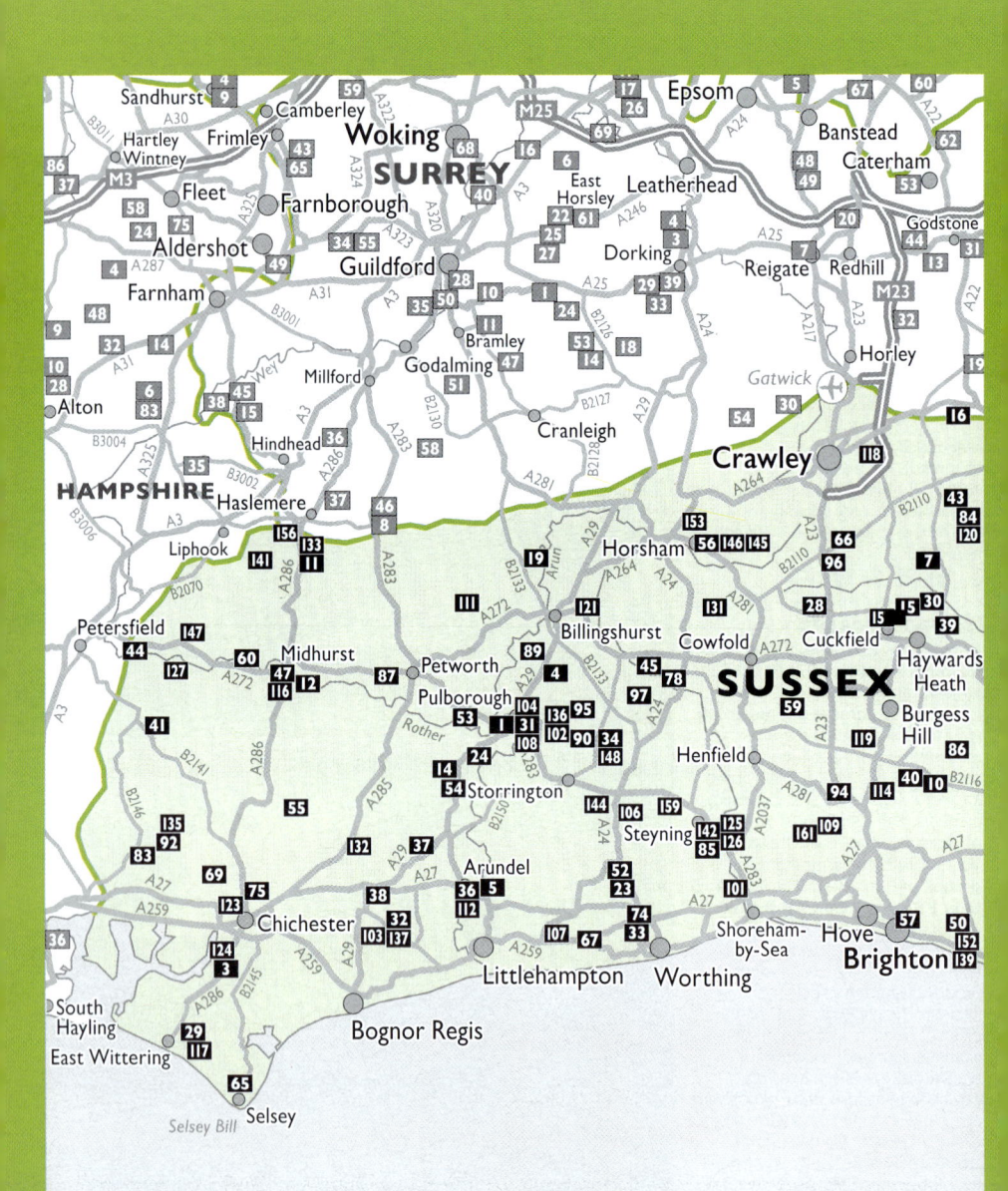

SUSSEX 513

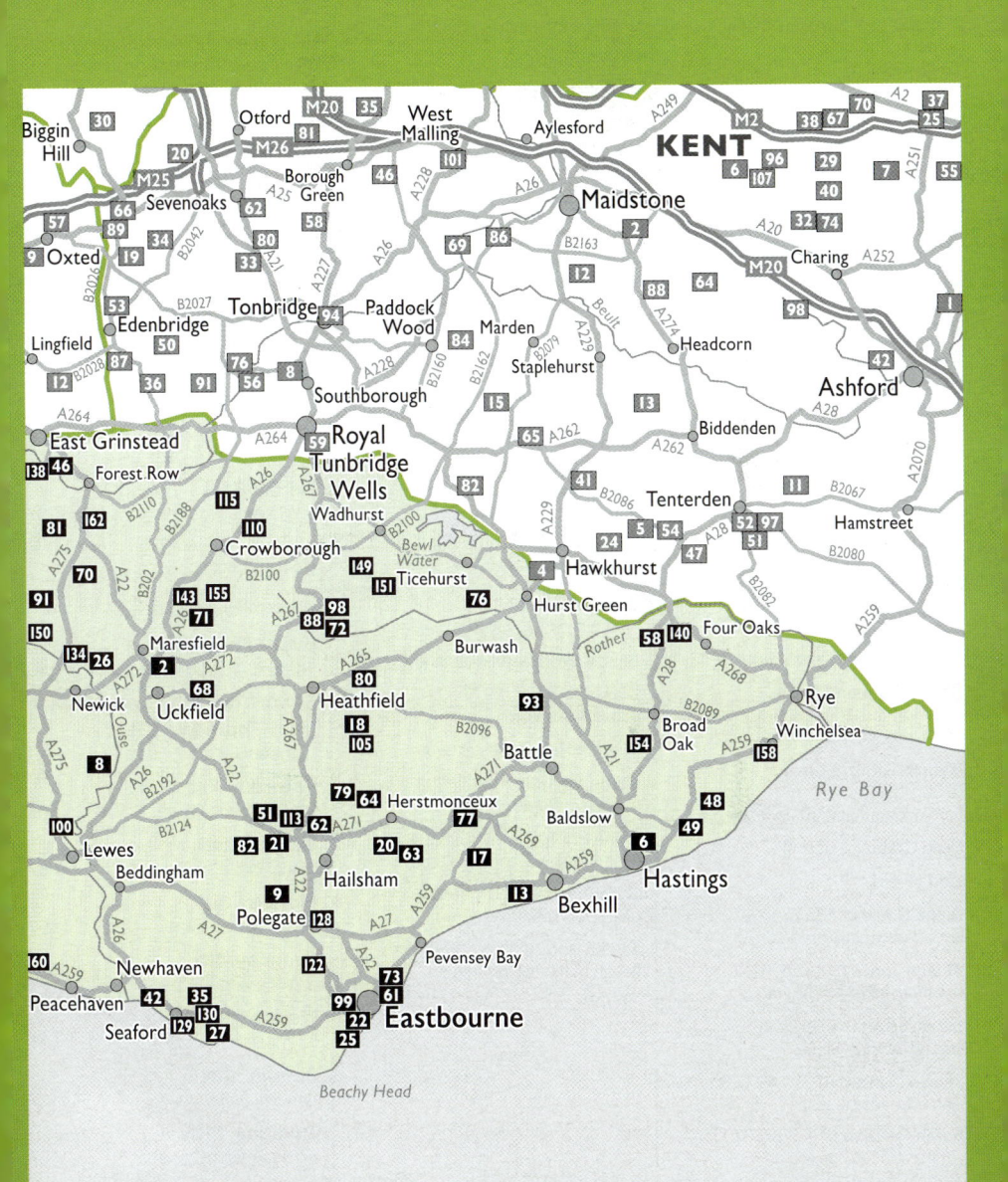

EAST & MID SUSSEX VOLUNTEERS

County Organiser, Booklet & Advertising Co-ordinator
Irene Eltringham-Willson
01323 833770
irene.willson@btinternet.com

County Treasurer
Andrew Ratcliffe 01435 873310
andrew.ratcliffe@ngs.org.uk

Publicity
Geoff Stonebanks 01323 899296
sussexeastpublicity@ngs.org.uk

Social Media
Nicki Crabb 07720 640761
nicki.crabb@ngs.org.uk

Social Media & Photographer
Kelly Whitaker Hughes
07920 402677
kelly.whitakerhughes@ngs.org.uk

Assistant County Organisers
Jane Baker 01273 842205
jane.baker@ngs.org.uk

Joan Ball
07976 349000
joanball53@gmail.com

Michael & Linda Belton
01797 252984
belton.northiam@gmail.com

Shirley Carman-Martin
01444 473520
shirley.carmanmartin@ngs.org.uk

Isabella & Steve Cass
07908 123524
oaktreebarn@hotmail.co.uk

Nicki Crabb (as above)

Linda Field

Diane Gould 01825 750300
lavenderdgould@gmail.com

Aideen Jones 01323 899452
sweetpeasa52@gmail.com

Susan Laing 01892 770168
splaing@btinternet.com

Jennie Maillard 07730 480308
jennie@maillard.me.uk

Sarah Ratcliffe 01435 873310
sarah.ratcliffe@ngs.org.uk

Dianna Tennant 01892 752029
tennantdd@gmail.com

@SussexNGSEast
@SussexNGS
@ngseastsussex

WEST SUSSEX VOLUNTEERS

County Organiser, Booklet & Advertising Co-ordinator
Maggi Hooper 07793 159304
maggi.hooper@ngs.org.uk

County Treasurer
Philip Duly 07789 050964
philipduly@tiscali.co.uk

Publicity
Kate Harrison 01798 817489
kate.harrison@ngs.org.uk

Social Media
Claudia Hawkes 07985 648216
claudiapearce17@gmail.com

Talks
Philip Duly (as above)

Booklet Distribution
Lesley Chamberlain 07950 105966
chamberlain_lesley@hotmail.com

Assistant County Organisers
Teresa Barttelot 01798 865690
tbarttelot@gmail.com

Sanda Belcher 01428 723259
sandambelcher@gmail.com

Emma Broda 07739 516178
emma.broda@gmail.com

Lesley Chamberlain (as above)

Diane Cotes 07789 565094
dirose8@me.com

Claudia Hawkes (as above)

Carrie McArdle 01403 820272
carrie.mcardle@btinternet.com

Fiona Phillips 07884 398704
fiona.h.phillips@btinternet.com

Susan Pinder 07814 916949
nasus.rednip@gmail.com

Teresa Roccia 07867 383753
teresa.m.roccia@gmail.com

@Sussexwestngs
@SussexWestNGS
@sussexwestngs

OPENING DATES

All entries subject to change. For latest information check
www.ngs.org.uk

Extended openings are shown at the beginning of the month.

Map locator numbers are shown to the right of each garden name.

January

Saturday 25th
5 Whitemans Close 157

Monday 27th
5 Whitemans Close 157

Wednesday 29th
5 Whitemans Close 157

Friday 31st
5 Whitemans Close 157

February

Snowdrop Festival

Every Thursday
The Old Vicarage 106

Every Thursday and Friday from Thursday 13th
Pembury House 114

Saturday 1st
5 Whitemans Close 157

Sunday 2nd
Manor of Dean 87

Monday 3rd
5 Whitemans Close 157

Tuesday 4th
5 Whitemans Close 157

Wednesday 5th
5 Whitemans Close 157

Sunday 9th
Sandhill Farm House 127

Tuesday 11th
5 Whitemans Close 157

Wednesday 12th
5 Whitemans Close 157

Thursday 13th
◆ Highdown Gardens 67

Friday 14th
5 Whitemans Close 157

Saturday 15th
5 Whitemans Close 157
Thursday 20th
Crosslands Flower Nursery 32

March

Every Thursday
The Old Vicarage 106
Every Thursday and Friday to Friday 7th
Pembury House 114
Tuesday 4th
Crosslands Flower Nursery 32
Sunday 9th
♦ Bates Green Garden 9
Manor of Dean 87
Tuesday 11th
Crosslands Flower Nursery 32
Saturday 15th
♦ Nymans 96
Sunday 16th
♦ Denmans Garden 38
Saturday 22nd
Down Place 41
♦ King John's Nursery 76
Sunday 23rd
Down Place 41
Saturday 29th
Limekiln Farm 82
Sunday 30th
Limekiln Farm 82
Peelers Retreat 112

April

Every Wednesday from Wednesday 23rd
Fittleworth House 53
Every Thursday
The Old Vicarage 106
Saturday 5th
Peelers Retreat 112
Sunday 6th
47 Denmans Lane 39
Friday 11th
The Garden House 57
Saturday 12th
Rymans 124
Sandhill Farm House 127

Sunday 13th
The Garden House 57
Newtimber Place 94
Penns in the Rocks 115
Rymans 124
Sandhill Farm House 127
Tuesday 15th
NEW The Old Rectory,
 Warbleton 105
Peelers Retreat 112
Wednesday 16th
NEW The Old Rectory,
 Warbleton 105
Friday 18th
Judy's Cottage Garden 74
Saturday 19th
Peelers Retreat 112
Monday 21st
47 Denmans Lane 39
The Old Vicarage 106
Saturday 26th
Banks Farm 8
NEW Duckyls 43
NEW Kotimaki 80
The Oast 98
Sunday 27th
Banks Farm 8
♦ Denmans Garden 38
NEW Duckyls 43
Manor of Dean 87
The Oast 98
Tuesday 29th
Peelers Retreat 112

May

Every Wednesday to Wednesday 14th
Fittleworth House 53
Every Thursday
The Old Vicarage 106
Thursday 1st
♦ Highdown Gardens 67
Saturday 3rd
Peelers Retreat 112
Sunday 4th
47 Denmans Lane 39
Stanley Farm 141
Terwick House 147
Monday 5th
47 Denmans Lane 39
Terwick House 147
Tuesday 6th
♦ Sheffield Park and Garden 134

Saturday 10th
96 Ashford Road 6
Cookscroft 29
Sunday 11th
Champs Hill 24
Hammerwood House 60
Mountfield Court 93
Penns in the Rocks 115
Tuesday 13th
Bignor Park 14
♦ Borde Hill Garden 15
Peelers Retreat 112
Wednesday 14th
Balcombe Gardens 7
Thursday 15th
Warnham Park 153
Friday 16th
The Cottage 31
Saturday 17th
96 Ashford Road 6
The Cottage 31
NEW Kotimaki 80
NEW Olivers 108
Peelers Retreat 112
NEW Pigeon Mead House 117
NEW The White House 155
Sunday 18th
Legsheath Farm 81
NEW Pigeon Mead House 117
NEW The White House 155
Saturday 24th
96 Ashford Road 6
54 Elmleigh 47
Grovelands 59
♦ King John's Nursery 76
♦ The Priest House 120
Sunday 25th
Bumble Farm 19
47 Denmans Lane 39
54 Elmleigh 47
Foxglove Cottage 56
Grovelands 59
Hollymount 71
9 Puttock Way 121
Monday 26th
Bumble Farm 19
Copyhold Hollow 30
47 Denmans Lane 39
54 Elmleigh 47
The Old Vicarage 106
9 Puttock Way 121
Tuesday 27th
Peelers Retreat 112
Friday 30th
Orchard Cottage 110

516 SUSSEX

Saturday 31st
The Old Rectory, Barnham 103
Orchard Cottage 110
Peelers Retreat 112
The Shrubbery 137
Skyscape 139
NEW Swallow Lodge 145

June

Every Wednesday from Wednesday 11th to Wednesday 18th
Fittleworth House 53

Every Thursday
The Old Vicarage 106

Sunday 1st
Brickyard Farm Cottage 17
51 Carlisle Road 22
Chelmsford Lodge 25
◆ High Beeches Woodland and Water Garden 66
Offham House 100
The Old Rectory, Barnham 103
Orchard Cottage 110
NEW Seaford Gardens North 129
The Shrubbery 137
Sienna Wood 138
Skyscape 139
Stroods 143
Tidebrook Manor 149

Thursday 5th
NEW The Old Manor 102
NEW Shorts Farm 136

Friday 6th
NEW Apuldram Roses 3

Saturday 7th
Alpines 2
◆ Farleys Sculpture Garden 51
Highlands 68
Kitchenham Farm 77
NEW Kotimaki 80
Lordington House 83
NEW The Old Manor 102
NEW 8 Rushy Mead 123
NEW Shorts Farm 136
NEW Swallow Lodge 145
Waterworks & Friends 154

Sunday 8th
4 Hillside Cottages 69
Lordington House 83
NEW Talma 146
Town Place 150

Monday 9th
Butlers Farmhouse 20

Tuesday 10th
Butlers Farmhouse 20
Peelers Retreat 112

Wednesday 11th
Kitchenham Farm 77
NEW The Old Rectory, Warbleton 105
Town Place 150

Thursday 12th
NEW The Old Rectory, Warbleton 105
NEW The Orchard 109
NEW Woodlands 161

Friday 13th
1 Pest Cottage 116
Wadhurst Park 151

Saturday 14th
NEW Alderbury 1
Bumble Farm 19
5 Coastguard Cottages 27
Hoopers Farm 72
NEW Milford Place 91
Oaklands Farm 97
Peelers Retreat 112
Wadhurst Park 151

Sunday 15th
NEW Alderbury 1
Bumble Farm 19
5 Coastguard Cottages 27
Down Place 41
Fairlight Hall 49
Hoopers Farm 72
1 Pest Cottage 116
NEW 8 Rushy Mead 123

Monday 16th
Down Place 41

Tuesday 17th
Bignor Park 14

Wednesday 18th
Town Place 150

Thursday 19th
◆ Clinton Lodge 26

Friday 20th
Parsonage Farm 111

Saturday 21st
Bexhill-on-Sea Trail 13
Durford Abbey Barn 44
Judy's Cottage Garden 74
◆ Knepp Castle 78
Luctons 84
Pine Tree Cottage 118
NEW Steyning Gardens 142

Sunday 22nd
Berlas 12
Durford Abbey Barn 44
The Folly 55
Herstmonceux Parish Trail 64

Pine Tree Cottage 118
Rymans 124
NEW Seaford Gardens South 130
NEW Steyning Gardens 142
Town Place 150
Warnham Park 153

Wednesday 25th
Luctons 84

Thursday 26th
64 Cuckfield Crescent 33
NEW Meadowside 90

Friday 27th
◆ St Mary's House Gardens 126

Saturday 28th
Balcombe Gardens 7
64 Cuckfield Crescent 33
Five Oaks Cottage 54
◆ King John's Nursery 76
◆ The Priest House 120
◆ St Mary's House Gardens 126

Sunday 29th
Balcombe Gardens 7
Findon Place 52
Five Oaks Cottage 54
Hellingly Parish Trail 62
Hollymount 71
Luctons 84
Town Place 150

July

Every Wednesday from Wednesday 9th to Wednesday 23rd
Fittleworth House 53

Every Thursday
The Old Vicarage 106

Tuesday 1st
Luctons 84

Thursday 3rd
NEW Meadowside 90

Friday 4th
NEW Apuldram Roses 3
NEW Lynwood 85
Saffrons 125

Saturday 5th
Winchelsea's Secret Gardens 158

Sunday 6th
East Grinstead Gardens 46
Old Well Cottage 107
Rose Cottage 122
Sayerland House 128
NEW Seaford Gardens North 129
Town Place 150

SUSSEX

Monday 7th
Cupani Garden 35

Tuesday 8th
Peelers Retreat 112

Thursday 10th
NEW 12 Keepers Wood 75

Friday 11th
NEW Lynwood 85
Nyetimber Manor 95
Saffrons 125

Saturday 12th
Peelers Retreat 112
Wiston House 159

Sunday 13th
Berlas 12
16 Hardy Drive 61
36 Jellicoe Close 73
NEW Seaford Gardens South 130

Tuesday 15th
Sullington Old Rectory 144

Wednesday 16th
Sullington Old Rectory 144

Thursday 17th
NEW 12 Keepers Wood 75
Oaklands Farm 97
NEW The Orchard 109
NEW Woodlands 161

Saturday 19th
5 Coastguard Cottages 27
NEW Kotimaki 80
NEW 2 Wanderdown Way 152

Sunday 20th
NEW Beardsland 10
5 Coastguard Cottages 27
The Hidden Garden 65
4 Hillside Cottages 69
NEW Talma 146
NEW 2 Wanderdown Way 152

Tuesday 22nd
Peelers Retreat 112

Wednesday 23rd
♦ Herstmonceux Castle Estate 63

Thursday 24th
Cumberland House 34
NEW 408 Falmer Road 50
Thakeham Place Farm 148
33 Wivelsfield Road 160

Saturday 26th
NEW 408 Falmer Road 50
Knightsbridge House 79
NEW The Old Rectory,
  Pulborough 104
33 Wivelsfield Road 160

Sunday 27th
NEW Architectural Plants 4
NEW The Beeches, Haslemere 11
Cumberland House 34
The Folly 55
Hollymount 71
NEW The Old Rectory,
  Pulborough 104
The Old Vicarage 106
NEW Shalford House 133
Thakeham Place Farm 148

August

Every Thursday
The Old Vicarage 106

Saturday 2nd
D & S Haus 36
Mayfield Gardens 88
NEW The Old Rectory,
  Pulborough 104

Sunday 3rd
D & S Haus 36
Mayfield Gardens 88
NEW The Old Rectory,
  Pulborough 104
Penns in the Rocks 115

Wednesday 6th
Fittleworth House 53
Kitchenham Farm 77

Thursday 7th
Bourne Botanicals 16

Saturday 9th
NEW Chalk Farm Flowers 23
Kitchenham Farm 77

Sunday 10th
Bourne Botanicals 16
NEW Chalk Farm Flowers 23
Champs Hill 24
NEW Pekes Manor 113
Pitfield Barn Cut Flower Farm &
  Studio 119

Saturday 16th
Holly House 70

Sunday 17th
Findon Place 52
4 Hillside Cottages 69
Holly House 70

Saturday 23rd
Butlers Farmhouse 20

Sunday 24th
NEW The Beeches, Haslemere 11
Butlers Farmhouse 20
The Folly 55
Hollymount 71
NEW Shalford House 133

Monday 25th
Durrance Manor 45
The Old Vicarage 106

Saturday 30th
Ditchling Garden Trail 40
Limekiln Farm 82

Sunday 31st
Limekiln Farm 82

September

Every Thursday
The Old Vicarage 106

Saturday 6th
The Cottage 31
Grovelands 59
NEW Kotimaki 80

Sunday 7th
Berlas 12
Grovelands 59
Parsonage Farm 111

Tuesday 9th
Bignor Park 14

Friday 12th
Wych Warren House 162

Saturday 13th
♦ King John's Nursery 76

Sunday 14th
Rymans 124

Sunday 21st
Meadow Farm 89
Tidebrook Manor 149

Sunday 28th
♦ High Beeches Woodland and
  Water Garden 66

October

Thursday 2nd
The Old Vicarage 106

Friday 3rd
Five Oaks Cottage 54

Saturday 4th
Five Oaks Cottage 54
NEW Kotimaki 80

Sunday 5th
♦ Bates Green Garden 9

Sunday 26th
♦ Denmans Garden 38

By Arrangement

Arrange a personalised garden visit with your club, or group of friends, on a date to suit you. See individual garden entries for full details.

Alpines	2
Berlas	12
Bourne Botanicals	16
Brickyard Farm Cottage	17
Brightling Down Farm	18
Butlers Farmhouse	20
Camberlot Hall	21
Champs Hill	24
Colwood House	28
Cosy Cottage, Seaford Gardens North	129
The Cottage	31
Crosslands Flower Nursery	32
Cupani Garden	35
Dale Park House	37
47 Denmans Lane	39
Down Place	41
Driftwood	42
Durrance Manor	45
54 Elmleigh	47
Fairlight End	48
Fittleworth House	53
The Folly	55
Foxglove Cottage	56
The Garden House	57
4 Hillside Cottages	69
Holly House	70
Hollymount	71
NEW 12 Keepers Wood	75
Legsheath Farm	81
Lordington House	83
Luctons	84
Malthouse Farm	86
Manor of Dean	87
Meadow Farm	89
Mitchmere Farm	92
Oaklands Farm	97
Ocklynge Manor	99
Old Erringham Cottage	101
The Old Rectory, Barnham	103
NEW The Old Rectory, Warbleton	105
The Old Vicarage	106
Orchard Cottage	110
Peelers Retreat	112
NEW 8 Rushy Mead	123
Rymans	124
Saffrons	125
Sedgwick Park House	131
Selhurst Park	132
Shepherds Cottage	135
The Shrubbery	137
Sienna Wood	138
South Grange	140
Town Place	150
4 Waterworks Cottages, Waterworks & Friends	154
Whitehanger	156
Winterfield, Balcombe Gardens	7
Wych Warren House	162

Cupani Garden

THE GARDENS

1 🆕 **ALDERBURY**
Church Hill, Pulborough, RH20 1AB. John & Marianne Dixon. *From A283 Lower St in Pulborough exit r'about to A29, Billingshurst. After 200 metres turn R onto Old Rectory Ln (Chequers Hotel on corner). Immed after turning, park in West Glebe Field on R. Walk down slope, across field following the signs.* **Sat 14, Sun 15 June (11-5). Adm £7, chd free. Tea, coffee & cake.**
A garden of just under 2 acres adjoining the East Glebe Field in the village. It is divided into a series of different rooms inc a large vegetable garden, a large and small greenhouse, an orchard, a duck pond, an area of lawn with ornamental beds, parterres with flowers in season and herb beds. Also, a large and unusual tree sculpture.
🐕 ☕ 🔊

2 **ALPINES**
High Street, Maresfield, Uckfield, TN22 2EG. Ian & Cathy Shaw, 07887 825032, Info@shaw.buzz. *1½ m N of Uckfield. Garden approx 150 metres N of Budletts r'about towards Maresfield. Blue Badge parking at garden, other parking in village approx 6 mins walk.* **Sat 7 June (11-5). Adm £6, chd free. Home-made teas & savouries.**
Visits also by arrangement 8 June to 31 Aug for groups of 6+.
A largely level 1 acre garden incorporating the ornamental and the edible. Offers riot of colour and scent over many months, especially early summer with large and rampant mixed borders, many scented roses, small mixed orchard, wildflower meadow, fruit cage and vegetable garden, shade, cottage and white borders, wildlife pond and bog garden. Pretty Victorian style greenhouse. Lots of spots to sit and relax. Wheelchair access over wide sweeps of lawn and gravel drive areas. Two steps down to greenhouse.
♿ 🐕 ✱ ☕ 🔊

3 🆕 **APULDRAM ROSES**
Birdham Road, Chichester, PO20 7EQ. Elizabeth Sawday, www.apuldramroses.co.uk. *2m S of Chichester. Located exactly opp the Dell Quay Rd on the L when travelling S. What3words app: nightcap.bumpy.laughs. Please arrive promptly for the talk at 2pm.* **Fri 6 June, Fri 4 July (2-5). Adm £12, chd free. Pre-booking essential, please visit www.ngs.org.uk for information & booking. Light refreshments.**
Spend a delightful afternoon listening to an informative talk on keeping your roses thriving. You will then have time to explore the rose garden, a summer paradise, especially from June to August when the roses are in full bloom. The garden transforms into a vibrant display of colours and fragrances during these months. The roses, meticulously cared for, showcase a stunning array of varieties, each with its unique charm and beauty. Plants for sale on site.
✱ ☕

4 🆕 **ARCHITECTURAL PLANTS**
Stane Street, North Heath, Pulborough, RH20 1DJ.
Mr Guy Watts, www.architecturalplants.com. *What3words app: jogged.fabric.land. Black & white bollards out the front, diagonally opp Hepworth Brewery.* **Sun 27 July (10-5). Adm £12, chd free. Tea, coffee & cake. Guided tours on the hour.**
Architectural Plants is home to an ensemble of captivating garden spaces designed to inspire you. Explore the Mediterranean lake garden and surrounding bankside walk tended by Head Gardener Colin and his apprentices. Italian cypress, olives, pines, hardy palms, spiky plants, and bamboo grove. The guided tour inc the large Acer house, the greenhouse of exciting and rare exotics, and a specialist Niwaki Production Zone. Prepare to enter exotica. Wheelchair access to the garden and lake view via grass lawns, and the plant nursery spans over a flat site.
♿ 🐕 ✱ 🚗 ☕ 🪑 🔊

5 ♦ **ARUNDEL CASTLE & GARDENS**
Arundel, BN18 9AB. Arundel Castle Trustees Ltd, 01903 882173, visits@arundelcastle.org, www.arundelcastle.org. *In the centre of Arundel, N of A27.* **For opening times and information, please phone, email or visit garden website.**
Ancient castle, family home of the Duke of Norfolk. 40 acres of grounds and gardens which inc hot subtropical borders, English herbaceous borders, stumpery, two glasshouses, walled flower and organic kitchen gardens, and Fitzalan Chapel white garden.
♿ 🚗 ☕ 🪑

6 **96 ASHFORD ROAD**
Hastings, TN34 2HZ. Lynda & Andrew Hayler. *Nr Alexander Park. From A21 (Sedlescombe Rd N) towards Hastings, take 1st exit on r'about A2101, then 3rd on L (approx 1m).* **Sat 10, Sat 17, Sat 24 May (1-4.30). Adm £4, chd free.**
Small (100ft x 52ft) Japanese inspired front and back garden. Full of interesting planting with many acers, azaleas and bamboos. Over 100 different hostas, many miniature ones. Also, an attractive Japanese Tea House and courtyard with fish pond. New Japanese bridge and pond in lower garden.
🐕 ✱ 🔊

129,032 people were able to access guidance on what to expect when a person is dying through the National Garden Scheme's support for Hospice UK this year.

SUSSEX 519

GROUP OPENING

7 BALCOMBE GARDENS
3m N of Cuckfield on B2036, 3m S of J10A on M23. Just N of Balcombe Stn, turn R into Newlands Rd leading to Oldlands Ave. Winterfield What3words app: tastings.estimate. inflating. **Wed 14 May, Sat 28, Sun 29 June (12-5). Combined adm £7.50, chd free. Home-made teas at Stumlet.**

NEW THE COPPICE
Oldlands Avenue, RH17 6LP. Carol & Sandy Jarvest-Chen.
STUMLET
Oldlands Avenue, RH17 6LW. Max & Nicola Preston Bell.
WINTERFIELD
Oldlands Avenue, RH17 6LP. Sarah & Ian Lamaletie, 07977 201637, sarah.lamaletie@yahoo.co.uk. **Visits also by arrangement 14 May to 29 June for groups of up to 30.**

Three quite different adjacent gardens on an easy walking trail. Winterfield is a long established plantsman's garden full of uncommon shrubs and trees, herbaceous borders, pond and wildlife area. Stumlet has evolved from being a 'work in progress' garden to an amazing, restful and special space.

There are places to sit and enjoy a little peace, scent and colour plus the interesting planting. The Coppice is a garden to watch develop over the coming yrs as it changes from a newly designed and part planted area to a completed inspirational one. The areas close to the house are planted and indicate the promise that is to come.

8 BANKS FARM
Boast Lane, Barcombe, Lewes, BN8 5DY. Nick & Lucy Addyman. 6m N of Lewes. From Barcombe Cross follow signs to Spithurst & Newick. 1st road on R into Boast Ln towards the Anchor Pub. At sharp bend carry on into Banks Farm. **Sat 26, Sun 27 Apr (11-4). Adm £5, chd free. Tea, coffee & cake.**
9 acre garden set in rural countryside. Extensive lawns and shrub beds merge with the more naturalistic woodland garden set around the lake. An orchard, vegetable garden, ponds and a wide variety of plant species add to an interesting and very tranquil garden. Refreshments served outside, so may be limited during bad weather. Wheelchair access to the upper part of garden. Sloping grass paths in the lower area.

9 ◆ BATES GREEN GARDEN
Tye Hill Road, Arlington, BN26 6SH. John McCutchan, 01323 485151, john@bluebellwalk.co.uk, www.batesgreengarden.co.uk. 3½m SW of Hailsham & A22. Midway between the A22 & A27, 2m S of Michelham Priory. Bates Green is in Tye Hill Rd (N of Arlington village), 350yds S of Old Oak Inn. Ample parking on hard-standing verges. **For NGS: Sun 9 Mar, Sun 5 Oct (10.30-3.30). Adm £7, chd £3.50. Home-made soup, cakes & scones plus light lunches in large insulated Bluebell Barn.** For other opening times and information, please phone, email or visit garden website.
This plantswoman's tranquil garden provides interest through the seasons. Woodland garden created around a majestic oak tree. Colour themed middle garden. Courtyard gardens with seasonal container displays. Front garden a spring and autumn joy with narcissi, primroses, violets then coloured stems and leaves of cornus and salix. Wildlife pond and wildflower meadow. Gardened for nature and wildlife. Spring visitors walk through a wild daffodil glade leading to the 24 acre ancient oak wood, home of the Arlington Bluebell Walk. Beatons Wood is managed for conservation

Shalford House

and diversity and autumn guests can enjoy spotting the abundant fungi within. Please visit www.ngs.org.uk for pop-up 'fungal foray' in October. Dogs not in garden but allowed in barn and woods. Wheelchair access to most areas. Mobility scooters to borrow free of charge. Accessible WC.

♿ ❀ 🚗 ☕ 🪑 🔊

10 NEW BEARDSLAND
97 Lewes Road, Ditchling, nr Hassocks, BN6 8TZ. Lynn & Clive Bush. ½ m E from the centre of Ditchling on the B2116. Situated at the eastern edge of Ditchling village on the B2116 between the recreation ground (parking available) & Spatham Ln. What3words app: snap.collides. amber. **Sun 20 July (12-5). Adm £7, chd free. Tea, coffee & home-made cakes.**
A constantly evolving country garden together with a 2 acre wildflower meadow, with views of the Downs and Ditchling Beacon. A colourful explosion of dahlias, delphiniums and assorted annuals and shrubs greet you, along with a border of vegetables where we have experimented by sowing from seed by the phases of the moon. There is a small orchard, a greenhouse and much more to explore.

☕ 🔊

11 NEW THE BEECHES, HASLEMERE
Square Drive, Haslemere, GU27 3LW. Mrs Bee Mack. Approx 2m S of Haslemere. A sharp narrow turning directly off the A286 (please take care). Heading S, Square Dr is at brow of hill to the L. Turn L again after ¼ m & follow road to R at bottom of hill. **Sun 27 July, Sun 24 Aug (1-5.30). Combined adm with Shalford House £8, chd free.**
3 acre informal garden linked to an attached 5 acre wood. With curving flower borders adjoining the lawns to the front of the house with meandering gravel paths. Mediterranean planting, low circular hedging and stone fountain to the rear. The hard landscaping at the back of the house melds into woodland softened with ferns, hostas and tree ferns.

♿ 🔊

12 BERLAS
Park Crescent, Midhurst, GU29 9ED. Mr & Mrs S Curzon-Hope, 07806 701186, suecurzonhope@hotmail.com. From the centre of Midhurst turn R from N or L from S, opp Angel Hotel. Berlas is on the L on Park Cres with lamppost outside. **Sun 22 June, Sun 13 July, Sun 7 Sept (1.30-4.30). Adm £5, chd free. Pre-booking essential, please visit www.ngs.org.uk for information & booking. Home-made teas.** Visits also by arrangement 29 May to 12 Sept.
150ft south west facing, sloping town garden, developed over 10 yrs by current owner. Hedges and trees planted, together with a wildlife pond (2020). This is a garden that showcases seasonal succession from early to late flowering prairie style planting. Two areas of grass kept as wild meadows. Collection of succulents, echeveria, and pelargoniums. Unusual pots and planters.

♿ ☕ 🔊

GROUP OPENING

13 BEXHILL-ON-SEA TRAIL
Bexhill & Little Common. Follow NGS signs to gardens from main roads. Tickets & maps available at each garden. All gardens not too far from Bexhill centre with the exception of The Small House which is in Little Common. **Sat 21 June (11-4). Combined adm £7, chd free. Home-made teas & light lunches at Westlands.**

THE CLINCHES
Collington Lane East, TN39 3RJ. Val Kemm.

64 COLLINGTON AVENUE
TN39 3RA. Dr Roger & Ruth Elias.

NEW **SHAMBLES**
202 Cooden Drive, TN39 3AH. Sylvia & John Brady.

SMALL HOUSE
Sandhurst Lane, TN39 4RG. Veronika & Terry Rogers.

WESTLANDS
36 Collington Avenue, TN39 3NE. Madeleine Gilbart & David Harding.

A beautiful trail of well designed mature and new gardens with specimen plants, shrubs and trees. Most have ponds with wildlife and fish, vegetable beds or fruit trees.

There is a combination of town, country, cottage and coastal, with a significant range of trees, roses, and mixed planting, focussing on attracting wildlife. Interesting sculptures and a Gothic folly are present in one of the gardens. It is worth noting that all gardens are continually changing and upgrading. Westlands on Collington Avenue will be serving refreshments which can be enjoyed sitting in the garden. There will be a European Folk Circle dance performances at Westlands and a Ukrainian Culbaba (Dandelion) dance at Clinches. A plant stand selling an array of plants, some live music and art for sale. Wheelchair access or partial access to most gardens.

♿ ❀ ☕ 🔊

14 BIGNOR PARK
Pulborough, RH20 1HG. The Mersey Family, www.bignorpark.co.uk. 5m S of Petworth & Pulborough. Well signed from B2138. Nearest villages Sutton, Bignor & West Burton. Approach from the E, directions & map available on website. **Tue 13 May, Tue 17 June, Tue 9 Sept (2-5). Adm £5, chd free. Home-made teas.**
11 acres of peaceful garden to explore with magnificent views of the South Downs. Interesting trees, shrubs and wildflower areas. The walled garden has been replanted with herbaceous borders and the Dutch garden has a new central obelisk and planting inc climbing roses, salvias and echinaceas. Temple, Greek loggia, Zen pond and unusual sculptures. Former home of romantic poet Charlotte Smith, whose sonnets were inspired by Bignor Park. Spectacular cedar of Lebanon and rare Lucombe oak. Wheelchair access to shrubbery and croquet lawn. Gravel paths in rest of garden and steps in stables quadrangle.

♿ 🐕 ☕ 🔊

The National Garden Scheme donated £281,000 in 2024 to support those looking to work in horticulture as well as those struggling within the industry.

522 SUSSEX

15 ♦ BORDE HILL GARDEN
Borde Hill Lane, Haywards Heath, RH16 1XP. Borde Hill Garden, 01444 450326, info@bordehill.co.uk, www.bordehill.co.uk. *1½ m N of Haywards Heath. 20 mins N of Brighton, or S of Gatwick on A23 taking exit 10a via Balcombe.* **For NGS: Tue 13 May (10-5). Adm £12.50, chd £8.50. For other opening times and information, please phone, email or visit garden website.**
Tranquil and picturesque, Borde Hill has been planted with passion by five generations of the Stephenson Clarke family. With rare and fine rhododendrons, magnolias, rose borders and champion trees, exploring the thirteen outdoor rooms is like travelling around the world in one garden. Wheelchair access to 17 acres of formal garden.
♿ 🐕 ✿ 🚗 NPC ☕ 🪑 ♪))

16 BOURNE BOTANICALS
The Bourne, Chesterfield Close, Furnace Wood, Felbridge, East Grinstead, RH19 2PY. Jackie & Andy Doherty *A264 between Copthorne & Felbridge. 1⅙ m from Felbridge. Parking in layby RH19 2QF on W bound A264 signed to Furnace Wood. Metrobus 400. Enter Furnace Wood via footpath R of barrier, 8 min walk to Bourne Botanicals.* **Thur 7, Sun 10 Aug (11-5). Adm £8. Pre-booking essential, please phone 07785 562558 or email bournebotanic@outlook.com for information & booking. Tea, coffee & cake.** Visits also by arrangement in Aug for groups of 15+.
A lush setting of huge bananas jostling alongside gunnera and arid beds of agave, yucca and cacti. A diverse tropical look garden with wildlife pond, stream and bog beds of carnivorous plants. Palms, tree ferns, tetrapanax and many unusual plants and quirky touches all set in an acre of woodland. Features inc 'Our Folly', a sunken garden. National Collection holder. Parking at property for disabled badge holders and those with mobility issues only.
♿ ✿ NPC ☕ ♪))

17 BRICKYARD FARM COTTAGE
Top Road, Hooe, Battle, TN33 9EJ. David & Grace Constable, 07740 447998, dc@constablespublishing.com. *From A269 turn R onto B2095, 2m on R. From A259 turn L onto B2095, 2½ m on L. Parking in field adjacent to garden.*

Sun 1 June (11-4.30). Adm £6, chd free. Tea, coffee & cake. Visits also by arrangement 15 May to 29 Aug for groups of 5 to 25.
A 4 acre garden started 24 yrs ago; stunning views, remarkable brick and stone follies, colourful mixed beds with alstroemeria and roses. Pine rockery surrounds pond. Topiary garden, pinetum, and a rhododendron and azalea walk leads to a planted parterre. Fruit and vegetables in cages. Orchard. Unique ruins in garden and also metal sculptures, made by garden owners. Rose-filled courtyard front garden where home-made teas will be served. Plentiful seating to admire the Sussex vista.
♿ 🐕 🚗 ☕ ♪))

18 BRIGHTLING DOWN FARM
Observatory Road, Dallington, TN21 9LN. Val & Pete Stephens, 07770 807060, valstephens@icloud.com. *1m from Woods Corner. At Swan Pub, Woods Corner, take road opp to Brightling. Take 1st L to Burwash & almost immed, turn into 1st driveway on L.* **Visits by arrangement 5 May to 26 Sept for groups of 12 to 35. Preferred days for visits Mon or Fri. Home-made teas inc.**
The garden has several different areas inc a Zen garden, water garden, walled vegetable garden with two large greenhouses, herb garden, herbaceous borders and a woodland walk. The garden makes clever use of grasses and is set amongst woodland with stunning countryside views. Winner of the Society of Garden Designers award. Most areas of garden can be accessed with the use of temporary ramps.
♿ D ☕

19 BUMBLE FARM
Drungewick Lane, Loxwood, Billingshurst, RH14 0RS. Will Carver. *Very well signed in the middle of Drungewick Ln.* **Sun 25, Mon 26 May, Sat 14, Sun 15 June (2-5). Adm £6, chd free. Home-made teas.**
Delightful large country garden. Passionately and imaginatively created by enthusiastic owner over the past 20 yrs. An interesting garden with a series of circular lawns surrounded by borders, full of mass drift, repeat planting of harmonious perennials, roses, shrubs, and more. A newly developed white garden, wisteria pergola, kitchen and cutting garden, fountains and various seating areas.
♿ ☕ ♪))

20 BUTLERS FARMHOUSE
Butlers Lane, Herstmonceux, BN27 1QH. Irene Eltringham-Willson, 01323 833770, irene.willson@btinternet.com, www.butlersfarmhouse.co.uk. *3m E of Hailsham. Take A271 from Hailsham, go through village of Herstmonceux, turn R signed Church Rd, then approx 1m turn R. Do not use SatNav!* **Mon 9, Tue 10 June (2-5). Adm £5, chd free. Sat 23, Sun 24 Aug (2-5). Adm £7.50, chd free. Home-made teas. Live jazz in Aug only.** Visits also by arrangement 10 Mar to 31 Oct. Discuss refreshment options on booking.
Is this one of the quirkiest gardens in Sussex? It might well be, we are certain you will have fun and enjoy the secret jungle garden, Cornish-inspired beach corners, rainbow border, not to mention the poison garden. C16 farmhouse in 6 acres of rural Sussex with South Downs in the distance; mainly wildflower meadow with an odd orchid. The garden is pretty in the spring, awash in primroses and violets. Plants for sale. Picnics welcome in June and Aug. Most of garden accessible by wheelchair.
♿ ✿ 🚗 🚙 ☕ 🪑 ♪))

21 CAMBERLOT HALL
Camberlot Road, Lower Dicker, Hailsham, BN27 3RH. Nicky & Paul Kinghorn, 07710 566453, nickykinghorn@hotmail.com. *500yds S of A22 at Lower Dicker, 4½ m N of A27 Drusillas r'about. From A27 Drusillas r'about through Berwick Stn to Upper Dicker & L into Camberlot Rd after The Plough pub, we are 1m on L. From A22 we are 500yds down Camberlot Rd on R.* **Visits by arrangement 16 June to 7 Sept for groups of 8 to 25. Adm £12, chd free. Tea & cake inc.**
A 3 acre country garden with a lovely view across fields and hills to the South Downs. Created from scratch over the last 11 yrs with all design, planting and maintenance by the owner. Lavender lined carriage driveway, naturalistic border, vegetable garden, shady garden, 30 metre white border and dahlia garden. Part-walled garden and summerhouse. Wheelchair access over gravel drive and some uneven ground.
♿ ☕ ♪))

22 51 CARLISLE ROAD
Eastbourne, BN21 4JR. Elaine & Nigel Fraser-Gausden, the3growbags.com. *200yds inland from seafront (Wish Tower), close to Congress Theatre.* **Sun 1 June (2-5). Combined adm with Chelmsford Lodge £4, chd free. Home-made teas.**
A secluded, award-winning, 75' x 65' garden with glorious early summer colour from an abundance of old roses, perennials, mixed beds and diverse planting. There is a small pond and areas for plants that love shade or sun. Special plants inc *Abutilon* and *Euphorbia mellifera* that enjoy the relatively mild microclimate of a below-street level space very close to the south coast.

23 NEW CHALK FARM FLOWERS
Roger's Lane, Findon, Worthing, BN14 0RE. chalkfarmflowers.com. *On A24 just S of Findon village. Take Roger's Ln directly at Findon Vale Garden Centre entrance. We are located by 1st farm gate on your L. Parking at farm, limited spaces at garden centre.* **Sat 9 Aug (9-5); Sun 10 Aug (10-4). Adm £6, chd free. Pre-booking essential, please visit www.ngs.org.uk for information & booking. Light refreshments.**
Tours and talks of sustainable working flower farm, run by two young horticulturalists with a passion for the environment. We are on a mission to spread the word about British grown flowers. A wide range of flowers grown across a 1 acre site. Fresh, chemical free bunches of flowers available. Enjoy refreshments with a view of the flower field. Wheelchair access over gentle slopes and, wide grassy and bark paths alongside flower farm growing beds.

In 2024, our donations to Carers Trust meant that 26,081 unpaid carers were supported across the UK.

Butlers Farmhouse

24 CHAMPS HILL
Waltham Park Road, Coldwaltham, Pulborough, RH20 1LY. Mrs Mary Bowerman, 01798 831205, info@thebct.org.uk, www.thebct.org.uk. *3m S of Pulborough. On A29 turn R to Fittleworth into Waltham Park Rd, garden 400 metres on R.* **Sun 11 May (11-5); Sun 10 Aug (2-5). Adm £6, chd free. Home-made teas. Visits also by arrangement 1 Mar to 5 Sept for groups of 10+.**
A natural landscape, the garden has been developed around three disused sand quarries with far-reaching views across the Amberley Wildbrooks to the South Downs. A woodland walk in spring leads you past beautiful sculptures, against a backdrop of colourful rhododendrons and azaleas. In summer the garden is a colourful tapestry of heathers, well-known for their abundance and variety. Exhibition 'Seeing the Downs' by renowned late Sussex artist Peter Iden in the Music Room on Sun 11 May. Optional combined garden and art exhibition entry £10 (pay on the day only).

25 CHELMSFORD LODGE
12 Granville Road, Eastbourne, BN20 7HE. Jane Stevens. *500yds from seafront (Wish Tower). From Congress Theatre take Carlisle Rd L at Granville Rd Xrds, then 100yds on R. Easy on-street parking.* **Sun 1 June (2-5). Combined adm with 51 Carlisle Road £4, chd free. Home-made teas at 51 Carlisle Road.**
A ¾ acre garden, which began in 1994, has developed each yr. It was once a former prep-school playing field and a neglected garden. Now, features inc lawns with herbaceous beds, mature and unusual trees, shrubs, formal beds around pond, rockery, fruit trees and soft fruit area.

26 ♦ CLINTON LODGE
Fletching, TN22 3ST. Lady Collum, 01825 722952, garden@clintonlodge.com, www.clintonlodgegardens.co.uk. *4m NW of Uckfield. Clinton Lodge is situated in Fletching High St, N of The Griffin Inn. Off road parking provided, weather permitting. It is important visitors do not park in street. Parking available from 11am.* **For NGS: Thur 19 June (11-5). Adm £7, chd free. Home-made teas from 12pm.**
No lunches. Cash only on the day. **For other opening times and information, please phone, email or visit garden website. Donation to local charities.**
6 acre formal and romantic garden overlooking parkland with old roses, William Pye water feature, double white and blue herbaceous borders, yew hedges, pleached lime walks, medieval style potager, vine and rose allée, wildflower garden, small knot garden and orchard. Caroline and Georgian house (not open).

27 5 COASTGUARD COTTAGES
Cuckmere Haven, Seaford, BN25 4AR. Mr Daniel Martin. *A259 turn S to Southdown Rd, turn 6th L onto Chyngton Rd edge of golf course, continue to Chyngton Way, at end take the R fork to the top, park & then walk 1m downhill to garden.* **Sat 14, Sun 15 June, Sat 19, Sun 20 July (10-5). Adm £5, chd free. Light lunches & refreshments.**
This iconic garden at Coastguard Cottages overlooking the Seven Sisters will be known to many from a distance, but this garden is rarely seen. Nestled on the cliff top in the South Downs National Park with sea views. Planted with native plants, poppies, herbs, vegetables and acanthus in June/July, it is a perfect setting for the owners sculpture and pottery display. An embryonic vegetable plot and beehives contribute to attracting wildlife to the garden. Note steep cliff drop, children to be supervised at all times. No level access.

28 COLWOOD HOUSE
Cuckfield Lane, Warninglid, RH17 5SP. Mrs Rosy Brenan, 01444 461352, rbrenan@me.com. *6m W of Haywards Heath, 6m SE of Horsham. Entrance on B2115 Cuckfield Ln. From E, N & S, turn W off A23 towards Warninglid for ¾m. From W come through Warninglid village.* **Visits by arrangement May to Sept for groups of 10 to 50. Adm £8, chd free. Light refreshments. Donation to Seaforth Hall, Warninglid.**
12 acres of garden with mature and specimen trees from the late 1800s, lawns and woodland edge. Formal parterre, rose and herb gardens. 100ft terrace and herbaceous border overlooking flower rimmed croquet lawn. Cut turf labyrinth and forsythia tunnel. Water features, statues and gazebos. Pets' cemetery. Giant chessboard. Lake with island and temple. Wheelchair access with gravel paths and some slopes.

29 COOKSCROFT
Bookers Lane, Earnley, Chichester, PO20 7JG. Mr J Williams, www.cookscroft.co.uk. *6m S of Chichester. At end of Birdham Straight A286 from Chichester, take L fork to East Wittering B2198. 1m on sharp bend, turn L into Bookers Ln, 2nd house on L. Parking available.* **Sat 10 May (11-4). Adm £5, chd free. Light refreshments.**
A garden for all seasons which delights the visitor. Started in 1988, it features cottage, woodland and Japanese style gardens, water features and borders of perennials with a particular emphasis on southern hemisphere plants. Unusual plants for the plantsman to enjoy, many grown from seed. The differing styles of the garden flow together making it easy to wander anywhere. Wheelchair access over grass, bark paths and unfenced ponds.

30 COPYHOLD HOLLOW
Copyhold Lane, Borde Hill, Haywards Heath, RH16 1XU. Frances Druce. *2m N of Haywards Heath. Follow signs for Borde Hill Gardens. With Borde Hill Gardens on L over brow of hill, take 1st R signed Ardingly. Garden ½m. Please park in the lane.* **Mon 26 May (12-4). Adm £5, chd free. Home-made teas.**
A different NGS experience in two north facing acres. The cottage garden surrounding C16 house (not open) gives way to slopes and steps up to woodland garden. Species primulas a particular interest of the owner. Stumpery. Not a manicured plot, but with a relaxed attitude to gardening, an inspiration to visitors.

31 THE COTTAGE
Potts Lane, Pulborough, RH20 2BT. Claire Denman, 07739 820712, Claire.denman1@yahoo.co.uk. *Potts Ln is a pedestrian lane off Lower St (A283) in Pulborough. The entrance is between two houses next to T-lights. Parking in Lower St public car park almost opp Potts Ln.*

Evening opening Fri 16 May (6-8). Adm £9, chd free. Wine. Sat 17 May (11-5). Combined adm with Olivers £9, chd free. Home-made teas. Sat 6 Sept (10-4). Adm £6, chd free. Tea, coffee & cake. Pre-booking essential, please visit www.ngs.org.uk for information & booking. Two hour timed slots on 17 May & 6 Sept. **Visits also by arrangement 13 May to 16 Sept for groups of 6 to 20.**
A quintessential English cottage garden, packed with a mix of perennials and bulbs on a potentially challenging multi layered site. Comprising four distinct rooms inc a small roof terrace, top terrace sitting above the house garden and a vegetable garden built in what was a small swimming pool. Every square inch has been used.
✿ ☕ 🔊

32 CROSSLANDS FLOWER NURSERY
Barnham Lane, Walberton, Arundel, BN18 0AX. Ben Cross, 07712 332141, crosslandsflowernursery@gmail.com, www.facebook.com/CrosslandsFlowerNursery. *4m W of Arundel. Midway between Barnham & Walberton down Barnham Ln, signed Crosslands Flower Nursery.* **Thur 20 Feb, Tue 4, Tue 11 Mar (10-12). Adm £10, chd free. Pre-booking essential, please visit www.ngs.org.uk for information & booking. Visits also by arrangement 3 Feb to 28 Mar for groups of 10 to 30.**
A 2 hr all access tour of a fourth generation, award-winning, sustainably run flower nursery with 3 acres of glasshouses filled to the brim with Sussex grown alstroemeria. There will be an opportunity to purchase flowers at the end of the tour.

33 64 CUCKFIELD CRESCENT
Worthing, BN13 2EB. The Allen Family. *Approx 2m from seafront & Worthing town. Bus routes stop S of Stone Ln, within a 5 min walk. Plenty of parking in Rogate Rd. Please be mindful of residents.* **Thur 26, Sat 28 June (10-4). Adm £5, chd free. Cream teas, home-made cakes & hot drinks.**
Relax and unwind in this tranquil, wildlife friendly town garden. Take a seat under the pergola, surrounded by a vast range of ferns and hostas. Walk along the short, winding path, enjoying the colour from the borders, and listen to the gentle sound of the water from the Koi pond as you wander through the rose covered arch into a grassed area with a wildlife pond and herbaceous border.
✿ ☕ 🔊

34 CUMBERLAND HOUSE
Cray's Lane, Thakeham, Pulborough, RH20 3ER. George & Jane Blunden. *At junction of Cray's Ln & The Street, nr St Mary's Church. Park at Thakeham Place Farm, 1 min walk away.* **Thur 24, Sun 27 July (2-5). Combined adm with Thakeham Place Farm £10, chd free. Home-made teas at Thakeham Place Farm.**
A Georgian village house (not open), next to the C12 church with a beautiful, mature ¾ acre English country garden. The garden comprises a walled garden laid out as a series of rooms with well-stocked flower beds, two rare ginkgo trees, and yew topiary. This leads to an informal garden with vegetable, herb, and fruit areas, pleached limes, and a lawn shaded by a copper beech tree. Wheelchair access through gate at right-hand side of house.
♿ 🐕 ☕ 🔊

Pigeon Mead House

35 CUPANI GARDEN
8 Sandgate Close, Seaford, BN25 3LL. Dr Denis Jones & Ms Aideen Jones OBE *From A259 follow signs to Alfriston, E of Seaford. R off Alfriston Rd onto Hillside Ave, 2nd L,1st R & 1st R. Park in adjoining streets. Bus 12A Brighton/ Eastbourne, get off Millberg Rd stop & walk down alley to garden.* **Mon 7 July (2-5). Adm £12, chd £5. Pre-booking essential, please phone 01323 899452, email sweetpeasa52@gmail.com or visit www.cupanigarden.com for information & booking. Home-made teas inc on 7 July. Opening with Seaford Gardens South on Sun 22 June, Sun 13 July. Visits also by arrangement 31 May to 31 July for groups of 6 to 15.**
Cupani is a tranquil haven with a delightful mix of trees, shrubs and perennial border. Courtyard garden, gazebo, summerhouse, water features, sweet pea obelisks and a huge range of plants. See TripAdvisor reviews. The garden has undergone major renovations in 2023/2024 and now inc a gravel garden, some more tropical planting and the old cutting garden has been replaced with planted troughs.

🐾 ✻ 🚗 ☕ »))

36 D & S HAUS
41 Torton Hill Road, Arundel, BN18 9HF. Darrell Gale & Simon Rose. *1m SW of Arundel town square. From A27 Ford Rd/ Chichester Rd r'about, take exit to Ford & immed turn R into Torton Hill Rd. Continue uphill & at large oak tree, keep L & we are on L going down the hill.* **Sat 2, Sun 3 Aug (12-5). Adm £6, chd free. Home-made teas.**
A lush rainforest/jungle garden, 25ft x 200ft, which the owners have planted from scratch over the last 10 yrs. Both front and rear gardens contain a mass of palms, bananas, bamboos and all manner of spiky and large luxuriant foliage. Normal rules are not followed, as the clashes of colour, shape and texture have driven its design. Surreal sculptures and some new features to delight. Tropical planting with lots of unusual plants, quirky sculptures and features.

☕ »))

37 DALE PARK HOUSE
Madehurst, Arundel, BN18 0NP. Robert & Jane Green, 01243 814260, robertgreenfarming@gmail.com. *4m W of Arundel. Take A27 E from Chichester or W from Arundel, then A29 (London) for 2m, turn L to Madehurst & follow red arrows.* **Visits by arrangement 19 May to 1 July for groups of 10+. Adm £6, chd free. Home-made teas.**
Set in parkland, enjoying magnificent views to the sea. Come and relax in the large walled garden which features an impressive 200ft herbaceous border. There is also a sunken gravel garden, mixed borders, a small rose garden, dreamy rose and clematis arches, an interesting collection of hostas, foliage plants and shrubs, and an orchard and kitchen garden.

🚗 ☕

38 ♦ DENMANS GARDEN
Denmans Lane, Fontwell, BN18 0SU. Gwendolyn van Paasschen. *5m from Chichester & Arundel. Off A27, ½ m W of Fontwell r'about.* **For NGS: Sun 16 Mar, Sun 27 Apr, Sun 26 Oct (11-4). Adm £10, chd £8. Pre-booking essential, please phone 01243 278950, email office@denmans.org or visit www. denmans.org for information & booking. Light refreshments. For other opening times and information, please phone, email or visit garden website.**
Created by Joyce Robinson, a horticulturalist and pioneer in gravel gardening and former home of influential landscape designer, John Brookes MBE. Denmans is a Grade II registered post-war garden renowned for its curvilinear layout and complex plantings. Year-round colour, unusual plants, structure and fragrance in the gravel gardens, faux riverbeds, intimate walled garden, ponds and conservatory. On site there is a plant centre with unusual plants for sale, a gift shop and Midpines Café offering breakfast, lunch, afternoon tea and a selection of sweet treats.

♿ 🐾 ✻ 🚗 ☕ »))

39 47 DENMANS LANE
Lindfield, Haywards Heath, RH16 2JN. Sue & Jim Stockwell, 01444 459363, jamesastockwell@aol.com, www. lindfield-gardens.co.uk/47denmans-lane. *Approx 1½ m NE of Haywards Heath town centre. From Haywards Heath Train Stn follow B2028 signed Lindfield & Ardingly for 1m. At T-lights turn L into Hickmans Ln, then after 100 metres take 1st R into Denmans Ln.* **Sun 6, Mon 21 Apr, Sun 4, Mon 5, Sun 25, Mon 26 May (1-5). Adm £7, chd free. Tea, coffee & cake. Visits also by arrangement 17 Mar to 31 May for groups of 5 to 50.**
This beautiful and tranquil 1 acre garden was described by Sussex Life as a 'garden where plants star'. Created by the owners over the past 20 yrs, it is planted for interest throughout the yr. Spring bulbs are followed by azaleas, rhododendrons, roses and herbaceous perennials. The garden also has ponds, vegetable and fruit gardens. Extensive choice of perennial and annual bedding plants plus home-made jams for sale. Most of the garden accessible by wheelchair with some steep slopes.

♿ ✻ 🚗 ☕ »))

GROUP OPENING

40 DITCHLING GARDEN TRAIL
Close to A23, 8m N of Brighton at the junction of the B2112 & B2116. No on road parking. Use car parks on B2116, West St, BN6 8TS (best),or Village Hall, BN6 8TT or Recreation Ground, BN6 8TY, on Lewes Rd. Maps available at The Sandrock gardens, High St. **Sat 30 Aug (11-4.30). Combined adm £8, chd free. Home-made teas at Meadow Cottage.**

COUM COTTAGE
The Sandrock, High Street, BN6 8TA. Valerie Winter.

MEADOW COTTAGE
24 Beacon Road, BN6 8UL. Yvonne Hennessy.

NEW PADDOCK END
Beacon Road, BN6 8UL. Catherine & David Lebrecht.

NEW PARDONS
78 East End Lane, BN6 8UR. John & Susie Godley.

SEPTEMBER COTTAGE
The Sandrock, High Street, BN6 8TA. Pamela Roy-Jones.

NEW WHITE RAILS COTTAGE
3 Common Lane, HBN6 8TJ. Philip Dunn & Veryan Greenwood.

Set within the South Downs National Park, Ditchling is a thriving village dating back to the Anglo-Saxon period. Today it is still home to artists, writers, and craftspeople, along with

SUSSEX 527

musicians and winemakers. The love and passion for gardening is evident in the six gardens opening. Five being in the village centre whilst White Rails Cottage is ½ mile walk away. Three of the gardens are mature, whilst the three new ones are at various stages of 'work in progress'. These are exciting projects, each different and complementing each other. Each garden has its own feel, united by a love of bees, birds, butterflies, and wildlife. Maybe even spot a hedgehog family or the very rare fungus *Sarcodontia crocea* at Meadow Cottage. The museum holds an internationally important collection of work by the artists and craftspeople who were resident over many yrs. The Horticultural Society was established in 1822 and is the oldest in the country. Public WC below the village hall.

✤ ☕ ◗))

41 DOWN PLACE
South Harting, Petersfield, GU31 5PN. Mrs David Thistleton-Smith, 01730 825374, selina@downplace.co.uk. *1m SE of South Harting. B2141 to Chichester, turn L down unmarked lane below top of hill. Coming from Chichester on B2141 take turning R just after the South Downs Way crossing the road.* **Sat 22, Sun 23 Mar, Sun 15, Mon 16 June (1.30-5.30). Adm £5, chd free. Home-made teas & cream teas. Visits also by arrangement Mar to end of July for groups of 15 to 40.**
Set on the South Downs with panoramic views out to the undulating wooded countryside. The garden merges seamlessly into its surrounding landscape with rose and herbaceous borders that have been moulded into the sloping ground. There is a well-stocked vegetable garden and walks shaded by beech trees which surround the natural wildflower meadow where various native orchids flourish. The wildflower meadow is covered in natural wild daffodils in April, cowslips in May, and six varieties of wild orchids, plus various other wild flowers from the end of May through to early July. Seeds from the meadow are used to regenerate devastated areas in the South Downs National Park. Substantial top terrace and borders accessible to wheelchairs.

♿ ✤ ☕ ◗))

42 DRIFTWOOD
4 Marine Drive, Bishopstone, Seaford, BN25 2RS. Geoff Stonebanks & Mark Glassman, 01323 899296, visitdriftwood@gmail.com, www.driftwoodbysea.co.uk. *A259 between Seaford & Newhaven. From Seaford, turn R into Bishopstone Rd, then immed L into Marine Dr, 2nd on R. Only park same side as house please, not on bend beyond the drive.* **Visits by arrangement 1 June to 3 Aug for groups of up to 25. Individuals welcome. Adm £6, chd free. Home-made teas.**
On BBC Gardeners' World in 2024 Monty Don said 'when it comes to growing conditions, I don't think you will find any garden in the land that is more different to Longmeadow than that belonging to Geoff Stonebanks'. The Sunday Times 2024 feature on age-proofing said 'visit this rejigged award-winning plot now opened up so the lush and varied plantings and theatrical vignettes are easier to appreciate'. Check out the 242 5-star reviews on TripAdvisor, awarded three successive Certificates of Excellence and four successive Travellers Choice Awards. Selection of Geoff's home-made cakes, all served on vintage china, on trays, in the garden. Sorry, no WC.

🐕 🚗 ☕ ◗))

43 NEW DUCKYLS
Selsfield Road, East Grinstead, RH19 4LP. Gia & Richard Thompson. *6m E of Crawley. At Turners Hill take B2028 S, 1m fork L to West Hoathly, turn L signed Gravetye Manor. Entry on Vowels Ln, 1st driveway on R, just after bend. Duckyls is larger house at end of drive. Limited parking.* **Sat 26, Sun 27 Apr (12-4). Adm £8, chd free. Pre-booking essential, please visit www.ngs.org.uk for information & booking. Tea, coffee & cake. Two hour timed slots at 12pm & 2pm.**
A recently renovated 15 acre garden with wonderful views across Sussex. Consisting of a rhododendron woodland, a newly planted orchard, ponds and a more formal secret garden. Mostly laid out in the 1920s and 30s by a dedicated plant collector and orchid breeder. Delight in the blazes of spring colour to be seen. Please note this garden inc steep slopes and many climbs. Suitable footwear is required.

☕ 🪑 ◗))

44 DURFORD ABBEY BARN
Petersfield, GU31 5AU. Mr & Mrs Lund. *3m from Petersfield. Situated on the S side of the A272 between Petersfield & Rogate, 1m from the junction with B2072.* **Sat 21, Sun 22 June (1.30-5.30). Adm £5, chd free. Home-made teas.**
A 1 acre plot with areas styled with cottage garden, prairie and shady borders set in the South Downs National Park with views of the Downs. Plants for sale and small art exhibition. Partial wheelchair access due to quite steep grass slopes.

♿ 🐕 ✤ ☕ ◗))

45 DURRANCE MANOR
Smithers Hill Lane, Shipley, RH13 8PE. Gordon Lindsay, 01403 741577, galindsay@gmail.com. *7m SW of Horsham. A24 to A272 (S from Horsham, N from Worthing), turn W towards Billingshurst. Approx 1¾ m, 2nd L Smithers Hill Ln signed to Countryman Pub. Garden 2nd on L.* **Mon 25 Aug (12-6). Adm £8, chd free. Home-made teas. Visits also by arrangement 1 May to 21 Sept for groups of 10 to 30. Home-made teas inc.**
This 2 acre garden surrounding a medieval hall house (not open) with Horsham stone roof, enjoys uninterrupted views over a ha-ha of the South Downs and Chanctonbury Ring. There are many different gardens here, Japanese inspired gardens, a large pond, wildflower meadow and orchard, colourful long borders and vegetable garden. There is also a Monet style bridge over a pond with water lilies.

♿ 🐕 ✤ 🚗 ☕ ◗))

Our donation to the Army Benevolent Fund supported 700 individuals with front line services and horticultural related grants in 2024.

Hollymount

GROUP OPENING

46 EAST GRINSTEAD GARDENS
7m E of Crawley on A264 & 14m N of Uckfield on A22. For Allotments park at Imberhorne Lane Car Park, disabled parking on site. For 5 Nightingale Cl & 7 Nightingale Cl park on Hurst Farm Rd. Roadside parking at 35 Blount Ave. **Sun 6 July (1-5). Combined adm £7, chd free. Tea, coffee & cake at 5 Nightingale Close.**

35 BLOUNT AVENUE
RH19 1JJ. Nicki Crabb.

IMBERHORNE ALLOTMENTS
RH19 1QX. Imberhorne Allotment Association, www.imberhorneallotments.org.

5 NIGHTINGALE CLOSE
RH19 4DG. Carole & Terry Heather.

7 NIGHTINGALE CLOSE
RH19 4DG. Gail & Andy Peel.

Imberhorne Allotments features 80 plots hosting a diverse range of planting, inc grapevines, various vegetables, fruits, and flowers. A worthwhile visit for anyone interested in grow your own. At 35 Blount Avenue, contemporary design blends seamlessly with lush and colourful plantings in this south facing town garden. The large borders are colour themed, complemented by tropical plants. The front garden is alive with vibrant dahlias and roses. 5 Nightingale Close is situated on a corner plot, showcasing beautifully landscaped gardens on two levels. The garden features vibrant and diverse plantings surrounding a naturalistic Koi pond, along with a productive fruit and vegetable patch, rose and herbaceous beds, and topiary trees. 7 Nightingale Avenue boasts a stunning array of roses and romantic flowerings that cascade down to a stream. This garden also inc a potager and a collection of bonsai. Plant sale at 35 Blount Avenue and 7 Nightingale Close. The Town Council hanging baskets and planting in the High Street are not to be missed and have achieved a Gold Medal from South and South East in Bloom. For steam train fans, the Bluebell Railway starts nearby.

✿ ☕ 🔊

47 54 ELMLEIGH
Midhurst, GU29 9HA. Wendy Liddle, 07796 562275, wendyliddle@btconnect.com. $\frac{1}{4}$ m W of Midhurst, off the A272, follow the yellow NGS signs. Plenty of parking off road on marked grass area. Reserved disabled parking at top of drive, please phone on arrival for assistance. **Sat 24, Sun 25, Mon 26 May (11-5). Adm £5, chd free. Tea, coffee, cakes & cream teas. Home-made elderflower cordial.** Visits also by arrangement 18 May to 31 Aug for groups of 10 to 20. $\frac{1}{5}$ acre property with terraced front garden, leading to a heavily planted rear garden which has plenty of seating and shaded areas, with majestic 130 yr old black pines. Shrubs, perennials, and packed with interest around every corner providing

all season colours. Many raised beds, numerous sculptures, vegetables in boxes, a greenhouse, pond and a large collection of tree lilies. Child friendly. Come and enjoy the peace and tranquillity in this award-winning garden, enjoy our little bit of heaven. Not suitable for large electric buggies.

& 🐕 ✿ 🚗 ☕ 🪑 »)

48 FAIRLIGHT END
Pett Road, Pett, Hastings, TN35 4HB. Chris & Robin Hutt, 07774 863750, chrishutt@fairlightend.co.uk, www.fairlightend.co.uk. *4m E of Hastings. From Hastings take A259 to Rye. At White Hart Beefeater turn R into Friars Hill. Descend into Pett village.* **Visits by arrangement 14 May to 12 Sept for groups of 12+. Tea, coffee & cake. Donation to Pett Village Hall.**
Gardens Illustrated said 'The 18th century house is at the highest point in the garden with views down the slope over abundant borders and velvety lawns that are punctuated by clusters of specimen trees and shrubs. Beyond and below are the wildflower meadows and the ponds with a backdrop of the gloriously unspoilt Wealden landscape'. Wheelchair access with steep paths, gravelled areas and unfenced ponds.

& 🐕 🚗 ♿ ☕

49 FAIRLIGHT HALL
Martineau Lane, Hastings, TN35 5DR. Mr & Mrs David Kowitz, www.fairlighthall.co.uk. *2m E of Hastings. A259 from Hastings towards Dover & Rye, 2m turn R into Martineau Ln. Entrance approx 650yds on L.* **Sun 15 June (10-4). Adm £10, chd free. Pre-booking preferred. Light refreshments at pop-up café (10-3). Lunches to pre-order via garden website.**
A restored stunning garden in East Sussex. The formal gardens extend over 9 acres and surround the Victorian Gothic mansion (not open). Features semitropical woodland avenues, a huge contemporary walled garden with amphitheatre and two 110 metre perennial borders above and below ha-ha with far-reaching views across Rye Bay. Home-made preserves, vegetables and cut flowers for sale. Most of the garden can be viewed by wheelchair. Please inform us on arrival, so we can direct you to disabled parking.

& 🐕 ✿ ☕ 🪑 »)

50 NEW 408 FALMER ROAD
Woodingdean, Brighton, BN2 6LG. Julie Christy. *S of Woodingdean. S on Falmer Rd B2123 towards Rottingdean. Through T-lights at Woodingdean & 408 is on L. Parking on Crescent Drive South & Happy Valley car park. Bus 22 to Briarcroft Rd or Bus 2 to bottom of Ridgway.* **Thur 24, Sat 26 July (11-5). Adm £4, chd free. Cakes. Vegetarian flans & salad. Open nearby 33 Wivelsfield Road.**
A quirky ¼ acre garden that sits between the South Downs and the sea. Jam packed with trees, a huge range of shrubs, a colourful palette of perennials and a bountiful vegetable patch. An ever increasing group of succulents has joined a sizeable collection of agapanthus. The use of Corten steel and a huge array of steel buckets, cans, and baths all planted up add to the unique feel of this garden.

✿ ☕ »)

51 ♦ FARLEYS SCULPTURE GARDEN
Muddles Green, Chiddingly, nr Lewes, BN8 6HW. Farleys House & Gallery Ltd, 01825 872856, info@leemiller.co.uk, www.farleyshouseandgallery.co.uk/sculpture-garden. *9m from Lewes, off A22. Turn L off A22 towards Eastbourne at BP garage at Golden Cross. After 1m turn R at T- junction. Farleys is on R. Free car park.* **For NGS: Sat 7 June (10-4.30). Adm £5, chd free. Tea, coffee & cake. For other opening times and information, please phone, email or visit garden website.**
Designed as different themed rooms for sculpture, Farleys garden presents our permanent collection of works chosen by photographer Lee Miller and surrealist artist Roland Penrose alongside works by contemporary guest sculptors. Over the yrs, giants, goddesses, mythical creatures and Roland's own work has populated the garden in the company of work by their artist friends. The visit also inc access to Farleys Gallery with two different exhibitions to enjoy. Locally baked cake, light salads, soup and refreshments will be available. You may recognise part of the garden as having been featured as the view through the window in the movie 'Lee' starring Kate Winslet.

🐕 🚗 ☕ 🪑 »)

SUSSEX 529

52 FINDON PLACE
Findon, Worthing, BN14 0RF. Miss Caroline Hill, www.findonplace.com. *Directly off A24 N of Worthing. Follow signs to Findon Parish Church & park through the 1st driveway on LHS.* **Sun 29 June, Sun 17 Aug (2-5). Adm £7, chd £5. Pre-booking essential, please visit www.ngs.org.uk for information & booking. Cream teas.**
Stunning grounds and gardens surrounding a Grade II listed Georgian country house (not open), nestled at the foot of the South Downs. The most glorious setting for a tapestry of perennial borders set off by Sussex flint walls. The many charms inc a yew allée, cloud pruned trees, espaliered fruit trees, a productive ornamental kitchen garden, rose arbours and arches, and a cutting garden.

🐕 ✿ 🚗 ☕ »)

53 FITTLEWORTH HOUSE
Bedham Lane, Fittleworth, Pulborough, RH20 1JH. Edward & Isabel Braham, 01798 865074, marksaunders66.com@gmail.com, www.racingandgreen.com. *2m E, SE of Petworth. Midway between Petworth & Pulborough on the A283 in Fittleworth, turn into lane signed Bedham just off sharp bend. Garden is 50yds along on the L. Plenty of car parking space.* **Every Wed 23 Apr to 14 May, Wed 11 June to 18 June, Wed 9 July to 23 July, Wed 6 Aug (2-5). Adm £5, chd free. Home-made teas. Visits also by arrangement 22 Apr to 8 Aug for groups of 8 to 40.**
3 acre tranquil, romantic, country garden with walled kitchen garden growing a wide range of fruit, vegetables and flowers inc a large collection of dahlias. Large glasshouse and old potting shed, mixed flower borders, roses, rhododendrons and lawns. Magnificent 115ft tall cedar overlooks wisteria covered Grade II listed Georgian house (not open). Wild garden, long grass areas and stream. The garden sits on a gentle slope, but is accessible for wheelchairs and buggies.

& 🐕 ✿ ☕ »)

54 FIVE OAKS COTTAGE
Petworth, RH20 1HD. Jean & Steve Jackman. *5m S of Pulborough. What3words app: partly.fuzzy.rashers. SatNav does not work! To ensure best route, we provide printed directions, please email jeanjackman@hotmail.com or call 07939 272443.* **Sat 28, Sun 29 June (2-5); Fri 3, Sat 4 Oct (2-4.30). Adm £6. Pre-booking essential, please visit www.ngs. org.uk for information & booking. Home-made teas (cash only).**
An acre of delicate jungle surrounding an Arts and Crafts style cottage (not open) with stunning views of the South Downs. Our unconventional garden is designed to encourage maximum wildlife with a knapweed and hogweed meadow on clay attracting clouds of butterflies, plus two small ponds and lots of seating. An award-winning, organic garden with a magical atmosphere.

55 THE FOLLY
Charlton, Chichester, PO18 0HU. Joan Burnett, 01243 811307, joankeirburnett@gmail.com, www.thefollycharlton.com. *7m N of Chichester & S of Midhurst off A286 at Singleton, follow signs to Charlton. Follow NGS parking signs. No parking in lane, drop off only. Parking nr the Fox Goes Free pub.* **Sun 22 June, Sun 27 July, Sun 24 Aug (2-4.30). Adm £5, chd free. Home-made teas. Visits also by arrangement 16 June to 9 Sept.**
Colourful cottage garden surrounding a C16 period house (not open), set in pretty downland village of Charlton, close to Levin Down Nature Reserve. Herbaceous borders well-stocked with a wide range of plants. Variety of perennials, grasses, annuals and shrubs to provide long season of colour and interest. Old well. Busy bees. Art studio open to visitors. Partial wheelchair access with steps from patio to lawn. Visitors with mobility issues can be dropped off at the gate. No dogs.

56 FOXGLOVE COTTAGE
29 Orchard Road, Horsham, RH13 5NF. Peter & Terri Lefevre, 01403 256002, teresalefevre@outlook.com. *East Horsham. At Horsham Stn, over bridge, at r'about 3rd exit (Crawley), 1st R Stirling Way, at end turn L, 1st R Orchard Rd. From A281, take Clarence Rd, at end turn R, at end turn L Orchard Rd. Street parking.* **Sun 25 May (11-5). Adm £6, chd free. Home-made teas inc vegan, gluten & dairy free cake. Visits also by arrangement 27 May to 4 July for groups of 12 to 30. Smaller groups or individuals can ask to join an existing visit.**
A ¼ acre plantaholic's garden, full of containers, vintage finds and quirky elements. Gravel paths navigate borders crammed with colourful planting, many salvias. A cosy summerhouse and deck, surprises at every turn! A water feature in a pebble circle, and two additional small ponds encourage wildlife. The end of the garden is home to climbers, drought tolerant planting and a plant nursery. A recently added gravel garden with a large, rusty metal arbour, called the Dome! Members of the Hardy Plant Society. A large selection of unusual plants for sale.

57 THE GARDEN HOUSE
5 Warleigh Road, Brighton, BN1 4NT. Bridgette Saunders & Graham Lee, 07729 037182, contact@gardenhousebrighton.co.uk, www.gardenhousebrighton.co.uk. *1½ m N of Brighton pier, Garden House is 1st L after Xrds, past the open market. Paid street parking. London Road Stn nearby. Buses 26 & 46 stopping at Bromley Rd.* **Fri 11, Sun 13 Apr (1-5). Adm £6, chd free. Home-made teas. Visits also by arrangement 3 Mar to 25 July for groups of 10+.**
One of Brighton's secret gardens. We aim to provide year-round interest with trees, shrubs, herbaceous borders and annuals, fruit and vegetables, two glasshouses, a pond and rockery. A friendly garden, always changing with a touch of magic to delight visitors, above all it is a slice of the country in the midst of a bustling city. Plants for sale.

58 ♦ GREAT DIXTER HOUSE, GARDENS & NURSERIES
Northiam, TN31 6PH. Great Dixter Charitable Trust, 01797 253107, www.greatdixter.co.uk. *8m N of Rye. Off A28 in Northiam, follow brown signs.* **For opening times and information, please phone or visit garden website.**
A vibrant, daring, and immersive garden with a C15 house restored by Sir Edwin Lutyens. Leading the way in ornamental gardening, gardening for biodiversity, and horticultural education. Created by the great gardener and garden writer Christopher Lloyd, OBE, VMH. Please see garden website for accessibility information.

59 GROVELANDS
Wineham Lane, Wineham, Henfield, BN5 9AW. Mrs Amanda Houston. *8m SW Haywards Heath. From Haywards Heath A272 W approx 6m, then L into Wineham Ln. House 1¾ m on L after The Royal Oak pub. 3m NE Henfield N on A281, R onto B2116 Wheatsheaf Rd, L into Wineham Ln. House ½ m on R.* **Sat 24, Sun 25 May, Sat 6, Sun 7 Sept (10-4.30). Adm £7, chd free. Tea, coffee & cake.**
A South Downs view welcomes you to this rural garden set in over an acre in the hamlet of Wineham. Created and developed by local landscape designer Sue McLaughlin and the owners, it is designed to delight throughout the seasons. Features inc mixed borders, mature shrubs and orchard. A vegetable garden with greenhouse and pond hide behind a tall clipped hornbeam hedge.

60 HAMMERWOOD HOUSE
Iping, Midhurst, GU29 0PF. Mr & Mrs M Lakin. *3m W of Midhurst. Take A272 from Midhurst, approx 2m outside Midhurst turn R for Iping. Over bridge, uphill to grassy junction, turn R. From A3 leave for Liphook, follow B2070, turn L for Milland & Iping.* **Sun 11 May (1-5). Adm £6, chd free. Home-made teas.**
Large south facing garden with lots of mature shrubs inc camellias, rhododendrons and azaleas. An arboretum with a variety of flowering and fruit trees. The old yew and beech hedges give a certain amount of formality to this traditional English garden. Tea on the terrace is a must with the most beautiful view of the South Downs. For the more energetic there is a woodland walk. Partial wheelchair access as garden is set on a slope.

61 16 HARDY DRIVE
Eastbourne, BN23 6ED. Deb Cornford. *E of Eastbourne, nr the Marina. Between Sovereign & Langley r'abouts. Going N turn R into Beatty Rd, in 300yds turn R into Hardy Dr.* **Sun 13 July (1-5). Combined adm with 36 Jellicoe Close £5, chd free.**
A small coastal town garden, made private by strategic planting and plenty of work. Filled with perennials, shrubs and climbers to give privacy and colour. Central to the garden is a magnificent 35 yr old Canary palm. The garden is well designed with lots of interest. An excellent example of what can be accomplished in a small garden resulting in an oasis of peacefulness and calm! Local cafés on Eastbourne seafront and in the harbour area.

GROUP OPENING

62 HELLINGLY PARISH TRAIL
What3words app: forks.standing. snowstorm. From A267 turn into B2104 & immed L into village, follow signs to gardens. Parking opp church green & in field by Brook Cottage & Cuckoo Trail. All gardens within walking distance.

Sun 29 June (11-5). Combined adm £8, chd free. Lunch & home-made teas at Brook Cottage. Ice-creams at Globe Place.

BROAD VIEW
Church Road, BN27 4EX.
Gill Riches.

BROOK COTTAGE
Mill Lane, BN27 4HD. Dr Colin Tourle MBE & Mrs Jane Tourle.

GLOBE COTTAGE
Mill Lane, BN27 4EY. Veronica Lee.

GLOBE PLACE
Mill Lane, BN27 4EY.
Emma & Simon Freedman.

MAY HOUSE
7 The Martlets, BN27 4FA.
Lynda & David Stewart.

POND COTTAGE
Mill Lane, BN27 4EY. Gill Nichols.

PRIORS COTTAGE
6 Church Path, BN27 4EZ.
Pat Booth.

PRIORS GRANGE
7 Church Path, BN27 4EZ.
Sylvia Stephens.

NEW ROSEMARY COTTAGE
5 Church Path, BN27 4EZ.
Fiona Dennis.

Nine gardens are opening in the delightful Sussex village of Hellingly. There is a pretty walled cottage garden with summerhouse and sunny terrace. A garden entered via a bridge over a large pond, perfect for wildlife with countryside views, and two cottage gardens overlooking the C12 Church of St Peter and St Paul. Another two gardens are in the heart of the village, one with a rose-filled front garden where the plant sale will be, and next door is an extensive garden still in development with beautiful trees and roses, and ice-creams for sale. On the other side of the village, a unique garden where lunches and teas will be served, incorporates the River Cuckmere, a sluice gate and a lush mix of perennials and mature trees. On the outskirts, an inspiring new-build garden has areas for sun, shade, climbers, and fruit trees, amid sounds of trickling water. Tickets and maps available on the green near church, at May House and Brook Cottage. Plant sale at Priors Grange. Wheelchair access to some gardens. Dogs on short leads.

♿ 🐕 ❄ ☕))

Architectural Plants

63 ♦ HERSTMONCEUX CASTLE ESTATE
Wartling Road, Hailsham, BN27 1RN. Bader College, Queen's University (Canada), 01323 833816, bc.events@queensu.ca, www.herstmonceux-castle.com. *9m NE of Eastbourne. Located between Herstmonceux & Pevensey on Wartling Rd. From Herstmonceux take A271 towards Bexhill. Turn R after Windmill Hill. If using SatNav enter Wartling Rd instead of postcode.* **For NGS: Wed 23 July (10-5.30). Adm £8, chd £3.50. Light refreshments in Tea Room.** For other opening times and information, please phone, email or visit garden website.
The Herstmonceux Castle Estate has formal gardens, woodland trails, meadows and lakes set around a majestic C15 moated castle. The gardens and grounds first opened for the NGS in 1927. Partial wheelchair access to formal gardens. A map showing an accessible route around the gardens can also be obtained from the ticket office.

& 🐕 ❋ 🚗 ☕ 🪑))

GROUP OPENING

64 HERSTMONCEUX PARISH TRAIL
Follow yellow NGS signs. Tickets & map available at each garden. Ticket covers all gardens. Not a walking trail. **Sun 22 June (12-5). Combined adm £7, chd free. Light refreshments at Hill House (2-5). Teas (12-5) & BBQ lunch (12-2) at The Windmill.**

THE ALLOTMENTS, STUNTS GREEN
BN27 4PP. Nicola Beart, Herstmonceux Allotments Association.

NEW FLITTERBROOK FLOWER FARM
West End, BN27 4NZ. Georgina Bollen, www.flitterbrookflowerfarm.co.uk.

HILL HOUSE
BN27 4RU. Maureen Madden & Terry Harland.

KERPSES
Trolliloes Lane, Cowbeech, BN27 4JG. Lynn & Peter Maguire.

LIME CROSS PINETUM & SECRET VINEYARD
BN27 4RS. Diana Tate, Victoria Tate & Helen Soudain, www.limecross.co.uk.

MERRIE HARRIERS BARN
Cowbeech, BN27 4JQ. Lee Henderson.

THE WINDMILL
BN27 4RT. Windmill Hill Windmill Trust, windmillhillwindmill.org.

Seven gardens inc a historic windmill and allotments. In Cowbeech there are two gardens: Merrie Harriers Barn is a garden with sweeping lawn and open countryside, colourful herbaceous planting and a large pond with places to sit and enjoy the view. Kerpses is a delightful mixture of mature trees, shrubs, herbaceous borders, vegetable garden, ponds and a meadow. In Stunts Green, The Allotments comprise 54 allotments growing a huge variety of traditional and unusual crops. Flitterbrook Flower Farm has an amazing collection of flowers for the retail market. At Lime Cross in Herstmonceux there is a Pinetum and Vinery with wine and mocktails, and Hill House has abundant roses, trees, shrubs and varied perennials, a greenhouse, and a wildlife pond with water lilies. Plenty of seating areas to sit and reflect and have tea. The historic Windmill is well worth a visit and where you can enjoy a BBQ lunch or tea.

☕))

65 THE HIDDEN GARDEN
School Lane (behind Selsey Library), Selsey, Chichester, PO20 9EH. Paul Sadler. *5m S of Chichester. Park behind Selsey Library or in front of the Academy School on School Ln. You will see The Bridge Support Centre, enter through the gate & The Hidden Garden is behind the centre.* **Sun 20 July (10-4). Adm £5, chd free. Tea, coffee & cake.**
The Hidden Garden is a community gardening project encouraging local people to become involved with growing fruit, vegetables, herbs and flowers as well as providing spaces for wildlife to thrive. The garden is open to people of all ages and abilities, organised by the Selsey Community Forum but looked after by a dedicated group of local volunteers.

🐕 ❋ ☕ 🪑))

66 ♦ HIGH BEECHES WOODLAND AND WATER GARDEN
High Beeches Lane, Handcross, Haywards Heath, RH17 6HQ. High Beeches Gardens Conservation Trust, 01444 400589, gardens@highbeeches.com, www.highbeeches.com. *5m NW of Cuckfield. On B2110, 1m E of A23 at Handcross.* **For NGS: Sun 1 June, Sun 28 Sept (1-5). Adm £11, chd £4. Tea, coffee & cake.** For other opening times and information, please phone, email or visit garden website.
25 acres of enchanting, landscaped woodland and water gardens with spring daffodils, bluebells and azalea walks, many rare and beautiful plants, an ancient wildflower meadow and glorious autumn colours. Picnic area. National Collection of Stewartias.

🚗 NPC ☕ 🪑))

67 ♦ HIGHDOWN GARDENS
33 Highdown Rise, Littlehampton Road, Goring-by-Sea, Worthing, BN12 6FB. Worthing Borough Council, highdown.gardens@adur-worthing.gov.uk, www.highdowngardens.co.uk. *What3words app: quiet.stages.camera. Off the A259 Littlehampton Rd heading E towards Worthing. Turn L up Highdown Rise. Nearest train station: Goring-by-Sea.* **For NGS: Thur 13 Feb (10-4.30); Thur 1 May (10-8). Adm by donation.** For other opening times and information, please email or visit garden website.
Highdown Gardens were created by Sir Frederick Stern. They are home to rare plants and trees, many grown from seed collected by Wilson, Farrer and Kingdon-Ward. A fully equipped glasshouse enables the propagation of this National Plant Collection. A visitor centre shares stories of the plants and people behind the gardens. An accessible path leads to a sensory garden with a secret sea view. Highdown is also offering Snowdrop Identification tours on the 13 Feb and Peony Identification tours on the 1 May (not for NGS), for more information and booking please see garden website. Accessible top pathway and lift to visitor centre, see garden website accessibility page for full details.

& ❋ 🚗 ☕

SUSSEX 533

68 HIGHLANDS
Etchingwood Lane, Framfield, Uckfield, TN22 5SA. Chris Brown, Head Gardener, www.instagram@ thesussexplanthunter. $1\frac{1}{2}$ m E of Uckfield. Leave Uckfield on B2102 (Framfield Rd). Bear L onto Sandy Ln. Turn L at Xrds with Etchingwood Ln. Entrance via field gate in 100 metres on R. Do not use postcode for SatNav, use Highlands. **Sat 7 June (10-4.30). Adm £9, chd free. Pre-booking essential, please visit www.ngs.org.uk for information & booking. Home-made teas.**
An 8 acre garden set around a house with C15 origins (not open), amid pasture and woodland. Intensively gardened beds near the house inc hot and pink beds and a white garden, are kept vibrant through waves of annuals planted through the perennials. These give way to meadow, orchard, ponds and woodland plantings.
✿ ☕ ᴗ)))

69 4 HILLSIDE COTTAGES
Downs Road, West Stoke, Chichester, PO18 9BL. Heather & Chris Lock, 01243 574820, chlock@btinternet.com. *3m NW of Chichester. From A286 at Lavant, head W for 1$\frac{1}{2}$ m, nr Kingley Vale.* **Sun 8 June, Sun 20 July, Sun 17 Aug (11-4). Adm £5, chd free. Home-made teas. Visits also by arrangement June to Aug.**
In a rural setting this stunning garden is densely planted with mixed borders and shrubs. Large collection of roses, clematis, fuchsias and dahlias, a profusion of colour and scent in a well maintained garden. Please visit www.ngs.org.uk for pop-up openings in June, July and August.
☕

70 HOLLY HOUSE
Beaconsfield Road, Chelwood Gate, Haywards Heath, RH17 7LF. Mrs Deirdre Birchell, 01825 740484, db@hollyhousebnb.co.uk, www.hollyhousebnb.co.uk. *7m E of Haywards Heath. From Nutley village on A22 turn off at Hathi Restaurant signed Chelwood Gate 2m. Chelwood Gate Village Hall on R, Holly House is opp.* **Sat 16, Sun 17 Aug (2-5). Adm £6, chd free. Home-made teas. Visits also by arrangement 1 May to 1 Sept for groups of up to 30.**
An acre of English garden providing views and cameos of plants and trees round every corner with many different areas giving constant interest. A fish pond and a wildlife pond beside a grassy area with many shrubs and flower beds. Among the trees and winding paths there is a cottage garden which is a profusion of colour and peace. Exhibition of paintings and cards by owner. Garden accessible by wheelchair in good weather, but it is not easy.
♿ 🐕 🚗 🏛 ☕ ᴗ)))

71 HOLLYMOUNT
Burnt Oak Road, High Hurstwood, Uckfield, TN22 4AE. Jonathan Hughes-Morgan, 07968 848418, jonnyhughesmorgan@gmail.com. *Exactly halfway between Uckfield & Crowborough, just off the A26. From A26 S of Crowborough or A272 between Uckfield & Buxted, follow sign to High Hurstwood. From N approx 2m down Chillies Ln take 1st L, from S 1$\frac{1}{2}$ m up Hurstwood Rd take 3rd R, $\frac{1}{2}$ m up on L.* **Sun 25 May, Sun 29 June, Sun 27 July, Sun 24 Aug (12-5). Adm £8, chd free. Home-made teas. Visits also by arrangement 30 Apr to 30 Sept for groups of 10+.**
A beautiful 7 acre garden centred around water. Streams run down the hill through waterfalls into ponds flanked by luscious planting. A huge variety of plants create interest from May through to Oct. Thick jungle borders flank the top garden while the beds further down are full of rhododendrons, acers, irises, day lilies and roses. There are pigs, alpacas, chickens and ducks. The secret garden is a must.
🐕 🏛 ☕ 🍴 ᴗ)))

72 HOOPERS FARM
Vale Road, Mayfield, TN20 6BD. Andrew & Sarah Ratcliffe. *10m S of Tunbridge Wells. Turn off A267 into Mayfield. Parking in the village & field parking at Hoopers Farm, TN20 6BD.* **Sat 14, Sun 15 June (11-5). Adm £6, chd free. Home-made teas. Opening with Mayfield Gardens on Sat 2, Sun 3 Aug.**
Large south facing garden with informal flowing layout. Colour themed island beds with mixed herbaceous and seasonal annual planting. Mature trees, flowering shrubs, rose beds, rose arbour, rock garden, secret garden and vegetable plot. Gravel paths lead through a richly planted area with lots of late season colour. Lawn conversion to wildflower meadow now in 3rd yr. Meadow walk to wildlife pond. Plant sales by Rapkyns Nursery. Local musicians will entertain in the garden on some of the dates. Wheelchair access to most of the garden.
♿ 🐕 ✿ ☕ ᴗ)))

73 36 JELLICOE CLOSE
Eastbourne, BN23 6DD. Amanda Haines. *E of Eastbourne, nr the Marina. Between Sovereign & Langley r'abouts. Going N turn R into Beatty Rd, in 300yds turn R into Hardy Dr, then 1st L into Jellicoe Cl, No.36 is at the top on RHS.* **Sun 13 July (1-5). Combined adm with 16 Hardy Drive £5, chd free.**
A new front and rear garden created over the last 5 yrs on shingle/beach reclaimed land. Mediterranean, cottage style garden with wildlife, ecology and sustainability at its heart. It is packed with trees, shrubs, perennial plants and a few exotics. There are winding paths, a gazebo and a potter's studio at the rear. Described by The Sunday Times as a 'sub-tropical paradise'. Local cafés on Eastbourne seafront and in the harbour area.
✿

74 JUDY'S COTTAGE GARDEN
33 The Plantation, Worthing, BN13 2AE. Mrs Judy Gordon. *Salvington. A24 meets A27 at Offington r'about, turn into Offington Ln, 1st R into The Plantation.* **Fri 18 Apr, Sat 21 June (10.30-3.30). Adm £5, chd free. Tea, coffee & cake.**
A beautiful medium sized cottage garden with something of interest all year-round. The garden has several mature trees creating a feeling of seclusion. The informal beds contain a mixture of shrubs, perennials, cottage garden plants and spring bulbs. There are little hidden areas to enjoy, a small fish pond and other water features. There is also a pretty log cabin overlooking the garden.
☕

In 2024 we awarded £232,000 in Community Garden Grants, supporting 89 community garden projects.

75 NEW 12 KEEPERS WOOD

Chichester, PO19 5XU. Mrs Sybille Bulloch, 07391 533741, sybulloch@gmail.com. *Northern outskirts of Chichester. What3words app: fortunate.garden.bliss.* **Thur 10, Thur 17 July (2-5). Adm £7, chd free. Pre-booking essential, please visit www.ngs.org. uk for information & booking. Home-made teas. Visits also by arrangement 11 July to 31 July for groups of 5 to 15. Adm inc refreshments for group visits only.**
A north facing, ¼ acre garden situated at the edge of the city, wedged between tall trees and open agricultural land was redesigned in 2017 to showcase its unique position. The result is a garden of different moods: Annabelle hydrangeas, a fern-packed woodland area, and a 90ft Piet Oudolf inspired prairie border, complemented by a majestic oak, a willow tipi, a pond, and a cut flower border.

76 ◆ KING JOHN'S NURSERY

Sheepstreet Lane, Etchingham, TN19 7AZ. Harry Cunningham, 01580 819220, harry@kingjohnsnursery.co.uk, www.kingjohnsnursery.co.uk. *2m W of Hurst Green. Off A265 nr Etchingham. From Burwash turn L before Etchingham Church, from Hurst Green turn R after church, into Church Ln, which leads into Sheepstreet Ln after ½ m, then L after 1m.* **For NGS: Sat 22 Mar, Sat 24 May, Sat 28 June, Sat 13 Sept (10-5). Adm £5, chd free. Light refreshments. For other opening times and information, please phone, email or visit garden website.**
Garden developed alongside the nursery, a romantic pond garden, gravel garden, long border, meadows and cutting garden. A garden of wild flowers and full of ideas. Garden is mostly flat, and areas with steps are generally accessible from other parts of the garden. Disabled WC.

77 KITCHENHAM FARM

Kitchenham Road, Ashburnham, Battle, TN33 9NP. Amanda & Monty Worssam. *5m S of Battle. S of Ashburnham Place from A271 Herstmonceux to Bexhill road, take L turn 500 metres after Boreham St. Kitchenham Farm is 500 metres on L.* **Sat 7, Wed 11 June, Wed 6,**
Sat 9 Aug (2-5). Adm £6, chd free. Home-made teas.
1 acre country house garden set amongst traditional farm buildings with stunning views over the Sussex countryside. Series of borders around the house and Oast House (not open). Lawns and mixed herbaceous borders inc roses and delphiniums. A ha-ha separates the garden from the fields and sheep. The garden adjoins a working farm. Wheelchair access to the garden. One step to WC.

78 ◆ KNEPP CASTLE

The Apple Store, nr Knepp Castle, off Pound Lane, West Grinstead, Horsham, RH13 8LJ. Sir Charles & Lady Burrell, www.knepp.co.uk. *8m S of Horsham. Entrance off Pound Ln following NGS signage. Parking on field nr to garden (200 metre walk).* **For NGS: Sat 21 June (10-3.30). Adm £15, chd free. Pre-booking essential, please visit www.ngs.org.uk for information & booking. Tea. Timed slots at 10am, 11.30am & 2pm. For other opening times and information, please visit garden website.**
The Walled Garden at Knepp has been transformed into a garden for biodiversity. With designers Tom Stuart-Smith and James Hitchmough, we have applied some of the principles we've learned from rewilding the wider landscape to this small, confined space to create a mosaic of dynamic habitats for wildlife. The croquet lawn is now a riot of humps and hollows, hosting almost 1000 species of plants. Lunches available at Knepp Wilding Kitchen, RH13 8NQ.

79 KNIGHTSBRIDGE HOUSE

Grove Hill, Hellingly, Hailsham, BN27 4HH. Andrew & Karty Watson. *3m N of Hailsham, 2m S of Horam. From A22 at Boship r`about take A271, at 1st set of T-lights turn L into Park Rd, new road layout here, so you need to take a L turn approx 150 metres from the lights & drive for 2⅔m, garden on R.* **Sat 26 July (2-5). Adm £7.50, chd free. Home-made teas.**
Mature landscaped garden set in 5 acres of tranquil countryside surrounding Georgian house (not open). Several garden rooms, spectacular herbaceous borders planted in contemporary style. Lots of all round colour with grasses and some magnificent specimen trees;
also partly walled garden. No card machine at this garden (poor phone signal). Wheelchair access to most of garden over gravel paths. Ask to park by house if slope from car park is too steep.

80 NEW KOTIMAKI

Tottingworth Park, Broad Oak, Heathfield, TN21 8UH. Mark Riches & John Jenkins. *Lane off A265 between Broad Oak & Burwash Common. Lane is 1m outside Broad Oak, nr Swife Ln, but opp side of A265. Telegraph pole next to lane marked with NGS sign, then follow NGS signs down lane. NB: SatNav may point to wrong lane.* **Sat 26 Apr, Sat 17 May, Sat 7 June, Sat 19 July, Sat 6 Sept, Sat 4 Oct (10-12). Adm £12, chd £6. Pre-booking essential, please visit www.ngs.org.uk for information & booking. Tea, coffee & biscuits inc. Talk about the garden at 10:30am.**
Large creatively planted gardens featuring a long double border within yew hedging, rockery, shade garden, exotic garden, pot garden, wildflower meadows, and kitchen garden. Emphasis on continuity of interest via imaginative mixed plantings of shrubs, climbers, perennials, bulbs, annuals and self-sowers; plus a varied collection of wisterias trained as shrubs, on trellis work, and on a pergola.

81 LEGSHEATH FARM

Legsheath Lane, nr Forest Row, RH19 4JN. Mr & Mrs Michael Neal, 01342 810230, legsheath@btinternet.com. *4m S of East Grinstead. 2m W of Forest Row, 1m S of Weirwood Reservoir.* **Sun 18 May (1.30-4.30). Adm £7, chd free. Home-made teas. Visits also by arrangement 4 May to 7 Sept. Donation to Holy Trinity Church, Forest Row.**
Legsheath was first mentioned in Duchy of Lancaster records in 1545. It was associated with the role of Master of the Ashdown Forest. Set high in the Weald with far-reaching views of East Grinstead and Weirwood Reservoir. The garden covers 11 acres with a spring fed stream feeding ponds. There is a magnificent davidia, rare shrubs, embothrium and many different varieties of meconopsis and *Abutilon*.

SUSSEX 535

82 LIMEKILN FARM
Chalvington Road, Chalvington, Hailsham, BN27 3TA. **Dr J Hester & Mr M Royle.** *10m N of Eastbourne. Nr Hailsham. Turn S off A22 at Golden Cross & follow the Chalvington Rd for 1m. The entrance has white gates on LHS. Disabled parking space close to house, other parking 100 metres further along road.* **Sat 29, Sun 30 Mar, Sat 30, Sun 31 Aug (2-5). Adm £8, chd free. Tea, coffee & cake in the Oast House. Talk at 3pm.**
The garden was designed in the 1930s when the house was owned by Charles Stewart Taylor, MP for Eastbourne. It has not changed in basic layout since then. The planting aims to reflect the age of the C17 property (not open) and original garden design. The house and garden are mentioned in Virginia Woolf's diaries of 1929, depicting a particular charm and peace that still exists today. Flint walls enclose the main lawn, herbaceous borders and rose garden. Nepeta lined courtyard. Informal pond and specimen trees inc a very ancient oak. Many spring flowers and tree blossom. New prairie-style garden with grasses and perennials. Physic garden with talk at 3pm about medicinal plants. Mostly flat access with two steps up to main lawn and herbaceous borders.

83 LORDINGTON HOUSE
Lordington, Chichester, PO18 9DX. **Mr & Mrs John Hamilton,** 01243 375862, hamiltonjanda@btinternet.com. *7m W of Chichester. On W side of B2146, ½m S of Walderton, 6m S of South Harting. Enter through white railings on bend.* **Sat 7, Sun 8 June (2-5). Adm £6, chd free. Tea, coffee & cake. Visits also by arrangement 9 June to 5 Sept for groups of up to 30.**
Early C17 house (not open) and walled gardens in South Downs National Park. Clipped yew, lawns, borders and fine views. Informal sunken garden. Vegetables, fruit and poultry in kitchen garden. Over 100 roses planted since 2008. Trees both mature and young. Lime avenue planted in 1973 to replace elms. Wildflower meadow outside walls, accessible from garden. Gardens overlook Ems Valley, farmland and wooded slopes of South Downs, all in AONB. Wheelchair access is possible, but challenging with gravel paths, uneven paving and slopes. Limited WC facilities. No disabled WC.

84 LUCTONS
North Lane, West Hoathly, East Grinstead, RH19 4PP. **Drs Hans & Ingrid Sethi,** 07787 523510, ingrid@sethis.co.uk. *4m SW of East Grinstead, 6m E of Crawley. In centre of West Hoathly village, nr church, Cat Inn & Priest House. Car parks in village.* **Sat 21, Wed 25, Sun 29 June, Tue 1 July (1.30-3.30). Adm £7, chd free. Pre-booking essential, please visit www.ngs.org.uk for information & booking. Tea, coffee & cake (cash only). Visits also by arrangement 2 June to 28 Aug for groups of 10 to 30.**
'A garden with everything', 'lots of unusual plants', 'stunning herbaceous borders', are comments of NGS and overseas garden tour visitors. 2 acres of Gertrude Jekyll style garden with herbaceous borders, wildflower orchard, swathes of spotted orchids, pond, roses, chickens, vegetables, herb garden, vine house, greenhouses, croquet lawn and shrubberies. WC facilities.

85 NEW LYNWOOD
Holland Road, Steyning, BN44 3GJ. **Debbie Chalmers.** *6m NE of Worthing. Exit r'about on A283 at S end of Steyning bypass into Clays Hill Rd. 1st R into Goring Rd, 4th L into Holland Rd. What3words app: surpasses.winner.evolution.* **Fri 4, Fri 11 July (12-5). Combined adm with Saffrons £8, chd free. Home-made teas at Saffrons.**
Medium sized garden with three distinct garden areas around an Edwardian house. Recently re-planted, colour-themed mixed borders of perennials and annuals inc flowers for cutting, eating and scent. Two lawned areas and two pot-filled patios, plus cedar wood greenhouse where many of the plants are raised from seed. Wheelchair access over gravel and grass.

86 MALTHOUSE FARM
Streat Lane, Streat, Hassocks, BN6 8SA. **Richard & Helen Keys,** 01273 890356, helen.k.keys@btinternet.com. *2m SE of Burgess Hill. From r'about between B2113 & B2112 take Folders Ln & Middleton Common Ln E (away from Burgess Hill); after 1m R into Streat Ln, garden is ½m on R. Please park carefully as signed.* **Visits by arrangement May to Sept**
for groups of 10 to 40. Home-made teas.
Rural 5 acre garden with stunning views to South Downs. Garden divided into separate rooms; box parterre and borders with glass sculpture, herbaceous and shrub borders, and mixed border for seasonal colour. Orchard with wild flowers leading to partitioned areas with grass walks, snail mound, birch maze and willow tunnel. Wildlife farm pond with planted surround. Partial wheelchair access over grass areas, some gravel paths, and steps tend to limit access to some parts.

87 MANOR OF DEAN
Tillington, Petworth, GU28 9AP. **Mr & Mrs James Mitford,** 07887 992349, emma@mitford.uk.com. *3m W of Petworth, just off A272. Car park accessed via New Rd. What3words app: unique.only.novels.* **Sun 2 Feb (2-4); Sun 9 Mar, Sun 27 Apr (2-5). Adm £5, chd free. Tea, coffee & cake. Visits also by arrangement 3 Feb to 18 May for groups of 20+.**
Approx 3 acres of traditional English garden with extensive views of the South Downs. Herbaceous borders, early spring bulbs, bluebell woodland walk, walled kitchen garden with fruit, vegetables and cutting flowers. NB under long term programme of restoration, some parts of the garden may be affected.

GROUP OPENING

88 MAYFIELD GARDENS
Mayfield, TN20 6AB. *10m S of Tunbridge Wells. Turn off A267 into Mayfield. Parking in the village, TN20 6BE & field parking at Hoopers Farm, TN20 6BD. A detailed map available at each garden.* **Sat 2, Sun 3 Aug (11-5). Combined adm £7, chd free. Home-made teas.**

ABBOTSBURY
Rob & Becky Morris.

NEW AIRLIE COTTAGE
Robert & Claire Montagu.

HOOPERS FARM
Andrew & Sarah Ratcliffe.
(See separate entry)

THE OAST
Mike & Tessa Crowe.
(See separate entry)

SOUTH STREET PLOTS
Val Buddle.

Mayfield is a beautiful Wealden village with tearooms, an old pub and many interesting historical connections. The gardens to visit are all within walking distance of the village centre. They vary in size and style with a wide range of shrubs, herbaceous and annual planting and inc wildflower meadows, wildlife ponds, fruit and vegetable plots and a childrens' play area. There are far-reaching, panoramic views over the beautiful High Weald.

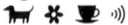

89 MEADOW FARM
Blackgate Lane,
Pulborough, RH20 1DF.
Charlie & Ness Langdale,
nesslangdale@icloud.com. *3m N of Pulborough. From Pulborough take A29 N. Just outside Pulborough L into Blackgate Ln signed to Toat. Continue on road for 1½ m. At sign for Scrase Farms keep going straight. Signed parking on R.* **Sun 21 Sept (1-5). Adm £7, chd free. Home-made teas.** Visits also by arrangement 1 May to 26 June for groups of 12 to 25.

2 acre garden, plus wildflower meadows, designed and planted from scratch by current owners. Colour themed beds inc double borders, formal pond, gravel garden and white garden. Pleached hornbeam avenue to the Sussex countryside. Walled garden provides fruit, cut flowers and vegetables. Orchard with hazelnut walk. Wildlife swimming pond with bog garden. New prairie bed.

90 NEW MEADOWSIDE
7 Finches Lane, West Chiltington, Pulborough, RH20 2PX. Kate Harrison. *3½ m from Pulborough via A283. No parking on Finches Ln or Little Hill. Other parking available within easy walking distance.* **Thur 26 June, Thur 3 July (10.30-4.30). Adm £6, chd free. Tea, coffee & cake.**

Designed to encourage wildlife, the formal areas are gradually being adapted. In the back garden, annual wild flowers have replaced box hedging, erigeron and chamomile have been allowed to self-seed between brick paths and paving; part of the lawn has become a wildflower area. A summerhouse looks out onto the fish pond and the deck has views over the wildlife areas and woodland beyond.

91 NEW MILFORD PLACE
Wyatts Lane, Horsted Keynes, Haywards Heath, RH17 7AH. Joanna Richardson, www.instagram.com/milfordplacegarden. *In the Weald, approx 5m NE of Haywards Heath. Visitor access via Sugar Ln/Hamsland. What3words app: rate.villager.learning. Park in paddock (uneven ground). Blue Badge holders only via house entrance, Wyatts Ln, RH17 7AH (sloping gravel drive).* **Sat 14 June (2-5). Adm £7.50, chd free. Home-made teas.**

A developing garden of 3⅓ acres with adjacent paddock, next to the Mid Sussex border path, and located in the High Weald, AONB. The house was built in 2021 with its terrace and retaining wall providing structure for the newly planted herbaceous beds. These are surrounded by borders and lawns relandscaped to blend with a variety of mature shrubs and trees. Sadly, not suitable for wheelchair access due to uneven ground.

47 Denmans Lane

SUSSEX

92 MITCHMERE FARM
Stoughton, Chichester, PO18 9JW. Neil & Sue Edden, 02392 631456, sue@mitchmere.co.uk. 5½m NW of Chichester. Turn off the B2146 at Walderton towards Stoughton. Farm is ¾m on L, ¼m beyond the turning to Upmarden. Please do not park on verge, follow signs for parking. **Visits by arrangement 8 Feb to 14 Nov. Adm £6, chd free. Min group charge £60. Tea, coffee & biscuits.** 1½ acre garden in lovely downland position, with a stream flowing through the garden most yrs when the Winterbourne rises. An orchard and unusual trees and shrubs, providing all yr colour and interest. Big areas of bulbs inc special snowdrops, a wildlife pond, a 'ruin' with a mosaic floor, terraces enclosed by yew hedges, and summer colour with roses and clematis. Optional 10 min walk down the long field beside the river, across the sleeper bridge, take the path through the copse with snowdrops up the steps into the new wood, then into the meadow and back to the garden. Wellies advisable. Dogs on short leads. Wheelchair access over gravel and grass.

93 MOUNTFIELD COURT
Robertsbridge, TN32 5JP. Mr & Mrs Simon Fraser. *3m N of Battle. On A21 London-Hastings; ½m NW from Johns Cross.* **Sun 11 May (2-5). Adm £7, chd free. Tea, coffee & cake.**
3 acre wild woodland garden with bluebell lined walkways through exceptional rhododendrons, azaleas, camellias, and other flowering shrubs. Fine trees and outstanding views. Stunning paved herb garden.

94 NEWTIMBER PLACE
Newtimber, BN6 9BU. Andrew & Carol Clay, 07795 346974, andy@newtimberholidaycottages.co.uk, www.newtimberplace.co.uk. *7m N of Brighton. From A23 take A281 towards Henfield. Turn R at small Xrds signed Newtimber in approx ½m. Go down Church Ln, garden is on L at end of lane.* **Sun 13 Apr (2-5.30). Adm £7, chd free. Home-made teas.**
Beautiful C17 moated house (not open). Gardens and woods full of bulbs and wild flowers in spring. Herbaceous border and lawns. Moat flanked by water plants. Mature trees, wild garden, ducks, and fish.

Wheelchair access across lawn to parts of garden, tearoom and WC.

95 NYETIMBER MANOR
Nyetimber Vineyard, Gay Street, Pulborough, RH20 2HH. Eric Heerema, sally.hughes@nyetimber.com, www.instagram.com/nyetimber. *West Chiltington. The postcode will take you to Lower Jordans Ln. Continue on Gay St & look for the Nyetimber Vineyard sign & gates.* **Fri 11 July (9.30-5.30). Adm £15, chd £7.50. Pre-booking essential, please visit www.ngs.org.uk for information & booking. Tea, coffee & cake in medieval barn. Timed slots at 9.30am, 11.30am, 1.30pm & 3.30pm.**
Nestled below the vineyards, The Manor garden at Nyetimber is one that is rarely glimpsed. This garden has everything from extensive herbaceous borders, to orchard, flower and rose garden, and courtyard. A tapestry of topiary, reflected in the lily ponds frame a beautiful view of the South Downs. Extensively redesigned and replanted in 2020, this newly establishing garden is one not to be missed. Cellar door operating for Nyetimber Wine. Wheelchair access to most areas. Some steps access, slopes and uneven ground. Disabled WC.

96 ♦ NYMANS
Staplefield Road, Handcross, RH17 6EB. National Trust, 01444 405250, nymans@nationaltrust.org.uk, www.nationaltrust.org.uk/nymans. *4m S of Crawley. On B2114 at Handcross signed off M23/A23 London-Brighton road. Metrobus 271 & 273 stop nearby.* **For NGS: Sat 15 Mar (10-5). Adm £19, chd £9.50. Adm subject to change. Light refreshments. For other opening times and information, please phone, email or visit garden website. Donation to Plant Heritage.**
One of NT's premier gardens with rare and unusual plant collections of national significance. In spring see blossom, bulbs and a stunning collection of subtly fragranced magnolias. The Rose Garden, inspired by Maud Messel's 1920s design, is scented by hints of old-fashioned roses. The comfortable yet elegant house, a partial ruin, reflects the personalities of the creative Messel family. Some level pathways. See full access statement on Nymans website.

97 OAKLANDS FARM
Hooklands Lane, Shipley, Horsham, RH13 8PX. Zsa & Stephen Roggendorff, 01403 741270, zedrog@roggendorff.co.uk. *S of Shipley village. Off the A272 towards Shipley, R at Countryman Pub, follow yellow signs. Or N of A24 Ashington, off Billingshurst Rd, 1st R signed Shipley, garden 2m up the lane.* **Sat 14 June, Thur 17 July (11-5). Adm £6, chd free. Home-made teas.**
Visits also by arrangement 19 Apr to 6 Sept for groups of 5 to 25.
Country garden designed by Nigel Philips in 2010. Oak lined drive leading to the house (not open) and farm opens out to an enclosed courtyard with pleached hornbeam and yew. The herbaceous borders are colourful throughout the yr. Vegetable garden with raised beds and greenhouse with white peach and vine. Wild meadow leading to orchard and views across the fields, full of sheep and poultry. Mature trees. Lovely Louise will be here with her special perennials for sale. Picnics welcome. Wheelchair access over gravel and brick paths, large lawn area and grassy paths.

98 THE OAST
Fletching Street, Mayfield, TN20 6TN. Mike & Tessa Crowe. *10m S of Tunbridge Wells. Turn off A267 into Mayfield. Parking along East St & in the village public car parks. Please do not park outside The Oast in Fletching St as it is very narrow.* **Sat 26, Sun 27 Apr (11-5). Adm £5, chd free. Home-made teas. Opening with Mayfield Gardens on Sat 2, Sun 3 Aug.**
A 1 acre garden in an idyllic High Weald setting with a beautiful view. Year-round interest, with highlights in spring and late summer/autumn. In April, over 4000 tulips and other spring bulbs bloom, while later in summer, dahlias, salvias, grasses, and asters are interplanted with colourful annuals. ½ acre wildflower meadow with old roses and orchard. Woodland-edge walk, wildlife pond, vegetables and soft fruit. Quality homegrown plants for sale.

99 OCKLYNGE MANOR
Mill Road, Eastbourne, BN21 2PG. Wendy & David Dugdill, 01323 734121, ocklyngemanor@hotmail.com, www.ocklyngemanor.co.uk. Take A22 (Willingdon Rd) towards Old Town, turn L into Mill Rd by Hurst Arms Pub. **Visits by arrangement Apr & May for groups of up to 25. Sorry, no refreshments.**
A hidden oasis behind an ancient flint wall. Informal and tranquil, ½ acre chalk garden with sunny and shaded places to sit. Use of architectural and unusual trees. Rhododendrons, azaleas and acers in raised beds. Garden evolved over 20 yrs, maintained by owners. Georgian house (not open), former home of Mabel Lucie Attwell. Wheelchair access over short gravel path before entering garden. Brick path around perimeter.

100 OFFHAM HOUSE
The Street, Offham, Lewes, BN7 3QE. Mr & Mrs P Carminger & Mr S Goodman. *2m N of Lewes on A275. Offham House is on the main road (A275) through Offham between the filling station & Blacksmiths Arms. On road parking off the main road, down by the Church. Limited parking at the house.* **Sun 1 June (1-5). Adm £7, chd free. Home-made teas.**
Romantic garden with fountains, flowering trees, arboretum, double herbaceous border and long peony bed. 1676 Queen Anne house (not open) with well knapped flint facade. Herb garden and walled kitchen garden with glasshouses, cold frames, chickens, sheep and ducks. A selection of pelargoniums and other plants for sale.

101 OLD ERRINGHAM COTTAGE
Steyning Road, Shoreham-By-Sea, BN43 5FD. Fiona & Martin Phillips, 07884 398704, fiona.h.phillips@btinternet.com. *2m N of Shoreham-By-Sea. From A27 Shoreham flyover take A283 towards Steyning. Take 2nd R into private lane. Follow sharp LH-bend at top, house on L.* **Visits by arrangement 26 May to 30 June for groups of 10 to 25. Home-made teas.**
Plantsman's garden set high on the South Downs with panoramic views overlooking the Adur valley. 1⅓ acres with flower meadow, stream bed and ponds, formal and informal planting areas with over 600 varieties of plants. Very productive fruit and vegetable garden with glasshouses. Many plants grown from seed and coastal climate gives success with tender plants.

102 NEW THE OLD MANOR
The Street, Nutbourne, Pulborough, RH20 2HE. Mr Frank & Mrs Erica Riddle. *2m E of Pulborough. Take A283 from Pulborough towards Storrington. Turn L down West Chiltington Rd then L down Nutbourne Rd. Go along The Street, pass The Rising Sun pub. Follow parking directions from a volunteer.* **Thur 5, Sat 7 June (12-5). Combined adm with Shorts Farm £8, chd free. Home-made teas at Shorts Farm.**
A Victorian allotment style kitchen garden has been recreated providing year-round vegetables, and fruit from strategically placed trees around the house. There are chickens and sometimes bottle-fed orphan lambs in the adjacent small field that abounds with wildflowers in the lower part. Look out for how the tiered levels have been used to provide niches for plants.

103 THE OLD RECTORY, BARNHAM
97 Barnham Road, Barnham, PO22 0EQ. Peter & Alexandra Vining, theoldrectory97@gmail.com. *8m E of Chichester. Between Arundel & Chichester at A27 Fontwell junction, take A29 road to Bognor Regis. Turn L at next r'about onto Barnham Rd. 30 metres after speed camera arrive at garden.* **Sat 31 May, Sun 1 June (10-4). Combined adm with The Shrubbery £6, chd free. Home-made teas. Visits also by arrangement 2 June to 6 June.**
Scratch built in June 2019 after the 300m² garden was removed down to 40cm, we then added fresh topsoil and re-turfed. By summer 2021 the garden was well established. Now, we have reached the final planning and planting stages 'we think'! Apart from replacing the odd failing plant (we all have them) we just keep things ship-shape as best we can. Wheelchair access through 90cm wide entrance, and no steps. Please advise if you need disabled parking.

104 NEW THE OLD RECTORY, PULBOROUGH
Old Rectory Lane, Pulborough, RH20 2AF. Claire Roscoe. *From A29, 200 metres from r'about to A283, enter Old Rectory Ln (Chequers Hotel on the corner) & pass the signboard listing all houses in the lane. The Old Rectory is the 1st house on your L.* **Sat 26, Sun 27 July, Sat 2, Sun 3 Aug (11-5). Adm £7, chd free. Tea, coffee & cake.**
A formal front garden with sunken centrepiece and rose and flower beds of approx ½ acre. Large rear garden consisting of small woods, croquet lawn with beds, natural swimming pond and large summerhouse, small orchard and meadow, and walled area by pickleball court. Many interesting trees inc a 500 yr old sweet chestnut.

105 NEW THE OLD RECTORY, WARBLETON
Kingsley Hill, Warbleton, TN21 9PT. Lord Barker Of Battle & George Prassas, sharneegates@hotmail.com, www.instagram.com/theoldrectorygarden. *5m S of Heathfield town centre. What3words app: weaved.throat. require takes you to the property's white front gate. Parking in the car park of the property opp (signed), in the lane, or by the church a 5 min walk away.* **Tue 15, Wed 16 Apr, Wed 11, Thur 12 June (11-4). Adm £9, chd free. Pre-booking essential, please visit www.ngs.org.uk for information & booking. Tea, coffee & cake. Visits also by arrangement 20 Jan to 6 Oct. Please contact Sharnee Gates, Head Gardener via email or Instagram.**
Nestled in the High Weald AONB, The Old Rectory garden was re-imagined by renowned designer Arne Maynard. His vision blends formal elements like yew and beech topiary, a knot garden, and herbaceous borders with wild flowers and rambling roses. A stream separates the formal garden from an orchard interplanted with roses and wild flowers. Over 3000 tulips bloom in spring. Other features inc cutting garden, pond, copse, meadows, pot displays, and gravel garden.

SUSSEX 539

106 THE OLD VICARAGE
The Street, Washington, RH20 4AS. Lady Walters, 07766 761926, meryl.walters@me.com, www.instagram.com/the_old_vicarage_washington. 2½ m E of Storrington, 4m W of Steyning. From Washington r'about on A24 take A283 to Steyning. 500yds R to Washington. Pass Frankland Arms, R to St Mary's Church. Car park available, but no large coaches. **Every Thur 6 Feb to 2 Oct (10-4). Adm £8, chd free. Pre-booking essential, please visit www.ngs.org.uk for information & booking. Self service light refreshments on Thurs (cash only) & picnics welcome. Mon 21 Apr, Mon 26 May, Sun 27 July, Mon 25 Aug (10-5). Adm £8, chd free. Purchase ticket in advance or at the gate on the day.** Home-made teas. **Visits also by arrangement 17 Mar to 2 Oct for groups of 12 to 30. No private group visits on Thursdays.**
Gardens of 3½ acres set around 1832 Regency house (not open). The front is formally laid out with topiary, wide lawn, mixed border and contemporary water sculpture. The rear features new and mature trees from C19, herbaceous borders, water garden and stunning uninterrupted views of the North Downs. The Japanese garden with waterfall and pond leads to a large copse, stream, treehouse and stumpery. Each yr 2000 tulips are planted for spring as well as another 2000 snowdrops and mixed bulbs throughout the garden. WC available. Wheelchair access to front garden, but rear garden is on a slope.
♿ 🐕 ☕ 🔊

107 OLD WELL COTTAGE
High Street, Angmering, Littlehampton, BN16 4AG. Mr N Waters. *Situated nr Angmering Manor Hotel & almost adjacent to the top of Weavers Hill in the High St. Look for the 'mushroom' shape tree! On road parking only, please be mindful of residents.* **Sun 6 July (11-4). Adm £5, chd free. Tea, coffee & cake.**
⅓ acre plot featuring topiary, formal areas and perennial borders. Framed within flint walls and surrounding the C16 to C18 cottage (not open) in the Angmering Conservation Area. Splendid holm oak and bay topiary trees, large espalier apple trees and a small kitchen garden. Lots of purples, whites and pinks.
☕ 🔊

108 NEW OLIVERS
Potts Lane, Pulborough, RH20 2AH. Mandy Faulkner. *Potts Ln is a pedestrian lane off Lower St (A283) in Pulborough. The entrance is between two houses next to T-lights. Parking in Lower St public car park almost opp Potts Ln.* **Sat 17 May (11-5). Combined adm with The Cottage £9, chd free. Pre-booking essential, please visit www.ngs.org.uk for information & booking. Home-made teas. Two hour timed slots at 11am, 1pm & 3pm.**
Olivers is a small cottage garden with old stone walls on two of its boundaries. The focus has been on simple planting to encourage wildlife where no chemicals are used. There are two ponds, one for fish and the other for the benefit of frogs and dragonflies. Where possible eco-friendly structures have been used to support climbing roses and clematis. A relaxing environment.
✿ ☕ 🔊

109 NEW THE ORCHARD
Dyke Lane, Poynings, Brighton, BN45 7AA. Ms Nigs Digby. *Take A281 off the A23 heading towards Henfield. 1m along, you will see signs for Poynings. Go straight into the village & look for signs to the garden. Street parking only. Very short drive to the other garden opening.* **Thur 12 June, Thur 17 July (11-5). Combined adm with Woodlands £7, chd free. Pre-booking essential, please visit www.ngs.org.uk for information & booking. Home-made teas. Two hour timed slots at 11am, 1pm & 3pm.**
This is a new garden, planted in autumn 2023 after finishing a new build on site. We have soft, prairie planting in the front and a rambling, informal cottage garden around the back, with a cutting bed, soft fruit, vegetables and a small natural pond. Stunning views of the South Downs.
♿ ☕ 🔊

110 ORCHARD COTTAGE
Boars Head Road, Boarshead, Crowborough, TN6 3GR. Jane & Ray Collins, 01892 653444, collinsjane1@hotmail.co.uk. *6m S of Tunbridge Wells, off A26. At T-junction, do not follow SatNav. Instead, turn L down dead end.* Orchard Cottage is at the bottom of the hill on LHS. **Fri 30, Sat 31 May, Sun 1 June (10-4). Adm £6, chd free. Tea, coffee & cake.** Visits also by arrangement 14 Apr to 30 June.
Mature 1½ acre plantaholic's garden with a large variety of trees and shrubs, perennials and bulbs, many unusual. Gardened organically. Mainly colour themed beds, planted informally. Small woodland, meadow and deep pond to encourage wildlife. Kitchen garden with raised beds. Hardy Plant Society member. Access via gravel drive with wide, gently sloping grass paths suitable for wheelchairs and mobility scooters. Drop-off in drive by prior arrangement.
♿ 🐕 ✿ 🚗 ☕ 🔊

111 PARSONAGE FARM
Kirdford, nr Billingshurst, RH14 0NH. David & Victoria Thomas. *5m NE of Petworth. Located between Petworth & Wisborough Green in the village of Kirdford. Opp side of the road from the turn to Plaistow. Use postcode RH14 0NG to reach Plaistow turning.* **Fri 20 June, Sun 7 Sept (2-6). Adm £10, chd free. Home-made teas.**
Major garden in beautiful setting developed over 30 yrs with fruit theme and many unusual plants. Formally laid out on grand scale with long vistas. C18 walled garden with borders in apricot, orange, scarlet and crimson. Topiary walk, pleached lime allée, tulip tree avenue, rose borders and vegetable garden with trained fruit. Turf amphitheatre, autumn shrubbery, yew cloisters and jungle walk. Wheelchair access to the whole garden with one step that can be avoided. Accessible WC.
♿ 🚗 ☕ 🔊

The National Garden Scheme donated over £3.5 million to our nursing and health beneficiaries from money raised at gardens open in 2024.

Meadowside

112 PEELERS RETREAT
70 Ford Road, Arundel, BN18 9EX.
Tony & Lizzie Gilks, 01903 884981,
timespan70@tiscali.co.uk. *1m S of Arundel. At Chichester r'about take exit to Ford & Bognor Regis onto Ford Rd. We are situated just before Maxwell Rd on the RHS.* **Sun 30 Mar, Sat 5, Tue 15, Sat 19, Tue 29 Apr, Sat 3, Tue 13, Sat 17, Tue 27, Sat 31 May, Tue 10, Sat 14 June, Tue 8, Sat 12, Tue 22 July (2-5). Adm £5, chd free. Home-made teas.** Visits also by arrangement 30 Mar to 28 Sept for groups of 5 to 28.
This inspirational space is a delight with permanent gazebos and comfortable seating to sit and relax, enjoying delicious teas. When cold we light the fire for our guests. Interlocking beds packed with year-round colour and scent, shaded by specimen trees, inventive water features and a range of quirky woodland sculptures.
🐕 🚗 ☕ 🔊

113 NEW PEKES MANOR
Nash Street, Golden Cross, Hailsham, BN27 4AD. Kildare & Sarah Bourke-Borrowes, www.pekesmanor.com. *5m from Hailsham, 1m E of A22 at Golden Cross. Turn off A22 at Golden Cross signed Gun Hill onto Nash St. In ¾m at triangle, L is Muddles Green & sharp R is Pekes. What3words*

app: pampering.ripen.toward. **Sun 10 Aug (2-5). Adm £6, chd free. Home-made teas.**
Pekes garden was created in 1908, surrounding a pre-Tudor Manor House (not open) and inc several distinct gardens. Spanning approx 2 acres the garden features an ancient pond, a formal front garden, large topiary lawn, rose border, column garden, and a walled garden. Pekes is a hospitality venue, so we aim to have something of interest in the gardens year-round.
☕ 🔊

114 PEMBURY HOUSE
Ditchling Road, Clayton, BN6 9PH. Nick & Jane Baker, www.pemburyhouse.co.uk. *6m N of Brighton, off A23. No parking at house. Car park opp church on Underhill Ln off A273. Height restrictor. Follow signs across playing field to footpath by railway to back gate. Good public transport. Avoid walking on road.* **Every Thur and Fri 13 Feb to 7 Mar (10.30-3.30). Adm £12, chd free. Home-made teas inc. Pre-booking essential, please visit www.ngs.org.uk for information & booking. Timed slots at 10.30am & 2pm.**
Depending on the vagaries of the season, hellebores and snowdrops are at their best in February and March. It is a country garden, tidy but not manicured. New work always

going on. Winding paths give a choice of walks through 3 acres of garden, which is in and enjoys views of the South Downs National Park. Suitable footwear, macs and winter woollies advised. A German visitor observed 'this is the perfect woodland garden'. Year-round interest. Plants for sale. Cash ideally.
🐕 ✱ ☕ 🔊

115 PENNS IN THE ROCKS
Groombridge, Tunbridge Wells, TN3 9PA. Mr & Mrs Hugh Gibson, www.pennsintherocks.co.uk. *7m SW of Tunbridge Wells. On B2188 Groombridge to Crowborough road, just S of Xrd to Withyham. For SatNav use TN6 1UX which takes you to the white drive gates, through which you should enter the property.* **Sun 13 Apr, Sun 11 May, Sun 3 Aug (2-6). Adm £7.50, chd free. Home-made teas. Cash only on the day.**
Large garden with spectacular outcrop of rocks, 140 million yrs old. Lake, C18 temple and woods. Daffodils, bluebells, azaleas, magnolia and tulips. Old walled garden with herbaceous borders, roses and shrubs. Stone sculptures by Richard Strachey. Part C18 house (not open) once owned by William Penn of Pennsylvania. Restricted wheelchair access. No disabled WC.
♿ ✱ ☕

SUSSEX 541

116 1 PEST COTTAGE
Carron Lane, Midhurst, GU29 9LF. Jennifer Lewin. *W edge of Midhurst behind Carron Lane Cemetery. Free parking at recreation ground at top of Carron Ln. Short walk on woodland track to garden, please follow signs.* **Fri 13, Sun 15 June (2-5). Adm £5, chd free.**
This edge of woodland, architect's garden of approx ¾ acre sits on a sloping sandy site. Designed to support biodiversity, a series of outdoor spaces connected with informal paths through lightly managed areas, creates a secret world tucked into the surrounding common land. The chosen planting palette is being adapted in response to changing weather patterns. Exhibition of architect's projects.

117 NEW PIGEON MEAD HOUSE
Earnley Manor Close, Earnley, Chichester, PO20 7JQ. Mr Adrian & Mrs Rachel Dadds. *5½ m SE of Chichester. What3words app: jots. gadget.toasted. 2 min walk from C13 Earnley Church.* **Sat 17, Sun 18 May (11-4). Adm £6, chd free. Pre-booking essential, please visit www.ngs.org.uk for information & booking. Tea, coffee & cake.**
A ⅓ acre plot about ¾ mile from the coast. South facing rear garden with a formal structure and informal mixed planting. Features inc a greenhouse, a formal lawn surrounded by beds and espaliered crab apples, a small labyrinth, and a shaded area. Family friendly space with places to sit and enjoy the garden. Front garden inc wildlife pond, a small meadow area, and a lovely, established magnolia tree.

118 PINE TREE COTTAGE
32 Mount Close, Pound Hill, Crawley, RH10 7EF. Zena & Barry Everest. *2m S of Gatwick. M23, J10 A264 to East Grinstead, 2nd exit at r'about, 4th exit at r'about to A220 Maidenbower, Three Bridges. 2nd exit at r'about, L at T-lights, 2nd L, 3rd L & L at T-junction. Park on road after house.* **Sat 21, Sun 22 June (11-4). Adm £5, chd free. Home-made teas.**
A multi-levelled ¼ acre plot divided into four distinct areas. All are planted with many colourful and unusual shrubs and perennials to complement our Sussex cottage. The front garden is enhanced with a fine-leafed lawn. The pond area is planted with exuberant and colourful plants. The 25ft stepped pergola, clothed with wisteria and clematis, sits between the pond and the terraced top garden. Partial wheelchair access.

119 PITFIELD BARN CUT FLOWER FARM & STUDIO
Chalkers Lane, Hurstpierpoint, nr Hassocks, BN6 9LR. Mrs Emma Martin, www.pitfieldbarn.co.uk. *Approach from B2117, Cuckfield Rd, turn into Chalkers Ln & we are the gate on the L just past the 30mph sign, close to Hurstpierpoint College.* **Sun 10 Aug (12-4). Adm £6, chd free. Light refreshments.**
We are passionate about British cut flowers at this working flower farm. We sow, grow and harvest seasonal, British cut flowers without chemicals or pesticides. Our seedlings are grown in peat free compost. We hand cut our flowers to order from what is available depending on the season. You can learn about the British flower market, how the garden works and our philosophy on Emma's tours. A converted barn and studio where various flower, art and craft workshops take place and café. Freshly cut bunches of seasonal flowers, local produce and gifts for sale. Wheelchair access over path from barn to second field and cut grass to other areas.

120 ♦ THE PRIEST HOUSE
North Lane, West Hoathly, RH19 4PP. Sussex Archaeological Society, 01342 810479, priest@sussexpast.co.uk, www.sussexpast.co.uk. *4m SW of East Grinstead, 6m E of Crawley. In centre of West Hoathly village, nr church & The Cat Inn. Car parks in village.* **For NGS: Sat 24 May, Sat 28 June (10.30-5.30). Adm £3, chd free. Tea, coffee & cake. For other opening times and information, please phone, email or visit garden website.**
C15 timber framed farmhouse with cottage garden on acid clay. Large collection of culinary and medicinal herbs in a small formal herb garden and mixed with perennials and shrubs in exuberant borders. Long established yew topiary and espalier apple trees provide structural elements. Traditional fernery and stumpery, recently enlarged with a small, secluded shrubbery and gravel garden. Be sure to visit the fascinating Priest House Museum, adm £1 for NGS visitors.

121 9 PUTTOCK WAY
Billingshurst, RH14 9ZJ. Emma & Simon Parker. *7m SW of Horsham. From the Hilland r'about to the N of Billingshurst, head E along the A272 (Hilland Rd) & take the 1st R turning into the estate (Rhodes Way). Take 2nd R onto Puttock Way.* **Sun 25, Mon 26 May (11-4). Adm £5. Pre-booking essential, please visit www.ngs.org.uk for information & booking. Home-made teas.**
A very small, sloping, new build garden which has been transformed from bare heavy clay into a series of spaces with interesting hard landscaping features. An unexpected cacophony of architectural shapes and textures greets you as you walk through the gate, a true plant lover's paradise. This space shows what can be achieved in a short space of time through hard work and passion.

122 ROSE COTTAGE
50 Wannock Lane, Willingdon, Eastbourne, BN20 9SD. Chris & Nick Ireland. *Between Eastbourne & Polegate on the A2270. From Eastbourne (A2270) turn L into Gorringe Valley Rd, at give way turn R. From Polegate turn R into Gorringe Valley Rd.* **Sun 6 July (1-5). Adm £5, chd free.**
The 1930s cottage nestles at the foot of the South Downs, and the 1066 trail starts nearby. This beautiful west facing, 200ft x 55ft rear garden has a wide selection of shrubs, herbaceous and perennials, plus trees. There are two small fish ponds, vegetable plot and greenhouses. Little nooks and seating areas provide interest and a sunny patio. There is interest for every type of gardener. Local cafés nearby.

In 2024, we celebrated 40 years of continuous funding for Macmillan Cancer Support equating to more than £19.5 million.

123 NEW 8 RUSHY MEAD
West Broyle, Chichester, PO19 3FW. Heather Millican, 07732 397756, heather.millican@btinternet.com. *Parking only available in car park adjacent to r'about on B2178 & entrance to Minerva Heights development. Walk through car park to High Meadow & onto Rushy Mead (100m).* **Sat 7, Sun 15 June (11-4.30). Adm £5, chd free. Pre-booking essential, please visit www.ngs.org.uk for information & booking. Tea, coffee & cake.** Visits also by arrangement 17 May to 26 July for groups of 6 to 15.
Created from scratch on a new build development this space has been transformed into a haven for bees, butterflies and birds. From an uninspiring turfed area it is now full of colour and interest. After attending a garden design course at nearby West Dean College, the owners created their own landscaping and planting plans, and within two yrs they have seen a remarkable transformation.

No steps to access the garden. While some paths are shingle and may be difficult, most of the garden can be enjoyed from the paved patio.

124 RYMANS
Appledram Lane South, Apuldram, Chichester, PO20 7EG. Zarina Chatwin, rymans.garden@gmail.com. *1m S of Chichester. If coming from A27, exit at Fishbourne r'about, following signs to Fishbourne. Take 1st L onto Appledram Lane South, house is 1m S.* **Sat 12, Sun 13 Apr, Sun 22 June, Sun 14 Sept (2-5). Adm £6, chd free. Tea, coffee & cake at St Mary's Church, Apuldram.** Visits also by arrangement 1 Apr to 20 Sept for groups of up to 25.
Walled and other gardens surrounding C15 stone house (not open). Featuring bulbs, flowering shrubs, roses, ponds, and potager, and many unusual and rare trees and shrubs. In late spring the wisterias are spectacular. Hybrid musk roses fill the walled garden in June and in late summer the garden is filled with dahlias, sedums, late roses, sages and Japanese anemones.

125 SAFFRONS
Holland Road, Steyning, BN44 3GJ. Tim Melton & Bernardean Carey, 07850 343516, tim.melton@btinternet.com, www.thetransplantedgardener.uk. *6m NE of Worthing. Exit r'about on A283 at S end of Steyning bypass into Clays Hill Rd. 1st R into Goring Rd, 4th L into Holland Rd. Park in Goring Rd & Holland Rd.* **Fri 4, Fri 11 July (12-5). Combined adm with Lynwood £8, chd free. Home-made teas.** Visits also by arrangement 16 June to 31 July for groups of 8 to 30.
Planted with an artist's eye for contrasts and complementary colours. Vibrant late summer flower beds of salvias, eryngiums, agapanthus, grasses and lilies attract bees and butterflies. A broad

Driftwood

lawn is surrounded by borders with maples, rhododendrons, hydrangeas and mature trees interspersed with ferns and grasses. The large fruit cage and vegetable beds comprise the productive area of the garden. One level garden with good access, except in very wet conditions.
&. 🐕 ✽ 🍵

126 ♦ ST MARY'S HOUSE GARDENS
Bramber, BN44 3WE. Roger Linton & Peter Thorogood, 01903 816205, info@stmarysbramber.co.uk, www.stmarysbramber.co.uk. *1m E of Steyning. 10m NW of Brighton in Bramber village, off A283.* **For NGS: Fri 27, Sat 28 June (2-5). Adm £8.50, chd free. Home-made teas. For other opening times and information, please phone, email or visit garden website.**
5 acres inc formal topiary, large prehistoric *Ginkgo biloba* and magnificent *Magnolia grandiflora* around enchanting timber-framed medieval house (not open for NGS). Victorian Secret Gardens inc splendid 140ft fruit wall with pineapple pits, Rural Museum, Terracotta Garden, Jubilee Rose Garden, King's Garden and circular Poetry Garden. Woodland walk and Landscape Water Garden. In the heart of the South Downs National Park. WC facilities. Wheelchair access with level paths throughout.
&. ✽ 🚗 🍵))

127 SANDHILL FARM HOUSE
Nyewood Road, Rogate, Petersfield, GU31 5HU. Rosemary Alexander. *4m SE of Petersfield. From A272 Xrds in Rogate take road S signed Nyewood & Harting. Follow road for approx 1m over small bridge. Sandhill Farm House on R, over cattle grid.* **Sun 9 Feb (12-4); Sat 12, Sun 13 Apr (1-4). Adm £8, chd free. Home-made teas.**
Front and rear gardens broken up into garden rooms inc small kitchen garden. Front garden with small woodland area, planted with early spring flowering shrubs, ferns and bulbs. White and green garden, large leaf border and terraced area. Rear garden has rose borders, small decorative vegetable garden, red border and grasses border. Snowdrop day on Sun 9 Feb. Home of author and principal of The English Gardening School.
🐕 ✽ D 🍵

128 SAYERLAND HOUSE
Sayerland Lane, Polegate, BN26 6QP. Penny & Kevin Jenden. *2m S of Hailsham, 1m N of Polegate. At Cophall r'about on A27 take A22, turn L at 1st turning (100yds). Follow through Bay Tree Ln, turn sharp L into Sayerland Ln. From N on A22 turn L into Bay Tree Ln before r'about.* **Sun 6 July (2-5.30). Adm £6, chd free. Home-made teas.**
Romantic, rambling, 5 acre garden surrounding listed Tudor house (not open). Several distinct garden areas all with an emphasis on a mix of annual and perennial naturalistic planting with many native plants and self seeders. A walled garden, rose garden, organic kitchen garden and a wild woodland area with many mature shrubs and trees inc a tulip tree and a very large fringe tree.
✽ 🍵))

GROUP OPENING

129 NEW SEAFORD GARDENS NORTH
Signed from the A259, gardens are located N of this road. Tickets & maps available at each garden. NB Not a walking trail. **Sun 1 June (12-5). Combined adm £8, chd free. Sun 6 July (12-5). Combined adm £7, chd free. Home-made teas at Whitehouse, Cosy Cottage & 129 Princess Drive.**

5 CLEMENTINE AVENUE
BN25 2UU. Joanne Davis.
Open on all dates

101 CLEMENTINE AVENUE
BN25 2XG. Mr John & Mrs Vanessa Kelly.
Open on all dates

COSY COTTAGE
69 Firle Road, BN25 2JA. Ernie & Carol Arnold, 07763 196343, ernie.whitecrane@gmail.com, www.facebook.com/CosyCottage69Garden.
Open on Sun 1 June
Visits also by arrangement 7 Apr to 30 June.

MADEHURST
67 Firle Road, BN25 2JA. Martin & Palo.
Open on all dates

NEW 129 PRINCESS DRIVE
BN25 2QT. Sue & Darrel Topp.
Open on all dates

NEW WHITEHOUSE
130 Firle Road, BN25 2JD. Jayne & Fred Bass.
Open on all dates

Six gardens open on the 1 June and five gardens open on the 6 July, see dates for each garden. Cosy Cottage, a garden over three levels with ponds, flowers, vegetables, and shrubs. Madehurst, a garden on different levels with mature planting. 5 Clementine Avenue, a garden over several levels with agave and succulents and great views over the downs. 101 Clementine Avenue, newly developing garden beautifully planted to attract wildlife, wide selection of hardy perennials, ferns, and hostas. 129 Princess Drive, new in 2025, inc ponds, small woodland area, herbaceous borders, covered seating area and colourful seasonal pots. Whitehouse, new in 2025, a large garden and main tea venue for the trail. Mature trees, herbaceous borders, gravel garden, herb bed, fruit cage, raised vegetable plot, plus wild area with apple trees. Plants for sale at Cosy Cottage on 1 June only.
🐕 ✽ 🍵))

Our 2024 donation to The Queen's Nursing Institute now helps support over 3,000 Queen's Nurses working in the community in England, Wales, Northern Ireland, the Channel Islands and the Isle of Man.

SUSSEX 543

GROUP OPENING

130 NEW SEAFORD GARDENS SOUTH
All gardens are signed off the A259. Six gardens are S of A259. Cupani & Allotments are N of A259. See individual entries for detailed directions. **Sun 22 June (11-5). Combined adm £9, chd free. Sun 13 July (12-5). Combined adm £8, chd free. Home-made teas at 34 Chyngton Road. Ice cream & cold drinks at Cupani. Tea & biscuits at 53 Southdown Road.**

BURFORD
Cuckmere Road, BN25 4DE.
Chris Kilsby.
Open on all dates

34 CHYNGTON ROAD
BN25 4HP. Maggie Wearmouth & Richard Morland.
Open on all dates

CUPANI GARDEN
8 Sandgate Close, BN25 3LL.
Dr Denis Jones & Ms Aideen Jones OBE.
Open on all dates
(See separate entry)

8 DOWNS ROAD
BN25 4QL. Mr Phil & Mrs Julie Avery.
Open on all dates

LAVENDER COTTAGE
69 Steyne Road, BN25 1QH.
Christina & Steve Machan.
Open on all dates

SEAFORD ALLOTMENTS
Sutton Drove, BN25 3NQ.
Peter Sudell.
Open on Sun 22 June

SEAFORD COMMUNITY GARDEN
East Street, BN25 1AD.
Seaford Community Garden.
Open on Sun 22 June

NEW 53 SOUTHDOWN ROAD
BN25 4PG. Eileen & Julian Counsell.
Open on all dates

Eight gardens open on 22 June and six gardens open on 13 July, see dates for each garden. Burford, a garden surrounded by mature trees, beds with a variety of herbaceous perennials inc iris. Vegetables, and an auricula theatre. 34 Chyngton Road, a mature garden, naturalistic planting, and colourful themed herbaceous borders. Fruit and vegetable area. Cupani, see individual entry. 8 Downs Road is a well-planted front garden that leads to a back garden with beautifully planted deep beds and large drifts of herbaceous perennials. Lawn, pond, vegetables, and shrubbery. Lavender Cottage, a flint walled garden with cottage, coastal and kitchen beds. Climb steps and enjoy views of Seaford Head. Relaxed planting to attract wildlife. Seaford Allotments has 189 plots with a wide range of planting and 100 yrs of cultivation. Wildlife meadow. Seaford Community Garden has a delightful walled garden with polytunnel, vegetable, flower beds and a pond. New for 2025, 53 Southdown Road, with a wrap-around maturing garden. Climbers, mature trees, and shrubs. Beds of perennial and annuals provide colour throughout.

131 SEDGWICK PARK HOUSE
Sedgwick Park, Horsham,
RH13 6QQ. Clare Davison,
01403 734930,
clare@sedgwickpark.com,
www.sedgwickpark.co.uk. *1m S of Horsham off A281. A281 towards Cowfold, Hillier Garden Center on R, then 1st R into Sedgwick Ln. At end of lane enter north gates of Sedgwick Park or west gate via Broadwater Ln, from Copsale or Southwater, off A24.* **Visits by arrangement Apr to June for groups of 10+. Home-made teas.**
Set in the grounds of Grade II listed Ernest George mansion, there are amazing views of South Downs, Chanctonbury Ring and Lancing College. Formal gardens by Harold Peto featuring 20 interlocking ponds, impressive water garden known as The White Sea. Large Horsham stone terraces and lawns look out onto clipped yew hedging and specimen trees. Herbaceous area and turf labyrinth. Some areas have been left to nature. Garden has uneven paving, slippery when wet, unfenced ponds and swimming pool.

132 SELHURST PARK
Halnaker, Chichester,
PO18 0LZ. Richard & Sarah Green, 01243 839310, mail@selhurstparkhouse.com. *8m S of Petworth. 4m N of Chichester on A285.* **Visits by arrangement 1 June to 8 Aug for groups of 10 to 30. Home-made teas.**
Come and explore the varied gardens surrounding a beautiful Georgian flint house (not open), approached by a chestnut avenue. The flint walled garden has a mature 160ft herbaceous border with unusual planting along with rose, hellebore and hydrangea beds. Pool garden with exotic palms and grasses divided from a formal knot and herb garden by espalier apples. Kitchen and walled fruit garden. Wheelchair access to walled garden, partial access to other areas.

133 NEW SHALFORD HOUSE
Square Drive, Kingsley Green,
GU27 3LW. Mr Paul Morrow & Mr Robert Beard. *2m S of Haslemere. A sharp narrow turning directly off from A286 (please take care). Heading S, Square Dr is at brow of hill to the L. Turn L again after ¼ m & follow road to R at bottom of hill.* **Sun 27 July, Sun 24 Aug (1-5.30). Combined adm with The Beeches £8, chd free. Home-made teas.**
A garden designer and plantsman's garden, set in 40 acres, with 10 acres of well maintained gardens created over 30 yrs. Featuring various herbaceous borders, ponds, a waterfall lake, and a 120 metre rill. Walled garden with large Alitex greenhouse with interesting plants inc acers, hostas, *Cornus kousa* and hydrangeas, all within a beautiful setting. A further 30 acres with arboretum and lake is perfect for picnics. Flat gravel areas with York stone terrace around the house with access to the main sloping lawns via gently sloping paths. Disabled WC.

134 ♦ SHEFFIELD PARK AND GARDEN
Uckfield, TN22 3QX. National Trust, 01825 790231,
sheffieldpark@nationaltrust.org.uk, www.nationaltrust.org.uk/sheffieldpark. *10m S of East Grinstead. 5m NW of Uckfield; E of A275.* **For NGS: Tue 6 May (10-4.30). Adm £16.15, chd £8. Light refreshments. For other opening times and information, please phone, email or visit garden website.**
Magnificent, landscaped garden laid out in C18 by Capability Brown and Humphry Repton covering 120 acres (40 hectares). Further development in the early yrs of this century by its owner Arthur G Soames. Centrepiece is original lakes with many rare trees

and shrubs. Beautiful at all times of the yr, but noted for its spring and autumn colours. National Collection of Ghent azaleas. Large number of champion trees, 87 in total. Light refreshments available in the Coach House Café and The Shant. Last entry 4.30pm. Garden largely accessible for wheelchairs, please call for information.

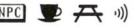

& 🐾 ✿ 🚌 NPC ☕ 🪑 »))

135 SHEPHERDS COTTAGE
Milberry Lane, Stoughton, Chichester, PO18 9JJ. Jackie & Alan Sherling, 07795 388047, milberrylane@gmail.com, www.instagram.com/drjackieblackman. 9½m NW Chichester. Off B2146, next village after Walderton. Cottage is nr telephone box & beside St Mary's Church. No parking in lane beside house. **Visits by arrangement Apr to Aug for groups of 10 to 30. Adm £15 pp inc home-made teas.** A compact terraced garden using the borrowed landscape of Kingley Vale in the South Downs. The south facing flint stone cottage (not open) is surrounded by a Purbeck stone terrace and numerous individually planted and styled seating areas. A small orchard under planted with meadow, lawns, topiary yew hedges, amelanchier, cercis and drifts of wind grass provide structure and year-round interest. Many novel design ideas and unusual perennial combinations suitable for a small garden. Ample seating throughout the garden to enjoy the views.

✿ D ☕

136 NEW SHORTS FARM
The Street, Nutbourne, Pulborough, RH20 2HE. Sarah & John Browne. 2m E of Pulborough. Take A283 from Pulborough towards Storrington. Turn L down West Chiltington Rd then L down Nutbourne Rd. Go along The Street, pass The Rising Sun pub. Follow parking directions from a volunteer. **Thur 5, Sat 7 June (12-5). Combined adm with The Old Manor £8, chd free. Home-made teas.** A ½ acre, classic cottage garden set around a C15 house of archaeological interest (not open). A thatched summerhouse, surrounded by herbaceous borders and lawned areas, separated by beds of perennial planting interspersed with occasional trees. There is a range of colour from early summer into late autumn, with some areas left wild. The garden has become more nature friendly over the yrs.

☕ »))

137 THE SHRUBBERY
140 Barnham Road, Barnham, PO22 0EH. John & Ros Woodhead, johnrosw@sky.com. Between Arundel & Chichester. At A27 Fontwell junction take A29 road to Bognor Regis. Turn L at next r'about onto Barnham Rd. After ½m the garden is 40 metres after the speed camera. **Sat 31 May, Sun 1 June (10-4). Combined adm with The Old Rectory £6, chd free. Home-made teas. Visits also by arrangement 2 June to 6 June for groups of 6 to 20.** A garden of ideas in a ¼ acre plot of mature trees, shrubs, wild flower lawn, roses, agapanthus, and dahlias leading to a walled back garden of mixed colourful borders, soft fruit, sculptures and a large collection of hostas.

& ✿ ☕ »))

Chalk Farm Flowers

138 SIENNA WOOD
Coombe Hill Road, East Grinstead, RH19 4LY. Belinda & Brian Quarendon, 07970 707015, belinda222@hotmail.com. *1m W of East Grinstead. Off B2110 East Grinstead to Turners Hill. Garden is ½m down Coombe Hill Rd on L.* **Sun 1 June (1-5). Adm £7, chd free. Tea, coffee & cake.** Visits also by arrangement May to Sept for groups of 15 to 50.
Explore our beautiful 4½ acre garden, picturesque lakeside walk and 6 acre ancient woodland. Start at the herbaceous borders surrounding the croquet lawn, through the formal rose garden to the lawns and summer borders stopping at the new Italian terrace, through the arboretum to the lake and waterfall and back past the exotic border, orchard and vegetable garden. Many unusual trees and shrubs. Possible sighting of wild deer inc white deer. Many interesting statues. Partial wheelchair access to many parts of the garden.
& ☕))

139 SKYSCAPE
46 Ainsworth Avenue, Ovingdean, Brighton, BN2 7BG. Lorna & John Davies. *From Brighton take A259 coast road E, passing Roedean School on L. Take 1st L at r'about to Greenways & 2nd R into Ainsworth Ave. Skyscape at the top on R. No. 52 bus on Sat & No. 57 on Sun.* **Sat 31 May, Sun 1 June (1-5). Adm £5, chd free. Home-made teas.**
250ft south facing rear garden on a sloping site with fantastic views of the South Downs and the sea. Garden created by owners over past 12 yrs. Orchard, flower beds, wildlife ponds and planting with bees and wildlife in mind. Full access to site via purpose built sloping path (not suitable for mobility scooters).
& 🐕 ❄ 🚗 ☕

140 SOUTH GRANGE
Quickbourne Lane, Northiam, Rye, TN31 6QY. Linda & Michael Belton, 01797 252984, belton.northiam@gmail.com. *Between A268 & A28, approx ½m E of Northiam. From Northiam centre follow Beales Ln into Quickbourne Ln, or Quickbourne Ln leaves A286 approx ½m S of A28 & A286 junction. Disabled parking at front of house.* Visits by arrangement 1 Mar to 19 Oct for groups of 5+. **Adm £6, chd free. Home-made teas.** Confirm refreshments at time of booking.

Hardy Plant Society members' garden with wide variety of trees, shrubs, perennials, grasses and pots arranged into a complex garden display for year-round colour and interest. Raised vegetable beds, wildlife pond, orchard, rose arbour, living gazebo. House roof runoff diverted to storage and pond. Small area of wild wood. An emphasis on planting for insects. We try to maintain nectar and pollen supplies and varied habitats for most of the creatures that we share the garden with, hoping that this variety will keep the garden in good heart. Home propagated plants for sale. Wheelchair access over hard paths through much of the garden, but steps up to patio and WC.
& ❄ 🚗 ☕

141 STANLEY FARM
Highfield Lane, Liphook, GU30 7LW. Bill & Emma Mills. *For SatNav please use GU30 7LN which takes you to Highfield Ln & then follow NGS signs. Track to Stanley Farm is 1m.* **Sun 4 May (12-5). Adm £5, chd free. Home-made teas.**
1 acre garden created over the last 15 yrs around an old West Sussex farmhouse (not open), sitting in the midst of its own fields and woods. The formal garden inc a kitchen garden with heated glasshouse, orchard, espaliered wall trained fruit, lawn with ha-ha and cutting garden. A motley assortment of animals inc sheep, donkeys, chickens, ducks and geese. Bluebells flourish in the woods, so feel free to bring dogs and a picnic, and take a walk after visiting the gardens. Wheelchair access via a ramp to view main part of the garden. Difficult access to woods due to muddy, uneven ground.
& 🐕 ❄ ☕))

GROUP OPENING

142 NEW STEYNING GARDENS
4m N of Shoreham by Sea. Tickets can be purchased at each garden & visited in any order. They will be signed on the day & detailed directions available on website. On-street parking. **Sat 21, Sun 22 June (10.30-5). Combined adm £8, chd free. Home-made teas at Nightingale House. Cashless payments at Brambletye only.**

BRAMBLETYE
25 Maudlyn Park Way, BN44 3PT. Nicola & Paul Middleton.

NIGHTINGALE HOUSE
Twittenside, BN44 3TW. Lynne Broome.

15 PENLANDS RISE
BN44 3PJ. Patsy Walton.

Steyning is a lively market town on the edge of the South Downs, home to many artists and crafts people. The three gardens open are all very different. Brambletye is a south facing garden designed with prairie effect to attract birds and pollinators, planted with bulbs, shrubs, herbaceous perennials and roses and a small sunken area of raised beds for vegetables and herbs. Nightingale House has a recently designed cottage style garden with both perennials and annuals. There is an attractive greenhouse and a bespoke metal screen covered in roses and clematis. 15 Penlands Rise is a small cottage garden which has evolved into a series of borders and island beds with narrow paths in between. There are roses, clematis, many salvias and perennials and a collection of over 100 pots some with hydrangeas but the majority with a colourful mix of annuals and tender plants.
☕))

143 STROODS
Herons Ghyll, Uckfield, TN22 4DB. Geraldine Ogilvy. *Located on A26 opp Clay Studio.* **Sun 1 June (12-4.30). Adm £7, chd free. Home-made teas.**
Nestled in the beautiful hills of Sussex, the garden is a peaceful space where ancient trees, an orchard and olive grove team carefully with curated herbaceous borders and meandering wildflower meadows, all attracting bees, butterflies and birds. The walled kitchen garden delivers delicious, traditional vegetables, embroidered with flowers and shrubs, plus the occasional wandering chicken.
& ☕))

144 SULLINGTON OLD RECTORY
Sullington Lane, Storrington, Pulborough, RH20 4AE. Oliver & Mala Haarmann. Jack Bryant, Head Gardener, jack@sullingtonoldrectory.com. *Travelling S on A24 take 3rd exit on Washington r'about. Proceed to Xrds on A283 for Sullington Ln & Water Ln. Take L onto Sullington Ln & garden located at the top.*

SUSSEX 547

Tue 15, Wed 16 July (9.30-5). Adm £10, chd free. Pre-booking essential, please visit www.ngs.org.uk for information & booking. Home-made teas. Two hour timed slots at 9.30am, 12pm & 2.30pm.
With a backdrop of stunning views of the South Downs, the naturalistic style of this beautiful country garden sits perfectly into the surrounding landscape. The rarely opened garden inc a potager, orchard, herb garden, mature trees and shrubs, South African themed border, newly extended large perennial borders, a profusion of grasses and experimental planting in the moist meadows. A range of home-made cakes, biscuits and light snacks, along with fresh coffee, a variety of teas and home-made apple juice. Head Gardener will be available for any Q&As. Wheelchair access to most areas.

145 NEW SWALLOW LODGE
St Leonard's Park, Horsham, RH13 6EG. Kathryn Shackleton. *E side of Horsham. What3words app: officials.spirit.chill. Please arrive promptly for your timed visit. Parking very limited, please ensure that you pre-book. Swallow Lodge is on R at the very end of Hampers Ln.* **Sat 31 May, Sat 7 June (12-5.30). Adm £5, chd free. Pre-booking essential, please visit www.ngs.org.uk for information & booking. Tea, coffee & cake. Timed slots at 12pm, 2pm & 4pm.**
Small rural and charming garden surrounded by fields, focusing on roses and delphiniums with a large cottage border and vegetable garden.

146 NEW TALMA
58 Pollards Drive, Horsham, RH13 5HH. Mr Mark & Mrs Susan Watts. *1m from Horsham town centre. 10-15 min walk from station. From Horsham Stn over railway bridge, 3rd exit at r'about onto B2195 Harwood Rd, 1st R into Stirling Way, then 1st L to Talma, 58 Pollards Dr.* **Sun 8 June, Sun 20 July (2-6). Adm £6, chd free. Tea, coffee & cake.**
Talma is a beautiful 1/3 acre garden which is in four parts. The front wild garden leads into a pretty cottage style area with small paths and little magical woodland walk. The main lawn has a gazebo and cutting border with a little gate going through to a small shady vegetable plot. Many surprises greet you as you explore this charming oasis. Wheelchair access restricted to the main lawn.

147 TERWICK HOUSE
Rogate, Petersfield, GU31 5BY. Mrs Fiona Dix. *2m N of Rogate village on road to Chithurst. Approx 1m E of Tullecombe Xrds on RHS. Roadside parking.* **Sun 4, Mon 5 May (2-5). Adm £6, chd free. Home-made teas.**
Wild woodland garden planted for spring interest some 40 yrs ago by plant collectors of rhododendron, azalea, camellia and acer, along winding steep paths to the south of the house. Notable garden for the extensive range of rhododendron cultivars, rare and unusual trees and shrubs. There is a collection of *Rhododendron yakushimanum* among many others; small pinetum and many specialist trees. Herbaceous planting is taking shape around the house (not open). Small potager garden off front driveway.

148 THAKEHAM PLACE FARM
The Street, Thakeham, Pulborough, RH20 3EP. Mr & Mrs T Binnington. *3m N of Storrington. The farm is at the E end of The Street, where it turns into Crays Ln. Follow signs down farm drive to Thakeham Place.* **Thur 24, Sun 27 July (2-5). Combined adm with Cumberland House £10, chd free. Tea, coffee & cake.**
Set in the middle of a working dairy farm, the garden has evolved over the last 35 yrs. Taking advantage of its sunny position on free draining greensand, the borders are full of sun loving plants and grasses with a more formal area surrounding the farmhouse (not open). In 2024 a new natural pond has been created in the wilder area of the garden to encourage wildlife.

149 TIDEBROOK MANOR
Tidebrook, Wadhurst, TN5 6PD. Edward Flint, Head Gardener. *Between Wadhurst & Mayfield. From Wadhurst take B2100 towards Mark Cross, L at Best Beech Ln, downhill past church on R, then take drive on L. From Mayfield take Coggins Mill Ln, follow for 2 1/2 m to Tidebrook, take drive on R.* **Sun 1 June, Sun 21 Sept (11-4.30). Adm £8, chd free.**
A welcome return for this beautiful 4 acre country garden developed over the last 20 yrs with outstanding views of the Sussex countryside. In the Arts and Crafts tradition, the garden features large mixed borders, intimate courtyards, meadows, hydrangea walk, kitchen garden with raised beds, a willow plat and a wild woodland garden. A lively and stimulating garden throughout the yr.

150 TOWN PLACE
Ketches Lane, Freshfield, Sheffield Park, RH17 7NR. Anthony & Maggie McGrath, 01825 790221, mcgrathsussex@hotmail.com, www.townplacegarden.org.uk. *5m E of Haywards Heath. From A275 turn W at Sheffield Green into Ketches Ln for Lindfield. 1 3/4 m on L.* **Sun 8, Wed 11, Wed 18, Sun 22, Sun 29 June, Sun 6 July (2-5). Adm £8, chd free.** Visits also by arrangement 9 June to 5 July.
A stunning 3 acre garden with a growing international reputation for the quality of its design, planting and gardening. Set round a C17 Sussex farmhouse (not open), the garden has over 400 roses, herbaceous borders, herb garden, white garden, topiary inspired by the sculptures of Henry Moore, an 800 yr old oak, potager, and a unique ruined Priory Church and Cloisters in hornbeam. Sorry, no dogs allowed, and no refreshments available. Picnics welcome. There are steps, but all areas can be viewed from a wheelchair.

48,000 people affected by cancer were reached by Maggie's centres supported by the National Garden Scheme over the last 12 months.

151 WADHURST PARK
Riseden Road, Wadhurst, TN5 6NT. Nicky Browne, wadhurstpark.co.uk. *6m SE of Tunbridge Wells. Turn R along Mayfield Ln, off B2099 at NW end of Wadhurst. Then turn L at Tidebrook Road & L at Riseden Rd.* **Fri 13, Sat 14 June (10-4). Adm £6, chd free. Home-made teas inc vegan & gluten-free cakes.**
The naturalistic gardens designed by Tom Stuart-Smith, created on a C19 site, situated within an 800 hectare estate managed organically to enhance its wildlife, cultural heritage and beauty. The gardens invite the wider landscape in with native woodland trees and ground cover, meadows and hedgerows, framing views to hills and lake. We strive to garden with a greater respect for the natural world. Features inc restored Victorian orangery, naturalistic gardens planted with mainly native species, meadows, potager and brownfield site. Due to uneven paths, please wear sensible shoes. Sorry no dogs. Wheelchair access to main features of garden. Some uneven surfaces over grass, cobbles and steps.

152 NEW 2 WANDERDOWN WAY
Ovingdean, Brighton, BN2 7BX. John Conlon & Chris Judge. *Located in Ovingdean village, E of Brighton, approx 5m from the city centre. By car A259 (E) from Brighton, or B2123 (Falmer Rd) from the A27. Bus No. 52 from Brighton alighting Ovingdean Stores, or No. 2 from Brighton alighting Ovingdean Rd.* **Sat 19, Sun 20 July (10-4). Adm £5, chd free. Tea, coffee & cake.**
A relatively new garden created almost from scratch five seasons ago. Adjacent to the South Downs National Park it is primarily a coastal chalk garden with wonderful downland views to the sea beyond. The planting reflects the location with an emphasis on colour and leaf form to create floral displays, which are showcased against a backdrop of subtropical plants and sculptural forms.

153 WARNHAM PARK
Robin Hood Lane, Warnham, Horsham, RH12 3RP. Mrs Caroline Lucas. *NW of Horsham. Turn in off A24 end of Robin Hood Ln, turn immed R by the large poster & follow signs.* **Thur 15 May, Sun 22 June**

(11-5). **Adm £6, chd free. Home-made teas (May). Ploughman's & home-made teas (June).**
The garden is situated in the middle of a 200 acre Deer Park, which has a very special herd of Red Deer husbanded by the Lucas Family for over 150 yrs. Borders with traditional planting and a kitchen garden that is prolific most of the yr. The rest of the garden comprises different spaces inc a small white garden, a Moroccan courtyard and a walled garden. There is also a woodland walk. WC available. Sorry, no dogs allowed.

GROUP OPENING

154 WATERWORKS & FRIENDS
Broad Oak & Brede, TN31 6HG. *6m N of Hastings. 4 Waterworks Cottages, Brede, off A28 by church & opp Red Lion, ¾m at end of lane. Sculdown, B2089 Chitcombe Rd, W off A28 at Broad Oak Xrds. Start at either garden, a map will be provided.* **Sat 7 June (10.30-4). Combined adm £6, chd free. Light refreshments at Sculdown.**

SCULDOWN
TN31 6EX. Mrs Christine Buckland.
4 WATERWORKS COTTAGES
TN31 6HG. Mrs Kristina Clode, 07950 748097, info@kristinaclodegardendesign.co.uk, www.kristinaclodegardendesign.co.uk. **Visits also by arrangement 9 June to 31 Oct for groups of 10 to 30.**

An opportunity to visit two unique gardens and discover the Brede Steam Giants 35ft Edwardian water pumping engines, and Grade II listed pump house located behind 4 Waterworks Cottages. Garden designer Kristina Clode has created her wildlife friendly garden at 4 Waterworks Cottages over the last 15 yrs. Delightful perennial wildflower meadow, pond, wisteria covered pergola and mixed borders packed full of unusual specimens with year-round interest and colour. Sculdown's garden is dominated by a very large wildlife pond formed as a result of iron-ore mining over 100 yrs ago. The stunning traditional cottage (not open) provides a superb backdrop for several colourful herbaceous borders and poplar trees. Plants for sale at 4

Waterworks Cottages. At Brede Steam Giants, accessible WC, and assistance dogs only (free entry, donations encouraged). At Sculdown, mobility cars to park in flat area at top of field.

155 NEW THE WHITE HOUSE
Redbridge Lane, Crowborough, TN6 3SR. Andrew & Gail Bourcier. *From the A26 turn at the sign for Rotherfield & Millbrook Industrial Estate, continue L on Sheep Plain, then R into High Broom Rd, R into Redbridge Ln. House is 300yds on L.* **Sat 17, Sun 18 May (11-4). Adm £6, chd free. Home-made teas.**
Sitting high on a hill with 180 degree panoramic views, overlooking the downs for 25 miles in an area of ANOB. Owned by the present owners family for over 100 yrs. Main garden has been redesigned to incorporate the borrowed landscape with herbaceous borders in a cottage garden style. The walled kitchen garden, featuring moongates, has been restored, containing a fruit cage, espalier trees, and raised vegetable beds.

156 WHITEHANGER
Marley Lane, Haslemere, GU27 3PY. Lynn & David Paynter, 07774 010901, lynn@whitehanger.co.uk. *What3words app: barman.funny.tango. Take A286 Midhurst Rd from Haslemere & after approx 2m turn R into Marley Ln (opp Hatch Ln). After 1m turn into drive shared with St Magnus Nursing & keep bearing L through the nursing home.* **Visits by arrangement 2 June to 17 Aug for groups of 8 to 25.**
Set in 6 acres on the edge of the South Downs National Park surrounded by NT woodland, this rural garden was started in 2012 when a new Huf house (not open) was built on a derelict site. Now there are lawned areas with beds of perennials, a serenity pool with Koi carp, a wildflower meadow, a Japanese garden, a sculpture garden, a woodland walk, a large rockery and an exotic walled garden.

SUSSEX 549

57 5 WHITEMANS CLOSE
Cuckfield, Haywards Heath, RH17 5DE. Shirley Carman-Martin. *1m N of Cuckfield. On B2036 signed Balcombe, Whitemans Cl is 250yds from r'about on LHS. No parking in Whitemans Cl. Buses stop at Whitemans Green, where there is also a large free car park.* **Sat 25, Mon 27, Wed 29, Fri 31 Jan, Sat 1, Mon 3, Tue 4, Wed 5, Tue 11, Wed 12, Fri 14, Sat 15 Feb (11-3.30). Adm £8.50, chd free. Pre-booking essential, please phone 01444 473520 or email shirley.carmanmartin@ngs.org.uk for information & booking. Home-made teas inc.**
This garden shows that winter need not be dull as there is much to see and enjoy in the depths of winter. Here in my garden I have collected many single and double snowdrops, hellebores, bulbs and other winter treasures, some not widely known. As it is a sheltered garden, yes, there are flowers to enjoy in January and early February. Come and see the enormous *Daphne bholua* that scents the garden for weeks on end at this time of yr.
❄ ☕

GROUP OPENING

58 WINCHELSEA'S SECRET GARDENS
Winchelsea, TN36 4EN. *2m W of Rye, 8m E of Hastings. Follow A259 from Rye or Hastings. Follow signs for central card payment point or pay cash at any garden gate.* **Sat 5 July (1-5). Combined adm £8, chd free. Home-made teas at Winchelsea New Hall.**

CLEVELAND PLACE
Sally & Graham Rhodda.

KENT CLOSE COMMUNAL GARDEN
Kent Close Residents.

KING'S LEAP
Philip Kent.

LOOKOUT COTTAGE
Anne Magee & David Richards.

MAGAZINE HOUSE
Susan Stradling.

NEW 2 MARITEAU HOUSE
Mary & Roger Tidyman.

NEW PORTOBELLO
Paul Williams.

NEW 1 ST GILES CLOSE
Charlotte & Paul Praeger.

NEW WHITE COTTAGE
Caroline & Jeremy Naylor.

Winchelsea continues to recruit fresh horticultural skills with yet more new gardens joining the group this yr. We offer secret walled gardens, roses, herbaceous borders and more. Nine gardens will open in the beautiful setting of the Cinque Port of Winchelsea. Explore the town with its magnificent church. Check winchelsea.com for the latest information on tours of our famous medieval cellars. If you are bringing a coach please contact ryeview@gmail.com, 01797 226524. Seven out of nine gardens are wheelchair accessible.
♿ 🐕 ❄ ☕ 🔊

59 WISTON HOUSE
Steyning Road, Wiston, BN44 3DD. Mr & Mrs R J Goring & Wilton Park, www.wistonestate.com. *1m NW Steyning. A24 Washington r'about, take A283 to Steyning. Driveway 2m on RHS.* **Sat 12 July (10.30-5.30). Adm £10, chd free. Tea, coffee & cake. Wiston Sparkling Wine will be available to purchase by the glass.**
Nestled at the foot of the South Downs within a landscaped park, Wiston House has a Victorian garden under restoration. Features inc a conservatory, terraced lawns with herbaceous borders, a cascade, woodland garden, Italian parterre, wildflower garden, walled vegetable garden and Victorian greenhouses. Wiston House will be open for guests to walk through the ground floor. St Mary's Church will be open. Wheelchair access over gravel paths.
♿ ☕ 🔊

60 33 WIVELSFIELD ROAD
Saltdean, Brighton, BN2 8FP. Chris Briggs & Steve Jenner. *From A259 at Saltdean turn onto Arundel Drive West, continue onto Saltdean Vale. Take the 6th turning on L, Tumulus Rd. Take 1st R onto Wivelsfield Rd, continue up steep hill, No. 33 is on the R.* **Thur 24, Sat 26 July (11-5). Adm £6, chd free. Tea, coffee & cake. Open nearby 408 Falmer Road.**
The garden, created in 2016, landscaped during 2017 and planting started later that yr. Split over three levels filled with colourful perennials, annuals, grasses, and succulents planted in the ground and in containers. The formal garden leads onto a wildflower meadow extending onto the downs, giving spectacular views of both the ocean and South Downs National Park. Front garden revamped in 2023.
🐕 ❄ ☕ 🔊

61 NEW WOODLANDS
The Street, Fulking, Henfield, BN5 9LT. Carolyn & Roger Loveless. *What3words app: defrost.massaging.slot. Please ignore SatNav. On E edge of Fulking, on sharp RH bend as approach from Poynings. Black & white chevrons on wall, walk down bridlepath. Limited street parking. Off-road parking approaching from Poynings & nr Shepherd & Dog pub a short walk away. Very short drive to other garden opening.* **Thur 12 June, Thur 17 July (11-5). Combined adm with The Orchard £7, chd free. Pre-booking essential, please visit www.ngs.org.uk for information & booking. Home-made teas at The Orchard. Two hour timed slots at 11am, 1pm & 3pm.**
Quiet location at the foot of the South Downs with lovely views and easy access for a walk. East, south and west facing with beautiful herbaceous perennials, alliums, shrubs, roses and grasses set against lawn, gravel and decking. Small pond, and tree owl and glass flower sculptures.
☕ 🔊

62 WYCH WARREN HOUSE
Wych Warren, Forest Row, RH18 5LF. Colin King & Mary Franck, 07852 272898, mlfranck@hotmail.com. *1m S of Forest Row. Proceed S on A22, track turning on L, 100 metres past 45mph warning triangle sign. Or 1m N of Wych Cross T-lights, track turning on R. Go 400 metres across golf course till the end.* **Fri 12 Sept (2-5). Adm £6, chd free. Tea, coffee & cake. Visits also by arrangement 9 May to 31 Oct for groups of 15 to 50. Please contact Mary by email.**
6 acre garden in Ashdown Forest, AONB, much of it mixed woodland. Perimeter walk all around property. Delightful and tranquil setting with plenty of space to roam, and various aspects of interest providing sensory and a relaxing visit. Ideal for forest bathing! Lovely stonework, specimen trees, three ponds, herbaceous borders, exotic bed, greenhouse and always something new on the go! Plants for sale and a great range of chutney and jams. Dogs on leads and children welcome. Partial wheelchair access by tarmac track to the kitchen side gate.
♿ 🐕 ❄ ☕ 🔊

WARWICKSHIRE
& West Midlands

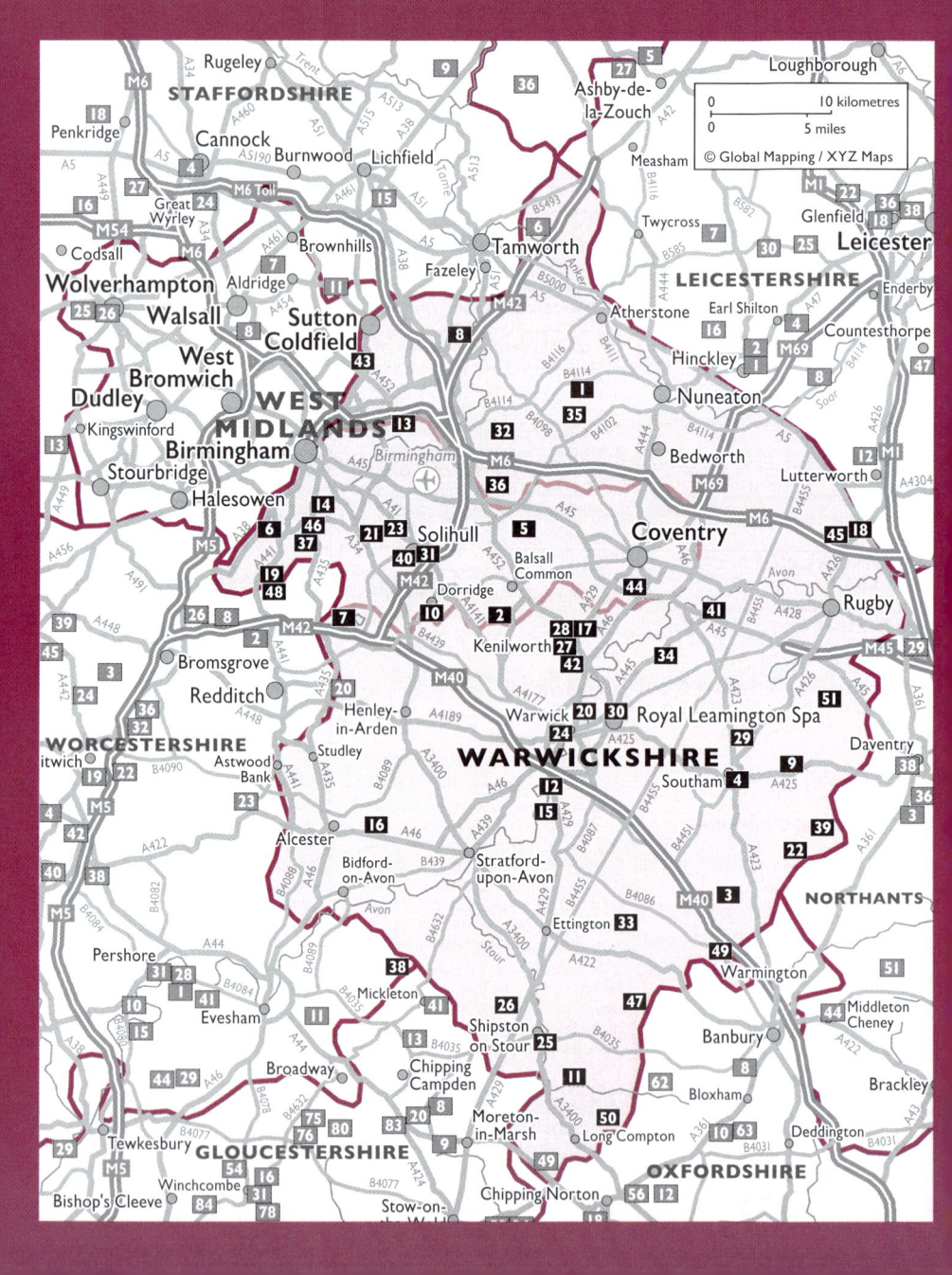

WARWICKSHIRE 551

VOLUNTEERS

County Organiser
Liz Watson
01926 512307
liz.watson@ngs.org.uk

County Treasurer
Ian Roberts
01926 864181
ian.roberts@ngs.org.uk

Publicity
Lily Farrah
07545 560298
lily.farrah@ngs.org.uk

Social Media
Jenny Edwards
07884 177889
jenny.edwards@ngs.org.uk

Booklet Co-ordinator
Hazel Blenkinsop
07787 005290
hazel.blenkinsop@ngs.org.uk

Booklet Advertising
Hugh Thomas
01926 423063
hugh.thomas@ngs.org.uk

Photographer
Annie Casey 07555 448109
annie.casey@ngs.org.uk

Assistant County Organisers
Jane Cerone
01827 873205
jane.cerone@ngs.org.uk

Jane Redshaw
07803 234627
jane.redshaw@ngs.org.uk

Isobel Somers
07767 306673
ifas1010@aol.com

Mick Wood
07773 334059
mick.wood@ngs.org.uk

@WarwickshireNGS
@WarksNGS
@warwickshirengs

OPENING DATES

All entries subject to change.
For latest information check
www.ngs.org.uk

Extended openings are shown at the beginning of the month

Map locator numbers are shown to the right of each garden name.

February

Snowdrop Openings

Sunday 9th
Fieldgate 17
2 St Nicholas Avenue 42

Saturday 15th
◆ Hill Close Gardens 24

April

Every Saturday and Sunday from Saturday 19th
◆ Bridge Nursery 9

Saturday 5th
◆ Castle Bromwich Hall Gardens 13

Sunday 6th
◆ Castle Bromwich Hall Gardens 13

Friday 18th
◆ Bridge Nursery 9

Monday 21st
◆ Bridge Nursery 9

Saturday 26th
6 Canon Price Road 12

Sunday 27th
Broadacre 10
6 Canon Price Road 12

May

Every Saturday and Sunday
◆ Bridge Nursery 9

Sunday 4th
Cedar House 15

Monday 5th
◆ Bridge Nursery 9

Sunday 11th
Beech Hurst 4
Cats Whiskers 14

Friday 16th
◆ Kenilworth Castle 27

Saturday 17th
6 Canon Price Road 12

Sunday 18th
Beech Hurst 4
Burmington Grange 11
6 Canon Price Road 12

Saturday 24th
Ilmington Gardens 26

Sunday 25th
Ilmington Gardens 26
Pebworth Gardens 38

Monday 26th
Bridge House 8
◆ Bridge Nursery 9
Pebworth Gardens 38

June

Every Saturday and Sunday
◆ Bridge Nursery 9

Sunday 1st
Hardwick Hill 22

Saturday 7th
6 Canon Price Road 12
Hall Green Gardens 21
Priors Marston Manor 39

Sunday 8th
6 Canon Price Road 12
Hall Green Gardens 21
Honington Gardens 25
NEW Lillington Road Gardens 30
Styvechale Gardens 44

Sunday 15th
Kenilworth Gardens 28
Maxstoke Castle 32
8 Rectory Road 40
Whichford & Ascott Gardens 50

Saturday 21st
NEW Forge House 18
NEW Heaton Road Gardens 23
NEW Swift House 45

Sunday 22nd
NEW Forge House 18
Marie Curie Hospice Garden 31
NEW Swift House 45
Warmington Gardens 49

Tuesday 24th
NEW Monksbridge 33

552 WARWICKSHIRE

Thursday 26th
NEW Monksbridge 33
Sunday 29th
Ansley Gardens 1
Berkswell Gardens 5

July

Every Saturday and Sunday
♦ Bridge Nursery 9
Tuesday 1st
NEW Monksbridge 33
Thursday 3rd
NEW Monksbridge 33
Saturday 5th
6 Canon Price Road 12
Packington Hall 36
Tysoe Gardens 47
Sunday 6th
Avon Dassett Gardens 3
Bournville Village 6
6 Canon Price Road 12
Tysoe Gardens 47
Saturday 12th
♦ Ryton Organic Gardens 41
NEW Thrive Birmingham 46
Sunday 13th
Old Arley Gardens 35

Saturday 19th
128 Green Acres Road 19
NEW 48 Varlins Way 48
Sunday 20th
Guy's Cliffe Walled Garden 20

August

Every Saturday and Sunday
♦ Bridge Nursery 9

September

Every Saturday and Sunday
♦ Bridge Nursery 9
Friday 5th
NEW 170 Station Road 43
Saturday 6th
♦ Ryton Organic Gardens 41
Sunday 7th
8 Rectory Road 40

October

Saturday 25th
♦ Hill Close Gardens 24

By Arrangement

Arrange a personalised garden visit with your club, or group of friends, on a date to suit you. See individual garden entries for full details.

Avening 2
10 Avon Carrow, Avon
  Dassett Gardens 3
Beech Hurst 4
Brackencote 7
Bridge House 8
Broadacre 10
6 Canon Price Road 12
Cedar House 15
The Croft House 16
36 Ferndale Road, Hall Green
  Gardens 21
19 Leigh Crescent 29
Oak House 34
Paul's Oasis of Calm 37
8 Rectory Road 40
69 Spring Lane, Kenilworth
  Gardens 28
Woolscott Barn 51

Thrive Birmingham

WARWICKSHIRE

THE GARDENS

GROUP OPENING

1 ANSLEY GARDENS
Ansley, CV10 9PS. *Ansley is situated W of Nuneaton, adjacent to Arley. Ansley is directly off the B4114. Tickets are available from the car park or in individual gardens.* **Sun 29 June (1.30-5.30). Combined adm £6. Tea, coffee & cake.**

NEW 14 BIRMINGHAM ROAD
Mr & Mrs Anna and Adam Smith.

25 BIRMINGHAM ROAD
Pat & David Arrowsmith.

59 BIRMINGHAM ROAD
Joan & Peter McParland.

NEW 261 BIRMINGHAM ROAD
Mr & Mrs Caroline Round.

NEW CHURCH FARM
Mrs Sally Goadby.

35 NUTHURST CRESCENT
Roger & Heather Greaves.

THE OLD POLICE HOUSE
Mike & Hilary Ward.

1 PARK COTTAGES
Janet & Andy Down.

NEW 397 TUNNEL ROAD
Mrs Karen Lucas and David Dalton.

Ansley is a small ex-mining village situated in north Warwickshire. In 2024 the village won Gold in the Britain in Bloom Competition so is well worth a visit. The nine gardens in and around the village that are opening are a selection of different styles and offerings and this year there are some new gardens opening. They range from a very small traditional cottage garden crammed with flowers and pots to larger gardens and those maximising the amazing views of the countryside. There are small new build gardens, a beautiful farmhouse garden complete with ducks and guinea fowl, small more mature gardens and a country garden with mature plants and ancient roses - something to inspire everyone. Most of the gardens are in the village with the opportunity to walk across the fields on public footpaths to the others if you are able. (There is parking available if not). The local Norman church will be open and the Morris Dancing Group will be entertaining visitors during the day.

2 AVENING
Oldwich Lane East, Kenilworth, CV8 1NR. Helen Jones, 07894 321919, hello@mygardenoasis.co.uk, www.mygardenoasis.co.uk. *8 m SE of Solihull & 5 m W of Kenilworth. Avening is at the end of College Ln, a short single-track lane off Oldwich Ln E which runs between Chadwick End and Fen End.* **Visits by arrangement 5 Apr to 28 Sept. Adm £5, chd free.**

Designed in 2009, this is a ¾ acre garden oasis in the West Midlands. It has been designed to attract wildlife and has a typical cottage garden feel. Features inc 2 ponds joined by a waterfall, wildflower meadow, wide mixed shrub/herbaceous border with a stepping stone path running through it and small vegetable plot. There are no steps in the garden, although some of the paths are unsuitable for wheelchairs.

GROUP OPENING

3 AVON DASSETT GARDENS
Avon Dassett, CV47 2AE. *7m N of Banbury. From M40 J12 turn L & L again onto the B4100, following signs to Herb Centre & Gaydon. Take 2nd L (signed) into bottom end of village. Please park in cemetery car park at top of hill, or where signed.* **Sun 6 July (1-5). Combined adm £7, chd free. Home-made teas.**

10 AVON CARROW
Anna Prosser, 07468 602078, annaprosser@cbemail.co.uk.
Visits also by arrangement Mar to Aug for groups of up to 20.

DASSETT HOUSE
Mrs Sarah Rutherford, dassettdwelling@gmail.com.

THE EAST WING, AVON CARROW
Christine Fisher & Terry Gladwin.

HILL TOP FARM
Mr D Hicks.

THE OLD RECTORY
Lily Hope-Frost.

SINCLAIR WITH THE SNUG
Mrs Deb Watts.

NEW SPIKES COTTAGE
Mrs Catherine Wahlberg.

Pretty Hornton stone village sheltering in the lee of the Burton Dassett hills. Wide variety of gardens inc cottage and stepped, with The Old Rectory mentioned in Domesday Book. Range of plants inc alpines, herbaceous, perennials, roses, climbers and shrubs. The gardens are on/off the main road through the village which is set on a long hill. We would be grateful if visitors could park in designated areas and not along the main road in the village. For 2025, we hope to run a shuttle service from top to bottom of the village, but this is not guaranteed. Plant sales, homemade teas, historic church open, and potters wheel display. Lunch available at the Yew Tree village pub, a Community-owned pub. Visit www.theyewtreepub.co.uk for details. Wheelchair access to most gardens, but parking not available at individual gardens. The village is set on a long hill.

4 BEECH HURST
3 Warwick Road, Southam, CV47 0HN. Michael and Sharon Mitchell, 01926 817559, michael@fmmitchell.net. *On R, ¼ to ½ m down Warwick Rd from A425 from Leamington Spa.* **Sun 11, Sun 18 May (2-5). Adm £5, chd free. Visits also by arrangement 1 Apr to 15 Sept for groups of 10 to 30. Tea on request for group visits only.**

Beech Hurst is a Regency House with an established 1¼ acre garden inc lawns, woodland areas, many mature and some historic trees, established shrubs, herbaceous borders and a recently added Japanese-inspired garden with a raked gravel bed and a variety of flowering cherries, acers, rhododendrons, azaleas and camellias. It also has a fine display of late winter and springtime bulbs. The property has a gravel drive.

WARWICKSHIRE

GROUP OPENING

5 BERKSWELL GARDENS
Berkswell, Coventry, CV7 7BB. Gordon Clark. *7m W of Coventry. A452 to Balsall Common & follow signs to Berkswell. Tickets & maps available at each garden. Car necessary to visit all gardens.* **Sun 29 June (11-6). Combined adm £7, chd free.**

NEW **27 BONNEVILLE CLOSE**
Mrs Lilian McGrath.

EMSCOT BARN
Mr Leigh & Mrs Sarah Mayers.

NEW **4 GIPSY LANE**
Mr Jamie & Mrs Sue Warner.

SPENCER'S END
Gordon Clark & Nicola Content.

THE TOWER HOUSE
Penny & David Stableforth.

NEW **5 WASTE LANE**
Mrs Jenny White.

Berkswell is a beautiful village dating back to Saxon times with a C12 Norman church and has several C16 and C17 buildings inc the pub. In 2014/15 the village was awarded Gold in the RHS Britain in Bloom campaign, plus a special RHS award in 2014 for the Best Large Village in the Heart of England. The gardens provide great variety with fine examples of small and large, formal and informal, wild, imaginatively planted herbaceous borders and productive vegetable gardens. Something for everyone and plenty of ideas to take home. Also open to visitors is the C12 Norman church and garden.

GROUP OPENING

6 BOURNVILLE VILLAGE
Birmingham, B30 1QY. Bournville Village Trust, www.bvt.org.uk. *Bournville. Gardens spread across 1,000 acre estate. Walks of up to 30 mins between some. Map available on the day. Parking: Bournville Garden Centre, (B30 2AE) & Rowheath Pavilion, (B30 1HH).* **Sun 6 July (11-5). Combined adm £5, chd free. Tea, coffee & cake.**

5 BLACKTHORN ROAD
Mr A & Mrs L Christie.

32 KNIGHTON ROAD
Mrs Anne Ellis & Mr Lawrence Newman.

MASEFIELD COMMUNITY GARDEN
Mrs Sally Gopsill, www.masefieldcommunitygarden.wordpress.com.

SELLY MANOR MUSEUM
Selly Manor Museum, www.sellymanormuseum.org.uk.

Bournville Village is showcasing four gardens. Bournville is famous for its large gardens, outstanding open spaces and of course its chocolate factory in a garden! We have a garden railway amongst bonsai, a traditional Tudor garden in a museum, a large mature cottage style suburban garden and an eco-friendly community garden. Free information sheet/map available on the day. For those with a disability, full details of access are available on the NGS website. Visitors with particular concerns with regards to access are welcome to call Bournville Village Trust on 0300 333 6540 or email: Communityadmin@bvt.org.uk a map will be available to download from www.bvt.org.uk nearer to the date and will be available on the day. Music, singing and food plants for sale available across a number of sites. Toilets at Selly Manor Museum.

7 BRACKENCOTE
Forshaw Heath Road, Earlswood, Solihull, B94 5JU. Mr & Mrs Sandy Andrews, 01564 702395/07710 107000, mjandrews53@hotmail.com. *From J3 M42 take exit signed to Forshaw Heath. At T-junc, turn L onto Forshaw Heath Rd, signed to Earlswood. Garden approx ½m on the L, before you get to Earlswood Nurseries.* **Visits by arrangement May to July for groups of up to 20. Adm £5, chd free. Tea, coffee & cake.**
A beautiful country garden with stunning wildflower meadow, full of orchids in spring and early summer. The 1¼ acre plot is surrounded by mature trees, with herbaceous borders enclosing a large circular lawn. Beyond this, the garden inc a brick and turf labyrinth, a rockery, a pond and bog garden as well as a large raised vegetable plot and garden buildings.

8 BRIDGE HOUSE
Dog Lane, Bodymoor Heath, B76 9JD. Mr & Mrs J Cerone, 01827 873205, janecerone@btinternet.com. *5m S of Tamworth. From A446 at Belfry Island take A4091 to Tamworth, after 1m turn R onto Bodymoor Heath Ln & continue 1m into village, parking in field opp garden.* **Mon 26 May (2-5). Adm £5, chd free. Tea, coffee & cake. Visits also by arrangement May to Sept for groups of 6 to 25.**
One acre garden surrounding converted public house. Divided into smaller areas with a mix of shrub borders, azalea and fuchsia, herbaceous and bedding, orchard, kitchen garden with large greenhouse. Pergola walk, arch to formal garden with big fish pool, pond, bog garden and lawns. Some unusual carefully chosen trees. Kingsbury Water Park and RSPB Middleton Lakes Reserve located within a mile.

9 ♦ BRIDGE NURSERY
Tomlow Road, Napton, Southam, CV47 8HX. Christine Dakin, 01926 812737, chris.dakin25@yahoo.com, www.bridge-nursery.co.uk. *3m E of Southam. Brown tourist sign at Napton Xrds on A425 Southam to Daventry Rd.* **For NGS: Fri 18 Apr (10-4). Every Sat and Sun 19 Apr to 28 Sept (10-4). Mon 21 Apr, Mon 5, Mon 26 May (10-4). Adm £3.50, chd free. Light refreshments.** For other opening times and information, please phone, email or visit garden website.
Clay soil? It can be very challenging but here is an acre of garden with an exciting range of plants which thrive in hostile conditions. Grass paths lead you round borders filled with many unusual plants, a pond and bamboo grove complete with panda! A peaceful haven for wildlife and visitors. Comments are often made about the tranquillity of the garden. Group visits welcome. The ground can be unsuitable for wheelchairs after a lot of rain.

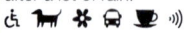

10 BROADACRE
Grange Road, Dorridge, Solihull, B93 8QA. John Woolman, 07818 082885, jw234567@gmail.com, www.broadacregarden.org. *Approx 3m SE of Solihull. On B4101 opp The Railway Inn. Plenty of parking.*

69 Spring Lane, Kenilworth Gardens

Sun 27 Apr (2-6). Adm £7, chd free. Home-made teas. All food is provided and served by Bentley Heath Country Market members. Visits also by arrangement.
Broadacre is a nature garden which we manage organically. Attractively landscaped with pools, lawns and trees, beehives, vegetable area and adjoining stream and wildflower meadows. Dorridge cricket club is on the estate. Lovely venue for a picnic. Dogs and children are welcome. Excellent country pub, The Railway Inn, at the bottom of the drive. Most areas are accessible.

11 BURMINGTON GRANGE
Cherington, Shipston-on-Stour, CV36 5HZ. **Mr & Mrs Patrick Ramsay.** *2m E of Shipston-on-Stour. Take Oxford Rd (A3400) from Shipston-on-Stour, after 2m turn L to Burmington, go through village & continue for 1 m, turn L to Willington & Barcheston, on sharp L bend turn R over cattle grid.* **Sun 18 May (2-6). Adm £7, chd free.**
Interesting plantsman's garden extending to about 1½ acres, set in the rolling hills of the North Cotswolds with wonderful views over unspoilt countryside. The garden is well developed considering it was planted 20 yrs ago. Small vegetable and picking garden, beautiful sunken rose garden with herbaceous and shrub borders. Orchard and tree walk with unusual trees.

12 6 CANON PRICE ROAD
Nursery Meadow, Barford, CV35 8EQ. **Mrs Marie-Jane Roberts,** 07775 584336. *1m from Warwick. From A429 turn into Barford. Park on Wellesbourne Rd & walk into Nursery Meadow by red phone box. No.6 is R in 1st close. Disabled parking by house.* **Sat 26, Sun 27 Apr (2-4.30). Adm £2, chd free. Sat 17, Sun 18 May, Sat 7, Sun 8 June, Sat 5, Sun 6 July (2-4.30). Adm £5, chd free. Tea, coffee & cake in the garden room or seating around the garden. Visits also by arrangement 1 Apr to 13 July. Tea, coffee, and cake are £4 extra per person.**
Unexpectedly large and mature garden with colour themed shrub and perennial plants immaculately grown. Separate areas for cut flowers, herbs, vegetables and 19 types of fruit, some fan trained. Spectacularly colourful patio pots, a small delightful rockery, pond and wildlife garden. There are many seating areas throughout. Cash only for plant sale. Access via a single slab path that joins a wide path through the garden.

13 ◆ CASTLE BROMWICH HALL GARDENS
Chester Road, Castle Bromwich, Birmingham, B36 9BT. **Castle Bromwich Hall & Gardens Trust,** 01217 494100, cbhallgardens@gmail.com, www.castlebromwichhallgardens.org.uk. *4m E of Birmingham centre. 1m J5 M6 (exit N only) What3words app: rated.cake.those.* **For NGS: Sat 5, Sun 6 Apr (10.30-4.30). Adm £6, chd £3. Light refreshments. For other opening times and information, please phone, email or visit garden website.**
10 acres of restored C17/18 walled gardens attached to a Jacobean manor (now a hotel), with a further 30 acres of historic parkland and nature reserve. Formal yew parterres, wilderness walks, summerhouses, holly maze, espaliered fruit and wild areas. Cream Tea in a Box, cafe and picnics all season. Paths are either lawn or rough hoggin - sometimes on a slope. Most areas generally accessible, rough areas outside the walls difficult when wet.

556 WARWICKSHIRE

4 CATS WHISKERS
42 Amesbury Rd, Moseley, Birmingham, B13 8LE. Dr Alfred & Mrs Michele White. *Opp back of Moseley Hall Hospital. Past Edgbaston Cricket ground straight on at r'about & up Salisbury Rd. Amesbury Rd, 1st on R.* **Sun 11 May (12-5). Adm £7, chd free. Light refreshments. cake, wine & soft drinks.**
A plantsman's garden developed over the last 40 yrs but which has kept its 1923 landscape. The front garden whilst not particularly large is full of interesting trees and shrubs; the rear garden is on three levels with steps leading to a small terrace and further steps to the main space. At the end of the garden is a pergola leading to the vegetable garden and greenhouse. Arisaema bed being developed in the hope of becoming a national collection.
❀ 🍵 ⋅))

5 CEDAR HOUSE
Wasperton, Warwick, CV35 8EB. Mr D Burbidge, 07836 532914, david.burbidge@burbidge.org.uk, www.cedarhousegardens.co.uk. *5 m from Warwick. Turn off A429 into Wasperton. There is only 1 road in the village. Continue for approx ½ m. What3words app: wool.parsnips. trickles.* **Sun 4 May (1.30-5). Adm £8, chd free. Home-made teas at Wasperton Village Hall. Visits also by arrangement 21 Apr to 31 Oct for groups of 15 to 25.**
Six acre former vicarage gardens, mature and exciting. Extensive Tulips and Rhododendrons in Spring - colourful herbaceous borders in Summer - brilliant colour in Autumn. Water meadow garden, woodland glade and walk with mix of young and mature specimen trees, inc two notable vintage trees, tranquil grass and bamboo area leading to the swimming pool garden. Lots of good seating areas. Interesting walks across the fields to the River Avon, Charlecote and Hampton Lucy. Cedar House is close to Warwick and Stratford upon Avon. Some gravel and woodchip paths.
♿ 🍵 ⋅))

6 THE CROFT HOUSE
Haselor, Alcester, B49 6LU. Isobel & Patrick Somers, 07767 306673, ifas1010@aol.com. *6m W of Stratford-upon-Avon, 2m E of Alcester, off A46. From A46 take Haselor turn. From Alcester take old Stratford Rd, turn L signed Haselor, then R at Xrds. Garden in centre of village. Please park considerately.* **Visits by arrangement May & June for groups of 5 to 30. Adm £7, chd free. Home-made teas.**
Almost an acre of trees, shrubs and herbaceous borders densely planted with a designer's passion for colour and texture. Hidden areas invite you to linger. Gorgeous scented wisteria on 2 sides of the house. Organically managed, providing a haven for birds and other wildlife. Frog pond, treehouse, small vegetable plot and a few venerable old fruit trees from its days as a market garden.
❀ 🍵

7 FIELDGATE
Fieldgate Lane, Kenilworth, CV8 1BT. Liz & Bob Watson. *Fieldgate is at the very bottom of Fieldgate Ln, on the corner next to the T-lights. Parking available at Abbey Fields car park & limited street parking on High St & Fieldgate Ln.* **Sun 9 Feb (12-4). Adm £3, chd free. Home-made teas in St Nicholas Church. Open nearby 2 St Nicholas Avenue. Combined adm £5. Opening with Kenilworth Gardens on Sun 15 June.**
Fieldgate is a ¼ acre town garden with lawns, herbaceous borders and formal ponds. It was remodelled by the owners in 2002 and has matured nicely. The borders contain a wide variety of plants and are colourful throughout summer and late into September with asters and dahlias. A small woodland area was created in 2021 planted with shade lovers, ferns and many snowdrops some of which are unusual. Kenilworth Castle is close by and there are pleasant walks in Abbey Fields. The Millennium Walk, starting at the castle is an hour's walk

14 Birmingham Road, Ansley Gardens

WARWICKSHIRE 557

through the Warwickshire countryside around the shore of the now drained Kenilworth Castle mere.

🐕 ✤ ☕ 🔊))

18 NEW FORGE HOUSE
Church Street, Churchover, Rugby, CV23 0EW. Mr Ed & Mrs Lesley Browne. *1m from J1 M6. In the village of Churchover on Church St.* **Sat 21, Sun 22 June (10-4). Combined adm with Swift House £5, chd free. Tea, coffee & cake at Swift House.**
A small well maintained village garden with a lawn, raised beds planted with shrubs and herbaceous perennials and a small pond to attract wildlife. There is large patio for entertaining and a summerhouse to enjoy the garden whatever the weather.

🐕 ☕

19 128 GREEN ACRES ROAD
Kings Norton, Birmingham, B38 8NL. Mr & Mrs Mark Whitehouse. *From the M42 J2 take the A441 towards Birmingham take the 2nd exit at r'about continue along the A441 for 3m Green Acres Rd is on the R next to Spar.* **Sat 19 July (10.30-4). Combined adm with 48 Varlins Way £5, chd free. Tea, coffee & cake.**
A small garden with lots of character full of interest and abundance of colour, inc various seating areas to enjoy different aspects and views. The garden has many different types of perennials, hostas, roses and dahlias. A fish pond, water feature plus many more points of interest. To access the garden, please follow signs to enter the garden from the rear.

✤ ☕ 🔊))

20 GUY'S CLIFFE WALLED GARDEN
Coventry Road, Guy's Cliffe, Warwick, CV34 5FJ. Sarah Ridgeway, www.guyscliffewalledgarden.org.uk. *Behind Hintons Nursery in Guy's Cliffe. Guy's Cliffe is on the A429, between N Warwick & Leek Wootton.* **Sun 20 July (10.30-3.30). Adm £4.50, chd free. Tea, coffee & cake.**
A Grade II listed garden of special historic interest, having been the kitchen garden for Guy's Cliffe House. The garden dates back to the mid-1700s. Restoration work started 11 yrs ago using plans from the early C19. The garden layout has already been reinstated and the beds, once more, planted with fruit, flowers and vegetables inc many heritage varieties. Part of the Peach House is being restored. The sunken Melon house is visible but not yet restored so not accessible. Original C18 walls. Fernery. Exhibition of artefacts discovered during restoration. 'No Dig' approach to all gardening activities Lots of signs describe different parts of the garden. Access, including wheelchairs, is through entrance of Hintons Nursery and paths through garden are accessible. WC with disabled access.

♿ 🐕 ☕ 🔊))

GROUP OPENING

21 HALL GREEN GARDENS
Hall Green, Birmingham, B28 9PH. *Off A34, 4m from city centre, 6m from M42, J4. Start at 65 Woodford Green Road, B28 8PH.* **Sat 7, Sun 8 June (1.30-5.30). Combined adm £5, chd free. Home-made teas at 111 Southam Road.**

36 FERNDALE ROAD
Mrs E A Nicholson, 01217 774921.
Visits also by arrangement 31 Mar to 30 Sept for groups of up to 30.

638 SHIRLEY ROAD
Dr & Mrs M Leigh.

111 SOUTHAM ROAD
Ms Val Townend & Mr Ian Bate.

65 WOODFORD GREEN ROAD
Mrs Maxine Chapman.

Four very different suburban gardens in leafy Hall Green with its beautiful mature trees and friendly residents. Our visitors love the unique atmosphere in each garden. It is such a perfect way to share a relaxing early summer saunter and pause for refreshments served by our brilliant catering team. We look forward to seeing you! 36 Ferndale Rd: Florist's large suburban garden, ponds and waterfalls, and fruit garden. 111 Southam Rd: Mature garden with well defined areas inc ponds, white garden and a majestic cedar. 638 Shirley Rd: Large garden with herbaceous borders, cutting patch, vegetables and greenhouses. 65 Woodford Green Rd: Much loved, small garden abounding in charming old teapots, bottle edging, and worn-out hiking boots now used as planters.

✤ ☕ 🔊))

22 HARDWICK HILL
Lower End, Priors Hardwick, Southam, CV47 7SP. Mrs Candida Kelly, www.candykelly.co.uk. *4½ SE of Southam. What3words app: piled. ever.tasty. Turn off A23 to Wormleighton. Turn L after Wormleighton and 1½ m later after village sign drive on R before bend. Please check for HS2 road closures.* **Sun 1 June (2-5). Adm £7.50, chd free. Home-made teas.**
The main lawn ends in a ha-ha with views stretching to the Malvern Hills. A 5 acre garden replanted and landscaped 20 yrs ago. Full of mature trees inc Copper Beeches, Corsican Pine and two Mulberry trees. Long borders lined with espaliered Malus Robusta by an ornamental pond that leads to a summerhouse with small wildflower meadow and beehives. A vegetable garden. A variety of hedging from wild roses, willow, weeping pear to buckthorn and hornbeam. Sadly the paths are gravel and there are various levels and so not suitable for wheelchairs.

✤ ☕ 🔊))

GROUP OPENING

23 NEW HEATON ROAD GARDENS
Solihull, B91 2DZ. *Heaton Rd is off main Warwick Road (A41) in central Solihull.* **Sat 21 June (1-5). Combined adm £5, chd free. Tea, coffee & cake at 67 Heaton Road.**

NEW 37 HEATON ROAD
Mrs Janet Barlow.

NEW 58 HEATON ROAD
Mr & Mrs Paula Fullard.

NEW 66 HEATON ROAD
Mr Robin Bone.

NEW 67 HEATON ROAD
Mr & Mrs Alan Thomas.

Four very different mature suburban gardens in central Solihull, with easy access from Birmingham and Warwickshire. Refreshments will be available. No. 37 has lawn, borders of flowering shrubs and water features. No. 58 has lawn and lots of well established flowering shrubs and Acers. Summer colour provided by variety of pots. No. 66 has large herbaceous borders, lots of flowering pots, fruit cage, raised vegetable beds and greenhouse full of cacti and succulents. No. 67 aims to provide all-year-round colour in borders with pergola leading to well-stocked fruit and vegetable garden.

🐕 ✤ ☕

558 WARWICKSHIRE

24 ♦ HILL CLOSE GARDENS
Bread and Meat Close, Warwick, CV34 6HF. Hill Close Gardens Trust, 01926 493339, hello@hcgt.org.uk, www.hillclosegardens.com. *Town centre. Follow signs to Warwick racecourse. Entry from Friars St onto Bread & Meat Cl Car park is by entrance next to racecourse. 2hrs free parking. Disabled parking outside the gates. What3words app: chat.apple.cute.* **For NGS: Sat 15 Feb, Sat 25 Oct (11-4). Adm £8.50, chd £1. Light refreshments.** For other opening times and information, please phone, email or visit garden website.
Restored Grade II Victorian leisure gardens comprising 16 individual hedged gardens, 8 brick summerhouses. Herbaceous borders, heritage apple and pear trees, C19 daffodils, over 100 varieties of snowdrops, many varieties of asters and chrysanthemums. Heritage vegetables. Plant Heritage border, auricula theatre, and Victorian style glasshouse. Children's garden. Wheelchair available. Please phone to book in advance.

& 🐕 ✱ 🚗 NPC ☕ 🔊

GROUP OPENING

25 HONINGTON GARDENS
Honington, Shipston-on-Stour, CV36 5AA. *1½ m N of Shipston-on-Stour. Take A3400 from Shipston on Stour, towards Stratford-upon-Avon, then turn R signed Honington. CV36 5AA.* **Sun 8 June (1.30-5.30). Combined adm £7, chd free.** Home-made teas on the Village Green within walking distance of car park, WC and the gardens.

THE GARDEN HOUSE
Mr & Mrs Andrew Sadleir.

THE GLEBE

HONINGTON HALL
B H E Wiggin.

MALT HOUSE RISE
Mr P Weston.

THE OLD COTTAGE
Donna Elliott.

THE OLD HOUSE
Mrs D Beaumont.

ORCHARD HOUSE
Mr & Mrs Monnington.

THE ORCHARD, HOME FARM
Mr Guy Winter.

ROSE COTTAGE
Mr & Mrs Andrew Sadleir.

C17 village, recorded in Domesday, entered by old toll gate. Ornamental stone bridge over the River Stour and interesting church with C13 tower and late C17 nave after Wren. 9 contrasting gardens. One with extensive lawns and fine mature trees with river and garden monuments. A plantsman's garden with unusual trees and shrubs creating year-round interest. A small, colourful and well-stocked garden, a developing garden with a hint of Japan, a typical cottage garden fit for a chocolate box cover. A secluded walled country garden with mixed perennial and annual planting, a structured cottage garden formally laid out with box hedging. A partially walled cottage garden with herbaceous borders. A traditional orchard with mown pathways and active beehives. Entrance payments by cash or card. Teas on the Village Green at Honington are a special feature of the afternoon. Car parking is free, please follow signs and be guided by stewards to car park area. Some of the smaller gardens have only partial wheelchair access.

& 🐕 🚗 ☕ 🔊

GROUP OPENING

26 ILMINGTON GARDENS
Ilmington, CV36 4LA. *8m S of Stratford-upon-Avon. 8m N of Moreton-in-Marsh. 4m NW of Shipston-on-Stour off A3400. 3m NE of Chipping Campden.* **Sat 24, Sun 25 May (12.30-5.30). Combined adm £10, chd free.** Home-made teas in Ilmington Community Shop, Upper Green on Sat, and at the Village Hall on Sun. Donation to Shipston Home Nursing.

THE BEVINGTONS
Mr & Mrs N Tustain.

FROG ORCHARD
Mr & Mrs Jeremy Snowden.

GRUMP COTTAGE
Mr & Mrs Martin Underwood.

ILMINGTON MANOR
Mr Martin Taylor.

MEADOW VIEW
Mr Geoff Davis.

RAVENSCROFT
Mr & Mrs Clasper.

STUDIO COTTAGE
Sarah Hobson.

Ilmington is an ancient hillside Cotswold village 2m from the Fosse Way with 2 good pubs. Start at Ilmington Manor (next to the Red Lion Pub); wander the 3 acre gardens with many roses, much topiary and a fish pond. Next go up Grump Street, above the Village Hall, to Ravenscroft's large, sculpture-filled garden with sloping vistas commanding the hilltop. Walk to nearby Frog Lane to view Frog Orchard's and The Studio's delightful gardens. Then walk down to the Bevington's many-chambered cottage garden at the bottom of Valanders Lane, and finally to the charming cottage gardens surrounding Meadow View in Back Street overlooking the Manor ponds and Berry Orchard. The traditional Ilmington Morris Dancers will be performing in the village on Sunday. Cash only please.

☕

---

27 ♦ KENILWORTH CASTLE
Castle Green, Kenilworth, CV8 1NG. English Heritage. *In Kenilworth off A46. Clearly signposted from the town centre, off B4103.* **For NGS: Evening opening Fri 16 May (5.30-7.30). Adm £20, chd free. Pre-booking essential, please email fundraising@english-heritage.org.uk or visit www.english-heritage.org.uk/visit/places/kenilworth-castle/events for information & booking. Light refreshments.** For other opening times and information, please email or visit garden website.
English Heritage in partnership with the National Garden Scheme is offering you the chance to visit gardens of Kenilworth Castle in the early evening when the site is closed to the public. At this exclusive event, you will meet a member of the garden team for a tour of the gardens, discover how the gardens are managed and experience the tranquillity and colourful planting of this historic garden.

& ☕

Our donation to Marie Curie this year equates to 17,496 hours of nursing care or 43 days of care in one of their nine hospices.

GROUP OPENING

28 KENILWORTH GARDENS
Kenilworth, CV8 1BT. *Fieldgate Ln, off A452.* Parking available at Abbey Fields or in town. Street parking is available. Tickets & maps at all gardens. Transport is necessary to visit all the gardens. **Sun 15 June (12-5.30). Combined adm £8, chd free. Home-made teas in St Nicholas Parochial Hall. Also light lunches.**

BEEHIVE HILL ALLOTMENTS
Kenilworth Allotment Association.

FIELDGATE
Liz & Bob Watson.
(See separate entry)

14C FIELDGATE LANE
Sandra Aulton.

KENILWORTH COMMUNITY GARDENS
Kenilworth Community Gardeners, www.facebook.com/kenilworthcommunitygardeners.

9 LAWRENCE GARDENS
Leo Lewis & Judith Masson.

23 LINDSEY CRESCENT
Mr John & Mrs Ruth Titley.

2 ST NICHOLAS AVENUE
Mr Ian Roberts.
(See separate entry)

1 SIDDELEY AVENUE
Clare Wightman,
www.instagram.com/wightmanclare.

69 SPRING LANE
Mr Chris Coton & Mr Nick Wood, 07443 642320,
homodimer@hotmail.com.
Visits also by arrangement 15 May to 20 Sept for groups of up to 30.

TREE TOPS
Joanna & George Illingworth.

1 VICARAGE GARDENS
Clive & Fran Dutson.

Kenilworth was historically a very important town in Warwickshire. It has one of England's best castle ruins, Abbey Fields and plenty of pubs and good cafes. There are 9 gardens open this year around the town plus allotments and the community gardens near the town centre. There are small, medium and large gardens with lots of variety - formal, prairie and cottage styles with trees, shrubs, herbaceous borders, ponds, many wildlife friendly features plus plenty of vegetables. Several of the gardens have won Gold in the Kenilworth in Bloom garden competition. Abbey Fields is an attractive park in the old part of town close to Kenilworth Castle and the Millennium Walk, starting here is an hour's walk through the Warwickshire countryside around the now drained Kenilworth Castle mere.

29 19 LEIGH CRESCENT
Long Itchington,
Southam, CV47 9QS. Tony Shorthouse, 01926 817192,
tonyshorthouse19@gmail.com. *Off the Stockton Rd in Long Itchington village.* **Visits by arrangement 23 June to 30 Sept for groups of 5 to 10. Adm £5, chd free. Tea.**
Discover a tropical garden where dappled sunlight filters through the green canopy above and sounds of a waterfall fills the air. A tropical garden, hidden in a Warwickshire village, densely packed with rare and unusual species, many raised from seed.

The Whichford Pottery, Whichford & Ascott Gardens

GROUP OPENING

30 NEW LILLINGTON ROAD GARDENS
Lillington Road, Leamington Spa, CV32 5YY. Mr Ian & Mrs Viv Roberts. *We are on the E side of Lillington Rd just S of the junc with Wathen Rd.* On street parking available. What3words app: frame.storm.gross. **Sun 8 June (1-5). Combined adm £5, chd free. Tea, coffee & cake.**

NEW **18 LILLINGTON ROAD**
Mr Steve & Mrs Vicky Bell.

NEW **32 LILLINGTON ROAD**
Mr Ian & Mrs Viv Roberts.

A great opportunity to see two different walled town gardens to the rear of a row of Victorian properties in the Lillington Road Conservation Area. The gardens feature flower filled, mixed herbaceous borders with trees and shrubs. Espaliered fruit trees and pleasant seating areas to enjoy the garden complete the picture and there is a signature Wollemi Pine at number 32. Both gardens are wheelchair accessible from the road.

560 WARWICKSHIRE

Monksbridge

31 MARIE CURIE HOSPICE GARDEN
Marsh Lane, Solihull, B91 2PQ. Mrs Do Connolly, www.mariecurie.org.uk/westmidlands. Close to J5 M42 to E of Solihull Town Centre. M42 J5, travel towards Solihull on A41. Take slip toward Solihull to join B4025 & after island take 1st R onto Marsh Ln. Hospice on R. Some onsite parking - plenty for blue badge holders. Sun 22 June (11-4). Adm £4, chd free. Light refreshments. The gardens contain two large, formally laid out patients' gardens, indoor courtyards, a long border adjoining the car park and a wildlife area with fairy garden and pond area. Children's games. The volunteer gardening team hope that the gardens provide a peaceful and comforting place for patients, their visitors and staff. The path to the fairy garden has a woodchip surface and may not be suitable for all wheelchair access.

32 MAXSTOKE CASTLE
Castle Lane, Coleshill, B46 2RD. Mr G M Fetherston-Dilke, www.maxstokecastle.com. Located in between Birmingham and Coventry. 2½ m E of Coleshill. The Castle drive is on Castle Ln (adjacent to the golf course). Sun 15 June (11-5). Adm £12, chd free. Pre-booking essential, please email events@maxstokecastle.com or visit www.maxstokecastle.com for information & booking. Home-made teas. Savoury options will also be available. Donation to other charities.
Five acres of garden and grounds with roses, herbaceous plants, shrubs and trees in the courtyard and immediate surroundings of this C14 moated castle. Tea and cakes; plant and gift stalls. Wheelchair access to the garden but not into the house.

33 NEW MONKSBRIDGE
Butlers Marston, Warwick, CV35 0NA. Mr & Mrs Piercey. Take lane signposted "Parish Church", car park is next to church. Tue 24, Thur 26 June, Tue 1, Thur 3 July (9-3). Adm £8, chd free.
Re-developed Victorian gardens inc herbaceous borders, parterre, kitchen garden, stone circle, Japanese garden and wildflower walks.

34 OAK HOUSE
Waverley Edge, Bubbenhall, Coventry, CV8 3LW. Helena Grant, 07731 419685, helena.grant@btinternet.com. 15 mins from Leamington Spa via the Oxford Rd/A423 & the Leamington Rd/A445 & the A46. Spaces for 5 cars only. Visits by arrangement Apr to Oct for groups of up to 10. Refreshments can be provided for a charge of £4.00 per person. Adm £6, chd free.
Tucked away next to Waverley Wood, Oak House enjoys a walled garden that has been landscaped and extended over 30 yrs. The garden is split on 2 levels with seating areas allowing for relaxed appreciation of every aspect of the garden, with peaceful places to sit, ponder and enjoy. A focal point is the large terracotta urn, over 60 yrs old, which delivers vertical interest and the summerhouse and arbour which face each other diagonally across the garden. The curved borders have a wide range of planting creating distinct areas which surround the lawn. There are over 80 different plant varieties giving year-round interest and creating a haven for birds and wildlife. Wheelchair access only on level path which runs round the house.

GROUP OPENING

35 OLD ARLEY GARDENS
Coventry, CV7 8FT. Enter Ansley Ln via B'ham Rd or Rectory Rd. Parking at the School. Transport may be required to visit all gardens. Sun 13 July (2-6). Combined adm £5, chd free. Tea, coffee & cake in Methodist Hall.

1 ELM GROVE
Ms Jane Taylor.

WARWICKSHIRE

HOLLYCROFT
Mr Lewis Hodges.

17 ST WILFREDS COTTAGES
VJ Eady.

35 ST WILFREDS COTTAGES
Mrs Justine Clee.

THE SCHOOL HOUSE
Mrs Pauline McAleese.

17 SPINNEY CLOSE
Mr David Cox.

Old Arley is an ancient village which appears in the Domesday book. More recently it was a small mining community and St Wilfreds Cottages were built in 1907 to accommodate the mine's supervisors and their families. The gardens around the village vary in style and size and the planting is varied, ranging from traditional cottage to more contemporary styles. Walking the route is 1½ miles so transport may be necessary.

36 PACKINGTON HALL
Meriden, nr Coventry, CV7 7HF.
Lord & Lady Guernsey,
www.packingtonestate.co.uk.
Midway between Coventry & B'ham on A45. Our main entrance is 400yds from Stonebridge r'about heading towards Coventry. Please use What3words app: dreamers. mandolin.portfolio as satnav often takes you to the wrong location. **Sat 5 July (11-5). Adm £7.50, chd free. Home-made teas on the terrace or in the Pompeiian Room if wet.**
Packington Hall is the setting for an elegant Capability Brown landscape. Designed from 1751, the gardens inc a serpentine lake, impressive Cedars of Lebanon, Wellingtonias and a 1762 Japanese bridge. There are also wildflower meadows, mixed terrace borders, and a recently restored walled garden. Wheelchair access is possible but please note there are no paths in the garden. The gravelled terrace, where teas are served, is easily accessible.

37 PAUL'S OASIS OF CALM
18 Kings Close, Kings Heath,
Birmingham, B14 6TP. Mr
Paul Doogan, 01214 446943,
gardengreen18@hotmail.co.uk.
4m from city centre. 5m from M42 J4. Take A345 to Kings Heath High St then B4122 Vicarage Rd. Turn L onto Kings Rd then R to Kings Cl.

Visits by arrangement May to Aug for groups of up to 15. Adm £3, chd free.
Garden cultivated from nothing into a little oasis. Measuring 18ft x 70ft. It's small but packed with interesting and unusual plants, water features and seven seating areas. The large piece of council land in front of the house has been cultivated.

GROUP OPENING

38 PEBWORTH GARDENS
Stratford-upon-Avon, CV37 8XZ.
www.pebworth.org/pebworth-open-gardens---national-garden-scheme.
7m SW of Stratford-upon-Avon. For parking & SatNav please use CV37 8XN. **Sun 25, Mon 26 May (1-5.30). Combined adm £7, chd free. Home-made teas at Pebworth Village Hall, served by The Pebworth and District WI. Coffee and soft drinks also available.**

ICKNIELD BARN
Sheila Davies.

JASMINE COTTAGE
Ted & Veronica Watson.

THE KNOLL
Mr & Mrs K Wood.

MEON COTTAGE
David & Sally Donnison.

ORCHARD HOUSE
David & Susan Lees.

PEBWORTH ALLOTMENTS
Les Madden.

Pebworth is a delightful village with thatched cottages and properties young and old. There are a variety of garden styles from cottage gardens to modern, walled and terraced gardens. Pebworth is topped by St Peter's Church which has a large ring of 10 bells, unusual for a small rural church. This year we have 6 gardens and the Pebworth Allotments opening, with scrumptious tea and cakes provided by the Pebworth WI in the village hall. The Pebworth Allotments have only been in existence a few years and residents have lovingly tended to them. Some of the Allotmenteers are real characters so do visit and have a chat, they have a wealth of knowledge. Partial wheelchair access in some gardens. Ramp available for village hall.

39 PRIORS MARSTON MANOR
The Green, Priors Marston,
CV47 7RH. Dr & Mrs Mark Cecil.
8m SW of Daventry. Off the A361 between Daventry & Banbury at Charwelton. Follow signs to Priors Marston, approx 2m. Arrive at T-junc with a war memorial on R. The manor will be on your L. **Sat 7 June (10-6). Adm £7, chd free. Tea, coffee & cake.**
Arrive in Priors Marston village and explore the manor gardens. Greatly enhanced by the present owners to relate back to a Georgian manor garden and pleasure grounds. Wonderful walled kitchen garden provides seasonal produce and cut flowers for the house. Herbaceous flower beds and a sunken terrace with water feature by William Pye. Lawns lead down to the lake and estate around which you can walk amongst the trees and wildlife with stunning views up to the house. Partial wheelchair access. Entrance through gravel courtyard.

40 8 RECTORY ROAD
Solihull, B91 3RP. Nigel & Daphne Carter, 07527 475759, npcarter@blueyonder.co.uk.
Solihull Town Centre. Located in the town centre: off Church Hill Rd, turn into Rectory Rd, bear L down the road, house on the R 100 metres down. **Sun 15 June (11.30-5.30). Adm £4, chd free. Home-made teas. Evening opening Sun 7 Sept (7-10). Adm £4. Wine.** Visits also by arrangement 16 June to 5 Sept for groups of 5 to 30.
Stunning town garden divided into areas with different features. A garden with unusual trees and intensively planted borders and an unusual folly. Walk to the end of the garden and step into a Japanese themed garden complete with pond, fish and traditional style bridge. Sit on the shaded decking area. A garden to attract bees and butterflies with plenty of places to relax. Japanese themed features, unusual folly and stunning moongate. Some steps; those with mobility issues may find access difficult.

562 WARWICKSHIRE

41 ♦ RYTON ORGANIC GARDENS
Wolston Lane, Ryton on Dunsmore, Coventry, CV8 3LG. Garden Organic, 02476 303517, enquiry@gardenorganic.org.uk, www.gardenorganic.org.uk. 5m SE of Coventry. From A45 take the exit signed Wolston with brown tourist signs for Ryton Gardens. **For NGS: Sat 12 July, Sat 6 Sept (1-5). Adm £5, chd free. Tea, coffee & cake.** For other opening times and information, please phone, email or visit garden website.
Garden Organic's inspirational and sustainable demonstration garden at Ryton contains a wonderful fruit and vegetable potager, together with several large ornamental flower beds. Packed full of ideas for gardens of all sizes, it features a large glasshouse, polytunnel, composting area, water features, no-dig and container gardens plus two National Plant Collections.
&. ✿ 🚌 [NPC] ☕ •))

42 2 ST NICHOLAS AVENUE
Kenilworth, CV8 1JU. Mr Ian Roberts. **Sun 9 Feb (12-4). Adm £3, chd free. Home-made teas in St Nicholas Church. Open nearby Fieldgate. Combined adm with Fieldgate £5. Opening with Kenilworth Gardens on Sun 15 June.**
The garden has been developed over the past 30 yrs. It has been transformed from an overgrown uninteresting patch to a mature and varied garden containing a wide selection of plants inc a collection of Snowdrops. It contains many features inc mixed borders, ponds, rockery, structures, mature trees and shrubs. All areas are interconnected by paths so the garden can be enjoyed at leisure.
☕ •))

43 NEW 170 STATION ROAD
Sutton Coldfield, B73 5LE. Mrs Jenny Ratcliff. *Sutton Coldfield, to the E of Birmingham. Location is easy to find just enter postcode B73 5LE into SatNav, or What3words app: tonic.drip.enter.* **Evening opening Fri 5 Sept (6.30-9). Adm £6, chd free. Light refreshments. Adm inc a glass of wine, small beer or soft drink. Additional drinks can be purchased by donation to the NGS.**
A typical suburban garden that has seen many changes over 30 yrs. From football pitch and adventure playground to a garden with different spaces. Inc scruffy bits, wildlife pond, vegetable garden with raised beds, shady area with fernery and well-stocked herbaceous beds and borders. Naturalised bulbs in the spring through to autumn hot colours. The garden is flat and accessible, however the drive is gravel which can be challenging for wheelchair users.
&. ☕ •))

GROUP OPENING

44 STYVECHALE GARDENS
Knoll Drive, Coventry, CV3 5DE. *Located on the S side of Coventry close to A45. Tickets & map available on the day from Church Room, St Thomas More Church Knoll Dr Coventry CV3 5DE.* **Sun 8 June (11-5). Combined adm £5, chd free. Tea, coffee & cake.**

11 BAGINTON ROAD
Ken & Pauline Bond.

105 BAGINTON ROAD
Parmjit and Jas Dhugga.

164 BAGINTON ROAD
Fran & Jeff Gaught.

59 THE CHESILS
John Marron.

66 THE CHESILS
Ami Samra & Rodger Hope.

16 DELAWARE ROAD
Val & Roy Howells.

An eclectic mix of lovely, mature suburban gardens. Enjoy their variety from kitchen garden to a touch of the exotic, restful gardens to a riot of colourful borders. Roses, water features, ponds, shady areas and more. Something for everyone and plenty of ideas for you to take home. One of the gardens was awarded garden of the year by a national newspaper. Relax in the gardens where a warm friendly welcome will await you. Plant sales and refreshments in some gardens. Additional gardens may be open on the day.
🐾 ✿ ☕ •))

45 NEW SWIFT HOUSE
The Green, Churchover, Rugby, CV23 0EP. Mr Richard & Mrs Denise Robinson. *1 m from J1 M6. One of the last houses if arriving in the small village of Churchover from the E / M6 / A426.* **Sat 21, Sun 22 June (10-4). Combined adm with**
Forge House £5, chd free. **Tea, coffee & cake.**
A mature 'old English' garden with large wildlife pond, wooded area, formal and informal areas and a great view over the Swift valley. Varied outdoor rooms with a surprise at every turn. The garden is built on a gentle slope and and not all areas are accessible with a wheelchair. Care with small children around the water features.
&. 🐾 🚌 ☕ •))

---

46 NEW THRIVE BIRMINGHAM
Vicarage Road, Kings Heath, Birmingham, B14 7TQ. Thrive, www.thrive.org.uk. *Located inside Kings Heath park. What3words app: prove.trio.fork.* **Sat 12 July (10.30-3). Adm £5, chd free. Tea, coffee & cake.**
The garden is a 2 acre site known historically as The Television Garden. Its rich heritage began in 1972 as a partnership between Birmingham City Council and television company ATV. Today, the gardens are used by Thrive, a national charity, who help to improve people's physical and mental health through gardening and horticulture. Some notable features of the garden inc wheelchair accessible raised beds, herbaceous borders, the timeless mature garden and several thriving ponds which are home to smooth newts. We are also fortunate to have three designer gardens, created by John Brookes, Bonita Bulaitis and Dan Pearson.
&. 🐾 ✿ ☕ •))

GROUP OPENING

47 TYSOE GARDENS
Tysoe, Warwick, CV35 0TR. *W of A422, N of Banbury (9m). E of A3400 & Shipston-on-Stour (4m). N of A4035 & Brailes (3m). Please park on the village Recreation Ground beside the Old Fire Stn CV35 0FF. What3words app: ports.exotic. general.* **Sat 5, Sun 6 July (2-6). Combined adm £7, chd free. Home-made teas at the Village Hall.**

5 AVON AVENUE
Penny & Rob Varley.

GARDEN COTTAGE & WALLED KITCHEN GARDEN
Sue & Mike Sanderson, www.twkg.co.uk.

1 JEFFS CLOSE
Miss Lucy Locke.

WARWICKSHIRE

NEW 12 OXHILL ROAD
Mrs Christine Tuffin.

NEW 2 PEACOCK LANE
Julie and Martin Smart.

NEW QUINTON HOUSE
Gill and Trevor Mouat.

NEW STANHOPE HOUSE
Alexandra and Alastair Murdie.

SUNNYSIDE
Ms Jennifer Cawood.

NEW WINDMILL VIEW
Heather Dowler.

Tysoe, an original Hornton stone village stands on the North East foothills of the Cotswolds below Edge Hill. Nine wonderful gardens open this year, five of which have never opened before. You can be sure that Tysoe will offer a happy atmosphere, some terrific teas at the village hall. Contactless payment available at the village hall for entrance tickets, cash payments can be made at all gardens. Cash only for plant sale and teas.

---

48 NEW 48 VARLINS WAY
Kings Norton, Birmingham, B38 9UX. Mr David Fernie. *A441 Birmingham Redditch Rd. Through Kings Norton. L at "Man on Moon" L at Bracken Way then L to park in Longdales Rd.* **Sat 19 July (10.30-4). Combined adm with 128 Green Acres Road £5, chd free.** Suburban garden with unusual collection of trees and shrubs with wildlife in mind. combined opening with 128 Green Acres Road which is a 15min walk away. Wheelchair access to lawn and main features.

GROUP OPENING

49 WARMINGTON GARDENS
Banbury, OX17 1BU. *5m NW of Banbury. Take B4100 N from Banbury, after 5m turn R across short dual carriageway into Warmington. From N take J12 off M40 onto B4100.* **Sun 22 June (1-5). Combined adm £6, chd free. Home-made teas at Warmington Village Hall.**

GOURDON
Jenny Deeming.

GREENWAYS
Tim Stevens.

LANTERN HOUSE
Peter & Tessa Harborne.

THE MANOR HOUSE
Mr & Mrs G Lewis.

THE ORCHARD
Mike Cable.

SPRINGFIELD HOUSE
Jenny & Roger Handscombe, 01295 690286,
jehandscombe@btinternet.com.

1 THE WHEELWRIGHTS
Ms E Bunn.

Warmington is a charming historic village, mentioned in the Domesday Book, situated at the NE edge of the Cotswolds in a designated AONB. There is a large village green with a pond overlooked by an Elizabethan Manor House (not open). There are other historic buildings inc St Michael's Church, The Plough Inn and Springfield House all dating from the C16 or before. There is a mixed and varied selection of gardens to enjoy during your visit to Warmington. These inc the formal knot gardens and topiary of The Manor House, cottage and courtyard gardens, terraced gardens on the slopes of Warmington Hill and orchards containing local varieties of apple trees. Some gardens will be selling homegrown plants. WC at village hall.

GROUP OPENING

50 WHICHFORD & ASCOTT GARDENS
Whichford & Ascott, Shipston-on-Stour, CV36 5PG. *6m SE of Shipston-on-Stour. For parking please use CV36 5PG. There is parking by the church. Parking also available at Wood House and roadside in Ascott.* **Sun 15 June (1.30-5). Combined adm £7.50, chd free. Home-made teas.**

ASCOTT LODGE
Charlotte Copley.

ASCOTT RISE
Carol & Jerry Moore.

BELMONT HOUSE
Robert & Yoko Ward.

LENTICULARS
Mrs Diana Atkins.

MURTON COTTAGE
Hilary & David Blakemore.

THE OLD RECTORY
Peter & Caroline O'Kane.

PLUM TREE COTTAGE
Janet Knight.

THE WHICHFORD POTTERY
Jim & Dominique Keeling,
www.whichfordpottery.com.

WOOD HOUSE
Mr and Mrs G James.

The gardens in this group reflect many different styles. The 2 villages are in an AONB, nestled within a dramatic landscape of hills, pasture and woodland, which is used to picturesque effect by the garden owners. Fine lawns, mature shrubs and interesting planning will all enrich your visit to our beautiful gardens. Many incorporate the inventive use of natural springs, forming ponds, pools and other water features. Classic cottage gardens contrast with larger and more classical gardens which adopt variations on the traditional English garden of herbaceous borders, climbing roses, yew hedges and walled enclosures. Partial wheelchair access as some gardens are on sloping sites.

---

51 WOOLSCOTT BARN
Woolscott, Rugby, CV23 8DB.
Neil Higginson, 07836 511495,
neilnrhigginson@btinternet.com,
www.instagram.com/neilhiggison.
2 m from Dunchurch. Take the A45 S from Dunchurch towards Daventry until R turn for Grandborough. After 1 m, go round a big bend & past manor house. Woolscott barn is 400m after manor house on L. **Visits by arrangement 31 Jan to 18 Aug. Adm £6, chd free. Tea, coffee & cake.**
A plantsman's garden set in 1½ acres a great variety of plants. Large areas of shade plantings. Over 300 different snowdrops, anemone nemorosa, Erythroniums, ferns and geraniums. A dwarf conifer rockery with a range of choice bulbs and herbaceous borders. Vegetable beds. Autumn brings mass plantings of Cyclamen to the party. There is a large area dedicated to propagation of more unusual plants. Please note that parking is limited, so kindly contact the owner beforehand to confirm availability.

WILTSHIRE

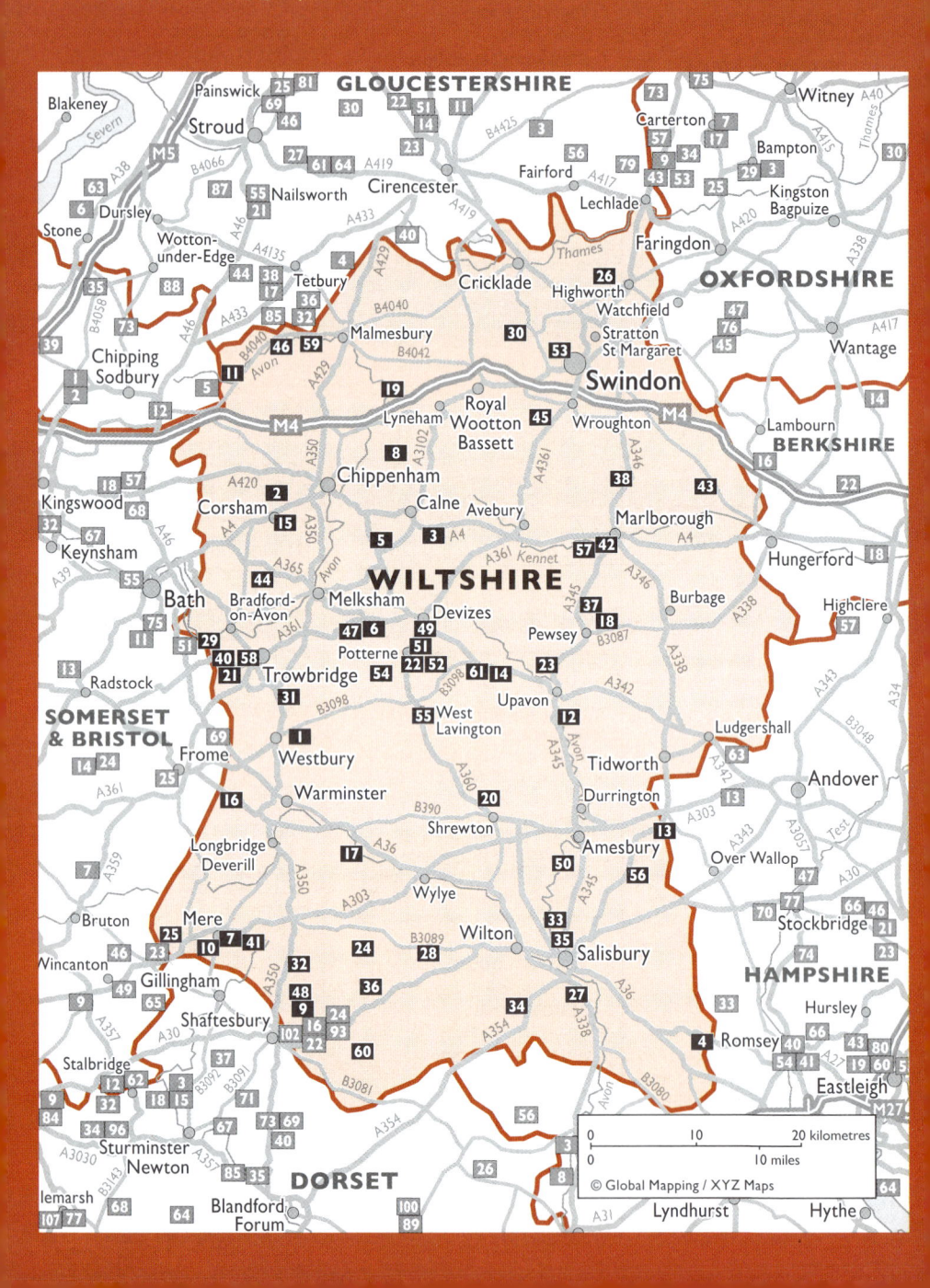

VOLUNTEERS

County Organisers
Ros Ford 07717 135028
ros.ford@ngs.org.uk

Alex Graham 07906 146337
alex.graham@ngs.org.uk

County Treasurer
Tony Roper 01249 447436
tony.roper@ngs.org.uk

Publicity
& Booklet Co-ordinator
Tricia Duncan 01672 810443
tricia.duncan@ngs.org.uk

Social Media
Maud Peters 07595 266299
maud.peters@ngs.org.uk

Assistant County Organisers
Sue Allen 07785 294153
sue.allen@ngs.org.uk

Sarah Coate 01722 782165
sarah.coate@ngs.org.uk

Annabel Dallas 01672 520266
annabel.dallas@btinternet.com

Andy Devey 07810 641595
andy.devey@ngs.org.uk

Jo Hankey 01722 742472
jo.hankey@ngs.org.uk

Julie Harding 07775 683163
julie.harding@ngs.org.uk

Jane Milligan 07771 901352
jane.milligan@ngs.org.uk

Alison Parker 07786 985741
alison.parker@ngs.org.uk

@WiltshireNGS
@Wiltshirengs

OPENING DATES

All entries subject to change.
For latest information check
www.ngs.org.uk

Map locator numbers are shown to the right of each garden name.

January

Wednesday 1st
Westcroft   56

Thursday 2nd
Westcroft   56

Thursday 9th
Westcroft   56

Thursday 16th
Westcroft   56

Saturday 18th
Westcroft   56

Sunday 19th
Westcroft   56

Thursday 30th
Westcroft   56

February

Snowdrop Openings

Saturday 1st
Westcroft   56

Sunday 2nd
Westcroft   56

Thursday 6th
Westcroft   56

Friday 7th
Westcroft   56

Thursday 13th
Westcroft   56

Thursday 20th
Westcroft   56

Saturday 22nd
Westcroft   56

Sunday 23rd
Westcroft   56

Thursday 27th
Westcroft   56

March

Thursday 6th
Westcroft   56

Thursday 13th
Westcroft   56

Sunday 23rd
Fonthill House   24

Sunday 30th
◆ Corsham Court   15

April

Wednesday 9th
Blackland House   3

Sunday 13th
Brow Cottage   6
◆ Corsham Court   15
Seend House   47

Wednesday 16th
Blackland House   3

Saturday 26th
Wellaway   54

Sunday 27th
Oare House   37
Wellaway   54

May

Friday 16th
Biddestone Manor   2

Saturday 17th
Winkelbury House   60

Sunday 18th
Knoyle Place   32
1 Southview   49
Trymnells   52
◆ Twigs Community Garden   53

Saturday 24th
Conock Manor   14

Sunday 25th
Hyde's House   28

Monday 26th
Cholderton Estate   13

Saturday 31st
NEW Caleston   9
Eastwell Manor   22

WILTSHIRE

June

Sunday 1st
Rookery Cottage 44

Wednesday 4th
Whatley Manor 59

Thursday 5th
Cadenham Manor 8
NEW Caleston 9

Saturday 7th
NEW Drax House 20
Horatio's Garden 27
NEW 20 Jubilee Estate 30
The Old Vicarage 39
West Lavington Manor 55

Sunday 8th
Burton Grange 7
The Chantry 10
Chisenbury Priory 12
Hannington Village Gardens 26
NEW 20 Jubilee Estate 30

Friday 13th
Salthrop House 45

Saturday 14th
Salthrop House 45

Sunday 15th
Dauntsey Gardens 19
Mawarden Court 35
North Cottage 36

Thursday 19th
NEW Preston Farmhouse 43

Sunday 22nd
Gasper Cottage 25

The Old Vicarage 40
Semley Grange 48
NEW 4 Westwood Road 58

Sunday 29th
Duck Pond Barn 21
Oare House 37

July

Sunday 6th
The Parish House 41
Teasel 50

Saturday 12th
Dane Brook 18

Sunday 13th
Dane Brook 18
Little Durnford Manor 33

Sunday 20th
Cherry Orchard Barn 11
♦ Twigs Community Garden 53

Sunday 27th
Corsley House 16
NEW Preshute Lane Gardens 42

August

Saturday 9th
NEW 20 Jubilee Estate 30

Sunday 10th
NEW 20 Jubilee Estate 30

Saturday 30th
NEW Ogbourne Manor 38

September

Saturday 6th
♦ Iford Manor Gardens 29

Sunday 7th
1 Southview 49

Saturday 13th
Wellaway 54

Sunday 14th
Wellaway 54

Sunday 21st
Brow Cottage 6

By Arrangement

Arrange a personalised garden visit with your club, or group of friends, on a date to suit you. See individual garden entries for full details.

Beggars Knoll Chinese Garden 1
Bluebells 4
Cadenham Manor 8
Chisenbury Priory 12
Cortington Manor 17
Falkners Cottage 23
Gasper Cottage 25
Kettle Farm Cottage 31
Manor House, Stratford Tony 34
Scots Farm 46
1 Southview 49
Teasel 50
Tristenagh House 51
West Lavington Manor 55
Westcroft 56
Westwind 57
Wudston House 61

Teasel

THE GARDENS

1 BEGGARS KNOLL CHINESE GARDEN
Newtown, Westbury, BA13 3ED. Colin Little & Penny Stirling, 01373 823383, silkendalliance@ talktalk.net. *1m SE of Westbury. Turn off B3098 at White Horse Pottery, up hill towards the White Horse for ¾m. Parking at end of drive for 10-12 cars.* **Visits by arrangement 2 June to 31 July for groups of 5 to 20. Only cash payments and cheques accepted. Adm £6, chd free. Tea, coffee & cake.**
A series of Chinese-style garden rooms, separated by elaborate gateways inc moongate, with mosaic paths winding past pavilions, ponds and many rare Chinese trees, shrubs and flowers. Relatively new, a tranquil Islamic-style tiled garden influenced by NW China. Potager full of flowers and vegetables. Spectacular views to the Mendips. Garden tours by owners inc in admission.

2 BIDDESTONE MANOR
Chippenham Lane, Biddestone, SN14 7DJ. Andy Smith, Head Gardener. *On A4 between Chippenham & Corsham turn N from A420, 5m W of Chippenham, turn S.* **Fri 16 May (11-4). Adm £8, chd free. Home-made teas and cakes.**
Cotswold stone C17 manor house (not open) with 5 acres of garden to enjoy. Lake, ponds, streams, arboretum, vegetable and cutting gardens and orchard. Formal front garden featuring box and yew topiary. Wheelchair access to most parts, a few steps.

3 BLACKLAND HOUSE
Quemerford, Calne, SN11 8UQ. Polly & Edward Nicholson, www.bayntunflowers.co.uk. *Situated just off A4. Use Google Maps. Enter the grounds through the side entrance signed St. Peter's Church & Blackland Park Deliveries. Opp The Willows on Quemerford.* **Wed 9, Wed 16 Apr (2-5). Adm £10, chd free. Pre-booking essential, please visit www.ngs.org.uk for information & booking. Home-made teas. Vegan & gluten free cakes. Tea & cakes charged at £5.** Donation to Dorothy House Hospice.

A wonderfully varied 5 acre garden adjacent to the River Marden (house not open). Formal walled productive and cutting garden, traditional glasshouses, rose garden and wide herbaceous borders. Interesting topiary, trained fruit trees, historic tulips (inc the National Collection of historic tulips) and other unusual spring bulbs. Certified organic with the Soil Association. Hand-tied bunches of flowers and Polly's new book 'The Tulip Garden' will be for sale. Partial wheelchair access, steps, grass and cobbles, wooden bridges, deep water.

4 BLUEBELLS
Cowesfield, Whiteparish, Salisbury, SP5 2RB. Hilary Mathison, 07709 205589, hilary.mathison@icloud.com. *SW of Salisbury. On main A27 road from Salisbury to Romsey. 1½m SE of Whiteparish, on A27, 100-200 m inside Wiltshire county boundary What3words app: centuries.baths.herbs.* **Visits by arrangement 19 Apr to 13 Sept for groups of 10 to 32. Space for 10-12 cars only. No parking on main road or nearby. Adm £5, chd free. Home-made teas. Wine & savoury bites for evening visits. Pls bring cash for refreshments.**
1½ acre garden in a rural setting. Small woodland has carpets of bluebells in season. Large front lawn surrounded by borders. Rear garden faces south and the design is contemporary to reflect the newly built house on site. Many tulips in spring throughout the garden, amongst the mainly perennial planting. Large vegetable area, fruit trees, inc espalier trees, 'stepovers' and 2 ponds. Partial wheelchair access.

5 ♦ BOWOOD WOODLAND GARDENS
Calne, SN11 9PG. The Marquis of Lansdowne, 01249 812102, houseandgardens@bowood.org, www.bowood.org. *3½m SE of Chippenham. Located off J17 M4 nr Bath & Chippenham. Entrance off A342 between Sandy Lane & Derry Hill Villages. Follow brown tourist signs.* **For opening times and information, please phone, email or visit garden website.**
This 30 acre woodland garden of azaleas, magnolias, rhododendrons and bluebells is one of the most exciting of its type in the country. From the individual flowers to the breathtaking sweep of colour, this is a garden not to be missed. With two miles of meandering paths, you will find hidden treasures at every corner. The Woodland Gardens are 2 miles from Bowood House & Gardens. They are open for six weeks during the flowering season from mid-April to early June (see website for full details).

6 BROW COTTAGE
Seend Hill, Seend, Melksham, SN12 6RU. Alexandra & James Gray, www.alexandragray.com. *2m W of Devizes on A361. Garden on L when coming from E, at top of Inmarsh Lane. Parking on green in village centre in Apr. Footpath via fields as marked by yellow signs. Parking in the field opp in Sept.* **Sun 13 Apr (1-5). Combined adm with Seend House £8, chd free. Sun 21 Sept (2-5). Adm £5, chd free. Home-made teas.**
A half acre contemporary cottage garden owned by a garden designer and created over the past 25 yrs. A garden of many harmonious parts inc lawns, well-stocked borders, topiary, potager, sunken pool garden, wildlife pond, short woodland walk, species bulb and wildflower lawn and canopied dining area. Open with Seend House in April and connected by a field footpath. Shuttle available. Wheelchair access over gravel driveway rather than steps from pedestrian gate on main road.

7 BURTON GRANGE
Burton, Mere, BA12 6BR. Sue Phipps & Paddy Sumner, www.suephipps.com. *What3words app: closes.part.standards. Take lane, signed to Burton, on A303 just E of Mere bypass. After 400 yds follow road past pond & round to L. Go past wall on R. Burton Grange entrance is in laurel hedge on R.* **Sun 8 June (11.30-5). Adm £5, chd free. Home-made teas.**
1½ acre peaceful garden, created from scratch since 2014. Lawns, borders, large ornamental pond, some gravel planting, vegetable garden, cutting garden and pergola rose garden, together with a number of wonderful mature trees.

WILTSHIRE

8 CADENHAM MANOR
Foxham, Chippenham,
SN15 4NH. Victoria & Martin
Nye, garden@cadenham.com,
www.cadenham.com. *B4069 from
Chippenham or M4 J17, turn R in
Christian Malford & L in Foxham.
On A3102 turn L from Calne or R
from Lyneham at Xrds between
Hilmarton & Goatacre. See map
www.cadenham.com/contact.*
Thur 5 June (2-7). Adm £10, chd free. Pre-booking essential, please visit www.ngs.org.uk for information & booking. Tea, coffee & cake. Visits also by arrangement 6 Mar to 30 Oct for groups of 15 to 40. Pre booking essential.
This glorious French-style 4 acre garden surrounds a listed C17 manor house with moats and a C16 dovecote Its many rooms are furnished with specimen trees, fountains and statues to focus the eye. Known for its stunning displays of old roses, it also has swathes of spring bulbs, wisteria, bearded iris, a water garden in the old canal, plus extensive vegetable and herb gardens.

9 NEW CALESTON
Semley, Shaftesbury, SP7 9AX.
Mark and Eloise Hawes. *From A350 take the turning to Semley, past village shop on R & follow road up towards Shaftsbury. Caleston is last house on L going out of the village. What3words app: courtyard. surpasses.lure.* **Sat 31 May, Thur 5 June (2-5). Adm £5, chd free. Pre-booking essential, please visit ngs.org.uk for information & booking. Tea, coffee & cake.**
A 3 acre woodland garden that has been developed over the last 20 yrs, planted with a mixture of mainly native tree species inc oak, birch and sweet chestnut. There are also some specimen trees planted such as tulip, paper handkerchief and a resistant elm! The garden has beautiful views across the Nadder Valley.

10 THE CHANTRY
Church Street, Mere, Warminster, BA12 6DS. Mr & Mrs Richard Wilson, instagram.com/thechantrygarden. *In the centre of Mere, turn down Angel Lane & follow it to the Cemetery Car Park (RHS) & through it into the field at the Chantry. Pedestrian access is via*

Church St. **Sun 8 June (1-5). Adm £7.50, chd free. Home-made teas.**
Medieval chantry house with large landscaped gardens (inc cottage and walled gardens) ponds, orchard, fields and woodland. Historical connection with celebrated Dorset poet William Barnes who wrote his most famous work 'My Orchard in Linden Lea' about the garden.

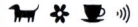

11 CHERRY ORCHARD BARN
Luckington, SN14 6NZ. Paul Fletcher & Tim Guard. *Cherry Orchard Barn is ¾m before the centre of SN14 6NZ at a T junction. Passing the Barn is ill-advised, as turning rapidly becomes difficult.* **Sun 20 July (1-5). Adm £5, chd free. Tea, coffee & cake.**
A charming one acre garden, created from the corner of a field, with open views of surrounding countryside. Containing seven rooms, three of which are densely planted with herbaceous perennials, each with individual identities and colour themes. The garden is described by visitors as a haven of tranquillity. Largely level access to all areas of garden. Some gravel paths.

12 CHISENBURY PRIORY
East Chisenbury, SN9 6AQ. Mr & Mrs John Manser, 07810 483984, peterjohnmanser@yahoo.com. *3m SW of Pewsey. Turn E from A345 at Enford then N to E Chisenbury, main gates 1m on R.* **Sun 8 June (2-5.30). Adm £10, chd free. Home-made teas.** Visits also by arrangement 2 May to 30 June.
Medieval Priory with Queen Anne face and early C17 rear (not open) in middle of 5 acre garden on chalk. Mature garden with fine trees within clump and flint walls, herbaceous borders, shrubs, roses. Moisture loving plants along mill leat, carp pond, orchard and wild garden, many unusual plants.

13 CHOLDERTON ESTATE
Kingsettle Stud, Cholderton Park, Cholderton, SP4 0DX. Henry & Felicity Edmunds. *Signed from the Cholderton Farm Shop on the A338 (Tidworth to Salisbury road) nr A303 junction.* **Mon 26 May (11.30-4.30). Adm £5, chd free. Tea, coffee & cake. Home-made teas in the courtyard at Kingsettle Stud, the**

Estate's Grade II listed stable block.
A striking Victorian walled garden featuring a peony walk dating over 100 yrs old and a working kitchen garden. Arboretum with wildlife garden, maze and numerous tree species. There are no stairs to access the garden but ground is uneven. The WCs are unfortunately not wheelchair accessible.

14 CONOCK MANOR
Conock, Devizes, SN10 3QQ.
Justin Kennedy. *5m SE of Devizes. Conock lies just off the A342 between the turnings for Urchfont & Chirton. Conock Manor is on the R side of the lane. What3words app: flap.emeralds.cashiers.* **Sat 24 May (11-4). Adm £8, chd free. Teas, coffee, cold drinks, cakes & pastries.**
A relaxed family garden embracing C18 architecture (inc a rustic dairy) and defined by its long, south facing wall. There are lawns and wildflower meadows, mixed borders and climbers, a magnolia grove and a vegetable garden with greenhouse. Evolving under the stewardship of Pip Morrison, the garden utilises a ha-ha to sit comfortably in the surrounding wooded parkland with views out to the surrounding hills and the Alton Barnes chalk-horse. Soft lawn, some gravel paths.

15 ♦ CORSHAM COURT
Corsham, SN13 0BZ. Lord Methuen, 01249 701610, staterooms@corsham-court.co.uk, www.corsham-court.co.uk. *4m W of Chippenham. Signed off A4 in Corsham.* **For NGS: Sun 30 Mar, Sun 13 Apr (2-5.30). Adm £5, chd £2.70.** For other opening times and information, please phone, email or visit garden website.
Park and gardens laid out by Capability Brown and Repton. Large lawns with fine specimens of ornamental trees surround the Elizabethan mansion. C18 bath house hidden in the grounds. Spring bulbs, beautiful lily pond with Indian bean trees, young arboretum and stunning collection of magnolias. Wheelchair (not motorised) access to house, gravel paths in garden.

WILTSHIRE 569

16 CORSLEY HOUSE
Corsley, Warminster, BA12 7QH. Glen Senk & Keith Johnson. *From Longleat on the A362 towards Frome turning 1st R on Deep Lane. Corsley House is ¼ m on R. The parkland entrance, where there is parking, is on R beyond the house.* **Sun 27 July (11-5). Adm £10, chd free. Tea, coffee & cake.**
A garden full of surprises to reflect the eclectic nature of a Georgian home with a secret Jacobean facade. A unique sculpted wave lawn and a truly exceptional walled garden. Many well preserved ancient outbuildings such as a potting and apple storage shed and a granary built on staddle stones. All gloriously overlooking the NT's Cley Hill.

17 CORTINGTON MANOR
Corton, Warminster, BA12 0SY. Mr & Mrs Simon Berry, simon.berry@berrycomputers.com. *5m S of Warminster. From Warminster, take rd thro Sutton Veny to Corton. Do not bear L into Corton but continue for ½ m. From A303, take A36, L to Boyton, cross railway and R at T-junction Continue for ¾ m.* **Visits by arrangement June to Sept for groups of 10+. Parking for 10 vehicles only. Adm £12, chd free. Refreshments by arrangement.**
4 acres of wild and formal gardens surround rose clad C18 manor house. Herbaceous border, yew bays with Portuguese laurel line the main lawn. Sweet pea arch opens to cutting garden, vegetable garden and orchard divided by yew hedges and formal pond garden. Lime avenue leads to river and wild pond from walled herb garden. Stable yard features pleached hornbeams and beech hedges.

18 DANE BROOK
Milkhouse Water, Pewsey, SN9 5JX. Peter & Gill Sharpe. *1m NE of Pewsey. From Pewsey take B3087 Burbage Rd. After approx ¾ m turn L to Milkhouse Water. Dane Brook is 1st on R after railway bridge.* **Sat 12, Sun 13 July (12.30-5). Adm £6, chd free. Home-made teas. Gluten free available. Donation to SSAFA, the Armed Forces Charity.**
Approx 1 acre of gardens, inc herbaceous beds, shrubs, trees, semi formal garden, roses, oxbow pond with planted banks and thatched summerhouse with Yorkstone patio.

Tree lined river walk runs the length of the garden, leading to shrubbery. Also lawns and paved areas with planted containers. Far reaching views from 2 acres of paddocks, with Jacob's sheep and rare breed chickens. Free range organic eggs. Vintage tractor, pop-up shop selling local crafts and sundries. Wheelchair accessible in dry weather with exception of pond and stream areas.

Our donation in 2024 has enabled Parkinson's UK to fund 3 new nursing posts this year directly supporting people with Parkinson's.

Cherry Orchard Barn

© Carole Drake

GROUP OPENING

19 DAUNTSEY GARDENS
Church Lane, Dauntsey, Malmesbury, SN15 4HT. Mr & Mrs Christopher Jerram. *5m SE of Malmesbury. Approach via Dauntsey Rd from Gt Somerford, 1¼m from Volunteer Inn Great Somerford.* **Sun 15 June (1-5). Combined adm £10, chd free. Home-made teas at Idover House. Cash only for admission & refreshments.**

THE COACH HOUSE
Col & Mrs J Seddon-Brown.

DAUNTSEY PARK
Mr & Mrs Giovanni Amati, 01249 721777, enquiries@dauntseyparkhouse.co.uk.

THE GARDEN COTTAGE
Miss Ann Sturgis.

IDOVER HOUSE
Mr & Mrs Christopher Jerram.

THE OLD COACH HOUSE
Tony & Janette Yates.

THE OLD POND HOUSE
Mr & Mrs Stephen Love.

THE OLD RECTORY
Mr Christopher & Mrs Claire Mellor-Hill, hello@theoldrectorydauntsey.com, www.theoldrectorydauntsey.com.

This group of 7 gardens, centred around the historic Dauntsey Park Estate, ranges from the Classical C18 country house setting of Dauntsey Park, with spacious lawns, old trees and views over the River Avon, to mature country house gardens and traditional walled gardens. Enjoy the formal rose garden in pink and white, old fashioned borders and duck ponds at Idover House, and the quiet seclusion of The Coach House with its thyme terrace and gazebos, climbing roses and clematis. Here, mop-headed pruned *Crataegus prunifolia* line the drive. The Garden Cottage has a traditional walled kitchen garden with organic vegetables, orchard, woodland walk and yew topiary. Meanwhile the 2 acres at The Old Pond House are both clipped and unclipped! Large pond with lilies and fat carp, and look out for the giraffe and turtle. The Old Coach House is a small garden with perennial plants, shrubs and climbers. The Old Rectory is a 2 acre garden adjoining the River Avon with mature trees, roses and shrubs.

20 NEW DRAX HOUSE
Orcheston, Salisbury, SP3 4RL. Mr & Mrs J Pugh. *12 m NW of Salisbury, just N of Shrewton in village of Orcheston. Turn off the A360 onto Orcheston Rd. At the Xrd turn L. Parking at the village hall approx 80 metres further into the village on R. Signs to Drax House from village hall.* **Sat 7 June (1.30-5.30). Adm £5, chd free. Home-made teas.**
Relaxed informal farmhouse garden with herbaceous border, small wildlife pond and some wilder areas. Walled kitchen garden with raised beds filled with vegetables and cutting garden. Several seating areas, some narrow and uneven paths and steps. Garden has been lovingly reclaimed over last 12 yrs with areas awaiting further work. The garden is still evolving.

21 DUCK POND BARN
Church Lane, Wingfield, Trowbridge, BA14 9LW. Janet & Marc Berlin. *9m SW of Bath. On B3109 from Frome to Bradford on Avon, turn opp Poplars pub into Church Lane. Duck Pond Barn is at end of lane. Big field for parking next door. No parking on the Farm.* **Sun 29 June (10-5). Adm £5, chd free. Tea, coffee & cake.**
Garden of 1.6 acres with large duck pond, lawns, ericaceous beds, dry bed, orchard, vegetable garden, big greenhouse, wood and wild areas of grass and trees with many wild flowers. Large dry stone wall topped with flower beds with rose arbour. 3 ponds linked by a rill in flower garden and large pergola in orchard. Set in farmland and mainly flat. Many interesting and rare succulents. Tea and cakes served outside in farm area. Wheelchair access to nearly all areas.

22 EASTWELL MANOR
Eastwell Road, Potterne, Devizes, SN10 5QG. Mr & Mrs Robert Hunt-Grubbe. *2½m S of Devizes. Stone pillars & black gates on W side of A360, 400 metres S of Potterne Xrds & George & Dragon. Entrance will be signed.* **Sat 31 May (1.30-5). Adm £8, chd free. Home-made teas.**
Eastwell Manor was built by the family in 1570 and is representative of a small manorial estate with its own brew house, granary and stables. The garden, based on terraces, features a banqueting house against a backdrop of woodland, with wonderful views to Salisbury Plain over water. Eastwell boasts various specialist trees and mature palms. There are uneven steps and limited wheelchair access.

23 FALKNERS COTTAGE
North Newnton, Pewsey, SN9 6LA. Anne & John Thompson-Ashby, 01980 630988, anne.thompsonashby@btinternet.com. *3m W Pewsey. SW from Pewsey on A345 direction Salisbury, exit 3 at Woodbridge r'about to Hilcott. Pass farm, next house on sharp L hand bend. Care turning R.* **Visits by arrangement 19 Apr to 14 Sept for groups of 10 to 25. Cream teas by arrangement. Adm £6.50, chd free.**
This 5 acre site inc a formal garden with colourful borders, topiary and box framed parterre and courtyard 'rooms' with contemporary sculpture. Behind the thatched barn lies a kitchen garden with hens. There is a meadow with ornamental trees, a small lake with a summerhouse on an island, a woodland, a wildlife pond and a bog garden. A short walk from the meadow is the C13 St James' Church.

24 FONTHILL HOUSE
Tisbury, SP3 5SA. The Lord Margadale of Islay, www.fonthill.co.uk/gardens. *13m W of Salisbury. Via B3089 in Fonthill Bishop. 3m N of Tisbury. Pls use Fonthill Park entrance. What3words app: creamed.moderated.passwords.* **Sun 23 Mar (12-5). Adm £8, chd free. Light refreshments. Sandwiches, quiches, cakes, soft drinks, tea, coffee & wine.**
Wonderful woodland walks with daffodils, rhododendrons, azaleas, shrubs and bulbs. Magnificent views, formal gardens. The gardens have been extensively redeveloped under the direction of Tania Compton and Marie-Louise Agius. The formal gardens are being continuously improved with new designs, exciting trees, shrubs and plants. Gorgeous William Pye fountain and other sculptures. Partial wheelchair access.

WILTSHIRE 571

25 GASPER COTTAGE
Gasper Street, Gasper Stourton, Warminster, BA12 6PY. Bella Hoare & Johnnie Gallop, 07812 555 883, bella.hoare@icloud.com, www.gaspercottage.com. *Nr Stourhead Gardens, 4m from Mere. Turn off A303 at B3092 Mere. Follow Stourhead signs. Go through Stourton. After 1m, turn R after phone box, signed Gasper. Parking before house on R, in field. House 2nd on R going up hill.* **Sun 22 June (11-5). Adm £7, chd free.** Visits also by arrangement 1 May to 12 Sept for groups of 10 to 20. Adm £14 & inc tea, coffee & cake.
Two acre garden, with stunning rural views. Luxurious mixed planting of perennials and shrubs with numerous hardy and tender annuals. Orchard embedded in a forest garden with a wildlife pond and model steam powered railway. Artist's studio surrounded by colour balanced planting and formal pond. Several seating areas. Can accommodate max 30 seater coach due to narrow lane.
)))

GROUP OPENING

26 HANNINGTON VILLAGE GARDENS
Hannington, Swindon, SN6 7RP. *Off B4019 Blunsdon to Highworth Rd by the Freke Arms. Park as directed by signs, in the street where possible, or opp Lushill House.* **Sun 8 June (10.30-5). Combined adm £10, chd free. Tea, coffee & cake in Hannington Village Hall.**

CHESTNUT HOUSE
Mary & Garry Marshall.

GLEBE HOUSE
Charlie & Tory Barne.

LUSHILL HOUSE
John & Sasha Kennedy.

QUARRY BANK
Paul Minter & Michael Weldon.

22 QUEENS ROAD
Jan & Pete Willis.

ROSE COTTAGE
Mrs Ruth Scholes.

STEP COTTAGE
Mr & Mrs J Clarke.

THE BUTLER'S COTTAGE
Alan & Laura Felton.

YORKE HOUSE GARDEN
Mr Miles & Mrs Cath Bozeat.

Hannington has a dramatic hilltop position on a Cotswold ridge overlooking the Thames Valley. A great variety of gardens, from large manor houses to small cottage gardens, many of which follow the brow of the hill and afford stunning views of the surrounding farmland. You will need lots of time to see all that is on offer in this beautiful historic village.

27 HORATIO'S GARDEN
Duke of Cornwall Spinal Treatment Centre, Salisbury Hospital NHS Foundation Trust, Odstock Road, Salisbury, SP2 8BJ. Horatio's Garden Charity, www.horatiosgarden.org.uk. *1m from centre of Salisbury. Follow signs for Salisbury District Hospital. Pls park in car park 10, which will be free to NGS visitors on the day.* **Sat 7 June (2-5). Adm £5, chd free. Tea & delicious cakes, made by Horatio's Garden volunteers, will be served in the Garden Room.**
Award winning hospital garden, opened in Sept 2012 and designed by Cleve West for patients with spinal cord injury at the Duke of Cornwall Spinal Treatment Centre. Built from donations given in memory of Horatio Chapple who was a volunteer at the centre in his school holidays. Low limestone walls, which represent the form of the spine, divide densely planted herbaceous beds. Everything in the garden is designed to benefit patients during their long stays in hospital. The garden is run by a Head Gardener and team of volunteers. Designer Cleve West has 9 RHS gold medals.

28 HYDE'S HOUSE
Dinton, SP3 5HH. Mr George Cruddas. *9m W of Salisbury. Off B3089 nr Dinton Church on St Mary's Rd. See signs & arrows.* **Sun 25 May (2-5). Adm £8, chd free. Home-made teas at Thatched Old School Room with outside tea tables.**
3 acres of wild and formal garden in beautiful situation with series of hedged garden rooms. Numerous shrubs, flowers and borders, all allowing tolerated wild flowers and preferred weeds, while others creep in. Large walled kitchen garden, herb garden and C13 dovecote (open). Charming C16/18 Grade I listed house (not open), with lovely courtyard. Every year varies. Free walks around park and lake. Steps, slopes, gravel paths and driveway.

29 ♦ IFORD MANOR GARDENS
Bradford-on-Avon, BA15 2BA. Mr Cartwright-Hignett. *7m S of Bath. Off A36, brown tourist sign to Iford 1m. From Bradford-on-Avon or Trowbridge via Lower Westwood Village (brown signs). Pls note all approaches via narrow single track lanes with passing places.* **For NGS: Sat 6 Sept (11-4). Adm £10. Pre-booking essential, please phone 01225 863146, email info@ifordmanor.co.uk or visit www.ifordmanor.co.uk for information & booking. Light refreshments in Iford Manor's award winning restaurant, or adjacent café & bakery. Children under 10 will not be admitted to the garden. For other opening times and information, please phone, email or visit garden website.**
Harold Peto's former home, this 2½ acre terraced garden provides timeless inspiration. Influenced by his travels, particularly to Italy and Japan, Peto embellished the garden with a collection of classical statuary and architectural fragments. Steep steps link the terraces with pools, fountains, loggias, colonnades, urns and figures, with magnificent rural views across the Iford Valley.

30 NEW 20 JUBILEE ESTATE
Purton, Swindon, SN5 4EU. Gavin & Ellen James. *NW of Swindon. From Station Rd, turn onto Witts Lane & follow this to Jubilee Estate on the L. Number 20 is on the R.* **Sat 7, Sun 8 June, Sat 9, Sun 10 Aug (10-4). Adm £5, chd free. Cream teas.**
Set in the picturesque village of Purton, this small cottage-style garden is a hidden gem packed with roses and planted for wildlife. Divided into different areas, with shaded pergola, sunny lawn and wildlife pond. Home-made cream teas are served on the patio. Not fully accessible due to gravel paths. Parking is limited so please be considerate.
)))

31 KETTLE FARM COTTAGE
Kettle Lane, West Ashton, Trowbridge, BA14 6AW. Tim & Jenny Woodall, 01225 753474, trwwoodall@outlook.com. *Kettle Lane is halfway between West Ashton T-lights & Yarnbrook r'about on S side of A350. Garden ½ m down end of lane. Limited car parking.* **Visits by arrangement 9 June to 10 Aug for groups of 20+. Adm £10, chd free. Admission inc home-made teas.**
Previously of Priory House, Bradford on Avon, which was featured on Gardeners' World, we now have a cottage garden that was featured in the August 2024 edition of The English Garden. The garden is full of colour and style, flowering from June to August. Bring a loved one/friend to see the garden and have tea. One or two steps.

32 KNOYLE PLACE
Holloway, East Knoyle, Salisbury, SP3 6AF. Lizie de la Moriniere. *What3words app: theme.poets.gadget. Turn off A350 into E Knoyle & follow signs to parking at Lower Lye. Walk 5 mins to Knoyle Place through village following signs.* **Sun 18 May (2-5). Adm £10, chd free. Home-made teas.**
Very beautiful and elegant garden created over 60 yrs by previous and current owners. Above the house there are several acres of mature rhododendron and magnolia woodland planting. Among the many different areas in this 9 acre garden is a box parterre, rose garden, vegetable garden and, around the house, a recently planted formal garden designed by Dan Combes. Sloping lawns and woodland paths, stone terrace.

33 LITTLE DURNFORD MANOR
Little Durnford, Salisbury, SP4 6AH. The Earl & Countess of Chichester. *3m N of Salisbury. Just N beyond Stratford-sub-Castle. Remain to E of R Avon at road junction at Stratford Bridge & cont towards Salterton for ½ m heading N. Entrance on L just past Little Durnford sign. What3words app: remark.collides.zones.* **Sun 13 July (2-5). Adm £5, chd free. Tea, coffee & cake in cricket pavilion within grounds.**
Extensive lawns with cedars, wildflower meadows, walled gardens, fruit trees, large vegetable garden, small knot and herb gardens. Terraces, borders, sunken garden, water garden, lake with islands, river walks, labyrinth walk. Little Durnford Manor is a substantial grade I listed, C18 private country residence (not open) built of an attractive mix of Chilmark stone and flint. Camels, alpacas, llama, pigs, pygmy goats, donkeys and sheep are all grazing next to the gardens.

34 MANOR HOUSE, STRATFORD TONY
Stratford Tony, Salisbury, SP5 4AT. Mr & Mrs Hugh Cookson, 01722 718496, lc@stratfordtony.co.uk. *4m SW of Salisbury. Take minor road W off A354 at Coombe Bissett. Garden on S after 1m. Or take minor road off A3094 from Wilton signed Stratford Tony & racecourse.* **Visits by arrangement 1 Apr to 5 Sept. Adm £10, chd free.**

Drax House

WILTSHIRE 573

Varied 4 acre garden with year-round interest. Formal and informal areas. Herbaceous borders, vegetable garden, parterre garden, orchard, shrubberies, roses, specimen trees, lakeside planting, winter colour and structure, many original contemporary features and places to sit and enjoy the downland views. Some gravel and uneven paving.

35 MAWARDEN COURT
Stratford Road, Stratford Sub Castle, SP1 3LL. **Alastair & Natasha McBain.** *2m WNW Salisbury. A345 from Salisbury, L at T-lights, opp St Lawrence Church.* **Sun 15 June (2-5). Adm £6, chd free. Tea, coffee & cake in pool pavilion.**
Mixed shrub and herbaceous borders set around C17 house (not open). Pergola walk, rose garden and white beam avenue down to River Avon, with pond pontoon and walk through newly planted woodland.

36 NORTH COTTAGE
Tisbury Row, Tisbury, SP3 6RZ. **Jacqueline & Robert Baker,** 01747 870019, baker_jaci@yahoo.co.uk. *12m W of Salisbury. From A30 turn N through Ansty, L at T-junction, towards Tisbury. From Tisbury take Ansty road. Car park entrance nr junction signed Tisbury Row.* **Sun 15 June (11-5). Adm £5, chd free. Home-made light lunches & teas.**
Walk through the vegetables to mown paths past wild flowers via pleached limes to the Cottage. Although modest there's variety, each part of the garden differs in style and feel but remains cohesive. From the intimacy of the garden explore the orchard, coppice, ponds and smallholding. Difficult to describe so do come see for yourself, and you will have a good home-made tea. There are also exciting metalwork sculptures, decorations and plant supports by Metal Menagerie and woodwork and ceramics by the garden owners. Please visit NGS website for extra pop-up open days.

37 OARE HOUSE
Rudge Lane, Oare, nr Pewsey, SN8 4JQ. **Rudge Estate.** *2m N of Pewsey. On Marlborough Rd (A345).* **Sun 27 Apr, Sun 29 June (2-6). Adm £8,**

chd free. **Tea, coffee & cake in the potting shed. Donation to The Order of St John.**
1740s mansion house later extended by Clough Williams Ellis in 1920s (not open). The original formal gardens around the house have been developed over the years to create a wonderful garden full of many unusual plants. Garden is undergoing a renaissance but still maintains split compartments each with its own individual charm; traditional walled garden with fine herbaceous borders, vegetable areas, trained fruit, roses and grand mixed borders surrounding formal lawns. The magnolia garden is wonderful in spring with some trees dating from 1920s, together with strong bulb plantings. Large arboretum and woodland with many unusual and champion trees. In spring and summer there is always something of interest, with the glorious Pewsey Vale as a backdrop. Partial wheelchair access.

38 NEW OGBOURNE MANOR
Ogbourne St. George, Marlborough, SN8 1SU. **Mr Andrew Tuckey.** *Please follow SatNav. The Manor is the most westerly house in the village beside the church.* **Sat 30 Aug (10-5). Adm £8, chd free. Home-made teas.**
The Manor House dates from 1619 and is built on the site of an ancient priory. The gardens have been extensively extended and improved by the present owners over the past 20 yrs and inc a parterre, swimming pool, tennis court, vegetable garden and stable block. Roses along the parterre walls and dahlias in the borders are particular features. Apart from a rich architectural history the house (not open) has more contemporary fame as the address from which the love letters were written as part of the successful WW2 deception featured in the book and film Operation Mincemeat.

39 THE OLD VICARAGE
Church Lane, Ashbury, Swindon, SN6 8LZ. **Mr David Astor.** *In the village of Ashbury, next to the church.* **Sat 7 June (10-3). Adm £5, chd free. Tea, coffee & cake.**
Within The Vale of the White Horse, Ashbury is a picturesque village with thatched cottages and a friendly atmosphere. Nestled between the village pub and St Mary's Church is

the garden of The Old Vicarage. The garden surrounds the house and is made up of a floriferous walled garden, a wildflower meadow, an extensive kitchen garden, filled with flowers, as well as vegetables, plus more.

40 THE OLD VICARAGE
Lower Westwood, Bradford-on-Avon, BA15 2AF. **Mrs Elizabeth Triggs.** *SW side of Bradford-On-Avon. Enter Lower Westwood, take turning opp the New Inn. 2nd house on R after the church. Parking outside the church.* **Sun 22 June (11-5). Adm £5, chd free. Home-made teas in the Parish Rooms next door between 2-5pm. Open nearby 4 Westwood Road.**
Large garden ($2/3$ acre) with lovely views to open countryside. A work in progress with a recently landscaped formal Italianate area featuring Mediterranean planting, a fruit and vegetable garden, small orchard, wild meadow, and a large family area set amongst prairie planting. Lunch available at the New Inn, 200 metres away, booking recommended. Flat, some areas of gravel.

41 THE PARISH HOUSE
West Knoyle, Mere, BA12 6AJ. **Alex Davies.** *What3words app: crucially.cheering.whirlwind. From E on A303 take signpost to West Knoyle at petrol station. Continue down hill & past church, take 1st R signed Charnage, continue 1m to end of lane. Parking in field on L.* **Sun 6 July (2-5). Adm £5, chd free. Tea, coffee & cake.**
The garden at The Parish House is small and south facing surrounded by hedges protecting it from the exposure of a high wide open landscape beyond. The garden is laid out with gravel to encourage a self-seeding natural look but there are also roses and herbaceous perennials as well. The look is held together with topiary. Beyond this garden there is a larger area of lawn, trees and developing bulb cover (Camassia). Large conservatory greenhouse containing mature Muscat grapevine and pelargoniums. Small vegetable garden. Level but gravel surfaces, some lawn.

WILTSHIRE

GROUP OPENING

42 NEW PRESHUTE LANE GARDENS
Preshute Lane, Manton, Marlborough, SN8 4HQ. *1m to W of Marlborough along A4, turn L at Manton Village sign. Continue over the bridge and take 1st L following Car Park signs. If arriving through Manton village turn R by pub.* **Sun 27 July (2-5). Combined adm £10, chd free. Tea, coffee & cake in the village hall opposite Greentrees.**

NEW GREENTREES
Chris Curtis.

NEW THE OLD POST OFFICE
Anna Marsden.

PEACOCK COTTAGE
Ian & Clare Maurice.

Three very different gardens each with their own distinct personality situated on Preshute Lane in the picturesque village of Manton. Peacock Cottage, the largest, has sweeping lawns with large herbaceous beds packed with summer colour, rose bed, mature trees, parterre, and wildflower area creating an interesting journey. An exotic bed sits near the house providing a lush, tropical oasis. Greentrees has an eclectic mix of herbaceous and shrub borders, trees, raised flower bed and various secret seating areas. Potted plants adorn the doorway on arrival. The Old Post Office is a thatched house with a contemporary and pretty small courtyard, consisting of a raised flower bed and private seating area.

43 NEW PRESTON FARMHOUSE
Preston, Marlborough, SN8 2HF. Shara Grylls. *1m SE of Aldbourne on B4192. Just beyond the small thatched toll cottage on L.* **Thur 19 June (12-4). Adm £8, chd free. Tea, coffee & cake.**
This glorious garden, with views over the surrounding countryside, has been created during the last 20 yrs with the help of designer Justin Spink and is divided into different areas. The parterre contains roses and magnolias, climbing roses tumble over arches, there are well-stocked herbaceous borders, a lawned area leading to the wildflower meadow and a small cutting garden all make this a wonderful garden to explore and enjoy. There is also a newly planted arboretum/pinetum.

44 ROOKERY COTTAGE
Coombe Lane, Atworth, Melksham, SN12 8NU. Lorraine MacFarlane. *3m from Bradford on Avon, Corsham or Melksham. Follow signs for Stonar School, pls drive slowly through the school grounds & follow yellow signs for car parking behind the school.* **Sun 1 June (1-5). Adm £5, chd free. Home-made teas.**
Delightful garden evolved by the owners over the past 40 yrs. Meander via the mown paths through beautiful trees and shrubs with unique features, many of which enable an abundance of wildlife. Different areas with gravel, where plants self seed and wild flowers thrive. The planting and artistic use of unusual containers will give you lots of inspiration. Not fully accessible because of uneven paths and different levels.

45 SALTHROP HOUSE
Basset Down, Wroughton, Swindon, SN4 9QP. Sophie Conran. *Driving W on M4, exit at J16, take 1st exit signed for Butterfly World, drive 2m, passing the golf course on your R, keep going up the hill, Salthrop House is the drive on the L.* **Fri 13, Sat 14 June (11-4). Adm £6.50, chd free. Home-made teas.**
Salthrop House is a manor house garden set on the edge of the Marlborough Downs. A tremendous variety of perennials, shrubs, borders and pots unfurl themselves across this romantic garden and surround the sweeping lawn. You can wind your way through the woodland paths, enjoy a moment of peace by the pond or visit the greenhouse and kitchen garden.

46 SCOTS FARM
Pinkney, Malmesbury, SN16 0NZ. Mr & Mrs Martin Barrow, 07947 792919, ljikob@gmail.com, www.Lawrencebarrow.com. *5m W of Malmesbury on B4040 towards Sherston. Take L at Pinkney Xrds, follow road over a bridge and up a hill.* **Visits by arrangement in July for groups of up to 30. Adm £8,** chd free. **We offer tea & cake for group visits.**
Across seven acres a colourful perennial border, a white garden, a Japanese Zen garden, a Mediterranean garden and follow a path through a wildflower meadow to a pottery studio and koi pond in this haven of tranquillity. Garden ware, pottery and sculptures on display. Most areas are wheelchair accessible although the meadow and Zen garden are via fields with paths mown through.

47 SEEND HOUSE
High Street, Seend, Melksham, SN12 6NR. Maud Peters, www.instagram.com/maud_seendgarden. *In Seend village. Nr church & opp PO. Parking on village green.* **Sun 13 Apr (1-5). Combined adm with Brow Cottage £8, chd free. Home-made teas at Brow Cottage.**
Seend House is a Georgian house with 6 acres of gardens and paddocks. Framed with yew and box. Highlights inc cloud and rose garden, stream lavender, view of knot garden from above, fountain with grass border, walled garden as well as formal borders. Amazing view across the valley to Salisbury Plain. There is a shuttle bus running between Seend House and Brow Cottage for the opening.

48 SEMLEY GRANGE
Semley, Shaftesbury, SP7 9AP. Mr & Mrs Reid Scott. *From A350 take turning to Semley, continue along road & under railway bridge. Take 1st R up Sem Hill. Semley Grange is 1st on L - parking on green.* **Sun 22 June (2-5). Adm £5, chd free. Light refreshments.**
Large garden recreated in last 10 yrs. Herbaceous border, lawn and wildflower meadow intersected by paths and planted with numerous bulbs. The garden has been greatly expanded by introducing many standard weeping roses, new mixed borders, pergolas and raised beds for dahlias, underplanted with alliums. Numerous fruit and ornamental trees introduced over last 10 yrs. Regret no dogs.

WILTSHIRE 575

49 1 SOUTHVIEW
Wick Lane, Devizes, SN10 5DR. Teresa Garraud, 01380 722936, tl.garraud@hotmail.co.uk. *From Devizes Market Place go S (Long St). At r'about go straight over, at mini r'about turn L into Wick Ln. Continue to end of Wick Ln. Park in road or roads nearby.* **Sun 18 May (1.30-4.30), open nearby Trymnells. Sun 7 Sept (1.30-4.30). Adm £5, chd free.** Visits also by arrangement 19 May to 13 Sept for groups of up to 20.
An atmospheric and very long town garden, full of wonderful planting surprises at every turn. Densely planted with pots near the house and large borders further up, it houses a collection of beautiful and often unusual plants, shrubs and trees, many with striking foliage. Colour from seasonal flowers is interwoven with this textural tapestry. 'Truly inspirational' is often heard from visitors.

50 TEASEL
Wilsford, Amesbury, Salisbury, SP4 7BL. Ray Palmer, 07785 233155, Ray.Palmer@fierarealestate.com. *2m SW of Amesbury in the Woodford Valley on western banks of R Avon which runs through the gardens.* **Sun 6 July (11-5). Adm £7, chd free. Home-made teas.** Visits also by arrangement 1 Apr to 1 Oct for groups of 15+.
Extensively developed since 2020, Teasel's 11 acres inc long herbaceous borders, a lake and ½ m riverside walk. Recently added potager, shrub border, hoggin pathways through orchard to fruit store, Monet inspired bridge, duck house on small pond, water lilies, specimen trees, chess pavilion and croquet lawn. Enjoy teas on the upper terrace with magnificent views of the garden and river.

51 TRISTENAGH HOUSE
23 Devizes Road, Potterne, Devizes, SN10 5LW. Andrew & Ros Ford, ros.ford@ngs.org.uk. *1m S of Devizes towards Salisbury on A360. Entrance through open wooden gates. What3words app: drifting.defensive.mini.* **Visits by arrangement May to July for groups of 5+. Adm £8, chd free. Home-made cakes, inc gluten free options.**
Garden of approx 2 acres, created over the past 20 yrs. Island beds with a mixture of herbaceous plants, bulbs, annuals and shrubs. Year-round structure provided by beech and yew hedges, box topiary and by mature beech and Scots pine trees. Small vegetable garden. Some gravelled areas with containers. Good views of valley from terrace. Wheelchair access to most parts of garden on grass paths. Access to terrace limited due to gravel. Some steps.

Semley Grange

WILTSHIRE

52 TRYMNELLS
1a Coxhill Lane, Potterne, Devizes, SN10 5PH. Linda Smith. *Coxhill Ln is opp George & Dragon pub. Trymnells is 2nd property on L & is at the top of a gravel drive. Parking at Potterne Village Hall, Some space on drive for those with limited mobility.* **Sun 18 May (12-5). Adm £5, chd free. Open nearby 1 Southview. Afternoon tea is available throughout the afternoon.**
Trymnells garden was started approx 8 yrs ago. It is now maturing and has many trees, shrubs, hedges and perennials. The garden is steep and slopes up from the property and reaches a steep bank at the very top. Sleepers, fences, walls and plants have imposed a sense of structure with bulbs and perennials providing wonderful colour.
♨ ⋯

53 ◆ TWIGS COMMUNITY GARDEN
Manor Garden Centre, Cheney Manor, Swindon, SN2 2QJ. TWIGS, 01793 523294, twigs.reception@gmail.com, www.twigscommunitygardens.org.uk. *From Gt Western Way, under Bruce St Bridges onto Rodbourne Rd. 1st L at r'about, Cheney Manor Industrial Est. Through estate, 2nd exit at r'about. Opp Pitch & Putt. Signs on R to Manor Garden Centre.* **For NGS: Sun 18 May, Sun 20 July (12-4). Adm £3.50, chd free. Home-made teas. For other opening times and information, please phone, email or visit garden website.**
Delightful 2 acre community garden, created and maintained by volunteers. Features inc 7 individual display gardens, ornamental pond, plant nursery, Iron Age round house, artwork, fitness trail, separate kitchen garden site, Swindon beekeepers and the haven, overflowing with wild flowers. Most areas wheelchair accessible. Disabled WC at TWIGS.
♿ 🐕 ✿ 🚗 ☕ 🪑 ⋯

54 WELLAWAY
Close Lane, Marston, SN10 5SN. Mrs P Lewis. *5m SW of Devizes. From A360, Devizes to Salisbury, R in Potterne just before George & Dragon pub. Through Worton. L at end of village signed to Marston, Close Lane ½ m on L.* **Sat 26, Sun 27 Apr, Sat 13, Sun 14 Sept (1-5). Adm £6, chd free. Home-made teas.**
Two acre flower arranger's garden comprising herbaceous borders, orchard, vegetable garden, ornamental and wildlife ponds, lawns and naturalised areas. Planted since 1979 for year-round interest. Shrubberies and rose garden, other areas underplanted with bulbs or ground cover. Springtime particularly colourful with daffodils, tulips and hellebores. Extensive autumn colour.
♿ 🐕 ✿ 🚗 ☕ ⋯

55 WEST LAVINGTON MANOR
1 Church Street, West Lavington, SN10 4LA. Andrew Doman & Jordina Evins, 07768 773856, andrewdoman01@gmail.com, www.instagram.com/westlavingtonmanor. *6m S of Devizes, on A360. House opp White St, where parking is available.* **Sat 7 June (11-6). Adm £12, chd free. We offer an extended lunch & tea menu inc wines, beer & other beverages. Seating nr to refreshment marquee.** Visits also by arrangement 2 Jan to 23 Dec. We are happy to welcome groups from anywhere around the world. Donation to West Lavington Youth Club and Nestling Trust.
A C15 manor house with spectacular 5 acre walled garden, established by Sir John Danvers, who brought the Italianate garden to the UK. Delightful aspects inc Laburnum walk, replanted herbaceous border, an authentic Japanese garden, new Mulberry rotunda, orchard with 25 different apple and pear species, an arboretum with outstanding specimen trees and lake with duck house. Partial wheelchair access.
♿ 🐕 🚗 ☕ 🪑 ⋯

56 WESTCROFT
Boscombe Village, nr Salisbury, SP4 0AB. Lyn Miles, 01980 610877/07787 852756, lynmiles@icloud.com, www.westcroftgarden.co.uk. *7m NE Salisbury. On A338 from Salisbury, just past Boscombe & District Social Club. Park there or in field opp house, or where signed on day. Disabled parking only on drive.* **Wed 1 Jan (11-4). Every Thur 2 Jan to 16 Jan (11-4). Home-made teas. Sat 18, Sun 19 Jan (11-4). Every Thur 30 Jan to 13 Mar (11-4). Sat 1, Sun 2, Fri 7, Sat 22, Sun 23 Feb (11-4). Adm £4, chd free. Home-made soups & teas, outside or undercover.** Visits also by arrangement 3 Jan to 31 Mar for groups of 15+.
Whilst overflowing with roses in June, in Jan and Feb the bones of this ⅔ acre galanthophile's garden on chalk are on show. Brick and flint walls, terraces, rustic arches, gates and pond add character. Drifts of snowdrops carpet the floor whilst throughout is a growing collection of well over 500 named varieties. Many hellebores, pulmonarias, grasses and seedheads add interest. Snowdrops (weather dependent) and snowdrop sundries for sale inc greetings cards, mugs, bags, serviettes, also chutneys and free range eggs.
✿ 🚗 ☕ ⋯

57 WESTWIND
Manton Drove, Manton, Marlborough, SN8 4HL. Kate Stewart-Hilliar, 07738 180759, westwindmanton@gmail.com. *1m W of Marlborough off A4. In Manton, bear R past Oddfellows Arms, then after 180 metres go L into Manton Drove. House is up the hill on the R.* **Visits by arrangement 19 May to 15 June for groups of up to 15. Max 5 cars. Adm £7, chd free.**
Working in harmony with nature, Westwind is a relaxed informal country garden set in 4 acres inc a 2½ acre meadow and woodland. It hosts the weekly outdoor learning for the village school and welcomes artists and photographers throughout the seasons. Westwind has an abundance of mature trees, beds full of herbaceous plants and 10 raised beds stuffed with colour from April to October.
🪑 ⋯

58 NEW 4 WESTWOOD ROAD
Trowbridge, BA14 9BR. Mrs Helen Hewlett. *Northern edge of the town off the Bradford-on-Avon Road. Plenty of parking in nearby residential roads, pls be considerate to local residents.* **Sun 22 June (11-5). Adm £5, chd free. Open nearby The Old Vicarage.**
New garden of approx 1 acre created over the last 4 yrs. Vegetable area with raised beds and espalier fruit trees, greenhouse. Small wildlife pond becoming established. Mixed herbaceous borders with roses. Small woodland area. Level ground but some uneven areas in the grass. No steps.
♿ ✿

59 WHATLEY MANOR

Easton Grey, Malmesbury, SN16 0RB. Christian & Alix Landolt, 01666 822888, reservations@whatleymanor.com, www.whatleymanor.com/gardens. *4m W of Malmesbury. From A429 at Malmesbury take B4040 signed Sherston. Manor 2m on L.* **Wed 4 June (2-6). Adm £9, chd free. Light refreshments in The Loggia Garden.** 12 acres of English country gardens with 26 distinct areas each with a strong theme based on colour, scent or style. Original 1920s Arts & Crafts plan inspired the design and combines classic style with more contemporary touches, inc specially commissioned sculpture. Dogs must be on a lead at all times. Hotel also open for lunch and full afternoon tea.

& 🐕 🛏 ☕ 🔊

60 WINKELBURY HOUSE

Berwick St John, Shaftesbury, SP7 0EY. Ian & Carrie Stewart. *5m E of Shaftesbury. From A30 follow sign to Berwick St John, after 1½m turn L into Woodlands Lane.* **Sat 17 May (2-5). Adm £7.50, chd free. Home-made teas.**
1½ acres with glorious views of surrounding countryside. The garden has evolved over last 8 yrs to inc kitchen garden with bothy and greenhouse, mown paths through informal areas, meadow planted with spring bulbs, 30m iris border, ha-ha, wildlife pond and bee friendly planting.

✿ ☕ 🔊

61 WUDSTON HOUSE

High Street, Wedhampton, Devizes, SN10 3QE. David Morrison, 01380 840965, djm@piml.co.uk. *Wedhampton lies on N side of A342 approx 4m SE of Devizes. House is set back on East side of village street at end of drive lined with a beech hedge.* **Visits by arrangement 1 June to 12 Sept for groups of up to 50. Light refreshments can be provided at additional cost of £5 per head. Adm £10, chd free.**
The garden was started in 2010, following completion of the house. It consists of formal gardens round the house, perennial meadow, pinetum and arboretum. Nick Macer and James Hitchmough, who have pioneered the concept of perennial meadows, have been extensively involved in aspects of the garden, which is still developing.

✿ ☕

Preston Farmhouse

WORCESTERSHIRE

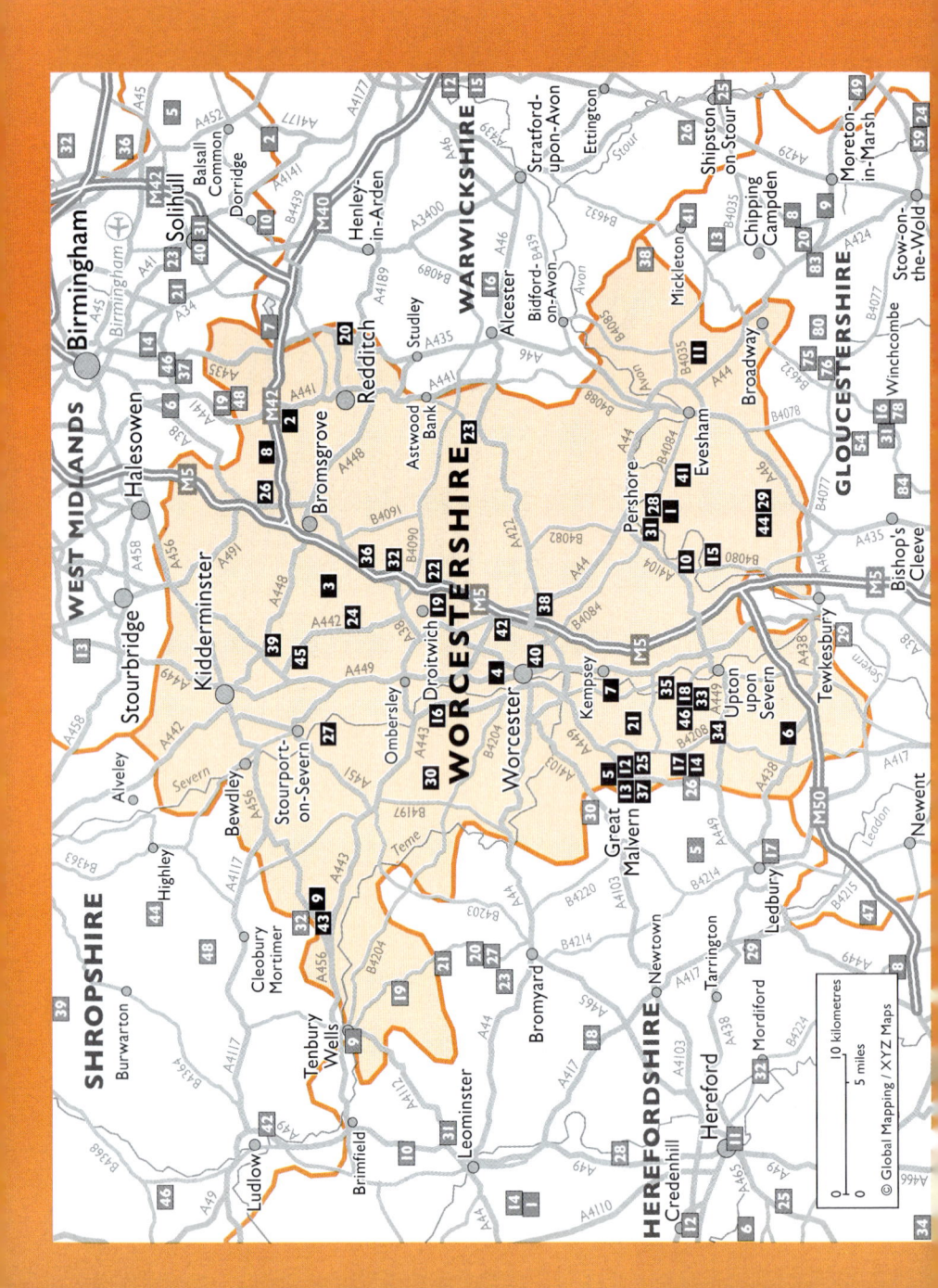

WORCESTERSHIRE 579

VOLUNTEERS

County Organiser
David Morgan 01214 453595
meandi@btinternet.com

County Treasurer
Doug Bright 01886 832200
doug.bright@ngs.org.uk

Publicity
Pamela Thompson 01886 888295
peartree.pam@gmail.com

Social Media
Brian Skeys 01684 311297
brian.skeys@ngs.org.uk

Booklet Co-ordinator
Steven Wilkinson & Linda Pritchard
01684 310150
steven.wilkinson48412@gmail.com

Assistant County Organisers
Andrea Bright 01886 832200
andrea.bright@ngs.org.uk

Brian Bradford 07816 867137
bradf0rds@icloud.com

John and Leslie Bryant
johnlesbryant@btinternet.com
01905 840189

Malcolm & Anne Garner
anne.restharrow@gmail.com
01684 310503

Lynn Glaze 01386 751924
lynnglaze@cmail.co.uk

Philippa Lowe 01684 891340
philippa.lowe@ngs.org.uk

Stephanie & Chris Miall
0121 445 2038
stephaniemiall@hotmail.com

Rachel Pryke
rachelgpryke@btinternet.com

David & Sandra Traynor
traynor@clickspeedphotography.co.uk

@WorcestershireNGS
@WorcsNGS

OPENING DATES

All entries subject to change.
For latest information check
www.ngs.org.uk
Map locator numbers are shown to the right of each garden name.

February
Snowdrop Openings
Wednesday 12th
Brockamin   7
Sunday 16th
Brockamin   7
Warndon Court   42

March
Wednesday 12th
◆ Cotswold Garden Flowers   11
Saturday 22nd
NEW   The Beehive   5
Sunday 23rd
Brockamin   7

April
Sunday 6th
Overbury Court   29
◆ Spetchley Park Gardens   38
Wednesday 9th
◆ Cotswold Garden Flowers   11
Saturday 12th
The Walled Garden & No. 53   40
Wednesday 16th
The Walled Garden & No. 53   40
Sunday 20th
Brockamin   7
Saturday 26th
The Alpine Garden Society   1
◆ Whitlenge Gardens   45
Sunday 27th
Hiraeth   19
◆ Whitlenge Gardens   45

May
Sunday 4th
The Dell House   14
Nimrod, 35 Alexandra Road   25
The Old Forge   28
Pear Tree Cottage   30
Monday 5th
The Dell House   14
Nimrod, 35 Alexandra Road   25
Saturday 10th
Eckington Gardens   15
Sunday 11th
Eckington Gardens   15
Monday 12th
The Dell House   14
Wednesday 14th
◆ Cotswold Garden Flowers   11
Thursday 15th
Madresfield Court   21
Saturday 17th
The Alpine Garden Society   1
Rothbury   37
Sunday 18th
Oak Tree House   26
Rothbury   37
Monday 19th
19 Winnington Gardens   46
Saturday 24th
Ravelin   33
Sunday 25th
2 Brookwood Drive   8
1 Church Cottage   10
Ravelin   33
Rothbury   37
Warndon Court   42
Monday 26th
1 Church Cottage   10
Oak Tree House   26
Ravelin   33
Rothbury   37

June
Sunday 1st
Hiraeth   19
Wednesday 4th
The Alpine Garden Society   1
The Dell House   14
Saturday 7th
Alvechurch Gardens   2
Pershore Gardens   31

WORCESTERSHIRE

Sunday 8th
Alvechurch Gardens	2
Birtsmorton Court	6
Pershore Gardens	31

Wednesday 11th
◆ Cotswold Garden Flowers	11

Saturday 14th
Elm Hill Cottage	16
Hanley Swan NGS Gardens	18
New House Farm	24

Sunday 15th
Elm Hill Cottage	16
Hanley Swan NGS Gardens	18
Warndon Court	42

Saturday 21st
Rest Harrow	34
Walnut Cottage	41
Wharf House	43

Sunday 22nd
Cowleigh Lodge	12
3 Oakhampton Road	27
Rest Harrow	34
Walnut Cottage	41
Wharf House	43

Friday 27th
NEW The Beehive	5

Saturday 28th
◆ Whitlenge Gardens	45

Sunday 29th
3 Oakhampton Road	27
◆ Whitlenge Gardens	45

July

Saturday 5th
New House Farm	24

Sunday 6th
2 Brookwood Drive	8
Holly Cottage	20
◆ Spetchley Park Gardens	38

Wednesday 9th
◆ Cotswold Garden Flowers	11

Saturday 12th
5 Beckett Drive	4

Sunday 13th
5 Beckett Drive	4
3 Oakhampton Road	27

Saturday 19th
Manor Cottage	22

Saturday 26th
Rothbury	37

Sunday 27th
3 Oakhampton Road	27
Rothbury	37

August

Saturday 2nd
Nimrod, 35 Alexandra Road	25
Rothbury	37

Sunday 3rd
Nimrod, 35 Alexandra Road	25
Rothbury	37

Wednesday 13th
◆ Cotswold Garden Flowers	11

Sunday 17th
3 Oakhampton Road	27

Saturday 23rd
◆ Morton Hall Gardens	23
◆ Whitlenge Gardens	45

Sunday 24th
3 Oakhampton Road	27
Pear Tree Cottage	30
◆ Whitlenge Gardens	45

Monday 25th
3 Oakhampton Road	27

Saturday 30th
Rest Harrow	34

Sunday 31st
Rest Harrow	34

September

Wednesday 10th
◆ Cotswold Garden Flowers	11
The Dell House	14

Saturday 13th
Ravelin	33

Sunday 14th
Ravelin	33

Sunday 21st
Brockamin	7

October

Monday 6th
19 Winnington Gardens	46

Wednesday 8th
◆ Cotswold Garden Flowers	11

Saturday 11th
Ravelin	33

Sunday 12th
Ravelin	33

By Arrangement

Arrange a personalised garden visit with your club, or group of friends, on a date to suit you. See individual garden entries for full details.

The Alpine Garden Society	1
Badge Court	3
5 Beckett Drive	4
NEW The Beehive	5
Brockamin	7
2 Brookwood Drive	8
Cherry Tree Barn	9
1 Church Cottage	10
Cowleigh Lodge	12
Cowleigh Park Farm	13
The Dell House	14
The Folly	17
Hanley Swan NGS Gardens	18
Hiraeth	19
Mantoft, Eckington Gardens	15
New House Farm	24
Nimrod, 35 Alexandra Road	25
Oak Tree House	26
3 Oakhampton Road	27
Overbury Court	29
Pear Tree Cottage	30
NEW Rashwood Care Home	32
Ravelin	33
Rest Harrow	34
Rhydd Gardens	35
Warndon Court	42
Wharf House	43
Whitcombe House	44
Willow Pond, Eckington Gardens	15
19 Winnington Gardens	46

70 inpatients and their families are being supported at the newly opened Horatio's Garden Northern Ireland, thanks to National Garden Scheme donations.

THE GARDENS

1 THE ALPINE GARDEN SOCIETY
Avon Bank, Wick, Pershore, WR10 3JP. The Alpine Garden Society, 01386 554790, ags@alpinegardensociety.net, www.alpinegardensociety.net. Wick, ½m from Pershore town. Take the Evesham Rd from Pershore over the River Avon, cont for ½ m & turn R for Pershore College, the garden is the 1st entrance on L. **Sat 26 Apr, Sat 17 May, Wed 4 June (11-4). Adm £4, chd free. Tea, coffee & cake.** Visits also by arrangement 7 Apr to 25 Sept for groups of 10+. Inspirational small garden next to the Alpine Garden Society office. The garden shows a wide range of alpine plants that are easy to grow in contemporary gardens over a long season. Visitors can see different settings to grow alpines, inc rock and tufa, scree, a dry Mediterranean bed, shade and sunny areas, also a dedicated alpine house, and many pots and troughs with alpines and small bulbs. Volunteers will be on hand on open days to provide more information, and planting demonstrations may be available on some dates. The garden slopes gently upwards with gravel paths which are accessible to wheelchairs with some assistance.

& ✱ ☕ »)

GROUP OPENING

2 ALVECHURCH GARDENS
Alvechurch, nr Birmingham, B48 7LG. Group Co-ordinators Janet & Martin Wright. *3m N of Redditch, 3m NE of Bromsgrove. Alvechurch is on the B4120 close to J2 of M42. Gardens are signed from all roads into the village. Pick up your map and ticket/wristband from Alvechurch Baptist Church Hall, Red Lion St, village centre.* **Sat 7, Sun 8 June (1-5). Combined adm £7.50, chd free. Tea, coffee & cake at Alvechurch Baptist Church Hall, Red Lion Street. There are also many cafés and pubs in the village.**

NEW 74 BEAR HILL
Vivien Morgan.

55 BIRMINGHAM ROAD
Roger & Sue Wardle.

43 BLYTHESWAY
Tony & Cheryl Godfrey.

28 CALLOW HILL ROAD
Janet & Martin Wright.

CORNER HOUSE
Janice Wiltshire.

THE MOAT HOUSE
Mike & Tracy Fallon.

RECTORY COTTAGE
Celia Hitch.

4 SNAKE LANE
Jason Turner & Paul Emery.

12 STATION ROAD
Mr & Mrs Bowen.

8 TRANTER AVENUE
Kevin Baker.

2 WHARF COTTAGE
Janette Poole.

1A WITHYBED LANE
Jean & Mike Collins.

WYCHWOOD HOUSE
Chris & Stephanie Miall.

Large village inc new development and historically interesting core with buildings spanning medieval to Edwardian and St Laurence Church dedicated in 1239 and refurbished in 1857 by William Butterfield. There is a selection of lovely open gardens ranging from a riverside previous rectory with waterfall to a corner plot gardened for wildlife. There are professionally landscaped terraced gardens and cottage gardens with lots of colour. Also a large moated garden on the site of the Bishop of Worcester's Summer Palace. Around the gardens there are mature trees, rose beds, shrubberies, herbaceous borders and fruit and vegetable beds. Some gardens inc sculptures. The gardens are walking distance from Alvechurch railway station (on the Cross-City Line 11 miles SW of Birmingham New Street).

✱ ☕ »)

3 Oakhampton Road

3 BADGE COURT
Purshull Green Lane, Elmbridge, Droitwich, WR9 0NJ. Stuart & Diana Glendenning, 01299 851216, dianaglendenning1@gmail.com. *5m N of Droitwich Spa. 2½ m from J5 M5. Turn off A38 at Wychbold down side of the Swan Inn. Turn R into Berry Ln. Take next L into Cooksey Green Ln. Turn R into Purshull Green Ln. Garden is on L.* **Visits by arrangement 2 June to 24 July for groups of 6 to 30. Adm £8, chd free.**
The 2½ acre garden is set against the backdrop of a C16 house (not open). There is something for all gardeners inc mature specimen trees, huge range of clematis and roses, lake with waterfall, stumpery, topiary garden, walled garden, Mediterranean Garden, specialist borders, long herbaceous border, large potager vegetable garden and Japanese Garden.
& ❋ ☕

4 5 BECKETT DRIVE
Northwick, Worcester, WR3 7BZ. Jacki & Pete Ager, 01905 451108, agers@outlook.com. *1½ m N of Worcester city centre. A cul-de-sac off the A449 Ombersley Rd. 1 m S of the Claines r'about on A449. SatNav WR3 7BZ.* **Sat 12, Sun 13 July (1-5). Adm £5, chd free. Home-made ice cream on sale. Visits also by arrangement 24 May to 31 July for groups of 10 to 20.**
An extraordinary town garden on the northern edge of Worcester packed with different plants and year-round interest guaranteed to give visitors ideas and inspiration for their own gardens. For more than 20 yrs visitors have enjoyed the unique and surprising features of this garden which has many planting schemes for a variety of situations.
❋ ☕))

5 NEW THE BEEHIVE
Halfkey Road, Malvern, WR14 1UL. Mrs Jane James, xjanejamesx@googlemail.com. *Edge of N Malvern towards Leigh Sinton. Halfkey Rd is approx halfway between Leigh Sinton and Malvern Link Top along B4503 Leigh Sinton Rd. The Beehive is approx 350 metres along Halfkey Rd on R. What3words app: lift.wages.manly.* **Sat 22 Mar, Fri 27 June (10.30-5). Adm £5, chd free. Tea, coffee & cake. Visits also by arrangement Mar to May for groups of 10 to 20.**
The Beehive is a country garden tucked away on the bend of Half Key and Hospital Road. It is an old farmhouse garden with chickens, a few beehives, and a small orchard. Up the drive leads into the more formal gardens around the house. Tea is available on the terrace with a lovely view of North Hill on the Malverns. Flat gardens with gravel paths.
& 🐕 ❋ ☕ 🪑))

6 BIRTSMORTON COURT
Birtsmorton, nr Malvern, WR13 6JS. Mr & Mrs N G K Dawes. *7m E of Ledbury. Off A438 Ledbury/Tewkesbury rd.* **Sun 8 June (2-5.30). Adm £9, chd free. Home-made teas.**
10 acre garden surrounding beautiful medieval moated manor house (not open). White garden, built and planted in 1997 surrounded on all sides by old topiary. Potager, vegetable garden and working greenhouses, all beautifully maintained. Rare double working moat and waterways inc Westminster Pool laid down in Henry VII's reign to mark the consecration of the knave of Westminster Abbey. Ancient yew tree under which Cardinal Wolsey reputedly slept in the legend of the Shadow of the Ragged Stone.
& ❋ ☕))

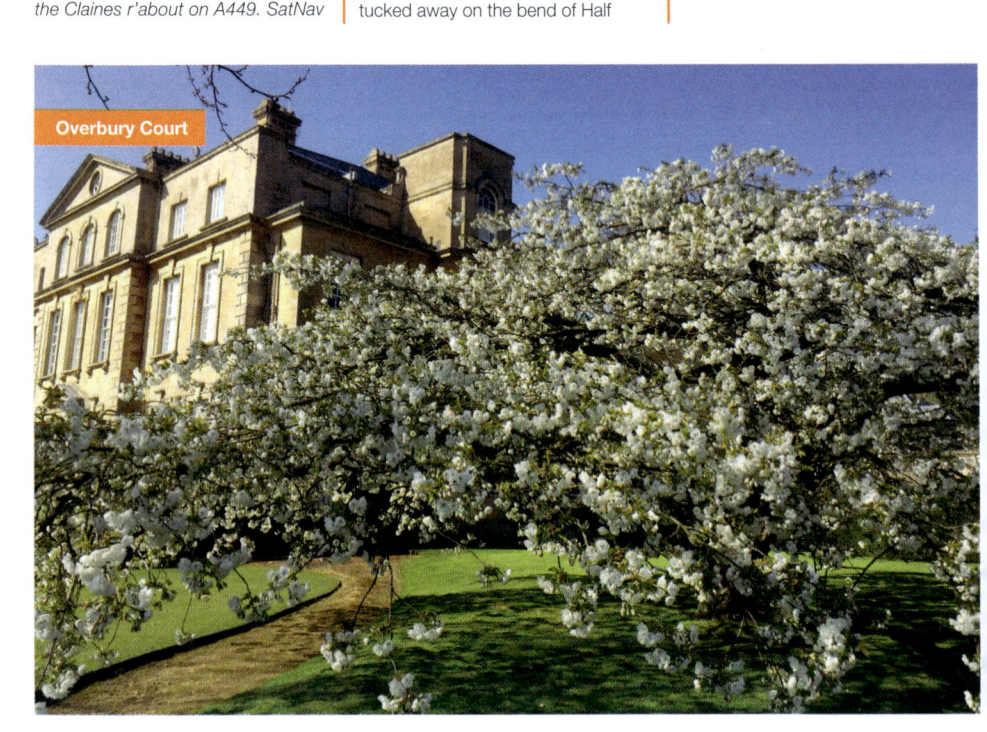

Overbury Court

7 BROCKAMIN
Old Hills, Callow End, Worcester, WR2 4TQ. Margaret Stone, 01905 830370, stone.brockamin@btinternet.com. *5m S of Worcester. ½ m S of Callow End on the B4424, on an unfenced bend, turn R into the car park signed Old Hills. Walk towards the houses keeping R.* **Wed 12 Feb (1-4); Sun 16 Feb (11-4); Sun 23 Mar, Sun 20 Apr, Sun 21 Sept (1-4). Adm £5, chd free. Home-made teas.** Visits also by arrangement 15 Feb to 15 Oct for groups of 10+. Donation to Plant Heritage.

1½ acre plantsman's garden situated next to common land. Informal mixed borders with a wide variety of hardy perennials where plants are allowed to self seed. Large collection of snowdrops. Plant Heritage National Collections of Pulmonarias, *Symphyotrichum novae-angliae* and some hardy geraniums. Open for snowdrops in Feb, daffodils and pulmonarias in March and April, geraniums in June and asters in September. Seasonal pond/bog garden and kitchen garden. Teas with home-made cakes and unusual plants for sale. An access path reaches a large part of the garden.

8 2 BROOKWOOD DRIVE
Barnt Green, Birmingham, B45 8GG. Mr Mike & Mrs Liz Finlay, 07721 746369, liz@lizfinlay.com. *5m N of Bromsgrove. Please park courteously in local roads or in village. Brookwood Dr is on R towards top of Fiery Hill Rd approx. ¼ m from station. Press the access button to open security gates if closed.* **Sun 25 May, Sun 6 July (10-4). Adm £5, chd free. Tea, coffee & cake. Refreshments £3 per person inc a choice of cakes and unlimited drinks.** Visits also by arrangement May to July for groups of 10 to 25.

A multi-themed mature garden with numerous water features and colourful borders. There is a formal white garden, wildlife pond and cutting garden surrounded by large rhododendrons which give a colourful display in late spring. Parking on Brookwood Drive for disabled only.

9 CHERRY TREE BARN
Southnett, Mamble, Kidderminster, DY14 9JT. Mr Ian & Mrs Julie Stackhouse, Stackhouse571@btinternet.com. *12m W of Kidderminster on the A456. Nearest motorway M5 J6. A456 from Kidderminster, past Mamble village approx 1m, garden on L up a track off main road. A456 from Tenbury Wells, past Broombank. Garden on R up a track off main road, follow signs.* **Visits by arrangement July & Aug for groups of 10 to 30. Refreshments inc in adm price. Adm £10, chd £5. Tea, coffee & cake.**

The garden has been planted out with a wide variety of trees and shrubs providing year-round interest. The main event are the herbaceous beds filled with a riot of colour from May onwards. There are two ponds, a bog garden inc stumpery, a rose bed, gravel garden, two azalea beds and a small woodland area. The rear garden offers wonderful views of the surrounding countryside.

10 1 CHURCH COTTAGE
Church Road, Defford, WR8 9BJ. John Taylor & Ann Sheppard, 01386 750863, ann98sheppard@btinternet.com. *3m SW of Pershore. A4104 Pershore to Upton Rd, turn into Harpley Rd, Defford. Don't go up Bluebell Ln as directed by SatNav, black & white cottage at side of church. Parking in village hall car park.* **Sun 25, Mon 26 May (11-5). Adm £6, chd free. Tea, coffee & cake.** Visits also by arrangement 8 Feb to 7 Sept for groups of 10 to 30.

True countryman's ⅓ acre cottage garden. Japanese style feature with 'dragons den'. Specimen trees, many rare and unusual plants, water features, perennial garden, vegetable garden, poultry, streamside bog garden. Wheelchair access to most areas, narrow paths may restrict access to some parts.

11 ♦ COTSWOLD GARDEN FLOWERS
Sands Lane, Badsey, Evesham, WR11 7EZ. Mr Bob Brown and Mr Edmund Brown, 01386 833849, info@cgf.net, www.cotswoldgardenflowers.co.uk. *Sands Ln is the last road on the L when leaving Badsey for Wickhamford. Garden is nearly ½ m down lane.* **For NGS: Wed 12 Mar, Wed 9 Apr, Wed 14 May, Wed 11 June, Wed 9 July, Wed 13 Aug, Wed 10 Sept, Wed 8 Oct (11-4). Adm £5, chd free. Light refreshments.** For other opening times and information, please phone, email or visit garden website.

The garden consists of one acre of stockbeds with many thousands of kinds of plants many of which are unusual and rare. Guided tours are available on NGS open days. Please note this is a working nursery and not a traditional garden. This garden proudly provided plants for the National Garden Scheme's Show Garden at Chelsea Flower Show in 2024.

12 COWLEIGH LODGE
16 Cowleigh Bank, Malvern, WR14 1QP. Jane & Mic Schuster, 07854 015065, dalyan@hotmail.co.uk. *7m SW from Worcester. From Hereford, turn R after Storridge church, follow road approx 2½ m, then L onto Cowleigh Bank. From Worcester R at Link Top - Hornyold Rd, R onto St. Peter's Rd, follow yellow signs.* **Sun 22 June (11-5). Adm £6, chd free. Tea, coffee & cake.** Visits also by arrangement 26 May to 11 July for groups of 10+.

The now mature one acre 'quirky' garden on the slopes of the Malvern Hills has a formal rose garden, grass beds, bamboo walk, colour themed beds, nature path leading to a wildlife pond, Acer bank and chickens. Large vegetable plot and orchard with views overlooking the Severn Valley. Explore the polytunnel and then relax with a cuppa and slice of home-made cake served with a smile. This is the 10th year of opening this developing and expanding garden. Visitors from previous years will be able to see the difference. Lots of added interest with staddle stones, troughs, signs and other interesting artefacts. The garden is definitely now a mature one.

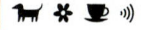

584 WORCESTERSHIRE

3 COWLEIGH PARK FARM
Cowleigh Road, Malvern, WR13 5HJ. John & Ruth Lucas, 01684 566750, info@cowleighparkfarm.co.uk, www.cowleighparkfarm.co.uk. *On the edge of Malvern. Leaving Malvern on the B4219 the driveway for Cowleigh Park Farm is on the R just before the derestrict speed sign. Coming from the A4103 we are on the L just after the 30mph sign.* **Visits by arrangement 14 Mar to 19 Oct. Adm £6, chd free. Tea, coffee & cake.**
The 1½ acre garden at Cowleigh Park Farm surrounds a Grade II listed timber framed former farmhouse (not open). Whilst no longer a farm, the property has views to adjacent orchards and inc lawns, spring fed ponds, a waterfall and stream. The focus in established beds and borders is to be wildlife and bee friendly. The garden contains multiple seating areas and a summerhouse. The whole garden can be viewed from wheelchair accessible places but some parts have steep grassy slopes that may not be accessible.

4 THE DELL HOUSE
2 Green Lane, Malvern Wells, WR14 4HU. Kevin & Elizabeth Rolph, 01684 564448, kande@dellhousemalvern.co.uk, www.dellhousemalvern.uk. *2m S of Gt Malvern. Behind former church on corner of Wells Rd & Green Ln. Small car park for those pre-booked. Approach downhill from Wells Rd. Don't use postcode in SatNav. What3words app: remember.shrub. robot.* **Sun 4, Mon 5, Mon 12 May, Wed 4 June, Wed 10 Sept (11-5). Adm £5, chd free. Pre-booking essential, please visit www.ngs. org.uk for information & booking. Tea, coffee & cake.** Visits also by arrangement Feb to Nov for groups of up to 20. Individuals or small groups welcome at short notice.
Two acre wooded hillside garden. Revived from a derelict state by the current owners over ten years, creating a garden natural in style and rich in variety. A former Victorian rectory garden containing magnificent specimen trees and historic garden buildings, and more recent additions of tree carvings and a model railway. Spectacular views from the terrace. Garden tours at 11:15am and 3:15pm. Partial wheelchair access.

Parking is on gravel with level access to the paved terrace with great views. Sloping bark paths, some quite steep.

GROUP OPENING

5 ECKINGTON GARDENS
Willow Pond, Pass Street, Eckington, WR10 3AX. Group Coordinator James Field. *One garden in Upper End 5th R off New Rd; Two gardens in Pass St which is 2nd R off New Rd. A4104 Pershore to Upton & Defford, L turn B4080 to Eckington. In centre, by war memorial turn L into New Rd.* **Sat 10, Sun 11 May (11-5). Combined adm £8, chd free. Home-made teas at Mantoft on Saturday 10 May and Quietways on Sunday 11 May.**

MANTOFT
Mrs Tupper, 07733 697076.
Visits also by arrangement May to Sept for groups of 5 to 30. Refreshments to be arranged direct with garden owner.

NEW QUIETWAYS
Mr Russell & Mrs Jude Stracey.

WILLOW POND
James Field & Mike Washbourne, 07970 962842, willowpondproperties@outlook.com, www.willow-pond.co.uk.
Visits also by arrangement Apr to Sept for groups of 5 to 30. Refreshments to be discussed with garden owner.

Three diverse gardens set in lovely village of Eckington. Mantoft: Wonderful ancient thatched cottage with 1½ acres of magical gardens. Fishpond with ghost koi, Cotswold and red brick walls, large topiary, treehouse with seating, summerhouse and dovecote, pathways, vistas and stone statues, urns and herbaceous borders. Willow Pond: Listed black & white cottage with 1 acre gardened for wildlife with lawn and long grass, herbaceous borders, water features and lots of large pots and places to sit and relax. Quietways: A mature and ever-changing fun-filled family garden with the grade II listed cottage at its heart. There are tree swings, wild areas, loose planting, containers and formal herbaceous beds. There is a raised vegetable garden, raised pond, areas of lawn with views of Bredon Hill with a rustic summerhouse,

shepherds hut as well as sculpture and other artistic elements. Gravel paths and grass areas.

6 ELM HILL COTTAGE
Sinton Green, Hallow, Worcester, WR2 6NU. Mr Michael & Mrs Tina Boughey. *4m NW of Worcester. Off A443. Take road to Sinton Green NGS sign (Dark Ln). Continue for 1 m and at 2nd Xrds, (NGS sign) turn R at the green, then follow NGS signs.* **Sat 14, Sun 15 June (1.30-5). Adm £5, chd free. Home-made teas. Gluten and dairy free cake available.**
Charming ¼ acre cottage garden surrounded by fields with views of Worcestershire. Mixed herbaceous planting, white borders, paved area with nod to the Mediterranean, a potted eucalyptus is surrounded by a selection of beds and pots overflowing with colour. Two espalier apples lead to borders with hardy geraniums, alliums, delphiniums, salvias, roses, peonies, clematis, iris, weigelas. Small vegetable area. A raised sitting area with views of the lakes, plus many more places to sit and not only enjoy the garden but also admire the views of the Worcestershire countryside. The area at the front of the house is laid to gravel. There is access by car to the start of the garden.

7 THE FOLLY
87 Wells Road, Malvern, WR14 4PB. David & Lesley Robbins, 01684 567253, lesleycmedley@btinternet.com. *Malvern Wells. 1½ m S of Great Malvern & 9m S of Worcester. 8m from M5 via J7 or J8. On A449, 0.7m N of B4209 & 0.2m S of Malvern Common. No parking restrictions on the A449 but parking off the main road is available on lay-by or side road opp the Common.* **Visits by arrangement 7 Apr to 6 July. Adm by donation. Tea, coffee & cake.**
A hillside garden in Malvern with three terraces and views over the Severn Vale. The first level has a potager with greenhouse, the second is a formal terrace and courtyard by the house, and the third is landscaped to create small cottage and scree gardens, stumpery and pergola under mature cedars. Planting inc climbers, spring plants and shrubs, roses, acers, hostas, succulents and ferns. The terraces all have seating and are linked

by both steps and winding paths. Garden art set amongst the plants and trees provides added interest.

GROUP OPENING

18 HANLEY SWAN NGS GARDENS
Hanley Swan, WR8 0DJ. Group Co-ordinator Brian Skeys, 01684 311297, brimfields@icloud.com, www.brimfields.com. *5m E of Malvern, 3m NW of Upton upon Severn, 9m S of Worcester & M5. From the B4211 towards Great Malvern & Guarlford (Rhydd Rd) turn L to Hanley Swan continue to Orchard Side WR8 0EA for entrance tickets & maps.* **Sat 14, Sun 15 June (1-5). Combined adm £7.50, chd free. Tea, coffee & cake at 19 Winnington Gardens. Visits also by arrangement 16 June to 29 Aug for groups of 10 to 20.**

NEW CHERRY TREE COTTAGE
Mr & Mrs Steve Gogerty.

MEADOW BANK
Mrs Lesley Stroud & Mr Dave Horrobin.

ORCHARD SIDE
Mrs Gigi Verlander, 01684 310602, gigiverlander@icloud.com.

THE PADDOCKS
Mr & Mrs N Fowler.

SUNDEW
Mr Nick & Mrs Alison Harper.

19 WINNINGTON GARDENS
Brian & Irene Skeys.
(See separate entry)

YEW TREE COTTAGE
Mr & Mrs Read.

7 gardens in the beautiful historic village of Hanley Swan all different in style and design. Entrance tickets and maps from Orchard Side. Wristbands valid for both days. Many wildlife features within the gardens with increasing environmental considerations, growing vegetables, fruit trees, herbs, perenials and exotics, cottage garden style plantings. C16 and C17 Black and White cottages (not open) sit in two of the gardens. Extended and individual garden descriptions are on the NGS website. Gardens with plenty of places to sit and enjoy your teas. One new garden and one returning this year. New planting schemes with in the group. Wildlife photographs and vintage garden tools on display. Hanley Swan is in a beautiful setting in the shadow of the Malvern Hills close to the Three Counties Showground, home of the RHS Spring Show. It is home to a school, shop, pub and pond with ducks and occasional swans.

Riverside Gardens at Webbs

19 HIRAETH
30 Showell Road, Droitwich, WR9 8UY. Sue & John Fletcher, 07752 717243, sueandjohn99@yahoo.com. *1m S of Droitwich. On The Ridings estate. Turn off A38 r'about into Addyes Way, 2nd R into Showell Rd, 500yds on R - Follow the yellow signs.* **Sun 27 Apr, Sun 1 June (1.30-4.30). Adm £4, chd free. Home-made teas.** **Visits also by arrangement 1 Apr to 29 Aug for groups of up to 30.**
⅓ acre gardens. The front has three barrels of ericaceous plants. A conifer bed, hydrangeas and a 300+ yr old olive tree, monkey puzzle, acers, silver birch and shrubs. The centre features a piece of Forest of Dean rock. A rose arch at one entrance. The rear garden is an oasis of colour created by numerous trees inc acers, weeping willow and weeping birch. Rose and hosta bed on one side and a numerous ferns on the other. Various statues and metal sculptures on display containing a variety of animals inc an alligator or crocodile (we're not sure which). A local minister has described the garden as 'a haven on the way to heaven'. Partial wheelchair access.

ਨ ✱ ☕

20 HOLLY COTTAGE
Gorcott Hill, Beoley, Redditch, B98 9EW. Mr Robin & Mrs Julie Boyce. *3m S of J3 M42. Take slip road from A435 (signed Ullenhall). Gorcott Hill is on the E side of A435, a no through road. Follow NGS signs to car parking.* **Sun 6 July (11.30-5). Adm £5, chd free. Tea, coffee & cake.**
½ acre garden that contains a cottage garden border, jungle area, formal garden, rose borders, small orchard, Mediterranean area with grapes, figs, olives and lavender, and all continually evolving. A pond for wildlife, and many seating areas. Our miniature donkeys look forward to seeing you, along with the chickens. Far reaching views of the Malverns, Abberley, and Bredon hills.

✱ ☕ ⊼))

21 MADRESFIELD COURT
Madresfield, Malvern, WR13 5AJ. Trustees of Lord Beauchamp's 1963 Settlement, 01684 573614, office@madresfield.co.uk, www.madresfieldestate.co.uk. *2m E of Malvern. Entrance ½ m S of Madresfield village, just outside Malvern.* **Thur 15 May (12-4). Adm £10, chd free. Tea, coffee & cake.**
Gardens mainly laid out in 1865, based on three avenues of oak, cedar and Lombardy poplar, within and around which are specimen trees and flowering shrubs. Meadows within the avenues abound in daffodils, and later, fritillaries, bluebells, cowslips etc. Recent rhododendron plantings. Holly hedge enclosure with 100m walk of peonies and irises, next to a crescent tunnel of pollarded limes. Overall a parkland garden of approx 60 acres. Tarmac main drive interspersed with gravel and grass paths. Accessible toilets available.

ਨ 🐕 🛏 ☕ ⊼))

22 MANOR COTTAGE
Hadzor, Droitwich, WR9 7DR. Mr Ian & Mrs Caroline Hancock. *Approx 10mins from either J5 or J6 from M5. J5: A38 S 1st L B4065 to L, B4090, under M5, R to Hadzor Ln for 1m / J6: A4538 to A38, R to island R on Adoyes Way R at island to Primsland Way R on Tagwell Rd L on Middle Ln 2nd L to Hadzor Ln.* **Sat 19 July (12.30-5.30). Adm £5, chd free. Tea, coffee & cake.**
We moved here 10 years ago to fulfil my desire to develop a garden large enough to keep us busy for years! The plot is just under an acre with borders surrounding the cottage. Large specimen trees and mixed hedges help give the garden structure. The pond is a definite pull to people and nature alike. We have many fruit trees, island beds and grasses. We hope to complete our Mediterranean courtyard and re-build the well in time for opening.

☕))

23 ♦ MORTON HALL GARDENS
Morton Hall Lane, Holberrow Green, Redditch, B96 6SJ. Mrs A Olivieri, 01386 791820, morton.garden@mhcom.co.uk, www.mortonhallgardens.co.uk. *13 m W of Stratford-Upon-Avon. In centre of Holberrow Green, at a wooden bench around a tree, turn up Morton Hall Ln. Follow NGS signs to gate opp Morton Hall Farm.* **For NGS: Sat 23 Aug (10-5). Adm £12, chd free. Pre-booking essential, please phone 01386 791820, email morton.garden@mhcom.co.uk or visit www.mortonhallgardens.co.uk for information & booking. Tea, coffee & cake inc gluten free & vegetarian options. For other opening times and information, please phone, email or visit garden website.**
Secluded private garden full of drama and colour: Seven garden rooms with bold landscapes and exquisite planting schemes guarantee a unique visit. Late summer borders are glorious, with brilliant and inspiring combinations. The elegant Japanese Garden and majestic Rockery offer an exciting contrast. Grand views over the Vale of Evesham complete the enthralling experience. Tulip Festival on 1st May bank holiday weekend. Visits by appointment from April to September. All visits must be pre-booked. See garden website for details. For NGS Open Day, click on the yellow banner on the Morton Hall Gardens homepage. Pre-booking closes at 8.30 am on 23.08.25. Only the formal gardens are suitable for wheelchairs.

ਨ 🚗 ☕

24 NEW HOUSE FARM
Kidderminster Road, Cutnall Green, Droitwich, WR9 0PW. Mrs Rachel Barnes, 01299 851013, barnes.p7@sky.com. *N of Droitwich Spa. S of Kidderminster. From either Droitwich or Kidderminster follow A442 until you reach the village of Cutnall Green. Yellow signs indicate separate parking and gardens.* **Sat 14 June, Sat 5 July (10-4). Adm £6, chd free. Tea, coffee & cake.** **Visits also by arrangement in June for groups of 10 to 50. Cheese and wine evening also available for groups.**
1 acre country garden surrounding Victorian farmhouse (not open), offering many old features, with new planting schemes and views over open countryside giving this garden a wealth of interest. The creativity is abundant due to the resident designer who runs an interior design/craft shop/workshops and Holiday let. Plenty of flat ground and lawned areas, some gravel pathways and steps.

ਨ 🐕 ✱ 🚗 🛏 ☕

25 NIMROD, 35 ALEXANDRA ROAD
Malvern, WR14 1HE. Margaret & David Cross, 01684 569019, margaret.cross@ifdev.net. *From Worcester A449. From Malvern Link, pass train stn, ahead at T-lights, 1st R into Alexandra Rd. From Great Malvern, go through Link Top T-lights (junc with B4503), 1st L.* **Sun 4, Mon 5 May, Sat 2, Sun 3 Aug (10.30-5).**

Adm £5, chd free. Home-made teas. Visits also by arrangement 6 May to 30 Sept.
Overlooked by the Malvern Hills, this peaceful garden is on two levels with mature trees, pond with stream, small wildflower meadow, shady woodland area, cottage garden, Japanese garden, rockeries, a New Zealand area and an arbour inspired by Geoff Hamilton. Elgar wrote some of the Enigma variations in a bell tent here. Colourful shrubs and trees in May and lots of flower colour in August. With help, the garden can be accessed by wheelchair, there are few steps but gravel paths and gradients. If advised we can offer closer parking.

⚅ 🐕 ✻ ☕ 🪑))

26 OAK TREE HOUSE
504 Birmingham Road, Marlbrook, Bromsgrove, B61 0HS. Di & Dave Morgan, 01214 453595, meandi@btinternet.com. *On main A38 midway between M42 J1 & M5 J4. Park in old A38 - R fork 250 yds N of garden or small area in front of Miller & Carter Pub car park 200 yds S or local roads.* **Sun 18, Mon 26 May (1.30-5). Adm £4, chd free. Tea, coffee & cake. Visits also** by arrangement May to July for groups of 10 to 40. Coach parties welcome but drop off only at garden (no coach parking).
Plantswoman's cottage garden overflowing with plants, pots and interesting artifacts. Patio with spring colour, azaleas, rhododendrons and acers, small pond and waterfall. Plenty of seating, separate wildlife pond, water features, rear open vista. Scented plants, hostas, dahlias, alpines and lilies. Conservatory with art by owners. Also: 'Wynn's Patch' - part of next door's garden being maintained on behalf of the owner.

☕))

27 3 OAKHAMPTON ROAD
Stourport-on-Severn, DY13 0NR. Sandra & David Traynor, 07970 014295, traynor@clickspeedphotography.co.uk. *Between Astley Cross Inn & Kings Arms. From Stourport take A451 Dunley Rd towards Worcester. In 1 m turn L into Pearl Ln. 4th R into Red House Rd, past the Kings Arms Pub, & next L to Oakhampton Rd. Extra parking at Kings Arms Pub.* **Sun 22, Sun 29 June, Sun 13, Sun 27 July, Sun 17, Sun 24, Mon 25 Aug (10-5.30). Adm £5, chd free. Home-made teas. Visits also by** arrangement 16 June to 31 Aug for groups of 5 to 20.
Beginning in March 2016 the plan was to create a garden with a decidedly tropical feel to inc palms from around the world, with tree ferns, bananas and many other strange and unusual plants from warmer climes that would normally be considered difficult to grow here as well as a pond and small waterfall. Not a large garden but you'll be surprised what can be done with a small space. Home-made cakes using eggs and honey from the neighbours whose bees visit the garden flowers.

✻ ☕

28 THE OLD FORGE
Main Street, Wick, WR10 3NZ. Sean & Elaine Young. *Wick Village. Off the B4084 between Evesham and Pershore. Postcode WR10 3NZ will take you onto Main St. Parking signs will be visible and the Old Forge is a short walk from the car park.* **Sun 4 May (1-6). Adm £5, chd free. Tea, coffee & cake.**
An evolving garden of approximately ⅓ of an acre with mixed herbaceous borders planted with a wide variety of trees, shrubs, perennials, grasses and bulbs. It features a long pergola and a moderately sized pond. To the rear is a courtyard with ornamental pond and vegetable and cutting garden. New Jungle garden for 2025.

☕))

29 OVERBURY COURT
Overbury, GL20 7NP. Sir Bruce Bossom & Penelope Bossom, 01386 725111, gardens@overburyenterprises.co.uk, www.overburyenterprises.co.uk. *5m NE of Tewkesbury. Overbury signed off A46. Turn off village road beside the church. Park by the gates & walk up the drive. What3words app: cars.blurs.crunches.* **Sun 6 Apr (11-4). Adm £5, chd free. Visits also by** arrangement Apr to Sept for groups of 10 to 20.
A 10 acre historic garden, at the centre of a picturesque Cotswold village, nestled amongst Capability Brown inspired Parkland. The Garden comprises vast formal lawns skirted by a series of rills and ponds which reflect the ancient plane trees that are dotted throughout the garden. The south side of the house has a formal terrace with mixed borders and yew hedging, overlooking a formal lawn with a reflection pool and yew topiary. Running parallel to the pool is a long mixed border which repeats its colours of silver and gold down to the pool house. Some slopes, while all the garden can be viewed, parts are not accessible to wheelchairs.

⚅ 🐕 🚗 ☕))

30 PEAR TREE COTTAGE
Witton Hill, Wichenford, WR6 6YX. Pamela & Alistair Thompson, 01886 888295, peartree.pam@gmail.com, www.peartreecottage.me. *13m NW of Worcester & 2m NE of Martley. From Martley, take B4197. Turn R into Horn Ln then 2nd L signed Witton Hill. Keep L & Pear Tree Cottage is on R at top of hill.* **Sun 4 May (11-5). Evening opening Sun 24 Aug (4-10). Adm £5, chd free. Home-made teas. Sun 24 Aug - Twilight Garden by Candlelight. Wine and Pimm's will be served after 6pm.** Visits also by arrangement May to Aug. Max of 10 cars preferred. Coaches by special arrangement.
A Grade II listed black and white cottage (not open) SW facing gardens with far-reaching views across orchards to Abberley Clock Tower. The ¾ acre garden comprises gently sloping lawns with mixed and woodland borders, shade and plenty of strategically placed seating. It not only exudes a quirky and humorous character but a thriving example of the world's rarest tree! A built in reclaimed cast iron range with Victorian tiled surround complete an unusual take on an outdoor kitchen! On the 4th May, the annual Plant Bonanza will take place at neighbouring garden 'Maranatha' in aid of the St Laurence Church. Barrels and Bells Clarinet Choir will be performing in Pear Tree Cottage Garden. Regret no picnics. Partial wheelchair access.

⚅ 🐕 ✻ ☕ 🪑))

In 2024, National Garden Scheme funding for Perennial supported 1,367 people working in horticulture.

GROUP OPENING

31 PERSHORE GARDENS
Pershore, WR10 1BG. Group Co-ordinator Sarah Charlton, www.visitpershore.co.uk. On B4084 between Worcester & Evesham, & 6m from J7 on M5. There is also a train stn to N of town. **Sat 7, Sun 8 June (1-5). Combined adm £7.50, chd free. Light refreshments at Holy Redeemer Primary School and Number 8 Community Arts Centre on High St. Refreshments at selected gardens as indicated on the map/ description sheet.**
Most years about 15 gardens open in Pershore. This small town has been opening gardens as part of the NGS for 50 yrs, almost continuously. Some gardens are surprisingly large, well over an acre, while others are courtyard gardens. All have their individual appeal and present great variety. The Abbey and the River Avon are some of the many points of interest in this market town. Tickets, which take the form of a wristband, map and garden descriptions, are valid for both days. They can be purchased a week before the event at 'Blue' in Broad St or at the Town Hall. On the weekend they can be bought at Number 8 Community Arts Centre in the High St and any open garden. Gardens are open all over the town inc Bridge St, Broad St, High St, Newlands, Defford Rd, Station Rd, Priest Ln and Hunter Rise. Parking available in car parks off Queen Elizabeth Dr and Asda car park. Both Free on Sunday only.

🐄 ✤ 🚗 🏠 ☕

32 NEW RASHWOOD CARE HOME
Rashwood, Droitwich, WR9 0BP. Ms Catherine Lines, 01527 861258, enquiries.rashwood@elizabethfinn.co.uk, www.elizabethfinn.co.uk. 1 m from J5 M5 follow signs for Droitwich. Sharp L after Robin Hood Pub. Rashwood Care Home is signposted at this turn. Drive to end of road. **Visits by arrangement May to Aug for groups of up to 20. Adm £8, chd free. Light refreshments.**
A 6½ acre landscaped garden, surrounding a large Queen Anne period house, designed as wildlife friendly due to the thriving population of woodland animals and our resident peacocks, with many seasonal flowering shrubs, mixed borders, sculptures, rose garden, mature trees inc redwoods, pine, beech and *Davidia Involucrata* (dove or handkerchief tree) plus a 100 yr old wisteria. Plenty of seating. Rashwood operates as a Nursing and Residential care home providing care where people can flourish, as part of the Elizabeth Finn Homes group. Most areas are wheelchair accessible. Disabled toilets available.

♿ 🐄 ☕ 🏠

33 RAVELIN
Gilberts End, Hanley Castle, WR8 0AS. Mrs Christine Peer, 01684 310215, caroline.peer@btinternet.com. *3m from Upton upon Severn, 5m from Malvern. From Worcester/Callow End B4424 or from Upton B4211 to Hanley Castle. Then B4209 to Hanley Swan. From Malvern B4209 to Hanley Swan. At pond/Xrds turn to Welland. ½ m turn L opp Hall, to Gilberts End.* **Sat 24, Sun 25, Mon 26 May, Sat 13, Sun 14 Sept, Sat 11, Sun 12 Oct (1-5). Adm £5, chd free. Cream teas. Visits also by arrangement Apr to Oct.**
This 60 yr evolving ½ acre garden with winding paths, hidden areas plentiful seating and views across fields and the Malvern Hills is a delight for gardeners, plant lovers and flower arrangers alike. Year-round colour and interest provided by a wide variety of unusual plants, hellebores, hardy geraniums, aconitum, heucheras, Michaelmas daisies, grasses and dahlias and a 55 yr old silver pear tree. Thought to be built on medieval clay pottery works in the royal hunting forest. Garden containing herbaceous and perennial planting with gravel garden, woodland area, pond and summerhouse . A quiz for children.

🐄 ✤ 🚗 ☕

34 REST HARROW
California Lane, Welland, Malvern, WR13 6NQ. Mr Malcolm & Mrs Anne Garner, 01684 310503, anne.restharrow@gmail.com. *4.6m S of Gt Malvern In un-adopted California Ln off B4208 Worcester Rd. From Gt Malvern A449 towards Ledbury, L onto Hanley Rd/B4209 signed Upton. After about 1m R (Blackmore Park Rd/B4209). After 1m R onto B4208. After ⅓ m R (California Ln). Garden 300 yds on L.* **Sat 21, Sun 22 June, Sat 30, Sun 31 Aug (1.30-5). Adm £6, chd free.**

Tea, coffee & cake. **Visits also by arrangement 25 June to 3 Sept for groups of 15 to 30.**
1½ acres developed over 18 yrs with five acre wildflower meadow, woodland and stunning borrowed views of Malvern Hills. Colourful and diverse flower beds, unusual plants, roses, alstroemeria, stocks and shrubs. Potager kitchen garden, fruit trees and rustic trellis made from our own pollarded trees. Sit, relax, enjoy the views or stroll down through the wildflower meadow to the wetland border area. Wheelchair access in garden but unsuitable down in field.

♿ ✤ ☕

35 RHYDD GARDENS
Worcester Road, Hanley Castle, Worcester, WR8 0AB. Bill Bell & Sue Brooks, 01684 311001, NGS@Rhyddgardens.co.uk, www.rhyddgardens.co.uk. *2km N of Hanley Castle. Gates 200 metres N of layby on B4211.* **Visits by arrangement. Adm £5, chd free.**
Two walled gardens and a 60ft greenhouse from the early 1800s set in six acres with wonderful views of the entire length of the Malvern ridge. One Walled garden is set out with formal paths and borders bounded by box hedging. We have planted fruit trees in espaliers and cordons as they would have been when the garden was first set out and have a nature area with walks and some woodland. Teas and homemade cakes on the lawn, or in the greenhouse if inclement weather. Self-guided tour leaflets available. Wheelchair access to the main walled garden with grass and paving paths. Parking near gates can be arranged in advance.

♿ 🏠 ☕

36 ♦ RIVERSIDE GARDENS AT WEBBS
Wychbold, Droitwich, WR9 0DG. Webbs of Wychbold, 01527 860000, www.webbsdirect.co.uk. *2m N of Droitwich Spa. 1m N of M5 J5 on A38. Follow tourism signs from M5 What3words app: regarding.clapper.* **For opening times and information, please phone or visit garden website.**
2½ acres. Themed gardens inc colour spectrum, tropical and dry garden, rose garden, vegetables, seaside garden, bamboozeleum and self-sufficient garden. Over the bridge is a natural garden with wildlife and seasonal interest with grasses and

Birtsmorton Court

perennials. We have a Woodland Walk - watch out for the Troll. There are willow wigwams and wooden tepees made for children to play in, a bird hide, the Hobbit House and a sleeping Miss Moss. Over The Bridge and Woodland Walk wheelchair accessible.

37 ROTHBURY
5 St Peter's Road, North Malvern, WR14 1QS. John Bryson, Philippa Lowe & David, www.facebook.com/RothburyNGS. *7m W of M5 J7 (Worcester). What3words app: departure.repaid.trip.* Turn off A449 Worcester to Ledbury Rd at B4503, signed Leigh Sinton. Almost immed take the middle road (Hornyold Rd). St Peter's Rd is $1/4$ m uphill, 2nd R. **Sat 17 May (11-5.30); Sun 18, Sun 25 May (1-5.30); Mon 26 May (10.30-5.30); Sat 26 July (11-5.30); Sun 27 July (1-5.30); Sat 2 Aug (11-5.30); Sun 3 Aug (1-5.30). Adm** £5, chd free. **Home-made teas inc gluten free and vegan options.** Set on slopes of Malvern Hills, $1/3$ acre plant-lovers' garden surrounding Arts & Crafts house (not open), created by owners since 1999. Dense planting with herbaceous borders, rockery, pond, small orchard. Siberian irises in May; magnificent Eucryphia glutinosa in July; Agapanthus in August. A series of hand-excavated terraces accessed by sloping paths and steps. Views and seats. Partial wheelchair access. One very low step at entry, one standard step to main lawn and one to WC. Decking slope to top lawn. Dogs on leads.

38 ◆ SPETCHLEY PARK GARDENS
The Estate Office, Spetchley Park, Worcester, WR5 1RS. Mr Henry Berkeley, 01905 345106, enquiries@spetchleyparkestate.co.uk, www.spetchleyparkestate.co.uk. *2m E of Worcester. On A44, follow brown signs.* **For NGS: Sun 6 Apr, Sun 6 July (10.30-5). Adm £10, chd £7.** For other opening times and information, please phone, email or visit garden website.

Surrounded by glorious countryside lays one of Britain's best kept secrets. Spetchley is a garden for all tastes and ages, containing one of the biggest private collections of plant varieties outside the major botanical gardens and weaving a magical trail for younger visitors. Spetchley is not a formal paradise of neatly manicured lawns or beds but rather a wondrous display of plants, shrubs and trees woven into a garden of many rooms and vistas. Features inc plant sales, gift shop and coffee shop serving homemade treats, and light lunches during the open season. Flat gravel paths, and grassed areas.

39 ♦ STONE HOUSE COTTAGE GARDENS
Church Lane, Stone, DY10 4BG. Louisa Arbuthnott, 07817 921146, louisa@shcn.co.uk, www.shcn.co.uk. *2m SE of Kidderminster. Via A448 towards Bromsgrove, next to church, turn up drive.* **For opening times and information, please phone, email or visit garden website.**
A beautiful and romantic walled garden adorned with unusual brick follies. This acclaimed garden is exuberantly planted and holds one of the largest collections of rare plants in the country. It acts as a shop window for the adjoining nursery. This garden was proud to provide plants for the National Garden Scheme's Show Garden at Chelsea Flower Show in 2024. Partial wheelchair access.
&♿ ❀ 🚌

GROUP OPENING

40 THE WALLED GARDEN & NO. 53
Rose Terrace, Worcester, WR5 1BU. Julia & William Scott. *Entry tickets from either garden. Close to the city centre, ½ m from the Cathedral. Via Fort Royal Hill, off London Rd. Park on 1st section of Rose Terrace or surrounding streets & walk 20yds down track to The Walled Garden.* **Sat 12, Wed 16 Apr (1-5). Combined adm £5, chd free. Tea, coffee & cake at The Walled Garden.**

53 FORT ROYAL HILL
Professor Chris Robertson MBE.

THE WALLED GARDEN
William & Julia Scott.

The C19 Walled Kitchen Garden is formal in layout, with relaxed planting. A peaceful historic garden in the city with a focus on chemical free planting especially herbs and their uses. Bees and a bee garden. Seating areas around the garden in shade and in the sun. No 53 a very small part-walled garden divided into three 'rooms', inc shade tolerant planting, a tranquil, 'secret' garden with containers and bee-friendly planting.
❀ ☕

---

41 WALNUT COTTAGE
Lower End, Bricklehampton, Pershore, WR10 3HL. Mr Richard & Mrs Janet Williams. *2½ m S of Pershore on B4084, then R into Bricklehampton Ln to T-junc, then L. Cottage is on R.* **Sat 21, Sun 22 June (2-5). Adm £6, chd free. Wine.**
1½ acre garden with views of Bredon Hill, designed into rooms, many created with high formal hedging of beech, hornbeam, copper beech and yew. There is a small 'front garden' with circular gravel path, well-stocked original garden area with wildlife pond and arches to the side of the house. Magnolia garden, mixed herbaceous beds and large area of unusual trees. Year-round interest and colour. Raised fish pond and stairway leading to roof-based viewing platform surrounded by roses. The garden continues to evolve with plenty of seating and interesting artefacts.
☕

---

42 WARNDON COURT
St Nicholas Lane, Worcester, WR4 0SL. Drs Rachel & David Pryke, 07944 854393, rachelgpryke@btinternet.com, www.rachelprykeartist.wordpress.com. *½ m from J6 of M5, Worcester N. St Nicholas Ln is off Hastings Dr.* **Sun 16 Feb (12-3). Adm £5, chd free. Sun 25 May, Sun 15 June (12-4). Adm £6, chd free. Home-made teas in St Nicholas Church Barn. For snowdrop opening hot chocolate and Welsh cakes available. Visits also by arrangement 17 May to 31 July for groups of 12+.**
A two acre family garden surrounding a Grade II listed farmhouse (not open) featuring a circular route with formal rose gardens, terraces, two ponds, pergolas, topiary (inc a scruffy dragon), pretty summerhouse, a potager and woodland walk along the dry moat and through the secret garden. It has bee-friendly wildlife areas and is home to great-crested newts and slow worms. Grade I listed St Nicholas Church will also be open to visitors. There will be an exhibition of original paintings, cards for sale and display of vintage cars. The gardens around the house can be accessed over lawns and down a slight slope to the potager. Disabled parking by the house.
♿ 🐕 ❀ ☕ 🔊

---

43 WHARF HOUSE
Newnham Bridge, Tenbury Wells, WR15 8NY. Gareth Compton & Matthew Bartlett, 01584 781966, gco@no5.com, www.wharf-house-gardener.blog. *Off A456 in hamlet of Broombank, between Mamble & Newnham Bridge. Follow signs. Do not rely on SatNav.* **Sat 21, Sun 22 June (10-5). Adm £7, chd free. Tea, coffee & cake. Visits also by arrangement May to Sept.**
Two acre country garden, set around an C18 house and outbuildings (not open). Mixed herbaceous borders with colour theming: white garden, bright garden, spring garden, canal garden, long double borders, intimate courtyards, a scented border, stream with little bridge to an island, vegetable garden. The garden is on several levels, with some uneven paths and only partial wheelchair access.
🐕 ❀ ☕ 🔊

---

44 WHITCOMBE HOUSE
Overbury, Tewkesbury, GL20 7NZ. Faith & Anthony Hallett, 01386 725206, faith.hallett1@gmail.com. *9m S of Evesham, 5m NE Tewkesbury. Leave A46 at Beckford to Overbury (2m). Or B4080 from Tewkesbury through Bredon/Kemerton (5m). Or small lane signed Overbury at r'about junc A46, A435 & B4077. Approx 5m from J9 M5.* **Visits by arrangement 5 Apr to 13 Sept for groups of up to 50. Coach parking available close by. Evening visits also possible. Coffee and cakes (am) home-made teas (pm), wine and canapés (evenings) all available by arrangement.**
An acre of colour from April-Sept in a peaceful shrub and herbaceous garden with mature and young trees inc weeping beech and catalpa. Spring fed stream bordered by water loving plants. Pastel colours merge with cool white and blue; later in the summer hot colours turn to mellow yellow. Lavender and lots of roses. Secret corners, arches, vines, figs, a vegetable parterre and benches for relaxation. C18 Listed Cotswold stone house (not open). Lovely village of Overbury with St Faith's Church dating from Norman times. Wheelchair access up gravel path through iron gate at south entrance. Also by double wooden gates at back of house by prior arrangement.
♿ 🐕 ❀ ☕ 🔊

WORCESTERSHIRE 591

45 ♦ WHITLENGE GARDENS
Whitlenge Lane, Hartlebury, DY10 4HD. Mr & Mrs K J Southall, 01299 250720, keith.southall@creativelandscapes.co.uk, www.whitlenge.co.uk. *5m S of Kidderminster, on A442. A449 Kidderminster to Worcester L at T-lights, A442 signed Droitwich, over island, ¼m, 1st R into Whitlenge Ln. Follow brown signs.* **For NGS: Sat 26, Sun 27 Apr, Sat 28, Sun 29 June, Sat 23, Sun 24 Aug (10-4.30). Adm £6.95, chd £2.95. Home-made teas in the adjacent tea rooms. Full menu from salads to hot meals, pies etc. Always a special of the day. For other opening times and information, please phone, email or visit garden website.**

Three acre show garden of professional garden designer inc large variety of trees, shrubs etc. Features inc a twisted brick pillar pergola, 2½ metres diameter solid oak moongate set into reclaimed brickwork, and a four turreted, mini moated castle folly with vertical wall planter set between two water falls, then walk through giant gunnera leaves into the Fairy Garden. There is a full size standing stone circle, a 400 sq metre turf labyrinth and a children's play/pet corner. Extensive plant nursery, Gift shop and large tearoom. Wheelchair access on a mix of hard paths, gravel paths and lawn.

46 19 WINNINGTON GARDENS
Hanley Swan, Hanley Swan, WR8 0DJ. Brian & Irene Skeys, 01684 311297, brimfields@icloud.com, www.brimfields.com. *5m E of Malvern, 3m NW of Upton upon Severn, 9m S of Worcester & M5. Yellow arrows from the village Xrds. What3words app: torso.directs. bonkers.* **Mon 19 May, Mon 6 Oct (11-3). Adm £4, chd free. Tea. Opening with Hanley Swan NGS Gardens on Sat 14, Sun 15 June. Visits also by arrangement 20 May to 14 Sept for groups of 5 to 20.**

19 Winnington Gardens is a small wildlife-friendly garden, planted in a series of garden rooms, for year-round interest from daffodils to dahlias. Redesigned green and white garden an oriental garden, an archway leads to a mixed border with iris, asters and hardy perennials, enclosed with shrubs, clematis and climbing roses. Fruit trees, developing more environmental and drought tolerant planting. A no-dig garden, the owner has been experimenting with peat-free compost for four years and now testing reduced fertiliser inputs to help control plant disease. There are several seats in the garden to sit and enjoy the surroundings and observe the birds on the feeders.

Morton Hall Gardens

© Clive Nichols

YORKSHIRE

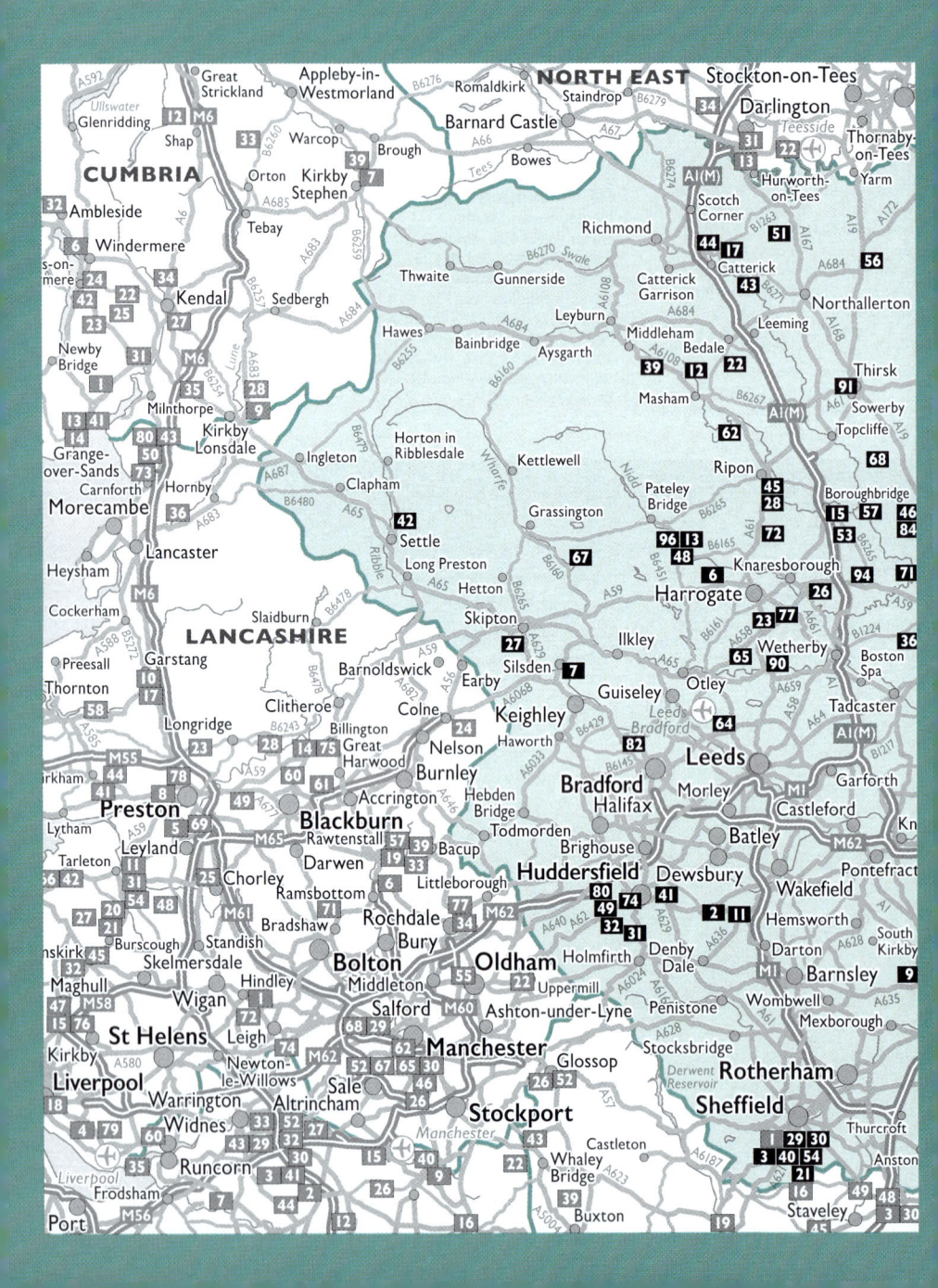

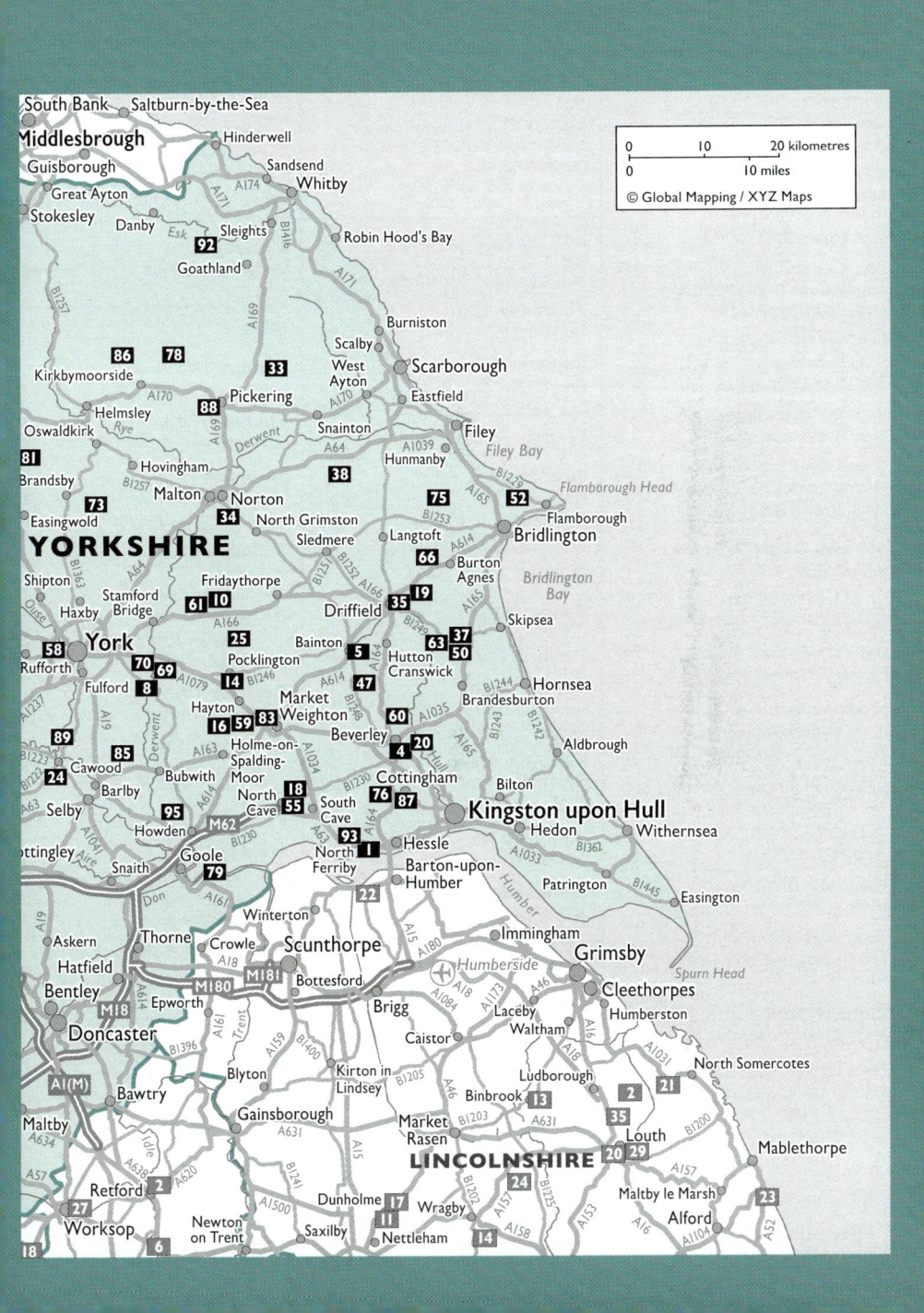

YORKSHIRE 593

VOLUNTEERS

County Organisers

East Yorks
Helen Marsden 07703 529112
helen.marsden@ngs.org.uk

North Yorks
Dee Venner 01765 690842
dee.venner@ngs.org.uk

South & West Yorks
Elizabeth & David Smith
01484 644320
elizabethanddavid.smith@ngs.org.uk

County Treasurer
Angela Pugh 01423 330456
angela.pugh@ngs.org.uk

Publicity & Social Media
Sally Roberts 01423 871419
sally.roberts@ngs.org.uk

Booklet Advertising
Sally Roberts (as above)

Group Visits Co-ordinator
Mandy Gordon 01423 331296
mandy.gordon@ngs.org.uk

Assistant County Organisers

East Yorks
Ian & Linda McGowan 01482 896492
ianandlinda.mcgowan@ngs.org.uk

Hazel Rowe 01430 861439
hazel.rowe@ngs.org.uk

Natalie Verow 01759 368444
natalieverow@aol.com

North Yorks
Annabel Alton 07803 907042
annabel.alton@ngs.org.uk

Jo Gaunt 07443 505291
jo.gaunt@ngs.org.uk

Susan Kerr 07952069419
susan.kerr@ngs.org.uk

South & West Yorks
Felicity Bowring 07773 647943
felicity.bowring@ngs.org.uk

Charlotte Cummins 07802 439051
charlotte.cummins@ngs.org.uk

Peter Lloyd 07958 928698
peter.lloyd@ngs.org.uk

@YorkshireNGS
@YorkshireNGS

OPENING DATES

All entries subject to change.
For latest information check
www.ngs.org.uk
Map locator numbers are
shown to the right of each
garden name.

February

Snowdrop Openings

Thursday 13th
Skipwith Hall 85

Sunday 16th
Devonshire Mill 14

March

Sunday 23rd
Fawley House 18
Goldsborough Hall 26

April

Sunday 6th
Clifton Castle 12
Ellerker House 16

Sunday 13th
Langton Farm 43
Southwood Hall 87

Saturday 26th
249 Barnsley Road 2
7 Low Westwood 49

Sunday 27th
249 Barnsley Road 2

Wednesday 30th
◆ Brodsworth Hall 9

May

Sunday 4th
Low Hall 48
The Ridings 75
Scape Lodge 80

Monday 5th
Saltmarshe Hall 79

Sunday 11th
◆ Jackson's Wold 38
Scape Lodge 80
◆ Stillingfleet Lodge 89
Whixley Gardens 94

Wednesday 14th
Primrose Bank Garden and Nursery 70

Friday 16th
◆ Shandy Hall Gardens 81

Sunday 18th
Galehouse Barn 24
Rudding Park 77

Sunday 25th
NEW Fern Lodge 20
Marton cum Grafton Gardens 53
115 Millhouses Lane 54

Monday 26th
Pilmoor Cottages 68

June

Sunday 1st
Lockington Gardens 47

Thursday 5th
Skipwith Hall 85

Saturday 7th
Old Sleningford Hall 62
Shiptonthorpe Gardens 83

Sunday 8th
Firby Hall 22
Hawthorne Cottage 31
Old Sleningford Hall 62
NEW Shipley Gardens 82
Shiptonthorpe Gardens 83

Tuesday 10th
The Manor, Birkby 51

Thursday 12th
The Priory, Nun Monkton 71

Friday 13th
◆ Shandy Hall Gardens 81

Sunday 15th
NEW Givendale House 25
◆ Jackson's Wold 38
Langton Farm 43

Wednesday 18th
Jervaulx Hall 39

Saturday 21st
Kirkwood Hospice 41

Sunday 22nd
Birstwith Hall 6
Goldsborough Hall 26
NEW Highfield 34
Langcliffe Hall 42
18 Riplingham Road 76
Yorke House & White Rose Cottage 96

Silvester House

Monday 23rd
| NEW Underhill Cottage | 92 |

Saturday 28th
| NEW Littlewood Cottage | 46 |
| NEW Silvester House | 84 |

Sunday 29th
NEW End House	17
Fern House, 5 Wold Road	19
Fernleigh	21
NEW Lime Tree House	44
Marton cum Grafton Gardens	53
Myton Grange	57
The Old Rectory	61
Paddock Wood	66
Prospect House	72

July

Tuesday 1st
| NEW ◆ Mount Grace Priory | 56 |

Sunday 6th
Beverley Gardens	4
Clifton Castle	12
Dacre Banks Gardens	13
Littlethorpe Manor	45
The Ridings	75
Sleightholmedale Lodge	86
Southwood Hall	87

Wednesday 9th
| Mires Beck Nursery | 55 |

Thursday 10th
| ◆ Parcevall Hall Gardens | 67 |

Saturday 12th
NEW Bilton Garth	5
33 Heights Drive	32
42 Main Street	50

Sunday 13th
NEW Inholmes House	37
42 Main Street	50
Saltmarshe Hall	79
Thirsk Hall	91

Wednesday 16th
| The Grange | 27 |

Saturday 19th
| Anne Turner Memorial Allotments | 1 |

Sunday 20th
Hawthorne Cottage	31
The Nursery	58
NEW Standfield Hall Farm	88

Monday 21st
| The Nursery | 58 |

Tuesday 22nd
| The Nursery | 58 |

Saturday 26th
249 Barnsley Road	2
90 Bents Road	3
6 Fulwith Avenue	23
7 Low Westwood	49

Sunday 27th
249 Barnsley Road	2
6 Fulwith Avenue	23
The Old Vicarage	63
Welton Lodge	93

Tuesday 29th
| The Manor, Birkby | 51 |

August

Sunday 3rd
Fern House, 5 Wold Road	19
Greencroft	28
Highfield Cottage	35
The Poplars	69
NEW Ridgewood	74

Wednesday 6th
| The Grange | 27 |
| NEW Standfield Hall Farm | 88 |

Saturday 9th
| Mansion Cottage | 52 |

Sunday 10th
| Mansion Cottage | 52 |
| St Mary's | 78 |

Saturday 16th
| Swindon House Farm | 90 |

Sunday 24th
128 Greystones Road	29
138 Greystones Road	30
NEW High Dalby House	33

Monday 25th
| Pilmoor Cottages | 68 |

Wednesday 27th
| Duncanne House | 15 |

15 Nab Wood Rise, Shipley Gardens

Thursday 28th
The Orchards 65

Friday 29th
The Orchards 65

Sunday 31st
Fernleigh 21

September

Sunday 7th
Bramble Croft 7
Southwood Hall 87

Sunday 14th
Hutton Wandesley Walled
 Garden 36
◆ Stillingfleet Lodge 89

Wednesday 17th
Jervaulx Hall 39

February 2026

Thursday 12th
Skipwith Hall 85

By Arrangement

Arrange a personalised garden visit with your club, or group of friends, on a date to suit you. See individual garden entries for full details.

90 Bents Road	3
Birstwith Hall	6
Bramble Croft	7
Bridge House	8
3 Church Walk	10
The Circles Garden	11
Devonshire Mill	14
Fawley House	18
Fern House, 5 Wold Road	19
Fernleigh	21
Firby Hall	22
Galehouse Barn	24
The Grange	27
Greencroft	28
138 Greystones Road	30
33 Heights Drive	32
NEW High Dalby House	33
Highfield Cottage	35
The Jungle Garden	40
The Manor, Birkby	51
Mansion Cottage	52

Marton cum Grafton Gardens	53
115 Millhouses Lane	54
The Nursery	58
The Old Priory	59
The Old Rectory	60
The Old Vicarage, Whixley Gardens	94
The Orchard	64
Pilmoor Cottages	68
The Poplars	69
Prospect House	72
Rewela Cottage	73
The Ridings	75
Scape Lodge	80
Skipwith Hall	85
Southwood Hall	87
Wressle Brickyard Farm	95
Yorke House & White Rose Cottage	96

THE GARDENS

1 ANNE TURNER MEMORIAL ALLOTMENTS
Church Road, North Ferriby, HU14 3AA. Anne Turner Allotments, www.nferribyallots.co.uk. *2 m W from Humber Bridge r'about. From Hull, A63 W from Humber Br to N. Ferriby junction. At village Xrds S towards parish church. Rail stn & cycle access available.* **Sat 19 July (11-5). Adm £5, chd free. Tea, coffee & cake at the Village Hall from 2.00pm.**
Allotments founded in 1902 by philanthropist Anne Turner for the local community celebrating 120 years of allotment gardening. There are 83 plots cared for by enthusiastic gardeners producing flowers, fruit and vegetables in an attractive setting. Competition sweet peas and dahlias in addition to homegrown produce. A protected woodland copse providing a wildlife sanctuary is currently being restored. Main paths accessible, some paths between plots too narrow for safe access.
&. 🐕 ✿ ☕ 🔊

2 249 BARNSLEY ROAD
Flockton, Wakefield, WF4 4AL. Nigel & Anne Marie Booth. *On A637 Barnsley Rd. M1 J38 or J39 follow signs for Huddersfield. Parking on Hardcastle Ln (WF4 4AR). Please park with consideration.* **Sat 26, Sun 27 Apr, Sat 26, Sun 27 July (1-5). Adm £5, chd free. Home-made teas.**
An elevated south facing garden with panoramic views. ⅓ of an acre garden packed with sun loving perennials and shrubs. The property is adorned with hanging baskets and surrounded by colour filled pots, creating the perfect chocolate box image. Relax on the patio and pergola areas or view the garden from the numerous seated viewing points. Massive plant sale. Disabled drop-off point at the bottom of the drive.
&. 🐕 ✿ ☕

3 90 BENTS ROAD
Bents Green, Sheffield, S11 9RL. Mrs Hilary Hutson, 01142 258570, h.hutson@paradiseregained.net. *3m SW of Sheffield. From inner ring road nr Waitrose, follow A625 (Ecclesall Rd). Bents Rd approx 3m on R.* **Sat 26 July (11-4). Adm £4, chd free. Light refreshments.**

Visits also by arrangement 27 July to 3 Aug. Light refreshments are offered for an additional fee.
Plantswoman's north east facing garden with many unusual species. Patio with alpine troughs for year-round interest and pots of colourful tropical plants in summer. Large conservatory with exotic plants. Mixed borders surround a lawn which leads to a second patio and mature trees underplanted with shade-loving plants. Many examples of maximum impact with minimal maintenance. Front garden and patio are wheelchair accessible. Back garden accessed via 6 steps with handrail, so unsuitable for wheelchairs.
🐕 ✿ ☕

GROUP OPENING

4 BEVERLEY GARDENS
30 St Giles Croft, Beverley, HU17 0DN. Mr and Mrs McIntyre. *Garden Lodge, Wylies Rd outside North Bar. 30 St Giles Croft, cul-de-sac off The Leases. Fern Lodge on Grovehill Rd which is near Flemingate Centre. 131-133 Keldgate on R from B1230/Queensgate r'bout.* **Sun 6 July (10.30-4.30). Combined adm £8, chd free. Light refreshments at Fern Lodge and Garden Lodge.**

NEW FERN LODGE
Mrs Lucy Dunham-Johnson.
(See separate entry)

GARDEN LODGE
Mr James Marritt.

131-133 KELDGATE
Sue McCallum & Gerard McElwee.

30 ST GILES CROFT
Mr and Mrs McIntyre.

Garden Lodge offers unexpected tranquillity behind high town walls with a satisfying mix of old and new styles. 30 St Giles Croft is a modern lawn-free walled garden with colourful borders, magnolias and wall shrubs. Fern Lodge plantsperson's organic garden. Arches, unusual hedges, trees, wildflowers create intimate spaces. 131-133 Keldgate is south facing walled garden with informal planting of trees, shrubs, perennials to all year interest. Careful attention given to encourage wildlife inc ponds, habitat piles and mini meadow.
&. ☕ 🔊

5 NEW BILTON GARTH
Back Street, Bainton, Driffield, YO25 9LL. Andrew Snee. *6 m SW of Driffield. Off A164 on W side of village, behind Bainton Stop cafe/bistro. Additional parking available on large lay-by on Main St a short walk away.* **Sat 12 July (11-4). Adm £6, chd free.**
Current owner started garden in 2013 (a former ¾ acre pony paddock) by planting young native trees and shrubs to provide basic structure and aspect. Over the years borders and island beds were created with many species of trees, shrubs and herbaceous plants. Large sloping gravel border. Features inc a renovated vintage tractor and treehouse. Plenty of seating areas to enjoy the different views.
&. 🐕 🔊

6 BIRSTWITH HALL
High Birstwith, Harrogate, HG3 2JW. Sir James & Lady Aykroyd, 01423 770250, ladya@birstwithhall.co.uk. *5m NW of Harrogate. Between Hampsthwaite & Birstwith villages, close to A59 Harrogate/Skipton road.* **Sun 22 June (2-5). Adm £5, chd free. Home-made teas. Visits also by arrangement 1 June to 15 July for groups of 10 to 50.**
Charming and varied four acre garden nestling in secluded Yorkshire dale. Formal garden and ornamental orchard, extensive lawns leading to picturesque stream and large pond. Walled garden and Victorian greenhouse.
&. 🐕 ✿ 🚗 ☕

129,032 people were able to access guidance on what to expect when a person is dying through the National Garden Scheme's support for Hospice UK this year.

7 BRAMBLE CROFT
Howden Road, Silsden, Keighley, BD20 0JB. Debbi Wilson, 07837 637862, deb2711@googlemail.com. *Next to Springbank Nursing Home, please park in Howden Rd. Steep access.* **Sun 7 Sept (11-4). Adm £4, chd free. Light refreshments. Visits also by arrangement 1 May to 20 Sept.** Bramble Croft's small hidden hillside artist's garden full of colour and texture and includes perennials, ferns, climbers, grasses and sculptures, lies on the edge of Silsden village. Wildlife encouraged with ponds, bird and insect boxes. Original paintings are on show and for sale in the new tranquil garden room. Terrace and outdoor covered dining patio. Seating available and WC.

✤ ☕

8 BRIDGE HOUSE
Main Street, Elvington, York, YO41 4AA. Mrs W C Bundy, 07974 277792, wendy@bundy.co.uk. *6m E from York ring road (A64). On B1128 from York, last house on R before bridge.* **Visits by arrangement 22 May to 22 July for groups of 5 to 40. Adm £6, chd free. Tea, coffee & cake.** Two acre garden carved out of the River Derwent's floodplain 40 yrs ago. It survives annual winter flooding of the river which can last up to many months. Formal rose garden, mixed borders, shrubbery, large pond surrounded by hostas and ferns. Productive kitchen garden and orchard. Various devices in kitchen garden used to keep above water level. Groups may book a talk about flooding with garden tour. Slopes to main garden are steep.

♿ 🐕 🚗 ☕

9 ♦ BRODSWORTH HALL
Brodsworth, Doncaster, DN5 7XJ. English Heritage. *In Brodsworth, 5m NW of Doncaster off A635 Barnsley Rd; from J37 of A1(M). Please follow brown tourist signs to Brodsworth, do not rely on SatNav directions.* **For NGS: Evening opening Wed 30 Apr (5.30-7.30). Adm £20, chd free. Pre-booking essential, please email fundraising@english-heritage.org.uk or visit www.english-heritage.org.uk/visit/places/brodsworth-hall-and-gardens/events for information & booking. Light refreshments.** For other opening times and information, please email or visit garden website.
Join our Head Gardener and expert gardens team for an exclusive evening tour. Step back in time to the 1860s through the extraordinary surroundings of Brodsworth Hall, exquisitely restored to their Victorian splendour. Enjoy awe-inspiring displays of colourful Victorian bedding surrounded by a vast collection of formal topiary and the wonders of the Fern Dell.

☕

10 3 CHURCH WALK
Bugthorpe, York, YO41 1QL. Barrie Creaser & David Fielding, 01759 368152, barriecreaser@gmail.com. *E of Stamford Bridge. On A166, 4m E of Stamford Bridge. Park outside Bugthorpe Church.* **Visits by arrangement for groups of 10 to 20. Refreshments inc in adm price. Adm £10, chd free. Tea, coffee & cake.**
Created in 2000, this garden has surprisingly mature trees and borders amalgamated in a quirky way to give depth and intrigue. The owners have developed a keen interest in growing from seed, resulting in plants for sale. Recently acquired old oak stump made into a table. Plenty of seating to appreciate the views. Garden wheelchair accessible, but gravel in courtyard. Please contact owners prior to arrival to ensure access to garden by car.

♿ ☕

11 THE CIRCLES GARDEN
8 Stocksmoor Road, Midgley, nr Wakefield, WF4 4JQ. Joan Gaunt, mandy.gordon@ngs.org.uk. *Equidistant from Huddersfield, Wakefield & Barnsley, W of M1. Turn off A637 in Midgley at the Black Bull Pub (sharp bend) onto B6117 Stocksmoor Rd. Park on road.* **Visits by arrangement Apr to Sept for groups of 5 to 20. Not Sundays. Adm £5, chd free. Teas provided by St Austin's Choir, Wakefield.**
An organic and self-sustaining plantswoman's ½ acre garden on gently sloping site overlooking fields, woods and nature reserve opposite. Designed and maintained by owner. Herbaceous, bulb and shrub plantings linked by grass and gravel paths, woodland area with mature trees, meadows, fernery, greenhouse, fruit trees, viewing terrace with pots. About 100 hellebores propagated from owner's own plants. South African plants, hollies, and small bulbs of particular interest.

☕

12 CLIFTON CASTLE
Ripon, HG4 4AB. Lord & Lady Downshire. *2m N of Masham. On road to Newton-le-Willows & Richmond. Gates on L just before turn to Charlcot.* **Sun 6 Apr, Sun 6 July (2-5). Adm £7, chd free. Home-made teas.**
Impressive gardens and parkland with fine views over lower Wensleydale. Formal walks through the wooded 'pleasure grounds' feature bridges and follies, cascades and abundant wildflowers. The walled kitchen garden is similar to how it was set out in the C19. Recent wildflower meadows have been laid out with modern sculptures. Gravel paths and steep slopes to river.

♿ 🐕 ☕ 🔊

GROUP OPENING

13 DACRE BANKS GARDENS
Nidderdale, HG3 4EW. www.yorkehouse.co.uk. *4m SE Pateley Bridge, 10 m NW Harrogate,10 m N Otley, on B6451. On-site parking at all gardens except Orchard House and at public car park opp the Royal Oak pub.* **Sun 6 July (12-5). Combined adm £10, chd free. Home-made teas at Yorke House and Low Hall. Visitors are welcome to picnic in the orchard at Yorke House.**

LOW HALL
Mrs P A Holliday.
(See separate entry)

NEW ORCHARD HOUSE
Mrs G Spain.

YORKE HOUSE & WHITE ROSE COTTAGE
Pat, Mark & Amy Hutchinson.
(See separate entry)

Dacre Banks Gardens are located in the beautiful countryside of Nidderdale and are designed to take advantage of the scenic Dales landscape. The gardens are linked by an attractive level walk along the valley, but each may be accessed individually by car. Low Hall has a romantic walled garden set on different levels around the historic C17 family home (not open) with herbaceous borders, shrubs, climbing roses, productive vegetable area and

Ridgewood

a tranquil water garden. The 2 acre garden at Orchard House contains perennial borders and attractive shrubs selected to attract a diverse wildlife population. Yorke House has extensive colour-themed borders, rambling roses and water features with beautiful waterside plantings. There are plentiful seating areas with attractive views. The newly developed garden at White Rose Cottage is specifically designed for wheelchair users and features a colourful cottage garden, woodland plantings and large collection of hostas. Picnic area at Yorke House. Full wheelchair access at White Rose Cottage. Main features accessible at Low Hall, Orchard House and Yorke House.

14 DEVONSHIRE MILL
Canal Lane, Pocklington, York, YO42 1NN. Sue & Chris Bond, 01759 302147, chris.bond. dm@btinternet.com. *1m S of Pocklington. Canal Ln, off A1079 on opp side of the road from the canal towards Pocklington.* **Sun 16 Feb (11-4.30). Adm £6, chd free. Tea, coffee & cake.** Visits also by arrangement 2 Feb to 31 Aug. Tea, coffee and cake inc in adm price for by arrangement visits.

Drifts of double snowdrops, hellebores and ferns surround the historic Grade II listed watermill (not open). Explore the two acre garden with mill stream, orchards, woodland, herbaceous borders, hen run and greenhouses. The old mill pond is now a vegetable garden with raised beds and polytunnel. Over the past 30 yrs the owners have developed the garden on organic principles to encourage wildlife.

15 DUNCANNE HOUSE
Roecliffe Lane, Boroughbridge, York, YO51 9LN. Colette & Tom Walker. *Off Roecliffe Ln leaving Boroughbridge, on L along small private drive, just before Boroughbridge Manor Care Home.* **Evening opening Wed 27 Aug (5.30-8.30). Adm £15, chd free. Pre-booking essential, please visit www.ngs.org.uk for information & booking. Wine and canapés.**
A secluded town garden, which borrows enclosure from surrounding gardens. From the front garden a birch glade leads to theatrical rear garden with water feature, sculptural grass bank, lawns, beds and two vistas terminated by treehouse and rustic tea pavilion. The product of a landscape architect and garden tour

operator team, who have lovingly developed the garden over the last 10 yrs. Wheelchair accessible via grass paths with some cross falls.

16 ELLERKER HOUSE
Everingham, York, YO42 4JA. Mr & Mrs M Wright, www.ellerkerhouse. weebly.com. *15m SE of York. 5½m from Pocklington. Just out of Everingham towards Harswell on R.* **Sun 6 Apr (10-4). Adm £7, chd free. Home-made teas. Savouries and sandwiches also served.**
5 acre garden of plant lovers' delight. Planted for all seasons with colour themed borders and many fine old trees. Daffodils, spring bulbs and alpines in stumpery around lake. Woodland walk of bluebells. Thatched oak hut and intimate seating. Shady borders planted with shrubs, ferns and hostas. Rose arbours planted with old English roses. Topiary garden. Entry inc rare plant fair with many plant stalls. See website for details. Most of the garden is accessible by wheelchair. Pop-up open days in June if building work done.

17 END HOUSE
High Row, Scorton, Richmond, DL10 6DH. Hilary Enevoldson. N of Caterick, 2 m E on B6271. In Scorton take road to Moulton, turn 1st L into Banks Ln. Parking at Lime Tree House. Walk 100 yds from parking back towards village, last entrance on R. **Sun 29 June (11-4). Combined adm with Lime Tree House £6, chd free.** Formally the village doctors' house and surgery. A large courtyard with planted containers leads through an arched opening into the secluded and intimate cottage garden with pond, mature trees and hedges, perennial and rose borders, kitchen garden. and summerhouse. Plant sales in the courtyard. Refreshments at Lime Tree House. Gates on left as you enter property, patio area also suitable for wheelchairs.

18 FAWLEY HOUSE
7 Nordham, North Cave, nr Brough, Hull, HU15 2LT. Mr & Mrs T Martin, 07951 745033, louisem200@hotmail.co.uk, www.nordhamcottages.co.uk. 15m W of Hull. Leave M62E at J38. L at '30' & signs: Wetlands & Polo. At L bend, turn R into Nordham, garden on RHS. From Beverley, B1230 to N Cave. R after church & over bridge on LHS. **Sun 23 Mar (12-5). Adm £6, chd free.** Home-made teas in beamed cottage tearoom with log burners. **Visits also by arrangement 10 Feb to 27 June for groups of 12 to 50. Tea is inc in adm price for by arrangement visits.**
Tiered, 2½ acre formal garden with lawns, mature trees, hedging, gravel pathways. Lavender beds, mixed shrub and hot double herbaceous borders. Apple espaliers, pears, soft fruit, produce and herb gardens. Terrace with pergola and vines. Sunken garden with white border. Further woodland area with naturalistic planting and spring bulbs. Quaker well, stream and spring with three bridges, ferns and hellebores near mill stream. Snowdrops and aconites early in year. Treasure hunt for children on open day. Self catering, accessible accommodation at Nordham Cottages. Wheelchairs welcome on pea gravelled terrace for garden views & teas. Tea room/WC have narrow entrance with step down.

19 FERN HOUSE, 5 WOLD ROAD
Nafferton, Driffield, YO25 4LB. Peter & Jennifer Baker, 01377 255224. N Nafferton. Follow directions rather than SatNav. From Driffield bypass to Nafferton on A614. Then 1st L & 1st L on Wold Rd. Park on street. **Sun 29 June (10-4), open nearby Paddock Wood. Sun 3 Aug (10-4). Adm £4, chd free. Visits also by arrangement 1 June to 7 Sept.**
Designed and developed by owners since 2019. This small garden feels spacious with over 50 varieties of fern amongst many other plants. Mixed planting in quirky containers, up trellises and walls. A pond, a living wall and 2 greenhouses, one entirely full of ferns and the other of house plants. Seats to view different aspects of a constantly evolving garden. Camomile and flagstone walkway. New garden room.

20 FERN LODGE
248 Grovehill Road, Beverley, HU17 0HP. Mrs Lucy Dunham-Johnson. Beverley town. Humber Br A164 cross Beverley Beck, r'bout 2nd L. York 1079, Wylies Rd, New Walkergate, past station L Grovehill Rd. Driffield A164 Swinemoor Rd, Aldi, r'bout R Grovehill R. **Sun 25 May (11-5). Adm £5, chd free. Light refreshments. Opening with Beverley Gardens on Sun 6 July.**
Organic plantsperson's garden wrapped around C19 cottage. Hedges, dead hedges, hornbeam obelisks, rose and pear archways, trees and many perennial plants create a series of intimate spaces to pause and relax. Central water feature, small wildflower areas and alpine troughs. Cornus Venus and Kousa in Spring. Small Katsura, large fig, Quince, Liquid Amber and other native trees. Access to some of the garden on narrow grass paths but can be viewed from other parts of the garden.

21 FERNLEIGH
9 Meadowhead Avenue, Meadowhead, Sheffield, S8 7RT. Mr & Mrs C Littlewood, 01142 747234, littlewoodchristine@gmail.com. 4m S of Sheffield. From city centre. A61, A6102, B6054 r'about, exit B6054. 1st R Greenhill Ave, 2nd R. From M1 J33, A630 to A6102, then as above. **Sun 29 June, Sun 31 Aug (11-5). Adm £4, chd free.** Home-made teas. **Visits also by arrangement 16 Apr to 14 Aug for groups of 10 to 30.**
Plantswoman's ⅓ acre cottage style suburban garden. Large variety of unusual plants set in different areas provide year-round interest. Several seats to view different aspects of garden. Auricula theatre, patio, gazebo and greenhouse. Miniature log cabin with living roof and cobbled area with unusual plants in pots. Sempervivum, alpine displays, collection of Epimedium and wildlife hotel. Over 30 peonies end of May. Wide selection of homegrown plants for sale. Animal Search for children.

22 FIRBY HALL
Firby, Bedale, DL8 2PW. Mrs S Page, rhp@firbyhall.com. ½ m along Masham Rd out of Bedale, follow sign to Firby. Hall gates on L after ½ m. What3words app: waitress.cornering. recently. **Sun 8 June (12-5). Adm £8, chd free.** Light refreshments in the Greenhouse set in the walled garden. **Visits also by arrangement 30 May to 27 Sept for groups of 12 to 20.**
The Hall sits in 4 acres with a walled garden to the north and 2 lakes to the south, the largest of which features a folly. The walled garden and greenhouse were restored in 2019. The main garden continues to undergo renovation: the ha-ha was restored during the 2020 lockdown as were the 110m long herbaceous beds. Ongoing work is now focused on the main west facing lawns. Some steps but most of the garden is wheelchair accessible.

23 6 FULWITH AVENUE
Harrogate, HG2 8HR. Vanda & David Hartley. 1½ m S of Harrogate. A61 (Harrogate-Leeds). From town centre straight over 2 r'abouts & main T-lights. 3rd L (Fulwith Mill Ln), lst R. **Sat 26 July (11-4.30); Sun 27 July (1-4.30). Adm £5. Pre-booking essential, please visit www.ngs.org.uk for information & booking. Light refreshments.**
From wall fountain to gothic folly, waterfall to Japanese tea garden, this small town garden has interest at every turn. The multi-layered planting provides a constantly changing tapestry of texture and colour.

YORKSHIRE 601

24 GALEHOUSE BARN
Bishopdyke Road, Cawood, Selby, YO8 3UB. Mr & Mrs P Lloyd and Mrs M Taylor, 07768 405642, junelloyd042@gmail.com. *On B1222 out of Cawood towards Sherburn-in-Elmet. On B1222 1m out of Cawood towards Sherburn in Elmet.* **Sun 18 May (12-5). Adm £4, chd free. Home-made teas.** Visits also by arrangement 1 May to 21 Sept for groups of 5 to 15. Refreshments and price to be determined by agreement.
The Barn: A plantaholic's informal cottage garden, created in 2015, to encourage birds and insects. Raised beds with tranquil seating area. The Farm: South facing, partly shaded varied herbaceous border. North facing exposed shaded border redeveloped 2017, ongoing for spring and autumn interest. Small experimental white garden. Raised beds for vegetables. Partial wheelchair access. Help available.
& 🐕 ✿ ☕))

25 NEW GIVENDALE HOUSE
Great Givendale, Pocklington, York, YO42 1TT. Matt Brash. *3 m N of Pocklington. What3words app: Sparks.Steams.Skyrocket. Parking below ha-ha, disabled access via main gates.* **Sun 15 June (10.30-4.30). Adm £6, chd free. Tea, coffee & cake.**
Approx 3 acres on SW edge of Wolds, giving stunning views of Vale of York and Pennines. House and garden owned by Garrowby Estate, built in C19, age of which is reflected in the established mature gardens, inc ha-ha. Gardens inc formal, herbaceous, shrub borders, vegetable patch and wildlife areas and many mature trees inc Sequoiodeae, Tilia, Quercus, Acer, Betula. St Ethelburga's Church, a Norman Church is also worth a visit at the other end of this small delightful village. Access for wheelchairs is possible via the main gate. Please contact on arrival and we will open these gates for access.
& 🐕 ☕))

26 GOLDSBOROUGH HALL
Church Street, Goldsborough, HG5 8NR. Mr & Mrs M Oglesby, 01423 867321, info@goldsboroughhall.com, www.goldsboroughhall.com. *2m SE of Knaresborough. 3m W of A1(M). Off J47 (A59 York-Harrogate). Spring: parking at Hall top car park. Summer: parking E of village in field off Midgley Ln. Disabled parking only at front of Hall.* **Sun 23 Mar, Sun 22 June (11-4). Adm £7.50, chd free. Light refreshments inc sandwiches, scones and cakes along with tea & coffee.** Donation to St Mary's Church, Goldsborough.
Historic 12 acre garden and formal landscaped grounds in parkland setting around Grade II*, C17 house, former residence of HRH Princess Mary, daughter of George V and Queen Mary. Gertrude Jekyll inspired 120ft double herbaceous borders, rose garden and woodland walk. Large restored kitchen garden with rill, fountain and large glasshouse which produces fruit and vegetables for the Hall's commercial kitchens. ¼ mile lime tree walk planted by royalty in the 1920s, orchard and flower borders featuring 'Yorkshire Princess' rose, named after Princess Mary. Gravel paths and some steep slopes.
& 🐕 ✿ 🛏 ☕))

27 THE GRANGE
Carla Beck Lane, Carleton in Craven, Skipton, BD23 3BU. Mr & Mrs R N Wooler, 07740 639135, margaret.wooler@hotmail.com. *1½ m SW of Skipton. Turn off A56 (Skipton-Clitheroe) into Carleton. Keep L at Swan Pub, continue to end of village then R into Carla Beck Ln.* **Wed 16 July, Wed 6 Aug (12-4.30). Adm £7.50, chd free. Light refreshments.** Visits also by arrangement July & Aug for groups of 20+. Donation to Sue Ryder Care Manorlands Hospice.
Over four acres of wonderfully varied garden set in the grounds of Victorian house (not open) with mature trees and panoramic views towards The Gateway to the Dales. The garden has been restored and expanded by the owners over the past three decades. Bountiful herbaceous borders with many unusual species, rose walk, parterre, mini-meadows and water features. Topiary and large greenhouse. Extensive vegetable and cut flower beds. Oak seating placed throughout the garden invites quiet contemplation - a place to 'lift the spirits'. Gravel paths and steps in some areas.
& ✿ 🛏 🚗 ☕

28 GREENCROFT
Pottery Lane, Littlethorpe, Ripon, HG4 3LS. David & Sally Walden, 01765 602487, s-walden@outlook.com. *1½ m SE of Ripon town centre. Off A61 Ripon bypass, signs to Littlethorpe, R at church. From Bishop Monkton take Knaresborough Rd towards Ripon then R to Littlethorpe.* **Sun 3 Aug (12-4). Adm £5, chd free. Cream teas.** Visits also by arrangement July & Aug.
½ acre country garden with long herbaceous borders packed with colourful late summer perennials, annuals and exotics. Circular garden with views through to large wildlife pond and surrounding countryside. Ornamental features inc gazebo, temple pavilions, formal pool, stone wall with mullions, gate to pergola and a water cascade.
& 🐕 ✿ 🚗 ☕

29 128 GREYSTONES ROAD
Greystones Road, Sheffield, S11 7BR. Tricia and Geoff Anderson. *2m S of Sheffield city centre. From Sheffield inner Ring Rd, W on A625 (Ecclesall Rd) for 1.8m; R onto Greystones Rd.* **Sun 24 Aug (10-4). Combined adm with 138 Greystones Road £6, chd free.**
A suburban, north facing garden on a steep hill. Natural springs create a damp habitat perfect for candelabra primulas, astilbes and meadowsweet and woodland plants inc ferns, Epimedium and foxgloves. Exposed spring, bespoke water feature and small wildlife pond. Cottage garden style. Collections of roses, geraniums and hostas mingle with Astrantia, Thalictrum, Achillea and Campanula.
☕

30 138 GREYSTONES ROAD
Sheffield, S11 7BR. Mr Nick Hetherington, 07706 236905, nick.hetherington@outlook.com. *From Sheffield inner Ring Rd, W on A625 (Ecclesall Rd) for 1.8m; R onto Greystones Rd.* **Sun 24 Aug (10-4). Combined adm with 128 Greystones Road £6, chd free. Tea, coffee & cake.** Visits also by arrangement 4 Aug to 28 Sept.
This typical, small suburban plot has been developed into a lovely garden over 20 yrs. It features many trees and acers combined with stunning late tender perennials inc banana plants, Ricinus, Canna, Agapanthus, Colocasia and dahlias. Several sculptures created by the owner are displayed amongst the plants. The garden has a tropical feel with splashes of colour, mainly orange and purple.
✿ ☕))

31 HAWTHORNE COTTAGE
21 Healey Houses, Netherton, Huddersfield, HD4 7DG. Mr & Mrs Peter Sargent. *Off Crosland Factory Ln, off the B6108 between Netherton & Meltham. From Meltham follow the B6108 N. Sharp R turn down to the valley on Crosland Factory Ln, take the next L after Siskin Gdns onto Healy Houses.* Sun 8 June, Sun 30 July (11-4). Adm £5, chd free. Pre-booking essential, please visit www.ngs.org.uk for information & booking. Tea, coffee & cake.

Hawthorne Cottage sits in Magdale with views toward Emley Moor in the far distance. There is a small front lawned area with a stream, herb garden and mixed planting of shrubs. The main lawn at the rear of the property is bordered by mixed beds of herbaceous plants and shrubs. The lawn extends into a small orchard on two levels. There is a stream and trough fountain with a number of sculptures by Mick Kirkby-Geddes. The dry stone walling is by Richard Clegg who has worked at RHS Chelsea. There is a slope into the garden. There is level access to most areas inc part of the allotment area.

& ❀ ☕))

32 33 HEIGHTS DRIVE
Linthwaite, Huddersfield, HD7 5SU. Dawn & Roy Meakin, 07825 184919, roymeakin7@btinternet.com. *4m SW of Huddersfield. From Huddersfield on A62 Manchester Rd for about 2m then fork L at T-lights, Cowlersley Ln, then Gillroyd Ln, all one road for 2m, parking on main road by bus shelter opp Heights Dr.* Sat 12 July (10-4). Adm £5. Tea, coffee & cake. Selection of home-made cakes with allergen labelling. Visits also by arrangement 5 May to 28 Sept for groups of 15+. Donation to Royal National Lifeboat Institute (RNLI).

Situated on a Pennine hillside is a quirky garden overlooking the Colne Valley. The plot has been carefully designed with a flower arranger's eye and offers many handmade bespoke features. The meandering paths draw the visitor's eye around the garden, within a wide range of different room settings. The garden has a range of modern and quirky twists, with a wonderful nod to tradition. Bespoke handmade creations nestled around the garden complementing the colour schemes of the plants, creating traditional and contemporary settings. Flower arranging demonstrations could be offered, please ask for details.

❀ 🚗 ☕

Givendale House

33 HIGH DALBY HOUSE
Dalby, Pickering, YO18 7LP. Linda and Ian Robinson, 01751 460001, ian@highdalbyhouse.com, www.highdalbyhouse.com. *Dalby Forest, North York Moors National Park. Enter Dalby Forest via Thornton Dale entrance barriers. Proceed for 2.2m, house on L.* **Sun 24 Aug (11-4). Adm £6, chd free. Pre-booking essential, please visit www.ngs.org.uk for information & booking. Home-made teas.** Visits also by arrangement.
Set in the heart of Dalby Forest, the garden comprises over six acres of a mix of woodland, small lake, wild areas, a cherry orchard, Labyrinth, formal borders including a RHS Tatton award-winning border. Newly-developed unique Trinity Garden with lively beck running through, crossing bridges and surrounding specimen trees. There are many places to sit, reflect and enjoy its variety.

34 HIGHFIELD
Beverley Road, Norton, Malton, YO17 9PJ. Ms C Stewart. *Malton. Drive entrance is on road between B1248 & Settrington. 100yds from B1248. What3words app: joke.unravel.important. Park in racing stable yard.* **Sun 22 June (10.30-4). Adm £5, chd free. Tea, coffee & cake.**
An informal garden set in the context of a North Yorkshire racing yard, Highfield Stables. The simple south facing garden is in 3 parts, terrace with borders near the house, then oval lawn surrounded by eccentrically planted trees and shrubs. In the distance, an old wild orchard with mown pathways, leading to fields with horses. Rose tunnel leads to vegetable garden and further young orchard. Famous racing stables.

35 HIGHFIELD COTTAGE
North Street, Driffield, YO25 6AS. Debbie Simpson, 07906 623432, debbie@simpsonhighfield.karoo.co.uk. *30m E of York. From A614/A166 into Driffield (York Rd, then North St.) Highfield Cottage is white detached house opp park next to an Indian takeaway.* **Sun 3 Aug (10-4). Adm £5, chd free. Tea, coffee & cake. Refreshments weather dependent as no inside seating.** Visits also by arrangement for groups of 10+.

A ¾ acre suburban garden bordered by mature trees and a stream. Structure provided by numerous yew and box topiary featuring a pergola and sculptures. Lawns with island beds, a small orchard and a fern and hosta area. The garden has been changed since joining the National Garden Scheme to create more distinctive areas and is slowly moving to white planting to provide contrast to the topiary.

36 HUTTON WANDESLEY WALLED GARDEN
Hutton Street, Hutton Wandesley, YO26 7NA. Christy & Sasha York, www.huttonwandesleystables.co.uk. *For SatNav use YO26 7NA. Once in Long Marston/Hutton Wandesley. Please follow signs from the main road down Hutton St to stables.* **Sun 14 Sept (10-4). Adm £6, chd free. Home-made teas in the stunning Event Barn. Lunches also served.**
Redesigned and re-landscaped in 2022 by the owner, Mrs Sasha York. Beautifully designed with a stunning planting scheme, it is hard to believe the garden is so young. The Walled Garden extends to 2½ acres with a quadrant design giving emphasis to the original design dated 1874. Four main areas comprise a perennial meadow, a parterre garden with 16 harmoniously planted parterres, a cutting garden with primarily annual flowers inc a stunning display of dahlias later in the season and large lawned area. Avenues are lined with *Pyrus salicifolia* and *Pyrus chanticleer*. Stunning throughout the year. Wheelchair friendly garden. Disabled facilities onsite.

37 INHOLMES HOUSE
Beeford, Driffield, YO25 8BG. Mr & Mrs Andy and Heather Mayo. *Between Beeford and North Frodingham. Located on B1249 ½ m out of Beeford on road to N Frodingham, large modern gates set back from the road. What3words app: stability.sparrows.warp.* **Sun 13 July (11-4). Adm £5, chd free. Tea, coffee & cake. Open nearby 42 Main Street.**
Country garden, 15 acres comprising native woodland, formal garden, deer and horse paddocks and fishpond with stream. Raised vegetable beds, greenhouse, orchard and chickens. Lawned area with specimen trees leading to lake and wetland habitat. Island and bridge to summerhouse. 1 mile woodland walk with seating and options for shorter loops. Wildlife haven. Site is flat with mowed grass paths.

38 ◆ JACKSON'S WOLD
Sherburn, Malton, YO17 8QJ. Mr & Mrs Richard Cundall, 07966 531995, jacksonswoldgarden@gmail.com, www.jacksonswoldgarden.com. *11m E of Malton, 10m SW of Scarborough. A64 E to Scarborough. R at T lights in Sherburn. Take the Weatherhorpe Rd. After 100 metres R fork to Helperthorpe & Luttons. 1m to top of hill. Turn L at garden sign. Do not use SatNav.* **For NGS: Sun 11 May, Sun 15 June (1-5). Adm £5, chd free. Tea, coffee & cake.** For other opening times and information, please phone, email or visit garden website.
Spectacular two acre country garden. Many old shrub roses underplanted with unusual perennials in walled garden. Woodland paths lead to further shrub and perennial borders. Lime avenue with wildflower meadow. Traditional vegetable garden inc roses and flowers with a Victorian greenhouse. Small adjoining nursery. Tours by appointment.

39 JERVAULX HALL
Jervaulx, Ripon, HG4 4PH. Mr & Mrs Phillip Woodrow. *Parking in the grounds of Jervaulx Abbey accessed from the A1608.* **Wed 18 June, Wed 17 Sept (12-5). Adm £7, chd free. Light refreshments.**
Eight acre garden adjacent to ruins of Jervaulx Abbey and inc Abbey Mill ruins with views of River Ure. Mixed borders and beds, croquet lawn, parterre, glasshouse. A small vegetable garden and fernery. Magnificent older trees and woodland areas with choice trees and shrubs planted in last ten years, inc magnolia, acer, Sorbus and Betula. Growing collection of contemporary sculptures.

40 THE JUNGLE GARDEN
124 Dobcroft Road, Millhouses, Sheffield, S7 2LU. Dr Simon & Julie Olpin, 07710 559189, simonolpin@blueyonder.co.uk. *3m SW of city centre. Dobcroft Rd runs between A625 & A621.* **Visits by arrangement 1 July to 18 Oct. Tea, coffee and home-made biscuits for £8, or cakes for £12, both inc adm fee. Adm £5, chd free. Donation to Sheffield Children's Hospital.**
Not a traditional garden, but a fascinating mature space of specialist interest using mainly hardy exotics creating a jungle effect. Long (250ft) narrow site, densely planted with mature trees and shrubs inc many Trachycarpus, European fan palms, large bamboos, several tree ferns, mature Eucalyptus and a number of species of mature Schefflera. The planting has a South East Asian theme.

41 KIRKWOOD HOSPICE
21 Albany Road, Dalton, Huddersfield, HD5 9UY. Julia Owen, www.thekirkwood.org.uk. *2m from Huddersfield town centre along A629. (Wakefield Rd) Follow Kirkwood Hospice signs L onto Dalton Green Rd then R onto Albany Road.* **Sat 21 June (11-3). Adm £3, chd free. Tea, coffee & cake inc a barbeque. Donation to The Kirkwood (Hospice).**
A peaceful space sitting in an acre of wonderful vistas and borders. Old favourites like Hydrangea Annabelle, nepeta, sedums along with scented roses. Our pond brings movement and sound to the area. The Kirkwood Potager supplies a fresh mix of herbs, salad and vegetables to our chef for to prepare for our patients. An organic garden full of interest and biodiversity where everything is recycled. Complete wheelchair accessibility.

42 LANGCLIFFE HALL
Langcliffe, Settle, BD24 9LY. www.instagram.com/nourish.hq. *1m N of Settle. Take B4679 from Settle up the hill for ½ m. Take RH turning onto Langcliffe Main St (signposted to Malham). Langcliffe Hall is on R.* **Sun 22 June (11-4). Adm £6, chd free. Home-made teas.**
Rambling gardens in the grounds of a historic, grade II listed Jacobean hall (not open). With a picturesque backdrop of the Yorkshire Dales,

explore winding paths leading you from the front of the house through secluded nooks filled with tumbling roses and fairytale charm. Wildflowers spill out of the formally structured garden, overflowing into the paths, lawns and steps. Features herbaceous borders, native wildflower meadows, a woodland walk, and a large walled garden filled with organic vegetables, cutting flowers and an apothecary garden growing native medicinal herbs.

43 LANGTON FARM
Great Langton, Northallerton, DL7 0TA. Richard & Annabel Fife. *5m W of Northallerton. B6271 in Great Langton between Northallerton & Scotch Corner.* **Sun 13 Apr (2-5); Sun 15 June (12-5). Adm £5, chd free. Home-made teas.**
Garden designer's organic garden created since 2000. Romantic flower garden with mixed borders, roses, poppies, Astrantias, delphiniums, white lilies and pebble pool. Formal and informal gravel areas, nuttery. Pear avenue underplanted with double helix of white daffodils.

44 NEW LIME TREE HOUSE
Banks Lane, Scorton, Richmond, DL10 6DG. Amanda Ramsay. *N of Caterick, 2 m E on B6271. In Scorton take road to Moulton, turn 1st L into Banks Ln. Parking at Lime Tree House.* **Sun 29 June (11-4). Combined adm with End House £6, chd free. Light refreshments.**
½ acre acre country garden on the edge of the village bordering farmland and wetlands. Meandering paths take you through garden rooms with clipped lawns, box topiary, colourful shrubs and perennials, exotic trees and garden ornaments. The unique pantile-roofed brick and glazed potting shed sports bird boxes and other paraphernalia.

45 LITTLETHORPE MANOR
Littlethorpe Road, Littlethorpe, Ripon, HG4 3LG. Mrs J P Thackray, www.littlethorpemanor.com. *Outskirts of Ripon nr racecourse. Ripon bypass A61. Follow Littlethorpe Rd from Dallamires Ln r'about to stable block with clock tower. Parking in adjacent field. See map on website.* **Sun 6 July (1.30-**

5). Adm £8, chd free. Home-made teas in marquee.
11 acres. Walled garden with herbaceous planting, roses and gazebo. Sunken garden with ornamental plants and herbs. Brick pergola with wisteria, blue and yellow borders. Formal lawn with fountain pool, hornbeam towers, yew hedging. Box-headed hornbeam drive with Aqualens. Large pond with classical pavilion and boardwalk. New contemporary Physic garden with rill, raised beds and medicinal plants. Gravel paths and some steep steps.

46 NEW LITTLEWOOD COTTAGE
Main Street, Alne, York, YO61 1TB. Mr & Mrs D Matthews. *4 m E of Easingwold just off the A19, 10 m N of York. From Easingwold (A19) Littlewood Cottage, The Fold, approx 4th house on L. Silvester House is the 8th house on L. Look out for the posters and balloons.* **Sat 28 June (1.30-5). Combined adm with Silvester House £6, chd free. Light refreshments at Whiteley's at Home with additional parking and WC facilities.**
Retired garden designer's garden. A small modern garden, on two levels created from scratch on a new development with open views and full of interesting plants such as ferns, hepaticas, epimediums, grasses, shrubs and small trees. Developed by the owners over the last 2 yrs, the garden has been created around the existing hard landscaping of porcelain flags and gabions laid by the developer. The garden is on two levels and with gravel paths.

GROUP OPENING

47 LOCKINGTON GARDENS
Driffield, YO25 9SR. *7m N of Beverley. South Glebe is located off Church Ln. What3words app: chess.nitrate.chariots. Penny Cottage on Thorpe. Gardens about 300yds apart.* **Sun 1 June (11-5). Combined adm £6, chd free. Tea, coffee & cake in Lockington Village Hall.**

PENNY COTTAGE
Mr John & Mrs Sue Rowson.

NEW 8 SOUTH GLEBE
Ms Stephanie Taylor.

Two small gardens in the village of Lockington. Penny Cottage - An interesting example of how to make best use of a small garden. Raised vegetable plot, fruit trees, path leads through planted shady area. Folly wall crammed with plants built by current owner, scree wadi through evergreens. Extensive collection of Hostas and Irises. A complete contrast to our companion garden. South Glebe, Lockington - A Contemporary East Yorkshire Garden Designed in 2013 by award-winning garden designer Matt Haddon. A modern garden created to be both easy to maintain and a pleasure to enjoy from every room in the house. Both the house and the garden have evolved together over the past decade, with thoughtful planting and design choices that ensure the space continues to thrive. These charming East Yorkshire gardens offers a peaceful retreat, showcasing how modern design can blend seamlessly with the surrounding landscape. Wheelchair accessible to most areas of the gardens. Cashless payments at 8 South Glebe only.

48 LOW HALL
Dacre Banks, Nidderdale, HG3 4AA. Mrs P A Holliday. *10 m NW of Harrogate. On B6451 between Dacre Banks & Darley, sign post to Low Hall.* **Sun 4 May (1-5). Adm £5, chd free. Home-made teas. Opening with Dacre Banks Gardens on Sun 6 July.**
Romantic walled garden set on differing levels designed to complement historic C17 family home (not open). Spring bulbs, rhododendrons and azaleas round tranquil water garden. Asymmetric rose pergola underplanted with auriculas and lithodora links the orchard to the garden. Vegetable garden and conservatory. Extensive herbaceous borders, shrubs and climbing roses give later interest. Bluebell woods, lovely countryside and farmland all around, overlooking the River Nidd. 80% of the garden can be seen from a wheelchair but access involves 3 stone steps.

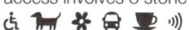

49 7 LOW WESTWOOD
Golcar, Huddersfield, HD7 4ER. Craig Limbert. $3\frac{1}{2}$ *m W of Huddersfield off A62. R at T-lights in Linthwaite signed 'Titanic Spa'. Park on road nr Titanic Spa. Garden is over canal bridge.* **Sat 26 Apr (11-3). Sat 26 July (10-4). Tea, coffee & cake. Adm £5, chd free.**
With 110 yds of canal frontage, this landscaped garden of $\frac{3}{4}$ acres has both flat and steeply sloping aspects with views across the Colne Valley. Mature lime tree walk, terraced herbaceous beds, pond and vegetable plot, contrasting shady and sunny sites. Daffodils and rhododendrons in the Spring. Late summer colour is plentiful. Kniphofia, ligularia, astrantia, agapanthus and hydrangeas.

In 2024 we awarded £232,000 in Community Garden Grants, supporting 89 community garden projects.

Underhill Cottage

50 42 MAIN STREET
North Frodingham, Driffield, YO25 8LG. Ms Beryl Fallows. *6m SE of Driffield. From Driffield take B1249 E for 6m. Garden on R, halfway through village. Street parking.* **Sat 12 July (10-4), open nearby Bilton Garth. Sun 13 July (10-4), open nearby Inholmes House. Adm £4, chd free.** Welcoming garden. Side path bordered with mix of herbs and flowers. Main garden created since 2019 designed with wildlife in mind. Paths wind through borders of shrubs, veg, herbs, fruit, herbaceous and trees. Tibouchina granulosa, peonies, roses, Astilboides tabularis and irises. Secluded sitting area by wall covered in wisteria, wild roses and clematis greenhouse. Pots inc eucomis, abutilon 'Kentish Belle'. Wheelchair access via path to rear garden. Further access across lawns.

51 THE MANOR, BIRKBY
Birkby Lane, Northallerton, DL7 0EF. Ginny and Jonathan McCloy, 07903 757250, ginny.lloyd@me.com. *7m NNW of Northallerton. On the A167, 5½m N of Northallerton turn L into Birkby Ln. ½ m along lane we are immed after St. Peter's Church.* **Tue 10 June, Tue 29 July (11-4.30). Adm £6, chd free. Tea, coffee & cake.** Visits also by arrangement 8 Apr to 30 July for groups of 10 to 25. C18 manor (not open) former rectory to adjacent church. 2½ acre gardens surrounded by mature trees. Extensive lawns, croquet lawn, mixed shrub and flower borders. Current owners have added new features – specimen trees, glasshouse, planned rose gazebo, and an elliptical shaped orchard with corten steel planters for flowers and vegetables. Meandering woodland path with curiosities for the observant. 10th June – Guided Walk (11.30am & 2pm) of adj Scheduled ancient settlement site of Birkby. Small supplementary fee. Stout shoes advisable. WC access for wheelchair users.

52 MANSION COTTAGE
8 Gillus Lane, Bempton, Bridlington, YO15 1HW. Polly & Chris Myers, 07749 776746, chrismyers0807@gmail.com. *2m NE of Bridlington. From Bridlington take B1255 to Flamborough. 1st L at T-lights - Bempton Ln, continue* through r'about and next R into Short Ln then L at end. L fork at church. **Sat 9, Sun 10 Aug (10-4). Adm £5, chd free. Light refreshments inc delicious sweet and savoury small plates.** Visits also by arrangement 25 May to 3 Aug for groups of 10 to 40. A truly hidden, private and secret garden with exuberant, packed, vibrant borders. Visitors' book says 'a veritable oasis', 'the garden is inspirational', with a surprise around every corner. Japanese influenced area, mini hosta walk, 100ft border, summerhouse and art studio. Vegetable plot, cuttery, late summer borders, bee and butterfly borders, deck and lawns. Sweet and savoury small plates served from the conservatory. Produce, plants and home made soaps for sale.

GROUP OPENING

53 MARTON CUM GRAFTON GARDENS
Marton cum Grafton, York, YO51 9QJ. Mrs Glen Garnett, 07901 592768, gwg01@talktalk.net. *2½ m S of Boroughbridge. Turn off the A168 or B6265 to Marton or Grafton, S of Boroughbridge.* **Sun 25 May, Sun 29 June (1-5). Combined adm £7, chd free.** Visits also by arrangement May & June for groups of 10 to 30.

ORCHARD HOUSE
Mr Rob & Mrs Lizzie Shepherd.

WELL HOUSE
Glen Garnett.

Two gardens in two adjacent rural villages within walking distance of each other. In Marton, Orchard House is a contemporary village garden with an abundance of features inc gravel garden, raised beds and extensive views across alpaca paddock. Well House in Grafton nestles under the hillside. A traditional English cottage garden with herbaceous borders, climbing roses and ornamental shrubs with a variety of interesting species. Paths meander through the borders to an orchard with chickens. Parking in Grafton. Refreshments at The Punch Bowl PH, Marton 01423 322519. Reservations advisable.

54 115 MILLHOUSES LANE
Sheffield, S7 2HD. Sue & Phil Stockdale, 01142 365571, phil.stockdale@gmail.com. *SW Sheffield nr Derbyshire border. Approx 4m SW of Sheffield City Centre. From city, follow A625 Castleton/Dore Rd, 4th L after Prince of Wales pub, 2nd L. Alternatively take A621 Baslow Rd. After Tesco garage take 2nd R, then 1st L.* **Sun 25 May (11-4.30). Adm £4, chd free. Light refreshments.** Visits also by arrangement May to Aug for groups of up to 30. Plantswoman's ⅓ acre south facing level cottage style garden with many choice and unusual perennials and bulbs, providing year-round colour and interest. Large collection of 60+ hostas, roses, peonies, iris and clematis with many tender and exotic plants inc aeoniums, echeverias, aloes, bananas and echiums. Seating areas around the garden. Many home-propagated plants for sale. Most of the garden is accessible for wheelchairs.

55 MIRES BECK NURSERY
Low Mill Lane, North Cave, Brough, HU15 2NR. Graham Elliott, www.miresbeck.co.uk. *Between N & S Cave. Do not follow SatNav if entering North Cave from the A63/M62. Through village, take S Cave Rd & reset SatNav. What3words app: amount.occupations.spades.* **Wed 9 July (10-4). Adm £5, chd free. Light refreshments.** Charity that provides horticultural work experience for adults with learning disabilities. 14 acre site features herbaceous borders, vegetable beds, dementia garden and Hull's official Garden of Sanctuary. We grow 500 herbaceous perennials, 50 herbs, 100 wildflowers for regional garden centres and heritage sites. For NGS visitors there are talks about the history and workings of MB, tours and woodland walk. Exclusive to NGS Visitors - Woodland walk, planting and history of the charity talks. Tarmac main paths, and compressed gravel side paths.

56 ◆ MOUNT GRACE PRIORY
Staddlebridge, Northallerton, DL6 3JG. English Heritage. *12 m N of Thirsk and 6 m NE of Northallerton, nr A19. Take care when turning off the dual carriageway. Look out for brown English Heritage direction signs ½ m before the turning.* **For NGS: Evening opening Tue 1 July (5.30-7.30). Adm £20, chd free. Pre-booking essential, please email fundraising@english-heritage.org.uk or visit www.english-heritage.org.uk/visit/places/mount-grace-priory/events for information & booking. Light refreshments.** For other opening times and information, please email or visit garden website.
Join our expert gardens team to explore the newly rejuvenated Arts and Crafts gardens and room-like spaces of the terraces and dell garden, with borders redesigned by award winning gardener Chris Beardshaw.
☕

57 MYTON GRANGE
Myton On Swale, York, YO61 2QU. Nick & Annie Ramsden. *15m N of York. From the N go through Helperby on York Rd. After ½ m follow yellow signs towards Myton. From the S leave A19 through Tollerton & Flawith. Turn L at Xrds.* **Sun 29 June (1-5). Adm £8, chd free. Home-made teas.**
This garden, attached to a Victorian farmhouse, once formed part of the Myton Estate. Size ¾ acre and adjacent to the River Swale. Inc a paved terrace garden, formal parterre, circular garden with mixed shrub and herbaceous border, lawn with topiary borders and new gravel garden. There will be a talk about the restored Victorian Stud Farm buildings, and history of the Myton Estate at 3pm.
🐕 ✽ ☕ 🔊

58 THE NURSERY
15 Knapton Lane, Acomb, York, YO26 5PX. Tony Chalcraft & Jane Thurlow, 01904 781691, janeandtonyatthenursery@hotmail.co.uk. *2½ m W of York. From A1237 take B1224 towards Acomb. At r'about turn L (Beckfield Ln). After 150 metres turn L.* **Sun 20, Mon 21, Tue 22 July (1-6). Adm £4, chd free. Home-made teas.** Visits also by arrangement June to Aug for groups of 10+. Visits can be themed depending on the season and can inc tastings.
A former suburban commercial nursery, now an attractive and productive one acre organic, private garden. Over 100 fruit trees, many in trained form. Many different vegetables grown both outside and under cover in 20 metres greenhouse. Productive areas interspersed with informal ornamental plantings and cut flower areas to provide colour and habitat for wildlife.
✽ ☕ 🔊

59 THE OLD PRIORY
Everingham, YO42 4JD. Dr J D & Mrs H J Marsden, 01430 860222, helen.marsden@ngs.org.uk. *15m SE of York, 6m from Pocklington. 2m S of A1079. On E side of village.* **Visits by arrangement 11 May to 30 June. Adm £10, chd free. Tea, coffee & cake.**
Two acre rural garden. Created in 1990s to enable self-sufficiency in vegetables, meat, most fruit, logs and timber. Walled vegetable garden, polytunnel and greenhouse. Borders planted to cope with sandy loam. Garden slopes down to natural bog garden. Dove tree, variegated tulip tree and various willows. Roughly mown pathway through woodland, along ponds, lake and lightly grazed pasture. Plenty wild flora and fauna.
♿ 🚗 ☕ 🔊

60 THE OLD RECTORY
Arram Road, Leconfield, Beverley, HU17 7NP. David Baxendale, 01964 502037, davidbax@newbax.co.uk. *Garden entrance on L 80yds along Arram Rd next to double bend sign before the church.* **Visits by arrangement 1 Jan to 30 May for groups of up to 10. Adm £7.50, chd free.**
Approx three acres of garden and paddock. The garden is particularly attractive from early spring until mid summer. Notable for aconites, snowdrops, crocuses, daffodils and bluebells. Later hostas, irises, lilies and roses. There is a small wildlife pond with all the usual residents inc grass snakes. Well established trees and shrubs, with new trees planted when required. Visitors are welcome to bring a picnic.
🪑

61 THE OLD RECTORY
Main Street, Bugthorpe, York, YO41 1QG. Dr & Mrs P W Verow. *4m E of Stamford Bridge. House 1st on R from A166 (York direction).* **Sun 29 June (10.30-4.30). Adm £5, chd free. Tea, coffee & cake.**
¾ acre country garden with views of Garrowby Hill and the Yorkshire Wolds. Mixed borders, ponds, gravel terrace, summerhouse, courtyard and many mature trees including arbutus unedo, paulownia and wing nut. Raised vegetable beds. Artist in the garden and herbaceous perennials and hostas for sale.
✽ ☕

62 OLD SLENINGFORD HALL
Mickley, nr Ripon, HG4 3JD. Jane & Tom Ramsden. *5m NW of Ripon. Off A6108. After N Stainley turn L, follow signs to Mickley. Gates on R after 1½ m opp cottage.* **Sat 7, Sun 8 June (12-3.30). Adm £7.50, chd free. Home-made teas.** Donation to other charities.
A large English country garden and award winning now rewilding permaculture forest garden. Early C19 house (not open) and garden with original layout. Wonderful mature trees, woodland walk and Victorian fernery, romantic lake with islands, watermill, walled kitchen garden, beautiful long herbaceous border, yew and huge beech hedges. Several plant and other stalls. Picnics around the mill pond very welcome. Of particular interest to anyone interested in permaculture. Reasonable wheelchair access to most parts of garden. Disabled WC at Old Sleningford Farm next to the garden.
♿ 🐕 ✽ ☕ 🪑 🔊

The National Garden Scheme donated £281,000 in 2024 to support those looking to work in horticulture as well as those struggling within the industry.

63 THE OLD VICARAGE
North Frodingham, Driffield, YO25 8JT. Professor Ann Mortimer. *From Driffield take B1249 E for approx 6m, garden on R opp church. Entrance at T-junc of road to Emmotland & B1249. From N Frodingham take B1249 W for ½m. Park in farmyard 50yds E opp side B1249.* **Sun 27 July (10.30-4.30). Adm £5, chd free. Home-made teas.**
1½ acre plantsman's garden, including rose garden, jungle, desert, nuttery, orchard, turf maze, winter, fountain, scented, kitchen gardens, glasshouses. Classic and modern statues, unusual trees and shrubs, large and small ponds, orchard, nuttery. Children's interest: 'Jungle Book', dinosaur and wild animals in the jungle. Neo-Jacobean revival house, built 1837, mentioned in Pevsner (not open). The land occupied by the house and garden was historically owned by the family of William Wilberforce.

64 THE ORCHARD
4A Blackwood Rise, Cookridge, Leeds, LS16 7BG. Carol & Michael Abbott, 01132 676764, michael.john.abbott@hotmail.com. *5m N of Leeds centre, 5 mins from York Gate garden. Off A660 (Leeds-Otley) N of A6120 Ring Rd. Turn L up Otley Old Rd. At top of hill turn L at T-lights (Tinshill Ln). Please park in Tinshill Ln.* **Visits by arrangement June & July for groups of 10+. Adm £5, chd free. Refreshments available on request.**
⅓ acre plantswoman's hidden oasis. A wrap around garden of differing levels made by owners using stone found on site, planted for year-round interest. Extensive rockery, unusual fruit tree arbour, oriental style seating area and tea house, linked by grass paths, lawns and steps. Mixed perennials, hostas, ferns, shrubs, bulbs and pots amongst paved and pebbled areas.

65 THE ORCHARDS
Crag Lane, Huby, Leeds, LS17 0BW. Joanne McCudden, www.instagram.com/harrogategardening. *Between Harrogate (8m) and Leeds (13m). Serviced well by Weeton train stn. From Harrogate Rd, in village of Huby, turn up Crag Ln or Strait Ln. The Orchards is near the top of the*

hill, opp the junc to Almscliffe Dr. 8min walk from train stn. **Thur 28, Fri 29 Aug (11-3). Adm £5, chd free. Tea, coffee & cake.**
Relaxed 2 acre family garden set into a hillside. Has an Arts and Crafts structure, with more recent contemporary planting by the award winning designer, Lizzie Tulip. Subtropical zone and greenhouse further down hill, growing a range of interesting plants and edibles. Arts and Crafts terracing, stone staircase, wildlife pond, woodland glade and giant plants feature as key features. Plant sale by Cliffbank Nursery. Square and Compass pub nearby for larger meals (please book).

66 PADDOCK WOOD
Driffield Road, Kilham, YO25 4SP. Chris and Emma Hobbs, www.instagram.com/paddockwoodgarden. *Next to Kilham Primary School.* **Sun 29 June (11-5). Adm £5, chd free. Tea, coffee & cake. Open nearby Fern House, 5 Wold Road.**
1¼ acre garden bordered by mature trees and beech hedges. Garden is a blend of established and recent planting. House surrounded by perennial borders. Lawn leads to mixed borders and ornamental pond created using unearthed old rockery. Beyond beech hedge, gravel herb garden, 50 year old greenhouse, rose garden and paved kitchen garden. Pottery for sale. WC facilities provided in local church. Most areas of the garden are accessible by wheelchair.

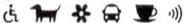

67 ◆ PARCEVALL HALL GARDENS
Skyreholme, Skipton, BD23 6DE. Walsingham College, 01756 720311, parcevallhallgarden@gmail.com, www.parcevallhallgardens.co.uk. *9m N of Skipton. Signs from B6160 Bolton Abbey-Burnsall rd or off B6265 Grassington-Pateley Bridge & at A59 Bolton Abbey r'about.* **For NGS: Thur 10 July (10-4.30). Adm £9, chd free. Tea, coffee & cake.** For other opening times and information, please phone, email or visit garden website.
The only garden open daily in the Yorkshire Dales National Park. 24 acres on a sloping south facing hillside in Wharfedale sheltered by mixed woodland. Terrace garden, rose garden, rock garden and ponds.

Mixed borders, spring bulbs, tender shrubs and autumn colour.

68 PILMOOR COTTAGES
Pilmoor, nr Helperby, YO61 2QQ. Wendy & Chris Jakeman, 01845 501848, cnjakeman@outlook.com. *20m N of York. From A1M J48. From B'bridge follow road towards Easingwold. From A19 follow signs to Hutton Sessay then Helperby. Garden next to mainline railway.* **Mon 26 May, Mon 25 Aug (11-4.30). Adm £5, chd free. Light refreshments. Visits also by arrangement.**
A year-round garden for rail enthusiasts and garden visitors alike. A ride on the 7¼' gauge railway runs through two acres of gardens and gives you the opportunity to view the garden from a different perspective. The journey takes you across water, through a little woodland area, past flower filled borders, and through a tunnel behind the rockery and water cascade. 1½ acre wildflower meadow and pond. Featuring a Clock-golf putting green.

69 THE POPLARS
Main Street, Newton upon Derwent, York, YO41 4DA. Peter & Christina Young, young.at.poplars@gmail.com, www.vimeo.com/showcase/10043886. *9m E of York. From A1079 at Wilberfoss, turn S towards Sutton upon Derwent. After ¾m, turn R into Newton, then L. Garden on R past pub.* **Sun 3 Aug (1-5). Adm £5, chd free. Tea, coffee & cake. Visits also by arrangement 1 June to 10 Aug for groups of 10 to 40.**
A plant lover's paradise. Over 100 different trees and shrubs around a Victorian house and barns provide structure and shelter for a succession of flowers through the seasons. Glasshouses full of tender plants that spill out into the gardens in summer. Meadow walk leads to two acre arboretum with over 200 woody species around a wildlife pond. Ceramic sculptures.

70 PRIMROSE BANK GARDEN AND NURSERY
Dauby Lane, Kexby, York, YO41 5LH. Sue Goodwill & Terry Marran, www.instagram.com/ primrose_bank_nursery. *4m E of York. At Junc of A64 & A1079 take road signed to Hull. After 3m, just as entering Kexby, turn R onto Dauby Ln, signed for Elvington. From the E travel on A1079 towards York. Turn L in Kexby.* **Wed 14 May (1-5). Adm £5, chd free. Home-made teas.**
Two acres of rare and unusual plants, shrubs and trees. Bulbs, hellebores and flowering shrubs in spring, followed by planting for year-round interest. Courtyard garden, mixed borders, summerhouse and pond. Lawns, contemporary rock garden, shade and woodland garden with pond, stumpery and shepherd's hut. New for 2025, sand beds and ongoing restoration of a 1902 carriage. Award-winning nursery. Poultry and Hebridean sheep. Dogs allowed on a short lead in car park and at designated tables outside the tearoom. Most areas of the garden are level and are easily accessible for wheelchairs. Accessible WC available.

71 THE PRIORY, NUN MONKTON
York, YO26 8ES. Mrs K Harpin. *9m W of York, 12m E of Harrogate. E of A1M J47 off A59 signed Nun Monkton.* **Thur 12 June (11-4). Adm £7.50, chd free. Tea, coffee & cake in greenhouse.**
Large and varied country garden surrounding William and Mary house (not open) at the confluence of the River Nidd and River Ouse. Featuring species trees, calm swathes of lawn, clipped yew, beech and box, formal rose garden and mixed borders. Area of soft perennial planting and informal parkland. Gravel paths.

72 PROSPECT HOUSE
Scarah Lane, Burton Leonard, Harrogate, HG3 3RS. Cathy Kitchingman, 07989 195773, cathyrk@icloud.com, www.abrightprospect.co.uk. *5m S of Ripon 5½m from A1, J48. Exit A61 signed Burton Leonard. Parking marshals on Station Ln. Drop off only for those with mobility issues outside Prospect House.* **Sun 29 June (12.30-4.30). Adm £5, chd free. Home-made teas. Visits also** by arrangement May to Aug for groups of 10+.
One acre walled garden with mixed herbaceous borders, ornamental pond and cutting garden beds. New planting and landscaping since 2019. Colour-themed borders, 'hot' border, physic bed, woodland area. Also mature hedging, trees and seasonal interest throughout. A renovated outhouse converted into a pretty potting area used for garden workshops. Coaches by arrangement only.

73 REWELA COTTAGE
Skewsby, YO61 4SG. John Plant & Daphne Ellis, 07711 555565, rewelacottage@gmail.com, www.rewelahostas.com. *4m N of Sheriff Hutton, 15m N of York. After Sheriff Hutton, towards Terrington, turn L towards Whenby & Brandsby. Turn R just past Whenby to Skewsby. Turn L into village. 500yds on R.* **Visits by arrangement 12 May to 31 Aug for groups of 10+. Adm £5, chd free. Home-made teas.**
Situated in a lovely quiet country village, Rewela Cottage was designed from an empty paddock, to be a labour saving, shade garden, using unusual trees and shrubs for year-round interest. Their foliage, bark and berries enhance the well-designed structure of the garden. The garden owner now specialises in growing and selling Hostas. Over 750 varieties of Hostas in the garden. Some gravel paths may make assistance necessary.

In 2024, our donations to Carers Trust meant that 26,081 unpaid carers were supported across the UK.

8 South Glebe, Lockington Gardens

74 NEW RIDGEWOOD
7 Park Drive South, Greenhead, Huddersfield, HD1 4HT. Mr Steve Cale and Ms Shireen Joshi. ½ m N of Huddersfield Town Centre. 3m from J23 M62. From M62 (J23) take A640 towards Huddersfield Town Centre. Turn R onto Park Ave then R again onto Park Drive South. From Huddersfield Ring Road take the 'Rochdale A640' turn off then L onto Park Ave. **Sun 3 Aug (12-4). Adm £5, chd free. Tea, coffee & cake.** South facing elevated garden with panoramic views. Originally designed in 1953 with stone tiered beds and terrace, the garden has been refreshed in recent years with a range of perennials, annuals, trees, and shrubs inc dahlias, salvias, agapanthus, grasses, and acers. Inc fruit and vegetable garden, paths, hens and wildlife friendly area.

75 THE RIDINGS
South Street, Burton Fleming, Driffield, YO25 3PE. Roy & Ruth Allerston, 01262 470489. *11m NE of Driffield. 11m SW of Scarborough. From Driffield B1249, before Foxholes turn R to Burton Fleming. From Scarborough A165 turn R to Burton Fleming.* **Sun 4 May, Sun 6 July (12-4). Adm £4, chd free. Tea, coffee & cake.** Visits also by arrangement Apr to July.
Secluded cottage garden with colour-themed borders surrounding neat lawns. Grass and paved paths lead to formal and informal areas through rose and clematis covered pergolas and arbours. Box hedging defines well-stocked borders with roses, herbaceous plants and trees. Seating in sun and shade offers vistas and views. Greenhouse and summerhouse. Terrace with water feature. Indoor model railway. Terrace, tea area and main lawn accessible via ramp.

76 18 RIPLINGHAM ROAD
Skidby, Cottingham, HU16 5TR. Mrs Mary Caldwell. *Between Beverley and Hull. From Humber Br A164 to Beverley L at Skidby r'about. From Beverley A164 to Humber Br R at Skidby r'about. Follow Main St past church then sch on L. Riplingham Rd straight ahead.* **Sun 22 June (2-5). Adm £5, chd free. Tea, coffee & cake.**
A small garden created by owner. The front has colour themed borders with dozens of pots. The rear planting creates a feeling of seclusion. From an octagonal lily pond paths radiate outwards under arches festooned in clematis leading to hidden corners. Borders overflow with trees, flowering shrubs, perennials, dozens of roses and hidden statues and ornaments. Productive greenhouse with soft fruit. Rear garden can be viewed in part from lower patio. Front garden accessible.

77 RUDDING PARK
Follifoot, Harrogate, HG3 1JH. Mr & Mrs Simon Mackaness, www.ruddingpark.co.uk. *3m S of Harrogate off the southern bypass A658. Follow brown tourist signs. Use hotel entrance.* **Sun 18 May (1-4). Adm £6, chd free. Tea, coffee & cake.**
20 acres of attractive formal gardens, extensive kitchen garden and lawns around a Grade I Regency House extended and now used as an hotel. Humphry Repton parkland. Formal gardens designed by Jim Russell with extensive rhododendron and azalea planting. Recent designs by Matthew Wilson featuring grasses and perennials.

78 ST MARY'S
Anserdale Lane, Lastingham, York, YO62 6TN. Mr Clemens & Mrs Johanna Heinrichs. *Lastingham village. Located close to St. Mary's Church & the Blacksmith Arms pub on route towards Hutton Le Hole. Parking on road side.* **Sun 10 Aug (12-5). Adm £7, chd free. Home-made teas in Lastingham Village Hall.**
Located within peaceful Lastingham Village with views towards the church. The garden has landscaped areas with grasses and perennials, meadows and lawns as well as formal structures and mature trees. There is a bog garden next to the beck with a natural waterfall. Newer additions are productive areas and a gravel garden. Garden inspired by Arts & Crafts having 10 different and enchanting areas. Only accessible to the upper garden. The stream areas are inaccessible to wheelchairs and visitors with mobility issues.

Ellerker House

YORKSHIRE 611

79 SALTMARSHE HALL
Saltmarshe, Howden, DN14 7RX.
Mark Chittenden, 01430 434920,
info@saltmarshehall.com,
www.saltmarshehall.com. *6m E of Goole. From Howden (M62, J37) follow signs to Howdendyke & Saltmarshe.* **Mon 5 May, Sun 13 July (10-4). Adm £5, chd free. Light refreshments available outside. Afternoon teas in Hall and picnic hampers available via pre-booking on garden website.**
Saltmarshe Hall sits within a 17 acre estate. Five acres of ornamental gardens, the remainder consisting of parkland and woodland. The gardens consist of herbaceous borders, an ornamental pond, walled garden, small orchard and lime avenue. Enjoy a pre-booked afternoon tea in the River Garden with its beautiful white floral palette. Wheelchair to the house via a ramp. Garden is accessed via gravel paths, narrow walkways and shallow steps.

&. 🐕 ❀ 🚐 ☕ ᐁ))

80 SCAPE LODGE
11 Grand Stand, Scapegoat Hill, Golcar, Huddersfield, HD7 4NQ. Elizabeth & David Smith, 01484 644320, elizabethanddavid.smith@ngs.org.uk, www.instagram.com/elizabethatscapelodge. *5m W of Huddersfield. From J23 or 24 M62, follow signs to Rochdale. From Outlane village, 1st L. At top of hill, 2nd L. Park at Scapegoat Hill Baptist Church (HD7 4NU) or in village. 5 min walk to garden. 303/304 bus.* **Sun 4, Sun 11 May (1.30-4.30). Adm £5, chd free. Home-made teas.** Visits also by arrangement 5 May to 31 May. Donation to Mayor of Kirklees Charity Appeal.
⅓ acre contemporary country garden at 1000ft in the Pennines on a steeply sloping site with far-reaching views. Gravel paths lead between mixed borders on many levels. Colour-themed informal planting sits comfortably in the landscape and gives year-round interest. Steps lead to a terraced kitchen and cutting garden. Gazebo, pond, shade garden, large collection of pots and tender plants.

❀ 🚗 ☕ ᐁ))

81 ♦ SHANDY HALL GARDENS
Thirsk Bank, Coxwold, York, YO61 4AD. The Laurence Sterne Trust, 01347 868465, info@laurencesternetrust.org.uk, www.laurencesternetrust.org.uk. *N of York. From A19, 7m from both Easingwold & Thirsk, turn E signed Coxwold. Park on road.* **For NGS: Evening opening Fri 16 May, Fri 13 June (6.30-8). Adm £5, chd free.** For other opening times and information, please phone, email or visit garden website.
Home of C18 author Laurence Sterne. Two walled gardens, one acre of unusual perennials interplanted with tulips and old roses in low walled beds. In old quarry another acre of trees, shrubs, bulbs, climbers and wildflowers encouraging wildlife, inc over 450 recorded species of moths. Features inc moth trapping demonstration. Partial wheelchair access. Gravel car park, steps down to Wild Garden.

&. 🐕 ❀ 🎪 ᐁ))

GROUP OPENING

82 NEW SHIPLEY GARDENS
Shipley, BD18 4HD. *Approx 2½ m N of Bradford city centre. 2½ m ESE of Bingley. From the A650 turn on to Nab Ln. (Shipley adjoins the UNESCO World Heritage site village of Saltaire).* **Sun 8 June (11-4). Combined adm £5, chd free. Home-made teas at 15 Nab Wood Rise and a pop-up café at 27 Staveley Road, hosted by 21 Co. The pop-up café is run by people with Down's Syndrome.**

NEW 1 GLENHURST ROAD
Mr & Mrs Harry and Sally Whittle.

NEW 15 NAB WOOD RISE
Kathryn Wilson.

NEW 24 STAVELEY ROAD
Mr & Mrs Simon and Sarojini Dunn.

NEW 27 STAVELEY ROAD
Mr & Mrs Rajiv and Shiela Puri.

Nestled in the heart of Yorkshire, Nab Wood, Shipley is where you can find our four suburban gardens, opening to celebrate Bradford City of Culture 2025. As a starting point on Staveley Rd BD18 4HD with ample parking you will find an acre garden, a plant lovers delight surrounding the house with mature herbaceous borders, a collection of Cornus & roses. At 27 Staveley Rd, the beds are enveloped by lush formal lawns whose owner invites you to walk here barefoot! They also have an interest in growing plants from seed resulting in plants for sale. Glenhurst Rd, has an abundance of Acers & Bamboo. A collection of Hostas including miniatures & mouse. Finally, a small hidden gem of herbaceous borders tucked away on Nab Wood Rise (no parking available). A paradise of pots, pergolas & planters where steps invite you down to the lower reaches of the garden. It is planted with wildlife in mind including a small pond. Each garden will feature ceramics & pottery from Hive, a community arts charity.

❀ ☕ ᐁ))

GROUP OPENING

83 SHIPTONTHORPE GARDENS
Shiptonthorpe, York, YO43 3PQ. *2m NW of Market Weighton. All 4 gardens are in main village on N side of A1079.* **Sat 7, Sun 8 June (11-5). Combined adm £8, chd free. Tea, coffee & cake in village hall.**

LANGDALE END
Di Thompson.

ORANMORE COTTAGE
Susan & Paul Kraus.

WAYSIDE
Susan Sellars.

YORK HOUSE
Tracey Baty.

Four contrasting gardens with different gardening styles, two of which survived and have thrived since being under flood water in 2023. Langdale End is an eclectic maze-like garden with a mix of contemporary and cottage garden styles, featuring tropical plants, an Asian inspired garden, water features and a pond. Wayside has artistically planted areas providing a variety of styles. Ever changing vegetable and fruit garden. Interesting old farm and garden implements. Pond and surroundings made for wildlife. Oranmore cottage is a surprising 'hidden garden' divided into two distinct areas featuring decorative architectural plants and carefully chosen herbaceous perennials. York House has a gravel bed, a shaded border, newly designed circular bed, raised vegetable beds, fruit and chattering hens. Wheelchair access limited in Langdale End.

&. ❀ 🚗 ☕ ᐁ))

84 NEW SILVESTER HOUSE
Main Street, Alne, York, YO61 1TB. Carole Marshall. *4 m E of Easingwold just off the A19 10 m N of York. From Easingwold (A19) Littlewood Cottage, The Fold approx 4th house on L, Silvester House is the 8th house on L. Lookout for the posters and balloons.* **Sat 28 June (1.30-5). Combined adm with Littlewood Cottage £6, chd free. Light refreshments at Whiteley's at Home with additional parking and WC facilities.**
A series of 'rooms' in about ¾ acre with clipped hedging, specialist acers, variety of hydrangeas, agapanthus, potted rhododendrons and colourful hanging baskets. A pond enclosed by ornamental railings is surrounded by naturalistic planting that attracts wildlife. A path leads through a selection of shrubs, roses and perennials, a vegetable garden and on to an orchard.

85 SKIPWITH HALL
Skipwith, Selby, YO8 5SQ. Sir Charles and Lady Forbes Adam, 07976 821903, rosalind@escrick.com, www.escrick.com. *9m S of York, 6m N of Selby. From York A19 Selby, L in Escrick, 4m to Skipwith. From Selby A19 York, R onto A163 to Market Weighton, then L after 2m to Skipwith.* **Thur 13 Feb (11-2). Light refreshments. Thur 5 June (1-4). Home-made teas. Adm £6, chd free. 2026: Thur 12 Feb. Visits also by arrangement 26 May to 30 June for groups of 10 to 50.**
4 acre walled garden of Queen Anne house. Mixture of historic formal gardens, some designed by Cecil Pinsent (worked largely in Italy in 1st half of the C20) and informal planting for wildlife. Woodland with variety of specimen trees and meadows woven to create a woodmeadow. No-dig kitchen garden with maze and pool, Italian garden, gravel garden, many roses. Orchard with trained fruit on walls. Gravel paths.

86 SLEIGHTHOLMEDALE LODGE
Fadmoor, YO62 7JG. Patrick & Natasha James. *6m NE of Helmsley. Parking limited in wet weather. Garden is 1st property in Sleightholmedale, 1m from Fadmoor.* **Sun 6 July (1-5). Adm £8, chd free. Home-made teas.**
A glorious south facing, three acre hillside garden with views over a peaceful valley in the North York Moors. Cultivated for over 100 yrs, wide herbaceous borders and descending terraces lead down the valley with beautiful, informal planting within the formal structure of walls and paths. The garden features roses, delphiniums and other classic English country garden perennials. In 2024, Sleightholmedale Lodge was awarded a commemorative plaque in recognition of its 75 years of opening for the National Garden Scheme.

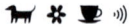

87 SOUTHWOOD HALL
Burton Road, Cottingham, HU16 5AJ. Kevin and Janet Barnes, 07976 605669, kevingasbarnes@icloud.com. *Two entrances: Burton Rd and from Southwood Rd, along Southwood Gardens. On street parking only. Please use this postcode: HU16 5EB.* **Sun 13 Apr, Sun 6 July, Sun 7 Sept (10-4). Adm £6, chd free. Light refreshments. Visits also by arrangement 1 May to 14 Sept for groups of 10+.**
Explore 1½ acres of secluded grounds surrounding this historic property. Spot the Alice in Wonderland sculptures in the Secret Walled Garden around a dipping pool and fountain. Enjoy teas in the formal front garden and parterre. View extensive driveway flower beds. Meander through the orchard, pottering garden, greenhouse and raised beds and marvel at the extensive composting area. Gardens are being continually developed. Wheelchair access possible in the grounds with assistance, all paths are gravel/grass, ramp available to access walled garden (2 steps).

88 NEW STANDFIELD HALL FARM
Westgate Carr Road, Pickering, YO18 8LX. Mike and Pam Sellers. *W of Pickering. From Helmsley on A170, through Middleton after Middleton Garage, 2nd R onto Westgate Carr Rd. From Pickering on A170 after A169 junction, 1 m L after bungalows.* **Sun 20 July, Wed 6 Aug (11-4). Adm £6, chd free. Home-made teas.**
Soil Association Organic Hidden Garden, developed by retired organic market gardeners from a 2 acre field. Expansive lawn with large pond, margins planted for wildlife, inlet and outlet stream flowing under bridge. Herbaceous borders. Copse of choice pines, acers and conifers, nuttery, area with wild flowers, woodland walk and variety of fruit and ornamental trees. Raised vegetable beds. Most of the garden is covered in firm grass. The toilet can not be accessed by a wheelchair nor are they suitable for the disabled.

89 ♦ STILLINGFLEET LODGE
Stewart Lane, Stillingfleet, York, YO19 6HP. Mr & Mrs J Cook, 01904 728506, vanessa.cook@stillingfleetlodgenurseries.co.uk, www.stillingfleetlodgenurseries.co.uk. *6m S of York. From A19 York-Selby take B1222 towards Sherburn in Elmet Ln village turn opp church.* **For NGS: Sun 11 May, Sun 14 Sept (1-5). Adm £7.50, chd £2. Home-made teas.** For other opening times and information, please phone, email or visit garden website.
Organic, wildlife garden subdivided into smaller gardens, each based on a colour theme with emphasis on use of foliage plants. Wildflower meadow, natural pond, 55 yd double herbaceous borders and modern rill garden. Rare breeds of poultry wander freely in garden. Adjacent nursery. Garden courses run all summer (see garden website.) Art exhibitions in the café. Gravel paths and lawn. Ramp to café if needed. No disabled WC.

90 SWINDON HOUSE FARM
Spring Lane, Kirkby Overblow, Harrogate, HG3 1HT. Penny Brook, 07770 916666, pennybrook65@gmail.com. *1m S of Kirkby Overblow village. From Spring Ln/Swindon Ln junc, the drive is exactly ½ m on R.* **Sat 16 Aug (11-4). Adm £5, chd free. Tea, coffee & cake. Home-made cakes with organic ingredients, fruit and herbs from the garden.**
An English country garden surrounded by farmland, with mixed perennial borders, a pond garden, orchard, roses, mature trees and native hedges, with wildlife at its heart. Wildflower areas have been created in the paddock together with re-wilding areas and paths mown through. A potager with espaliers, raised willow hurdle beds for vegetables and cut flowers, thyme

YORKSHIRE

path and small camomile lawn. Parking for wheelchair users so that all areas are accessible.

91 THIRSK HALL
Kirkgate, Thirsk, YO7 1PL. Willoughby & Daisy Gerrish, 01845 444455, info@thirskhall.com, www.thirskhall.com. *In the centre of Thirsk. On Kirkgate, next to St Mary's Church.* **Sun 13 July (11-4). Adm £7, chd free. Tea, coffee & cake.**
Thirsk Hall is a Grade II listed townhouse completed by John Carr in 1777 (not open). Behind the house the unexpected 20 acre grounds inc lawns, herbaceous borders, kitchen gardens, walled paddocks and parkland. The present layout and planting are the result of a sensitive restoration, blending formal and informal beds, shrubbery and mature trees. Sculpture Park.

92 NEW UNDERHILL COTTAGE
Underhill, Glaisdale, Whitby, YO21 2PJ. Bob Doncaster and Bev Shepherd. *8m W of Whitby, N Yorkshire. Turn off A171 from S to Egton or from N to Lealholm. Follow signs to Glaisdale.* **Mon 23 June (11-4). Adm £5, chd free. Light refreshments.**
2 acre garden with a large lower garden carved out of a steep slope begun in 2012. From the upper terrace meandering paths and steps lead through a variety of mixed borders, sculptures, viewing platforms and bespoke ornamental railings forged by the local blacksmith. Informal planting of garden favourites, trees, shrubs, roses and the less common. Classic front garden and vegetable garden.

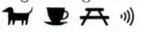

93 WELTON LODGE
Dale Road, Welton, Brough, HU15 1PE. Brendon Swallow, 07792 345858, manager@weltonlodge.co.uk. *11 m W of Hull nr A63. From A63 take exit for Welton, Elloughton & Brough. Immed turn R at junc. Straight through village, to Xrds and straight on. Garden on R after 10yds.* **Sun 27 July (10-4). Adm £5, chd free. Tea, coffee & cake.**
Welton Lodge is a Grade II listed house occupying 1½ acres in the beautiful village of Welton and

features a series of tiered gardens. The top lawn features a newly renovated Gazebo and arbours, leading to a tranquil formal pond with shaded semi-circular seating. The renovated walled kitchen gardens have espaliers of fruit trees and vines around formal lawns and flower beds and a 20m orangery. Block paved ramp leads to gravelled access to lower and upper gardens without steps. Steep upper garden access.

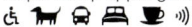

GROUP OPENING

94 WHIXLEY GARDENS
York, YO26 8AR. *8m W of York, 8m E of Harrogate, 6m N of Wetherby. 3m E of A1(M) off A59 York-Harrogate. Signed Whixley.* **Sun 11 May (11-4.30). Combined adm £8, chd free. Home-made teas at The Old Vicarage.**

COBBLE COTTAGE
John Hawkridge & Barry Atkinson.

LABURNUM FARM
David & Rachel Lindley.

THE OLD VICARAGE
Mr & Mrs Roger Marshall, 01423 330474, biddymarshall@btinternet.com. *Visits also by arrangement 1 May to 1 July.*

Attractive rural yet accessible village nestling on the edge of the York Plain with beautiful historic church and Queen Anne Hall (not open). The gardens span the village with good footpaths. A plantsman's and flower arranger's garden at Cobble Cottage has views to the Hambleton Hills. In the centre of the village the garden at Laburnum Farm has been developed over the last eight years with formal parterre at the front and mixed herbaceous borders and a small courtyard leading to an orchard and paddock to the rear. Close to the church is The Old Vicarage with a ¾ acre walled flower garden overlooking the old deer park. The walls, house and various structures are festooned with climbers creating the atmosphere of a romantic English garden. Wheelchair access to The Old Vicarage only.

95 WRESSLE BRICKYARD FARM
Newsholme, Goole, DN14 7JX. Ms Elizabeth Shutt, 01757 630193, shutt872@btinternet.com. *3m from Howden M62 Junction, 10m from Selby. From M62 follow signs to Selby on A63. In 3m turn R to Wressle. From York/Selby on A19 take A63 signed Hull. In 7m turn L to Wressle.* **Visits by arrangement 15 June to 17 Aug for groups of 10 to 25. Adm £10, chd free. Home-made teas.**
One acre garden with EW&B standard gauge railway and 1930s station. Formal garden with lawns, mature trees, borders and pots of summer colour. Old orchard leads to fountain garden. Two large natural ponds, bog garden and mature trees inc weeping copper, beech and spindle. Bandstand, polytunnel and greenhouse for fruit/vegetable and species geraniums. Botanical illustrations in studio.

96 YORKE HOUSE & WHITE ROSE COTTAGE
Dacre Banks, Nidderdale, HG3 4EW. Pat, Mark & Amy Hutchinson, 01423 780456, pat@yorkehouse.co.uk, www.yorkehouse.co.uk. *4m SE of Pateley Bridge, 10m NW of Harrogate, 10m N of Otley. On B6451 near centre of Dacre Banks. Car park on site.* **Sun 22 June (11-4.30). Adm £6, chd free. Cream teas. Visitors welcome to use picnic area in orchard. Opening with Dacre Banks Gardens on Sun 6 July. Visits also by arrangement 15 June to 20 July for groups of 10+.**
Award-winning English country garden in the heart of Nidderdale. A series of distinct areas flowing through two acres of ornamental garden. Colour-themed borders of herbaceous perennials, roses and shrubs. Natural pond and stream with delightful waterside plantings. Large collection of Hosta. Secluded seating areas and attractive views. Adjacent cottage garden designed for wheelchair access. Special exhibition of Steve Blaycock's naturalistic sculptures. All main features and car parking accessible to wheelchair users.

CHANNEL ISLANDS

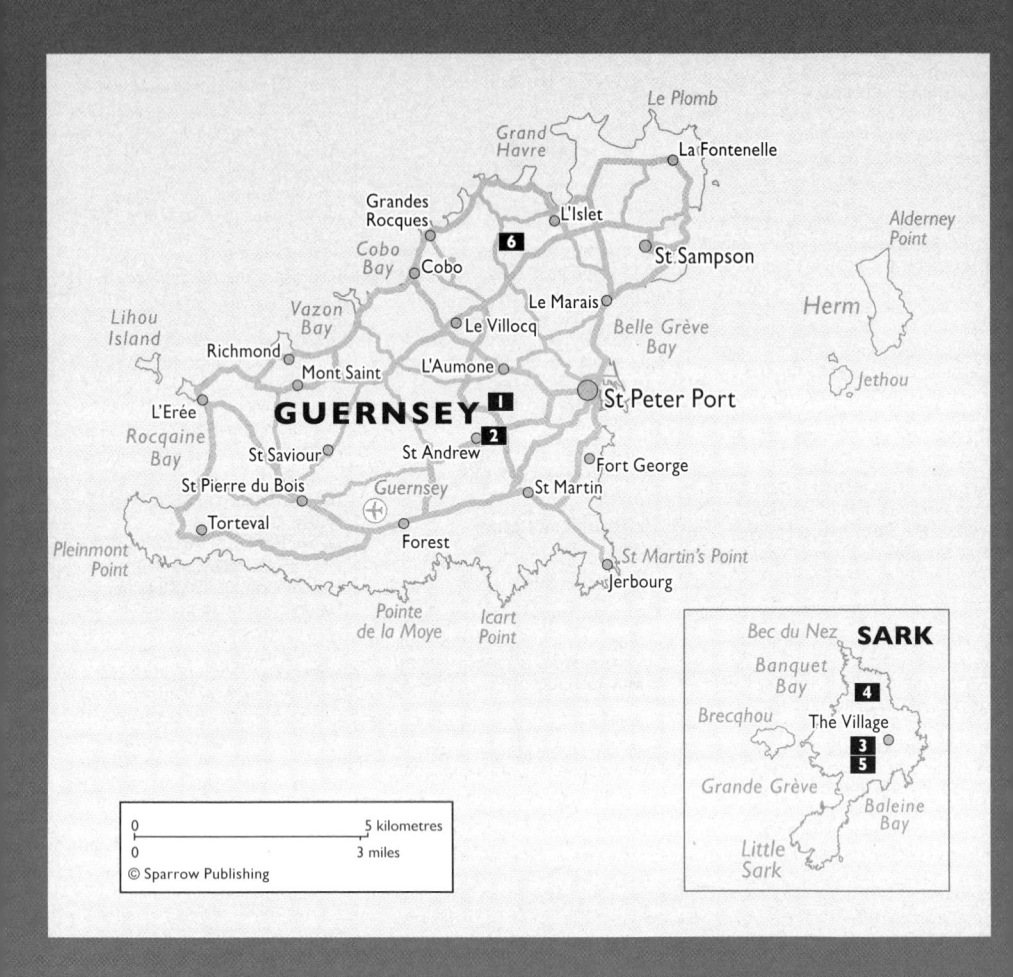

VOLUNTEERS

Area Organiser
Patricia McDermott
patricia.mcdermott@gov.gg

Publicity
Alison Carney
alison.carney@gov.gg

Booklet Coordinator
Ellie Phillips
ellie.phillips@gov.gg

@National Garden Scheme Guernsey

… CHANNEL ISLANDS 615

OPENING DATES

All entries subject to change. For latest information check www.ngs.org.uk

Map locator numbers are shown to the right of each garden name.

June

Saturday 7th
◆ La Seigneurie 3
La Tour 4
Le Grand Dixcart 5

Sunday 8th
La Tour 4
Le Grand Dixcart 5

Saturday 14th
NEW Highfields 1
NEW La Croute De Bas 2
NEW Les Vieilles Salines 6

Sunday 15th
NEW Highfields 1
NEW La Croute De Bas 2
NEW Les Vieilles Salines 6

By Arrangement

Arrange a personalised garden visit with your club, or group of friends, on a date to suit you. See individual garden entries for full details.

NEW Les Vieilles Salines 6

THE GARDENS

1 NEW **HIGHFIELDS**
Les Ruettes, St Andrew, Guernsey, GY6 8UG. Mrs Jaine Dowding. *Perry's Guide p24 B1. From the Rohais turn onto Le Foulon by The Doghouse. Continue along past the Foulon Cemetery on L then take the next L hand lane which is Les Ruettes.* **Sat 14, Sun 15 June (2-5). Adm £5, chd free. Tea, coffee & cake. Open nearby La Croute De Bas.**
Although not a large garden, it is full of interest with a mix of well established shrubs, perennials and annuals. There are several places to sit, relax and enjoy the planting which has generally a loose organic feel although some areas are more stylised, such as the new covered arbour. There is also a small greenhouse, a vegetable area and a corten steel water feature.

2 NEW **LA CROUTE DE BAS**
Route De St Andrew, St Andrew, Guernsey, GY6 8TX. Mrs Liz Harrison-Beck. *Next door to Rangers Football Club.* **Sat 14, Sun 15 June (12-6). Adm by donation. Home-made teas. Open nearby Highfields.**
Predominantly an open lawn with a croquet pitch surrounded by hedges, flower borders, greenhouse attached to a barn and summerhouse. The front garden has a cottage take and over the road is a recently planted (2021) orchard with a variety of fruit trees.

3 ◆ **LA SEIGNEURIE**
Sark, Guernsey, GY10 1SF. Sarah Beaumont, gardens@laseigneuriedesercq.uk, www.laseigneuriedesercq.uk. *Follow signs to La Seigneurie, or ask any local for directions.* **For NGS: Sat 7 June (10-5). Adm £8, chd £2. Open nearby Le Grand Dixcart. Lunch booking is advisable (01481 832233). For other opening times and information, please email or visit garden website.**
The gardens are a place to relax, unwind and find inspiration. There are 4 diverse acres to explore and an on site café and restaurant to enjoy. The Walled Garden is one of the finest of its kind in the Channel Islands and has regularly won awards for its planting schemes and diversity of flora.

4 **LA TOUR**
Sark, Guernsey, GY10 1SF. Sébastien & Marie-Agnès Moerman. *At the north of the Island, following Rue du Fort.* **Sat 7 June (9-4), open nearby La Seigneurie. Sun 8 June (9-4), open nearby Le Grand Dixcart. Adm by donation.**
La Tour is surrounded by hedges of roses, mainly pink and white. In front of the house there is a formal rose garden with roses from David Austin, pink and white. An organic vegetable garden has been created behind the greenhouse. At the back of the house, there is a pond with water lilies surrounded by roses of all colours, also from David Austin.

5 **LE GRAND DIXCART**
Sark, Guernsey, GY10 1SD. Helen Magell, 01481 832943, helen@horse.gg, www.legranddixcart.com/gardens. *Next to Stocks Hotel. Take the boat from Guernsey to Sark & follow the signs to Stocks Hotel. From the hotel continue up Dixcart Ln towards La Coupée & Le Grand Dixcart is on your R.* **Sat 7, Sun 8 June (11-3). Adm £5, chd £2.50. Tea, coffee & cake. Home-made jam.**
The gardens surround an old farmhouse and date from 1565. They are formed into five distinct areas over 2 acres and are cultivated for beauty, wildlife and food. There is a large mandala style permaculture area providing many different vegetables and cutting flowers alongside habitats for wildlife, ponds, lawns, herbaceous borders, two glasshouses, woodland, sculptures and an orchard. Wheelchair access around Sark can be difficult but once you are actually at the gardens there are just grassy slopes and paths.

6 NEW **LES VIEILLES SALINES**
Rue Du Clos, L'Islet, St Sampson, Guernsey, GY2 4FN. Mrs Liz Downing, 07781 121566, Buzzadowning@gmail.com. *What3Words: Longitude.cuckoos.stuff. Perry's Guide 9H1. From L'islet Xrds towards M&S. Take 1st R into Marrette Ln which leads into Rue du Clos. Pass Dowding signs company on L. Look for a bungalow called Brentwood after a lamp post on the R. The driveway is immed after that.* **Sat 14 June (10-6). Adm £5. Sun 15 June (10-6). Adm £5, chd free. Home-made teas. Visits also by arrangement Apr to Sept.**
This 3 acre garden has been developed over 30 yrs to provide year-round interest and colour. A border inspired by the Augusta golf course contains a variety of azaleas & rhododendrons. The garden includes perennial borders, a fruit & vegetable garden, managed woodland, a stumpery, dry river area a wildflower meadow and some fine specimen trees. A good example of sustainable gardening. Wheelchair users can access patio and refreshment area, with view of garden.

NORTHERN IRELAND

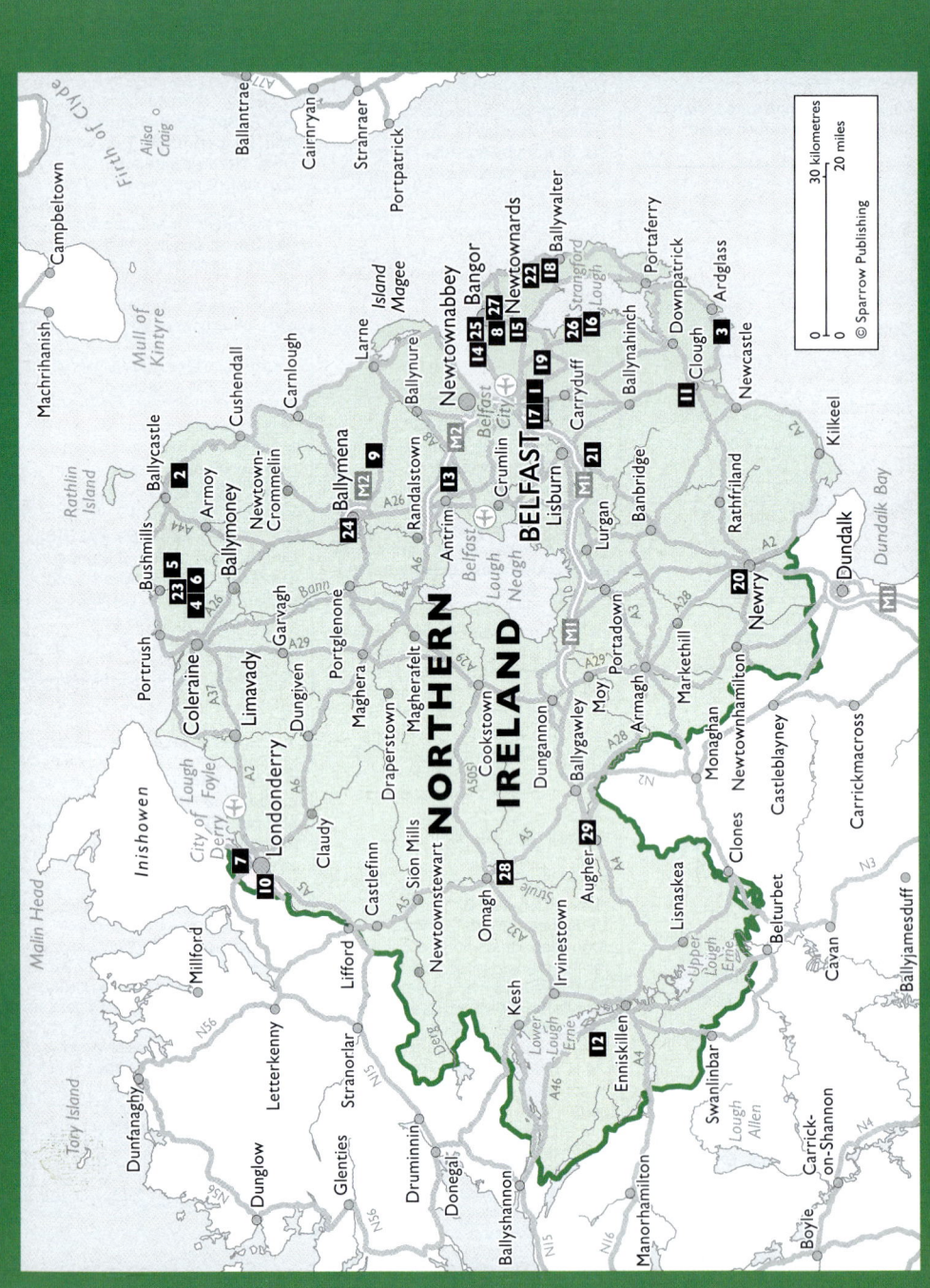

VOLUNTEERS

Area Organiser
Rosslind McGookin
02825 878848
rosslind.mcgookin@ngs.org.uk

Area Treasurer
Ann Fitzsimons
07706 110367
ann.fitzsimons@ngs.org.uk

Assistant Area Organisers
Pat Cameron
07866 706825
pat.cameron@ngs.org.uk

Kaye Campbell
07739 095840
kaye.campbell@ngs.org.uk

Patricia Clements
07470 474527
patricia.clements@ngs.org.uk

Fionnuala Cook
02840 669669
fionnuala.cook@ngs.org.uk

Patricia Corker
07808 926779
pat.corker@ngs.org.uk

Trevor Edwards
07860 231115
trevor.edwards@ngs.org.uk

Will Hamilton
02890 825967
will.hamilton@ngs.org.uk

Jackie Harte
07977 537842
jackie.harte@ngs.org.uk

Sally McGreevy
07871 427025
sally.mcgreevy@ngs.org.uk

Margaret Orr

Joy Parkinson
07792 801510
joy.parkinson@ngs.org.uk

@ngsnorthernireland
@ngsnorthernireland

OPENING DATES

All entries subject to change.
For latest information check
www.ngs.org.uk
Map locator numbers are
shown to the right of each
garden name.

February

Snowdrop Openings
Saturday 15th
Benvarden Gardens 4
Billy Old Rectory Peace Garden 5
Sunday 16th
Benvarden Gardens 4
Billy Old Rectory Peace Garden 5

April
Saturday 12th
◆ Brook Hall Estate & Gardens 7
Sunday 13th
◆ Brook Hall Estate & Gardens 7
Saturday 26th
35 Sheridan Drive 25
Sunday 27th
35 Sheridan Drive 25

May
Saturday 3rd
Clandeboye Estate 8
Sunday 4th
Clandeboye Estate 8
Saturday 17th
Horatio's Garden Northern Ireland 17
Saturday 24th
Brockagh Wood 6
Sunday 25th
Brockagh Wood 6
Saturday 31st
Tattykeel House Garden 28

June
Sunday 1st
Tattykeel House Garden 28
Saturday 14th
Billy Old Rectory Peace Garden 5
Sunday 15th
Billy Old Rectory Peace Garden 5
Saturday 21st
NEW Pheasant Hill 22
Sunday 22nd
NEW Pheasant Hill 22
Saturday 28th
The McKelvey Garden 20
Sunday 29th
The McKelvey Garden 20

July
Saturday 5th
Old Barrack House Garden 21
Sunday 6th
Old Barrack House Garden 21

August
Saturday 16th
NEW 9 Devenish Church Road 12
Sunday 17th
NEW 9 Devenish Church Road 12
Friday 22nd
Rustic Garden at 14 Woodgrove 24
Saturday 23rd
NEW Drumacalaugh Brae 13
Rustic Garden at 14 Woodgrove 24
Sunday 24th
NEW Drumacalaugh Brae 13
Rustic Garden at 14 Woodgrove 24
Monday 25th
Rustic Garden at 14 Woodgrove 24
Saturday 30th
Helen's Bay Organic 14

February 2026
Saturday 14th
Benvarden Gardens 4
Billy Old Rectory Peace Garden 5
Sunday 15th
Benvarden Gardens 4
Billy Old Rectory Peace Garden 5

NORTHERN IRELAND

By Arrangement

Arrange a personalised garden visit with your club, or group of friends, on a date to suit you. See individual garden entries for full details.

Adrian Walsh Belfast Garden	1
13 Ballynagard Road	2
The Barn Gallery and Rose Gardens	3
Brockagh Wood	6
Clayburn	9
Creevagh House	10
NEW Cumran House	11
NEW Drumacalaugh Brae	13
The Henry's Garden	15
NEW The Hill, Ballymorran Bay	16
Iona Cottage Garden	18
NEW Ivydene	19
The McKelvey Garden	20
10 Riverside Road	23
NEW 35 The Straits, Lisbane	26
NEW 24 Tadworth	27
Tattykeel House Garden	28
NEW Tullybroom	29

24 Tadworth

THE GARDENS

1 ADRIAN WALSH BELFAST GARDEN
59 Richmond Park, Stranmillis, Belfast, BT9 5EF. Adrian Walsh, 07808 156856. *From the r'about at Stranmillis College & going along the Stranmillis Rd towards Malone Rd, Richmond Park is the 2nd exit on the L. No 59 is on the L.* **Visits by arrangement June to Oct for groups of 5 to 20. Adm £5, chd free.**
Described by Shirley Lanigan, in 'The Open Gardens of Ireland', as a garden that 'has become a favourite horticultural destination', and 'a veritable sea of plants', this is an imaginatively designed naturalistic city garden that combines a vibrant mix of annuals, perennials, grasses, shrubs and trees set within a formal layout.

2 13 BALLYNAGARD ROAD
Ballyvoy, Ballycastle, BT54 6PW. Tom & Penny McNeill, 07754 190687, pennymcneill@yahoo.co.uk. *3m outside Ballycastle. Drive through Ballycastle, pass hotel on L, 2nd exit on r'about to Cushendall. From Ballyvoy drive ¾ m, Ballynagard Rd is on R. Drive ¾ m. Arrive at 1st bungalow on R.* **Visits by arrangement 1 June to 29 Aug for groups of up to 10. Adm £5.**
A challenging ½ acre site 400ft above sea level with stunning rural and sea views. Designed to meet prevailing environmental conditions and to protect each section from severe winds. Seasonal planting with mature shrubs and rockery on a terraced site create cosy contrasting rooms with seating area. Regret unsuitable for young children due to steep paths through rockery.

3 THE BARN GALLERY AND ROSE GARDENS
49 Rossglass Road South, Killough, Downpatrick, BT30 7RA.
Mr Bernard Magennis, 02844 842082, bernardjjmagennis@hotmail.com, www.facebook.com/barngalleryandrosegardens. *2m E of Tyrella Beach. From Clough on A2 6 m. After Minerstown turn R signed St John's Point. From Killough A2 1.8 m turn L. Park opp Our Lady Star of the Sea Church, then 2 min walk. Limited disabled parking at garden.* **Visits by arrangement June to**
Sept for groups of up to 15. Refreshments upon request. **Adm £6, chd free.**
From a garden originally planted with 300 roses, the 'rose walk' leads uphill to a stunning viewpoint across the Bay to Newcastle, Kilkeel and the Mournes. The downhill path leads through herbaceous planting and dahlias to a white garden, and a planting of sunflowers when in season. Original stone built farmyard, fishpond, waterfall, rockery, herbaceous perennials etc. Artist's studio and gallery.

4 BENVARDEN GARDENS
Benvarden Road, Ballybogey, Ballymoney, BT53 6NN.
Hugh Montgomery, www.benvarden.co.uk. *Between Ballybogy & Derrykeigan, N.Antrim. From Ballymoney head toward Portrush, in the village of Ballybogey turn R into the Benvardin Rd after ½ m (before the River Bush) the Gardens are on your R.* **Sat 15 Feb (12-5); Sun 16 Feb (1-5). Adm £5, chd free. Light refreshments in Stableyard Tearoom. Open nearby Billy Old Rectory Peace Garden. 2026: Sat 14, Sun 15 Feb.**
The garden at Benvarden has been enclosed since the mid C17, most probably evolved from a semi-fortified Bawn. It is shown on a 1788 map soon after the neighbouring rhomboid cobbled courtyard was built. Bought by the Montgomery family in 1797, it was transformed into a modern walled garden with the bawn wall faced with brick and the height raised to the present 16ft, with paths and beds laid out. From the pond, paths lead to the banks of the River Bush, well-known as the river which leads to the Bushmills Distillery, the world's oldest whiskey, and here the river is spanned by a splendid bridge, built by Robert James Montgomery, who survived the charge of the Heavy Brigade in the Crimean war.

5 BILLY OLD RECTORY PEACE GARDEN
5 Cabragh Road, Castlecat, Bushmills, BT57 8YH. Mrs Meta Page. *Ballymoney bypass straight at Kilraughts Rd take 2nd R to B66 sign Dervock turn L (B66) sign Bushmills through Derrykeighan after 2.3 m at Castlecat, R sign Billy ½ m & L - Haw Rd at Church R -Cabragh Rd.* **Sat 15, Sun 16 Feb (1-5).**
Light refreshments. Open nearby Benvarden Gardens. **Sat 14, Sun 15 June (1-5)**. Home-made teas. **Adm £5, chd free.** Limited refreshments at snowdrop opening. **2026: Sat 14, Sun 15 Feb.**
A mature 3 acre garden on an historic site. Front of the Georgian Rectory is a lawn with shrubs, pond and summerhouse. Integrated into the garden are 20 small peace gardens. See guide for further information. There is the Old Orchard Nature Garden comprising of one acre. Tea on the lawn for all visitors provided by N.I.K.R.F.

6 BROCKAGH WOOD
47 Benvardin Road, Ballybogy, Ballymoney, BT53 6NN. Mr Shaun Boyd, 07973 682319, shaunboyd2020@gmail.com. *From Ballymoney take road to Portrush. At Ballybogey turn R onto Benvarden Rd. 1½ m on L.* **Sat 24, Sun 25 May (1-5). Adm £5, chd free.** Light refreshments. **Visits also by arrangement 26 May to 31 July for groups of 10+.**
Living better with nature. A rewilding habitat created during lockdown 2020. This 15 acre site inc a two acre pond, native wildflower meadows, marginal plants, water lilies, moorhens, mallard ducks and little grebes. The 1 mile undulating walk around the perimeter of Brockagh Wood will enrich our lives and help us to reconnect with Mother Nature. Key to a happy and healthy life. Wheelchair access is available to the main pond but not the perimeter walk around Brockagh Wood.

70 inpatients and their families are being supported at the newly opened Horatio's Garden Northern Ireland, thanks to National Garden Scheme donations.

7 ♦ BROOK HALL ESTATE & GARDENS
65-67 Culmore Road,
Londonderry, BT48 8JE.
Mr Gilliland, 02871 358968,
info@brookhall.co.uk,
www.brookhall.co.uk. *3m N of Derry, Londonderry. From the Culmore r'about off the Foyle Bridge, take the exit towards Moville (A2). Continue on the Culmore Rd (A2) for 1m to the entrance on the R.* **For NGS: Sat 12, Sun 13 Apr (2-5). Adm £5, chd free. Light refreshments in the Visitors Centre, check on the day for additional refreshment locations. For other opening times and information, please phone, email or visit garden website.**
Brook Hall Estate & Gardens is a C18 demesne, home to one of the finest private arboretums in the north west of Ireland with unique collections of conifers, rhododendrons, magnolias and camellias. The C17 walled garden on the edge of the River Foyle once used to feed the people of the City of Derry, now home to many of the gardens magnolia and camellia collections. Hard surface paths suitable for wheelchairs and prams through the arboretum and gardens. Please note that some paths may be quite steep.
& 🚗 ☕ ♪)

8 CLANDEBOYE ESTATE
Bangor, BT19 1RN. Mrs Karen Kane, www.clandeboye.co.uk. *Clandeboye Estate Bangor Co Down. Main entrance is off the main Belfast to Bangor A2 circa 2m before Bangor.* **Sat 3, Sun 4 May (2-5.30). Adm £10, chd free. Pre-booking essential, please visit www.ngs.org.uk for information & booking. Tea, coffee & cake at the Banqueting Hall.**
A series of intimate walled gardens adjoin the courtyard and house. These inc the delightful Bee Garden, the Chapel Walk and the intimate Conservatory Garden.
🐑 ✤ 🚗 ☕ ♪)

9 CLAYBURN
30A Ballynulto Road, Glenwherry, Ballymena, BT42 4RJ. Judith & Hugh Jackson, 07539 712991. *What3words app: schematic. composers.remedy. From the A36 Ballymena to Larne Rd, ½ m E of its junc with B94, turn L onto Ballynulto Rd. The garden is 0.8m on the R.* **Visits by arrangement 14 June to 14 Sept for groups of up to 10. Adm £8, chd free. Refreshments available by arrangement.**
Clayburn has been transformed from an exposed site in the shadow of Slemish Mountain to become a low maintenance prairie style garden. Shrubs, grasses and insect attracting perennials along with traditional hedging and many dry stone walls. Also incorporated are numerous trees providing both windbreaks and habitat for many bird species.
☕

10 CREEVAGH HOUSE
63 Letterkenny Road,
Londonderry, BT48 9XQ.
Mr William & Mrs Elma Lynn, 07771 608084,
wlynn_geology@hotmail.com. *3m S of Derry-Londonderry. On Letterkenny Rd (N40). From lower deck Craigavon Bridge turn L to Letterkenny. Pass settlement at Nixon's Corner then ½ m with entrance on R (white gates).* **Visits by arrangement 21 Apr to 31 May for groups of up to 25. Adm £7, chd free.**
A mature garden set in 2½ acres of woodland surrounding a Georgian house c1780 (not open). Variety of trees and shrubs most notably a collection of rhododendrons, camellias and azaleas with mature trees, some dating from the construction of the house. Easy access with a network of level gravel or grass paths with a profusion of bluebells in late April/early May. Some remnants of United States naval hospital in the grounds from 1943 to 1945. Owner can provide information on request. By arrangement, owner can be available for short introductory talk to groups. Wheelchair access to main features.
&

11 NEW CUMRAN HOUSE
231, Newcastle Road, Seaforde, Downpatrick, BT30 8SQ. Mrs Polly Hughes, 02844 811217. *Between Seaforde and Clough, Co Down. Access is via a long (700 metres) lane from the Newcastle Rd. From Seaforde turn R after 750 metres. From Clough turn L after 500 metres.* **Visits by arrangement Mar to Aug for groups of up to 15. Adm £5, chd free.**
A mature garden planted with colourful herbaceous plants and shrubs, surrounding a charming house built in 1840. Stunning views of the Mournes enhance the drifts of snowdrops and daffodils at the start of the year followed by Euchryphia displays in August.

12 NEW 9 DEVENISH CHURCH ROAD
Monea, Enniskillen, BT74 8GE.
J and G Thompson. *5½ m NW of Enniskillen. From Enniskillen take A46 to Belleek, after approx 1 m turn L (B81 to Derrygonnelly) After 5 m, just before Monea, turn R onto Devenish Church Rd. No 9 is last bungalow on L.* **Sat 16, Sun 17 Aug (2-5). Adm £5, chd free.**
Just 17 yrs on from a neglected site with poor soil, this delightful small garden now contains sunny sitting areas and many flowering plants. Bulbs, perennials and climbers, intermingled with roses and shrubs are planted to provide all year colour. Annuals grown in a cutting bed are used to fill gaps when the perennials finish and a glut of salads and vegetable are produced in raised beds.
& ☕

13 NEW DRUMACALAUGH BRAE
76 Rathmore Road, Dunadry, Antrim, BT41 2HX. Mr John & Mrs Marsha McKendry, 07785 337957, john@rathmore.org. *Off Loughanmore Rd (B95) between Antrim and Parkgate.* **Sat 23, Sun 24 Aug (12-5). Adm £5, chd free. Tea, coffee & cake.** Visits also by arrangement 1 Apr to 22 Aug.
Several acres inc a mill dam and wallsteads that used to house a waterwheel. Garden was designed to complement the existing typography with the expert guidance of Jonnie Campbell of the neighboring Landscape Centre. The garden is accessible by many pathways and should be a haven of tranquillity. Much of the garden is now mature as we have been custodians for over 40 yrs.
& 🐑 🚗 ☕ ♪)

14 HELEN'S BAY ORGANIC
Coastguard Avenue, Helen's Bay, BT19 1JY. Mr John McCormick, www.helensbayorganic.com. *Off Craigdarragh Rd. Coming from A2 (Main Belfast-Bangor road). Drive 200 metres past the railway bridge on Craigdarragh Rd then turn L onto Coastguard Ave. Go over 2 speed bumps & enter 1st farm gate on L.*

Sat 30 Aug (2-5). Adm £5, chd free. Tea, coffee & cake in the garden provided by Community Garden Volunteers.
An urban market garden, established in 1991, producing over 50 varieties of organic vegetables for direct retailing. Also hosts a community garden and allotments which inc an extensive range of fruit and vegetables. An ideal space to get ideas to combine flowers, fruit, food and biodiversity in your garden.

15 THE HENRY'S GARDEN
5 Aldergrange Avenue, Newtownards, BT23 4FY. Mr Victor & Mrs Roz Henry, 02891 826764, victhenry@aol.com. *From Dundonald follow A20 to r'about at Ards Shopping Centre. Take 1st exit onto Blair Mayne Rd North. Turn L onto Manse Rd. Turn R to Aldergrange Park then R into Aldergrange Ave. Turn R to No 5.* **Visits by arrangement 24 May to 31 July for groups of 10 to 40. Adm £6, chd free.**
An abundance of plants and wildlife await you at this multi award winning large urban garden. Tropical ginger lilies and banana plants give the garden an exotic feel. Roses, agapanthus, clematis, succulents give colour and scent. The pond adds more wildlife activity to the garden. A selection of tree ferns tower and flourish, adding interest, texture and a jungle feel to this area of the garden. Partially suitable for wheelchairs.

16 NEW THE HILL, BALLYMORRAN BAY
36 Ballymorran Road, Killinchy, Newtownards, BT23 6UE. Mr Leslie & Mrs Yvonne Murray, 07974 256540. *From Comber take A22 Killyleagh Rd. At Balloo xrds turn L onto Beechvale Rd through Killinchy village onto Whiterock Rd. Ballymorran Rd 1st on R. Proceed to Lough, turn L at No.36 (on stone).* **Visits by arrangement 11 Aug to 31 Aug for groups of up to 20. Max 5 cars. Adm £5, chd free.**
Large, informal garden on the shores of Strangford Lough established over 40 yrs. Consists of a wide variety of herbaceous plants, perennials, shrubs, trees and is a delight in all seasons. A 'wild' border edges the tennis court and a small pond provides a habitat for frogs and newts. An overall ambiance of tranquillity pervades.

17 HORATIO'S GARDEN NORTHERN IRELAND
Musgrave Park Hospital, Stockmans Way, Belfast, BT9 7JB. Mr Matthew Lee, www.horatiosgarden.org.uk/the-gardens/horatios-garden-northern-ireland. *Off Stockmans Ln, Balmoral. Off Stockmans Ln turn into Stockmans Way - signed Musgrave Park Hospital the garden is to the rear of the Withers Orthopaedic Centre.* **Sat 17 May (1-5). Adm £5, chd free. Tea, coffee & cake.**
Horatio's Garden Northern Ireland is a beautiful, accessible, restorative garden located at the heart of the Spinal Cord Injuries Unit (SCIU) at Musgrave Park Hospital in Belfast. Designed by nine-time RHS Chelsea Gold Medal winner Andy Sturgeon, the garden supports people adjusting to life-changing spinal injuries from across the entirety of Northern Ireland. Designed for patients, their friends and families, and NHS staff spending time at the Spinal Cord Injuries Unit (SCIU) at Musgrave Park Hospital in Belfast. Full wheelchair access throughout the garden.

35 The Straits, Lisbane

18 IONA COTTAGE GARDEN
14C Cardy Road, Greyabbey, Newtownards, BT22 2LS. Mr Darren & Mrs Victoria Colville, 07793 672653, victoria.colville@googlemail.com. *From North Ards 4 m down Portaferry Rd, turn L onto Mount Stewart Rd. After 3 m, sharp R turn onto Cardy Rd. Immed on R go down concrete lane. Go over 3 speed bumps to 2nd lane, 14C on R.* **Visits by arrangement. Weekends only for June visits. Adm £5, chd free.**
A relaxed, environmentally friendly country cottage garden which has been under development for the past 10 yrs. The garden, which inc herbaceous borders, kitchen garden and cut flower garden is pesticide free with wildlife friendly habitats such as pond, log piles, bird boxes and meadow. Some natural exposed rock areas and slightly uneven terrain. Fantail doves fly freely. Most of the garden has wheelchair access.
& ❀

19 NEW IVYDENE
64 Ballystockart Road, Comber, Newtownards, BT23 5QY. Mr Robert Russell, robertrussellbally@gmail.com. *Located between Dundonald and Comber. From Dundonald, take A22 (Comber Rd). After approx 2m, turn R at Hill Head Rd, then 200yds turn L to Ballystockart Rd. Drive ½ m, garden is on L after the quarry.* **Visits by arrangement June to Aug for groups of up to 8. Adm £10, chd free.**
A charming plant lover's garden surrounding an Irish farmhouse dating from 1850 (not open). Consists of 1½ acre of gardens arranged into rooms together with a 2 acre wildflower meadow with mowed pathway.
🐾 ❀

20 THE MCKELVEY GARDEN
7 Mount Charles North, Bessbrook, Newry, BT35 7DW. Mr William & Mrs Hilary McKelvey, 02830 838006. *In the village of Bessbrook. Enter village from Millvale Rd. Turn L at Morrow's Garage. 300 yds up hill past terraced houses turn L through gate.* **Sat 28, Sun 29 June (2-5). Adm £5, chd free. Home-made teas in Town Hall during open weekend. Visits also by arrangement 1 May to 30 Aug for groups of up to 50.**
A connoisseurs garden situated in a village setting containing snowdrops, alpine crevice beds, salvias and a large collection of clematis planted among herbaceous and shrub borders. Can also be accessed by a side entrance.
& ❀ 🚗 ☕

21 OLD BARRACK HOUSE GARDEN
7 Main Street, Hillsborough, BT26 6AE. Mr & Mrs Ken & Dawn McEntee. *Situated at the bottom of Main St in Royal Hillsborough, opp the Parish Church.* **Sat 5, Sun 6 July (2-5). Adm £5, chd free. Home-made teas.**
Old Barrack House garden is in essence a secret garden, hidden behind the Grade I listed house. Venturing down the alley between the houses you reach the yard and barn, subtly changed and improved to create charming pebbled terraces and garden areas. Dawn's creative instinct is much in evidence. Plants and flowers are chosen for height, form and leaf colour in relation to the ambiance of each area. Most of garden has wheelchair access.
& ❀ 🚗 ☕

22 NEW PHEASANT HILL
41 Woburn Road, Millisle, BT22 2HY. Mr & Mrs Rosie and Denis Colwell. *From Millisle follow A2 to Ballywalter for 0.8 m. Turn R up Woburn Rd for 0.7 m. No.41 is on RHS.* **Sat 21, Sun 22 June (10-5). Adm £5, chd free. Home-made teas.**
14 yr old garden with mixed planting on an exposed site, enjoying countryside views. Planted in the cottage style, it contains mature trees with protection from wind a priority. The owner is passionate about propagation, recycling and accommodating wildlife. Although relatively young, the garden has matured and complements the surrounding landscape. There will be a large plant sale.
& ❀ 🚗 ☕ 🔊

Drumacalaugh Brae

23 10 RIVERSIDE ROAD
Bushmills, BT57 8TP. Mrs Pam Traill, 02820 731219, pmtraill@gmail.com. $1\frac{1}{2}$ m from Bushmills on Riverside Rd, off the B66. Turn L by Drum Lodge, 100 yds further on R beware ramps. **Visits by arrangement 8 Feb to 20 Sept. Adm £5, chd free.**
Rambling cottage garden with unusual shrubs, deep borders, spring garden with aconites snowdrops and scillas, rockery and arboretum.

❀

24 RUSTIC GARDEN AT 14 WOODGROVE
14 Woodgrove, Ballymena, BT43 5JQ. Colin & Gill Agnew. $1\frac{1}{2}$ m N of B'mena on the B'money Rd At r'about turn L onto the Carnburn Rd. Turn R onto the Carniny Rd then L onto the Woodtown Rd. Woodgrove is the 1st cul-de-sac on the R. **Fri 22, Sat 23, Sun 24, Mon 25 Aug (10-8). Adm £5, chd free. Pre-booking essential, please phone 07920 832216/07710 577732 for information & booking.** Tea, coffee & cake.
The Rustic Garden is a suburban garden bordered to the north by the Antrim countryside. Features inc a small pond and stream with marginal planting and a modest collection of hydrangea species. Well established trees help to create a natural canopy under which a sunken fernery has been developed. Ornamental grasses and agapanthus thrive in the south facing aspect of the garden. There are water features, mature ornamental trees and quirky recycling artwork.

☕

25 35 SHERIDAN DRIVE
Helen's Bay, Bangor, BT19 1LB. Prof Desmond and Mrs Amy Archer. *Located between Bangor and Holywood, Co. Down. A2 to Craigdarragh Rd, Helen's Bay, and 2nd L to Sheridan Dr. The garden is on the sea side.* **Sat 26, Sun 27 Apr (2-5.30). Adm £6, chd free.**
Two acre garden along Belfast Lough. Developed over 50 yrs from a challenging site with a stream, small pond and steep inclines. The garden features Japanese maples, magnolias, azaleas, hydrangeas, unusual trees inc *Cornus controversa* 'Variegata', *Cercidiphyllum japonicum* and *Parrotia persica*.

🔊

26 NEW 35 THE STRAITS, LISBANE
Comber, Newtownards, BT23 6AQ. Mrs Olwen Sheridan, 07721 880137, olwensheridan@hotmail.co.uk. *4 m S of Comber towards Killinchy on A22. In the village of Lisbane, turn into The Straits (opp The Old Post Office Tea Shop). No.35 is situated on R after $\frac{1}{2}$ m. Garden entrance on L at top of a long lane.* **Visits by arrangement June to Aug for groups of up to 30. Adm £5, chd free.**
Nestled in the Co Down countryside with wrap-around views of Strangford Lough and Scrabo Tower, this 7 yr old garden of approx 1 acre comprises well-stocked and herbaceous shrub borders. A delightful Bothy, come potting shed provides an enchanting foil for an impressive display of pots and window boxes. In development is a vegetable garden and lawn area. Wheelchair access to most parts of the garden.

♿ 🚗

27 NEW 24 TADWORTH
Bangor, BT19 7WD. Mr Paul Bittle, 07850 677074, bittle.paul@yahoo.com. *Bangor, Co. Down. At the Gransha Rd r'about take the 3rd exit onto the Gransha Rd, past Bangor Grammar School on the R, after the T-lights turn R into Tadworth and take the next R.* **Visits by arrangement July to Oct for groups of 5 to 8. Adm £5, chd free.**
Bangor Jungle is an urban tropical garden where exotic plants thrive despite the cool UK climate. Divided into four individual areas (courtyard, gravel, north, and west garden), this hidden gem showcases bold plant combinations inc tree ferns, palms, banana trees and unusual species typically grown indoors. A lush paradise of experimentation, intrigue and beauty.

❀ 🔊

28 TATTYKEEL HOUSE GARDEN
115 Doogary Road, Omagh, BT79 0BN. Mr Hugh & Mrs Kathleen Ward, 02882 249801, tattykeelhouse@hotmail.com, www.tattykeelhouse.com/gardens. *Approx $2\frac{1}{2}$ m from Omagh on the S side of the A5 Omagh to Ballygawley Rd. There's a sign outside the entrance Tattykeel House & Studio.* **Sat 31 May, Sun 1 June (2-5). Adm £5, chd free.** Home-made teas. **Visits also by arrangement 2 May to 31 Aug for groups of up to 50.**
Borders brimming with blossom and lush planting are seamlessly offset by sweeps of well tended lawn in the carefully choreographed garden at Tattykeel House' as described by Conrad McCormick (Irish Garden Magazine Aug 2024). The garden features in 'The Open Gardens of Ireland' by Shirley Lanigan. The $1\frac{1}{2}$ acres inc sheltered seating areas, a Japanese inspired area, and many climbers. Partially suitable for wheelchairs.

♿ 🚗 🛏 ☕

29 NEW TULLYBROOM
48 Tullybroom Road, Clogher, BT76 0UW. Mr Alan Beatty, 07713 851777, alanwbeatty@gmail.com. *Do not rely on Satnav. Road signs are Corick Rd. Access via the A4. Midway between Augher & Clogher - at sign for Corick House Hotel turn L (from Clogher), R (from Augher). Pass hotel and at the Xrds go straight over. Garden $\frac{1}{4}$ m on R.* **Visits by arrangement 2 June to 10 Sept for groups of 5 to 25. Adm £5, chd free.**
$\frac{1}{2}$ acre intensively planted garden developed over the last 30 yrs in rural setting with borrowed landscape of green-fields and surrounding hills, inc Knockmany, burial site of Queen Anya, an ancient Queen of Ireland. Plantspersons/flower arrangers garden featuring mostly shrubs and herbaceous - many unusual. Features inc borders, small courtyard, gravel area and stone troughs. Most of the garden is accessible to wheelchair users.

♿ ❀

The National Garden Scheme donated over £3.5 million to our nursing and health beneficiaries from money raised at gardens open in 2024.

WALES · CYMRU

Map of Wales showing regions: Gwynedd & Anglesey, North East Wales, Ceredigion, Powys, Carmarthenshire & Pembrokeshire, Glamorgan, Gwent. Neighbouring areas: Cheshire & Wirral, Shropshire, Herefordshire, Somerset, Bristol Area & S. Glos.

The areas shown on this map are specific to the organisation of The National Garden Scheme. The Gardens of England, listed by area, precede the Gardens of Wales.

CARMARTHENSHIRE & PEMBROKESHIRE

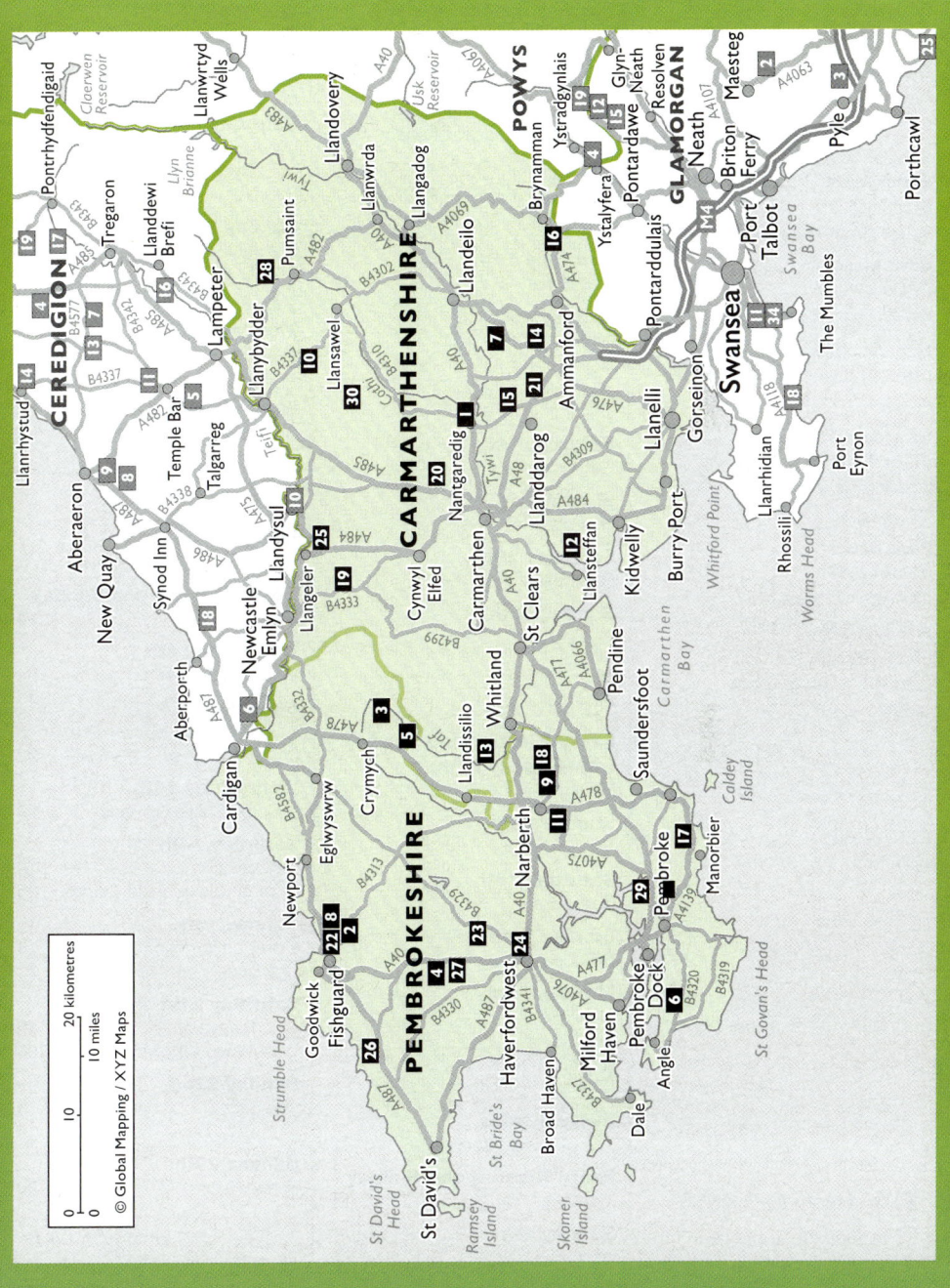

VOLUNTEERS

County Organisers
Jackie Batty
01437 741115
jackie.batty@ngs.org.uk

County Treasurer
Graeme Halls
07484 775553
graeme.halls@ngs.org.uk

Assistant County Organisers
Elena Gilliatt
01558 685321
elenamgilliatt@hotmail.com

Gayle Mounsey
07900 432993
gayle.mounsey@gmail.com

Mary-Ann Nossent
07985 077022
maryann.nossent@ngs.org.uk

Liz and Paul O'Neill
01994 240717
lizpaulfarm@yahoo.co.uk

Social Media
Paula Davies
07967 125881
paula.davies@ngs.org.uk

Fran Rumbelow
07862 736341
fran.rumbelow@ngs.org.uk

@CarmsandPembsNGS
carmsandpembsngs

OPENING DATES

All entries subject to change.
For latest information check
www.ngs.org.uk
Extended openings are shown at the beginning of the month.
Map locator numbers are shown to the right of each garden name.

February

Saturday 15th
Gelli Uchaf   10

Sunday 16th
Gelli Uchaf   10

March

Saturday 1st
Gelli Uchaf   10

Sunday 2nd
Gelli Uchaf   10

Saturday 29th
Gelli Uchaf   10

Sunday 30th
Gelli Uchaf   10

April

Every Tuesday and Sunday from Sunday 27th
Moelfryn   14

Sunday 13th
Treffgarne Hall   27

Saturday 19th
Gelli Uchaf   10

Sunday 20th
Gelli Uchaf   10

Monday 21st
Moelfryn   14

May

Every Sunday
NEW   Annwyn Arboretum   1

Every Tuesday and Sunday
Moelfryn   14

Sunday 4th
Treffgarne Hall   27

Monday 5th
Moelfryn   14

Sunday 18th
Cold Comfort Farm   4
House On Stilts   12

Wednesday 21st
Cold Comfort Farm   4

Friday 23rd
Dwynant   7

Saturday 24th
Dwynant   7
NEW   Dyffryn Mill   9
Gelli Uchaf   10

Sunday 25th
Dwynant   7
NEW   Dyffryn Mill   9
Gelli Uchaf   10

Monday 26th
Dwynant   7
Moelfryn   14

Wednesday 28th
Cold Comfort Farm   4

June

Every Sunday
NEW   Annwyn Arboretum   1

Every Tuesday and Sunday
Moelfryn   14

Wednesday 4th
Cold Comfort Farm   4

Sunday 8th
◆ Dyffryn Fernant   8
Pont Trecynny   22

Wednesday 11th
◆ Upton Castle Gardens   29

Saturday 14th
Gelli Uchaf   10
Skanda Vale Hospice Garden   25

Sunday 15th
Cold Comfort Farm   4
Gelli Uchaf   10

Saturday 21st
NEW   Pantybara   19
West Wales Willows   30

Sunday 22nd
Cae Bach   3
NEW   Pantybara   19

Sunday 29th
Pentresite   20

CARMARTHENSHIRE & PEMBROKESHIRE

July

Every Sunday
NEW Annwyn Arboretum 1

Every Tuesday and Sunday
Moelfryn 14

Thursday 3rd
Pont Trecynny 22

Saturday 5th
Gelli Uchaf 10
NEW ◆ Scolton Manor 23

Sunday 6th
Gelli Uchaf 10
Norchard 17
NEW ◆ Scolton Manor 23
Treffgarne Hall 27

Saturday 19th
Dwynant 7

Sunday 20th
Dwynant 7

Saturday 26th
NEW Corseside Nursery 6
Neuadd y Felin 16

Sunday 27th
Neuadd y Felin 16

August

Every Sunday
NEW Annwyn Arboretum 1

Every Tuesday and Sunday
Moelfryn 14

Monday 4th
Pont Trecynny 22

Sunday 10th
Cae Bach 3

Monday 25th
Moelfryn 14

September

Every Tuesday and Sunday to Tuesday 16th
Moelfryn 14

Saturday 6th
NEW ◆ Scolton Manor 23

Sunday 7th
◆ Dyffryn Fernant 8
NEW ◆ Scolton Manor 23

By Arrangement

Arrange a personalised garden visit with your club, or group of friends, on a date to suit you. See individual garden entries for full details.

NEW Annwyn Arboretum 1
NEW Bridgend Inn 2
Cae Bach 3
Cold Comfort Farm 4
Cornerstone House 5
Dwynant 7
Gelli Uchaf 10
Grove of Narberth 11
House On Stilts 12
Llwyngarreg 13
Moelfryn 14
The Old Rectory 18
Pentresite 20
Pen-y-Garn 21
Pont Trecynny 22
Shoals Hook Farm 24
Stable Cottage 26
Treffgarne Hall 27
Ty'r Maes 28

Pantybara

THE GARDENS

1 NEW ANNWYN ARBORETUM
Four Season Health Club, Nantgaredig, SA32 7NY.
Mr William Berry, 01267 590011, enquiries@annwyn.co.uk, www.annwyn.co.uk. 7m E of Carmarthen. At Xrds of A40 & B4310 in Nantgaredig head N for 1/2 m and follow signs for 'Four Seasons'. Go up the drive, turn L and park where indicated. **Every Sun 4 May to 31 Aug (9-4). Adm £5, chd free. Tea, coffee & cake.** Visits also by arrangement 1 May to 1 Sept. Discuss refreshments when booking.
A 10 acre Arboretum (formerly a 9 hole golf course), planted 40 years ago with an extensive collection of common and unusual trees. These inc redwoods, southern beeches, limes, handkerchief tree and *Magnolia macrophylla*. Beautiful views over the Tywi valley with lots of fun things to explore inc a treasure hunt. Some uneven paths, so good footwear recommended.

2 NEW BRIDGEND INN
Bridge Street, Llanychaer, Fishguard, SA65 9TB.
Mrs Sorrel Arnold, 01348 875648. 2m SE of Fishguard. From Fishguard, take B4313 to Llanychaer. From Haverfordwest, take A40 towards Fishguard. After Letterston, take 2nd Trecwn turning on R. Follow road for about 2m until junc with B4313, turn L. **Visits by arrangement June to Sept for groups of up to 12. Even one or two visitors are welcome. Adm £4, chd free. Light refreshments.**
Recently established and hidden behind pub front, discover a richly planted Japanese garden with pond and lawn areas. There are water features, raised beds, pergolas and arches. Variety of acers, wisteria, grasses, clematis, succulents, water lilies and bog plants, azaleas, ferns and much more to explore. An eclectic mix planted with skill and design flair- the dream of a passionate gardener.

3 CAE BACH
Hermon, Glogue, nr Crymych, SA36 0DS. Liz & Will North, 01239 831663, elizabethmmnorth@gmail.com. 2m SE of Crymch. From Crymych take Hermon Rd at Ysgol Bro Preseli, at T-junc in Hermon, turn L. Cae Bach is 300 yds on R. Disabled parking only at house, other parking signposted in village. **Sun 22 June (11-5), open nearby Pantybara. Sun 10 Aug (11-5). Adm £5, chd free. Tea, coffee & cake.** Visits also by arrangement 15 June to 20 July for groups of up to 25. Discuss refreshments when booking.
A 1½ acre newly established garden designed to attract wildlife, particularly bees and butterflies. Wander through the garden and discover herbaceous borders, ponds, grasses and our Japanese garden with rill. Our rose garden has 50 varieties, and don't miss the greenhouse, exotic area, conifer and heather area. We also have a wildflower meadow area, vegetable and fruit trees and fruit cage. Most areas wheelchair accessible.

4 COLD COMFORT FARM
Wolfscastle, Haverfordwest, SA62 5PA. Judy & Paul Rumbelow, 07809 560409, judy.rumbelow@gmail.com, www.facebook.com/people/Cold-Comfort-Plants/100042072915115. 7m N of Haverfordwest. Signed off A40 at Wolfscastle. Turn towards Hayscastle at Wolfe Inn. 1m along lane on L. **Sun 18, Wed 21, Wed 28 May, Wed 4, Sun 15 June (11-4). Adm £5, chd free. Home-made teas.** On weekday openings there will be an option of light lunch as well as home-made teas. Visits also by arrangement May to July for groups of up to 50. Discuss refreshments when booking.
Five acres of wildflower meadow alongside wrap around farm garden and small plant nursery. Perennial beds, showcasing interesting perennials from nursery stock, rockery, gravel garden, raised beds, greenhouses, polytunnel and compost. Welcoming garden under development on sloping plot, full of planting ideas for windy and difficult conditions. Outstanding views of the Preseli Mountains.

5 CORNERSTONE HOUSE
Glandwr, Whitland, SA34 0XY. Ruth Swaffield, 01994 419683, ruth.swaff@gmail.com. 3.8m S of Crymych. From Narberth, N on A478 for approx 11 m, turn R at the sign for Glandwr. From Cardigan S on the A478 for approx 11 m turn L, 1m down hill turn R. **Visits by arrangement 18 May to 7 Sept.** Discuss refreshments when booking. **Adm £4, chd free.**
A rural sloping garden of an acre which features a pond, small sunken garden and a gravel area, patio and seating areas, and view of hills. A path leads through a wisteria covered pergola and shrubbery to another pergola with hops and climbing roses leading to a sun house. The garden contains many rhododendrons and azaleas. Fruit trees and low hedges separate the fruit cage and vegetable gardens.

6 NEW CORSESIDE NURSERY
Angle, Pembroke, SA71 5AA.
Mrs Sandra Williams, www.corsesidenursery.com. 6m S of Pembroke. Take B4319 from Pembroke to Angle, cont. onto Clay Ln (B4320) to Angle village. We are >2½ m past the Speculation Inn. If you reach Freshwater W Beach or the refinery, you've gone too far. **Sat 26 July (10-4). Adm £5, chd free. Tea, coffee & cake.**
1½ acre eclectic tropical garden nestled in the Pembrokeshire countryside with stunning sea views. Wander winding paths to discover secret spaces filled with vibrant succulents and exotic plants. Spot planters made from recycled beach finds and garden treasures. Each corner blends tropical charm with seaside allure, offering a unique escape for garden enthusiasts and tranquillity seekers. Corseside Nursery is an RHS Gold Medal winning Nursery. Sections of our RHS exhibitions have been re-created at the Nursery and can be viewed by visitors. Corseside also has an impressive display of Echium flowers each year.

CARMARTHENSHIRE & PEMBROKESHIRE   629

7 DWYNANT
Golden Grove, SA32 8LT. Mrs Sian Griffiths 14m E of Carmarthen, 3m from Llandeilo. Take B4300 Llandeilo to Carmarthen. Take L turn to Gelli Aur, pass church & vicarage then 1st R onto Old Coach Rd. Dwynant is approx ¼m on R. **Fri 23, Sat 24, Sun 25, Mon 26 May, Sat 19, Sun 20 July (11-5). Adm £5, chd free. Pre-booking essential, please phone 07502 539737 or email sian.41@btinternet.com for information & booking. Cream teas.** Visits also by arrangement Apr to Sept for groups of 5 to 20. Limited parking therefore car sharing is appreciated.
A ¾ acre garden set on a steep slope designed to sit comfortably within a verdant countryside environment with beautiful scenery and tranquil woodland setting. A garden with lily pond, selection of plants and shrubs inc azaleas, rhododendrons, hydrangeas, and rambling roses set amongst a carpet of bluebells. Seating in appropriate areas to enjoy the panoramic view and flowers. For accommodation visit www.airbnb.co.uk/rooms/31081717

8 ◆ DYFFRYN FERNANT
Llanychaer, Fishguard, SA65 9SP. Christina Shand & David Allum, 01348 811282, christina@dyffrynfernant.co.uk, www.dyffrynfernant.co.uk. 3m E of Fishguard, then ½m inland. A487 E, 2m from Fishguard turn R towards Llanychaer. Follow lane for ½m, entrance on L. Look for yellow garden signs. **For NGS: Sun 8 June (12-5), open nearby Pont Trecynny. Sun 7 Sept (12-5). Adm £10, chd free. Hot drinks machine in the library.** For other opening times and information, please phone, email or visit garden website.
Magical 2.4 ha garden, evolving from wilderness and ancient rocky landscape. Distinctively planted areas leading down to marsh and woodland, against backdrop of the Preselis. RHS Partner Garden. Planting inc: tulips, primulas, *Camassias*, *Wisteria alba*, orchard fruit blossom, roses. Peonies and *Embothrium coccineum*, salvias, dahlias, *Hedychium*, *Canna*, *Colocasia*, *Ricinus*, and ornamental grasses. Disabled parking near house (please note garden has gravel paths and steep slopes). Coach visits by arrangement via a minibus transfer. Member Great Gardens of West Wales.

9 NEW DYFFRYN MILL
Llanmill, Narberth, SA67 8UE. Mrs Abigail Hart. 2½m E of Narberth. Follow signs to Narberth crematorium, go past crem on L. ½m downhill, signed parking on farmyard in Llanmill village. 10 min walk to garden. Limited parking at house for disabled visitors. **Sat 24, Sun 25 May (1-5). Adm £5, chd free. Tea, coffee & cake.**
A rural garden which makes the most of its stunning setting. 'Rewilding' on a postage stamp with lake, pond, boggy scrapes and woodland planted in 2019. Hostas, ferns, corydalis, astilbes, epimediums abound and giant water tanks turned into planters to soften old industrial mill building. Wisteria and rambling roses, shrubbery, orchard, 'hot' slate bed. Wander along the river and through woodland.

10 GELLI UCHAF
Rhydcymerau, Llandeilo, SA19 7PY. Julian & Fiona Wormald 5m SE of Llanybydder. 1m NW of Rhydcymerau. From the B4337 in Rhydcymerau take minor road opp bungalows. After 300yds turn R up track. Limited parking so essential to phone or email first. **Sat 15, Sun 16 Feb, Sat 1, Sun 2, Sat 29, Sun 30 Mar, Sat 19, Sun 20 Apr, Sat 24, Sun 25 May, Sat 14, Sun 15 June, Sat 5, Sun 6 July (10.30-5). Adm £6, chd free. Pre-booking essential, please phone 01558 685119, email thegardenimpressionists@gmail.com or visit www.thegardenimpressionists.com/visiting-the-garden for information & booking.** Visits also by arrangement 15 Feb to 6 July for groups of 10 to 25. Please discuss refreshments when booking.
This 1½ acre garden complements our C17 Longhouse and 11 acre smallholding. In the garden trees and shrubs are underplanted with thousands of snowdrops, crocus, cyclamen, and daffodils, together with many rhododendrons, skimmias, clematis, rambling roses and hydrangeas. There are several wildflower hay meadows, wildlife ponds, stream and shepherd's hut to explore beyond the main garden. Extensive views and seats to enjoy them. Year-round flower interest with naturalistic plantings. Two ponds and stream.

11 GROVE OF NARBERTH
Molleston, Narberth, SA67 8BX. 01834 860915, events@grovenarberth.co.uk, www.grovenarberth.co.uk. 2m S of Narberth. From A40 between Whitland and Haverfordwest, take A4075 towards Tenby. Go past Oakwood Theme Park, turn L on the A4115 towards Templeton. L turn at brown sign for Grove approx 2m later. **Visits by arrangement 1 Feb to 22 Dec. Cream Teas (additional £12 pp) may be booked in advance. Adm £7, chd free.**
The garden is framed by ancient oaks and towering beeches, and from our hillside glade you can enjoy views across the rolling Pembrokeshire countryside to the Preseli Hills. 26 acres of woodlands, meadows and gardens, inc an historic walled garden, kitchen garden, and cut flower garden. Extensive woodland walks through the grounds, which inc some steep slopes and undulating paths.

12 HOUSE ON STILTS
Rotten Pill Road, Ferryside, SA17 5TN. Paula & Iain Davies, 07967 125881, paulapdavies@gmail.com, www.instagram.com/paulapdavies. 9 m SW of Carmarthen. A484 towards Kidwelly. At Llandyfaelog junc turn R towards Ferryside. Follow until 'Welcome to Ferryside' sign. Follow NGS signs to garden for drop off only or parking at rugby club (7 min walk). **Sun 18 May (1-5). Adm £5, chd free. Tea, coffee & cake.** Visits also by arrangement 25 May to 22 June for groups of up to 20. Smaller parties welcome alongside larger groups. Please discuss refreshments when booking.
A ⅓ acre garden surrounds a mid-century modern house resembling a bird hide nestled in a rural estuary setting. A garden designed with an artist's eye, subtle colour palette, form and texture. A mosaic of different habitats for wildlife, from a large pond at the rear to a dry cockle shell garden to the front. An emphasis on promoting biodiversity, whilst creating a relaxing space for people. Coastal front garden, wildlife pond

with viewing deck, bog garden, native hedging, summerhouse (for sheltering from the rain), slopes planted with shrubs, perennials, wildflowers, bulbs and edibles, wild area with log pile etc. Potting shed and propagation area. Compost corner.

13 LLWYNGARREG
Llanfallteg, Whitland, SA34 0XH. Paul & Liz O'Neill, 01994 240717, lizpaulfarm@yahoo.co.uk, www.llwyngarreg.co.uk. *19m W of Carmarthen. A40 W from Carmarthen, turn R at Llandewi Velfrey, 2½m to Llanfallteg. Go through village, garden ½m further on: 2nd farm on R. Car park in bottom yard on R.* **Visits by arrangement Feb to Oct. Adm £7, chd free. Tea, coffee & cake. Discuss refreshments when booking.**
Llwyngarreg is always a work in progress, delighting plant lovers with its many rarities inc primulas, many huge bamboos with *Roscoeas, Hedychiums* and salvias extending the season through to autumn colour. Trees and rhododendrons are underplanted with perennials. The sunken garden and gravel gardens contain unusual exotics. Springs form a series of linked ponds across the main garden, providing colourful bog gardens. Fruit and vegetables, composting, numerous living willow structures, mobiles and quirky installations made largely from garden findings, swing, chickens, goldfish. Partial wheelchair access.

14 MOELFRYN
Llandeilo Road, Castel y Rhingyll, Gorslas, Llanelli, SA14 7LU. Elaine & Graeme Halls, 07484 775553, revelainehalls@gmail.com. *Between Crosshands and Llandeilo on A476. On A476 N of Gorslas and S of Carmel. Yellow arrows at gate. What3words app: indeed. noise.hedgehog.* **Mon 21 Apr (10.30-4.30). Every Tue and Sun 27 Apr to 16 Sept (10.30-4.30). Mon 5, Mon 26 May, Mon 25 Aug (10.30-4.30). Adm £4, chd free. Tea, coffee & cake.** Visits also by arrangement Apr to Sept for groups of 2 to 15.
A ⅓ acre taking account of its Welsh hillside. Aesthetically pleasing, this eco-friendly garden has much to discover. From herbs, fruit and veg to shrubs and perennials, trees, mini meadow and orchard. Plants to note inc cranesbills, hydrangeas, clematis and wisteria. We also have cold frames, wormery, hot bin, pond, stumpery, and a propagation area. Hen keeping and holding advice can be given. Grassy and slate chipping paths lead you on, with something to attract and inspire both new and well-seasoned gardeners. Lots of quirky areas and every twist and turn reveals something more. A tranquil, life-affirming and inspiring space.

15 ♦ NATIONAL BOTANIC GARDEN OF WALES
Middleton Hall, Llanarthne, SA32 8HN. 01558 667149, www.botanicgarden.wales. *Between Cross Hands & Carmarthen. From Carmarthen take A48 E, after 8m take slip road signed B4310 to Nantgaredig. Follow brown signs.* **For opening times and information, please phone or visit garden website.**
Dedicated to conservation, horticulture, science, education, leisure and the arts, the National

National Botanic Garden of Wales

Botanic Garden of Wales features the Great Glasshouse, Tropical House, Walled Garden, a working farm, Waun Las Nature Reserve and British Bird of Prey Centre. Set in a historical Regency landscape of over 500 acres, it hosts a programme of events and activities throughout the year.

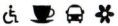

16 NEUADD Y FELIN
Neuadd Road, Garnant, Ammanford, SA18 1UF. **Terry & Sara Knight.** *On A474, 5m W of Pontardawe, 5m E of Ammanford. Access to garden from Nant Gwinau Rd. Turn R as you enter Garnant on A474 from Pontardawe. From Ammanford direction turn L just before you leave Garnant on A474.* **Sat 26, Sun 27 July (10.30-4.30). Adm £5, chd free. Home-made teas.**
A mature two acre smallholding with many different areas of interest. A large garden with sloping perennial beds and rose garden. There is a large dahlia display, mature shrubs and shaded planted areas. We have a 40 foot white wisteria climbing a pergola and wildlife and fish ponds. Wander through the meadow on the willow walk and explore the riverside walk with seated area. Located on the site of an old C14 watermill.

17 NORCHARD
The Ridgeway, Manorbier, Tenby, SA70 8LD. **Ms H Davies.** *4m W of Tenby. From Tenby, take A4139 for Pembroke. ½m after Lydstep, take R at Xrds. Proceed down lane for ¾m. Norchard on R.* **Sun 6 July (1-5). Adm £6, chd free. Tea, coffee & cake.**
Historic gardens at a Medieval hall nestled in tranquil location and sheltered by an ancient oak woodland. Strong structure with formal and informal areas. Early walled gardens, restored Elizabethan parterre, ornamental kitchen garden, subtropical planting and orangery. 1½ acre orchard of old (many local) varieties. Young arboretum and meadow looking towards grist mill. Extensive collections of roses, daffodils and tulips. Millpond with moorhens and ducks. Partial wheelchair access. Access to lower level of the kitchen garden via steps only.

18 THE OLD RECTORY
Lampeter Velfrey, Narberth, SA67 8UH. **Jane & Stephen Fletcher**, 01834 831444, jane_e_fletcher@hotmail.com. *3m E of Narberth. Next to church in Lampeter Velfrey. Parking in church car park.* **Visits by arrangement 1 Mar to 22 Sept. Adm £4, chd free. Please discuss refreshments when booking.**
Behind a formal front garden the woodland garden is a green hollow of historic charm; wildlife welcoming, with ancient and newly planted trees and shrubs. Spring brings snowdrops, daffodils and bluebells to the woodlands. Later rhododendrons, hydrangeas, acers, roses, daisies and geraniums bring pops of colour to the green backdrop. Approx two acres inc veg, ponds and unique garden buildings.

19 NEW PANTYBARA
Velindre, Llandysul, SA44 5XT. **Mrs Helen Maxwell,** www.instagram. com/rural_creator. *4m S of Newcastle Emlyn. From Newcastle Emlyn take B4333 towards Cynwyl Elfed. After 4m turn sharp L on unmarked road. Garden is 0.7m down this lane on R. What3words app: skater.target.massaging.* **Sat 21 June (12-4). Sun 22 June (12-4), open nearby Cae Bach. Adm £5, chd free. Home-made teas.**
An acre of garden on a sloping south facing hillside 250m high and terraced on several levels with dry stone walls. Designed to provide year round interest, to benefit wildlife, provide food and as a setting for our home. The garden consists of a pond, bog garden, rockeries, perennial beds, mixed borders, dry stone walls and vegetable gardens. Additional parking on yard at Blaen Bran Farm opposite garden.

20 PENTRESITE
Rhydargaeau Road, SA32 7AJ. **Gayle & Ron Mounsey,** 07900 432993, gayle.mounsey@gmail.com. *4m N of Carmarthen. Take A485 heading N out of Carmarthen, once out of village of Peniel take 1st R to Horeb & cont for 1m. Turn R at NGS sign, 2nd house down lane.* **Sun 29 June (11-5). Adm £5, chd free. Tea, coffee & cake. Visits also by arrangement May to Sept.**
Approx two acre garden developed over the last 18 years with extensive lawns, colour filled herbaceous and mixed borders, on several levels, a bog garden and magnificent views of the surrounding countryside. There are many unusual trees, shrubs and herbaceous plants, with an interesting collection of hydrangeas This garden is south facing and catches the south westerly winds from the sea. The garden features statutory by James Doran-Webb. Check the National Garden Scheme website for additional dates.

21 PEN-Y-GARN
Foelgastell, Cefneithin, SA14 7EU. **Mary-Ann Nossent & Mike Wood,** 07985 077022, maryann.nossent@ngs.org.uk, www.instagram.com/pen_y_garn. *10m SE Carmarthen, A48 N from Cross Hands. Take 1st L to Foelgastell R at T-junc 300 metres sharp L, 300 metres 1st gateway on L. A48 S Bot. Gdns turning r'about R to Porthythyd 1st L before T-junc. 1m 1st R & 300 metres on L.* **Visits by arrangement 22 Mar to 31 July for groups of up to 20. Parking is limited so car sharing is essential. Adm £4, chd free. Home-made teas.**
1½ acres set in former limestone quarry sympathetically developed to sit within the landscape, with five distinct areas cultivated herbaceous borders and wild no mow lawns. A shady area with woodland planting and wild ponds; no dig kitchen garden; terraced borders with shrubs and herbaceous planting; lawns and pond. The garden is on several levels and steep in places. It sits on a bedrock of limestone so has both cultivated and wildflowers that thrive on this soil type.

In 2024, we celebrated 40 years of continuous funding for Macmillan Cancer Support equating to more than £19.5 million.

22 PONT TRECYNNY
Garn Gelli Hill, Fishguard, SA65 9SR. Wendy Kinver 1½ m N of Fishguard. Driving up the hill from Fishguard to Dinas turn R ½ way up the rd & follow signs. SatNav will take you to a lay-by opp the garden, please ignore as we are on the other side. **Sun 8 June (1-4). Open nearby Dyffryn Fernant. Thur 3 July, Mon 4 Aug (1-4.30). Pre-booking essential, please phone 01348 873040 or email wendykinver@icloud.com for information & booking. Adm £5, chd free. Visits also by arrangement 26 May to 25 Aug for groups of 10 to 30.**
A diverse garden of 3½ acres. Meander through the meadow planted with native trees, pass the pond and over a bridge which takes you along a path, through an arboretum, orchard and gravel garden and into the formal garden full of cloud trees, exotic plants and pots, which then leads you to the stream and vegetable garden.

23 NEW ◆ SCOLTON MANOR
Bethlehem, Haverfordwest, SA62 5QL. 01437 731328, scolton.enq@pembrokeshire.gov.uk, www.scoltonmanor.co.uk. 6m outside Haverfordwest. On B4329 Cardigan Rd, brown-signed off A40 from both Haverfordwest & Fishguard. **For NGS: Sat 5 July (10-4), Sun 6 July, open nearby Treffgarne Hall, Sat 6, Sun 7 Sept (10-4). Adm £5, chd free. Light refreshments at Edie's tearoom. For other opening times and information, please phone, email or visit garden website.**
We recently acquired a collection of 60 salvia varieties (from Lamphey Walled Garden) now sited within our working walled garden. This features organic produce and flowers, a willow arch, pineapple house, perennial borders and arboretum. A Tree Nursery of endangered native trees from West Wales, grown from seed for local groups to plant. The Walled Garden is part of 'One Historic Garden' scheme. Scolton Manor comprises of 60 acres of park and woodland surrounding a Victorian Manor House, with a Welcome Centre, Bee-keeping Centre, sculpture trail, tearoom, play areas and gift shop. Access in Walled Garden and majority of grounds, some restrictions in Manor House.

Disabled toilets and baby-changing facilities available.

24 SHOALS HOOK FARM
Shoals Hook Lane, Haverfordwest, SA61 2XN. Karen & Robert Hordley, 07712 268899, shoalshook@icloud.com. From A40 take B4329 to H/west town centre (Prendergast). Before fork with Fishguard Rd, turn L into Back Ln, turn L to Shoals Hook Ln. 1m, property on L. What3words app: clips.november.samplers. **Visits by arrangement 21 Apr to 15 Sept for groups of up to 14. Visits from Mon-Thurs only. Please discuss refreshments when booking. Adm £5, chd free.**
Approx six acre garden on our smallholding. Designed and made by ourselves over 29 years. Inc flower borders, veg garden, fruit trees, woodland walk, lake garden and specimen trees. Planted for the different seasons and to encourage wildlife. Many spring bulbs at the start of the year, ending with a late summer prairie style grass garden area.

25 SKANDA VALE HOSPICE GARDEN
Saron, Llandysul, SA44 5DY. brotherfrancis@skandavalehospice.org, www.skandavalehospice.org. Between Carmarthen & Cardigan. On A484, in village of Saron, 13m N of Carmarthen. **Sat 14 June (11-4.30). Adm £4, chd free. Home-made teas.**
Tranquil garden of approx 1 acre, built for therapy, relaxation and fun. Maintained by volunteers, lawns and glades link garden buildings with willow spiral, wildlife pond, borders, sculptures and stained glass. Blue and gold planting at entrance inspires calm and confidence, leading to brighter red, orange and white. Hospice facilities open for viewing. A garden for quiet contemplation, wheelchair friendly, with lots of small interesting features. For accommodation please visit www.skanda-hafan.com/en

26 STABLE COTTAGE
Rhoslanog, Mathry, Haverfordwest, SA62 5HG. Mr Michael & Mrs Jane Bayliss, 01348 837712, michaelandjane1954@michaelandjane.plus.com. Between Fishguard and St David's. Heading W on A487, turn R at Square & Compass sign. ½ m, at hairpin take track L. Stable Cottage on L with block paved drive. **Visits by arrangement 1 May to 13 July for groups of up to 12. Discuss refreshments when booking. Adm £4, chd free.**
Garden extends to approx ⅓ of an acre. It is divided into several smaller garden types, with a seaside garden, small orchard and wildlife area, scented garden, small vegetable/kitchen garden, and two Japanese areas - a stroll garden and courtyard area.

27 TREFFGARNE HALL
Treffgarne, Haverfordwest, SA62 5PJ. Martin & Jackie Batty, 01437 741115, jmv.batty@gmail.com, www.instagram.com/battyplanting. 7m N of Haverfordwest, signed off A40. Go up through village & follow road round sharply to L, Hall ¼ m further on L. **Sun 13 Apr, Sun 4 May (1-5). Sun 6 July (1-5), open nearby Scolton Manor. Adm £5.50, chd free. Home-made teas. Visits also by arrangement Mar to Sept. Please discuss refreshments when booking.**
Stunning hilltop location with panoramic views: Grade II listed Georgian house (not open) provides formal backdrop to garden of four acres with wide lawns and themed beds. A walled garden, with double rill and pergolas, planted with a multitude of borderline hardy exotics. Summer border, gravel garden, heather bed, stumpery. woodland area and new rose garden. Planted for year-round interest. The planting schemes seek to challenge the boundaries of what can be grown in Pembrokeshire. Gravel paths not wheel-friendly. Some steps.

28 TY'R MAES
Tyr Maes, Farmers, Llanwrda, SA19 8JP. John & Helen Brooks, 01558 650541, johnhelen140@gmail.com. *7m SE of Lampeter. 8m NW of Llanwrda. From Llanwrda 1½ m N of Pumsaint on A482, 1st L after turn to Ffarmers. From Lampeter 1st R after Springwater Lakes. Garden entrance 30yds down lane. Please use postcode SA19 8DP with SatNav.* **Visits by arrangement Mar to Oct. Adm £6, chd free. Home-made teas. Discuss refreshments when booking.**
A four acre garden with splendid views. Herbaceous and shrub beds, formal design, exuberantly informal planting, full of cottage garden favourites and many unusual plants. Wildlife and lily ponds; fascinating arboretum with over 200 types of tree; particular focus on rhododendron, magnolia and hydrangea cultivars. Gloriously colourful from early spring till late autumn. Wheelchair note: Some gravel paths.

& 🐕 ❋ 🚗 ☕

29 ♦ UPTON CASTLE GARDENS
Cosheston, Pembroke Dock, SA72 4SE. Prue & Stephen Barlow, 01646 689996, info@uptoncastle.com, www.uptoncastlegardens.com. *4m E of Pembroke Dock. 2m N of A477 between Carew & Pembroke Dock. Follow brown signs to Upton Castle Gardens through Cosheston.* **For NGS: Wed 11 June (10-4.30). Adm £7.50, chd free. Home-made teas.** For other opening times and information, please phone, email or visit garden website.
Privately-owned, listed, historic gardens and arboretum of 35 acres surround C13 castle (not open). Terraces of herbaceous borders and formal rose garden with over 150 roses provide constant summer interest. Walled productive kitchen garden, chapel garden with millennial yew. Rare magnolias, rhododendrons, camellias, and new hydrangea beds. Woodland with rare and champion trees. RHS Partner Garden. Walk on the Wild Side: Woodland walks funded by C.C.W. and Welsh Assembly Government. Medieval chapel as featured on Time Team. Partial wheelchair access.

& 🐕 ❋ 🚗 🚙 ☕ 🏛

30 WEST WALES WILLOWS
The Mill, Gwernogle, SA32 7SA. Justine & Alan Burgess, www.facebook.com/WestWalesWillows. *3m from Brechfa. On A40 at Nantgaredig, take B4310 to Brechfa. ½ m after Brechfa, turn L towards Gwernogle. After 2½ m pass Chapel on R, up steep hill & bear R. Take 1st R & The Mill is on the R.* **Sat 21 June (10-4). Adm £4.50, chd free. Tea.**
Located in a scenic valley, halfway up a mountain, the National Plant Collection of *Salix* (willow) is set in a sloping field with grass pathways. Approx 260 varieties are on show, inc varieties for pollinators, autumn colour, bio fuel, hedging and windbreaks. The field also has sample living willow structures on display inc domes, tepee, long arch/tunnel, hedges and a new arbour.

[NPC] ☕ 🔊

Dyffryn Mill

CEREDIGION

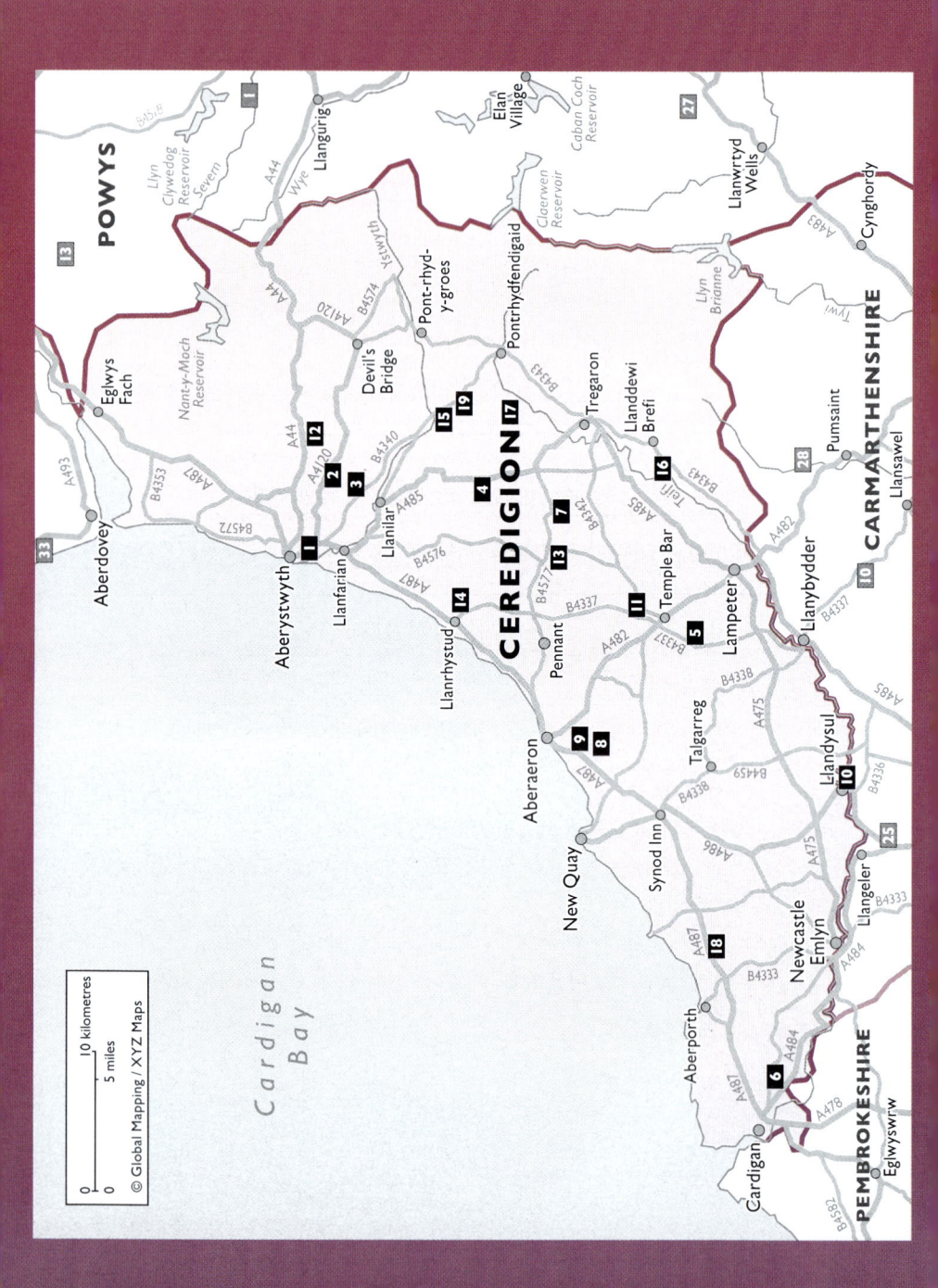

CEREDIGION

VOLUNTEERS

County Organiser
Stuart Bradley
07757 799553
stustart53@outlook.com

County Treasurer
Elaine Grande
01974 261196
elaine.grande@ngs.org.uk

Publicity
Shelagh Yeomans
07796 285003
shelaghyeo@hotmail.com

Social Media
Samantha Wynne-Rhydderch
07899 911483
samantha.wynne-rhydderch@ngs.org.uk

Assistant County Organisers
Gay Acres
01974 251559
gayacres@aol.com

Joanna Kennaugh
07872 451821
joanna.kennaugh@ngs.org.uk

David & Gill Shepherd
01545 574916
lymphoedemamidwales@btinternet.com

@Ceredigion Gardens
@ceredigion_ngs

OPENING DATES

All entries subject to change. For latest information check **www.ngs.org.uk**

Map locator numbers are shown to the right of each garden name.

April

Monday 21st
Bryngwyn 2

Sunday 27th
NEW The Hidden Garden 10

May

Sunday 11th
Llanllyr 11

Sunday 18th
Bwlch y Geuffordd 3

Saturday 24th
NEW Y Felin 19

Sunday 25th
NEW Y Felin 19

June

Sunday 1st
Rhos Villa 16

Thursday 5th
Bryngwyn 2

Saturday 7th
Bryngwyn 2
NEW Temple Bar Farm 18

Sunday 8th
NEW Temple Bar Farm 18

Sunday 15th
Ffynnon Las 9

Sunday 22nd
Llanllyr 11

Sunday 29th
Rhos Villa 16

July

Saturday 19th
NEW Cilbronnau Mansion 6
Penybont 15

Sunday 20th
Aberystwyth Allotments 1
NEW Cilbronnau Mansion 6
Penybont 15

Sunday 27th
NEW Felinfach House 8

August

Sunday 3rd
NEW Penelton 14

Sunday 10th
◆ Cae Hir Gardens 5

Sunday 24th
NEW The Hidden Garden 10

September

Sunday 14th
NEW Cwrt Mawr 7

By Arrangement

Arrange a personalised garden visit with your club, or group of friends, on a date to suit you. See individual garden entries for full details.

Bwlch y Geuffordd Gardens 4
NEW Cilbronnau Mansion 6
Ffynnon Las 9
NEW The Hidden Garden 10
Llanllyr 11
Melindwr Valley Bees,
  Tynyffordd Isaf 12
Pencnwc 13
Penybont 15
Tanffordd 17
NEW Temple Bar Farm 18
NEW Y Felin 19

THE GARDENS

1 ABERYSTWYTH ALLOTMENTS
5th Avenue, Penparcau, Aberystwyth, SY23 1QT. Aberystwyth Town Council. *On S side of R.Rheidol on Aberystwyth by-pass. Froma N or E, take A4120 between Llanbadarn & Penparcau. Cross bridge then take 1st R into Minyddol. Allotments ¼ m on R.* **Sun 20 July (1-5). Adm £5, chd free. Home-made teas.**
There are 47 plots in total on two sites just a few yards from each other. The allotments are situated in a lovely setting alongside River Rheidol close to Aberystwyth. Wide variety of produce grown, vegetables, soft fruit, top fruit, flowers, herbs and a newly created wildlife pond. There will be surplus plants and produce available, with donations gratefully received. Refreshments will be provided by the local Scout Group. Grass and gravel paths throughout. Car parking available. For more information contact Brian Heath 01970 617112.

2 BRYNGWYN
Capel Seion, Aberystwyth, SY23 4EE. Mr Terry & Mrs Sue Reeves. *5m E of Aberystwyth on A4120. On the A4120 between the villages of Capel Seion & Pant y Crug. Parking for up to 15 cars available on site. What3words app: elephant.sunflower.forks.* **Mon 21 Apr, Thur 5, Sat 7 June (2-5). Adm £5, chd free. Home-made teas.**
Managing our land for wildlife is at the heart of all we do. As a result of conservation work and tree planting, habitat has been restored to such, that numbers and diversity of wildflowers and wildlife have increased. Explore along mown paths through traditional wildflower-rich hay meadows. Small orchard containing Welsh heritage apples and pears. Wildflower seeds are available for sale. Find us on Facebook at 'Wildlife and Photographic Days Aberystwyth'.

The Hidden Garden

3 BWLCH Y GEUFFORDD
New Cross, Aberystwyth, SY23 4LY. Manuel & Elaine Grande. *5m SE of Aberystwyth. Off A487 from Aberystwyth, take B4340 to New Cross. Garden on R at bottom of small dip. Parking in lay-bys opp house.* **Sun 18 May (10.30-4.30). Adm £5, chd free. Tea, coffee & cake.**
Landscaped hillside 1½ acre garden, fine views of Cambrian Mountains. Embraces its natural features with different levels, ponds, mixed borders merging into carefully managed informal areas. Banks of rhododendrons, azaleas, bluebells in spring. Full of unusual shade and damp-loving plants, flowering shrubs, mature trees, clematis and climbing roses scrambling up the walls of the old stone buildings. Partial wheelchair access only to lower levels around house. Some steps and steep paths further up the hillside.

4 BWLCH Y GEUFFORDD GARDENS
Bronant, Aberystwyth, SY23 4JD. Mr & Mrs J Acres, 01974 251559, gayacres@aol.com, bwlch-y-geuffordd-gardens.myfreesites.net. *12m SE of Aberystwyth, 6m NW of Tregaron off A485. Take turning opp village sch in Bronant for 1½m then L up ½m uneven track.* **Visits by arrangement. Adm £5, chd £2.50. Tea.**
1000ft high, three acre, constantly evolving wildlife and water garden. An adventure garden for children. There are a number of themed gardens, inc Mediterranean, cottage garden, woodland, Oriental, memorial and jungle. Plenty of seating. Unique garden sculptures and buildings, inc a cave, temple, gazebo, jungle hut, treehouse and willow den. Fantasy and adventure dragon hunt. Garden is wildlife rich, particularly insects and birds. Gravel paths and some steps but alternate route possible for wheelchair users.

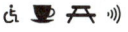

5 ♦ CAE HIR GARDENS
Cribyn, Lampeter, SA48 7NG. Julie & Stuart Akkermans, 07538 789180, caehirgardens@gmail.com, www.caehirgardens.com. *5m W of Lampeter. Take A482 from Lampeter towards Aberaeron. After 5m turn S on B4337. Garden on N side of village of Cribyn.* **For NGS: Sun 10 Aug (10-5). Adm £7.50, chd £2.50. Tea, coffee & cake.** For other opening times and information, please phone, email or visit garden website.
A Welsh garden with a Dutch history, Cae Hir is a true family garden of unassuming beauty, made tenable by its innovative mix of ordinary garden plants and wildflowers growing in swathes of perceived abandonment. At Cae Hir the natural meets the formal and riotous planting meets structure and form. A garden not just for plant lovers, but also for design enthusiasts. Five acres of fully landscaped gardens. Tearoom serving a selection of homemade cakes and scones and a 'Soup of the Day'. Limited wheelchair access.

6 NEW CILBRONNAU MANSION
Llangoedmor, Cardigan, SA43 2LP. Lyn and Roger Bushell, 07817 944593, bushellroger962@gmail.com. *2m E of Cardigan. Situated on the B4570, 2m from Cardigan. Turn down track between the 2 lodge houses and drive carefully- there are ramps to help with drainage.* **Sat 19, Sun 20 July (11-4). Adm £5, chd free. Tea, coffee & cake.** Visits also by arrangement May to Sept for groups of 5 to 12.
The 2½ acre garden inc a courtyard cottage garden, Mediterranean and gravel gardens, vegetable plots, lawns, beds and borders, all at various stages of development. There are a number of yews, ancient oaks, beech and Wellingtonia. The garden is on three levels, connected by grass slopes. Most, but not all, areas are accessible to wheelchair users in dry conditions.

7 NEW CWRT MAWR
Llangeitho, Tregaron, SY25 6QJ. Pauline Gorissen & Philip Levy. *Approx 2m from the village of Llangeitho. From Llangeitho, turn L at sch signed Penwuch. Garden 1½m on R, ¼m up track. From Cross Inn take B4577 past Penwuch Inn. R after brown sculptures in field. Garden ¾m on L, ¼m up track. What3words app: uttering.stardom.warms.* **Sun 14 Sept (11-4.30). Adm £5, chd free. Light refreshments.**
Nestled in ancient woodlands with Cambrian Mountain views, this mature garden offers tranquillity with two ponds linked by a meandering stream flanked by varied plants. Enjoy terraced flower beds, a woodland walk, and a vibrant cut flower garden with dahlias and other blooms. Raised beds feature numerous hydrangeas and perennials. Seating areas let you take in the garden from many perspectives. The woodland walk and some seating areas are not accessible for wheelchairs.

8 NEW FELINFACH HOUSE
Oakford, Llanarth, SA47 0RP. Andrew and Rachael McInnes. *Between New Quay and Aberaeron. A short distance off the A487. Turn off A487 at Llwyncelyn (near the Petrol Stn) following signs towards Oakford. After approx 1m turn R into car park. What3words app: slept.towns.sweetened.* **Sun 27 July (11-5). Adm £5, chd free. Tea, coffee & cake.**
Explore this acre of productive country garden with a variety of elements inc large lawned area, vegetables, flower borders, fruit trees, polytunnel and greenhouses. There is a wildlife pond with water lilies leading to a woodland walk and gentle flowing stream. Poultry pen and a variety of wild birds. Wooded area is not suitable for wheelchair access.

9 FFYNNON LAS
Ffosyffin, Aberaeron, SA46 0HB. Liz Roberts, 01545 571687. *A short distance off the A487. 1m S of Aberaeron. Turn off A487 opp The Forge Garage in Ffosyffin, 300m up the road take the L turn at the T junc.* **Sun 15 June (12-5). Adm £5, chd free. Tea, coffee & cake.** Visits also by arrangement 14 June to 26 July for groups of up to 15. Open by arrangement according to owners availability. Donation to Pancreatic Cancer Research.
A two acre garden that has been in the making for over 15 years, Ffynnonlas is a beautiful area that delivers on many different aspects of gardening. There are large lawns, several beds of mature shrubs and flowers. A small lake and two smaller ponds that are separated by a Monet style bridge with lilies. There is a wildflower meadow, a work in progress that has spectacular wild orchids in spring. A rockery with water cascade, vegetable garden with raised beds. For wheelchair users, please note there are grass paths and level ground.

10 NEW THE HIDDEN GARDEN
Farmyard Farm, Dol Llan Road, Llandysul, SA44 4RL. 01559 363389, sales@farmyardnurseries.co.uk, www.facebook.com/FarmyardNurseries. *Head towards Llandysul and find the petrol stn (Valley Services). Follow brown signage to Farmyard Nurseries. Approx. 1m up the road opp the garage.* **Sun 27 Apr, Sun 24 Aug (10-4). Adm £5, chd free. Tea, coffee & cake.** Visits also by arrangement 1 Jan to 19 Dec. Guided tours available. Donation to Plant Heritage.
A large, serene woodland garden with extensive plantings to complement the existing natural trees and shrubs. Numerous paths lead to, a small lake with many ducks in residence, the 'hobbit house' and adjoining large stumpery, and the acer grove. Hydrangeas and hellebores are widespread with masses of spring bulbs. Great care has been taken to give all year round interest.

11 LLANLLYR
Talsarn, Lampeter, SA48 8QB. Mrs Loveday Gee & Mr Patrick Gee, 01570 470900, lgllanllyr@aol.com. *6m NW of Lampeter. On B4337 to Llanrhystud. From Lampeter, entrance to garden on L, just before village of Talsarn.* **Sun 11 May, Sun 22 June (2-6). Adm £5, chd free. Tea, coffee & cake.** Visits also by arrangement 7 Apr to 27 Sept.
Large early C19 garden on site of medieval nunnery, renovated and replanted since 1989. Discover the large pool and bog garden as well as a formal water garden. There are also rose and shrub borders, gravel gardens, and a beautiful rose arbour. Wander through the allegorical labyrinth and mount, all exhibiting fine plantsmanship. Year-round appeal, interesting and unusual plants. Visit our spectacular rose garden planted with fragrant old fashioned shrub and climbing roses. Specialist Plant Fair by Ceredigion Growers Association. Garden mostly flat for wheelchair users.

12 MELINDWR VALLEY BEES, TYNYFFORDD ISAF
Capel Bangor, Aberystwyth, SY23 3NW. Vicky Lines, 01970 880534, vickysweetland@googlemail.com, www.the-heartened-homestead.co.uk. *From Aberystwyth take L turn off A44 at E end of Capel Bangor. Follow this road round to R until you see sign with Melindwr Valley Bees.* **Visits by arrangement 2 June to 3 Aug for groups of up to 10. Adm £5, chd free. Home-made teas. Cream teas £5 each.**
A bee farm dedicated to wildlife with permaculture and forest garden ethos. Fruit, vegetables, culinary and medicinal herbs and bee friendly plants within our wildlife zones. Beehives are situated in dedicated areas and can be observed from a distance. Ornamental and wildflower areas in a cottage garden theme. Formal and wildlife ponds. Vintage tractors and other machinery on show.

13 PENCNWC
Penuwch, Tregaron, SY25 6RE. Ms Andrea Sutton, 01974 821413, andreasutton@uclmail.net. *7m W of Tregaron on B4577. On the B4577, where the B4576 turns off in direction of Bwlchllan. Turning is opp Bear's Hill cottage. Driveway to Pencnwc is 100yds from the Tregaron Road on R.* **Visits by arrangement for groups of up to 5. Adm £5, chd free.**
7½ acre landscape garden 900ft up with view of Irish Sea between long bare hill and treed hill. Stone and slate house is in the centre. Land reaches out in a star shape around, all sloping down to marshland, now holding a large lake with boathouse. Springs are collected into hillside pools that run to the lake. Woodland, wildlife, especially birds. Walks, bridges, dry stone walls and castles, seats. Gorgeous lake. Excellent examples of dry stone walling inc a castle wall.

14 NEW PENELTON
Llanrhystud, SY23 5BA. Mr Arthur Newman. *½m from Llanrhystud in the village of Cwm Mabws. From Llanrhystud take the B4337. Take the 2nd L turn signed Cwm Mabws. The garden is approx ¼m on the L with parking opp.* **Sun 3 Aug (11-4.30). Adm £5, chd free. Tea, coffee & cake.**
A two acre garden recently recovered and replanted, benefitting from established large trees. Comprising of interesting herbaceous and shrub plantings in island beds, in addition to impressive borders beside a long, south facing stone garden wall . Highly productive vegetable garden, polytunnel and small orchard. Two small ponds add to the charm and tranquillity of an inspirational garden.

15 PENYBONT
Llanafan, Aberystwyth, SY23 4BJ. Norman & Brenda Jones, 01974 261737, tobrenorm@gmail.com. *Ystwyth Valley. 9m SE of Aberystwyth. B4340 via Trawscoed towards Pontrhydfendigaid. Over stone bridge. ¼m up hill. Turn R along Lane/Ystwyth Trail past ex forestry houses.* **Sat 19, Sun 20 July (11-5.30). Adm £5, chd free. Home-made teas.** Visits also by arrangement May to Aug.
Carefully designed hillside country garden next to the Ystwyth Forest overlooking the valley. An acre of interest with continuity of colour and textures from spring bulbs and bluebells, rhododendrons and azaleas through May, roses from June and a Mediterranean summer feel with swathes of lavender, grapevines and lots of different hydrangeas in bright blues, whites and pinks. Designed and landscaped for colour and texture. Seats with stunning views over fields, woodland, valley and hills. Red kites, buzzards and sheep wander. Sloping ground means only partial wheelchair access.

16 RHOS VILLA
Llanddewi Brefi, Tregaron, SY25 6PA. Andrew & Sam Buchanan. *Between Olmarch and Llanddewi Brefi. From Lampeter, take the A485 towards Tregaron. After Llangybi turn R opp junc for Olmarch. The property can be found on the R after 1½m.* **Sun 1, Sun 29 June (10.30-4.30). Adm £5, chd free. Tea, coffee & cake.**
A ¾ acre garden creatively utilising local materials. Secret pathways meander through sun and shade, dry and damp. A variety of perennials and shrubs are inter-planted to create interest at every turn and throughout the year. A productive vegetable and fruit garden with semi-formal structure contrasts the looser planting through the rest of the garden. Interesting and beautifully crafted pitch cobble paths and walls constructed from local stone.

Temple Bar Farm

17 TANFFORDD
Swyddffynnon, Ystrad Meurig, SY25 6AW. Jo Kennaugh & Stuart Bradley, 07872 451821, stustart53@outlook.com. *1m W of Ystrad Meurig. 5m E of Tregaron. Tanffordd is ¼m from Swyddffynnon village on the road to Tregaron. Please do not follow SatNav.* **Visits by arrangement May to Sept for groups of up to 25. Limited parking. Car share required. Adm £5, chd free. Tea, coffee & cake. Soft drinks and ice cream also available.**

Wildlife garden, rich in biodiversity, set in a five acre smallholding with large pool. The garden inc a small woodland area and beds of shrubs and herbaceous planting containing more unusual plants. Vegetables, polytunnel and poultry enclosures with chickens and ducks. Wander along to meet the friendly donkeys and ponies who share a buttercup filled field in late spring and early summer.

18 NEW TEMPLE BAR FARM
Sarnau, Llandysul, SA44 6QU. Jenny & Teifi Davies, 01239 811079, jennydavies3@live.co.uk. *Located on A487 between villages of Sarnau & Tanygroes. Situated 8m N of Cardigan & 14m S of Aberaeron on A487. Turn into side road at junc. What3words app: measure. household.printing.* **Sat 7, Sun 8 June (11-4). Adm £5, chd free. Tea, coffee & cake.** Visits also by arrangement 14 Apr to 31 July for groups of up to 10.

Interesting garden on a farm. Planting areas wherever space allows! Spring bulbs, bog garden, auricula theatre, foxglove and tree lupin walk, mixed perennial beds and many containers nestling in original farmyard. We have a herd of rare Ancient Cattle of Wales plus an important Iron Age Fort (Cadw) on our land, with amazing views over three counties, Cardigan Bay, Preseli Mountains and Welsh countryside. Parking in field.

19 NEW Y FELIN
Tynygraig, Ystrad Meurig, SY25 6AE. Brian and Hilary Malaws, 07779 801968, hilary.malaws@btinternet.com. *10m SE of Aberystwyth via B4340. Pass Tynygraig village sign, branch R signed Swyddffynnon, turn R 70 metres before house Ty Chwarel. What3words app: positives. remembers.clown.* **Sat 24, Sun 25 May (1-5). Adm £5, chd free. Tea, coffee & cake.** Visits also by arrangement 1 May to 26 June for groups of up to 20.

A two acre garden set within a 14 acre wooded landscape with historic industrial features, inc a former corn mill and pond. Caradog Falls 100ft waterfall can be seen from the garden. The garden inc masses of rhododendron, azalea, camellia and magnolia with many other unusual trees and shrubs. There are woodland walks through a fragment of temperate rainforest to the waterfall. Mill pond, old mill with waterwheel. Old mine level now a cave.

GLAMORGAN

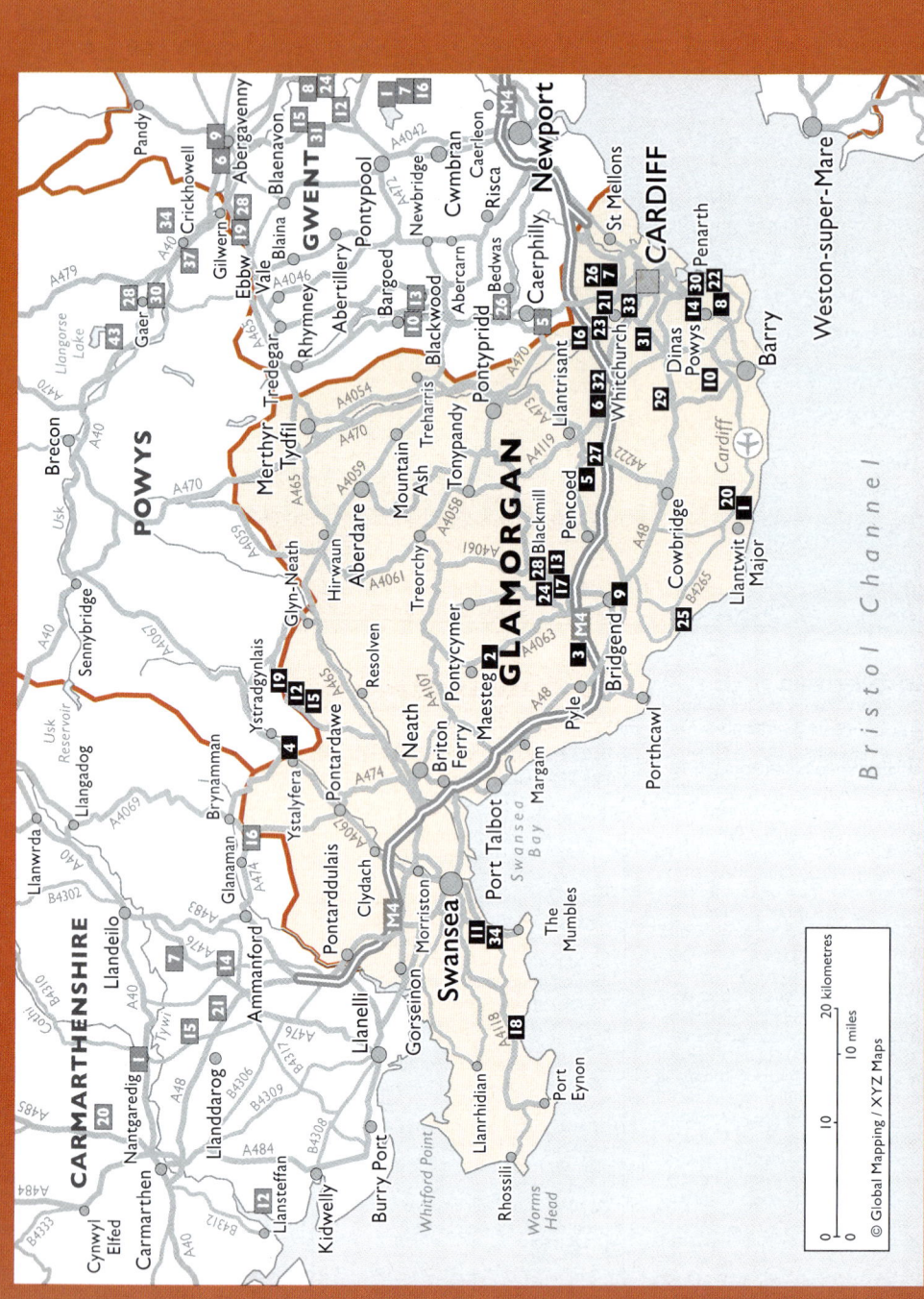

VOLUNTEERS

County Organiser
Rosamund Davies 01656 880999
rosamund.davies@ngs.org.uk

County Treasurer
Steven Thomas 01446 772339
steven.thomas@ngs.org.uk

Publicity
Bernadette Nicholas 07815 449568
bernadette.nicholas@ngs.org.uk

Social Media – Instagram
Sue Deary 01656 720833
suedeary888@gmail.com

Social Media – Facebook
Sarah Boorman 07969 499967
sarah.boorman@ngs.org.uk

Booklet Co-ordinator
Rosamund Davies
(as above)

Talks Co-ordinator
Frances Bowyer 02920 892264
frances.bowyer@ngs.org.uk

Health and Gardens Co-ordinator
Miranda Workman 02920 766225
miranda.parsons@talktalk.net

Assistant County Organisers
Cheryl Bass 07969 499967
cheryl.bass@ngs.org.uk

Sol Blytt Jordens 01792 391676
sol.blyttjordens@ngs.org.uk

Sarah Boorman (as above)

Pam Creed
pam.creed@ngs.org.uk

Janet Evans 07961 542452
janetevans54@me.com

Tony Leyshon 07896 799378
anthony.leyshon@icloud.com

Ceri Macfarlane 01792 404906
ceri@mikegravenor.plus.com

Derek Price 07717 462295
derekprice7@btinternet.com

Marie Robson
mariedrobson@gmail.com

@ngsglamorgan

OPENING DATES

All entries subject to change.
For latest information check
www.ngs.org.uk
Map locator numbers are shown to the right of each garden name.

February

Sunday 16th
Slade 25

May

Saturday 3rd
9 Willowbrook Gardens 34
Sunday 4th
9 Willowbrook Gardens 34
Sunday 11th
NEW 112 Heol Heddwch 12
NEW Llwyn-Onn 15
Saturday 17th
16 Hendy Close 11
Saturday 24th
NEW Bronygarn House 2
Sunday 25th
Old Froglands 20
Monday 26th
NEW Bronygarn House 2
Friday 30th
100 Pendwyallt Road 23
Saturday 31st
17 Maes y Draenog 16
100 Pendwyallt Road 23

June

Sunday 1st
17 Maes y Draenog 16
Saturday 7th
NEW Heol Laethog 13
Penarth Gardens 22
64 Western Drive 33
Sunday 8th
185 Pantbach Road 21
Penarth Gardens 22
64 Western Drive 33
Friday 13th
V21 Community Garden 31

Saturday 14th
Boverton House 1
Sunday 15th
22 Dan-y-Coed Road 7
Saturday 21st
Boverton House 1
Tal-Y-Fan Farm 28
Sunday 22nd
Cefn Cribwr Garden Club 3
Creigiau Village Gardens 6
Tal-Y-Fan Farm 28
Saturday 28th
Hen Felin & Swallow Barns 10
Horatio's Garden Cardiff 14
Sunday 29th
Hen Felin & Swallow Barns 10
38 South Rise 26
12 Uplands Crescent 30
Monday 30th
38 South Rise 26

July

Friday 4th
Mulberry Hill 18
Saturday 5th
Dinas Powys 8
Sunday 6th
Dinas Powys 8
NEW 90 Grove Road 9
Mulberry Hill 18
12 Uplands Crescent 30
Saturday 12th
Uplands 29
Sunday 13th
Maes-y-Wertha Farm 17
Sunday 20th
Swn y Coed 27
Saturday 26th
16 Hendy Close 11
Sunday 27th
Rose Cottage 24

August

Saturday 9th
4 Clyngwyn Road 4
Sunday 10th
4 Clyngwyn Road 4
12 Uplands Crescent 30
Sunday 17th
Waunwyllt 32

August

Sunday 24th
12 Uplands Crescent 30

Sunday 31st
Coed Cae Farm 5

February 2026

Sunday 15th
Slade 25

By Arrangement

Arrange a personalised garden visit with your club, or group of friends, on a date to suit you. See individual garden entries for full details.

NEW Bronygarn House 2
Coed Cae Farm 5
22 Dan-y-Coed Road 7
Hen Felin & Swallow Barns 10
16 Hendy Close 11
17 Maes y Draenog 16
Nant Melyn Farm 19
Swn y Coed 27
12 Uplands Crescent 30
64 Western Drive 33
9 Willowbrook Gardens 34

Waunwyllt

THE GARDENS

1 BOVERTON HOUSE
Boverton, Llantwit Major, CF61 1UH. Mr John Wainwright. *Boverton, at the E end of Llantwit Major. Garden entrance is approx 50m E of the Boverton Post Office. Please follow yellow NGS signs.* **Sat 14, Sat 21 June (10.30-4). Adm £4.50, chd free. Home-made teas.**
A walled garden next to the River Hoddnant, recently brought back to use. Formerly an orchard and kitchen garden, the garden has a unique character and has been designed to create a beautiful garden space and encourage wildlife, whilst retaining its unique historic character. There is a raised kerb to enter from the road which may require assistance. Thereafter level grass throughout.
&. 🐕 🍽))

2 NEW BRONYGARN HOUSE
Station Street, Maesteg, CF34 9AL. Dr Noel Thomas and Alina Ascari, 01656 737358, nthomas@doctors.org.uk. *Please follow NGS yellow signs to Station St. and Bronygarn House, trees over pavement and garden wall, with further signs to house.* **Sat 24, Mon 26 May (12-5). Adm £5, chd free. Light refreshments. Visits also by arrangement 15 May to 1 Sept for groups of up to 8.**
Enjoyed by four generations of same family over 160 years. Many interesting mature trees, young fruit trees, rhododendrons, ponds, numerous rose bushes and standards, and much else of interest, even in the wilder areas. Lawn used for tennis in last century, now smaller and left unmown in parts, wildflowers encouraged. We live and let live, encourage all wildlife, try to garden organically.
❋ 🍽

GROUP OPENING

3 CEFN CRIBWR GARDEN CLUB
Cefn Cribwr, Bridgend, CF32 0AP. www.cefncribwrgardening club.com. *5m W of Bridgend on B4281.* **Sun 22 June (11-5). Combined adm £6, chd free. Tea, coffee & cake in the village hall. WC facilities also available and will have stalls selling plants and crafts.**

13 BEDFORD ROAD
Mr John Loveluck.

2 BRYN TERRACE
Alan & Tracy Birch.

CEFN CRIBWR GARDEN CLUB ALLOTMENTS
Cefn Cribwr Garden Club.

77 CEFN ROAD
Peter & Veronica Davies & Mr Fai Lee.

15 GREEN MEADOW
Tom & Helen.

6 TAI THORN
Mr Kevin Burnell.

3 TY-ISAF ROAD
Mr Ryland & Mrs Claire Downs.

Cefn Cribwr is an old mining village atop a ridge with views of Swansea to the west, Somerset to the south and home to Bedford Park and the Cefn Cribwr Iron Works. The village hall is at the centre with teas, cakes and plants for sale. The allotments are to be found behind the hall. Children, art and relaxation are just some of the themes to be found in the gardens besides the flower beds and vegetables. There are also water features, fish ponds, wildlife ponds, summerhouses and hens adding to the diverse mix in the village. Themed colour borders, roses, greenhouses, recycling, composting and much more. The chapel grounds are peaceful with a meandering woodland trail. Visitors may travel between gardens courtesy of the Glamorgan Iron Horse Vintage Society.
❋ 🍽))

4 4 CLYNGWYN ROAD
Ystalyfera, Swansea, SA9 2AE. Paul Steer, www.artinacorner.blogspot.com. *Heading on A4067 from Swansea or Brecon, stay on A4067 until r'about to Tesco. Take 3rd exit off mini r'about. Turn L up Commercial St, take 2nd R for Alltygrug Rd.* **Sat 9, Sun 10 Aug (11-3). Adm £4, chd free. Tea, coffee & cake.**
The Coal Tip Garden is a small personal space created in order to help us relax. Its main character is enclosure and a sense of rest. It is not a flowery garden but is formed out of shrubs and trees - forming a tapestry of hedging with arches and niches being cut out in order to place seats and sculpture and to produce a visual rhythm. A key philosophy is using native perennials. An intimate space designed for rest, contemplation and creativity.
🐕 🍽))

5 COED CAE FARM
Llanharan, Pontyclun, CF72 9NH. The Liley Family, 07967 580099, jeremy@farmtrack.wales. *M4 J34 or J35 on the A473. Turn off A473 at gates/stone pillars of Llanharan Manor House, approx. ½ m E of village of Llanharan. Farm track has passing places. What3words app: reputable.casino.shorthand.* **Sun 31 Aug (11-5). Adm £6, chd free. Tea, coffee & cake. Visits also by arrangement May to Sept for groups of 5 to 12.**
While it's the garden you come to view, your first instinct will be to stop and admire the panoramic views over the countryside. The gardens are laid out for all seasons, bulbs and herbaceous in shrub borders. Water features with cascades down to a pond, surrounded by mixed borders and trees, offering shade. A native woodland with a large pond offers alternative areas in the gardens. Please ask to park in yard where there is wheelchair access into the garden and tea tent.
&. 🐕 🍽 🛋))

---

70 inpatients and their families are being supported at the newly opened Horatio's Garden Northern Ireland, thanks to National Garden Scheme donations.

GLAMORGAN 643

GROUP OPENING

6 CREIGIAU VILLAGE GARDENS
Maes Y Nant, Creigiau, CF15 9EJ. W of Cardiff (J34 M4). From M4 J34 follow A4119 to T-lights, turn R by Castell Mynach Pub, pass through Groes Faen & turn L to Creigiau. Follow NGS signs. **Sun 22 June (11-5). Combined adm £7, chd free. Home-made teas at 28 Maes y Nant.**

28 MAES Y NANT
Mike & Lesley Sherwood.

26 PARC Y FRO
Mr Daniel Cleary.

WAUNWYLLT
John Hughes & Richard Shaw.
(See separate entry)

Creigiau Village Gardens - three vibrant and innovative gardens. Each quite different, they combine some of the best characteristics of design and planting for modern town gardens as well as cottage gardens. Each has its own forte; Waunwyllt's ½ acre is divided into garden rooms; 28 Maes y Nant, cottage garden planting reigns; 26 Parc y Fro is newly planted with wildlife at its heart. Enjoy a warm welcome, home-made teas and plant sales.

7 22 DAN-Y-COED ROAD
Cyncoed, Cardiff, CF23 6NA. Alan & Miranda Workman, 07764 614013, miranda.parsons@talktalk.net. *Dan y Coed Rd leads off Cyncoed Rd at the top & Rhydypenau Rd at the bottom. No 22 is at the bottom of Dan y Coed Rd. There is street parking & level access to the R of the property.* **Sun 15 June (11-5). Adm £5, chd free. Tea, coffee & cake.** Visits also by arrangement 1 Apr to 21 Sept for groups of 8 to 20.
A medium sized, much loved garden. Owners share a passion for plants and structure, each year the lawn gets smaller to allow for the acquisition of new features. Hostas, ferns, acers and other trees form the central woodland theme as a backdrop is provided by the Nant Fawr woods. Year-round interest has been created for the owner's and visitor's greater pleasure. There is a wildlife pond, many climbing plants and a greenhouse with cacti, succulents and pelargoniums. There is wheelchair access to the garden patio area only.

GROUP OPENING

8 DINAS POWYS
Barry Road, Dinas Powys, CF64 4TS. *Approx 6m SW of Cardiff. Exit M4 at J33, follow A4232 to Leckwith, onto B4267 & follow to Merry Harrier T-lights. Turn R & enter Dinas Powys. Follow yellow NGS signs.* **Sat 5, Sun 6 July (11-5). Combined adm £6, chd free.** Donation to Dinas Powys Voluntary Concern, Dinas Powys Community Library & Vale Foodbank.

21 CARDIFF ROAD
Rob & Pam Creed.

23 CARDIFF ROAD
Eoghan Conway & David Manfield.

32 LONGMEADOW DRIVE
Julie & Nigel Barnes.

30 MILLBROOK ROAD
Mr & Mrs R Golding.

32 MILLBROOK ROAD
Mrs Judy Marsh & son, Tim Marsh.

NIGHTINGALE COMMUNITY GARDENS
Keith Hatton.

5 SIR IVOR PLACE
Ceri Coles.

WEST CLIFF
Alan & Jackie Blakoe.

There are many gardens to visit in this small friendly village, all with something different to offer. Displays of vegetables and fruit in the community garden, gardens with exuberant planting providing yearlong interest, wildlife ponds, chickens and a mini vineyard. There will also be plants for sale and refreshments in the different gardens. There are many restful and beautiful areas to sit and relax. Good wheelchair access to all gardens.

9 NEW 90 GROVE ROAD
Bridgend, CF31 3EF. Miss Claudia Scicluna and Mr John Doran. *20m W of Cardiff. Turn into Grove Rd from Ewenny Rd. Travel down Grove Rd, no. 90 is the last one on the R before reaching Merthyr Mawr Rd.* **Sun 6 July (10-3). Adm £4.50, chd free. Tea, coffee & cake.**

A cottage garden surrounded by a purple beech hedge making the garden private. The garden wraps around the house from the front door right round to the secret garden at the back of the house. Bright red *Crocosmia* and pink, purple and white *Dierama* (Angels fishing rod) are a feature in the summer. All set around a wildlife pond full of dragons flies and frogs. The main garden is on one level, although some paths may be a bit narrow past the water butts.

GROUP OPENING

10 HEN FELIN & SWALLOW BARNS
Vale of Glamorgan, Dyffryn, CF5 6SU. Janet Evans & Rozanne Lord, 07961 542452, janet.evans54@me.com. *3m from Culverhouse. Cross r'about take the A48 up the hill to St Nicholas. L at T-lights, past Dyffryn. House, R at T-junc & follow the road to big yellow NGS signs.* **Sat 28, Sun 29 June (11-6). Combined adm £5, chd free.** Visits also by arrangement 31 Mar to 31 Oct for groups of 10+.
Yr Hen Felin: Beautiful cottage garden with stunning borders, breathtaking wildflower meadows, oak tree with surrounding bench, 200 year old pig sty, wishing well, secret garden with steps to river, lovingly tended vegetable garden and chickens, sheep and alpacas. Mill stream running through garden with adjacent wildflowers. The Barns: Cross the bridge over the river to enter The Barns garden of about four acres. The area around the house is formal with mixed herbaceous borders, and a rose walk to a small secluded pond. The meandering paths pass small garden rooms and raised beds for vegetables, run alongside the River Waycock through an orchard of heritage, apple trees, plums, and cherries, and finally through woods, reaching a large pond with water lilies, dragonflies, pontoon with seating and summerhouse. Teas and cakes are available from the house with seating in the herb garden, and a sale of original water colours. NB Unprotected river access, children must be supervised. Wheelchair access possible to most areas of the two gardens. The bridge has steps however so wheelchair access between the gardens is via the lane.

V21 Community Garden

16 HENDY CLOSE
Derwen Fawr, Swansea, SA2 8BB. Peter & Wendy Robinson, 07773 711973, robinsonpetel@hotmail.co.uk. Approx 3m W of Swansea. A4067 Mumbles Rd follow sign for Singleton Hosp. Then R onto Sketty Ln at mini r'about. Turn L then 2nd R onto Saunders Way. Follow yellow NGS signs. Please park on Saunders Way if possible. **Sat 17 May, Sat 26 July (2-5). Adm £6, chd free.** Visits also by arrangement 17 May to 30 July for groups of 10+.
Originally the garden was covered with 40ft conifers. Cottage style, some unusual and mainly perennial plants which provide colour in spring, summer and autumn. The garden is an example of how to plan for all seasons. Visitors say it is like a secret garden because there are a number of hidden places. Plants to encourage all types of wildlife in to the garden.

12 NEW 112 HEOL HEDDWCH
Seven Sisters, Neath, SA10 9AE. Sharon Preddy. *Approx 10m from Neath. From A465 take slip road to Blaendulais. 3rd exit on r'about to A4109. Follow yellow signs.*

From A4067 go R onto A4421, 2nd turn R after 2m. Turn R onto A4109. What3words app: explain. relishes.pound. **Sun 11 May (1-5). Combined adm with Llwyn-Onn £6, chd free.**
A small mature Balinese style front garden comprising of pond, jungle hut and palms.

GROUP OPENING

13 NEW HEOL LAETHOG
Bryncethin, Bridgend, CF32 9JE. Ms Sue Deary. *Follow the common road from Bryncethin for approx 2m & approx 1m from Heol Y Cyw. What3words app: straying. scavenger.trial.* **Sat 7 June (11-5). Combined adm £5, chd free.** Home-made teas.

NEW 8 RAILWAY TERRACE
Mr Jason & Mrs Tammy Cheung.

9 RAILWAY TERRACE
Ms Sue Deary.

NEW 10 RAILWAY TERRACE
Mr William & Mrs Megan Gwilliam.

A row of former miners cottages on the common between Bryncethin and Heol Y Cyw, known as Heol Laethog or Tyn'Waun locally. All have uninterrupted views of the common with a large green in front with a park at the end. Three gardens opening, all typical cottage gardens with vegetables, fruit and flowers. Front south facing gardens and rear gardens accessed by a small lane at the back.

129,032 people were able to access guidance on what to expect when a person is dying through the National Garden Scheme's support for Hospice UK this year.

646 GLAMORGAN

14 HORATIO'S GARDEN CARDIFF
University Hospital Llandough, Penlan Road, Llandough, CF64 2XX. Owen Griffiths, www.horatiosgarden.org.uk/the-gardens/horatios-garden-wales. Turn into the University Hospital Llandough from the main road and keep going straight. The garden is raised on the R of the road, just past the visitor's car park. **Sat 28 June (11-4). Adm £5, chd free. Pre-booking essential, please visit www.ngs.org.uk for information & booking. Tea, coffee & cake.**
Sarah Price's design was inspired by the Welsh landscape. The planting is naturalistic and gentle featuring valerian, poppies, field maple, and crab apples. The garden is adorned with climbers such as clematis, grapes, and roses. Circular openings within the perimeter fence frame the countryside and sea in the distance. It provides beneficiaries with a beautiful place to spend time in year-round. Fully wheelchair accessible.
& ❊ ☕

15 NEW LLWYN-ONN
1e Bynteg, Seven Sisters, Neath, SA10 9ET. Mr Lyn Jenkins. *9m N of Neath on A4109. Take M4 J43, on the A465 towards Neath / Merthyr Tydfil. Take turn onto A4109 towards Aberdulais/Crynant. Stay on the A4109 to Seven Sisters.* **Sun 11 May (1-5). Combined adm with 112 Heol Heddwch £6, chd free. Tea, coffee & cake.**
LLwyn-Onn is set in the shadow of Bannau Brycheiniog (Brecon Beacons). This serene garden has a small arboretum, woodland walk, oriental garden, pergola, pond, shrub and perennial borders. Take time to appreciate this peaceful garden and the many features of this thoughtfully planned six acre garden.
☕ 🎵

16 17 MAES Y DRAENOG
Tongwynlais, Cardiff, CF15 7JL. Mr Derek Price, 07717 462295, derekprice7@btinternet.com. *N of M4, J32. From M4 J32, take A4054 into village. R at Lewis Arms pub, up Mill Rd. 2nd R into Catherine Dr. Park in signed area (no parking in Maes y Draenog). Follow signs to garden.* **Sat 31 May, Sun 1 June (12-5). Adm £5. Tea, coffee & cake.** Visits also by arrangement 30 May to 15 June for groups of 6 to 16.
A hidden garden, in the shadow of Castell Coch, fed by a mountain stream, with a wooden footbridge to a naturalised, woodland area. There are wonderful late spring flower displays set against a woodland backdrop. Developed over many years with a wide variety of lavender beds and herbaceous borders, summerhouse, patios, greenhouse and vegetable area. A good variety of plants in different borders around house. Rear of house is set against woodland and fields, while front areas have mature roses and herbaceous plants, borders. Not suitable for young children and partial access for wheelchair users.
& ❊ 🚗 ☕ 🛏

17 MAES-Y-WERTHA FARM
Bryncethin, CF32 9YJ. Stella & Tony Leyshon. *3m N Bridgend. Follow sign for Bryncethin, turn R at Masons Arms. Follow sign for Heol-y-Cyw garden about 1m outside Bryncethin on R.* **Sun 13 July (12-7). Adm £7, chd free. Home-made teas. Pimms available.**
A three acre hidden gem outside Bridgend. Entering the garden you find a small Japanese garden fed by a stream, this leads you to informal mixed beds and enclosed herbaceous borders. Ponds and rill are fed by a natural spring. A meadow with large lawns under new planting gives wonderful vistas over surrounding countryside. Mural in the summerhouse by contemporary artist Daniel Llewelyn Hall. His work is represented in the Royal Collection and House of Lords. Fresh handmade sandwiches available and live music all afternoon.
& 🎵 🚗 ☕

18 MULBERRY HILL
Penmaen, Gower, Swansea, SA3 2HQ. Mrs Sian Burgess. *10m W of Swansea. A4118 to Penmaen. Turn at church. Car Park after cattle grid can be used for visiting garden(300 yds). Limited parking at Mulberry Hill.* **Fri 4, Sun 6 July (1-5). Adm £6, chd free. Tea, coffee & cake.**
Elements of a Victorian garden with some original features. Hidden behind a high wall is a garden of "rooms" with sea views: a yew tunnel and flower beds surround a fish pond; a terrace with borders leads down to a lawn and herbaceous borders and eventually to a lower garden with pond, bog garden and meadow area. Mature trees, hedges and shrubs throughout.
❊ 🛏 ☕ 🎵

19 NANT MELYN FARM
Seven Sisters, Neath, SA10 9BW. Mr Craig Pearce, cgpearce@hotmail.co.uk. *From M4 J43 take A465 towards Neath. Exit for Seven Sisters at r'about take 3rd exit, 6m for Seven Sisters you come to Pantyffordd sign, turn L under low bridge.* **Visits by arrangement 30 June to 1 Sept. Adm £5, chd free. Light refreshments.**
A spacious interesting garden with many features which inc a stunning natural waterfall, a meandering woodland stream covered by a canopy of entwined trees, a picturesque Japanese garden, beautiful lawned areas with winding pathways.
& 🐕 ❊ 🛏 ☕

20 OLD FROGLANDS
Llanmaes, Llantwit Major, CF61 2XY. Dorne & David Harris. *5m S of Cowbridge. From Llantwit Major by pass B4265 go E & turn L at t-lights into Eglwys Brewis Rd. Take 1st L. Old Froglands is 1st house on the R. What3words app: meaning,danger.barstool.* **Sun 25 May (1-5). Adm £5, chd free. Tea, coffee & cake.**
One acre farmhouse cottage garden with woodland and stream. 'Rooms' are linked by bridges and patios. Ponds and natural water features provide a playground for chickens to roam freely. Wetland areas provide a habitat for primula candelabras, ferns and hostas. Kitchen garden now productive. Wellies required if wet. It is difficult to move around the garden in a wheelchair on a wet day.
& 🐕 ❊ ☕ 🛏

21 185 PANTBACH ROAD
Rhiwbina, Cardiff, CF14 6AD. Kate & Glynn Canning. *Situated $\frac{1}{2}$m from Heol-y -Deri in the heart of Rhiwbina.* **Sun 8 June (12-5). Adm £5, chd free. Home-made teas.**
An Urban Retreat in the heart of Cardiff. The garden, once overgrown wasteland, turned into an ongoing lockdown' project in 2020 for owners Kate and Glynn. Although still in its infancy, the garden features raised beds, a formal rose garden and a central water feature. The winding path is framed by standard roses, borders and lawns.
& ☕ 🎵

77 Cefn Road, Cefn Cribwr Garden Club

GROUP OPENING

22 PENARTH GARDENS
Penarth, CF64 3HY. *Follow yellow signs to Lower Penarth.* **Sat 7, Sun 8 June (10-5). Combined adm £6, chd free. Tea, coffee & cake at 27 Victoria Road.**

2 BERKLEY DRIVE
Ian & Jane Hydon.
Open on all dates

23 PLYMOUTH ROAD
Mrs Nicola Griffiths.
Open on Sat 7 June

5 ROSEBERRY PLACE
Cathryn Mayo.
Open on all dates

SEAFIELD HOUSE
Anja Ernest.
Open on all dates

27 VICTORIA ROAD
Emma Berry.
Open on all dates

VICTORIA SQUARE COMMUNITY GARDEN
Friends of Victoria Square,
www.friendsofvictoriasquare.org.
Open on Sat 7 June

During the Victorian Era, Penarth was known as the 'Garden by the Sea'. Come and visit a selection of traditional and contemporary town gardens all within walking distance of each other. There is also a chance to visit an exciting community garden in the grounds of All Saints Church.

23 100 PENDWYALLT ROAD
Whitchurch, Cardiff, CF14 7EH.
Near M4 J32. Cul-de-sac on opp side of road to Village Hotel. Take narrow road opp side of road to Whitworth Sq. Go uphill past blocks of flats (Odet Court and Greenmeadow Court). **Fri 30, Sat 31 May (12-5). Adm £5, chd free.**
Three large areas- across the road, in front and back of house form a garden without lawns. Intensively planted to encourage wildlife. Ornamental trees inc Japanese maples, shrubs, and bamboos. Long pergola with clematis, wisteria, rose. Two huge ponds, one of which has windows to view the koi.

24 ROSE COTTAGE
32 Blackmill Road, Bryncethin, Bridgend, CF32 9YN. Maria & Anne Lalic, www.instagram.com/scarecrowcottagewales. *1m N of M4 J36 on A4061. Follow A4061 to Bryncethin. Straight on at mini r'about for approx 400 metres. Just past used car garage, turn R onto side road & park on grass. Do not block the track as farmer requires access.* **Sun 27 July (12-5). Adm £4, chd free. Tea, coffee & cake.**
If you want a proper garden with manicured borders and Latin plant names, maybe Rose Cottage isn't the place for you. We have a traditional Welsh working cottage garden with jumbled flower beds, a herb yard, seasonal growing of fruit and vegetables, ideas borrowed from permaculture, no-dig and companion planting to help us with our simple, sustainable and self-reliant way of life. Our pop-up tearoom sells tea, coffee and home-made cakes. Main path and gateways suitable for wheelchairs. Some paths are loose stone or narrow and bark chipped. These are uneven and care should be taken.

Mulberry Hill

25 SLADE
Southerndown, CF32 0RP.
Rosamund & Peter Davies,
rosamund.davies@ngs.org.uk,
www.instagram.com/
sladewoodgarden. *5m S of Bridgend. M4 J35 Follow A473 to Bridgend. Take B4265 to St. Brides Major. Turn R in St. Brides Major for Southerndown, then follow yellow NGS signs.* **Sun 16 Feb (1.30-4). Adm £7, chd free. Home-made teas.**
Hidden away, Slade garden is an unexpected jewel to discover next to the sea with views overlooking the Bristol Channel. The garden tumbles down a valley protected by a belt of woodland. In front of the house are delightful formal areas a rose and clematis pergola and herbaceous borders. From terraced lawns great sweeps of grass stretch down the hill enlivened by spring bulbs and fritillaries. Heritage Coast wardens will give guided tours of adjacent Dunraven Gardens with slide shows every hour from 2pm (May opening only). Partial wheelchair access.

26 38 SOUTH RISE
South Rise, Llanishen, Cardiff, CF14 0RH. Dr Khalida Hasan. *N of Cardiff. From Llanishen Village take Station Rd past train stn and go R down The Rise. Or further down onto S Rise directly. Following yellow signs.* **Sun 29, Mon 30 June (10-4). Adm £5.50, chd free. Tea, coffee & cake. Cakes & South Asian savouries (e.g. samosa, chick pea chaat) available.**
An inner city garden backing on to Llanishen Reservoir gradually establishing with something of interest and colour all year-round. Herbaceous borders, vegetables and fruit plants surround central lawn. Wildlife friendly; variety of climbers and exotics. In front shrubs and herbaceous borders to a lawn. Stepping stones leading to children's play area and vegetable plot also at the back. Wheelchair access to rear from the side of the house.

27 SWN Y COED
Tyla Garw, Pontyclun, CF72 9HD.
Mair & Owen Hopkin,
07434 096410,
mair.hopkin@icloud.com. *Near Pontyclun. M4 J34. Onto A4119, r'about take 1st exit to A473, straight over next r'about. Through t-lights, L at r'about, at next r'about 2nd L follow yellow signs.* **Sun 20 July (11-4). Adm £6, chd free. Tea, coffee & cake inc gluten and dairy free options.** Visits also by arrangement 31 May to 24 Aug for groups of 6+. Suitable for minibus parking.
This family friendly garden started from a blank canvas eight years ago, initially laid to lawn. Raised vegetable beds were installed and a 75m natural hedge planted along the side boundary to encourage wildlife. This was supplemented with fruit trees, flower and herb borders to attract insects. The lawn provides a clearing to the surrounding forestry attracting a variety of birds. Disabled parking on drive. Ramped access to rear patio and WC. Path adjacent to herb border and lawn access in dry weather.

GLAMORGAN 649

28 TAL-Y-FAN FARM
Blackmill, Bridgend, CF35 6UD. Suzanne, 07721 385633, skchurchill100@hotmail.co.uk. *Between Llangeinor and Blackmill. Accessed via A4093 between Llangeinor & Blackmill. Take turning opp the hanging sign for the Llangeinor Arms & follow the yellow signs. Access is along a private gravel road crossing the common.* **Sat 21, Sun 22 June (10.30-5). Adm £6, chd free. Light refreshments. Cakes, home-made scones, tea coffee and cold drinks and snacks.**
Elevated country garden with stunning 360 degree views over the Bristol Channel to the Devon coastline; situated in an isolated location. David Austin roses are the main attraction in the garden it has a parterre and rose arch, surrounded by 180 year old beech trees. Currently under development Japanese pond and bridge. There is a large seating area with glass balustrade to enjoy the views. We have pigs, alpaca, chickens, geese and turkeys - I also run a small campsite and glamping in the adjacent paddock. Access onto terrace area with views over the garden and far reaching coastal views.

& 🛏 ☕ 🔊))

29 UPLANDS
Gwern-y-Steeple, Peterston Super Ely, CF5 6LG. David Richmond. *12m W of Cardiff. From the A48 between St Nicholas & Bonvilston take the Peterston Super Ely turning & follow yellow arrow. Park at small green near Gwern-y-Steeple sign.* **Sat 12 July (12-5). Adm £4, chd free. Home-made teas.**
Uplands has a rustic heart within a cottage garden design. The front garden has vegetables and fruit beds. The back was planted in 2019, which was once all grass. There are four main herbaceous borders, young fruit trees, ornamental grasses, ferns, shrubs and roses, with many places to relax and enjoy the garden. Medium sized greenhouse and several sculptures located around the garden.

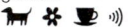

🛏 ❄ ☕ 🔊))

30 12 UPLANDS CRESCENT
Llandough, Penarth, CF64 2PR. Mr Dean Mears, 07910 638682, dean.mears@ntlworld.com. *Head for Llandough Hosp & a small turning. Tall banana plants clearly visible in the front garden. Follow NGS signs.* **Sun 29 June, Sun 6 July, Sun 10, Sun 24 Aug (2-4.30). Adm £5, chd free.** Visits also by arrangement 5 May to 30 Sept for groups of up to 15.
An exotic small garden full of unusual and large plants and a pond. Banana plants, tree ferns, gunnera, *Tetrapanax* and a foxglove tree surround the garden. Ferns, *Phormium, Brunnera, Brugmansia, Cordyline* and giant reed add interest to the garden. An area of potted tropical plants, *Brugmansia, Canna, Alocasia, Colocasia, Strelitzia* and palms add to the significant variety of exotic plants.

❄ 🔊))

31 V21 COMMUNITY GARDEN
Sbectrwm, Bwlch road, Cardiff, CF5 3EF. Mr Roy Bailey, www.V21.org.uk. *3m W of central Cardiff. From the A48 turn R onto St Fagans Rd. Continue onto Norbury Rd leading to Finchley Rd & Bwlch Rd.* **Fri 13 June (10-4). Adm £5, chd free. Tea, coffee & cake at the on-site café.**
The V21 Community Garden is developed and maintained by people with learning disabilities. The garden is designed to be an accessible learning environment. The garden has a newly developed herbaceous flower border, a spring garden, a wildlife pond, bog garden and areas for growing fruit and vegetables. There is also a large polytunnel and glasshouse to extend the growing season. Wheelchairs access via main paths.

& 🛏 ❄ ☕ 🔊))

32 WAUNWYLLT
Pant y Gored, Creigiau, Cardiff, CF15 9NF. John Hughes & Richard Shaw. *Heol Pant y Gored, Creigiau.* **Sun 17 Aug (11-5). Adm £5, chd free. Tea, coffee & cake. Opening with Creigiau Village Gardens on Sun 22 June.**
Waunwyllt is a garden of approx ½ an acre, divided into several 'garden rooms'. Winding paths lead the visitor through a tranquil garden set against a woodland backdrop with many secluded seating areas along the way and something of interest around every corner. Colour coordinated borders and strong design contribute to an attractive and stylish garden.

❄ ☕ 🔊))

33 64 WESTERN DRIVE
Cardiff, CF14 2SF. 07511 744976. *Gabalfa Cardiff. A470 - Manor Way W along Birchgrove Rd to Whichchurch. R at t-lights along College Rd. L at r'about, across next r'about to NGS sign. A48 Western Ave past LLandaff, at Tesco lights turn L.* **Sat 7 June (10.30-6); Sun 8 June (2-5). Adm £4, chd free. Light refreshments.** Visits also by arrangement 24 May to 27 July for groups of up to 10.
Interesting small, town garden in a city suburb. Pretty garden with something of interest for everyone. Water feature, pebble garden and mixed perennial borders inc species roses, English, rambler and climbing roses. Wildlife pond with small waterfall. Cordon fruit trees. Many species of birds visit the garden. Nearby walks and cycle paths. Established hedgerow and trees. Concrete drive access to front garden with concrete path access to back garden. Well behaved dogs on leads.

& 🛏 ❄ ☕ 🔊))

34 9 WILLOWBROOK GARDENS
Mayals, Swansea, SA3 5EB. Gislinde Macpherson, 01792 403268, ngs@willowgardens.idps.co.uk. *Nr Clyne Gardens. Go along Mumbles Rd to Blackpill. Turn R at Texaco garage on Mayals Rd. At the top of Clyne Park, turn R into Westport Ave. Willowbrook Gardens is 2nd turning on the L up Westport Ave.* **Sat 3 May (12.30-5.30); Sun 4 May (12.30-5). Adm £5, chd free. Home-made teas.** Visits also by arrangement.
Informal ½ acre mature garden on acid soil, designed to give natural effect with balance of form and colour between various areas linked by lawns; unusual trees suited to small suburban garden, especially conifers and maples; rock and water garden. Sculptures, ponds and waterfall.

& 🛏 ❄ ☕

GWENT

VOLUNTEERS

County Organiser
Debbie Field
01873 832752 / 07885 195304
wenalltisaf@gmail.com

County Treasurer
David Warren
01873 880031
david.warren@ngs.org.uk

Publicity
Penny Reeves
01873 880355
penny.reeves@ngs.org.uk

Gilly Jenks
07753 604296
gillyjenks1@gmail.com

Social Media
Mike & Tina Booth
07921 128169
christinabooth@me.com

Roger Lloyd
01873 880030
droger.lloyd@btinternet.com

Booklet Co-Ordinator
Veronica Ruth
07967 157806 / 01873 859757
veronica.ruth@ngs.org.uk

Assistant County Organiser
Suzanne George
01443 837708
philandsuzannegeorge@gmail.com

Tim Haynes
07738 236899
tim.haynes@hotmail.co.uk

Jenny Lloyd
01873 880030 / 07850 949209
jenny.lloyd@ngs.org.uk

Veronica Ruth
(as above)

@gwentngs
@GwentNGS
@gwentngs

OPENING DATES

All entries subject to change.
For latest information check
www.ngs.org.uk

Map locator numbers are shown to the right of each garden name.

January

Sunday 26th
Bryngwyn Manor   4

February

Snowdrop Openings
Saturday 1st
Bryngwyn Manor   4

March

Sunday 30th
Bryngwyn Manor   4
Llanover   15

April

Sunday 20th
The Old Vicarage   21
Saturday 26th
Park House   22
Sunday 27th
High Glanau Manor   11

May

Saturday 3rd
Longhouse Farm   17
Sunday 4th
Longhouse Farm   17
Saturday 10th
Glebe House   8
Sunday 11th
Glebe House   8
Sunday 18th
Monmouth Gardens   18
Saturday 24th
Hillcrest   13

Sunday 25th
Baileau   2
Hillcrest   13
Old Llangattock Farm   20
Monday 26th
Hillcrest   13

June

Sunday 1st
Cwm Farm   7
Long Owl Barn   16
Wenallt Isaf   28
Friday 6th
◆ Wyndcliffe Court   30
Saturday 7th
Rockfield Park   23
◆ Wyndcliffe Court   30
Sunday 8th
Rockfield Park   23
Sunday 15th
Chapel Gardens   6
Highfield Farm   12
Sunday 22nd
The Caerphilly Miners Community Centre - Climate Change Garden   5
Saturday 28th
Little Caerlicyn   14
Usk Open Gardens   27
Sunday 29th
Little Caerlicyn   14
Usk Open Gardens   27

July

Sunday 6th
Hillcrest   13
Sunday 13th
Birch Tree Well   3
The Growing Space Garden   9
Highfield Farm   12
Saturday 19th
14 Gwerthonor Lane   10
Sunday 20th
14 Gwerthonor Lane   10
NEW Woodbine House   29
Saturday 26th
Ty Isaf Farm   26
Sunday 27th
Ty Isaf Farm   26

August

Sunday 3rd
April House 1
Hillcrest 13

Sunday 10th
Highfield Farm 12

Sunday 17th
Neuadd Stone Barn 19

September

Sunday 7th
Hillcrest 13

Sunday 14th
Highfield Farm 12

By Arrangement

Arrange a personalised garden visit with your club, or group of friends, on a date to suit you. See individual garden entries for full details.

Birch Tree Well 3
Bryngwyn Manor 4
Highfield Farm 12
Hillcrest 13
Little Caerlicyn 14
Llanover 15
Rockfield Park 23
Trostrey Lodge 24
The Tump 25
Wenallt Isaf 28
Y Bwthyn 31

11 The Gardens, Monmouth Gardens

THE GARDENS

1 APRIL HOUSE
Coed y Paen, Usk, NP15 1PT.
Charlotte Fleming. *2m W of Usk. From Usk bridge go S towards Caerleon. Take 1st R towards Coed y Paen & go uphill for 1.9m. Garden is on L. SatNav gets you here. What3words app: enormous.eliminate.civic.* **Sun 3 Aug (11-5). Adm £5, chd free. Pre-booking essential, please visit www.ngs.org.uk for information & booking. Home-made teas.**
One acre site with glorious views over the Usk Valley and Wentwood Forest. Garden developed over past 20 years from bramble thicket and dairy pasture. Large herbaceous border, bog and shrub borders, wildlife pond. Fruit and vegetables.

2 BAILEAU
Llantilio Crossenny, Abergavenny, NP7 8TA. Sue Wilson & Seb Gwyther. *Between Llantilio Crossenny & Treadam. Please follow the yellow NGS signs. What3words app: dislikes. piglet.views.* **Sun 25 May (11-4). Adm £5, chd free. Tea, coffee & cake.**
A mature cottage style garden around an ancient farmhouse (not open). Packed with fruit and vegetables, the garden inc a rose walk, a crab apple walk, herbaceous borders, a circular ornamental vegetable garden and an old orchard. Activities for children and dogs welcome. Plenty of spots for a picnic. Views to Blorenge and Sugarloaf Mountains. Baked goods, light lunches, drinks and treats for sale, making creative use of abundant produce from the garden.

3 BIRCH TREE WELL
Upper Ferry Road, Penallt, Monmouth, NP25 4AN.
Jill Bourchier, 01600 775327, gillian.bourchier@btinternet.com. *4m SW of Monmouth. From Monmouth on B4293, turn L (Penallt/Trelleck) After 2m turn L to Penallt. In village turn L at Xrds & follow yellow signs. Lanes are single track & steep. What3words app: alerting.dramatic. blues.* **Sun 13 July (2-5). Adm £5, chd free. Home-made teas. Visits also by arrangement 7 Apr to 30 Sept for groups of up to 25.**
Situated in the heart of the Lower Wye Valley, amongst the ancient habitat of woodland, rocks and streams, these three acres can be viewed from a lookout tower. The garden features bluebells, specialist hydrangeas as well as unusual plants and trees attracting butterflies, bees and insects. An addition this year is the newly planted Reflective Garden with a brookside walk featuring many ferns. For the nimble footed only (children welcome under supervision).

4 BRYNGWYN MANOR
Bryngwyn, Raglan, NP15 2JH. Peter & Louise Maunder *2m W of Raglan. Take B4598 (old Abergavenny - Raglan Rd signed Clytha). Turn S between the 2 garden centres. House ¼ m up lane on L. Use NP15 2JH for SatNav or What3words app: fond.haggle. like.* **Sun 26 Jan, Sat 1 Feb, Sun 30 Mar (11-4). Adm £5, chd free. Pre-booking essential, please phone 01291 691485 or email louiseviola@live.co.uk for information & booking. Tea, coffee & cake. Visits also by arrangement 1 Jan to 12 July for groups of 15 to 40.**
A relaxed three acre garden featuring snowdrops, daffodil walk, mature trees, walled parterre garden, mixed borders, lawns, ponds and shrubbery. Family friendly afternoon out, with children's activities, loads of space to run about, and scrumptious teas. Ground is uneven and mainly grass paths. Please contact owner with any concerns.

5 THE CAERPHILLY MINERS COMMUNITY CENTRE - CLIMATE CHANGE GARDEN
Watford Road, Caerphilly, CF83 1BJ. Caerphilly Miners Centre for the Community, www.caerphillyminerscentre.co.uk.
What3words app: often.hunter.occupy From Ystrad Mynach: A469 to Caerphilly follow A468/A469 then 1st exit onto St Cenydd Rd. From Newport: M4 J32 take A470 exit Cardiff(N)/Merthyr Tydfil A468 then A469 turn onto Watford Rd. **Sun 22 June (11-4). Adm £4, chd free. Tea, coffee & cake.**
A climate change garden promoting carbon reduction, biodiversity, health and wellbeing. There is a stumpery; wildlife pond; children's wildlife and play area in the wildflower meadow; a drought resistant rear garden; plus borders planted to demonstrate sustainability in all weathers, attract pollinators and local fauna; alongside a dahlia border which aims to show how easy it is to grow cut flowers in our climate. Wheelchair accessible paths at top of the front garden. Accessible slope to the rear garden.

GROUP OPENING

6 CHAPEL GARDENS
Abergavenny, NP7 7BE. Mary Barkham and Gary Smith. *Access via Avenue Rd, Abergavenny. On street parking only. Please follow signs to individual gardens that will guide you to the 3 gardens. Pentre Rd is very narrow so please don't drive down it. What3words app: crabmeat.contoured.implanted* **Sun 15 June (11-5). Combined adm £8, chd free. Pre-booking essential, please visit www.ngs. org.uk for information & booking. Tea, coffee & cake. Refreshments only served at Chapel Farm House.**

THE CHAIN, 90 CHAPEL ROAD
Sarah Price.

CHAPEL FARMHOUSE
Mary Barkham and Gary Smith.

ROCK VILLA, 111 CHAPEL ROAD
Veronica Ruth and Rod Cunningham.

These gardens are opening for the second time as Chapel Gardens and have been developed with the same ethos of encouraging wildlife and pollinators. The Chain: A two acre Victorian walled garden created by award winning garden designer, Sarah Price. With a wide range of habitats for wildlife to thrive, this garden is a must see. It has been gardened experimentally over the last ten years and was created especially for the beauty of nature and wildlife. Chapel Farm House: A stunning 1½ acre garden with an ancient orchard and wildlife pond. A wildflower meadow and new prairie garden are spectacular. Chapel Farm House also has formal front and courtyard gardens. Rock Villa: Developed over 25 years, this garden is organically cultivated. With purple beech hedges, roses and clematis, this garden is the very essence of a town garden. Some areas may not be accessible for those with mobility difficulties, such as the Secret Garden at The Chain.

GWENT 653

654 GWENT

7 CWM FARM
Coedypaen, Pontypool, NP4 0TB. Lee & Louisa Morgan. *2m from Usk towards the village of Coed y Paen. Take turning to Coed-y-paen from Llanbadoc or Llangybi follow yellow signs. From Cwmbran Crem take Tre-Herbert Ln towards Llangybi, turn to Coed-y-Paen. What3words app: tailwind.client.restore.* **Sun 1 June (11-5). Combined adm with Long Owl Barn £10, chd free. Tea, coffee & cake.**
Nestled in the Usk Valley, the garden of this C16 smallholding has been created over the last 10 years. Set in two acres, perennial borders and wildflower areas are contrasted against structural elements of topiary and hedging. A large pond and stream is surrounded by a wild meadow with mown paths and a Victorian style greenhouse stands within a vegetable garden. Most of the garden is suitable for a wheelchair.

8 GLEBE HOUSE
Llanvair Kilgeddin, Abergavenny, NP7 9BE. Mr & Mrs Murray Kerr. *5m SW of Abergavenny. Midway between Abergavenny & Usk on B4598. What3words app: fortunes.spreading.reeling.* **Sat 10, Sun 11 May (2-6). Adm £6, chd free. Home-made teas.**
Borders bursting with spring colour inc tulips, narcissi, and alliums. South facing terrace with wisteria and honeysuckle, decorative vegetable garden and orchard densely underplanted with succession of bulbs. Some topiary and formal hedging in 1½ acre garden in wonderful setting of Usk valley AONB. St Mary's church, Llanfair Kilgeddin will also be open to view famous Victorian scraffito murals. Some gravel and gently sloping lawns.

9 THE GROWING SPACE GARDEN
Mardy Park Resource Centre, Hereford Road, Mardy, Abergavenny, NP7 6HU. Jim Quinn. *The rear of Mardy Park Resource Centre. 1½ m N of centre of Abergavenny, on the Hereford Rd opp the Crown & Sceptre public house. What3words app: create.shudders.knees.* **Sun 13 July (10-4.30). Adm £5, chd free. Tea, coffee & cake.**
The gardens are laid out around disabled access paths, herbaceous borders, a prairie-style border, and fruit and vegetable beds. There is also a tropical border and large raised beds. We have two polytunnels and a small craft and carpentry workshop. The gardens are tended by a hard working team of volunteers of mixed ability and ages from 18 to 96. Adjoining parkland is perfect for a picnic. Woodland and the River Gavenny. Good access for wheelchair users. There is a hand rail as garden is on a slight slope.

10 14 GWERTHONOR LANE
Gilfach, Bargoed, CF81 8JT. Suzanne & Philip George. *8m N of Caerphilly. A469 to Bargoed, through the T-lights next to sch then L filter lane at next T-lights onto Cardiff Rd. 1st L into Gwerthonor Rd, 4th R into Gwerthonor Ln. What3words app: bless.input.famed.* **Sat 19, Sun 20 July (11-6). Adm £5, chd free. Light refreshments.**
The garden has a beautiful panoramic view of the Rhymney Valley. A real plantswoman's garden with over 800 varieties of perennials, annuals, bulbs, shrubs and trees. There are numerous rare, unusual and tropical plants combined with traditional and well loved favourites (many available for sale). A small wildlife pond adds to the tranquil feel of the garden.

11 HIGH GLANAU MANOR
Lydart, Monmouth, NP25 4AD. Mr & Mrs Hilary Gerrish, 01600 860005, helenagerrish@gmail.com, www.highglanaugardens.com. *4m SW of Monmouth. Situated on B4293 between Monmouth & Chepstow. Turn R into private road, ¼ m after Craig-y-Dorth turn on B4293.* **Sun 27 Apr (2-5.30). Adm £6, chd free. Home-made teas.**
Listed Arts and Crafts garden laid out by H Avray Tipping 100 years ago. Original features inc impressive stone terraces with far-reaching views over the Vale of Usk to Blorenge, Skirrid, Sugar Loaf and Brecon Beacons. Pergola, herbaceous borders, Edwardian glasshouse, rhododendrons, azaleas, tulips, orchard with wildflowers. Originally open for the National Garden Scheme in1927. Garden guidebook by owner, Helena Gerrish, available to purchase. Garden lovers cottage to rent.

12 HIGHFIELD FARM
Penperlleni, Goytre, NP4 0AA. Dr Roger & Mrs Jenny Lloyd, 01873 880030, jenny.plants@btinternet.com, highfieldfarmgarden.co.uk. *4m W of Usk, 6m S of Abergavenny. Turn off the A4042 at Goytre Arms, over railway bridge, bear L. Garden ½ m on R. From Usk off B4598, turn L after Chain Bridge, then L at Xrds. Garden 1m on L. What3words app: copper.single.forensic.* **Sun 15 June, Sun 13 July, Sun 10 Aug, Sun 14 Sept (11-4). Adm £7, chd free. Tea, coffee & cake. Visits also by arrangement 1 June to 28 Sept for groups of 5 to 40.**
Highfield Farm Garden is a celebration of plants. There are over 1400 cultivars, with many rarities, densely planted over three acres and set within the majestic Monmouthshire landscape. It offers an exuberant display across the seasons, providing an intimate, immersive experience with a diverse array of herbaceous, shrubs and trees. Huge sale of plants from the garden. Live music. Art sale. Access to almost all garden without steps.

13 HILLCREST
Waunborfa Road, Cefn Fforest, Blackwood, NP12 3LB. Mr M O'Leary, 01443 837029, olearymichael18@gmail.com. *3m W of Newbridge. B4254/A469: T-junc turn L to B'wood. At x-road take lane ahead. 1st on L at top of hill. A4048/B4251: cross Chartist Bridge, 2nd exit on 2 r'bouts. End of road turn L & immed R onto Waunborfa. What3words app: view.fall.brush* **Sat 24, Sun 25, Mon 26 May, Sun 6 July, Sun 3 Aug, Sun 7 Sept (11-6). Adm £5, chd free. Light refreshments. Visits also by arrangement Apr to Sept.**
A cascade of secluded gardens of distinct character over 1½ acres with a naturalistic approach in some areas. Magnificent, unusual trees, interesting shrubs, perennials and annuals. Choices at every turn, visitors are well rewarded as hidden delights and surprises are revealed. Well placed seats encourage a relaxed pace to fully appreciate the garden's treasures. Tulips in April, glorious blooms of the Chilean firebushes, handkerchief tree and cornuses in May and many trees in their autumnal splendour. Lowest parts of garden not accessible to wheelchairs.

4 LITTLE CAERLICYN
Caerlicyn Lane, Langstone, Newport, NP18 2JZ. Mrs Katharine Notley, 07793 122936, lc.flowerfarm@gmail.com, www.lcflowerfarm.co.uk. *Off the A48 from Newport towards Penhow/ Chepstow. Just over 2m from the Coldra r'about (M4 J24). Please follow yellow signs up Caerlicken Ln. What3words app: builds.encloses. tickling.* **Sat 28, Sun 29 June (11-4). Adm £5, chd free. Home-made teas.** Visits also by arrangement for groups of 6 to 15.
Small flower farm and gardens around renovated Tudor cottage and barn, situated on a steep hillside. Four distinct areas, perennials, roses, grape vines and wildflower areas and an ancient mulberry tree plus bees and woodland walk. Protecting and promoting of wildlife is central to this garden whose owners follow a no dig approach. Amazing views over the Severn Estuary.

6 LONG OWL BARN
Coedypaen, Pontypool, NP4 0TB. Mike & Tina Booth, www.instagram.com/michaelbooth1963. *2m W of Usk, 1m from Llandegveth reservoir. Take turning to Coed-y-paen from Llanbadoc or Llangybi follow yellow signs. From Cwmbran Crem take Tre-Herbert Ln towards Llangybi, turn to Coed-y-Paen. What3words app: crispier.racing. achieving.* **Sun 1 June (11-5). Combined adm with Cwm Farm £10, chd free. Tea, coffee & cake.**
In a rural setting with extensive views, there are meandering paths, colourful borders and wildlife areas with plenty to explore in a little over an acre. Small orchard, ponds, a vegetable plot and greenhouse. Extensive perennial beds full of colour. Sloping ground makes some areas inaccessible. Uneven steps and loose surface paths throughout.

7 LONGHOUSE FARM
Penrhos, Raglan, NP15 2DE. Mr & Mrs M H C Anderson. *Midway between Monmouth & Abergavenny. 4m from Raglan. Off Old Raglan/ Abergavenny rd signed Clytha. At Bryngwyn/Great Oak Xrds turn towards Great Oak - follow yellow NGS signs from red phone box down narrow lane. What3words app: cake. audibly.oxidation.* **Sat 3, Sun 4 May (2-5.30). Adm £6, chd free. Home-made teas.**
Spacious two acre country garden with colourful borders, interesting trees, shrubs and productive vegetable garden. Discover the natural pond, house and barns covered with roses and vines. A roundabout with un-named ancient Perry Pear tree surrounded by bulbs and seasonal plants. Woodland walk around a series of spring fed ponds with wonderful views of hidden parts of Monmouthshire.

5 LLANOVER
Abergavenny, NP7 9EF. Mr & Mrs M R Murray, 07753 423635, elizabeth@llanover.com, www.llanovergarden.co.uk. *4m S of Abergavenny, 15m N of Newport, 20m SW Hereford. Garden is off the A4042 in Llanover, opp the bus stop. What3words app: flash.ready.limits.* **Sun 30 Mar (2-5). Adm £8, chd free. Home-made teas.** Visits also by arrangement May to Oct.
Benjamin Waddington, the direct ancestor of the current owners, purchased the house and land in 1792. Subsequently he created a series of ponds, cascades and rills which form the backbone of the 15 acre garden as the stream winds its way from its source in the Black Mountains to the River Usk. There are herbaceous borders, a drive lined with *Narcissi*, spring bulbs, wildflowers, a water garden, champion trees and two arboreta. The house (not open) is the birthplace of Augusta Waddington, Lady Llanover, C19 patriot, supporter of the Welsh language and traditions. Gravel and grass paths and lawns. No disabled WC.

Neuadd Stone Barn

GROUP OPENING

18 MONMOUTH GARDENS
Monnow Street, Monmouth, NP25 3EN. Central Monmouth. Parking at Monnow St Car Park. What3words app: rejoin.shape.hindering. Please follow signage throughout Monmouth to the gardens. **Sun 18 May (11.30-5.30). Combined adm £10, chd free. Home-made teas at North Parade House and St Johns.**

CORNWALL HOUSE, 58 MONNOW STREET
Jane Harvey and John Wheelock. www.historichouses.org/house/cornwall-house/visit.

11 THE GARDENS
Mrs Cheryl Cummings, www.cherylcummingswildgardenwriting.co.uk.
&

THE NELSON GARDEN
The Nelson Garden Monmouth, www.nelsongarden.org.uk.

NORTH PARADE HOUSE
Tim Haynes & Lisa O'Neill.

ST JOHNS
Simon & Hilary Hargreaves.

Five very different town gardens open under the banner of Monmouth Gardens. The Nelson Garden dates back to Roman times, and as the name suggests has links with Lord Nelson. St Johns, in Glendower St is a charming walled garden which has undergone extensive restoration with a sunken central lawn and deep herbaceous borders. Entrance to both these gardens is via Chippenham Fields. Cornwall House opens with the group for the second time this year. The beautiful walled garden and productive kitchen garden date from the C17. North Parade House is a hidden gem with a surprisingly large and secluded walled garden with mature specimen trees, herbaceous borders and a kitchen garden. Another garden opening for the second time this year is a re-wilding project by garden designer Cheryl Cummings. Range of different gardening styles in town gardens. Plant sales at the Nelson Garden. Tickets available at each garden along with maps to aid visitors. Some gardens may not be accessed by wheelchair users due to steps at the entrances.

19 NEUADD STONE BARN
Church Road, Gilwern, Abergavenny, NP7 0HF. Mrs Katherine Franklin, www.brambleandbombus.co.uk. Out of Gilwern past Llanelly Church. From the middle of Gilwern, follow Church Rd, past the Church on the R and follow the yellow signs. What3words app: compress.envelope.sparrows. **Sun 17 Aug (11-5). Adm £5, chd free. Home-made teas.**
Recently established flower farm which is part of a working farm. The site is in an AONB and has breathtaking views of the three hills surrounding Abergavenny. A huge array of perennial and annual flowers are grown for cutting and sale.

20 OLD LLANGATTOCK FARM
Llangattock Vibon-Avel, Monmouth, NP25 5NG. Dr Cherry Taylor, www.cherrysnodiggarden.co.uk. 4m W of Monmouth. From Monmouth, take the B4233 towards the Hendre. Continue through the S-bend and on for a few miles, turning R opp post box. Proceed up lane and follow the yellow signs to the garden. What3words app: difficult.tunes.lush. **Sun 25 May (2-5). Adm £6, chd free. Home-made teas.**
The 10 year old 1½ acre garden is no dig, organic, wildlife-friendly and constantly evolving. There are copious flower beds, vegetable gardens, a large pond, greenhouses, a polytunnel, substantial herb terraces, meadows and an orchard. There are many wildlife features like logs piles and dead hedges, plus plenty of seating and far-reaching views. Steps, slopes, uneven gravel and woodchip paths. Garden is evolving all the time and has changed considerably since opening in 2019. Used multiple times by Charles Dowding and other garden influencers to run courses.

21 THE OLD VICARAGE
Penrhos, Raglan, Usk, NP15 2LE. Mrs Georgina Herrmann. 3m N of Raglan. From A449 take Raglan exit, join A40 & move immed into R lane & turn R across dual carriageway. Follow yellow NGS signs. What3words app: salad.tungsten.crucially. **Sun 20 Apr (2-5.30). Adm £5, chd free. Light refreshments.**
This will be our 20th garden opening for the National Garden Scheme, and probably our last, so please come and visit. The emphasis in 2025 will be our trees of many varieties and ages, as well as some fine topiary, setting off the newly painted Victorian vicarage (1867) with its wonderful views. There are shrubs, spring flowers, a parterre, kitchen garden, wildlife areas and ponds.

22 PARK HOUSE
School Lane, Itton, Chepstow, NP16 6BZ. Professor Bruce & Dr Cynthia Matthews. From M48 take A466 Tintern. At 2nd r'about turn L B4293. After blue sign Itton turn R Park House is at end of lane. Parking 200 metres before house. From Devauden B4293 1st L in Itton. **Sat 26 Apr (10-5). Adm £5, chd free.**
Approximately one acre garden with large vegetable areas and many mature trees, rhododendrons, azaleas, camellias in a woodland setting. Bordering on Chepstow Park Wood. Magnificent views over open country.

23 ROCKFIELD PARK
Rockfield, Monmouth, NP25 5QB. Mark & Melanie Molyneux, 07803 952027, melmolyneux@yahoo.com. On arriving in Rockfield village from Monmouth, turn R by phone box. After approx 400yds, church on L. Entrance to Rockfield Park on R, opp church, via private bridge over river. What3words app: blueberry.cabin.bind. **Sat 7, Sun 8 June (10.30-4). Adm £7, chd free. Tea, coffee & cake on the terrace.**
Visits also by arrangement 30 Apr to 31 July for groups of 8 to 30.
Rockfield Park dates from C17 and is situated in the heart of the Monmouthshire countryside on the banks of the River Monnow. The extensive grounds comprise formal gardens, meadows and orchard, complemented by riverside and woodland walks. Possible to picnic on riverside walks. Main part of gardens can be accessed by wheelchair but not steep garden leading down to river.

24 TROSTREY LODGE
Bettws Newydd, Usk, NP15 1JT. Frances Pemberton, trostrey@googlemail.com. 4m W of Raglan. 7m E of Abergavenny. Off old A40 (B4598) Abergavenny - Raglan. 1m S of Clytha Gates & 1½ m N of Bettws Newydd. What3words app: blip.ants.operated. **Visits by arrangement 1 May to 1 Sept for groups of 8 to 24. Tea, coffee & cake.**

GWENT

Wander over the ha-ha and through the C18 listed iron gate which leads to the tall tulip tree, you will find a delightful walled garden full of colour and imagination. Poppies, herbs, vines, roses and honeysuckle thread through the box topiary all attractive to bees and insect life. Home artworks and packets of flower seeds available, all to help the bees.

25 THE TUMP
Penallt, Monmouth,
NP25 4AQ. Mr Doug and Mrs Sue Hilton, 07899 995822, bucklandlake@hotmail.com. *3m S of Monmouth Town. From A40 take B4293 in 3½ m turn L for Narth and Whitebrook. Follow signs to L at. Same turn is 1m N of Trellech on B4293 on R. What3words app: torn.measuring.edge.* **Visits by arrangement 14 June to 22 June for groups of up to 12. Adm £5, chd free. Light refreshments.**
Nine acres of mixed habitat, sloping meadows surrounded by mature trees, views, mown paths, orchard areas, two large ponds, stream, stone circle and exhibition of wildlife and wildflower paintings in art studio. Four years into rewilding from grazing land by quadruple gold award gardening for wildlife winners. Emphasising the importance of building up the understory of grassland and mixed habitat.

26 TY ISAF FARM
Pandy Mawr Road, Bedwas, Caerphilly, CF83 8EQ. Mrs Linda Davies, 07429 529161. *3m N of the centre of Caerphilly. From A468 at Caerphilly head towards Bedwas & then Pandy-Mawr Rd. Follow NGS yellow signs. The postcode will take SatNav users to the area, then follow the yellow signs. What3words app: clash.swims.down* **Sat 26, Sun 27 July (11-4). Adm £5, chd free. Light refreshments.**
This garden, on a working farm, surrounds the Grade II listed sub-medieval farmhouse and barn. The garden is being revitalised with the renovation of beds and development of areas such as the wildlife pond. The ancient yew is a magnificent feature as are the stone walls surrounding areas of the garden. A naturalistic approach to planting and spectacular far-reaching views.

GROUP OPENING

27 USK OPEN GARDENS
Maryport Street, Usk, NP15 1BH. www.uskopengardens.uk. *Main car park postcode is NP15 1AD. From M4 J24 take A449 for 8m N to Usk exit. Signposts to free parking around town. Blue badge parking in main car parks. Map of gardens provided with ticket.* **Sat 28, Sun 29 June (10-5). Combined adm £10, chd free. Donation to local charities.**
Usk's floral public displays are a wonderful backdrop to the gardens. Around 10 to 15 private gardens opening. Gardeners' Market with interesting plants. Lovely day out for all the family with lots of places to eat and drink inc places to picnic. Wheelchair accessible gardens and gardens are noted on map. Available from the ticket desks at the free car park at Usk Memorial Hall (NP15 1AD).

28 WENALLT ISAF
Twyn Wenallt, Gilwern, Abergavenny, NP7 0HP. Tim & Debbie Field, 07885 195304, wenalltisaf@gmail.com. *3m W of Abergavenny. Between Abergavenny & Brynmawr. Leave the A465 at Gilwern & follow yellow NGS signs through the village. Do not follow SatNav. What3words app: sensibly.gone.connects.* **Sun 1 June (2-6). Adm £6, chd free. Tea, coffee & cake. Home-made cakes inc gluten and lactose free. Visits also by arrangement May to Oct for groups of 8+. Refreshments and guided talk by the owner inc in adm.**
A hidden gem of nearly three acres owner designed in sympathy with its surroundings and the challenges of being 650ft up on a north facing hillside. Far-reaching views of the magnificent Black Mountains, mature trees, rhododendrons, viburnum, spectacular hydrangeas, herbaceous borders, vegetable garden, small polytunnel, orchard, chickens, bees. Child friendly with plenty of space to run about.

29 NEW WOODBINE HOUSE
Monmouth Road, Usk, NP15 1QY. Mr Jonathan Stephens FLS. *Off Cwrt Bryn, Derwen. From Usk, take the Monmouth Rd. At t-lights take L fork signed Gwehelog. After the one-way, in 50yds turn R into Cwrt Bryn Derwen. Kerbside parking on Monmouth Rd. What3words app: dairy.went.requiring.* **Sun 20 July (11-5.30). Adm £5, chd free. Tea.**
A hidden naturalistic garden extending to about 2½ acres. Woodland walks with quirky features at every turn. A lake, dug and landscaped by the owners with an island, a boathouse, well established gunnera, and ferns. Quite an amazing area developed over a number of years, a children's paradise, not a traditional garden.

30 ♦ WYNDCLIFFE COURT
St Arvans, NP16 6EY. Mr & Mrs Anthony Clay, 07710 138972, sarah@wyndcliffecourt.com, www.wyndcliffecourt.com. *3m N of Chepstow. Off A466, turn at Wyndcliffe signpost coming from the Chepstow direction. What3words app: merely.piano.healers.* **For NGS: Fri 6, Sat 7 June (2-5). Adm £10, chd free. Pre-booking essential, please visit www.ngs.org.uk for information & booking. Home-made teas.** For other opening times and information, please phone, email or visit garden website.
Exceptional and unaltered garden designed by H. Avray Tipping in 1922. Explore the Arts and Crafts 'Italianate' style garden inc stone summerhouse, terracing and ponds. Yew hedging and topiary, sunken garden, rose garden, bowling green and woodland. Walled garden new in 2023 for Charles III coronation. Renaissance mural and vine shaded arbour. Rose garden designed by Sarah Price.

31 Y BWTHYN
Pencroesoped, Llanover, Abergavenny, NP7 9EL. Jacqui & David Warren, 01873 880031, warrens.ybwthyn@gmail.com. *6m S of Abergavenny, just outside Llanover. What3words app: admire.blogs.layover.* **Visits by arrangement 2 Aug to 10 Aug for groups of 10 to 30. Adm inc refreshments and garden tour by the owner. Adm £12. Home-made teas.**
There's plenty to see in this beautiful 1½ acre garden, with sweeping vistas across the garden and into the countryside beyond. Colourful mixed borders, gravel garden, lawns, pond and bog garden, kitchen garden and greenhouse, meadow areas and a magnificent veteran oak. Small house history and art exhibitions too. Most garden routes are step-free. Some grass slopes and narrow gravel paths. Sorry, no wheelchair access to the WC.

GWYNEDD & ANGLESEY
GWYNEDD A MÔN

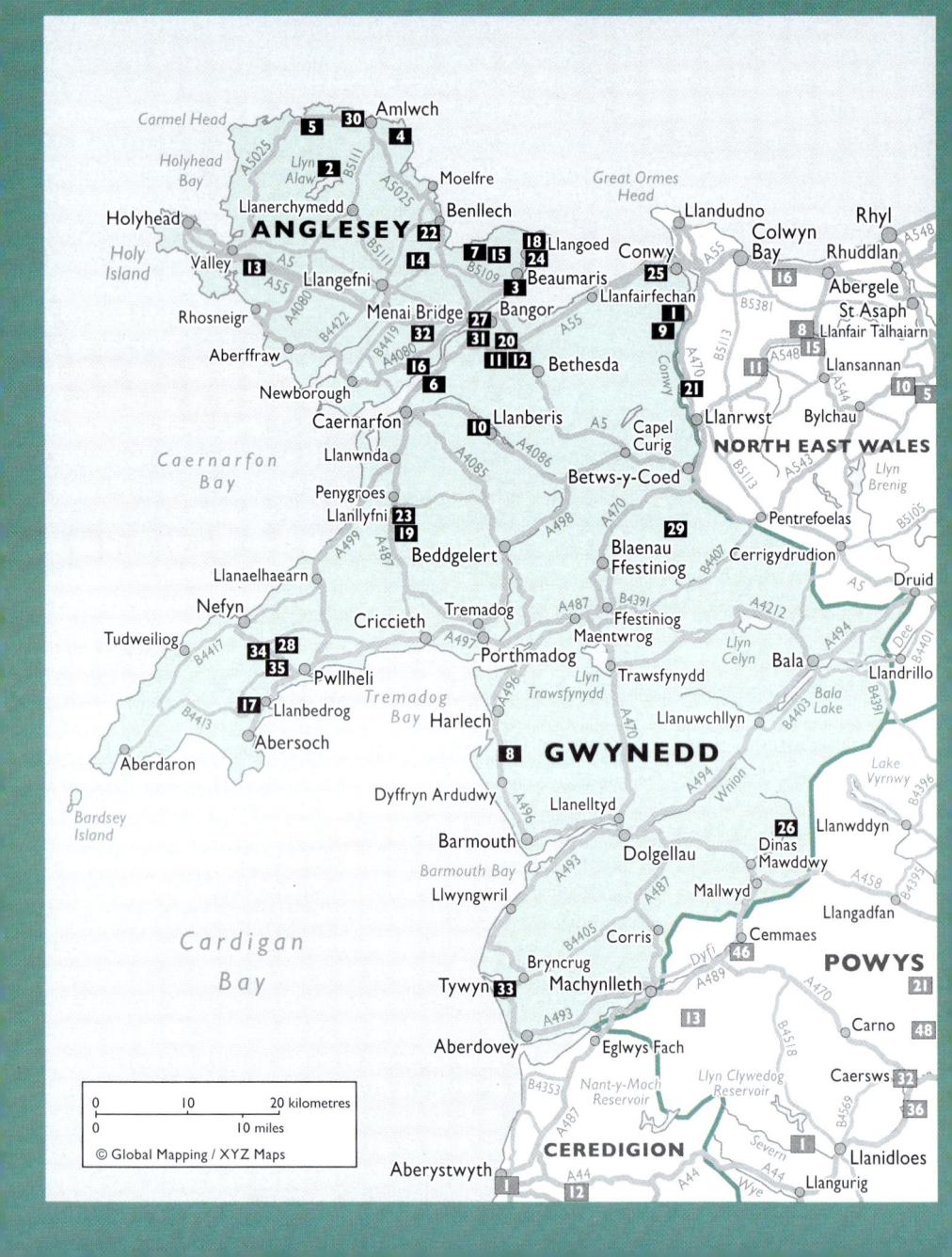

VOLUNTEERS

County Organiser
Kay Laurie
07971 083361
kay.laurie@ngs.org.uk

Heather Broughton
07747 737237
heather.broughton@ngs.org.uk

County Treasurer
Chris Clark
07760 174154
chris.clark@ngs.org.uk

Publicity
Position vacant

Booklet Co-Ordinator
Heather Broughton
(as above)

Photographer
Gary Phillips
07742 892743
gaphll@aol.com

Social Media
Katie Holmes
07552 957009
katie.holmes@ngs.org.uk

Assistant County Organisers
Hazel Bond
07378 844295
hazelcaenewydd@gmail.com

Janet Jones
01758 740296
janetcoron@hotmail.co.uk

Delia Lanceley
01286 650517
delia@lanceley.com

@gwyneddandangleseyngs
@ngs.gwyneddandanglesey

OPENING DATES

All entries subject to change.
For latest information check
www.ngs.org.uk

Map locator numbers are shown to the right of each garden name.

April

Sunday 27th
Maenan Hall   21

Wednesday 30th
◆ Plas Cadnant Hidden Gardens   27

May

Saturday 3rd
Llanidan Hall   16

Sunday 4th
Sunningdale   30

Sunday 11th
Glan Llyn   10

Saturday 17th
NEW Plas Pont y Crybin   28

Sunday 18th
Cyplau   8
Tyn Y Pant   34

Sunday 25th
Gwaelod Mawr   13
NEW Y Felin Rhyd Hir   35

June

Saturday 14th
NEW Bedlwyn   1
◆ Crûg Farm   6
Ty Cadfan Sant   33

Sunday 15th
◆ Pensychnant   25
Ty Cadfan Sant   33

Saturday 21st
Llanidan Hall   16
Llwydiarth   17
NEW Llys Ifor   19
NEW Nant Noddfa   23

Sunday 22nd
Cyplau   8
Llwydiarth   17

Saturday 28th
Mynydd, Cors Goch   22

July

Saturday 5th
Llanidan Hall   16

Saturday 12th
Llanddona Village Gardens   15

Sunday 13th
◆ Pensychnant   25
Treborth Botanic Garden, Bangor University   31

Saturday 19th
Caswallon   4
Sunningdale   30

Sunday 20th
Glan Llyn   10

Sunday 27th
Maenan Hall   21
Tyn Y Pant   34

August

Sunday 3rd
NEW Plas Pont y Crybin   28

Sunday 17th
NEW The Granary   11
NEW Growing for Change Organic Market Garden   12

Sunday 31st
Llwyn Onn   18
The Old School   24

September

Saturday 6th
NEW Castle Court   3
NEW Y Felin Rhyd Hir   35

Sunday 7th
Gwenfro Uchaf   14
◆ Plannwch y Plas   26

660 GWYNEDD & ANGLESEY

By Arrangement

Arrange a personalised garden visit with your club, or group of friends, on a date to suit you. See individual garden entries for full details.

Cae Newydd	2
NEW Cuddfan	7
Gilfach	9
Gwenfro Uchaf	14
Llwydiarth	17
Llys-y-Gwynt	20
Plasglasgwm	29
Sunningdale	30
Trefnant Bach	32
Ty Cadfan Sant	33
Tyn Y Pant	34
NEW Y Felin Rhyd Hir	35

THE GARDENS

1 NEW BEDLWYN
Tyn-Y-Groes, Conwy, LL32 8SR. Mr Stan & Mrs Vivien Watson-Jones. *2m S of Conwy. B5106 S from Conwy castle for 2m. Pass the Groes hotel on your R & sign for Hen Efail on your L. From Llanrwst: N on the A470 & turn L for Tal-y-Cafn. Travel for 1m then turn R at Red Lion.* **Sat 14 June (11-4). Adm £4, chd free. Home-made teas.**
Quiet location with wildlife in mind. Stunning views to the Carneddau Mountains. Cottage garden with plenty of seating to enjoy the garden or to bird watch. An acre field of woodland and meadow walks which is a haven for bees. Parking in field on dry days or top of road. Picnic tables in the field. Wheelchair access to most of the garden.
&♿ 🐕 ❀ ☕ 🔊

2 CAE NEWYDD
Rhosgoch, Amlwch, LL66 0BG. Hazel & Nigel Bond, 07378 844295, nigel@cae-newydd.co.uk. *3m SW of Amlwch. A5025 from Benllech to Amlwch, follow signs for leisure centre & Lastra Farm. Follow yellow NGS signs (approx 3m), car park on L.* **Visits by arrangement 14 Feb to 30 Sept. Small coaches only due to access. Adm £5, chd free. Tea, coffee & cake. Refreshments may be self serve.**
An informal country garden of 2½ acres which blends seamlessly into the open landscape with stunning views of Snowdonia and Llyn Alaw. Variety of shrubs, trees and herbaceous areas, large wildlife pond, polytunnel, greenhouses. Collections of fuchsia, pelargonium, cacti and succulents. An emphasis on gardening for wildlife throughout the garden, lots of seating to enjoy this peaceful space. Hay meadow with cut paths, beehives, visit in February and March to see snowdrops and hellebores. Garden area closest to house suitable for wheelchairs.
♿ 🐕 ❀ ☕ 🔊

3 NEW CASTLE COURT
Beaumaris, LL58 8AL. Janine and Stephen Walters. *Castle Court is next to Beaumaris Castle in town centre. Public parking on The Green. No parking at the garden.* **Sat 6 Sept (11-4). Adm £5. Tea, coffee & cake in The Serenity Garden, at St. Mary's Church, LL58 8AA.**
Castle Court is a 200+ year old walled garden set in a plot of approximately ⅓ acre. It is immediately adjacent to Beaumaris Castle in the beautiful town of Beaumaris. Entrance is at the rear of the garden from a contemporary double garage. A large lawn opens onto large herbaceous borders, a mini "Wood", hosta garden, a "Hedge Shed" with roof platform and a front courtyard. An area of calm and surprising privacy. The Serenity Garden, a quiet oasis in the middle of Beaumaris. Ancient church open, garden recently adopted by community volunteers.
♿ 🐕 ❀ ☕ 🔊

4 CASWALLON
Llaneilian, Amlwch, LL68 9NN. Julian & Gillian Sandbach. *Mynydd Eilian. From the A5025 take the turning to Pengorffwysfa near Amlwch, the garden will be signed from this village. It is a single track lane. Plenty of parking.* **Sat 19 July (10-4.30). Adm £5, chd free. Home-made teas.**
In 2018 we bought Caswallon, house and garden in complete need of renovation. House now finished our energy is dedicated to restoring the large historic gardens. Under years of undergrowth we have discovered formal gardens, small woodland dells, a walled garden, an ancient well, meandering paths, crumbling dry stone walls, steps carved into bedrock, everyday is an adventure, always more to discover.
☕ 🔊

5 NEW CESTYLL
Cemaes Bay, LL67 0AA. Nuclear Decommissioning Authority. *1½m W of Cemaes Bay. Parking at Wylfa Power Stn Visitors Centre. Accessible off of the A5025. Shuttle bus or footpath walk to garden entrance. What3words app: gratuity. stretch.symphonic.* **Please check the National Garden Scheme website for more openings. Adm by donation. Light refreshments at Wylfa Power Station Visitor Centre.**
Cestyll Garden lies just along the coast from the Wylfa nuclear site, overlooking Porth y Felin between Cemaes and Cemlyn Bays. Created in 1922 it has been cared for since 1983 by Wylfa/ Nuclear Decommissioning Authority. Traversed by the Afon Cafnan and divided by streams and bridges, it is a rocky garden featuring a large variety of plants, some original planting.
🐕 ☕ 🔊

6 ◆ CRÛG FARM
Griffiths Crossing, Caernarfon, LL55 1TU. Bleddyn & Sue Wynn-Jones, 01248 670232, sue@crug-farm.co.uk, www.crug-farm.co.uk. *2m NE of Caernarfon. Main A487 Caernarfon to Bangor road. Do not join new by-pass At R'about follow signs for local traffic. Brown tourist sign Crûg Farm Plants.* **For NGS: Sat 14 June (11-4). Adm £5, chd free. Tea, coffee & cake. For other opening times and information, please phone, email or visit garden website.**
Renowned plant collectors' garden of three acres which are grounds to old country house (not open). Explore different areas inc walled, woodland and Crûg gardens which are filled with unusual and shade loving plants and trees, many not seen in cultivation before. Chelsea Gold Medallists and winners of the President's Award. Partial wheelchair access.
♿ ❀ ☕ 🔊

7 NEW CUDDFAN
Llanddona, Beaumaris, LL58 8TR. Mrs Jacquie Blakeley, 07836 549361, jacqueline.blakeley@btinternet.com. *What3words app: echo.animate.lilac. Enter Llanddona from Beaumaris, turn L signposted Pentraeth. Head towards Wern y Wylan (single track lane with passing places). After 1m enter Wern y Wylan. After ⅕m Cuddfan is on R.* **Visits by arrangement Apr to Oct for groups of up to 10. Adm £8, inc**

refreshments. Chd, free.
Cuddfan, ('Hideway' in English) a garden in the Japanese style features a range of mature cloud pruned pine, acer, ginko and other trees with rocks, ponds and meandering paths in the Japanese tradition. The design with its constrained palette has colour bursts from azaleas in season. It connects with nature incorporating symbolic Japanese aesthetics highlighting the natural landscape.

8 CYPLAU
Llanbedr, LL45 2ND.
Ms Jacqueline Gilleland. *7m NW Barmouth. From Barmouth A496 direct to Llanbedr. From Harlech 3m on A496 to Llanbedr.* **Sun 18 May, Sun 22 June (12-4). Adm £5, chd free.** Home-made teas.
Under an acre of intensely planted hillside garden created over 24 years. Twisting pathways with steps lead to small garden areas. Inc topiary, cloud pruned yew, tsunami heather hedge, box and *Ilex crenata*. Multi stemmed and shaped shrubs, ornaments and sculptures. Superb sea views in hillside garden. Vegetable garden with fruits. This garden is a way of living to encourage nature and enjoy peace. Relax and listen to a choir in the garden.

9 GILFACH
Rowen, Conwy, LL32 8TS.
James & Isoline Greenhalgh, isolinegreenhalgh@btinternet.com. *4m S of Conwy. At Xrds 100yds E of Rowen S towards Llanrwst, past Rowen Sch on L, turn up 2nd drive on L.* **Visits by arrangement 20 Apr to 31 Aug. Adm £4, chd free. Refreshments to be discussed when booking.**
An acre of country garden on south facing slope with magnificent views of the River Conwy and mountains; set in 35 acres of farm and woodland. Collection of mature shrubs is added to yearly; woodland garden, herbaceous border and small pool. Spectacular panoramic view of the Conwy Valley and the mountain range of the Carneddau.

10 GLAN LLYN
Llanberis, Caernarfon, LL55 4EL.
Mr Bob Stevens. *On A4086, ½ m from Llanberis village. Next door to the Gallt y Glyn Hotel (Pizza & Pint Restaurant) opp DMM factory.* **Sun 11 May, Sun 20 July (11-4). Adm £5, chd free. Tea, coffee & cake.**
A three acre woodland edge garden inc two acres of woodland, wildlife ponds, stream, wildflower area, raised sphagnum bog garden, two green roofs, four glasshouses for cacti, succulents and geophytes. Australasian and South African beds, sand bed, many unusual trees, shrubs and herbaceous perennials. The garden is on fairly steep sloping ground. Regret, no wheelchair access to the woodland.

11 NEW THE GRANARY
Felin Hen Road, Bangor, LL57 4BB. Dr Maya Nedeva. *Located between Bangor and Tregarth. Leave A55 at J11 & take A4424 (services). Turn L onto B4409. Garden on L. Drop off only at garden. Parking at Moelyci, a 10-15 mins walk down Lon Las Ogwen.* **Sun 17 Aug (11-4). Adm £5, chd free. Tea, coffee & cake. Open nearby Growing for Change Organic Market Garden.**
A 2½ acres garden with a lot of rare and unusual plants from around the world, many grown from seed with a special interest in Australasian and xeric plants. This would not be a Welsh garden without many ferns, inc tree ferns. Discover a large pond in the front garden and many palms, yuccas and a rockery in the back garden. Limited wheelchair access as part of the garden is on a slope.

Plas Pont y Crybin

12 NEW GROWING FOR CHANGE ORGANIC MARKET GARDEN

Felin Hen Road, Tregarth, Bangor, LL57 4BB. Mr Paul Gordon-Roberts, www.facebook.com/GrowingForChangeMaesg. *4m from Bangor. At A55 Junc11 follow the signs for services. Drive past services & continue for ½ m passing under a green footbridge. Take next L & continue for 100 metres. Entrance on R.* **Sun 17 Aug (11-4). Adm by donation. Home-made teas at The Granary garden, access via Lon Las Ogwen. Open nearby The Granary.**
Organic Market Garden with delicious, seasonal produce. Through sharing the wonder and joy of nurturing plants in a supportive environment, people in recovery from substance abuse or mental health issues develop new skills with Growing for Change during their recovery journey. Their produce is so good they supply local restaurants. Our production follows a distinct process, with dedicated araes for seed sowing, propagation, washing and packing. Lunches and savouries available at Blas Lon Las cafe by market garden. Wheelchair access to polytunnels and some of garden.

13 GWAELOD MAWR

Caergeiliog, LL65 3YL. Tricia Coates. *6m E of Holyhead. ½ m E of Caergeiliog. From A55 J4. R'about 2nd exit signed Caergeiliog. 300yds, Gwaelod Mawr is 1st house on L.* **Sun 25 May (11-4). Adm £5, chd free. Home-made teas.**
A two acre garden created by owners over 30 years with lake, large rock outcrops and palm tree area. Spanish style patio and wonderful laburnum arch in May which leads to sunken garden and wooden bridge over lily pond with fountain and waterfall. Peaceful Chinese orientated garden offering contemplation. Separate Koi carp pond. Abundant seating throughout. Garden is mainly flat, with gravel and stone paths. No wheelchair access to sunken lily pond area.

14 GWENFRO UCHAF

Lon Gwenfro, Talwrn, Llangefni, LL77 8JD. Ms Karen Hillyer, gwenfrouchaf@yahoo.com. *4m NE from Llangefni towards Llanbedrgoch and Red Wharf Bay.* *From Bridge take A5025 towards Amlwch; go through Pentraeth, turn L to Llanbedrgoch after layby; Take 2nd L onto Lon Gwenfro, follow signs for 1m. Limited parking.* **Sun 7 Sept (11-5). Adm £5, chd free. Light refreshments inc home-made soup, teas and cakes using garden produce. Gluten and dairy free options available. Visits also by arrangement 12 Apr to 15 June for groups of up to 10.**
Discover two ½ acres of formal and informal areas with encroaching nature and great views; with wild meadow walks, trees, hedgerows and stream; a kitchen garden, lean-to greenhouse, orchard and apiary, divided by hedges and stonewall terracing with steps. All paths are mown, with one slate path down slope to house and lawn, teas, seating and fire pit. Food and nature focused. A collection of 15 apple and pear tree varieties. Honey from the apiary for sale and possibly other garden produce (herbs, juice, fruit) depending on availability. Parking may be restricted.

GROUP OPENING

15 LLANDDONA VILLAGE GARDENS

Beaumaris, LL58 8TU. Gardens of Llanddona Residents. *3m from Beaumaris. From Beaumaris take B5109 for 1m turn R at T-junc. 2 m to Llanddona.* **Sat 12 July (11-4). Combined adm £5, chd free. Home-made teas will be served all day at Cefn Farm and Y-Gilsach gardens. Owain Glyndwr Pub (Pre-booking for lunch advised 01248 810710).**
Llandonna, one of the highest villages in Anglesey sits between Red Wharf Bay and the Menai Strait. Some of the gardens need shelter from strong winds but have a sunny location with spectacular views. The gardens often have rocky outcrops, but many plants do well. Llanddona has a variety of gardens, from small to quite large with different gardening styles. Drop in to see a smallholding with some carefully tended vegetables, Jacob's sheep and a working pottery studio; rocky garden with a wildlife area and views towards Holyhead mountain; cottage gardens; a colourful garden with pots and greenhouse and former chapel built c. 1840 with a large garden in the early stages of restoration. Most will be within a short walk of each other. Regret, no dogs in some gardens due to livestock. The more accessible gardens will be shown on the map provided on the day.

16 LLANIDAN HALL

Brynsiencyn, Llanfairpwllgwyngyll, LL61 6HJ. V Marchant. *5m E of Llanfair Pwll. From LlanfairPG follow A4080 towards Brynsiencyn for 4m. After Hooton's farm shop on R take next L, follow lane to gardens.* **Sat 3 May, Sat 21 June, Sat 5 July (10-4). Adm £6, chd free. Donation to RSPCA.**
Walled garden of 1¾ acres. Physic and herb gardens, ornamental vegetable garden, herbaceous borders, water features, spring bulb display, many varieties of old roses in June and well established summer perennials. Sheep, rabbits and hens to see. Children must be kept under supervision. Llanidan Old Church open for viewing. Regret, no dogs or refreshments. Hard gravel paths and gentle slopes.

17 LLWYDIARTH

Mynytho, Pwllheli, LL53 7RW. David & Anne Mitchell, 07973 968207, anne@wishawcountrysports.com. *Garden on main road through Mynytho village. 5½ m from Pwllheli 3½ m from Abersoch.* **Sat 21, Sun 22 June (12-5). Adm £5, chd free. Home-made teas. Visits also by arrangement 19 May to 30 Sept for groups of 6 to 30.**
Just four years ago this garden was an overgrown field, but now with hedges, trees, shrubs, grasses, perennials and roses planted, it is already developing character and interest. A large wildlife pond, filled with aquatic plants and surrounded with tons of sandstone, dug from the field itself, now makes a stunning rockery. There is a lush green Mediterranean style back yard.

18 LLWYN ONN

Penmon Village, Beaumaris, LL58 8SG. Paul Richardson & Pauline Williams, *3m NE of Beaumaris. Pass Beaumaris Castle on coast road. After 1.7m turn R to Penmon and follow yellow signs.* **Sun 31 Aug (11-4). Combined adm with The Old School £5, chd free. Tea, coffee & cake.**

The garden benefits from coastal and mountain views, and inc some three acres of deciduous woodland, originally planted by a local estate owner in the C19, mostly with beech. We have protected the remaining old trees, encouraged natural regeneration, and enriched the woodland with some plantings. The garden we created inc lawns, herbaceous borders, and a small wildlife pond.
&))

19 NEW **LLYS IFOR**
Ffordd Pont Lloc, Nebo, Caernarfon, LL54 6EL.
June Burrough,
www.juneburrough.co.uk. *Come to the village square, & Ffordd Pont Lloc is by the bus stop opp the sch. We are 2nd house on the R. What3words app: shuttled. jugs.airship.* **Sat 21 June (11-4). Combined adm with Nant Noddfa £5, chd free. Home-made teas.** Set in beautiful countryside, Llys Ifor is a landscaped garden with glades, seated areas, artwork, and a variety of vegetables, trees and flowers. With views of Snowdonia, it is bordered by a small river. In nine years, the two acres of fields has transformed into a mix of vegetable and flower garden, wildlife woodland havens, a polytunnel, and a pond - all connected by slate paths. Combination of wildlife haven, pond, vegetables and medicinal and edible herbs.
🐕 ✼ 🍵))

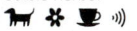

20 **LLYS-Y-GWYNT**
Pentir Road, Llandygai, Bangor, LL57 4BG. Jennifer Rickards, 07799 893418,
mjrickards@gmail.com. *3m S of Bangor. 300yds from Llandygai r'about at J11, A5 & A55, just off A4244. Follow signs for services (Gwasanaethau). Turn off at No Through Rd sign, 50yds beyond. Do not use SatNav.* **Visits by arrangement. Adm £5, chd free. Tea, coffee & cake.**
Interesting, harmonious and very varied two acre garden inc magnificent views of Snowdonia. An exposed site inc Bronze Age burial cairn. Winding paths, varied levels planted to create shelter, year-round interest, microclimates and varied rooms. Ponds, bridge and other features use local materials and craftspeople. Wildlife encouraged, well organised compost. Good family garden with visiting peacocks.

Parts of the garden are wheelchair accessible.
♿ 🚗 🍵

21 **MAENAN HALL**
Maenan, Llanrwst, LL26 0UL. Mrs Mclaren & Family. *2m N of Llanrwst. On E side of A470, ¼m S of Maenan Abbey Hotel.* **Sun 27 Apr, Sun 27 July (10.30-5). Adm £5, chd free. Light refreshments inc lunches and afternoon tea. Catering for dietary needs.**
Superbly beautiful four hectares on the slopes of the Conwy Valley. Dramatic views of Snowdonia, set amongst mature hardwoods. Both the upper part, with sweeping lawns, ornamental ponds and retaining walls, and the bluebell carpeted woodland dell contain copious specimen shrubs and trees, many originating at Bodnant. Magnolias, rhododendrons, camellias, pieris, cherries and hydrangeas, amongst many others, make a breathtaking display. Upper part of garden accessible but with fairly steep slopes.
♿ 🐕 ✼ 🍵 🪑))

22 **MYNYDD, CORS GOCH**
Llanbedrgoch, LL76 8TZ.
Mr Wyn & Mrs Ann Williams. *2m N of Pentraeth, ½ m N of Llanbedrgoch next to Cors Goch nature reserve. From Pentraeth take L turn to Llanbedrgoch, thru village. Parking is on R side of road after ¼ m, almost opp short track to garden. From B5108 turn at sign for Llanbedrgoch, parking on L.* **Sat 28 June (11-4). Adm £5, chd free. Tea, coffee & cake.**
An acre garden planted with trees, mature shrubs, perennials, heathers and bulbs. Another three acres devoted to wildlife inc a pond and a copse. Wildflower meadow with a good show of wild orchids.
🐕 🍵))

23 NEW **NANT NODDFA**
Nebo, Caernarfon, LL54 6RY. Teri Shaw and Bob Pethers. *What3words app: puddings.curve.huddled.* **Sat 21 June (11-4). Combined adm with Llys Ifor £5, chd free. Home-made teas at Llys Ifor.**
Set in countryside down a narrow lane, Nant Noddfa's garden covers approximately three acres and has been established over 20 years, transforming fields into a haven for wildlife. Paths wander among the many trees where you will discover polytunnels, a greenhouse, veg

beds, an orchard, beehives, a pond and patio by the house. All grown organically with sustainability in mind.
🐕 ✼ 🍵))

24 **THE OLD SCHOOL**
Penmon Village, Beaumaris, LL58 8RU. Kay Laurie. *3m NE of Beaumaris. Pass Beaumaris Castle on coast road, after 1.7m turn R to Penmon and follow yellow signs.* **Sun 31 Aug (11-4). Combined adm with Llwyn Onn £5, chd free. Light refreshments at The Old School inc hot drinks and savouries. Home-made Teas with cakes at Llwyn Onn.**
Created from brambly wilderness since 2015, the garden is on unforgiving rocky remains of quarried stone from building the Old School. South facing, views of Menai Strait. Sheltered from westerly winds dry, free draining soil suits agapanthus; ginger lilies; salvias and enormous echiums. Winding paths, steep in parts, mean accessibility is limited. Biomass heated greenhouse: An ongoing project. Sea and Mountain views. Historic Old School. Use of recycled materials for structures.
✼ 🍵))

25 ♦ **PENSYCHNANT**
Sychnant Pass, Conwy, LL32 8BJ. Pensychnant Foundation; Warden Julian Thompson, 01492 592595, jpt.pensychnant@btinternet.com, www.facebook.com/pensychnant. *2½ m W of Conwy at top of Sychnant Pass. From Conwy: L at Lancaster Sq into Upper Gate St; after 2½ m, Pensychnant's drive signed on R. From Penmaenmawr: fork R by shops, up Sychnant Pass; after walls at top of Pass, U turn L into drive.* **For NGS: Sun 15 June, Sun 13 July (11-5). Adm £4, chd free. Tea, coffee & cake. For other opening times and information, please phone, email or visit garden website.**
Wildlife garden with diverse herbaceous cottage garden borders surrounded by mature shrubs, banks of rhododendrons, ancient and Victorian woodlands. 12 acre woodland walks with views of Conwy Mountain and Sychnant. Listen out for woodland birds. Picnic tables, archaelogical trail on mountain. A peaceful little gem. Large Victorian Arts and Crafts house (open) with art exhibition. Partial wheelchair access, please phone for advice.
♿ ✼ 🍵))

26 ◆ PLANNWCH Y PLAS
Dinas Mawddwy, Machynlleth, SY20 9AQ. Mr Michael Hennessy, plannwchyplas@gmail.com, www.facebook.com/people/Plannwch-Y-Plas/100069190334855. *Travelling from Mallwyd, pass through the village and at the Red Lion Pub go straight across 200 yds to the garden. Coming from Dolgellau, turn in to the village, take 1st L.* **For NGS: Sun 7 Sept (10-4). Adm by donation. Tea, coffee & cake.** For other opening times and information, please email or visit garden website.
A community garden in Dinas Mawddwy, created to provide a growing and communal space where people can grow, chat and relax. A garden for production of food and connect with nature, with raised beds and a space for wildflowers. The pond and woodland is a haven for wildlife, packed with native and nonnative species of trees and shrubs. History of the Plas Dinas site and woodland tours available. There is a ¼ mile walk through the woodland and pond area. Explore a children's play area on the site. Historical guided tours available throughout the open day.

27 ◆ PLAS CADNANT HIDDEN GARDENS
Cadnant Road, Menai Bridge, LL59 5NH. Mr Anthony Tavernor, 01248 717174, plascadnantgardens@gmail.com, www.plascadnantgardens.co.uk. *½ m E of Menai Bridge. Take A545 & leave Menai Bridge heading for Beaumaris, then follow brown tourist information signs. SatNav not always reliable.* **For NGS: Wed 30 Apr (12-5). Adm £10, chd free.** For other opening times and information, please phone, email or visit garden website. Donation to Wales Air Ambulance.
Early C19 picturesque garden undergoing restoration since 1996. Valley gardens with waterfalls, large ornamental walled garden, woodland and early pit house. Also Alpheus water feature and Ceunant (Ravine) which gives visitors a more interesting walk featuring unusual moisture loving alpines. Recently voted one of the nation's favourite gardens. Restored area following flood damage. Guidebook available. Visitor centre open. Partial wheelchair access. Steps, gravel paths and slopes. Access statement available.

Accessible Tea Room and WC.

28 NEW PLAS PONT Y CRYBIN
Llannor, Pwllheli, LL53 8LZ. Ralph Martin and Xiaoqing Li. *3m NW of Pwllheli. Go N out of the village of Llannor. Keep L at a fork in the road, where the main road bends round to the R. Our drive is the 1st drive on the L. What3words app: branched.releases.dose.* **Sat 17 May, Sun 3 Aug (10-4.30). Adm £5, chd free. Pre-booking essential, please visit www.ngs.org.uk for information & booking. Tea, coffee & cake.**
This is a two acre mixed garden with flowerbeds, woodland, fruit trees, a vegetable garden and a large greenhouse with cacti and succulents. A spring visit is recommended for cactus flowers, and a later visit for garden flowers. Morning or afternoon pre-booked visits only, as there is limited parking.

29 PLASGLASGWM
Penmachno, Betws-Y-Coed, LL24 0PU. Mr Peter & Mrs Tamsyn Gallimore, 01690 760181, office@plasglasgwm.co.uk, www.plasglasgwm.co.uk. *5m from Betws y Coed. Turn off the A5 at Conwy Falls Cafe onto the B4406 to Penmachno. Once in Penmachno, please follow the brown tourism signs for Plasglasgwm for 1m.* **Visits by arrangement 18 Apr to 28 Sept for groups of up to 18. Please discuss refreshments when booking. Adm £5, chd free.**
Discover a hidden place tucked away in the foothills of Snowdonia. Five acres of gardens and grounds created by the owners over 30 years at this historic mountain farm. Hedges of yew, box and beech complement mixed and herbaceous borders, a re-introduced orchard, natural woodland and natural areas. Wander along the pathways to discover all the secret corners of this C16 farm holding. Yew and box hedging, box parterre, orchard, woodland walks, stream, bridges, seating areas and cafe.

30 SUNNINGDALE
Bull Bay Road, Bull Bay, Amlwch, LL68 9SD. Mike & Gill Cross, 01407 830753, mikeatbb@aol.com. *1½ m NW of Amlwch. On A5025 through Amlwch towards Cemaes.*

Just after the Trecastel Hotel. No parking at the house. **Sun 4 May, Sat 19 July (12-6.30). Adm £5, chd free. Home-made teas.** Visits also by arrangement June & July for groups of 10+. Refreshments can be arranged on booking.
Located on a headland overlooking the Irish sea, there are spectacular views, wildflowers and sheer drops with seating. The garden has many paths to take; discover raised fishpond and wildlife ponds, with plants jostling together and constantly evolving. Wander through the woodland but don't miss the hosta area with rill, raised veg beds complete with compost area and arches with climbers. Access to private headland and a completely different atmosphere in the rear garden. A 70 year old laburnum. Different rooms within the garden and many paths and surprises to be found. Ideas for other gardeners. Wheelchair access to front garden only.

31 TREBORTH BOTANIC GARDEN, BANGOR UNIVERSITY
Treborth, Bangor, LL57 2RQ. Natalie Chivers, www.treborth.bangor.ac.uk. *On the outskirts of Bangor towards Anglesey. Approach Menai Bridge from Upper Bangor on A5 or A55 J9 & travel towards Bangor for 2m: At Antelope Inn r'bout turn L before entering the Menai Bridge. What3words app: cleanest.flocking.witless.* **Sun 13 July (2-5). Adm £4, chd free. Tea, coffee & cake inc vegan & gluten free options.**
Owned by Bangor University and used as a resource for teaching, research, public education and enjoyment. Treborth comprises planted borders, species rich natural grassland, ponds, arboretum, Chinese garden, ancient woodland, and a rocky shoreline habitat. Six glasshouses provide specialised environments for tropical, temperate, orchid and carnivorous plant collections. Partnered with National Botanic Garden of Wales to champion Welsh horticulture, protect wildlife and extol the virtues of growing plants for food, fun, health and wellbeing. Wheelchair access to some glasshouses and part of the garden. Woodland path is surfaced but most of the borders only accessed over grass.

32 TREFNANT BACH
Anglesey Bees, Llanddaniel Fab, Gaerwen, LL60 6ET. Dafydd & Dawn Jones, 07816 188573, dafydd@angleseybees.co.uk, www.angleseybees.co.uk. $^2/_5$ m from the centre of Llanddaniel Fab. A5 from LlanfairPG, $1^1/_2$ km W, turn L for Llanddaniel. Village centre, by bus shelter follow signs down farm track. Parking onsite. Alternatively park in village & 10 min walk. **Visits by arrangement 5 Apr to 27 Apr for groups of 5+. Adm £5, chd free. Light refreshments. Specific dietary requirements can be catered for by prior arrangement.** An eight acre smallholding which is a pollinator and wildlife sanctuary. Spring-fed pond with islands. Honeybee friendly woodland and lakeside walks. Apiary. Spring bulbs and honeybee specific herbaceous borders. Orchard, soft fruit, raised vegetable bed. Meadows grazed with Shropshire tree-friendly sheep. Apiary and Anglesey Bees centre for beekeeping training and experiences. Local honey for sale. Very gentle slopes, short-mowed grassed or hard paths. Refreshment area accessible with hard surface. Regret WC unsuitable for wheelchair access.

& 🐑 ❀ 🏠 ☕ 🪑

33 TY CADFAN SANT
National Street, Tywyn, LL36 9DD. Mrs Katie Pearce, 07816 604851, katie@tycadfansant.co.uk. *A493 going S & W: Turn L into one way, garden ahead. Bear R, parking on 2nd L. A493 going N: 1st R in 30mph zone, L at bottom by garden, parking 2nd L.* **Sat 14 June (2-5.30). Cream teas. Sun 15 June (11.30-3.30). Light refreshments. Adm £5, chd free. Pulled pork baps at lunchtime. Drinks and home-made cakes in addition to cream teas. Visits also by arrangement 30 Mar to 28 Sept. Refreshments and bee keeping advice by arrangement.** Large eco friendly garden. In the front, shrubbery, mixed flower beds and roses surround a mature copper beech. Six steps lead to the largely productive back garden which has an apiary in the orchard, fruit, vegetables, flowers and a polytunnel. Plenty of seating throughout. Seasonal produce available, honey and preserves, plants. Bee keeper present, information on environmentally friendly gardening. Partial wheelchair access due to steps to rear garden.

& ❀ ☕ 🪑

34 TYN Y PANT
Boduan, Pwllheli, LL53 6DT. Mrs Elizabeth Broadbent, 01758 720587, royandlizbroadbent@hotmail.co.uk. *Off the A497 between Pwllheli and Nefyn. On the A497 travelling from Pwllheli, turn L opp St Buan's Church, (from Nefyn R) after approx 500 metres. Sharp R into our driveway which has the house name clearly displayed.* **Sun 18 May, Sun 27 July (11-4.30). Adm £5, chd free. Tea, coffee & cake. Visits also by arrangement 5 May to 30 Sept for groups of up to 20.** A tranquil, rural garden developing on a tight budget around mature trees, shrubs and ponds. Highlights inc kitchen garden, flower beds, bluebell banks, a mini woodland walk and plenty of seating. New features for 2025 inc a fernery and 75sqm mixed border. We garden organically and reuse and recycle to benefit wildlife and the environment. The main garden is wheelchair accessible. There are areas of gravel and paths that may not be suitable.

& 🐑 ❀ 🏠 ☕ 🪑

35 NEW Y FELIN RHYD HIR
Efailnewydd, Pwllheli, LL53 8TN. Mr & Mrs Carol and Adrian Priest, 07756 115138, adrian.priest2908@gmail.com, www.facebook.com/p/Y-Felin-Rhyd-Hir-100067562478855. *Situated on the B4415 between Efailnewyedd and Rhydyclafdy. What3words app: refreshed.windy.braked.* **Sun 25 May, Sat 6 Sept (11-3.30). Adm £5, chd free. Tea, coffee & cake. Visits also by arrangement May to Sept for groups of 15 to 40. Discuss refreshments when booking.** Y Felin Rhyd Hir (Melin Bodfel) is a stone built water-powered corn mill. The composite overshot waterwheel, with cast iron shrouds has been fully renovated. It was supplied by a now restored mill pond to the north of the mill, fed from the Afon Rhyd-hir via a 1.7 km long leat. The site has extensive grounds, newly landscaped garden, pond, Victorian style glasshouse, vegetable beds and orchard.

🐑 ❀ 🚗 🏠 ☕ 🪑

Y Felin Rhyd Hir

NORTH EAST WALES

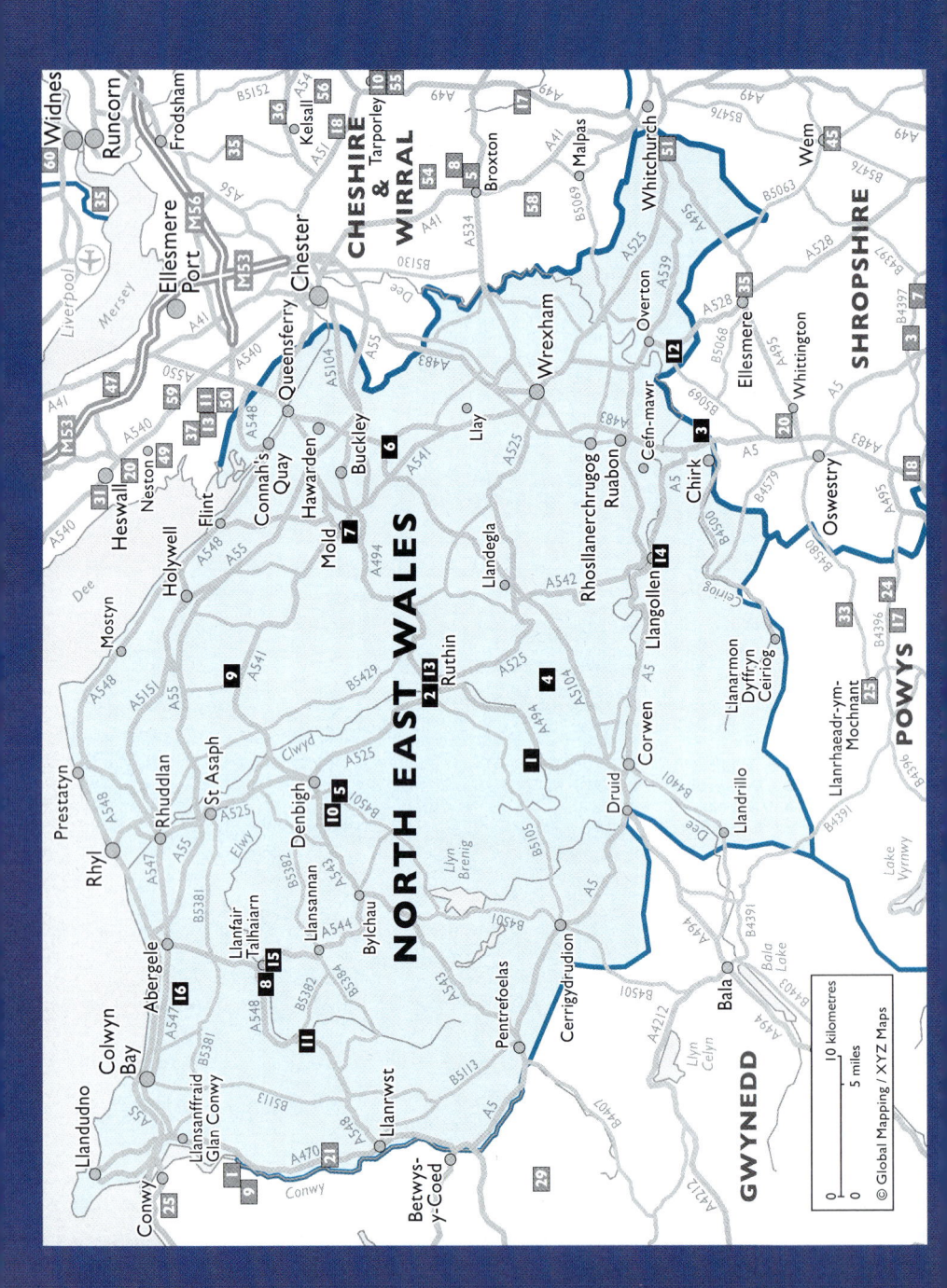

VOLUNTEERS

County Organiser
Jane Moore
07769 046317
jane.moore@ngs.org.uk

County Treasurer
Helen Robertson
01978 790666
helen.robertson@ngs.org.uk

Booklet Co-ordinator
Position vacant
Please email hello@ngs.org.uk
for details

Assistant County Organisers
Fiona Bell
07813 087797
bell_fab@hotmail.com

Iris Dobbie
01745 886730
iris.dobbie@ngs.org.uk

Pat Pearson
01745 813613
pat.pearson@ngs.org.uk

@North East Wales NGS

OPENING DATES

All entries subject to change.
For latest information check
www.ngs.org.uk
Map locator numbers are
shown to the right of each
garden name.

March

Snowdrop Openings
Wednesday 19th
Aberclwyd Manor 1

April

Wednesday 2nd
Aberclwyd Manor 1

Wednesday 16th
Aberclwyd Manor 1

Saturday 19th
Glasfryn Hall 9

Sunday 20th
Glasfryn Hall 9

Monday 21st
Glasfryn Hall 9

Wednesday 30th
Aberclwyd Manor 1

May

Monday 5th
Dibleys Nurseries 4

Saturday 10th
Tudor Cottage 16

Sunday 11th
Tudor Cottage 16

Wednesday 14th
Aberclwyd Manor 1

Saturday 17th
NEW Knolton Hall 12

Sunday 18th
Brynkinalt Hall 3

Sunday 25th
Hafodunos Hall 11

Wednesday 28th
Aberclwyd Manor 1

June

Sunday 8th
Bron y Gaer 2
Nantclwyd y Dre 13

Wednesday 11th
Aberclwyd Manor 1

Sunday 15th
Gwaenynog 10

Wednesday 25th
Aberclwyd Manor 1

Friday 27th
◆ Plas Newydd 14

July

Wednesday 9th
Aberclwyd Manor 1

Wednesday 23rd
Aberclwyd Manor 1

August

Wednesday 6th
Aberclwyd Manor 1

Wednesday 20th
Aberclwyd Manor 1

September

Wednesday 3rd
Aberclwyd Manor 1

Sunday 7th
Brynkinalt Hall 3

Wednesday 17th
Aberclwyd Manor 1

By Arrangement

Arrange a personalised garden visit
with your club, or group of friends,
on a date to suit you. See individual
garden entries for full details.

Aberclwyd Manor 1
Dolhyfryd 5
Dove Cottage 6
Fron Haul 7
Garthewin 8
NEW Primrose Cottage 15

THE GARDENS

1 ABERCLWYD MANOR
Derwen, Corwen, LL21 9SF. Mr & Mrs G Sparvoli, 01824 750431, aberclwydgarden@outlook.com. *7m from Ruthin. Travelling on A494 from Ruthin to Corwen. At Bryn SM Service Stn turn R, follow sign to Derwen. Aberclwyd gates on L before Derwen. Do not follow SatNav directions.* **Wed 19 Mar, Wed 2, Wed 16, Wed 30 Apr, Wed 14, Wed 28 May, Wed 11, Wed 25 June, Wed 9, Wed 23 July, Wed 6, Wed 20 Aug, Wed 3, Wed 17 Sept (11-4). Adm £5, chd free. Cream teas.** Visits also by arrangement 19 Feb to 24 Sept for groups of 10 to 25.
A four acre garden on a sloping hillside overlooking the Upper Clwyd Valley. The garden has mature trees with snowdrops, fritillaries and cyclamen. An Italianate garden of box hedging lies below the house ponds, perennials, roses and an orchard are also to be enjoyed within this cleverly structured area. Mass of cyclamen in September and spring flowers. Mostly flat with some steps and slopes.

2 BRON Y GAER
Castle Street, Ruthin, LL15 1DP. Mr Richard Chamberlain. *120yd up Castle St from the Square on the R.* **Sun 8 June (11-4). Combined adm with Nantclwyd y Dre £7, chd free.**
A real secret garden. Hidden from the bustle of town, and nestled next door to Nantclwyd y Dre. This garden has beautiful cottage garden planting, a small collection of medicinal herbs and seating by a quiet reflective pool. Good wheelchair access, but please be aware that the garden has two low steps.

3 BRYNKINALT HALL
Brynkinalt, Chirk, Wrexham, LL14 5NS. Iain & Kate Hill-Trevor, www.brynkinalt.co.uk. *6m N of Oswestry, 10m S of Wrexham. Come off A5/A483 & take B5070 into Chirk village. Turn into Trevor Rd (beside Mary's Church). Cont past houses on R. Turn R on bend into Estate Gates. N.B. Do not use postcode with SatNav.* **Sun 18 May, Sun 7 Sept (11-4). Adm £6, chd free. Tea, coffee & cake.**
A five acre ornamental woodland shrubbery, overgrown until recently, now cleared and replanted, rhododendron walk, historic ponds, well, grottos, ha-ha and battlements, new stumpery, ancient redwoods and yews. Also two acre garden beside Grade II* house (see website for opening), with modern rose and formal beds, deep herbaceous borders, pond with shrub, mixed beds, pleached limes and hedge patterns. Home of the first Duke of Wellington's grandmother and Sir John Trevor, Speaker of House of Commons. Stunning rhododendrons and formal West Garden. Major film location for Lady Chatterley's Lover.

Hafodunos Hall

Aberclwyd Manor

4 DIBLEYS NURSERIES
Cefn Rhydd, Cricor, Llanelidan, Ruthin, LL15 2LG. Lynne Dibley, www.dibleys.com. *7m S of Ruthin.* Follow brown signs off A525 nr Llysfasi College. What3Words app: screaming.topples.submits. **Mon 5 May (10-4). Adm £6, chd £1. Light refreshments. Donation to Plant Heritage.**
An eight acre woodland garden with a wide selection of rare and unusual trees set in beautiful countryside. In late spring there is a lovely display of rhododendrons, magnolias, cherries and camellias. Much of our grassland promotes native wildflowers. Our ¾ acre commercial glasshouses are open showing a display of streptocarpus and other rare houseplants. Houseplant shop. Partial wheelchair access to glasshouses, uneven ground and steep paths in arboretum and elsewhere.

5 DOLHYFRYD
Lawnt, Denbigh, LL16 4SU. Captain & Mrs Michael Cunningham, 01745 814805, virginia@dolhyfryd.com, www.dolhyfrydgardens.com. *1m SW of Denbigh. On B4501 to Nantglyn, from Denbigh - 1m from town centre.* **Visits by arrangement for groups of 10+. Adm by donation. Light refreshments.**
Established garden set in small valley of River Ystrad. Acres of crocuses in late Feb to early Mar. Paths through wildflower meadows and woodland of magnificent trees, shade loving plants and azaleas; mixed borders; walled kitchen garden. Many woodland and riverside birds, inc dippers, kingfishers, grey wagtails. Many species of butterfly encouraged by new planting. Much winter interest, exceptional display of crocuses. Wheelchair users will need to negotiate gravel paths and some steep slopes.

6 DOVE COTTAGE
Rhos Road, Penyffordd, Chester, CH4 0JR. Chris & Denise Wallis, 01244 547539, dovecottage@supanet.com. *6m SW of Chester. Leave A55 J35 take A550 to Wrexham. Drive 2m, turn R onto A5104. From A541 Wrexham/Mold Rd in Pontblyddyn take A5104 to Chester. Garden opp train stn.* **Visits by arrangement 1 July to 1 Sept for groups of 5 to 25. Adm £5, chd free. Tea.**
Approx 1½ acre garden, shrubs and herbaceous plants set informally around lawns. Established vegetable area, two ponds (one wildlife), summerhouse. Raised board walk through planted woodland area. Wheelchair access via gravel paths.

7 FRON HAUL
Denbigh Road, Mold, CH7 1BL. Mr David & Mrs Hilary Preece, 07966 080032, dglynnep@gmail.com. *We are a yellow house, opp the entrance to Bailey Hill. For SatNav please use 'Shire View, Mold' rather than the postcode.* **Visits by arrangement May to Sept for groups of 5 to 20. Adm £5, chd free. Light refreshments.**
Approximately ⅔ acre garden created around 1870, possibly under Edward Kemp's guidance, and may be considered the oldest 'domestic' garden in Mold. The general layout and many original features remain. It comprises herbaceous borders, a small orchard, lawns, a pond and a wisteria covered walkway. There is also a wooded area with a number of old yew trees dating back to Victorian times. Disabled parking available, please call in advance. Access to garden via terraced area, the garden is on a slope and some paths are uneven.

8 GARTHEWIN
Llanfairtalhaiarn, LL22 8YR.
Mr Michael Grime, 01745 720288,
michaelgrime12@btinternet.com.
6m S of Abergele & A55. From Abergele take A548 to Llanfair TH & Llanrwst. Entrance to Garthewin 300yds W of Llanfair TH on A548 to Llanrwst. **Visits by arrangement 1 Apr to 1 Nov. Adm £6.**
Valley garden with ponds and woodland areas. Much of the eight acres have been reclaimed and redesigned providing a younger garden with a great variety of azaleas, rhododendrons and young trees, all within a framework of mature shrubs and trees. Old Theatre and Chapel open.

9 GLASFRYN HALL
South Street, Caerwys, Mold, CH7 5AF. Mrs Lise Roberts, www.orielglasfryn.com. *Follow signs for Caerwys from the A55 N Wales expressway or the A541 Mold/ Denbigh Rd. Garden is at Oriel Glasfryn Gallery, which is clearly signed at the S end of the town.* **Sat 19 Apr (10-5); Sun 20, Mon 21 Apr (10-4). Adm £5, chd free. Tea, coffee & cake in the Horsebox cafe. Ice-cream and alcoholic beverages also available. Seating is outdoors. No picnics.**
Victorian villa set in three acres of gardens with an interesting variety of mature trees, beds, tea house, pond and parterre. Horsebox café serving on the croquet lawn with its stunning views of the Clwydian hills. The property is also home Oriel Glasfryn Gallery, featuring work by leading Welsh artists. The 2025 open gardens coincide with the spring exhibition meaning the house will be open. The gardens are on level ground and most areas can be accessed by wheelchair.

10 GWAENYNOG
Denbigh, LL16 5NU. Major & Mrs Tom Smith. *1m W of Denbigh. On A543, Lodge on L, ¼m drive.* **Sun 15 June (2-5.30). Adm £5, chd free. Home-made teas.**
Two acres inc the restored walled garden where Beatrix Potter wrote and illustrated the Tale of the Flopsy Bunnies. Also a small exhibition of some of her work. Long herbaceous borders and island beds, some recently replanted, espalier fruit trees, rose pergola and vegetable area. C16 house (not open) visited by Dr Samuel Johnson during his Tour of Wales. Wheelchair users will need to negotiate grass paths.

11 HAFODUNOS HALL
Llangernyw, Abergele, LL22 8TY.
Dr Richard Wood, www.facebook.com/hafodunoshall. *1m W of Llangernyw. Halfway between Abergele & Llanrwst on A548. Signed from opp Old Stag pub. Parking available onsite.* **Sun 25 May (12-4). Adm £6, chd free. Tea, coffee & cake in the Victorian conservatory.**
Historic garden undergoing restoration after 30 years of neglect, surrounds a Sir George Gilbert Scott Grade I listed Hall, derelict after arson attack. Unique setting with a ½ mile tree-lined drive, formal terraces, woodland walks with ancient redwoods, laurels, yews, lake, streams, waterfalls and a gorge. Wonderful rhododendrons. Most areas around the hall are wheelchair accessible by gravel pathways. Some gardens are set on slopes with rough woodland paths.

12 NEW KNOLTON HALL
Oswestry Road, Overton, Wrexham, LL13 0LG. Mr and Mrs Edward Chantler. *5m N of Ellsemere, 8m S of Wrexham. Take the B5069 towards Oswestry. Pass Knolton Cheese farm & do not turn R down the unmade road. Driveway on R by black & white gate lodge. What3words app: starring.bounding. orbit.* **Sat 17 May (10-4). Adm £5, chd free. Tea, coffee & cake.**
Situated on the banks of the Shellbrook and the River Dee this five acre garden has beautiful views of the Lower Dee Valley. The garden has many mature trees underplanted with snowdrops, fritillaries and bluebells. A tiered Italianate garden of box hedging lies below the house and shrubs, ponds, perennials and roses. Abundance of spring flowers, rhododendrons and magnolia. It is possible to access the top of the garden by wheelchair although there are changes in levels and small steps to negotiate.

13 NANTCLWYD Y DRE
Castle St, Ruthin, LL15 1DP.
Denbighshire County Council, www.denbighshire.gov.uk/ nantclwyd-y-dre-ruthin. *100yds from the square. 100yd along Castle St from the square on the R. Access via alleyway to side of house. Nearest parking Market St or Dog Ln car park.* **Sun 8 June (11-4). Combined adm with Bron y Gaer £7, chd free. Tea, coffee & cake. Gluten free and non dairy options available.**
With far-reaching views over Ruthin and the Clwydian Range, this Grade II listed walled garden was the former kitchen garden for Ruthin Castle. The garden features elements from three distinct periods; Medieval aspects inc an orchard with wildflowers, hedges, a nuttery, and vegetable beds representative of the C17 and C19 additions such as a glasshouse and herbaceous borders. One of the oldest timber framed town houses in Wales and the Lord's garden first mentioned in 1282 is thought to pre-date the structure, C17 summerhouse. Most of the garden is wheelchair accessible but with gravel paths.

14 ♦ PLAS NEWYDD
Llangollen, LL20 8AW.
Denbighshire County Council, 01978 862834, plasnewydd@ denbighshire.gov.uk, www.instagram.com/plasnewyddllan. *Follow brown sign from A5 in Llangollen. Hill St is steep.* **For NGS: Fri 27 June (10-3). Adm by donation.** For other opening times and information, please phone, email or visit garden website.
Plas Newydd, home to the famous Ladies of Llangollen (1780-1831), boasts a picturesque grade II* garden with a formal parterre, intricate topiary, and a Gorsedd stone circle (C19). A serene woodland walk follows the Cyflymen stream. The garden features a stunning rose collection, inc varieties cherished by the Ladies, offering a blend of history and natural beauty.

15 NEW PRIMROSE COTTAGE
Water Street, Llanfairtalhaiarn, Abergele, LL22 8SB. Mrs Elizabeth Thorburn, 07502 610916, elizabethprimrose@icloud.com. *6m from Abergele on A548. From Swan Sq, with post office on R, walk and look L for a wide footpath. Primrose Cottage can be found halfway up hill to the L and before the handrail. What3words app: firewall.deflect.*

insects. **Visits by arrangement 1 May to 23 June for groups of up to 20. Tea, coffee & cake.**
Small cottage garden on south west facing sloped site, terraced with stone walls and steps to different areas- inc wildlife pond, raised ponds, gravel planting, small herbaceous borders, lawned area, mini orchard, Japanese style courtyard and seating areas. Lovingly developed over the years, still making mistakes and and still a work in progress.

16 TUDOR COTTAGE
Isallt Road, Llysfaen, Colwyn Bay, LL29 8LJ. Mr & Mrs C Manifold. 1½m SE of Old Colwyn. Turn S off A547 between Llandulas & Old Colwyn. Up Highlands Rd for ½m, R onto Tan-y-Graig. Ignore SatNav, ¾m to swings. Take Isallt Rd on far R. **Sat 10, Sun 11 May (2-5). Adm £5, chd free. Home-made teas.**
¾ acre garden on different levels set amongst natural rock faces. Unusual and varied planting featuring cottage, scree, Japanese, shade and bog gardens. Display bedding, an abundance of colourful pots and baskets, together with quirky statues, ponds, bridges and a folly. Lovely views from upper level. Some uneven paths and steep steps. Care required. Children must be supervised by an adult at all times please.

48,000 people affected by cancer were reached by Maggie's centres supported by the National Garden Scheme over the last 12 months.

Glasfryn Hall

POWYS

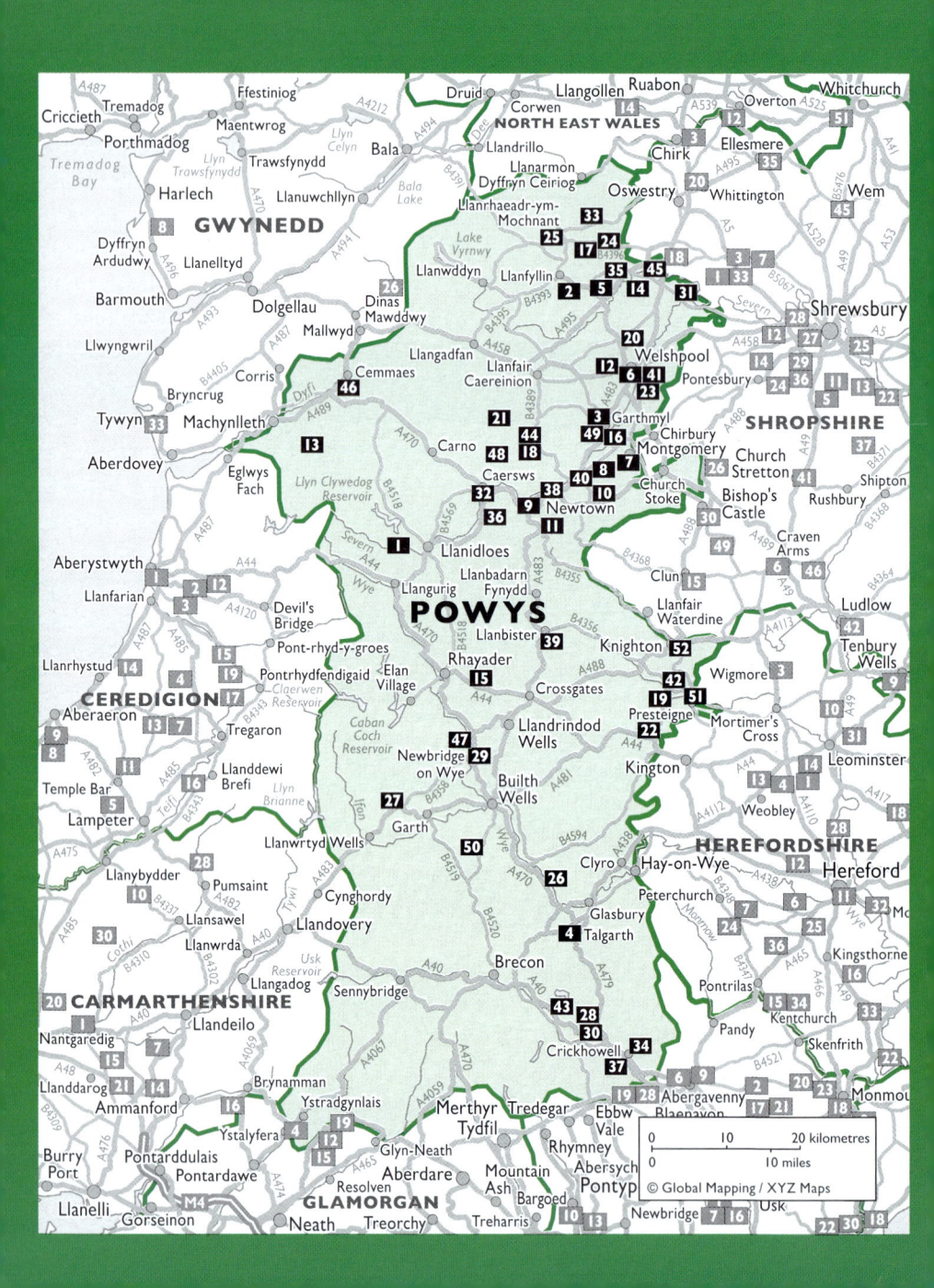

POWYS

VOLUNTEERS

North Powys County Organiser
Susan Paynton 01686 650531
susan.paynton@ngs.org.uk

County Treasurer
Jude Boutle 07702 061623
jude.boutle@ngs.org.uk

Publicity
Sue McKillop 07753 289701
sue.mckillop@ngs.org.uk

Gill Powell 07968 250364
gill.powell@ngs.org.uk

Simon Quin 07958 915120
simon.quin@ngs.org.uk

Talks
Helen Anthony 07986 061051
helen.anthony@ngs.org.uk

Social Media
Nikki Trow 07958 958382
nikki.trow@ngs.org.uk

Booklet Co-ordinator
Position Vacant

Assistant County Organisers
Simon Cain 07958 915115
simon.cain@ngs.org.uk

Elizabeth Fairhead 07824 398810
elizabeth.fairhead@ngs.org.uk

Georgina Newson 01686 689306
georgina.newson@ngs.org.uk

Kate Nicoll 07960 656814
kate.nicoll@ngs.org.uk

South Powys County Organiser
Owen Hughes 07711 198123
owen.hughes@ngs.org.uk

Temporary County Treasurer
Jude Boutle 07702 061623
jude.boutle@ngs.org.uk

Publicity Officer and Talks
Gail Jones 07974 103692
gail.jones@ngs.org.uk

@powysngs
@powysngs

OPENING DATES

All entries subject to change. For latest information check **www.ngs.org.uk**

Extended openings are shown at the beginning of each month

Map locator numbers are shown to the right of each garden name.

April
Wednesday 30th
Vaynor Park　　　　　　　　49

May
Sunday 4th
NEW Bronllys Court　　　　4
Saturday 10th
◆ Dingle Nurseries & Garden　12
Garregllwyd　　　　　　　　15
Sunday 11th
◆ Dingle Nurseries & Garden　12
Garregllwyd　　　　　　　　15
Saturday 17th
Llanrhaeadr Ym Mochnant Gardens　　　　　　　　　25
Sunday 18th
Treberfydd House　　　　　43
Saturday 24th
Bachie Uchaf　　　　　　　2
Sunday 25th
Bachie Uchaf　　　　　　　2
Llwyn Madoc　　　　　　　27
Llysdinam　　　　　　　　29
Monday 26th
Garthmyl Hall　　　　　　　16
Llanstephan House　　　　26
Saturday 31st
Clawdd-Y-Dre　　　　　　　7
◆ Gregynog Hall & Garden　18

June
Sunday 1st
Clawdd-Y-Dre　　　　　　　7
◆ Gregynog Hall & Garden　18
The Neuadd　　　　　　　34

Saturday 7th
The Malthouse　　　　　　31
The Rock House　　　　　39
Tremynfa　　　　　　　　45
Sunday 8th
NEW Bronllys Court　　　　4
The Malthouse　　　　　　31
The Rock House　　　　　39
Tremynfa　　　　　　　　45
Saturday 14th
Llwynau Mawr Farm　　　　28
Maes Llechau　　　　　　　30
Sunday 15th
Plum Tree Cottage　　　　37
Saturday 21st
NEW Dolwen　　　　　　　13
Sunday 22nd
NEW Dolwen　　　　　　　13
Saturday 28th
Ash and Elm Horticulture　　1
Sunday 29th
Ash and Elm Horticulture　　1
Llangedwyn Hall　　　　　24

July
Every day from Saturday 26th
◆ Welsh Lavender　　　　50
Sunday 6th
NEW Bronllys Court　　　　4
NEW Gwernfyda　　　　　21
NEW Leighton Gardens　　23
Tynrhos　　　　　　　　　47
Tyn-y-Graig　　　　　　　48
Saturday 12th
Ponthafren　　　　　　　　38
NEW Ty Cwm Dyfi　　　　46
Sunday 13th
Ponthafren　　　　　　　　38
NEW Tregynon Gardens　　44
NEW Ty Cwm Dyfi　　　　46
Saturday 19th
Cultivate Community Garden　9
Sunday 20th
Eve's Garden　　　　　　　14
Willowbrook　　　　　　　51
Sunday 27th
Berriew Village Gardens　　3
◆ Bryngwyn Hall　　　　　5

August

Friday 1st
◆ Welsh Lavender　　　　　　　50

Saturday 2nd
Moel y Gwelltyn Ucha　　　　　33

Sunday 3rd
Moel y Gwelltyn Ucha　　　　　33

Sunday 10th
NEW　Guilsfield Gardens　　　20

Saturday 16th
1 Church Bank　　　　　　　　6

Sunday 17th
1 Church Bank　　　　　　　　6

Saturday 30th
NEW　14 St Mary's Place　　　41

Sunday 31st
NEW　14 St Mary's Place　　　41

September

Sunday 7th
Cwm-Weeg　　　　　　　　　11

October

Saturday 11th
◆ Dingle Nurseries & Garden　12

Sunday 12th
◆ Dingle Nurseries & Garden　12

Saturday 18th
◆ Gregynog Hall & Garden　　18

Sunday 19th
◆ Gregynog Hall & Garden　　18

By Arrangement

Arrange a personalised garden visit with your club, or group of friends, on a date to suit you. See individual garden entries for full details.

1 Church Bank	6
Cuckoo Hall	8
Cwm Sidwell	10
Eve's Garden	14
Garregllwyd	15
NEW Glan Yr Afon	17
NEW The Grove	19
The Hymns	22
Llysdinam	29
The Meadows	32
The Neuadd	34
NEW The Old Pottery	35
Plas Dinam	36
Ponthafren	38
Rock Mill	40
Tranquility Haven	42
Tyn-y-Graig	48
Willowbrook	51
1 Ystrad House	52

The Grove

THE GARDENS

1 ASH AND ELM HORTICULTURE
Cae Felyn, Old Hall, Llanidloes, SY18 6PW. Emma Maxwell, www.ashandelm.co.uk. *3m from Llanidloes. At Llanidloes Market Hall turn R on Shortbridge St over river & stay on this road for 3m. Garden on L.* **Sat 28, Sun 29 June (11-3). Adm £5, chd free. Tea, coffee & cake. Range of cakes, seasonal fruit and home-made elderflower cordial.**
Diverse five acre market garden; flowers, vegetables, fruit, nuts and plants grown using agroecological techniques that nurture nature. Enjoy wandering through the extensive cut flower garden or explore the one acre orchard, home to a family of barn owls. See wide range of seasonal vegetables growing in the polytunnels, glasshouse and in the field or just relax by one of the wildlife pools. Talks through the day on growing principles. Wheelchair access via grass paths.
& 🐾 ❋ ☕ 🔊

2 BACHIE UCHAF
Bachie Road, Llanfyllin, SY22 5NF. Glyn & Glenys Lloyd. *S of Llanfyllin. Going towards Welshpool on A490 turn R onto Bachie Rd after Llanfyllin primary sch. Keep straight for ⅕m. Take drive R uphill at cottage on L.* **Sat 24, Sun 25 May (12-4). Adm £5.50, chd free. Home-made teas.**
Inspiring and colourful hillside country garden. Gravel paths meander around extensive planting and over streams cascading into ponds. Specimen trees, shrubs, rhododendrons and azaleas aplenty and a vegetable garden. Enjoy the wonderful views from one of the many seats; your senses will be rewarded.
🐾 ☕ 🔊

GROUP OPENING

3 BERRIEW VILLAGE GARDENS
Berriew, Welshpool, SY21 8BA. www.berriew.com. *A483 5m S Welshpool. From Welshpool take A483 S for approx 4m. Turn R onto B4390. Cont through village & turn R to car park at sch. Map & adm tickets at car park. All within walking distance of car park.* **Sun 27 July (12-5). Combined adm £7, chd free. Home-made teas at Community Centre.**

NEW 5 CAE CELYN
Gillian James.
1 GLAN YR AFON
Ms Lesley Ellis.
26 MAES BEUNO
Helen & Kristian Hickson-Booth.
THE OLD COURT HOUSE
Michael Davis & Andrew Logan.
NEW RECTORY BARN
Oliver and Sarah Hill.
NEW 2 SCHOOL ROOM COTTAGES
Jo Barton.
UPPER RECTORY
Kerry and Paul Huber, www.upperrectory.co.uk.

The picturesque village of Berriew is on the Montgomeryshire Canal with the River Rhiew flowing through its heart. Black and white cottages, church, pub, shops and Andrew Logan Museum of Sculpture. Seven very different gardens (three new openers): The Old Court House has an idyllic situation on banks of River Rhiew terrace with metal staircase by Berriew sculptor/metalworker William O'Brien, raised beds for soft fruits and vegetables. Upper Rectory with multiple vegetable beds. 1 Glan yr Afon colourful small garden with pergola covered in grape vine. 5 Cae Celyn riverside garden with small orchard and wonderful views. 26 Maes Beuno edibles and flowers mix of an allotment and cottage style of gardening. Rectory Barn herbaceous borders, vegetable patch, orchard area. 2 School Room Cottages haven for both plants and wildlife with wonderful views and pollinator-attracting plants. All the gardens are buzzing with bees, butterflies, and other beneficial insects. Partial wheelchair access.
& ❋ 🚗 ☕ 🔊

4 NEW BRONLLYS COURT
Bronllys, Brecon, LD3 0LF. Amanda-Jane Page, www.instagram.com/thefloralark. *8m from Hay-on-Wye and Brecon off A438. Parking on surrounding roads. What3words app: mammoth.displays.sunflower.* **Sun 4 May, Sun 8 June, Sun 6 July (11-4). Adm £5, chd free. Tea, coffee & cake.**
Floral Ark at Bronllys Court is a magical food and medicine garden beside the beautiful Black Mountains; it is a place where people can deeply connect with plants, trees and fungi. Medicinal trees and plants, ceremonial circles, and pollinator-friendly wildlife areas all in one acre. Sculpture and tree discovery trails by grass and bark paths with uneven ground. A 30-min talk at 12noon: Extraordinary Experiences in Nature. Children's activities available.
🐾 ❋ ☕ 🪑 🔊

5 ◆ BRYNGWYN HALL
Bwlch-y-Cibau, Llanfyllin, SY22 5LJ. Auriol Marchioness of Linlithgow, www.bryngwyn.com. *3m SE Llanfyllin. From Llanfyllin take A490 towards Welshpool for 3m turn L up drive just before Bwlch-y-Cibau.* **For NGS: Sun 27 July (12-5). Adm £7, chd free. Home-made teas.** For other opening times and information, please visit garden website.
Stunning Grade II* listed nine acre garden with 60 acres parkland design inspired by William Emes. Woodland garden, shrubbery, rose garden, restored herbaceous borders, meadows and serpentine lake. Unusual trees, shrubs and unique Poison Garden.
& 🐾 🚗 ☕ 🔊

6 1 CHURCH BANK
Welshpool, SY21 7DR. Mel & Heather Parkes, 01938 559112, melandheather@live.co.uk. *Centre of Welshpool. Church Bank leads onto Salop Rd from Church St. Follow one way system, use main car park then short walk. Follow yellow NGS signs.* **Sat 16, Sun 17 Aug (12-5). Adm £4, chd free. Home-made teas.** Visits also by arrangement Apr to Aug for groups of 5 to 30.
An intimate jewel in the town with many interesting plants and unusual features where the sounds of water fill the air. Densely planted garden with Gothic arch and zig zag path leading to shell grotto, bonsai garden and fernery. Explore the ground floor of this C17 barrelmakers cottage and museum of tools and memorabilia.
🐾 ☕

7 CLAWDD-Y-DRE
Lions Bank, Montgomery, SY15 6PT. **Nadine and Daniel Roach and Geoff Ferguson.** *From centre of Montgomery (parking) proceed up hill along Church Bank, past St Nicholas Church. Turn R into Lions Bank past Spider Cottage.* **Sat 31 May, Sun 1 June (2-5). Adm £5, chd free. Home-made teas.**
Sitting on the old town walls, this well established ¾ acre garden features mature trees, yew hedging and landscaped rockeries. Gravel pathways lead to a manicured lawn and a productive orchard with both fruit and nut trees. Displaying a wide range of shrubs and herbaceous perennials the garden also boasts a delightful gazebo with stunning panoramic views across the valley to the Shropshire Hills. Children's quiz.

8 CUCKOO HALL
Abermule, Montgomery, SY15 6LD. **Gill and Cliff Plowes,** 01686 630209, gillian.plowes@gmail.com. *3m W of Montgomery. From Newtown A483 N approx 3m, turn R B4386 signposted Abermule/Clun/Montgomery. At r'bout take L (B4385) to Montgomery, after 0.2m over bridge immed R towards Llandyssil. Follow yellow signs.* **Visits by arrangement 16 May to 29 July for groups of 12 to 32. Adm £6, chd free. Tea, coffee & cake.**
1½ acre garden developed and designed by retired nursery owners and RHS gold medallists. Semi mature trees with island beds, mature grasses with shrubs give permanent structure: three wildlife ponds, streamside garden, rose pergola, herbaceous borders inc Robert's bed, inspired by a young boy who left a legacy of love. Colour co-ordination foremost in mind during the design to give a flowing feel. Wheelchair access to the majority of the garden.

9 CULTIVATE COMMUNITY GARDEN
Pendinas, Llanidloes Road, Newtown, SY16 4HX. www.cultivate.uk.com. *A489 W from centre Newtown adjacent to Newtown College & Theatre Hafren.* **Sat 19 July (10-3). Adm £4.50, chd free. Tea, coffee & cake.**
Thriving two acre community garden run by local food hub, Cultivate. Extensive range of vegetables, herbs and fruit growing on communal plots and 'micro-allotments'. Lawns to relax on and wildlife area with pond. Managed by Cultivate volunteers with help from our partners Montgomery Wildlife Trust, Tir Coed and students from Neath Port Talbot college. Look out for the turf-roofed roundhouse, amazing colourful mural, and trained apple trees and our no-dig vegetable beds. Polytunnels and lots of compost heaps. Wheelchair access to main parts of garden. Accessible compost toilet.

10 CWM SIDWELL
Kerry, Newtown, SY16 4NA. **Jan Rogers,** 07772 414783, janetrogers62@hotmail.co.uk. *6m E Newtown. From Newtown take A489. After 4m turn L on B4368. After 1½ m turn R signed Goetre Follow yellow arrows.* **Visits by arrangement June to Sept for groups of up to 20. Adm £4, chd free. Home-made teas.**
Cottage garden with lovely views brought back from the wilderness over the last couple of years. Roses, sweet peas, herbaceous perennials, vegetable garden and cut flower garden all grown from seed. Pockets of colour whichever way you look. Pond and chickens. Flower and vegetable seedlings for sale.

11 CWM-WEEG
Dolfor, Newtown, SY16 4AT. **Dr W Schaefer & Mr K D George,** 01686 628992, wolfgang@cwmweeg.co.uk, www.cwmweeg.co.uk. *4½ m SE of Newtown. Off bypass, take A489 E from Newtown for 1½ m, turn R towards Dolfor. After 2m turn L down asphalted farm track. Do not follow SatNav.* **Sun 7 Sept (2-5). Adm £6, chd free. Cream teas and home-made cakes available.**
A 2½ acre garden set within 24 acres of wildflower meadows and bluebell woodland with stream centred around C15 farmhouse. Formal garden in English landscape tradition with vistas, grottos, sculptures, stumpery, lawns and extensive borders terraced with stone walls. Translates older garden vocabulary into an innovative C21 concept. Covered seating area in the large Garden Pavilion. Extensive woodland walks along stream with several bridges. The tower/mausoleum under construction. Partial wheelchair access. For further information please see garden website.

12 ♦ DINGLE NURSERIES & GARDEN
Welshpool, SY21 9JD. **Mr & Mrs D Hamer,** 01938 555145, info@dinglenurseriesandgarden.co.uk, www.dinglenurseryandgarden.co.uk. *2m NW of Welshpool. Take A490 towards Llanfyllin & Guilsfield. After 1m turn L at sign for Dingle Nurseries & Garden. Follow signs & enter the Garden from adjacent plant centre.* **For NGS: Sat 10, Sun 11 May, Sat 11, Sun 12 Oct (9-5). Adm £3.50, chd free. Tea & coffee available. For other opening times and information, please phone, email or visit garden website.**
4½ acre internationally acclaimed RHS partner garden on south facing site, sloping down to lakes. Huge variety of rare and unusual trees, ornamental shrubs and herbaceous plants give year-round interest. Set in the hills of mid Wales this beautiful well known garden attracts visitors from Britain and abroad. Plant collector's paradise.

13 DOLWEN *NEW*
Aberhosan, Machynlleth, SY20 8SD. **Scott and Teym Vere Hunt.** *3½ m SE Machynlleth. From Machynlleth A489 E for ½ m. Turn R on Forge Rd. At Forge turn L over bridge & continue for 2½ m.* **Sat 21, Sun 22 June (11-4). Adm £5. Tea, coffee & cake.**
C18 cottage Dolwen (White Meadow) has ⅓ acre pretty hillside cottage garden with upper and lower levels sloping down to River Dulas. Roses, clematis and herbaceous borders, lots of pots, chickens and beehives. Wildlife pond alive with dragonflies, newts and frogs. Lots of seating areas throughout. Beautiful stained glass for sale made by the owner.

14 EVE'S GARDEN
The Old Stackyard, Cefn-Y-Coed, Llansantffraid, SY22 6TB. **Emyr Wigley,** 01691 828360. *2m S Llansantffraid. Across bridge out of Llansantffraid on B4393 in direction of Shrewsbury. Turn R for Deuddwr & follow signs to garden.* **Sun 20 July (11-5). Adm £5, chd free. Home-made teas. Visits also by arrangement July to Sept for groups of 5 to 99.**
Deep borders filled with roses,

fuschias, pelargoniums, annuals and flowering shrubs surround the house which is itself adorned with pots, hanging baskets and climbing roses. At the back there is a lawn with Japanese maples and a kitchen garden for vegetables, fruit and cut flowers. A home-made greenhouse with tomatoes completes this vibrant garden made in memory of the owner's wife. Level paths throughout the garden for wheelchair access.

& ❀ 🚗 ☕))

15 GARREGLLWYD
Nantmel, Rhayader, LD6 5PE.
Stephanie Morgan, 07425 358550, samorgan100@hotmail.com. *5m E of Rhayader. From Rhayader take A44 E for 3½m to Nantmel. Turn L by Dolau Chapel signed Abbeycwmhir. Follow lane for 1½ m then turn R by red warning triangle signed Garregllwyd. Follow track for ½ m.* **Sat 10, Sun 11 May (12-5). Adm £5, chd free. Tea, coffee & cake.** Visits also by arrangement Apr to Sept for groups of 5+.
A three acre landscaped garden at 1000' with stunning panoramic views of mid Wales. Large ponds with abundance of wildlife, unusual specimen trees, daffodils, bluebells, rhododendrons and raised vegetable beds and greenhouses growing seasonal veg. Designed to cope with exposed altitude with minimal maintenance and to encourage wildlife. Variety of seating areas to enjoy the ever changing weather conditions.

🐑 ❀ ☕ 🪑))

16 GARTHMYL HALL
Garthmyl, Montgomery, SY15 6RS.
Julia Pugh, 01686 639401, hello@garthmylhall.co.uk, www.garthmylhall.co.uk. *On A483 midway between Welshpool & Newtown (both 8m). Turn R 200yds S of Nag's Head Pub.* **Mon 26 May (1-5). Adm £5, chd free. Tea, coffee & cake.**
Grade II listed Georgian manor house (not open) surrounded by five acres of grounds. 100 metre herbaceous borders, newly restored one acre walled garden with gazebo, circular flower beds, lavender beds, wildflower meadow, pond, two fire pits and gravel paths. Fountain, three magnificent cedar of Lebanon and giant redwood. Partial wheelchair access. Accessible WC.

& 🐑 🚗 🚌 ☕))

17 NEW **GLAN YR AFON**
Llangedwyn, Oswestry, SY10 9LQ.
Nick & Gill Powell, 07968 250364, gill.powell@ngs.org.uk. *10m W of Oswestry. From Llynclys x-roads (A483) follow B4396 towards Llanrhaeadr YM. After approx 5m turn L at T-junc by Llangedwyn Sch. Over river bridge, take next R: cottage is 4th property on L.* **Visits by arrangement May to Aug for groups of 6 to 20. Adm £5, chd free. Tea, coffee & cake.**
500 year old cottage in an acre sloping plot overlooking the Tanat Valley. Large decked area with pergola and arbour. Pond with cascade, productive orchard, raised beds and greenhouse. Steep steps to summerhouse with far-reaching views. Extensive shrub and perennial plantings. Small paddock bordered by natural wooded stream. Steeply sloping site unsuitable for wheelchair users. Limited parking: extra space at Craft Mill (5 min walk).

☕ 🪑))

18 ♦ GREGYNOG HALL & GARDEN
Tregynon, Newtown, SY16 3PL.
The Gregynog Trust, 01686 650224, enquiries@gregynog.org, www.gregynog.org. *5m N of Newtown. From Newtown A483 N turn L B4389 for Tregynon/ Llanfair Caereinion (car parking charge applies).* **For NGS: Sat 31 May, Sun 1 June, Sat 18, Sun 19 Oct (10-4). Adm by donation. Light refreshments in Courtyard Cafe.** For other opening times and information, please phone, email or visit garden website.
Gardens are Grade I listed due to association with the C18 landscape architect William Emes. Set within 750 acres, a designated National Nature Reserve with SSSI, there is parkland with small lake and traces of a water garden. A mass display of rhododendrons, azaleas and unique yew hedge surround the sunken lawns. Unusual trees, woodland walks and arboretum. Good autumn colour. Lily lake 750 acres of estate to explore with marked woodland walks. Two areas of SSSI, National Nature Reserve and part of Wales' National Forest. Wheelchair access via some gravel paths, accessible path being built around the lily lake.

& 🐑 🚗 🚌 ☕ 🪑

19 NEW **THE GROVE**
Presteigne, LD8 2NS.
grovegarden82@gmail.com. *Nr Presteigne. 3m W of Presteigne on the B4357, between Beggar's Bush & Whitton.* **Visits by arrangement 5 July to 10 Aug for groups of 10 to 40. Adm £10.**
Stunning seven acre garden divided into large defined areas, each with its own mood and planting style. Beautiful walled garden, courtyard garden, stunning grass garden, very productive vegetable plot and greenhouse. Arboretum with 200+ varieties of tree. Riverside walk and unique sculptures complement the planting. Around every corner there are surprises and delights to discover. For garden clubs, as an introduction to a visit, a 1hr presentation 'The Evolution of Grove Garden: One Step at a Time'. Discuss when booking if presentation is required.

☕

GROUP OPENING

20 NEW **GUILSFIELD GARDENS**
Guilsfield, Welshpool, SY21 9ND. *3m N of Welshpool. From Welshpool A490 N 1⅗m. Turn R on B4392 for Guilsfield. Pass Derwen Garden Centre on R. Adm tickets & parking at Guilsfield sch approx ½ m on L.* **Sun 10 Aug (12-5). Combined adm £6, chd free. Home-made teas at The Old School, SY21 9NQ.**

NEW **21 ACREFIELD AVENUE**
Keith and Rhian Wall.

NEW **31 ACREFIELD AVENUE**
Janet Powell.

NEW **1 COED Y GLYN**
Midge Bocking.

NEW **THE MILL**
Richard and Frances Birkett.

A new group of four delightful gardens in Guilsfield village. 21 Acrefield: Mature trees, shrubs and a nature reserve form backdrop to beautifully maintained garden. Extensive gravel area, with a collection of roses, echinacea, begonias, and bedding. Shaded and sunny seating areas. 31 Acrefield: Cottage-garden style borders, wealth of planters contain hostas, ferns, summer bedding, hydrangeas and more. 1 Coed y Glyn: Interesting all-the-year-round garden featuring many roses, shrubs, annuals and perennials. Clematis and climbers over walls, arches and pergolas. Small pool, several seating areas sited so garden can be appreciated to the full. The Mill: A water-powered corn mill in use until the 1960's. Mill leat now an area of damp and water-loving plants. Meandering paths, mature trees inc many acers, fruiting *Cornus kousa* var. *Chinensis*, lodgepole pine and more. Pond, shady area, rockery and pleasant seating areas. All wildlife friendly. Wheelchair access at 21 Acrefield Avenue and 1 Coed-y-Glyn; front gardens of 31 Acrefield Ave and The Mill.

21 NEW GWERNFYDA
Cefn Coch, Welshpool, SY21 0AQ. Helen Parker. *5m SW Llanfair Caereinion. From Llanfair Caereinion take B4389 S for ¼ m. Turn R signed Cefn Coch. Turn L at Cefn Coch Inn, entrance 1m on L.* **Sun 6 July (1-5). Adm £4.50, chd free. Home-made teas.**
A country garden surrounded by fields with pretty views and a small stream running through. At the heart of the ¾ acre garden sits a pretty C16 house and barns. The mix of cottage garden, vegetable garden, stream and naturalistic areas make this a haven for wildlife. Enjoy the sound of the stream, the views and the peace.

22 THE HYMNS
Walton, Presteigne, LD8 2RA. E Passey, 07958 762362, thehymns@hotmail.com, www.thehymns.co.uk. *5m W of Kington. Take A44 W, then 1st R for Kinnerton. After approx 1m, at the top of small hill, turn L (W).* **Visits by arrangement 31 Mar to 30 Sept. Adm £6, chd free.**
In a beautiful setting in the heart of the Radnor valley, the garden is part of a restored C16 farmstead, with long views to the hills, and the Radnor Forest. It is a traditional garden reclaimed from the wild, using locally grown herbs and seeds, and with a herb patio, wildflower meadows and a short woodland walk. It is designed for all the senses: sight, sound and smell.

GROUP OPENING
23 NEW LEIGHTON GARDENS
Welshpool, SY21 8HH. Catherine Williams. *Approx 1½ m E of Welshpool. From A458 turn at Buttington church/ Green Dragon, follow B4388 1½ m. From Welshpool, B4381to Leighton approx 1m. R at T-junc ⅖ m on L. Parking, tickets & map at Leighton Village Hall.* **Sun 6 July (11-5). Combined adm £6, chd free. Home-made teas at Leighton Village Hall.**

NEW BRIARWOOD
Pat and Laura Poole.

NEW CAE BERLLAN
Catherine Williams.

NEW OAK HOUSE
Annie and Ian Corke.

NEW OAKWOOD
Roger Clegg.

NEW PROVIDENCE HOUSE
Wendy Edwards.

NEW 6 REDWOOD CLOSE
Terry and Hilary Lomas.

NEW THE WHITE HOUSE
Robert and Margaret Landgrebe.

The small communities of Leighton and Hope, originally part of the Victorian Naylor Estate, are surrounded by gorgeous views of the Mid Wales countryside inc Powis Castle, Offa's Dyke, and The Redwoods. The collection of gardens encompasses a range of styles, sizes, and approaches. Leighton Church and the buildings of the Model Farm (now Yorton Stud) provide a back drop and there are many delightful walks around the area. Parking also available at the Grade II* listed Holy Trinity Church which will be open to look around. Shuttle Bus between gardens available. Children's quiz, colouring table and community playground at village hall.

24 LLANGEDWYN HALL
Llangedwyn, Oswestry, SY10 9JW. Nicholas Williams-Wynn, llangedwyn.co.uk. *8m SW of Oswestry. From Oswestry, A483 S for 3½ m, turn R at Llynclys x-roads turn W on to the B4396 towards Llanhaeadr-ym-Mochnant. Continue approx 5m to the village of Llangedwyn.* **Sun 29 June (12-4). Adm £6, chd free. Home-made teas.**

Beautiful four acre formal terraced garden on three levels, designed and laid out in late C17 and early C18. Unusual herbaceous plants, sunken rose garden, small water garden, walled kitchen garden and woodland walk. Fantastic views over the surrounding countryside with the C18 Cadw listed octagonal Stallion House. Woodland walks, summerhouse, formal ponds and newly planted arboretum.

GROUP OPENING
25 LLANRHAEADR YM MOCHNANT GARDENS
Market Street, Llanrhaeadr Ym Mochnant, Oswestry, SY10 0JN. *The village is 12m W of Oswestry on the B4580. Parking and tickets at Village Hall in Back Chapel St. Additional parking in Park St.* **Sat 17 May (12-5). Combined adm £6, chd free. Home-made teas in Llanrhaeadr ym Mochnant Public Hall, Back Chapel Street.**

NEW 5 HAFAN Y DORLAN
Ms Janet Edwards.

NEW ISFRYN
Stephen Hopper.

PLAS YN LLAN
Kate & Fergus Nicoll.

ROCK HOUSE
Mrs Pauline Kirby.

TRE TYLLUAN
Mr Peter Carr.

The lively village of Llanrhaeadr ym Mochnant is set on the edge of the Berwyn Mountains with local shops and beauty spots such as the famous waterfall, Pistyll Rhaeadr. We have a selection of small village gardens offering a range of styles from cottage, courtyard, terrace and prairie style plantings. Innovative use of small spaces, often steeply sloping down to the beautiful River Rhaeadr. All of the gardens attract a multitude of wildlife: birds, bees, bats and butterflies. Some have trained fruit trees and productive vegetable plots, as well as pots of bulbs for late spring interest. Local coffee shop Gegin Fach will be open for light lunches. The Wynnstay Arms offers a carvery lunch which would need to be booked in advance. Many show the challenges of working in steeply sloping gardens. Open Studio at Isfryn.

5 Cae Celyn, Berriew Village Gardens

26 LLANSTEPHAN HOUSE
Llanstephan, Llyswen, LD3 0YR. Lord & Lady Milford. *10m SW of Builth Wells. Leave A470 at Llyswen onto B4350. 1st L after x-ing river in Boughrood. From Builth Wells leave A470, Erwood Bridge, 1st L. Follow signs.* **Mon 26 May (1-5). Adm £5, chd free. Tea, coffee & cake. Visitors are welcome to bring a picnic.**
A 20 acre garden, first laid out almost 200 years ago and in the present owner's family for more than a century. Featuring a Victorian walled kitchen garden and greenhouses, 100 year old wisteria, woodland walks punctuated by azaleas and rhododendrons, specimen trees and immaculate lawns. Beautiful and celebrated views of Wye Valley and Black Mountains.

27 LLWYN MADOC
Beulah, Llanwrtyd Wells, LD5 4TT. Patrick & Miranda Bourdillon, 01591 620564, miranda.bourdillon@gmail.com. *8m W of Builth Wells. On A483 at Beulah take road towards Abergwesyn for 1m. Drive on R. Parking on field below drive- follow yellow signs.* **Sun 25 May (2-5.30). Adm £6, chd free. Cream teas.**
Terraced garden in a glorious wooded valley, overlooking a stunning lake. Yew hedges and a rose garden with pergola. The gardens slope down away from the house and are at their best when the rhododendrons and azaleas are out. Guided walks to the other side of the lake are available for the fit and adventurous to see ducks, geese, red kite, heron and, if you are really lucky, otters too.

28 LLWYNAU MAWR FARM
Cwmdu, Crickhowell, NP8 1RS. Dr Pauline Ruth. *N of Tretower on edge of Cwmdu. Travelling N turn L at the Farmers Arms pub in Cwmdu, through the village and then follow the signs to Llwynaumawr. Llwynaumawr Farm is the 300 year old barn. Parking will be signposted.* **Sat 14 June (10-4). Combined adm with Maes Llechau £10, chd free. Tea, coffee & cake.**
Old barn beautifully located on Beacons Way facing south with fantastic views of Black Mountains. Since October 2022, Pauline has been working on an established garden with productive vegetable plot, two acre orchard of rare apples, pears, plums, damsons, cherry, crabapple and walnut. Woodland walks. Climbing roses, fig and vine. Borders and wildflower area. Multiple seating areas to enjoy. Stream, mown paths, dry stone walling, arbour, greenhouses, ancient pears, free range hens, wildflowers and pollinators.

29 LLYSDINAM
Newbridge-on-Wye, LD1 6NB. Sir John & Lady Venables-Llewelyn & Llysdinam Charitable Trust, 07748 492025, llysdinamgardens@gmail.com, www.llysdinamgardens.org. *5m SW of Llandrindod Wells. Turn W off A470 at Newbridge-on-Wye; turn R immed after x-ing River Wye. Entrance is up the hill.* **Sun 25 May (2-5). Adm £5, chd free. Cream teas. Visits also by arrangement 15 Jan to 16 Dec.**
Llysdinam Gardens are among the loveliest in mid Wales, especially noted for a magnificent display of rhododendrons and azaleas in May. Covering some six acres, they command sweeping views down the Wye Valley. Successive family members have developed the gardens over the last 150 years to inc woodland with specimen trees, large herbaceous and shrub borders and a water garden, all of which provide varied, colourful planting throughout the year. The Victorian walled kitchen garden and extensive greenhouses grow a wide variety of vegetables, hothouse fruit and exotic plants. Wheelchair access via gravel paths.

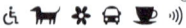

30 MAES LLECHAU
Cwmdu, Crickhowell, NP8 1SB. Drs Douglas and Alison Paton. *5m NW of Crickhowell. A40 from Crickhowell at 4½m turn into the lane on R. Follow to T-junc, turn L Maes Llechau is on the R. From Brecon 1st L off A40 after Bwlch, to Maes Llechau after 1m.* **Sat 14 June (10-4). Combined adm with Llwynau Mawr Farm £10, chd free. Tea, coffee & cake. Savoury options available.**
We moved to Maes Llechau, translated as 'field of slate' in 2016 having converted a long-barn into our home. Developed from scratch, the 1½ acres of verdant garden inc perennial borders, meadows, orchard, new woodland and vegetable garden. Maes Llechau draws from the borrowed landscape of the Black Mountains.

31 THE MALTHOUSE
Llandrinio, Llanymynech, SY22 6SG. Veronica and Alec White. *On B4393, in Llandrinio Village. Between the Punchbowl Pub & Llandrinio Church. Car park opp entrance drive. Parking for disabled at the house.* **Sat 7, Sun 8 June (1-5). Adm £6, chd free. Home-made teas. Gluten, dairy free and vegan cakes available.**
Walled kitchen garden dating from the C17, adjacent to Llandrinio Hall (Grade II listed building). Restored and planted by present owners over the last 20 years. A long herbaceous border, vegetable parterres, interesting range of C17 pig sties, fruit trees, beehives, long view to the Breidden Hills. Garden is flat and wheelchair accessible.

32 THE MEADOWS
Carno Road, Caersws, SY17 5JA. Pete & Lesley Benton, 07929 038936, bentlesl@aol.com. *7m W of Newtown. From Newtown A489 for 6m, turn R for Caersws. Cont thru village onto Carno Rd. ½m on L, red brick house. From Carno 6m on A470 on R.* **Visits by arrangement 9 June to 31 Aug for groups of up to 20. Afternoon or evening bookings. Discuss refreshments when booking. Adm £4, chd free.**
South facing level country garden on village edge. Although compact, there is a large variety of shrubs, perennials and annuals, some unusual, packed into beds and 100+ containers. Interesting themed areas, quirky recycled objects and plenty of scented, restful seating areas, in open and under cover. Optional Quiz to discover the more unexpected. Limited space on drive, additional parking can be arranged. Wheelchair users will need to navigate some gravel paths.

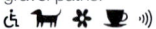

33 MOEL Y GWELLTYN UCHA
Llansilin, Oswestry, SY10 7QX.
Mr Nick & Mrs Sue Roberts. *8m W of Oswestry. Follow yellow NGS signs from St Silin's Church Llansilin. Garden less 2½ m W of Llansilin on B4580 towards Llanrhaeadr-ym-Mochnant. Garden ¼ m from parking area accessed via a farm track.* **Sat 2, Sun 3 Aug (1.30-5.30). Adm £6, chd free. Home-made cakes, teas and coffee.**
South facing terraced cottage garden at 900ft on steep hillside in stunning location; fabulous views towards Rodney's Pillar and Long Mountain. Colourful, floriferous: roses, shrubs, pots and herbaceous perennials. We also have a vegetable plot. The garden and pond offer a haven for birds, insects and lots of other wildlife. Seats enable you to pause, relax and enjoy the scenery. Courtesy transport from parking area to the garden for those with mobility issues. Enjoy refreshments whilst taking in the extensive views. Accessible toilet available. Homemade jams and chutneys for sale. Cash sales only.

34 THE NEUADD
Llanbedr, Crickhowell, NP8 1SP.
Philippa Herbert, 01873 812164, philippaherbert@gmail.com. *1m NE of Crickhowell. Leave Crickhowell by Llanbedr Rd. At junc with Great Oak Rd bear L, cont up hill for approx 1m, garden on L. Ample parking.* **Sun 1 June (2-6). Adm £6.50, chd free. Home-made teas in the courtyard. Visits also by arrangement 1 May to 1 Sept for groups of up to 12.**
The late Robin Herbert and his wife Philippa started work on the garden at The Neuadd in1999 and planted many unusual trees and shrubs in the dramatic setting of the Bannau Brycheiniog National Park. One of the major features is the walled garden, with both traditional and decorative planting of fruit, vegetables and flowers. Circuit walks of the garden. Spectacular views, water feature, rare trees and shrubs and a great plant stall and teas. Most of the garden is accessible for wheelchair users, but some steep paths.

35 NEW THE OLD POTTERY
Foel Farm, Llansantffraid, SY22 6UA. Graeme Slack and Karen Chadwick, graemeslack2013@talktalk.net. *7m SW of Oswestry. 8m N of Welshpool.*

From A483 at Llynclys x-road turn R A495 W towards LLansantffraid. At Lion pub turn R towards Llanfechain. 80 metres past Cain's vets on L. **Visits by arrangement Apr to Oct for groups of 12 to 20. Adm £6, chd free.**
The garden has developed over the last few years. Plants abound with colour during most seasons. In spring we see spring bulbs, hellebores, *Pulmonaria* and magnolias followed by azaleas and young rhododendrons; then come the perennials, flowering shrubs and much more. There are two small ponds one for wildlife the other with goldfish. A main feature in the garden is a railway bridge.

36 PLAS DINAM
Llandinam, Newtown, SY17 5DQ. Eldrydd Lamp, 07415 503554, eldrydd@plasdinam.co.uk, www.plasdinamcountryhouse.co.uk. *7½ m SW Newtown. Garden located on A470.* **Visits by arrangement 3 Mar to 27 Nov for groups of 15+. Monday- Thursday only. Adm £5.50, chd free. Home-made teas.**
12 acres of parkland, gardens, lawns and woodland set at the foot of glorious rolling hills with spectacular views across the Severn Valley. A host of daffodils followed by one of the best wildflower meadows in Montgomeryshire with 36 species of flowers and grasses inc hundreds of wild orchids; Glorious autumn colour with *Parrotias, Liriodendrons, Cotinus* etc. Millennium wood. Explore the new Remarkable Tree Walk which inc eight champion trees. From 1884 until recently the home of Lord Davies and his family (house not open). Paths and house are wheelchair accessible.

37 PLUM TREE COTTAGE
Ffawyddog, Crickhowell, NP8 1PY.
Mr & Mrs Bennett. *1m S of Crickhowell. From Crickhowell cross the river and then R by Vine Tree. Follow the road into Llangattock and take the 1st R after the Horseshoe pub. Follow yellow signs up hill to Ffawyddog common.* **Sun 15 June (12-4). Adm £6, chd free. Home-made teas.**
This large cottage garden in the heart of the Brecon Beacons National Park is around ¾ acre and comprises a shaded area, herbaceous borders, vegetable beds and wild areas. Wild orchids grow freely in unmown

grass along with other wildflowers. The garden is organic and free of herbicides and pesticides. Borders have wide range of traditional and unusual plants. Uncultivated areas have been allowed to encourage wildlife. Large greenhouse for raising and growing plants. Adjacent to Ffawyddog Common, an AONB.

38 PONTHAFREN
Long Bridge Street, Newtown, SY16 2DY. Ponthafren Association, 01686 621586, admin@ponthafren.org.uk, www.ponthafren.org.uk. *Park in main car park in town centre, 5 mins walk. Turn L out of car park, turn L over bridge, garden on L. Limited disabled parking, please phone for details.* **Sat 12 July (11-4); Sun 13 July (1-4). Adm by donation. Tea, coffee & cake. Visits also by arrangement Apr to Sept for groups of 5 to 20.**
Ponthafren is a registered charity that provides a caring community to promote positive mental health and wellbeing for all. Open door policy so everyone is welcome. Interesting community garden on banks of River Severn run and maintained totally by volunteers: sensory garden with long grasses, herbs, scented plants and shrubs, quirky objects. Productive vegetable plot. Lots of plants for sale. Covered seating areas positioned around the garden to enjoy the views. We received a Community Garden Grant in 2023. Partial wheelchair access.

39 THE ROCK HOUSE
Llanbister, LD1 6TN. Jude Boutle & Sue Cox. *10m N of Llandrindod Wells. Off B4356 just above Llanbister village. What3words app: jousting.radically.iron.* **Sat 7, Sun 8 June (12-5). Adm £5, chd free. Home-made teas. Gluten free and vegan cakes available.**
About an acre of informal mature hillside garden, with views over the Radnorshire Hills. Over 30 years we have created wildlife ponds, a bluebell meadow, laburnum arch and have recently revamped the vegetable garden. An example of what can be achieved 1000ft up a Welsh hillside.

40 ROCK MILL
Abermule, Montgomery, SY15 6NN. Rufus & Cherry Fairweather, 01686 630664, fairweathers66@btinternet.com. *1m S of Abermule on the Kerry Rd (B4368) on LHS. Best approached from the village as there is an angled entrance into field for parking.* **Visits by arrangement 2 May to 31 May for groups of 10 to 30. Adm inc cream tea. Adm £10.**
A river runs through this magical three acre award-winning garden in a beautiful wooded valley. Discover colourful borders and shrubberies, specimen trees and terraces. Take a stroll along woodland walks, bridges and extensive lawns. You'll find fishponds, an orchard, herb and vegetable beds, roundhouse and remnants of industrial past (corn mill and railway line). There is much to explore.

41 NEW 14 ST MARY'S PLACE
Union Street, Welshpool, SY21 7PF. Jill Rock. *Centre of Welshpool below St Mary's Church. Car park behind town hall, cross road, turn R and house is just past cafe on L. Follow yellow NGS signs.* **Sat 30, Sun 31 Aug (11-5). Adm £4, chd free.**
Interesting secret town garden on two levels behind house. Steep steps to first level with paved area made from floors of older houses once on the site. Large acers, potted hostas and studio with wisteria and jasmine growing up it. Steps to side of studio to higher level with views of Welshpool mainly planted with perennials. Seating areas. Unusual varieties of plants and interesting pots. Very steep steps sturdy footwear required.

42 TRANQUILITY HAVEN
7 Lords Land, Whitton, Knighton, LD7 1NJ. Val Brown, 01547 560070, valerie.brown1502@gmail.com. *Approx 3m from Knighton & 5m Presteigne. From Knighton take B4355 after approx. 2m turn R on B4357 to Whitton. Car park on L by yellow NGS signs.* **Visits by arrangement May to Aug for individuals and groups up to 30. Adm £5, chd free.**
Amazing Japanese inspired garden with borrowed views to Offa's Dyke. Winding paths pass small pools and lead to Japanese bridges over natural stream with dippers and kingfishers. Sounds of water fill the air. Enjoy peace and tranquillity from one of the seats or the Japanese Tea House. Dense oriental planting with Cornus kousa 'Satomi', acers, azaleas, unusual bamboos and wonderful cloud pruning.

43 TREBERFYDD HOUSE
Llangasty, Bwlch, Brecon, LD3 7PX. Sally Raikes, 07748 155484, sally@treberfydd.com, www.treberfydd.com. *6m E of Brecon. From Abergavenny on A40, turn R in Bwlch on B5460. Take 1st L towards Pennorth & cont 2m along lane. From Brecon, turn L off A40 in Llanhamlach towards Pennorth. Go through Pennorth, 1m on L.* **Sun 18 May (12.30-5.30). Adm £6.50, chd free. Home-made teas.**
Grade I-listed Victorian Gothic house with 10 acres of grounds designed by W A Nesfield. Magnificent cedar of Lebanon, towering Atlantic cedars and other notable historic trees, Victorian rockery, herbaceous border and manicured lawns ideal for a picnic. Wonderful views of the Black Mountains. Plants available from commercial nursery in grounds - the Walled Garden Treberfydd. 30 minute self-guided tree tour and shorter version is wheelchair friendly. Tours of the house during the NGS open day (limited numbers on each tour, £2.50) conducted by a member of the Raikes family. Easy wheelchair access to areas around the house, but herbaceous border only accessible via steps.

GROUP OPENING

44 NEW TREGYNON GARDENS
Tregynon, Newtown, SY16 3EH. Liz Davies. *6m N Newtown. From Newtown: A483 N. After 3m turn L onto B4389 to Tregynon. Adm tickets & parking in Community Centre car park. Follow yellow NGS signs.* **Sun 13 July (1-5). Combined adm £6, chd free. Home-made teas at Parson's Field.**

NEW MAES ADERYN
Karen Trow.
NEW 48 PARC HAFOD
Tracy Evans and Ian Pugh.
PARSON'S FIELD
Liz Davies, www.facebook.com/p/Parsons-Field-Tregynon-100081300246740.

NEW 7 TAN Y LLAN
Michelle Zizka.
NEW 19 TAN Y LLAN
Anne Allen.

A trail of five small gardens (four new) with a range of styles: inc plantswoman's garden with unusual plants, gravel gardens, productive fruit and vegetable gardens, rose garden and a beautiful Community Garden with wildflower meadow. The centre of village retains its old charm with Rectory, Church House and the old School displaying traditional mid Wales half timber framed black and white dwellings. Visit beautiful St Cynon's church.

45 TREMYNFA
Carreghofa Lane, Llanymynech, SY22 6LA. Jon & Gillian Fynes. *Edge of Llanymynech village. From Oswestry, S on A483 to Welshpool. In Llanymynech turn R at Xrds (car wash on corner). Take 2nd R then follow yellow NGS signs. 300yds park signed field, limited disabled parking nr garden.* **Sat 7, Sun 8 June (1-5). Adm £6, chd free. Tea, coffee & cake. All cakes and scones home-made. Some gluten free options available.**
South facing one acre garden developed over 17 years. Old railway cottage set in herbaceous and raised borders, patio with many pots of colourful and unusual plants. Garden slopes to productive fruit and vegetable area, ponds, spinney, unusual trees, wild areas and peat bog. Patio and seats to enjoy extensive views inc Llanymynech Rocks. Pet ducks on site, Montgomery canal close by. Homegrown plants and home-made jams for sale.

46 NEW TY CWM DYFI
Cemmaes, Machynlleth, SY20 9PR. Melanie Pepper & Wayne Fisher-Edwards. *7m NE of Machynlleth. From Machynlleth take A489 NE for $5^{3}/_{5}$m then A 470 N for $2^{2}/_{5}$m to Cemmaes. Parking at Penrhos Arms & disabled parking at house. What3words app: rooting. black.emeralds.* **Sat 12, Sun 13 July (12-5). Adm £5, chd free. Tea, coffee & cake.**
Discover an acre garden combining different styled zones with emphasis

47 TYNRHOS
Newbridge-on-Wye, Llandrindod Wells, LD1 6ND. Clare Wilkinson. *1m NW Newbridge-on-Wye. From A470 take B4518 (signed Beulah). After 400yds, cross bridge & turn R for Llysdinam. Proceed up the hill for 1m, Tynrhos is on L.* **Sun 6 July (1.30-5.30). Adm £5, chd free. Home-made teas.**
A ¾ acre family cottage garden lying at approx 800ft with views over the Wye Valley. Mainly herbaceous planting with summer annuals and pots. Vegetable plot with greenhouse leading to orchard, fields and wildlife pond. Cobbled area to terrace. Wheelchair access to rear garden over grass. Paths are a mix of grass and gravel.

48 TYN-Y-GRAIG
Bwlch y Ffridd, Newtown, SY16 3JB. Simon & Georgina Newson, 07989 855925, simon.newson@yahoo.com. *4m N Caersws. B4568 from Newtown: Turn R after Aberhafesp. At fork bear L past community centre, then at x-roads turn R. At next fork bear L. Go over cattle grid take 1st R onto rough track.* **Sun 6 July (11-5). Adm £5, chd free. Home-made teas. Visits also by arrangement 31 May to 4 July for groups of up to 15.**
Plant-person's garden at 300m elevation with views of surrounding hills. Varied borders and hectare of stunning indigenous wildflower meadow managed for biodiversity sits around a large pond and woodland. Garden planted to achieve different moods inc a herb area, bright, white and pastel borders, rose garden, farmyard borders, fernery, fruit trees and vegetable beds. Open studio. Partial wheelchair access. Grass paths, some steps, most can be avoided. Disabled visitors may be dropped off at house.

SPECIAL EVENT

49 VAYNOR PARK
Berriew, Welshpool, SY21 8QE. Mr & Mrs William Corbett-Winder. *5m S Welshpool. Leave Berriew going over bridge & straight up the hill on the Bettws Rd. Entrance to Vaynor Park is on R ¼m from speed derestriction sign.* **Wed 30 Apr (2-4.30). Adm £25, chd free. Pre-booking essential, please visit www.ngs.org.uk for information & booking. Home-made teas in the stables.**
Spectacular five acre garden set in parkland with Medieval oaks. Stunning display of over 3000 tulips on long Victorian archery lawn flanked by herbaceous borders with *Geums, Anemones, Erysiums,* alliums, *Lunaria* and *Hesperis.* Woodland with rhododendrons inc forrestii, magnolias, euphorbias, *Trilliums, Erythroniums* and bluebells. Tulips in urns close to house contrast with clipped box and yew topiary. A limited number of tickets have been made available for this special one-day event kindly hosted by William and Kate Corbett-Winder. Meet in the courtyard for an introductory talk, followed by a guided tour accompanied by Kate and her gardener Rupert Redway.

50 ♦ WELSH LAVENDER
Cefnperfedd Uchaf, Maesmynis, Builth Wells, LD2 3HU. Nancy Durham, 01982 552467, farmers@welshlavender.com, www.welshlavender.com. *Approx 4½m S of Builth Wells & 13m N from Brecon Cathedral off B4520. The farm is 1⅓m from turn signed Farmers' Welsh Lavender.* **For NGS: Daily Sat 26 July to Fri 1 Aug (10-4). Adm £5, chd free. Pre-booking essential, please visit www.ngs.org.uk for information & booking. Tea, coffee & cake.** For other opening times and information, please phone, email or visit garden website.
The farm, situated at 1100ft high in the hills of mid Wales, offers spectacular views in all directions. Jeni Arnold's stylish wild planting of the steep bank above the ever popular wild swimming pond is a riot of colour. Walk through the fields of blue lavender at their peak. The farm is a bumblebee haven with its wild flower area, orchards and a vegetable garden. Learn how the distillation process works, and visit the farm shop to try body creams and balms made with lavender oil distilled on the farm. Swim in the pond before enjoying coffee, tea and light refreshments. Partial wheelchair access. Large paved area adjacent to coffee, teas and shop area easy to negotiate.

51 WILLOWBROOK
Knighton Road, Presteigne, LD8 2ET. Fiona Collins & David Beech, 07867 385694, fm.collins@hotmail.co.uk. *Outskirts of Presteigne on B4355 towards Knighton, turning L just before the bridge.* **Sun 20 July (12-5). Adm £5, chd free. Home-made teas. Visits also by arrangement June to Aug.**
Begun in 2013, yew hedges create garden rooms and vistas in this approx ¼ acre garden. Discover the pergola cottage garden planted with climbing roses and wisteria. There is a formal 'Italian' style pond garden and a double 'hot' summer border. Roses, box parterre, a rill flowing into a sunken garden. Kitchen garden with raised vegetable beds, fruit trees, soft fruit. Greenhouses, polytunnel. Wheelchair access via level grass and gravel paths.

52 1 YSTRAD HOUSE
1 Church Road, Knighton, LD7 1EB. John & Margaret Davis, 01547 528154, jamdavis1258@outlook.com. *At junc of Church Rd & Station Rd. Take the turning opp Knighton Hotel (A488 Clun) travel 225yds along Station Rd. Yellow House, red front door, at junc with Church Rd. Enter by side gate in Station Rd.* **Visits by arrangement 15 June to 15 Sept for groups of up to 25. Adm £5, chd free. Home-made teas.**
A town garden behind a Regency Villa of earlier origins. A narrow entrance door opens revealing unexpected calm and timelessness. A small walled garden with box hedging and greenhouse lead to broad lawns, wide borders with soft colour schemes and mature trees. More intimate features: pots, urns and pools add interest and surprise. The formal areas merge with wooded glades leading to a riverside walk. Croquet on request. Lawns and gravelled paths mostly flat, except access to riverside walk.

Plant Heritage
CONSERVING THE DIVERSITY OF GARDEN PLANTS

More than sixty gardens that open for the National Garden Scheme are holders of a Plant Heritage National Plant Collection. These gardens carry the NPC symbol. Through the National Collections, Plant Heritage members are safeguarding 95,000 different plants for the future by growing them, recording them and sharing them. Find out more: www.plantheritage.org.uk.

Aster & related genera (autumn flowering)
The Picton Garden, Herefordshire

Astilbe
Marwood Hill Garden, Devon

Astrantia
Norwell Nurseries, Norwell Gardens, Nottinghamshire

Buddleja (hardy spp. & cvs.)
Longstock Park Water Garden, Hampshire

Calendula spp.
Ryton Organic Gardens, Warwickshire

Camellia (autumn & winter flowering)
Green Island, Essex

Camellia japonica
Antony Woodland Garden & Woodland Walk, Cornwall

Camellia & Rhododendron (introduced to Heligan pre 1920)
The Lost Gardens of Heligan, Cornwall

Carpinus
Sir Harold Hillier Gardens, Hampshire

Carpinus betulus cvs.
West Lodge Park, London

Catalpa
West Lodge Park, London

Ceanothus
Eccleston Square, London

Cercidiphyllum
Sir Harold Hillier Gardens, Hampshire
Hodnet Hall Gardens, Shropshire

Chrysanthemum (hardy)
Norwell Nurseries, Norwell Gardens, Nottinghamshire
Hill Close Gardens, Warwickshire

Citrus
Shortgrove Manor Farm, Herefordshire

Codonopsis & related genera
Woodlands, Lincolnshire

Colchicum
East Ruston Old Vicarage, Norfolk

Convallaria
Kingston Lacy, Dorset

Cornus
Sir Harold Hillier Gardens, Hampshire

Corokia
Mona's Garden, London

Corylus
Sir Harold Hillier Gardens, Hampshire

Cotoneaster
Sir Harold Hillier Gardens, Hampshire

Cyclamen (excl. persicum cvs.)
Higher Cherubeer, Devon

Dierama spp.
Yew Tree Cottage, Staffordshire

Dionaea
Beaufort, Shropshire

Echium spp. & cvs. from the Macaronesian Islands
Renishaw Hall & Gardens, Derbyshire

Erica & Calluna (Sussex heather cvs.)
Nymans, Sussex

Erythronium
Greencombe Gardens, Somerset

Eucalyptus spp.
The World Garden at Lullingstone Castle, Kent

Eucryphia
Whitstone Farm, Devon

Euonymus (deciduous)
The Place for Plants, East Bergholt Place Garden, Suffolk

Fraxinus
The Lovell Quinta Arboretum, Cheshire

Gaultheria (incl Pernettya)
Greencombe Gardens, Somerset

Geranium phaeum cvs. & primary hybrids
The New Barn, Leicestershire

Geranium sanguineum, macrorrhizum & x cantabrigiense
Brockamin, Worcestershire

Geum cvs.
1 Brickwall Cottages, Kent

Hamamelis
Sir Harold Hillier Gardens, Hampshire

Hamamelis cvs.
Green Island, Essex

Heliotropium
Hampton Court Palace, London

Heritage Seed Library (vegetable)
Ryton Organic Gardens, Warwickshire

Hilliers (plants raised by)
Sir Harold Hillier Gardens, Hampshire

Hoheria
Abbotsbury Subtropical Gardens, Dorset

Hypericum sect. Androsaemum & Ascyreia spp.
Holme for Gardens, Dorset

Hypericum spp. & cvs.
Sir Harold Hillier Gardens, Hampshire

Iris ensata
Marwood Hill Garden, Devon

Jovibarba
Fir Croft, Derbyshire

Juglans
Upton Wold, Gloucestershire

Lapageria rosea (& named cvs.)
Roseland House, Cornwall

Lewisia
'John's Garden' at Ashwood Nurseries, Staffordshire

Ligustrum
Sir Harold Hillier Gardens, Hampshire

Lithocarpus
Sir Harold Hillier Gardens, Hampshire

Malus (ornamental)
Barnards Farm, Essex

Metasequoia
Sir Harold Hillier Gardens, Hampshire

Narcissus cvs. (bred & introduced by Noel Burr)
Bourne Botanicals, Sussex

Narcissus cvs. (bred & introduced by the Rev G H Engleheart)
2 Holmwood Cottages, Suffolk

Nymphaea
Bennetts Water Gardens, Dorset

Pennisetum spp. & cvs. (hardy)
Knoll Gardens, Dorset

Peperomia cvs.
Meveril Lodge, Derbyshire

Photinia
Sir Harold Hillier Gardens, Hampshire

Pinus
Sir Harold Hillier Gardens, Hampshire

Pinus spp.
The Lovell Quinta Arboretum, Cheshire

Polypodium (hardy cvs.)
The Picton Garden, Herefordshire

Polystichum
Greencombe Gardens, Somerset

Pterocarya
Upton Wold, Gloucestershire

Pulmonaria cvs.
Brockamin, Worcestershire

Quercus
Chevithorne Barton, Devon
Sir Harold Hillier Gardens, Hampshire

Quercus (Sir Bernard Lovell collection)
The Lovell Quinta Arboretum, Cheshire

Rhododendron (Ghent Azaleas)
Sheffield Park and Garden, Sussex

Rhododendron (Colonel Stephenson Clarke's collection at Borde Hill)
Borde Hill Garden, Sussex

Rhus
The Place for Plants, East Bergholt Place Garden, Suffolk

Rosa (Hybrid Musk intro by Pemberton & Bentall 1912-1939)
Dutton Hall, Lancashire, Merseyside & Greater Manchester

Rosa (rambling)
Moor Wood, Gloucestershire

Salix
West Wales Willows, Carmarthenshire & Pembrokeshire

Salvia (tender)
Kingston Maurward Gardens and Animal Park, Dorset

Salvia (microphylla & relatives)
Highview House, Norfolk

Sambucus
Cotswold Garden Flowers, Worcestershire

Sarracenia
Beaufort, Shropshire

Sarracenia spp. & cvs. (incl. Adrian Slack hybrids)
The Hidden Garden, Ceredigion

Saxifraga sect. Ligulatae spp. & cvs.
Waterperry Gardens, Oxfordshire

Saxifraga sect. Porphyrion subsect. Porophyllum
Waterperry Gardens, Oxfordshire

Sempervivum
Fir Croft, Derbyshire

Sorbus
Ness Botanic Gardens, Cheshire

Sorbus (British endemic spp.)
Blagdon, Northumberland

Stewartia
High Beeches Woodland and Water Garden, Sussex

Streptocarpus
Dibleys Nurseries, North East Wales

Symphyotrichum (Aster) novae-angliae
Brockamin, Worcestershire

Symphytum
Ryton Organic Gardens, Warwickshire

Taxodium spp. & cvs.
West Lodge Park, London

Toxicodendron
The Place for Plants, East Bergholt Place Garden, Suffolk

Tulbaghia spp. & subspp.
Marwood Hill Garden, Devon

Tulipa (historic tulips)
Blackland House, Wiltshire

Vaccinium
Greencombe Gardens, Somerset

Yucca
Spring View, Burwell Village Gardens, Cambridgeshire
Renishaw Hall & Gardens, Derbyshire

Scotland's GARDENS Scheme
OPEN FOR CHARITY

Visit Scottish gardens open for charity

Explore nearly 400 secret gardens in beautiful Scotland, from tiny urban oases to grand Scottish estates and castle gardens.

scotlandsgardens.org

SC049866

Pictured: Gardyne Castle

Acknowledgements

Each year the National Garden Scheme receives fantastic support from the community of garden photographers who donate and make available images of gardens: sincere thanks to them all. Our thanks also to our wonderful garden owners who kindly submit images of their gardens.

Unless otherwise stated, photographs are kindly reproduced by permission of the garden owner.

The 2025 Production Team: Vicky Flynn, Louise Grainger, Vince Hagan, Sarah Hosker, Kay Palmer, Christina Plowman, Helena Pretorius, George Plumptre, Gail Sherling-Brown, Laura Steel, Catherine Swan, Georgina Waters, Anna Wili.

The moral right of the author has been asserted. All rights reserved. No part of this publication may be reproduced, stored in a retrieval system, or transmitted, in any form, or by any means, without the prior permission in writing of the publisher, nor be otherwise circulated in any form of binding or cover other than that in which it is published and without a similar condition including this condition being imposed on the subsequent purchaser.

A CIP catalogue record for this book is available from the British Library.

ISBN: 978-1-0369-0531-6

Designed by Level Partnership
Cover designed by lydiafee.co.uk
Maps by Mary Spence © Global Mapping and XYZ Maps
Printed and bound in the United Kingdom by PCP Ltd

WORLD LAND TRUST™
www.carbonbalancedpaper.com
CBP021465